MACMILLAN
ENCYCLOPEDIA
OF
WORLD SLAVERY

MACMILLAN
ENCYCLOPEDIA
OF
WORLD SLAVERY

VOLUME 2

Edited by

Paul Finkelman
Joseph C. Miller

MACMILLAN REFERENCE USA
SIMON & SCHUSTER MACMILLAN
NEW YORK

SIMON & SCHUSTER AND PRENTICE HALL INTERNATIONAL
LONDON   MEXICO CITY   NEW DELHI   SINGAPORE   SYDNEY   TORONTO

Simon & Schuster Macmillan
1633 Broadway
New York, NY 10019-6785

PRINTED IN THE UNITED STATES OF AMERICA

1 2 3 4 5 6 7 8 9 10

LIBRARY OF CONGRESS CATALOGING-IN-PUBLICATION DATA

Macmillan encyclopedia of world slavery / edited by Paul Finkelman,
  Joseph C. Miller.
      p.   cm.
    Includes bibliographical references (p.   ) and index.
    ISBN 0-02-864607-X (set : lib. bdg. : alk. paper). — ISBN
0-02-864780-7 (Vol. 1 : lib. bdg. : alk. paper). — ISBN 0-02-864781-5
(Vol. 2 : lib. bdg. : alk. paper).
    1. Slavery—Encyclopedias.   I. Finkelman, Paul, 1949– .
II. Miller, Joseph Calder.   III. Macmillan Reference USA (Firm)
HT861.M24   1998
306.3′62′03—dc21   98-30610
                                                           CIP

This paper meets the requirements of ANSI/NISO Z39.48-1992 (Permanence of Paper)

Maps

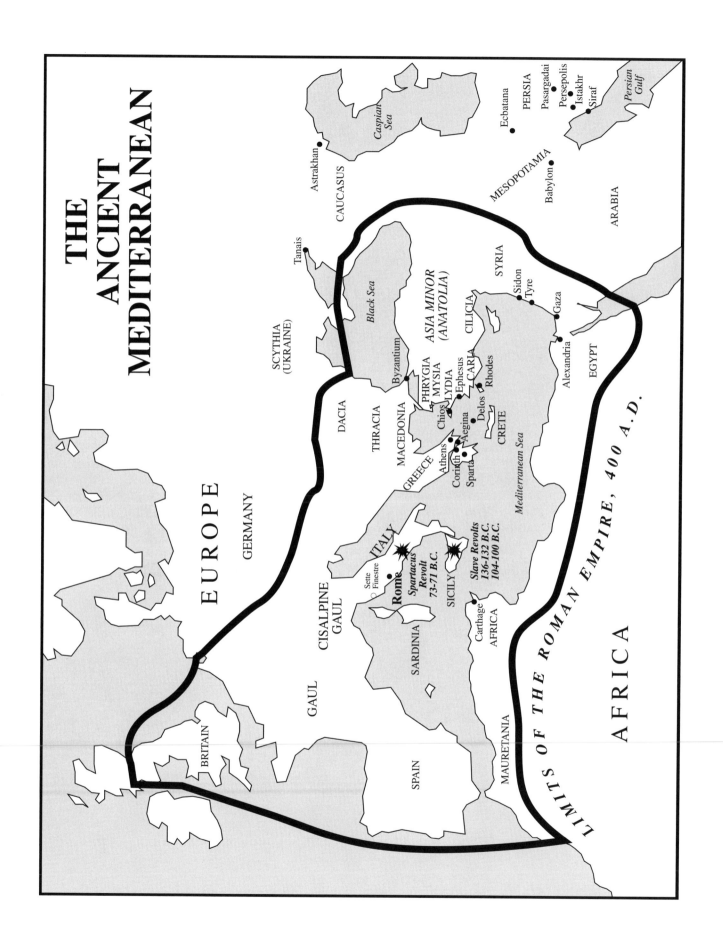

THE ANCIENT MEDITERRANEAN

EUROPE

GERMANY

BRITAIN

GAUL

CISALPINE GAUL

ITALY

Sette Finestre

Rome

Spartacus Revolt 73-71 B.C.

Slave Revolts 136-132 B.C. 104-100 B.C.

SARDINIA

SICILY

SPAIN

Carthage

AFRICA

MAURETANIA

AFRICA

SCYTHIA (UKRAINE)

DACIA

THRACIA

MACEDONIA

GREECE

Athens

Corinth

Sparta

Aegina

Chios

Delos

CRETE

Tanais

Black Sea

Byzantium

PHRYGIA

MYSIA

LYDIA

Ephesus

CARIA

Rhodes

ASIA MINOR (ANATOLIA)

CILICIA

SYRIA

Sidon

Tyre

Gaza

Alexandria

EGYPT

Mediterranean Sea

Astrakhan

Caspian Sea

CAUCASUS

MESOPOTAMIA

Babylon

ARABIA

Ecbatana

PERSIA

Pasargadai

Persepolis

Istakhr

Siraf

Persian Gulf

LIMITS OF THE ROMAN EMPIRE, 400 A.D.

EUROPE 500-1500

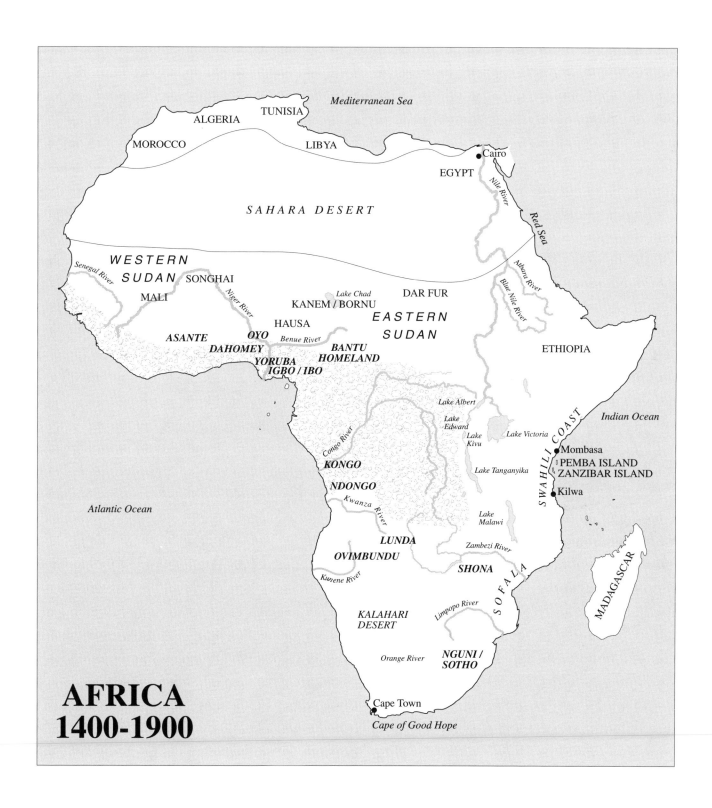

Mediterranean Sea

MOROCCO   ALGERIA   TUNISIA

LIBYA

Cairo

EGYPT

Nile River

Red Sea

SAHARA DESERT

Senegal River

WESTERN
SUDAN   SONGHAI

MALI

Niger River

KANEM / BORNU

Lake Chad

DAR FUR

Abara River

Blue Nile River

HAUSA

Benue River

EASTERN
SUDAN

ASANTE   OYO

DAHOMEY

YORUBA

IGBO / IBO

BANTU
HOMELAND

ETHIOPIA

Lake Albert

*Lake
Edward*

*Lake
Kivu*

Lake Victoria

Indian Ocean

SWAHILI COAST

Mombasa
PEMBA ISLAND
ZANZIBAR ISLAND

Congo River

KONGO

NDONGO

Kwanza River

Lake Tanganyika

Kilwa

Atlantic Ocean

LUNDA

OVIMBUNDU

Kunene River

*Lake
Malawi*

Zambezi River

SHONA

SOFALA

MADAGASCAR

KALAHARI
DESERT

Limpopo River

Orange River

NGUNI /
SOTHO

Cape Town

Cape of Good Hope

AFRICA
1400-1900

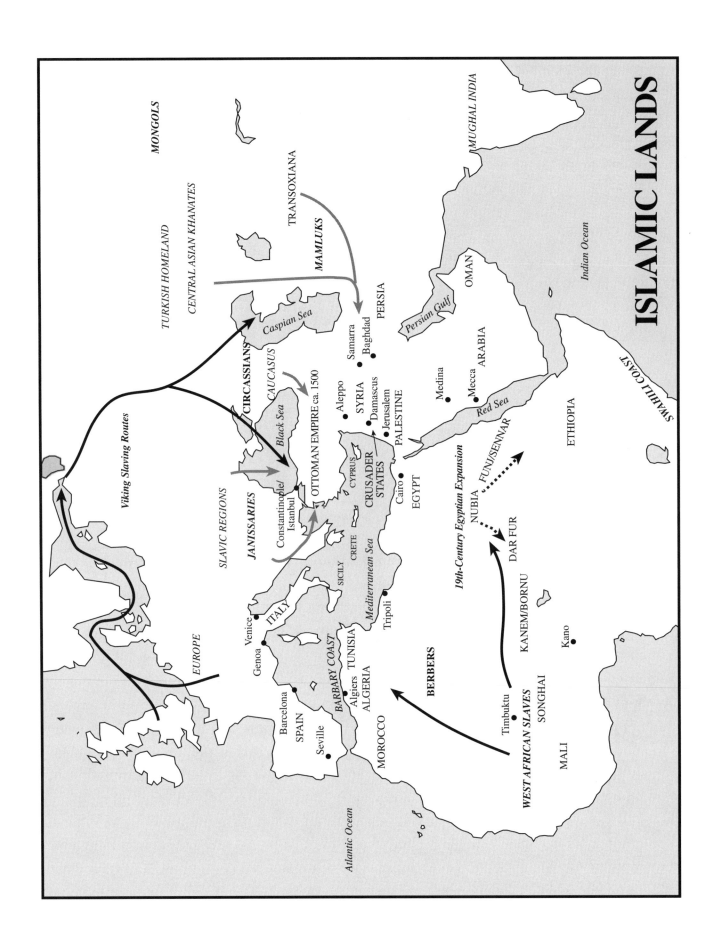

ISLAMIC LANDS

MONGOLS

MUGHAL INDIA

TURKISH HOMELAND

CENTRAL ASIAN KHANATES

TRANSOXIANA

MAMLUKS

Caspian Sea

PERSIA

Indian Ocean

OMAN

Persian Gulf

Samarra

Baghdad

CIRCASSIANS

CAUCASUS

OTTOMAN EMPIRE ca. 1500

Black Sea

Aleppo

SYRIA

Damascus

Jerusalem

PALESTINE

Medina

Mecca

ARABIA

Red Sea

Viking Slaving Routes

SLAVIC REGIONS

JANISSARIES

Constantinople/
Istanbul

CYPRUS

CRUSADER
STATES

Cairo

EGYPT

ETHIOPIA

SWAHILI COAST

19th-Century Egyptian Expansion

NUBIA

FUNJ/SENNAR

DAR FUR

CRETE

SICILY

Mediterranean Sea

KANEM/BORNU

Kano

EUROPE

Venice

ITALY

Genoa

Tripoli

Barcelona

SPAIN

BARBARY COAST

TUNISIA

Algiers

ALGERIA

MOROCCO

BERBERS

Timbuktu

SONGHAI

WEST AFRICAN SLAVES

MALI

Seville

Atlantic Ocean

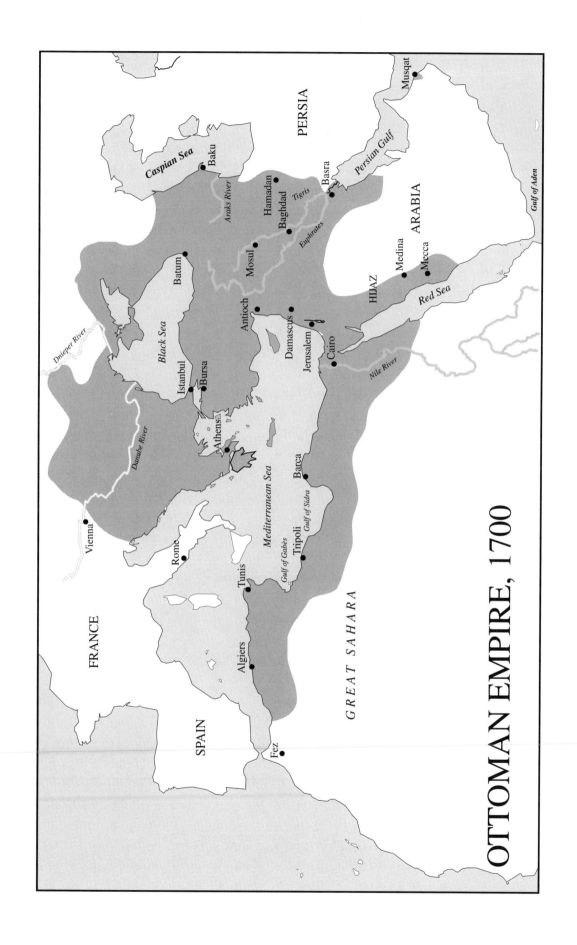

OTTOMAN EMPIRE, 1700

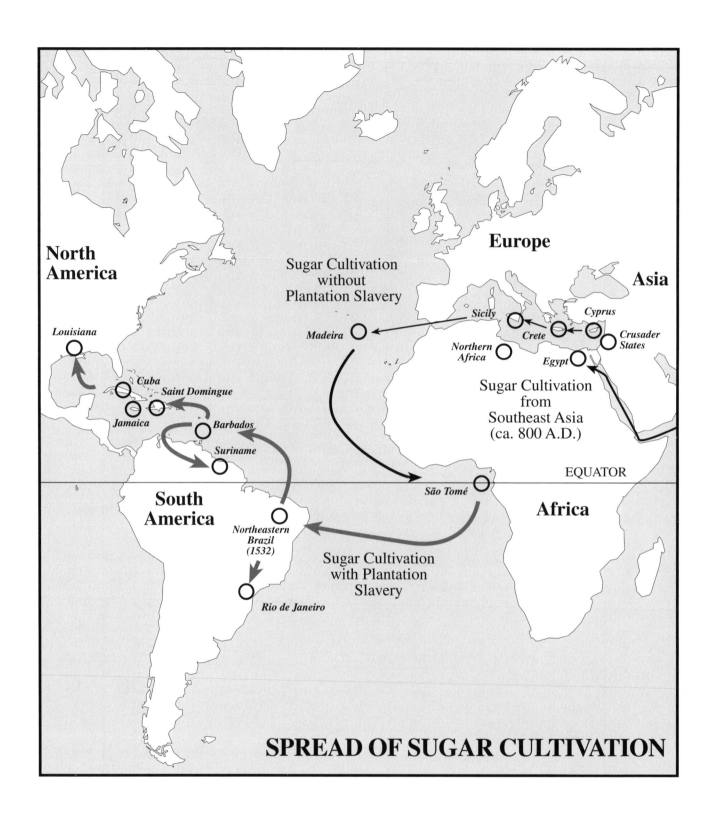

SPREAD OF SUGAR CULTIVATION

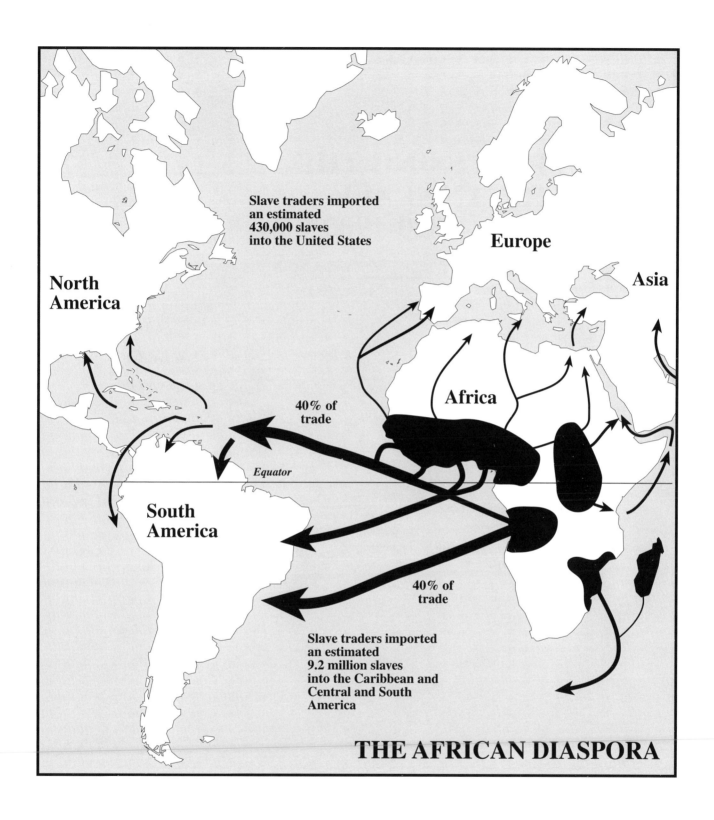

Slave traders imported an estimated 430,000 slaves into the United States

Europe

Asia

North America

Africa

40% of trade

Equator

South America

40% of trade

Slave traders imported an estimated 9.2 million slaves into the Caribbean and Central and South America

THE AFRICAN DIASPORA

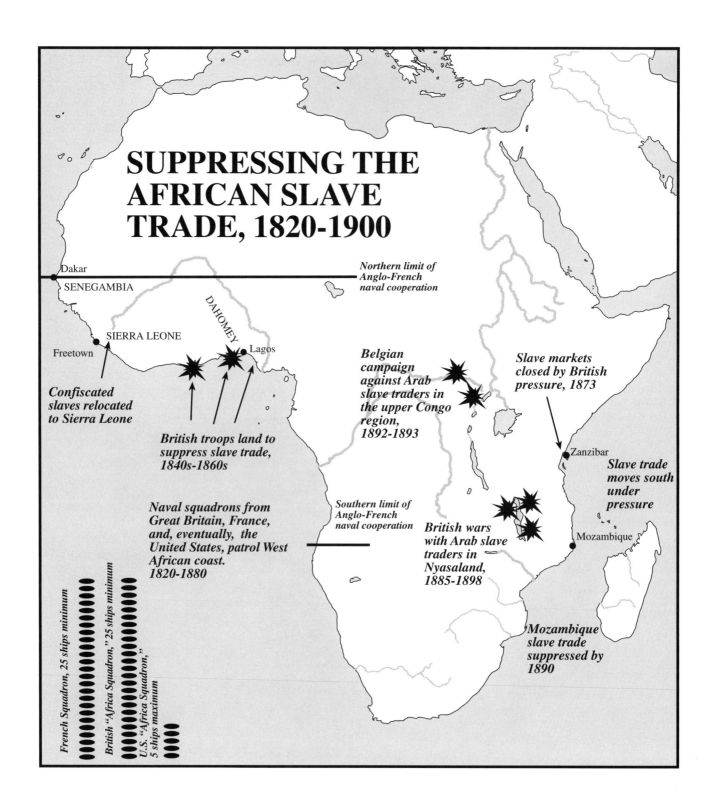

SUPPRESSING THE AFRICAN SLAVE TRADE, 1820-1900

Dakar

Northern limit of Anglo-French naval cooperation

SENEGAMBIA

DAHOMEY

SIERRA LEONE

Lagos

Freetown

Confiscated slaves relocated to Sierra Leone

British troops land to suppress slave trade, 1840s-1860s

Belgian campaign against Arab slave traders in the upper Congo region, 1892-1893

Slave markets closed by British pressure, 1873

Zanzibar

Slave trade moves south under pressure

Mozambique

Naval squadrons from Great Britain, France, and, eventually, the United States, patrol West African coast. 1820-1880

Southern limit of Anglo-French naval cooperation

British wars with Arab slave traders in Nyasaland, 1885-1898

Mozambique slave trade suppressed by 1890

French Squadron, 25 ships minimum

British "Africa Squadron," 25 ships minimum

U.S. "Africa Squadron," 5 ships maximum

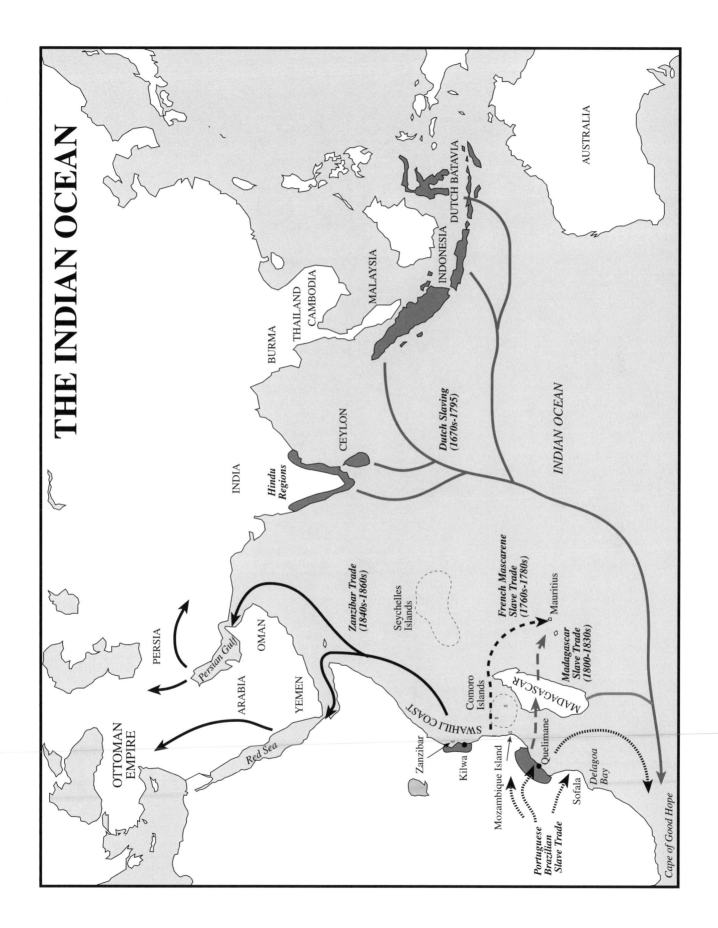

THE INDIAN OCEAN

AUSTRALIA

DUTCH BATAVIA

INDONESIA

MALAYSIA

CAMBODIA

THAILAND

BURMA

CEYLON

Hindu Regions

INDIA

Dutch Slaving (1670s-1795)

INDIAN OCEAN

PERSIA

Persian Gulf

OMAN

ARABIA

YEMEN

OTTOMAN EMPIRE

Red Sea

Zanzibar Trade (1840s-1860s)

Seychelles Islands

French Mascarene Slave Trade (1760s-1780s)

Mauritius

Madagascar Slave Trade (1800-1830s)

Comoro Islands

MADAGASCAR

SWAHILI COAST

Zanzibar

Kilwa

Mozambique Island

Quelimane

Sofala

Delagoa Bay

Portuguese Brazilian Slave Trade

Cape of Good Hope

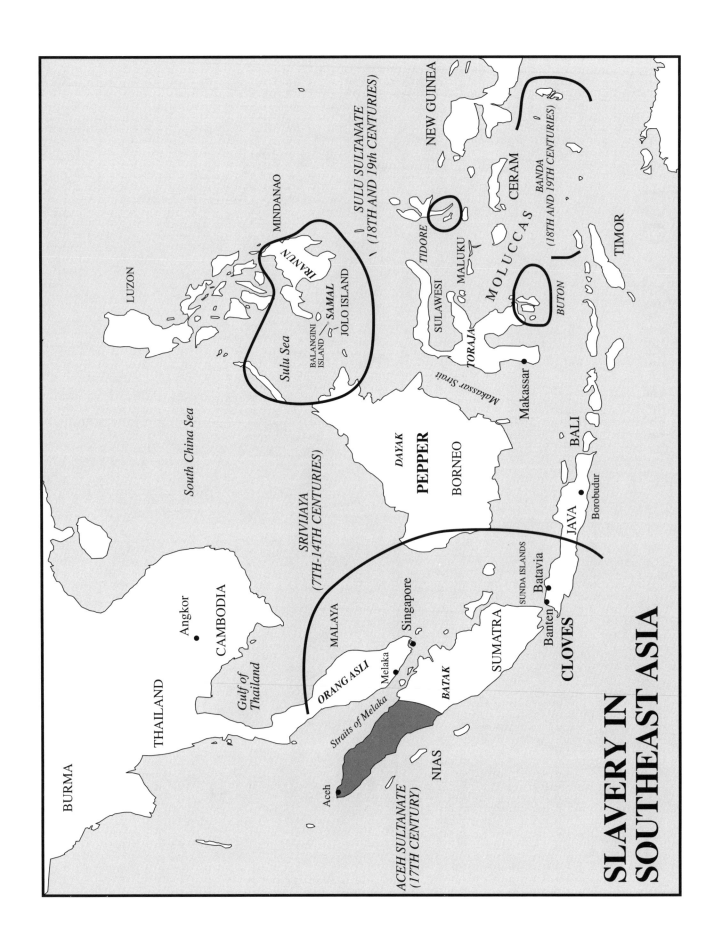

SLAVERY IN SOUTHEAST ASIA

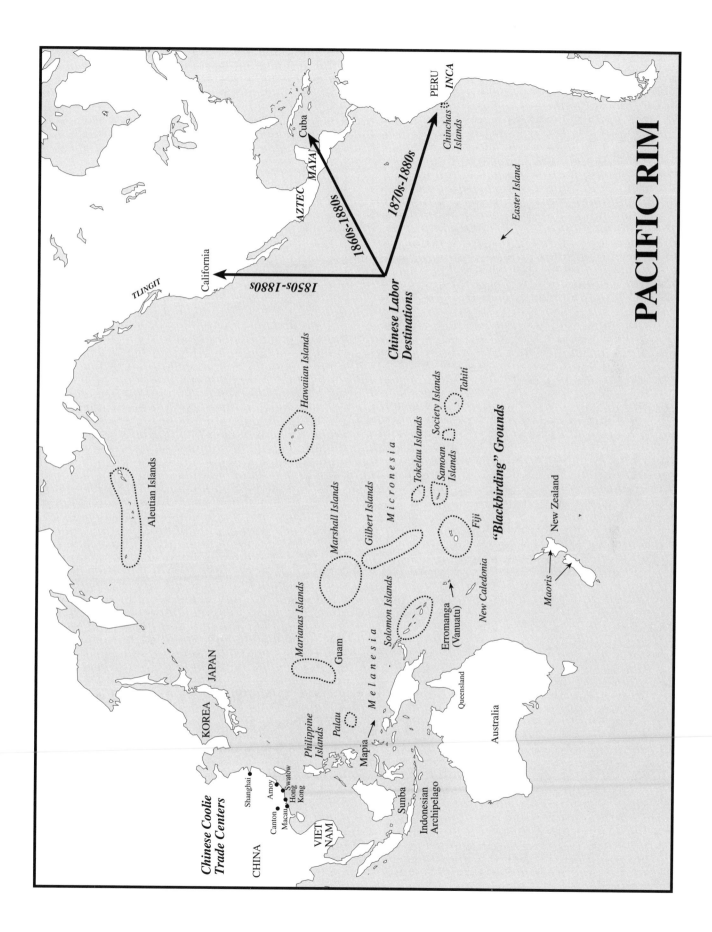

PACIFIC RIM

Chinese Coolie
Trade Centers

CHINA

VIET
NAM

Shanghai
Amoy
Canton
Macau
Swatow
Hong Kong

KOREA

JAPAN

Philippine
Islands

Palau

Mapia

M e l a n e s i a

Marianas Islands

Guam

Marshall Islands

Gilbert Islands

M i c r o n e s i a

Solomon Islands

Sumba

Indonesian
Archipelago

Australia

Queensland

New Caledonia

Erromanga
(Vanuatu)

Fiji

"Blackbirding" Grounds

Samoan
Islands

Tokelau Islands

Society Islands

Tahiti

Maoris

New Zealand

Aleutian Islands

Hawaiian Islands

TLINGIT

California

AZTEC

MAYA

Cuba

1860s-1880s

1850s-1880s

1870s-1880s

PERU   INCA

Chinchas
Islands

Easter Island

Chinese Labor
Destinations

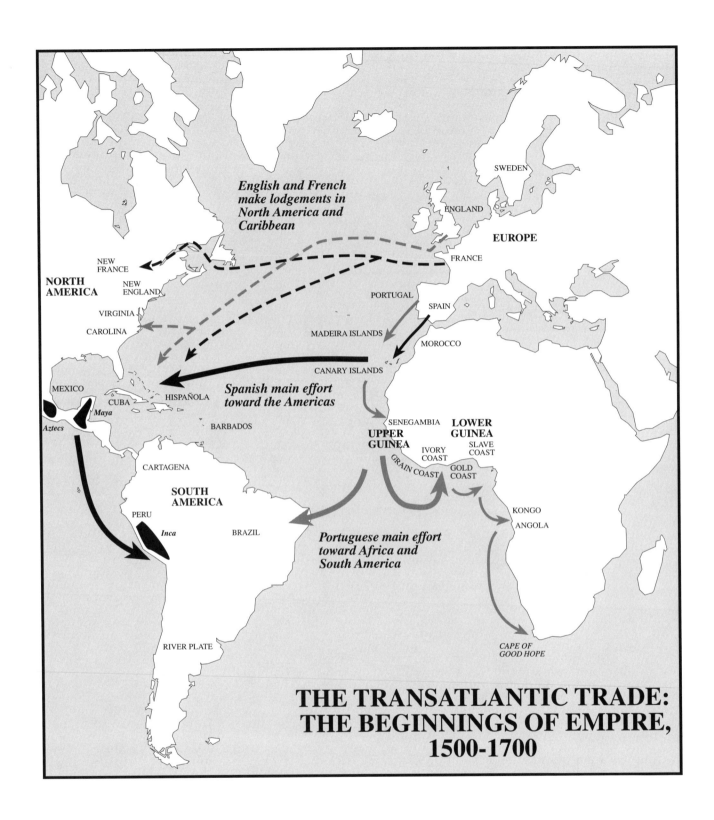

English and French make lodgements in North America and Caribbean

EUROPE

SWEDEN

ENGLAND

FRANCE

NORTH AMERICA

NEW FRANCE

NEW ENGLAND

VIRGINIA

CAROLINA

PORTUGAL

SPAIN

MADEIRA ISLANDS

MOROCCO

CANARY ISLANDS

MEXICO

CUBA

Maya

HISPAÑOLA

Aztecs

BARBADOS

Spanish main effort toward the Americas

SENEGAMBIA

LOWER GUINEA

UPPER GUINEA

IVORY COAST

SLAVE COAST

GRAIN COAST

GOLD COAST

CARTAGENA

SOUTH AMERICA

PERU

Inca

BRAZIL

KONGO

ANGOLA

Portuguese main effort toward Africa and South America

RIVER PLATE

CAPE OF GOOD HOPE

THE TRANSATLANTIC TRADE: THE BEGINNINGS OF EMPIRE, 1500-1700

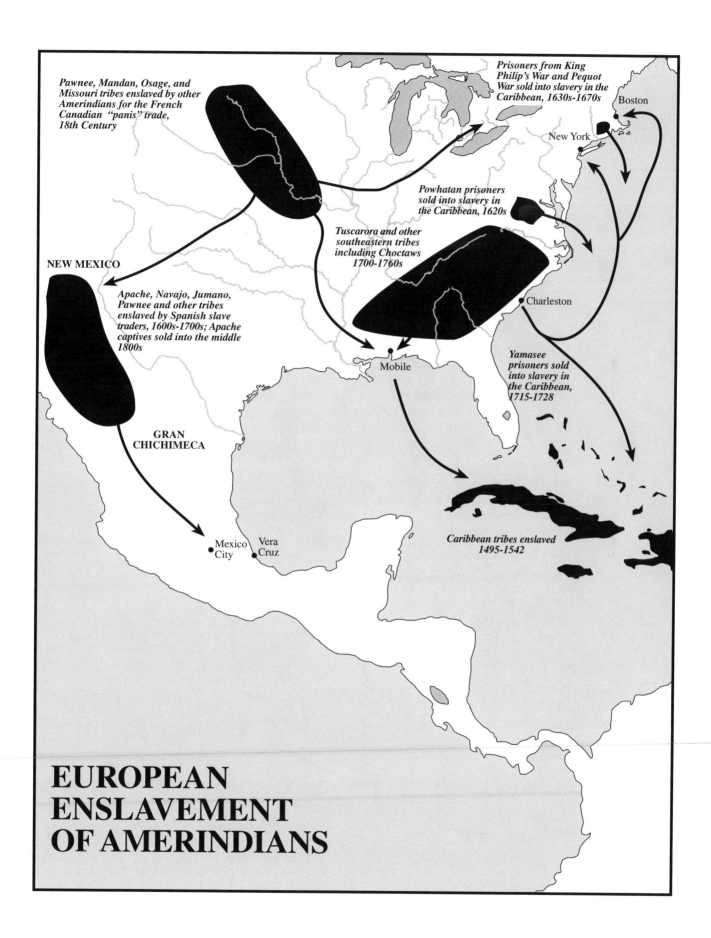

Pawnee, Mandan, Osage, and
Missouri tribes enslaved by other
Amerindians for the French
Canadian "panis" trade,
18th Century

Prisoners from King
Philip's War and Pequot
War sold into slavery in the
Caribbean, 1630s-1670s

Boston

New York

Powhatan prisoners
sold into slavery in
the Caribbean, 1620s

Tuscarora and other
southeastern tribes
including Choctaws
1700-1760s

NEW MEXICO

Charleston

Apache, Navajo, Jumano,
Pawnee and other tribes
enslaved by Spanish slave
traders, 1600s-1700s; Apache
captives sold into the middle
1800s

Yamasee
prisoners sold
into slavery in
the Caribbean,
1715-1728

GRAN
CHICHIMECA

Mobile

Mexico
City

Vera
Cruz

Caribbean tribes enslaved
1495-1542

EUROPEAN
ENSLAVEMENT
OF AMERINDIANS

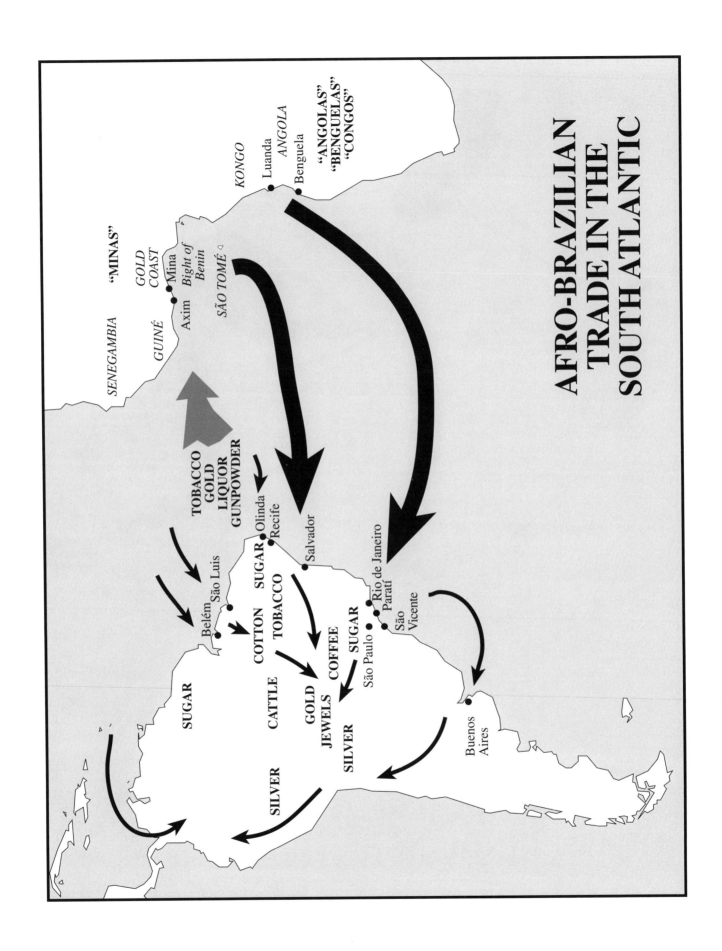

AFRO-BRAZILIAN TRADE IN THE SOUTH ATLANTIC

SENEGAMBIA

GUINÉ

"MINAS"

GOLD COAST

Axim • Mina Bight of Benin ▽

SÃO TOMÉ ▽

KONGO

Luanda • ANGOLA

Benguela •

"ANGOLAS"
"BENGUELAS"
"CONGOS"

TOBACCO
GOLD
LIQUOR
GUNPOWDER

Belém • São Luis

Olinda
Recife

SUGAR

Salvador •

Rio de Janeiro
Paratí
São Vicente •

COTTON
TOBACCO

SUGAR

CATTLE

COFFEE

GOLD
JEWELS

São Paulo •

SILVER

SUGAR

SILVER

SILVER

Buenos Aires •

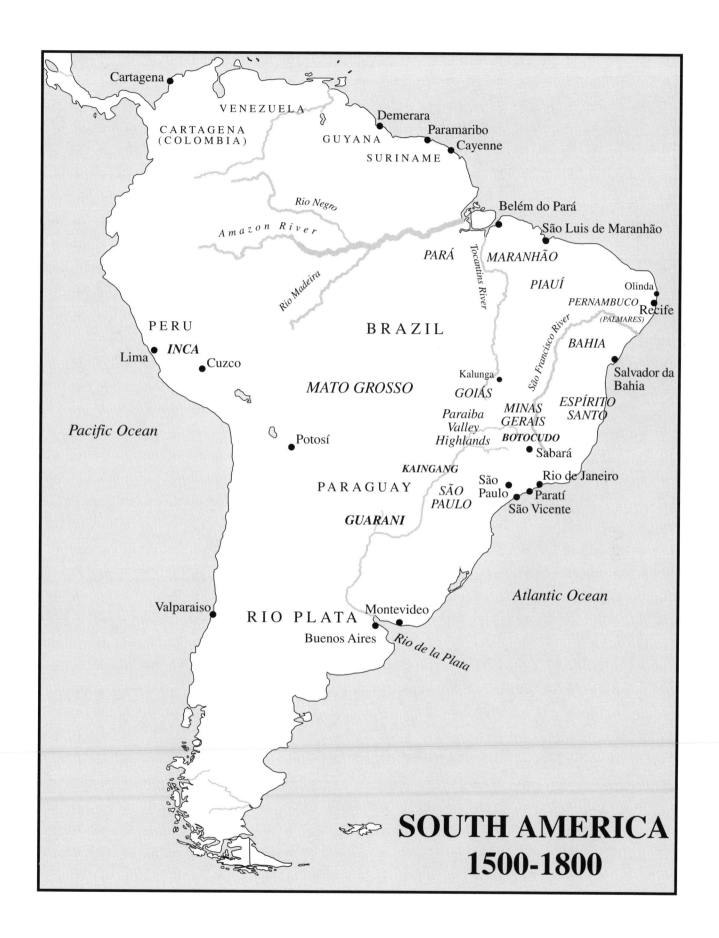

Cartagena

VENEZUELA
CARTAGENA
(COLOMBIA)

Demerara
GUYANA
Paramaribo
SURINAME
Cayenne

Rio Negro

Amazon River

Belém do Pará

São Luis de Maranhão

Rio Madeira

PARÁ

Tocantins River

MARANHÃO

PIAUÍ

Olinda

PERNAMBUCO
(*PALMARES*)

Recife

PERU

INCA

BRAZIL

BAHIA

Lima

Cuzco

MATO GROSSO

Kalunga

GOIÁS

São Francisco River

BAHIA

Salvador da Bahia

Pacific Ocean

MINAS GERAIS

ESPÍRITO SANTO

Paraiba Valley Highlands

BOTOCUDO

Potosí

Sabará

KAINGANG

Rio de Janeiro

PARAGUAY

SÃO PAULO

São Paulo

Paratí

São Vicente

GUARANI

Atlantic Ocean

Valparaiso

RIO PLATA

Montevideo

Buenos Aires

Rio de la Plata

SOUTH AMERICA
1500-1800

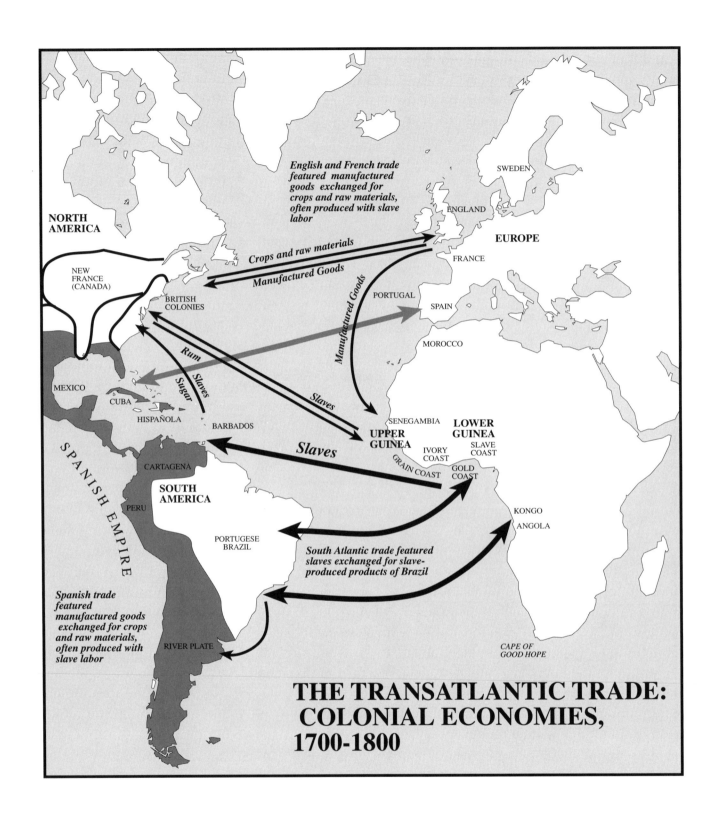

THE TRANSATLANTIC TRADE:
COLONIAL ECONOMIES,
1700-1800

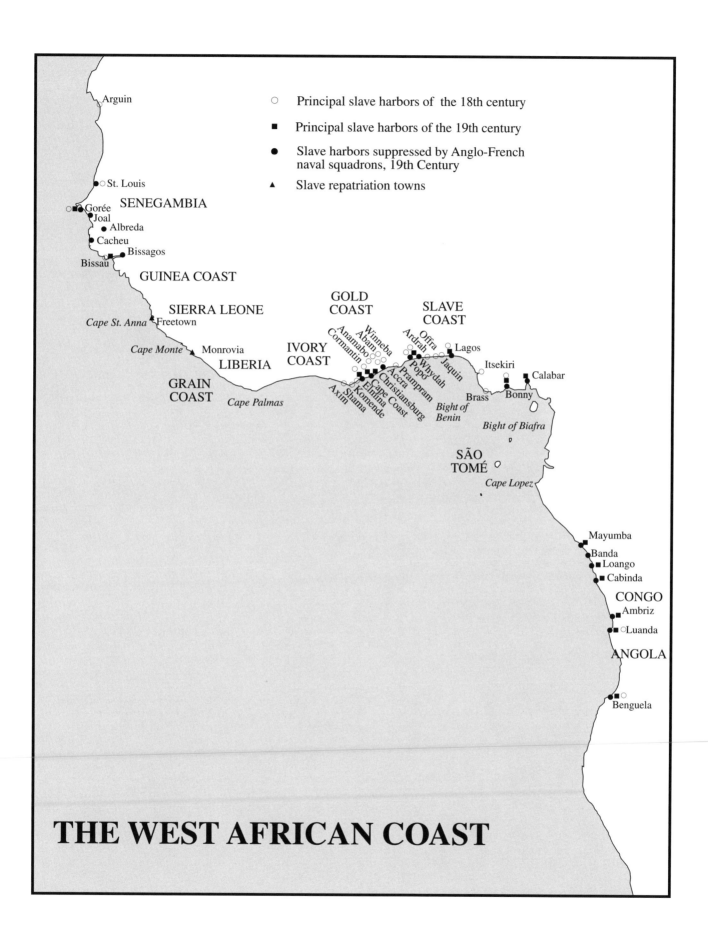

○   Principal slave harbors of the 18th century

■   Principal slave harbors of the 19th century

●   Slave harbors suppressed by Anglo-French naval squadrons, 19th Century

▲   Slave repatriation towns

Arguin

St. Louis

Gorée
Joal
Albreda
Cacheu
Bissagos
Bissau

SENEGAMBIA

GUINEA COAST

SIERRA LEONE

Cape St. Anna   Freetown

Cape Monte   Monrovia

LIBERIA

GRAIN COAST

Cape Palmas

IVORY COAST

GOLD COAST

Cormantin
Anamabo
Abam
Winneba
Accra
Pranpram
Christiansburg
Cape Coast
Elmina
Komende
Shama
Axim

SLAVE COAST

Ardrah
Offra
Popo
Whydah
Jaquin
Lagos

Itsekiri

Brass

Bight of Benin

Bonny

Calabar

Bight of Biafra

SÃO TOMÉ

Cape Lopez

Mayumba
Banda
Loango
Cabinda

CONGO

Ambriz

Luanda

ANGOLA

Benguela

THE WEST AFRICAN COAST

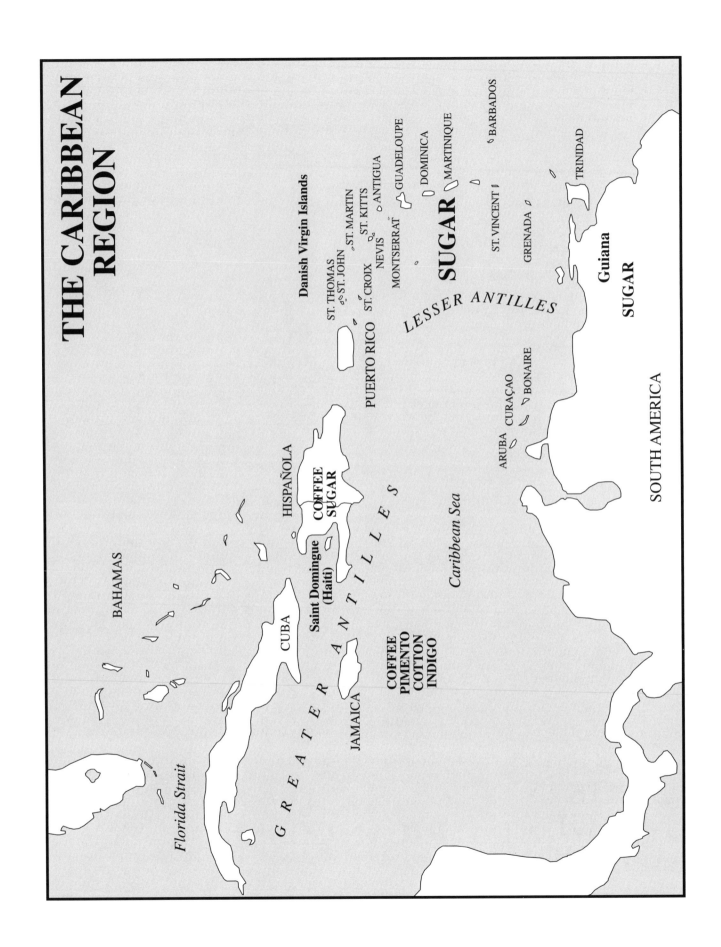

THE CARIBBEAN REGION

Florida Strait

BAHAMAS

CUBA

GREATER ANTILLES

JAMAICA

**COFFEE
PIMENTO
COTTON
INDIGO**

HISPAÑOLA

**Saint Domingue
(Haiti)**

**COFFEE
SUGAR**

Caribbean Sea

Danish Virgin Islands

ST. THOMAS
ST. JOHN
ST. MARTIN
ST. KITTS
ST. CROIX
NEVIS
MONTSERRAT
ANTIGUA
GUADELOUPE
DOMINICA
MARTINIQUE

PUERTO RICO

SUGAR

LESSER ANTILLES

ARUBA CURAÇAO
BONAIRE

BARBADOS

TRINIDAD

ST. VINCENT

GRENADA

Guiana
SUGAR

SOUTH AMERICA

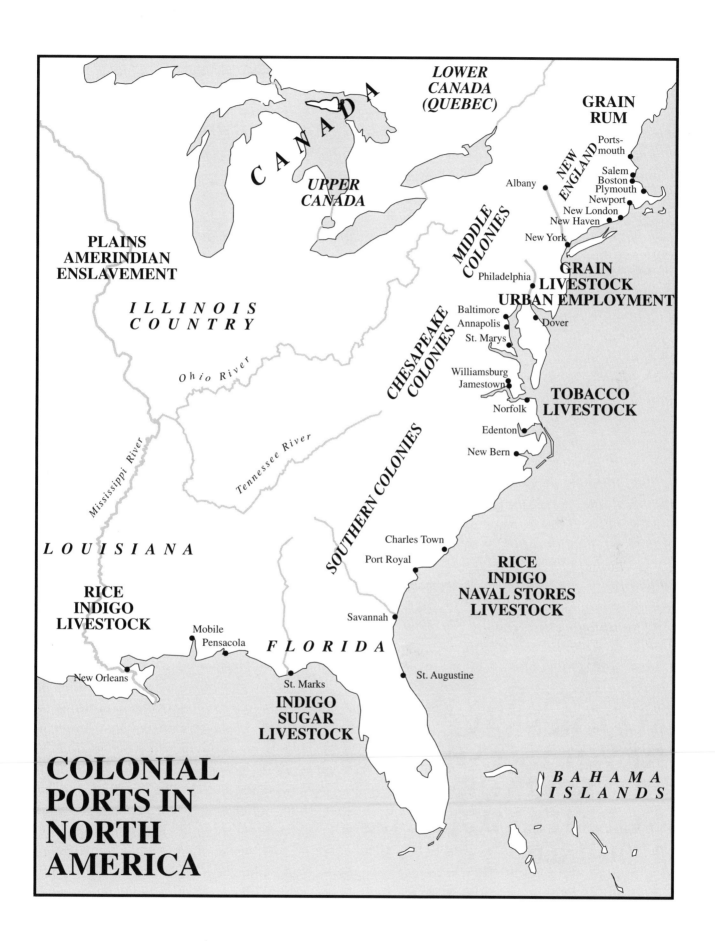

LOWER
CANADA
(QUEBEC)

GRAIN
RUM

CANADA

UPPER
CANADA

PLAINS
AMERINDIAN
ENSLAVEMENT

*ILLINOIS
COUNTRY*

Ohio River

*MIDDLE
COLONIES*

*NEW
ENGLAND*

Albany

Ports-
mouth
Salem
Boston
Plymouth
Newport
New London
New Haven
New York

Philadelphia

GRAIN
LIVESTOCK
URBAN EMPLOYMENT

Baltimore
Annapolis
St. Marys

Dover

*CHESAPEAKE
COLONIES*

Williamsburg
Jamestown

Norfolk

TOBACCO
LIVESTOCK

Edenton

Tennessee River

New Bern

SOUTHERN COLONIES

Mississippi River

LOUISIANA

RICE
INDIGO
LIVESTOCK

Mobile
Pensacola

FLORIDA

New Orleans

St. Marks

Charles Town
Port Royal

RICE
INDIGO
NAVAL STORES
LIVESTOCK

Savannah

St. Augustine

INDIGO
SUGAR
LIVESTOCK

COLONIAL
PORTS IN
NORTH
AMERICA

*BAHAMA
ISLANDS*

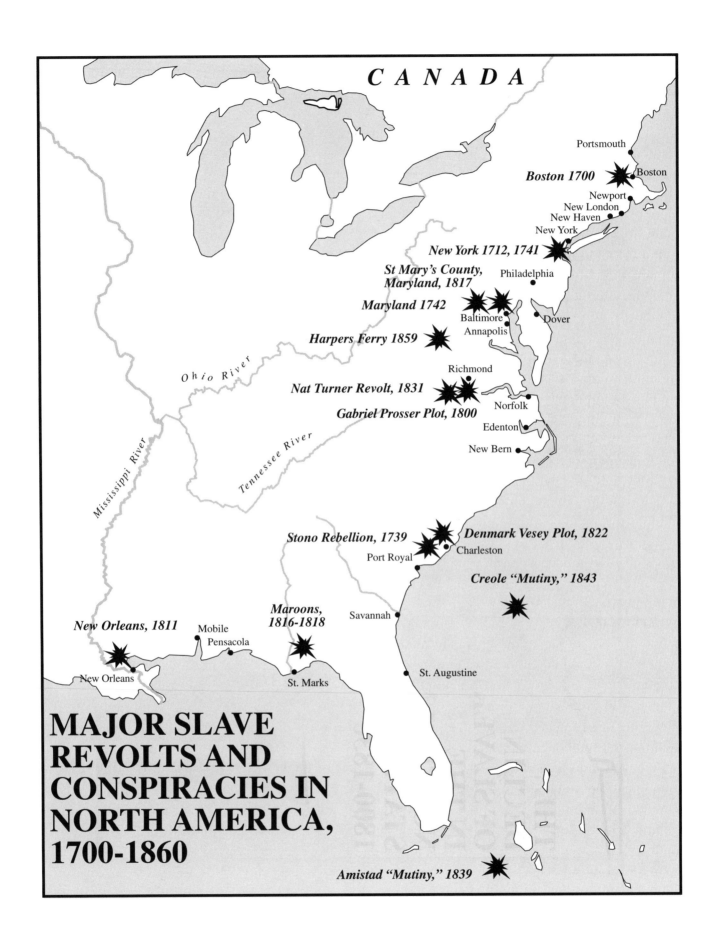

CANADA

Portsmouth

Boston 1700 Boston

Newport
New London
New Haven

New York

New York 1712, 1741

*St Mary's County,
Maryland, 1817*

Philadelphia

Maryland 1742

Baltimore
Annapolis

Dover

Harpers Ferry 1859

Richmond

Nat Turner Revolt, 1831

Norfolk

Gabriel Prosser Plot, 1800

Edenton

New Bern

Ohio River

Tennessee River

Mississippi River

Stono Rebellion, 1739 *Denmark Vesey Plot, 1822*

Port Royal Charleston

Creole "Mutiny," 1843

Savannah

*Maroons,
1816-1818*

New Orleans, 1811 Mobile

Pensacola

St. Augustine

New Orleans St. Marks

MAJOR SLAVE
REVOLTS AND
CONSPIRACIES IN
NORTH AMERICA,
1700-1860

Amistad "Mutiny," 1839

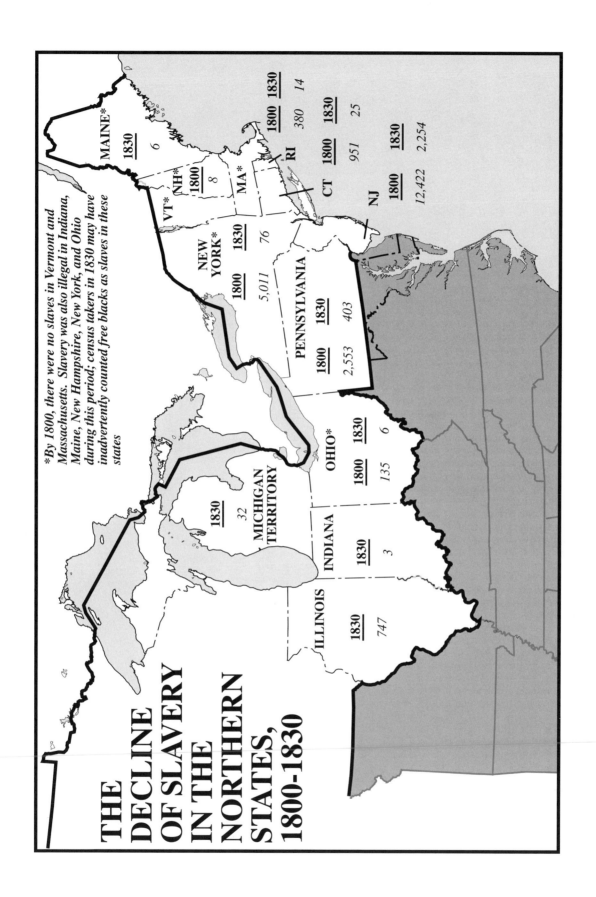

THE DECLINE OF SLAVERY IN THE NORTHERN STATES, 1800-1830

*By 1800, there were no slaves in Vermont and Massachusetts. Slavery was also illegal in Indiana, Maine, New Hampshire, New York, and Ohio during this period; census takers in 1830 may have inadvertently counted free blacks as slaves in these states

MAINE*
1830
6

NH*
1800
8

VT*

MA*

RI **1800** **1830**
380   14

CT **1800** **1830**
951   25

NJ **1800** **1830**
12,422 2,254

NEW YORK*
1800 **1830**
5,011   76

PENNSYLVANIA
1800 **1830**
2,553   403

OHIO*
1800 **1830**
135   6

MICHIGAN TERRITORY
1830
32

INDIANA
1830
3

ILLINOIS
1830
747

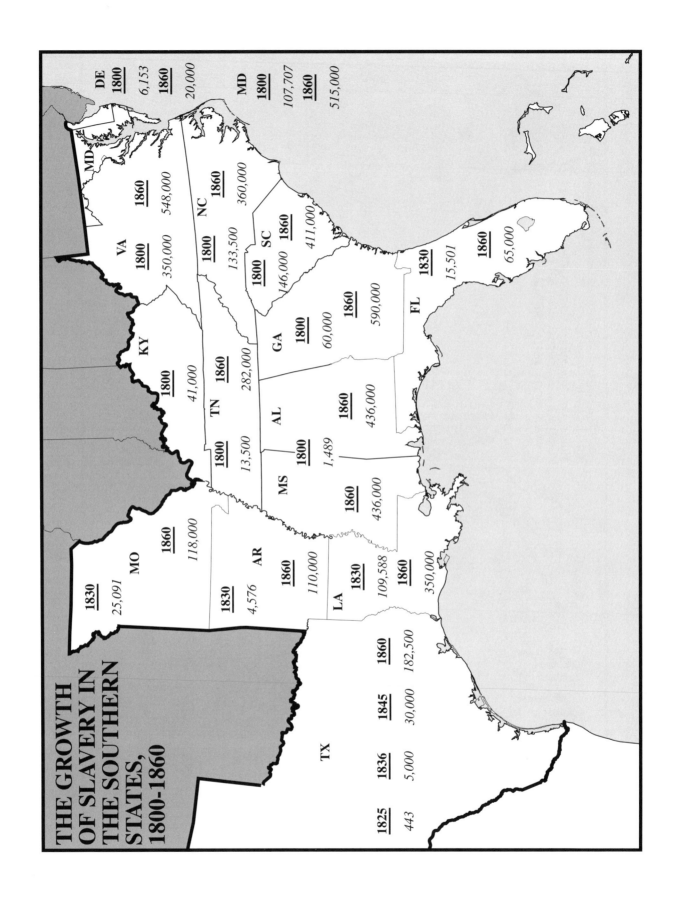

THE GROWTH
OF SLAVERY IN
THE SOUTHERN
STATES,
1800-1860

DE
1800 6,153
1860 20,000

MD
1800 107,707
1860 515,000

VA
1800 350,000
1860 548,000

NC
1800 133,500
1860 360,000

SC
1800 146,000
1860 411,000

FL
1830 15,501
1860 65,000

GA
1800 60,000
1860 590,000

KY
1800 41,000

TN
1800 13,500
1860 282,000

AL
1800 1,489
1860 436,000

MS
1800 1,489
1860 436,000

MO
1830 25,091
1860 118,000

AR
1830 4,576
1860 110,000

LA
1830 109,588
1860 350,000

TX
1825 443
1836 5,000
1845 30,000
1860 182,500

MD

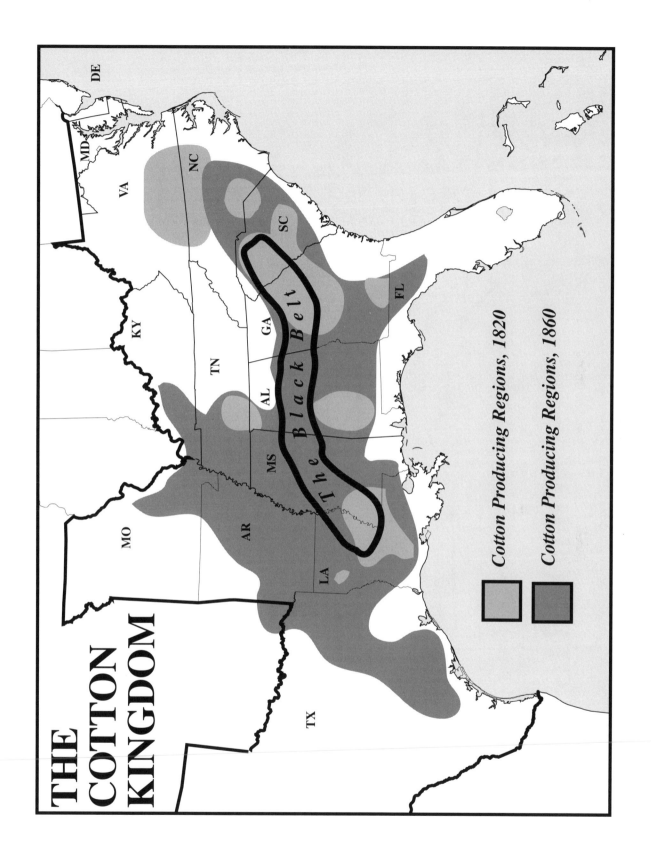

THE COTTON KINGDOM

DE
MD
VA
NC
SC
FL
KY
TN
GA
AL
The Black Belt
MS
AR
MO
LA
TX

Cotton Producing Regions, 1820

Cotton Producing Regions, 1860

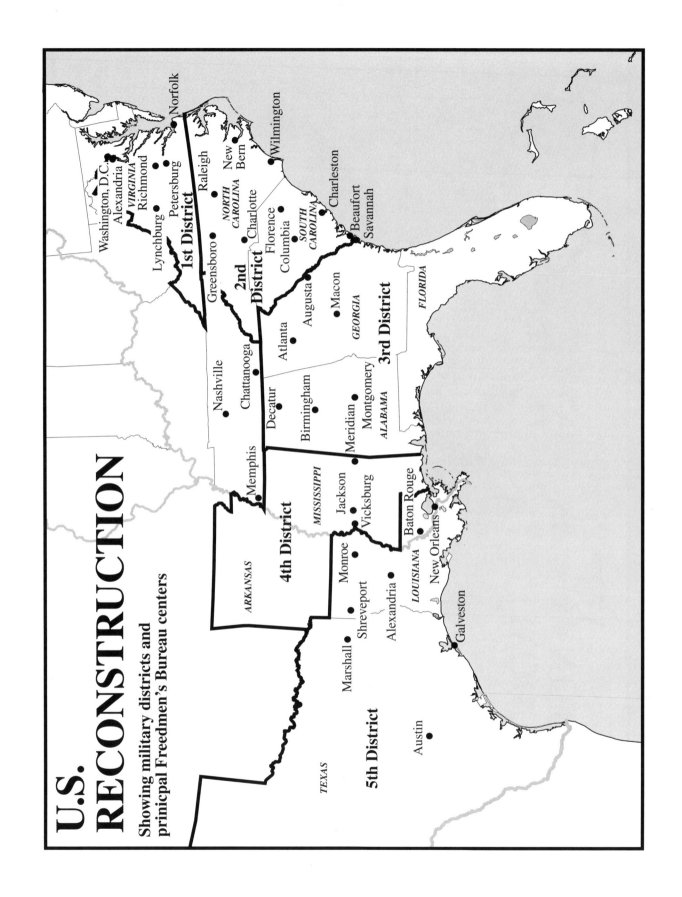

U.S. RECONSTRUCTION

Showing military districts and prinicpal Freedmen's Bureau centers

1st District

2nd District

3rd District

4th District

5th District

VIRGINIA

NORTH CAROLINA

SOUTH CAROLINA

GEORGIA

FLORIDA

ALABAMA

MISSISSIPPI

ARKANSAS

LOUISIANA

TEXAS

Washington, D.C.
Alexandria
Richmond
Lynchburg
Petersburg
Norfolk
Raleigh
Greensboro
New Bern
Charlotte
Wilmington
Charleston
Florence
Columbia
Augusta
Beaufort
Savannah
Macon
Atlanta
Nashville
Chattanooga
Decatur
Birmingham
Montgomery
Meridian
Memphis
Jackson
Vicksburg
Baton Rouge
Monroe
Shreveport
New Orleans
Alexandria
Marshall
Galveston
Austin

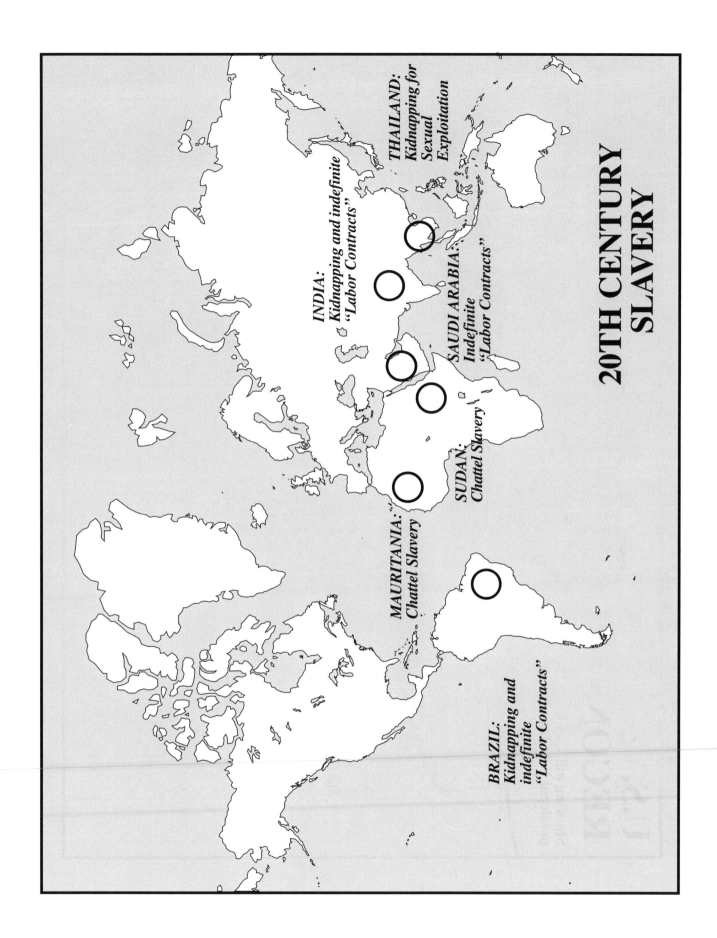

20TH CENTURY SLAVERY

INDIA:
Kidnapping and indefinite
"Labor Contracts"

THAILAND:
Kidnapping for
Sexual
Exploitation

SAUDI ARABIA:
Indefinite
"Labor Contracts"

SUDAN:
Chattel Slavery

MAURITANIA:
Chattel Slavery

BRAZIL:
Kidnapping and
indefinite
"Labor Contracts"

L

Labor Systems

This entry includes the following articles: Contract Labor; Convict Labor in Australia; Convict Leasing in the United States; Coolies; Corvée; Forced Labor; Indentured Labor (Seventeenth-Century); Indentured Labor (1834–1960); Penal Servitude. *See also* Field Labor; International Labor Organization; Nazi Slave Labor.

Contract Labor

The first substantial numbers of workers came to the United States in the colonial era as unfree indentured servants who voluntarily signed agreements that set employment terms of five to seven years. Between the Revolution and the Civil War indentured servitude practically disappeared. After the Civil War, however, many employers contracted directly with European immigrant workers. Although contract laborers never composed the bulk of immigrants to the United States, U.S. trade unions deemed such laborers a threat to the "American standard of living," and the unions succeeded in 1885 in having Congress outlaw the importation of contract labor (the Foran Act). Contract labor proved a much more successful and substantial alternative to slave and free labor in the Caribbean sugar islands and in significant segments of eastern and southern Africa, where millions of eastern and southern Asians worked on plantations and mines in a form of indentured servitude.

Although contract labor had been rendered illegal in the United States, it continued to exist informally after 1885, sometimes in violation of the law. Substantial numbers of Asian, Pacific Island, and Italian immigrants came to the United States after signing agreements with labor contractors who, typically, promised the laborers transportation and jobs in return for a percentage of their wages. Because contract laborers owed a part of their wages to the *padrone* (Italian for "patron" or "employer") and because they often had to purchase room and board from the padrone and were not free to quit work at will, critics characterized contract labor as a form of slavery. Contract labor, however, was not comparable in any strict sense to chattel slavery. Contract laborers entered into agreements voluntarily, served for a contracted period of time, and broke their contracts.

At the end of the twentieth century, contract labor continues to exist in the United States in two forms. Many of the migrant workers who harvest crops, especially those who enter the United States as temporary immigrants, are employed by labor contractors who function much in the manner of classical padrones. Other more highly educated and skilled workers sign agreements with temporary employment agencies or directly with employers to serve as self-employed contract workers rather than as waged or salaried employees.

See also CHATTEL SLAVERY; PEONAGE. *See also the other articles in this entry.*

A padrone supervises the work of a group of migrant cranberry pickers in Burlington County, New Jersey, in 1938. [Library of Congress/Corbis]

BIBLIOGRAPHY

ERICKSON, CHARLOTTE. *American Industry and the European Immigrant, 1860–1885.* 1957.
PECK, GUNTHER. "Reinventing Free Labor: Immigrant Padrones and Contract Laborers in North America, 1885–1925." *Journal of American History* 83 (1996): 848–871.

Melvyn Dubofsky

Convict Labor in Australia

As a system of labor, convict labor, as it was employed in Australia, is often compared to African slavery. From the inception of penal colonies in Australia in 1787, convict laborers outnumbered free laborers and made up the majority of Australia's population to the 1820s. These bonded laborers faced circumstances similar in many ways to those of African slaves; still, the two institutions exhibited obvious differences.

Like African slaves, the laborers were not free to travel as they pleased. Decisions regarding their labor or their personal lives were made by others. Convict laborers were not owned; they were assigned to work either for free men or the state. The free men to whom the convicts' labor was contracted could not legally punish the laborers. Punishment was carried out by the state. Solitary confinement, flogging, and hanging were common methods of punishment, but extreme physical abuse was not as widespread as among African slaves in the Americas.

Fifty percent of Australia's convicts were sentenced to seven-year terms, 25 percent to life. Neither race nor religion determined their status as unfree laborers in Australia, only their socioeconomic circumstances or decisions made at home in England. The majority were from poor families, and most of them had previously been convicted of some crime (usually theft) in a court of law before being banished to the penal colonies. Unlike African slaves, the beneficiaries of this system paid no official costs for convict labor. Even the cost of the convicts' transportation to the colony was paid by England.

See also other articles in this entry.

BIBLIOGRAPHY

MERIVALE, HERMAN. *Lectures on Colonization and Colonies.* 1861.
ROBSON, L. L. *The Convict Settlers of Australia.* 1965.

Perry L. Kyles Jr.

Convict Leasing in the United States

Forced labor comes in many forms. For half a century after the U.S. Civil War, persons convicted of crimes were not sentenced to prisons but were leased to perform labor for corporations and individuals. Because convict leasing arose immediately after the destruction of slavery, because most of the convicts were black, and because the practice perpetuated forms of labor discipline arising in slavery times, some observers, past and present, have identified leasing as a form of slavery.

This system was not slavery, however. Indeed, differences between it and slavery are pronounced. The fundamental conditions of slavery—permanence, natal alienation (being cut off from ancestors and descendants), and complete dishonor (no socially recognized name or independent existence)—did not obtain for leased convicts. Though the material conditions of their lives were at least as bad as these of slaves had been, convicts were not shorn of their civil rights or subjected to the "social death" Orlando Patterson identified as central to the condition of slavery. Nor does leasing conform to the categories economic historians use to explain slavery. Generally, prison populations were leased in the aggregate, whereas slaves were purchased individually. And while slave maintenance and monitoring costs had to cover the entire slave community, including the aged, the infirm, and children, lessees of convicts paid only for productive workers. Finally, slave labor was much more productive than convict labor. Leased convict labor was generally reckoned by contemporaries as being about three-fourths as productive as free labor, a figure confirmed in available wage data.

Convicts work on a Florida farm around 1910. [Corbis-Bettmann]

See also ECONOMIC INTERPRETATION OF SLAVERY; PATTERSON THESIS.

BIBLIOGRAPHY

LICHTENSTEIN, ALEX. *Twice the Work of Free Labor: The Political Economy of Convict Labor in the New South.* 1996.
MANCINI, MATTHEW J. *One Dies, Get Another: Convict Leasing in the American South, 1866–1928.* 1996.
MCKELVEY, BLAKE. "Penal Slavery and Southern Reconstruction." *Journal of Negro History* 23 (1935): 153–179.
PATTERSON, ORLANDO. *Slavery and Social Death: A Comparative Study.* 1982.

Matthew J. Mancini

Coolies

From the mid-1840s to 1874 several hundred thousand *coolies* sailed from China to labor in the haciendas, factories, plantations, and mines of the Americas and the British Empire. Virtually all males, they were drawn by demand for cheap labor in countries ending slavery, like Peru and Cuba, as well as by economies suffering labor shortages as a result of suppression of the slave trade. China's large population, coupled with political and economic turmoil, encouraged peasants to emigrate. Macao, a Portuguese colony on China's southern coast, was the most important center of the trade.

Like the African slave trade, the coolie trade employed force and inhumanity. While coolies were contracted nominally voluntary immigrants, exchanging years of labor for transportation, many were simply kidnapped by *crimps* (coolie brokers). Others were deceived about their destination, term of service, or the work they would do, or had been strong-armed after losing at rigged games of chance.

Conditions in Macao's *barracoons* (preembarkation holding pens) and on the so-called devil ships were harsh. Aboard, coolies lived behind bars in overcrowded quarters; ships featured punishment cages and flogging pillars. Provisions were meager; many died of thirst. Brutal conditions led to suicides, mutinies, and escape attempts; mortality en route sometimes exceeded 30 percent. Arrival brought no deliverance: if the coolies had not been purchased in advance, they were sold on the open market. Men worked daily in cotton fields or guano beds for up to twenty hours per day. Those who resisted were whipped, mutilated, chained, or put in stocks.

Nevertheless, the coolie system differed from the harshest forms of chattel slavery. First, because it lasted only a single generation, coolie labor was not institutionalized to the same degree; for example, few children were born into it, and some coolies survived their contracted bondage to die free.

More important, the trade was condemned rather than legitimated by law. In 1871 the world learned that when the *Delores Ugarte* caught fire en route from Macao to Peru, the crew sealed their coolie passengers below and abandoned ship. The next year, coolies on the *Maria Luz*, in port in Yokohama, appealed to Japanese authorities for help; Japan ultimately determined that they were being held involuntarily and unlawfully. When such incidents underscored the trade's brutality and stripped from it its patina of consent, governments enforced laws against it. Hong Kong refused to service coolie ships. Chinese authorities severely punished crimps, and the Chinese navy blockaded Macao. In 1874, under pressure, Portugal ended its participation in the trade. Meanwhile, China developed a system of foreign consuls to protect its citizens laboring overseas.

Many Chinese émigrés in this period probably were not coolies. In the United States, for example, the Chinese were exploited and suffered governmental and private mistreatment. However, most lived in free states like California; only a handful replaced slaves. Claims that the Six Companies and other tongs effectively owned the immigrants were exaggerations propounded by opponents of Chinese immigration. While Chinese who borrowed money for passage

The harbor at Macao as it appeared during the height of the coolie trade. [*Ballou's Pictorial Drawing Room Companion/* Corbis]

might suffer if they did not repay it, generally they were not bought and sold or compelled to work in particular occupations or locales.

See also SLAVE TRADE.

BIBLIOGRAPHY

CAMPBELL, PERSIA CRAWFORD. *Chinese Coolie Emigration to Countries within the British Empire.* 1923.
CHING-HWANG, YEN. *Coolies and Mandarins: China's Protection of Overseas Chinese during the Late Ch'ing Period (1851–1911).* 1985.
The Cuba Commission Report: A Hidden History of the Chinese in Cuba. 1993. Introduction by Denise Helly.
DANIELS, ROGER. *Asian America: Chinese and Japanese in the United States since 1850.* 1988.
IRICK, ROBERT L. *Ch'ing Policy toward the Coolie Trade (1847–1878).* 1982.
STEWART, WATT. *Chinese Bondage in Peru: A History of the Chinese Coolie in Peru, 1849–1874.* 1951. Reprint, 1970.
TAKAKI, RONALD. *Strangers from a Different Shore: A History of Asian Americans.* 1989.

Gabriel J. Chin

Corvée

The French word *corvée* literally means "forced labor." As a system of labor mobilization for the construction of national projects, it seems to have been both universal and, almost, infinite. Historian Nathan J. Brown suggests that the pyramids in Egypt were built using corvée labor and that corvée was still in existence in parts of Asia, perhaps in a modified form, as late as 1995. It is somewhat ironic, as the historian Martin J. Klein notes, that the element that separates

corvée most clearly from outright slavery is that only free members of a society were, and are, subject to it while slaves, who were usually outsiders and by definition not free, normally were not. There are exceptions to this, but where slaves were liable to corvée, the exactions were much lower. According to historian David Feeny, slaves in Siam at the start of the nineteenth century only owed eight days a year compared with a maximum of six months for at least one class of free citizens.

As a traditional, and essentially local, method of labor mobilization, corvée does not seem to have generated much peasant unrest even though the exactions could be onerous at times and the system allowed for exactions to be made at all levels by local officials. Because richer members of society always had the opportunity to buy, or bribe, their way out of service, corvée's greatest impact was on the lowest socioeconomic classes, whose apparent lack of resistance seems to have several possible explanations. On the positive side, corvée seems to have been designed to accommodate at least some of the interests of the lower classes. For example, in Siam although some groups owed the king up to six months' labor a year, they were required to work only for one month at a time, and they did not work during the planting or harvesting periods. However, military service in times of war was no doubt an exception to this. Local public work schemes such as water control could be seen as something from which they themselves directly benefitted.

On the other hand, peasant resistance traditionally has been based on avoidance rather than violence, and there are examples of this type of opposition to corvée duties. A Siamese land register of 1867 shows that some 60 percent of the supposedly eligible males had listed themselves as officials, monks, or slaves or as mentally ill in order to render themselves ineligible for the corvée. In 1864 many Malays simply moved rather than be recruited to build a road across the isthmus. And in 1882 huge numbers of Javanese migrated to the Malayan Peninsula to avoid Dutch exactions. Peasants could also frustrate corvée requirements by less direct methods. The contemporary literature is littered with complaints about the poor work skills of corvée laborers, and according to historian Cannon Hickey, while employed in what seems to have been the most detested form of corvée labor, porterage (carrying people and goods from place to place), they were not above surreptitiously lightening their loads by, among other things, boring small holes into the casks of wine that they carried.

Incoming colonial powers and indigenous authorities often attempted to use corvée labor to develop their expanding states within a capitalist framework, and as Brown notes, their very success seems to have led, often directly, to the collapse of the system itself. In Egypt forced labor had been used to expand the nation's irrigation system during the agricultural slack period. This eventually resulted in the perennial commercial cropping of the Nile Delta and the concomitant call for a permanent labor supply. This demand was more efficiently met by paid, rather than forced, labor.

The change from forced labor to wage work was clearly supported by the British authorities. Lord Cromer, British consul-general in Egypt from 1883 to 1907 stated that he was prepared to accept that compulsory labor would, under certain circumstances, be required for public works, but when it was "employed for private profit, (it was) wholly unjustifiable and (was) synonymous with slavery." In other parts of the colonial world, peasant avoidance was so successful that it brought the more commercial aspects of the system to an end. For example, as a result of the massive Malay peasant migration, described by scholar James C. Scott, the Wan Mat Saman Canal project begun in 1885 had to be dug using paid Chinese labor. And the inability of untrained Siamese corvée armies to resist French-led forces at the end of the nineteenth century essentially marked the end of the use of this system for national defense.

A more intricate picture of the use of corvée labor can be drawn from historian Bruno Lasker's description of its use by the Dutch in the Dutch East Indies. Here corvée labor was officially divided into three separate categories: *panjendiensten*, which was occasional labor owed to native officials and which became a substitute for the salaries of indigenous local officials, thus saving the state money; *heerendiensten*, which was compulsory labor on public works; and *desadiensten*, which was compulsory labor on local village projects. Aside from reducing expenditure on the administrative infrastructure, the system promoted stability by appearing to restore control of lands to indigenous local leaders. However, by creating this vested local interest in the maintenance of the system, the Dutch also made reform difficult. When *heerendiensten* was abolished in 1893 by the central Dutch East Indies authorities, many local officials simply continued to employ existing labor practices by claiming that the corvée duties came under the definition of *desadiensten*, which remained in place for at least another ten years. And, in the outer islands especially, it remained possible to meet tax demands with labor rather than cash until at least 1941.

One other set of special circumstances, war, has often led to the major use of corvée labor. Twentieth-century examples include the French use of Indochinese labor in Europe during World War I, the Japanese indigenous labor corps of World War II in Southeast Asia, and the Vietnamese use of Cambodians to lay mines along the Thai-Cambodian border following their defeat of the Pol Pot regime.

During the twentieth century, international opposition to forced labor grew, and in 1947 France, the last major colonial power to take this step, abolished corvée except under special circumstances, which included "serving a sentence under common law." It is here, within penal systems perhaps more than anywhere else, that the system still persists in the late twentieth century. However, it does surface occasionally in its rather more traditional form. Anthropologist Holger Bernt Hansen notes that as recently as July 1992 the residents of the Luwero Triangle in Uganda complained that "whenever a government official is to visit their area they are subjected to forced labor. They are forced to abandon their work to clear public roads." Newspaper reports on conditions in Burma (Myanmar) seem to indicate quite clearly that the regime in power in 1995 used forced labor under abysmal conditions to carry supplies for its troops as well as on the construction of national projects such as a petrol pipeline to Thai refineries and the building of roads.

See also SOUTHEAST ASIA; THAILAND.

BIBLIOGRAPHY

BROWN, NATHAN J. "Who Abolished Corvée Labor in Egypt and Why?" *Past and Present* 144 (1994): 116–137.

DAVIES, PAUL, and NIC DUNLOP. *War of Mines: Cambodia, Landmines and the Impoverishment of a Nation.* 1994.

FEENY, DAVID. "The Demise of Corvée and Slavery in Thailand, 1782–1913." In *Breaking the Chains: Slavery, Bondage, and Emancipation in Modern Africa and Asia,* edited by Martin A. Klein, 1993.

HANSEN, HOLGER BERNT. "Forced Labor in a Missionary Context: A Study of Kasanvu in Early Twentieth-Century Uganda." In *The Wages of Slavery: From Chattel Slavery to Wage Labor in Africa, the Caribbean, and England,* edited by Michael Twaddle. 1993.

HICKEY, CANNON. *Sons of the Mountains.* 1982.

INTERNATIONAL LABOR CONFERENCE. *Forced Labor: Report and Questionnaire.* 1929.

KLEIN, MARTIN A. "Introduction: Modern European Expansion and Traditional Servitude in Africa and Asia." In *Breaking the Chains: Slavery, Bondage, and Emancipation in Modern Africa and Asia,* edited by Martin A. Klein. 1993.

LASKER, BRUNO. *Human Bondage in Southeast Asia.* 1950.

MURRAY, MARTIN J. *The Development of Capitalism in Indochina, 1870–1940.* 1980.

PASUK PHONGPAICHIT and CHRIS BAKER. *Thailand Economy and Politics.* 1995.

SCOTT, JAMES C. *Weapons of the Weak: Everyday Forms of Peasant Resistance.* 1985.

David Booth

Forced Labor

In everyday use the phrase *forced labor* is the most general term—along with *involuntary servitude*—used to encompass the widest set of sociohistorical and legal categories: slavery, traditional labor duties (for example, feudal corvée), compulsory military service, indentured servitude and articled apprenticeship, penal servitude, mandatory labor by prisoners of war, compulsory nonmilitary service, alternative national service, peonage, and slave labor, as well as contract labor under certain conditions.

As a term of art in the social sciences today, however, "forced labor" has become virtually synonymous with "slave labor," where the ownership of an individual by private citizens is not a feature, but where a group or class of persons (usually an extremely large number) are forced to perform involuntary labor. Such labor is often, but not always, compelled by and done for the state, and the conditions of such labor are usually, but not always, appalling.

Again, the social sciences have tended to exclude from the definition of "forced labor" those categories of involuntary servitude that admit of more precise definition. Chattel slavery, indentured servitude and apprenticeship, compulsory military service and alternative nonmilitary service, peonage, traditional labor duties, and penal servitude are usually not included within the scope of forced labor. It is worth noting, however, that their exclusion cannot be regarded as absolute. Traditional labor duties such as the feudal corvée, by which arrangement serfs—and in some parts of Europe, otherwise-free peasants—were compelled in certain seasons of the year to work on repairs of the roads, gained some wide degree of societal acceptance for long periods of time in the Middle Ages and beyond. The corvée in France was not completely abolished until the French Revolution, but there is evidence that peasant acceptance of the institution had begun to wane a considerable time before its actual abolition.

In like manner, we may assume that in the obscure centuries from late antiquity to the High Middle Ages, many institutions like the corvée, which became over time generally accepted features of feudalism, began as forced labor imposed by threat upon a recalcitrant rural population by the conquering tribes. The same might be said of the labor on the great projects of the state in the "hydrological empires" that Karl Wittfogel used as his models for "oriental despotism." In the ancient empires of Egypt, China, India, and Mesopotamia, peasants were required to labor on the canals, levees, and other hydrological projects that provided water for agriculture.

As with other feudal institutions, one finds evidence of later acceptance of such arrangements by the peasantry in general, but it is difficult not to imagine that these traditional institutions too began as slave labor imposed by a unifying conqueror from within or an invading conqueror from without.

While penal servitude is not generally included in the category of forced labor, perhaps the infamous chain gangs of the southern United States should be considered since they did not always represent penal servitude in the strictest sense. In theory, persons who had committed crimes and had been sentenced were forced to labor on highways or other construction projects or on public farms while in leg irons and often under atrocious conditions. Investigations of chain gangs revealed corruption and brutalities, including deliberate murders, beatings, and malnutrition. When labor was needed, furthermore, there is evidence that in many counties police authorities and judges conspired to supply the demand by arresting and convicting Negroes and poor whites on trumped-up charges.

The twentieth century has witnessed forced labor on a massive scale, especially with the rise of totalitarian powers and with the exigencies of the Second World War. Nazi Germany, Stalin's Russia, and imperial Japan employed forced labor by millions of political prisoners, prisoners of war, and impressed conquered people.

In Nazi Germany during the Second World War, 2 million prisoners of war from Eastern Europe—mostly Russians—were utilized as slave labor by the regime. By 1944 over 7.5 million civilians from occupied nations were transported to Germany and forced to toil under appalling conditions.

In the Soviet Union between 1923 and 1954, massive numbers of persons were rounded up by the Soviet secret police for incarceration and forced labor in the innumerable camps that dotted the Russian landscape (especially in Siberia—the so-called Gulag Archipelago). Prisoners of war were included in the population of the gulag, but the vast majority were persons charged with political or ideological crimes, especially those imprisoned during Stalin's great purges of the 1930s. Inadequate clothing in sub-zero conditions and inadequate rations combined with grueling toil and barbarous mistreatment led to the deaths of millions. The slave labor camps mined rare minerals (including gold), cut and processed timber, and caught and prepared fish, among other things, and many economists calculate that the system of forced labor in Soviet society contributed an enormous amount to overall economic production.

In Soviet Russia, with the death of Joseph Stalin in 1954, the state ceased to condemn people to the gulag solely to instill terror in the masses or in order to achieve goals through the employment of slave labor. Nonetheless, the gulag continued on a reduced scale, supplied with slave labor not only by the condemnation of common criminals but also by imprisoning religious practitioners, those guilty of "economic crimes," and political dissidents. With the collapse of the Soviet Union and with Russia's abandonment of communism, conditions have improved in the camps, and with the legalization of religious activity and the embrace of capitalism and democracy, noncriminal incarcerations have massively declined. The camps were still operating in the late twentieth century, however.

In other communist regimes, especially Cuba, China, and Vietnam, slave labor was regularly employed and on a fairly large scale. In Vietnam and China, with their relative liberalization, the size of slave-labor-camp populations has declined, but such institutions still perform important economic functions for the state, and since these regimes' moves toward capitalism have not been coupled with democratization, political dissidents still face imprisonment. In Cambodia, with the fall of communism, slave labor has ceased, but under Pol Pot's regime in the 1970s, when one to two million people were killed, virtually the entire population was forced into slave labor camps in a radical utopian attempt to instantaneously de-urbanize and communize society.

Imperial Japan, under the strains of the war in the Pacific, utilized allied prisoners of war and impressed civilians from conquered nations to build fortifications and infrastructures in the expanded Japanese empire.

The defendants during a session of the International Military War Crimes Tribunal in Tokyo. [Hulton-Deutsch Collection/Corbis]

Tens of thousands of such slave laborers died constructing the infamous Bangkok-to-Rangoon railroad. Thousands of women, Korean, Chinese, and others, were forcibly dragooned by the Japanese army to serve as comfort women—slave prostitutes who were raped by dozens or even hundreds of soldiers daily.

The employment of slave labor and the mistreatment of slave laborers figured in the indictments of the Nazi leaders at Nuremburg and of Japanese leaders before the International Military War Crimes Tribunal in Tokyo, as well as in numerous trials of lesser Axis functionaries subsequently pursued by the Allies.

The International Labor Organization of the United Nations adopted a resolution in 1957 condemning all uses of forced labor throughout the world, but the practice has not completely disappeared. With the collapse of much of the communist world, forced labor by states is now greatly reduced, but some forced labor in the private sector persists.

In the carpet industry of India, for example, young children are often sold into temporary slavery, which tends to end when they reach early adulthood, and in the remaining communist regimes some forced labor endures.

Historically, imperialism has sometimes utilized forced labor. Throughout the Spanish involvement in the New World, for example, Amerindians were forced to labor for the crown or for individual colonists. When Christopher Columbus became governor of the island of Hispaniola, one of his first acts was to require that, under severe penalty, each adult native bring in a specified quantity of gold. The silver mining operations at Potosi on the South American mainland sent enormous quantities of the precious metal to the mother country, mined by the forced labor of the aboriginal population.

Imperial powers continued to use conscript labor for public works projects of a sufficient magnitude in the nineteenth and twentieth centuries. In Egypt and India especially such labor was often used by British colonial authorities, who often chose to employ already existing local laws and practices, rather than to enact conscription statutes within the body of English law.

See also CHATTEL SLAVERY; COMFORT WOMEN IN WORLD WAR II; MILITARY SLAVES; PEONAGE.

BIBLIOGRAPHY

CONOT, ROBERT E. *Justice at Nuremberg.* 1983.
CONQUEST, ROBERT. *The Great Terror: Stalin's Purges of the Thirties.* 1968.
TOLSTOY, NIKOLAI. *Stalin's Secret War.* 1981.
TUSA, ANN, and JOHN TUSA. *The Nuremberg Trial.* 1986.
WITTFOGEL, KARL A. *Oriental Despotism: A Comparative Study of Total Power.* 1957.

Patrick M. O'Neil

Indentured Labor (Seventeenth-Century)

Thousands of Europeans were integrated into the colonial system as indentured servants. Contracting as workers, such persons came out from Europe with the hope of achieving in colonial society those socioeconomic benefits denied them at home. They came mainly to enjoy a wider range of personal freedoms and to raise their social status by accumulating wealth. To these ends, most were prepared to offer their labor to unknown employers in wholly unfamiliar territory. As voluntary migrants, they were motivated not by any collective patriotic or nationalist cause but by unmitigated self-interest—the dominant ideological force in capitalist socioeconomic culture.

Indentured servitude emerged as the principal mode by which colonies recruited laborers who were financially unable to sponsor their transatlantic migration. There were four main ways in which the contractual relationship was established. First, employers or their agents recruited individuals and made the legal arrangements necessary for their transportation to the colony as servants. Second, merchants or their agents recruited laborers, contracted them as indentured servants, and on arrival in the colonies auctioned the indentures to colonists. This was by far the most common method. Third, political prisoners, convicts, and others were transported by the state for civil or criminal offenses, and the relevant government body sold individuals as indentured servants to specified merchants, who resold the indentures to colonists. Fourth, individuals paid for their own passage and indentured themselves on arrival in the colonies. This method ensured shorter lengths of service and allowed the servant greater control over contractual conditions.

Despite the existence of the fourth alternative, the terms of most indenture contracts were the result of economic calculations made by merchants and colonial employers. Merchants wanted to profit by marketing servants; employers sought to ensure that their marginal revenue exceeded marginal cost. During the period up to the American Revolution, employers calculated that they could recover their investment in servant labor within three years of servitude.

The earliest system of commodity production in the colonies was built on the labor of these indentured servants. Consequently, white servitude is of cardinal importance in understanding the development of colonial society and economy. To clear forested land and initiate production, colonists had to look outward for a labor supply. Unlike the Spanish in the New World, the French, Dutch, and English first looked to their homeland. The African slave trade was not fully established in the early seventeenth century, and it was virtually monopolized by the Iberians. The price of African slaves was prohibitively high, and northern Europeans were neither familiar with nor committed to black slavery as a basic institution. These factors contributed to dependence upon home labor.

It was a common practice in seventeenth-century Europe for farmers to hire servants by the year for agricultural and artisan work. The logical next step, therefore, was to demand labor from Europe under temporary indenture, not for a year but for between three and ten years. Employers would pay passages and feed, clothe, and shelter servants in return for their labor. At the end of the indenture, in a practice consistent with the labor culture of Europe, the servant would receive a "freedom due" of money or a piece of land.

Servants, then, paved the way for the emergence of the revolutionizing plantation economy and the large-scale absorption of African slaves. By the 1660s, slaves had become indispensable to continued economic growth. This change ushered in the rapid decline of indentured servitude as an important economic institution. Servants subsequently shared their material deprivation, and its corresponding sociopolitical oppression, with slaves. Officially sanctioned antiblack racist ideologies, which degraded all manual labor by linking it directly with slavery, rapidly pervaded colonial society, rendering servants anomalous. The final marginalization of indentured servitude therefore must explained in terms of developments in both labor markets, and in relation to socioideological trends.

Colonial indentured servitude represented a significant departure from the traditional European systems of apprenticeship and domestic servitude, while retaining their fundamental conceptual and structural features. The primary colonial adaptations were sufficiently radical, in the case of the Caribbean, to allow us to conceive of indentured servitude there as a new and different institution. The traditional values and ideologies of paternalistic master-servant relations were not retained. Planters did not think of their servants, socially or emotionally, as integral parts of the family or household, but instead viewed them as an alienated commodity which could be recruited and exploited best within the legal framework of traditional servitude.

Having abandoned the moral responsibility of precapitalist ideology, masters enforced an often violent social domination of servants by the manipulation of oppressive legal codes that mirrored structurally antagonistic relations. These legal provisions reflected an overtly economic concept of labor, a radical departure from the "moral economy." Indentured servitude, in spite of the fact that it was entered into voluntarily by most servants, was maintained by the systematic application of legally sanctioned force and violence. Its social content, as reflected in plantation life, differed drastically from what laborers had anticipated when they signed contracts in their hometowns and villages. They found themselves powerless as individuals, without honor or respect, and driven into commodity production not by any inner sense of moral duty but by the outer stimulus of the whip. They possessed one right—to complain to legal authorities about breaches of contract, particularly excessive violent abuse. But this right, which by custom was also available to black slaves in some societies, had little or no mitigating effect on their overall treatment.

White indentured servitude became a training ground where planters obtained the skills and attitudes necessary for a rapid and unproblematic transition to large-scale black slavery. At the point of transition, some features of chattel slavery were already established, particularly an advanced market view of labor. The sensitivity of early planters to market forces was the basis of these developments. The shift from white to black labor was primarily a response to market forces, but some of the important ideologies and social relations necessary for slavery had already been established within indentured servitude. These were further developed as it became necessary to intensify the exploitation of resources during the early years of sugar production in the Caribbean.

An indenture did not make the servant a slave. At the end of the time stated in the contract, the servant became free. In addition, the offspring of servants were born free, and this in itself distinguished servitude from slavery. The distinguishing mark of slavery was not the loss of liberty, political or civil, but the perpetuity and the almost absolute character of that loss, whether voluntary or involuntary. A large number of servants, however—especially transported political prisoners, convicts, adjudged rogues, beggars, and other defenseless poor people—were used by planters as "life servers"—a commutation of a death sentence or life imprisonment. They were stripped of any honor within society and were violently subordinated. An attempt was also made to impose a measure of perpetuity within servitude by means of bonding to masters or vestries the illegitimate offspring of servants until they reached the age of twenty-one, as compensation for the cost of their upbringing. Ultimately, however, traditional ideological constraints of the imported European labor culture kept planters from deriving from servitude the full benefits offered by chattel slavery.

Many servants, nonetheless, experienced their plantation servitude as a form of enslavement, and they responded much as black slaves did. They ran away, both within and outside of the colonies, for temporary respite from labor as well as to sever their relations with their employers permanently. Planters saw servants, particularly the Irish, as a dangerous political element and took measures to police their activities. What planters feared most, given the servants' persistent rebelliousness, was a full-fledged alliance of servants and slaves in a rebellion. They guarded against this possibility by disarming servants, searching the houses of servants and slaves at frequent intervals, and preventing their easy association. Servants, then, not only posed a labor problem but fomented crises in the daily management of estates. As a result, master-servant relations were characterized generally by mutual distrust, tension, and sporadic violent encounters.

For most servants, especially those without a special skill, the transition from servitude to freedom cannot have been a meaningful emancipation. For most, unemployment and seasonal employment, along with diminishing levels of material welfare, were the common results. Skilled servants managed to maintain part of their privileged status in spite of the corrosive effects of slavery, but even for this minority, reduced socioeconomic expectations were the norm over the century. Few managed to accumulate capital sufficient to purchase land or other forms of property, and those who occupied low-level offices within government were exceptional.

A result of diminishing expectations and realizations was that fewer laborers were registered in European ports for the Americas. During the period between 1715 and the American Revolution, Jamaica was by far the favored West Indian colony for the British. A register of 3,257 servants who departed from London between 1720 and 1732 shows this: Jamaica, 1,146; Maryland, 918; Virginia, 223; Antigua, 165; Pennsylvania, 423, Barbados, 31. Only Saint Lucia and Nevis in the West Indies trailed behind Barbados, with 24 and 22 respectively.

The social experience of servants during the rise and demise of the institution was quite unlike the success, glory, and excitement recorded for property holders. Former servants were landless, and their share of the accumulated colonial wealth, as measured by any criterion, was minimal; also, their participation in the planter-dominated sociopolitical democracy was marginal. Their social existence and experiences, in stark contrast to their flamboyant masters' extravagant display of wealth and power, may be summed up best by the term *alienation*.

See also CARIBBEAN REGION; ECONOMICS OF SLAVERY; PLANTATIONS.

BIBLIOGRAPHY

BECKLES, HILARY. "The Colours of Property: Brown, White and Black Chattels and Their Responses on the Caribbean Frontier." In *Slavery and Abolition*, Vol. 15, No. 2. 1994.

———. "Plantation Production and 'White Proto-Slavery': White Indentured Servants and the Colonisation of the English West Indies, 1624–1645." *The Americas* 41 (1985).

———. "English Parliament Debates 'White Slavery' in Barbados, 1659." *Journal of the Barbados Museum and Historical Society* 36 (1982).

———. "'A Riotous and Unruly Lot': Irish Indentured Servants and Freemen in the English West Indies, 1644–1713." *William and Mary Quarterly* 47 (1990).

———. *White Servitude and Black Slavery in Barbados 1627–1715*. 1989.

BECKLES, HILARY, and ANDREW DOWNES. "The Economics of Transition to the Black Labor System in Barbados, 1639–1680." *Journal of Interdisciplinary History* 18, no. 2 (1987).

BERLEANT-SCHILLER, RIVA. "Free Labor and the Economy in Seventeenth Century Monsterrar." *William and Mary Quarterly* 46 (1989).

DUNN, RICHARD. *Sugar and Slavery: The Rise of the Planter-Class in the English West Indies, 1624–1713*. 1972.

GALENSON, DAVID. "The Market Evaluation of Human Capital: The Case of Indentured Servitude." *Journal of Political Economy* 89 (1981).

———. *White Servitude in Colonial America: An Economic Analysis*. 1981.

PUCKREIN, GARY A. *Little England: Plantation Society and Anglo-Barbadian Politics, 1627–1700*. 1984.

SMITH, ABBOT. *Colonists in Bondage: White Servitude and Convict Labor in America, 1607–1776*. 1947.

———. "The Transportation of Convicts to the American Colonies in the Seventeenth Century." *American Historical Review* 39 (1933–1934).

Hilary McD. Beckles

Indentured Labor (1834–1960)

Indentured (or contract) labor is generally associated with the great migrations from the seventeenth century to the beginning of the nineteenth century, when the "poor Protestants of Europe" were mobilized to provide the workforce necessary for opening up the Americas. Less well-known is the second wave of indenture, which was rather different from its predecessor. When slavery and indenture coexisted, there was a racial divide: slavery was for blacks and indenture for whites. With the gradual dismantling of chattel slavery, white workers moved progressively into freer forms of labor and the institution of indenture became a device to mobilize a nonwhite labor force in tropical and subtropical areas. The second wave of indenture, in other words, was the logical successor to slavery but no less a racial category than before: white servitude was transformed into brown, black, and yellow servitude. The second wave of indenture began in 1834, replacing the freed slaves on sugar plantations in the British Caribbean. Spreading to many other parts of the globe, the indenture system involved well in excess of 2 million workers and lasted in some places until the 1950s.

The second wave of indentured labor involved diverse areas of recruitment and scattered places of employment, all of which were organized differently. Tropical plantations and mining ventures in the New World faced a chronic labor shortage with the progressive abolition of slavery. Although slavery had involved higher initial costs, planters had preferred it to indenture. Slaves were, they felt, more productive; and slaves—and their offspring—were held permanently. Indentured laborers, on the other hand, were only on contract and had to be freed at the end of their terms and replaced by new workers. At the same time indenture was preferable to relying on free labor, despite high recruiting costs: at least the planter had the worker for a lengthy, if definite, period, thus stabilizing the workforce, just as the fixed wage stabilized costs. Finally, the penal clauses in the contract allowed for much greater control than could be exercised over free laborers. Removed from the support systems of their own communities and vulnerable in other ways, indentured laborers stayed and obeyed in ways that free laborers would not have tolerated (as the Norwegians in Hawaii demonstrated).

The migration of indentured labor was both intercontinental and intraregional. By far the largest single source was the Indian subcontinent, which provided more than 1.3 million workers to places as far apart as the Caribbean, Fiji, Mauritius, East Africa, and Natal. China provided 386,000 and Japan another 85,000. Non-Asian sources include Africa and the Pacific islands. The major destination was the British Caribbean, which received almost 530,000 indentured workers. Mauritius was the single largest recipient, taking some 450,000 workers, overwhelmingly East Indian. As colonial empires developed, the migration of indentured labor increasingly became confined within these empires. The intraregional streams of migration were predominantly within Asia and the Pacific islands (including Queensland); the former predominantly involved Chinese and Indians (to Burma, Ceylon, and Malaya), and the latter Melanesians. Some 56,000 Europeans enlisted—mostly Portuguese from the poverty-stricken Azores and Madeiras, who went to the Caribbean and Hawaii. Their motivation was overwhelming to escape economic deprivation and to a lesser extent, political persecution. One simply took one's chances.

Conditions of service varied widely. Peru and parts of the Caribbean had a grim reputation, whereas Queensland, at least after the mid-1880s, enacted and enforced a degree of protective legislation. Whatever the variations, indentured servitude was nevertheless a form of unfree labor: indentured workers had no say over the terms and conditions of their contracts and no control over the choice of employer; they typically endured harsh material conditions; they were subject to corporal punishment; and they had diminished civil rights. Indentured workers also typically suffered high mortality rates, largely through being transported to different epidemiological environments where they lacked immunity against a range of respiratory and gastrointestinal infections. Indeed, there is some correlation between disease and labor costs, as the case of Fiji demonstrates. Employers initially preferred imported Pacific islanders, who were cheaper to transport and whose wages were lower. But eventually the East Indians were recognized as the cheapest option. Not only did East Indians pay for their food from their wages (whereas islanders were provided with rations) but the recruiting costs were spread over five years (as against three years) and, furthermore, East Indians suffered a much lower mortality rate.

Estimating the cost of the trade in indentured laborers is difficult because of variations over time, even within a given labor flow. What needs to be stressed is that recruiting and transport represented a sizable proportion of all-inclusive labor costs. In Queensland in 1901, for example, the cost of employing a single indentured individual was estimated at just over 96 pounds sterling over his or her three-year term. In round figures transport and repatriation cost £26, wages £24, food and lodging £32, and other costs £14.

As a form of labor relations, indentured servitude had contradictions. Superficially, the provisions of indenture seemed to serve employers admirably. The fixed term of service kept the laborers at the workplace. The stipulated wage, together with a prohibition against forming trade unions, helped stabilize costs, discouraged strikes, and ruled out collective bargaining. In addition, employers could usually rely on state support because the local legislatures were dominated by planters and because colonial administrations depended on plantations and other tropical enterprises for the bulk of state revenues. But there was a catch. Given a lack of job satisfaction and other incentives, and without the alternative of being able to dismiss unsatisfactory workers, planters took the line of least resistance and fell back on coercive strategies. This in turn fueled workers' resentment, which required yet more coercion to contain.

The institution of indenture gradually died out in the twentieth century, although in some places (such as Papua New Guinea) there was more indentured servitude in the twentieth century than the nineteenth. When it was eventually laid to rest; basically in the 1950s, it had long been an anachronism, frowned upon by the international community. Its legacy lies in multicultural societies in the Caribbean, Africa, and the Pacific islands, where the descendants of indentured laborers form segments of so-called pluralistic societies. In some places they have done well—for example, the Japanese in Hawaii dominate the state legislature, and Trinidad has had its first East Indian prime minister. But mostly the descendants of the immigrant laborers are discriminated against politically and economically.

Although the institution of indenture is legally a thing of the past, labor systems reminiscent of indenture persist in one way or another in various parts of the world: slavery or slavelike conditions continue in Brazil; child labor is still common in India and Pakistan; and until recently aboriginal workers on outback cattle stations (i.e., ranches) in Australia were provided with "tucker" (food) instead of wages. Such arrangements, widespread as they are, share the coercive and highly controlled features of indentured servitude in colonial regions.

See also CARIBBEAN REGION; HAWAII; HEADRIGHT SYSTEM.

BIBLIOGRAPHY

EMMER, P. C., ed. *Colonialism and Migration: Indentured Labor before and after Slavery.* 1986.
MOORE, CLIVE, JACQUELINE LECKIE, and DOUG MUNRO, eds. *Labour in the South Pacific.* 1990.
NORTHRUP, DAVID. *Indentured Labor in the Age of Imperialism, 1834–1922.* 1995.
SAUNDERS, KAY, ed. *Indentured Labour in the British Empire, 1834–1920.* 1984.

Doug Munro

Penal Servitude

Penal servitude as a system of punishment for crime dates from the late Middle Ages. In the ancient world, of course, criminals were sometimes sold into slavery, but it was with the rise of slave-rowed galleys that a consistent system of penal servitude evolved.

In penal servitude, confinement or exile is combined with forced labor. In the late eighteenth century, Britain, France, and Russia began creating penal colonies where persons convicted of serious crimes would be exiled and put to hard labor. In czarist Russia, labor camps were established in Siberia, and over 200,000 prisoners worked in these camps. Under the Soviet regime that followed the Romanovs, millions labored in these camps under appalling conditions with extremely high mortality rates—especially under Stalin from the 1930s to the early 1950s.

In the British empire, with the loss of the American colonies, Australia became the locus for numerous

A librere, *one of the free men left to live out their lives in Guiana after the French penal colony was dissolved.* [Hulton-Deutsch Collection/Corbis]

penal colonies, the last of which were abolished only in the late 1850s. More than 160,000 convicts were transported. The French Empire established penal colonies in Guiana (Devil's Island) for convicts from metropolitan France and from the other colonies. This system was officially abolished in 1938, but the coming of World War II delayed its actual liquidation.

In the United States, under the so-called "Auburn system," which originated at Auburn Penitentiary in upstate New York, solitary confinement was combined with industrial labor. The purpose of this system was threefold: punishment, rehabilitation, and cost-cutting.

In the postbellum South, the infusion into the penal system of large numbers of blacks, who were once dealt with by the discipline of the plantations, strained the inadequate prisons and helped to bring about the "convict lease system." Under this system, industrialists, planters, and contractors bid for the labor of convicts. Conditions of life under the convict lease system were often horrendous. Malnutrition, overwork, and brutality were common.

Perhaps the best known aspect of this system was the chain gang, in which convicts marched to work chained to one another and carried on their work shackled, usually in leg-irons, overseen by armed men, often prison trustees. The image of the chain gang became associated with slavery, for the majority of convicts were black, and people saw their shackles and brutal conditions as corresponding to the worst aspects of chattel slavery in the old South.

When involuntary servitude was forbidden by the ratification of the Thirteenth Amendment in 1865, a specific exception was made for servitude imposed in punishment for a crime for which the criminal had been convicted through the due process of the law. Nonetheless, the practices that arose under the convict lease programs across the South constituted a violation of the spirit, if not the letter, of the Thirteenth Amendment, especially in those southern counties where prosecutions seemed to rise and fall with the demand for convict labor.

As a result of opposition from free labor and the reforming spirit, which triumphed for a time under Progressivism, the convict leasing system was abolished in many states, for example, Tennessee (1893–1897), South Carolina (1895), and Louisiana (1898–1901). North Carolina, however, did not abolish the system until the 1930s.

See also CHATTEL SLAVERY; GULAG.

BIBLIOGRAPHY

BOURDET-PLEVILLE, MICHEL. *Justice in Chains: From the Galleys to Devil's Island.* Translated by Athon Rippon. 1960.

CARLETON, M. T. *Politics and Punishment.* 1971.

CARTER, D. T. *Convict Lease.* 1964.

ROBSON, LLOYD L. *The Convict Settlers of Australia: An Enquiry into the Origins and Character of the Convicts Transported to New South Wales and Van Diemen's Land, 1787–1852.* 1965.

Patrick M. O'Neil

Las Casas, Bartolomé de   [1474–1566]

Spanish Dominican friar; chonicler of slavery in Spanish America.

After becoming a priest in Spain, Bartolomé de Las Casas left for the New World, landing in Santo Domingo in 1502. He then received an *encomienda*, which entitled him to collect the royal tribute from an allotment of Indians. As an *encomendero*, or holder of an *encomienda*, Las Casas also could compel these Indians to labor in his behalf. Although laws set limits on this labor, few people agreed on their interpretation. Furthermore, the crown possessed weak enforcement powers in the New World and needed to placate *encomenderos* in order to encourage colonization. These factors led to widespread abuses against Indians. Witnessing firsthand the decimation of Indian populations in Santo Domingo and Cuba, Las Casas renounced his *encomienda* in 1514 and dedicated the rest of his life to the protection of Indians. In late

1519 he won royal approval for the peaceful settlement of the Tierra Firma coast at Cumaná in present-day Venezuela. At Cumaná, however, Las Casas was unable to curtail Spanish slavers, who continued to capture Indians to ship to Santo Domingo. Forced to seek help from the viceroy in Santo Domingo, he departed from Cumaná in late 1521, thereby escaping harm when Indians attacked and destroyed the mission in 1522. The failure of the Tierra Firma mission did not diminish Las Casas's zeal. After joining the Dominican order in 1524, he wrote the first versions of *History of the Indies* and *The Apologetic History of the Indies*, which, along with his later work, *Short Account of the Destruction of the Indies*, described the region and its people while publicizing Spanish abuses and atrocities committed against Indians. He also influenced Pope Paul III's *Bulla Sublimis Deus* (1537), which, by asserting the rationality of Indians and their eligibility to become Christians, undercut legal and moral arguments favoring their enslavement and exploitation. In 1540 he returned to Span where he persuaded the crown and imperial officials to enact laws protecting Indians. The resulting New Laws, decreed in 1542, addressed Las Casas's concerns by expressly forbidding coerced Indian labor in behalf of *encomenderos*.

Bartolomé de Las Casas. [Library of Congress/Corbis]

However, strong resistance from Spaniards in the Americas plus the crown's own desire to mine precious ores rendered the New Laws much less effective than Las Casas had demanded. Instead, the crown eventually replaced the *encomienda* with the *repartimiento*, a system of labor allotment in which royal authorities exercised much greater control. While in Spain, Las Casas also received crown approval to convert Indians as Bishop of Chiapas. In Chiapas, however, he faced intense hostility from Spaniards who used Indian labor, thus forcing him to leave the region prematurely. In 1547 he returned to Spain and, in 1550, delivered his important polemic against the Spanish theologian and historian Juan Ginés de Sepúlveda, who advocated the Aristotelian doctrine of "slaves by nature." Although at one time Las Casas had advocated substituting African slaves for coerced Indian labor, he had renounced that concept. Las Casas spent his remaining years organizing missions, defending the equality of Indians, and writing.

See also AMERINDIAN SOCIETIES; ARISTOTLE.

BIBLIOGRAPHY

FRIEDE, JUAN, and BENJAMIN KEEN, eds. *Bartolomé de Las Casas in History: Toward an Understanding of the Man and His Work.* 1971.
HANKE, LEWIS. *Aristotle and the Amerian Indians: A Study in Race Prejudice in the Modern World.* 1959.

John J. Crocitti

Latter-day Saints, Church of Jesus Christ of

From its origin in the antebellum nineteenth-century United States of America, the Church of Jesus Christ of Latter-day Saints (commonly nicknamed Mormons; referred to here as L.D.S. or Saints) has opposed slavery. Its history, however, has been closely tied to, and very much misunderstood concerning, slavery.

The L.D.S. church came into being as a restoration of original, or "primitive," biblical Christianity, rather than as yet another reformation of existing denominations. The church was organized in upstate New York in 1830. Most early converts were originally from New England and had little sympathy for slavery. The *Book of Mormon* and other L.D.S. scriptural texts condemned slavery in principle and practice and warned of the impending consequences of its continuation.

Had the L.D.S. church remained a small northern institution, it might have escaped later conflicts and persecutions, but from its inception active proselytizing efforts produced a relatively rapid expansion of membership. Also, revelations to its first prophet, Joseph Smith, guided the church into frequently suc-

cessful but politically unpopular cooperative economic practices and a migration to the city of Independence in Jackson County, Missouri, beginning in 1831. Despite the practice of slavery in Missouri, this area and other areas in the state were understood by the Saints to be central to long-term preparations for the eventual millennial return of Jesus Christ to the earth. The Saints were never radical abolitionists. Perhaps because they had themselves been repeatedly robbed of their properties and assaulted by mobs, they did not advocate violence or government expropriation without compensation. Nevertheless, this move into Missouri put the church onto a collision course with some of American slavery's most radical proponents.

Immigration fed by continuing conversions to the church fueled their proslavery neighbors' suspicions of the expanding L.D.S. population in western Missouri. Apart from predictable tensions between slaveholders and antislavery Northerners, the rapid expansion of the Saints' population was seen as a threat. The comparative efficiency of capital accumulation for land acquisition, which their cooperative economic system made possible, meant that a considerable amount of land was purchased quickly. Consequently, the L.D.S. community also had substantial potential to become a Free-Soil voting block. These questions and the religious differences that produced persecutions elsewhere were sufficient to motivate mob reactions in and of themselves, but the character of L.D.S. conversions raised another issue.

It has long been understood that an editorial which appeared in the first L.D.S. newspaper published in Missouri, *The Evening and Morning Star*, was the catalyst that led to the Saints' expulsion from the Missouri frontier. The editorial, titled "Free People of Color," begins with this admonition:

> To prevent any misunderstanding among the [L.D.S.] churches abroad, respecting Free people of color, who may think of coming to the western boundaries of Missouri, *as members of the church*, we quote the following clauses from the laws of Missouri. [Italics added.]

There followed a recitation of the laws restricting the rights of free blacks. These Missouri laws severely threatened nonslave black populations within the state. The laws were similar to limits that were developed in all the slave states of the United States after the Nat Turner rebellion (August 1831) and were designed to prevent further slave revolts.

This editorial became the pretext for personal violence, the destruction of their press, and the expulsion of the Saints from Jackson County (October–November 1833). The L.D.S. took their expulsion to

Joseph Smith. [Corbis-Bettmann]

be a result of their own failures and the proslavery mob's misreading of the editorial, somehow construing it to be an encouragement for free blacks to move into the state. It is virtually impossible, however, for it to have been so read. A much more fundamental conflict was involved. It is clear from the text that the church elsewhere was quite accepting of converts with African ancestry—or in other words it was, and intended to remain, an integrated church. This was the really unacceptable fact that revealed the irreconcilable gap between the Saints and the proslavery Missouri mobs, who would have understood this implication of the text quite accurately.

Joseph Smith's "Revelation and Prophecy on [the Civil and subsequent] War" (25 December 1832) had left no room for optimism on the question of slavery among the Saints. Continuing proslavery persecutions drove the Saints out of northern Missouri in the winter of 1838–1839. On 27 October 1838 Missouri Governor Boggs proclaimed to the militia, "The Mormons must be treated as enemies, and must be extermi-

nated or driven from the state, if necessary for the public peace."

The Saints escaped to Nauvoo, Illinois, and built a new city in this antislave state. Problems between the L.D.S. and Missourians continued. Then, in May of 1844, a month before Joseph Smith was martyred, he became a candidate for president of the United States in order to bring a platform of issues on religious liberty and other questions into the national dialogue. His platform was published in the L.D.S. newspaper *Times and Season* on 15 May 1844. Concerning slavery, Smith stated,

> Petition also, ye goodly inhabitants of the slave states, your legislators to abolish slavery by the year 1850, or now, and save the abolitionist from reproach and ruin, infamy and shame. Pray Congress to pay every man a reasonable price for his slaves out of the surplus revenue arising from the sale of public lands [note this was the position later taken by Ralph Waldo Emerson], and from the deduction of pay from the members of Congress. Break off the shackles from the poor black man, and hire them to labor like other human beings; for "an hour of virtuous liberty on earth, is worth a whole eternity of bondage! . . . Oh! then, create confidence! restore freedom!—break down slavery! banish imprisonment for debt, and be in love, fellowship and peace with all the world!

During the years from 1846 to 1848 the Saints would be driven from antislavery Illinois as well. Among other things their beliefs in continuing revelations, an open canon of scriptures, cooperative (anticapitalist) economics, and modern prophets were equally unacceptable to their persecutors. In early 1846 the L.D.S. community began its emigration from the United States to what was then Mexican territory (Utah). They left with the hope of escaping persecutions entirely, but manifest destiny and U.S. expansion, through the war with Mexico beginning in 1846, brought the Saints once again under U.S. jurisdiction and persecution. Cooperative economics and unpopular religious teachings continued to be primary reasons for persecution, and these drew the church directly back into the problems of antebellum slavery. Utah, as the state of Deseret, applied for statehood in 1849 but was denied admission; California was admitted as a free state, maintaining a senatorial "balance" of votes between free and slave states. As a provision of the Compromise of 1850, Utah and New Mexico were admitted as territories with the question of slavery to be decided by local election. As a result, popular sovereignty and states' rights became primary concerns in Utah, not for slavery but for statehood and protection from persecution. In practice, slave-owning converts to Mormonism arriving in Utah were very strongly encouraged by church leaders to manumit their slaves.

In 1852 the longstanding coalition of anti-Mormon forces found a new pretext with which to justify their continuing persecutions. With the public announcement by the L.D.S. church of the restored biblical practice of "plural" or "celestial" marriage (polygyny), the anti-Mormon forces gained national attention and a new alliance. They were accepted into the 1854 coalition of Whigs, Democrats, and Free-Soilers that had become the Republican party, and from the 1856 presidential election onward the party adopted as a key plank the "abolition of the twin relics of barbarism: slavery and polygamy." This political equation of slavery and polygamy forced the L.D.S. in Utah, who were denied the national vote or any representation owing to the imposition of territorial status on the state, to seek in political self-defense an alliance with Southerners despite their continuing institutional and personal objections to slavery. In 1857 President James Buchanan attempted to co-opt the Republican platform's polygamy issue with his ill-fated and transparently unjustified "Utah" war (also called the Contractor's War), which the Eastern media came to label "Buchanan's blunder." The defensive alliance between the L.D.S. community and southern states'-rights advocates was weakened after the end of the Civil War and the coming of emancipation, but some southern Democrats still took the church's defense into the 1880s.

One other factor needs to be treated with regard to the L.D.S. community's perspective on slavery. For many years before the Saints' arrival in Utah, both Spanish and Mexican traders and Ute raiders had been carrying on a traffic in kidnapped Native Americans, selling them as slaves to Mexican settlers from New Mexico to California. As early as 1851, Brigham Young, as governor of the territory, had arrested and tried some of the former slavers and reported on this to the territorial legislature in 1852. Ute war parties were a greater risk. They would kill captives on the spot if the Saints would not purchase them. In those cases the legislature authorized settlers to use ever scarce capital, livestock, and even guns to purchase such captives into a kind of indentured servitude, while they worked to prevent such captures. The territory lacked funds to compensate settlers, and it was usually impossible to determine the children's origins or return them to their families. There were standards as to how the children were to be cared for, educated, and set free in a fixed amount of time, and how much work could be expected from them in return.

Indentured servitude had been part of the experience of many European ancestors of Saints who had come to the United States, and while abuses could occur, this system appeared to most to be a more or less equitable method of compensation for the ransoms paid. It was never a popular solution to the problem and was apparently almost as objectionable as chattel slavery itself was to members of the church in general, but until the raiding could be suppressed, indenture certainly was preferable to allowing the captives to be killed. Some children were adopted by Mormon families, and some married into the families who ransomed them. In all, some fifty to sixty cases of purchase have been reported.

The L.D.S. church also showed no tolerance for slavery or similar conditions after the U.S. Civil War and even maintained integrated congregations in the Republic of South Africa while apartheid was being practiced in that country.

See also UTAH.

BIBLIOGRAPHY

ALLEN, JAMES B., and GLEN M. LEONARD. *The Story of the Latter-day Saints.* 1976.

ARRINGTON, LEONARD J., and DAVIS BITTON. *The Mormon Experience: A History of the Latter-day Saints.* 1979.

CHURCH OF JESUS CHRIST OF LATTER-DAY SAINTS. *The Book of Mormon: Another Witness for Jesus Christ.* 1981.

———. *The Doctrine and Covenants of the Church of Jesus Christ of Latter-day Saints.* 1981.

EMBRY, JESSE L. "Mormonism." In *Gale Encyclopedia of Multicultural America,* edited by Judy Galens, Anna Sheets, and Robyn V. Young. 1995.

LARSON, GUSTAVE O. *The "Americanization" of Utah for Statehood.* 1971.

LDS Collectors Library '97. CD-ROM and search engine containing over 1400 L.D.S. works, including L.D.S. scriptures, other church publications, hundreds of books, and academic journals. 1996.

LUDLOW, DANIEL, ed. *Encyclopedia of Mormonism.* 1992.

MAY, DEAN. "Mormons." In *Harvard Encyclopedia of American Ethnic Groups,* edited by Stephan Thernstrom. 1980.

PHELPS, W. W., ed. *The Evening and Morning Star.* 1833.

Times and Seasons . . . of the Church of Jesus Christ of Latter-day Saints. 1844.

Gordon C. Thomasson

Law

This entry includes the following articles: Law and Legal Systems; Ancient Middle East; Ancient Israel; Germanic Law and Peoples; Ancient Greece; Ancient Rome and Byzantium; Islamic Law; Slavery Cases in English Common Law; English Common Law in England and the American Colonies; Roman Law in the New World; Overview of U.S. Law; U.S. North; U.S. South.

Law and Legal Systems

All slaveholding societies with written legal codes developed a distinct body of law to accommodate the needs of masters and the peculiar disabilities and limitations on slaves. Many societies created laws and legal rules to separate slaves from the main population, to mark them as "dishonored" persons who had in effect suffered "social death."

Some societies required special marks or special clothing for slaves. Mesopotamian law, for example, required slaves to have a distinctive haircut, which would set them apart from others. In ancient Israel Hebrew male slaves who chose that status (usually in order to remain with a slave wife) had an ear pierced. Traditional Chinese law had elaborate sumptuary provisions, setting out the kinds of clothing members of various classes could wear, thus ensuring that nobles, slaves, and everyone in-between would be easily identifiable by their garb. Islamic law, on the other hand, required that masters dress slaves as well as they dressed themselves. And in ancient Rome, no visible distinctions were required. In fact, since Roman slavery was never based on either race or ethnicity, many slaves acted on a day-to-day basis like free people, except when some act or event highlighted their true status.

Except for a small number of Indian slaves, mostly in the sixteenth and seventeenth centuries, all slaves in the New World were of black African ancestry, and most blacks were slaves. Thus no special clothes or other markers were needed, because their race made black people presumptively slaves. New Orleans, however, was an exception: it had a very large free black population, and a city ordinance required free blacks to wear a brass badge so that all people of African ancestry without badges would be clearly recognized as slaves.

All slave-owning societies understood that slaves were first and foremost property. Islamic law, Roman law, and U.S. law all explicitly recognized the right of masters to sell, trade, or give away slaves. Legal records from the ancient world show that slaves were constantly bought and sold, like other forms of property. Biblical law is explicit: the slave is described as the master's "money" or "property." Similarly, all societies recognized that slaves could be passed on to heirs at the death of the master.

The law surrounding the sale of slaves provided buyers with some protections. Contracts for the sale of slaves from the ancient Near East, dating from as early as 500 B.C.E., had clauses guaranteeing that the slaves did not have leprosy or epilepsy and that they would not run away. Some 2,500 years later, slave purchasers in the United States sued the seller when slaves ran away immediately after sale or appeared to be diseased. In antebellum Louisiana the law assumed that a slave was healthy and not a habitual runaway; purchasers who discovered otherwise could recover the sale price through an action known as redhibition. Islamic law allowed prospective buyers to examine only the face of a slave, but a purchaser who found undisclosed defects could return a slave.

Laws differed dramatically with regard to limitations on the education and use of slaves. In Rome, the law did not limit how a master might use or train a slave, and Roman slaves were often highly educated; most of the physicians in the city of Rome may have been slaves. Similarly, in Islamic law a slave might hold public office, including serving as a provincial governor or a military officer. In the U.S. South, by contrast, masters were prohibited from teaching slaves to read and write, and slaves were banned from many professions, including pharmacy, medicine, and printing. In the early colonial period slaves served as soldiers, but they were later forbidden to act in that capacity, or indeed to own weapons. Many masters in the South nevertheless educated certain slaves because it was convenient to have some slaves who were skilled and literate.

Slave societies rarely regulated sexual contact between female slaves and male masters. Most slave societies seem to have recognized the right of the male master to use his slaves for sexual purposes. This was apparently true in ancient Israel for foreign slaves; and Mosaic law also noted that when an Israelite man sold his daughter into slavery she should "not go out as the male slaves do—" rather, she was to be used by the master or "for his son." Under Islamic law a master had an absolute right to treat his female slave as a concubine. However, Islamic law, and to a lesser extent Mosaic law, also regulated sexual relations in a variety of ways. For example, a Muslim master could not have sexual relations with a slave woman who was also a wet nurse for his children. Roman law does not seem to comment on this question, but that is because, as the private property of the owner, a slave woman could be compelled to do whatever the master wished. In China male slaves were punished more harshly for sexual relations with free women than if the illegal sex had been between free people. It was illegal for a free male to have sex with another person's slave, but male Chinese masters, like masters in all other cultures, apparently had unimpeded sexual access to their own slaves. The laws of the U.S. South generally prohibited extramarital or nonmarital sexual relations and also banned interracial sex. But, except for a few fornication cases in the early seventeenth century, there are no known cases of white men charged for sexual activity with their own slaves. Rape of a slave by an owner, or any white, was legally impossible. There is no indication that white men, other than owners, were ever prosecuted or sued for sexual involvement with slaves they did not own.

Marriage between master and slave, or between a free person and a slave, was also a concern in many legal systems. In the ancient Near East, legal codes usually allowed slaves to marry free persons, and their children would be considered free, though with a somewhat lower status than the children of two non-slave parents. Biblical law, for example, specifically allowed for the marriage of a "captive" woman by a warrior-captor, but only after a month in which the woman had time to mourn her lost family and community. Israelites (as noted above) could also sell their daughters into slavery, to be taken as wives (or concubines) by the purchaser or his sons. The Germanic codes forbade marriage between slaves and free people. In China the T'ang, Ming, and Ch'ing codes all prohibited marriages between slaves and free people. A male T'ang slave marrying a free woman was subject to a year and a half of penal servitude, and of course the marriage was annulled. In the American South slaves could not legally marry at all, and so there was no question of masters marrying their slaves. Furthermore, of course, whites could not legally marry people of African ancestry. Free blacks could, however, purchase slaves, emancipate them, and marry them.

The children of slave couples were considered slaves by the laws of almost every slave society. In ancient Rome and throughout the Americas, the child of a slave woman was a slave, no matter what the status of the father might have been. As a result, in the American South many white men owned their children and the children of their sons and other male relatives.

The rules on marriage between slaves also varied. The ancient codes and the codes of the Germanic peoples during the fifth and sixth centuries usually gave legal recognition to slave marriages. Roman law, on the other hand, did not recognize slave marriage, because slaves had no legal personality. Mosaic law and Islamic law both recognize slave marriage, which was legal with the permission of the master. Various schools of Islamic law allowed male slaves either two or four wives. In ancient Israel, the master of an Israelite male slave (who served for only six years) could allow his slave to marry a slave woman whom he also

owned. However, at the end of his servitude, the Hebrew slave had to choose between freedom without his wife or lifetime slavery with his wife and any children they had. Roman Catholic canon law also recognized slave marriage. The laws of the Spanish and Portuguese colonies of the New World allowed slaves to marry, even against the will of their masters. Slaves in Latin America were also legally able to marry free people. However, in the New World these laws were often ignored by masters who found it economically necessary to sell slaves. In the English colonies and the United States slave marriage was never given legal recognition, because a marriage is a contract, and slaves were not legally persons and therefore could not enter into contracts. Still, slaves in the United States were often married by a clergyman if the master was religious. They might also be married by the master or in a slave wedding. Recognizing the lack of legal respect for their union, slaves often took vows "until death or sale do us part." Although none of the southern states recognized slave marriages, they did allow free blacks to live as married people with slaves. After the Civil War most of the former slave states gave ex post facto recognition to slave marriages, declaring them valid.

All slave societies struggled with issue of testimony by slaves in courts. In Rome and among the Germanic people, slaves were sometimes tortured before their testimony was allowed. In the United States slaves could always testify against other slaves, and in some states they could testify against free blacks, but they could never testify against whites.

The treatment of slaves varied from place to place and time to time, but the state rarely interfered in how masters treated their slaves. In almost all societies a master might kill a slave without fear of legal consequences, unless the killing was blatant, intentional, and so brutal as to shock the community. Throughout most of the history of Rome it was not illegal for a master to kill a slave. A stranger killing someone else's slave was subject to monetary damages for the value of the dead slave; but killing a slave was not murder in Rome. Islamic law did not punish masters who harmed their slaves, though a judge could compel a master to sell a slave to someone else if the charge of excessive cruelty was proved. There was no punishment at all if the master killed the slave. In the United States the accidental death of a slave through punishment was not considered criminal. A few southern masters were prosecuted for killing their slaves, and at least one master was executed, but these were cases of extreme and shocking brutality—and even gross brutality and torture were not always sufficient to bring about legal action, because in the United States slaves could not testify against whites. Thus when the only witnesses to a crime were slaves, the crime would go unpunished; for example, it was simply impossible to prosecute any free person for the rape of a slave, because the victim could not offer any testimony. By 1830 all jurisdictions in the U.S. South banned certain kinds of punishments, like castration, cutting off limbs, and branding, but in the colonial period such punishments were legal, just as they had been in Rome and most other slave cultures. In general, American law accepted the position taken by Chief Justice Thomas Ruffin of North Carolina in *State v. Mann* (1829), that "The slave, to remain a slave, must be made sensible, that there is no appeal from his master; that his power is in no instance, usurped; but is conferred by the laws of man at least, if not by the law of God."

An exception to the general permissiveness about cruelty and punishment seems to be ancient Israel. If an Israelite master hit a slave, knocking out a tooth or an eye, the master had to immediately emancipate the slave—"an eye for an eye, a tooth for a tooth," was transformed into "freedom" for an eye or a tooth. Mosaic law subjected a master to the death penalty if a slave died immediately after punishment, on the theory that such a killing was intentional. But if the slave survived punishment for "a day or two" and then died, the law assumed that the death was accidental, because no man would intentionally destroy his property.

Although slaves were property everywhere, they were also people who, like other humans, accumulated property of their own. In Rome a slave was entitled to control wealth, property, and even other slaves through a fund known as a *peculium*. Roman slaves accumulated their peculium through gifts from the master, by earning outside money, and even from inheritance from others. But "technically the peculium belonged to the slave's master, since a slave could own nothing" (Watson, 1987). In the United States the law had no such concept, and thus a slave could never legally control property. Most southern states prohibited slaves from buying anything without the explicit (sometimes written) permission of the owner, on the theory that any money in a slave's possession belonged to the owner. In reality, of course, slaves everywhere, including the United States, used money and bought all kinds of goods and products.

What slaves everywhere most wanted to purchase was their own liberty. Here too the law differed significantly from place to place. Islamic law recognized a written contract, known as a *kitāba*, in which a slave was guaranteed freedom after the payment of an agreed-upon sum. This could be paid in installments or in a lump sum. Once a contract was in place, a master could not sell a slave, and if a slave was female, the master was prohibited from having sexual relations with her. In Rome a slave might contract with a master to purchase freedom with the peculium. However, such an agreement was never enforceable in the courts. In the United States, courts would never enforce a contract for self-purchase, on the dual rationale that the slave could not make a contract and any money the slave accumulated already belonged to the master. However, many slaves did gain their freedom through self-purchase when their masters agreed and then—without coercion by the courts—kept the bargain and manumitted the slave.

Law of course regulated manumission. Manumission in fact created an interesting, almost unique, problem in law: it turned a piece of property into a person who was not property. Islamic law made manumission very easy, involving simply a public verbal declaration by a competent master that a slave was free. Roman law also made manumission relatively easy. Moreover, almost uniquely among slave societies, Rome allowed former slaves to become full citizens. At the other extreme was the U.S. South, which by the antebellum period (after 1820) made manumission increasingly difficult. By the 1850s masters wishing to free slaves in Virginia, North Carolina, and most of the deep South had to remove the slave to a free jurisdiction either before or after manumission.

The more legalistic societies—especially Rome, Islamic societies, ancient Israel, and the United States—created elaborate laws and interpretations to regulate human bondage. Such legal rules and regulations made sense because they separated slaves from free people. Most of these societies understood, even if they rarely articulated it, that slavery was unnatural even if it was common or possibly universal. To make people into property required ingenuity and deft legal minds. For at least three millennia such jurists, lawyers, legislators, theologians, and legal philosophers in Asia, the Near East, Europe, Africa, and the Americas worked to create laws and precedents to support a system that could turn human beings into things. While the specific rules differed from place to place, the overall notion that law was necessary to preserve and protect slave property seems to have been accepted everywhere.

See also ANCIENT ROME; BIBLE; CHINA; CONCUBINAGE; ISLAM; MANUMISSION; PECULIUM; SEXUAL EXPLOITATION.

BIBLIOGRAPHY

CARMICHAEL, CALUM. *The Spirit of Biblical Law.* 1996.
COBB, THOMAS R. R. *An Inquiry into the Law of Negro Slavery.* 1858.

FINKELMAN, PAUL. *The Law of Freedom and Bondage: A Casebook.* 1986.

———, ed. *Slavery and the Law.* 1997.

Holy Bible. New Revised Standard Version. 1989.

MACCORMACK, GEOFFREY. *The Spirit of Traditional Chinese Law.* 1996.

MORRIS, THOMAS D. *Southern Slavery and the Law, 1619–1860.* 1996.

WATSON, ALAN. *Roman Slave Law.* 1987.

———. *Slave Law in the Americas.* 1989.

Paul Finkelman

Ancient Middle East

The portrait of slavery revealed in the ancient Middle Eastern legal texts is of an institution of marginal importance to the economy and involving few persons. Both males and females appear as slaves. Slavery could be imposed as a penalty, especially for defaulting debtors, but self-sale was also possible, as was child-sale, and many slaves were prisoners of war.

The legal texts came from kings and people serving kings, although in the case of the Old Testament, the authors were people associated with prophets who opposed the central government. Although we refer to these texts as codes, most were used for teaching just behavior, were not invoked in courts of law, and were rarely referred to in letters.

Legal texts from southern Mesopotamia in modern Iraq include the so-called Ur-Nammu Code from around 2100 B.C.E., the Lipit-Ishtar Code from 1930 B.C.E., the code of Eshnunna from 1770 B.C.E., the massive code of Hammurabi from 1752 B.C.E., and a Neo-Babylonian collection from before 700 B.C.E. Also connected to these traditions are the Hittite Code from 1500 B.C.E. in Turkey and the Middle-Assyrian Code from 1100 B.C.E. in northern Iraq. The legal material in the Old Testament, dating from the first millennium B.C.E., appears closely related to such texts.

In Mesopotamia slaves could be marked with a tattoo or brand bearing their owner's name, and they could be made to wear a slave haircut. A barber who cut the slave haircut off was supposed to have his hand amputated in punishment.

Slaves sometimes entered marriages with free persons, and the children were regarded as free, though they might not inherit from a free father if there were other children from a free wife. Offspring of marriages between two slaves probably were slave, and the Eshnunna Code provides for the master's seizing of a child given by a slave girl to a free person. It was possible to free one's slaves, though in one case a slave had to pay twice his value in order to purchase freedom. It is not clear if there was an identifiable group of freedmen in these societies.

Slaves were punished more severely than others in these societies, and the losses of slaves were less important to the legislators. In the Hittite Code a slave might be punished less severely than the freeborn for a theft but more harshly for casting a magic spell.

In legal texts the gods were invoked in a general way, to assert that the weak were to be protected. But religious sanction for slave holding was not emphasized. Rather, the texts assumed that class divisions were part of the fabric of urban life, which had been bestowed upon humans at the beginning of time by the gods.

Documents from the practice of law, available by the thousands and dating from many periods, show that the privileges of slaves were limited. For example, in the twelve appeals by slaves challenging their status, recorded around 2030 B.C.E., no slave was granted freedom. But there seemed to be no problem for slaves to bring suit in court.

Slaves sometimes had considerable economic freedom but could be punished for acting as receivers of stolen property. Legislators also wanted to punished the "uppity" slave woman who might claim equality with her mistress.

A detail from Hammurabi's Code depicts Hammurabi receiving the law from Shamash, the sun god. [Gianni Dagli Orti/Corbis]

Neo-Babylonian slave sales from the sixth century B.C.E. provided guarantees against the slave's being discovered to be of free status, against escape and sudden death, and sometimes offered a hundred-day guarantee that the slave was not afflicted with leprosy and epilepsy. Slaves usually lived in family units, but children as young as four years old were sold separately. There is little evidence for manumission in this late period, and the numbers of slaves in the Persian period 539–331 B.C.E were much greater than in earlier times.

There also was a great mass of unfree people whose legal and economic status may not have been uniform. Sometimes they could be sold along with their land, though usually not separately from it. Some scholars maintain that the presence of the unfree defined these societies as slave societies, but most observers doubt it is useful to think of them as dominated by compelled labor. Free peasants were always economically much more important than the unfree.

Israelite texts envisioned a time limit for slavery, and Hammurabi imposed a three-year term for debt slavery of debtors' relatives. In Israel there was also an ethnic limitation; Israelite slaves were supposed to serve only for a seven-year term and then be set free, while foreign slaves served for life.

See also ANCIENT MIDDLE EAST; HAMMURABI'S CODE.

BIBLIOGRAPHY

DANDAMAEV, MUHAMMAD A. *Slavery in Babylonia*. 1984.
DRIVER, GODFREY R., and JOHN C. MILES. *The Babylonian Laws*. 2 vols. 1960.
MENDELSOHN, ISAAC. *Slavery in the Ancient Near East*. 1949.
ROTH, MARTHA T. *Law Collections from Mesopotamia and Asia Minor*. 1995.

Daniel C. Snell

Ancient Israel

The ancient Israelites began their national history with the Exodus from Egypt, where they had been slaves. Biblical law commanded that the Hebrews remember their enslavement: "Remember that you were a slave in the land of Egypt, and the Lord Your God freed you from there with a mighty hand and an outstretched arm" (Deuteronomy, 5: 15). This experience of enslavement and redemption helped temper Hebrew slave law; but as with other peoples of the ancient Near East, this experience with slavery did not make the ancient Israelites into abolitionists. The pre-Israelite ancestors, Abraham, Isaac, and Jacob, had all been owners of slaves and servants. Mosaic law modified, regularized, and ameliorated slavery but did not condemn it.

A breast plate for the Scroll of the Law includes the commandments flanked by Moses and Aaron. [Hulton-Deutsch Collection/Corbis]

Mosaic law provided for various types of slaves: male Hebrew slaves serving for a term of years; male Hebrew slaves for life; female Hebrew slaves, sold to be a concubine or a wife; and foreign slaves, either captured in battle or purchased. Exodus 21: 2–6 provides the basic rules for the Hebrew slave. Leviticus 25: 44–46 provides for the non-Hebrew slave.

Usually Hebrew slavery was more like indentured servitude than slavery as it is generally understood. A male Hebrew could become a slave either by selling himself into slavery or, in the case of a thief who was unable to make restitution, by order of a court. A Hebrew could sell himself into slavery only for a period of six years. A Hebrew who sold himself to a fellow Hebrew would attain freedom automatically after the expiration of six years from the time of sale, or at the onset of the jubilee year (once every fifty years). In addition, a Hebrew slave could attain freedom through self-redemption by repayment to the master of his purchase price less the value of service already given. In each of these three cases the manumission did not require the assent of the master. In addition, a master could voluntarily manumit a Hebrew slave. If a master died without leaving a male descendant, the master's slaves went free. If a Hebrew sold himself to a non-Hebrew or a convert, he became free upon the death of the master without regard to the existence of the master's offspring.

If a Hebrew was reluctant to leave his master's household and wished to remain a slave, he could be brought before judges to declare his intention. If the slave persisted with his request, his master would bore a hole in the slave's ear with an awl and, with that mark, the slave would be bound in servitude for life. One incentive to remain a slave involved marriage. While Hebrew slaves were to go free after six years, they were to leave slavery as they entered it. Thus, if married before enslavement, the slave was to be emancipated as married; if single, the slave was to leave single. If a master allowed a male slave to marry one of his female slaves, at the jubilee the husband would have to choose between freedom without his wife and children or permanent enslavement with his new family. The Mosaic law held: "But if the slave declares, 'I love my master, my wife, and my children; I do not wish to go free' then his master shall take him before God. He shall be brought to the door or the doorpost, and his master shall pierce his ear with an awl; and he shall then remain his slave for life" (Exodus, 21: 5–6).

A female Hebrew could be sold into slavery only by her father, and only during childhood. She could not sell herself. Like a male Hebrew slave, she became free at the end of six years, at the onset of a jubilee year, by payment of the remaining cost of her original purchase price, or by a bill of manumission drafted by her master. Unlike the male slave, the female slave became free upon the death of her master even if he had a male descendant. At the time a female slave reached puberty, if she consented to marriage the master had the obligation of either marrying her, betrothing her to his son, or freeing her immediately. If she married, she gained the same status as a freeborn wife.

Biblical slavery for non-Hebrews, however, was more like conventional slavery. Leviticus 25: 44–46 provides that:

> Such male and female slaves as you may have—it is from the nations round about you that you may acquire male and female slaves. You may also buy them among the children of aliens resident among you, or from the families that are among you, whom they begot in your land. These shall become your property: you may keep them as a possession for your children after you, for them to inherit as property for all time. Such you may treat as slaves.

In addition to purchase, slaves could be acquired legally through warfare and capture. Thus, Deuteronomy 120: 11–14 provides that when a town surrenders to the Israelites without a battle, "all the people present there shall serve you at forced labor." However, if the town is taken in battle, then all the men are to be killed and the women and children are to be taken "as your booty." Such laws governing capture and enslavement seem to have been common throughout the ancient Near East and might be properly seen as the accepted international law of the time and region.

The laws of acquisition of non-Hebrew slaves do not distinguish between males and females. The methods of obtaining title to a non-Hebrew slave are the same as those for obtaining title to land: by the payment of money, by transfer of a deed, or by an act of possession. Examples of an "act of possession" include doing work for the vendee or being physically led by the vendee, which is called "drawing." Unlike the Hebrew slave, the non-Hebrew slave does not gain freedom at the coming of a particular date. In fact, the Bible provides, "These shall become your property . . . for all time."

This biblical provision suggests that a non-Hebrew slave must remain in bondage, even against the will of the master. In reality, the biblical commandment did little to prevent Hebrew masters from freeing their non-Hebrew slaves. Prior to the destruction of the Second Temple in the first century C.E. manumission of slaves was encouraged. Slaves were frequently emancipated, and an emancipated slave was free to marry a freeborn Hebrew. There is some indication that emancipation was specifically encouraged for the purpose of marriage. The Talmud contains advice remembered from an earlier period: "If your daughter has become nubile, manumit your slave and give her to him in marriage." A deed from the colony of Elephantine in the fifth century B.C.E. gives us an example of manumission in that period. The deed shows that manumission at that time required a two-step process. The master Zakkur wanted to liberate his slave, Yedoniah. Instead of giving Yedoniah a deed of manumission directly, Zakkur transferred ownership of Yedoniah to a third party, Uriah, on condition that Uriah liberate Yedoniah. The deed contained provisions for severe penalties if Yedoniah remained in slavery.

Only in the second century C.E. was the biblical verse used to discourage emancipation. At this time rabbis were concerned that freed slaves might tell tales of Jewish life to Romans. Rabbi Akiba ruled that manumission of slaves violated a positive commandment. This ruling, however, never gained a foothold among a majority of rabbis.

It is difficult to determine the number of slaves in an ancient Hebrew household. Ezra 2: 64–65 and Nehemiah 7: 67 indicate that among the 42,360 exiles who returned from Babylonian captivity 7,337 were slaves. These figures suggest that one slave per household would have been common.

From the time of Abraham slaves owned by the Hebrews were to be circumcised (Genesis, 17 11–13). Following circumcision the slave became a partial member of the household. Slaves were required to obey the laws of the sabbath and could not be required to tasks that would violate the sabbath. They were both required and entitled to join in festival celebrations. For non-Hebrew slaves, however—unlike freeborn members of the household—biblical law imposed no other religious duties.

Aside from ensuring a day of rest for the slave as well as other members of the household, biblical law provided some protection against physical abuse. If a master killed a slave and the slave died immediately, the master could be punished, on the theory that such a blow was intentional. However, if the slave lived "a day or two" and then died, the master was not criminally liable ("the assailing shall go unpunished"), on the theory that "he is the other's property" (Exodus, 21: 20–21) and that therefore the death was an accident, because presumably most masters would not intentionally destroy their property. If a master knocked out the eye of a slave, or a tooth, or inflicted a serious injury to any other part of the body which could not be restored to its normal condition, the slave was to be freed immediately. This is a modification of the penalty of "an eye for eye, a tooth for a tooth," the compensation for harming free people. For slaves, the law became freedom for an eye, freedom for a tooth. (Exodus, 21: 26–27) A slave was subject to punishment for violating the criminal laws to the same extent as a free member of the community.

Unlike many other ancient cultures, biblical Israel was not a slave society. Indeed, in many ways, the experience in Egypt made the laws of ancient Israel hostile to slavery, even though they recognized the institution. Many of the laws favored freedom. Illegal enslavement of any free people within the community was harshly punished: "If a man is found to have kidnapped a fellow Israelite, enslaving him or selling him, that kidnapper shall die. Thus you will sweep out evil from your midst" (Deuteronomy, 24: 7). The ease of manumission also illustrates this hostility to slavery. One indication is the requirement that injured slaves be manumitted. Another is the biblical injunction to free Hebrew slaves after six years, which was directly tied to the Exodus from Egypt. Thus, the biblical lawgiver declares: "For they are My servants, whom I freed from the land of Egypt; they may not give themselves over into servitude" (Leviticus, 25: 42). Tied to this was an injunction to treat Hebrew slaves with compassion: "You shall not rule over him [a Hebrew slave] ruthlessly; you shall fear your God" (Leviticus, 25: 43). Also unusual was the treatment of fugitive slaves. Deuteronomy (23: 16–17) declared, "You shall not turn over to his master a slave who seeks refuge with you from his master. He shall live with you in any place he may choose among the settlements in your midst, wherever he pleases; you must not ill-treat him." It is unclear from the text whether this admonition applied only to slaves from other nations who escaped into Israel. But in any case the law illustrated the tension between slavery, in a culture surrounded by other slave societies, and a people whose national identity was deeply rooted in the experience of escaping bondage.

See also BIBLE; JEWS; JUDAISM; LABOR SYSTEMS; MANUMISSION.

BIBLIOGRAPHY

COBIN, DAVID M. "A Brief Look at the Jewish Law of Manumission." *Chicago-Kent Law Review* 70 (1995): 1339–1348.
FALK, ZE'EV W. *Introduction to Jewish Law of the Second Commonwealth*, vol. 2. 1978.
———. "Manumission by Sale." *Journal of Semitic Studies* 3, no. 127 (1958).
JACKSON, BERNARD J. "Biblical Laws of Slavery: A Comparative Approach." In *Slavery and Other Forms of Unfree Labor*, edited by Léonie Archer. 1988; pp. 86–101.
MENDELSOHN, I. *Legal Aspects of Slavery in Babylonia, Assyria, and Palestine. A Comparative Study, 3000–500 B.C.* 1932.
MIELZINER, MOSES. "Slavery amongst the Ancient Hebrews" (1865). In *Moses Mielziner—His Life and Works*, edited by Ella McKenna Friend Mielziner. 1931.
Tanakh—a New Translation of the Holy Scriptures according to the Traditional Hebrew Text. 1985.
URBACH, E. E. "The Laws Regarding Slavery as a Source for Social History of the Period of the Second Temple, the Misnah and Talmud." In *Papers of the Institute of Jewish Studies London*, vol. 1, edited by J. G. Weiss, 1964.

David M. Cobin
Paul Finkelman

Germanic Law and Peoples

The invaders of the western European part of the Roman Empire in the fourth to sixth centuries C.E. were primarily people referred to as Germans—in contrast to the Celts (including the Gauls), who had penetrated all parts of western Europe in the first millenium B.C.E. The Celts had orginated in eastern and central Europe and slowly moved west; as they moved west, the Germans moved into the areas they vacated. Some Germanic peoples moved west more or less directly from eastern Europe, others first southeast from earlier homes in Scandinavia and northern Europe before going west. By the time of Caesar, Germanic peoples had penetrated as far west as the Rhine River and what is now western Switzerland, and a few Germanic groups had crossed into Gaul and became involved in Caesar's Gallic wars, sometimes as friends of the Romans, sometimes as foes. Caesar was sufficiently impressed by the warlike qualities of the Germans that he took the time to build a temporary bridge across the Rhine and to lay waste a band of territory to the east of the river, to discourage the Germans from interfering in the new Roman province of Gaul.

Establishment of the Germanic Kingdoms

During the first three or four centuries C.E., Germanic peoples continued to move in small or large confederations, which were constantly changing and constantly warring with one another, always seeking new land. Some of these people were still pastoralists, but most supported themselves with a fairly primitive form of agriculture. Much of the area was heavily forested, and the forest had to be cut down before fields could be created. The Germanic plow was too light to till the heavy soil very deep; and since these people had no knowledge of fertilizer or fallow plots, the fields soon wore out and the group would need to move on to another place.

Contacts between Germans and Romans, especially in trade, became frequent and routine along the Rhine-Danube frontier. The Romans had many things that the Germans wanted, such as exotic food, pottery dishes, weapons, and especially coins. The Germans did not have much offer in return; but furs, amber (from the Baltic shores), and slaves were in demand. Slaves were the commodity most sought, and the Germans had plenty of them to offer, as a result of the constant wars among the various confederations and the sale of prisoners of war. Through this trade, the Germans living close to the Roman frontier were influenced by Roman dress, food, jewelry, eating utensils, weapons, and coinage. They were not, however, influenced much by urban institutions—there were no towns in the German territory. In fact, the Germans had little interest in town life; their interest was in the empire's agricultural land. To the Germans, the lighter soil of the empire, in contrast with their own heavier soil, was a great temptation: fields were already cleared, and a light plow was sufficient.

Roman traders were common in the Germanic world (especially near the Roman frontier) before the migrations began. But Germans were also common in the Roman world as slaves and freedpersons. As individuals, they were no threat; the Romans were willing to accept conquered people who acculturated. Manumission was common, and a freed slave became a Roman citizen and melted into the general population. In the third century, Germans as individuals and as groups were allowed to join the Roman army—recruits from the more romanized, more pacifistic provinces having become fewer. After some years of service, during which the Germans learned Latin, the language of the army, they were usually rewarded with Roman citizenship and land. Thus the late Roman empire included many people of Germanic birth who had essentially assimilated. By the fourth century, even some commanders of the Roman army were German by birth or descent.

Germanic groups had been living up against the Rhine-Danube, sometimes crossing over when the garrisons were weak but always pushed back by the Roman army, until the late fourth century, when developments in Asia speeded up organized German attempts to settle within the empire. This catalyst was the appearance out of Asia of the Huns, riding on horseback and easily overcoming the armies of the southeastern-most Germans, the Goths, which consisted mainly of infantry. The eastern Goths (Ostrogoths) fells under Hunnic domination, but the western Goths (Visigoths) were allowed to cross the Danube frontier into the eastern part of the Roman Empire. Mistreatment by Roman authorities and mutual misunderstanding led to long-drawn-out conflict and a sack of Rome in 410 before the Visigoths were allowed to settle in southwestern Gaul in Aquitaine in 418. The Visigoths lost Aquitaine to the Franks in 507, but by that time they had crossed the Pyrenees into Spain and established a kingdom there. The Visigothic kingdom would be overthrown only in 711 by Muslims (Moors) from North Africa.

Meanwhile the Roman army of the Rhine had been recalled to face the Visigothic threat, leaving the Rhine frontier undefended. A number of Germanic people forced their way across about 406, including among others, the Burgundians, who headed directly south to establish a kingdom first at Worms (until it was overthrown by the Huns), before being allowed to settle in the mid-Rhone region in 443 as federate allies of Rome. This kingdom would be defeated by the Franks in the early sixth century and thereafter constituted a partially autonomous area of the Frankish kingdom.

All these movements of Germanic peoples were a direct or indirect result of the progress of the Huns under Attila from eastern to central Europe and into the eastern part of Gaul. The Huns were defeated in 451 by a Roman field army strengthened by contingents of allied Visigoths, Burgundians, and Franks, and thereafter the Huns turned south, intending to sack Rome. But Attila's days of greatness were over: the sack of Rome was deflected by Pope Leo I, Attila himself died shortly thereafter, and struggles over the succession destroyed the power of the Huns, who retreated eastward toward Asia. This retreat freed those Germanic peoples who had been forced to join the Hunnic army.

Among the people so freed were the Ostrogoths, who sought entry into the eastern Roman empire. Like their predecessors, the Visigoths, the Ostrogoths were shunted from place to place until the early 490s, when they were encouraged to go west and take Italy from the German Odoacer, who had dethroned the last western Roman emperor in 476. Accordingly the Ostrogoths entered Italy, overthrew Odoacer, and established a kingdom that lasted until 552, when it was destroyed by the eastern Roman (Byzantine) army of the emperor Justinian. These fierce Gothic wars left the Italian peninsula devastated and restless under heavy Byzantine taxation. The unstable situation invited intervention, and another Germanic people, the Lombards, invaded in 568 to establish the last of the Germanic kingdoms on western Roman soil. The kingdom would be conquered by the Franks under Charlemagne in 774.

In the meantime, two other Germanic states were established that were destined to survive many vicissitudes through the Middle Ages and into the modern world: France and England. The Franks were a Germanic people who had been allowed to settle, in the mid-fourth century, just west of the Rhine River in an abandoned part of northeast Gaul, on the condition that they would protect that part of the frontier against further entry by other Germans. In the early fifth century, when the Rhine army was recalled to protect Italy against the Visigoths, more groups of Franks, each under its own leader or king, pushed over into northeast Gaul. They fought one another until the accession of Clovis to the kingship of one group in the late fifth century. Clovis defeated and eliminated all his rivals and started on a career of conquest to the west and south that would bring almost all of present-day France under the control of his descendants. His famous successor in the eighth century, Charlemagne, would extend Frankish control to northern Spain, to northern and central Italy, and deep into eastern Germany. Although the Frankish lands would divide in many ways in the coming years, a recognizable integrated France would appear by the end of the Middle Ages.

In the fifth century, the Anglo-Saxon Germans began to move from the Danish peninsula and the lowlands immediately to the west, entering Britain, the island that had been abandoned by Rome a few years before. There migrations were spread out over the mid-fifth through sixth centuries: the Anglo-Saxons were not one people but came over in small groups, establishing small kingdoms that were constantly at war with one another. First one kingdom predominated and then another, until another series of invasions (Norse in the north and Danes in south) wiped out all of them except Wessex in the southwest. Wessex survived, and under its leadership England was unified and had established a strong centralized government by the time of the Norman invasion in the late eleventh century. The Norman invasion brought radical changes in landholding and social relations, but the basic governmental organization remained; and after several centuries during which French was the language of the ruling class, the native tongue, English, emerged as the language of the kingdom.

Germanic Institutions and Slavery

The primary living unit among the Germans was the family, consisting of father, mother, children (unmarried daughters and minor sons), and other dependents. The father represented all the members of this group at law. For purposes of waging feuds, satisfying the justice system, and inheritance, a larger kin group was recognized. In general, the kin group was more important in the northern kingdoms, were Roman influence was weak; it was less important in the southern areas, where the Roman influence was stronger. This is seen primarily in "self-help" in conflict resolution: the family and the larger kin group were necessary to get satisfaction before the courts in the remote northern kingdoms, which had no strong centralized government and therefore no police power. In the more southerly kingdoms, the strong, centralized Roman empire was reflected in stronger Visigothic and Lombard governments. There, although self-help was still important, a well-organized judicial system and some police power made reliance on the larger kin group unnecessary.

The Germanic invasions of the empire were not primarily military expeditions but movements of confederations of family groups seeking better land. Unless a Roman army was at hand to protect them, the civilian inhabitants did not put up much resistance other than to retreat inside the walls of fortified towns. If no Roman field army repelled a German advance, or if the Germans persisted in spite of military setbacks, the empire eventually gave in and entered into a treaty, allowing the Germans to settle in a province in return for taking over military protection of the area. The Germanic king thus replaced the Roman provincial governor and became the head of the provincial government. So long as there was an emperor in the west, the Germanic state thus created was theoretically subordinate to Rome. After 476, however, the Germanic states were for all practical purposes independent.

These new states had a combined Roman and Germanic population, but lack of evidence makes it difficult to know how Roman or how Germanic their governments were. They were protected by the king and his retinue, plus military service when necessary by all German freedmen. Undoubtedly, a Germanic king would have utilized some parts of the existing Roman administration. However, as the western empire slowly disintegrated in the fifth century, Roman officials were not replaced, and inevitably provincial administration became less Roman and more German. Roman versus German influence is important, because the best sources of information about Germanic slavery (after *Germania*, written in the first century by the Roman historian Tacitus) are the Germanic law codes—recorded principally in the fifth and sixth centuries, though with later additions. Do these codes reflect genuine Germanic custom, as the present discussion will assume? Or do they reflect Germanic custom as interpreted by scribes with some training in Roman law? Or are they simply redactions of Roman provincial law?

When the presence of the Germans in a province was formally settled, a division of property followed. The exact process is much debated, but most probably a landed estate and its workers would be divided between a Roman and a German proprietor. The Germans arrived in family groups that included dependent slaves and half-free workers who would join the dependent workers already present, slaves and half-free *coloni*—men and their families who were technically free but unable to leave the land. In the late empire, because there were few war captives to purchase as slaves, Roman agricultural slaves were settled in families on landed estates, where their condition was little different from that of the *coloni*. Germanic half-free men and women lacked legal competence and had a value between that of slaves and freedpersons, but somewhat closer to that of slaves. Roman landholders were not happy to divide their property, but there was little resistance, partly because the Germans had a reputation for being warlike but also because the population had been declining since the third century and there was plenty of land for all—especially in the southern areas, where the Germans were a small minority.

The slavery revealed by the Germanic law codes is very similar to premigration slavery. Germanic slaves were very much a part of the family, legal dependents of their lord. Except possibly in the case of slaves who came with distributed land, there was not likely to be much physical difference between slaves and the lord's family, since the sources of slaves were such that there was little likelihood of enslaving persons of different ethnic background. People could be born slaves, they could be captured in war and sold as slaves, could become slaves voluntarily in order to survive, or could be enslaved for debt by a judicial ruling.

To avoid feuds, the Germanic codes provided for the assessment of *wergeld* ("man worth") in cases of homicide or composition (i.e., compensation) for lesser violent acts, theft, or other misdeeds. Wergelds and compositions were set so high that they would have been especially difficult for an ordinary person to pay without the help of kin or a lord (if the person was a member of a retinue). Judicially imposed slavery was recognized by all of the Germanic states; it was sometimes temporary, in the case of smaller assessments, but sometimes permanent, in the case of larger ones. Permanent slavery is often associated with the phrase "Let the man found guilty pay with his life." That is, a successful accuser could legally kill the opponent (take revenge) or enslave the opponent (take compensation); the latter was encouraged. This use of the legal system to create slaves in the Germanic states was quite distinct from anything in the late Roman Empire.

King Euric of the Visigoths had Roman jurists compile a code of laws, commonly known as the Code of Euric, which was the earliest Germanic code. [Michael Nicholson/ Corbis]

All the Germanic codes (Burgundian, Visigothic, Frankish, Anglo-Saxon, and Lombard, plus the later Ripuarian, Alamannian, and Bavarian) assigned a "value" to the slave, somewhat comparable to wergeld. A slave's value depended on his or her personal standing and abilities. Among the Anglo-Saxons and Visigoths, it was determined partly by the rank of the slave's lord or master and partly determined by the slave's own training and function. Among the other Germans, value was determined primarily by training and function although the king's slaves were always most valuable. Germans distinguished two general categories by employment: household slaves (*servi ministeriales*) and field slaves (*servi rustici*). Within these categories, value was determined by responsibility—the chief household slave was valued higher than the one who assisted him or her, the chief herder was more valuable than the assistant herder, and so forth. Injuries to slaves were assigned compensation just as injuries to freemen were, although in the slave's case the compensation went to the lord rather than to the slave, just as a free dependent's compensation accrued to the head of his or her family or to a patron.

Only the Lombard and Visigothic laws go into great detail about pursuit of runaway slaves, manumission, or the status of freedmen and freedwomen. This is perhaps not surprising, since there was considerable survival of Roman law in Lombard Italy and Visigothic Spain.

Germanic slaves were essentially part of their lord's family and were classed legally as dependents not very different from minor sons, unmarried daughters, or half-free peasants (*originarii, aldii, lidi*). The actual living conditions of the Germanic slave might not differ significantly from that of the Roman slave, but Germanic slaves did have more legal protection. As noted, injuries to slaves were compensated for by monetary payments, the payment going of course to the lord rather than to the slave—but the same was true of compensation for injuries to free persons who were not legally competent. (Occasionally the legally dependent person, whether slave, half-free, or free, might receive the compensation—these instances usually involved dishonorable treatment of one kind or another.) Slave marriages were recognized and were the subject of important negotiations between lords if the slaves belonged to different masters. At least in written law, a married slave woman was protected against rape by her lord. Mistreatment (including rape) of another man's slave, whether married or not, was regulated by law, and compensation was assigned to the master. There are no references in the laws to any restrictions on a lord's treatment of his or her own slaves except the provision against rape of a married slave woman—and even then, how could her case be brought before a court if her master was her legal representative?

In the case of freedmen accused of some offense (and sometimes free women, although women were usually represented by their fathers or husbands), two forms of proof were used. Compurgation involved taking an oath, accompanied by "oath helpers." The ordeal was usually boiling water (the accused was required to plunge an arm into a cauldron of boiling water and pull out a stone), although combat (*camfio*—duelling) was used by the Lombards. It was supposed that God would intervene to demonstrate the truth: the oath calls directly upon God; the ordeal relies on God to give the innocent a "clean" wound or a victory. With slaves, neither compurgation nor combat was used—the former was only for persons of good reputation and the latter only for persons of high status. Usually, a slave was subjected to the ordeal of boiling water, but the Franks used an ordeal by lot—the accused chose something at random, like opening a book to any page so that a priest could interpret the text revealed (again, this was an appeal to God). A slave (in general, unlike a free person) could be subjected to torture, not as a form of proof but in an attempt to get at the truth: a confession, or evidence against his or her lord. For convicted free persons, punishment consisted largely of paying compensation, although the death penalty could be imposed for very serious offenses such as treason, and loss of a hand was imposed for offenses such as forgery or counterfeiting. For a slave, punishment was physical punishment—the lash, castration, or death.

The Frankish laws make it quite clear that a lord could intervene on a slave's behalf. If the punishment was set at 120 lashes, the lord could "spare the slave's back" by the payment of 120 pence or 3 solidi; castration could be bought off by a payment of 240 pence or 6 solidi. Evidently the death penalty could not be countered by a lord, although before a conviction progressed to punishment, a lord could postpone the application of torture for some time by delaying tactics (Frankish law allowed delays in most judicial proceedings). And finally, an accuser who did proceed to torture had to provide a slave of his or her own as security, in case the accused slave should die under torture without confessing.

Almost all of the Germanic codes provide for marriage between dependents and between a dependent and a free person. Marriage between a slave and a free person was not possible, however. If a free woman married her slave or freedman, both were punished very severely. A man could not enter into a legal marriage with either his own slave or someone else's slave unless she was first manumitted. If a free man kept another man's slave as a concubine, her children became the slaves of her lord unless the man purchased them and freed them. If a man kept his own slave as a concubine, her children became his own slaves unless he manumitted them. Only the Lombards recognized manumitted children as "natural" offspring who shared with legitimate children in an inheritance, though with a much smaller portion. Freemen could marry half-free women and produce free offspring. Half-free women could marry slaves, and normally their offspring became slaves of the father's lord, although if the man and woman belonged to different lords, the marriage and the disposition and status of the offspring were subject to negotiation. Given that free could marry half-free and half-free could marry slave, legal status must have become very complicated after several generations.

The church was very much a part of slavery. Long before the establishment of the Germanic states, the church has absorbed slaveholding into its teachings. Both the Old and the New Testament refer to slavery without condemning it, and those who spread early Christianity laid more emphasis upon being content with the position into which one was born than on any basic human rights. Slaves were accepted as Christians, but that did not imply legal or economic equality. Officials of the church (e.g., bishops or abbots) were subject to the laws of the state regarding their own slaves. The church acquired slaves as secular persons did, but it also received gifts of land, with workers, since under Roman law, people could dispose of property in any way they liked, usually by testament. In the early Germanic states, family property (that obtained in the general distribution) descended according to fixed rules of inheritance, which precluded leaving land and workers to the church, although this ban did not apply to other kinds of property (such as special land grants from the king in return for services). Later, under pressure from the church, most of the Germanic states eventually removed the ban, and the church became one of the greatest slaveholders.

Manumission was recognized by all the Germanic codes and was encouraged by the church as a good work. Manumission could grant complete freedom, with no further tie to the former lord; or it might be limited during the lord's lifetime, to be absolute on his death; or a freed slave might become a sort of client of the former lord, with the lord inheriting the wealth of a former slave who died without leaving legitimate heirs. But church law limited a cleric's freeing of church slaves, and thus slavery lasted longer on some ecclesiastical estates than on secular estates.

In law, Germanic slavery seems to have been a fairly benign institution. But, still, a slave was property—even the provision that lords could offer some support for an accused slave was justified on the ground that the lords were protecting their property. Also, when medieval texts mention "emancipation," they mean only manumission; the concept of emancipation in its modern sense did not exist then.

See also ANCIENT ROME; CHRISTIANITY; MEDIEVAL EUROPE, SLAVERY AND SERFDOM IN; SLAVE TRADE.

BIBLIOGRAPHY

AMORY, PATRICK. *People and Identity in Ostrogothic Italy, 489–554.* 1997.
ATTENBOROUGH, F. L. *The Laws of the Earliest English Kings.* 1922.
DREW, K. F. *The Burgundian Code.* 1949.
———. *The Laws of the Salian Franks.* 1991.
———. *The Lombard Laws.* 1973.
KING, P. D. *Law and Society in the Visigothic Kingdom.* 1991.
PELTERET, DAVIS A. E. *Slavery in Early Mediaeval England.* 1995.
RIVERS, THEODORE JOHN. *Laws of the Alamans and Bavarians.* 1977.
TACITUS. *The Agricola and the Germania.* Translated by H. Mattingly. 1970.
THOMPSON, E. A. *The Early Germans.* 1965.

Katherine F. Drew

Ancient Greece

The Greeks believed that justice and law had originated with the god Zeus, but they did not believe that the god had handed down a specific body of laws. Human lawgivers dominate the early legal history of the Greek polis and range from such mostly legendary seventh-century figures as Zaleucus (Locri in Southern Italy), Lycurgus (Sparta), and, perhaps, Draco (Athens) to the historical Athenians Solon (ca. 594 B.C.E.) and Cleisthenes (508–507 B.C.E.). These men were seen as acting in accordance with divine justice but were not merely conduits of divinely revealed laws. In Athens, from the early fifth century, laws were enacted by the sovereign legislative body of all citizens (*ekklesia*) or, after the late fifth century, by a group of officials called "lawmakers" (*nomothetai*), supervised by six magistrates called "law guardians" (*thesmothetai*). The Greeks had decided as early as the mid-seventh century that the best laws were those written down.

Apart from the fragmentary fifth-century Gortyn (Crete) corpus and Athenian attempts (in the late fifth and early fourth centuries) to eliminate duplication and lack of clarity, few systematic codifications are known. It is Athenian law about which the best information exists, although even for these laws no complete text has survived. Our knowledge of Athenian laws in general and of those relating to slavery in particular comes from quotations (sometimes explicitly labeled "a law of Solon"); from speeches written for delivery by litigants in the courts or in the popular assembly (*ekklesia*), mostly dating from the fourth century B.C.E.; from references in tragedies, comedies, and histories; and from one or two manuals on household and estate management. Inscriptions—the most reliable records—supply a small amount of additional data, including some about manumission of slaves. Plato, Aristotle, and a few other philosophers offer additional material, although it is sometimes normative rather than descriptive.

Greek laws in general—apart from those that organized the polity—and courts were primarily responses to the need to deal with conflict or dangerous individual behavior with which the private sphere was unable to cope. Thus homicide laws stemmed the twin dangers to the community of blood pollution and blood feud. Except when it involved slaves owned communally (by the polis or the temples), the Greeks generally took slavery to be a natural condition and a private matter affecting property. The polis limited its intrusions to a number of key areas.

One major area was the desire to maintain the distinctions between free and servile. To judge by the screed of a conservative Athenian (early fourth century B.C.E.) known only as "the Old Oligarch," it was precious hard to distinguish a slave from a free man in Athens (though not elsewhere, apparently) by dress or behavior. Here the object was to distinguish those things forbidden to slaves but part of the normal rights of free citizens. Thus, slaves in Athens were forbidden to attend the popular assembly, the focal point of citizen participation. The law denied that slaves had any legal identity or power of action. Social behavior was also regulated, so that the law enjoined slaves from working out in the communal exercise facilities. This extended to sexual behavior as well: slaves could not be the active (i.e., penetrating) lovers of young boys or of free women; the former relationship would have given slaves a dominant role over a free person, and the latter, in addition, would threaten inheritance lines and claims to citizenship. Slaves might have religious rites and festivals of their own, but they were generally barred from those of the community.

A second purpose of civic intervention in slavery was to maximize owners' control of and responsibility for slaves and, simultaneously, to limit illicit or dangerous acts by slaves. Thus in any legal action involving slaves, they could not act on their own but required a "protector" (prostates), usually but not always the owner. Also, a slave could not be the object of the action. Legally, masters had full responsibility for their slaves; the master had to bring a private suit (under the laws pertaining to property) against anyone who injured or killed a slave. Likewise, if the slave did something wrong or injurious to a third party, the owner bore the responsibility for any cost or restitution that ensued from the private action. The state's interest in ensuring that slaves' testimony would be as reliable as possible required that such slaves be routinely tortured before giving their evidence.

The polis also intervened to limit the master's power over the slave, but only to some small extent. Under normal circumstances, the degree to which owners or third parties subjected slaves to physical violence or sexual abuse was not regarded as an area for community intervention. In general, in Athens—unlike some other poleis—third parties were not free to abuse, injure, or kill other people's slaves. Should someone other than the owner do so, the law went so far as to enforce, as far as possible, any compensation to the owner required by a private action. While owners were not supposed to kill their slaves, except for the most extraordinary reasons, they sometimes did. So far as can be told, no penalty normally applied. Both categories of killers, however, posed a threat to the community by their act, so the state demanded that they undergo ritual purification, thereby freeing the community from blood pollution and its potentially dire consequences. In Sparta, the state—the communal owner, in theory, of all *helots* (slaves)—took an entirely different and essentially extralegal approach to this particular problem: each year, the chief magistrates (*ephor*) declared war on all the helots, so that if a Spartan citizen killed any slave this would be an act of war and would not incur the blood pollution of murder.

See also ANCIENT GREECE; TORTURE.

BIBLIOGRAPHY

GAGARIN, M. *Early Greek Law.* 1986.
HANSEN, M. H. *The Athenian Democracy in the Age of Demosthenes.* 1991.
HARRISON, A. R. W. *The Law of Athens.* Vol. 1. 1968.
HOPKINS, K. *Conquerors and Slaves.* 1978.
MacDOWELL, D. M. *Law in Classical Athens.* 1978.
WEDEMANN, T. *Greek and Roman Slavery.* 1981.

Gerald E. Kadish

Ancient Rome and Byzantium

The story of Roman law begins, fairly reliably, with a sort of codification known as the Twelve Tables (451–450 B.C.). Its ancient life ends with the codification, or compilation, of Emperor Justinian in the years A.D. 529 to 534, known as the *Corpus Iuris Civilis*. This consisted of an introductory textbook for law students called the *Institutes*, a selection from the writings of the jurists (of whom more below) called the *Digest* or *Pandects*, and a collection of imperial enactments called the *Code*; Justinian's own legislation (*Novels*) was added. Justinian's reign also traditionally marks the start of the Byzantine Empire, the heir in the eastern

Mediterranean of the Roman Empire. This empire finally disappeared with the fall of Constantinople in 1453. So Roman law and Byzantine law have a continuous life of nineteen hundred years, and their separate influences have continued into the twentieth century.

The Twelve Tables was a code dealing with procedure and private law; it was largely composed of existing custom. It was statute (*lex*), that is, formal legislation passed by the centuriate assembly, the most important assembly of the Roman Republican constitution. As in the modern world, statute was the most direct and authoritative source of law, and new legislation overrode previous statute. So important were the Twelve Tables to lawyers of later generations that they were often referred to simply as *lex*; other legislation would be named specifically. At the end of the Republic in the first century B.C., they could still be described as the source and origin of all Roman law. This was true in that their interpretation and development by the jurists, along with some later legislation, comprised the *ius civile*, the state law peculiar to citizens, in contrast to the *ius honorarium*, the law specifically developed by the praetor, the magistrate in charge (from 366 B.C.) of all private jurisdiction whether the case sprang from state or praetorian law. The term *ius civile* was also used by Cicero to mean private law, as contrasted with public law. In legal writings the *ius civile*, as specifically Roman law, is often contrasted with the *ius gentium*, the law of all peoples. Slavery, although some held it to be contrary to the *ius naturale*, was an institution of the *ius gentium*—it was universal in the ancient Mediterranean world—but actual methods of making or freeing slaves were institutions of the *ius civile*. Thus in the Republic law was created by the assemblies, by the praetor, and by the jurists as well as by custom.

Legislation after the Twelve Tables, although supreme where relevant, was never the dominant method of developing law; indeed, most legislation was not concerned with private law. The praetor, advised by the jurists, was able to modify the law through his edict. This was issued each year, perhaps with some revisions, when a new praetor was elected, and it offered remedies for the claims people brought before him. Some pleas were clearly based directly on existing law (*ius civile*), as when somebody claimed ownership of a slave or that his slave had been burned by the wrongful act of somebody else, a case where a remedy was laid down by the *lex Aquilia*. Others were based on analogy, as when an owner claimed that his slave—although not burned or directly injured—had been denied food and starved to death. Actions granted for cases such as this were called actions on the facts or analogous actions (*actiones in factum, ac-*

tiones utiles), and they rested on the praetor's authority as a magistrate.

The praetor's authority gave him other powers as well. He was able, for instance, to deny a remedy to someone who had, on the face of it, a right, such as a freedman suing his patron or somebody pursuing a gambling debt. He will also have denied a remedy to an owner claiming the services of a slave who had been freed informally; such a slave was said (before the *lex Junia*, probably of Augustus, created the intermediate status of Junian Latin) to be free under the protection of the praetor. Manumission with the correct formality made a former slave—male or female—a citizen, a result unique in the Mediterranean world of antiquity. However, without the necessary formality a purported manumission had no effect in strict law. Formal manumission in the Republic was achieved in any of three ways: at the quinquennial census the slave owner would omit to list the slave as a member of the household; a claim would be made before the praetor in which a third party and the owner colluded in maintaining that the slave was being held wrongfully, that he or she was actually a free person; or an owner could free a slave in his or her will. In the Empire the census ceased to be taken, but the other two methods continued. In the later (Christian) Empire informal manumission gradually became equated with the formal methods, but it is not clear whether this was owing to changes in moral attitude or simply to a greater philosophical stress on the will of the actor in a legal transaction. In the interests of good faith and equity the praetor did not allow an owner or his heir to go back on his word. The slave could behave as a free man while he lived, working where he wished and acquiring property; however, when he died, all that he had acquired reverted to his owner as though it had been a personal fund, or peculium.

The end of the Republic—which one may perhaps date to 27 B.C., when Augustus claimed to have restored it—did not see any immediate change in the sources of law. The first emperors made use of assembly legislation; the praetor's edict did not disappear. The emperors preferred at first not to make new law directly, although they might use their status as magistrates for some reforms, as when Claudius (A.D. 41–54) issued an edict saying that slaves abandoned by their owners on grounds of ill-health were to become Junian Latins. During the first century A.D. resolutions of the senate replaced assembly laws as a form of direct legislation. But imperial enactments, whatever form they took, steadily grew in importance and by the end of the second century had become the only source of new direct law, although the old remained in force unless repealed. The jurists, however, continued in their advisory role to citizens, magistrates, of-

A session of the Roman Senate. [Corbis-Bettmann]

ficials, and emperors; they also published authoritative writings.

The explanation of why juristic writings were universally accepted as a source of law goes back to the time of the Twelve Tables. At that period the interpretation of law was in the hands of the college of pontiffs, a small group of patricians whose religious functions did not prevent them from taking leading parts in politics and war. Each year they appointed one of their number to be responsible for private law. The views of such men would readily be accepted as binding on those who consulted them, whether magistrates or private persons. Furthermore, their interpretation could change, thus making new law. During the third century B.C. the pontiffs ceased necessarily to be patricians, and other leading figures in the state began to interpret the law; "jurist" was their new name. The Republican jurists were nearly all members of the senate, the three-hundred-member body composed mostly of former magistrates, who in a way represented the state, as in the phrase *senatus populusque romanus* (the senate and people of Rome). Thus their moral authority continued to be enormous, as so often they had been or might become magistrates. In the Empire the jurists continued to hold the old magistracies or else were appointed as senior imperial officials; nevertheless, their authority as jurists was clearly dependent on their knowledge and their acceptance by their peers, rather than stemming from any particular post.

Jurists' law was primarily casuistic, arguing towards principle from the facts of the case (real or imaginary) that was before them. This is one reason for the clear distinction in Roman thought between jurisprudence and philosophy. Because of their social status one can safely assume that all the jurists had some philosophical training as part of their education and that they were familiar with doctrines such as Stoicism. Natural law was not, however, a concept which interested the jurists, as jurists, although they described such institutions as transfer of ownership by delivery as "natural." When they considered a specific institution, such as the slaves contained in a dowry (*servi dotales*), they worked out rules based on the two sets of rights, the husband's current rights and the wife's residuary rights, but they did not theorize about this double ownership. The slaves were owned by the husband while the marriage endured, and he could manumit them, but if he did so, he was normally liable to his wife for the diminution in the value of the dowry. Interestingly, a husband was liable for his ill-treatment of dotal slaves, even if he was habitually brutal to his own. In this respect a higher standard was required than the care he took in his own affairs. He was entitled to the fruits of the dotal slaves' labor and acquired whatever they earned or did for him; however, while jurists such as Julian and Paul held that casual acquisitions increased the value of the dowry, Pomponius thought it depended on the intention of the donor or testator.

The Roman Empire, in the colonial or geographical sense, was already close to its widest extent at the end of the Republic. Southern Britain was to be added under Claudius, and the province of Raetia was to fill the gap between the Rhine and the Danube. Rome, however, governed—rather as the British did in India—by giving local authorities responsibility for most administration in a province, while a Roman governor was responsible for law and order and the defense of the frontiers. All provinces of the Empire accepted slave owning, although the economic, as opposed to the social, importance of slavery was much more restricted in most of the provinces than it was in Italy. Roman notions came to dominate everywhere—extraordinary notions such as that a freed slave should normally become a citizen, or that there was no need for slave law since the rules governing dependent members of a family sufficed—except where a slave was to be viewed as a chattel, when the ordinary law of property operated. There were, of course, a few exceptions: The killing of a slave could be treated as murder (probably from the time of Sulla in the 80s B.C.), although an owner would be more likely to prefer treating the murder as a wrongful act, for which he could receive compensation. Under legislation passed by the emperors Hadrian and Antonious Pius, an owner became criminally responsible for deliberately killing his slave; however, an owner's right to severely punish his own slave would have made such a restriction relatively limited in practice. Meanwhile, when an owner was murdered in mysterious circumstances, the whole slave household was put at risk. Custom probably dictated that all the slaves should

be put to death for failing to prevent the killing of the owner. The Silanian resolution of the Senate (SC Silanianum), circa A.D. 10, laid down that all slaves of the household were to be tortured to discover the actual criminal; it also permitted the punishment—even death—of all those slaves who had failed in their duty by not preventing the killing.

There were no spheres of activity closed to slaves, except military service and politics. The prospects of any individual slave depended on the humanity and wealth of the owner, not on any attitude of the state. Classical Roman law was essentially the law of Italy until A.D. 212, when an edict of Emperor Caracalla gave citizenship, and therefore the use of Roman law, to all free inhabitants of the Empire. Greek or Hellenistic institutions survived to some extent, if only as local custom, but the Theodosian Code of A.D. 438 seems to accept a high degree of uniformity in legal practice. Postclassical Roman law had become the common law of the whole Empire, even if it was not exclusive. By this time too government had everywhere become direct, in a hierarchy with the emperor at its head.

In the later Roman Empire, dating from the reign of Constantine (312–337), the only lawgiver was the emperor. The jurists had disappeared, although of course there remained legal advisers in the civil service, law professors in the schools, and advocates and judges in the courts. Constantine's legalization of Christianity made no immediate difference to the private law, and certainly none to the status of slaves. Slavery remained embedded in the law throughout the Roman period. In the fifth century, law schools (in almost the modern sense) were founded at Beirut and Constantinople. Here Justinian found the jurists who could still read Latin, although his own legislation after the *Corpus Iuris* was all in Greek.

In the Byzantine Empire the sole lawgiver was the emperor; he was God's viceroy on earth with the duty to maintain in peace and war—war against Persian or Arab unbelievers—the empire willed by God. The East, in contrast with the West, maintained the single law of a single state, with its single source. There were some changes in the written sources of this law, but its continuity was never put into question; Byzantine law was founded on the *Corpus Iuris Civilis*. Justinian had forbidden commentaries on his codification, particularly on the *Digest*, which contained much argument, but translations, with other aids for a Greek-speaking public, were rapidly produced. Several of the compilers, and other professors contemporary with the publication of the *Corpus*, wrote summaries and abridgments of the *Digest* and the *Code*; Theophilus, in particular, wrote an extended Greek version of the *Institutes* known as the *Paraphrase*. Some time after

Marcus Antoninus, nicknamed Caracalla. [Charles and Josette Lenars/Corbis]

Basil proposed to restore and update Justinian's legislation, in some cases abrogating it. He issued the *Procheiron* (Manual; also called *Procheiros Nomos* or *Enchiridion*), designed to replace the heretical *Ecloga* as a guide to Justinian. The language was entirely Greek, with Greek equivalents rather than translations for many technical terms. His name was given to the *Basilica*, a major compilation in sixty books; this now became the basis of legal study, with many *scholia* (glosses) as well as epitomes. Justinian's law was still in force; this was the updated version with excisions and additions. Within each title, dealing with its own topic, relevant extracts (using Greek translations or abridgments) from the *Digest, Code, Novels,* and *Institutes,* were put together, usually in the original order; some extracts from the *Procheiron* were also included, as well as commentary from the work of Theophilus and others of the sixth century.

In the eleventh century there was something of an intellectual revival. The *Ecloga ad Procheiron mutata* was published; there was a glossing in greater depth of the *Basilica*—although there was never a standard gloss as in the West—and various handbooks were written. Under Constantine Monomachus (1042–1054) a chair of law was again set up at Constantinople; advocates and notaries qualified there. Canon law almost ousted secular law as an intellectual study in the twelfth century, but some epitomes and manuals continued to be produced. Of these the best known is the *Hexabiblos* (*Six-Book-Work*), published by a judge called Constantine Harmenopoulos around 1345; it updated the *Procheiron*, and included some canon law. It was actually in force in Greece from its independence in 1828 until the coming into force of a Greek Civil Code in 1946.

See also ANCIENT ROME; BYZANTIUM; PECULIUM; TORTURE.

BIBLIOGRAPHY

BUCKLAND, W. W. *The Roman Law of Slavery.* 1908.
FRESHFIELD, E. H., trans. *A Manual of Eastern Roman Law: The Procheiros Nomos.* 1928.
———. *A Manual of Later Roman Law: The Ecloga ad Procheiron Mutata.* 1927.
———. *A Manual of Roman Law: The Ecloga.* 1926.
———. *A Revised Manual of Roman Law: Founded on the Ecloga Privata Aucta.* 1927.
HONORÉ, T. *Tribonian.* 1978.
JOLOWICZ, H. F., and B. NICHOLAS. *Historical Introduction to the Study of Roman Law.* 1972.
ROBINSON, O. F. *The Sources of Roman Law.* 1997.
VAN DE WAL, N., and J. H. A. LOKIN. *Historiae Iuris Graeco-Romani Delineatio.* 1985.
WATSON, A. *Roman Slave Law.* 1987.

                                        O. F. Robinson

the death of Justinian, someone perforce known as "Anonymous" wrote, among other things, notes on the *Digest* which may have used other passages of the excerpted jurists. But the *Corpus* seems almost at once to have become too much for the courts to handle.

Under Leo III (717–741) and his son Constantine the Arabs were defeated and pushed eastward to make their capital in Baghdad. In the sphere of law the *Ecloga* (Selection) was published as a working guide to Justinian's legislation; it describes itself as selections from the *Institutes, Digest, Code,* and *Novels.* In penal law mutilation seems officially to have replaced the death penalty for many crimes. Slavery as an institution remained embedded in the law, although there were attempts to prevent Christians from being held as slaves; for example, a slave who entered the religious life with the consent of his owner was thereby automatically free. Leo's reign also saw the start of the Iconoclastic movement, from which the Empire was only recovering under the next great legislators, Basil I (867–886) and Leo VI (886–912).

Islamic Law

Of all the civilizations that have incorporated the institution of slavery, few have accorded the slave as many legal protections as Islam. At the same time, Islamic civilization has been one of the most resistant to extirpating slavery.

Religious Rules

Slavery was embedded in the social and legal structure of pre-Islamic Arabia. Most slaves were African, and Mecca was a primary center for the slave trade. Captives in war were either enslaved or put to death. In his religious transformation of Arabia, Muhammad (ca. A.D. 570–632) maintained but reformed many social structures. Slavery was one of them. In the Koran, the pre-Islamic practice of prostituting one's slaves is expressly forbidden; fair treatment and adequate maintenance are mandated. With the consent of the master, slaves may marry, and Muslim slaves are even permitted to marry free persons. In fact, the Koran encourages masters to provide spouses for morally upright slaves. In the fivefold scale of moral action in Islam—that which is compelled, laudatory, neutral, blameworthy, or forbidden—owning slaves is neutral, but manumitting them is a laudable act with direct benefits to the emancipator in the afterlife.

The moral attitude of the Koran toward slavery was extended in later traditions ascribed to Muhammad. Slaves could be asked to work only to the extent that they were physically able. They were not to be abused, and they were to be fully fed and clothed. Atonement for abusing a slave was accomplished by manumission. The widespread practice of concubinage was addressed by the promise of heavenly reward for a master who freed and then married his slave concubine. To gain heaven, the slaves on their part must be loyal and trustworthy.

The Law

The *shari'a*—classical Islamic law—developed over the two centuries after the death of Muhammad into a number of major legal schools within the dominant Sunni wing of Islam. Within the Shari'a, the law on slavery reached a new level of complexity and sophistication.

Like Roman law, the shari'a recognizes that human freedom comes from nature and that slavery is only a practice permitted by law. Slaves may be obtained as booty in a lawful war (i.e., a jihad declared by the caliph), by sale, or by birth to a slave mother. Depending on the circumstances, defeated soldiers were enslaved, killed, held for ransom, offered conversion, or allowed to live as a protected population.

An engraving depicts the revelation to Muhammad. [Corbis-Bettmann]

Under the shari'a, no one can be reduced to slavery either voluntarily or by debt. There is no permanent class of slaves. Apparently, the religious doctrine in favor of emancipation meant that the demand for new slaves continued on a high level. Thus, although legally only non-Muslim captives in a war could be reduced to slavery, in fact the need for slaves was met by raids on the periphery of the empire mediated by the network of Arab slave traders, and captives were Muslim well as non-Muslim.

Property Law

For the most part, the shari'a, drawing an analogy with animals, treats the slave as a species of property casuistically. The entire range of the Islamic law of sales, ownership (single or joint), inheritance, bailment, pledge, and deposit applies to the slave, as to most other forms of property.

Understandably, the law of sales as applied to slaves is among the most highly developed. The following are examples. The seller need cover only the loins of a slave being sold. It is up to the purchaser to provide the kind of clothing required by the law. Should the seller attempt to make a female slave more attractive by putting jewelry on her (obviously a common practice), the jewels are not included in the sale unless stipulated.

A right of inspection by the potential buyer is limited to the face, but the purchaser has the option of returning the slave if defects that were not stipulated at the time of the sale are later discovered. Such defects include disease, deformity, bad teeth, marriage, impotence, promiscuity (for the male), excessive wine drinking, madness, left-handedness (if the right hand is too weak to carry on tasks), having been a runaway, or having been convicted of a criminal offense. Defects voiding the sale of a female include being illegitimate, having committed fornication, being pregnant, or having borne a child. Other defects in a female encompass lack of menses, overeating, hidden scars, poor eyesight, and not being beautiful if she was sold as such. A purchaser forgoes the right to return a slave if he engages in sexual intercourse with or otherwise uses the slave twice; or if he lends or rents out the slave; if he offers the slave for sale; or if he punishes the slave in a way that leaves a permanent mark.

Personal Law

Status.   Even though slaves were a species of property, they had some limited personal rights. Four kinds of slavery are recognized in the shari'a: (1) *'abd*, the classic form of chattel slavery; (2) *mudabbar*, a slave with a guarantee of emancipation at the death of the master (owner); (3) *umm am-walid*, a female slave who obtains the emancipation at the master's death by bearing a child acknowledged by the master as his own; and (4) *mukatab*, a slave granted a contract for emancipation by his master in return for a specified sum.

A *mukatab* may own property, including other slaves, and is civilly liable for his transactions. A master may also allow other types of slaves to engage in a trade. Such a slave and the master are jointly responsible for the slave's debts, but the property the slave may acquire is the master's. In addition, a master may confer legal agency upon a slave, whose actions then bind the master. Masters are forbidden to sell a *mudabbar* or *umm am-walid* slave, though they may change the slave's status to a *mukatab* or may choose to emancipate the slave before the master's death. A *mukatab* may be sold only with the master's permission. At the death of the master, the law regards the emancipation of the *muddabbar* and *umm am-walid* slaves as bequests of the property of the slaves to themselves. Consequently, their value is regarded as part of the one-third of the estate that the deceased is allowed to give away by bequest.

Treatment.   Owner's must maintain a slave in food and clothing roughly equal to that which they provide for themselves. If an owner fails to do this, slaves have a right to work for their own sustenance. If the slave is incapable of work, the owner is required either to maintain him or to sell him. Although masters own the offspring of their female slaves, they are not permitted to separate young slave children from their parents or near relatives. If a master abuses his slave, there is no personal liability, but the *qadi*, or judge, may compel such a master to sell the slave to another person. Apparently, there is no legal remedy whatsoever if a master kills his slave.

A master may not make a female slave his concubine if she is within the degrees of relation that would be prohibited to him in marriage. Similarly, a female slave who suckles a master's child is sexually forbidden to him.

Marriage and Divorce.   There is not moral or legal prohibition against concubinage between a master and his female slave, but no man can marry his own slave unless he frees her first and thereby changes her status. Female owners are not permitted any sexual connection with their slaves. The Hanafi school in Sunni Islam allows a free man to marry another person's slave even through the children will be owned by the slave's master. The Shafi'i school is stricter: no man able to pay the marriage dower for a free woman can marry a slave. The schools differ on the status of additional wives. The Hanafis allow a man already married to a slave to marry a free woman, but they forbid any man married to a free woman to marry a slave as an additional wife. The Shafi'i and Maliki schools will permit such a marriage if the man himself is a slave.

Except in the Maliki school, every slave needs the permission of the master to marry. A master may contract marriage of a female slave without her consent. (The schools differ as to whether the master has the same right in regard to male slaves.) Whether married by permission or compulsion, however, the married female slave remains in the household of the master, and the husband may claim only reasonable access to his wife. A master loses his right of concubinage over his married slave. Should the master permit the slave to dwell with the husband, the husband is liable for her care and maintenance. Liability for payment of the dower by a male slave devolves upon him, the husband; but if he is unable to pay it, the master is responsible. The master, of course, may sell the slave to discharge the dower debt to the slave's wife. If a male slave marries a free woman, he is responsible for her maintenance, and if he fails in his duty, the master may sell the slave to pay the debt. A male slave can marry up to the legal limit of four wives, except in the Hanafi school, where he is limited to two.

If a woman who was married while she was a slave becomes free, she has a right, under the Hanafi school, to void the marriage because she is now free of the requirement of the master's consent and can make the decision as a sui generis person. Similarly, if she married without her owner's consent, the marriage is illegal, but it becomes legal the moment she is freed, for the impediment of the master's lack of consent is no longer present. If a free man marries a slave without the owner's consent, and the husband has sexual relations with her (technically, the marriage, being illegal, is not thereby consummated), the husband must pay his promised dower to the master as a form of damages. It follows that if the husband had no relations until after the slave was free, then the marriage would have been legalized and truly consummated, and the dower is due then to the wife.

In general, the rules concerning divorce are the same for slaves as for free persons. However, if a free person married to a slave purchases that slave, the marriage is immediately voided, no formula for divorce being necessary or permitted.

Emancipation.   Any adult, competent master may free a slave by any verbal formulation signifying the intent to do so. Emancipation procured by fraud is effective, but not if procured by duress. In some interpretations of the law, partial emancipation is considered total emancipation. Other jurists hold that slaves who are partially emancipated become *mukatab* and have the right to work out the rest of their freedom by labor as indentured servants. Similar differences arise when a co-owner of a slave emancipates his or her portion. By a legal fiction, a slave may purchase himself and is thereby immediately freed, but he remains indebted and must pay the amount stipulated.

Any acknowledged child of a slaveowner is free as of conception and has equal rights with the master's legitimate children. The slave mother of an acknowledged child of a master is free upon the master's death. According to some interpretations, a master cannot deny paternity of a child born to a virtuous female slave within his household. If a person by sale, gift, or inheritance obtains a slave who is within the range of relations prohibited to him by marriage, such a slave is immediately freed. A master also has the option of directly freeing the unborn child of his pregnant slave without affirming his paternity, and the emancipation of a female slave pregnant by any man frees her unborn child as well.

Criminal and Civil Liability.   A slave enjoys less protection and less liability than a free person for criminal acts, except homicide. Except in the Hanafi school, a free man who kills a slave is subject to the law of retaliation. Likewise, a slave may be killed in retaliation for killing a free man. But the right of retaliation is not permitted if a slave suffers only bodily injury from another. Instead, damages are due to the owner. Likewise, in most cases, a slave is not subject to the same degree of punishment for criminal acts such as adultery or intoxication as a free Muslim would be. Civilly, a master is responsible for damages caused by negligent acts of his slave.

Practice

In an empire stretching from West Africa to the East Indies, and over a history extending well past a millennium, the variations in slaveholding practices went beyond the limits of the shari'a, although the sacred law exerted major constraints. Islamic law, historically understood, comprehends more than the formulas of the shari'a. It includes custom as well as the positive law of the state. In highly developed societies where slavery was already established, such as the Hausa in West Africa, Islamic rules melded with the traditions already in place.

For much of the history of Islam, slavery was a vigorous and ubiquitous part of Islamic empires and principalities. Wars of conquest, raids across the Mediterranean, piracy, and forays into Slavic territories, as well as the ever-present capture, sale, and trade of Africans, provided a virtually unceasing supply of slaves. In the Middle East, agricultural slavery was rare, the institution being limited to urban areas, households (household slavery included the widespread practice of concubinage), trading centers, the bureaucracy, and the military. Classes of educated slaves, artisans, and eunuchs were part of the economy and the social structure. For slaves, conversion to Islam for the slaves was highly attractive, since manumitting Muslim slaves was a common practice.

Throughout Islam, slavery continued unabated until fairly late in the nineteenth century, when, particularly under pressure from the British, Islamic authorities began to restrict it by law. By the 1870s, slavery had been legally abolished in India, Russia, and the French and Dutch possessions. A long process of enfranchisement was completed in the same decade in Tunisia, Egypt, and the Ottoman Empire. In East Africa however, slavery was not legally prohibited until shortly before World War I. The North African slave trade continued into the twentieth century, and despite its universal prohibition under international law, it was not legally abolished in Saudia Arabia until 1962 and in Muscat and Oman until 1970. In fact, slavery is still practiced widely in Mauritania and has resurfaced in the Sudan, where a genocidal war against the non-Muslim Nubians has produced thousands of black slaves, children in particular.

See also ISLAM; OTTOMAN EMPIRE.

BIBLIOGRAPHY

"'Abd." In *The Encyclopaedia of Islam,* new ed., vol. 1. 1975.
ANDERSON, NORMAN. *Law Reform in the Muslim World.* 1976.
COULSON, NOEL J. *A History of Islamic Law.* 1964.
CRONE, PATRICIA. *Slaves on Horses: The Evolution of the Islamic Polity.* 1980.
FISHER, ALLAN G. B., and HUMPHREY J. FISHER. *Slavery and Muslim Society in Africa: The Institution in Saharan and Sudanic Africa and the Trans-Saharan Trade.* 1970.
HAMILTON, CHARLES. *The Hedaya.* 1791.
KHALIL, SIDI. *Maliki Law.* 1916. Reprinted 1980.
MAKRIS, G. P. "Slavery, Possession and History: The Construction of Self among Slave Descendants in the Sudan." *Africa* 66 (1996): 159–182.
NAWAWI. *Minhaj et talibin: A Manual of Muhammadan Law according to the School of Shafi.* 1941.
OCHSENWALD, W. "Muslim-European Conflict in the Hijaz: The Slave Trade Controversy, 1840–1895." *Middle Eastern Studies* 16 (1980): 115–126.
RAHIM, ABDUR. *Muhammadan Jurisprudence.* 1911.
SCHACHT, JOSEPH. *An Introduction to Islamic Law.* 1964.
———. *The Origins of Muhammadan Jurisprudence.* 1950.
WILLIS, JOHN RALPH. *Slaves and Slavery in Muslim Africa,* vol. 1: *Islam and Ideology of Enslavement.* 1985.

David Forte

Slavery Cases in English Common Law

The common law of England had for centuries rejected the condition of slavery, but when the creation and expansion of the British Empire began, courts of common law strove to reconcile the new colonial institution with the doctrines and procedures of English common law.

This process was necessarily piecemeal and sporadic, rather than planned and systematic. Cases came to the courts as they naturally arose in the give-and-take of commercial activity and social interaction.

The question of "trover" arose early in common-law cases. Trover is a common-law action for the value of property or chattels improperly converted to the use of another.

For trover to apply to a slave, the slave had to be regarded as property in law. In *Butts v. Penny* (1677), trover was allowed for a group of a hundred Negro slaves because, the court reasoned, the Negroes were infidels, the subjects of an infidel prince, and were regularly traded as merchandise among merchants. These facts established there was sufficient property in the Negroes to allow trover. *Noel v. Robinson* (1687) upheld the same principle as *Butts.*

Gelly v. Cleve (1694) likewise found for trover in a Negro boy slave, but the court based its decision upon the fact that the boy was a heathen. It is suspected, furthermore, that the boy was a resident of America, as is also believed to have been true in the case of *Butts.* In *Chamberline v. Harvey* (1696–1697), however, the court refused to allow trover to lie for a Negro, citing Chief Justice Holt to the effect that trover cannot lie for any Negro. The court denied that a slave was chattel, asserting that a slave was a special class of servant. The master could recover only for the loss of the services of the slave (*per quod servitium amisit*—for services lost, in the phrase of the law), not for the value of the slave.

In *Smith v. Brown and Cooper* (early 1700s), Chief Justice Holt was prepared to find for the plaintiff in an *indebitatus assumpsit* (i.e., a claim of a debt owed and promised, in consideration, to be paid), but he insisted that the court papers be amended to specify that although the sale had taken place in London, the slave was domiciled in Virginia, where slavery was legal. The intervention of the attorney general, however, ended the attempted emendation, when he informed the court that in Virginia slaves were transferrable only by deed.

In *Smith v. Gould* (1708), furthermore, the court held that trover could not lie with a Negro slave because an owner did not enjoy an absolute property right in him—for example, he could not legally kill him as he might an ox. Chief Justice Lord Hardwicke broke with the tendency in the slave-trover cases by holding, in *Pearne v. Lisle* (1749), that trover will lie with a Negro slave, since "it is as much property as any other thing." Rather disingenuously, Lord Hardwicke held that his opinion in *Pearne* was not at odds with earlier cases such as *Smith v. Gould* and *Smith v. Brown and Cooper,* because the earlier cases dealt with "Negroes" who were not stipulated to be slaves in the official court papers.

Of all the cases of slave law heard by British courts, the two most famous are undoubtedly *Somerset v. Stewart* (1772) and *The Slave, Grace* (1827). The irony, perhaps, is that while *Somerset* is often seen as an unprecedented "bolt from the blue" and *The Slave, Grace* is often interpreted as cutting back on the implications of the *Somerset* doctrine, there were ample precedents for *Somerset,* and the outcome of *The Slave, Grace* was well in line with the judicial findings in *Somerset.*

In *Somerset v. Stewart,* the slave Somerset sued for and won his freedom as a result of his presence in England. Somerset's master unsuccessfully attempted to compel him to return to Jamaica, but Lord Mansfield and the court held that slavery was so odious and contrary to nature that only the positive law could sanction it. In England, villeinage had been the only "slavery" recognized by the common law, and that had disappeared with the death or emancipation of all who had been subject to it. Somerset, therefore, was a free man.

Smith v. Brown and Cooper had partially anticipated *Somerset* in that Chief Justice Holt had declared that as soon as a Negro entered into England he became free, for one could be a villein in England, but not a slave. The jointly rendered advisory opinions of the attorney-general Sir Philip Yorke, and the solicitor-general Talbot (1729) stood against the trend, however, for they held that his presence in Great Britain or Ireland did not free a slave, any more than the Christian baptism of a slave freed him from servitude. This joint advisory opinion seems to have been politically motivated and to have had very limited basis in law, arguing mainly by analogy from the established principle that conversion and baptism did not free one who was already enslaved.

In *Sheddan v. a Negro* (1757), a Scottish case, a black slave from Virginia, who had been apprenticed to an artisan in Scotland by his master, was in the process of being forcibly returned to Virginia when the court granted a hearing on the status of the slave. The death of the slave alone intervened to prevent a trial on the issue.

In *Shanley v. Harvey* (1762), Shanley, as executor of the estate of Margaret Hamilton, sought the return of the Negro slave Joseph Harvey, whose mistress had freed him and given him a substantial sum of money. Lord Chancellor Henly found for Harvey, stating that by setting foot on English ground he was free. Clearly, *Shanley* anticipated the result of *Somerset*, except that the Negro was physically at liberty at the time of the suit, and it was the estate of an owner, rather than the owner, which sought to vindicate its claim of ownership.

Finally, in *The Slave, Grace*, an admiralty case involving the claim for liberty of a slave who had resided in England but had voluntarily returned to Antigua, where she was a slave, Lord Stowell held that the freedom which the slave could have claimed while in England amounted to the right not to be forcibly removed from the realm. Having voluntarily returned to Antigua, Grace's status as a slave under that colony's laws allowed her to be held as a slave.

Again, although many scholars have seen *The Slave, Grace* as an unprecedented abandonment of the full implications of the *Somerset* doctrine, the opinion of the court cited ample precedents, including *King v. Thomas Ditton* (1785) in which Lord Mansfield himself stated that the only issue involved in *Somerset* was "whether a slave would be taken from this country in irons and carried back to the West Indies, to be restored to the dominion of his master?" and *Williams v. Brown* (1802), which also denied the transmarine application of the *Somerset* doctrine.

The prejudice of English common law was in favor of freedom and against captivity, but that presumption had always had its limitations. The law's presumption of liberty never prevented the execution within the realm of sales of slaves and contracts for the labor of slaves held in venues where slavery was legal. The presumption also did not require the application of *Somerset* doctrine in transmarine colonies, and it did not prevent the erection of the legal infrastructure for slavery within various colonies of the British Empire.

The latter limitation rested on the theory that the colonies were the king's possessions through conquest in war and that acts of Parliament and common law did not apply within them, except as the king should freely grant, or as an act of Parliament should explicitly provide.

See also SLAVE GRACE; SOMERSET V. STEWART.

BIBLIOGRAPHY

BUSH, JONATHAN A. "The British Constitution and the Creation of Slavery." In *Slavery and the Law*, edited by Paul Finkelman. 1997.

CATTERALL, HELEN TUNNICLIFF, ed. *Judicial Cases Concerning American Slavery and the Negro*, vol. 1. 1926.

Patrick M. O'Neil

English Common Law in England and the American Colonies

Slavery in the British Empire received its legal form, in large part, from the English common law, and the same continued to prove true in post-Revolutionary America, where all states but Louisiana used it as the basis of their most fundamental civil and criminal law.

Common law is that great body of law in the Anglo-American tradition which derived not from statutes but rather from usages and customs of immemorial antiquity recognized in court decisions.

Equity was formally separated from common law throughout much of history, at least in part because different courts held these jurisdictions. The courts of the King's Bench, Common Pleas, and Exchequer were the judicial sources of the common law, while equity jurisdiction rested in the Court of Chancery, derived from the authority of the Lord Chancellor—the "Keeper of the King's Conscience." Equity applied established principles of fairness and justice to modify the rigidity of common law, as well as to provide equitable interpretation of statutory enactments.

The applicability of common law to the colonies was at first a matter of controversy. The theory of the English law held that as conquered territory, these colonies were governed at the king's pleasure and did not, as a matter of right, receive the statutory and common law of England. Eventually, however, the issue became academic, as Britain did extend both codes of law to its American colonies.

Slavery had ended in England during the reign of Edward VI (1547–1553), and the British Parliament and the common-law and equity courts at Westminster had created little systematic slave law for the slaveholding colonies or for the slave trade that was carried out in British ships. Colonial slavery was created by common law, court decisions, and statutes. It also developed out of the practices of individual masters, who without any legal authority enslaved their black indentured servants. Retrospectively, colonial legislation and court decisions recognized and regulated such actions.

While the slave trade remained legal, it required little recognition by common law, because admiralty law was based on Roman law, not English common law. The only common-law body of doctrines that might be seen as relevant to slavery was associated with medieval "villeinage"—common-law serfdom—but there were enormous differences between serfdom and slavery, such as the residual rights of the villein to religion, property, inheritance, formation of a family, and freedom from sale.

One of the first questions that arose in common law was whether slaves constituted real property or personal property (chattels)—categories governed by very different rules and procedures. Originally, there was a split among the various colonies over this issue, but eventually all came to treat slaves as chattels. When South Carolina defined slaves as real estate in 1690, the English Privy Council disallowed it. In 1705, however, Virginia, passed a law making the slaves of farmers or plantation owners realty; and a law of 1728 allowed them to be included in the entailment of estates, which protected the interests of successive legitimate heirs.

Next, the outer limits of state power were set by common law, so that, for example, any master (or any other person) who deliberately killed a slave might face a charge of murder (sometimes with the possibility of the death penalty in certain jurisdictions) or of manslaughter. However, southern courts also held that a slave had no rights to respond to insult, nondeadly assault, or minor forms of battery from a white person. Similarly, a white person might be justly provoked by a slave acting violently or impolitely to a white person. For example, in *State v. Tackett* (1822) the North Carolina Supreme Court reversed the murder conviction of a white person who had killed someone else's slave, asserting that Tackett had the right to introduce evidence showing that the deceased slave had been notoriously rude to whites. Significantly, however, southern courts also ruled that slaves had a common-law right to defend themselves—even to the point of killing whites—if threatened with deadly force.

The common-law principle of *respondeat superior* ("let the master answer") played a major role in the obligations of the masters. Under this rule, a master bears financial obligation for injuries and damages caused by servants in carrying out their duties. If, for example, a coach driver—through carelessness—injures someone, the driver's employer must pay to compensate for the damages. The theory behind this legal doctrine had a dual justification: (1) The master normally had financial resources, while the servant ordinary had little. (2) The master had a positive duty to control the activities of employees. However, starting with *Snee v. Trice* (1802), the South Carolina courts rejected the application of this rule to slaves. Most southern states followed South Carolina's lead. Southern courts, dominated by slave owners, thus altered the common law to protect masters from liability for the negligence of their slaves, unless the negligent slave acted under the immediate supervision of his master or the master's white agent or overseer.

Since many customs regarding the treatment of slaves were not specifically sanctioned in medieval villeinage, common-law jurists tended to interpret many rules of slavery as private arrangements rather than public law.

Sometimes colonial courts would simply follow Roman law, on the understanding that civil law had elaborate rules concerning slavery, whereas common law had none; but the pattern was haphazard rather than systematic. In South Carolina, in the case of *Guardian of Sally, a Negro v. Beaty* (1792), the courts refused to apply civil law to a dispute about slavery; but in *Bynum v. Bostick* (1812), a case involving the establishment of a trust to free a slave, Roman law was applied. In *State v. Jones* (1821), the Supreme Court of Mississippi refused to exonerate the killer of a slave on the proffered grounds of the Roman law's grant of absolute dominion; but in Mississippi, in *George, a slave v. State* (1859)—a case involving the rape of one slave by another—Roman law was used.

Even when slaves were not designated as real estate, however, an analogy between real property and slave property was entertained by the courts in order to apply useful common-law concepts to issues involving slave property. In *Hetton v. Caston* (1831), Judge John O'Neall of South Carolina entertained an action of trespass involving the severe beating of a slave by a hirer. In Florida, furthermore, in *McLeod v. Dell* (1861), the question arose whether slaves—unlike land under common-law—could pass by a nuncupative will. Chief Justice Charles H. DuPont concluded they could not.

Interstate succession in the realm was provided for by the English Statute of Distributions of 1670, and many colonies followed its provisions, with partible inheritance a consequence and slave families often divided to fulfill legal requirements.

Under common law, all personal property, including slaves, could be bequeathed as the owner chose;

The Court of Common Pleas in London around 1808. [Historical Picture Archive/Corbis]

but there were legal devices—such as excecutory devices, entails, remainders, and trusts—whereby the right of an heir to liquidate an estate could be restricted or eliminated.

Colonial jurisprudence on slavery often modified the established common law as well. In Virginia, in *Edwards v. Hughes* (1730), the presumption that there can be no remainder in a chattel was overturned in regard to slaves on the theory that the remainder was granting the use for a time of the slave property rather than assigning the thing itself.

In the nineteenth century, trusts had become an important means of securing property from seizure for debt. In a case in Virginia, *Gile v. Mallicotte* (1738), the question arose whether a testator could bequeath slaves not yet born. When a remaind is set up with one party receiving the income of the slave for life, do children born to these slaves belong to the tenant for life or ought they to pass to the remainderman? The Maryland Supreme Court in *Holmes v. Mitchell* (1850)

held for the remainderman, as did *Tims v. Potter* (1780s) in North Carolina, and *Murphy v. Riggs* (1819) in Kentucky.

Common law required that a widow receive a life-interest in one-third of real property owned by her husband during their marriage, and by the early eighteenth century it adopted the rule that one-third of personal goods should also pass to the widow. In *Herndon v. Herndon's Adm'rs.* (1958), the Missouri courts decided that children born to a slave who was possessed by the wife as part of her dower went with the mother, rather than remain part of the descendant's estate.

In *Fitzhugh v. Foote* (1801), a Virginia court of appeals—in ordering rectification of the amount of dower given to a widow—directed that young slave children could not be separated from their mothers.

With slaves designated as chattel, there was little to forestall their seizure for debt. Some wills provided that slaves of estates be hired out to pay debts, rather than break up estates in order to sell chattels to pay debts. The Chesapeake colonies utilized a three-tier system with land entirely protected, slaves semiprotected, and ordinary chattels entirely unprotected from seizure for debt. Even in places where they were defined as real estate, slaves were still liable to sale for debts. In Virginia, in *Tucker v. Sweney* (1730) and *Goddin v. Morris* (1732), the court held that although slaves constituted a special category, when other personalty was sold, slaves could also be sold to satisfy obligations of an estate, including obligations to an heir or legatee. In North Carolina, in *Holderness v. Palmer* (1858), an executor was upheld in selling some land of the estate rather than its slaves. The court held that the sale was because of exigent circumstances; and if some slaves, rather than land, had been sold, the purposes of the testator in keeping slaves together would have been frustrated.

In Kentucky, in *Logan v. Withers* (1830), the court held that slaves were realty and that legal title transferred immediately to the devisee, although in *Anderson v. Irvine* (1845), the court held that slaves were assets.

Under warranty, law, common law generally turned to the maxim *caveat emptor* (let the buyer beware); nonetheless, there were limits to this principle. Deliberate deception constituting fraud was one such limit, as, of course, was the concept of merchantability, which protected an absolute minimum standard implicit in the sale of an item.

In *Waddill v. Chamberlayne* (1735), a Virginia court found for the plantiff in a suit over the sale of a slave with an incurable disease who proved of little worth. In *Timrod v. Shoolbred* (1793), a South Carolina court found, in the case of the slave who soon afterward died of smallpox, that a maxim of Roman law applied—"A sound price raises a warranty of the soundness of the thing sold." In *Rouple v. M'Carty* (1795), the court held to a doctrine that where a case is doubtful, the contract is to be maintained. In *Watson v. Boatwright* (1845), the court utilized the fact of an agreed discount in the price of a slave to apply *caveat emptor;* and in *Rodriques ads. Habersham* (1843) the court utilized the formal refusal of the seller to agree to a warranty before the sale in order to apply that principle.

In Alabama, in *Caldwell v. Wallace* (1833), the court held that the mental soundness of a slave was warrantied in any sale where notice of unsoundness was not given. In North Carolina, in *Sloan v. Williford* (1843), the court attempted to set a more precise standard of mental competence. Slaves are warrantied not only against idiocy but against any weakness of reason rendering them incapable of comprehending and performing the common duties of slaves.

The decision in *Martin v. Martin* (1842), in Virginia, included an explanation of why the English remedy of detinue, which had mostly been replaced by trover, had been revived in the colonies: this was because of the attachment often felt between slaves and master. In that case, as in an earlier case in South Carolina, *Brown v. Gilliland* (1813), specific execution of contract was required. In two later cases, *Rees v. Parish* (1825) and *Farley v. Farley* (1826) in South Carolina, the courts declined to require specific performance of contract; but in *Sarter v. Gordon* (1835), *Harry v. Glover* (1837), and *Young v. Burton* (1841), the courts returned to that remedy.

In *Wilson and Trent v. Butler* (1813), the Virginia court granted an injunction against the seizure and sale of "family" slaves conveyed in trust. As to the mortgage of chattels, Chancellor James Kent's *Commentaries on American Law* held that personal property could be subject to mortgage. In *Overton v. Bigelow* (1832) in Tennessee, the court, following Kent, pronounced slaves open to mortgage.

Another issue that naturally arose was the right of redemption of mortgaged property. Until the 1820s,

James Kent. [Library of Congress/Corbis]

twenty years had been the time limit for redemption of a slave. In 1822, a Virginia court, in *Roberts Admin. v. Cockee, Ex'r. of Thompson*, held thirteen years too great a passage of time to claim redemption. Kentucky and Arkansas courts set a five-year limitation. By statute, Georgia set four years and Alabama set six.

In regard to the escape of mortgaged slaves, in *Webb and Foster v. Patterson* (1846), a Tennessee court held that where a slave owner knew that a slave had a tendency to flee, the creditor did not bear the costs of recovery. In *Kees v. Yewell* (1834), Kentucky courts held that when flight occurred, the creditor bore the loss; but in this case—unlike *Webb*—there was no evidence of foreknowledge on the part of the debtor. In Maryland, in the case of *Evans v. Merrikin* (1836), the court found that offspring born to mortgaged slaves were the property of the mortgagee.

Finally, common law had to deal with slave hiring, which formed a not inconsiderable aspect of the system. The law the court selected was that of bailments, modified to the peculiarities of the institution of slavery and to the needs of individual contractors bailee and bailor through the element of contract.

The early law of bailments was set down by Sir William Jones in *An Essay on the Law of Bailments* (1781) and by Joseph Story in *Commentaries on the Law of Bailments* (1832). Because the common law of bailments had been so sparse, Jones had to import ideas from civil law.

In Virginia, in *Georgia v. Elliot* (1806), the court decided that when a slave became sick the tenant still had to pay for the hire; but in the case of death of a slave through no fault of the tenant, the owner bears the loss of the hire.

In *Harris v. Nicholas* (1817), the Virginia courts held a tenant not to be liable despite his overseer's having killed a hired slave, since the overseer's action was unauthorized misconduct. In *Hicks v. Parham, Ex'r.* (1817), the Tennessee Supreme Court found that the faultless death of a hired slave did not justify a refund to the tenant. The Alabama Supreme Court in *Outlaw and McClellan v. Cook* (1824) found the tenant liable for the loss when a slave was disabled by an accidental wound; and in *Helton v. Caston* (1831), the South Carolina appeals court found an action for trespass to lie with the owner when the tenant was abused or damaged the property.

As to the rights and powers of the hirers of slaves, *Harrison v. Murrell* (Kentucky, 1827) upheld the owner's right to collect for the whole contract when the slave died, although without any fault on the part of the hirer. *Harmon v. Fleming* (Mississippi, 1852) and *Lennard v. Boynton* (Georgia, 1852) concluded similarly. Other state courts found the opposite—*Dud-

geon v. Teass* (Missouri, 1846), *Townsend v. Hill* (Texas, 1857) and *Alston v. Balls* (Arkansas, 1852).

The common law as it was received from its English sources was modified and expanded to treat the problems posed by slavery in the American colonies and in the states that succeeded them. No catalogue of the influences of the common law could be complete without mention of a case that was to play an influential role in the comity between the slave and free states. In *Somerset v. Stewart* (1772), Lord Mansfield, Chief Justice of the Court of the King's Bench, found that the plaintiff Somerset could not be forcibly removed from the realm by the master who had brought him to England. Mansfield found that slavery was so contrary to nature that only positive law could give it existence. The force of the *Somerset* doctrine was somewhat blunted by *The Slave, Grace* (1827), an admiralty case which held that Grace could not claim her freedom on account of her residence in Britain, because she had voluntarily returned with her master to the British West Indies—her slave status had reattached itself upon her reentry into that jurisdiction.

These two cases, but especially *Somerset*, would help to set patterns in the comity between slave state and free state and conflict-of-laws doctrine during the entire antebellum period of United States history.

See also SLAVE GRACE; SOMERSET V. STEWART.

BIBLIOGRAPHY

BUSH, JONATHAN A. "The British Constitution and the Creation of American Slavery." In *Slavery and the Law*, edited by Paul Finkelman. 1997.

FINKELMAN, PAUL. *The Law of Freedom and Bondage: A Casebook*. 1986.

JENKS, EDWARD. *The Book of English Law*, 6th ed. Edited by P. B. Fairest. 1967.

METCALFE, O. K. *General Principles of English Law*, 11th ed. Edited and revised by Gavin McFarlane. 1980.

MORRIS, THOMAS D. *Southern Slavery and the Law, 1619–1860*. 1996.

The Slave, Grace, 2 Haggard Admiralty (G.B.) 94 (1827).

Somerset v. Stewart, Loft (G.B.) 1 (1772); 20 Howell St. Tr. (G.B.) 1 (1772).

Patrick M. O'Neil

Roman Law in the New World

The term *civil law* is used in various senses, in contrast to military law, criminal law, or canon law. But in the context of slavery the contrast is with common law, the law applied in Anglo-American jurisdictions. In this sense, civil law refers to those systems found in states that accepted the Byzantine emperor Justinian

I's compilation of Roman law, the *Corpus Juris Civilis* (529–534 A.D.) as authoritative or at least directly highly persuasive in whole or in part. In North America civil law, including slave law, was thus to be found in the Spanish, French, Portuguese, and Dutch colonies.

This *Corpus Juris Civilis* was in four parts. The *Code* was a large collection of imperial enactments dating from the second century to the time of Justinian himself. The *Digest*, twice as long as the *Code* (in the standard edition it occupies around two thousand printed pages), contained fragments of the writings of the Roman jurists from the first century B.C. until about 235 A.D. The *Institutes* was a textbook for law students, and it was promulgated as statute in 533. The *Novels*, or *Novellae* ("New Constitutions") was a collection of Justinian's own enactments, issued after the main work of codification of Roman law was complete. This last is of little significance for subsequent legal development, partly because of its substance, largely because the "constitutions" were written in Greek and hence long could not be read in the Latin West.

The reception of Roman law in European states and its application in the New World took various forms, and the extent of its influence differed from place to place. But in all cases the reception was monumental. It should be noted that here we are concerned with the period from the twelfth century on, before the great European codes of law.

In Spain the reception of Roman law had begun even before Justinian and resulted in the great Visigothic Code (654), which began as the law of one small people but, after the peninsula was retaken from the Moors, came to be dominant in the region. The Visigothic Code was translated into Castilian in the mid-thirteenth century as the *Fuero Juzgo*, which was in force to a greater or lesser extent throughout all Spain. The greatest legal achievement of the Spanish Middle Ages was *Las Siete Partidas* (The Seven Parts), an enormous compilation largely based on Justinianian Roman law. The final shape of *Las Siete Partidas* was probably fixed around 1265. *Las Siete Partidas* were confirmed as law by the *Leyes de Toro* of 1505.

By ingenious reasoning, medieval jurists manipulated the rules of Roman private property law on a topic called *accessio* (accession) in order to come up with the doctrine that when territories of infidels were acquired by a Christian prince they were automatically incorporated by accession into his lands. The territories in the New World granted to Spain thus became in law part of Castile and were therefore governed by Castilian laws including *Las Siete Partidas*. Hence, much Roman law came to the Spanish colonies, and those colonies were also the object of much subsequent legislation from Spain itself. Be-cause Spain had slaves, slavery was dealt with in *Las Siete Partidas*; thus one can almost say that Spain's colonies had slave law before they had slaves.

Much more than Spain, France was a land of customary law, with each district having its own system of binding custom. In the south, the so-called "land of written law," the custom was Roman law itself, as modified in each place by subsequent custom. In the north, the "land of customary law," Roman law was not directly accepted as custom. Still, much Roman law was incorporated into the individual local customs. Even more to the point, throughout France the customs left many gaps. When these had to be filled, jurists and judges borrowed from elsewhere—from neighboring customs, from the Custom of Paris, or from Roman law. Roman law was accepted by different localities on three bases: as the written law of France supplementing local customs when they failed; as incorporating "right reason"; and as the common law of France, wherein customs were treated as local variations that were to be interpreted restrictively.

A great unifying force for law in France and its colonies was the most influential French law book for centuries, Jean Domat's *Les Loix civiles dans leur ordre naturel* (The Civil Laws in Their Natural Order) first published between 1689 and 1697. Domat's aim was to set out a system of Christian law for all of France, arranged so as to be easily understood. In this unifying book Roman law dominates. Though the Louisiana *Digest* of 1808 postdates the colonial period, the prominence among its sources of works such as Domat's treatise and *Las Siete Partidas* testifies to their importance in colonial days.

Basically, the law to be applied in the French North American colonies was the Custom of Paris. There were no slaves in France; hence there was no slave law in the Custom of Paris. Notably, the French home government took considerable interest in legislation for the colonies. When slavery was introduced into Louisiana and the Antilles, it came to be regulated by royal edict from Paris, resulting in the compilation known as the *Code Noir* (Black Code) of 1742. This code, not made in the colonies, is very directly based on Roman law. Preliminary work on it was, however, done in the Antilles, and local conditions had an impact on policing regulations and on relations between owner and slave.

The so-called Dutch colonies were technically possessions of the Dutch West India Company, not of the United Provinces. By its charter of 1621, the law to be applied to the Company was the common law of the United Provinces of the Dutch Republic, or such of that common law as was approved by the governing body of the company, but legal procedure was to be as short as possible. The law of the colonies, therefore, was not identical to that which obtained in any particular one of the seven provinces, but took its form from that which was most generally accepted in all of them. The seven provinces, each having its own legal system, had received Roman law in different ways and to different extents. The most heavily Romanized was Friesland, followed by Holland. The most influential Dutch law books of the seventeenth century were written for Holland and Friesland by Hugo Grotius and Ulrich Huber respectively.

There were no slaves in the Dutch Republic, and so no common law of slavery. Still, by the charter of the Dutch West India Company, contract law and trading generally were to be governed by the "common written law"; and "written law" meant Roman law, not custom. By skillful and deliberate misinterpretation "trading" was taken to include slavery. Accordingly, though this was not officially stated, Roman slave law was applied practically in its entirety. There was some subsequent local modification, but this was almost entirely concerned with policing.

Portugal's American colonies were incorporated into the state by *accessio*. The main Portuguese laws were a poor codification, the *Ordenaçoes Filipinas* (1643), which remained in force for more than three centuries, even after Brazil became independent. There were slaves in Portugal, and the *Ordenaçoes* contained some rules governing the practice, but not enough. But the *Ordenaçoes* provided that gaps in secular law were to be filled from the *Corpus Juris Civilis*; hence the dominant law for slavery in Portuguese America was again Roman law.

Thus, the civil law systems of slavery in the American colonies varied among themselves, but the law of the English colonies had characteristics that set them markedly apart from all the rest.

Two masters were not regulated by the influence of the *Corpus Juris Civilis*: policing regulations, because the Roman rules were not, and are not, known; and relations between master and slave were not regulated, because Roman law did not in general get involved in these.

The main issues of slave law in the colonies of civil law countries were settled under the guidance of Roman law. Thus, enslavement was still determined by birth to a slave mother or by capture in a just war (which was not defined in the Roman legal sources). Because Roman slavery was not racist, though American slavery was, racism is not prominent in slave law. Again, Roman law regulated in detail acquisitions by the master through his slaves and his liability for contracts made by his slaves. The relevant actions were available in the colonies, and appear most prominently in the French *Code Noir*. Most important, perhaps, Roman law generally allowed owners to free slaves without great formality, with little state intervention, and with no cause stated. Therefore, ease of manumission long remained the norm in the colonies of civil law countries.

See also ANCIENT ROME; CARIBBEAN REGION; CODE NOIR; MANUMISSION; NETHERLANDS AND THE DUTCH EMPIRE; PORTUGAL; SPAIN.

BIBLIOGRAPHY

ELKINS, STANLEY. *Slavery, a Problem in American Institutional and Intellectual Life.* 1959. Reprint, 1968.
TANNENBAUM, FRANK. *Slave and Citizen: The Negro in the Americas.* 1946.
WATSON, ALAN. *Roman Slave Law.* 1987.
———. *Slave Law in the Americas.* 1989.

Alan Watson

Overview of U.S. Law

Slavery provided an extremely contentious concern in U.S. law from the very foundation of the republic. The Declaration of Independence made statements, both direct and oblique, that were highly significant for slavery.

States

The vast majority of laws regulating slaves and slavery were state—not federal—enactments, of course, and by far the greatest number of judicial proceedings involving slavery were heard in state courts. The rules under which slavery was regulated in the various states were a mixture of custom, common law, and statutory enactments. For many of the states, all of these sources of regulation could be traced back to colonial times. Generally, it is not an exaggeration to say that up until 1865 laws pertaining to slavery in the states had become increasingly more restrictive and severe.

Certain rules were universal, of course. In theory, nobody could kill or maim a slave—whether the perpetrator be another slave, a free man, or even the master. Theoretically, the willful, unjustified killing of a slave was punishable by death. In practice, many murderers escaped punishment because of a lack of proof, jury nullification, or the claim that death inadvertently resulted from "reasonable chastisement."

Slaves, in general, were not permitted to appear as witnesses except against other slaves. Slaves could not bear or possess arms. They could not travel in many localities without a written pass from the master or his overseer. They could not contract valid marriage, nor did their parental rights supersede the plenary power of the master.

Slaves were subject to all state laws, although in common practice, masters were expected to punish minor transgressions so as to spare communities excessive legal expenses.

Although slaves were sometimes considered real estate, more commonly, and almost always after the Revolution, they were considered chattels—that is, movable property. They could be bought, sold, given away, inherited, and forcibly sold to pay debts of the owner.

As time went on, many states forbade anybody to teach slaves to read, and manumission (voluntarily freeing a slave) was made more difficult in most southern states. By the 1850s many southern states prohibited manumission of a slave by will. Some states required that a slave be taken out of the state to be freed, while others required that a manumitted slave leave the state within a year or less. Some required the reenslavement of freed slaves who did not leave the state. Most slave states also prohibited free blacks from entering their jurisdiction. On the eve of the Civil War, Arkansas required that all free blacks living in the state either leave the state or choose masters. Other states, meanwhile, were debating these issues.

Declaration of Independence

Among the abuses of King George III, Thomas Jefferson listed that "[h]e has excited domestic insurrection among us"—in reference to fears of servile uprisings triggered by British inducements to slaves to gain freedom by fighting for the crown (for example, Lord Dunmore's Proclamation). As written by Jefferson, the list of the king's abuses included a denunciation of George III for permitting the slave trade and for his veto of colonial enactments aimed at suppressing that commerce. John Adams termed this passage of the Declaration of the Independence a "vehement philippic against negro slavery," but it was ultimately omitted because the Continental Congress found it too divisive for a cause whose adherents included many slaveowners.

By far the most relevant passage of the Declaration of Independence for slavery was that well-known sentence with which the second paragraph opens: "We hold these truths to be self evident: that all men are created equal; that they are endowed by their creator with certain unalienable rights; that among these are life, liberty, and the pursuit of happiness. . . . "

Historians, political philosophers, and legal scholars have debated what kind of equality and protection of life, liberty, and pursuit of happiness could be reconciled with slavery, for Jefferson himself and many of

A plaque of the Declaration of Independence, signed by the forefathers of the United States of America on 4 July 1776. [Library of Congress/Corbis]

his fellow delegates held slaves. Dr. Samuel Johnson, the famous English author and lexicographer, attributed the paradox of the declaration's proclamation of equality and its author's keeping of slaves to hypocrisy: "How is it that we hear the loudest yelps for liberty among the drivers of negroes?"

John C. Calhoun, the U.S. statesman and political philosopher, claimed that Jefferson meant to assert the equality of all men including Negroes, but that science had since demonstrated the inherent inequality of the races. Chief Justice Roger Taney, of course, in the *Dred Scott* (1857) decision simply denied that Jefferson or his contemporaries would have intended blacks to be included within the category of men possessing equality of status or unalienable rights.

The dominant scholarly view of equality and rights within the Declaration of Independence interprets these within their original Lockean context. In John Locke's political philosophy—upon which Jefferson heavily relied—man in the presocial condition (the "state of nature") has rights under natural law and the laws of God, but he requires the institutions of a society to protect those rights. In the state of nature, man enjoyed complete equality, for there was no subordination—no ruler and subject, no master and slave. Once man entered the social contract, however, the natural equality of the state of nature was abandoned to hierarchical roles of civil society. Slavery itself was justified as a less evil way of dealing with captives of war, in preference to slaying them.

Whatever the true reading of equality and rights within the Declaration of Independence, there is no denying that in the decades between adoption of the declaration and the ratification of the Thirteenth Amendment, the seeming discrepancies between the rhetoric of that document and the legal and historical realities of slavery would fascinate and torment the minds of the American public engaged in the political discourse of that day.

Articles of Confederation

In the Articles of Confederation, which received their final ratification on 1 March 1781, there was no direct mention of slavery, but some passages clearly were relevant to the issue. Article IV extended all the privileges and immunities enjoyed by the citizens of a state to the "free inhabitants of each of these states, paupers, vagabonds, and fugitives from justice excepted. . . . " Article IX declared that requisitions from each state would be "in proportion to the number of white inhabitants in such state," and the same article imposed a restriction on the treaty-making power of the United States in Congress assembled, preventing it "from prohibiting the exportation or importation of any species of goods or commodities, whatsoever." A fair construction of the latter prohibition would acknowledge it a barrier to any treaty restricting the international slave trade.

The Treaty of Paris of 1783, which ended the American War of Independence, pledged each party to return to the other any property that had been confiscated during the war. The Congress of the Articles of Confederation lacked the power to force the states to comply, especially with regard to the return of confiscated Tory lands, while the crown refused to return slaves who had been freed, under Lord Dunmore's Proclamation, since the British argued that a freed slave was a person, not chattel property.

On 13 July 1787 the Congress passed the Northwest Ordinance, which provided for territorial government in the land ceded by Great Britain under the Treaty of Paris. Accordingly, Article VI forbade slavery, except in cases of criminal punishment, and provided further for the rendition of fugitive slaves. Article V permitted the people of the territory to form up to five states, and specified that to be admitted to the Union, these states must be republican and "in conformity to the principle contained in these articles." When the laws Congress had previously passed were voided by adoption of the Constitution, Con-

gress reenacted the Northwest Ordinance as a federal statute. Despite the unequivocal mandate of the ordinance, slavery continued in the territory well into the new century, and a series of court cases in successor states were required to extinguish slavery in what became Indiana and Illinois.

U.S. Constitution

In the years between adoption of the Declaration of Independence and the convening of the Constitutional Convention in Philadelphia in 1787, slavery had become more contentious among states than was previously the case, and abolition was in the air in many states of the North. In Massachusetts, for example, a set of cases concerning the slave Quock Walker—including *Walker v. Jennison* (1781), *Jennison v. Caldwell* (1781), and *Commonwealth v. Jennison* (1783)—held that the Massachusetts constitution had abolished slavery. Pennsylvania began a complicated journey to total emancipation by the passage in 1780 of "An Act for the Gradual Abolition of Slavery."

Slavery was not the most contentious issue at the convention, however; that distinction belonged to controversy between big states and small states over representation. Nevertheless, slavery-related conflicts arose over several sections of the Constitution. Indeed, during the convention James Madison claimed that the "real differences" between the states were caused by slavery.

How slaves were to be enumerated for the apportionment of representation and direct taxes proved thorny. Northerners wished to count slaves as persons for assessment of taxes but not for representation, while southerners demanded the reverse. The Three-Fifths Compromise required that slaves be counted as three-fifths of a person for both purposes, and Congress was forbidden to levy direct taxes except in proportion to such an enumeration—with no amendment to alter this before 1808. In reality, southern states benefited enormously from this compromise, since no significant direct taxation was ever undertaken during slavery's existence.

Congressional power "[t]o provide for calling forth the militia to execute the laws of the Union, suppress insurrections, and repel invasions"; the powers of the president as commander in chief of the army, navy, and federalized militias; and the guarantee clause, which required the United States to protect states from domestic violence, were well recognized as provisions applying to servile insurrection. Other provisions that became significant in future political struggles over slavery, such as Congress's plenary power over the federal capitol district and its authority over the territories, were not particularly remarked on at the time.

Significantly, congressional power over international commerce was restricted in regard to the slave trade. Congress was forbidden to outlaw it or levy taxes in excess of ten dollars per slave before 1808, and this restriction was entrenched by a rare limitation upon the amending power. Northern and southern solidarity broke over conflicting economic interests. On key votes over the slave trade the New England states voted with the deep South in return for South Carolina's support for a provision allowing Congress to regulate commerce by a simple majority. Virginia, on the other hand, had a surplus of slaves and recognized that ending the slave trade would increase the value of its slaves.

The "full faith and credit" clause, with its demand for comity between the states and its grant of congressional empowerment, had significant implications when the Union became ideologically divided over slavery.

Lastly, although the "fugitive slave" clause, which required rendition of slaves fleeing into another state—any state statutory or constitutional provision notwithstanding—did not provoke serious objection at the Constitutional Convention, it later became a source of friction between states.

Fugitive Slave Laws

In 1791 issues of extradition of fugitives from justice and rendition of fugitive slaves became entangled together, resulting in the Fugitive Slave Act of 1793. When Virginia refused the Pennsylvania governor's request for extradition of three men who kidnapped the runaway John Davis, Pennsylvania appealed to President George Washington. The Fugitive Slave Act of 1793 followed, regularizing rendition under the fugitive slave clause.

The constitutionality of the law (adopted February 1793) might have been questioned, for although the "full faith and credit" clause grants Congress enforcement powers, no empowerment appears concerning rendition. The act provided a five-hundred-dollar fine for anyone "knowingly and wilfully obstruct[ing]" rendition and permitted civil damage suits (state or federal) for loss to the owner. The owner or his agents could capture a runaway, applying to any federal or state judge or "any magistrate of a county, city or town corporate" for a certificate of removal at a hearing, with evidence oral or through affidavit.

When the act passed, no federal officeholder questioned its constitutionality, but half a century later, in *Prigg v. Pennsylvania* (1842), the Supreme Court examined that question. Edward Prigg had been convicted for kidnapping in 1837 because he did not have state and federal certificates of removal as required by an 1826 Pennsylvania statute. In reversing the conviction, Associate Justice Joseph Story held the Pennsylvania act to be unconstitutional because regulation of the rendition of fugitive slaves rested exclusively with Congress. Justice Story found a right of "self-help" independent of the requirement of a federal certificate, so that an owner or agent could remove a fugitive if it were accomplished without violence. Furthermore, Justice Story held that Congress could not compel state officials to enforce federal statutes, although he exhorted such officials to assist federal authorities for harmony in the Union.

Although some scholars have seen *Prigg* as proslavery, as did most opponents of slavery at the time, its ultimate effects were otherwise. As opposition to slavery intensified throughout the North, few state officials would actively cooperate with rendition. This led to southern demands for a new fugitive slave statute. This demand was finally satisfied by the Fugitive Slave Act of 1850, passed as part of the Compromise of 1850.

By the late 1840s the noncooperation of state officials, the activities of the Underground Railroad, and violent resistance by blacks and whites alike to slave catching had convinced many of the inadequacy of the 1793 law. Even the eloquent northern champion of the Union Daniel Webster admitted that in the matter of rendition, southern compliants of northern violations of the constitutional compact had merit.

The 1850 law was harsh, lacking any provision for the testimony of the alleged fugitive, allowing arrests without warrant, requiring only summary hearings, and holding the testimony of an owner or his agent sufficient to send an alleged fugitive to the South. The law allowed for the appointment of commissioners in every country. The commissioners were empowered to enforce the law, grant certificates of removal, and call on federal marshals or the army to aid them. The law provided up to one thousand dollars in fines and six months' imprisonment for interference.

As many on both sides of the Mason-Dixon Line had prophesied, the 1850 enactment produced more antislavery agitation than it gave real aid for rendition. Covert resistance to capture, overt violence (including rescue efforts by mobs), political agitation, and state "personal liberty" statutes became major roadblocks to successful slave catching, while Harriet Beecher Stowe's *Uncle Tom's Cabin*, as well as innumerable articles and pamphlets, inflamed public sentiment in the North. On 15 February 1851 the fugitive slave Shadrach was detained for a hearing before the U.S. Commissioner in Boston but was released by a mob of free blacks.

In 1851 *In re Thomas Sims*, heard before Commissioner George T. Curtis in Boston, provided the first genuine exposition of legal and constitutional objec-

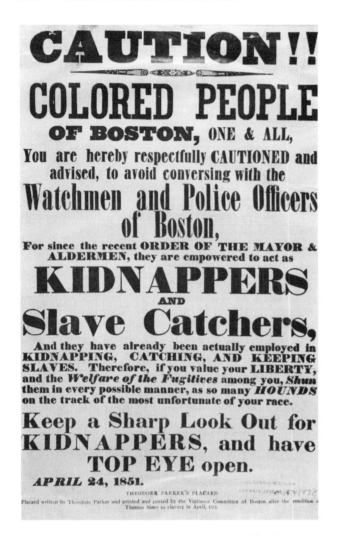

Placard written by Theodore Parker and issued by the Vigilance Committee of Boston after the rendition of Thomas Sims to slavery in April 1851. [Corbis-Bettmann]

tions to the Fugitive Slave Act of 1850, although Sims was ultimately returned to Georgia. Points against the act included (1) that given the judicial character of the office, commissioners were not appointed according to Article III; (2) that the act denied both parties their right to trial by jury; (3) that evidence from state courts should be inadmissible because Congress lacked authority to confer judicial authority on state courts; (4) that Congress was not constitutionally authorized to pass the act. None of these objections prevailed.

U.S. v. Hanway (1851) saw a charge of treason prosecuted against Castner Hanway both for refusing to aid a group of slave catchers and for refusing to prevent enraged blacks from attacking them. It was also alleged that Hanway incited the black resistance that led to the death of Edward Gorsuch, the leader of the slave catchers. The presiding judge, U.S. Associate Jus-

tice Robert C. Grier, instructed the jury that refusal of assistance under the statute could not constitute treason, and acquittal followed.

Legal resistance by states to acts performed under color of the statute dramatically increased. After the prosecution of thirteen rescuers of the fugitive Jerry (or William Henry) in federal court, an Onondaga County grand jury in Syracuse, New York, indicted Marshal Henry W. Allen for kidnapping for his role in initially seizing William Henry. New York State Supreme Court Judge R. P. Marvin, in his charge to the trial jury, upheld the constitutionality of the 1850 law and held that a U.S. marshal could not be arrested by New York for enforcing a federal law. Acquittal followed.

In re Anthony Burns (1854) and the associated cases, *U.S. v. Stowell* and *Ela v. Smith*, did not raise new legal issues, but the spectacular events surrounding them made them noteworthy. When Burns, a Virginia runaway, was confined in Boston, an enormous mob attacked the jail, causing the death of a policeman. Before the emergency was over, artillery, units of marines, and legions of law enforcement officials occupied the courthouse square, and Burns was placed abroad a revenue cutter for rendition.

In *In re Booth* (1854) and associated cases, the physical struggles of slave catching clearly took second place to judicial battles between the federal and state courts. In 1854 the fugitive slave Joshua Glover was seized and held in the Milwaukee County jail. A mob, allegedly led by Sherman Booth, forced the jail and freed Glover. Booth was then arrested by U.S. Marshal Ableman.

In re Booth saw the Wisconsin Supreme Court free Booth because he was arrested without a warrant supplied by a judge. Rearrested under a proper warrant, Booth was unsuccessful in applying to the state supreme court for habeas corpus. Booth was then convicted in a federal trial. At that point, having applied again for habeas corpus, Booth was freed by the state supreme court, which declared the 1850 act unconstitutional. However, under Chief Justice Roger Taney, the U.S. Supreme Court, in *Ableman v. Booth*, declared that state courts could not overrule federal courts and that federal laws were the law of the land.

In *U.S. v. Bushnell* and *U.S. v. Langston* (1859), the leaders of a mob rescue of an alleged fugitive slave were convicted of interference with the act. The prospective prosecution in Ohio state courts of two Kentuckians and two federal officials for kidnapping, however, led to a compromise that saw all parties freed. In *U.S. v. Hossack* and *U.S. v. Stout*, a federal district court convicted both men of leading a rescue of a fugitive slave from a federal courtroom, although both received extremely light sentences. *U.S. v. Gordon*

(1861) saw the conviction of the Reverend George Gordon, president of Iberia College in Ohio, for leading a crowd in preventing the rendition of a fugitive. Gordon unsuccessfully sought a review by the Supreme Court; he obtained a pardon from President Lincoln instead.

During the Civil War federal policy toward fugitive slaves changed abruptly. Initially, Union officers returned fugitives to their Confederate masters. As the war progressed, however, the executive policies of President Lincoln and a series of confiscation acts by Congress led to an end of rendition to rebel masters.

Sometimes abolitionists aiding slaves were not charged under the 1793 or the 1850 acts but were prosecuted for stealing slaves. In *Drayton v. U.S.* (1849) Daniel Drayton appealed his conviction for larceny for attempting to transport seventy-six slaves from the District of Columbia to the North. The circuit court overturned his conviction, finding that a charge of larceny required proof that slaves had been stolen for personal use or profit. After two further trials Drayton agreed to plead to transportation charges. Fined ten thousand dollars, he remained in jail until he was pardoned by President Millard Fillmore in 1852.

In re William Chaplin (1851) involved a charge of larceny for attempting to smuggle two runaways from the District of Columbia to Pennsylvania. Freed in the District of Columbia on six thousand dollars bail, Chaplin was turned over to Maryland and held in lieu of an extraordinary bail of twenty-five thousand dollars, which was ultimately paid by abolitionist friends.

International Slave Trade

The 1808 prohibition of the international slave trade, by the Slave Trade Prohibition Act of 1807, was poorly enforced, as were the supplementary acts of 1818, 1819, and 1820. The U.S. Navy lacked sufficient ships to patrol the long southern coastline, and U.S. diplomats refused to allow the Royal Navy to search U.S. ships suspected of slaving.

Although the prohibition act provided for the execution of slavers for piracy, the usual federal action taken against the slave trade consisted of the confiscation of the ship and its cargo.

There were many uncomplicated seizures, such as *U.S. v. La Costa* and *U.S. v. Smith* (1820), but there were quite complex cases as well. In *U.S. v. the La Jeune Eugenie* (1822), Justice Joseph Story heard the case of the claim by Robert Stockton for award of a slave ship he had captured off the African coast while it flew the French flag. There was strong suspicion that French ownership was a fiction to shield U.S. owners. With true ownership unverifiable, Justice Story ruled the ship forfeited to the appropriate government because Stockton's prize claim required proving U.S. ownership. Story ordered forfeiture to France in order to avoid further Franco-American litigation.

The 1858 *Echo* cases, including *In re Bates*, dealt with the capture of the *Echo* in waters near the Florida Keys by a U.S. brig. A habeas corpus hearing was followed by the trial of the sixteen crew members for slaving; all were acquitted in what must be judged jury nullification.

The 1860 cases of *The Wanderer* and *U.S. v. Corrie* involved confusion over the ownership of a slaver vessel. In the argument before District Judge Peleg Sprague, the original owner, Charles A. L. Lamar, claimed *The Wanderer* on the grounds that it was not conclusively proven to be a slaver and had, in any case, been stolen from him. The crew also claimed the vessel in payment of their accrued wages, while the United States claimed forfeiture for slaving. The government prevailed. Judge Sprague declared that the odiousness of the trade and the widespread use of deceptions required that forfeiture be rigorously enforced.

Two of the most important and tangled cases related to the slave trade, however, were the cases known as *The Antelope* and *The Amistad*. In 1820 the *Antelope*, flying the revolutionary flag of José Artiga—the founder of the Uruguayan Republic—was captured off the northeastern coast of Florida with two hundred eighty slaves aboard. The disposition of the case took eight years and involved the Supreme Court, both houses of Congress, two U.S. presidents—James Monroe and John Quincy Adams—and many of their respective cabinet ministers.

The *Antelope* had done some slaving, but the crew had also seized slaves in raids upon Spanish and Portuguese vessels. It was clear that the slaves taken from Africa were to be freed, but their number and their identities were impossible to determine with certitude. In addition, the courts had to determine the legality of the slave trade in international law in order to ascertain the status of the pirated Iberian slaves. If the slave trade was not contrary to international law, then the owners of the pirated slaves had a right to reclaim their property, in that they had not willfully violated the U.S. ban on that trade within U.S. jurisdiction or by U.S. citizens. Did the right to reclaim lost slaves reside in diplomatic personnel, as had been ruled in a different case, *The Bello Corunnes*, in regard to ordinary species of property?

Complicating the case still further were the claims for costs by the U.S. marshal into whose custody the slaves had been placed. Who should pay these costs? Did the marshal have a lien against all the Africans until his expenses were reimbursed, or was a lien against the Africans directly enslaved by the *Antelope* repugnant to their status as persons?

In the end, the Supreme Court upheld the legality of the slave trade in international law except as domestic law might prohibit it. It was also held that actual owners, rather than diplomats, must apply for recaptured slaves, given the frauds routinely practiced. Eventually, a number of slaves were repatriated to the new Liberian colony founded by the Colonization Society to live as free men. The remainder were awarded to their Spanish owners and sold to a U.S. citizen in order to pay costs incidental to the case. The questionable option of the use of a lottery to determine which slaves were to be returned to the Spanish was avoided.

For all the legal complexities of the *Antelope* case, the case of the *Amistad* raised far greater sectional passions. In 1839 a U.S. revenue cutter intercepted the *Amistad*, whose crew now consisted of Africans who had successfully risen up against their recent enslavement. The *Amistad* was a Spanish schooner that had left Havana with fifty-three slaves. During the trip the slaves rebelled, killing all but two of the crew. Captured off Long Island by a U.S. warship, the *Amistad* and its cargo were claimed as salvage.

For the defenders of slavery, the slaves were rebels, mutineers, and murderers. For the southern mind, with its fear of servile insurrection, the drama of the *Amistad* was nothing short of nightmarish. The rebels had to be hanged or returned to the Spanish or, at least, sold to reward the recoverer. For abolitionists, the issue was the natural right of men to be free and to defend their freedom when it was unjustly taken.

In law, the defenders of the Africans held that there was strong evidence that all or most of the slaves had been enslaved in Africa, contrary to the laws of all the Atlantic powers, including Spain. Their captivity was illegal, even as the abolitionists held it to be immoral under natural law and the laws of God. Justice Story, the author of a scholarly treatise on conflict-of-laws theory, wrote the decision for the Africans, denying that U.S. courts had to accept the position of Spanish authorities on the status of Africans of the *Amistad*. The blacks were repatriated to Africa.

Slavery in the Territories

The South had entered the constitutional compact with little concern for questions of population. Virginia was the most populous state in the Union, and the greater geographic size of the southern states promised a population equal to or greater than that of the North. With the advent of industrialization and urbanization, however, the North excelled in population growth and came, thereby, to dominate the House of Representatives and, potentially at least, the

presidency. The Senate became the essential redoubt of southern interests.

In addition to political power, the South needed new lands for the cultivation of its crops, especially for cotton, the repeated cultivation of which depleted the soil. This led to projects for expansion through foreign policy: the Louisiana Purchase, expansionistic designs on Spanish territory in the War of 1812, plans to annex Cuba by purchase or Santo Domingo by treaty, Central American filibustering expeditions, the annexation of Texas and Florida, and the great land grab at the end of the Mexican-American War.

Domestically, annexations alone were insufficient to assure southern parity or hegemony. The new territories had to became slave territories if they were to mature into slave states. The first crisis came in 1820, when Maine, a noncontiguous region of Massachusetts, sought statehood, as did frontier Missouri. The Compromise of 1820 simply allowed the entry of the two states—Missouri (slave) and Maine (free)—and extended a line from the mouth of the Ohio River across the continent, with slavery prohibited above the line (Missouri excepted) and slavery allowed below it.

With the annexations of vast tracts of land at the end of the Mexican-American War, controversy arose over the relationship of the new lands to slavery. By the Compromise of 1850, the Missouri Compromise line was recognized as determinative for the new territories, California was admitted as a free state, a tough fugitive slave law was passed, and the slave trade was banned in the District of Columbia.

The territorial divisions of this compromise did not settle matters for long, since the land allotted for slavery was overwhelmingly arid or semiarid, highly unsuitable for the intensive agriculture necessary to sustain slavery. In 1854 the Kansas-Nebraska Act was passed, allowing the residents of each territory to decide for or against slavery at the time of their entry into the Union, thus modifying the Compromise of 1850. Practically, this produced a virtual rehearsal for civil war in "Bleeding Kansas," where pro- and antislavery forces attacked each other with deadly consequences.

Dred Scott Case

The greatest single legal case to come out of these territorial divisions was the 1857 *Dred Scott* decision of the Supreme Court. In *Dred Scott v. Sandford*, Dred Scott and his family pursued their claims for freedom from the state courts of Missouri to the U.S. Supreme Court under Chief Justice Roger Taney.

Scott's personal claim was based upon the fact that he had been taken by his master from his domicile in the slave state of Missouri to free territory in the North

Dred Scott. [Corbis-Bettmann]

(later to become Minnesota), which under the Compromise of 1820 was closed to slavery. He had voluntarily returned to Missouri, but several years later he sued for his freedom under the assumption that residence in free territory had granted him free status.

By a vote of seven to two, the high court found that Scott was not free, but few of those voting in the majority were in agreement as to why. First, the court held it lacked jurisdiction to even hear the case because Negroes—slave or free—were not citizens and thus Scott had no right to sue in federal court.

The court, however, went on to examine the substance of Scott's claim, despite its denial of its own jurisdiction in the suit. The court found that the Compromise of 1820—and by implication that of 1850—was unconstitutional. Justice Taney reasoned that the federal government lacked municipal authority within the territories, and thus, it lacked the power to outlaw slavery therein. In addition, Taney claimed that the property rights of the slaveholder, under the Fifth Amendment, would be infringed by denying him the right to bring this particular species of property into the territories.

As law, *Dred Scott* had little effect beyond its denial of freedom to Scott and his family; and even they were purchased and freed by white friends of Scott.

Politically, however, *Dred Scott* produced a firestorm, inflaming northern and southern opinion alike and contributing fuel to the coming secession crisis. The prestige of the Supreme Court itself was damaged for a considerable time by the adverse reaction to this infamous case.

Emancipation

With the advent of the secession crisis and the Civil War, the federal government tentatively moved against slavery. A congressional act abolished slavery in the District of Columbia and the territories, providing compensation. By a series of executive orders and two congressional confiscation acts, the Union army was instructed to confiscate slaves used in the furtherance of the Confederate war effort and to refuse rendition of the fugitive slaves of rebel masters.

Immediately following the Union victory at Antietam, President Lincoln announced his intention to free the slaves of rebel masters who continued to repudiate their allegiance as of 1 January 1963. On that date the Emancipation Proclamation took effect, but its effect was limited by certain legal and political considerations. The legal justification of the proclamation rested in the right of the president, under his war powers as commander in chief, to seize contraband used in furtherance of the rebellion; therefore, the legal force of the proclamation could only apply to those actually in rebellion.

To remedy this, on 15 December 1865 the Thirteenth Amendment was ratified by the requisite number of states, and became part of the U.S. Constitution, ending slavery absolutely, immediately, and without compensation. Legislation on slavery did not end with the Thirteenth Amendment, however, for criminal statutes have often been passed to punish those holding slaves.

In another sense, much of the civil rights legislation that has been passed from the Reconstruction era to the present can be interpreted as attempting to undo the badges and insignia of slavery that were thrust upon the black race. Similarly, the Fourteenth and Fifteenth Amendments may be understood as undoing the fullest implications of *Dred Scott*, granting the full measure of citizenship and political rights to all races.

See also AMISTAD; CONSTITUTION, U.S.; DRED SCOTT V. SANDFORD; EMANCIPATION; FUGITIVE SLAVE LAWS, U.S.; LOCKE, JOHN; NORTHWEST ORDINANCE.

BIBLIOGRAPHY

FINKELMAN, PAUL. *The Law of Freedom and Bondage: A Casebook.* 1986.

————. *Slavery and the Founders: Race and Liberty in the Age of Jefferson.* 1996.

————. *Slavery in the Courtroom: An Annotated Bibliography of American Cases.* 1985.

JONES, HOWARD. *Mutiny on the "Amistad": The Saga of a Slave Revolt and Its Impact on American Abolition, Law, and Diplomacy.* 1987.

NOONAN, JOHN T., JR. *The Antelope: The Ordeal of the Recaptured Africans in the Administrations of James Monroe and John Quincy Adams.* 1977.

Patrick M. O'Neil

U.S. North

On the eve of the Revolution, all the American colonies allowed slavery. The northern colonies had slave codes and rules that were similar to those of the South: slaves could not testify against free people; only people of African ancestry could be enslaved; the status of "slave" was inheritable; and slaves could be sold, deeded away, and inherited. Slaves' marriages were not recognized by law, and slaves could own no property in their own right. The children of slave mothers were born slaves. Like the South, colonies in the North regulated trade with slaves and had curfews for blacks, slave and free, that did not apply to whites.

The northern colonies' laws regarding slavery were less harsh in some ways than those of the South. Northern masters were legally able to free their slaves, while southern masters were usually prohibited from doing so. For example, in 1703 Massachusetts passed legislation allowing, though regulating, the private manumission of slaves. Such benevolence was prohibited in Virginia until 1782. And although slaves in the North were routinely punished more harshly than free people, there were generally fewer capital offenses for slaves in the North than the South. In colonial Massachusetts a slave could be whipped for striking a white; in some parts of the South the punishment for such an infraction might be death or savage corporal punishment.

During the Revolution all the northern states prohibited the African slave trade. None of these states ever resumed the trade, and some of them vigorously sought to prevent the use of their ports to outfit ships for the trade.

The Revolution undermined slavery in much of the North. Most of the northern states allowed blacks to enlist in the militias raised for the war effort and passed laws or promulgated rules allowing masters to enlist their slaves, take the slaves' enlistment bounties, and at the same time emancipate them. According to one leader in Massachusetts, during "the revolution-war, the *publick opinion* was so strongly in favour of the abolition of slavery, that in some country towns, votes were passed in town-meetings, that they would have no slaves among them" ("The Tucker-Belknap Correspondence on Slavery in Massachusetts," in *The Collections of the Massachusetts Historical Society for the Year M,DCC,XCV*, 1795, pp. 191–211). In Massachusetts slaves gained freedom through a combination of constitutional provisions, judicial decisions, and a culture that made slave owning unacceptable. New Hampshire and the fourteenth state, Vermont, ended slavery in the same way. All the new northern states after 1800 banned slavery in their constitutions, although Illinois allowed some forms of bondage and the short-term use of slaves in some industries.

Pennsylvania (1780), Connecticut (1784), Rhode Island (1784), New York (1799), and New Jersey (1804) ended slavery through gradual emancipation statutes. The laws provided that the children of all slave women were to be considered free from birth but indentured to the owners of their mothers for periods ranging from eighteen to twenty-eight years. Because of these laws slavery lingered into the 1840s for a few individuals in some of these states, even though most blacks were free. Thus some slave codes remained on the books in this period, regulating the treatment of slaves and crimes committed by and against slaves. In general, these laws provided increasingly mild rules for the governing of slaves. In 1780, for example, Pennsylvania declared that all blacks convicted of crimes, slave as well as free people, would be "adjudged, corrected and punished, in like manner" as "other inhabitants of the states." In 1788 Pennsylvania forbade masters to remove their slaves from the state or to separate married couples by more than ten miles. These laws also led to improved conditions for free blacks, whose numbers increased throughout the North after the Revolution. Thus in 1780 Pennsylvania allowed free blacks to testify against whites, and in the same year Massachusetts allowed blacks to vote, hold office, and serve on juries on the same basis as whites.

In 1788 Pennsylvania provided special penalties for anyone who kidnapped free blacks and removed them from the state. At the same time, however, Pennsylvania allowed masters to recover runaway slaves in the state. In 1793 the national government passed the first federal fugitive slave law, which provided minimal protection for free blacks seized by slave catchers. By the mid-1820s most northern states had passed "personal liberty" laws to protect their free black population from kidnapping or illegal enslavement. These laws were not designed to prevent the return of actual fugitives, but they did impede the process. In the 1830s courts in New Jersey and Pennsylvania intervened on behalf of blacks whose status as fugitives was dubious. In *Prigg v. Pennsylvania* (1842) the U.S. Supreme Court ruled that any state statutes interfering with the return of a fugitive slave were unconstitutional. Following this decision a number of states adopted new personal liberty laws that prohibited state officials from participating in the return of fugitive slaves. These laws often meant that slave owners could not recover their runaway slaves because they could not place the slaves in local jails while trying to return them to the South.

To limit the effect of these new personal liberty laws, Congress passed the Fugitive Slave Law of 1850, which provided for federal officials to help ensure the return of runaway slaves. In 1854 the supreme court of Wisconsin declared this law unconstitutional and ordered the federal marshal to release from custody the abolitionist Sherman Booth, who had helped a slave escape from the custody of his master. In *Ableman v. Booth* (1859) the U.S. Supreme Court reversed the Wisconsin decision and upheld the constitutionality of the 1850 law. In upstate New York and northern Ohio, prosecutors charged slave owners and federal marshals with kidnapping for their unsuccessful attempts to seize fugitive slaves. These prosecutions went nowhere, because they were in fact at odds with federal law, but they do indicate the profound hostility many northerners had to the fugitive slave laws.

While northern states could not constitutionally interfere with the return of fugitives, they could and did liberate slaves voluntarily brought into their jurisdiction. Pennsylvania's gradual emancipation act of 1780 extended to the freeing of any slave brought into the state, but it gave visiting masters a grace period of six months before the rule went into effect. In 1799 New York passed a similar law but allowed masters to visit the state with their slaves for up to nine months. Implicit in both statutes, however, was the notion that the states had the authority to emancipate any slaves the moment a master brought them into the state. In *Commonwealth v. Aves* (1836) the supreme judicial court of Massachusetts ruled in precisely this way, holding that any slaves voluntarily brought into that state were immediately free. This opinion was written by Chief Justice Lemuel Shaw, the most respected state judge in the nation. Shaw argued that the slave was immediately free "because by the operation of our laws, there is no authority on the part of the master, either to restrain the slave of his liberty whilst here, or forcibly to take him into custody in order to secure his removal." Within a few years most of the North had adopted Shaw's rule. New York repealed its nine-month law in 1841, and Pennsylvania got rid of its six-month rule in 1847. By 1860 every free state but Illinois, Indiana, and New Jersey had, through either legislation or judicial action, endorsed this rule.

In 1852 a trial court in New York ordered the release of eight slaves who had been brought into the state from Virginia by Jonathan and Juliet Lemmon. The Lemmons had entered New York only to change boats for a direct passage to New Orleans. They planned to be in the state for only a few days. Nevertheless, the New York court ruled that their slaves became free the moment the Lemmons voluntarily brought them into the state. In *Lemmon v. People* (1860) New York's highest court upheld this ruling. This case was the high point of the use of law by reformers in the North to attack slavery whenever it was within their reach. Had the Civil War not begun a year later, it is likely that the Supreme Court would have heard the case and, given its proslavery jurisprudence, reversed the New York decision.

By the eve of the Civil War slavery was illegal in all of the North. Most of the free states had adopted legislation to protect free blacks and prohibit their officials from cooperating in the return of runaway slaves. All but three immediately emancipated any slaves, other than fugitives, who entered the state. With the exception of Indiana, Illinois, and Oregon, all of the states also allowed the unrestricted migration of free blacks, although only in New England (except for Connecticut) could free blacks vote on the same basis as whites. Everywhere in the North the law assumed that all persons were free—the polar opposite of the law of the South, where all blacks were assumed to be slaves.

See also FUGITIVE SLAVE LAWS, U.S.; MILITARY SLAVES.

BIBLIOGRAPHY

FINKELMAN, PAUL. *An Imperfect Union: Slavery, Federalism, and Comity.* 1981.
MORRIS, THOMAS D. *Free Men All: The Personal Liberty Laws of the North, 1780–1861.* 1974.
ZILVERSMIT, ARTHUR. *The First Emancipation: The Abolition of Slavery in the North.* 1967.

Paul Finkelman

U.S. South

The slave is a peculiar creature: wholly property, yet wholly a person. This anomaly appears prominently in the law of the antebellum U.S. South. As a Kentucky court stated in *Turner v. Johnson* (1838), "[S]laves are property and must, under our present institutions, be treated as such. But they are human beings, with like passions, sympathies, and affections with ourselves." To construct slave law, then, lawmakers acknowledged the dual nature of slaves and borrowed freely from laws concerning inert chattels and animals, as well as from rules regarding servants, employees, and free persons. The outcome was a set of sophisticated legal doctrines that supported the southern way of life. Yet, just as slave law combined elements of other sorts of law, so too did it yield principles that were eventually applied elsewhere, particularly in laws regarding commerce, employment, personal injury, and livestock.

Overview

Scholars have documented and analyzed various aspects of southern slave law, usually focusing on leading cases or laws from one state but sometimes tackling the entire body of law. The English common law of property, along with certain principles that arose in English chancery courts, formed a foundation. The French and Spanish influence in Louisiana—and, to a lesser extent, Texas—meant that Roman (or civil) law offered building blocks there as well. Despite certain formal distinctions, slave law as practiced differed little between common-law and civil-law states. Through much of the South's history, the law classified slaves as personal chattels for most purposes. In early days and in some jurisdictions, the law sometimes considered slaves as real estate, especially for purposes of sale, taxes, and inheritance.

These sorts of broad classifications cloak the complexities of southern slave law, however. Slave law governed roughly five areas: interactions between slave owners and contractual partners, rights and duties of noncontractual parties toward others' slaves, masters' treatment of slaves, slave crimes, and slave status. For each, legislatures crafted guidelines for affected parties, whereas courts applied statutes and created common law to cope with ambiguities.

Masters made numerous contractual arrangements involving slaves. Often, these were intended to increase the profitability or decrease the risk associated with slave ownership. Masters sold or hired out slaves when workloads were light at home, sent slaves to market or distant plantations aboard common carriers, insured slaves against accidents and disease, and employed overseers to supervise slaves. Statutes and common law guided the formation of such contracts; courts interpreted them and determined liability in the event of breach.

Although contracts controlled some relationships between slave owners and others, many interactions were far more casual—or accidental—in nature. Masters suffered property losses through slaves' injuries and escapes; these losses often occurred through the negligence or willful acts of third parties. Opponents of bondage helped slaves escape, shady traders stole slaves, patrollers shot runaways, home owners killed trespassers, jailers neglected slave prisoners, and common carriers offered a means of flight as well as a menace to life and limb. Here again, legislators responded with statutes that required people to care for

others' slaves and, in some instances, instituted criminal penalties. Judges administered laws and assigned liability for losses.

Just as masters worried about the injuries others might inflict on their slaves, so did others fear the mischief of mistreated slaves. People expected malnourished slaves to steal produce and livestock. They dreaded violence by slaves. Southerners also had mixed feelings about kindly masters, especially masters who freed slaves. The preamble to Delaware's Act of 1767 conveys one prevalent view: "[I]t is found by experience, that freed [N]egroes and mulattos are idle and slothful, and often prove burdensome to the neighborhood wherein they live, and are of evil examples to slaves." Accordingly, masters sometimes fell afoul of the criminal law when they neglected, brutalized, indulged, or manumitted their slaves. Certainly slave owners enjoyed great freedoms. North Carolina Chief Justice Thomas Ruffin expressed the sentiments of many southerners when he wrote in *State v. Mann* (1829), "The power of the master must be absolute, to render the submission of the slave perfect." Still, slave masters had to live under legal rules intended to protect southern society generally.

Southern law governed slaves as well as slave owners and their adversaries. What few due process protections slaves possessed stemmed from a desire to grant rights to masters. And slaves faced harsh penalties themselves for their crimes. Preserving property mattered, but when slaves stole, rioted, set fires, or killed free people, the law sometimes had to subvert the property rights of masters in order to punish slaves as persons and to preserve slavery as a social institution. In the course of conserving slavery, the southern legal system tended to identify race with status. During slavery's heyday, skin color was prima facie evidence of bondage or freedom.

Sales

Because the United States banned the importation of foreign slaves in 1808, owners who wanted more slaves had to rely on inheritance, natural increase, domestic purchase, or the small number of African slaves illegally smuggled into the United States after the ban took effect. Domestic slave sales therefore flourished in the nineteenth century, taking place at the hands of traders or resulting from estate and bankruptcy auctions. The South developed detailed laws to govern such transactions.

Some of this law consisted simply of enforcing contracts. Vendors often offered explicit warranties of a slave's title, soundness, or specific characteristics. Sellers of slaves, like sellers of other goods, generally had to abide by such warranties. If a slave turned out other

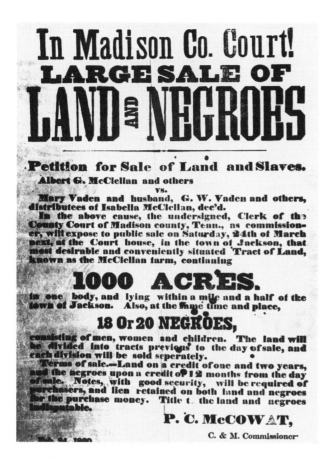

An advertisement from 24 February 1860 guarantees that title to the land and Negroes being sold is indisputable. [The National Archives/Corbis]

Much sales law dealt with more ambiguous circumstances. Legally, slave sellers were responsible for their representations, required to disclose known defects in their wares, and often liable for unknown defects, as well as bound by explicit contractual language. These rules stand in stark contrast to the doctrine of caveat emptor commonly applied in antebellum cases involving commodity sales. In fact, they more closely resemble certain provisions of the modern Uniform Commercial Code. Some scholars have argued that antebellum commercial law as a whole departed from caveat emptor more in the South than the North. Still, southern law offered greater protection to slave buyers than to buyers of other goods, in part because slaves were complex commodities with characteristics not easily ascertained by inspection. For example, courts interpreted contractual language more sympathetically for buyers of slaves than purchasers of horses.

Sales law in South Carolina and Louisiana stands out. South Carolina was extremely pro-buyer, presuming that any slave sold at full price was sound. If a buyer could not observe (and was not told of) a defect but had paid the price of a sound slave and could prove that the defect existed at the time of sale, he was entitled to damages or rescission. Buyers in Louisiana enjoyed extensive legal protection as well. A sold slave who later manifested an incurable disease or vice—such as a penchant for flight—could generate a redhibitory suit, the civil law action that entitled a purchaser to rescind a sale. Slave buyers in other states had less protection, perhaps because many residents not only bought slaves but also sold them to traders, often for export. Traders, who earned their livelihood buying and selling slaves, naturally needed less legal protection than ordinary buyers.

Touting the skills, health, trustworthiness, fecundity, or age of a slave nonetheless bound sellers in many jurisdictions, regardless of whether an explicit warranty existed. In a case during the Civil War era, *Miller v. Gaither* (1867), a seller in Kentucky even bore liability for what was essentially an implied warranty of fitness for a particular purpose. Here, the seller represented his slave Henry (absent at the time of sale) as a suitable substitute for duty in the Union army, yet Henry was actually underweight, underage, and too short. Implied warranties did not, however, extend to "moral" character or to representations made by slaves.

As well as being responsible for their own representations, slave sellers had to disclose nonobvious flaws. But obvious defects precluded recovery of damages, and courts refused to grant relief to slave buyers who had been told of flaws. Southern law also expected buyers to account for special perils associated with human property: buyers usually could not win

than warranted, the seller either had to pay damages (usually equaling the market value of the promised property) or repossess the slave and refund the purchase price. Vendors did not, however, pay damages for slaves warranted sound when new owners mistreated them. In the Arkansas case of *Pyeatt v. Spencer* (1842), for example, Pyeatt warranted his slave Sophia as sound. The buyer, Spender, claimed Sophia was insane because she talked to herself and frequently ran away. Yet Spencer had whipped Sophia severely shortly after the purchase, salted her wounds, staked her to the ground naked, and taunted her over the loss of her children. Although a jury initially awarded Spencer damages, an appellate court reversed and remanded the case.

In addition to warranties, other specific clauses sometimes appeared. Sentimental ties led some sellers to discount prices if buyers agreed to keep slaves in the neighborhood or hold families together. A buyer who broke his word had to repatriate the slave to the agreed-upon location or disgorge all profits from any subsequent sale.

damages for slaves who committed suicide shortly after the sale, or for slaves emancipated by the federal government.

One other intriguing aspect of sales law deserves mention. What if a slave were seized and sold unlawfully by someone other than his master? In these circumstances, southern courts often decided that the slave owner was entitled to the return of his slave rather than to mere money damages because, as a court in North Carolina stated in *Williams v. Howard* (1819), "[F]or a faithful or family slave, endeared by a long course of service or early association, no damages can compensate; for there is no standard by which the price of affection can be adjusted, and no scale to graduate the feelings of the heart."

Hiring

Slave hiring was common in the U.S. South. Although scholars quarrel about the extent of hiring in agriculture, most agree that hired slaves frequently worked in manufacturing, construction, mining, and domestic service. Hired slaves and free persons often labored side by side.

The bond worker and the free worker both faced a legal obligation to behave responsibly on the job. Yet the law of the workplace differed significantly for the two. When free laborers suffered injuries and brought suit, judges nearly always dismissed the charges or accepted one of three defenses by the employer: contributory negligence, assumption of risk, or the fellow-servant rule (which exculpates employers when coworkers cause an accident). The law governing fatalities was even grimmer: once the industrial age began to flourish, the United States adopted the reasoning in the English case *Baker v. Bolton* (1808). Under *Baker*, a tort died with the victim. In contrast, slave owners often recovered damages for injuries to hired slaves. And, because the "victim" in a slave-hiring case was the master, courts did not apply the *Baker* rule.

Essentially, people had a duty to treat hired slaves the same as slaves they owned. Hirers retained vast authority to direct and discipline slaves; otherwise, they might not get the work they had paid for. A court made clear in *State v. Mann* (1829) that North Carolina hirers had the same power as masters. Despite the fact that the hirer in *Mann* had shot a slave in the back, the court refused to entertain criminal charges because battery by masters—even temporary masters—was not indictable. Masters naturally feared exploitation of slaves working out of their sight, however, and often specified tasks and work locations in contracts. Hirers paid for losses when they violated such clauses, even if slaves had been disobedient, sui-

cidal, drunk, or careless. Negligent hirers also paid for escaped slaves. But courts split the difference when hired slaves employed by nonnegligent hirers fled or fell ill. Such hirers paid wages for escaped and idle sick slaves, medical bills, and any costs of pursuit. Yet they did not typically pay wages for slaves who died or reimburse masters for the value of escaped slaves. In short, judges who could not pinpoint fault made legal rules that discouraged two things: ill treatment and slack supervision by contractual hirers, and underhanded dealings by masters who otherwise might have tried to hire out sickly and escape-prone slaves. People who employed slaves without the masters' consent did not enjoy this evenhanded treatment, however. They paid for losses arising from escapes or injuries, regardless of fault. The law therefore upheld the authority of slave owners. In most jurisdictions, civil sanctions promoted workable slave-hiring arrangements. Rarely, courts applied criminal penalties in cases of extreme cruelty to hired slaves.

Southern law placed duties upon those who hired slaves, yet it also recognized the characteristics that slaves shared with free workers: human intelligence, volition, and ability to avoid danger. If hired slaves were hurt or killed through their own carelessness, the loss fell on their owners as long as the employer had complied with the contract. As North Carolina Chief Justice Thomas Ruffin reasoned in *Heathcock v. Pennington* (1850), "[A] slave, being a moral and intelligent being, is usually as capable of self preservation as other persons. If an owner let his slave for a particular purpose . . . [he] must have foreseen these risks and provided for them in the hire. . . ." Similarly, courts relieved employers of liability when slave owners knew about the risks of jobs their slaves were to perform. Still, southern courts scrutinized arguments based on contributory negligence and assumption of risk more closely when the victim was valuable property owned by the plaintiff. And courts almost uniformly rejected the fellow-servant rule in slave cases because slaves could not negotiate wages, report or reprimand negligent coworkers, testify in court, or quit their jobs.

The divergent law for slave and free workers does not necessarily imply that free workers suffered: empirical evidence shows that nineteenth-century free laborers received at least partial compensation for the risks of jobs. Indeed, the tripartite nature of slave-hiring arrangements suggests why antebellum laws appeared as they did. Whereas free persons had direct work and contractual relations with their bosses, slaves worked under terms designed by others. Free workers arguably could walk out or insist on different conditions or wages. Slaves could not. The law therefore offered substitute protections. Still, the powerful interests of slave owners may also mean that they simply were more successful at shaping the law. Postbellum developments in employment law—in the North and South—in fact paralleled earlier slave-hiring law, at times relying upon slave cases as legal precedents.

Common Carriers

Public transportation figured in slave law in three circumstances: when masters sent slaves on journeys aboard common carriers, when common carriers accidentally injured or killed slaves, and when slaves escaped on trains, boats, or stagecoaches. As elsewhere, the law in this area both borrowed from and established precedents for other areas.

Slaves, like other chattels, constituted valuable cargo on common carriers. Unlike inanimate goods, slaves could escape from danger. But cargo they nonetheless were—unlike free passengers, slaves embodied large and easily calculated property values. Consequently, southern law regarding slave transport struck a balance between laws governing goods and passengers. Carriers of commodities typically faced strict liability for losses, unless the loss came about through an act of God or a public enemy. Antebellum carriers involved in the injury of free passengers, on the other hand, often got off scot-free. And slaves had to take reasonable care in avoiding accidents while traveling but generated damages for their masters when common-carrier operators negligently injured them. Postbellum passenger plaintiffs, like employees, borrowed from slave law to buttress their arguments.

Not only were passenger slaves sometimes hurt, but slaves also suffered wounds or death in accidental collisions. Train accidents in particular figure prominently. Although some state statutes held railroad companies strictly liable for injuries to livestock, legal authorities flatly refused to do the same when slaves were hurt. In fact, early court opinions favored transportation interests in railroad mishaps involving any person, slave or free. But over time, southern courts modified liability rules: common-carrier defendants that had failed to offer slaves—even negligent slaves—a last clear chance to avoid accidents ended up paying damages to slave owners. Slave owner plaintiffs won several cases in the decade before the Civil War when engineers failed to warn slaves off the tracks. This "last-clear-chance" rule did not generally apply to free victims until the twentieth century.

Besides being harmed when slaves died or were injured by common carriers, masters lost valuable property when slaves escaped. Sometimes slaves impersonated free blacks; sometimes they simply stowed away. Before 1840, laws generally spread blame among parties. From the early days, however, state legislatures in border states and states with navigable interstate waterways tended to set more stringent standards for owners and operators of public transportation. By the late 1840s and early 1850s, virtually all southern states imposed strict legal duties upon common carriers to prevent slaves from escaping. After the war, courts seemed more concerned with salvaging the fortunes of former slave owners than evaluating blame. Even when defendants had displayed no negligence, courts were inclined to award damages for slaves who had escaped via common carrier shortly before war's end.

Governments and Government Officials

Government cannot be sued without its consent. In antebellum days, federal and state governments, officials, and employees enjoyed virtual immunity from suit. Few people pursued lawsuits against local government before the late 1800s and even fewer won, especially in the South. Instead, disgruntled plaintiffs usually sued local officials for injuries sustained when defendants did their jobs.

As in other antebellum cases, lawsuits brought by slave owners against local governments almost never generated damages. Judges cited three reasons: police actions intended to preserve public peace should not create public liability, owners of negligent slaves did not deserve compensation, and government should not pay for injuries attributable to the negligence of public officials. Some states forestalled lawsuits by passing statutes that entitled masters to partial compensation for slaves killed while rebelling. Still, some slave owners brought suit against governments. Only in Georgia, and only in slave cases, did Justice Joseph Lumpkin depart from sovereign immunity. Masters elsewhere who tried to dodge the justifications for immunity sometimes brought actions in eminent domain—again, unsuccessfully. Here, plaintiffs argued that the government unjustly deprived slave owners of property when it convicted slaves of crimes. In one such case (*U.S. v. Amy*, 1859), U.S. Supreme Court Chief Justice Roger Taney responded tartly, "A person, whether free or slave, is not taken for public use when he is punished for an offense against the law . . . and the loss which the master sustains in his property . . . necessarily arises from its twofold character, since the slave, as a person, may commit offenses which society has a right to punish for its own safety, although the punishment may render the property of the master of little or no value. But this hazard is invariably and inseparably associated with the description of the property."

In contrast to antebellum governments, local officials sometimes lost in court. The negligence of sheriffs and jailers generated personal liability in numerous slave (and nonslave) cases. Antebellum sheriffs also faced responsibility for the acts of underlings. In fact, the first use of the principle of *respondeat superior*—when a person answers for the acts of his agent or subordinate—arose with sheriffs' deputies.

Public officials were responsible for slaves in one unique circumstance: Southern jails often served as slave warehouses. Many states provided procedures to imprison captured fugitives. Compliance with procedure protected one from liability, but noncompliance could generate damage awards or fines. Some states also passed statutes allowing masters to commit slaves to jail for safekeeping. Here, negligence standards typically applied to jailers.

Slave Patrollers

Public officials were not the only persons legally entitled to supervise slaves. In lieu of a standing police force, every southern state except Delaware passed legislation to establish and regulate countywide citizen patrols. County courts usually had local administrative authority; court officials appointed three to five men per patrol from a pool of white male citizens

to serve for a specified period. Typically, patrol duty ranged from one night per week for a year to twelve hours per month for three months. Not all white men had to serve: judges, magistrates, ministers, and sometimes millers and blacksmiths were exempt. So were those in the higher ranks of the state militia. In many states, courts had to select from adult males under a certain age, usually forty-five, fifty, or sixty. Some states allowed only slave owners or householders to join patrols. Patrollers typically earned fees for captured fugitive slaves and exemption from road or militia duty, as well as hourly wages.

Keeping order among slaves was the patroller's primary duty. Statutes set guidelines for appropriate treatment of slaves and often imposed fines for unlawful beatings. In rare instances, patrollers had to compensate masters for lost wages when slaves were injured. For the most part, however, patrollers enjoyed quasi-judicial or quasi-executive powers in their dealings with slaves.

Overseers

The southern overseer was the linchpin of the large slave plantation. He ran daily operations and served

Slave patrollers look over the passes of slaves who are traveling along a Louisiana road. [Library of Congress/Corbis]

as a first line of defense in safeguarding whites. The vigorous protests against drafting overseers into military service during the Civil War reveal their significance to the South.

Accordingly, southern law regarded overseers as an essential element of slave control. Yet slaves were too valuable to be left to the whims of frustrated, angry overseers. Overseers, like hirers, had implicit duties toward slaves. Injuries caused to slaves by overseers' cruelty (or immoral conduct) usually entitled masters to recover damages. In a few cases, overseers confronted criminal charges as well as civil proceedings. And brutality by overseers naturally generated responses by their victims; at times, courts reduced murder charges to manslaughter when slaves killed abusive overseers.

Strangers

Whether they liked it or not, many southerners dealt daily with slaves. Southern law shaped these interactions among strangers, awarding damages more often for injuries to slaves than injuries to other property or persons, shielding slaves more than free persons from brutality, and generating convictions more frequently in cases involving stolen slaves than in other criminal cases. The law also recognized more offenses against slave owners than against other property owners because slaves, unlike other property, succumbed to influence.

Across the South, strangers hurt and killed slaves in efforts to protect other property. Many former slaves later recalled stealing food, for example, especially hens and hogs. Sometimes they did so out of hunger, sometimes for spite, sometimes at their masters' bidding. Burglarized home owners responded by shooting at intruders, finding at times that they had injured valuable property. Courts awarded damages to slave owners in many such cases. Kentucky gave home owners a bit more discretion, however; the reason was stated by the court in *Gray v. Combs* (1832): "[T]he rights of self defen[s]e are so dearly cherished and so well maintained by the sentiments of our population." Like Kentucky, Louisiana allowed some residents—freeholders—to shoot at trespassing slaves under certain circumstances. Even with these exceptions, antebellum southern law favored masters of errant slaves far more than free persons who trespassed. Mississippi allowed home owners to use force in ejecting trespassers, even to the point of killing them, and Texas permitted killing in defense of property of slight value. Most southern states let citizens set spring guns to protect their belongings. Long after the Civil War, states finally begin to institute official measures to shield petty thieves. Courts in Louisiana and Iowa

even used cases of chicken stealing by slaves as precedents after World War I to convict defendants of manslaughter or assault.

Despite restrictions on protecting property from slave trespassers, strangers could discipline slaves in many circumstances and defend themselves physically from slaves. Still, they faced civil and criminal penalties for wanton assaults. Slaves hurt when fleeing from menacing strangers usually created civil liability for their injurers as well, and slaves who defended themselves against threatening outsiders sometimes earned reprieves. One Florida court took especial pride in such rulings, saying in *McRaeny v. Johnson* (1849), "[I]n cases of injury to the peculiar species of property, the American courts, by a spirit of enlightened humanity. . . have extended a more enlarged protection than prevails in the case of mere chattels." By comparison, free persons virtually never recovered civil damages or saw criminal sanctions applied in assault cases. Southerners thought many assaults and murders were acts of passion or self-defense that society could not or should not deter. Those few southerners indicted for assault, battery, manslaughter, or murder of a free person brought successful defenses under the notorious Tennessee case of *Grainger v. State* (1830), which essentially excused the killing with a deadly weapon of an unarmed assailant. The Mississippi case of *Ex parte Wray* (1856) significantly expanded justifiable circumstances for self-defense. In most of the antebellum South, the rule was to "stand one's ground" against an assailant, rather than the customary northern rule of a "duty to retreat." Texas retained the "stand one's ground" rule until 1973.

Just as assaults on slaves generated civil damages and criminal penalties, so did stealing slaves to sell them or help them escape to freedom. Many southerners considered stealing slaves worse than killing fellow citizens. The counterpart to helping slaves escape—picking up fugitives—also created laws. States offered rewards to defray the costs of capture or passed statutes requiring owners to pay fees to "slave catchers." Although slave stealing was considered a heinous crime, several states also passed statutes to punish the theft of livestock, particularly horses and cattle. In contrast to laws surrounding slaves and animals, selling a free black into slavery carried almost no penalties. Some states even punished free blacks for petty crimes by enslaving them.

Besides hurting slave owners by shooting trespassers and by assaulting and stealing slaves, people injured masters indirectly. Paramount among the South's concerns were persons who weakened masters' authority by offering liquor to slaves, allowing slaves to gather together, and trading with slaves. Most states prohibited the sale of spirits to slaves and passed statutes to outlaw slave assemblies. In both instances, defendants faced civil damages as well as criminal punishment. Many states passed laws about transactions with slaves, forbidding people to sell, give, or deliver poison to slaves and imposing fines on people who bought from slaves. However, some states, like slave-rich Virginia and South Carolina, did allow slaves to trade with the consent of their masters.

Masters and Slaves

As in other areas of law, the law governing master-slave interactions reflected the complex character of slaves. Like cattle and horses, slaves were living chattel property. Yet slaves were also humans, often considered as much a part of the family circle as children, apprentices, and domestic help. And slaves also substituted for free laborers. By the nineteenth century, household heads had far more power over the bodies of their slaves, relatives, and livestock than the bodies of their employees. In part, the differences in allowable physical punishment had to do with the substitutability of other means of persuasion. Instead of physical coercion, antebellum employers could legally withhold all wages if a worker did not complete all agreed-upon services. No such alternative mechanism existed for family members, animals, or slaves. The tools of the market did not work at home.

In spite of the necessary subjugation entailed by slavery, the law—particularly in the thirty years before the Civil War—limited owners somewhat. Southerners feared that unchecked abuse of slaves could lead to unpleasant scenes of pilfering, public beatings, and

A Florida slave is bound and struck with a wooden paddle in public in 1845. [Library of Congress/Corbis]

insurrection. Because slaves had no legal standing, only criminal actions made sense when masters hurt their own slaves. Many states required masters to give adequate food and clothing to slaves, just as states later required livestock owners to tend to their animals and—much later—made household heads provide for their families. Most states stopped short of permitting people to kill slaves; North Carolina, Alabama, Mississippi, and Virginia were willing to convict masters who had murdered their own slaves. Colonial South Carolina and Georgia restricted nonfatal abuse as well as murder, although Virginia, North Carolina, Maryland, and Delaware did not. Later on, the codes of ten southern states instituted fines or imprisonment for cruel masters. In *State v. Hoover* (1839) a North Carolina court even sentenced a slave owner to death for killing his own slave. The *Hoover* court was appalled at the defendant's barbaric behavior—he had beaten his slave with clubs and iron chains, scourged her, and forced her to work unceasingly even when she was in the late stages of pregnancy and immediately after she delivered a child.

Still, prosecuting a master was extremely difficult because often the only witnesses were slaves, who could not testify against a white person, or the master's wife, who could not testify against her husband. In most cases, any official punishment was far less extreme than that administered by the *Hoover* court. In the Virginia case of *Souther v. Commonwealth* (1851), for example, a slave owner beat his slave, then burned him and rubbed red pepper into his burnt flesh, tortured him, and finally strangled him. Souther was found guilty only of second-degree murder and received a five-year prison sentence. (Harriet Beecher Stowe used the *Souther* case in her research for *Uncle Tom's Cabin*.)

Southern law did encourage benevolence, at least if it tended to supplement the lash and shackle. Court opinions in particular indicate the belief that good treatment of slaves could enhance labor productivity, increase plantation profits, and reinforce sentimental ties. Allowing slaves to control small amounts of property, even if statutes prohibited it, was an often-sanctioned practice. As a North Carolina court put it in *Waddill v. Martin* (1845), "[T]hese slight indulgences are repaid by the attachment of the slave to the master and his family, by exerting his industry and honesty, and a spirit to make and save for the master as well as himself." Courts also permitted slaves small diversions, such as Christmas parties and quilting bees, despite statutes that barred slave assemblies.

The master's ultimate kindness was to bestow freedom. The South allowed manumission in part because it was inherent in the rights of property owners. During the Revolutionary period, some southern leaders also believed that manumission was consistent with the ideology of the new nation. Manumission occurred only rarely in colonial times, mushroomed during the Revolution, then ebbed after the early 1800s. Virginia is a case in point. The state legislature passed a law in 1782 allowing private manumission within the state. From 1782 to 1806, as many as thirty thousand slaves gained their freedom. After 1806 the legislature vacillated as to whether newly freed slaves could remain in Virginia. The 1852 Virginia constitution finally prohibited in-state manumission.

By the 1830s most southern states had begun to restrict manumission, often requiring newly freed slaves to leave the state. Postmortem manumissions especially caused consternation, as South Carolina Chancellor Job Johnston complained in *Gordon v. Blackman* (1844): "This is another one of those cases . . . in which the superstitious weakness of dying men [proceeds] from an astonishing ignorance of the solid moral and scriptural foundations upon which the institution of slavery rests, and from a total inattention to the shock which their conduct is calculated to give to the whole frame of our social policy." States passed a variety of laws designed to limit manumissions. Some required former masters to file indemnifying bonds with state treasurers so governments would not have to support indigent former slaves. Some instead required former owners to contribute to ex-slaves' upkeep. Many states limited manumissions to slaves of a certain age who were capable of earning a living. A few states made masters emancipate their slaves elsewhere or encouraged slave owners to bequeath slaves to the Colonization Society, which would then send the freedmen and freedwomen to Liberia. Former slaves sometimes paid fees on the way out of town to make up for lost property tax revenue; they often encountered hostility and residential fees on the other end as well. By 1860 most southern states had banned in-state and postmortem manumissions, and some had enacted procedures by which free blacks could voluntarily become slaves. Arkansas even passed a law requiring free blacks to either leave the state or choose a master.

In addition to constraints on manumission, laws restricted other actions of masters and, by extension, slaves. Masters generally had to maintain a certain ratio of white-to-black residents upon plantations. Some laws barred slaves from owning musical instruments or bearing firearms. All states refused to allow slaves to make contracts or testify in court against whites. About half of the southern states prohibited masters from teaching slaves to read and write (among them North Carolina, though it did allow slaves to learn rudimentary mathematics). Although masters could use slaves for various tasks and responsibilities, they typically could not order slaves to compel pay-

ment, beat white men, or sample cotton. Nor could slaves hire themselves out to others, although such prohibitions were often ignored by masters, slaves, hirers, and public officials. Owners faced fines and civil damages if their agent slaves caused injuries. In some jurisdictions, masters even paid for losses arising from willful acts (particularly theft) committed by their slaves. In this last respect, the law placed greater responsibility on owners of slaves than on masters of servants.

Manumission Cases and Freedom Suits

Southern courts heard scores of cases involving claims of freedom on the part of slaves. These cases can be divided roughly into three categories: litigation of the manumission of slaves through wills; suits by blacks who claimed to have been illegally enslaved; and suits by slaves who claimed to have become free through some act of their masters.

Almost all southern states strictly regulated manumission. Typical was Virginia, which before 1782 prohibited any master from freeing a slave inside the state. Until 1782 a master could free a slave only by removing the slave from the state. However, in 1782 the law changed and allowed masters to free healthy adult (but not old) slaves within the state. Initially the Virginia courts acted favorably on such wills. In *Pleasants v. Pleasants* (1799) the Virginia court ruled in favor of Robert Pleasants, a Quaker who was trying to enforce the wills of his father and his brother, which were designed to manumit their slaves. Despite an obvious violation of the rule against perpetuities in the will, the Virginia court ruled in favor of freedom for the slaves. After 1806 Virginia no longer allowed in-state manumission, although local courts were able to grant exemptions until the 1852 Virginia Constitution banned any in-state manumissions.

Some masters used the American Colonization Society to free their slaves by sending them out of the country. In *Elder v. Elder's Ex'or* (1833) the Virginia court liberally interpreted the law to allow an executor to rent out slaves to pay the debts of an estate, and then to send the slave overseas. However, in *Bailey et al. v. Poindexter's Executor* (1858) the court read the language of a will in the most narrow way possible in order to deny liberty to Poindexter's slaves. The will had provided that the slaves should be able to choose whether they wanted to remain in Virginia as slaves or go to Liberia as free people. The court ruled slaves could not make a legal decision, and thus the will was void because it attempted to take the slaves wishes into consideration. By the 1850s most of the South frowned on manumission, and most judges likewise opposed it when they could. In *Cleland v. Waters* (1855)

Chief Justice Joseph Henry Lumpkin of Georgia upheld a will emancipating slaves outside of the state but took the opportunity to lecture the legislature on the "mischief" of allowing such wills.

In addition, many claims for freedom made by slaves were based on residence in a free state. Early on, southern courts had rules that slaves who lived in free states with the consent of their masters gained their liberty. Thus, in *Harry v. Decker and Hopkins* (1818) the Mississippi court found that a slave who had lived in Indiana was free. The Mississippi court found it "an unquestioned rule, that courts must lean 'in favoreum vitae et libertatis' [in favor of life and liberty]." In *Rankin v. Lydia* (1820), *Winny v. Whitesides* (1824), and *Lunsford v. Coquillon* (1824) the courts in Kentucky, Missouri, and Louisiana reached similar decisions with respect to slaves who had lived in Indiana and Illinois. However, by the 1850s many slave state courts had rejected this theory. In *Scott v. Emerson* (1852) the Missouri Supreme Court rejected more than a dozen precedents, decided in the previous twenty-eight years, and held that the slave Dred Scott, who had lived in Illinois and the Wisconsin Territory, was not free. The U.S. Supreme Court upheld this result in *Dred Scott v. Sandford* (1857). Here the Court ruled that a black person—even if free—had no rights under the U.S. Constitution. This was a decision most slave states applauded.

A similar change in jurisprudence took place with certain other kinds of claims of freedom. In *Gobu v. Gobu* (1802), *Hudgins v. Wrights* (1806), and *Adelle v. Beauregard* (1810) the courts in North Carolina, Virginia, and Louisiana found that persons of mixed ancestry or uncertain legal status were free. However, after 1830 southern courts showed increasing hostility to such claims. *Maria and Others v. Surbaugh* (1824) illustrates this. In his 1790 will, which he wrote the year he died, the Virginia master William Holiday declared that his slave Mary should be free when she turned thirty-one. The Virginia court ruled that her children, born after the will was probated but before she turned thirty-one, were not free. It is easy to imagine the Virginia court that decided *Hudgins v. Wrights* or *Pleasants v. Pleasants* finding a legal argument sufficient to free Mary's children. In *Mitchell v. Wells* (1859) Mississippi's highest court held that Nancy Wells was not free under Mississippi law, even though her late father had taken her to Ohio and filed manumission papers with an Ohio court. In some of the most outrageous language of any American opinion, the Mississippi court declared that Ohio had no more right to free a black than it did "to confer citizenship on the chimpanzee or the ourang-outang (the most respectable of the monkey tribe)." No longer did Mississippi or most other slave states, "lean 'in favoreum vitae et libertatis.'"

Slave Criminals

Slaves, like other residents of the antebellum South, committed a host of crimes ranging from arson to theft to homicide. Other crimes by slaves included violating curfew, attending religious meetings without a master's consent, and running away. Indeed, a slave was not permitted to leave the master's farm or business without the owner's permission. In rural areas, a slave was required to carry a written pass to leave the master's land.

Southern states imposed numerous punishments for slave crimes, including prison terms, banishment, whipping, castration, and death. In most states the criminal law for slaves (and blacks generally) was noticeably harsher than for free whites; in others, slave law as practiced resembled that governing poorer white citizens. Particularly harsh punishments applied to slaves who had allegedly killed their masters or who had committed rebellious acts. Southern colonies considered this an act of treason and resorted to burning, drawing and quartering, and hanging.

Originally, many jurisdictions tried to spirit criminal slaves out of the state. But southern states quickly caught on and began to ban slave imports or to check for criminal backgrounds of imported slaves. Transportation soon gave way to capital punishment for many slave crimes. Most states simultaneously implemented policies of compensating slave owners—at least those who lived in the state—for part of the value of executed slaves. These policies reduced incentives to conceal slaves' crimes or sell criminals to unsuspecting buyers. Yet lawmakers did not want people to abuse the state's generosity, so owners could not recover full value or coerce slaves to confess.

Besides prohibiting coerced confessions, southern states adhered to various other criminal procedures for slaves. Slave defendants were allowed attorneys, in part because the alternative would have been self-representation. Slaves generally had jury trials, though obviously not of their peers. And slaves could testify against other slaves, although supportive testimony by one slave in defense of another carried little weight.

Status

By the end of the seventeenth century, the status of blacks—slave or free—tended to follow the status of their mothers. Generally, "white" persons were not slaves, but Native Americans and African-Americans could be. (One odd case was the offspring of a free white woman and a slave: the law bound these people to servitude for thirty-one years.) Conversion to Christianity could set a slave free in the early period, but this practice quickly fell by the wayside.

Even before the American Revolution, southern law largely identified skin color with status. Those who appeared to be African or of African descent were generally presumed to be slaves. Virginia was the only state to pass a statute that actually classified people by race: essentially, it considered those with one-quarter or more black ancestry as black. Other states used informal tests: one-quarter, one-eighth, or one-sixteenth black ancestry might categorize a person as black. In turn, the law used visual evidence of "blackness" as prima facie evidence of slavery.

Even if blacks could prove that they were free, they enjoyed not much higher status than slaves (except in Louisiana, to some extent). Many southern states forbade free persons of color to become preachers, sell certain goods, tend bar, stay out past a certain time of night, or own dogs, among other things. Federal law, of course, denied black persons citizenship under the *Dred Scott* decision (1857).

Conclusion

The South's legal system, like its politics, social customs, and religious practices, strengthened the shackles of slavery and reinforced racial stereotyping. As such, it was undeniably evil. Yet, by protecting property, slave law necessarily sheltered the persons embodied within it. In a sense, the apologists for slavery were right: slaves sometimes fared better than free persons because someone powerful had a stake in their well-being.

What is more, lawmakers, as they crafted laws to preserve property rights, had to consider the intelligence and volition of slaves. Slavery therefore created legal rules that could potentially apply to free persons as well as to those in bondage. Consequently, people who argued vigorously on behalf of ordinary consumers, workers, and victims of accidents or assaults sometimes turned to slave cases and codes for guidance. Many legal principles we now consider standard, particularly in personal injury cases, in fact had their origins in slave law.

See also AMERICAN COLONIZATION SOCIETY; MANUMISSION; PLEASANTS V. PLEASANTS; STATE V. MANN.

BIBLIOGRAPHY

BODENHAMER, DAVID J., and JAMES W. ELY, eds. *Ambivalent Legacy: A Legal History of the South.* 1984.
CATTERALL, HELEN T., ed. *Judicial Cases concerning American Slavery and the Negro.* 5 vols. 1926.
FINKELMAN, PAUL. *An Imperfect Union: Slavery, Federalism, and Comity.* 1981.
———. *Slavery and the Law* (1997).
———, ed. *Slavery, Race, and the American Legal System, 1700–1872.* 16-vol. facsimile series. 1988.
———, ed. *State Slavery Statutes.* 354 microfiches and guide. 1989.
FLANIGAN, DANIEL J. *The Criminal Law of Slavery and Freedom, 1800–1868.* 1987.
FRIEDMAN, LAWRENCE M. *History of American Law.* 1985.
GOODELL, WILLIAM. *The American Slave Code.* 1853.
HIGGINBOTHAM, A. LEON, JR. *In The Matter of Color, Race, and the American Legal Process: The Colonial Period.* 1978.
HINDUS, MICHAEL S. *Prison and Plantation.* 1980.
HOLT, WYTHE, ed. *Essays in Nineteenth Century American Legal History.* 1976.
HORWITZ, MORTON J. *The Transformation of American Law, 1780–1860.* 1992.
HURD, JOHN C. *Law of Freedom and Bondage in the United States.* 2 vols. 1858.
MONKKONEN, ERIC H., ed. *Crime and Justice in American History: The South.* 2 parts. 1992.
MORRIS, THOMAS D. *Southern Slavery and the Law, 1619–1860.* 1996.
NASH, A. E. KEIR. "Reason of Slavery: Understanding the Judicial Role in the Peculiar Institution." *Vanderbilt Law Review* 32 (January 1979): 7–218.
SCARBOROUGH, WILLIAM K. *The Overseer: Plantation Management in the Old South.* 1966.
SCHAFER, JUDITH K. *Slavery, the Civil Law, and the Supreme Court of Louisiana.* 1994.
STROUD, GEORGE M. *A Sketch of the Laws Relating to Slavery in the Several States of the U.S.A.* 1856.
TUSHNET, MARK V. *The American Law of Slavery, 1810–1860: Considerations of Humanity and Interest.* 1981.
WAHL, JENNY B. *The Bondsman's Burden: An Economic Analysis of the Common Law of Southern Slavery.* 1997.
WHEELER, JACOB D. *A Practical Treatise on the Law of Slavery.* 1837.
WIECEK, WILLIAM M. "The Statutory Law of Slavery and Race in the Thirteen Mainland Colonies of British America." *William and Mary Quarterly* 34 (April 1977): 258–280.
ZAINALDIN, JAMIL S. *Law in Antebellum Society.* 1983.

Jenny Bourne Wahl

Lay, Benjamin and Sarah

Quakers and U.S. abolitionists.

Born in England, Benjamin (1681–1759) and Sarah (?– ca. 1740) Lay moved to Barbados in 1718 for business reasons, whereupon they became interested in the plight of the island's many slaves. Their attempts to share their Quaker faith and to ameliorate the miserable condition of the slaves antagonized white Barbadians to the point that in 1731 the Lays were constrained to leave Barbados and settle near Abington, Pennsylvania. At that time many Delaware Valley

Friends owned slaves, and Benjamin, fully supported by Sarah, expended much energy protesting that fact. On one occasion he fasted for forty days and almost died. On another he stood with one leg bared in deep snow outside a meeting house, in imitation of the half-clad slaves owned by many of his coreligionists. On yet another occasion he kidnapped a Quaker child to demonstrate the deleterious effects of the slave trade on black families. At the 1738 Philadelphia Yearly Meeting he harangued those Friends who owned slaves and then stabbed a Bible with a sword to represent what slavery did to bondsmen. The hollowed-out book held a bladder full of red liquid and its bloodlike contents were sprinkled on many of the outraged attendees, who promptly expelled him from the meeting.

Benjamin Lay wrote numerous antislavery pamphlets, the most important one being *All Slave-keepers, That Keep the Innocent in Bondage, Apostates Pretending to Lay Claim to the Pure and Holy Christian Religion* (1737). These protests, although not immediately successful, laid the groundwork for the 1754 decision of the Philadelphia Yearly Meeting to denounce the ownership of slaves.

See also ABOLITION AND ANTISLAVERY MOVEMENTS; PERSPECTIVES ON SLAVERY; QUAKERS.

BIBLIOGRAPHY

ROWNTREE, C. BRIGHTWEN. "Benjamin Lay (1681–1759)." *Journal of the Friends' Historical Society* 33 (1936): 3–19.
SODERLUND, JEAN R. *Quakers and Slavery: A Divided Spirit.* 1985.

Charles W. Carey Jr.

League of Nations

The Covenant of the League of Nations, which entered into force in 1920, did not expressly state that slavery was illegal. However, the eradication of slavery and the slave trade was one of the first issues addressed by the league. The league promulgated the Slavery Convention, compiled annual reports on the status of slavery throughout the world, and dispatched a commission of inquiry to investigate conditions in Liberia, where slavery had been reported.

The abolition of slavery was first raised in the Assembly of the League of Nations in 1922 by the representative from New Zealand. Although a questionnaire regarding the status of slavery was distributed to member nations, only fifteen out of fifty-two members responded. In 1924, a Temporary Slavery Commission was created to study and report on the extent of slavery throughout the world. It held two sessions. After its second session in 1925, it submitted a report to the assembly in which it outlined the areas of the world where slavery existed.

The commission reported that slave raiding was prevalent in the Sahara, where nomads attacked other nomadic tribes and villages for the purpose of capturing people to be used or sold as slaves; and that slave trading was openly practiced in the Arabian peninsula, where most of the slaves were African. The commission recommended that slavery be outlawed in every nation and that international agreements be entered into to combat slave raiding, the slave trade, and forced labor. One suggested agreement would have declared the transport of slaves privacy—an illegal act—thereby permitting ships to pursue and capture ships flying the flags of other nations suspected of carrying slaves. No such agreement was ever promulgated.

However, a Slavery Convention was promulgated in 1926. Among other things, the Slavery Convention provided that each nation forward to the league an annual report of any laws and regulations enacted pursuant to the convention. In 1932, a permanent Advisory Committee of Experts on Slavery was formed to receive these reports and compile reports of its own on the existence of slavery.

In 1930, an Inquiry Commission was sent to Liberia—the only case in which the league investigated the existence of slavery in an individual country. The commission was made up of Dr. Cuthbert Christy, the league appointee; Dr. Charles Spurgeon Johnson, the appointee of the United States; and Arthur Barclay, a former president of Liberia, who was appointed by Liberia. It heard testimony from civilians and local officials and collected public and private documents. On 8 September 1930, it submitted a report that documented the existence of slavery, pawning, and compulsory labor. In 1931, the league appointed a Liberian Committee, which compiled a second report confirming the findings of the first and submitting a Plan of Assistance for the reorganization of Liberia with the aid of foreign money and advisors. Negotiations between the Liberian government and the league continued for three years, after which Liberia executed part of the plan under threat of expulsion from the league.

The commission made several recommendations, including education of the indigenous peoples and reorganization of the political structure. As a result of the commission's findings, the Liberian president and vice president and several other high officials resigned, and laws prohibiting many of the abuses found by the commission were adopted. Liberia also requested from the league expert and financial assistance in reforming the country. The Liberian Committee that was formed put together a plan of assistance for the reorganization of the country through the aid of foreign advisors and loans.

Negotiations between the committee and the Liberian government lasted for three years. The problems were lack of money and the fact that neither the Liberian government nor the Firestone Plantation Company really wanted to institute the suggested reforms. In 1925, the government had signed an agreement with the Firestone Rubber Company and the Finance Corporation of America, a company set up by Firestone, whereby Firestone agreed to loan the government five million dollars in exchange for the lease of one million acres to be used for rubber plantations. The agreement prohibited the government from borrowing anywhere else without the permission of the corporation.

In 1934, the committee withdrew its offer after concluding that Liberia had rejected the plan of assistance. However, faced with threats of expulsion from the league for permitting slavery in violation of the covenant, Liberia eventually executed part of the plan by inviting foreign advisors and making a temporary agreement with the Finance Corporation as had been suggested by the committee.

See also AFRICA; LIBERIA; SLAVERY CONVENTION.

BIBLIOGRAPHY

AD HOC COMMITTEE ON SLAVERY. U.N. ECONOMIC AND SOCIAL COUNCIL. *The Suppression of Slavery: Memorandum Submitted by the Secretary General.* 1951.
BURTON, MARGARET ERNESTINE. *The Assembly of the League of Nations.* 1941.
REDMAN, RENEE COLETTE. "The League of Nations and the Right to Be Free from Enslavement: The First Human Right to Be Recognized as Customary International Law." *Chicago-Kent Law Review* 70, no. 2(1994): 759.

Renee C. Redman

Legacy of Slavery

See Africa.

Legislation and Legal Cases

See Civil Rights Act of 1866; Civil Rights Act of 1875; Dred Scott v. Sandford; Law; Pleasants v. Pleasants; Prigg v. Pennsylvania; Slave Grace; Somerset v. Stewart; State v. Mann.

Liberator, The

See Garrison, William Lloyd.

Liberia

The Republic of Liberia began as a settlement for freed slaves under the auspices of the American Colonization Society and the United States government in 1822. At that time, the area that was to become Liberia was inhabited by at least sixteen ethnic groups. Most of these peoples had probably begun arriving in the area about 400 years before, at about the same time the Portuguese first made contact with the coast. Although the local groups did not develop the extensive trading network of other West African peoples, several, notably the Vai, Manes, and Kru, were involved in the Atlantic slave trade. It is estimated that 300,000 of the 5.6 million slaves taken by Great Britain between 1690 and 1807 from the coastal region that became Liberia were from that area originally. In 1807, the slave trade escalated as a result of a rise in the price of slaves created by Great Britain's ban against participation in the trade by British citizens. There is evidence that the Kru were still engaged in the Atlantic slave trade as late as 1848.

The slaves were obtained through raids on interior groups as well as from the coastal peoples themselves. Like most West African groups, coastal societies included several forms of servitude. Indentured laborers were debtors who worked until the debt was paid. Pawns were people, often children, who were given in servitude to a third party for an indefinite period in exchange for payment. The pawned person was never compensated, was held without any rights, and in practice, was never redeemed. When the pawn was not from the same ethnic group as the pawn holder, he was often essentially a domestic slave. Domestic slaves were also obtained through war, as punishment for the commission of serious crimes, through purchase, or by birth to slaves or a slave woman.

The local leaders of the coastal region initially refused to sell land to the settlers from the United States because they feared that such a settlement would interfere with the slave trade. However, a coastal strip of land at Cape Mesurado (now Monrovia) about 130 miles long by 40 miles wide was finally bought by Lieutenant Robert Field Stockton of the United States Navy in exchange for goods valued at less than three hundred dollars.

The first settlement was followed by several others, and about 12,009 United States blacks were sent to Liberia between 1822 and 1867. In addition, about 5,700 Africans taken from slave ships captured by the U.S. Navy were sent to the new settlements. Some of these settlements formed the Republic of Liberia in 1847.

Until World War II, Liberia consisted of two distinct groups of inhabitants: the indigenous peoples and the descendants of the U.S. slaves known as Americo-Liberians. The Americo-Liberians lived in the forty-mile-wide strip along the coast that had been bought by the United States government, and the indigenous groups lived in the interior.

Article I of the 1848 Constitution of the Republic of Liberia states that "[t]here shall be no slavery within this Republic. Nor shall any . . . person resident therein, deal in slaves either within or without this Republic, directly or indirectly." However, beginning in at least 1890, the Liberian government permitted and eventually ran a contract labor system that recruited and supplied indigenous labor forced to work under oppressive conditions for government officials and foreign employers. For example, in 1890, Liberian laborers worked on the Panama Canal and served in the French Colonial Army. In 1897, the Liberian legislature granted a German company a concession whereby the company was permitted to recruit laborers from the indigenous population. In 1900, the owners of the Spanish Cocoa Plantation in the Spanish colony of Fernando Po (now Bioko), an island off the coast of Cameroon, began recruiting Liberian laborers. In 1908, the Liberian legislature forbade such forced recruitment but only within two coastal coun-

ties. In 1912, the government created a Labor Bureau that had the responsibility for recruiting native labor for domestic and foreign purposes.

In 1929, Liberia's contract labor system came to the attention of the League of Nations, which was investigating the extent of slavery throughout the world. An inquiry commission sent to Liberia in 1930 found that conditions of slavery, pawning, and forced labor existed. It reported that the government did not enforce the prohibitions against slavery found in the Liberian constitution among the indigenous peoples of the interior, where both inter- and intra-group domestic slavery existed. The commission also found that Americo-Liberians had circumvented Article I's prohibition against slavery by abusing the native people's system of pawning. In Liberia, the price for a pawn was the same as that for a slave. The only distinction was the type of token that was passed—a leopard's tooth for a freeborn and a piece of metal or a mat for a born slave.

The commission also concluded that the recruitment and shipment of native labor to Fernando Po constituted conditions analogous to slavery, which tended to acquire the status of slavery. In 1928, an agreement had been made by a group of Liberians

Refugee families from Arkansas wait at the Mount Olivet Baptist Chapel in New York City for transportation to Liberia around 1880. [Library of Congress/Corbis]

pursuant to which laborers were recruited and shipped to the Spanish colony. The colony agreed to pay the laborers, and to provide food, housing, and medical services, in exchange for two years of labor. The commission found that few, if any, of the laborers went voluntarily to Fernando Po. It also reported that the laborers rarely received payment, and when they did, it was for much less than they were due.

The commission found that the indigenous peoples were also forced to work on an extensive network of roads being built throughout Liberia, most of which led from one military station to another. Local chiefs were required to furnish certain numbers of laborers and were fined if they failed. Most high government officials owned huge plantations of rubber, coffee, cocoa, rice, or vegetables where much of this labor was conscripted.

The League of Nations offered a Plan of Assistance for the reorganization of Liberia with the aid of foreign money and advisors. Liberia eventually adopted part of the plan.

See also ABOLITION AND ANTISLAVERY MOVEMENTS; AMERICAN COLONIZATION SOCIETY; LABOR SYSTEMS; LEAGUE OF NATIONS; SLAVERY CONVENTION; SLAVE TRADE.

BIBLIOGRAPHY

BEYAN, AMOS J. *The American Colonization Society and the Creation of the Liberian State: An Historical Perspective, 1822–1900.* 1991.
———. "Transatlantic Trade and the Coastal Area of Pre-Liberia." *Historian* 57, no. 4 (1995) 757–768.
LIEBENOW, J. GUS. *Liberia: The Evolution of Privilege.* 1969.
REDMAN, RENEE COLETTE. "The League of Nations and the Right to Be Free from Enslavement: The First Human Right to Be Recognized as Customary International Law." *Chicago-Kent Law Review* 70, no. 2 (1994): 759.
SHICK, TOM W. *Behold the Promised Land: A History of Afro-American Settler Society in Nineteenth-Century Liberia.* 1980.
SUNDIATA, IBRAHIM K. *Black Scandal: America and the Liberian Labor Crisis, 1929–1936.* 1980.

Renee C. Redman

Libreville

As the French reluctantly joined Britain's efforts to suppress the slave trade in the Atlantic during the 1840s, they sought a place on the African coast to land the slaves they had "recaptured" from ships they interdicted on the high seas. They settled on the Gabon estuary, near the equator in central Africa. There they displaced twelve Mpongwe clans, numbering some seven thousand people, who had prospered through selling captives from the river's banks. After the French secured their control of the right bank of the river, naming their center Fort Aumale (where, nearby, Protestant and Roman Catholic missionaries had settled after 1842), the Mpongwe continued to broker slave exports from the opposite shore.

Paralleling the English resettlements of freed slaves in Freetown, Sierra Leone, and of freedmen from the United States colonizing Liberia, Gabon was seen by the French as a site to exhibit the fruits of their 1848 revolution by forming a settlement of freed slaves who would fulfill another need: labor. The new republic would make a virtue out of necessity.

The first group of 261 recaptured slaves were mostly Vili (from Angola and Cabinda), seized on the *Elizia* off the coast of Cabinda and initially resettled on Gorée Island off Senegal. The French naval decree of 16 August 1849 charged that the new "Libreville" settlement in Gabon would be "both Christian and French," and ordered the twenty-seven ex-slaves still in Senegal to be brought to Gabon—many against their will.

A supervised election among these "Librevillois" or "colons" was followed by a mass marriage of fifteen couples celebrated by Monseigneur Bessieux on 6 October. Although a few other freed slaves later trickled into the colony, Mpongwe oral traditions and French archives corroborate the fact that all the Librevillois were assimilated by the Mpongwe within a few years. Nevertheless, Libreville remained the name for the city that expanded on Mpongwe ancestral lands, and later became the capital of the Republic of Gabon.

See also LIBERIA; SIERRA LEONE.

BIBLIOGRAPHY

BUCHER, HENRY H. "Libery and Labor: The Origins of Libreville Reconsidered." In *Paths toward the Past: African Historical Essays in Honor of Jan Vansina*, edited by Robert W. Harms, Joseph C. Miller, et al. 1994.

Henry Bucher Jr.

Lincoln, Abraham   [1809–1865]

U.S. president.

Abraham Lincoln was never an abolitionist or a believer in racial equality. Well into the Civil War, he thought slavery might end gradually, with compensation for slave owners and colonization outside the United States for the former slaves. Yet Lincoln's antislavery position was strong enough that his election to the presidency was intolerable to most of the South. The result was complete, uncompensated destruction of American slavery, and the arming of former slaves

Abraham Lincoln. [Oscar White/Corbis]

against former masters. After Lincoln's death, former slaves were granted U.S. citizenship.

When the Civil War began, Lincoln saw the political and constitutional necessity of defining the aim of the U.S. government as preserving the Union. He needed the support of northern "war Democrats" and of the nonseceding border slave states. He also believed that it would be unconstitutional for him to interfere with slavery where state law permitted it. Yet in 1858 he had posed the central problem: could the nation survive half-slave and half-free?

Slaves in the Confederate states forced the issue by fleeing to the northern lines. Their swelling numbers, pressure from antislavery northern whites, and the need to prevent foreign powers from recognizing the Confederacy led Lincoln to use his wartime authority as commander in chief to proclaim emancipation within the Confederacy on January 1, 1863. The Emancipation Proclamation actually freed nobody immediately, but it made abolition a war aim for the North: slavery would be totally destroyed if the United States won the war. As with emancipation, Lincoln presided over rather than initiated the entry of black men into the Union army. Yet Lincoln understood that his role in ending slavery marked his great claim to a place in history.

See also CIVIL WAR, U.S.; EMANCIPATION.

BIBLIOGRAPHY

FRANKLIN, JOHN HOPE. *The Emancipation Proclamation.* 1963.
QUARLES, BENJAMIN. *Lincoln and the Negro.* 1962.

Edward Countryman

Literature of Slavery

This entry includes the following articles: U.S. Literature; British Literature; Dutch Literature; French Literature; Spanish Literature; African Literature; Caribbean Literature; Brazilian and Portuguese Literature.

U.S. Literature

John Smith's comment on a "dutch man of warre that sold us twenty Negars" in his *Generall Historie of Virginia, New England, and the Summer Isles* (1624) is the earliest known reference in English to slavery in the territory of what was to become the United States. Since then, white and black Americans have treated slavery extensively in novels, poetry, drama, and controversial literature. Harriet Beecher Stowe's antislavery novel *Uncle Tom's Cabin* (1852) and Margaret Mitchell's Confederate romance *Gone with the Wind* (1936), despite their divergent representations of slavery, have been the most popular American novels of the nineteenth and twentieth centuries. Black writers have created the genre of the slave narrative, or autobiography, of which the *Narrative of the Life of Frederick Douglass* (1845) is perhaps the best known example.

Literature of Slavery and by Slaves in Early America (1688–1830)

The *Narrative of the Uncommon Sufferings and Surprizing Deliverance of Briton Hammon* (1760), the first slave narrative to be published in North America, was told by an enslaved sailor from Boston. Hammon survived shipwreck and capture by Indians in a twelve-year-odyssey that ended with his return to his master and his thanks to God for his deliverance. This focus on spiritual autobiography thus resembles an Indian captivity narrative. Another work in this vein is *A Narrative of the Lord's Wonderful Dealings with John Marrant, a Black* (1785), written by a New York slave. By establishing black access to salvation and mastery of written language, these works paved the way for openly antislavery autobiographies, such as Venture Smith's, which was published in Connecticut in 1798. Smith had been enslaved as a child and brought to America, where he purchased his freedom after years of hard work and broken promises by whites. His themes are the industry and respectability of slaves and freedmen and slaveholders' abuses of power.

Controversial literature of slavery began in colonial North America with a petition by German-speaking Quakers in 1688. Quaker antislavery literature would appear throughout the pre-1830 period, written by such figures as Benjamin Lay, John Woolman, and Anthony Benezet in the eighteenth century and, in the early national period, by Benjamin Lundy, publisher of the weekly newspaper *The Universal Genius of Emancipation*. The earliest New England literary exchange on the subject of slavery occurred with Samuel Sewall's *The Selling of Joseph* (1700), an antislave trade pamphlet, with a rejoinder by Joseph Saffin.

New England also produced the first poetry by a slave, Lucy Terry's "Bars Fight" (1746), about an Indian skirmish. Jupiter Hammon (1711–1800), an enslaved clerk of a New York merchant, urged slaves to accept their earthly lot and concentrate on heavenly salvation in "An Evening Thought" (1760). Phillis Wheatley (1753–1784) also stressed spiritual themes

The title page of Phillis Wheatley's book Poems on Various Subjects, Religious and Moral, *published in London in 1773.* [Library of Congress/Corbis]

but criticized whites for failing to recognize black spiritual equality. Wheatley was manumitted in Massachusetts just as her *Poems on Various Subjects* (1773) appeared in print.

Early American novels occasionally depicted slavery. Royall Tyler's *The Algerine Captive* (1797), though centered on a white man's captivity in North Africa, touches on plantation life in the southern United States. The Virginian George Tucker's *Valley of the Shenandoah* (1824) presents slaveholders as benevolent and slaves as loyal and obedient but also describes a slave auction in uncompromising terms; nonetheless, Tucker's overall tone is ameliorationist. James Fenimore Cooper's *The Spy* (1821) has a slave character, Caesar, who is an early embodiment of white stereotypes of slaves as loyal, superstitious, and unintentionally comical.

Slavery Literature in Antebellum America (1830–1860)

Slave narratives became prominent in antebellum literature, along with anti- and proslavery novels. These narratives touched off a tremendous struggle over how to represent slavery, slaveholders, slaves, and free people of color. Defenders of slavery presented southern plantation life as harmonious, orderly, and productive, with chivalrous and benevolent planters presiding over loyal if childlike slaves in an atmosphere of mutual affection. Slave narratives and antislavery novels attacked these images at every point, portraying slavery as brutal and dehumanizing, coarsening for slaveholder and slaves alike, sapping initiative, corroding morals, and destroying trust and mutuality.

Slave narratives focused on the unrestrained power of the slaveholder and on the slave's battle to resist despair through inner strength and self-definition as a person of worth. Frederick Douglass expressed resistance through a fight with a slave-breaking master and maintained hope by teaching himself to read. The power of literacy is also evoked in Solomon Northup's *Twelve Years a Slave* (1852), a narrative of a freeborn kidnapping victim whose escape turned on his writing a letter to a friend in New York. Northup also depicted slaveholders as uninterested in innovation because of their control of black labor, a theme echoed in travelers' accounts of the South, from Tocqueville's *Democracy in America* (1835) through Dickens's *American Notes* (1842), to Frederick Law Olmstead's *The Cotton Kingdom* (1861).

Whatever their provenance, slave narratives asserted slaves' superior morality. None achieved this more strikingly than Harriet Jacobs's *Incidents in the Life of a Slave Girl* (1861). Jacobs's story is one of virtuous resistance to a master's attempt to sexualize his power.

Her initial resistance was followed by escape, years in hiding in her grandmother's attic, and eventual freedom. Other narratives offered frankly escapist themes, such as William and Ellen Craft's *Running a Thousand Miles for Freedom* (1850), the tale of a light-skinned slave woman who traveled by passing for a white man, with her husband accompanying her in the role of valet. Other noteworthy narratives include those of Charles Ball, Henry Bibb, Henry "Box" Brown, William Wells Brown, Josiah Henson, Lunsford Lane, and J. W. C. Pennington. During the Civil War, two narratives of emancipation in wartime were written by ex-slave women: Elizabeth Keckley, onetime dressmaker to both Mary Todd Lincoln and Varina Davis; and Susie King Taylor, who described the transition to freedom in the Sea Islands of South Carolina. The last slave narratives were collected by the Federal Writers' Project of the WPA during the 1930s.

White writers produced fictional accounts presented as autobiography, such as Mattie Griffiths's *Autobiography of a Female Slave* (1857) and Richard Hildreth's more novelistic *Archy Moore* (1836), whose protagonist escapes slavery in Virginia to become a British privateer in the War of 1812.

Black-written novels dealing with slavery appeared in the 1850s. Frederick Douglass elaborated on militant resistance in *The Heroic Slave*, a story loosely based on an 1841 shipboard slave mutiny. Martin R. Delany's (1812–1885) central character in *Blake; or, The Huts of America* (1859) conspires at an international slave insurrection. William Wells Brown (1816–1884) highlighted miscegenation and racial injustice in *Clotel; or, The President's Daughter* (1853). In this novel, Clotel, the child of Thomas Jefferson by his black housekeeper, is promised freedom but sold and eventually drowns in the Potomac, hounded to death by slave catchers and an antiblack street mob.

Finally, the slave narrative inspired Harriet Beecher Stowe, who drew on Josiah Henson's autobiography in creating *Uncle Tom's Cabin*. Stowe strove with mixed success to present slaves who were resolute and ingenious, such as Eliza Harris, who flees to freedom across the icy Ohio River. Uncle Tom is a Christlike figure of steadfast faith, gentleness, and simplicity. Stowe's slaveholders are fatally flawed, ranging from the genteel but decadent St. Clare to the demonic Simon Legree, Tom's murderer. *Uncle Tom's Cabin* was an immense popular success, as both novel and play, but southerners reacted with fury and energy, generating a subgenre, the "anti-Tom" novel. Mary Eastman's *Aunt Phillis' Cabin* (1852) and Caroline Hentz's *The Planter's Northern Bride* (1854) describe paternal planters surrounded by loving slaves, with an occasional free black who repents his misery and longs again to be a slave.

A poster advertises the sale of Uncle Tom's Cabin *by Harriet Beecher Stowe.* [Corbis-Bettmann]

These proslavery writers employed themes that descended from George Tucker in the 1820s through his successors, among them John Pendleton Kennedy (1795–1870). Kennedy was a Baltimorean whose *Swallow Barn* (1832) and *Horse-Shoe Robinson* (1835) sentimentally depicted slavery and plantation life. The South Carolinian William Gilmore Simms (1806–1870) sprinkled his romances with comical slaves who frequently demonstrated their faithfulness by refusing offers of freedom.

The proslavery poet William Grayson (1788–1863) contrasted contented and well-treated slaves with overworked, miserable white factory workers in "The Hireling and The Slave" (1854). Black poets offered another point of view. George Moses Horton (1797–1883), a North Carolina slave, expressed his yearnings in *Hope of Liberty* (1829), while freeborn Frances Ellen Watkins Harper's (1825–1911) "The Slave Auction" (1854) searingly described that institution. James M. Whitfield (1823–1878) rejected American slave society, urging black colonization in *American and Other Poems* (1853).

William Grayson's proslavery vision found full expression in prose controversalist George Fitzhugh (1806–1881), whose *Sociology for the South* (1854) and *Cannibals All!* (1857) lauded slavery as a natural institution and declared free labor an aberration and failure. James Henry Hammond stressed slavery's role in maintaining a conservative republic of property-holding whites, while Thomas Roderick Dew held that slavery was critical for continuing economic development.

An outpouring of antislavery prose campaigned for slavery's abolition as a brutal and economically irrational institution. The free black David Walker urged slaves to rebel in *Walker's Appeal* in 1829. Most editors, such as Douglass, Delany, and William Lloyd Garrison (1805–1879) in his *The Liberator* (1831–1865), and the authors Theodore Weld and Sarah Grimké in *American Slavery As It Is: The Testimony of a Thousand Witnesses* (1839), disavowed violence.

Black historians also denied the assertion that Africans were natural slaves. J. W. C. Pennington's *A Text Book of the Origins and History &c. & c. of the Colored People* (1841) demonstrated that colonial whites created slavery before blacks were in America, and Hosea Easton's *Treatise on the Intellectual Character, and Civil and Political Condition of the Colored People of the United States* (1837) showcased ancient Egypt as a story of African achievement.

Antebellum drama's most popular rendering of slavery was the minstrel show, a mixture of dance, song, and comedy in which white actors blacked their faces to play slaves. Catering to northern white audiences, minstrelsy derided slaves as foolish "Jim Crows," while free blacks were seen as dandified "Zip Coons." Minstrelsy was a mainstay of the American musical stage from the 1840s to the early twentieth century.

Late Nineteenth- and Early Twentieth-Century Literature

Literature concerning slavery long survived the institution's demise in 1865. Local colorists like John Esten Cooke, Sidney Lanier, and Thomas Nelson Page sustained the stereotype of the faithful and contented slave. Page's *In Ole Virginia* (1887) puts "Marse Chan," a cavalier admired by his slaves, at center stage. This literature reached its apotheosis in Margaret Mitchell's *Gone with the Wind* (1936), still popular today. Joel Chandler Harris (1848–1908) echoed these stereotypes with his Uncle Remus in *Uncle Remus: His Songs and His Sayings* (1881), black folktales in dialect. The collection is best known for the Br'er Rabbit stories.

Mark Twain's Jim, in *Huckleberry Finn* (1884), is a fairly complex rendering of a slave in postbellum mainstream literature. Jim is superstitious and sentimental but is also purposefully trying to gain freedom. Twain's *Pudd'nhead Wilson* (1893) plays on the absurdity of race-based slavery in a tale involving a free white baby switched in the cradle with a nearly white slave infant.

Paul Lawrence Dunbar. [Corbis-Bettmann]

The black poet Paul Dunbar (1872–1906) used dialect to present a conflictual portrait of slavery in *Lyrics of Lowly Life* (1896), as did novelist Charles Chesnutt (1858–1932), with his Uncle Julius McAdoo, in *The Conjure Woman* (1899). The writers of the Harlem Renaissance, interested in celebrating African-Americans' culture and in challenging racism in U.S. society—concepts embodied in the term "the New Negro"—mostly eschewed the direct delineation of slavery. Nonetheless, they captured its psychological heritage with power, as can be seen in Langston Hughes's "Negro Mother" (1931). Research into black history and culture generated such testimonies as James Weldon Johnson's *Book of American Negro Spirituals* (1925), Arna Bontemps and Langston Hughes's *Book of Negro Folklore,* and the anthropological works of Zora Neale Hurston.

Slavery in Middle to Late Twentieth-Century Literature

White literature finally began to abandon the stereotypes of the proslavery plantation novel and the Confederate romance when William Faulkner's *Absalom! Absalom!* (1936) offered the conniving and bestial Thomas Sutpen as a counterpart to the genteel planter. In 1940 Willa Cather's *Sapphira and the Slave Girl* put slaveholders in an unflattering light, emphasizing slavery's impact on women, white and black.

William Styron's *The Confessions of Nat Turner* (1967) broke new ground in treating a slave insurrection sympathetically; still, many black writers criticized Styron's portrayal of Turner as simplistic and tinged with racism.

Beginning in the 1960s, black writers attempted to recapture slave experiences in works such as Margaret Walker's *Jubilee* (1966), Ernest Gaines's *Autobiography of Miss Jane Pittman* (1971), and Alex Haley's *Roots* (1976). The literature of slavery achieved full mainstream recognition with the awarding of the Nobel Prize for Literature to the African-American Toni Morrison, whose best-known novel, *Beloved* (1987), evokes antebellum antislavery novels in an imaginative reconstruction of a historical event. Morrison based *Beloved* on the story of a fugitive slave mother who killed her own daughter to prevent the child's recapture and return to slavery.

See also DOUGLASS, FREDERICK; HENSON, JOSIAH; JACOBS, HARRIET; SLAVE NARRATIVES; STOWE, HARRIET BEECHER; WALKER, DAVID.

BIBLIOGRAPHY

CARETTA, VINCENT, ed. *Unchained Voices: An Anthology of Black Authors in the English-Speaking World of the Eighteenth Century.* 1996.

DAVIS, CHARLES T., and HENRY LOUIS GATES JR. *The Slave's Narrative.* 1985.

DAVIS, DAVID BRION. *The Problem of Slavery in the Age of Revolution, 1770–1823.* 1975.

———. *The Problem of Slavery in Western Culture.* 1967.

GATES, HENRY LOUIS, JR. *Figures in Black: Words, Signs, and the "Racial" Self.* 1987.

VAN DEBURG, WILLIAM L. *Slavery and Race in American Popular Culture.* 1984.

WHITLOW, ROGER. *Black American Literature: A Critical History.* 1973.

T. Stephen Whitman

British Literature

Literature reflects the society from which it springs. Persuading people of the evils of slavery motivated many British religious writers, particularly Quakers and their allies among Methodists and evangelical Anglicans. But references to slavery and abolition arise in other British literary sources as well. Some of these writings may also have been intended to persuade. Yet many authors were not widely read in their day (Blake, for example), and even popular works may have done no more than entertain. Still, twentieth-century commentators can at least use literature to map out the mores and assumptions of an author's community.

Shakespeare's most obvious use of slaves occurs in *The Tempest* (1611). Here appear several stock characters familiar from ancient comedy. Ariel is the clever slave who sometimes surpasses the master and eventually gains freedom. Caliban is the sullen, lying, plotting slave who ends up in his proper servile place. Ferdinand temporarily endures slavery but emerges as his true self: a free man. Slaves and slavery are used primarily as devices to get a laugh or teach a lesson.

A century after Shakespeare, slaves emerge as characters in some of the best-known early novels. Most of these works suggest occasional sympathy for slaves and an understanding of the desire for freedom, but they cast no doubt on the morality of slavery as an institution. The development of the novel itself was influenced by Aphra Behn's *Oroonoko* (1688). Behn, the first Englishwoman to make her living as a writer, tells the story of an African prince enslaved in South America.

Among the early novelists who wrote of slaves are Daniel Defoe and Tobias Smollett. In his economic writings Defoe takes slavery for granted and in his fiction he portrays slavery as moral—if used efficiently. *Robinson Crusoe* (1719) is a case in point. Crusoe is captured in West Africa but escapes with the help of the faithful Moorish boy Xury. Xury's reward? Crusoe binds him to a Portuguese ship's captain for ten years, using the money to set up a sugar plantation in Brazil. In the most famous part of the novel, Crusoe sets out for Africa to buy more slaves in a speculative scheme. Perhaps as punishment for his reckless imprudence, his ship founders and Crusoe is stranded off Trinidad. After years of isolation, he meets the savage Friday, then returns to find that his well-managed slave plantation has turned a handsome profit. Smollett, like Defoe, takes slavery as given. His rogue hero in *Roderick Random* (1748) finds adventure as a surgeon bound for the coast of Guinea. His ship picks up 400 Negroes, selling them for a tidy sum in Paraguay. Random expresses relief at "being freed from the disagreeable lading of negroes" to whom he "had been a miserable slave."

About the time Lord Mansfield issued his ruling in the Somerset case, British literature began to strike a more compassionate tone. A passage in Laurence Sterne's *Tristram Shandy* (1767) refers to the "poor negro girl" who flaps away flies rather than kill them. Says Uncle Toby, "She had suffered persecution but learnt mercy." Toby goes on to suggest that the Negro has a soul and should be treated kindly. Slavery seemed undesirable, but inevitable. William Blake denounces slavery and oppression in "Visions of the Daughters of Albion" (1793), but in "The Little Black Boy" (1789) he suggests that only death can free the boy's "white

The meeting with Friday is depicted in a rendering of a stage performance of Daniel Defoe's Robinson Crusoe. [Leonard de Selva/Corbis]

soul" and make him resemble the little English boy, who "will then love" him. Rather than express humane sentimentality about the plight of the slave, some works, like the anonymous *Jonathan Corncob* (1788), resort to satire, lumping slavery in with the other evils of the world. *Corncob* talks of an earthquake in Barbados that kills 661 people and 5,018 black cattle. "Cattle" cleverly refers both to livestock (745 oxen) and to chattel slaves (4,273 Negroes).

Early nineteenth-century writings, particularly by the romantic poets, reveal an increasing revulsion against slavery and a celebration of antislavery efforts. A pair of Wordsworth's poems herald the accomplishments of the man who secured passage of the bill to abolish the slave trade ("To Thomas Clarkson," 1807) and of the former slave who led the Haitian revolution ("To Toussaint L'Ouverture," 1803). New World planters are portrayed as depraved beings who meet unhappy ends (for example, George Staunton in Sir Walter Scott's *The Heart of Midlothian*, 1816); their offspring are symbols of crass materialism (for instance, Miss Swartz in William Thackeray's *Vanity Fair*, 1848). The popular journals of the actress Fanny Kemble

(who married and then divorced the southern slave owner Pierce Butler) give firsthand accounts of the evils of slavery in the United States.

By midcentury, British writers could assume an antislavery consensus among their readers. Yet this did not necessarily signal enthusiasm for the abolitionist cause, as Thomas Carlyle's *The Nigger Question* (1849) and Charles Dickens's *Bleak House* (1852) show. Dicken's Mrs. Jellyby is obsessed with schemes to improve conditions in Borrioboola-Gah, on the left bank of the Niger, while her house remains squalid and her children are hungry and unclothed. She has fine eyes, writes Dickens, but they "look a long way off—as if they could see nothing but Africa." Although slavery remained an evil as the American Civil War approached, British authors began to focus more upon pressing social problems at home.

See also CLARKSON, THOMAS; TOUSSAINT-LOUVERTURE.

BIBLIOGRAPHY

BOWRA, M. *The Romantic Imagination.* 1950.
DYKE, E. *The Negro in Romantic Thought.* 1942.
NOVAK, M. E. *Economics and the Fiction of Daniel Defoe.* 1962.

RICE, C. D. "Literary Sources and the Revolution in British Attitudes to Slavery." In *Anti-Slavery, Religion, and Reform: Essays in Memory of Roger Anstey,* edited by C. Bolt and S. Drescher. 1980; pp. 319–334.

SYPHER, WYLIE. *Guinea's Captive Kings: British Anti-Slavery Literature of the Eighteenth Century.* 1942.

Jenny Bourne Wahl

Dutch Literature

Despite H. J. Niebohr's pioneering comparative work, *Slavery as an Industrial System* (1910), Dutch studies of slavery—with a few notable exceptions—languished until the 1970s. The interest of the Dutch in their western colonies had always been overshadowed by concerns with their more profitable possessions in Southeast Asia—for example, Colbrander's three-volume *Koloniale Geschiedenis* (1925–1926) devoted only four percent of its pages to "the West." But with Indonesian independence after World War II, Dutch scholars began to turn their attention to Suriname and the Caribbean, contributing a number of significant works to the study of New World slavery and its aftermath. H. Hoetink's *Het patroon van de oude Curaçaose samenleving* (1958), an analysis of Curaçao as a relatively mild (nonplantation) slave society, and his *The Two Variants in Caribbean Race Relations* (1967), a controversial exploration of the contrastive "Iberian" and "North-West European" variants of race relations in New World slave societies, represent two milestones from this period of renewed scholarly interest in the Caribbean.

Eighteenth- and nineteenth-century general histories of Suriname, the most important slave colony of the Dutch, contain a good deal about slavery—Jan Jacob Hartsinck's *Beschrijving van Guiana of de Wilde Kust in Zuid-Amerika* (1770), David de Ishak Cohen Nassy's *Essai historique sur la colonie de Surinam* (1788), and J. Wolbers's *Geschiedenis van Suriname* (1861) are representative examples. In the twentieth century, two very different works by Surinamers, Anton de Kom's searing anticolonial indictment *Wij slaven van Suriname* (1934) and sociologist R. A. J. van Lier's scholarly *Frontier Society* (1971, orig. 1949) laid the groundwork for a number of recent studies of Suriname slavery, the most penetrating of which are undoubtedly Gert Oostindie's *Roosenburg en Mon Bijou* (1989) and Alex van Stipriaan's *Surinaams Contrast* (1993). A collection edited by Gert Oostindie, largely written by Dutch scholars (*Fifty Years Later: Antislavery, Capitalism and Modernity in the Dutch Orbit*, 1995), debates antislavery in the Netherlands and the Dutch colonial world, adding to our understanding of the cause of abolitionism more generally. Meanwhile, Dutch scholars of the Atlantic slave trade—Pieter

Emmer, Ernst van den Boogart, and others, as well as Dutch-born Johannes Postma—have transformed our knowledge of the Dutch role in transatlantic commerce. Recent Dutch studies of marronage and maroon societies include major contributions, particularly for Suriname.

In terms of *belles lettres*, Dutch literature on slavery has been most closely explored by A. N. Paasman in *Reinhart: Nederlandse Literatuur en Slavernij ten tijde van de Verlichting* (1984), which takes off from a late-eighteenth century epistolary novel set in Demerara—Elisabeth Maria Post's *Reinhart* (1791–1792)—to explore Dutch views of slavery in literature from 1625 to 1823. English-language versions of Suriname folk literature (songs, folktales, poems), much of it arising out of slavery, are presented in Jan Voorhoeve and Ursy M. Lichtveld's *Creole Drum: An Anthology of Creole Literature in Surinam* (1975).

See also CARIBBEAN REGION; MAROONS; NETHERLANDS AND THE DUTCH EMPIRE.

BIBLIOGRAPHY

LICHTVELD, U. M., and J. VOORHOEVE. *Suriname: Spiegel der vaderlandse kooplieden.* 1980.

OOSTINDIE, GERT G. "Historiography on the Dutch Caribbean: Catching Up?" *Journal of Caribbean History* 21 (1987): 1–18.

POSTMA, JOHANNES. *The Dutch in the Atlantic Slave Trade, 1680–1815.* 1990.

Richard Price

French Literature

The French reading public became increasingly aware of the injustice of slavery in the eighteenth century. Fueling the interest sparked by Du Tertre, Labat, and other seventeenth-century chroniclers of French colonization, popular philosophical works of the Enlightenment such as the baron de Montesquieu's *L'Espirit des lois* (1748), Abbé Raynal's *Histoire des deux Indes* (1770), Louis-Sébastien Mercier's *L'An 2440* (1771), and the marquis de Condorcet's *Réflexions sur l'esclavage des nègres* (1781) made slavery one of the most significant social and literary topics of the time. Those works highlighted the cruelty and injustice of slavery, warned of *marronage* and slave revolts, and pleaded for more enlightened colonial policies and enforcement of the *Code Noir*, instituted in 1685 under Louis XIV to ensure humane treatment of slaves but never strictly observed. Committed to preserving European property, the inefficiency of the slavery system notwithstanding, writers took the moderate position of advocating amelioration of the slaves' lot instead of abolition. In novels and short fiction also the French turned their attention to slavery, following the immense popularity of *Oroonoko*, written by the English novelist Aphra Behn and first translated in 1745. That novel began the current of *littérature négrophile*, in which black characters were depicted as possessing heroic qualities. The idealized, exotic image of Africans that resulted appears in such eighteenth-century works as Jean-François Saint Lambert's *Ziméo* (1769), Joseph La Vallée's *Le Nègre comme il y a peu de blancs* (1789), and Germaine de Staël's *Mirza* (1795). Olympe de Gouge's *L'Esclavage des noirs*, performed at the Comédie-Française in 1789, and numerous other dramatic works, mainly melodramas, contained this idealized image of slaves, which appealed greatly to mass audiences. The depiction of slaves as tragic heroes reflected preromantic trends of sentimentalism or exoticism and expressed new literary themes of alienation or exclusion. Works about slavery declined sharply, however, after the slave uprisings and massacres of whites in Saint Domingue and Guadeloupe in the 1790s. Those events also effectively silenced the abolitionist movement for several decades.

In the nineteenth century the subject of slavery reflected trends toward romanticism and socially committed literature. *De la littérature des nègres* (1808) by the Abbé Grégoire was one of the few works addressing injustices toward slaves during the era of Napoleon, whose negrophobic policies Staël opposed in several short essays. The subject regained popularity in 1823, when the French Academy proposed slavery and the slave trade as the subject for the prize in poetry, which was won by Victor Chauvet for his poem "Néali, histoire africaine." Another significant poem from this time is Marceline Desbordes-Valmore's "La Veillée du nègre" (1825). Victor Hugo's *Bug-Jargal* (1826), Prosper Mérimée's *Tamango* (1829), and other works in prose, poetry, and theater of the romantic period continued to dwell on slavery as an expression of themes of melancholy, social injustice, exile, and rebellion. In *Ourika* (1823) Claire de Duras provided a sympathetic treatment of an African woman whose plight echoes Duras's own alienation as a woman. George Sand also addressed injustice toward subjects of oppression: in *Indiana* (1832) she showed how oppression similarly affects women and persons of color; in an influential review in *La Presse* in December 1852, she praised Harriet Beecher Stowe's *Uncle Tom's Cabin*, thereby contributing to the great popularity of Stowe's novel in France. Other nineteenth-century works, such as Eugène's Sue's *Atar Gull* (1831) and Lamartine's play *Louverture* (1850), recounted the horrors of the transatlantic passage or deplored the condition of slaves. In the few works published by persons of color in the nineteenth century—for example, short stories by the New Orleans writer Victor Séjour and novels by Alexandre Dumas such as *Georges*—the complex nature

of mulatto identity is explored. Emeric Bergeaud's *Stella* (1859), the first Haitian novel, recounts life under slavery and the quest for independence.

Considerations of slavery in twentieth-century French Caribbean literature focus on themes of heroism, national identity, and gender. Efforts to assert black identity during and after the "negritude" movement have led to numerous works on leaders of the Haitian revolution: Touissant Louverture is the subject of works by Aimé Césaire (1960) and Edouard Glissant (1963); Henri Christophe figures in Césaire's play *La tragédie du roi Christophe* (1963). Other works—Simone Schwarz-Bart's *Pluie et vent sur Télumée Miracle*, Daniel Maximin's *L'isolé soleil* (1981), Patrick Chamoiseau's *Texaco* (1992), Raphaël Confiant's *Eau de café* (1991)—delve into the past to restore a collective memory and contribute to healing what Caribbean authors see as the traumas of alienation and oblivion resulting from slavery. Still other works focus on the

Alexandre Dumas (the elder). [Hulton-Deutsch Collection/Corbis]

role of women: their lives under slavery in Maryse Condé's *Moi, Tituba sorcière* (1986); their neglected role as revolutionary heroes in André Schwarz-Bart's *La mulâtresse solitude* (1972); and their forgotten contributions to culture and society in Marie Chauvet's *La danse sur le volcan* (1957).

See also CARIBBEAN REGION; ENLIGHTENMENT; FRANKLIN, BENJAMIN, AND THE MARQUIS DE CONDORCET; GRÉGOIRE, HENRI, BISHOP; MAROONS; MONTESQUIEU; RAYNAL, G.-T.-F. DE, ABBÉ.

BIBLIOGRAPHY

ANTOINE, RÉGIS. *Les Ecrivains français et les antilles des premiers pères blancs aux surréalistes noirs.* 1978.
DAYAN, JOAN. *Haiti, History, and the Gods.* 1995.
HOFFMAN, LÉON-FRANÇOIS. *Le Nègre romantique.* 1973.
KADISH, DORIS Y., and FRANÇOISE MASSARDIER-KENNEY, eds. *Translating Slavery: Gender and Race in French Woman Writers, 1783–1823.* 1994.

Doris Y. Kadish

Spanish Literature

Literature of slavery falls into two categories: abolitionist literature and historical reconstructions written after abolition (1886). Poems, plays, and novels have been written about slavery, and in the twentieth century the subject has been treated in opera, operetta (*Cecilia Valdés*), and film (Tomás Gutiérrez Alea's *The Last Supper*).

While authors from Spain and many Spanish-American countries used their literary skills to oppose slavery, often under constraints of government censorship, literature on slavery is primarily a Cuban phenomenon, owing to the central importance of the institution to Cuba, as a sugar producer. In addition, the novel, which lends itself to description and examination of an institution like slavery, became a dominant genre in Spanish America only in the 1830s. By then, with the exception of Cuba and Puerto Rico, Spanish-American countries had won their independence and abolished slavery, and their literature focused on European and romanticized Indian, not African, elements of their emerging national cultures.

In Cuba, the most important works of the nineteenth century used slavery not only to advocate abolition but also as a metaphor for ongoing political subjugation to Spain. A slave's account of his life, *Autobiografía de un esclavo* (Autobiography of a Slave, 1839) by Juan Francisco Manzano, and the novel *Francisco* (written 1838, published 1880) by Anselmo Suárez y Romero, were translated for the use of English abolitionists. Although their antislavery message was often blurred by romanticism, the novels *Sab* (1841)

by Gertrudis Gómez de Avellaneda, and Cirilo Villaverde's *Cecilia Valdés* (first part 1839, second part 1882) still had to be published outside of Cuba. *Cecilia Valdés* told a true story of the son of a slaving merchant who fell in love with a mulatto woman, not knowing that she was his half sister; the novel powerfully captured the multiple worlds of nineteenth-century Cuba and the tragedy of racism in a racially diverse, socially divided society and became the foundational masterpiece of Cuban literature.

Other Cuban antislavery novels are Antonio Zambrana's *El negro Francisco* (1873), modeled on *Francisco*; and *La campana del ingenio* (The Bell of the Sugar Mill, 1883), by Julio Rosas (the pseudonym of Franciso Puig). Martín Morúa Delgado, the "black Zola," planned a cycle of novels about slavery but wrote only two: *Sofía* (1891) and *La familia Unzúazu* (The Unzúazu Family, 1901).

The antislavery play *El mulato* (The Mulatto) by Alfredo Torroela (1845–1879) was staged in Mexico, where, like other Cuban plays, it could escape the surveillance of the Spanish censor. Among poems that denounced slavery are "Blanco y negro" (Black and White) by Diego Vicente Tejera (Cuba, 1844–1903); "El último esclavo" (The Last Slave) by Manuel Serafín Pichardo (Cuba, 1865–1937); "La libertad" (Liberty) by Manuel Atanasio Fuentes (Peru, 1820–1890); and "El esclavo muerto" (The Dead Slave) by José Martí (1853–1895), Cuba's most famous poet and patriot.

In the twentieth century, slavery continued as a prime metaphor for political oppression, and its interracial implications emerged as defining aspects of Cuban national identity. In poetry, "Ballad of the Two Grandfathers" and "The Grandfather," by Nicolás Guillén (1902–1989), respectively, depicted the history of conquistadors and slaves in African rhythms and the lasting African heritage in pure Spanish sonnet form. The powerful "I Love my Master" by Nancy Morejón (1944–) captures the rage produced by sexual and cultural subjugation. Historical novels like *El negrero* (The Slaver, 1933), by Lino Novás Calvo (1905–1983) used nineteenth-century motifs to speak of contemporary politics; and *The Kingdom of This World* (1949), about the Haitian revolution, by Alejo Carpentier (1904–1980) introduced a type of "magical realism" inspired by African spiritism. After the Cuban revolution, Miguel Barnet's *Autobiography of a Runaway Slave* (1966) based on interviews with a 104-year-old former slave, created a bibliography that became a best-seller as a novel celebrating the revolutionary contributions of blacks to the island's society. *Los guerrilleros negros* (The Black Guerrillas, 1979) by César Leante (1928–), also published in the Castro era, depicted nineteenth-century runaway slave communities (*palenques*) as protorevolutionary. More recently,

José Martí. [Corbis-Bettmann]

and grotesquely, *Graveyard of the Angels* (1987) by Reinaldo Arenas (1943–1990) parodies *Cecilia Valdés*—a literary icon—and implicitly rejects other sacred cows of Cuban culture, including Castro's ideology. Arenas continues the Cuban tradition of invoking slavery as a metaphor to oppose political oppression.

See also ABOLITION AND ANTISLAVERY MOVEMENTS; CUBA.

BIBLIOGRAPHY

LUIS, WILLIAM. *Literary Bondage: Slavery in Cuban Narrative.* 1990.
WILLIAMS, LORNA V. *The Representation of Slavery in Cuban Fiction.* 1994.

Gustavo Pellón

African Literature

Two of the earliest novels from sub-Saharan Africa—Félix Couchoro's *L'esclave* (1929) and Paul Hazoumé's *Doquicimi* (1938)—raise issues that have continued to be explored throughout twentieth-century African literature: (1) the complex social hierarchies within African societies that make it difficult to define slave status in Africa, and (2) the parallels between the subordination of women as wives and various slavelike social statuses. Until recently, Couchoro and Hazoumé have been largely ignored in the critical literature, mainly because of the lack of anticolonial sentiment in their narratives. This points to a third issue common in literary treatments of slavery by African writers: the depiction of the horrors of the overseas slave trade and its metaphorical parallels with oppressive colonial and postcolonial political regimes.

Characters with a disadvantaged status as less than a full kin member appear in many novels. The incidental figure of Ikemefuna, who is killed as a sacrifice in Chinua Achebe's *Things Fall Apart* (1959), is typical of slavelike figures depicted without comment. In contrast, Elechi Amadi (*The Slave*, 1978) and Abdulrazak Gurnah (*Paradise*, 1994) explore the experience of individuals living within an unfree status. Amadi's tale of *osu* slavery among the Igbo of Nigeria deals with the status and obligation of the descendants of a man who took refuge as a shrine slave. Set in early colonial Tanganyika, Gurnah's novel describes the life of Yusuf, a child pawned to a wealthy trader, whom he sees alternately as an uncle and as a master.

Buchi Emecheta's *The Slave Girl* (1977) explores a similar situation, the life of Ojebeta, sold by her older brother to a wealthy trader in Onitsha, Nigeria. Gender relations and sexual abuse are central themes, despite the irony of the relative wealth of slavery in town versus the poverty of rural freedom. Ojebeta flees with a man who ultimately redeems her but subjects her to the oppression of marriage, while Emecheta comments that with marriage, "Ojebeta . . . was changing masters." *Anowa* (1970), a play by Ama Ata Aidoo, parallels the use of slaves and wives as subordinates as it follows a young Ghanaian woman's marriage to the "wrong" man to its tragic end. In *Anowa*, the culturally deviant husband insists on buying slaves rather than marrying co-wives to help attain the prosperity that is within the couple's reach.

Aidoo's play also touches African complicity in the overseas trade in slaves and the emergence of an African comprador class allied with European colonial interests. That broader picture was first expressed in literature through the works of Africans who produced personal narratives of their experience as slaves. Two of the best-known narrators were Phillis Wheatley (*The Poems of Phillis Wheatley*, 1966) and Olaudah Equiano (*The Life of Olaudah Equiano or Gustavus Vassa, the African*, 1989). Twentieth-century writers such as Ayi Kwei Armah (*Two Thousand Seasons*, 1973) and Yambo Ouologuem (*Bound to Violence*, 1968) have not hesitated to express their rage at historically unequal relations between African rulers and ruled, Arab conquerors and Africans, and European colonizers or neocolonialists and Africa and the continuing ramifications of these relations.

See also AFRICA; EQUIANO, OLAUDAH; SLAVE NARRA-
TIVES; SLAVE TRADE; WHEATLEY, PHILLIS.

BIBLIOGRAPHY

JOHNSON, LEMUEL A. "The Middle Passage in African Literature: Wole Soyinka, Yambo Ouologuem, Ayi Kwei Armah."
African Literature Today 11 (1980): 62–84.
OGUDE, S. E. "Slavery and the African Imagination: A Critical Perspective." *World Literature Today* 55 (1981): 21–25.

Edna G. Bay

Caribbean Literature

In the Caribbean, slavery is both an issue in identity
politics (who is a Caribbean; who has the right to
speak as one), and a set of images (loyal slave, heroic
rebel, bestial savage). It is part and parcel of Europe's
quarrel with itself, this epistemological debate of
"same" and "other" by which the West has long defined the "primitive" in opposition to the "civilized."
Thus, one cannot speak of a literature of slavery without evoking its double, a literature on slavery.

Whether Spanish-born Bartolomé de Las Casas
pleads the cause of Indians by demanding the importing of African labor (*The Tears of the Indians,* 1552); or
Enlightenment philosopher Denis Diderot calls for a
black liberator-cum-avenger, a "new Spartacus" (*L'Encyclopédie,* vol. 5, 1774); whether William Blake produces shocking engravings on slave mistreatment for
John Stedman's *Narrative of a Five Year's Expedition
against the Revolted Negroes of Surinam* (1796); or
Britain's William Wilberforce brings the slave trade
to an end in 1807 after nineteen years of effort, the
conquered were not allowed to speak for themselves
(*Incas: The Royal Commentaries,* written in 1609 by Gar-
cilaso de la Vega, born of a Spanish father and an
Inca mother, might be considered the exception). In
Karl Marx's often quoted conclusion to the preface
of his *Eighteenth Brumaire of Louis-Bonaparte* (1851), he
states, "they cannot represent themselves; they must
be represented."

Instead, the paternalistic benevolence of masters
speaks for the slaves and for itself, as do the perfunc-
tory regrets of poets, for whom slavery is a theme but
not a reality (Wordsworth comes to mind). The thread
runs through many a Rousseauistic fable of the eighteenth century (the much translated Saint Lambert's
1769 *Zimeo* is one), as well as, in succeeding centuries,
the multiple translations and reprints of the complacent master-text, Aphra Behn's 1688 *Oroonoko; or, the
Royall Slave.* Characters are rendered heroic precisely
by their exceptional virtues; their race brothers, by
implication, deserve their fate. The wrenching memories of home by Ibo-born, Caribbean-enslaved Olau-

An actor portrays the role of Oroonoko in a stage version of
the novel by Aphra Behn. [Hulton-Deutsch Collection/
Corbis]

dah Equiano (*The Interesting Narrative,* 1789) only
serve to perpetuate romanticized clichés which, by
the end of the nineteenth century, verge on melo-
drama. The fact that in this literature, descriptions of
the physical characteristics of slaves do not always distinguish between native American or native African is
a clear indication that, in the encounter with its others, Europe remains primarily interested in itself.
The infatuated slave who gives up his life for the master's daughter (Victor Hugo's *Bug-Jargal,* written in
1822), is twin to the "noble savage" pining for a Castil-
lean aristocrat in the Cuban Manual de Jesus Galvan's
Enriquillo: or, the Cross and the Sword (1879). Expressing
the alternative view of slaves, travelers' reports recon-
firmed perceptions of the bestiality of the justly enslaved (to wit, Oxford Professor James Anthony

Froude's 1888 *English in the West Indies; or, the Bow of Ulysses*).

Although *Froudacity* (1889), by J. J. Thomas of Trinidad, had already gone a long way toward establishing Caribbean claims to full humanity and the complacent focus eventually shifted with emancipation (for Cuba, the wrenching runaway tale of Esteban Montejo's 1840 *Autobiography;* or, for Jamaica, the remarkable evenness of Mary Seacole's 1857 *The Wonderful Adventures of Mrs. Seacole*), it would take almost another century for Caribbeans to move from under the "victim or hero" dichotomy. In 1938 Trinidad's C. L. R. James wrote *Black Jacobins: Toussaint Louverture and the San Domingo Revolution,* a vibrant homage proving once and for all that the conquered now speak for themselves:

> I made up my mind that I would write a book in which Africans, or people of African descent, instead of being the object of other people's exploitation and ferocity, would themselves be taking action on a grand scale and shaping others to their needs. (*Black Jacobins,* "Preface," vii).

Haiti, where in the words of Martinican poet Aimé Césaire, "Negritude rose for the first time and stated that it believed in its humanity" (*Cahier d'un retour au pays natal,* 1937), would give modern Caribbean literature its most compelling self-representation yet with Toussaint and Christophe—uncanny incarnations of Diderot's avengers. It also laid the foundation for an Afrocentric cultural nationalism that would eventually sweep all of the black diasporic world: Negritude.

See also EQUIANO, OLAUDAH; TOUSSAINT-LOUVERTURE.

BIBLIOGRAPHY

CÉSAIRE, AIMÉ. *Discours sur le colonialisme.* 1955. Translated as *Discourse on Colonialism.* 1972.
COOMB, ORDE, ed. *Is Massa Day Dead?* 1974.
DABYDEEN, DAVID, ed. *The Black Presence in English Literature.* 1985.
FANON, FRANTZ. *Peaux noires, masques blancs.* 1952. Translated as *Black Skins, White Masks.* 1967.
FRANCIS, ARMET. *Children of the Black Triangle.* 1989.
KENNEDY, ELLEN CONROY, trans. *The Negritude Poets: An Anthology of Translations from the French.* 1989.
WILLIAMS, ERIC. *Capitalism and Slavery.* 1944.

Clarisse Zimra

Brazilian and Portuguese Literature

Given Portugal's early and continuous involvement in the Atlantic slave trade and the millions of Africans taken to Brazil, it is surprising that relatively few Portuguese literary works deal with slavery. In Portugal, a few minor slave characters appear, primarily in plays, during the sixteenth and early seventeenth centuries. Most literary references to slavery after that period appear in the works of two Afro-Brazilian poets who emigrated to Portugal, Domingos Caldas Barbosa (1738?–1800) and Gonçalves Crespo (1846–1883). From the late eighteenth century on, Portuguese intellectuals, distrustful of British pressure to end slavery and the slave trade, tended to view the issues as geopolitical rather than humanitarian.

There are far more references to slavery in Brazilian literature, beginning in the sixteenth century. Many of those references support African slavery as an alternative to the enslavement of Amerindians. The two most important texts of the seventeenth century are the "Twenty-Third Sermon on the Rosary" of Father Antônio Vieira (1608–1697), an enormously influential figure in both Portugal and Brazil, and the poems of Gregório de Matos (1633–1696). While Vieira concluded that African slavery was the unpardonable sin that had led God to punish Portugal by destroying much of its empire, Matos portrayed women of color, whether slave or free, as lascivious erotic objects— still a deeply embedded stereotype in Brazilian culture.

For much of the eighteenth and early nineteenth centuries, Brazil's millions of slaves were almost invisible in its literature. As in Portugal, there was no literary campaign against the slave trade, which British naval pressure halted in 1850. The most famous protest against the traffic, "The Slave Ship" of Antônio de Castro Alves (1847–1871), was not written until 1868—eighteen years after the trade ended.

Antislavery literature finally developed in Brazil after 1850, but only a handful of novels and plays and a few dozen poems were published before the institution was abolished in 1888. While nineteenth-century Brazil produced a number of important writers of African descent, few of them were active in the abolitionist movement; the major exceptions are Luís Gama (1830–1882) and José do Patrocínio (1854–1905). The two antislavery stories of the nation's greatest writer, Joaquim Maria Machado de Assis (1839–1908), who was also descended from slaves, were not published until well after 1888. Some Brazilian abolitionist texts presented idealized slave characters like those found in European and North American works; the most important of these are the poems of Castro Alves; *Mother* (1859), a play by José de Alencar (1829–1877); and *The Slave-Girl Isaura* (1875), a novel by Bernardo Guimarães (1825–1884). Many other works, however, took a more sharply negative view of slaves, arguing that they were inherently violent and immoral; slavery, which required close contact with these dangerous creatures, thereby threatened the physical and moral survival of white Brazilians. The most influential of these negative texts was *Victims or Executioners*

(1869), by Joaquim Manuel de Macedo (1820–1882). This tendency, reinforced by a series of naturalist novels published between 1881 and 1895, inevitably influenced whites' attitudes toward freedmen after abolition.

See also ABOLITION AND ANTISLAVERY MOVEMENTS; BRAZIL; PERSPECTIVES ON SLAVERY; PORTUGAL.

BIBLIOGRAPHY

BROOKSHAW, DAVID. *Race and Color in Brazilian Literature.* 1986.

CONRAD, ROBERT EDGAR, ed. *Children of God's Fire: A Documentary History of Black Slavery in Brazil.* 1983.

HABERLY, DAVID T. *Three Sad Races: Racial Identity and National Consciousness in Brazilian Literature.* 1983.

MAROTTI, GIORGIO. *Black Characters in the Brazilian Novel.* 1987.

SAYERS, RAYMOND S. *The Negro in Brazilian Literature.* 1956.

David T. Haberly

Locke, John   [1632–1704]

British philosopher and political scientist.

For John Locke—whose political theories were mostly set forth in his *Two Treatises of Government*—slavery, which consisted of being under someone's absolute power and which was a condition that could never be

John Locke. [Corbis-Bettmann]

voluntary, was an issue near the core of his political philosophy. By his definition, slavery was "nothing else, but the State of War continued, between a lawful Conqueror, and a Captive." Voluntary acceptance of slavery, political or chattel, by those enslaved could never create a moral obligation to obey. Such obligation could only be established where slavery had been imposed as just punishment of crime. This opinion directly contradicted Thomas Hobbes's theory of the contractarian origins of society—that is, in a covenant between the individual and the sovereign, whereby the individual, leaving the state of nature and entering society, surrenders all rights to the sovereign and receives back only such rights (and only for so long a time and under such circumstances) as the sovereign is pleased to bestow.

Locke denied the binding nature of the Hobbesian covenant because, he reasoned, persons could not pledge through the social contract, in a morally binding manner, to place themselves under absolute power. Locke utilized two moral principles to place limits upon such power—one cannot make a morally binding agreement to do that which is wrong, and in the maxim of the law, "Nobody is able to give what he does not have" (*nemo potest dare quid non habet*).

Since one does not have the right to kill oneself, one cannot give the sovereign the right to do so. Such right as the sovereign has to take life comes from the surrender to him of the right to do justice and to defend oneself, a right enjoyed in the state of nature. From this surrender of power, the sovereign derives the right to impose the death penalty (or any lesser punishment) and to engage in just war, but he enjoys no right over life otherwise.

The slave or the subject of a tyranny has no property right in law to his own life, liberty, or estate, for the tyrant's or master's power supersedes any such right. Locke defended ordinary chattel slavery when it arises from capture in just war—a standard position in early modern European moral philosophy. Slavery, like tyranny, was seen as a continuation of the state of war, where only power counted.

Many scholars have questioned how Locke could possibly have believed the fiction of capture in just war to vindicate slave trading in Africa, where expeditions penetrated into the interior of the continent with the explicit aim of capturing and enslaving tribesmen or purchasing slaves from their own kings.

Locke's acceptance of African chattel slavery arose from the an anthropologically unjustified view of Africa as a continent of universal misery and tyranny. That view permitted one to see slavery as no infringement of the rights of Africans. In 1669 Locke wrote "The Fundamental Constitutions of Carolina"—most likely in collaboration with his patron, the Earl of

Shaftesbury. Sections One Hundred Nine and One Hundred Ten of that organic law seem in radical contradiction to one another. Section One Hundred and Nine states "No person whatsoever shall disturb, molest, or persecute another, for his speculative opinions in religion, or his way of worship"—a rule quite in concert with the sentiments expressed in Locke's famous *Letter on Toleration.* Section One Hundred and Ten, however, provided that "Every freeman of Carolina, shall have absolute power and authority over his negro slaves, of what opinion or religion soever." Locke seems to have recognized the inherent contradiction between the status of chattel slave and the possession of any guaranteed liberty, even religious freedom.

In the years prior to Locke's draft of this constitution, a controversy raged in the British West Indies over the claim of some clergy to the right to baptize and to preach to slaves, even contrary to the wishes of their owners.

Locke's political philosophy in general, as well as his views on slavery, had enormous influence, especially in the Anglo-American legal tradition. The Constitution has Lockean influences, and Jefferson's Declaration of Independence is a direct echo of Locke. Even today, political theorists as divergent as the libertarian Robert Nozick and the liberal John Rawls utilize central elements from Locke's political philosophy in formulating their own theories.

See also ENLIGHTENMENT; HOBBES, THOMAS; LAW; PHILOSOPHY.

BIBLIOGRAPHY

LOCKE, JOHN. *Two Treatises of Government: A Critical Edition with an Introduction and Apparatus Criticus.* Edited by Peter Laslett. 1963.

Patrick M. O'Neil

Long, Edward   [1734–1813]

Proslavery planter-historian of Jamaica.

Edward Long was born, was educated, and began practicing law in England. When his father died in Jamaica in 1757, he went there to administer his family's property at Longville. He became a judge in Jamaica's Vice-Admiralty Court before ill health forced his permanent return to England in 1769, and a retirement devoted to historical study.

Long's principal work, *The History of Jamaica* (1774) contains a sustained argument for the legitimacy of slavery both in theory, drawing on historical precedence and the fundamental antagonisms between the top and bottom in hierarchical social orders, and

as the institution then existed in the British West Indies. Here, Long used overtly racist justifications, characterizing Africans and their Jamaican descendants as barbarous savages incapable of being civilized and the colored, or "mulatto," population as depraved mongrels. His similarly jaundiced conception of Africa depicted a brutal slave system there, from which the Atlantic slave trade had rescued those now enslaved within what he claimed was the benign patriarchy of West Indian sugar plantations. Long had earlier marshaled these arguments to attack Lord Mansfield's decision in the case of the slave James Somerset (*Somerset v. Stewart*). *Candid Reflections* (1772) casts Long's racism in extraordinarily vituperative terms, while the anxieties and frustrations planters and slaveowners felt at the ruling in this case account for the book's splenetic tone.

Long formulated his ideology, which other West Indian planter-historians, most notably Bryan Edwards, subsequently echoed, to counter increasing abolitionist sentiment in Britain. His arguments thus concentrated on defending slavery and the slave trade within the particular context of the British West Indian sugar plantation economy in the eighteenth century, but Britain's proslavery lobby continued to champion his ideas until emancipation came (1834). Long's views found renewed currency among proslavery ideologues in the U.S. South.

See also CARIBBEAN REGION; PERSPECTIVES ON SLAVERY; .SOMERSET V. STEWART.

BIBLIOGRAPHY

EDWARDS, BRYAN. *The History, Civil and Commercial, of the British Colonies in the West Indies.* 3 vols. 1793. Reprint, 1972.
LEWIS, GORDON K. *Main Currents in Caribbean Thought: The Historical Evolution of Caribbean Society in Its Ideological Aspects.* 1983.
LONG, EDWARD. *Candid Reflections upon the Judgement lately awarded by the Court of King's Bench, in Westminster-Hall, on what is commonly called the Negro Cause, by a Planter.* 1772.
———. *A Free and Candid Review of a Tract, Entitled "Observations on the Commerce of the American States."* 1784.
———. *The History of Jamaica.* 3 vols., 1774. Reprint, 1972.
Papers Relating to Jamaica, presented by C. E. Long. British Library, London.

Roderick A. McDonald

Louisiana

Slavery was a fact of life in Louisiana before the 1699 planting of the French colony. Native American tribes enslaved captives from rival nations, and French set-

Table 1. Slave and Free Populations in Louisiana, 1810–1860.

Year	Free White	Free Colored	Slave	Total
1810	34,311	7,585	34,660	76,556
1820	73,383	10,476	69,064	153,407
1830	89,441	16,710	109,588	215,739
1840	158,457	25,502	168,452	352,411
1850	255,491	17,462	244,809	517,762[1]
1860	357,629	18,647	331,76	708,002[2]

1. Total free households in 1850 = 49,101.
2. Total free households in 1860 = 63,992.

tlers followed suit. Like the British to the east, however, they found Indian slavery too problematic. By 1706 officials were proposing a two-for-one exchange of the colony's red slaves for black ones from the islands. Native American enslavement did continue, with a small but steady influx of western Indians sold by the Spanish into French Louisiana, but no more than a few hundred ever existed in the colony at any time. In the 1770s Indian slavery was banned.

Louisiana's African-American slaves far outnumbered their Indian counterparts, but slavery's progress lagged in comparison with Britain's North American colonies. As elsewhere, its growth was closely tied to agricultural progress. The first slave ships landed in 1719, but importation rarely occurred after 1731. During that period fewer than six thousand Africans were brought in, principally from the Senegambia. Without government support until agricultural production could be stabilized, since the staple crops (indigo, tobacco, corn, rice) were very labor-intensive, the colony frequently lacked basic foodstuffs to support new slaves. While colonists clamored for them, anticipating the wealth slaves would bring, they could not afford them.

New Orleans, history's fabled slave-trading center, did not earn that reputation until after the American Revolution, when sugarcane and cotton transformed the Louisiana economy. Thereafter, large-scale agricultural production had three centers: the east bank of the lower Mississippi River between New Orleans and Baton Rouge; the almost state-long alluvial plain of the Mississippi's west bank; and the rich valley of the Red River. Sugarcane dominated below Baton Rouge; cotton ruled along the Red and the upper west bank of the Mississippi. In between, mixed production reflected landowner preferences. While these re-

gions were first occupied by the colonial French, they still offered abundant acreage to Americans who arrived after the Revolution and the Louisiana Purchase of 1803.

The limited size of the colony's slave population, as well as Latin social attitudes and the influence of the Roman Catholic Church, produced relatively humanitarian slave laws. Under the Code Noir of 1724, the slave was treated as a person with limited rights, rather than as a piece of property. Slave marriages were encouraged, spouses could not be separated by sale, and children under fourteen could not be parted from their mothers. Freedom was a status slaves had the right to purchase; when owners balked, slaves could petition for government intervenors to set their value and facilitate the sale. Countless owners permitted slaves to bear arms as hunters and soldiers; in the latter capacity, black males fought valiantly in several Indian campaigns and in the Spanish campaigns of the American Revolution as well.

The extent to which this social and political climate ameliorated the everyday burdens of slavery remains debatable. As slave numbers increased late in the colonial period, as plantations spread from village out-

A potential buyer at an 1855 Louisiana auction inspects the slaves for sale. [Corbis-Bettmann]

skirts to distant areas with minimal pastoral supervision, and as Anglo-Americans poured into Louisiana bringing different values, slave life significantly deteriorated. Church unions, which were the only legal form of marriage for any race in colonial Louisiana, became rare for slaves; civil marriages remained nonexistent. On the cotton plantations the lifestyle of the labor force differed little from elsewhere in the South. But on sugarcane plantations, demands on labor during grinding and processing season were notoriously extreme. Despite Louisiana's reputation as a dumping ground for excess slaves from older states, the numerical growth of the slave population during the American regime actually underperformed several new Anglo-American states. Between the first and last of Louisiana's antebellum censuses (1810 and 1860), the number of enslaved blacks grew one-hundredfold (34,660 to 331,726)—a seemingly significant number until compared, for example, with the thousandfold growth of Anglo-Alabama in that same period.

Although slavery was not an exclusively white-over-black situation in any state, black and mixed-black slave owners in Louisiana significantly outnumbered those in other North American societies. Their proliferation primarily stemmed from the century of liberal manumission and economic opportunity under French and Spanish regimes. One extended family of freed slaves turned masters, at its peak, owned some five hundred slaves and more than eighteen thousand acres in the rich Red River Valley. However, as the state moved further away from its colonial Latin roots, its institution of slavery increasingly shifted toward Anglo-American norms.

See also CODE NOIR. *See also the individual entries on the other states of the United States.*

BIBLIOGRAPHY

SCHAFER, JUDITH K. *Slavery, the Civil Law, and the Supreme Court of Louisiana.* 1994.
TAYLOR, JOE GRAY. *Slavery in Louisiana.* Edited and with an introduction by Kimberly Hanger. 1988.

Gary B. Mills

Lovejoy, Elijah P. [1802–1837]

Abolitionist and free-speech advocate.

Born in Maine to a Congregational minister and his wife, Elijah Parish Lovejoy attended college at Waterville (Colby College), graduating with honors in 1826. Heading to Saint Louis, Missouri, in 1827, Lovejoy opened a school and eventually became a partner of T. J. Miller, publisher of the *Saint Louis Times.* Al-though he was an advocate of other humanitarian causes, Lovejoy did not express interest in abolitionism until after attending Christian revivals in 1832. He studied for the ministry at Princeton Theological Seminary, returning to Saint Louis in 1833 as a preacher and as the editor of a new Protestant newspaper, the *Saint Louis Observer*; at the *Observer* he drew both praise and criticism for his outspoken critique of Catholicism. By 1835, Lovejoy began to denounce slavery, becoming a proponent of gradual emancipation. Throughout the 1830s, his denunciation of slavery intensified, though he hesitated to describe himself as an abolitionist. In April 1837, Lovejoy publicly condemned the lynching of a free black man for the alleged murder of a white sheriff. The conservative judge, Luke E. Lawless, did not indict a single defendant for the lynching, but blamed Lovejoy and the *Observer* for disrupting the community over the antislavery issue. The next day, Lovejoy denounced the judge in print, whereupon a large mob surrounded the newspaper's offices, destroying nearly everything.

This event precipitated Lovejoy's relocation to Alton, Illinois, that same year. There, he published the *Alton Observer*. On 7 November 1837, a proslavery mob, made up mostly of people from Missouri, attacked the building that housed Lovejoy's press and killed Lovejoy while he was defending it. Lovejoy's murder electrified the abolitionist movement and became a rallying point for free speech. Lovejoy, the abolitionists' first martyr, became a symbol for northern opponents of slavery. Lovejoy's murder was especially

A lynch mob attacks and burns the warehouse of Godfrey Gilman and Elijah Lovejoy in Alton, Illinois, on the night of 7 November 1837. [Library of Congress/Corbis]

important because it illustrated the threat that slavery posed, not only to blacks but also to the civil liberties of white northerners.

See also ABOLITION AND ANTISLAVERY MOVEMENTS.

BIBLIOGRAPHY

GILL, JOHN. *Tide without Turning: Elijah P. Lovejoy and Freedom of the Press.* 1958.
SIMON, PAUL. *Freedom's Champion: Elijah Lovejoy.* 1994.
TABSCOTT, ROBERT W. "Elijah Lovejoy: Portrait of a Radical," *Gateway Heritage* 8, no. 3 (1987–1988): 32–39.

David A. Reichard

Lundy, Benjamin   [1789–1839]

U.S. abolitionist and editor.

A native of New Jersey, Lundy first encountered slavery in 1809 while working as a saddlemaker's apprentice in Wheeling, Virginia. In 1816 he founded the Union Humane Society as an instrument to oppose racial discrimination in the North and began working for the creation of a national antislavery organization. In 1821 he founded *The Genius of Universal Emancipation,* one of the first abolitionist newspapers.

During the 1820s Lundy was a tireless advocate of emancipation in the United States. He believed that the best solution to the problem of slavery involved colonization, and between 1825 and 1835 he attempted unsuccessfully to establish freedmen's colonies in Haiti, Canada, and Mexico. In 1828, while promoting colonization on a lecture tour of the North, he met William Lloyd Garrison, who eventually became abolitionism's most prominent figure, and in the next year Lundy persuaded Garrison to join *The Genius* as associate editor. Garrison's fiery articles involved the paper in several lawsuits and the two parted company shortly thereafter.

In 1835 Lundy ceased publishing *The Genius* and moved to Philadelphia, Pennsylvania, where he founded *The National Enquirer and Constitutional Advocate of Universal Liberty,* another abolitionist newspaper. He opposed the admission of Texas to the Union on the grounds that it would perpetuate slavery. In his effort to prevent the admission of Texas, Lundy provided John Quincy Adams, at the time an

Benjamin Lundy. [*Dictionary of American Portraits*]

abolitionist congressman, with much of the factual material for his antiannexation speeches. In addition, Lundy wrote *The War in Texas* (1836). In 1838 he sold *The National Enquirer,* moved to Illinois, and resumed publishing *The Genius* until his death.

See also ABOLITION AND ANTISLAVERY MOVEMENTS; AMERICAN COLONIZATION SOCIETY; EMANCIPATION; GARRISON, WILLIAM LLOYD.

BIBLIOGRAPHY

PEASE, JANE H., and WILLIAM H. PEASE. *Bound with Them in Chains: A Biographical History of the Antislavery Movement.* 1972.

Charles W. Carey Jr.

M

Madagascar

See East Africa.

Maine

Because it was a province of the state of Massachusetts until it entered the Union as a separate state in 1820, much of the history of slave jurisdiction in Maine is simply that of Massachusetts.

The rocky soil and short growing seasons of Maine agriculture were unsuitable to slavery, and the lack of large international harbors excluded Maine from serious participation in the Atlantic slave trade. As a result, there were virtually no slaves at any time within this territory.

The issue of slavery was raised by the case of Quock Walker, a Negro slave who sued his alleged master, Nathaniel Jennison of Barre, Massachusetts, for assault and battery after Jennison beat Quock in the course of a violent recapture of the alleged slave. The events in this affair led to a series of cases, including *Walker v. Jennison* (1781), *Jennison v. Caldwell* (1781), and *Commonwealth v. Jennison* (1783). The result of these cases was the judicial abolition of slavery in the Commonwealth of Massachusetts, including the province of Maine, when the state supreme court under Chief Justice William Cushing held that the "free and equal clause" of the Massachusetts Declaration of Rights had effectively abolished slavery throughout the state, rendering it unconstitutional.

When, as a result of the Missouri Compromise (also known as the Compromise of 1820), Maine entered the Union as a free state, its first constitution declared that "all men are born equally free and independent." A legislative act of 1821, furthermore, forbade the removal of "any person lawfully residing and inhabiting" in the state of Maine, although this does not appear to have been aimed at frustrating legitimate recapture under the fugitive slave clause of the U.S. Constitution. However, acts passed in 1838 and 1855, and two passed in 1858, were in fact designed to frustrate the implementation of the federal fugitive slave laws of 1793 and 1850.

See also MASSACHUSETTS; MISSOURI COMPROMISE.

BIBLIOGRAPHY

CUSHING, JOHN D. "The Cushing Court and the Abolition of Slavery in Massachusetts: More Notes on the 'Quock Walker Case.'" In *The Law of American Slavery*, edited by Paul Finkelman. 1987.
FINKELMAN, PAUL. *The Law of Freedom and Bondage: A Casebook.* 1986.
———, ed. *An Imperfect Union: Slavery, Federalism, and Comity.* 1981.

Patrick M. O'Neil

Malaya

The institution of slavery was an integral component of precolonial Malay society in the Malay peninsula. Sultans and important chiefs often owned more than a hundred slaves, and virtually all aristocratic families and prosperous commoner families owned at least some. Having a large contingent of slaves and other dependents conferred prestige on the head of the household.

Islam, which forbids Muslims from enslaving fellow Muslims, spread through Malaya beginning in the fourteenth century, and Muslim Malays introduced legal distinctions between non-Muslim "slaves" (*abdi, hamba*) and Muslim "debt slaves" or "debt bondsmen" (*orang berhutang*). Technically, debt slaves were free persons, but in practice they were little different from ordinary slaves.

Slaves came from a variety of sources. Raiding parties of coastal and immigrant Malays attacked aboriginal (*orang asli*) villages and camps in the interior of the peninsula, killing the men and older women and seizing the young women and children. Slave traders captured or bought large numbers of slaves in Bali, Celebes, Borneo, Mindanao, Sumatra, and other islands of the Indonesian archipelago, and brought them to Malayan ports. Malay Muslim pilgrims and Arab merchants also bought small numbers of African slaves in the slave market at Mecca. Some Malays were slaves in all but name. The *orang hulur* consisted of Malay criminals who surrendered their freedom to sultans to avoid physical punishment. In addition, sultans and powerful chiefs could seize any commoner women they desired and force them to serve as concubines, maids, or nurses. If the women were married, their husbands and children became slaves as well. Younger women were expected to offer themselves as sexual partners and possible wives to attract young free men to serve in the ruler's bodyguard or militia.

Slaves were legally classified as private property and had no rights or protections from the state. Owners could choose to abuse them or treat them like family members. Anyone who injured or killed a slave was legally required to pay compensation to the slave's owner. Children born to slaves also became the property of their parents' owner. Owners could sell, give away, or bequeath their slaves like any other movable property. Occasionally, owners freed their slaves or stipulated that the slaves be freed after the owners' death.

Debt slaves were people who were unable to repay borrowed money or goods and therefore forfeited their freedom to their creditors. Most debt slaves were Malay commoners who had borrowed money or food from aristocrats. Some impoverished people voluntarily entered debt slavery in the hope of obtaining food, shelter, work, or a spouse. Sultans and chiefs could enslave commoners at will by fabricating claims of debt or imposing unpayable fines for trumped-up offenses. Spouses and children of debt slaves became slaves as well, on the principle that families were collectively responsible for their members' debts. In theory debt slaves could gain their freedom by paying off their debt, but in practice they had no way to accumulate funds, because their masters could lay claim to all their earnings. People could buy debt slaves by paying off the slave's debt to the previous owner.

Most domestic slaves (including debt slaves) lived in their master's household, performing all the menial chores and manual work that members of the aristocratic class considered beneath their own dignity. Females prepared food, cleaned house, washed clothes, split firewood, carried water, and looked after children. Males served as craftsmen, gardeners, messengers, personal servants, guards, and militia members. Some slaves, usually married couples, lived outside their owner's household, working the owner's fields and orchards and producing most of the food for the master's family, dependents, and guests. Other slaves worked in their masters' commercial enterprises, including tin mines, plantations, and trade. Some of these slaves were permitted to conduct business on their own behalf as well as for their masters. The most successful even owned their own slaves.

Royal slaves (*hamba raja*) formed a privileged class, because, as royal property, any offense against them was considered an insult to the sultan. Consequently, they acquired a reputation for abusing the populace with impunity. In trade-based kingdoms like Malacca, sultans used their slaves to manage their merchandise, work on the docks, and crew their ships.

Malaya's precolonial kingdoms depended heavily on slavery. Because the population was sparse, labor was hard to get; so slaves were the most valuable possession a person could have. The labor of slaves, along with the taxes and corvée labor of Malay commoners, supported the aristocratic class and enabled its members to live in the ease and luxury that symbolized their superiority. Some slaves contributed directly to the rulers' power by serving in their militias and as their bodyguards. Although the proportion of slaves in the population was relatively low (about 7 percent in Perak state in 1874), they were crucial to the power and prestige of sultans, chiefs, and other aristocrats.

As the British extended their influence in the Malay states in the late nineteenth century, they pressured the sultans to abolish slavery. Economic changes also undermined slavery. The British brought in contract laborers from China, the Dutch East Indies (modern Indonesia), and India to work in the expanding colonial mining and plantation industries, and it became cheaper to employ these immigrant workers than to maintain slaves. The British forced the sultan of Perak to abolish slavery in 1883, and all other states soon followed suit, though it lingered on in disguised forms long after abolition. Some household slaves declined to leave their masters following emancipation.

The institution of slavery has had little enduring effect on Malay society. Any stigma attached to the descendants of slaves has virtually disappeared over succeeding generations. However, the Malayan aborigines still fear and mistrust outsiders, especially Malays, and keep alive stories of slave raiding and other past abuses in their oral traditions.

See also DEBT PEONAGE; SLAVE TRADE; SOUTHEAST ASIA.

BIBLIOGRAPHY

ENDICOTT, K. "The Effects of Slave Raiding on the Aborigines of the Malay Peninsula." In *Slavery, Bondage and Dependency in Southeast Asia*, edited by Anthony Reid. 1983.
GULLICK, J. M. *Indigenous Political Systems of Western Malaya.* 1958.
MATHESON, V., and M. B. HOOKER. "Slavery in the Malay Texts: Categories of Dependency and Compensation." In *Slavery, Bondage and Dependency in Southeast Asia*, edited by Anthony Reid. 1983.
MAXWELL, W. E. "The Law Relating to Slavery among the Malays." *Journal of the Straits Branch of the Royal Asiatic Society* 22 (1890): 247–297.
SULLIVAN, PATRICK. *Social Relations of Dependence in a Malay State: Nineteenth Century Perak.* 1982.

Kirk Endicott

Mamluks

See Enslavement, Methods of; Islam; Military Slaves; Ottoman Empire.

Manumission

This entry includes the following articles: Ancient Rome; United States; Latin America.

Ancient Rome

Manumission played a large role in Roman slavery, especially among the domestic and urban slaves who dominate the evidence. The promise of freedom motivated slaves to work hard, behave well, and save their money, although for the average slave the chance of obtaining freedom may not have been great. Roman slavery was perhaps unique in that ex-slaves became citizens.

Frequency of Manumission

The Romans were often prejudiced against foreigners, but their slavery lacked the racist element that would condemn the freeing of slaves. The manumission of a slave was considered a joyful occasion: in a letter (*Epistulae ad Familiares* 16.16) Quintus Cicero, the orator's brother, reports that he "jumped for joy" on hearing of the manumission of Cicero's trusted and highly educated slave, Tiro. Indeed, especially during the republic, many slaves came from the Greek eastern Mediterranean, whose high culture the Romans generally admired. The manumission of hardworking slaves was at least an ideal.

Cicero in *Philippic* 8.11 implies that "good and deserving" slaves would commonly attain freedom a few years after being captured. Literary and legal sources are full of references to manumission and to ex-slaves. In Italian epitaphs that unambiguously indicate status, ex-slaves outnumber those who died as slaves. This tendency becomes more pronounced as the age at death increases beyond thirty. Records on papyri in Roman Egypt show a similar pattern. Such evidence has encouraged some scholars to describe Rome as an "open" slave society, in which slavery was a transitional state that preceded incorporation into the community.

The incorporation of ex-slaves into the citizen population is indeed a striking feature of Roman slavery. Nevertheless, problems with the evidence for frequent manumission as well as other considerations support a darker picture. To begin with, thirty was a relatively old age in a society with high mortality, such as Rome. By age thirty a slave might have been working for twenty years and had already exceeded the average life expectancy at birth. In addition, both literary sources and epitaphs are likely to focus on domestic slavery at the expense of its agricultural counterpart, and on successful ex-slaves rather than impecunious or recalcitrant slaves.

Slave owners most contact with and most interest in their domestic staffs rather than the agricultural slaves on their estates. Also, the overwhelming majority of epitaphs come from large cities. In contrast, the promise of manumission is conspicuously absent from Cato's and Varro's works on farming—though Columella does mention manumission. Rich ex-slaves were conspicuous, and they were usually resented. They too probably show up in literature to an extent disproportionate to their numbers. In general, ex-slaves are more likely than slaves to have had the wherewithal and the motivation to commemorate themselves by means of epitaphs. Thus their representation in such texts does not accurately reflect the respective numbers of slaves and ex-slaves. The counterexample of Brazilian slavery shows that a highly visible ex-slave culture—certainly the case at Rome—is entirely compatible with a small percentage of slaves who actually gain freedom.

Although the chance for manumission could not have served its well-attested motivational function unless some attained freedom, slaves' prospects of manumission must have varied considerably, according to the occupation of the individual slave. Skilled slaves or domestic slaves with access to their masters had a fair chance of liberation. So did slaves involved in commerce or a business. On the other hand, agricultural slaves on a distant estate had little chance to make money and might never—or only rarely—have seen their masters. Such slaves, the vast majority, were less likely to have been freed.

Reasons for Manumission

Freeing slaves was considered a generous display of wealth. Masters also might gain economic benefits from manumission, or at least not lose much. They were freed from having to support aging or unproductive slaves. They could recoup their initial investment if a slave bought his or her freedom. They might even continue to derive profit from the ex-slave, if the slave contracted at the time of manumission to continue to do work for them, to perform *operae*. In many cases, the ex-slave's estate would revert to the master. Finally, masters could benefit indirectly from state subsidies, during periods when ex-slaves were allowed to enroll for the grain dole.

Testamentary manumission enabled masters to retain the use of their slaves while alive and to be sure of grateful mourners at their funerals. The importance of this last motive should not be exaggerated: Kathleen Atkinson (1966) points out that for a spectacular funeral "grateful heirs would be a better investment than grateful new *liberti* [ex-slaves]." Slaves were unlikely to kill their master to hurry the process along, since all slaves, innocent or guilty, in the house of a murdered master were executed.

The possibility of manumission encouraged hard work and good behavior, especially for those slaves upon whose skilled or independent labor slaveholders especially relied. Such slaves could save their money and eventually buy their freedom. This incremental progress toward freedom allowed the incentive for good behavior to be spread out over time. Slaves who managed businesses or had opportunities for tips were most likely to be able to save money. Some other slaves were given a wage to spend or to save for their freedom. Seneca writes that slaves paid for their freedom "from the *peculium* they've acquired by cheating their stomachs" (*Epistle* 80.5). Once a price had been agreed on, it was considered an abuse for a master to renege (Tacitus, *Annals* 14.42.1; Justinian, *Digest* 40.1.5). Slaves seem usually to have paid about or above market value for their freedom. Ex-slaves often bought freedom for their relatives.

Slaves might also be liberated for services to their owners. The *lex Aelia Sentia,* which prohibited manumission of slaves under age thirty or by masters under age twenty, listed conditions that would justify exceptions: saving a master's life or reputation could bring freedom; masters could free slaves to whom they were

*This detail from a late-second-century floor mosaic depicts gladiatorial combat. A gladiator who survived combat in the arena and repeatedly demonstrated strength and daring could win the coveted wooden sword (*rudis*) from the emperor, signifying his liberation.* [Roger Wood/Corbis]

related by blood; masters could free their teachers or their foster mothers; and women could be freed in order to marry their masters—such freedwomen could not marry anybody else without their ex-master's permission.

In practice, a wide range of other services could gain a slave freedom after age thirty. Columella (*Res Rustica* 1.8.19) recommends freeing a slave women who had raised four children. The fictional freedman Trimalchio pleased both this master and his mistress sexually. He was not only freed but made heir to the estate (Petronius, *Satyricon* 75–76). Since close kin had the *beneficium abstinendi*—that is, the right to refuse to inherit an insolvent estate, a slave might also be instituted as a person's heir in such a case to bear the infamy of bankruptcy proceedings, public auctions, and the like.

On occasion the state freed slaves without the permission of their masters. The *Volones*, slave volunteers, were freed after service against the Carthaginians in the late third century B.C.; their masters were eventually compensated. In the civil wars of the late republic, rival generals or factions would promise freedom to slaves to raise supporters, and Sulla (ca. 138–78 B.C.) freed many of the slaves of his murdered political enemies. Informers, usually in cases of treason, could obtain their freedom from the state. Finally, the emperor Claudius ruled that sick slaves abandoned by their masters were free if they recovered.

Copius evidence indicates that slaves could free themselves by running away. The cities of the empire, with their large ex-slave populations, could easily swallow up a fugitive slave. Measures taken against desertion provide evidence for its occurrence: runaways were often branded on recapture; in the countryside, we find evidence of chain gangs and cells fitted with manacles; Cicero petitioned several well-connected friends to track down a fugitive in another province of the empire; finally, "slave catchers" must have tracked down some slaves, although they appear in legal texts primarily as the perpetrators of a variety of frauds. Escape beyond the boundaries of Roman rule would ensure freedom from Roman slavery, but the empire was large and potential dangers, including reenslavement, awaited rootless fugitives.

Laws Governing Manumission

The three principal legal methods of granting manumission probably go back at least to the time of the Twelve Tables in the fifth century B.C. Since the state had an interest in the creation of a new citizen, these forms of manumission originally involved a representative of the state. Manumission could be performed *censu*, by enrollment in the list of Roman citizens; *tes-*tamento, by a will originally ratified by a special assembly; or *vindicta*, probably by a collusive suit by a third party for the liberty of the slave. Manumission *censu* seems to have been rare in the classical period. Manumission *vindicta* required the presence of a magistrate, if only briefly: for example, a praetor could witness a manumission on the way to the baths. Governors could witness manumissions in the provinces, but they were busy and seldom did so. Opportunities for manumission *testameno* were obviously limited. All three methods were associated with a tax of 5 percent to be paid by the ex-slave. This tax was a source of government income for seven centuries, starting in the fourth century B.C. This tax, along with the inconvenience of formal manumission, encouraged masters to manumit their slaves informally. Although such slaves could try to appeal to the praetor against reenslavement, they had no civic rights and could not contract a legal marriage or have legitimate children. On their death, their property, still a *peculium*, would revert to their masters.

The *lex Junia* (probably 25 or 17 B.C., but perhaps A.D. 19) regularized the status of such slaves. Informally manumitted slaves gained the status of the old Latin allies of Rome and were called *Junian Latins*. Although Junian Latins had no testamentary rights, they could gain full citizenship by contracting a legitimate marriage and presenting a one-year-old child to the praetor. Later, Junian Latins could gain citizenship by actions such as building large grain ships or houses at Rome, or serving six years in the police at Rome.

The *lex Fufia Caninia* (2 B.C.) imposed a sliding scale to limit the proportion of a master's slaves who could be freed by will: the larger the total number of slaves, the smaller the proportion who could be freed: five out of a household of ten slaves could be freed, but only one hundred out of five hundred or more slaves. The *lex Fufia Caninia* limited only testamentary manumission rather than manumission in general. This may be because the Roman state traditionally curbed ostentatious funerals and tried to preserve estates. This law would also have cut down on the number of ex-slaves without ties to former owners.

The *lex Aelia Sentia* (A.D. 4) also restricted manumission. Owners could not formally free slaves—and thus give them citizenship—until the owner was twenty and the slave was thirty years old. A number of exceptions allowed slaveholders to free slaves to whom they were closely related or who had saved their lives or reputations. Slaves who had been punished by torture, branding, or fighting in the arena were permanently barred from formal manumission and thus from citizenship. Manumission for the purpose of defrauding creditors or an ex-master was also prohibited. The *lex Aelia Sentia* would have made formal manumission more difficult to achieve. The law seems to have been primarily concerned with ensuring that immoral or undeserving slaves did not obtain citizenship.

This series of laws governed manumission for five centuries, but their basic tendency and their internal consistency remain controversial subjects. Earlier in the twentieth century, scholars tended to accept Suetonius's claim that the emperor Augustus wanted to preserve the ethnic purity of the Roman population (Suetonius, *Augustus* 40). But the *lex Junia,* as well as the Augustan *lex Julia de maritandis ordinibus* and *lex Papia Poppaea,* encouraged ex-slaves to marry citizens and have children. In general, the laws regularized manumission and tended to restrict it, lest it be employed to what might be regarded as an excessive or inappropriate degree.

See also ANCIENT ROME; FREEDMEN; LAW; PECULIUM.

BIBLIOGRAPHY

ATKINSON, KATHLEEN M. T. "The Purpose of the Manumission Laws of Augustus." *Irish Jurist,* n.s. 1 (1966): 356–374.

BRADLEY, K. R. *Slaves and Masters in the Roman Empire: A Study in Social Control.* 1987.

BUCKLAND, W. W. *The Roman Law of Slavery.* 1908.

GARDNER, JANE F. "The Purpose of the Lex Fufia Caninia." *Echoes du Monde Classique/Classical Views* 35, n.s. 10 (1991): 21–39.

PATTERSON, ORLANDO. *Slavery and Social Death.* 1982.

TREGGIARI, SUSAN. *Roman Freedmen during the Late Republic.* 1969.

WATSON, ALAN. *Roman Slave Law.* 1987.

WEAVER, P. R. C. "Where Have All the Junian Latins Gone? Nomenclature and Status in the Early Empire." *Chiron* 20 (1990): 275–305.

WIEDEMANN, THOMAS E. J. "The Regularity of Manumission at Rome." *Classical Quarterly* 35 (1985): 162–175.

Peter Hunt

United States

Nothing exposes the complexity and contradictions of chattel bondage more than the act of manumission. Manumission, the freeing of individual slaves (as distinguished from general emancipation, the liberation of all slaves) was the slave owner's right, and masters made much of the inability to bestow freedom on their slaves. Manumission thus revealed the power of the owner and the utter dependence of the slave, who, as property, could be disposed of as the slave owner wished. But manumission almost always took place at the slave's behest, and thus it also revealed the ability of slaves, at least in some instances, to shape their own destiny, even against the slave owner's will. Indeed, in the case of one particular form of manumission, self-purchase, the initiative moved from the master to the

An 1817 New York City manumission certificate signed by Mayor Jacob Radcliff and Richard Riker, the city recorder. [Corbis-Bettmann]

slave, making the slave more than an equal partner in the process of securing freedom. But no matter what its particular form, manumission—as a contract between master and slave—conceded to the slave an equality that the slave owner would rarely admit.

Like other property transactions, manumission was regulated by the state through executive pronouncements, legislative enactments, and judicial injunctions. The state's involvement in manumission, however, went far beyond the normal regulation of property transactions, thus confirming slavery as a distinctive form of property, asserting that others besides the slave owner had an interest in the slave, and conceding the slave's humanity. Manumission took a variety of forms, since property could be transferred in any number of ways. Slaves could be freed by deed or by testament, both of which could be encumbered by stipulations by owners, by the state, and sometimes even by slaves. Slave owners often made manumission contingent on the slaves' good behavior, on special payments, and on the former slaves' continued probity and their fidelity to the former master, the master's family, and others. The state added its own requirements, often denying slaves critical rights as subjects or citizens even when liberty was granted. Slaves, for their part, tried to negotiate special terms, which provided protection and sometimes annuities after liberation.

Because both slave owner and slave found these regulations burdensome and inconvenient, they often acted outside the law. Extralegal and illegal manumission became so common in some places that they eclipsed legal freeing of slaves. Such extralegal and illegal manumissions were sometimes recognized de facto and were occasionally legalized retroactively, so that they gained the force of law.

The fact that the law was often bent by slave owners and slaves points to the dual purpose of manumission. From the perspective of the slave owner, manumission was a means of rewarding slaves, and thus a way to assure the slaves' continued loyalty and obedience even after they had been freed. Upon occasion, slaveholders promised future freedom in order to extend the life of slavery and, in a crisis, to ensure its survival. In short, manumission was another weapon in the slaveholder's armory, much like the lash or Christmas gifts. From the slave's perspective, however, manumission had a very different meaning. As a source of freedom, it was just as much a means of resisting enslavement as flight or rebellion.

Manumission was thus yet another outcropping of the ongoing struggle between slave owner and slave, with all the trials and tribulations this contest entailed. What was true of slave society generally was also true for the slave societies that emerged in mainland North America, most of which became incorporated as the United States in the late eighteenth century.

The history of manumission followed the history of slavery in mainland North America, reflecting the constant pulls and pushes of resistance and accommodation. In general, manumission was more open when and where the commitment to slavery was weak. In such circumstances, the line between free and slave was porous, and slaves crossed it frequently. However, as the commitment to slavery grew, the regulation of manumission became more restrictive and manumission itself was less frequent.

In outline, the history of manumission in mainland North America between the first arrival of slaves in the sixteenth century and the final emancipation of 1865 can be divided into three periods. In the years prior to the development of the plantation, manumission was generally open and easy. There were few colonial regulations, especially in the seventeenth century, and what regulations existed were often ignored or circumvented. Slaves were eager to be free, and many masters consented, granting slaves their freedom or allowing them to purchase it. Approximately one-fifth to one-quarter of the African and African-American population gained freedom.

The growth of the plantation—in the Chesapeake region at the end of the seventeenth century, in the lowcountry at the beginning of the eighteenth century, in the lower Mississippi Valley at the end of the eighteenth century, and in the Northern colonies in the middle years of the eighteenth century—saw a tightening of regulations concerning manumission. Through executive, legislative, or judicial decrees, various colonial governments stripped slaveholders of exclusive control over manumission and required them to secure prior approval. Often this approval was contingent upon a bond for the slave's future good behavior and compelled the immediate removal of freed slaves beyond the boundaries of the colony. With the passage of such regulations, manumission declined sharply, as did the proportion—and sometime the absolute number—of free black people.

The age of revolutions, roughly the years between 1770 and 1810, saw a reversal of this trend, with a liberalization of manumission laws. Led by Quakers and then others, who were inspired by the words of the Declaration of Independence and the Declaration of the Rights of Man, slaveholders took advantage of these laws and manumitted slaves in record numbers. In the northern states, this presaged a general emancipation. Emancipation never received serious consideration in the states, territories, and colonies to the South, but in the upper South there was a sharp increase in the number of manumissions, particularly in the states of Delaware, Maryland, and Virginia. In 1782, for example, Virginia passed legislation allowing masters to manumit adult slaves, and they did so in substantial numbers. A small increase was also registered in the lower South during this period.

With the failure of general emancipation outside the northern states, slavery gained new life. During the early years of the nineteenth century, with Virginia leading the way in 1805, manumission laws were tightened, and the number of slaves who gained their freedom declined. In the years thereafter, as the commitment to slavery grew, many southern states—particularly those in the lower South—prohibited manumission entirely, and manumission became solely an illegal or extralegal practice.

Within this general chronology of manumission, regional variations developed, which were shaped by the demography, geography, and economies of various slave societies in mainland North America. Among the most important variations were those in the French and Spanish settlements of the Caribbean rim, especially Louisiana. In Louisiana manumission was increased by reliance on black soldiers to protect the colony from internal as well as external enemies and by the influence of French and (after 1763) Spanish law and custom, within the context of a slow developing plantation economy. Particularly important in this regard were the *siete partidas* and the *coartación*—the latter an amalgam of customary practices that had gained the force of law in Spanish America in the eighteenth century. These gave slaves the power to initiate their own manumission through negotiations with their owners. Once the process of self-purchase began, it transcended the relationship between master and slave, and a slave's right to freedom could not be denied, even in the face of an owner's opposition. If a slave owner refused to negotiate freedom, the slave—or any interested party, for that matter—could petition the governor's court and have a *carta de libertad* issued, thereby requiring the owner to manumit when the stipulated price was paid. The *carta,* moreover, remained in force no matter how many times a slave was sold or traded, and any contribution the slave had made toward freedom had to be recognized by future owners. Owners who refused to negotiate with their slaves could be brought before a judicial tribunal, which would fix a price for slaves to buy themselves.

As slaves in Louisiana grasped the implications of Spanish law and—most important—came to appreciate the willingness of Spanish officials to enforce it, more and more slaves took advantage of the new opportunities. Although voluntary, master-inspired manumissions outnumbered those initiated by slaves who reported to the Spanish law during the first decade of Spanish rule, the proportion of slave-initiated manumissions increased steadily during the 1780s. Drawing up their own resources and joining together with free people of color, slaves opened negotiations to buy their own liberty and that of their families and friends. If owners rejected the slaves' proposals to buy their way out of bondage, slaves did not hesitate to invoke their legal rights.

As events in Louisiana demonstrate, the law alone did not free a single slave. Freedom depended upon both master and slave and sometimes involved close bargaining between the two. Certain general patterns emerged. Slaves who lived in close contact with their owners had a better chance of being manumitted than those who knew their owners indirectly or not at all. Practically, this meant that slaves held in small units on farms or in cities had a better opportunity to be manumitted than those who lived on plantations, because working closely with the owner gave slaves a chance to ingratiate themselves and request freedom. Thus house servants, messengers, and artisans had a greater chance for freedom than field hands. Among these favored groups, women who formed a sexual liaison with their owners, and their mixed-race children, had the greatest opportunity for freedom. More women than men, and more people of mixed descent and light color than people of unmixed African origins and darker color, gained their freedom.

In this undated nineteenth-century illustration, a plantation owner named George Shelby is shown giving his slaves their liberty. [Corbis-Bettmann]

The pattern for slaves who purchased themselves differed from the pattern for those who depended largely, although rarely solely, on their owners' largess. Urban slaves with connections to the house and workshop—house servants and artisans—had the greatest opportunity to gain freedom through self-purchase. However, the balance was not nearly as heavily weighed toward women and people of color.

General patterns of manumission also changed over time in mainland North America, reflecting, among other things, the slaveholder's motives in manumitting. Masters who acted for personal reasons—because of their affection for or debt to particular slaves—generally freed only a few selected slaves. These were disproportionately women and light-skinned people—often their wives, mistresses, children, and others with whom they had close ties. Masters who acted for ideological reasons, such as a revulsion against slavery itself or a desire to extend the life of slavery—often freed slaves indiscriminately, sometimes in large numbers, liberating men as well as women and black people as well as brown.

The diverse pattern of manumission was reflected in the growth of the free black population, which itself became an important force in the process of manumission. Free people of color spent enormous sums and much of their time and energy buying their families and friends out of bondage. But "self-purchase" was a misnomer, since the act of purchasing liberty was almost always collective, requiring the cooperation of large numbers of people beginning with family members and extending to the larger black community and sometimes to benevolent whites. Indeed, when manumission was restricted and prohibited by law, they often purchased slaves and held them as de facto free people, manumitting in fact despite the legal prohibition. Such clandestine manumissions suggest the complexity of the process of freeing the slaves, and of the institution which made property of men and women.

See also COARTACIÓN; CONCUBINAGE; EMANCIPATION; LAW; PLANTATIONS; QUAKERS; SIETE PARTIDAS.

BIBLIOGRAPHY

BERLIN, IRA. *Slaves without Masters: The Free Negro in the Antebellum South.* 1974.
HANGER, KIMBERLY S. *Bounded Lives, Bounded Places: Free Black Society in Colonial New Orleans, 1769–1803.* 1977.
NASH, GARY B., and JEAN R. SODERLUND. *Freedom by Degrees: Emancipation in Pennsylvania and Its Aftermath.* 1991.
OLWELL, ROBERT. "Becoming Free: Manumission and the Genesis of a Free Black Community in South Carolina." *Slavery and Abolition* 17 (1996).
WHITE, SHANE. *Somewhat More Independent: The End of Slavery in New York City, 1770–1810.* 1991.
WHITMAN, T. STEPHEN. *The Price of Freedom: Slavery and Manumission in Baltimore and Early National Maryland.* 1997.

Ira Berlin

Latin America

Africans entered southern Portugal and Spain with Muslim armies in the eighth century, and long-term interaction and lenient manumission practices created sizable free black populations in cities such as Lisbon, Seville, Cádiz, and Valencia. Manumitted persons in those cities filled accepted economic, social, and religious roles and, in fifteenth-century Seville, even minor political positions.

Medieval Iberian law, transplanted in the fifteenth century to the Americas, acknowledged a slave's juridical and moral personality and defined the rights and obligations of both slaves and masters. Because slavery was not exclusively based on race, Africans were treated like slaves of other races and ethnicities who had been captured in "just wars," had been condemned, or had sold themselves into slavery to escape debt or destitution.

Iberian law considered slavery an unnatural condition and therefore provided many avenues out of bondage. Castilian law, codified in the thirteenth century and entitled the *Siete Partidas,* permitted slaves to report a master's abusive behavior to the court, which, if verified, resulted in his removal from that owner and sale to another master. A slave could also earn freedom for meritorious service to the state, which might include betraying conspiracies, denouncing crimes, performing heroic acts, or rendering military service. If an owner named a slave as his or her heir or if the owner named the slave as guardian for his heirs, the slave became free. The medieval ideal of charity toward "miserable classes" also led owners to manumit favored slaves, often in their wills. Furthermore, law and custom permitted slaves to hold and transfer property (*peculium*) and purchase their own freedom or that of relatives or friends.

Although Iberian law also applied to Latin America, distinctive demographic, economic, and sociopolitical conditions transformed slavery in the colonies. Unacculturated Africans, consequently, did backbreaking labor in the mines and on plantations and ranches with little hope of manumission. Because of older metropolitan slave relations, their access to legal and religious protections, and their integration into a cash economy, urban slaves in the Americas received better treatment than their rural counterparts and had more opportunities for manumission.

Many urban slaves in Latin America earned manumission through self-purchase. They worked in a *jornal* (day wage) system that allowed them to hire out their own time and live independently in return for an agreed-upon payment to their owners. Owners not only gained income but also avoided many of the responsibilities of feeding, sheltering, clothing, and providing medical care for their slaves. Slaves enjoyed some autonomy and also earned funds for their self-purchase. Although both sexes used the *jornal* system, male slaves had the advantage over females because they had skills in higher-paid occupations such as masonry, carpentry, blacksmithing, and tailoring, while women more often worked as lower-paid laundresses, domestics, wet nurses, and cooks.

Iberian slave owners in the Americas often accepted reimbursement of the slave's original purchase in exchange for freedom. Brazilian masters were legally compelled to free slaves providing such reimbursements. In the Spanish colonies of the circum-Caribbean, this customary arrangement was legalized. If an owner refused to allow self-purchase, a slave could initiate a legal action called *coartación,* by which the court intervened to determine the slave's "just price." Once the court set that price, the slave moved beyond a master's control and could live and work independently and make installments on his or her freedom at the stipulated price. Slaves bought their freedom with personal income accrued through self-hire, loans, or gifts—often from lay religious brotherhoods to which they belonged. Slaves earned money by raising animals and foodstuffs; by fishing, oystering and hunting; and by gathering wild fruits, firewood, and hay to huckster in the markets and through the streets. Others produced and sold a wide variety of craft items. Upon full payment of the mandated sum the court issued a notarized manumission or *carta de libertad* (*carta de alforria* in Portuguese).

Those manumitted were most often urban, mulatto, female, or minors; many of the latter group were freed by their white fathers. Colin Palmer's analysis of parish registers from late-sixteenth-century Mexico City showed that over 70 percent of the freed population were women and that mulattoes formed over 80 percent of the freed population, regardless of gender. Frederick Bowser's study of Mexico City manumissions of the late sixteenth and early seventeenth centuries also found that 62 percent involved women and children and only 8 percent were granted to adult males. Bowser's study of Peruvian manumissions yielded similar results: females formed 67 percent of the freed population and adult males only 3 percent. The average age of manumitted persons in eighteenth-century Bahia was only fifteen.

With more women than men becoming free and because children followed the legal condition of their mother, natural reproduction soon became more important than manumission to the growth of free black populations, which by the eighteenth century were sizable throughout Latin America. Free black populations grew even faster and larger in Brazil than in Spanish America, although Brazil continued a massive importation of Africans until legally closing the slave trade in 1850.

Whereas fond or pious masters often freely manumitted women and children (some of whom may have been their concubines and offspring) and even aged slaves, they were less inclined to liberate more valuable and potentially threatening adult males. Adult males, however, often manipulated geopolitical and religious contests in the Americas to advantage. Spain's inability to defend its far-flung empire led its territorial governments to manumit adult male slaves who joined local militia units. From the sixteenth century on, freed black militias defended Spain's interests not only throughout the Caribbean but also in more remote arenas such as the Philippines. Spain even manumitted maroons (whom it first tried to extirpate) if they would swear loyalty and defend the Spanish crown against its many enemies, including Indians, Europeans, and pirates.

After numbers of fugitive slaves from Carolina requested baptism in the "true faith" and religious sanctuary in Spanish Florida, Charles II issued a royal proclamation on 7 November 1693, "giving liberty to all . . . the men as well as the women . . . so that by their example and by my liberality others will do the same." Thus, medieval obligations of religious sanctuary and freedom for conversion were transformed into state strategy. In the eighteenth century Spain extended the offer of religious sanctuary throughout the circum-Caribbean and began to manumit the slaves who were fleeing Protestant enemy territories such as Jamaica, Curaçao, and Saint Croix if they reached Spanish territory and requested conversion. Military leaders on both sides of the Spanish American wars of independence freed large numbers of slaves in return for their military service. Once independence was achieved in the early nineteenth century, most Latin American nations abolished slavery; by this time free blacks already far outnumbered slaves. Brazil did not abolish slavery until 1888, and Cuba abolished it only in 1886.

Although socioreligious imperatives once were the primary reason for Iberian manumissions, in Latin America manumission and, finally, emancipation were driven more by a combination of economic and political motivations that varied in time and place. Scholars contrast the open manumission systems of Spanish and Portuguese America with the absence of similar opportunities in British America, where after a brief but more fluid and multiracial beginning, slavery quickly hardened into a perpetual condition to which only persons of African descent were consigned. In the same process self-purchase and manumission were first discouraged and later forbidden, keeping the class of free blacks in the British colonies small and making the eventual abolition of slavery more difficult.

See also COARTACÍON; FREEDOM; MAROONS; PECULIUM; SELF-PURCHASE; SPAIN.

BIBLIOGRAPHY

COHEN, DAVID W., and JACK P. GREENE, eds. *Neither Slave nor Free: The Freedmen of African Descent in the Slave Societies of the New World,* 1972.

DAVIS, DAVID BRION. *Slavery and Human Progress.* 1984.

KLEIN, HERBERT S. *African Slavery in Latin America and the Caribbean.* 1986.

LANDERS, JANE G., ed. *Against the Odds: Free Blacks in the Slave Societies of the Americas.* 1996.

PHILLIPS, WILLIAM D., JR. *Slavery from Roman Times to the Early Atlantic Trade.* 1985.

TANNENBAUM, FRANK. *Slave and Citizen: The Negro in the Americas.* 1946.

Jane G. Landers

Maori

Slavery in Maori society before the Europeans landed in New Zealand was not common, leading some eighteenth-century visitors to the Bay of Islands in northern New Zealand to conclude that slavery did not exist at all. One of the early visitors, Le Dez, as cited by Anne Salmond, deduced from the invisibility of enslaved captives that Maori "warfare must be cruel," and the Maori practice of killing prisoners does seem to be one reason for the apparent scarcity of slaves. This inference is contradicted by Raymond Firth's assertion that a "mark of a chief was generally the number of slaves he had in his household"; however, because Firth does not date the period he is referring to, he may be describing the postcontact era, when the economic usefulness of retaining captives as slaves increased. A. P. Vayda, using contemporary sources, suggests that before contact with Europeans significantly altered the indigenous society, less than 10 percent of Maoris lived in slavery. But even this figure should be treated as a guess, because the number of slaves in each community varied, and because no count was possible. There are also reports of entire communities being "enslaved to," that is, under the *mana,* or "dominion," of other, more powerful, groups, but these clearly refer to vassalage rather than slavery.

Most accounts suggest that the fate of captives taken in battles—the main source of slaves—was precarious. It was believed by many Maori that being taken prisoner resulted in such a great loss in *tapu,* or status, that

Maori warriors, armed with spear, hatchet, and rifle, display ritualistic tattoos. [*Gleason's Pictorial Drawing Room Companion/*Corbis]

many would go out of their way to ensure that their captors would kill them on the spot, and sometimes parents killed their own children rather than allow them to become captives. Many of those who survived to reach their captors' village faced vengeful slaughter by women who had lost their men in the battle. Also, the limited nature of the subsistence economy of many Maori tribes meant that acquiring numerous slaves would restrict, rather than expand, their resource base. According to Te Rangi Hiroa, however, at times captives were deliberately taken to do menial work, though this may have been in raids rather than full-scale battles.

Prisoners who became slaves lived in conditions no more onerous than those of lower-class individuals born in that tribe. Their main occupation appears to have been helping prepare food and carrying out other duties characterized as "woman's work," which *tapu,* or high-status, warriors could not perform, and carrying food for raiding parties. The slave's lack of *tapu* allowed them to perform tasks that others would find polluting, thus creating their economic value to the community. Conversely, it prevented their being used for tasks restricted to those who had not lost their *tapu* status, such as canoe building. Tasks that lacked *tapu,* and involved the participation of the whole community, such as agriculture, often saw chiefs working considerably harder than their slaves.

The only physical brutality to which slaves were exposed was that their "owner" could kill or sacrifice them in a fit of anger or on a whim. For example, J. S. Polack, a nineteenth-century observer, noted how one chief tried out each new musket he acquired on one of his unsuspecting slaves. There is some dispute as to how often slaves were chosen for a sacrifice. Elsdon Best notes that communities occasionally offered slaves but preferred freemen, with their much higher *tapu*, for matters important to the tribe as a whole. Te Rangi Hiroa notes two sacrifices associated with the death of a chief that involved slaves. In the first a slave belonging to the deceased chief would be killed so that his soul would accompany the chief's on its journey to the next world. In the second, from the north Auckland area, a number of slaves would be cooked and placed on a stage or platform in pots next to the body of the chief to provide him with sustenance on his journey after death. However, human sacrifices seem to have been relatively rare in New Zealand in comparison with the rest of Polynesia.

The other distinctive form of "punishment" that slaves suffered, especially if they had high *tapu* before capture, was the total loss of that status upon becoming enslaved. Maori, and in particular males, were bound by *tapu* rules of purity, and any infringement of them could be life-threatening. Although captives, or slaves, thus lost their *tapu* protection from supernatural pollution, Maori ideology offered no explanation for their continued survival.

Once they were enslaved, the captives were usually abandoned by their relatives as dead, and very few rescue attempts were launched against their captors, who had demonstrated their martial superiority. The slaves' lack of alternatives encouraged them to assimilate into their new "kin" groups, usually by marrying a woman of the new society. Being chosen by a woman from the captors' group as her husband seems often to have been a matter of life and death for many captive warriors. The slaves accepted their new identity so strongly that they would return to fight their natal tribesmen on behalf of their captors. Although the children of a slave-freeborn marriage did not inherit slave status and were considered free members of the tribe, they did not become part of its official genealogy, and they may well have been teased as the descendants of slaves. The low status of children of these marriages applied even if the mother had been a high chieftainess before being enslaved and the father had been one of the conquering chiefs.

Very high-status captives appear, at least sometimes, to have retained their standing even as slaves. For example, Te Rangi-i-paia II, wife of a Ngati Potou chief, was captured in 1820 by the renowned chief Pomare, who then made her his wife. When he wished to make peace with her original tribe in 1823, he sent her as an emissary, a strategy that took advantage of her standing among her own people and demonstrated his own respect for them. The maneuver succeeded no doubt because she retained some of her status with the Ngati Potou. However, she returned to Pomare, perhaps reflecting the transfer of group membership imposed on captives.

As contact with Europeans increased in the latter part of the eighteenth century, Maori chiefs gained economic opportunities, and slaves were put to work cutting timber, raising pigs, or growing provisions as trade goods, and at least some of the female slaves were sent to work as prostitutes on whaling ships. From this trade the chiefs frequently sought yet more muskets, which would further increase their power and allow them to capture even more slaves, who could then be used to extend the labor force of the tribe.

As producers of wealth, slaves also became valuable in themselves and were occasionally exchanged for muskets among the tribes; slaves tended to move north and muskets south reflecting the greater contact with Europeans in the North Island. Trade with the Europeans did have its macabre side, though: around the 1820s the popularity of shrunken heads as a trade item in Sydney led to several chiefs killing some of their slaves to make a profit. (Shrinking heads for preservation was an old Maori custom that allowed warriors to bring home at least a part of a brother warrior who had died in battle.)

Slavery in Maori society did not entail the degree of exploitation associated with enslavement in capitalist economies. In the subsistence economy of the pre-European period, although slaves did provide a small source of extra labor, their main value seems to have been that they were not bound by *tapu* rules. After the Europeans introduced new food sources—animals and plants—and new forms of agriculture, slaves did gain economic value, but even this was limited because the freemen of the tribe often continued to work harder than the slaves.

See also HUMAN SACRIFICE; PACIFIC ISLAND SOCIETIES.

BIBLIOGRAPHY

BEST, ELSDON. *The Maori.* 1924.
———. *The Maori As He Was: A Brief Account of Maori Life As It Was in the Pre-European Days.* 1924. Reprint, 1974.
FIRTH, RAYMOND. *Primitive Economics of the New Zealand Maori.* 1929.
ORANGE, CLAUDIA, ed. *The People of Many Peaks: The Maori Biographies from the Dictionary of New Zealand Biography, 1769–1869.* Vol. 1. 1991.
PATTERSON, ORLANDO. *Slavery and Social Death: A Comparative Study.* 1982.
POLACK, J. S. *Manners and Customs of the New Zealanders.* Vol. 2. 1840. Reprint, 1976.
REED, A. W. *An Illustrated Encyclopedia of Maori Life.* 1963.

SALMOND, ANNE. *Two Worlds First: Meetings between Maori and Europeans, 1642–1772.* 1992.

TE RANGI HIROA. *The Coming of the Maori.* 1949. Reprint, 1966.

VAYDA, A. P. *Maori Warfare.* 1960.

David Booth

Maroons

The English word "maroon" (like French and Dutch *marron*, as well as English *Seminole*) derives from Spanish *cimarrón*—itself based on an Arawakan (Taino) Indian root. As used by the colonists, *cimarrón* originally referred to domestic cattle that had taken to the hills in Hispaniola, but it was soon being used also for American Indian slaves who escaped from the Spaniards. By the end of the 1530s, the word had taken on strong connotations of "fierceness," of being "wild" and "unbroken," and was used primarily to refer to African-American runaways.

Maroon communities existed throughout plantation America, from Brazil to Florida, from Peru to Texas. Usually called *palenques* in the Spanish colonies and *mocambos* or *quilombos* in Brazil, these new societies ranged from small bands that lasted less than a year to powerful states with thousands of members that survived for generations and, sometimes, for centuries. Today, the descendants of maroons still form semi-independent communities in various parts of the Americas—in Suriname, French Guiana, Jamaica, Colombia, Belize, Honduras, and elsewhere—remaining proud of their maroon origins and, in some cases at least, faithful to the distinctive cultural traditions that were forged during the earliest days of African-American history.

During the past several decades, scholarship on maroons has flourished, as new research has done much to dispel the myth of the docile slave. The extent of violent resistance to enslavement has been carefully documented—from the revolts in the slave factories of West Africa and mutinies during the Middle Passage to organized rebellions that began to sweep most colonies within a decade after the arrival of the first slave ships. There has also been growing attention to the pervasiveness of various forms of "day-to-day" resistance—from simple malingering to subtle but systematic acts of sabotage.

Maroons and their communities hold a special place in the study of slavery. While they were, from one perspective, the antithesis of all that the institution stood for, they were at the same time a widespread and embarrassingly visible part of all slave systems. Just as the very nature of plantation slavery implied violence and resistance, the wilderness setting of early New World plantations made marronage and maroon communities a ubiquitous extension of it. The large number of detailed newspaper advertisements placed by masters for runaway slaves attests to the level of planter concern, while at the same time affording the critical historian one important set of sources for establishing the profiles of maroons, which varied significantly by historical period and country. Not all individual maroons fled to the hinterlands. Many, especially skilled slaves, escaped to urban centers and successfully melted into the freedman population, while others became maritime maroons, fleeing by fishing boat or other vessel across international borders.

Planters generally tolerated repetitive or periodic truancy when it was motivated by temporary goals such as visiting a friend or lover on a neighboring plantation (so-called *petit marronage*). But within the first decade of the existence of most slaveholding colonies, the most brutal punishments—amputation of a leg, castration, suspension from a meathook through the ribs, slow roasting to death—had been reserved for long-term, recidivist maroons. Marronage on the grand scale, with individual fugitives banding together to create communities of their own, struck directly at the foundations of the slave system, presenting military and economic threats that often taxed the colonists to their limits.

Maroon communities, whether hidden near the fringes of the plantations or deep in the forest, lived in symbiosis with the plantation world, periodically making raids for firearms, tools, and women, often reuniting in freedom families that had formed during slavery. In a remarkable number of cases, beleaguered colonists were forced to sue their former slaves for peace. In Brazil, Colombia, Cuba, Ecuador, Hispaniola, Jamaica, Mexico, and Suriname, for example, the colonists reluctantly offered treaties that recognized the freedom that maroon communities had won, acknowledged their territorial integrity, and made provisions for meeting their economic needs, in return for an end to hostilities against the plantations and an agreement to return future runaways. Of course, many maroon societies never reached such accommodations, having been defeated by armies sent against them, and even when treaties were proposed they were sometimes refused or quickly violated. Nevertheless, new maroon communities seemed to appear almost as quickly as old ones were exterminated, and they remained, from a colonial perspective, the "chronic plague," the "gangrene" of many slave societies right up until abolition.

In most cases, the initial maroons in any New World colony hailed from a wide range of societies in West and Central Africa—and they shared neither language nor other major aspects of culture. Their collective task, once they had successfully escaped into the forests or swamplands or mountains, was nothing less than to create new communities and institutions, largely via a process of inter-African cultural syncretism. Those scholars, mainly anthropologists, who have examined contemporary maroon life most closely agree that such societies are often uncannily "African" in feeling but at the same time largely devoid of directly transplanted systems. However "African" in character, no maroon social, political, religious, or aesthetic system can be reliably traced to a single, specific African ethnic provenience—they reveal rather their syncretistic composition, forged in the early meeting of peoples bearing diverse African (as well as European, and Amerindian) cultures in the dynamic setting of the New World.

Marronage represented a major form of resistance, whether accomplished by lone individuals, by small groups, or in great collective rebellions. Throughout the Americas, maroon communities stood out as a heroic challenge to white authority, as the living proof of the existence of a slave consciousness that refused to be limited by the masters' conception or manipulation of it. It is no accident that throughout the Caribbean today, the historical maroon—often mythologized into a larger-than-life figure—has become a touchstone of identity for the region's writers, artists, and intellectuals, the ultimate symbol of resistance to oppression and the fight for freedom. And it is no small irony that today, the living descendants of these same maroons must fight hard and continually in order to avoid objectification by urban elites as figures that are at once heroic and ultimately obsolete.

See also CARIBBEAN REGION; CUBA; RESISTANCE, DAY-TO-DAY; REBELLIONS AND VIOLENT RESISTANCE; SLAVE REPUBLICS; SURINAME

BIBLIOGRAPHY

CRATON, MICHAEL. *Testing the Chains: Resistance to Slavery in the British West Indies.* 1982.

DUHARTE JIMÉNEZ, RAFAEL. *Rebeldía esclava en el Caribe.* 1992.

GENOVESE, EUGENE D. *From Rebellion to Revolution: Afro-American Slave Revolts in the Making of the New World.* 1979.

HEUMAN, GAD, ed. *Out of the House of Bondage: Runaways, Resistance, and Marronage in Africa and the New World.* 1986.

PRICE, RICHARD. *Maroon Societies: Rebel Slave Communities in the Americas.* 3rd ed. 1996.

Richard Price

Marriage of Slaves

See Ancient Rome; Ancient Greece; Family, U.S.; United States.

Marxism

This entry includes the following articles: Theory of Slavery; Historiography of Slavery.

Theory of Slavery

The Marxist theory of slavery begins with the thought of Georg Wilhelm Friedrich Hegel, who saw slavery not simply in moral terms but also in its role in the development of human civilization. Karl Marx (1818–1883) and Friedrich Engels (1820–1895) saw slave and master as the first genuine classes to arise out of primitive society. Slavery, which began with the taking of prisoners of war, quickly extended to include members of the tribe. A degree of wealth production was necessary to support slavery, and the increase in wealth and its appropriation into private property necessitated the institution of the state.

Marx saw slavery as historically justified, that is, justified by the role that it played in the appropriate stage of human development. Once a full-blown capitalist economic order was established, however, slavery became a relic—in contradiction to the underlying institutions of capitalism, whose dominant ideology was free labor. Marx and Engels, personally, were both quite opposed to the slavery of their day and decried its inhumanity and oppressiveness.

Karl Marx. [Corbis-Bettmann]

The classes of master and slave were disappearing in Marx's day, as were all other intermediate classes, and mankind was dividing into the two great classes: bourgeoisie and proletariat.

In his mature philosophy Marx distinguished between systems by the means they employed to extract surplus value from their workers. In the slave-master relationship the methods were often direct and brutal. In all slave societies the master enjoys the right of physical chastisement of the slave, and the state intervenes to sanction the slave if he resists the master or rebels. When the followers of the slave Spartacus rose up, they were killed in battle or crucified along the Via Appia by the Roman state.

Slavery has been almost universal throughout most of human history, but it has been the dominant mode of production for only very limited periods, such as in Greco-Roman antiquity in the Mediterranean basin and in the American South and Brazil in the first half of the nineteenth century. Although slavery existed in the Germanic and Celtic societies to the north of the Mediterranean world, the slave element of these societies never formed the dominant mode of wealth production, and the same could be said of the Asiatic societies to the east.

Throughout much of the history of Marxist thought, no significant innovations occurred in the interpretation of slavery, but with the creation of a generation of Marxist scholars who were more concerned with utilizing Marxist theory as a heuristic tool rather than in defending any particular conclusions or ideological positions, a wealth of new insights was offered.

Marxist scholars in the late twentieth century have been less determined to maintain ideological purity and more interested in genuinely explaining the phenomenon of slavery and the slave-dominated modes of production. Moses I. Finley, a distinguished historian of ancient slavery, has recognized the difficulties of including all societies within the slave mode of production. In the Roman Empire, for example, the slave-dominated societies of Italy and Greece were quite different from the dependent labor forces in the northern and western provinces. The slaves of the western and northern provinces of the Roman Empire were not themselves commodities (that is, they were not subject to sale, and they often owned the tools of production themselves). Finley correctly raised the theoretical question of whether the inclusion of two so different forms of slavery could be meaningfully classed as one system of production.

In studying traditional slavery in Africa and Asia, Marxist anthropologists have had to alter significantly the definition of slavery. Claude Meillassoux broke with ideological orthodoxy to the extent of denying that any general theory exists which permits an en-tirely adequate definition of slavery and denying further that slavery is only a relationship of production. To meet the difficulties inherent in the problem of developing a Marxist interpretation of slavery, Professor J. L. Watson has proposed that as many modes of production as prove necessary to explain the complexity of social reality should be theorized.

The rise of modern slavery has presented special problems for Marxist theory, as it seems a throwback to earlier modes of production and in contradiction to the free-labor ideology which characterizes the capitalistic mode of production, as Marx himself noted in his *Grundrisse*. The contradiction implicit in the coexistence of the capitalistic and slave modes of production is amply demonstrated, according to the Marxist theorists, by the ease with which slavery was ended by constitutional amendment at the end of the U.S. Civil War. This contrasts sharply with the prolonged transformation of Greco-Roman slavery into medieval serfdom by a process still very much in dispute.

For the Marxist the true test of whether a society is within the slave mode of production lies not in the absolute number of slaves or in the percentage of slaves in the general population but rather in the relative amount of wealth produced by means of their labor.

See also FINLEY, MOSES I.; PHILOSOPHY.

BIBLIOGRAPHY

DOCKES, P. *La Libération médiévale.* 1979.
ENGELS, FRIEDRICH. *The Origin of the Family, Private Property and the State: In Light of the Researches of Lewis H. Morgan.* Edited by Eleanor Burke Leacock. 1972.
FINLEY, MOSES I. *Ancient Slavery and Modern Ideology.* 1980.
————. *Economy and Society in Ancient Greece.* 1982.
GARLAN, Y. *Les Esclaves en Grèce ancienne.* 1982.
MARX, KARL, and FRIEDRICH ENGELS. *Basic Writings on Politics and Philosophy.* Edited by Lewis S. Feuer. 1959.
MEILLASSOUX, C., ed. *L'esclavage en Afrique précoloniale.* 1975.
RADER, MELVIN. *Marx's Interpretation of History.* 1979.
SOWELL, THOMAS. *Marxism: Philosophy and Economics.* 1985.
WATSON, J. L., ed. *Asian and African Systems of Slavery.* 1980.

Patrick M. O'Neil

Historiography of Slavery

Karl Marx himself was not an expert on slavery in the Americas, yet his ideas have framed the important questions pursued by historians of this topic. The resonance of his work is due to the inherent contradiction American slavery posed to the Marxist ideology, which professed faith in a path-dependent world history. Marx saw history as an evolving class struggle between "freeman and slave, patrician and plebeian, lord and serf, guildmaster and journeyman," and, during his own time, between the bourgeoisie and wage laborers. The fact that American slavery emerged simultaneously with European wage labor presented a historical puzzle. Marx himself recognized this tension, casting the capitalist planters in America as "anomalies within a world market based on free labor."

Slavery in the New World exhibited both feudalistic and capitalistic qualities. Both Marxist and non-Marxist historians have delineated planters as capitalists in their orientation toward markets and as precapitalists in their adherence to an antiquated mode of production through their ownership of slaves. This duality not only directed the scholarship of slavery but also helped make it one of the most important areas of historical research. Marxist thought has molded three areas of slavery research: (1) the role of slavery in the rise of global market economies; (2) the unique social and economic relationship between masters and slaves; and (3) the constant class struggle embedded in slavery.

The most direct applications of Marxist philosophy to the history of slavery are studies that connect the ruthless plantation economy to the development of modern capitalism. Eric Williams was the first modern historian to argue that the success of Britain's industrial revolution was directly linked to capital accumulated through the trade in slaves and slave-manufactured produce. Williams, echoing Marx, interpreted this connection in terms of historical stages, with a slave-based mercantilist period giving way to a capitalist era of free trade and free labor. He argued that the entire sugar plantation complex allowed for an accumulation of capital that in turn funded the great fortunes of Bristol and Liverpool. These funds were reinvested in capital stock and equipment, thereby enabling the transformation of Britain's household industries into a factory-centered economy.

Elizabeth Fox-Genovese and Eugene Genovese, in *Fruits of Merchant Capital*, also linked the development of the modern world economy to the emergence of slavery. But unlike Williams, they deemphasize slavery in the industrialization of Europe. Instead, they treat the enslavement of Africans as a retrograde step in the evolution of capitalism. European "merchant capital" affected the early modern economy in contradictory ways, changing the modes of production on both sides of the Atlantic. Although this capital acted to dissolve European feudalism, it also acted as a reactionary force in the world economy by funding, and thereby spreading, the brutal seignorial system of slavery in the Americas. This contradictory force produced a white ruling class of a "new type, at once based on slave relations of production and yet deeply embedded in the world market."

The second area of Marxist research has centered on the relationship between master and slave in the context of the seignorial plantation economy. Eugene Genovese, in several other works, has discussed how planters were antibourgeoise in their consolidation of power and prestige at the expense of productivity, efficiency, and profitability. Planters, in fact, limited their economic and social development because they "could not accept the idea that the cash nexus offered a permissible basis for human relations" (Genovese, 1967). This emphasis on power and the control of labor through nonmarket mechanisms also appears in the work of Orlando Patterson. His comparative history of slave societies is founded on Marx's notion that slavery is "first and foremost a 'relation of domination.'" Violence and power, according to many Marxists, were essential motivating forces, used to extract the maximum surplus labor from slaves.

Manuel Moreno Fraginals, in his book *The Sugarmill*, explored the larger implications of the violence associated with managing slaves. He concluded that the system of organizing labor under slavery was incompatible with the integration of new technologies into the slave-based economy. Industrial machinery demanded a vigilant workforce that required positive incentives in order to be productive. Consequently, slavery was destined to be eclipsed as newer technologies were pursued and implemented.

Marx's influence can also be seen in the historians' approaches to the study of slaves' resistance against the master class. Research in the last twenty years has focused on elements of slave ideology, a subject first seriously considered in C. L. R. James's *Black Jacobins* over fifty years ago. But whereas James described Haitian slaves as appropriating a European enlightenment philosophy, today's scholars speak of a common, independent antislavery ideology among slaves. Hilary Beckles contends that the period of slavery in the British West Indies was a constant, evolving struggle that can be considered a "200 Years' War." Slaves expressed their beliefs through sabotage, infanticide, suicide, murder, and—eventually—rebellion.

The unifying thread in the Marxist approach to slavery is its emphasis on historical stages. Whether it be the study of the world economy, plantation economy, or slave resistance, Marx-inspired historiography casts its analysis in terms of periods. Determining if the American slave system fit into a capitalistic or feudalistic era has been a challenge to Marxists who wish to make sense of an anomaly within the progression of world history. In pursuing this goal, these historians have set an agenda for understanding slavery in Latin America, North America, and the Caribbean.

See also CARIBBEAN REGION; ECONOMIC INTERPRETATION OF SLAVERY; ECONOMICS OF SLAVERY; HISTORIOG-

RAPHY OF SLAVERY; PATTERSON THESIS; PLANTATIONS; REBELLIONS AND VIOLENT RESISTANCE.

BIBLIOGRAPHY

BECKLES, HILARY McD. "Caribbean Anti-slavery: The Self-Liberation Ethos of Enslaved Blacks." *Journal of Caribbean History* 22 (1988): 1–19.

FOGEL, ROBERT W., and STANLEY L. ENGERMAN. *Time on the Cross: The Economics of American Negro Slavery.* 1974.

FOX-GENOVESE, ELIZABETH, and EUGENE D. GENOVESE. *Fruits of Merchant Capital: Slavery and Bourgeois Property in the Rise and Expansion of Capitalism.* 1983.

GENOVESE, EUGENE D. *The Political Economy of Slavery: Studies in the Economy and Society of the Slave South.* 1961, 1967.

JAMES, C. L. R. *The Black Jacobins: Toussaint Louverture and the San Domingo Revolution.* 1938.

MORENO FRAGINALS, MANUEL. *The Sugarmill: The Socioeconomic Complex of Sugar in Cuba.* 1976.

PATTERSON, ORLANDO. *Slavery and Social Death: A Comparative Study.* 1982.

WILLIAMS, ERIC. *Capitalism and Slavery.* 1944, 1964.

David Ryden

Maryland

African servitude began in Maryland with the birth of Lord Baltimore's colony in 1634: one of the original settlers, Father Andrew White, brought with him a black servant who may have been a slave. Until the 1660s, the status of Africans was ambiguous; some Africans became free after a term of servitude, but others remained slaves for life. Slaves made up 3 percent of the population in 1658.

In 1664, the colonial assembly established lifelong servitude as the norm for Africans and for future children of slave mothers. These laws were passed after the arrival of slaveholding immigrants from Barbados and may reflect the influence of these newcomers. Throughout most of the seventeenth century, Maryland imported few slaves, relying instead on white indentured servants to cultivate its staple crop of tobacco. But as fewer whites entered the colony after 1680, slave buying increased, especially after the abolition of the Royal Africa Company's monopoly on the trade in 1698. By 1710 slaves made up about 25 percent of the colony's population.

Slave Demographics in Maryland

At first, slaves in Maryland failed to reproduce themselves, partly because of a high ratio of men to women, partly because of harsh work and exposure to unfamiliar diseases. By the second quarter of the eighteenth century, Maryland's slave population began to increase naturally, as sex ratios became more even and the slaves acquired immunities to local diseases. By 1783, Maryland's approximately 100,000 slaves made up one-third of its population and were more numerous than in any other state except Virginia. The legislature could abolish the African slave trade without fear of a shortage of black workers. Thereafter, Maryland became a slave-selling state. Tens of thousands of blacks were marched to Kentucky. Thousands more were shipped from Baltimore and smaller ports on the Chesapeake—at first to South Carolina and Georgia, and by the 1810s to Alabama and Louisiana. The domestic trade, combined with extensive manumissions after 1790, led to a slow decline in slaves' numbers, despite continued natural increase. In 1860, Maryland had 87,000 slaves, about 13 percent of its people. Slaveholders numbered about 16,000, about one out of every six white households.

Slaves were distributed unevenly across the state. The tobacco-growing counties along the lower western shore of the Chesapeake had black majorities. On the eastern shore, slaves made up a quarter to a third of the population. But in the counties bordering Pennsylvania, only 10 to 15 percent of residents were slaves.

The Life and Work of Slaves in Maryland

Maryland's first African slaves chiefly grew tobacco. They lived in groups of eight to twenty in a "quarter," that is, an area encompassing houses, outbuildings, livestock, and surrounding tobacco fields. By the 1750s, planters were using slaves to grow wheat, corn, and vegetables, and to tend livestock, especially on the eastern shore. Others began to use slaves as craft workers and industrial laborers, performing tasks that ranged from carpentry or cooperage to ironmaking and shipbuilding. Overall, slaves' work intensified in the eighteenth century and included more "night work," such as corn milling and tobacco processing, especially for black women. Beginning in the 1780s, slaves took part in the dynamic expansion of Baltimore, which by 1810 was the third largest city in the nation. Thousands of African-Americans worked in Baltimore as craftspeople, sailors, carters, day laborers, domestics, and washerwomen, and they were often hired out by rural owners to city employers.

Despite the uprooting that resulted from the slave trade and in-state migrations, many blacks developed and maintained strong families. In the religious sphere, Maryland's blacks embraced Methodism in great numbers from the late eighteenth century onwards, and helped found the African Methodist Episcopal church in Baltimore in the early nineteenth century. By 1860, Baltimore became home to 25,000

Table 1. Slavery and Emancipation in Maryland, 1790–1860.

Year	Slaves	Free Blacks	% Blacks Enslaved	Whites	Total
1790	103,036	8,043	93	208,649	319,728
1800	105,635	19,587	85	216,326	341,548
1810	111,502	33,927	77	235,117	380,546
1820	107,327	39,730	73	260,223	407,280
1830	102,994	52,938	66	291,108	437,040
1840	89,737	62,078	59	318,204	470,019
1850	90,368	74,723	55	417,942	583,033
1860	87,189	83,942	51	515,918	687,049

free blacks, the largest concentration of free people of color in the United States.

Manumission and Black Freedom in Maryland

Between 1790 and 1860, Maryland's free blacks increased from eight thousand to eighty-three thousand. They accounted for 49 percent of all blacks in the state in 1860, a much higher share than in any other slave state except Delaware. Blacks gained freedom through manumission, a legal action whereby a master gave or sold freedom to a slave. Most manumissions granted in Maryland before 1790 came from Quakers or Methodists, who saw slaveholding as evil. In 1789, the state assembly debated, but rejected, a bill to abolish slavery by gradually freeing slave children born after 1790. Still, private manumission became far more widespread in the 1790s, as slavery's profitability became less certain. This was due in part to the increased risk of blacks' running off to Pennsylvania, which had adopted a gradual Abolition Act in 1780. Masters increasingly allowed slaves to work their way out of slavery, and slaves often paid for their own liberation with money acquired as incentive payments from employers in return for extra labor. By 1830, a third of the state's blacks had become free. Thereafter, rising slave prices coupled with white hostility toward free blacks slowed the pace of emancipation. In the 1830s, Maryland's whites legislated the expenditure of public funds for the transportation of free blacks to the colony of Liberia to prevent the erosion of slavery at home. But blacks strongly opposed colonization, and only a few thousand persons ever migrated to Liberia.

The Destruction of Slavery in Maryland

Overt rebellion against slavery was rare in colonial Maryland, but slaves seized opportunities to flee to freedom with British forces during both the Revolutionary War and the War of 1812. The British organized a regiment of such black fugitives in 1814, transplanting them to Trinidad and elsewhere after the war. In the antebellum era, some Maryland slaves escaped to northern states and became prominent abolitionists. Frederick Douglass, J. C. Pennington, and Henry Highland Barnet all began life in slavery in Maryland. Josiah Henson, the model for Harriet Beecher Stowe's Uncle Tom, had been a slave in Maryland, as had the heroic conductor on the Underground Railroad, Harriet Tubman.

The Civil War brought the institution of slavery tumbling down in Maryland. Thousands of slaves fled their masters to find freedom working for and fighting as United States troops. In November of 1864, Maryland's voters narrowly approved a new constitution that ended slavery, just two hundred years after its original statutory enactment by the colonial assembly.

See also DEMOGRAPHY OF SLAVES IN THE UNITED STATES; DOUGLASS, FREDERICK; ESCAPE; LIBERIA; MANUMISSION; METHODISM; QUAKERS; STOWE, HARRIET BEECHER; TUBMAN, HARRIET.

BIBLIOGRAPHY

FIELDS, BARBARA JEANNE. *Slavery and Freedom on the Middle Ground: Maryland during the Nineteenth Century.* 1985.

KULIKOFF, ALLAN. *Tobacco and Slaves: The Development of Southern Cultures in the Chesapeake, 1680–1800.* 1986.

WALSH, LORENA. "Slave Life, Slave Society, and Tobacco Production in the Tidewater Chesapeake, 1620–1820." In *Cultivation and Culture: Labor and the Shaping of Slave Life in the Americas,* edited by Ira Berlin and Philip D. Morgan. 1993.

WHITMAN, T. STEPHEN. *The Price of Freedom: Slavery and Manumission in Baltimore and Early National Maryland.* 1997.

T. Stephen Whitman

Massachusetts

In 1636 judges in Massachusetts colony sentenced an Indian to lifetime slavery, although the resulting condition of state servitude seems to be more a seventeenth-century equivalent of life in prison than private slavery. After the Pequot war (1637), Massachusetts enslaved a number of captured Indians and sold some to other colonies. In 1638 ten black slaves arrived, but three whites were also sentenced to penal "slavery," suggesting that the term had not acquired a precise definition in this period. Other whites were later sentenced to "slavery" but released. In 1641 a colonial law declared that no one could be kept as a slave, except for "lawfull captives taken in just warrs, and such strangers as willingly sell themselves, or are sold to us."

Despite these early instances of enslavement, slavery never became significant in Massachusetts, where cultural, economic, religious, and demographic factors undermined its value to society. Nor did race determine civil status, although Massachusetts was a maritime center and some slave traders were based there throughout the colonial period. The black population of colonial Massachusetts was 3 percent at most, and many of these were indentured servants or free people.

In 1700 a Puritan lawyer, Samuel Sewell, wrote one of the first attacks on slavery, *The Selling of Joseph*. By the time of the Revolution, substantial popular opposition to slavery appeared in Massachusetts. During the Revolution many slaves left their masters to join the army; other masters manumitted their male slaves so that they could enlist. In 1778 the people of the new state rejected a proposed constitution, at least in part because it did not end slavery. Part I, Article I, of the state constitution of 1780 declared, "All men are born free and equal, and have certain natural, essential, and unalienable rights; among which may be reckoned the right of enjoying and defending their lives and liberties." In the Quock Walker cases (1781 and 1783) Massachusetts courts interpreted this clause as having ended slavery in the state. In reality, by this time public hostility had already destroyed the institution. In 1836, in *Commonwealth v. Aves,* the supreme judicial court of Massachusetts held that any slave brought into the state immediately became free. *Aves* became the leading American case on slave transit and was followed by most Northern courts. Massachusetts thus became one of the most racially egalitarian states in the country, having almost no discriminatory legislation. Antebellum blacks in Massachusetts voted, held public office, served on juries, and practiced law. In *Roberts v. Boston* (1850) a state court decision upheld

William Lloyd Garrison. [Library of Congress/Corbis]

segregated schools, but by 1855 the legislature had prohibited them.

In 1831 a revitalized antislavery movement led by William Lloyd Garrison began in Massachusetts. By the 1840s, Massachusetts was one of the leading antislavery states in the nation. In 1843, the legislature prohibited the use of any state facility or the action of any state official for the removal of a fugitive slave. In 1851 a mob freed a slave, Shadrach, who had been seized as a fugitive; in 1854 a mob failed to liberate another fugitive, Anthony Burns, and after a dramatic week-long hearing he became the last slave removed from Massachusetts.

During the Civil War Massachusetts pushed for the enlistment of black troops, and its 54th Regiment became the most famous black unit of the war. Throughout this period politicians from Massachusetts campaigned for an end to slavery and advocated the equality of blacks.

See also BURNS, ANTHONY; GARRISON, WILLIAM LLOYD; MASSACHUSETTS ANTI-SLAVERY SOCIETY; SEWALL, SAMUEL.

BIBLIOGRAPHY

FINKELMAN, PAUL. "Legal Ethics and Fugitive Slaves: The Anthony Burns Case, Judge Loring, and Abolitionist Attorneys." *Cardozo Law Review* 17 (1996): 1793–1858.

GREENE, LORENZO. *The Negro in Colonial New England*. 1942.
HORTON, JAMES, and LOIS HORTON. *Black Bostonians: Family Life and Community Struggle in the Antebellum North*. 1974.

Paul Finkelman

Massachusetts Anti-Slavery Society

In late fall 1831, William Lloyd Garrison convened a series of meetings to gather support in the Boston area for immediate emancipation. Out of these meetings emerged the New England Anti-Slavery Society in early 1832. As the abolitionists' strength grew in the region, state-level societies were formed, and the original core group renamed itself the Massachusetts Anti-Slavery Society in 1835. Garrison's heavy influence over the society caused increasing internal tensions as he vociferously denounced both religious and political institutions as proslavery and endorsed such radical causes as women's rights and pacifism. Opponents of the Garrisonians quit the Massachusetts Anti-Slavery Society in 1839 and formed their own body, the short-lived Massachusetts Abolition Society. This acrimonious split presaged the division of the national abolitionist movement into Garrisonian and anti-Garrisonian wings. The Massachusetts Anti-Slavery Society remained firmly under the control of Garrison and his closest associates, including Wendell Phillips, Maria Weston Chapman, Francis Jackson, and Edmund Quincy. In the mid-1840s, the society condemned all political activity, asserting that because the Constitution was proslavery, voting or running for office implied endorsement of the legality of slavery. Similarly, the society called on the northern states to cut all ties with the slaveholding South. The Massachusetts society held a well-attended annual meeting each January and published an annual report on the progress of abolitionist activities throughout the country. The society also hired traveling lecturers such as Frederick Douglass, Henry Clarke Wright, Parker Pillsbury, Abby Foster, and Stephen S. Foster. During the Civil War, strong disagreements occurred when Garrison encouraged the society to give unquestioning support to the administration of President Abraham Lincoln. These quarrels culminated in 1865, when Garrison quit the society. Phillips and others kept it alive for as few more years as a vehicle for Massachusetts abolitionists to lobby for more legislative protection of the freedpeople of the South.

See also ABOLITION AND ANTISLAVERY MOVEMENTS; GARRISON, WILLIAM LLOYD; PHILLIPS, WENDELL.

BIBLIOGRAPHY

BROOKE, ELAINE. "Massachusetts Anti-Slavery Society." *Journal of Negro History* 30 (1945): 311–330.

DUMOND, DWIGHT LOWELL. *Antislavery: The Crusade for Freedom in America*. 1961.
FRIEDMAN, LAWRENCE J. *Gregarious Saints: Self and Community in American Abolitionism, 1830–1870*. 1982.

John R. McKivigan

Masters and the Master Class

See Perspectives on Slavery.

Material Culture in the United States

The daily lives of slaves in the United States were filled not only with the drudgery of forced labor in fields of tobacco, cotton, rice, and sugarcane but also with tasks associated with the manufacture and use of domestic objects. When the day's assigned work in the fields was completed, more tasks remained to be done in the quarters. There were meals to prepare as well as numerous chores associated with the maintenance and upkeep of a house. While slaves had relatively few possessions, they did have the usual household equipment required to feed and cloth themselves, as well as the furniture needed for sitting, sleeping, and storage. This modest assemblage of artifacts constituted the core of the slaves' domestic material culture. In these things can be read a narrative marked by the themes of endurance, adjustment, survival, resistance, and memory.

Women's Household Artifacts

Cooking, the primary domestic task for women, was done in the fireplace using mainly large cast iron pots suspended from hooks, a frying pan, and occasionally some metal skewers. Other implements such as mortars and pestles, grindstones, and sieves were used to prepare the foods for cooking; a fork and a ladle would be needed to serve them. Preparing meals also required a number of containers such as pails, basins, casks, barrels, and crocks, all of which were used to store water, meal, and other foodstuffs until they were needed. Archaeological excavations at selected slave quarter sites reveal the presence of all sorts of ceramic wares, ranging from rough earthenware bowls to fine porcelain plates. While many of these artifacts were provided by the plantation owner, slaves themselves added to their inventory of kitchen utensils and containers by crafting such items as dippers, cups, spoons, and bowls from calabash gourds.

Because slave women were often expected to spend some part of the evening producing cloth, cabins frequently contained spinning wheels and sometimes a

Two female slaves (one smoking a pipe) sit by the fireplace in a slave shanty near Petersburg, Virginia. [Corbis-Bettmann]

loom as well. The common custom in Virginia was to make cloth and then use it to provide each field hand with four sets of clothing: two cotton outfits for summer, and two woolen suits for winter. A family of ten people might have as many as forty sets of clothes. (In other areas cloth was imported from New England and then sewn into shirts, pants, dresses, and other garments.) Not only did this supply of apparel represent a significant achievement on the part of slave women, but the sheer number of shirts, pants, shifts, jackets, and stockings would fill up much of the standard twenty-by-sixteen-foot cabin.

Slave women also produced bedcovers, mainly quilts and blankets. Not only do quilts provide warmth for their users, but their production could become the occasion for significant celebrations. Former slave Julia Banks recalled that her people

> would go from one plantation to another and have quiltings and corn huskings. And they would dance. They used to go six or seven miles afoot to corn huskings and quiltings. And those off the other plantation would come over and join in the work. And they would nearly always have a good dinner.

The quilts created in the context of such occasions were the products of a cooperative design process that manifested communal rather than individual aesthetic choices. Such quilts might be the culmination of a long series of processes: planting, cultivating, harvesting, carding, spinning, dyeing, weaving, piecing, and finally quilting. It is no wonder that finishing a quilt was a moment of great joy.

Men's Household Artifacts

In the quarters, slave men were charged with the maintenance of their houses. This included keeping roofs from leaking and the walls in good repair. The men who were particularly skilled at woodworking also constructed furniture. One of the more typical types of beds was built into the corner of a room with two sides attached to the walls of the cabin and the other two meeting at a post in the middle of the floor. Strung with cord, this frame supported a mattress tick that was usually filled with corn shucks. Short stools were often fashioned for sitting near the fire, but the more gifted artisan might produce rocking chairs and even items of case furniture, like chests of drawers or armories. Yach Stringfellow, who had been a slave in Texas, recalled:

> In the long winter days the men sat round the fire and whittle wood and make butter paddles and troughs for the pigs and ax handles and hoe handles and box traps and figure-four traps. They make combs to get the wool clean for spinning.

Such efforts yielded not only items that were useful for carrying out the work of the plantation but also artifacts that enhanced the quality of life in the quarters.

Much of the material culture of slavery reflects a concerted effort by African-Americans to survive the oppressive conditions of their captivity. But in addition to preparing their own food, making their clothes, and maintaining, if not building, their houses, men's skills also proved to be a valuable means of generating cash for a plantation's owner. George Mason, owner of Gunston Hall in Virginia, had on his estate slave carpenters, coopers, sawyers, tanners, blacksmiths, weavers, knitters, and even a distiller. This crew produced the essential materials and implements needed to operate the plantation: dwelling houses, barns, stables, gates, plows, shoes, casks, all manner of iron implements, shoes, and numerous types of garments. Any surplus goods were sold, at a considerable profit, to other estates.

A large plantation like Gunston Hall was thus more than an agricultural estate. Given the number of skilled artisans among George Mason's workforce, the plantation was also an industrial village, producing timber, charcoal, leather, barrels, cloth, yarn, chains, and other hardware. While the manufacture of goods for export was usually carried out in a set of specialized workshops located close to the plantation owner's residence, some production tasks, particularly those that involved the harvesting of raw materials, also could be carried out in the slave quarters. A 1726 inventory of a Maryland plantation revealed that one of the slave houses contained the following tools: a crosscut saw, a hand saw, a froe, two augers, a draw knife, a set of wedges, and a broad axe. Apparently one of the seven slaves living in this cabin was sawyer, tasked with producing supplies of shingles and fence posts.

Technical and Commercial Artifacts

Not only did planters sell the items produced by their slave artisans, they also sold their slaves' labor by hiring skilled slaves out to neighboring plantations for given periods of time. But while such activities proved financially advantageous for the slave owner, they could have a different impact among the slaves. The chance to leave the plantation and their owner's immediate supervision provided slaves with the opportunity for a measure of liberation, even if only for a brief time. In 1825, one of Thomas Jefferson's highly skilled slaves, a carpenter named John Hemings, was hired out to work on the roof of an elaborate mansion house—a complicated job which took much longer than was expected. When Jefferson sought to retrieve his slave carpenter, Hemings balked, claiming that the job was too important to abandon. He wrote a letter to Jefferson saying that he hoped "to be able to let you know when I shall finish and when to

send for me." This episode illustrates the skill, well-developed sense of self-worth, and desire for autonomy on the part of the slave.

When slaves were encouraged to develop mechanical skills they generally manifested an attitude of self-assurance. On a Georgia rice plantation, Charles Lyell observed of a team of slave carpenters who were installing a complex set of irrigation gates that they addressed their owner as if they were his equal. "Their manner of speaking to him," Lyell wrote, "is as independent as that of English artisans to their employers." At another Georgia estate, plantation mistress Fanny Kemble reported that two woodworkers had built a canoe during their "leisure time." This was a sturdy vessel, which they rowed to the nearby town of Darien and sold for the considerable sum of sixty dollars. Such a handsome financial reward signaled to these men that craft skill was a potential pathway to independence. More remarkable are the large stoneware storage jars (some with a capacity of over thirty gallons) made by a South Carolina slave known only as Dave. Not only did he fashion durable vessels essential for preserving and storing the large amounts of food that were kept in plantation commissaries, but he also wrote messages on their sides. Usually taking the form of witty rhymes in couplet form, Dave's words had political significance because, after 1837, it was illegal for a slave to be taught how to read and write. A literate slave should have been sold out of the state, and yet Dave continued to sign and date his wares with his distinctive poetic inscriptions until 1860. Knowing how valuable his pots were to the white community, he openly defied the law. Dave understood that his craftsmanship granted him an exemption from the restrictions of the slave codes, and to judge from the number of his verses, he clearly exulted in his triumph.

African Influences on Craft Production

While most of the artifacts made and used by slaves conformed to the types and modes that were also used by whites, there were some noteworthy instances where African traditions were maintained. One case involves earthenware containers discovered at the sites of many coastal South Carolina plantations. These vessels were dubbed "colono-ware" and thought at first to have been the invention of Indians, but it is now certain that they were made by enslaved Africans during the seventeenth and eighteenth centuries. Because these bowls are too small to have been practical for serving food, they have been linked to African medicinal practices. The Mande-speaking peoples of West Africa, for example, maintain that remedies, in order to be effective, must be prepared in or consumed from a small clay pot. While planters provided their slaves with basic kitchen utensils, the Africans remained indifferent to ancestral traditions for medicine. The artifactual evidence clearly shows that many of the early generations of slaves recalled how to make the African types of vessels required for an effective cure. Since the plantation owners did not object to these earthenware vessels, the slaves simply carried on what might be termed an immigrant practice. Only with the passing of the African-born from the slave population in the first half of the nineteenth century does the production of colono-ware decline and, finally, disappear from the scene.

Another craft tradition based on African precedents is the making of coiled-grass baskets. Found in the coastal regions of South Carolina and Georgia, these baskets evolved on plantation estates devoted to the production of rice, a staple common in Africa but little known in Europe. It was therefore the enslaved African workers who best understood the crop and its requirements for cultivation and harvest. Because of their expertise, slaves were allowed to take the lead in developing the means for preparing the crop for market. Not too surprisingly, they used mortars and pestles of African design to separate the grain from its tough outer husk, and round, tray-like baskets to separate the kernels of rice from the useless chaff. Known as "fanners," these baskets were identical to the baskets made in the rice-cultivating homelands from which these captive Africans had been taken.

First noted in 1690, this type of basketry is still produced today in several African-American communities. Given the changes that are expected to occur over the course of three centuries, the tradition has been considerably modified. In addition to the work baskets, a newer category, called a "show basket," developed, probably during the early nineteenth century. It is the show basket mode that is seen most often today at numerous roadside stands near Charleston, South Carolina. The forms of these contemporary show baskets vary with the personal inspiration of their makers, but old-style work baskets, even rice fanners, may be obtained upon request. The tradition of coiled basketry remains quite vibrant, and even though considerable experimentation is allowed, the practice remains firmly rooted in a common history: many basketmakers acknowledge that the baskets "come from Africa."

That the banjo is descended from African sources is quite surprising to many. In the twentieth century this distinctive instrument has been linked almost exclusively with rural white America, particularly with those who live in the southern mountains. The contemporary banjo is factory-made, with metal strings and fittings, and offers almost no clues to its planta-

tion origins. Yet no less an authority than Thomas Jefferson wrote in 1781, "The instrument proper to them [his slaves] is the banjar, which they brought hither from Africa."

The earliest banjos were very different from their modern counterparts and, indeed, looked very much like African instruments. The plantation banjo consisted of a hollowed-out calabash gourd covered with some type of animal skin. An unfretted neck was attached to the gourd and the instrument was fitted with gut strings. The early banjo was essentially a drum combined with a guitar. It produced a highly percussive music because the strumming fingers constantly struck the drum-like cover of the sound chamber. While the modern banjo is very different in form and construction, it retains the distinctive "thrumping" sound when played—an echo of Africa.

With the rise of farcical blackface theatricals during the nineteenth century, in which banjo music featured prominently, the instrument came to be seen by black Americans as a badge of shame. Consequently African-Americans abandoned the banjo, thus allowing white southerners to claim it as their own. There is considerable irony in the tale of the banjo, for the so-called "pure mountain sound" that it is said to produce was without a doubt first heard on African soil. The banjo has become, by and large, an unacknowledged Africanism in the American cultural scene.

Encoded in the material culture of slavery are messages of despair and hope, memory and loss. Africans were brought to southern plantations fully equipped

A slave in Virginia accompanies his singing with a banjo as others listen. [Corbis-Bettmann]

with an inventory of ideas, values, and skills, but only a small portion of their fund of traditions was judged by slaveholders as valuable—the coiled-grass baskets used to clean rice would be one example. Other artifacts which did not intrude too far upon the cultural order of the master class, like the colono-ware pots, lingered in the background and finally dropped from sight with the passing of the elders who fully understood their utility.

Inexorably, Africans were transformed by the practice of chattel slavery into African-Americans, and in the process the things that slaves made and used changed as well. Their material culture became less about holding on to thoughts of a former homeland and more concerned with how to endure and survive the current situation. One senses in the testimony of ex-slave Abram Sells a survivor's courage: "Us even make our own plow line out of cotton and if us run short of cotton sometime made them out of bear grass and we make buttons for us clothes out of little round pieces of gourds and cover them with cloth." Folded into this description of resourcefulness is the unmistakable pride of someone who can seemingly make something out of nothing. There is also the resolve to succeed, an attitude that surely would be needed by any person facing the prospects of bondage.

See also ARCHAEOLOGY OF SLAVERY; ARTISANS; CLOTHING, U.S.; FOOD AND COOKING; HOUSING.

BIBLIOGRAPHY

CAMPBELL, EDWARD D. C., and KYM S. RICE, eds. *Before Freedom Came: African-American Life in the Antebellum South.* 1991.
FERGUSON, LELAND. *Uncommon Ground: Archaeology and Early African America, 1650–1800.* 1992.
FOSTER, HELEN BRADLEY. *"New Raiments of Self": African American Clothing in the Antebellum South.* 1997.
JOYNER, CHARLES. *Down by the Riverside: A South Carolina Slave Community.* 1984.
ROSENGARTEN, DALE. *Row upon Row: Sea Grass Baskets of the South Carolina Lowcountry.* 1986.
VLACH, JOHN MICHAEL. *The Afro-American Tradition in the Decorative Arts.* 1990.
———. *By the Work of Their Hands: Studies in Afro-American Folklife.* 1991.

John Michael Vlach

Mauritius and Réunion

Mauritius, also known as the Île de France between 1721 and 1810, and Réunion, known as the Île de Bourbon from 1670 to 1848, are the principal islands in the Mascarene group located in the southwestern Indian Ocean east of Madagascar. Although Arab or Swahili sailors probably visited Mauritius and Réu-

nion before 1500, the islands were unknown to the European world until Portuguese explorers reached the Indian Ocean early in the sixteenth century. The Mascarenes remained uninhabited until 1638, when the Dutch East India Company (VOC) made the first of several attempts to colonize Mauritius. The French Compagnie des Indes occupied the neighboring Île de Bourbon in 1670. Following abandonment of Mauritius by the Dutch in 1710, colonists from the Île de Bourbon settled the island in 1721. In 1767 the French crown took control of the Îles de France et de Bourbon from the bankrupt Compagnie. The islands remained a French colony until they were captured by the British in 1810. The Treaty of Paris in 1814 ceded Mauritius and its dependencies to Britain, while the Île de Bourbon was returned to French control.

Slaves were first introduced into the Mascarenes by the Dutch during their attempts to colonize Mauritius during the seventeenth century. Slavery did not become an important social and economic institution, however, until the eighteenth century. Only 5,000 of an estimated 160,000 slaves imported into the Mascarenes between 1670 and 1810 reached the islands before 1729. Over the next forty years the Compagnie des Indes continued to monopolize the slave trade to the Mascarenes, importing an average of one thousand slaves a year.

The decision to open Port Louis (Mauritius) in 1769 to free trade by all French nationals allowed colonists to engage in slave trading on their own account. The local demand for servile labor increased steadily during the late eighteenth century and contributed to a dramatic expansion of the East African and Malagasy slave trades. An estimated eighty thousand slaves reached the islands between 1769 and 1793 at an average rate of three thousand a year except for the years 1791 to 1793, when imports climbed to five thousand a year. The 1793 decree that abolished slavery throughout the French colonial empire was ignored in the Mascarenes, and the slave trade continued unabated. Despite the disruptions caused by the Anglo-French wars of the revolutionary and Napoleonic eras, another thirty-five thousand slaves were landed in the islands before the British conquest in 1810.

The slaves imported into the Mascarenes before 1810 came from throughout the Indian Ocean world and beyond. Forty-five percent of these bondmen arrived from Madagascar, while 40 percent were shipped from Mozambique and East Africa, 13 percent originated in India, and 2 percent were of West African origin. Small numbers of Malayan and Indonesian slaves also reached the islands during the eighteenth century. Census data indicate that an average of two male slaves were imported for every female slave, a sex ratio comparable to that for the transatlantic slave trade at the same time.

Formal abolition of the legal slave trade to Mauritius and its dependencies in 1811 and to the Île de Bourbon in 1818 did not, however, bring an end to the Mascarene trade. The importance of servile labor to the islands' economy, and especially to the sugar industry on the islands that began to develop rapidly after 1815, soon made the Mascarenes notorious as a center of illegal slave trading. The clandestine trade to Mauritius commenced soon after its capture by the British and lasted into the mid-1820s. The Île de Bourbon likewise became a center of illicit slave trading after France formally abolished the slave trade to its colonies in 1818.

The number of slaves imported into Mauritius after 1810 remains a subject of informed speculation. Contemporary observers estimated that at least thirty thousand slaves found themselves illegally on the island by the early 1820s, despite governmental attempts to suppress the trade that brought them there. Census data from this era, although problematic, indicate not only that these minimum estimates are reasonable but also that the number of slaves introduced illicitly into Mauritius and its dependencies (especially the Seychelles) was actually significantly higher. Projections based upon these data suggest that perhaps as many as fifty-two thousand slaves reached the island between 1811 and the late 1820s. Reports from this era indicate that the Mauritian trade peaked between 1815 and 1819 and that Madagascar was initially the single most important source of illegal slaves. By 1820 the treaties banning the export of slaves that Britain had signed with Radama I, the ruler of the kingdom that controlled much of Madagascar, forced slave traders to concentrate their activities along the East African coast, especially at Kilwa and Zanzibar.

Modern scholarship suggests that forty-five thousand slaves were landed illegally on the Île de Bourbon between 1817 and 1848. Population figures indicate that this clandestine trade flourished during the 1820s. The number of slaves reaching the colony began to decline after 1830, and illicit slaving appears to have largely ceased by 1840. On the Île de Bourbon, as on Mauritius, the complicity of local officials contributed to the illegal trade's early success.

Slaves in the Mascarenes during the eighteenth and early nineteenth centuries served in various capacities—as sailors, fishermen, harbor and shipyard workers, and household servants—but the great majority produced foodstuffs for local consumption and naval stores needed by French naval squadrons and privateers operating in the Indian Ocean. Slave labor was also important to the attempts during the eighteenth century to encourage the production of tropical commodities for export. While schemes to grow cotton, indigo, and spices enjoyed little success, the Île de Bourbon became a modest exporter of coffee before a series of devastating cyclones destroyed many of the island's coffee trees early in the nineteenth century. Slave owners in the Mascarenes, like their counterparts elsewhere in the colonial world, assigned stereotypical attributes to their slaves, with the result that they often employed Indians and Malays, who were perceived as being more intelligent and less suited to physical labor than other slaves, as domestic servants and skilled craftsmen, while slaves of African and Malagasy origin usually worked as field hands. The development of the islands' sugar plantations during the 1810s and 1820s led to increasing numbers of slaves being employed in sugar production.

Detailed information about many aspects of Mascarene slave life is scarce, especially during the eighteenth century. Early nineteenth-century observers often characterized the slave regime on Mauritius as particularly brutal, even by contemporary standards. Complaints filed by slaves with the Protector of Slaves appointed by Britain during the early 1830s confirm that, for many Mauritian bondmen, overwork and ill treatment were an integral part of their lives. Demographic evidence sheds additional light on the harshness of life for many Mascarene slaves. As in other plantation colonies, the number of slave deaths exceeded the number of births, often by a substantial margin. Between 1814 and 1832, for example, the birth and death rates among Mauritian government slaves averaged 26.1 and 51.5 per thousand, respectively. The conditions under which Mauritian slaves lived became a subject of considerable concern to British reformers and abolitionists during the 1820s as they sought to ameliorate slaves' living and working conditions throughout the British Empire.

Contemporary records shed more light on two areas of slave life: manumission and marronage. Reports from Mauritius indicate that fewer than 0.2 percent of the island's slaves were manumitted each year between 1767 and 1824, and that women and children accounted for three-fourths of all those freed. Maroon registers reveal that adult males accounted for 80 percent or more of all fugitive slaves on Mauritius, that a majority of desertions lasted less than one month, and that desertions by groups of two or more slaves declined between the late eighteenth century and the early 1830s, from approximately 40 percent to about one-fifth of all desertions. Marronage rates on the island rose from 4 to 5 percent each year during the late eighteenth century to 11 to 13 percent of the slave population from 1821 through 1826. By the 1820s there are also indications that the ideology of marronage had become more complex as increas-

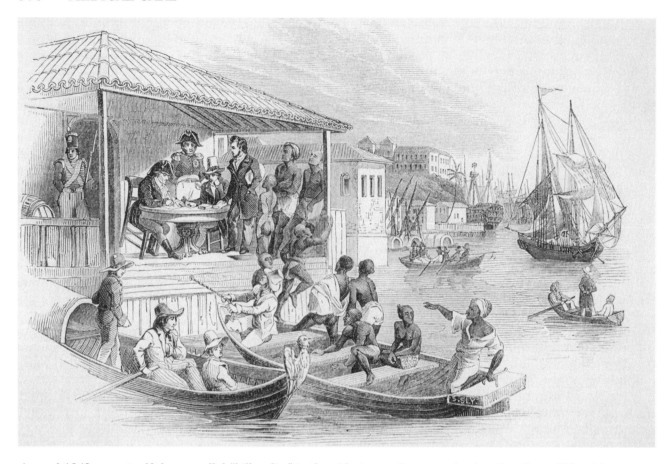

Around 1842 a group of laborers, called "hill coolies" in the mid-nineteenth century, land at the colony of Mauritius to work for merchants and planters. Though not strictly slavery, the condition produced similar human grievances. [*Illustrated London News*/Corbis]

ingly creolized slaves relied upon temporary flight from their masters as a tactic to secure better working conditions and as a means of maintaining important social relationships beyond the confines of their master's estate.

Opposition from the local planter class delayed the abolition of slavery in Mauritius until 1 February 1835, some six months after the 1833 Act of Abolition took effect in Britain's other colonies. The colony's 66,613 new freedmen, like those elsewhere in the British empire, were required to serve their former masters as "apprentices" for a further period of up to six years. Their apprenticeship ended on 31 March 1839. On Réunion, 60,800 men, women, and children were freed from the chains of legal servitude on 20 December 1848 in the wake of France's abolition of slavery throughout its colonial territories.

See also DEMOGRAPHIC ANALYSIS OF SLAVES AND SLAVERY; EAST AFRICA; SLAVE TRADE.

BIBLIOGRAPHY

ALLEN, RICHARD B. *Slaves, Freedmen, and Indentured Laborers in Colonial Mauritius.* 1999.

BARKER, ANTHONY J. *Slavery and Antislavery in Mauritius, 1810–1833.* 1996.

FILLIOT, J.-M. *La traite des esclaves vers les Mascareignes au XVIIIᵉ siècle.* 1974.

FUMA, SUDEL. *L'esclavagisme à La Réunion, 1794–1848.* 1992.

Richard B. Allen

Medical Care

See Health.

Medieval Europe, Slavery and Serfdom in

What is known about medieval slavery comes primarily from the law codes: the Theodosian Code and its derivative Breviary of Alaric for those regions in the south where Roman law prevailed, and the various Germanic codes (Burgundian, Frankish, Lombard, and Anglo-Saxon, plus the later Riparian, Bavarian, and Alamannic) for those areas where Germanic law was in effect. Roman law distinguished sharply between slave and free and did not recognize any status in between, although the condition of the small free farmers (known as *coloni*) on large estates, bound to the land they cultivated since the early fourth century, might seem to blur the distinction. Germanic law (except the Visigothic, which was heavily influenced by Roman law) recognized a status between slave and free that is usually translated as "half-free." In practice Roman *coloni* merged with Germanic half-free in regions where Germanic law prevailed.

Western Europe

Germanic slavery resembled Roman slavery in its use of both domestic and agricultural slaves but integrated them more closely into the familial structures of society. The Germanic slave had considerable protection at law as a legal dependent of the master, like minor sons, unmarried daughters, and even wives, and injuries to a slave by others fell under the same compensation scheme that governed these free dependents. Usually the master, not the slave, received the compensation, but the same held true for free dependents. The Germans had never used gang slaves, since their fields in Germany had been cleared from the forest, were small, and had to be moved frequently. So German agricultural slaves lived in families, although not necessarily on a plot of land—some of them were swineherds, cowherds, or goatherds or performed other rural tasks. German household slaves were not numerous but were highly regarded and had a higher value than agricultural slaves.

In the Germanic kingdoms that were established in the western part of the Roman Empire, the Roman and German forms of slavery remained distinct for some time, a distinction made possible by a legal culture that tended to recognize the validity of various "national" laws. In some parts of Europe (in southwestern France, the central Rhone area extending east into what is now western Switzerland, west to Spain, and south into parts of Italy) the Roman legal tradition remained strong, and Roman law was the law of the courts. Germanic law prevailed in other parts of western Europe (England, northern France, the Low Countries, Alamannia, Bavaria, and most of northern and central Italy). But the era of the Germanic kingdoms was brought to an end by the career of Charlemagne (768–814), who united not only the various parts of France and western Germany but also part of Spain, Saxony, and two-thirds of Italy into a Frankish Carolingian Empire. Each part of this empire retained its own law, but Charlemagne issued a number of capitularies (laws) that added imperial law to the various codes issued by the earlier Germanic kings. The capitularies were not much concerned with slavery, so the older codes remained in effect. But slav-

Charlemagne. [Corbis-Bettmann]

ery was affected by changes that came after Charlemagne, as his successors proved much less able than he, and their weaknesses coincided with the beginning of a new series of migrations—Scandinavians from the north, Hungarians from the east, and Saracens (Muslims) from the south. Charlemagne had managed to keep the first waves of these invasions at bay, but his successors lost control and defense fell into the hands of the local lords. Slavery was less effectively protected by these petty rulers, and the institution declined in the tenth and eleventh centuries, although it continued into the twelfth century in England and some places in France, like the Loire Valley, where it survived on the estates of abbeys and other ecclesiastical establishments.

The church, as one of the largest landholders of the Middle Ages, was involved in the slave labor system. Much of its land had come in the form of gifts from rich and poor. These gifts accumulated in the "dead hand" of the church, which was a never-dying institution and thus never had an heir. Gifts of land came with the land's workers—slave, half-free, or free. The church accepted slavery without qualm, for it taught that one should be satisfied with one's lot, although it did encourage other landlords to manumit slaves as a "good work." However, church law strictly limited a cleric's capacity to free any slaves, since that would involve a loss of church property. And so church lands tended to lag behind secular estates in accepting change in the status of the labor force, although on some church lands, such as the Cistercian abbeys, the policies were very forward-looking and involved efforts to improve agricultural production in order to provide the largest income possible. If churchmen wrote about slavery at all, it was to encourage kings to issue laws to prevent Jews from acquiring Christian slaves, or laws to prohibit the export of Christian slaves to areas that were still heathen.

Secular lords manumitted by a simple statement in the presence of witnesses, by testament, or before a church altar. The act of manumission could bring full freedom, or it might continue the slave's services until the lord's death, or it might continue the familial tie that made the former lord or the lord's heirs the freedman's heir if the freedman died without direct heirs.

As slavery declined in western Europe, slave exports increased to meet the demands of the Islamic world. In the ninth and tenth centuries this trade was in Christian or Jewish hands. Slaves were captured when Hungarian incursions were turned back by the German rulers, who thus claimed the mantle of Roman emperors in the tenth century and were later known as Holy Roman emperors. The Hungarians settled in the Danube valley east of the German principalities, but German expansion continued east and southeastward into the Balkan peninsula. So many Slavic people were enslaved in the conflicts accompanying German expansion that the word for slave in the vernaculars changed from the Latin *servus* to forms of the ethnonym "slave."

At a rate that varied from time to time and from place to place, slavery was replaced by another sort of servile labor adapted to the post-Carolingian manorial system. This system expanded greatly in the eleventh and twelfth centuries as a result of technological and economic innovations, like a heavier wheeled plow; a horse collar that allowed plows to be pulled by horses rather than the much slower oxen; the stirrup; horseshoes; watermills and windmills; and the three-field system that improved production by allowing cultivation of two out of three fields each year (rather than the earlier one out of two), the third lying fallow. Increased food supplies encouraged a population expansion, international trade revived, and towns grew as outlets for the food produced. Landlords responded by opening up new fields and offering concessions to induce peasants to leave their old holdings. Personal freedom was one such concession, although mobile peasants still owed rents and some labor. Large domains, formerly worked by slaves or hired workers, were broken up into hereditary tenures, consisting of a small homestead and varying numbers of strips in each of the three fields. These were bestowed on peasant families, creating a manor that included the three fields, a village containing the homesteads, some common land, a church, and the lord's house. Some of these peasant families were slave in origin, some half-free, and some free who were eager to have the protection of a strong lord. The slave families tended to owe services as well as rent for their land; the free might owe rent only. But when tenures fell vacant and were regranted or purchased by other cultivators, free families might end up holding servile tenures and servile families free tenures. Since all were subject to the lord's manorial court, all were regarded as servile. Various terms were used to describe these workers, but the terms most frequently used were "serf," from the Latin *servus,* meaning slave; and "villein," from the Latin *villanus,* meaning country person. The new servile peasants were free in their persons but bound to their tenures, and the tenures were hereditary. They were no longer subject to the public courts but instead were subject to their lord's manorial court, attended by the heads of the peasant families. Their dependency was emphasized by their inability to enter into contracts without their lord's permission. So the development of serfdom, as distinct from slavery, is associated with improved agricultural productivity, the spread of manorial system based on three-field rotation, the breakup of centralized authority, and the creation of a feudal aristocracy.

Legal reforms of the eleventh and twelfth centuries reduced the role of the family in the administration of justice and further lessened reliance on agricultural slavery in western Europe by eliminating an important local source of slaves. On the continent these reforms were associated with the revival of classical Roman law, whose justification of the prince as the source of law attracted centralizing rulers; in England a royal law, usually referred to as common law, developed. Before, the family brought criminal charges and the family was compensated. Virtually any injury or death could be compensated by paying a set amount or by becoming a slave if one could not pay. Under the reformed law, families no longer brought suits in criminal matters and were not compensated. Some form of physical punishment or monetary fine to the state replaced judicially imposed slavery.

Slavery and Serfdom in England

Roman domination and slavery under Roman law came to an end in the earth fifth century, leaving behind a Romano-Celtic society romanized in its upper ranks but primarily Celtic in the lower layers. There is virtually no evidence about slavery from the sub-Roman period, but there is no reason to think that slavery disappeared, even with the breaking up of a centralized authority that could enforce the slave laws.

A number of Germans appeared even before Roman political authority in Britain declined. These may have been brought over in the late fourth to early fifth century as bands of mercenaries to shore up the last Roman garrisons. But before the fifth century ended, bands of Germans began to arrive, perhaps at first by invitation of one of the sub-Roman rulers who sought more reinforcements for his army. Tales about the richness of the southeast part of Britain may have attracted the northern Germanic settlers. At any rate, these Anglo-Saxon migrations from the continent to Britain continued from the mid-fifth to the late sixth century.

Since slavery was well established under Germanic law and since the Anglo-Saxons came over in kindred groups as well as war bands, slaves surely came with the families who arrived. In England (as it may be called from then on, rather than Britain) the Germans encountered a primarily Celtic resident population. In general, it would seem that the more Romanized part of the population retreated west rather than submit to the Anglo-Saxons, but during the conquest the bulk of the population was killed, enslaved, or reduced to some lesser form of servitude. By the time of the first Anglo-Saxon laws, issued by Aethelbehrt of Kent at the beginning of the seventh century, the existence of these slaves was taken for granted. Aethelbehrt's laws are difficult to interpret, but they seem to indicate separate hierarchies of freemen and slaves. While the wergeld (that is, the human worth) of the free depended on their own positions in the hierarchy, the value of slaves depended on the position of their lords as well as on the slave's function.

The sources of slaves in Anglo-Saxon England were the same as those of the continental Germanic kingdoms: capture in war (or purchase of war captives), birth to an enslaved mother, voluntary servitude, and debt slavery, whether the debt was incurred for economic reasons or by reason of the failure to pay compensation judicially assessed. Slavery by means of capture in warfare continued after the Anglo-Saxon conquest, since the small kingdoms that emerged fought among themselves until a larger territorial unit emerged; these larger units engaged each other until one was destroyed or internal unrest led to overthrow of the ruling dynasty. At any rate, there was no cessation in the availability of local slaves, and only in the strongest of these small states, such as Wessex or Mercia under Offa, was there adequate machinery to overcome the problem of slaves who ran away to neighboring enemies. Hence slavery in England before the eighth century was a rather weak institution. The ranks of the slaves were reduced by manumission, which, as elsewhere, was easily accomplished and ranked by the church as a "good work," by disease, or by running away or being lured away. The Scandinavian invasions of the eighth and ninth centuries destroyed the little kingdoms in the north, and weakened slavery as a result. To the south, the kingdoms fell to Danish conquest until only Wessex in the southwest was left. Wessex too was threatened but under Alfred began to push the Danes back, and Alfred's successors united the former Anglo-Saxons as England under a Wessex dynasty. This England was a well-organized kingdom by the end of the tenth century that gave slavery a new life there at the very time that it began to disappear on the continent. English slavery lasted throughout the eleventh century, although by the end of that century the same technological and economic developments already cited for western Europe, added to the replacement of public hundred courts by private manorial courts in the wake of the Norman conquest in 1066, were causing a decline. The laws still continued to refer to slaves by the Latin term *servus* throughout most of the twelfth century, although by that time the terms *servus* and *villanus* were increasingly interchanged.

The End of Serfdom in Western Europe (including England)

Serfdom slowly replaced slavery in western Europe beginning in about the tenth century. Although, by the twelfth century, the process was nearly completed north of the Pyrenees and north of the Alps, this process was never completed in the countries bordering the Mediterranean Sea. Agricultural slavery could be found on some of the islands, such as the Balearics, until the early modern period. Domestic slavery could be found in Spain and Italy until the seventeenth and eighteenth centuries. The increased hostilities between Christian and Muslim that resulted from the Crusades put enslaved Muslims (or presumed Muslims) in significant numbers on the slave markets. Conversely, Muslims captured Christians and sold them in North African markets if they could not be ransomed.

But even in these southern countries (with the exception of a few islands) serfdom in one of its varying forms replaced agricultural slavery at varying times. Serfdom in turn declined by the end of the Middle Ages, for a number of reasons. First, population increased between the eleventh century and the end of the thirteenth century. Peasants (serfs or villeins) held hereditary tenures, but even in those areas that recognized the prior rights of either the eldest or the youngest son to inherit land, peasant families usually managed to carve out something for other children, with the inevitable tendency for plots to become smaller, until some of them could no longer support a family. At the same time, towns were growing and offered jobs for artisans and people who provided services. Children not provided for on the manor were attracted to the towns, where if they remained for a year and a day (or some such period of time), they were accepted as freemen, leading to the saying that "town air breathes free." Landlords could demand the return of any serfs they found, but generally there were too many mouths to feed on the manor, and many serfs successfully escaped to freedom. Thus towns provided an alternative to life on the manor for those who held no land.

Population increase led to cultivation of marginal lands that soon wore out. At about the same time, a series of natural disasters (drought or unceasing rain) led to crippling famines in the earth fourteenth century. Population growth had ceased by the middle of the fourteenth century when another disaster struck between 1348 and 1350: bubonic plague, usually called the black death. The plague seriously decreased populations in much of western and central Europe as it returned again and again throughout the rest of the fourteenth century. Although the plague attacked all classes of the population, it hit the laboring classes hardest, since they could not flee to isolation. In the countryside whole villages might disappear. Landlords and employers were desperate for workers, and legislative attempts (such as the Statute of Laborers in England, 1351) were made to force the remaining workers to continue to work on the same terms as before.

This legislation was aimed primarily at workers, urban and rural, who were "for hire." These were the lowest category of worker. The urban workers were not members of the guilds but unskilled workers in industry or households. The rural workers were those

In this engraving by Wenzel Hollar (1607–1677), peasants work on a plot of ground in the shadow and under the protection of a feudal castle. [Corbis-Bettmann]

with no land or insufficient land who depended on being hired to work the lord's share of strips in the fields. This legislation was impossible to enforce, and landlords and other employers made concessions that undermined serfdom. To obtain workers, higher wages had to be offered. Peasants who held tenures might find it to their advantage to abandon their holdings and go where higher wages were offered. To keep the peasants on the manor, lords reduced the number of services required and lowered rents.

At approximately the same time, the jurisdiction of manorial courts was being threatened by the extension of justice administered by increasingly powerful monarchs in France and England in order to divert proceeds into royal coffers. And when the royal courts extended their jurisdiction to protect peasant tenures, the authority of the lords and their manorial courts over serf tenants on their lands was seriously compromised. To meet the increasing cost of bureaucratic government, royal governments preferred free peasants, who could be taxed, over serfs protected by their lord's court.

By the end of the fifteenth century, serf-like manorial dues were nearly gone, although pockets of serfdom lingered on into the sixteenth century and in a few instances the seventeenth, primarily in areas distant from urban influences. Agricultural production became more and more specialized for sale in urban and then international markets, and even in the countryside industrial production absorbed more and more of the people. Serfdom was out of place in this world, which was rapidly becoming capitalist.

Slavery and Serfdom in Central and Eastern Europe

It is difficult to draw a line distinguishing the development of agrarian institutions in western Europe on the one hand and central and eastern Europe on the other. The term *central and eastern Europe* is misleading because of a western-influenced transitional zone—extending east to the Baltic lands through northern and western Poland, Bohemia, Hungary, Slovakia, Slovenia, and Croatia. To the south and east of this area (in south Poland, Romania, Bulgaria, Serbia, and European Russia), agrarian development followed an eastern pattern, since part of this region was under Mongolian or Turkish control until the seventeenth century. There, as serfdom was disappearing in the west toward the sixteenth century, a noncapitalist form of serfdom or enforced labor (corvée) developed.

Very little is known about slavery in eastern Europe before the tenth century, when references to slavery and the slave trade appear. The main factor seems to be the sparse population. Slavs had moved into central and eastern Europe from Asia as the Germanic peoples moved east, but the Slavs were not numerous, and the area to be settled was vast. Settlements were village communities more or less clustered around a "fort" where a ruler or the ruler's representative lived, with local nobles taking up residence there from time to time. The community, not the individual or the family, was responsible for feeding and maintaining the fort, including entertainment of the lord when the court came to visit. Pasturing was more important than in the west. Agriculture was very primitive, and land wore out rapidly. Since the peasant huts were very fragile, it was easy to abandon a village and build another, probably not very far away.

These peasants were not slaves, and they were not bound to the soil—but individuals had no right to land, and there were no hereditary holdings, since the village community distributed land and paid tribute owed to the local ruler. The peasant could move, but since there were no markets, there was no reason

to move or even to try to improve production; thus agricultural production was stagnant. The principal export of the region, therefore, was a slave trade that began in the ninth to tenth centuries. Raids organized in the ports against the villages of distant lordships produced captives who were sold to international slave traders, who transported them to southern European ports whence they could be shipped in large numbers to Muslim Spain. From there, large numbers were sent on to other parts of the Muslim world. So the sparse population in eastern Europe was depleted further by the medieval slave trade.

Beginning in the tenth century Germans pushed back to the east in a movement that involved some nobles, some town dwellers, and some peasants. A noble or a town dweller would receive a grant of land from a large eastern landholder (secular or ecclesiastical) with special privileges to bring immigrants along to work it. Germans and Hollanders were especially welcome because of their experience in felling forests and draining marshes. Peasants who had been serfs on their previous tenures were attracted by the promise of freedom to move, and by low rents. As a result, Slavic lands adjoining Germanic lands acquired considerable knowledge of western agricultural technology and organization of production by use of the manorial system. These settlers produced much more than the slavic agricultural villages and soon exported surpluses. Where the Germanic influence was strong enough, even the native Slavs came to resemble western peasant producers. The German-influenced manors specialized in grain, raw wool, fish farming, and meat, since the east had always devoted more land to the raising of livestock than the west. Other eastern landlords with access to waterways or close to urban markets in the west converted their domains to specialized production (grain in the Baltic area, mining and fish farming in Bohemia, cattle and sheep raising in Hungary) and in some cases took away the peasants' land in favor of immigrants. Since the labor supply was low, these more eastern landlords imposed heavier and heavier labor demands on the surrounding peasantry to produce surpluses on their domains. These pressures, in the absence of monarchical authority concerned to protect peasants as taxpayers, allowed a serfdom that in the more eastern areas permitted lords to buy and sell serfs at will. These restraints prevailed until the reform movements of the late eighteenth and nineteenth centuries.

This increased force used by eastern landlords in managing their domains was partly a result of increased opportunities for export to the west, but it was also provoked by the growing political power of eastern aristocrats (Poland being the extreme example), their increased numbers, and the discrepancy between their incomes and the costly western-influenced life-style they regarded as necessary to the status they claimed. Western aristocrats felt this discrepancy also but found it politically impossible to re-enserf the peasantry, so they turned to capitalistic enterprises that required little labor, such as raising sheep for wool.

In the east, the legal position of the peasant declined as aristocratic landlords obtained legislation or decrees depriving peasants of their freedom of movement, and the village community lost its ability to intervene between lord and peasant. Especially in the more eastern plain, the serf was essentially chattel until the great reform movements that slowly developed out of the French Revolution brought emancipation beginning in the late eighteenth century and concluding with the emancipation of the Russian serfs in 1861. Unfortunately, legal emancipation did not always significantly improve the economic status of the peasant.

See also LAW; SLAVS.

BIBLIOGRAPHY

BONNASSIE, PIERRE. *From Slavery to Feudalism in South-Western Europe.* 1991.
The Cambridge Economic History of Europe. Vol. 1, *The Agrarian Life of the Middle Ages,* 2nd ed., edited by M. M. Postan. 1966.
DOCKÈS, PIERRE. *Medieval Slavery and Liberation.* 1982.
FRANTZEN, ALLEN J., and DOUGLAS MOFFAT, eds. *The Work of Work: Servitude, Slavery and Labor in Medieval England.* 1994.
GUNST, PETER. *Agrarian Development and Social Change in Eastern Europe, Fourteenth–Seventeenth Centuries.* 1996.
MISKIMIN. HARRY A. *The Economy of Later Renaissance Europe, 1460–1600.* 1977.
PELTERET, DAVID A. E. *Slavery in Early Mediaeval England from the Reign of Alfred until the Twelfth Century.* 1955.
TOPOLSKI, JERRY. *The Manorial Economy in Early-Modern East-Central Europe.* 1994.
WALLERSTEIN, IMMANUEL. *The Modern World-System: Capitalist Agriculture and the Origins of the European World-Economy in the Sixteenth Century.* 1974.

Katherine Fischer Drew

Mediterranean Basin

From the end of the Roman Empire to the beginning of European expansion in the Atlantic, slavery in the Christian Mediterranean was reinforced by contact with the highly developed urban slavery in the Muslim areas. Varieties of slavery are readily apparent in both Islam and western Christendom. Because of the many ways they were employed, slaves cannot be fit-ted neatly into a single category, nor do they form a distinct social class or caste. Even though all slaves suffered similar legal, emotional, and ideological disabilities, there were gradations in their material circumstances.

Slaves continued to perform household service in the Christian Mediterranean throughout the Middle Ages. Such slaves were usually assigned to nonproductive service tasks. As servants, guards, and sexual partners, their primary function in many cases was to demonstrate the wealth and luxury enjoyed by their owners. Yet with domestic slavery as well, there were exceptions and variations. In the preindustrial world most manufacturing was artisan production, which took place in workshops within the homes of the artisans, where a few domestic slaves might aid their artisan owners and collectively make a significant impact on production. Other variations—such as slaves as business agents, state-owned slaves, and military slaves—were present in the Roman period, and they appear at certain times and places in the Islamic world but far less frequently in medieval and Renaissance Europe.

Large-scale, or gang, slavery, which we associate with the late Roman Republic and early Roman Empire and with Latin American and United States slavery, was not present at all in medieval Europe. It was exceptional in the Islamic world, occurring in particular places at particular times (such as in lower Mesopotamia in the early years of Islamic expansion). For the medieval West and for the Islamic world in the same period, small-scale slavery was the norm. In western Europe a progressive ruralization of society and the economy followed the end of the Roman Empire. Cities declined and the population increasingly moved to rural estates and agricultural villages. As a consequence, slavery lost much of its former importance.

Large-scale agricultural slavery was feasible only when the government was strong enough to keep slaves from fleeing their masters to obtain freedom and when a flourishing market system allowed specialized commodities to be sold in the towns for money. In early medieval Europe both features were lacking. The governments were weak and the market economy was restricted. With the cities and their markets in decline, the lords made their manors as self-sufficient as possible. The lords dispensed with the use of slaves and secured a more dependable, contented, and cheaper labor force by granting improved conditions to their workers and giving them security of tenure and individual houses and plots.

The laborsaving devices invented or adopted in the early Middle Ages, and in general use by the mid-eleventh century, also helped reduce the need for slave labor. These included better plows, harnesses that permitted horses and oxen to pull heavier loads and to be harnessed in tandem, horseshoes for better traction, and water mills. They reduced human labor requirements, as did the larger and more powerful draft animals, products of centuries of selective breeding. As a consequence of these changes, slavery ceased to be the normal pattern for rural labor in western Europe.

Domestic slavery continued, although we do not know much about its specifics in the early Middle Ages. Cities and towns, as well as the larger manors, provided places of employment for skilled slaves. Artisan wares were produced in the towns in small artisan shops owned by free people and worked at times by slaves. On the estates, too, slave artisans, especially textile workers, labored under the direction of the higher class of the lords' slaves. Specialized occupations on the manor—managers, record keepers, smiths, messengers, soldiers, beekeepers, and experts in cattle raising—were often filled by the lord's dependents, either slave or semifree, who had the same servile legal status as the agricultural laborers but who through their skills attained a better and more highly regarded status.

The assimilation of the formerly free and the slave into a more or less uniform class of serfs was substantially complete by the twelfth century. Language altered as the new social realities were recognized. The word "serf" comes from the Latin word *servus,* "slave," but the medieval serf was far different in status from the *servus* of the Romans. Administrators, whose written language was Latin and whose training was in Roman law, simply applied the word the Romans had used to describe their lowest class to indicate the lowest class of medieval society. The word *servus* (and its feminine equivalent, *ancilla*) was transformed so completely from its original meaning that it could no longer be used to describe true chattel servitude and ceased to be used in France around the early twelfth century. To describe the true slaves, a new word was coined, derived from the most numerous ethnic group in the medieval slave trade: the Slavs (slave in English, *esclave* in French, *esclavo* in Spanish, *escravo* in Portuguese, *schiavo* in Italian, and *Sklave* in German). At the same time, the word "serf" came to be used exclusively to describe dependent peasants.

In the late Middle Ages Europe's economy continued to develop and strengthen. Slavery was still present, although agricultural production throughout most of Europe was carried out by the labor of serfs or free peasants. Domestic and artisan slavery continued, particularly in Italy and the Iberian peninsula—the European areas in greatest contact with the Islamic world.

Several developments stimulated a rise in the use of slaves in western Europe in the later Middle Ages. In the eleventh century western European crusaders established a series of states in Syria and Palestine that lasted until the late thirteenth century. The presence of the crusader states allowed a greatly expanded commercial activity by Italian merchants, the most active participants in the slave trade. More importantly, Europeans gained a taste for cane sugar. From the Muslims of Syria and Palestine, they learned the techniques for the cultivation and refining of cane sugar. With the end of the Crusades, Europeans introduced sugarcane planting and refining to several parts of southern Europe. At first, labor on European sugar estates was either slave or free; the identification between sugar production and slave labor became complete only in the sixteenth century.

In the early Middle Ages legal systems varied by kingdom or city-state and drew on a combination of Germanic customs and surviving portions of Roman law. In the late Middle Ages Europeans recovered and assimilated into their legal systems the entirety of Roman law, with its elaborate regulations for slaves. In Iberia, for example, the Castilian king Alfonso X in the mid-thirteenth century produced a new law code for his kingdom, known as the Siete Partidas, with heavy influences derived from Roman law. The Siete Partidas had a significant influence in late medieval and early modern legislation on slavery in Spain, both for the home countries and for the American colonies, and thereby ensured that many Roman rules for slavery entered Spanish law.

Another late medieval influence that heightened the use of slaves was the black death of the mid-fourteenth century. The plague originated in central Asia and was brought to the Crimea across caravan routes in 1346. Two years later it entered Italy and spread to the rest of western Europe, killing about a third of the European population in the greatest catastrophe Europe had known. Because of the high death rate, the workers who survived could easily find good jobs in the countryside or in the cities. They could not be induced to become household servants. Death had not spared the elite, but the rich who remained had a larger supply of money available, as fortunes were consolidated through inheritance. Those with money needed servants, and in the absence of free workers willing to accept domestic service, they turned to slaves.

Slavery thus persisted throughout the Middle Ages in Europe, preserved from Roman times and reinforced continually by contact with the Islamic world. Nonetheless, slavery in the medieval period was less important in terms of numbers and economic significance than it had been in the ancient world or than it would be in the Americas in later times.

See also MEDIEVAL EUROPE, SLAVERY AND SERFDOM IN.

BIBLIOGRAPHY

BLOCH, MARC. *Slavery and Serfdom in the Middle Ages.* 1975.
BONNASSIE, PIERRE. *From Slavery to Feudalism in Southwestern Europe.* 1991.
DOCKÈS, PIERRE. *Medieval Slavery and Liberation.* 1982.
HEERS, JACQUES. *Esclaves et domestiques au Moyen Age dans le monde méditerranéen.* 1982.
PHILLIPS, WILLIAM D., JR. *Slavery from Roman Times to the Early Transatlantic Trade.* 1985.
VERLINDEN, CHARLES. *L'esclavage dans l'Europe médiévale.* 2 vols. 1955 and 1977.

William D. Phillips, Jr.

Melon, Jean-François   [1675–1738]

French economist, lawyer, and writer.

Born in Tulle, Melon trained as a lawyer in Bordeaux and, in 1715, moved to Paris, where he held a variety of positions before becoming a secretary and financial advisor to the regent. His *Essai politique sur le commerce* (1734), praised by Voltaire as "the work of an intellectual, a citizen, and a philosophe," was widely read in France and soon translated into English. In this treatise Melon conceded that "Equality amongst Men is a Chimera, which can scarce bring forth an ideal Commonwealth," though there remained important "degrees" to all "subordinations." According to Melon, under "the wise Regulations of Louis XIV in the Code Noir," slavery in the French West Indies was as well-regulated and humane a system of governance as any the world had seen. Educated by benevolent owners, permitted to earn "a peculium," and cared for in their "indigent old age," these bondsmen possessed "an advantageous Compensation preferable to the Liberty, which is now engaged by Domestick Servants, Soldiers, and Persons hired to serve in our Colonies."

While hopelessly naive about the true nature of French colonial slavery, Melon vigorously opposed power relations grounded in "cruelty" and "barbarity." Unlike many of his contemporaries, he recognized the insidious nature of white racial prejudice and lamented the fact that "do what we can, we love Europeans better than Africans." Ultimately Melon concluded that for slavery to continue to exist in the French West Indies, it must cease being based on the subservience of the "negro" to "white people." Racism, not slavery, posed the greatest challenge to his lofty ideals.

See also CODE NOIR; ENLIGHTENMENT; PERSPECTIVES ON SLAVERY.

BIBLIOGRAPHY

MELON, JEAN-FRANÇOIS. *A Political Essay upon Commerce.* Translated by David Bindon. 1738.
REBIÈRE, ALPHONSE. *Jean-François Melon l'economiste.* 1896.

Eric Robert Papenfuse

Memorials

The creation of "sites of memory"—plaques, monuments, sculpture, and sometimes entire historical structures or communities—which commemorate slavery has largely been carried out in Africa and the Americas in the last two centuries. Classical monument builders depicted captured slaves trudging into bondage or cowering before imperial military power on the columns of Roman emperors, but these are monuments to conquest, not memorials of slavery. Indeed, slavery as a social and economic institution went largely unquestioned for most of human history; thus, it also went without memorials. (Of course, with modern hindsight we might choose to reinterpret, say, the Roman Coliseum, as a memorial to the slaves who died there.) With the rise of antislavery movements in the eighteenth century and the self-emancipation of enslaved peoples through rebellion in the nineteenth century, opportunities arose to pay tribute to those who struggled against, and endured the indignity of, oppression.

Not surprisingly, the theme of emancipation as well as monuments to individual emancipators accounts for many of the memorials of slavery. In the United States, Frederick Douglass and Abraham Lincoln stand out as the most frequently honored emancipators. Funded entirely by freedmen and women, sculptor Thomas Ball's Emancipation Monument (1876) in Washington, D.C., depicts Lincoln standing before the kneeling figure of a freed slave. Among the many Douglass memorials is the Frederick Douglass Monument (1899) in Rochester, New York. The Shaw Memorial in Boston, Massachusetts, honoring the Fifty-fourth U.S. Colored Troops Regiment and their white commander, might also be considered a monument to black emancipation. By the late 1990s plans were under way for a monument to African-American Civil War soldiers to be built in Washington, D.C.

Sites related to the Underground Railroad have also provided a variation on the themes of resistance and emancipation in the United States and Canada.

A detail from the Shaw Memorial. [Lee Snider/Corbis]

Memorials range from a massive seven-ton Underground Railroad Monument in Battle Creek, Michigan, to an early 1990s memorial in Syracuse, New York, commemorating the site where white and black abolitionists rescued fugitive slave William Henry (also known as Jerry) from the city's jail in 1851. In the center of the Oberlin (Ohio) campus is a railroad track protruding from the ground with a plaque declaring that this is where the Underground Railroad ended. Canada also pays homage to the Underground Railroad, mainly through sites related to communities of ex-slaves and famous escapes. A typical memorial site is the John Brown Meeting House/First Baptist Church in Chatham, Ontario, where John Brown and some of his followers planned the Harpers Ferry raid.

Revolutionaries were also potential emancipators. Where large-scale rebellions occurred and sometimes succeeded, such as occurred in the West Indies, leaders of rebellions have been especially esteemed. Jamaica, for instance, honors several revolutionaries, who are also official National Heroes. Sam Sharpe Square in Montego Bay pays tribute to the leader of the 1831 Christmas Rebellion, and Paul Bogle and George William Gordon, leaders of the Morant Bay Rebellion, share a monument at the National Shrine, George VI Memorial Park in Kingston.

The memorialization of slave revolutionaries in the United States has been more controversial. While whites held a monopoly on political and cultural power, such memorials had little chance of approval. In fact whites often proposed and erected memorials to loyal and docile slaves, such as the United Daughters of the Confederacy's proposed memorial to the faithful southern "mammy." Despite the erection of several statues of John Brown—at least one of which was constructed by blacks—and the preservation of sites associated with him, he remains a controversial figure. Black revolutionaries Denmark Vesey and Nat Turner remain largely unheralded. Gabriel's Rebellion, a planned insurrection in Virginia in 1800, was recently commemorated by the erection of two historic highway markers, and the Spring Park Historic Site in Henrico County interprets this event. Revolts against slavery as well as the slave trade are the theme of the Amistad Memorial in New Haven, Connecticut, where the Mende tribesmen who seized the slave ship *La Amistad* were initially charged with mutiny and murder.

The legacy of the slave trade is a significant part of the historical fabric of West Africa, and several former points of embarkation memorialize the trade, including Gorée Island in Senegal, Elmina and Cape Coast Castles in Ghana, and Ouidah in Bénin. Gorée Island's La Maison des Esclaves is a point of pilgrimage for many belonging to the African diaspora. Ouidah features the Road of the Slaves and the Memorial to Slavery at Zoungbodji. One of the most unusual memorials to the slave trade lies beneath the waters near Key West, Florida. In 1993 members of the National Association of Black Scuba Divers placed a plaque near the underwater wreck of the *Henrietta Marie,* an English slave ship discovered by treasure hunter Mel Fisher. The memorial commemorates the suffering of those who died in the Middle Passage.

Memorials to slave communities, to burial sites, and to institutions in the New World have emerged in the late twentieth century. A Slave Memorial (1983), created by Howard University students, stands at the slave cemetery at Mount Vernon, Virginia, paying homage to the hundreds of bondsmen and women who lived, toiled, and died there. Cemetery sites have engendered considerable debate in recent years, prompting calls for proper memorialization of the dead at sites like New York's African Burial Ground, on which a federal building was supposed to have been built. The many memorials to slavery that continue to be planned will in all likelihood continue to spark controversy and pique public interest.

See also MUSEUMS AND HISTORIC SITES.

BIBLIOGRAPHY

BERNEY, K. A., and TRUDY RING, eds. *International Dictionary of Historic Places.* 5 vols. 1996.

BURNSIDE, MADELINE. *Spirits of the Passage: The Transatlantic Slave Trade in the Seventeenth Century.* 1997.

CHASE, HENRY. *In Their Footsteps: The American Visions Guide to African-American Heritage Sites.* 1994.

CURTIS, NANCY C. *Black Heritage Sites: An African American Odyssey and Finder's Guide.* 1996.

Gorée: Island of Memories. 1985. Compiled by the staff of UNESCO from documentary sources.

SAVAGE, BETH L., ed. *African American Historic Places: National Register of Historic Places, National Park Service.* 1994.

SAVAGE, KIRK. *Standing Soldiers, Kneeling Slaves: Race, War, and Monument in Nineteenth-Century America.* 1997.

Gregg D. Kimball

Memory and History

The place slavery should receive in the annals of the American people, the perspectives from which it should be approached, and the legitimacy and validity of the material to be examined are questions that are still being discussed. The first mainstream professional historians were southerners, who viewed slavery as a major factor in the development of southern society, stressing, as Ulrich B. Phillips did, its paternalistic character and its civilizing function. Memories of plantation life were all the more firmly implanted as the system came to an abrupt end in the bloodiest war in the nation's history. Antebellum society was praised for efficiency, management skills, and a sophisticated lifestyle, and for the splendor of its architectural, artistic, and intellectual accomplishments. This homage was echoed not only in monographs and local histories but also in monuments, memorials, and collections. Not only plantation records and diaries and the testimony of contemporary visitors and travelers were taken into account, but also visual sources and material culture.

More than a century after emancipation, plantation homes are still visited, and many have become museums. Ditties and songs, which first found their way into the minstrel tradition, are still remembered. Photography and fiction, children's literature, and textbooks have contributed to the creation of a mythic "old South" with the plantation as the central metaphor, obliterating what should not be remembered. If the descendants of the masters have participated in this romanticization in their memoirs, paradoxically,

A tour guide dressed in period costume tells the history of Melrose Plantation in Natchez, Mississippi. [Kelly-Mooney Photography/Corbis]

ex-slaves have also done so. Evoking the antebellum years at a time when the Great Depression was creating more problems in their lives, some considered slavery with nostalgia, if we are to believe the reminiscences of ex-slaves collected by the Works Progress Administration. During this same era, the documentary reliability of the nineteenth-century fugitive slave narratives was questioned because of their function in antislavery propaganda. Ever since the Civil War, efforts have been made to restore the South to its former grandeur, and to merge history and memory harmoniously.

Yet the moral issue that slaveholding posed to the nation has played a great part in the shaping of another form of historical consciousness and memory. The issue was raised mainly by northerners and abolitionists; it was rarely voiced by sons of planters, who had a sense of their birthright as owners of land and chattels. The pressing idea that if all people were free and equal, slaves should also have been endowed with the inalienable right to liberty has haunted many a conscience and has led historians to examine antislavery thought and the role of blacks themselves in this critique of the peculiar institution.

The most significant change in the forging of a history and memory of slavery probably occurred when more attention was given to the striving of slaves and free blacks for liberty and learning. The dominant historical view of slavery was challenged, and its assumption of slaves' inferiority and incapacity to shape their own destiny was questioned. Race and, later, gender were seen as major factors, but additional elements that raised disturbing issues were also brought into the picture—the overseer, slaves without masters, black and Indian slaveowners, and interaction between Indians and slaves.

Because of the influence of such works as W. E. B. DuBois's *Souls of Black Folk* (1903), slaves came to be considered as makers of history who could take action, create institutions, and produce a culture that found expression in an impressive body of tales, songs, and artifacts. Slaves who because of their illiteracy had been ignored in a history based essentially on written records now received credit for the oral, musical, and pictorial tradition which they had managed to establish and through which history and memory had been passed on. In the 1990s slave religion, family, community, culture, and lore have become the focus of much scholarly work.

Since the "black power" movement, the concept of black history, first presented in the 1930s by such scholars as Carter Woodson and John Hope Franklin, has flourished. According to this concept, it is necessary to look at untapped sources, listen to previously unheeded voices, record memories, and create archives—and to introduce all this material into university and school curricula. The idea, however, has received a wide range of interpretations and diverse emphases, such as inclusion in American history versus separateness and consideration of the whole diaspora versus an Afrocentric perspective. Each interpretation has dealt differently with slavery: stressing inequities, horrors, and cultural death or stressing continuity with the African past; seeing slavery as a shameful experience that should be forgotten or glorifying the slaves' resilience and their achievements. Whatever the orientation, however, the concept has increased African-Americans' pride in their past and has contributed to an African-American identity.

These debates have to be seen in a larger context—a reexamination of the nature of historical inquiry. Who writes history? Who are its actors? The most intriguing question has been about the dynamics of history and memory and the interaction between their personal, collective, and national aspects. This has informed attitudes toward slavery: How much should be remembered or told? And since there are so many contending memories and stories, which ones should be taken into account? For example, should the focus be on those that evoke tension and antagonism or on those that record affective and intellectual ties between slaves and masters?

After having long distrusted memory and oral sources, scholars are listening to new black voices and are also being more attentive to women. Present-day African-Americans have looked into the memory of their grandparents. Voices from the Caribbean or Latin America have also been heard, leading to exploration of the Middle Passage, the slave trade, and the complex communication between Europe, Africa, and the New World. After having been dismissed as documentary evidence, the slave narrative as a genre has once again gained recognition as a valid vehicle of memory in historical perspective.

The question of slavery has gone well beyond the limits of scientific inquiry into the realm of the imaginary and the symbolic. To the pro-Confederate vision characteristic of *Gone with the Wind*, black novelists from Margaret Walker and Ernest Gaines to Toni Morrison and Charles Johnson have opposed an "inside" vision of slavery and of the Middle Passage. Such television offerings as *Roots* and *The Autobiography of Miss Jane Pittman*, and film treatments such as Steven Spielberg's *Amistad*, provide correctives to the blatantly racist *Birth of a Nation*. These authors and filmmakers have begun to reconstruct the history of slavery, "recollecting" scattered fragments of the past and dramatizing the intricate process of forgetting or remembering. White and black Americans are trying to come to terms with this section of their past, with a sense of guilt and shame or of grief and tragedy. A larger place has been given to slavery in the quest for "sites of memory."

Narratives by slaves and ex-slaves have been among these sites, showing that the interplay of history and memory yields many truths out of which to build a collective record and gives insights into how slavery has shaped sensibilities and worldviews. Writers and artists have claimed the right to delve into recesses where memories lie buried. Transmission and "passing on" have become crucial issues, and so have the notions of heritage, ancestry, and genealogy. Many places or events are being revisited: plantation houses, slave quarters, markets, and graveyards. Memorials and monuments, such as those erected to Crispus Attucks in Boston and to Lincoln in Washington, themselves have a history, and these landmarks assume new meaning when they become the chosen sites for other memorable moments, as some did during the civil rights era. New sites are constantly being created. Storytelling, sermons, song and dance, quilts, artifacts, and paintings are stored in the collective memory in honor of the ancestors who dared create them against daunting odds; the work of such predecessors serves as an inspiration for new images and ideas. The will to remember is strong now, as is the desire to preserve. A calendar of commemorative events is set to celebrate the past, and many institutions, families, churches, and community organizations participate actively in this process of recollection and retrieving. This reconstruction of the history and memory of slavery is taking place worldwide: the African forts of Gorée in Senegal and Elmina in Ghana and the European ports of Liverpool and Nantes have been acknowledged as major memorial landmarks.

The different actors seem to become reconciled with a past they cannot escape and yet were unwilling to confront. Slavery finds a new place in American history and memory: an era that is not so much disturbing as it is meaningful, and a moment that can provide clues to an understanding of the nation's past and future.

See also DU BOIS, W. E. B.; LITERATURE OF SLAVERY; MIDDLE PASSAGE; MUSIC BY SLAVES.

BIBLIOGRAPHY

BLASSINGAME, JOHN W., ed. *Slave Testimony: Two Centuries of Letters, Speeches, Interviews, and Autobiographies.* 1977.

CAMPBELL, EDWARD D. C., and KYM S. RICE, eds. *Before Freedom Came: African American Life in the Antebellum South.* 1991.

FABRE, GENEVIÈVE, and ROBERT O'MEALLY, eds. *History and Memory in African-American Culture.* 1994.

RAWICK, GEORGE P., ed. *The American Slave: A Composite Autobiography.* 1972–1979.

SINGLETON, THERESA A., ed. *The Archaeology of Slavery and Plantation Life.* 1985.

Geneviève Fabre

The Lincoln Memorial served as a background for the 1963 March on Washington. [Flip Schulke/Corbis]

Mercado, Tomás de   [fl. 1560–1580]

Spanish theologian and writer.

Tomás de Mercado was born in Seville, Spain, but migrated to Mexico, where he became a Dominican friar and studied theology. His major work is the *Suma de Tratos y Contratos*, first published in 1569, reissued in 1587, and translated into Italian in 1591. Mercado wrote as a moral philosopher, examining the dynamics of sixteenth-century commerce in the Atlantic economy. The next to last chapter of his book discusses slavery and the slave trade.

Mercado accepted the theoretical legitimacy of slavery, holding that people could be enslaved as captives of war, as punishment for crimes, or by self-sale. Even the sale of children by their parents, resting as it did on paternal authority, was legal for Mercado. But he noted that the actual practices of the Atlantic slave trade were morally indefensible and inevitably involved all participants in grievous sins.

In Mercado's view, the prices offered for slaves in Africa stimulated warfare, raiding, and kidnapping, and also induced judges and fathers to abuse their power by selling criminals or children into slavery for trumped-up reasons. Mercado also condemned conditions in slave pens and slave ships as inhumane. These circumstances rendered any participation in the slave trade a deadly sin, even though buying and selling slaves was not inherently wrong. Mercado's emphasis on the greed of slave traders and on the endangerment of the slaveholder's soul thus anticipated by two hundred years the eighteenth-century criticisms of the slave trade.

See also ABOLITION AND ANTISLAVERY MOVEMENTS; LITERATURE OF SLAVERY; SLAVE TRADE.

BIBLIOGRAPHY

BLACKBURN, ROBIN. *The Making of Colonial Slavery, 1492–1800*. 1997.
DAVIS, DAVID BRION. *The Problem of Slavery in Western Culture*. 1966.

T. Stephen Whitman

Mesopotamia

See Ancient Middle East.

Methodism

Originally a movement to reform the colonial-era Anglican Church, the Methodist Episcopal Church began its life as a separate denomination in the flush of post–Revolutionary War antislavery sentiment. In keeping with the strong expectations of the times, the original Methodist discipline condemned the "buying and selling of men, women, and children" and resolved that members who bought and sold slaves "shall be expelled." Because of southern complaints little effort was taken to enforce this rule, however. Methodism experienced considerable expansion in its first half century, becoming the second-largest denomination in the nation. To maintain this rate of growth in the face of changing southern attitudes toward slavery, the Methodists gradually abandoned prohibitions on slave owning. By the 1820s such a policy was maintained only in the ministry, and there only in states permitting manumission. Methodist leaders feared that a stronger antislavery stand would cause masters to bar the denomination's itinerant preachers from access to their slaves and weaken the church's ability to further ameliorate slave treatment.

Thanks to the denomination's enthusiastic preaching and singing styles, the Methodists' missionary efforts among the slaves had great success. Also early in the nineteenth century, two small all-black denominations, the African Methodist Episcopal and the African Methodist Episcopal Zion churches, were founded to protest racially discriminatory practices in the main denominations. Generally barred from access to the slaves, the African Methodist ministers recruited members from the free black population of the border and northern states.

The U.S. abolitionist movement arose during the 1830s as a by-product of the upsurge of revivalism popularly known as the Second Great Awakening. These religiously inspired abolitionists demanded that the churches testify to slavery's inherent sinfulness by barring slave owners from their communion and fellowship. While the abolitionists recruited many individual Methodists in the 1830s, their early labors bore little fruit in changing the church's official position. In the 1830s Methodist abolitionists pushed for enforcement of their church's long ignored disciplinary condemnation of slavery. Methodist abolitionists held denominational antislavery conventions and founded a permanent national organization, the American Wesleyan Anti-Slavery Society, in October 1840.

Despite financial and propaganda assistance from non-Methodist abolitionists, the Methodist abolitionists made little progress. A large majority of delegates at the Methodists' General Conference of 1836 publicly resolved that they were "decidedly opposed to modern abolitionism." By the time of the 1840 General Conference, abolitionists had made major inroads in annual conferences in New England and upstate New York. Abolitionist petitions for stronger wording of the discipline against "buying or selling" slaves, however, were overwhelmingly rejected by the General Conference. With the official machinery of the denomination turned against them, Methodist abolitionists, led by the Reverend Orange Scott, began seceding in November 1842 to form a new Methodist church promoting abolition. The resulting Wesleyan Methodist Connection grew within two years to nearly fifteen thousand members in churches from Michigan to New England.

Ironically, the Wesleyans' bolt preceded a similar southern secession from the Methodist Episcopal Church by less than two years. Despite their rejection of abolitionism, Methodist church councils continued to pay lip service to their conservative antislavery heritage by endorsements of African colonization and by missionary work among the slaves. The conservatives' conciliatory policy was put to the test at the Methodist General Conference of 1844. Bishop James O. Andrew of Georgia had recently become a slaveholder through inheritance. Andrew wanted to resign his office, but southern militants desired to make this a test of one of the few still respected antislavery rules of the church. Although eighteen northern delegates sided with the South, the conference voted 110 to 68 to suspend Andrew from his episcopal duties as long as he continued to own slaves. Outraged southerners immediately seceded to form the Methodist Episcopal Church, South. Efforts to arrange an equitable division of properties failed, and the old and new churches became contentious rivals for the loyalty of congregations in the upper South. At least four thousand slaveholding Methodists from the border states retained their allegiance to local conferences of the Northern Methodist Episcopal Church.

The disputes over church property and the border state congregations intensified antinorthern sentiment in the new Methodist Episcopal Church, South. A movement began to repeal all negative references to slaveholding in the church discipline. Older, conservative Methodist leaders successfully resisted this effort at the 1851 and 1854 General Conferences, but the militant proslavery faction was victorious in 1858. Southern Methodists frequently denounced the North as morally corrupted by infidel abolitionism and supported political steps to break up the Union. In 1860 the South Carolina Annual Conference, for example, formally endorsed "resisting Northern domination" by secession. Simultaneously, during the 1840s and 1850s, the Methodist Episcopal Church, South, conducted a highly successful missionary effort among southern blacks. Despite white paternalism and loose supervision slaves and free blacks forged their own brand of Methodism that would achieve institutional independence after the Civil War.

Abolitionists continued their agitation of the northern Methodist Episcopal Church, but a coalition of northern conservative and border state delegates blocked debate on strengthening church rules against slaveholding at the 1848 and 1852 General Conferences. At the 1856 conference antislavery delegates from New York, Ohio, and Wisconsin managed to place under consideration four resolutions intended to strengthen church discipline against slaveholding, but none received the required three-fourths approval.

In the 1850s antislavery church members forced open the columns of their denomination's official periodicals by debating the political as well as moral aspects of slavery-related issues. A younger generation of antislavery Methodists, such as Gilbert Haven, became active supporters of the Republicans and their platform of not extending slavery into the territories.

This politically inspired growth of antislavery feelings, in turn, encouraged a younger generation of churchmen to revive efforts toward strengthening religious antislavery practices. The coming of the Civil War irrefutably demonstrated to northerners the moral corruption inherent in a slaveholding society. In 1860 the Methodist General Conference amended the church discipline to declare the "holding of human beings as chattels" as grounds for expulsion from fellowship. Conservatives, however, weakened this ruling by convincing the general conference to label it merely "advisory." Four years later the Methodists rescinded all qualifications on this judgment and also endorsed a federal immediate-emancipation program. During and after the Civil War northern Methodists conducted missionary efforts to attract the freed blacks to their denomination. Such efforts were compromised by the century's end by the desire of northern church leaders for reunion with their southern white counterparts, which was finally achieved in 1939.

See also ABOLITION AND ANTISLAVERY MOVEMENTS; ANGLICANISM.

BIBLIOGRAPHY

CARWARDINE, RICHARD J. *Evangelicals and Politics in Antebellum America.* 1993.
MATHEWS, DONALD G. *Slavery and Methodism: A Chapter in American Morality, 1780–1845.* 1965.
MCKIVIGAN, JOHN R. *The War against Proslavery Religion: Abolitionism and the Northern Churches, 1830–1865.* 1984.

John R. McKivigan

Mexico

See Amerindian Societies.

Michigan

Slavery was part of Michigan's heritage when the United States assumed control over this section of the Northwest Territory in 1796. Earlier, the area had been governed by the British as part of Canada from 1763, and prior to that it had been a colony of New France. Slavery existed under both regimes. Though no evidence has surfaced to indicate exactly when slavery became anchored under French rule, an ordinance was passed in the territory in 1709 permitting the purchase and sale of all Indians and blacks. In 1724 Louis XV established the *Code Noir ou Recueil de Règlements,* which mandated the baptism and education of all slaves in the Apostolic Roman Catholic faith. This was the first written record dealing with slavery in the Michigan Territory.

Britain acquired the area in 1763, after the Seven Years' War, and continued to allow the practice. In

1783, under terms of the Treaty of Paris, the Northwest Territory and its slaves passed from Britain to American control. The sixth article of the U.S. Northwest Ordinance of 1787, however, declared slavery illegal in the area that included Michigan. Nevertheless, slavery remained in the territory well after the turn of the century, prompting heated debate and violence between advocates and opponents of slavery.

Ultimately, agitation over slavery subsided following the War of 1812. Authorities let the institution diminish with the death of those slaves held in captivity after 1807. By 1830 there were still 788 slaves in the region at the time of the fifth census. During that time there were thousands of blacks in the territory; some were slaves, but the vast majority were free blacks endeavoring to give meaning to freedom.

Michigan entered the union in 1837 with a constitution that absolutely prohibited any form of slavery. In 1855 the state passed a personal liberty law to protect free blacks from being kidnapped. The state was a haven for runaway slaves, in part because it was so distant from slave catchers. Cass County in southwestern Michigan had one of the largest percentages of blacks in any county in the North. Many were legally free, but many were fugitives openly living as free people. By the mid-1850s the state was politically controlled by Republicans opposed to the spread of slavery into the western states.

See also CODE NOIR; NORTHWEST ORDINANCE.

BIBLIOGRAPHY

FINKELMAN, PAUL. *Slavery and the Founders: Race and Liberty in the Age of Jefferson.* 1996.
FRANKLIN, JOHN HOPE, and ALFRED A. MOSS. *From Slavery to Freedom: A History of African Americans.* 7th ed. 1994.
KOOKER, ARTHUR RAYMOND. "The Antislavery Movement in Michigan, 1796–1840: A Study in Humanitarianism on an American Frontier." Ph.D. diss., Michigan State University, 1941.

Matthew C. Whitaker

Middle East

See Ancient Middle East; Modern Middle East.

Middle Passage

The expression Middle Passage now often refers to the maritime phase of the slaves' voyages from Africa to the Americas—the time in between their capture and their sale, the two wrenching transitions in the lives of people torn from their native land and condemned for the rest of their lives to survive among strangers. Histories of the Atlantic trade commonly employ the phrase to designate chapters devoted to the conditions endured below the decks of the slave ships at sea, at least since the foundational *Black Cargoes* published in 1962 (Daniel Mannix, with Malcolm Cowley). One quantitative survey of slaves' lives and deaths at sea appropriately bore *Middle Passage* as its title (Klein, 1978).

The term originated early in the eighteenth century with quite another sense. English mariners first followed complex sailing routes to deliver manufactured goods to the African coast. They then carried hundreds of Africans to the West Indies (or, less often, to the North American colonies) on the easterly trade winds of the middle latitudes; finally, they loaded New World produce, or departed in ballast with planters' bills of exchange, and set out for England along the Gulf Stream across the North Atlantic. These mariners came to call the middle slave-carrying leg of this three-phase venture the "middle passage." The pattern as a whole subsequently became known as the "triangular trade."

Historians have learned a great deal about the lives—and deaths—of the slaves at sea, the sense in which this essay discusses the Middle Passage. Pitifully few captives learned to write or told their stories to literate sponsors who preserved the narratives of their experiences, but a greater number of captains left accounts sympathetically revealing what the slaves endured. Government and business records bearing on twenty-seven thousand known slaving voyages reveal even more, though only in the aggregate. The picture drawn from them is not a happy one.

The slaves' lives hung in a delicate balance that slaving captains had to maintain, between assigning the limited room in their holds to captives worth cash in the Americas or giving the valuable space over to provisions—food and especially water—to sustain their human cargoes at sea. The holds of the ships reflected this trade-off, being divided by "a deck" constructed—often while lying at anchor along the African coast—at a height judged suitable to stow food below yet adequate to meet the needs of the captives chained above in the "slave deck" thus created. Pressures for profit often produced both inadequate supplies in the hold and extremely cramped conditions for the slaves. A famous abolitionist diagram showed bodies crowded shoulder-to-shoulder and front-to-back, so close together on the slave deck that they could not move; other reconstructions of those ships show an imaginative variety of techniques of "tight-packing." Delays in making landfall brought death from dehydration, if not starvation, to measurable numbers of slaves. In one horrifying extreme instance, the officers of the ship *Zong,* upon encountering

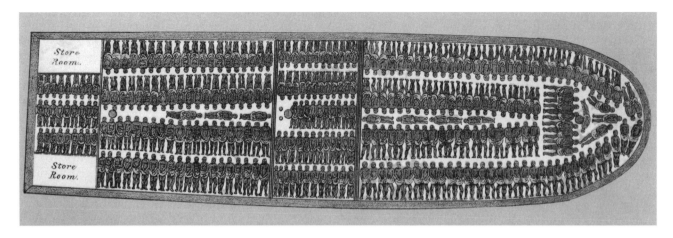

A diagram of the lower deck of a slave ship (drawn for the slave-trade debates in Parliament) illustrates how closely packed the slaves were to allow transportation of as many as possible to maximize profits. The model for the drawing is believed to be a ship called the Brooks. *[Corbis-Bettmann]*

delays at sea, cast living slaves overboard to recover insured "losses at sea" rather than absorb the unrecoverable cost of deaths that they expected would otherwise follow, from lack of enough food and water to sustain their captives. The first laws regulating slavers tackled these deadly abuses by limiting the number of slaves carried per ton of capacity—a measure that, significantly, included the hold space devoted to water and food.

Slaves boarded the ships already weakened by weeks, sometimes months, of insufficient nourishment along the African paths to the coast, sickened by exposure to lowland coastal disease environments to which those from higher, drier regions in the interior had no immunities, and demoralized by the emotional trauma they had suffered. The crowded conditions and inadequate provisions aboard the ships gained lethal power under these circumstances. Sickness was common, most often dysenteries and other "fluxes" acquired from spoiled water supplies, but also scurvy. Slavers bemoaned deaths that they attributed to "fixed melancholy" (as the English termed it), a despondent lethargy that seemed inevitably fatal. Once wrongly thought to be sleeping sickness, and also interpreted as profound depression from the psychological shock of the abuses slaves experienced, torpor of the sort reported also characterizes terminal dehydration and malnutrition.

In the southern Atlantic voyages from Angola to Brazil, communicable diseases like smallpox surged in epidemic proportion through the holds in waves that followed corresponding droughts in west-central Africa. To treat these, and many other, threats to the profits of the venture arising from the vulnerability of the slaves, ships carried surgeons charged to care for them, and some also employed American slaves knowledgeable in African healing technology. Ships' surgeons, particularly in the English trade, were prompt to experiment with inoculation techniques against smallpox in the 1770s, and they introduced vaccination after 1800 to good effect.

The average two- or three-masted slaver carried about three hundred prisoners, although many small sloops and other single-masted vessels carried cargoes of eighty or one hundred, and a few large ships sailed with five hundred and more captives. The smaller vessels exposed everyone on board to the vagaries of the sea, and captains found that oversized vessels required so much time in port to fill their holds with slaves that the first ones purchased began to sicken and die before the traders could complete their purchases. Africans sold (and slaving captains also preferred to buy) almost twice as many men as women; children were not common on the Middle Passage. On some ships crews herded the boys and men below decks and locked up the women and girls separately in the forecastle; such segregation by gender was intended at least as much to make the females available to the crew for sexual gratification as it was to allow for minimal privacy. Iron shackles restrained the men: so symbolic of the trade were chains and other irons that nineteenth-century antislave-trade squadron commanders were authorized to condemn as a slaver any ship thus equipped, even if they found no human cargo aboard at the time of seizure.

In spite of these precautions, slaves still managed to revolt, though seldom with success. The victory of the slaves aboard the *Amistad*, a small craft ferrying slaves from Havana to eastern Cuba in 1839, which culminated in their being freed by the Supreme Court of the United States in 1841, was unusual in that they gained control of the vessel and survived. That others, even occasionally, managed to escape their fetters, overcome language barriers to coordinate an attack, assault heavily armed crews, and attempt to operate a complex piece of unfamiliar equipment reveals the desperation that they must have felt. In every part of Africa the Europeans seem to have been regarded as cannibals: the huge copper pots on the decks of the ships, used to prepare the gruel commonly fed to the cargo, took on a terrifying aspect in the light of these expectations. Other reports asserted that the cowrie shells that Europeans paid along the Slave Coast grew on the carcasses of captives thrown overboard. In Angola slaves believed that the Portuguese distilled red wine from the blood of their predecessors, boiled the soft, white cheese imported from Brazil from their brains, and burned their bones to make gunpowder from the ashes. The crews of the ships experienced terrors of their own, outnumbered ten or fifteen to one as they were by prisoners they feared as much as they despised them. Naval architects in the 1780s designed specialized vessels with high barricades extending far out beyond the gunwales to protect the ship's wheel and the captain's and offi-

cers' quarters to the rear from the forward deck with its hatches leading below to the slaves.

Beyond the terrors of being locked in dark, airless confinement, captives not too dazed or weak to notice their surroundings suffered conditions deeply offensive to every sense. Naked or covered crudely with rags, they could not preserve elementary decency. The dysenteries, often bloody, vomit from panic and from seasickness, and perspiration flowing in the close, humid atmosphere heated by hundreds of bodies covered everyone in filth. Crews made periodic attempts to clean and fumigate slave decks, but the burning tar and vinegar they employed could only have sharpened the stench. Other ships at sea could identify passing slavers by the ghastly smells that trailed them far downwind.

Death in numbers great enough that the Portuguese knew slave ships as "floating tombs" (*tumbeiros*) was the final experience of many of the Africans chained beneath their decks. Traders arranged business strategies to avoid owning the captives at the periods of greatest mortality, that is, during the Middle Passage. Losses on the maritime passage may have averaged 20 percent or more during the sixteenth century, before the slavers worked out effective techniques of carrying

A slaver walks among the cargo of enslaved Africans during the Atlantic crossing. [Library of Congress/Corbis]

human cargoes safely; by the eighteenth-century peak of slave-carrying, mortality was declining toward 10 percent, and less in some sectors of the trade. By the nineteenth century fast, well-equipped, furtive slavers evading Britain's antislavery squadron averaged losses below 5 percent. For normal crossings—ranging from thirty-five days on the shortest routes (Angola to Brazil) to eighty or ninety days on longer routes (to the Caribbean, or North America)—deaths at the 10 percent level represented annual rates in the range of four hundred per thousand and more, that is, fifteen to twenty-five times greater than mortality among less stressed, "normal" populations. Yet these mortality ratios rise even higher when compared with those for groups of vital young men and women who were not enslaved. The psychological burden of being landed alive after such decimation at sea, beyond the "social death" imposed by enslavement itself, can only be surmised from our knowledge of modern survivors of genocide.

See also AMISTAD; SLAVE TRADE.

BIBLIOGRAPHY

ALLISON, ROBERT J., ed. *The Interesting Narrative of the Life of Olaudah Equiano, Written by Himself.* 1995.
CURTIN, PHILIP D. *The Atlantic Slave Trade: A Census.* 1969.
———, ed. *African Remembered: Narratives by West Africans from the Era of the Slave Trade.* 1967.
ELTIS, DAVID, DAVID RICHARDSON, STEPHEN D. BEHRENDT, and HERBERT S. KLEIN, eds. *The Atlantic Slave Trade: A Database on CD-ROM Set and Guidebook.* 1998.
FEELINGS, TOM. *The Middle Passage.* 1995.
JONES, HOWARD. *Mutiny on the* Amistad*: The Saga of a Slave Revolt and Its Impact on American Abolition, Law, and Diplomacy.* 1986.
KLEIN, HERBERT S. *The Middle Passage: Comparative Studies in the Atlantic Slave Trade.* 1978.
MANNIX, DANIEL P., and MALCOLM COWLEY. *Black Cargoes: A History of the Atlantic Slave Trade, 1518–1865.* 1962.
MILLER, JOSEPH C. "Overcrowded and Undernourished: Techniques and Consequences of Tight-Packing in the Portuguese Southern Atlantic Slave Trade." Condensed in *De la traite à l'esclavage,* edited by Serge Daget. 1988, vol. 2, pp. 395–424.
———. *The Way of Death: Merchant Capitalism and the Angolan Slave Trade, 1730–1830.* 1988.
RICHARDSON, DAVID. "The Costs of Survival: The Transport of Slaves in the Middle Passage and the Profitability of the 18th-Century British Slave Trade." *Explorations in Economic History* 24, no. 2 (1987): 178–196.

Joseph C. Miller

Military Slaves

This entry includes the following articles: Muslim Military Slavery; African Military Slaves in the Americas.

Muslim Military Slavery

The institution of military slavery is a paradox, marked by ambiguities in status and power; the distinctions between freedom and servitude, power and powerlessness are blurred. It is as much a social category as a legal classification, with a specific history in place and time. Military slavery as an institution is distinct from the use of individual slaves in military roles. Daniel Pipes, in *Slave Soldiers and Islam: The Genesis of a Military System* (1981), has given this broad definition: "A 'military slave' is a person of slave origins who undergoes acquisition in a systematic manner, followed by training and employment as a soldier. This term does not apply to all slaves who fight in wars, but only to those whose lives revolve around military service. The military slave keeps this appellation even after he attains legal or real freedom. 'Military slavery' is the system which acquires, prepares, and employs military slaves."

The institution has been a tool of statecraft in many Muslim societies. It had its origin in the Abbasid caliphate in the ninth century after Christ (the third century in the Muslim calendar, which dates from the hegira) and was replicated by a succession of Muslim dynasties and states from Spain to India. Military slavery assumed central political importance in Mamluk Egypt and the Ottoman Empire (both beginning in the thirteenth century after Christ—seventh century A.H.). In its latter stages in the nineteenth century after Christ, before it was completely replaced in the Islamic heartlands by conscripted national armies, military slavery played a critical role in both the expansion of and the resistance to European colonial empires in many parts of Sudanic and eastern Africa.

Origins of Military Slavery

Max Weber proposed an evolutionary role for military slavery in the development of the "patrimonial state," whereby the ruler built up an army and an administrative system based on kinsmen, clients, and slaves loyal only to himself. Weber cited ancient Egypt as the earliest example of large-scale use of military slaves. This date has since been disputed, and it is now generally accepted that the first organized, systematic and sustained recruitment, training, and use of military slaves occurred in the Middle East after the foundation of the Muslim caliphate. A precedent was set during the initial Muslim conquests of the Umayyad period (A.D. 661–750; 41–132 A.H.) by recruitment into the army of the freed slaves of defeated enemies and the non-Arab clients (*mawla*) of the new Arab elite.

It was only with the civil wars of the eighth and ninth centuries after Christ (the second and third centuries A.H.)—which led to the establishment of the

Abbasid caliphate and the displacement of the Arab feudal elite by a largely Iranian elite—that an army of slaves taken from outside the Muslim world and placed under the direct command of the caliph became a central feature of the Muslim state. The brother caliphs, Mamun and Mutasim (A.D. 813–842; 198–227 A.H.), initiated the recruitment of slaves from the newly conquered Transoxania region of central Asia, and subsequently of Turks taken in raids from the northern borders of Muslim domains. Placed under their own commanders, garrisoned in the new capital of Samarra, and provided with wives, the new slave soldiers (mamluks) were isolated from the old Abbasid army and came under the personal patronage of the caliph, who resided among them. A standing army of slaves under centralized control replaced earlier tribal armies of Islam, with their regional loyalties.

Different reasons have been given for the origins and persistence of the mamluk system in Islam. David Ayalon, in his pioneering studies of mamluk society (1979), ascribed its origin to the Muslim project of Islamizing the world through jihad (holy war or struggle). The rapid early conquests outstripped the manpower reserves the Arabian peninsula could supply, necessitating recruitment of non-Arabs, and eventually non-Muslims, into the army. This need was met by taking slaves from the densely populated areas of Central Asia, the Caucasus, and Transcaucasus. The martial character of these peoples accounted more than the slave status of the soldiers for the success and durability of the mamluk system and for its adoption by a succession of Muslim states down through the centuries.

Two other historians, Daniel Pipes and Patricia Crone (1980), argue that the adoption of the mamluk system was not owing to its intrinsic strengths but stemmed from inherent weaknesses in the Islamic political system. It is Pipe's contention that Islam set impossibly high political ideals. It requires a government to enforce religious law (*sharia*) and create an environment in which Muslims can live lives prescribed by *sharia*. But the civil wars which followed the establishment of the first caliphate violated the ideal of the Muslim community (*umma*) as a united whole, in which war between believers was prohibited. Failure of government to live up to the public ideals of Islam led devout Muslim subjects to withdraw from active participation in government. This alienation forced the Abbasid caliphs to turn to soldiers recruited from the marginal areas of the empire, first as mawla and then as mamluks. The system of military slavery provided the most efficient way for the caliphs to acquire and control these marginal soldiers.

Crone argues that the institution of military slavery was not so much the product as the cause of this alien-ation. The mamluk system was created from a fusion of two previously discrete factors: the servile status of slaves and clients and the alien origin of mercenaries. The personal dependence of the mamluk on the ruler created a bond of loyalty and obedience that made for an effective fighting unit as long as that bond lasted. But since slave armies are essentially private in character, this bond of loyalty could not always be transferred to successor rulers. When it was not transmitted, armies revolted, allegiance was transferred to rivals, new private slave armies were raised by contenders for power, the caliphate disintegrated, and new regional dynasties arose. The adoption of the mamluk system of slave soldiers by a succession of medieval Islamic states led to the loss of control of the state to the mamluks, further deepening the divide between rulers of the state and the nonpolitical elite of urban merchants, rural landowners, and religious authorities.

Essential Features of Military Slavery

Detailed studies of the origins of military slavery and the mamluk system have established the essential features of the institution, which can be found in varying degrees and combinations wherever it was practiced in the Middle East and Africa. Military slavery defined and regulated relations between a central state and its peripheries, and between a ruler and his slave soldiers. The systematic acquisition of military slaves through raiding, tribute, or purchase was a state activity. As such it was a means by which the state destabilized communities beyond its borders or exerted political control over marginal (and in most cases, non-Muslim) peoples living within or just outside its direct authority. Military slaves were owned not by ordinary people but by governments, rulers, officials, or provincial leaders. They were trained and garrisoned separately from free elements of the army. Foreign origin, isolation, deracination, and cultural dissociation were all essential in providing a new exclusively military identity for captive boys and young men, transforming them into highly trained soldiers and Muslims, and at the same time keeping them separated from the main population of the polity and maintaining their dependence on and loyalty to the ruler or patron. There was thus no potential conflict of loyalty when they were employed to collect taxes and police the free Muslim subjects of the state.

Military slaves were racially diverse. The Buyids (A.D. 932–1062; 320–454 A.H.) significantly increased the use of Turkish slaves. Fatimid Egypt (A.D. 909–1171; 297–567 A.H.) raised its army from Slav, Turkish, Berber, and African slaves. The janissaries of the Ottoman Empire were acquired mainly in tribute from

An officer of the janissaries (early eighteenth century).
[Historical Picture Archive/Corbis]

the Christian peoples of the Caucasus, the Transcaucasus, and southern Russia, and many of them were also exported to Mamluk Egypt. The slave cavalrymen of the Funj sultanate in the Sudan during the seventeenth and eighteenth centuries were captured in raids or taken in tribute from the African peoples of the Nuba mountains and the Sudan-Ethiopian foothills. Because a continuous supply of slaves was needed in order to perpetuate the institution, those states that effectively controlled the supply of slaves could have an impact on the armies of other states. In the ninth century the independent Aghlabid dynasty of Tunisia retained its own African slaves and ceased to send them to the Abbasids in Iraq; this accounts for the decline of Africans in the Abbasid armies. In the nineteenth century the Ottoman embargo on the sale of mamluks to Muhammad Ali's Egypt was one factor in his decision to seek a source of supply elsewhere by conquering the Sudan.

The legal status of enslaved soldiers often changed, but an ambiguous servile social status remained. Manumission frequently accompanied incorporation into the army, but it was not universally provided, and it became less common as time went on. Manumission did not imply that the commander gave up real control over his ex-slaves; and even free men who joined the corps of military slaves voluntarily were regarded as the ruler's slaves. Slave status accompanied the profession of soldier, whatever the legal or formal position of the individual soldier, whether he was manumitted by his master or freed himself. Only in the Mamluk dynasty of Egypt, where there was no sultan, was manumission part of the rite of passage that marked the slave's completion of military training and his formal induction into the army.

The ruler's long-term reliance on his military slaves meant that he, too, was dependent on them and never willingly relinquished his control. This dependence became the source of the slave soldiers' access to power and enhanced status; this was the true paradox of their enslavement. Being part of a corps of military slaves and being instruments of the ruler's authority meant that slave soldiers could achieve positions of power and social superiority denied to many of free birth—so much so that the eighteenth-century Scottish explorer of the Blue Nile, James Bruce, remarked that in the Funj sultanate of Sennar slavery was "the only true nobility." But even though military slaves could effectively free themselves over the course of time through the exercise of power, their position depended on maintaining their loyal subordination as the ruler's soldiers. Thus although military slaves were attached to the ruling elite, they were never fully integrated into it. Their position in society required a patron. When slave armies mutinied, they usually did so to throw off one patron in favor of another.

Military slavery was not just a feature of the medieval period in the Middle East. Military slaves were used to establish new dynasties in seventeenth- and eighteenth-century Muslim Africa. The Abid al-Bukhari, a corps of some fifteen thousand soldiers at its height, was created by Mawlay Ismail to help establish and consolidate his Alawi dynasty in Morocco (1672–1727). It was composed entirely of marginalized peoples, either confiscated slaves or Haratin, the dark-skinned autochthonous landless farmers and artisans of southern Morocco. They were stationed in separate garrisons, provided with slave and Haratin wives, maintained through subsidies and grants from the state, and bound to the sultan personally by an oath of holy service, which he took along with them. The Abid al-Bukhari freed the sultan from exclusive dependence on tribal levies, which had proved unreliable when confronted by Ottoman musketeers, but it also brought him into conflict with the free population of Morocco and the religious authorities, who attempted to declare the new army illegal. Upon Ismail's death the Abid al-Bukhari transferred their loyalty to his sons and played an active, if disruptive, role in the interregnum from 1727 to 1757. After that, they were disbanded.

The Abid al-Bukhari do not seem to have been a product of large-scale state slave raiding. In the eastern Sudanic states of Dar Fur and Sennar (both founded in the sixteenth century) slave raiding and slave trading were state monopolies, and both states, at different times, raised slave armies. These were of more lasting importance in Sennar than in Dar Fur. In Sennar the sultan's slave soldiers were mounted on horses and provided with armor, both also obtained by the state through trade. They were used not only to expand the state's boundaries in war and to raid the non-Muslim peripheries for more slaves, but also to collect tribute from the free Muslim nomads subject to the state. The importance of the Funj sultan as a patron, even if only nominal, continued when real power passed to the slave cavalry of the Hamaj regents in the late eighteenth century.

The Transformation of Military Slavery

During the early nineteenth century slave armies in the Islamic heartlands of the Middle East were replaced by conscript national armies, organized on the Napoleonic model and trained in modern European warfare. The entrenched power of the military slaves was such that this replacement was accomplished only by force, with the massacre of the Mamluks of Egypt by Muhammad Ali in 1811, and of the janissaries in Turkey by the sultan's new army in 1826. But as the old forms of military slavery disappeared in the central Islamic capitals, they were revived in new forms throughout the Nile Valley and Sudanic Africa as a direct result of Muhammad Ali's creation of an Egyptian African empire. These latter-day slave armies became racially specific, composed almost exclusively of black Africans. With the international acceptance of the language of emancipation in the nineteenth century, colonial governments referred to these soldiers as legally free, but actual freedom came only gradually. Their transformation into armies of free conscripts was not completed until the early twentieth century, and in many countries the descendants of these soldiers form distinct social groups whose servile origins are remembered today.

Muhammad Ali, an Albanian mercenary among the Ottoman troops sent to regain Egypt after Napoleon's invasion, attempted to rival his Ottoman overlord by raising a slave army of his own, through the conquest of the Sudan in 1820 and the subjugation of the sultanate of Sennar. Slaves captured for this new army came initially from the same slaving areas hunted by Sennar. Egypt's Muslim subjects in the Sudan were able to ally with their new rulers by participating in annual slave raids and paying tribute to Egypt in slaves. Muhammad Ali's plan for a new Sudanese slave army failed for three reasons: the high mortality of the first batch of slave conscripts sent to Egypt, the low population of the Sudan compared with Egypt, and the adoption of a competing Napoleonic model for a parallel Egyptian conscript army. Muhammad Ali pursued his imperial ambitions in the Middle East with a modern army of conscript Egyptian peasantry, but Egypt's more successful efforts in carving out and maintaining an African empire were based mainly on the slave battalions of Sudanese riflemen. It was in part with these troops that Egypt was able to open up new areas for commercial exploitation in the southern Sudan in the 1840s and 1860s, which in turn opened up new slaving reservoirs.

Muhammad Ali thus maintained a modern military formation—the rifle-armed infantry—through the older institution of military slavery. This combination was adopted by commercial adventurers who took advantage of Egypt's opening up of the southern Sudan. Private armies of slave riflemen were organized and raised by the ivory trading companies of European, Turkish, Egyptian, and northern Sudanese merchants operating in the South from the 1850s through the 1870s. These private armies became so powerful that they challenged Egypt's control in parts of its own African empire until their suppression in 1878–1879.

The destruction of these private armies had long-term ramifications. One such army, under Rabih ibn Fadlallah, escaped west and established a mobile empire that conquered the Sudanic kingdom of Bornu before being defeated by the French in 1900. Some slave soldiers from the commercial companies were incorporated into the Egyptian forces; others ultimately found employment in the army of Muhammad Ahmad al-Mahdi, the leader of the successful religious revolt of 1881–1885 against Egyptian rule in the Sudan.

The Sudanese Mahdiyya (1881–1898) was the most recent period in which slave armies played a significant role in the establishment of a Muslim state or the expansion of an empire. Britain occupied Egypt in 1882 and reorganized the army, but it retained the Sudanese slave battalions during the long confrontation with the Mahdist state across Egypt's frontiers between 1885 and 1896, and finally in the reconquest of the Sudan from 1896 to 1898. Soldiers of the old slave battalions and private armies fought in both the Mahdist and the Egyptian armies during this time, often changing sides. The soldiers' slave status was not officially acknowledged; in fact, from the 1860s on, Egypt, and later Britain, asserted that the soldiers were all emancipated. But in every other way they resembled classical mamluks: the soldiers were drawn exclusively from the slave stratum of society or from reservoirs of enslaveable peoples; they were conscripted mainly through war; men were "recruited for life" and branded; children were trained as soldiers from an early age; and garrisons were kept separate from the free population. Both the Egyptian and the Mahdist armies were socially stratified into free and unfree, and this stratification followed racial lines.

Military slaves turned up in early colonial armies in other parts of Africa. Sudanese soldiers were sold by Egypt to Germany to suppress the Bushiri rising in German East Africa (Tanganyika) in 1888 and formed the nucleus of German's colonial army there. Other groups of Sudanese soldiers, cut off in the Great Lakes area by the Mahdiyya, were recruited into the Imperial British East Africa Company in 1891 and subsequently helped Britain secure its hold on Uganda and Kenya. In East Africa, the Sudanese soldiers maintained themselves by undertaking their own slave raids, taking both women and children as captives. (The children were often trained by their captors and later absorbed into the army.) This was the foundation of the modern Nubi (from "Nubian") community of East Africa.

Pacification and civil administration in Britain's Sudanese and East African territories in the early twentieth century brought military slavery in this region to an end. With the suppression of the slave trade, the development of a policy of returning agricultural slaves to their masters, and the gradual elimination of the legal status of slave, the reservoir of slave recruits disappeared. The conscription of war captives, hostages, and other prisoners into the army during the pacification period in the Sudan delayed the establishment of a settled civil administration in many areas of the non-Muslim South. Of greater political significance is the fact that Britain never succeeded in establishing its own rulers as the patrons of slave soldiers, whose loyalty they could command. The last revolt of Sudanese battalions under British command was the mutiny of 1924, reasserting loyalty to the Egyptian khedive. The old slave battalions were completely disbanded by 1930 and replaced by territorially recruited units, with links to the rural tribal elite of the local native administration. The descendants of the slave soldiers formed a racially and socially distinct community. Some continued to pursue the military profession, but with the rise of Arab nationalist politics in the modern Sudan, most faced social exclusion and political marginalization.

The ambiguities of status, which were essential features of the classical institution of military slavery, are evident even in this final transformation from slave soldier to free conscript. Men became soldiers through an initial act of enslavement or capture. The military institutions of which they were a part perpetuated themselves through further acts of enslavement until they were superseded by parallel organizations in which military service was based on a specified term of conscription or voluntary enlistment. The military slaves' personal freedom—whether formally or informally granted—was qualified by the requirement of their continued service in the army. They had access to power by virtue of belonging to the coercive arm of government, but their exercise of power was restricted by physical segregation in separate garrisons or colonies and by social exclusion. Thus they were neither completely servile nor completely free.

See also EGYPT; ISLAM; JANISSARIES; NORTH AFRICA; OTTOMAN EMPIRE; SLAVS.

BIBLIOGRAPHY

AYALON, DAVID. *The Mamluk Military Society: Collected Studies.* 1979.

CRONE, PATRICIA. *Slaves on Horses: The Evolution of the Islamic Polity.* 1980.

HILL, RICHARD. *Egypt in the Sudan, 1820–1881.* 1959.

HILL, RICHARD, and PETER HOGG. *A Black Corps d'Elite: An Egyptian Sudanese Conscript Battalion with the French Army in Mexico, 1863–1867, and Its Survivors in Subsequent African History.* 1995.

HOLT, PETER M. *The Mahdist State in the Sudan, 1881–1898.* 2nd ed. 1970.

JOHNSON, DOUGLAS H. "The Structure of a Legacy: Military Slavery in Northeast Africa." *Ethnohistory* 36 (1989): 72–88.

———. "Sudanese Military Slavery from the Eighteenth to the Twentieth Century." In *Slavery and Other Forms of Unfree Labour,* edited by Leonie Archer. 1988.

MAKRIS, G. P., "Slavery, Possession and History: The Construction of the Self among Slave Descendants in the Sudan." *Africa* 66 (1996): 159–182.

MARSOT, AFAF LUTFI AL-SAYYID. *Egypt in the Reign of Muhammad 'Ali.* 1984.

MEYERS, ALLEN R. "Class, Ethnicity, and Slavery: The Origins of the Moroccan 'Abid." *International Journal of African Historical Studies* 10 (1977): 427–442.

———. "Slave Soldiers and State Politics in Early 'Alawi Morocco, 1668–1727." *International Journal of African Historical Studies* 16 (1983): 39–48.

O'FAHEY, R. S. *State and Society in Dar Fur.* 1980.

PIPES, DANIEL. *Slave Soldiers and Islam: The Genesis of a Military System.* 1981.

SAVAGE, ELIZABETH, ed. *The Human Commodity: Perspectives on the Trans-Saharan Slave Trade.* 1992.

SOGHAYROUN, IBRAHIM EL ZEIN. *The Sudanese Muslim Factor in Uganda.* 1981.

SPALDING, JAY. *The Heroic Age in Sinnar.* 1985.

WEBER, MAX. *The Theory of Social and Economic Organization.* Translated and edited by A. M. Henderson and Talcott Parsons. 1947.

Douglas H. Johnson

African Military Slaves in the Americas

African slaves not only built New World societies but also—throughout the Americas, from the introduction of slavery to its end—defended these societies in conflicts, wars, and issues of social control. Thousands of armed enslaved Africans, along with free blacks and mulattoes, served in the armies and police forces of almost all the colonies, and additional numbers were employed for many other military purposes. However, as David Brion Davis has commented, "Unfortunately, the question of the effects of war on slavery has not received the detailed study it deserves."

Slaves had been used as soldiers much earlier in the ancient world and during the medieval period—for example, in the Roman Empire and the Middle East. They had also been used by monarchs in Africa; in fact, an African ruler was likely to prefer slaves as soldiers because their dependence evoked loyalty and because, through constant training, they had become proficient fighters. For centuries, slaves brought back from black Africa by Arab traders were especially prized as soldiers.

In the Americas too, African slaves and free blacks were valued for their military skills. Some slaves arrived in America as veterans of African armies; sometimes they represented whole units that had been captured in battle. At first, the Spanish and Portuguese (who had a tradition of military slaves dating back to medieval Iberia) used slaves mainly in emergencies, as personal military aides, and as auxiliaries on expeditions. But blacks were so effective as soldiers that many became part of European units fighting in the Americas, some being integrated into white forces and others being formed into their own units; they proved to be skillful and loyal troops.

Military service inspired loyalty in slaves for several reasons. It could lead to liberation from slavery, or at any event from servile treatment. It tended to promote dignity, human rights, and equality, if for no other reason than that in battle there was often little distinction between free and slave. Moreover, the military achievements of slave troops demonstrated to whites—and especially to imperial officers and colonial officials—the humanity and talents of blacks, whether slaves or free. As a result, military service contributed to an earlier end to slavery, and it mitigated discrimination in some postslavery societies. Spanish and British leaders, both military and political, noted the incongruity of a slave's fighting for imperial causes, and proving his superiority as a soldier, while he himself was denied freedom. Some officers reported that they had moderated their personal racism after serving with slave soldiers. And colonists, as well as the slaves themselves, observing white prisoners guarded by proud uniformed, armed blacks, had to reconsider their image of the passive, dominated slave. Free black soldiers also contributed to the undoing of slavery, since many of them had gained their freedom through military service. A war gave slaves a chance to run away and join the enemy; many were recruited with the promise of manumission, which was often fulfilled. In addition, the military fostered integration of units and roles.

For instance, the British West India regiments, made up of black slaves, deeply impressed Caribbean legislatures and planters. Indeed, attitudes changed even in the Confederacy. In 1865, when the Confederate army started enlisting slaves, the Southern politician Howell Cobb acknowledged, "You cannot make soldiers of slaves or slaves of soldiers. . . . The day you make soldiers of them is the beginning of the end of the revolution. If slaves make good soldiers, our whole theory of slavery is wrong." In sum, the military became a liberating institution, not just freeing individual slaves but freeing entire regions from the system of slavery.

Europeans also respected the military talents of Africans who formed communities of escaped slaves, such as the Black Maroons of Jamaica, Cimarrons of Panama, Sambo-Mosquitos of Nicaragua, Esmereldas Zambos of Peru, Black Caribs of Saint Vincent, Bush Negroes of Surinam, and numerous *quilombos* in Brazil. These maroon groups were formidable military entities, and they sometimes allied themselves with colonial forces to catch runaway slaves, fight Indians, and repel foreign invaders. The Europeans much preferred to have maroons as allies than as adversaries.

In time of war, racial consciousness and distinctions between master and slave usually took second place to loyalty, shared ambitions, and expedience. Whites joined enslaved blacks, free blacks, Indians, and people of mixed ancestry to fight other whites, blacks, and Indians.

Initially, the North American colonies armed slaves and free blacks reluctantly, because the English had less experience than the Iberians in trusting slaves. Black troops did fight on both sides in the American Revolution, but later the federal government and the states greatly restricted any military use of blacks. (This was in contrast to Latin America and the Caribbean, where the colonial and imperial authorities and national governments steadily increased their use of black soldiers and, over time, integrated them into white forces.) However, although the American colonies started with many laws forbidding weapons for slaves and free blacks, exceptions quickly devel-

The participation of slaves in the American Revolution is commemorated in Emanuel Leutze's painting of George Washington crossing the Delaware. Prince Whipple (third from the left), a former slave who was emancipated when he joined the army, attended Washington for that crossing on Christmas night 1776. [Corbis-Bettmann]

oped and often became the rule. Slaves were allowed to have weapons to defend a master; or when they were employed as guards, cowboys, hunters, or policemen; or when they were serving in a militia chasing runaway slaves or fighting Indians; or in emergencies, invasions, and wars. As slaves were found to be faithful and effective fighters, more and more trust was placed in them.

When a New World government used armed slaves in an emergency, they were sometimes the crucial factor in victory—as in 1710, when some 7,000 Portuguese and 7,000 armed slaves and free blacks defended Rio de Janeiro from a French invasion; and in the Yamasee war of 1715, when 400 armed blacks, mostly slaves, joined 600 Englishmen to fight Indians. Slaves were also important, fighting on both sides, in many English invasions, including Cartagena in 1585, Santo Domingo and Jamaica in 1654, the French West Indies in 1759, Havana in 1762, and Nicaragua in 1779.

In most colonies African-American slaves were also employed in various paramilitary roles; they were bodyguards, watchmen, military agents, interpreters, overseers, spies, messengers, scouts, guides, trackers, drummers, army suppliers, military servants and nurses, bearers, construction workers, artisans, teamsters, auxiliary soldiers, "pioneers" (army workers attached to units), and sailors on merchant ships and

men-of-war (mainly because often there were too few white sailors). Beyond such service in governmental forces, some free blacks fought as pirates and some blacks fought as slaves of European pirates, becoming known especially as marksmen. Slave and free black soldiers were also used in private armies.

Slaves and Free Blacks in the Militia

In general, the Spanish colonies and Brazil used armed slaves and free black soldiers in militia units sooner, and in greater numbers, than the English, Dutch, or French colonies of North America and the Caribbean. As early as the 1500s, the militias of the Spanish colonies included slaves and free blacks. In 1600 Panama had a free black militia company of 100 men, and other Spanish colonies had comparable units, many with slave troops serving side by side with free blacks. From the 1600s on, Cuba's militias had more free blacks than whites; the Cuban militias were usually separated into black, white, and *pardo* (mulatto) companies. In Peru it was mostly black militia troops who put down a revolt by the Túpac Amarú Indians in 1780. Records from colonial Mexico are filled with accounts of struggles by *pardo* companies and their colored officers for the honors and privileges that they claimed equally with white units.

In Portuguese Brazil blacks were part of the militias early in the 1600s. As in Cuba, the Brazilian militias were normally divided into black, white, and mulatto units, although white companies often had some mulatto troops and even some black and slave troops. Slaves and free blacks in the militia of Pernambuco were decisive in defeating a Dutch invasion in the 1640s, especially the slave company of the famous black officer Henrique Dias. Later, many black companies were called "Henriques" in his honor. In Brazil most officers of black companies were themselves black, but some black officers in white companies were legally white, having had themselves declared so in court. The Portuguese king ordered the integration of all the militias in the 1730s.

In the British West Indies, which had too few whites to defend the islands during the recurrent wars between European colonial powers, blacks often filled the gaps in the militias. By 1660 there were hundreds of armed slaves and free blacks in the militia of English Barbados, equal to the number of whites. By 1800 some separate black companies in Barbados had black noncomissioned officers; by 1830 some had black officers.

The first black officer of an English colonial militia unit was Juan Loyola, a runaway Spanish slave. Loyola had led his ex-slave comrades in defecting to the British when they invaded Jamaica in the 1650s. His reward was freedom and a life appointment as captain of his own free militia company. Jamaica soon had many free blacks enrolled in its militia. The Jamaican black militia helped defeat runaway slaves several times: in the First Maroon War of the 1730s, Tackey's slave rebellion of 1760, and the Second Maroon War of 1795. By the 1790s Jamaica's militia was 40 percent black, and some parishes had a majority of blacks and mulattoes; one of them was two-thirds black. In 1797 Jamaica's militia had 263 white, 92 mulatto, and 31 black sergeants.

Such racial mixing in the military was typical of most of the English colonies in the Caribbean. For example, in the early 1700s Antigua reported that it had 32 "trusty slaves," mostly armed, in each militia unit with "Negro leaders": all had uniforms, received medical attention, and were eligible for ten pieces of eight if wounded and freedom if they "served with distinction." In 1774 smaller islands in the British West Indies had hundreds of free blacks and mulattoes "under arms in the militia," most of them former slaves, many freed for their military service. There were also thousands of armed slaves in special units and slaves who were ready to be armed when needed.

The Dutch colonies of Suriname, Demerara, Essequibo, and Berbice had slaves as rangers, as well as blacks in their militias. By 1823 the militia in Berbice had a majority of black soldiers and some black officers. In almost all these colonies, the militia offered slaves the prospect of both liberation and social mobility.

Massachusetts and Connecticut had some blacks in their militias by 1652, perhaps as slave laborers; Rhode Island had some blacks and free blacks by 1667. In 1708 South Carolina had 950 whites and an equal number of blacks serving in its militia; many of these blacks were armed slaves serving with their masters, and several hundred had been conscripted by the governor from planters in South Carolina or from nearby colonies. In 1704 a law in South Carolina ordered that militia slaves be armed, and also that they be freed for meritorious service—as many were in the Tuscarora and Yamasee Indian wars a few years later. Virginia allowed armed free blacks in its militia by 1730. A century later, however, blacks were barred from southern militia units; in fact, in some states they were barred until the 1890s.

In the French colonies the free black and mulatto militias were the main military force throughout most of the colonial era, but slaves were also sometimes armed to help in defense. In 1693 the governor of Guadeloupe, where there were few free blacks, obtained 300 guns to arm slaves to defend the island—"a milestone in white-black relations," according to one historian, because it was apparently the first large-scale use of armed slaves by the French in the Caribbean. Service in the military was mandatory for free blacks and mulattoes.

Such military experience was probably important in the Haitian revolution. It was used against whites in the 1790s to make Haiti independent; and shortly thereafter it was used by the Haitian mulattoes in their war against the blacks, though the mulattoes failed despite the fact that most Haitian blacks, as slaves, had little militia training. The free black militia of New Orleans had a glorious record under French and Spanish rule in the 1700s and for a few years under the Americans after 1803 before it was pressured out of existence in the 1820s.

Special Professional Military Units of Slaves

To catch runaways, early slave police forces were employed; these were called *cuadrilleros* in Peru and *capitães do mato* (field captains) or bushwackers in Brazil; in the French colonies free black and mulatto officers were called *maréchaussées*. Beyond this, eighteenth-century governors and assemblies in the Caribbean colonies established units of slave troops for special purposes.

In the Maroon wars Jamaica had the Black Shot, companies of armed "trusty" slaves, noted for tracking and bush fighting. In the 1700s, both British and French colonies set up local black corps of armed slaves for defense against each other and other foreign attackers. French Guadeloupe had three such companies in 1701, and Martinique had 3,000 troops in these corps by 1780. During the American Revolution the British formed the South Carolina Corps from slaves fleeing loyalist areas; this unit was taken to the Caribbean to help defend British islands. In the 1770s in his famous account of Suriname—a British-occupied colony—Captain John Stedman highly praised the Black Rangers, which consisted of freed slaves. He described them as "infinitely preferable to the European scarecrows," English soldiers who were mostly sick with fevers. In 1793 Dominica had a Loyal Dominican Black Corps of five hundred slave troops. When the British captured French Domingue—also in 1793—they enlisted slave corps of *chausseurs* in many parishes; examples include the York Cavalry, the Prince of Wales's Regiment, and the Royal Legion. Saint Kitts raised more than 1,000 slaves for defense, in addition to its black and white militias; Tobago formed its Black Yagers.

In the 1790 the English colonies were especially anxious to raise slave corps to repel the French slave forces that were capturing some British islands. Accordingly, the British formed Black Ranger units, mobile slave corps that could be taken where needed to fight throughout the Caribbean. They even formed such units in the French and Dutch colonies they captured, basing the new units on existing slave corps like the Royal Trinidad Rangers and the Dutch South American Rangers and keeping their white and black officers.

Slaves in Regular Forces

Other slaves and free blacks served in regular imperial army units throughout the colonial era, under conditions ranging from integrated artillery units to segregated cavalry companies of blacks. The thousands of slaves, free blacks, and mulattoes who fought for imperial or nationalist forces in the Spanish-American revolutions served with white troops as well as in colored regiments of their own.

Slave officers gained freedom, and then social mobility, more often in Latin countries than in the English colonies. The first record of a black officer in the Americas—a captain—is from 1531 in Peru. A few years later there were two black captains in Chile; there were many more, especially in Cuba, during the 1600s and 1700s. Many of the officers in the Spanish-American revolutions were black, and they included some generals. However, before the 1820s there were few black officers in Brazil or in the French or British

Caribbean, and before World War II there were few in the United States

Slave soldiers achieved the most prestige and the most equal treatment in the British West India Regiments raised in the 1790s to defend Britain's possessions against the French, who were led by the great mulatto general Victor Hugues and employed slaves widely in their forces. The British organized these regular imperial army units entirely of slaves purchased directly off ships from Africa, because many white soldiers in the islands were dying of malaria and yellow fever—tropical diseases to which Africans were mostly immune. The English had found their colonial ranger slave forces inadequate to confront the French, and the planters were reluctant to see their slaves moved as troops to other islands. New slaves, it was found, could be trained into excellent fighting men under white officers; many of these slaves had experience as warriors in Africa, and all were anxious to avoid plantation labor. They received the honorable status of soldiers, equal to white troops with regard to uniforms, weapons, diet, and general treatment; and they retired as free men with military pensions.

Slavery ended in most of Latin America before 1820 and in the British West Indies by the 1830s, and so ended the units made up of slaves. But the emancipated troops of these colonies and new nations continued fighting; actually, their number increased, and again their exploits demonstrated their military skill and their patriotism and contributed to reducing racial prejudice. The West India Regiments eventually became a majority of the British units garrisoning the West Indies; they helped the English forces stop the Atlantic slave trade in Africa and establish British authority there. Like colonial forces in most regions, they fought for the Allies in World War I.

In the nineteenth century, Spanish-controlled Cuba created first a militia company and then an imperial regular unit of free blacks on equal footing with the Spanish army forces, but in Cuba there were few slaves in the military. As the institution of slavery withered away in the 1880s, Brazil's army, consisting significantly of blacks and mulattoes, turned against slavery and refused to enforce the laws concerning it.

In the American Revolution both sides used slave troops successfully; but afterward the United States eliminated almost all slave and free black forces, though black troops and sailors did fight in the War of 1812. The Southern states had almost no black units in the nineteenth century. By contrast, during the Civil War the North (after two years' delay) accepted the enlistment of black troops, two-thirds of whom were runaway slaves; without them, as President Lincoln later said, the Union would not have won the war. Even in the racially charged atmosphere of the United

RECEIPT.

CERTIFICATE OF APPRAISEMENT.

SURGEONS' CERTIFICATE.

NEGRO IMPRESSMENT RECEIPT AND APPRAISEMENT CERTIFICATE DURING THE CIVIL WAR.

A slave impressment receipt and appraisement certificate issued during the U.S. Civil War. [Corbis-Bettmann]

States, the military opened a path to personal freedom for thousands of slaves and—in part through their efforts—won the emancipation of millions more. Some of these freed slave troops went on to become the celebrated Buffalo Soldiers, who fought in the conquest of the American West and in the Spanish-American War. However, the U.S. armed forces were slow to welcome blacks into their ranks, and it was only in the twentieth century that they came to follow the path of integration that had been opened earlier throughout the hemisphere. It should be noted, though, that once the U.S. armed forces did commit themselves to integration, they became probably the institution most likely to foster upward mobility for talented, patriotic blacks.

See also ANCIENT ROME; BRAZIL; CARIBBEAN REGION.

BIBLIOGRAPHY

ANDREWS, GEORGE REID. *The Afro-Argentines of Buenos Aires, 1800–1900.* 1980.

BOWSER, FREDERICK P. *The African Slave in Colonial Peru, 1524–1650.* 1974.

BUCKLEY, ROGER NORMAN. *Slaves in Red Coats: The British West India Regiments, 1795–1815.* 1979.

CAULFIELD, JAMES E. *One Hundred Years' History of the Second West India Regiment.* 1896.

ELLIS, ALFRED BURDEN. *The History of the First West India Regiment.* 1885.

GEGGUS, DAVID P. *Slavery, War, and Revolution: The British Occupation of San Domingue, 1793–1798.* 1982.

KUETHE, ALLAN J. *Military Reform and Society in New Granada, 1773–1808.* 1978.

MCALISTER, LYLE N. *The "Fuero Militar" in New Spain, 1764–1800.* 1974.

MCCLOY, SHELBY T. *The Negro in the French West Indies.* 1976.

MCCONNELL, ROLAND C. *Negro Troops of Antebellum Louisiana.* 1968.

STEDMAN, JOHN. *Narrative of an Expedition against the Revolted Negroes of Surinam.* 1971.

THORNTON, JOHN. *Africa and Africans in the Making of the Atlantic World.* 1992.

VOELZ, PETER M. *Slave and Soldier: The Military Impact of Blacks in the Colonial Americas.* 1993.

Peter M. Voelz

Mill, John Stuart   [1806–1873]

British philosopher.

John Stuart Mill was one of a few British intellectuals who supported the Union immediately following the outbreak of the U.S. Civil War. Many members of the British upper class supported the Confederacy because they either had interests in the manufacture of cotton goods or they held the mistaken notion that the war was a dispute about tariffs. Following the Trent Affair in November 1861, when a U.S. Navy warship boarded a British vessel on the high seas and removed two Confederate officials, prosouthern sentiment swept Great Britain to the point that many advocated declaring war on the United States. Mill understood that slavery had caused the war and strove mightily to convince his fellow countrymen of this fact. In "The Contest in America" (*Fraser's Magazine*, February 1862), he argued that the war was a struggle between good and evil and that the North fought for the cause of righteousness while the South sought to restore slavery into British colonial possessions. He praised John Brown's raid on Harpers Ferry, denied that the South had any more right to secede from the Union than a highwaymen had to avoid punishment for his crimes, and declared that if Great Britain entered the war she should do so on the side of the North.

Mill's persuasive argument influenced many British intellectuals, particularly John Elliott Cairnes. Cairnes's book *The Slave Power* (1862–1863), which diluted considerably the British public's support for the Confederacy and helped to keep Britain out of the war, was dedicated to Mill.

See also BROWN, JOHN.

John Stuart Mill. [Corbis-Bettmann]

BIBLIOGRAPHY

PACKE, MICHAEL ST. JOHN. *The Life of John Stuart Mill.* 1954.

Charles W. Carey Jr.

Miners

This entry includes the following articles: Greek and Roman Mines; U.S. Mines.

Greek and Roman Mines

Greek and Roman mines produced huge profits both for the states that controlled them and for individuals. This wealth played a crucial and well-known role in classical history, but we know little about the slaves who typically worked the mines.

Most famously, public income from the silver mines around Laurium paid for the Athenian fleet that won the battle of Salamis in the Persian War (480 B.C.). From ten to forty thousand slaves may have worked at Laurium during its peak in the fourth century B.C.; recent scholarship tends to favor the lower number. Individual operations at Laurium might have employed only fifty slaves, often rented rather than pur-

chased. The renters paid a daily rate and were responsible for supporting the slaves and maintaining their numbers. The Athenian general and politician Nicias (d. 413 B.C.) owned one thousand of these profitable slaves. The family of Thucydides (late fifth century B.C.) had interests in the gold and silver mines around Amphipolis. These same mines, lost and never recovered by Athens, eventually helped fund Macedonia's rise under Phillip and Alexander the Great. This treatment of Greek mining, however, will concentrate on the better-known and more intensely studied mines at Laurium.

Although Italy was rich in iron, Rome derived its precious metals from its empire. Spain was particularly valuable for its minerals, especially gold and silver. The Romans also acquired and further developed mining operations already begun by the Carthaginians. By the second century B.C. forty thousand slaves were reportedly working in the silver mines of New Carthage alone (Strabo, *Geography* 3.2.10; Diodorus, 5.36). Mining in Roman Spain peaked in the first and second century after Christ and declined in the late empire.

Although some free Athenians may have worked in the silver mines, either alongside their slaves or for hire, our sources, such as Xenophon (*Ways and Means 4*), talk mainly of slave miners. Roman mining, on the other hand, spanned a millennium and a vast and varied empire. Different types of labor, usually forced, were employed. During the empire condemnation to the mines was a punishment for lower-class people convicted of serious offenses; convicts were often transported long distances to mines in need of labor. Prisoners of war and purchased slaves were common and often made up the majority of the mine workers. Wage labor is documented in Spain and in the gold mines of Dacia, modern Transylvania. In the late empire, people were bound to mining, as to other professions.

A relief from near Linares in Spain shows a gang of nine miners going down to work. The tallest man, the overseer, seems to be carrying a truncheon. They all wear leather aprons. One carries a pick, another a lamp. Other tools such as shovels, hammers, chisels, and crowbars have been found. A variety, albeit limited, of tasks can be inferred from these items. In addition, slaves worked screw pumps and waterwheels; drainage was a common problem that evoked some of Rome's most ingenious technology. Finally, comparative studies suggest that more slaves worked at rinsing, processing, and refining the ore than on the mining itself. Although the design of mines was sophisticated, most of the work was unskilled; training seems to have been "on the job." Mine slaves in Athens seem to have been rented at a single standard price.

Condemned criminals and, occasionally, Roman soldiers worked in mines without special training.

In many periods mine slaves were readily replaceable, and they were treated accordingly. Diodorus Siculus (5.38 cf. 3.12–14) describes the working of the Roman mines in Spain: "The slaves working the mines produce for their masters unbelievable wealth, but they wear out their bodies both by day and by night. . . . Many die because of the exceptional hardships they endure." Diodorus details the harsh treatment of mine slaves in a rhetorical condemnation of greed and of the unnaturalness of mining. His claim that the slaves were given no rest, day or night, only reflects that they worked in shifts, probably of about ten hours, around the clock. Conditions also varied depending on the operator, whether state or individual, of the particular mine and the replacement cost of slaves.

Archaeology and other sources, however, generally confirm Diodorus's grim picture of the life and work of slave miners. Shackles are often found. Mine slaves were also typically branded to hinder their escape. In some Roman mines, slaves were even housed underground. Extremely few mine slaves ever recovered their freedom. We can assume the inevitable whips of slavery as well as the truncheon of the Linares relief. At the end of the second century after Christ, Laurium experienced one of the rare slave rebellions of classical antiquity. The mine slaves killed their overseers, seized nearby Suniun, and plundered the countryside until they were suppressed. The substantial military presence around Roman mines was probably aimed as much at keeping the recalcitrant workforce in line as at protecting the valuable ore and metal.

The cramped quarters and poor ventilation of ancient mines were particularly horrible. Some shafts in Laurium were 300 feet deep; Roman mines contain shafts of 650 feet and levels 3,000 feet across. Parallel shafts, cross galleries, and other measures were used to ensure air movement. Nevertheless, the remains of suffocated miners attest to occasional complete failures of ancient technology; discomfort and difficulty breathing must have been common. When the technique of breaking down the rock with fire was used, ventilation became even more difficult. Extremely low and narrow passages also exacerbated this problem. At Laurium, for example, the galleries were never much more than 3 feet high and sometimes as low as 2 feet. Mine slaves had to lie on their backs or sides as they worked. The broken ore then had to be passed hand to hand, since movement was so difficult. The air in these narrow galleries must have been foul with dust from the excavation, and from lamp smoke. From such places and such work came much of the wealth of Greece and Rome.

See also ANCIENT GREECE; ANCIENT ROME.

BIBLIOGRAPHY

DAVIES, J. G. "Diodorus Siculus, iii. 12–14; v. 36–38." *Journal of Hellenic Studies* 75 (1955): 153.
EDMONDSON, J. C. *Two Industries in Roman Lusitania.* 1987.
HEALY, J. F. *Mining and Metallurgy in the Greek and Roman World.* 1978.
LAUFFER, SIEGFRIED. *Die Bergwerkssklaven von Laureion.* 1979.

Peter Hunt

U.S. Mines

Slavery played a critical role in mining ventures across the southern and western United States during the nineteenth century. Southern mine owners, both individual and corporate, rented or owned slaves that proved invaluable in maintaining their operations. From eastern Virginia to the Mississippi Valley to California, black slaves mined coal, lead, and gold. Many of these black miners were unskilled laborers hired away from nearby plantations, but some slaves developed such prodigious mining skills that their owners risked bringing them into free territory when they shifted their operations there. In short, slavery and southern mining became inseparable during the antebellum period.

The first utilization of slave labor in mining occurred in Virginia's eastern bituminous coal fields. The early "coal pits," as they were called in the British fashion, probably began operation in the 1740s. By the beginning of the nineteenth century Virginia was the nation's leading producer of coal—in no small part due to slave labor either owned or hired out by mine operators. The risk of cave-ins and floods, and the presence of toxic atmospheres, fires, and combustible gases made Virginia coal mining a particularly dangerous occupation. A single explosion in 1839 killed forty-five black miners and two white overseers. These risks made the owners of plantations reluctant to lease their slaves for work in the mines, and shortages in the industry's work force—especially of skilled hands—constantly threatened the Virginia's coal industry. Hazardous conditions also affected the management of slaves working in mines. Overseers combined brutal discipline with small incentives such as cash rewards to keep black miners productive, but runaways and the threat of violent uprisings were widespread among bonded miners. Despite the resistance of both owners and slaves to mining, the total number of slaves employed in the coal industry hovered between one and two thousand for most of the antebellum era, and enslaved miners toiled in eastern Virginia's mines through the end of the Civil War.

Western Virginia's antebellum salt industry also depended upon the labor of bondsmen. After the first coal mine opened to supply mineral fuel for salt mining in 1817, the number of slaves in the Kanawha Valley salt industry increased steadily until it reached its peak of 3,140 slaves in 1850. In fact, the rate of growth of slaves in that area increased much more rapidly than that of the white population. Slaves worked in all facets of manufacturing salt, which included a number of slaves listed by Kanawha Valley firms as "coal diggers." The combination of danger and the demand for experienced hands exacted higher prices in rents and demonstrated the necessity of slave labor in Virginia's salt industry.

Lead mining was another industry that used slave labor extensively. In the early nineteenth century, lead mines in both southwestern Virginia and Missouri employed slaves. By 1819, slaves made up the majority of Missouri's 1,100 lead miners. As lead mining operations spread across the Mississippi Valley, so did the use of slaves. In fact, black slaves mined lead during the industry's early years in northwestern Illinois and southwestern Wisconsin. When they first migrated to those areas, southern entrepreneurs found that the skill and experience of their slaves outweighed the risk of bringing them to free territory.

The gold rush in western North Carolina of the 1820s and 1830s created another center of slave mining. In 1833, for example, one county in North Carolina alone saw five thousand slaves used in gold mining. The use of slave labor combined well with the boom and bust cycle of gold mining—owners could move their bonded miners with them from field to field. For example, when the gold mines in western North Carolina failed, mine operators simply shifted their entire operation to newly opened gold fields in eastern Virginia, northern Georgia, and even California. By the 1850s, several hundred slaves worked in the gold fields of California, and the successful relationship between slavery and mining became a favorite argument for southern politicians in favor of extending slavery to western territories. Even after California entered the United States as a free state in 1850, some slave labor persisted in the gold regions, as the bonded miners were purposely kept uninformed of their situation.

The compatibility of slavery and mining continued to surface during the political debate between southern expansionists and free soilers of the 1850s, but the commitment to slavery among mine operators themselves seemed more a matter of economic efficiency than racial ideology. Unfortunately, little is known about the attitudes and experiences of those who actually worked in the mines. The prevalence of cash incentives for enslaved miners suggests that owners placed a high value upon their labor, but the constant presence of runaways also indicates that despite their efficiency, black slaves often resisted working in the mines.

See also INDUSTRIAL SLAVES; UNITED STATES.

BIBLIOGRAPHY

INSCOE, JOHN CUNNINGHAM. *Mountain Masters, Slavery and the Sectional Crisis in Western North Carolina.* 1989.
LAPP, RUDOLPH M. "The Negro in Gold Rush California." *Journal of Negro History* 49 (April 1964): 81–98.
LEWIS, RONALD L. *Coal, Iron, and Slaves. Industrial Slavery in Maryland and Virginia, 1715–1865.* 1979.
STAROBIN, ROBERT S. *Industrial Slavery in the Old South.* 1970.
STEALEY, JOHN E., III. *The Antebellum Kanawha Salt Business and Western Markets.* 1993.

Sean Adams

Minnesota

Although the Missouri Compromise and Northwest Ordinance declared the territory that is now Minnesota free, this region was not isolated from slavery. Slaves passed through the region with southern businessmen and with southern families on vacation. Army officers stationed at Fort Snelling, on the confluence of the Mississippi and Minnesota Rivers, also brought slaves, and few white residents questioned the presence of enslaved men and women at the army post. The post's first commander, Colonel Josiah Snelling, kept a slave to wait on his family, and other officers hired out and sold slaves to one another. Slaves who lived there, however, doubted the legality of their enslavement and filed lawsuits that challenged their status as slaves in a free territory.

The most famous such lawsuit was that of Dred and Harriet Scott, who lived at Fort Snelling for two years as slaves belonging to the army post's surgeon. Even before the Scotts' landmark case was heard by the Supreme Court, however, another Fort Snelling slave, named "Rachel," argued in court that her time at the army post made her a free woman. Her case made its way to the Missouri Supreme Court, which in 1836 ruled in Rachel's favor and set her free.

Slavery also became entangled in the issue of Minnesota statehood. Congressional debate over the future of slavery in the Kansas and Nebraska territories delayed Minnesota's admission to the Union in the 1850s. Even after Minnesota achieved statehood in 1858, with a constitution that prohibited slavery, abolitionism was not unanimous in this state whose settlers were a mix of emigrants from New England and from the South. Slavery divided candidates in the first election of state officials, while proprietors of Minnesota's hotels and resorts objected to antislavery laws that would alienate southern patronage. Outspoken abolitionists such as Reverend Henry M. Nichols and Jane Grey Swisshelm, editor of the *St. Cloud Visitor*, were frequently targets of proslavery backlash, which included the destruction of Swisshelm's newspaper offices in 1858. The Civil War brought new hope for Minnesota abolitionists, however, who successfully pushed the legislature to condemn proslavery southern secessionists in January 1861.

See also DRED SCOTT V. SANDFORD; KANSAS-NEBRASKA ACT; MISSOURI COMPROMISE; NORTHWEST ORDINANCE.

BIBLIOGRAPHY

BLEGEN, THEODORE C. *Minnesota: A History of the State.* 1975.
HESS, JEFFREY A. "Dred Scott: From Fort Snelling to Freedom." *Historic Fort Snelling Chronicles* no. 2 (1975): 1–6.
KLEMENT, FRANK. "The Abolition Movement in Minnesota." *Minnesota History* 32 (1951): 15–33.

Amy E. Murrell

Miscegenation

Though Europeans and Africans engaged in sexual activity with one another from their earliest years of contact in the fifteenth century, only in 1864 did David Croly, a journalist, coin the term "miscegenation" to refer to such activity, in a piece of campaign propaganda for the Democratic Party in its efforts to defeat Abraham Lincoln's bid for reelection as President of the United States. Prior to 1864 Euro-Americans in the United States generally referred to this kind of sexual contact as "amalgamation." It is wholly appropriate that "miscegenation" was invented in the United States, as sexual connections between people of European and African descent could have been an issue of concern only in American societies where Americans constructed artificial categories and hierarchies of "race" as foundations for their slave-based socioeconomic orders. Without the notion that race defined human differences justifying a condition of servitude, sexual activity between human beings of different skin colors would have been entirely irrelevant.

Until sometime in the seventeenth century, Europeans premised their own sense of superiority to Africans primarily upon religious rather than racial distinctions. Clearly, Africans had darker skin and different physiognomies than Europeans, but Europeans originally found African non-Christian religious beliefs more disturbing to their sensibilities than the relative degree of melanin in African skin or the variance of African facial features from their own. Over the course of the seventeenth and eighteenth centuries, as Euro-American colonists took increasing advantage of the economic opportunities offered by the perceived efficiency of using Africans as chattel slaves, and as increasing numbers of Africans converted to Christianity, Europeans developed the idea that Africans comprised an entirely distinct "race" of people, easily justifying the notion that Africans were also an "inferior" race by the (circular) logic that their enslavement in the Americas proved their inferiority.

Every Euro-American slave society, in the desire to maintain some phenotypically evident distinction between slaves and free people, legally and culturally sanctioned against the sexual "mixing" of whites and blacks that threatened to blur that distinction. But not every society defined the "races" identically, nor did every society attach the same significance to racial difference. Statutes and public perception regarding miscegenation varied accordingly. In the United States, where economic growth (especially in southern states) depended heavily on black slave labor, whites developed a nearly dichotomous black-white racial order in which being black almost always meant being a slave. Whites, wanting to believe in their own absolute control over both their slaves and their sexual urges, feared the racial intermixture, which demonstrated the breakdown of such control and which threatened to undermine the unequal socioeconomic order they had so carefully built. While whites failed to stop interracial sexual activity, they frowned severely upon miscegenation as an impure mixing of races meant to remain separate. They supported cultural condemnation with legal regimes that, by the end of the seventeenth century, expressly forbade interracial marriages and financially or physically punished whites caught engaging in sexual activity with blacks.

In Latin American societies, however, a high degree of racial intermixture existed within and between the European, African, and Native American populations (the last of which was much larger in Central and South America than in North America). This intermixture preceded race-based definitions of difference and blurred the later association of color with social control. The Europeans in these societies constructed more flexible orders, recognizing numerous intermediate somatic categories between "white" and "black." While elite Latin Americans frowned upon sexual relations with lesser orders, the complexities of racial hierarchies in these societies and the inexact correlation between race and slavery made it more difficult for legislative and judicial officials to define separation on the basis of race and to punish crossing the boundaries by miscegenation.

The status of children produced by interracial sexual liaisons varied by society accordingly. Throughout the Americas, women transmitted slave status. In

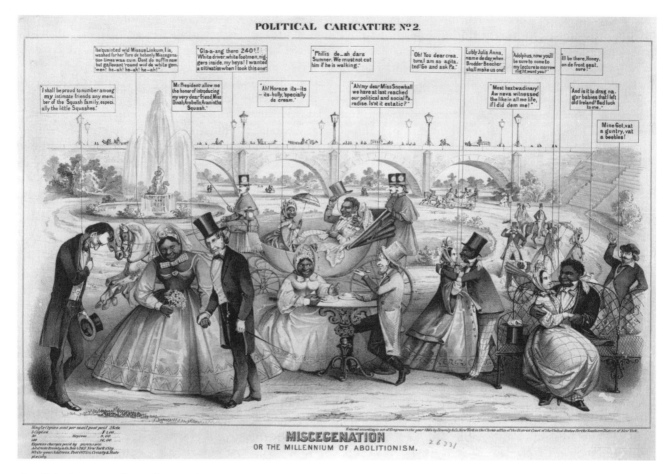

A political cartoon shows the switching of social and economic roles—as well as the rise of interracial marriage (miscegenation)—that opponents of abolition claimed would occur if slavery was ended. [Library of Congress/Corbis]

the United States, miscegenation most frequently involved white slave owners and their female slaves, sometimes yielding a situation where free white men owned their own children. In some cases fathers favored or emancipated these "mulatto" children, and mulattoes were far more likely than individuals of solely African ancestry to be free, educated, and owners of property. But in most cases, whites categorized people of mixed ancestry as nothing other than "black" and presumed them, almost always correctly, to be slaves. Mulattoes generally faced intense hostility from whites, who perceived that their very existence marked white failure to maintain strict racial order. In the many-tiered Latin American societies, meanwhile, people of mixed ancestry manipulated the racial hierarchy to gain social privileges from their lighter skin color.

After the abolition of slavery in every American society, fear and condemnation of sexual intermixture survived as one of that institution's legacies of racism. Though few nations in the Americas currently maintain racial distinctions in their laws, the people of every society continue to confront their own discomfort with interracial sexual relations.

See also GENDER RELATIONS; LAW; SEXUAL EXPLOITATION.

BIBLIOGRAPHY

DEGLER, CARL N. *Neither Black nor White: Slavery and Race Relations in Brazil and the United States.* 1971.

JOHNSTON, JAMES HUGO. *Race Relations in Virginia and Miscegenation in the South, 1776–1860.* 1970.

JORDAN, WINTHROP. *White over Black: American Attitudes toward the Negro, 1550–1812.* 1968.

WILLIAMSON, JOEL. *New People: Miscegenation and Mulattoes in the United States.* 1980.

Joshua D. Rothman

Missionaries

Missionaries have been a regular part of the history of world slavery. Clerics and lay people alike, from virtually every major world religion, have been involved in the issues raised by buying, selling, and holding human beings in thralldom. Before the advent of the South Atlantic system in the late fifteenth century, Africans and many other indigenous peoples were enslaved on a substantial scale by many Islamized peoples, ranging from the Ottoman Turks of the Mediterranean to the Berber and Arab raiders of the empires of the western Sudan, Ghana, Mali, and Songhay, and their rivals and successors, in wars and sieges that were frequently portrayed as having a religious dimension. Yet Muslims, be they Arab or non-Arab, did not usher in this series of events. Slaveholding and commerce were key elements of the ancient world, flourishing in the Fertile Crescent, the Levant, and the various Mediterranean constituents of the Greco-Roman synthesis, on the one hand, as well as in the great states of Asia, on the other. Thus, no one society or civilization can either claim credit or escape blame for slavery's ubiquity. And it is in the religious realm that the coexistence of slavery and the dissemination of faith traditions promising deliverance from mortal sin or frailty with all its attendant contradictions makes the toil of missionaries so compelling.

Before 1500 Christian missionary activity centered around the concept of containing the enemies of Christendom, the most powerful of which were practitioners and proselytizers of Islam. In literal and figurative combat with Muslim armies throughout the Crusades, Christian kings, typically in tandem with the Bishop of Rome (or pope) in the West and his allies in the East, crafted strategies to stave off Islamic influence in Europe and to retake Jerusalem.

Preoccupied by "barbarians" in their own backyard and fearful of Muslim encroachment beyond their borders, the leaders of Christendom built upon the established tradition of proselytism, which had formed a vital part of the activities of the early Christians, especially the companions of Jesus, the Twelve Apostles. In and out of the clergy true believers close to the seats of power in the capitals of the Christian states began to form societies intended to spread the gospel and recruit supporters beyond the boundaries of Christendom's core.

In the course of this endeavor, some came to believe that somewhere past the limits of the world they knew there existed a kingdom which was led by a Christian called Prester John. Some felt this kingdom lay in Asia, while others were convinced it was in east Africa, perhaps in Ethiopia, a land about which Europe had knowledge: Italy sent missionaries there on a quest for allies that both succeeded and failed. It succeeded, for two Italian Christians did, in fact, reach the Ethiopian court; it failed when the monarch elected not to allow them to return home for several years, and one perished in captivity. This search

formed part of the background for the broader desire of Prince Henry the Navigator of Portugal's House of Avis to find a way around Islamic influence in the Mediterranean by looking first at the West African coast as he contemplated securing a passage to the Indies.

After 1500 Portugal experienced its *século maravilhoso* ('marvelous century'), as its maritime innovations led it to a position of prominence in the establishment of what Charles Boxer termed a "seaborne empire." Beginning with the conquest of Ceuta in 1415, and in stages over the next two decades, ships flying Portuguese colors made their way down the Atlantic coast of Africa. By the end of the fifteenth century, these had made contact with Benin in present-day Nigeria and Kongo in present-day Angola and by the early sixteenth century had established factories, or trading posts, on the Indian Ocean coast of southeast and eastern Africa en route to the Indies. Imposing liabilities to trade, these voyages were accompanied by clerics who hoped to convert the indigenes to Christianity. As the merchants, or factors, on the coast insinuated themselves into local society, they also often purchased "surplus" persons, typically those captured in warfare or guilty of social crimes. It was not unknown for clerics to engage in this lucrative commerce, even if ostensibly proselytizing.

Meanwhile, Portugal's sometime rival, sometime ally, and sibling Catholic kingdom, Spain, was carving out spheres of influence in the New World, using missionaries to help as well. In short order, ecclesiastical debates ensued over whether indigenes in the New World and Africa had souls (Juan Ginés de Sepúlveda vs. Bartolomé de las Casas) and, therefore, what should be the church's attitude toward enslaving this or that "heathen" group. Sepúlveda felt that Indian enslavement via "just war" was morally right; in Mexico Las Casas earned plaudits for his ringing defenses of beleaguered Native Americans; Africans, however, found few defenders at this stage and thus continued to be regarded as well-suited for enslavement.

The Spanish sought to convert Native Americans even as they enslaved them, these two trends occurring simultaneously in the fifteenth and sixteenth centuries. Dominican friar Bartolomé de Las Casas suggested that Africans be used in lieu of Native American slaves in order to forestall the obliteration of the Caribs; in time, however, Las Casas became an advocate of black conversion, emerging as the first important critic of slavery in the Spanish Empire.

Portugal, whose African sphere was protected by the 1494 Treaty of Tordesillas and the Line of Demarcation, did "plant" Christianity in the Kongo kingdom in the early 1500s, but this created as many problems as it solved, for it both exacerbated preexisting factional tensions in and beyond the Kongo court and was neutral on slaving. In fact, Portuguese traders were far more effective in supporting and expanding the sale of Africans in Kongo and elsewhere, in spite of occasional conversions; missionary labors in Africa had to await the advent of the second Great Awakening in the latter eighteenth century.

With England's entry in the New world and a globalization of the European system between the sixteenth and eighteenth centuries, when slaving was vital, the contradiction between human sale and the quest for human souls struck many as galling. While the overall humanitarian dimension of this should not be exaggerated, several societies sprang up to share the "good news" of Christianity, including the Society for the Preservation of the Gospel in Foreign Parts (SPG, later known as the Society for the Promotion of Christian Knowledge or SPCK), which, initially interested in Native Americans, subsequently turned its attention to Africa and the conversion of African slaves in the English New World. After Mungo Park's expedition in the late eighteenth century, more and more missionary societies, first and foremost in England, then across Europe, and later in North America, began to follow suit, linking humanitarian and spiritual concerns, especially trying to undo some of the damage wrought by African slave trading. This found reflection in the establishment of Sierra Leone in the last quarter of the eighteenth century by British antislave interests, who saw Christ, commerce, and industry as means to end slavery. Cinqué (Singbe), leader of the rebellion on the slave ship *Amistad,* returned to Sierra Leone as a missionary in 1842. Sponsored by the Union Missionary Society, started by blacks in Hartford, Connecticut, Cinqué's missionary companions established the American Missionary Association.

The emergence of a very different American Colonization Society (ACS) gave rise to a somewhat similar social experiment, the adjacent resettlement colony of Liberia. Whereas Sierra Leone was envisioned by British humanitarians as a step on the way to ending Britain's involvement in the Atlantic slave trade, Liberia's colonists were spurred by an unlikely alliance of pro- and antislave elements, who shared a pessimism about the future prospects of freedpeople within the boundaries of the United States. There the resemblance between these two contiguous resettlement colonies ended. Yet the ACS did play a part in the expansion of Christianity in Africa undertaken by proselytizers of African descent, an early instance of the indigenization of what for most would long remain an alien religious tradition. Recaptives James "Holy" Johnson and Samuel Ajayi Crowther, both Yoruba former slaves born in western Nigeria, rose to become Protestant Bishops after "seasoning" terms in Sierra Leone, staging area for Nigeria's Christian missions (though the former eventually broke away to pursue an independent interpretation of the gospel emphasizing what he termed the "African Personality," while the latter conformed to an early colonial standard). This thrust, along with the mid-nineteenth-century zeal to "discover" Africa, led missionaries from all over Europe and the United States into Africa, the most famous being the Scot David Livingstone, whose endeavor to substitute "legitimate" or "free trade" for slaving inspired countless imitators in the British Isles and beyond and made his life legendary.

More than mere proselytism; however, as laudable as were the examples set by some missionaries, their success or failure was often more the result of local conditions than the strength of their appeals. Those Africans most susceptible to the blandishments of conversion were slaves, persons who had lost faith in the strength of their institutions or who found themselves removed from the social settings in which their lineages or descent groups, the building blocks of African society, were sources of esteem and social power. Many missionaries were often effective because their compounds were protected from the depredations of slave raids, and the price for their protection was frequently conversion.

David Livingstone, Scottish explorer and medical missionary, reads the Bible to two African men in 1874. [Corbis-Bettmann]

Missionaries both spurred and retarded social progress in contradictory utterances and behavior. Some noted missionaries served as apologists for slavery, claiming that the peculiar institution was actually beneficial for Africans, delivering them from "barbarism" and "heathen ignorance." Indeed, both Africans and African-Americans were often swayed by this curious type of logic. Among the more remarkable of Africa's missionary pioneers was Johannes Capitein, enslaved in what is now Ghana, West Africa, in the seventeenth century. Manumitted and baptized as a Dutch Reformed Church cleric, the mature Capitein wrote an eloquent, deeply ironic defense of African enslavement stressing this notion of deliverance. Similar themes appeared in sermons and texts by African converts like the late-eighteenth-century slave mariner and later British abolitionist Olaudah Equiano and myriad African-American missionaries well into the twentieth century. Among the latter was the distinguished pan-Negro and pan-African theorist Bishop Alexander Walters, who argued that "a Divine Providence" brought Africans to America as slaves so that their progeny might return to spread Christianity and thus contribute to the "uplift" of the black race. This messianic impulse, by which Africa's overseas diaspora returns to rescue it, a central theme of twentieth-century black nationalist thought, was most certainly at least partially rooted in slavery.

See also CHRISTIANITY; EQUIANO, OLAUDAH; LAS CASAS, BARTOLOMÉ DE; SLAVE TRADE.

BIBLIOGRAPHY

ALLISON, ROBERT J., ed. *The Interesting Narrative of Olaudah Equiano Written by Himself.* 1995.

BOXER, CHARLES R. *The Portuguese Seaborne Empire, 1415–1825.* 1969.

JONES, HOWARD. *Mutiny on the* Amistad: *The Saga of a Slave Revolt and Its Impact on American Abolition, Law and Diplomacy.* 1987.

LUNENFELD, MARVIN, ed. *1492, Discovery, Invasion, Encounter. Sources and Interpretations.* 1991.

THOMAS, HUGH. *The Slave Trade: The Story of the Atlantic Slave Trade, 1440–1870.* 1997.

THORNTON, JOHN. *African and Africans in the Making of the Atlantic World, 1400–1680.* 1992.

WALTERS, ALEXANDER. *My Life and Work.* 1917.

David H. Anthony III

Mississippi

In 1860 the United States had 3,953,760 slaves out of a total population of 31,443,321 persons. Slavery was practiced in only fifteen of the thirty-three states and by little more than 20 percent of the South's 8,099,760 whites. But in Mississippi, one of the country's most rural and heaviest slaveholding states, nearly one-half of the families held slaves.

In 1802 Georgia gave up its claim to its western territories, which included Mississippi, and Mississippi was admitted into the union on 10 December 1817, with "no prohibition against slavery." Two-thirds of Mississippi remained unsettled by whites as late as 1820, and some of the interior was still frontier in 1850. Between 1820 and 1850 white settlers from the eastern states rushed into the soil-rich region. Mississippi was hot and humid, with adequate rainfall, and there was seldom any freezing weather, snow, or ice. By 1860 more than half of Mississippi was occupied, mostly by cotton growers whose slaves outnumbered them and accounted for 55.2 percent of the state's population. At over $800 apiece, Mississippi's slaves were worth $550 million in 1860.

By 1860 slave gangs were common in the deep South, including Mississippi. Some 49.2 percent of the families in Mississippi owned slaves. Slaveholders averaged 14.1 slaves per owner. Half the owners held 6 or more slaves, 20 percent owned 15 to 47 slaves, 5 percent held 50 to 199, and 0.12 percent owned 200 or more. One planter owned 500.

Slaveholding was especially heavy in the delta of the Mississippi River. The Yazoo delta was an alluvial bed, a basin of 7,065 square miles, some 4,520,600 flat acres derived from Mississippi River mud deposits. Between 1819 and 1860 swamps were cleared and levees built to plant more cotton. Some 43,000 bales of cotton were produced in 1820; the number reached 483,504 bales by 1840. The delta counties had 50 to 90 percent slaves by 1850. Issaquena County had 92 percent slaves in 1860. Slaves outnumbered whites in four counties in the delta, which stretched from south of Memphis to Vicksburg.

Mississippi's slaves often were supervised by white overseers and Negro drivers who made sure that everyone did a full day's work picking cotton. Adult male slaves were expected to pick at least 150 pounds daily; women and teenage slaves were expected to pick at least 100 pounds. Some slaves could pick over 300 pounds. An acre produced one or two bales (400 or more pounds of deseeded cotton), and each slave could produce five to six bales per crop. Because the cotton season lasted most of the year, slaves got some relief only during the brief cold months. Mississippi slaves also worked at building railroads and in textiles, lumber, and cotton gins.

In frontierlike Mississippi the "peculiar institution" was a harsh labor system, a social institution in which slavery and tyranny went hand in hand. The types of slaves included field hands (80 percent of the women; 75 percent of the men), house servants, artisans,

Table 1.   Slave and Free Population of Mississippi, 1800–1860.

	1800	1810	1820	1830	1840	1850	1860
Free blacks	182	240	458	519	1,366	930	773
Slaves	3,489	17,088	32,814	65,659	195,211	309,878	436,631
Whites	5,000	23,000	42,000	70,000	179,000	296,648	354,674
Owners	–	–	–	–	–	23,116	30,943

Source: The Negro in the United States, 1790–1915 (1968).

industrial workers, and a few urban slaves. Slaves began work at sunup and returned to their quarters after sundown. They worked five and a half days or more per week, especially during the cotton harvest season. Four to five slaves usually lived in a one-room cabin of about two hundred square feet, with a central fireplace for heat and cooking. Bedding was straw or feather pallets on the floor, or, rarely, crude post beds made by the slaves. Because of the warm climate, a slave's annual issue of clothing consisted of two hats, two pairs of shoes (heavy "brogans"), and two pairs of pants and two shirts or wool or calico dresses. Negro mortality was higher than that of whites. Infant mortality was especially high because of pneumonia, whooping cough, cholera, bowel disorders, and various other diseases caused by hard work, poor housing, insufficient diet, and often no health care.

Mississippi farmers focused on cash crops and had to import much of the food for the labor force. Because food rationing was more critical on Mississippi's plantations, some masters fed their slaves well, and some did not. Food for slaves consisted of fat pork (bacon), cornmeal, molasses, rice, vegetables (peas, potatoes, and corn), fruits from local orchards when available, and wild game. Sometimes industrious slaves used what money they earned working for neighboring farmers to buy better clothes, some sugar, coffee, and flour. Coffee drinking was common among slaves of all ages. On Mississippi's large plantations, the slaves' life was hard and their life expectancy was short—less than forty-five years.

Because of the whites' Negrophobia—perpetual fear of the Negro majority—Mississippi's laws regarding slavery and race were notoriously harsh. Slave codes required written permission to leave the farm, imposed ten lashes for wandering away, and prohibited possession of firearms, sale of goods to other slaves, and assembly. No area of Mississippi had fewer than 10 percent slaves, and because the Negro majority was a constant threat, Mississippi whites imposed brutal codes, which included death as a com-

mon punishment. Masters in the upper South often issued the unsettling threat to a misbehaving slave that he would be "sold down to Mississippi." Escape was difficult because Mississippi's plantations were many miles apart, and the notorious slave patrols ("patty-rollers") were frequent and brutal in their punishment of blacks. Moreover, the state was surrounded by other slave states and the wide Mississippi River.

The isolated slaves had to create a world of their own beyond reflections of the white families' culture. The slave family served as the foundation for the Negro's survival of slavery. Negroes entertained themselves by sitting outside the cabins after work, singing, dancing, and engaging in religious practices. Most Christian slaves in Mississippi were Methodists and Baptists. Blacks outnumbered whites in the Natchez Baptist Church. Many Muslim slaves were brought from West Africa directly to Mississippi. They were not however, allowed to continue their Islamic religious practices. Ibrahima, a son of Sori, king of the Fulbe people in Guinea, was among the Muslim slaves in Mississippi. Ibrahima had been sold from the import city of New Orleans to Natchez, which was a chief slave market. He was nicknamed "prince" by other slaves and eventually was freed and returned to his country in Africa. Although one planter built a Gothic-style church and hired a preacher for his slaves, most Mississippi slaveholders did not promote religion; some slaves, therefore, had their own secret "brush arbor" churches in the woods.

Negroes yearned for freedom and resisted slavery as best they could—by claiming to be too sick to work, by making mules go lame, and by breaking tools, for example. Some slaves talked back, slowed the pace of work, ran into the woods and stayed there for days, and even conspired to kill their masters. In 1835 twenty-one blacks and whites were hanged for an alleged slave conspiracy in Mississippi.

In racially conservative Mississippi there was little antislavery sentiment, hardly any cases of manumission, and few free blacks. Mississippi never had more

A sidewheel steamboat approaches the dock of a nineteenth-century cotton plantation along the Mississippi River. [Library of Congress/Corbis]

than 930 free Negroes, and the numbers declined by 17 percent between 1850 and 1860. Even the small number of urban Negroes suffered a decline. In Natchez blacks numbered 3,031 in 1850 but only 2,138 in 1860. Yet Mississippi had a chapter of the American Colonization Society for the export of manumitted Negroes to Liberia, Africa; Negro settlers named one of the Liberian provinces Mississippi. All of the manumissions in the state of Mississippi took place before fanatical agitation against southern slavery by northern abolitionists began.

In January 1861 Mississippi joined the Confederacy. Some 17,896 Mississippi blacks joined Union army regiments, including the Third U.S. Colored Cavalry, in the nearby Union-occupied states of Tennessee, Arkansas, and Louisiana. On 22 May 1865 Confederate Mississippi surrendered to the Union army. In December 1865 the Thirteenth Amendment to the national Constitution ended slavery, freeing over 436,000 blacks in Mississippi. However, violence by whites and outmigration by slaves caused Mississippi's black population to decline by 12 percent by 1866.

See also CONFEDERATE STATES OF AMERICA; DEMOGRAPHY OF SLAVES IN THE UNITED STATES; LAW; UNITED STATES.

BIBLIOGRAPHY

ALFORD, TERRY. *Prince among Slaves: The True Story of an African Prince Sold into Slavery in the American South.* 1977.
BRANDON, ROBERT L. *Cotton Kingdom of the New South.* 1967.
GENOVESE, EUGENE D. *From Rebellion to Revolution: Afro-American Slave Revolts in the Making of the Modern World.* 1979.
HARRIS, WILLIAM C. *Presidential Reconstruction in Mississippi.* 1967.
SYNDOR, CHARLES S. *Slavery in Mississippi.* 1933.
WILEY, BELL I., ed. *Slaves No More: Letters from Liberia, 1833–1869.* 1980.

Bobby L. Lovett

Missouri

In 1860, when there were 3,953,760 slaves out of 31,443,321 persons in the United States, Missouri was an Upper South slave state, one in which slaveholding was practiced to a moderate degree. (Slavery was permitted in only fifteen of the thirty-three states, and only a little more than 20 percent of the South's 8,099,760 whites owned slaves.) Missouri was unique, however, because it bordered the free territories of the Northwest. The famous (or infamous) Dred Scott Supreme Court case (1857) was centered around a Missouri slave family.

The first black codes in the Missouri territory were introduced in 1724 and 1769 under the Spanish. In 1803, when the territory was purchased from France, blacks, mostly slaves, made up 1,320 of Missouri's 10,340 inhabitants. Slaves were brought into Missouri by white settlers from Kentucky, Tennessee, and eastern slave states. Missouri had a southern flavor also because by 1850 not more than 20 percent of its population consisted of European immigrants. When Congress formally admitted Missouri to the union in March of 1821, the state's constitution forbade any legislative interference with slavery.

Slave gangs were not common in Missouri, where the average holding of slaves was only 5.7 persons in 1860. Slaves represented no more than 2 percent of the total population of the north end of the state. They were most numerous in the river lands (3 to 27 percent of the population), moderate in numbers in central Missouri, and least common in the mountainous areas. Missouri slaves mined lead and iron deposits and raised tobacco, hemp, corn, cattle, other livestock, wheat, and some cotton in the extreme southeast counties. The largest slave plantations were in Sainte Genevieve and Cooper counties.

The settlement of Missouri was marked by an effort to extend the plantation system into a place not really suited to the cultivation of staple crops. Unfavorable climate and soil, especially for growing large amounts of cotton, forced owners to sell surplus slaves to the cotton belt states, making Missouri a slave-exporting state, like Kentucky and Tennessee. In 1860 24,320 owners (12.7 percent of white families) held 114,931 slaves (9.7 percent of Missouri's total population). Slaves cost $800 to $1,000 each and rented for between $100 and $150 a year. Many slaves were hired for mining operations. Slave-hiring practices were common in Saint Louis, where blacks worked in the steamboat and shipping industries. The types of slaves included field hands (80 percent women; 75 percent men), house servants, artisans, and industrial and urban workers.

A slave's day began at sunup and ended after sundown. In the industries of cotton and tobacco, the slaves worked five and a half days or more per week, especially during harvest time. Four to five slaves usually shared one-room cabins measuring about 200 square feet, with a central fireplace for heat and cooking. Bedding was usually straw or feather pallets on the floor, but crude post beds were occasionally made by the slaves. Annual issues of clothing were typically two hats, two pairs of shoes, and two pair of pants and two shirts or wool or calico dresses.

Slaves frequently used money they earned to buy additional clothing and a few luxury items when visiting local towns. One slave recalled that he and his fellows used what money they earned to buy Sunday clothes, sugar, coffee, and flour (they drank coffee everyday and had biscuits once a week). Blacks and their children suffered and died more often than whites from pneumonia, whooping cough, cholera, and bowel disorders. These and other diseases were caused by hard work, poor housing, inadequate diet, and poor health care. Some masters fed their slaves well, and some did not. Mattie J. Jackson, a Missouri slave, recalled that her stepfather was sold after asking for adequate food to feed his family of six. Food for slaves consisted of fat pork (bacon), corn meal,

---

Table 1. Slave and Free Population of Missouri, 1810–1860.

	1810	1820	1830	1840	1850	1860
Free blacks	607	347	569	1,574	2,618	3,572
Slaves	3,011	10,222	25,091	58,240	87,422	114,931
Whites	17,000	56,000	115,000	324,000	592,662	1,063,081
Owners	–	–	–	–	16,781	24,320

Source: The Negro in the United States, 1790–1915 (1968).

molasses, some vegetables (peas, potatoes, and corn), fruits from local orchards, and rabbits, fish, and opossums, among other wild game.

Slaves created a world of their own. They entertained themselves by sitting outside the cabins after work, singing, dancing, betting on cock fights and horse races, gambling, having parties, and holding religious services. Not only did slaves attend church with religious masters, many blacks held their own religious services in secret places called brush arbors. Blacks in Saint Louis had two separate churches by 1850.

Free blacks were always present but unwanted in the Missouri territory. The new state constitution granted licenses for them to remain in Missouri but prohibited the exercise of voting privileges. Free blacks had no civil rights and were required to carry "free papers." Any new migration of free blacks into Missouri was prohibited. Yet many of Missouri's free blacks lived in the busy port city of Saint Louis, where they and the urban slaves drove drays or served as barbers, cooks, house servants, laundresses, artisans, common laborers, or boat hands. Between 1820 and 1860 the free black population grew to 1,046, or 2.6 percent of the total population of Saint Louis. By 1860 free blacks numbered only 3,572 (3 percent) of Missouri's black population.

After the Civil War newly freed slaves migrated to St. Louis, where they were warmly welcomed by the city's black residents, many of whom had lived there as free people. [Corbis-Bettmann]

Slavery in Missouri denied personal freedom and encouraged racism. The Missouri slave codes required that slaves obtain written permission to leave the farm, and ten lashes were administered as punishment for wandering away. Slaves were prohibited from owning firearms or selling possessions to other slaves. Assemblies were banned, and slave patrols were used to control the slave population—though they were much less frequent in Missouri than in Mississippi, for example. Still, the slaves resisted these harsh and inhumane conditions however they could: they broke their tools, slowed the work pace, made trouble in the slave quarters, feigned sickness, ran away for days on end, and sometimes even assaulted their masters. Whenever possible, they did extra work to earn enough money to buy their own freedom and that of their relatives.

Antislavery societies and a free-labor movement sought either to end slavery or at least to stop its expansion in Missouri. For a time, masters could manumit slaves and resettle them in free states. There was an active Missouri Emancipation Society by the 1860s. Abolitionist John Brown and Underground Railroad operators helped many Missouri slaves to escape to adjacent free states, especially Iowa and across the river to Illinois.

During the Civil War Missouri remained in the Union. Some 8,344 blacks from Missouri served in the Union army. Slavery was ended in Missouri by state proclamation on 11 January 1865.

See also BROWN, JOHN; DRED SCOTT V. SANDFORD; KANSAS; MISSOURI COMPROMISE; UNITED STATES.

BIBLIOGRAPHY

BRYAN, JOHN A. "The Blow Family and Their Slave Dred Scott." *Bulletin of the Missouri Historical Society* 4 (1948): 223–231.

OBERHOLZER, EMIL. "The Legal Aspects of Slavery in Missouri." *Bulletin of the Missouri Historical Society* 6 (1949): 139–160, 333–351, 540–546.

TREXLER, HENRY A. *Slavery in Missouri, 1804–1865.* 1914.

Bobby L. Lovett

Missouri Compromise

In 1803 the Louisiana Purchase gave the United States a vast expanse of western land. The treaty guaranteed the right of its residents, most of whom lived in the southernmost quarter, to own slaves, and in 1812 Louisiana was admitted to the union as a slave state. The question of whether slavery should be permitted in the sparsely populated northern reaches of the Purchase remained unanswered until 1819, when the territory of Missouri, of whose residents approximately one-sixth were slaves, applied for statehood. Northern

Congressmen, fearful that the North's free labor system would be overwhelmed politically and economically if slavery were allowed to spread throughout the Purchase, refused to admit Missouri unless it amended its constitution to provide for gradual emancipation. In retaliation, when the northern part of Massachusetts applied for admission as the state of Maine later that year, southern Congressmen threatened to defeat its statehood bill.

In 1820 the impasse was solved when the Missouri Compromise, a single bill proposing the admission of Missouri as a slave state and Maine as a free state, passed the Senate. The bill also prohibited slavery in the Purchase north of 36°30′, Missouri's southern border, a provision that was debated hotly in the House of Representatives before passing that body.

The Missouri Compromise governed the expansion of slavery in the United States until 1850, when attempts to organize the Mexican Cession gave rise to the concept of popular sovereignty, whereby a territory's status as slave or free was determined by its residents rather than Congress.

See also COMPROMISE OF 1850.

BIBLIOGRAPHY

FEHRENBACHER, DON E. *Sectional Crisis and Southern Constitutionalism.* 1995.

Charles W. Carey Jr.

Modern Middle East

From the perspective of the Middle East, the "modern" period begins in the early nineteenth century. With regard to slavery, the modern Middle East turned increasingly to slave workers at the same time that "modernity" in western Europe and the Americas meant replacing slaves with free and contract workers. In the Ottoman Empire, including its semi-independent Egyptian province, and in Safavid and Qajar Persia (contemporary Iran) at that time, merchants and entrepreneurs responded to growing commercial prosperity by developing very old Muslim practices of slavery in the region not only to increase production but also to surround themselves with servants who could enhance the comfortable lifestyles they enjoyed from their profits.

As the merchants and landholding notables prospered on their growing trade with Europe, they distanced themselves from the ruling authorities (Ottoman sultans and Persian shahs), and they imported increasing numbers of Africans as slaves to support their economic independence. Africans, in particular, were available cheap owing to wars in Africa, sparked by the introduction of modern weaponry, and a "boom" in imports of Africans between 1840 and 1860, which doubled and tripled the numbers of captives reaching the Muslim heartlands. Annual totals rose from the range of five thousand to around fifteen thousand. Those from west and central Africa arrived through Tunisia and Libya (Tripoli and Benghazi), while east Africans came down the Nile through Cairo and Alexandria continuing through Ethiopia to the Red Sea ports, or they came from the Swahili towns of the Indian Ocean coast (Mogadishu, Mombasa, Malindi, and Zanzibar) through the Red Sea and the Persian Gulf. Slaves from southern Asia (the Sind Valley and Baluchistan) also arrived through the Persian Gulf. The Black Sea was the source for Circassians, Georgians, and Armenians; slaves from Central Asia came across the Caspian Sea and overland from Afghanistan. Over a million people may have reached the Middle East as slaves during the nineteenth century.

Early in the nineteenth century entrepreneurs in the Middle East employed these slaves in the growing commercial sectors of the economy: white males in middle-level military and administrative positions and as household guards; African males particularly as soldiers, menial office-staff workers, market porters, and dockworkers—only occasionally as agricultural laborers. Black and white women alike served their masters in domestic capacities as household servants, wet nurses, governesses, and concubines. They gave an aristocratic air to the nouveaux riches of the cities. By the middle of the century, commercial development had spread to agriculture; entrepreneurs then employed slaves in large-scale production of opium, cotton, silk, tobacco, and foodstuffs. Slaves were also set to work digging and maintaining irrigation canals and excavating mines that produced ores for export. International restrictions on imports of central Asians gradually increased the proportion of Africans among domestic slaves. Still, the proportion of slaves in the urban populations was not large by American standards; an 1867 census in Tehran (Qajar Iran) recorded a population of 147,000 among whom 3 percent were male and female "black slaves" and 10 percent were described as domestic servants.

Royal and notable parties, aware of the independent-minded commercial classes thriving in their realms, found it possible to cooperate with European abolitionists in limiting, and then largely eliminating, the trade that fed Middle Eastern slavery during the second half of the nineteenth century. Modern weaponry gradually reduced the reliance of the regimes on the elite corps of slave soldiers that had formerly been typical in the area. In 1846 the Tunisian and Persian regimes both issued formal prohibitions of further imports, followed by the Ottoman sultan in 1857 and Egypt in 1877. Only Arabia failed to act, although several coastal towns there restricted the movement of slaves through their ports. Abolition raised complex political issues throughout the region, since antislavery pressure also came from European sources, such as the Brussels Act of 1890, and endorsement of it seemed to amount to collaboration with foreign imperialist ambitions. Still, by the last decades of the nineteenth century, the annual volume of imports had dropped to around ten thousand, and by the eve of World War I, it is estimated to have been fewer than three thousand slaves each year. High mortality among slaves and failure to reproduce slave children—since Muslims married slave women who bore them children and freed the offspring—reduced the surviving slave population. Tehran's recorded 800,000 residents by that time included fewer than fifteen hundred (0.2%) enslaved Africans.

With the post–World War I consolidation of liberal constitutionalism in the former Ottoman provinces and in Qajar Persia, "new" intermediate classes of professionals, bureaucrats, and military officers brought antislavery policies to the fore in Middle Eastern politics. Pan-Islamic congresses in Cairo in 1926 and again in 1964 in Mogadishu condemned the "evils" of the slave trade and slavery on religious and legal grounds, acknowledging the personal corruption that stemmed from holding slaves and citing the portions of Islamic law (*sharia*) that prescribed "correct" behavior toward fellow Muslims, "strangers," and even "infidels." However, Europe-based international organizations continued to report young African and Indian girls being brought into the region as late as World War II, albeit in small numbers. Saudi Arabia issued its first major decree against slavery and the slave trade in 1962, and Mauritania became the last Muslim nation in the world to abolish legal slavery in 1980.

See also EGYPT; ISLAM; LAW; OTTOMAN EMPIRE.

BIBLIOGRAPHY

CLARENCE-SMITH, WILLIAM GERVASE, ed. *The Economics of the Indian Ocean Slave Trade in the Nineteenth Century.* 1989.
ERDEM, Y. HAKEN. *Slavery in the Ottoman Empire and Its Demise, 1800–1909.* 1996.
GORDON, MURRAY. *Slavery in the Arab World.* 1989.
HOURANI, ALBERT. *A History of the Arab Peoples.* 1991.
LEWIS, BERNARD. *Race and Slavery in the Middle East: An Historical Enquiry.* 1990.
PIPES, DANIEL. *Slave Soldiers and Islam: The Genesis of a Military System.* 1981.
RICKS, THOMAS M. "Slaves and Slave Traders in the Persian Gulf, 18th and 19th Centuries: An Assessment." *Slavery and Abolition* 9, no. 3 (December 1988): 60–70.
SHAW, STANFORD J., and EZEL KURAL SHAW. *History of the Ottoman Empire and Modern Turkey.* Vol. 2, *Reform, Revolution, and Republic, 1808–1975.* 1977.
TOLEDANO, EHUD R. *The Ottoman Slave Trade and Its Suppression: 1840–1890.* 1982.
WILLIS, JOHN RALPH. *Slaves and Slavery in Muslim Africa.* Vol. 1, *Islam and the Ideology of Enslavement.* 1985.

Thomas M. Ricks

Montejo, Esteban   [1860–1973]

Runaway Cuban slave; the subject of an important biographical study.

Born a slave in Cuba in 1860, Esteban Montejo was 103 when he told the story of the first forty years of his life to Miguel Barnet, a Cuban writer now regarded as one of the founders of the testimonial genre (*testimonio*) in Latin American letters. The result of their collaboration was *Biography of a Runaway Slave*, the fascinating first-person account of a man who escaped slavery as a teenager, lived briefly as a maroon in the forests of central Cuba, and, after emancipation, worked as a day laborer on sugar plantations and fought in the rebel forces during the Second War of Independence (1895–1898). The *Biography* is by far one of the richest records we have of life as a slave, a maroon, a just-liberated freedman, and an independence fighter in Cuban, Caribbean, and Latin American history. It is also among the best examples of a genre that allows the marginalized to recount significant details of their lives in their own words.

Displaying an amazingly sharp memory, Montejo recalls poignant events of his life as a child and young adult. He paints a compelling picture of what it was like to be poor and black in late-nineteenth-century Cuba. He tells of the hardships and indignities of slavery on a sugar plantation, but his recollections of slavery are not all bitter. In rich detail, he also recounts the pastimes, ceremonies, courtships, and other pleasures that made the suffering a bit more tolerable. His escape into the forest, he adds, was an act of individual rebellion. Montejo spent an unspecified period living alone in the forest—unlike other maroons, who sought protection and solace in numbers. Although he lacked companionship and suffered great deprivation, he nonetheless portrays this experience as a time of introspection and communion with nature.

Sometime between 1880 and 1886 Montejo came out of the forest and into a world transformed by emancipation. The bulk of the *Biography* focuses on the next fifteen or twenty years of his life. During these years he sold his labor on various sugar estates. He describes in colorful detail the life of freedmen and other waged workers at a time when the abolition of slavery and the adoption of the central mill system were revolutionizing the Cuban sugar industry. During these years Montejo had, by his own account, numerous affairs with women, but, surprisingly, he does not devote more than a few sentences to any of them. His descriptions of Afro-Cuban religious beliefs and practices are more richly drawn, as are his tales of combat action with the revolutionary forces. Especially memorable were his actions under the black general Antonio Maceo.

With commending the *Biography* as an invaluable historical source that helps unlock a critical period in Cuban history, some scholars have recently questioned Miguel Barnet's motives for ending his life story of Esteban Montejo at a relatively early age. In this way, they argue, Barnet avoided, among other things, having to deal with Montejo's later involvement with the Partido Independiente de Color (PIC), an Afro-Cuban party that, in striving for equality with whites, became the object of the Cuban government's scorn and fury. A campaign of repression against the PIC culminated in a massacre of black Cubans in 1912, an episode that few scholars, no matter what position they take on the Cuban revolution of 1959, have been eager to discuss or study. In denying this claim, Barnet has argued that Montejo's life after 1902 or 1904 was unexceptional, or at least reveals much less about the historical experiences of working-class Cubans than does his story of slavery, escape, and armed rebellion.

See also: CUBA; SLAVE NARRATIVES.

BIBLIOGRAPHY

BARNET, M. *Biography of a Runaway Slave.* Rev. ed. Translated by W. N. Hill. 1994.
———. "The Untouchable Cimarrón." *New West Indian Guide/Nieuwe West-Indische Gids* 71, nos. 3 and 4 (1997): 281–289.
ZEUSKE, M. "The Cimarrón in the Archives: A Re-Reading of Miguel Barnet's Biography of Esteban Montejo." *New West Indian Guide/Nieuwe West-Indische Gids* 71, nos. 3 and 4 (1997): 265–279.

Francisco A. Scarano

Montesquieu, Charles-Louis de Secondat de   [1689–1755]

Philosopher and magistrate.

An aristocratic jurist, president of the appeal court of Bordeaux, Montesquieu initiated the Enlightenment's critique of slavery, though with an ambivalence still difficult to interpret. A leading citizen of a

Charles-Louis de Secondat de Montesquieu. [Library of Congress/Corbis]

slave-trading port that served as the booming center of French colonial trade, he wrote curiously little about the contemporary expansion of black slavery and far more about slavery as an abstract concept or as an institution of times past. Although he attacked traditional moral justifications for slavery, his writings provided a new utilitarian one, and like most philosophes he did not advocate abolition.

Montesquieu's satirical *Lettres persanes* (1721) condemned the destructiveness of American slavery but identified it with conditions of work in Spanish mines—not on Caribbean plantations, which he ignored. His book praised the productivity of Roman slavery and adopted an ambiguous stance toward colonization. The encyclopedic *L'espirit des lois* (1748) rejected previous legal and philosophic justifications for slavery, claiming it corrupted slave and owner. Enslavement was not a just alternative to killing war captives, nor a legitimate means for religious conversion. Neither self-sale nor Aristotle's theory of natural slavery had a rational basis. Central to *L'espirit des lois*, however, was a concept of environmental determinism that linked law to climate and led Montesquieu to suggest that the use of slaves was reasonable in tropical climates, where free people supposedly shunned

MORTALITY IN THE NEW WORLD   613

labor. Ironic passages in which he stated that if Africans were fully human, Europeans might cease to appear Christian, have been variously read as powerfully mordant, as frivolous, and by Pierre Pluchon (*Nègres et juifs* [1984]) as genuinely racist. Montesquieu advocated only very limited protections for slaves.

Though preceded by the sixteenth-century theorist Jean Bodin, Montesquieu was the first major philosopher to condemn slavery. Highly respected in the eighteenth century, his name gave authority to subsequent abolitionist arguments, but it was also used by proslavery writers.

See also ENLIGHTENMENT; PERSPECTIVES ON SLAVERY.

JAMESON, RUSSELL P. *Montesquieu et l'esclavage: Étude sur les origines de l'opinion antiesclavagiste en France au XVIII siécle.* 1911.

LAFONTANT, JULIEN J. *Montesquieu et le problème de l'esclavage dans l'Espirit des lois.* 1979.

David Geggus

Mormons

See Latter-day Saints, Church of Jesus Christ of; Utah.

Morocco

See North Africa.

Mortality in the New World

As more detailed demographic information has become available on slave regimes in the Western Hemisphere, a central problem has emerged: why did the slave population of the United States grow at a rapid rate, doubling from natural increase roughly every thirty years, while those elsewhere failed to reproduce their numbers? Both fertility and mortality contributed, but differential mortality was probably the most important factor.

Mortality rates and average stature summarize health conditions. Little direct information is available on slave mortality prior to the nineteenth century because vital registration systems often did not exist and few plantation documents describing births or health have survived. Thus, much of our knowledge is confined to the later years of the institution, when various registration systems were designed to monitor slavery.

Given the diversity of circumstances in the Western Hemisphere, it is not surprising that the health of slaves varied considerably by time period and colony.

Prior to the eighteenth century, colonies outside North America experienced an excess of deaths over births as high as 5 percent, suggesting a crude death rate as large as 7 or 8 percent, and possibly more. Slave mortality was particularly high in frontier colonies, where a large inflow of imports from Africa was needed to achieve population growth. In most colonies, however, the natural increase of the slave population remained negative until emancipation. Rates of natural decrease were also lower in colonies such as Jamaica and the Bahamas, where the climate was less tropical.

In the United States slave population, births exceeded deaths by the early 1700s, and near the end of the century the rate of natural increase approached 2 percent. Demographic models estimated from census data suggest that the crude death rate may have been 3.5 to 4.0 percent in the nineteenth century.

Evidence from stature confirms the general pattern of health observed in mortality rates. Average height, which measures a population's history of net nutrition (diet minus claims on the diet made by maintenance, disease, and work), is a sensitive indicator of health. As adults, slaves in the United States attained 159 centimeters (females) to 171 centimeters (males), which placed them near the twentieth percentile of modern National Center for Health Statistics (NCHS) height standards (the U.S. children were much smaller, falling below the first percentile of the same standards). In the Caribbean, native-born women were 153 to 156 centimeters and men were 162 to 164 centimeters, or in roughly the first to the eighth percentile of NCHS standards.

Explanations for the different health experiences include the effect of the disease environment, work, and diet. Some medical care, such as smallpox inoculations, may have been beneficial, but physicians and midwives who lacked knowledge of the germ theory of disease also spread infections. Several studies reveal a strong association between the main crop grown by slaves and mortality rates. In the Caribbean, deaths were often much higher on sugar plantations compared with those occurring on cotton plantations, and within the United States, mortality rates were higher on rice and sugar farms as opposed to those where cotton or tobacco were grown. The general link between mortality and labor on sugar plantations points to hard work as an important factor, but the connection with rice farming indicates that low, swampy areas also adversely affected health. Whatever the underlying mechanism, the lack of sugar production and the minor role of rice farming in the United States were boons for health.

The slave diet was almost certainly better in the United States. With abundant land resources, food was relatively cheap and the types of foods available were often quite diverse, nutritionally rich combinations of Old and New World products. In contrast, most of the arable land in the sugar colonies was devoted to cane production, and planters therefore relied significantly on food imports, mainly from the United States. As a result, the slave diet was less varied, was more expensive, and probably lost nutritional value during shipment and storage.

Contrasting economic histories were also relevant for slave mortality. Europe's sweet tooth fueled a rapid growth of the sugar industry, and to keep up with growing demand they acquired colonies, imported slaves, and cleared land. After very difficult journeys, the slaves often arrived in poor health, and this combined with hard work on sugar plantations and encounters with new diseases in the Western Hemisphere led to high mortality rates. To keep up with ever-growing demand, even more slaves were imported, which further elevated death rates.

Unable to produce commercial quantities of sugar until the 1820s (and then only in southern Louisiana), the colonial economy of the southern United States emphasized tobacco and, to a lesser extent, rice. Unlike the demand for sugar, the demand for these products grew slowly. Cotton eventually became king in the nineteenth century, but only after the slave trade was closed in 1808. Thus, the United States imported few slaves, and most of the health problems associated with rapid importation were avoided.

See also DEMOGRAPHY AND DEMOGRAPHIC THEORIES OF SLAVERY; DEMOGRAPHY OF SLAVES IN THE UNITED STATES; FOOD AND COOKING; HEALTH.

BIBLIOGRAPHY

FOGEL, ROBERT WILLIAM. *Without Consent or Contract.* 1989.
HIGMAN, BARRY W. *Slave Populations of the British Caribbean, 1807–1834.* 1984.
KIPLE, KENNETH F., ed. *The African Exchange: Toward a Biological History of Black People.* 1988.

Richard H. Steckel

Movies

See Film and Television, Slavery in.

Murder of Slaves

In the *Federalist Papers,* Alexander Hamilton, defending the Three-Fifths Compromise in the Constitution, observed that under United States law a slave is sometimes a person and sometimes property. One of Hamilton's prime examples of this legal personhood was in the matter of murder—for when slaves are murdered, as well as when they are thought to have committed murder, the law treats them not as chattel property but as persons.

Most systems of legal slavery throughout history have had some means, formal or ad hoc, by which the authorities could restrain excessive abuse of slaves, particularly the gratuitous infliction of death. In some cases, this has reflected the slave society's recognition of the ultimate humanity of the slave, or it has been part of society's own psychological and moral defenses of that system, but in other cases it has reflected nothing more than the interest of society in avoiding servile insurrection.

In ancient Athens, killing a slave could sometimes bring criminal prosecution, for in Plato's *Euthyphro,* Socrates debates with Euthyphro about the nature of the good and of justice, after Euthyphro has just come from the law courts after bringing charges against his own father for causing the death of one of the father's own slaves.

In the Roman republic and in the early empire, it was not illegal to kill one's own slaves, for the slave was under the *dominium* of the master, which included the power of life and death. Gladiators, for example, were often slaves who had been trained to face death in staged public combat, but, out of concern for rebellions, the state took a limited interest in excessive cruelty to slaves. The first and second centuries B.C. had seen slave rebellions, including the spectacular uprising led by Spartacus, which had ultimately required three Roman armies to suppress.

Every large city had a prefect with the authority to intervene against the excessively cruel treatment of slaves. The Stoic philosopher Seneca recounted how the emperor Augustus had prevented the exsanguination of a boy slave in a garden pond filled with giant lampreys. The cruel, rich master, who was Augustus's host, had intended to punish the boy for accidentally breaking a goblet by throwing him into the infamous pool. Augustus also ordered the pool filled in.

In the Old Testament, under the ancient Hebrew law of slavery, it was provided that a master who knocked out the eye or the tooth of a slave was required to free that slave (Exodus 21: 26–27). A master who killed a slave under chastisement was to be punished (Exodus 21:20) but the punishment was not specified. It was further provided that if a slave survived for one or two days after mistreatment, there was to be no punishment, because the destruction of a slave damaged a master financially (Exodus 21: 21), and therefore, the Biblical law assumed no master would intentionally kill his slave.

Under the common law of England, which was the underlying law of all the original colonies, the deliberate killing of anyone was punishable as murder, and so the killing of a slave under immoderate chastisement was also indictable as manslaughter. As most colonies matured, the common law of slavery was supplemented by statute law, with the law of homicide sometimes altered in regard to slaves.

Often problems arose through defects in the wording of the statutes, but the most common problem was the indifference of authorities and the unwillingness of grand juries to indict and petit juries to convict whites for abuse of blacks. As late as 1848, in central South Carolina, a crippled slave was chained in an outhouse in freezing weather in wet clothing. He was found strangled in his own chains, but no prosecution resulted.

Death under "correction" did not always lead to an accusation of murder, of course, for the law recognized the category of death by misadventure. Michael Dalton, in *The Countrey Justice,* a popular guide for justices of the peace in colonial Virginia, explained that if a schoolmaster, parent, or slavemaster corrected a charge in a reasonable manner and the charge happened to die therefrom, this would not be accounted murder.

In 1669, Virginia adopted a law that excused the death of a slave if it resulted from correction at all, with no requirement that the correction had to be reasonable or moderate. By an act of 1723, protection was extended to anybody who should happen to kill a slave because of the latter's provocation. These statutes represented a great weakening of common-law protections.

An act of 1774 in North Carolina provided a single year's imprisonment for the willful murder of a slave, but it also provided that a killer who was not the master had to pay the value of the slave in compensation.

In 1690, South Carolina passed an ordinance which excused death resulting from correction but which also provided three month's imprisonment and a payment of £50 to the owner if the slayer was someone other than the owner. When Georgia first permitted slavery in 1740, common law on slave homicide was applied, as it had been in Maryland and Delaware, where no special statutes on the subject were ever enacted.

Concerning differentiation of guilt and punishment among persons of various relations to a slave who had been killed, the master or the master's designee was given the widest latitude of action under the law. A free white man who stood in no particular relationship to the slave was next in protected status. A slave who killed another slave could be exculpated only by demonstrating necessary self-defense or having acted on the command of the master.

A FREEHOLDER'S COURT. Page 197.

A slave is about to be hanged in 1855, following the verdict of a "freeholder's court." [Library of Congress/Corbis]

Finally, a recurrent problem for the law was to set standards of murder and manslaughter in regard to the killing of a slave. This distinction was further complicated by decisions like that of Judge Colcock of South Carolina in *State v. Raines* (1826), which held that under state law there could be no manslaughter of a slave.

By the late antebellum period most southern states, either by statute, precedent, or both, had made it a crime to murder a slave. In *State v. Reed* (1823) the North Carolina Supreme Court upheld the conviction and death penalty of a white person who had been indicted at common law for murdering a slave. In *State v. Hoover* (1839) the North Carolina court upheld a death sentence for an owner who had tortured his own slave with the "most brutal and barbarous whippings, scourgings and privations." These cases illustrate the willingness of southern courts to impose the death sentence for whites who had murdered slaves, but they are also unusual. More common, were cases like *Souther v. Commonwealth* (1851), in which the Virginia court upheld the conviction of an owner who had tortured a slave to death over a two-day period. The court declared this was the most "atrocious and wicked cruelty" ever found in Virginia's jurisprudence. Despite these circumstances, Souther was given only a five-year sentence for manslaughter. Similarly, in *State v. Tackett* (1829) the North Carolina court reversed the conviction of a white man who had ambushed and killed a slave who was known to be unruly. Thus, while the law formally protected the slave from murder, in reality only in the most extreme cases were whites actually punished or executed for killing slaves.

See also LAW.

BIBLIOGRAPHY

FINKELMAN, PAUL. *The Law of Freedom and Bondage: A Casebook.* 1996.
MORRIS, THOMAS D. *Southern Slavery and the Law, 1619–1860.* 1996.
TUSHNET, MARK. *The American Law of Slavery.* 1981.

Patrick M. O'Neil

Museums and Historic Sites

The preservation and the interpretation of archives, artifacts, and structures related to slavery have a century-long history. The home of Frederick Douglass in the Anacostia neighborhood of Washington, D.C., was preserved after his death in 1895 as the "black Mount Vernon"; the home of the British abolitionist William Wilberforce in Kingston upon Hull has been

Students tour the Washington, D.C., home of Frederick Douglass. [Kelly-Mooney Photography/Corbis]

a museum dedicated to the history of slavery and its abolition since 1906. At the Jamestown Ter-Centennial Exposition (1907) in Virginia, organizers of the Negro Building mounted an exhibition with tableaux that showed the black odyssey in America. In the early twentieth century a number of black scholars and collectors in the United States accumulated materials that formed the basis for institutional collections such as the Schomburg Center for Research in Black Culture in New York and the Moorland-Springarn Collection at Howard University.

Beyond these early efforts at collecting and preservation, the post–World War II era has seen an explosion of public history about people of African descent. The liberation of African nations from colonial rule, the struggle against legal segregation in America and South Africa, and black freedom movements in general contributed to a greater awareness of black culture and the history of slavery. The opening of museums and historic sites to the interpretation of slavery has stimulated a broad public discussion of the institution.

Several nations in western Africa maintain historical sites and museums that tell the story of the Atlantic slave trade including Gorée Island, Senegal, Elmina and Cape Coast Castles, Ghana, and Ouidah, Benin. Gorée Island and the Ghanaian Castles became UNESCO World Heritage Sites in 1978 and 1979 respectively. Historical interpretation of the trans-Saharan slave trade seems to be less well developed, although the slave pens in Tunis, Tunisia, have apparently survived as a tourist site.

Conflicts over the interpretation of Ghana's coastal forts and castles reveal different perspectives on the interpretation of slavery. In 1994 Ghana opened the Cape Coast Castle Museum featuring the exhibition "Crossroads of People, Crossroads of Trade," developed in collaboration with the Smithsonian Institution. The exhibition discusses the slave trade, but within the context of Ghana's larger history. African-Americans, both tourists and those who have chosen to live in Ghana, view the castles as powerful monuments to the slave trade—sacred places that should not be "cleaned up"—and some protested the renovation of the castle and the exhibition. Ghanaians, while understanding the role the castles played in the slave trade, view slavery as simply one phase of a much longer national saga and see the castles as part of their overall tourist industry.

Several European and American museums also have taken steps to document the slave trade. In 1994 the Merseyside Maritime Museum in Liverpool, England, opened its new Transatlantic Slavery Gallery with the exhibition "The Transatlantic Slave Trade: Against Human Dignity": and issued a major publication of the same name. In the United States, the exhibition "A Slave Ship Speaks: The Wreck of the Henrietta Marie" opened at the Historical Museum of Southern Florida in 1997 with plans to travel to a number of other American museums. Artifacts from the *Henrietta Marie,* an English slave ship that sank near Key West, Florida, in 1701, form the core of the exhibition.

Perhaps the most sweeping attempt to interpret the slave trade for the public is the "Slave Route" project spearheaded by the World Tourism Organization and UNESCO. First proposed in 1994, the project seeks to inventory, evaluate, and preserve slave trade sites and promote tourism to these destinations. Originally an African initiative, the project is now set to expand into the Americas and the Caribbean.

In the United States the rise of black consciousness movements in the 1960s prompted a growing call for university programs, archives, and museums of African-American culture and history. New collecting institutions sprang up, such as the Amistad Research Center, now based in New Orleans on the campus of Tulane University. One of the earliest American exhibitions that dealt with slavery, "Out of Africa," was mounted by the Anacostia Museum, a neighborhood museum in Washington, D.C., connected to the Smithsonian Institution. In the 1970s museums specifically dedicated to African-American history opened in many cities and localities, including Philadelphia, Los An-

geles, and Wilberforce, Ohio, and all tackled issues related to slavery. A museum dedicated to the Underground Railroad was completed in Cincinnati, Ohio, at the end of the twentieth century. Historians supported these developments with detailed historical research on slavery in specialized collections and in colonial, national, and local archives.

Somewhat later, mainstream American museums began to appreciate the growing scholarship of and audience for African-American history and life. A flurry of local exhibitions on slavery in the 1980s was followed by synthetic shows such as "Before Freedom Came: African-American Life in the Antebellum South," a major traveling exhibition sponsored, ironically, by the Museum of the Confederacy in Richmond, Virginia.

The development of slavery studies also has revolutionized the interpretation of historical places. In the past, American plantation tours fixated on the impressive mansions of masters and rarely, if ever, discussed the source of the planter's wealth or their human chattel. While such narrow interpretations are still all too common, many plantation sites are now fully committed to interpreting the system of slavery and slave culture. Colonial Williamsburg's reconstruction of slave housing at the Carter's Grove plantation and its commitment to ongoing dramatic and living history programs related to slavery throughout its historic area is one of the most publicized examples. Plantations sites in the Caribbean and in Central and South America nations are also doing pioneering work interpreting slavery for visitors.

Perhaps the most challenging issue facing museums and historic sites is the integration of the history of slavery into the overall story of a country or community. One early and innovative exhibition, "'Negro Cloth': Northern Industry and Southern Slavery," opened in 1981 at the visitor center of the Boston National Historical Park and later formed the basis for "The Loom and the Lash," a 1983 exhibition at the Museum of Rhode Island History. Produced by the Merrimack Valley Textile Museum (now the American Textile History Museum in Lowell) and sponsored by several other Boston-area institutions, the show connected cotton production in New England with slavery in the southern United States. Likewise, the Merseyside Maritime Museum's exhibition on the transatlantic slave trade explicitly linked the wealth of Liverpool to the horrors of the Middle Passage by revealing that local notables, for whom many of the town's streets are named, were deeply implicated in the trade. Some white residents protested this very personal approach. Just as in the case of the slave castles of Ghana, the placing of slavery in a central position within a community's larger history still sparked debate in the late twentieth century.

See also AMISTAD; DOUGLASS, FREDERICK; PLANTATIONS; SLAVE TRADE; WILBERFORCE, WILLIAM.

BIBLIOGRAPHY

BRUNER, EDWARD M. "Tourism in Ghana: The Representation of Slavery and the Return of the Black Diaspora." American Anthropologist 98 (June 1996): 290–304.

BURNSIDE, MADELINE. Spirits of the Passage: The Transatlantic Slave Trade in the Seventeenth Century. 1997.

CAMPBELL, EDWARD D. C., and KYM RICE, eds. Before Freedom Came: African-American Life in the Antebellum South. 1991.

Ghana: The Chronicle of a Museum Development Project in the Central Region. 1997.

HORTON, JAMES OLIVER, and SPENCER W. CREW. "Afro-Americans and Museums: Towards a Policy of Inclusion." In History Museums in the United States: A Critical Assessment. 1989.

HUTCHINSON, LOUISE DANIEL. Out of Africa: From West African Kingdoms to Colonization. 1979.

SAVAGE, BETH L., ed. African American Historic Places: National Register of Historic Places, National Park Service. 1994.

TIBBLES, ANTHONY, ed. Transatlantic Slavery: Against Human Dignity. 1994.

VLACH, JOHN MICHAEL. Back of the Big House: The Architecture of Plantation Slavery. 1993.

Gregg D. Kimball

Music about Slavery

Music about slavery covers a multitude of genres and ranges from the slave era to the end of the twentieth century. It encompasses not only the spirituals or "sorrow songs," as designated by Dr. W. E. B. Du Bois but classical works such as Giuseppe Verdi's grand opera Aïda.

The subject of slavery has fascinated composers, known and unknown, since time immemorial. It was as vital for conscripts doing gang labor for Egypt's pharaohs to ease their burdens by fashioning tuneful phrases to assuage their anguish as it was for their latter-day cousins in the fields and on the wharves of Mississippi, Alabama, Virginia, Georgia, the Carolinas, the Antilles, Brazil, Spanish America, Africa, Iberia, India, and the Muslim world.

But the manner in which slavery as a topic has been treated musically is immensely variegated. Verdi's Aida, for example, first performed in Cairo in 1871, draws on the then-contemporary fascination with ancient Egypt that swept early nineteenth-century Europe. Utilizing a libretto by Antonio Ghislanzoni and Camille du Locle, it was inspired by a prose sketch crafted by Egyptologist Auguste Mariette to celebrate the exploits of the khedive Ismail, the most ennobling of which deeds was the impending opening of the great Suez Canal. As such, it treats Egypt mostly as a backdrop and slavery primarily as a dramatic device.

By contrast, the music shaped by slaves themselves is typically rooted in the starker realities of day-to-day existence as the property of others. In the North American context this includes everything from the secular field hollers, work songs, ring shouts, and lighter reels, to the more sacred spirituals. In the Caribbean as well as the U.S. South, slave music often contained ironic and satirical elements functioning as social commentary, most notably in the case of caiso, or calypso, as it came to be known, as well as songs and folkways that poked fun at the master class in the plantation societies of the New World.

Much of the modern interest in spirituals as a genre is due in large part to the activity of African-American composers and performers reworking the idiom, beginning with the Fisk Jubilee Singers, who traveled the world in the late nineteenth century and helped inspire several generations of emulators from Harry Burleigh to Nathaniel Dett, from James and Rosamond Johnson in the compositional sphere to performers such as Roland Hayes, Marian Anderson, Paul Robeson, and, more recently, Leontyne Price, Simon Estes, Kathleen Battle, and Jessye Norman.

Though more than a century has intervened since the lyrics printed by Thomas Wentworth Higginson and fifty years since the appearance of W. F. Allen's Slave Songs of the United States, the power of these collections remains clear. "Let My People Go" or "Go Down Moses," evoking images of biblical slavery, has long been favorite not only in the United States but universally among mass and elite audiences alike. Anderson and Battle have performed and recorded "Ride on, King Jesus," clearly the same text and melody as Higginson's "Ride on, Kind Savior." Following in the Hayes, Anderson, and Robeson tradition, Price and her high-profile apostles, sopranos Norman and Battle, as well as the bass baritone Estes, have often included spirituals in their recitals. Jazz composer and master percussionist Max Roach's 1968 classic "Members Don't Get Weary" is in effect a reworking of Allen's "Oh, Brothers, Don't Get Weary."

Direct survivals of slavery can be discerned in the call-and-response work songs and blues associated with road-gang labor, most notably in southern prisons. One famous hero of such songs, the legendary John Henry ("the Steel-Driving Man"), is often linked to slavery, although railroader John Henry was actually a free man. While this idiom had diminished with transformations in social attitudes toward convict labor, the post-1995 resurgence of chain gangs in Alabama, Texas, and Arizona may change this.

Leontyne Price sings the role of Aïda, pleading with Pharaoh for the lives of her fellow Ethiopian slaves, in a 1981 production. [Ira Nowinski/Corbis]

Popular music, theater, musicals, and Hollywood films have frequently contained songs evocative of slavery. These range from efforts to recreate the sonorities and settings of slave musicians—either in solo performance or choral ensembles piloted by talented choir masters Hall Johnson, Eva Jessye (who for several decades directed every *Porgy and Bess* ensemble), Leonard DePaur, and Jester Hairston—to burlesque-like renditions of varying degrees of authenticity. Some could be heard in films made by skilled, often sympathetic aficionados of African-American song, like King Vidor's powerfully emotional cinematic offering of 1929 *Hallelujah!*, featuring majestic choral arrangements directed by Eva Jessye.

Dance hall and stage performances with slave subjects are often of two broad types: first, the multitude of airs, ditties, and parodistic treatments of African or black diasporic slave life that found expression in the minstrel tradition; second, popular songs composed by Broadway or "Tin Pan Alley" lyricists, inspired by slavery elsewhere in the world. Literary interest in Africa and Africans was evident in England by the seventeenth century, motivated in large part by the slave trade. During the next century this gave rise to a largely emulative tradition of Negro impersonation. By the late eighteenth century, with reaction still rooted in England's encounter with Africa, the publication of explorer Mungo Park's *Travels* in 1799 stimulated further interest in Africa and Africans, extending from the schoolhouse to the pub and ultimately the popular stage. In time this gave rise to such "pathetic" songs as William Cowper's "The Negro's Complaint," "The Desponding Negro" by John Collins and William Reeve, and "The Negro Slave" by C. J. Pitt and V. De Cleve, among others.

In short order, as "Ethiopian Delineators," North American white actors like Dan Emmett and Thomas "Daddy" Rice donned blackface to create a caricature of the black slave. They devised hundreds of songs that left an indelible mark upon American life, reinforcing the stereotype of slavery as benevolent and portraying black folk as docile, lazy, and childlike. For much of the century 1830 to 1930 these shows and the images associated with them set the tone for the ways in which many Americans (and non-Americans) viewed black people. Indeed, black actors and singers were often forced to wear burnt cork well into the 1920s. Among the most well-known blackface performers of African descent was Bert Williams, an actor, singer, and stage entertainer, who often appeared in Ziegfeld's *Follies.*

No less noteworthy are the myriad depictions of slave life that tended toward the nostalgic, such as James Bland's "Carry Me Back to Old Virginia," the state's ode from 1940 until the 1990s. Bland, a northern African-American minstrel, exploited familiar plantation themes in his song; by the 1990s his lyrics had provoked a paroxysm of rage among the commonwealth's African-American residents, causing the governor to abandon it. Stephen Foster, a northerner, though white, also left behind a substantial oeuvre of stereotypical plantation songs treating slavery and slaves in a monolithic, atavistic manner. Nonetheless, such anthems as "Old Man River," from Jerome Kern's 1927 stage musical and 1936 film *Showboat,* although rife with romantic slave imagery and condescending terms like "darky," could be reinterpreted by a few apt lyrical substitutions like the interventions made by Paul Robeson and his savvily engagé accompanists in recitals and concert tours in the forties and fifties.

Yet popular cinema, particularly the musical genre, is a treasure trove of stereotypes on slavery. *The King and I,* by Richard Rodgers and Oscar Hammerstein II, contains a play within a play depicting a stage performance of *Uncle Tom's Cabin,* as well as a key subplot involving two lovers in slavelike subordination to the King of Siam. Harriett Beecher Stowe's melodramatic saga was a favorite subject of popular thespians, with or without musical accompaniment. When music was included, it often reflected the influence of minstrelsy.

Outside the United States Afro-Brazilian and Afro-Latin musics (Cuban *batá* drumming, Puerto Rican *danza,* Dominican merengue, Colombia *cumbia* and *marimbula,* and others) have each built upon instrumentation and performance traditions rooted in both African and slave precedents. Drumming, ensemble singing, call-and-response vocalization patterns, and reproduction of sacred and secular texts preserved in large part by the persistence of secret societies have been key to the resilience of these styles. Many of these genres have found new audiences both at home and outside in the emergence of a market for "world music" that includes the samba and *capoeira* of Brazil, Afro-Latin salsa, and the amalgams of Jamaican reggae (truly the quintessential music of the African Diaspora), Trinidadian *soca* (a mix of "soul" and "calypso") and allied *zouk* music of Haiti. Interestingly, these hybrid genres have fed back to Africa, sparking the blues of Mali's Ali Farka Touré, the reggae of South Africa's Lucky Dube and Burkina Faso's Alpha Blondi, and a host of others.

Rita Moreno portrayed Tuptim in the 1956 movie musical The King and I. *Tuptim was sent to the king of Siam as a gift from the prince of Burma. Before trying to escape, she helped stage the story of* Uncle Tom's Cabin *(under the title* The Small House of Uncle Thomas*) for visiting European dignitaries.* [UPI/Corbis-Bettmann]

Beyond the boundaries of the Western Hemisphere, the category of slave music extends to populations whose appearance and presence is still readily recognizable as part of the legacy of a servile past. In Morocco the Gnawa, descended from Western Sudanese Fulani and the Bambara of Mali and Guinée (Guinea), were spirited north as slaves in the sixteenth century, though they continue to migrate voluntarily today. Gnawa are clearly identifiable by their darker hue and distinctive attire and by their hypnotically rhythmic trance music played on the lutelike *gimbri,* accompanied by singing, the double-reeded *ghaita,* hand claps, and drums, in ceremonies liked to Sufism. Similarly, the Tihama coastal plain of North Yemen is home to performers who migrated across the Red Sea from Somalia, Ethiopia, and Sudan, most of whom belong to the *akhdam* caste, at the lowest rung of the social ladder. They have traditionally found work as entertainers and menial laborers, snake-charmers, fortune tellers, and magicians, but above all as professional itinerant musicians for hire.

See also LITERATURE OF SLAVERY; MUSIC BY SLAVES; SPIRITUALS.

BIBLIOGRAPHY

The Afro-Arabian Crossroad: Music of the Tihama on the Red Sea, North Yemen. Lyrichord Records, ca. 1982.

CHARTERS, ANN. *Nobody: The Story of Bert Williams.* 1970.

FISHER, MILES MARK. *Negro Slave Songs in the United States.* 1969.

HIGGINSON, THOMAS WENTWORTH. *Army Life in a Black Regiment.* 1962.

HUGHES, LANGSTON, and MILTON MELTZER. *Black Magic: A Pictorial History of Black Entertainers in America.* 1967.

LOTT, ERIC. *Love and Theft: Blackface Minstrelsy and the American Working Class.* 1993.

NATHAN, HANS. *Dan Emmett and the Rise of Early Negro Minstrelsy.* 1962.

OSBORNE, CHARLES. Notes to a recording of Giuseppi Verdi's opera, *Aïda.* RCA Victor. 1971.

ROBERTS, JOHN STORM. *Black Music of Two Worlds.* 1973.

TOLL, ROBERT C. *Blacking Up: The Minstrel Show in Nineteenth Century America.* 1974.

TOTO LA MOMPOSINA Y SUS TAMBORES. *Colombia: Musique de la côte Atlantique.* A.S.P.I.C. France. N.d.

David H. Anthony III

Music by Slaves

Because slaves have been taken from virtually every human race and society, it would seem that only two generalizations can be made with any certainty about the origins and forms of slave music. In places where slaves came from a cultural background similar to that of their masters, as was the case throughout most of Asia and Africa, or where slaves came from so many different cultural backgrounds that no one background predominated, as was the case in the slave societies of Europe and the Middle East, the music made by slaves was indistinguishable from the music made by their masters. In other places, such as the slave societies of the Western Hemisphere, the interaction between slaves and masters resulted in the development of distinctive musical forms that drew in varying degrees from the cultural backgrounds of both slaves and masters.

Little evidence exists to support the first generalization. As for the second generalization, it seems reasonable to assume that the Slavs, who inhabited one of the world's great population reservoirs for slaves and who were exported throughout Europe and the Middle East in such great numbers that they gave their name to the most extreme condition of unfree labor, carried with them their own distinctive vocal and instrumental music. However, the lack of evidence to support this contention suggests that perhaps enslaved Slavs did indeed abandon their native music. On the other hand, sufficient documentation exists to trace the origins of slave music in the New World to the musical forms of Africans, who inhabited the world's other great population reservoir for slaves. Consequently, any informed discussion of the distinctive musical forms and genres created by slaves must begin and end with the musical contributions of African slaves who were transplanted to the region around the Caribbean.

The roots of Afro-American slave music were in West Africa, where music focused on rhythm rather than melody. Tribes such as the Fon, Fulani, Mandingo, and Yoruba utilized a wide variety of percussion instruments, especially drums. These drums came in various shapes—cylinders, cones, barrels, goblets, kettles, frames, mushrooms, beehives, or hourglasses—and were made from wood, carved tree trunks, metal, clay, bone, ivory, and gourds. Some drums had multiple heads, some were covered on the bottom as well as on the head, and some were played with the hands instead of with sticks. Other percussion instruments included rattles, scrapers, concussion sticks, shakers, bull roarers, and mirlitons, membraneous devices that could be attached to other instruments or voices to create a buzzing sound. Many of these percussion instruments appeared in the New World shortly after the arrival of African slaves. West Africans also possessed a number of other musical instruments, although the only ones that seem to have crossed the Atlantic Ocean are the flute; the marimba, a xylophone with a gourd resonator for each slab or key; and the banjar, a bow lute with a shallow drum resonator that slaves in the United States transformed into the modern-day banjo.

When Africans arrived in the New World, they came into contact with European music. These two distinctive forms of music could not have been more different from each other; whereas European music focused on sophisticated melodies, complicated harmony, key tonality, and chord progressions, African music featured intricate rhythms and heterophony, the simultaneous performance of the same melodic line, with slight individual variations, by a number of performers.

Slaves seem to have preserved their native musical traditions most completely in their religious celebrations. In the Bahia region of eastern Brazil, where a majority of the population was descended from West Africans, the music associated with the religious cult known as *candomblé* was virtually indistinguishable from the music used in Yoruba spirit-worship ceremonies. The Yoruba influence also made itself felt in the musical rituals of the *santería* and *lucumi* cults in Cuba, while the Dahomean musical influence was strong in the *shango* cult, which flourished in Trinidad. The music associated with voodoo rituals in Haiti and other Caribbean islands, where the vast majority of the population was descended from Africans, is derived with little embellishment from Fon religious music.

In the southern United States, slaves adapted their religious music to European forms to a greater degree than did slaves in Latin America, probably because slaves constituted a smaller percentage of the population throughout most of the South. Nevertheless, even though slaves sang English Protestant hymns, they did so in ways that were decidedly African. Slaves eschewed the decorous harmonizing that characterized English choirs in favor of spontaneous, simultaneous improvisations on the main melody line by two or more singers and the call-and-response pattern so characteristic of African vocal music. Because the use of percussion instruments was greatly restricted after the 1740s by masters—who were afraid that the slaves' "talking drums" were devices for fomenting insurrection—slaves attending church meetings compensated by clapping their hands and stamping their feet.

Eventually, slaves in the United States began composing their own religious songs, known as spirituals. Many spirituals, although by no means all, expressed faith in the Lord and hope for a better future, and some evoked the miraculous way in which the Lord had led the Hebrews out of bondage in Egypt to the promised land. Not surprisingly, many of these songs had a double meaning; what the master often innocently supposed was a song simply praising the Lord was often a surreptitious song about freedom. Harriet Tubman, the famous rescuer of slaves, often communicated by means of spirituals and is said to have used the following song to let slaves know she was in the neighborhood:

Dark and thorny is de pathway
Where de pilgrim makes his ways;
But beyond dis vale of sorrow
Lie de fields of endless days.

Another song, innocently titled *Steal Away to Jesus,* in which "Jesus" was a code word for "freedom," was supposedly written by the slave preacher turned insurrectionist Nat Turner. Other songs combined a spiritual message with practical advice on how to attain freedom. A good example of this type of song is "Follow the Drinking Gourd." The gourd refers to the Big Dipper, a constellation that points to the North Star, the primary navigational aid available to runaways. One line in this song counselled slaves that "the Old Man [God] is a-waiting for to carry you to freedom, if you follow the drinking gourd."

Music also led some slaves to freedom in a more direct way. The most interesting example involved the slaves of a Kentuckian named Graham, Reuben and Henry, who had been trained at Graham's expense as professional musicians. After performing for four years with Graham's written permission throughout the South as well as in Ohio and Indiana, in 1841 the two slaves made use of their passes to work their way across the North to Canada and to freedom.

Slaves made music in their secular lives as well, and often sang while working. Among the wide variety of work songs were tunes to be sung while chopping sugarcane, picking or hoeing cotton, drawing water, and plowing, as well as special songs that were sung only at quitting time. Frequently, these songs served as a means of regulating the work pace of a gang of slaves and were therefore encouraged by slave owners and overseers. Slaves employed in such diverse nonagri-

Cover art for "The Fugitive's Song," an antislavery song written by former slave Frederick Douglass. [Corbis-Bettmann]

cultural occupations as lumbering, manning river boats, building levees, manufacturing chewing tobacco or iron, and working on the railroad had special work songs that regulated the rhythm of the work while also relieving tedium.

The interaction between African and European musical genres can also be seen in the recreational music of slaves. Although it was unknown in Africa, the fiddle became a popular instrument among bondsmen in the United States. In time, slaves developed enough proficiency with this instrument that they were often employed by their masters to play at dances and balls for the entertainment of whites; a slave named Sy Gilliat became the official fiddler of the state dances at Williamsburg, Virginia. Slave music became so popular among whites in the United States that in the early nineteenth century, a form of music known as minstrelry developed. Minstrel shows featured white musicians masquerading as blacks, who sang and played what were known as "Negro tunes." The rumba, which originated among Afro-Cuban slaves, combined verses in Spanish and certain features of European music with neo-African polyrhythms. In Puerto Rico slaves developed a musical form similar to the rumba known as bomba.

After emancipation, slave music evolved into other forms of popular music. In the United States, a number of genres including blues, jazz, rhythm and blues, and rock and roll trace their roots to the music of slaves. In the Caribbean, the evolution of slave music resulted in such forms of musical expression as calypso and reggae.

See also SPIRITUALS.

BIBLIOGRAPHY

BORROFF, EDITH. *Music in Europe and the United States: A History.* 1990.
MANUEL, PETER, with KENNETH BILBY and MICHAEL LARGEY. *Caribbean Currents: Caribbean Music from Rumba to Reggae.* 1995.
MERRIMAN, ALAN P. *African Music in Perspective.* 1982.
ROBERTS, JOHN STORM. *Black Music of Two Worlds.* 1974.
SOUTHERN, EILEEN. *The Music of Black Americans: A History.* 1971.

Charles W. Carey Jr.

Muslims

See Islam.

Myanmar (Burma)

See Southeast Asia.

N

Nabuco de Araujo, Joaquim [1849–1910]

Brazilian abolitionist.

Joaquim Nabuco de Araujo was given the same name as his father, a wealthy slave owner and Brazilian senator who cosponsored the Rio Branco Law, or Law of Free Birth. Passed in 1871, this law guaranteed freedom at age twenty-one for all children born to slave mothers after that year. While in law school, Nabuco wrote abolitionist articles for his father's political party newspaper, and in 1879 he was elected to the Chamber of Deputies. Dissatisfied with the slow pace of gradual emancipation, he introduced legislation that same year calling for the complete abolition of slavery within ten years. In 1880, following the legislature's overwhelming rejection of this proposal, Nabuco founded the Brazilian Antislavery Society and a monthly abolitionist newspaper. Denied re-election in 1881, he moved to London, England, where he wrote *O Abolicionismo* (*Abolitionism*, 1883).

Nabuco's book attacked slavery by outlining its debilitating effect on the economic and social development of Brazil, which after 1880 was the only country in the New World where slavery still existed legally. He emphasized slavery's role in retarding progress in the interior and its negative influence on the inculcation of national patriotism among the lower classes. The following year he wrote a series of abolitionist articles under the pen name Garrison. Written at a time when abolitionism was at low ebb in Brazil, Nabuco's works contributed significantly to the abolition of slavery in the Brazilian state of Amazonas in 1884, the lib-eration of all slaves over age sixty in 1885, and the complete emancipation of Brazil's remaining 700,000 slaves in 1888.

See also ABOLITION AND ANTISLAVERY MOVEMENTS; BRAZIL; BRAZILIAN ANTISLAVERY SOCIETY; LAW.

BIBLIOGRAPHY

NABUCO, CAROLINA. *The Life of Joaquim Nabuco.* Translated by Ronald Hilton. 1950.
NABUCO, JOAQUIM. *Abolitionism: The Brazilian Antislavery Struggle.* Translated by Robert Conrad. 1977.

Charles W. Carey Jr.

Names and Naming

Ralph Ellison wrote in *Shadow and Act* (1953), "It is through our names that we first place ourselves in the world. Our names, being the gift of others, must be made our own" (p. 147). Perhaps unintentionally, Ellison described the process of acculturation by which Africans became African-Americans and the extent to which their names, and naming practices in particular, reflected the means by which slaves took appellations given them by their owners and, over time, "made them their own."

Scholars of slavery have in recent years come to recognize the names and naming of slaves as a meaningful gauge by which to assess a number of aspects of slave life and culture and how they changed over time. In *Kinship and the Social Order* (1969), the anthropologist Meyer Fortes observed that the naming practices of any society "epitomize personal experiences, historical happenings, attitudes to life, and cultural ideas and values"; and this is particularly true of African-American slaves. Extensive plantation records over several generations, combined with records from churches, manumission societies, slave traders, and estate settlements, provide a vast pool of data from which one can trace patterns and trends in slave names in the American South from the colonial period through emancipation.

Most evidence indicates that children born in America were probably named by their own parents. Recognizable patterns of changes in names and naming practices are evident from the mid-eighteenth century through the early nineteenth century and on to the 1860s. They reflect a process of acculturation by which generations of slaves, ever farther removed from the direct influence of the first Africans to be enslaved and transplanted, adapted more and more the culture of their masters, eventually creating a culture and value system all their own. The names they gave their children provide a constant, if limited, index of that process over time.

To their captors, slaves remained nameless from the time of their capture until their purchase by American masters. Quite a few slaves were allowed to keep their original African names or names assigned them elsewhere (as reflected by the frequency of Spanish and Portuguese names among the earliest slaves in Virginia and the Carolinas). Throughout the colonial period, as many as one-fifth of the slaves in the Carolinas retained African names. (Quash, Cuffee, Mingo, Sambo, Mustapha, and Sukey were among the most common.) Slaves often transferred those names to later generations in modified form, or they followed African traditions, such as giving basket or day names, or names reflecting the birth order of siblings. Both Peter Wood and Charles Joyner have used the names and naming patterns among coastal South Carolina slaves to measure the extent of African linguistic and cultural holdovers and the dynamics of creolization through which the Gullah dialect emerged.

Though masters may well have given newly purchased slaves names that were whimsical, satirical, or condescending in intent, the frequent appearance of classical names—Venus, Cato, Hercules, Bacchus, Pompey—reflect the planters' education, and their libraries. While such names continued to appear well after slave parents themselves took over the naming of their children, the parents had many other sources, traditions, and beliefs to draw on. They sometimes chose a name denoting the weather at the time of a child's birth or some distinctive feature of a child's

appearance. Geographical names were common, as were the names of ships and ports, either distant or nearby. Beginning in the early nineteenth century, biblical names became far more prevalent among slaves, a reflection of widespread Christianization of slave communities and the greater exposure of slaves to the Bible.

If the names slaves chose for their children reflect certain aspects of their worldview, values, and priorities, the patterns by which such names were perpetuated from one generation to another provide valuable insight into other aspects of slave life and culture. For the few plantations from which full, multigenerational slave records have survived, slave names serve as a useful index to the structure of slave families. Herbert Gutman found extensive kinship networks among slaves and saw in the multigenerational recurrence of male names, in particular, an indication that bonds between children and grandparents, and even great-grandparents, were often strong. He argued as well that the frequency with which fathers' names were given to sons suggests more viable two-parent households among slaves than most historians have acknowledged.

Cheryll Cody's extensive examination of individual slave communities in South Carolina and John Inscoe's work on naming practices in North and South Carolina suggest that matrilineal naming—the passing on of mothers' and grandmothers' names to daughters and granddaughters—was nearly as common as patrilineal naming, and far more common among slaves than among their owners. The frequency with which all such names were repeated may imply the very opposite of Gutman's conclusion about the stability of family structure: it may have been the uncertainty of such bonds, and the likelihood of separation of slave parents from their children, that inspired the parents to bestow familiar names.

Finally, the changes in African-American names that accompanied emancipation are indicative of new priorities and identifies among freedmen and freedwomen. As slaves, blacks perpetuated African names, classical names, or other unusual names from one generation to the next, creating a distinctive nomenclature unlike that of southern whites. Once they were freed, however, assimilation replaced acculturation, and the acquisition of last names and more traditional anglicized versions of their first names became a high priority for most African-Americans. Their choices of last names also suggest far more of an effort to relate to the mainstream white culture, and their greater stake in it.

The full-scale process of assimilation made even more apparent just how distinctive an identity African-

Americans had created for themselves as slaves, a reflection of both their willingness and their ability to create a culture all their own.

See also FAMILY, U.S.

BIBLIOGRAPHY

CODY, CHERYL. "Naming, Kinship and Estate Dispersal: Notes on Slave Family Life on a South Carolina Plantation, 1786–1833." *William and Mary Quarterly* 39 (January 1982): 192–211.

———. " 'There Was No Absalom on the Ball Plantation': Slave-Naming Practices in the South Carolina Low Country, 1720–1865." *American Historical Review* 92 (June 1987): 563–596.

GUTMAN, HERBERT G. *The Black Family in Slavery and Freedom, 1750–1925.* 1976.

INSCOE, JOHN C. "Carolina Slave Names: An Index to Acculturation." *Journal of Southern History* 59 (November 1983): 527–554.

JOYNER, CHARLES. *Down by the Riverside: A South Carolina Slave Community.* 1984.

WOOD, PETER. *Black Majority: Negroes in Colonial South Carolina from 1670 through the Stono Rebellion.* 1975.

John C. Inscoe

Narratives, Slave

See Slave Narratives.

Native Americans

This entry includes the following articles: Enslavement of Native Americans; Slaveholding by Native Americans.

Enslavement of Native Americans

Enslavement of Native Americans took two distinct forms: individuals were taken captive by another native group, or Indians were forced to labor for Europeans on plantations and in mines.

Warfare between native peoples often resulted in the taking of captives. Warriors unlucky enough to be captured suffered torture and death in order to assuage the grief of those who had lost relatives in battle. Usually, though, noncombatant captives (women and children) were spared to perform menial tasks for their captors, such as gathering wood and water; thus their status was that of "slaves."

Native Americans seized members of other societies for social rather than economic purposes. In many cases, slaves played an anomalous role. Because they did not belong to a family or clan, they enjoyed none of the benefits or protections that numerous relatives provided; slaves could be killed without fear of retaliation. Therefore, they strengthened group identity among their captors by demonstrating the perils of not belonging to a clan. However, a slave could gain a legitimate position within the clan and the wider community if clan members—usually the highest-ranking women—accepted a captive for adoption. For some groups, such as the seventeenth-century Iroquois, taking captives and subsequently adopting them augmented a population diminished by European diseases. This became the principal impetus for Iroquois warfare against other Indians. Slaves and adoptees contributed to the subsistence-level economy of their new society, but the accumulation of material wealth was not a primary goal, except among Indian groups on the Northwest Coast.

The arrival of Europeans in North America transformed aboriginal slavery from a social to an economic institution. All of the European colonial powers

Hernando de Soto's capture of the fortified Indian town of Alibano, Mississippi, on the Yazoo River in 1541.
[Library of Congress/Corbis]

sought Indian slaves. Spanish exploration along the coasts of North America and in the interior resulted in the seizure of Indians. Although Spain legally outlawed Indian slavery with the publication of the New Laws in 1542, Spaniards continued to enslave Indian peoples on the fringes of their empire. During Hernando de Soto's *entrada* through the Southeast, hundreds of natives were apprehended for use as pack carriers; other Spanish expeditions shipped Indian captives to Spain, Cuba, and Mexico. The silver mines of northern Mexico demanded a large labor force, which was supplied principally by Indian slaves. In the New Mexico area, Spanish colonizers seized Native American slaves by use of the doctrine of a "just war"; "hostile" Indians were subdued through war, and the captives were enslaved. Additionally, Spaniards purchased from the Apaches and Comanches slaves who had been captured through raids on other Indian peoples. Whether under the *encomienda*, or tribute, system utilized throughout Spain's possessions or in the Catholic missions of California, the Southwest, and the Southeast, Indian people supplied the Spanish demand for labor in North America.

English colonizers also enslaved Native Americans. They sent mainland Indian slaves by the hundreds to plantations in the West Indies after wars with Native Americans such as the Powhatan Uprisings (1622 and 1644) in Virginia, the Pequot War (1637) and King Philip's War (1675–1676) in New England, and the Tuscarora War (1711–1713) in North Carolina. Indian slaves also labored alongside Africans on English plantations in North America, particularly in the Southeast. Landowners in early Virginia, for instance, initially sought Indian labor for use on their burgeoning tobacco fields. Such face-to-face contact encouraged cultural borrowing, notably in language and material culture, and intermarriage between Native Americans and African slaves.

Nothing did more to disrupt the native Southeast in the late seventeenth and early eighteenth centuries than the English slave trade. Encouraged by traders from South Carolina, groups such as the Catawbas, Cherokees, and Chickasaws raided their neighbors for captives to sell to the English as slaves. "No imployment pleases the Chickasaws so well as slave Catching," observed the trader Thomas Nairne in 1708. He explained that the capture and sale of an Indian slave to the English brought a Chickasaw warrior honor, a gun, ammunition, a horse, a hatchet, and a suit of clothes. Such material incentives proved irresistible. Armed with guns, Chickasaw and Creek slave raiders condemned about 2,000 Choctaws to slavery in South Carolina and the West Indies. From 1703 to 1708, more Indians than Africans were enslaved in South Carolina—1,050 compared with 1,000. The arrival of the French on the Gulf Coast in 1699, and the subsequent acquisition of firearms by the Choctaws, helped to stop large-scale slave raids. It was the adoption of African slavery and the growing importance of the trade in deerskins, however, that definitively ended the Indian slave trade in the Southeast.

By the middle of the eighteenth century, Indian slavery was a declining institution. Nevertheless, slaves with Native American ancestry toiled in the South until the Thirteenth Amendment to the Constitution freed all persons in bondage.

See also AMERINDIAN SOCIETIES.

BIBLIOGRAPHY

CRANE, VERNER W. *The Southern Frontier, 1670–1732.* 1929.
GUTIÉRREZ, RAMON A. *When Jesus Came, the Corn Mothers Went Away: Marriage, Sexuality, and Power in New Mexico, 1500–1846.* 1991.
MOORE, ALEXANDER. *Nairne's Muskhogean Journals: The 1708 Expedition to the Mississippi River.* 1988.
PERDUE, THEDA. *Slavery and the Evolution of Cherokee Society, 1540–1866.* 1979.

Greg O'Brien

Slaveholding by Native Americans

Some Native Americans, particularly those living in southeastern North America, began to enslave African-Americans toward the end of the eighteenth century. The British established incentives, particularly payments in manufactured goods, to reward Native Americans for catching and returning runaway African slaves. That encouraged Indians to use Africans as vehicles for economic gain. Always cognizant of the values and ideas of their Euro-American neighbors, Indians noticed the racial antipathy European colonists felt toward Africans. Indians resisted being placed in a similar category with Africans, and they adopted notions of racial hierarchy as a result. At their own initiative, some southern Indians acquired African slaves for use as translators and as cultivators of livestock herds and subsistence crops.

After the American Revolution, the U.S. government applied increasing pressure on Indians in the South to expand their production of cash crops, such as cotton, which stimulated Indian use of African slave labor. Such efforts on the part of President George Washington's administration and subsequent administrations appeared most clearly in the "civilization" program forced upon Indians beginning in the 1790s. Implemented by the U.S. government, the "civilization" program encouraged the adoption of African slavery by Indians. U.S. government officials and Protestant missionaries tried to transform native peoples culturally into white men through the adoption of Christianity, cash-crop farming, and patriarchal values. Indian men who sought equality with white society bought slaves for use in their fields and eventually enacted formal slave codes protecting their rights as property owners. By so doing, they enhanced their personal economic standing while radically changing southeastern Indian traditions of matrilineal land ownership and inheritance. Indian women, who were ordinarily the farmers, took up household chores, while men, who considered agricultural labor to be "women's work," were able to employ African slaves instead. With the spread of the cotton boom to the deep South in the early nineteenth century, some Native American slave owners became wealthy planters owning dozens of slaves.

The Cherokees provided the most dramatic example of the adoption of mainstream Euro-American commercial values and slavery in the early nineteenth century. The numbers of African slaves among the Cherokees rose from 583 in 1809 to 1,592 in 1835. A small minority of Cherokee men held these African slaves, but the slaveholders' importance in matters of Cherokee-American relations grew steadily. As these men replaced the traditional Cherokee notion of communal land ownership with plantations growing cotton and other crops for sale on regional and international markets, they established themselves as an economic elite. These wealthy men centralized the Cherokee government under a written constitution and enacted laws that protected their rights as property holders, including land and slaves. Additionally, they established paternal inheritance, generated business contracts, and placed questions of national importance—such as land cessions—under their control. They used their position to combat U.S. pressure to remove Indians west of the Mississippi River. Thus, acquiring slaves and other markers of elite white society encouraged Cherokee planters to seek preservation of the Cherokee nation as the best way to uphold their own claims to land and other property. In the end, however, a few Cherokee elites surrendered to U.S. demands for removal, thus initiating the Trail of Tears so devastating to the majority of Cherokees.

Other Indian groups responded to African-Americans in different ways from the Cherokees. The Seminoles, for example, counted hundreds of runaway African-Americans among their population. These former slaves among the Seminoles enjoyed a semiautonomous existence, with their own towns and leaders. African-Americans fought alongside their Seminole brethren in the fight against removal (1835–1842), and many of them then accompanied the

John Ross, the principal chief of the Cherokee Indians for nearly forty years, had become a wealthy farmer and slave owner in Georgia by the time he participated in the creation of the written constitution for the Cherokee nation in 1827. [Library of Congress/Corbis]

Seminoles to Indian Territory and continued a semi-independent existence.

When removal took southeastern Indians west of the Mississippi River in the 1830s, their use of African slaves persisted and grew. By the time of the Civil War the Cherokees owned over four thousand African-American slaves. Indians who possessed slaves naturally sided with the Confederacy during the war, but deep divisions arose within the Indian nations over the issue. Both the Creeks and Cherokees fought their own civil wars over which side to support in the war, and native slave owners fled south to the Choctaw nation, where slavery remained safe, or to Texas. Native Americans in Indian Territory freed their slaves as the Civil War ended, but their freedmen, like former slaves throughout the South, found promises of equality and opportunity lacking. Debt peonage awaited most freed slaves, whether they had been owned by Native Americans or whites.

See also AMERINDIAN SOCIETIES.

BIBLIOGRAPHY

LITTLEFIELD, DANIEL F., JR. *Africans and Creeks: From the Colonial Period to the Civil War.* 1979.

———. *Africans and Seminoles: From Removal to Emancipation.* 1977.

PERDUE, THEDA. *Slavery and the Evolution of Cherokee Society, 1540–1866.* 1979.

PERDUE, THEDA, and MICHAEL D. GREEN. *The Cherokee Removal: A Brief History with Documents.* 1995.

Greg O'Brien

Nat Turner's Rebellion

See Turner, Nat.

Natural Law

In the "Letter from Birmingham Jail," Martin Luther King Jr. cites St. Augustine and St. Thomas Aquinas to support the principle that "an unjust law is no law at all." American abolitionists condemned slavery in the name of a "higher law" that took precedence over the Constitution; but only since the Enlightenment has the concept of natural law been employed to condemn slavery unequivocally. Older theories of natural law either justified slavery or described it as an unavoidable evil in an imperfect world.

In Book V of the *Ethics,* Aristotle distinguishes between what is "just by convention" and what is "just by nature," which "has the same force everywhere and does not depend on what we regard or do not regard as just." But it is Cicero (106–43 B.C.) who gives the concept of natural law its classic form: "True law is right reason in agreement with nature; it is of universal application, unchanging and everlasting; it summons to duty by its commands, and averts from wrongdoing by its prohibitions . . . And there will not be different laws at Rome and at Athens, or different laws now and in the future, but one eternal and unchangeable law will be valid for all nations and all times . . ." (*Republic* III, xxii). Natural law is thus (1) based upon universal human nature (as distinguished from the diverse characters of particular peoples); (2) eternal (unlike conventional law, which can be deliberately changed); and (3) knowable through natural reason (thus distinguishable from, though compatible with, law based on divine revelation). It does not substitute for the enacted laws of each people; rather it functions as a standard against which to judge the justice of enacted law. A law which contradicts natural law is "no law at all."

The concept of natural law as such neither requires nor condemns slavery but instead shapes the form that any justification or condemnation would take. Under natural law slavery could not be justified merely by invoking a "right of conquest" by which the vanquished preserves his life in exchange for servitude. Natural-law justifications of slavery would have to refer to

human nature and human reason. Thus, if certain human beings are by nature deficient in reason—as Aristotle claims in Book One of the *Politics*—they can be justly enslaved. Conversely, if all human beings are by nature capable of reason, slavery can be condemned in the name of natural law.

Cicero sees no contradiction between slavery and natural law: "The master's restraint of his slaves is like the restraint exercised by the best part of the mind, the reason, over its own evil and weak elements. . . ." Like Aristotle, however, Cicero admits that not all those held in slavery are justly slaves: "For there is a kind of unjust slavery, when those who are capable of governing themselves are under the domination of another" (*Republic* III, xxv).

Saint Augustine (354–450 A.D.) follows Cicero's description of natural law but gives it an entirely different significance. Cicero believed that the standard set by natural law was at least approximated by the laws and customs of the Roman republic in its better times. For Augustine, Rome—like all earthly cities—was founded on injustice from the beginning. In *The City of God* (XIX, 21) Augustine contrasts Cicero's own ideal of earthly justice with the reality of Roman practice. But Augustine holds no hope for reform; true justice cannot be found in the "city of man" but only in the spiritual "city of God."

It is in this spirit that Augustine discusses slavery: it contradicts natural law, but there is no remedy for it in this world. "By nature, in the condition in which God created man, no man is the slave either of man or of sin" (XIX, 15). But when sin entered the world, slavery came into existence. It is worse to be a slave to sin than to man. Those held in slavery, even to wicked masters, should be patient and loyal "until all injustice disappears and all human lordship and power is annihilated, and God is all in all."

Saint Thomas Aquinas (1225–1274) sought to synthesize Christian revelation with the natural philosophy of Aristotle in order to restore to human life and human law its proper dignity within the framework of Christianity. Aquinas distinguishes between four types of law: eternal, divine, natural, and human. Natural law is consistent with divine law (revelation) but unlike the latter can be known through natural reason. Human law must be based upon natural law; it can add particulars not specified in natural law but cannot contravene it (*Summa Theologica* I, 94–97).

Where does this leave slavery? Slavery does not follow directly from natural law but can be practiced without violating natural law. In original nature there was neither servitude nor private property, but both "were devised by human reason for the benefit of human life" (*Summa Theologica* I, 94). In describing this "benefit," Aquinas follows Aristotle: to carry out their ideas, intelligent men require other men, "robust in body and deficient in mind" (*Commentary on the Politics* I, 19–24), who benefit from being ruled.

The Aristotelian/Platonic philosophers of medieval Islam—including al-Farabi (ca. 878–ca. 950) and Avicenna (Ibn Sina; 930–1037)—likewise accepted slavery. Islamic law prohibited enslavement of fellow Muslims but permitted enslavement of unbelievers; no racial or ethnic distinctions were made. In the writings of the philosophers, however, the category of unbeliever merges with that of Aristotle's natural slave and acquires a racial and ethnic character. According to al-Farabi, it is just to make war upon "those who do not submit to slavery and servitude . . . for whom it is best and most fortunate that their place in the world should be that of slaves" (*Aphorisms of the Statesman* 62; see also Lewis, *Race and Slavery*, pp. 54–55).

Turning to early modern Europe, Jean Bodin (1529–1596) was the first political theorist to call for the abolition of slavery, which he claims violates natural law and threatens public order. Bodin was an advocate of absolute monarchy and a theorist of sovereignty in the century before Hobbes. But Bodin's sovereign, unlike that of Hobbes, is bound by natural law: the "absolute power" of the sovereign "only implies freedom in relation to positive laws, and not in relation to the law of God" (*Six Books:* 1, VIII). Bodin refutes the arguments of Aristotle and others that slavery is natural. The ubiquity of the institution does not prove that it is natural; the cruel practice of human sacrifice was likewise universal in former ages. "Such things show how little the laws of nature can be deduced from the practices of men, however inveterate, and one cannot on these grounds accept slavery as natural." Slavery also threatens public order because rebels, promising liberty to slaves, can "throw the whole state into confusion" (*Six Books:* 1, II–V).

For Hugo Grotius (1583–1645), in contrast, the ubiquity of slavery was indeed a mark of its legitimacy: it is part of the "law of nations" established by the practices of states and therefore exists by a kind of universal consent. Grotius concedes that "by nature . . . no human beings are slaves." But just as a people can subject itself to a king, an individual can legitimately sell himself into slavery to preserve his life after capture in war or to obtain subsistence when no other is available (*Law of War and Peace:* Book 2, V, and 3, VII). Despite his commitment to natural law, Grotius's defense of slavery is difficult to distinguish from the right of the stronger.

The concept of a "higher law" was crucial to the antislavery movement in the United States. For William Lloyd Garrison the preamble to the Declaration of Independence takes precedence over the Constitu-

Hugo Grotius. [Corbis-Bettmann]

tion. William Seward repudiates the Fugitive Slave Act in the name of "the law of nature, written on the hearts and consciences of freemen," which is "a higher law than the Constitution."

In conclusion: the concept of natural law is compatible with a wide range of religious and political perspectives on slavery. However, once it is decided that slavery is unjust, natural law can provide a powerful engine for abolition because of its claim to supersede all existing laws.

See also ARISTOTLE; ENLIGHTENMENT; LAW; PHILOSOPHY; RIGHTS OF MAN; THOMAS AQUINAS.

BIBLIOGRAPHY

ARISTOTLE. *Nicomachean Ethics.* Translated by Martin Ostwald. 1962.
———. *The Politics.* Translated by Carnes Lord. 1984.
AUGUSTINE OF HIPPO. *City of God.* Translated by Henry Bettenson. 1972.
BODIN, JEAN. *Six Books of the Commonwealth.* Translated by M. J. Tooley. 1955.
CICERO. *The Republic.* Translated by C. W. Keyes. 1928.
AL-FARABI. *Aphorisms of the Statesman.* Translated by D. M. Dunlop. 1961.
GARRISON, WILLIAM LLOYD. "No Compromise with Slavery (Public Address, 14 February 1854).
GROTIUS, HUGO. *The Law of War and Peace.* Translated by Louise R. Loomis. 1949.

KING, MARTIN LUTHER, JR. "Letter from Birmingham Jail." In *Why We Can't Wait*. 1964; pp. 76–95.

LEWIS, BERNARD. *Race and Slavery in the Middle East: An Historical Inquiry*. 1990.

SEWARD, WILLIAM. Speech in U.S. Senate, 11 March 1850.

THOMAS AQUINAS. *Commentary on the Politics*. Translated by Ernest Fortin and Peter O'Neill. In *Medieval Political Philosophy*, edited by Ralph Lerner and Muhsin Mahdi.

———. *Summa Theologica*. Questions 90–97.

James H. Read

Nazi Slave Labor

In their case against leading Nazi figures held before the International Military Tribunal in Nuremberg, Allied prosecutors charged the defendants with four counts: a common plan or conspiracy to commit crimes against peace, war crimes, and crimes against humanity, and the commission of said crimes. Under war crimes, the indictment states that

> during the whole period of the occupation by Germany of both the Western and the Eastern countries it was the policy of the German Government and the German High Command to deport able-bodied citizens from such occupied countries to Germany and to other occupied countries for the purpose of slave labor upon defense works in factories, and in other tasks connected with the German war effort.

Such a policy, the Allied prosecutors argued, constituted a flagrant violation of the Hague Convention and was thus punishable under international law. In the subsequent war-crimes trials held in Nuremberg (1946–1949), U.S. military tribunals also charged and convicted German governmental, SS, and military officials, as well as leading industrialists, of participation in the Nazi slave-labor program.

The term *slave labor* well conveys the notion of coercion, which was an essential part of the system of foreign-labor deployment in Nazi Germany, yet it is imprecise and fails to explain the complexities of this program. Among those who fell under this system were voluntary laborers from German-allied and -conquered nations, workers forcibly recruited from occupied countries, prisoners of war, and concentration camp prisoners. Each of these disparate groups was subject to different German laws and regulations, and the place that each occupied within the Nazi racial hierarchy greatly affected their treatment.

At the height of the Nazi foreign-labor program in 1944, there were about eight million foreign civilians and POWs at work in the German Reich. In addition, there were more than one-half million concentration camp prisoners working in various wartime economic enterprises. These figures, however, provide only a partial picture of the Nazi foreign-labor program, because they neither include the many civilians (including ghetto inhabitants) who were compelled to perform forced labor in their native countries nor identify the total number of individuals who were deported to Germany during the war.

The Nazi foreign-labor program, as recent scholarship has shown, did not develop out of a premeditated plan or as a preconceived war aim; rather, it was more a temporary solution to a severe manpower shortage. The crisis first developed in the late 1930s when Germany had largely recovered from the devastating effects of the Great Depression and was embarked upon a path to military and economic expansion. Through large public works projects, rearmament, and military conscription, and by encouraging women to leave the workplace, unemployment disappeared, but in key economic sectors, such as agriculture and industry, there was a growing labor shortage that threatened to disrupt Hitler's preparations for war.

To resolve this manpower crisis, the Nazi regime turned more and more to the recruitment of foreign labor and toward mobilizing other sectors of the German population. In the two years from 1936 to 1938, the number of registered foreign workers increased from less than 230,000 to almost 400,000, yet this increase did little to ameliorate the situation. In mining, production stagnated or declined in certain areas, while in agriculture the harvests suffered. By 1939 some Nazi officials calculated that one million additional workers were needed to cover the labor shortage.

In addition to foreign labor, the Nazis looked to exploit the labor of concentration camp prisoners and impoverished Jews. Until 1938, when the SS established a number of its own economic enterprises, labor in concentration camps was used almost exclusively to brutalize the prisoners; it served no real economic function. In the years just prior to the invasion of Poland, however, the Nazi concentration camp system expanded both in the numbers of prisoners and in the number of camps. The SS established new concentration camps, such as Mauthausen, Gross Rosen, Neuengamme, Buchenwald, Ravensbrück, and Flossenbürg, near stone quarries or with SS-owned factories so that prisoner labor could be exploited in arduous tasks. At the same time, the Gestapo and the Criminal Police carried out massive arrests of individuals deemed to be "asocial" and "workshy" and placed over ten thousand of them in concentration camps, where they could be "reeducated" through hard work. Here they joined thousands of political prisoners, Jews, Jehovah's Witnesses, homosexuals, and criminals. In 1939 Nazi camps held some twenty-five thousand people.

Slave labor was used in this former brick factory at Neuengamme, a Nazi concentration camp during World War II. [Ira Nowinski/Corbis]

Beginning in 1938, Jews were also conscripted for forced labor. After systematically depriving many Jews of their livelihood and assets, the Nazi regime decreed that those Jews receiving welfare or unemployment benefits would now be subject to conscription for labor on state or local construction projects or with private firms. By mid-1939 there were over thirty Jewish labor camps in Germany.

During the Second World War the manpower crisis in Germany became acute as a result of the conscription of almost thirteen million German men into the armed forces. Unwilling on ideological grounds to bring more women into the workplace, the Nazis turned more and more to the deployment of foreign labor. Indeed, the German wartime economy became so dependent upon foreign labor that by 1945 almost 25 percent of the country's workforce was made up of non-German nationals. In agriculture it was close to 50 percent, and in some industries the figure was almost 33 percent. Nazi political leaders, however, viewed the mass deployment of foreign laborers during the war merely as a temporary expedient and feared the consequences of "racial mixing" between Germans and others, particularly Slavs.

With the speedy victory over Poland and the need to prepare for war in the West, the Nazi regime began deploying large numbers of Polish civilians and POWs to bring in the harvests. By the end of 1939, some three hundred thousand Polish prisoners of war and about forty thousand civilians were brought to Germany to work on farms, yet these measures failed to fill the manpower shortage. In the fall and winter of 1939–1940, recruiters first tried to solicit volunteers and then began forcibly conscripting workers in the German-administered territory (General Government) in occupied Poland, where all Poles and Jews were subject to compulsory labor. Reich officials demanded that at least one million Polish men and women be sent to Germany, and to attain such goals, German authorities in occupied Poland established quotas for each district. When the requisite number of "volunteers" did not appear, SS and police units organized terror actions in the cities and countryside, surrounding noncompliant villages or seizing nonregistered workers on the street. Though such policies engendered resistance against the German occupiers, they proved to be successful in providing labor for the Reich; in August 1944 the number of Polish workers in Germany reached 1.7 million.

Military victory in western Europe provided Nazi Germany with even more foreign labor. In spring 1941 there were over one million POWs and several hundred thousand civilians from the occupied West deployed in agriculture and industry. In addition, Italy provided Germany with manpower in exchange for badly needed raw materials. Reich labor officials also decreed that all able-bodied German Jews between the ages of 15 and 65 were to be conscripted for forced labor. Such additional manpower proved to be crucial as the German military prepared for the invasion of the Soviet Union.

Basing their plans on the blitzkrieg tactics that had been so successfully employed in Poland and in western Europe, the German military envisioned the rapid defeat of the USSR. As a consequence, Nazi officials made no plans to bring Soviet workers to the Reich and instead counted on the quick return of demobilized German soldiers to the workplace. Indeed, Hitler expressly prohibited the use of Soviet POWs for forced labor in Germany. Advancing rapidly into the Soviet Union, German army troops and the SS mobile killing squads carried out a brutal occupation policy, which had little to do with economic rationale. Jews, Gypsies (Roma), and communist party functionaries were singled out for extermination, while Soviet POWs were intentionally left to die in camps. Of the 3.3 million Soviet POWs who fell into German hands in 1941, about 2 million perished by February 1942 because of the calculated brutality with which they were treated, the lack of proper housing and food, and disease.

By the late fall of 1941, the German military realized that their hopes of a swift victory in the East were illusory; Germany found itself in a protracted war for which it was ill prepared. To gain badly needed manpower, Hitler reversed his earlier position and ordered the deployment of Soviet workers to the Reich. As in Poland, German recruiters first sought volunteers, and when this failed to produce the requisite number of workers, they began forcibly conscripting labor. The brutal Nazi policies in the occupied Soviet territory produced predictable results: the partisan movement gained crucial popular support, and there were almost three million Soviet workers in the Reich in 1944.

In 1942 Germany stood at the crossroads. Though its forces still occupied much of Europe, losses on the eastern front had increased, the war had spread to North Africa, Great Britain stood undefeated in the West, and the United States had just joined the hostilities. Faced with such an impossible situation, Hitler moved to rationalize the operation of the war economy. He appointed Albert Speer as Minister of Munitions to prioritize and increase production and to distribute raw material and named Fritz Sauckel as Plenipotentiary General for the Utilization of Labor to centralize the allocation of labor. To satisfy Germany's growing demands for manpower, Sauckel launched four major recruiting campaigns that brought millions of foreign laborers to the Reich.

Within his concentration camp empire, Heinrich Himmler also moved to increase wartime production by establishing the SS Economic and Administrative Main Office. From 1942 to 1945 the SS dramatically increased the prisoner population from approximately 110,000 to over 700,000 and created a network of hundreds of satellite camps linked to the major concentration camps. German industrial enterprises, eager to find sources of cheap labor, leased concentration camp prisoners from the SS. Brutality and economic exploitation went hand in hand. In the fall of 1942, the German Justice Ministry arranged with Himmler to deliver thousands of prisoners (criminals, Jews, Gypsies, Poles, and others) held in penal institutions to SS concentration camps for "extermination through labor." The SS worked tens of thousands of prisoners to death in constructing underground tunnels and factories, in quarries, and in other industrial enterprises.

In spite of Germany's need to boost wartime armaments production in the face of defeat, the Nazis refused to abandon their genocidal policies. Although the economy was suffering from a shortage of manpower, the SS murdered millions of Jews, many of whom had been working in war-related enterprises. In the extermination camps of Belzec, Treblinka, Sobibor, and Chelmno, only a few thousand prisoners were kept alive to sort the property looted from the new arrivals and to carry out the disposal of the victims' corpses: the overwhelming majority of prisoners were dispatched immediately to the gas chambers, without regard to their work skills or capabilities. At Auschwitz-Birkenau SS doctors and other personnel carried out "selections," separating those Jews who were capable of working from those deemed unfit. Elderly persons, young children, and pregnant women were singled out for immediate extermination, while those hired out to German industries often survived for only a few months.

Nazi racial and political ideology also greatly determined how foreign laborers in the Reich were treated. Reich officials viewed workers from western Europe as being "racially" akin to Germans and feared that any harsh treatment of these laborers would outrage public opinion in their home countries and thus jeopardize German foreign policy. Unlike western European workers, who received the same wages as their German counterparts, those from Poland and the Soviet Union were subject to severe discriminatory regulations. Beginning in 1940, Poles—and later Jews, Gypsies, and Soviet workers—had to pay a "social compensation tax" amounting to 15 to 20 percent of their earnings. Polish and Soviet laborers also had to wear special badges on their clothing as a sign of their inferior status and could be executed for having sexual relations with German women. During the war perhaps thousands of eastern European workers were put to death for such offenses. Polish and Soviet women who gave birth had to turn over their babies to special children's homes, where frequently they were left to die from calculated neglect. German authorities severely punished even minor infractions by eastern European workers and in the final weeks of the war, the Gestapo executed thousands of foreign workers.

When the war in Europe ended in May 1945, millions of displaced persons were left scattered throughout the former Reich, many of them foreign laborers who had been forcibly deported from their homelands. Allied victory brought repatriation to most of these workers and prosecution for some German officials and industrialists who had participated in the slave labor program. In Nuremberg the International Military Tribunal found both Albert Speer and Fritz Sauckel guilty of such crimes; Speer was sentenced to twenty years' imprisonment, while Sauckel was executed. In the subsequent war crimes trials held in Nuremberg, U.S. military tribunals convicted a number of leading German officials, including Erhard Milch, a field marshal in the Luftwaffe, and Oswald

Pohl, the head of the SS Economic and Administrative Main Office, of participation in the Nazi slave-labor program. In addition, these tribunals sought to punish leading German industrialists for their role. In 1947/1948 prominent members of the Krupp steel and munitions works, the Friedrich Flick heavy industrial concern, and I. G. Farben, a major chemical conglomerate, were found guilty of exploiting the labor of foreign conscript workers and concentration camp prisoners. Of these convicted German industrialists, most received rather lenient sentences, and some of these sentences were subsequently reduced. Beginning in the 1950s, some victims of Nazi persecution, especially those who had worked without pay in concentration camps, began filing suits against those German companies that had profited from their labor. Since then, a number of German enterprises have agreed to settlements with their former "slave laborers," but the quest for just compensation continued into the last years of the century.

See also LABOR SYSTEMS.

BIBLIOGRAPHY

BELLON, BERNARD P. *Mercedes in Peace and War: German Automobile Workers, 1903–1945.* 1990.

BLACK, PETER. "Forced Labor in the Concentration Camps, 1942–1944." In *A Mosaic of Victims: Non-Jews Persecuted and Murdered by the Nazis,* edited by Michael Berenbaum. 1990.

BROWNING, CHRISTOPHER R. "Nazi Germany's Initial Attempt to Exploit Jewish Labor in the General Government: The Early Jewish Work Camps 1940–1941." In *Die Normalität des Verbrechens: Bilanz und Perspektiven der Forschung zu den nationalsozialistischen Gewaltverbrechen,* edited by Helge Grabitz, Klaus Bästlein, and Johannes Tuchel. 1994.

FERENCZ, BENJAMIN B. *Less Than Slaves: Jewish Forced Labor and the Quest for Compensation.* 1979.

GELLATELY, ROBERT. *The Gestapo and German Society: Enforcing Racial Policy, 1933–1945.* 1990.

GRUNER, WOLF. "*Terra incognita?* The Camps for 'Jewish Labor Conscription' (1938–1943) and the German Population." *Yad Vashem Studies* 24 (1994): 1–41.

HAYES, PETER. *Industry and Ideology: IG Farben in the Nazi Era.* 1987.

HERBERT, ULRICH. *Hitler's Foreign Workers: Enforced Foreign Labor in Germany under the Third Reich.* 1997.

———, ed. *Europa und der "Reicheinsatz": Ausländische Zivilarbeiter, Kriegsgefangene und KZ-Häftlinge in Deutschland, 1938–1945.* 1991.

HOMZE, EDWARD L. *Foreign Labor in Nazi Germany.* 1967.

———. "Nazi Germany's Forced Labor Program." In *A Mosaic of Victims: Non-Jews Persecuted and Murdered by the Nazis,* edited by Michael Berenbaum. 1990.

KWIET, KONRAD. "Forced Labour of German Jews in Nazi Germany." *Leo Baeck Institute Yearbook* 36 (1991): 389–410.

SIEGFRIED, KLAUS-JÖRG. "Racial Discrimination at Work: Forced Labour in the Volkswagen Factory, 1939–1945."

On 7 July 1945 former slave laborers are given their ration of bread, supplied by the United Nations Relief and Rehabilitation Administration, before they start the journey back to their homes. [UPI/Corbis-Bettmann]

In *Confronting the Nazi Past: New Debates on Modern German History*, edited by Michael Burleigh. 1996.

Trial of the Major War Criminals before the International Military Tribunal. 1947–1949.

Trials of War Criminals before the Nuernberg Military Tribunals. 1949–1953.

Steven Luckert

Near East

See Ancient Middle East; Modern Middle East.

Netherlands and the Dutch Empire

Slavery was illegal in the Dutch Republic (United Provinces) when the state was recognized by international treaty in 1648. Efforts to establish slave markets at the ports of Amsterdam and Middelburg had been firmly rejected by local authorities. The Dutch West India Company initially rejected participation in the transatlantic slave trade, but as Holland's global commercial empire expanded the Dutch became more accepting of slavery and its profits.

No one seemed to object when Dutch officials purchased and employed slaves at the various commercial stations and colonies in the burgeoning seventeenth-century Dutch overseas empire. Dutch colonists in Indonesia (the Dutch East Indies) imported large numbers of slaves from various Indian Ocean littorals, primarily from Asian vendors. The Dutch East India Company was only marginally involved in shipping slaves from Madagascar and East Africa either to Indonesia or to the Cape Colony, South Africa, where returning East India ships and slave ships of other nations dropped off slaves in small numbers.

Dutch shippers later played a more significant role in the transatlantic slave trade, although their level of participation in terms of volume remained considerably lower than that of the English, Portuguese, and French. In total, Dutch ships carried between 500,000 and 540,000 enslaved persons from the African continent to various destinations in the Western Hemisphere, mostly Suriname (Dutch Guiana).

The chief agent of Dutch slaving in the Atlantic was the Dutch West India Company, which had a monopoly of this trade from its inception in 1621 until the 1730s, when free traders were allowed to enter the traffic. In 1730 the company's monopoly was limited to the Gold Coast (Ghana) in Africa and the Guiana region in South America, and the company monopoly was terminated by the end of that decade.

It has often been assumed that the Dutch were involved in the Atlantic slave trade as early as 1619, when the Virginian chronologer John Rolfe reported that "... a Dutch man of Warre ... sold us 20 negars." But this was most likely an isolated case of disposing of captives from an intercepted Spanish or Portuguese ship. There were other cases of private slave shipments early in the seventeenth century that were not part of a systematic involvement in the slave traffic. Only after the conquest of northern Brazil in 1630, and of Portugal's African stations shortly thereafter, did the West India Company become deeply involved in the slave trade. During the next two decades, Dutch ships carried more than thirty thousand slaves to Brazil.

Experience with the traffic and the lure of profits encouraged continued involvement. After loss of Brazil in 1654, directors of the Dutch West India Company found a new market for slaves in the Spanish American colonies. Since Spain originally had no access to the sub-Saharan African coastline, its colonies relied on foreign vendors to supply slaves through the so-called *asiento* trade. The Dutch, by contrast, had driven the Portuguese from most of the African Atlantic coasts and had easy access to slaves. They also had a large merchant marine and abundant capital to finance the traffic. Thus they became the chief suppliers of forced labor to the Spanish colonies, mostly via a depot at the island of Curaçao. Approximately sixty thousand slaves reached Spanish America through Dutch intervention and by Dutch ships. The Antilian island of St. Eustatius also served also as a slave depot for the Dutch illicit trade with the Spanish colonies, as well as with the French islands in the Antilles during times of war.

By the second half of the seventeenth century, the Dutch had established plantation settlements on the Guiana or Wild Coast, at the Berbice and Demerara rivers (present day Guayana), and at the Suriname river. During the eighteenth century, these settlements expanded and demands for slave labor grew, because Dutch citizens had little inclination to emigrate to tropical regions. Suriname became the largest and most important of these settlements. Initially, sugar was cultivated in the colony, but other crops like coffee, cotton, and cacao were added and shipped to the Netherlands. During the eighteenth century, Suriname became the principal slave market for Dutch slave traders, with a total of approximately 180,000 African slaves landed there before 1795.

With declining access to foreign markets and the loss of the *asiento* to the English in 1713, the Dutch share of the Atlantic slave trade decreased significantly during the early eighteenth century. During the 1730s, this forced them to follow the example of other European nations and replace the company monopoly with free trade practices. In the ensuing competitive environment, free traders used smaller vessels but han-

Near a row of slave quarters stands an obelisk that once directed ships to the settlement on Bonnaire, part of the Netherlands Antilles. [Bradley Smith/Corbis]

By 1795 the Dutch slave trade ground to a halt as a result of international political tensions generated by the revolution in France. Britain captured most of the Dutch colonies and completely dominated the Atlantic slave traffic. Under diplomatic pressure from Britain, the Dutch formally ended their participation in the Atlantic slave trade in 1815. Despite their relatively late entrance and early withdrawal from the traffic, the Dutch delayed abolishing the institution of slavery in their colonies. Not until 1863 did royal decree abolish slavery in the Dutch Caribbean and Suriname.

See also CARIBBEAN REGION; INDONESIA; SURINAME.

BIBLIOGRAPHY

DEN HEIJER, HENK. *Goud, ivoor en slaven, 1674–1740.* 1997.

OOSTINDIE, GERT, ed. *Fifty Years Later: Antislavery, Capitalism, and Modernity in the Dutch Orbit.* 1995.

POSTMA, JOHANNES M. *The Dutch in the Atlantic Slave Trade, 1600–1815.* 1990.

ROSS, ROBERT. "The Last Years of the Slave Trade to the Cape Colony." *Slavery and Abolition* 9, no. 3 (1988): 209–219.

Johannes Postma

dled more consignments. This change in strategy, combined with the expansion of Suriname, produced a new high point in the volume of the Dutch slave trade during the 1760s. Altogether, free traders shipped more than 200,000 slaves across the Atlantic.

The Dutch presence on the African Coast was concentrated on the Gold Coast, where they maintained ten to twelve fortified trading stations that initially focused on the acquisition of gold. When the Dutch began to buy slaves, they purchased them primarily on the Slave Coast to the east and to a lesser extent along the central African coast north of the Congo River. After 1700 the Gold Coast also became a primary slave-exporting region, and after 1730 Dutch free traders began to acquire slaves from the regions to the west of the Gold Coast, primarily from Liberia and the Ivory Coast.

With shipments of slightly over half a million slaves, the overall Dutch share in the Atlantic trade was nearly five percent of the total, far behind the major slaving nations of Portugal, England, France, and Spain. But during the relative short period of Dutch involvement (1630–1795) their participation may have reached ten percent, and during the last quarter of the seventeenth century they may have been the dominant slave trading power.

New Hampshire

African slaves were present as early as 1645 in New Hampshire. According to the provincial records, it was legal to enslave whites, blacks, and native people who had been taken in "just wars" and those who "willingly sell themselves or are sold to us." Clear distinctions soon evolved, however, between the customary practice of limiting indenture for whites and imposing perpetual servitude upon people of color.

New Hampshire's laws of 1714 and 1715 resembled slave codes adopted throughout the Americas during the period: they limited the mobility, fraternization and autonomy of Indians, blacks, and mulattos, regardless of their condition of servitude. It is notable that laws affecting slaves generally applied equally to free blacks and other nonwhites. There were no laws restricting literacy. New Hampshire was unique for this period in having as a capital offense the murder of a slave by an owner. The law, however, was never applied.

While little is known about the enslavement of native people by European settlers, there is ample evidence of African and black American slaves in colonial New Hampshire. Probate and church baptismal records document white ownership of slaves. Newspapers advertised the sale of children and adults recently arrived from Africa and the West Indies, the sale of American-born slaves, and notices of rewards for the return of runaway slaves.

Running away was one means of self-liberation. Most slaves apparently either purchased their own freedom or negotiated manumission by their owners during the period of economic decline after the Revolutionary War. In 1779, twenty Portsmouth slaves, identifying themselves as Africans, petitioned the state legislature for their freedom and for an end to the practice of slavery. The petition was tabled. One of its sponsors was Prince Whipple, a slave since childhood of General William Whipple, a signer of the Declaration of Independence.

General emancipation was gradual and personalized, based on individual circumstances, until the end of the eighteenth century. Although the new state constitution declared "all men are born equally free and independent," it was the legislature's removal of a tax on human chattel in 1789 that implied an end to slavery.

William Wells Brown, Abby Kelley, Horace Mann, Charles Lennox Remond, William Lloyd Garrison, and Frederick Douglass were among the abolitionists who were on the speakers' circuit throughout New Hampshire. Often they were met by angry proslavery mobs at the lecture halls and were forced to curtail their appearances. A few women's antislavery societies were active throughout the state. President Franklin Pierce, a Democrat from New Hampshire, was committed to uphold states' rights and signed into law the Kansas-Nebraska Act.

Despite New Hampshire's economic dependency on the fruits of southern black labor, both white and black recruits fought in the Union Army during the Civil War. In addition to their involuntary role as personal servants in nonblack regiments, New Hampshire slaves and free men also served as enlistees in every war, beginning with the French and Indian wars. Several were in the all-black Fifty-fourth Massachusetts Regiment.

Many Portsmouth-built ships were directly engaged in the Atlantic and American coastal slave trade, continuing even after slavery had ended in the North. The *Nightingale* was called the "prince of slavers" because of its elegant appearance and speed. Shipments of slaves typically were exchanged in the West Indies for sugar and rum to be brought to New England ports. In addition, merchants supplied affluent residents of the New Hampshire seacoast with imports such as mahogany, rosewood, indigo, and rice produced by enslaved laborers on West Indian and southern plantations. Meanwhile, New Hampshire's textile mills were fueled with cotton from the South; a course fabric called "niger cloth" was, in turn, sold to plantation owners.

Franklin Pierce. [Library of Congress/Corbis]

In colonial New Hampshire, one, two, or three slaves would live within a household; rarely were there more than three servants. The term "servant" was used for indentured servants, hired help, and slaves. Although not all slave owners were wealthy, most were. Servant quarters would be in the attic or a back room of the owner's residence. Types of work required, whether primarily agricultural or mercantile, would change with the seasons. Men, both slaves and free blacks, also were employed in maritime industries, on shore and at sea. Women performed the varied and rigorous tasks required to maintain the well-being of the owners' families, and to entertain the political leaders and social gentry passing through the international port of Portsmouth.

The largest number of slaves lived in Rockingham County, particularly in the thriving seaport of Portsmouth. In 1767 Portsmouth slaves numbered 187, representing four percent of the total population of the town and one-third the number of slaves in all of New Hampshire. By 1790 the number of slaves reported in all of the state had decreased to 158, while the combined number of enslaved and free blacks was six-tenths of one percent (787) of the total (141,899). From that time until the present, the proportionate number of blacks living in the state has remained small and has not changed significantly.

See also DOUGLASS, FREDERICK; GARRISON, WILLIAM LLOYD; KANSAS-NEBRASKA ACT. *See also the individual entries on the other states of the United States.*

BIBLIOGRAPHY

CUNNINGHAM, VALERIE. "First Blacks of Portsmouth." *Historical New Hampshire* 44 (1989): 180–201.
SAMMONS, MARK, and VALERIE CUNNINGHAM. *Portsmouth Black Heritage Trail: A Resource Book.* 1996.

Valerie Cunningham

New Jersey

Enslaved Africans first appeared here in 1630 at Pavonia, an ill-fated plantation across the river from New Amsterdam and in the Swedish colony of New Amstel on the Delaware River. In subsequent decades, enslaved blacks accompanied their pioneer masters to outposts in East Jersey. Conquest of the region by the English in 1664 opened New Jersey to greater white settlement and slavery. Quakers in the south and west Jersey counties, Scot, Irish, Dutch, Huguenot, New Englanders, and Anglicans all found labor needs more compelling than any religious scruples. In fact, northern European religions acquiesced in slave trading and chattel bondage by using the "fortunate fall" thesis, which contended that African slaves in contact with Christianity were better off than their free counterparts. By 1680 masters in East Jersey owned over 120 bondspeople. Laws governing slaves were local, but by 1704 the colonial legislature enacted a *code noir* (black code), identifying Africans as slaves. Clauses added in 1714 denied free blacks ownership of property and mandated a £200 bond for any emancipation, effectively foreclosing any grants of freedom.

The first colonial census in New Jersey in 1726 enumerated 2,581 slaves, or 8 percent of the total population. By 1745 there were 4,606 enslaved Africans in the colony. New Jersey had no duty on slaves and so traders often landed and sold captive Africans in the colony or smuggled them overland to Philadelphia and New York. East Jersey counties such as Bergen, Monmouth, and Somerset relied heavily on slave labor to support their agricultural economies. Although there were few "gentlemen's farms" with dozens of slaves, the general pattern was a few slaves per farm, though masters were often related. Males predominated and worked year-round planting, cultivating, and harvesting grain crops, chopping firewood, and performing innumerable other tasks, often with white free wage laborers. Other blacks worked at mines or as artisans.

Black resistance to slavery was common. Uprisings were few, though a massive effort failed in Somerset in 1734, and Jersey blacks were implicated in the 1741 New York conspiracy. There were constant instances of flight, poisonings, and brutal attacks on masters. At first antislavery attitudes were rare, but by the 1750s the Society of Friends (Quakers) campaigned against enslavement and forced members to sell or emancipate their chattel. Most Friends chose gradual emancipation, popularizing this reform. During the American Revolution, hundreds of Jersey blacks fled to freedom behind the British lines and later settled in Nova Scotia and Sierra Leone.

After the American Revolution, the New Jersey Society for the Abolition of Slavery, composed of Quakers and liberal Anglicans, spearheaded the drive to end slavery and assist blacks active in the cause. By 1790 roughly 20 percent of New Jersey's 14,185 blacks were free. Dutch-dominated Bergen county rejected this movement; there, only 193 of 2,493 blacks were free. In 1804, after years of negotiation, the state legislature finally enacted a gradual emancipation act, which awarded freedom after twenty-one years of service to females and after twenty-five years to males. Blacks born before 4 July 1804 were slaves for life. Slavery died stubbornly in New Jersey. Bergen masters petitioned anxiously for repeal of the abolition act. As late as 1830 there were still 2,221 slaves in East Jersey. Masters bequeathed slaves to their children, advertised for fugitives, and registered newborns to ensure full use of their bondage. A court case in 1846 succeeded in changing the status of slaves to lifetime indentured servants; in 1860, eighteen blacks were still enslaved. The Fifteenth Amendment finally ended servitude in New Jersey in 1870.

See also ABOLITION AND ANTISLAVERY MOVEMENTS; CODE NOIR; DEMOGRAPHY OF SLAVES IN THE UNITED STATES; EMANCIPATION IN THE UNITED STATES, ESCAPE; QUAKERS.

BIBLIOGRAPHY

HODGES, GRAHAM RUSSELL. *Slavery and Freedom in the Rural North: African Americans in Monmouth County, New Jersey, 1660–1865.* 1977.
WRIGHT, GILES G. *Afro-Americans in New Jersey: A Short History.* 1988.

Graham Hodges

New Mexico

While chattel slavery was uncommon, forced Indian labor, an active trade in captives, and indentured servitude created an eclectic and ambiguous system of bonded labor in New Mexico. Even before the arrival of the first Spaniards, raiding for captives was part of the native landscape. With the Spanish *entrada* in the sixteenth century, Spanish colonial officials conscripted Pueblo labor for public works (*repartimiento de indios*), Pueblo labor supported Franciscan missionaries, and the Spanish crown allotted certain settlers the right to extract tribute in goods and labor (the system of *encomienda*) from particular Pueblos as reward for colonization. Abuse of Indian labor played a major role in precipitating the Pueblo Revolt of 1680, in which the Spanish were ejected from New Mexico until nearly the end of the century. After the Spanish reconquest in 1692–1696, the Spaniards' conscription of Indian labor lessened.

However, well into the nineteenth century, pueblo and Spanish settlements became targets of Apache, Ute, and Comanche raids, which occasionally resulted in the taking of captives, especially women and children. While some historians have described captivity as akin to slavery, noting an active captive slave trade, others have suggested that captives were primarily incorporated into their host societies, becoming cultural bridges among the various native and, later, Hispano populations of the region.

Hispano communities worked actively to redeem captives as part of their efforts at Christianization. One scholar estimates that between 1700 and 1850, nearly 3,000 nomadic Indians were redeemed in New Mexico, roughly 10 to 15 percent of New Mexico's colonial society. While many captives were purchased at local trade fairs to become servants (*criados*) in Spanish or mestizo households, others were sold into slavery. Thus there was intense competition for control of this trade. Although redemption of captives declined in the nineteenth century, historians estimate that by the 1860s, there were between 600 and 3,000 Indian servants in New Mexico, many becoming lifelong members of the households in which they lived.

Debt peonage, which tied debtors to their creditors as laborers for varying periods of time, was also common. Many New Mexican Hispanos defined peonage as a labor contract, permitting debtors to fulfill obligations in a cash-poor economy; but after New Mexico was conquered by the United States peonage became a target of Euro-American critics of slavery. This pressure prompted the territorial supreme court to declare peonage illegal in 1867, though the practice continued for many years thereafter.

Finally, a small number of African slaves had arrived with the Spanish from the beginning of the colonial period. After conquest by the United States, other slaves accompanied their southern masters. The U.S. Congress allowed slavery in the New Mexico Territory under the Compromise of 1850, and in 1859 the territorial legislature enacted a slave code. However, the numbers of these slaves was small. The 1860 census, for example, reported only 40 slaves of African descent in New Mexico. Congress prohibited slavery in New Mexico and other U.S. territories in 1862.

See also COMPROMISE OF 1850; LABOR SYSTEMS; NATIVE AMERICANS; PEONAGE; PUBLIC WORKS.

BIBLIOGRAPHY

BROOKS, JAMES F. "'This Evil Extends Especially to the Feminine Sex': Negotiating Captivity in the New Mexico Borderlands." *Feminist Studies* 22, no. 2 (Summer 1996): 279–309.

MURPHY, LAWRENCE R. *Anti-Slavery in the Southwest: William G. Kephart's Mission to New Mexico, 1850–1853.* 1978.

TAYLOR, QUINTARD. "African Americans in the Enchanted State: Black History in New Mexico, 1539–1990." In *History of Hope: The African American Experience in New Mexico,* edited by Thomas Lark. 1996.

WEBER, DAVID J. *The Spanish Frontier in North America.* 1993.

David A. Reichard

New York

The Dutch West India Company brought the first enslaved Africans to New Amsterdam in 1626 to clear the land, build the fort, and provide general labor. They were emancipated in the 1640s, but later arrivals were not so fortunate. Searching for an economic base for the struggling colony, Governor Petrus Stuyvesant made New Amsterdam the leading slave depot in North America by the 1650s. When the English con-

Petrus (Peter) Stuyvesant. [Corbis-Bettmann]

quered the colony in 1664, it had 800 Africans, all but 75 of whom were enslaved.

Though the colony was not a main destination for the slave trade, its number of Africans increased to 2,258, or 10 percent of the total population. Traders brought enslaved blacks from Madagascar, the West Indies, and, after 1714, directly from the west African coast. The state legislature enacted a harsh slave code in 1704 and augmented it after the slave revolt of 1712 forbidding free blacks to own property and requiring £200 bond for emancipation. After that, nearly all blacks in New York were enslaved.

The slave trade and natural increase brought the number of enslaved Americans in New York to 7,231 by 1731 and to 13,548 by 1756. There were three demographic patterns. The first, urban slavery, was characterized by small numbers per household, primarily female slaves, especially in New York City, and paternalism. Surprisingly, more slaves lived in Albany than in New York City in the late colonial period. The second, rarer pattern was the large farm, epitomized by Frederick Phillips's manor in Westchester, which employed over sixty slaves. The third pattern, which predominated, was the small farm; outlying counties such as Suffolk, Westchester, and Kings utilized enslaved blacks as their labor force. Kings County was over one-third black in the 1740s. By 1771, nearly twenty thousand enslaved blacks lived and worked in New York, by far the greatest number north of the Chesapeake.

Black resistance was constant in New York. A major uprising in 1712 was followed by a widespread conspiracy in 1741, but this was brutally repressed. Runaways, attacks on masters, and insubordination were common problems. The ethnic diversity and dependence on slave labor ensured that despite anxieties, antislavery was weak in New York. Reform-minded Anglicans attempted to ameliorate enslavement by protecting blacks against brutality or tried to inculcate Christianity in blacks through charity schools. The New York Meeting of the Society of Friends was far more conservative than its counterpart in Philadelphia. During the American Revolution, hundreds of New York blacks joined the British side; in 1783 more than three thousand blacks from all over the east coast departed New York for Nova Scotia. Over one-fifth were from New York.

After the American Revolution, slavery again flourished. Antislavery groups such as the Anglicans and the Quakers were regarded with suspicion. Despite the influence of the New York Manumission Society, little headway was made against enslavement until 1799, when the legislature passed a weak gradual emancipation act, which freed slaves born after 4 July 1799, after twenty-one years of bondage for females and twenty-five years for males, effectively costing them their productive years. Masters were compensated by a clause paying them to maintain freed infant slaves; by 1808, compensation payments burdened state budgets.

Despite gradual emancipation, slavery died very slowly in New York. In rural regions masters held tightly to slaves until the 1820s. Sensitive to this, Governor Daniel D. Tompkins in 1817 pushed through legislation that ended all enslavement in the state on 4 July 1827, a date celebrated widely by the black population.

See also ANGLICANISM; NEW YORK MANUMISSION SOCIETY; QUAKERS; PANICS.

BIBLIOGRAPHY

MCMANUS, EDGAR. *A History of Negro Slavery in New York.* 1966.
WHITE, SHANE. *"Somewhat More Independent": The End of Slavery in New York City, 1770–1810.* 1991.

Graham Hodges

New York Manumission Society

In January 1785 Anglicans and Quakers, who opposed slavery in the new American republic, formed the New York Manumission Society. The society served several purposes. First, using verbal persuasion, letters, and readings of the essay on slavery by the English abolitionist Thomas Clarkson, the society sought to convince slave owners of the virtues of gradual emancipation. It also lobbied the New York State legislature to abolish slavery and in 1792 summoned a convention of similar organizations from other states, a meeting that marked the inception of the national movement to end slavery. The society claimed that between 1792 and 1814 it liberated 429 African-American slaves and provided a registry for free blacks wishing to leave precious freedom papers in a secure place. Finally, it acted as a political conduit between black voters and the Federalist Party. Blacks acquired antislavery materials from the society, which distributed three hundred copies of Clarkson's essay and Granville Sharpe's reports on the fledgling colony in Sierra Leone. The society paid for publication of "Slavery" (by someone called only "A Free Negro"), an important early black abolitionist appeal, which appeared in the *American Museum* in 1788.

Slave ownership by key members was a sharp contradiction of the society's liberalism. Important statesmen and philanthropic members, including the future chief justice John Jay, Judge James Duane, and Senator Rufus King, proposed legislation favoring abolition of slavery while retaining their own bond servants.

Nearly all planned gradual emancipation for their slaves, a process that could take twenty years.

These practices have spurred recent historians to view the society very critically. Shane White has asserted that the Manumission Society did nothing to end slavery in New York. Another argument contends that the society forced free blacks into accepting dependent status by requiring registration before black children could attend the African Free School.

The society won an important victory in the late 1790s by ending the New York City government's practice of correcting disorderly slaves at the request of their masters. This method, a carry-over from the colonial period, was widely used in the 1790s. According to a city report in 1799, the law was also used regularly to bring runaway slaves from other areas into the Bridewell jail to await their masters' retrieval. That year the Manumission Society successfully petitioned the city government to end the practice. Also in 1799 the society spearheaded the state decision to enact a gradual emancipation law, which insured the eventual extinction of slavery in New York State. In succeeding years its ardor cooled, though Governor Daniel D. Tompkins, long a member, pushed through legislation in 1817 that ended slavery forever ten years later.

The society's significance lies not so much in its members' halting neocolonial liberalism as in its support for African-Americans' legal actions for freedom, in its hotminded vigilance against dangerous slave catchers, in its lobbying recalcitrant slave masters, and as a registry for precious freedom papers. The society earned an important victory by convincing the municipal government to halt the practice of disciplining slaves.

See also ABOLITION AND ANTISLAVERY MOVEMENTS; CLARKSON, THOMAS; NEW YORK; SHARP, GRANVILLE.

BIBLIOGRAPHY

ALEXANDER, ARTHUR J. "Federal Officeholders in New York State as Slave Holders, 1789–1805." *Journal of Negro History* 28 (1943): 326–350.

WHITE, SHANE. *Somewhat More Independent: The End of Slavery in New York City, 1770–1810.* 1991.

Graham Hodges

New Zealand

See Maori; Pacific Island Societies.

Nguni

See Southern Africa.

Nile River

See Egypt; Northeast Africa.

Nóbrega, Manuel da   [1517–1570]

Portuguese Jesuit missionary.

Manuel da Nóbrega, who devoted his energies to Christianizing Brazilian Indians and protecting them from enslavement, arrived in Brazil in 1549 and immediately petitioned the governor to free a number of unjustly enslaved Indians—that is, those who were willing to become Christians and also refrained from cannibalism. As part of his campaign against Indian captivity, Nóbrega urged clerics to deny confession to settlers guilty of unjust enslavement. He also advised the Portuguese crown and its colonial officials against the Spanish-American practice of allotting Indian labor to conquistadors and settlers. Instead, he advocated gathering Indians in villages where Jesuit clergy would Christianize and pacify them while overseeing their labor. Nóbrega's ideas influenced Mem de Sá, governor of Brazil from 1558 to 1572, who approved the Jesuit system of villages. Three years before his death, Nóbrega issued a strong indictment against Indian enslavement, the *Caso de Consciência*. In this

Daniel D. Tompkins. [Oscar White/Corbis]

treatise Nóbrega discredited the practice of Indians' selling themselves or their children into slavery. Citing oppression and threats from settlers, Indian misery and naiveté, and deception by both parties, he called for strict restrictions on this method of enslavement. The *Caso de Consciência* led to the first significant Portuguese law favoring Indian liberty (1570). Nóbrega limited his antislavery efforts to Indians. Indeed, his acquisition of African slaves to work on Jesuit lands in Brazil implies that he condoned African slavery.

See also BRAZIL.

BIBLIOGRAPHY

LEITE, SERAFIM. *Breve itinerário para una biografia do P. Manual da Nóbrega.* 1955.
———. *Novas páginas de História do Brasil.* 1962.

John J. Crocitti

Norris, Robert   [?–1791]

English defender of the slave trade.

Robert Norris traded in West Africa from the mid-1750s to the 1780s; his travels there included a visit to the Dahomean ruler in 1772. Norris shared his knowledge about the slave trade with abolitionist Thomas Clarkson for Clarkson's *Essay on the Slavery and Commerce of the Human Species* (1786), an influential attack on the trade. But Norris's *Short Account of the African Slave Trade Collected from Local Knowledge, from Evidence at the Bar of Both Houses of Parliament, and from Tracts Written Upon that Subject* (1787) defended the trade, as Norris did when he represented Liverpool traders in appearances before governmental investigative committees in the late 1780s.

Norris agreed with navy men that the slave trade, by employing British sailors, maintained a reservoir of skilled seamen that the royal navy could use in wartime; thus slavery contributed to British security. Norris also linked the trade to national greatness and subjects' rights, claiming that

> the principle which has raised the commerce and navigation of this country . . . is the *right* which every man . . . possesses, to carry on his own business, in the way most advantageous to himself . . . , without any sudden interruption in the pursuit of it; and [with] the . . . steady protection of the laws.

Finally, Norris told horrific stories about life in Dahomey, in an effort to make the slave trade seem comparatively humane for blacks. Norris's work helped defeat abolition or significant regulation of the slave trade in the 1780s and early 1790s.

See also CLARKSON, THOMAS; SLAVE TRADE.

BIBLIOGRAPHY

DAVIS, DAVID BRION. *The Problem of Slavery in the Age of Revolution, 1770–1823.* 1975.
STEPHEN, SIR LESLIE, ed. *Dictionary of National Biography.* 1885–1901.

T. Stephen Whitman

North Africa

This entry includes the following articles: Morocco; Sahara Region. *Related articles may be found at the entries* Africa; Central Africa; East Africa; Northeast Africa; Slave Trade; Southern Africa; West Africa. *See also the note accompanying the entry* Africa *for further information about the organization of these entries.*

Morocco

In late-nineteenth-century Morocco, European observers found *'abid* (singular, *'abd*)—that is, slaves—everywhere. Women were household domestics, concubines, and factory workers; men were artisans, shop assistants, and transporters. Both were cultivators and herders. Male slaves managed property for absentee masters and served in armies of powerful chiefs. Most notable were the men, women, and children owned by the Sultan himself—said to number in the thousands.

'Abid married and had children. It was difficult for Europeans to differentiate between them and the poor, the *haratin* (singular, *hartani, hartania*), and the recently freed slaves. (*Haratin* sometimes means a freed slave, but more often, in the Moroccan context, means a free person; *hurr*, "second," and *thani*, "rank.") Slaves were generally better off than, and considered themselves superior to, these groups. The urban poor constituted a growing class in misery, who resented the safety net masters provided to slaves and freed slaves brought into the labor market. Haratin occupied different social niches. In cities like Fez, they ranged from blond and blue-eyed to jet-black with Negroid features; they could work as skilled artisans, they could be wealthy traders, and could even be married into free families. But in the south they were almost exclusively dark-skinned and Negroid and worked as cultivators; their communities—at one time indigenous to the region—had clearly welcomed many slaves into their ranks over the centuries.

Slaves who developed a self-identity as members of the families who owned them felt superior to the haratin, who had no pedigree and no protectors. Slaves were relieved by their masters of the responsibilities and expectations imposed on nonslaves; and this kind of patronage relationship extended to freed slaves, who often remained in the household even after manumission. Thus this was not slavery as Europeans thought they knew it, and most nineteenth-century observers were hesitant even to apply the term.

Slavery in Morocco dates from at least Roman times. Morocco was the province of Mauritania Tingitane; prisoners from the incessant wars were enslaved as laborers and domestics, and enslaved captives (only a few of whom were black) may have constituted between 8 percent and 20 percent of the population. In the post-Roman era, as trans-Saharan commerce with the agricultural regions south of the desert (the Sudan, in Muslim times) grew, the region—whose frontiers shifted frequently—became an important source of African as well as Berber slaves, first supplying Constantinople, and later, from about the eighth century, the expanding Islamic world.

This world was fragmented, and its internal ruptures gave added impetus to commercial dynamics. Revolt by the Kharijites (a dissident sect of the Shia believers, who were followers of Ali in the secession dispute after the Prophet's death) led to the establishment of Sijilmassa (Saharan southeastern Morocco) around 750; its commercial importance as a source of sub-Saharan gold and labor established the pivotal role of the Maghrib al-Aqsa (the western Maghreb) in the international Muslim economy. Berber Almoravids from the desert (eleventh century) capitalized on the gold trade to finance a new empire extending into Spain and across the Sahara. Sijilmassa and its sub-Saharan counterpart, Awdagust, housed wealthy merchants, landowners, and thousands of slaves, who worked in the fields, provided domestic service, and traveled with caravans.

The Almoravids' conquest of the Maghreb al-Aqsa heartland was achieved by creating the *hasham,* a special royal horse cavalry of 2,000 black slaves and 250 purchased Andalusian Christians. This model was replicated by the Almoravids' successors, the twelfth-century Almohads' abid al-Maghzen, "slaves of the state." Both the Almoravids and the Almohads frequently faced rebellion by desert Berbers, providing their armies with legitimate opportunities to enslave the Berber women and children so much in demand in eastern markets. This era also marked the beginning of a trade in slaves from the sub-Saharan Sudan to Europe via the Maghreb and Andalusia, which would continue into the fifteenth century.

With the decline of the unifying force of the Almohads (late thirteenth century), distinguishing features of the domestic development of Maghrib al-Aqsa emerged. North of the Anti-Atlas Mountains, urban culture reflected Andalusian and Oriental influences: female slaves were domestics and concubines; castrated male slaves—eunuchs—were harem keepers and administrators for the sultan; males were servants and laborers in the royal stables and on farms. The southern plains of the Wadi Sous and Dra'a looked to the Sahara as a source of culture and economic strength: haratin and slaves populated farming villages and a growing number of *zwaya* (religious centers); in the Wadi Dra'a and oases of Tafilelt-Sijilmassa and Tuat, they cultivated date-palm groves.

From the rise of the Muslim Saadien dynasty (sixteenth century), through the Alawites (from the seventeenth century), sultans fought these fragmenting tendencies, seeking to concentrate power in a court and an army capable of rivaling the Ottomans. Slaves of diverse origins remained central to palace life: concubines, wet nurses, and mothers of royal children; male soldiers (including Christian prisoner-slaves); eunuch harem keepers and administrators. The Saadien conquest of Songhay, south of the Sahara, in 1591 was led by a former Christian freed slave, and the soldiers included many such slaves. The great Alawite sultan Mulay Ismail (1672–1727, himself born of a slave mother), created a veritable black slave army, the 'Abid al-Bukhari. Resembling the Ottoman *devshirme* more than the earlier Almoravid or Almohad guards, the 'abid were to become a self-reproducing class: slave soldiers were given wives, and their children were brought up in palace service. Male slaves in the kingdom were requisitioned (for a nominal remuneration) from their masters. Haratin and blacks of uncertain origin were also dragooned, causing the *'ulamma* (Islamic legal scholars) of Fez to object vigorously (and in vain) that the sultan was enslaving free Muslims, a contravention of *sharia,* Islamic law. Slaves who were obtained directly from the Sudan continued to supplement the slave corps on a regular basis. Following Moulay Ismail's death, the 'abid soon became political powers unto themselves, and consequently, many met the same fate as their overly ambitious Ottoman counterparts, the janissaries. This royal slave culture extended to local centers of power, including the zwaya, which never ceased to challenge the centralizing tendencies of maghzen authority.

During the nineteenth century, the most significant influence on Moroccan slavery was not European abolitionism but rather French colonial conquests to the east (the Ottoman regencies, Algeria and Tunisia) and south (the West African Sudan). As the French occupied Mediterranean coastal regions and extended their presence into the desert, traditional markets supplying sub-Saharan Africans as slaves (e.g., Tuat) closed. Annual slave imports to southern Morocco increased from the 1860s to the 1880s to between four thousand and seven thousand; merchants in Timbuktu began training slaves in Islam and Arabic to raise their sale price in the north. Royal tax revenues

In Tangier, Morocco, around 1900, a young man stands while his female slave sits at his feet. [Michael Maslan Historic Photographs/Corbis]

drew heavily on these sales; on occasion, markets were leased out like tax farms (where local notables bid on the right to manage and profit from the sultan's lands in exchange for agreed-upon rent revenues).

In the 1890s French conquests succeeded in closing off the Sudan as a source of slaves, but Moroccan slavery continued, turning to local supplies. In the face of severely reduced imports, Moroccan merchants encouraged intertribal raids to obtain Berber prisoners, mostly women and children; haratin cultivators were the favored prey of locally organized kidnapping parties (often with the consent of local chiefs or caids); and in the Sous, slaves were raised for domestic sale. Even the sultan, the single largest proprietor of humans, marketed his excess slaves. Resale of southern slaves in northern markets became a profitable and growing business.

By 1912, when the French established a formal protectorate over the Moroccan monarchy, European abolitionists had succeeded in forcing the sale of slaves from public markets to private courtyards. A subsequent questionnaire on the "condition of slavery" affirmed Europeans' impression that Moroccan slavery was not "real," that slaves were "a veritable part of the family" and of Muslim culture. In 1922, a colonial government circular emphasized that administrators were to reinforce the freedoms the *sharia* advocated and protect those who claimed such rights. Marketing slaves was illegal, though slavery itself was not. Kidnapping of children was still common in the south in the 1930s; domestic slavery, including concubinage, continued in towns and villages. It was only in the 1940s that freed slaves and haratin gradually replaced slaves per se. The vast majority of unskilled manual and menial labor created by the colonial economy was the domain of this new underclass. Men and women managed to buy property and even establish small businesses. Those who could found work with the French administration; haratin in particular were adept at parleying this opportunity into political advantage. Freed slaves generally maintained contact with their former families for assistance with customary needs like marriage expenses, credit, and legal problems.

Twentieth-century distinction between haratin and freed slaves may in part be a product of that recent period of social transition. But difficult economic circumstances during the 1950s pushed both groups to emigrate from the south in search of work. Whereas northern cities had frequently absorbed such population influxes, and their haratin populations occupied as many economic niches as they represented racial mixes, southern society was less accustomed to having a servile population with direct access to independent revenue. The differential investment between the advantaged north and the largely marginalized south—first by the colonial regime, then by the independent Moroccan regime (from the 1960s)—exacerbated the social tension between blacks and indigenous Berbers. Emergent discrepancies between the increasing material wealth of non-noble families and their lack of a comparable increase in social and political status have not been lost on local politics. Contemporary democratic elections promise to play increasingly on this tension.

As the twentieth century neared its end, there seemed to be some interest in reviving annual slave *moussem* (fairs) as cultural events. This celebration of the slave heritage was a development of some import, whose significance in terms of social identity is not yet clear. The contemporary "slave" was just as likely to be a suit-clad young migrant returning from France or a college-educated woman in jeans and African braids, as a retired soldier or an elderly farmer settled in the local village. Slavery—broadly understood as the basis of many identities in the Moroccan context—seemed poised to carry yet another generation into the twenty-first century.

See also AFRICA; CONCUBINES; EUNUCHS; MODERN MIDDLE EAST; OTTOMAN EMPIRE; SLAVE TRADE.

BIBLIOGRAPHY

BARBOUR, BERNARD, and MICHELLE JACOBS. "The Mi'raj: A Legal Treatise on Slavery by Ahmad Baba." In *Slaves and Slavery in Muslim Africa*, vol. 1, edited by J. R. Willis. 1985.

BATRAN, A. A. "The 'ulama of Fas, Mulay Ismail, and the Issue of the Haratin of Fas." In *Slaves and Slavery in Muslim Africa*, vol. 2, edited by J. R. Willis. 1985.

BINEBINE, MAHI. *Le Sommeil de l'esclave*. 1992. A novel, reportedly autobiographical.

ENNAJI, MOHAMMED. *Soldats, domestiques et concubines: L'esclave au Maroc au XIXe siècle*. Preface by Ernest Gellner. 1994.

———. "Vols d'esclaves et rapts de personnes libres: Un aspect des rapports socieux au Maroc du XIXe siècle." *Bulletin economique et social du Maroc*, special issue, "En hommage à Paul Pascon," nos. 159–161 (1988): 211–223

HUNWICK, JOHN. "Black Africans in the Mediterranean World: Introduction to a Neglected Aspect of the African Diaspora." In *The Human Commodity: Perspectives on the Trans-Saharan Slave Trade*, edited by Elizabeth Savage. 1992.

MCDOUGALL, E. ANN. "A Sense of Self: The Life of Fatma Barka (Southern Morocco)." *Canadian Journal of African Studies* 32, no. 3 (1998).

"An Old Missionary"; "Some Slaves in Morocco." In *The Moslem World*, vol. 26. 1968.

PELLOW, THOMAS. *The History of the Long Captivity and Adventures of Thomas Pellow, in South Barbary*. 1739. Reprint, 1973.

SCHROETER, DANIEL J. "Slave Markets and Slavery in Moroccan Urban Society." In *The Human Commodity: Perspectives on the Trans-Saharan Slave Trade*, edited by Elizabeth Savage. 1992.

E. Ann McDougall

Sahara Region

"Sahara" is more than a geographic or climatic descriptor. The sand, the mountains, the river valleys (*wadi*), the oases were realities that focused economic activity around oasis and *wadi* agriculture, mineral extraction, commerce, and above all pastoralism. But how work was done and by whom was a function of the social order, one which evolved over time to produce a complex structure ranging from degrees of "freedom" and "nobility" to absolute nonfreedom and slavery. Over the centuries, this society extended networks of religious, political, and social relations into the Sahelian frontiers, that is, the desert's edge. Thus, to be Saharan, whether noble or slave, did not always mean living in the Sahara.

The early Sahara was not a desert at all. A population of black, Negroid cultivators and Berber small-stock pastoralists flourished during its "wet phase" (ca. 5000–2000 B.C.). Gradual desiccation pushed both groups to Sahelian margins, leaving pockets of sedentary 'blacks" where water tables permitted. These were probably the first Saharan slaves, hunted by Libyan Berber slave-raiders using the horse-drawn chariots recorded in second-millennium rock art, for use in the Libyan Fezzan or export to Egypt. The entry of the camel to Saharan trade (fourth century after Christ) allowed Romans and Byzantines to regularize commerce and to push it into "sudanic" (black) Africa. A shift from horse rearing to camel rearing permitted some Berber tribes, often under pressure from new arrivals in the northern regions, to repopulate the desert. When North African Muslim merchants began to invest in Saharan trade in the eighth century, Berbers possessed the means of transport, the desert salts desired by Sudanese slave merchants, and the slaves who mined the salt. They were well positioned to exploit the expanding market.

Contemporary Arabic writers grouped widely dispersed Berbers clans into *znaga* (Sanhaja or "veiled people" from Libya west to the Atlantic), and Lamta or Massufa (in the central region, between Timbuktu and Fezzan). In the ninth and tenth centuries, *znaga* controlled Awdagust, the southern-Saharan terminus of the flourishing slave trade with Sijilmassa, and the Lamta-Massufa were developing a similar trade to Fezzan. These latter were the ancestors of the Tuareg *Imashaghen* (the "noble and free"). Their capital, Tadmakka, was like Awdaghust and several other oasis communities that shared a distinctively "urban" culture: multiracial, and "international," with thousands of slaves. Concubines, domestic workers, artisans, and artists, they were initially of Ethiopian and Slavic origin, but increasingly, they arrived from the Sudan. These communities also absorbed remnants of indigenous peoples into various servile categories. As Islam took root, these towns welcomed scholars and *telamidh* (students) who established centres of learning (*zawiya*). By the twelfth and thirteenth centuries, sedentarized clans (*Ineslemen* among the Tuareg, *zawaya* among the *znaga*) were specializing in teaching, cultivating, and trading.

Nevertheless, the medieval Sahara was overwhelmingly pastoral. The unsettling migrations of powerful "Arab" camel-raisers, the Banu Hassan, into *znaga* society in the thirteenth and fourteenth centuries accentuated this character. (The purely Arab origins of the Banu Hassan have been under considerable dispute.) *Znaga* herders established client relations with them or turned to the pacific activities of the *zawaya*; *hassani* became synonymous with "warrior" and lent its name (*hassanyya*) to the distinctive Arabic-Berber dialect which evolved in the western regions. Whereas Tuareg identity and language (*tamashek*) remained primarily Berber and Tuareg political culture reflected connections with Egypt and the Ottomans, *znaga* society remained rooted in Almoravid traditions—integrated with the political economy of the Maghrib al-Aqsa (western Maghrib). Timbuktu, a seasonal camp on the Niger River bend where Tuareg slaves looked after their masters' goods, grew into a pivotal intellectual, cultural, and commercial center between these Saharan worlds.

Between the fifteenth and eighteenth centuries, several external developments reshaped their context: the establishment of Portuguese traders on the Atlantic coast gave rise to an east-west flow of Sudanese slaves from markets as far inland as Timbuktu; the rise of Ottoman military and economic power in the North and Middle East created an unprecedented demand for Africans as slave soldiers, concubines, and domestic workers; and the Alawite dynasty in Morocco extended its political influence into the Sahara, stimulating slave raids and increased slave trading. The large military states lying to the south of the desert—Mali, Songhai, and Kanem-Bornu—struggled continuously to rebuild centralized polities during this era and in the process produced regular supplies of slave prisoners for all three networks.

In the desert in the late sixteenth and seventeenth centuries, droughts were catalysts of further change. Poor herders sought patrons, and *zawaya* and *Ineselemen,* led by miracle-performing *shaykhs* ("chiefs") with access to diversified resources among their various followers, were well positioned to play that role. They established new *zawiya,* and by at least the eighteenth century these clerical interests were expanding into the floodwater lands of the Senegal and Niger Rivers. *Telamidh* provided initial support for these activities, but slave labor sustained them. In some cases, slaves who worked year-round on their *shaykh's* behalf were freed. Their status was recognized as entailing continued mutual obligations. Among western Saharans, these freed slaves were *haratin* (from *hurr*, "free"; and *thani,* "second rank"); among the Tuareg, where *haratin* referred to servile groups of uncertain, but generally not slave, origin, *ighawalen, bella,* and *buzu* were among the terms used.

In the nineteenth century, European pressures on Ottoman imports of slaves led to the closing of major Middle Eastern and North African markets; only Morocco openly merchandised slaves. The French conquest of West Africa after the 1840s was meant to suppress slavery and to encourage production of cotton, grain, peanuts, and gum by free laborers. But Islamic jihads (holy wars) across the sahel continued to send thousands of slave prisoners to market annually, well into the 1890s. Slave exports to Morocco flourished, as did the western Saharan economy. Saharans purchased slaves to cultivate date-palm groves, harvest gum, and mine salt. In response to French colonial markets for exportable commodities. Saharans settled colonies of *haratin* and *bella* to grow cash crops in the Sahel and their *'abid, haratin* and *bella* also worked along the Niger and Senegal Rivers, in the salt and transport industries. Effectively, slaves facilitated the integration of desert and Sahelian economies.

As colonial pacification followed conquest, the number of marketable slaves fell, and Saharans intensified raiding and kidnapping along the desert edge to maintain a slave labor force on which they had come to depend. The victims, generally women and children, were mostly destined to stay in the Sahara. As became apparent to colonial authorities early in their administration, female slaves played a special role in Saharan society. The traditional custom of fattening noble girls at puberty in preparation for marriage (*gavage*) impaired their physical ability for successful pregnancy and childbirth. And strict enforcement of Muslim morality concerning sexual behavior could reduce women's fertility when material conditions necessitated delaying or avoiding marriage. Colonial and contemporary evidence confirms what must have been true then: slave women had babies more successfully, and more often, than their noble mistresses. As Islamic law provided that a child born of a slave concubine and her master was legally free, such children thereby became noble Saharans. By the colonial era, slavery had become essential to the material and social reproduction of Saharan society.

It took the French over thirty years (ca. 1900–1930s), to "pacify" the Sahara. Administrators aggressively attempted to suppress slave marketing but adopted more subtle policies regarding slavery itself. The regime needed labor to develop the colonial economy and exercised pressure on owners to contribute their male slaves to the ranks of a new working class. Saharan masters were relatively compliant, having no intention themselves of laboring; in any case freed slaves remained attached to the family. But masters were less acquiescent when French administrators extended protection to colonies of *haratin* and *bella* against customary exactions and when these same authorities encouraged former dependents to migrate into arable lands further south.

Domestic slavery was different again. Masters resisted freeing women, as that was tantamount to giving up access to children. They could count on French administrators not to know a slave from a wife from a concubine. And among the Tuareg, the language of slavery—masters and mistresses were "fathers" and "mothers," and married slaves had "parents-in-law"—complicated even identifying slavery. Moreover, fictive relations carried real obligations: masters fed, clothed,

Twentieth-century slaves stack slabs of salt in the desert. [Hulton-Deutsch Collection/Corbis]

and took legal responsibility for slaves. The law notwithstanding, authorities tended to leave this perceived Muslim paternalism alone.

Nor did slaves always seek freedom. Women feared losing the children to whom they had no legal right, or finding themselves destitute. Women in any case always belonged to someone—a father, brother, husband, or master. But they were not without power. They used their right to freedom as a lever to negotiate the terms of their service, and sometimes the status of their children, with their masters. Slaves, especially women, were also feared because of their all-powerful pagan magic. This aspect of Saharan slavery had become entrenched in the nineteenth century with the importation of numerous Bambara war captives produced in the jihads; as recently as the 1950s French administrators resorted to the use of "specialist" *sufi shaykhs* to exorcise communities paralyzed by fear of sorcery.

In the Sahara, the end of French rule in 1960 intensified ethnic and social conflict. In Mali and Niger, the new governments were Sahelian descendants of the victims of generations of raiding; nomadic Saharans who rejected their authority were subject to policies approximating genocide. The effects of drought-induced sedentarization and impoverishment in the 1970s rendered the material differences between noble and slave almost imperceptible. In the 1980s former masters' expectations of tribute emerged as painful reminders of past realities largely because sedentarized *bella* had weathered the crisis better than the pastoralists. In Mauritania power passed to the Saharans. Not only had their *haratin* enriched themselves, but some had also become masters: possessing slaves was a concrete difference between the slave and the freed slave. In independent Mauritania, *haratin* continued to exercise economic influence and even had some political voice, although real power remained in the hands of the nobles. Most important, cultivable land worked by *haratin* remained the property of masters. *Haratin* who identified with their noble family and benefited from that identity to obtain resources had no wish to associate themselves with slaves. This disunity weakened attempts by various antislavery groups to achieve a stronger political voice for *haratin* and recently freed slaves.

The fact that slavery was (again) abolished by the Islamic republic of Mauritania in 1980 did not fundamentally change that situation. Most significantly, it did not address the question of resources—how masters were to be compensated, how slaves were to be propertied—in one of the poorest countries in the world. "Slavery" no longer exists, but the conditions that continued to support it through the colonial era are changing only slowly: consciousness of being noble and being servile continues to govern social relations, political sensitivity to charges of "permitting slavery" distorts both government policy and the importance of external critics, and that same sensitivity makes "slavery" a useful political lever for groups seeking more of a voice. In this new era of democracy, slavery's most important impact may well be its demographic legacy: former slaves are too numerous and too visible to be ignored.

See also AFRICA; CONCUBINAGE; SLAVE TRADE.

BIBLIOGRAPHY

BAIER, STEPHEN, and PAUL E. LOVEJOY. "The Tuareg of the Central Sudan: Gradations in Servility at the Desert Edge (Niger and Nigeria)." In *Slavery in Africa: Historical and Anthropological Perspectives,* edited by Suzanne Miers and Igor Kopytoff. 1977.

BERNUS, EDMOND, and SUZANNE BERNUS. "L'évolution de la conditions servile chez les Touaregs saheliens." In *L'esclavage en Afrique précoloniale,* edited by Claude Meillassoux. 1975.

DUNBAR, ROBERTA ANN. "Slavery and the Evolution of Nineteenth-Century Damagaram (Zinder, Niger)." In *Slavery in Africa: Historical and Anthropological Perspectives,* edited by Suzanne Miers and Igor Kopytoff. 1977.

FISHER, ALLAN G. B., and HUMPHREY J. FISHER. *Slavery and Muslim Society in Africa: The Institution in Saharan and Sudanic Africa and the Trans-Saharan Trade.* 1970.

KEENAN, JEREMY. *The Tuareg: People of Ahaggar.* 1977.

MCDOUGALL, E. ANN. "Setting the Story Straight: Louis Hunkarin and un Forfait Colonial." *History in Africa* 5, no. 16 (1989): 285–310.

———. "A Topsy-Turvy World: Slaves and Freed Slaves in the Mauritanian Adrar, 1910–1950. In *The End of Slavery in Africa,* edited by Suzanne Miers and Richard Roberts. 1988.

———. "The View from Awdaghust: War, Trade, and Social Change in the Southwestern Sahara, from the Eighth to the Fifteenth Century." *Journal of African History* 26 (1985): 1–31.

MERCER, JOHN. *Slavery in Mauritania Today.* 1982.

OULD CHEIKH, ABDEL WEDOUD. "L'évolution de l'esclavage dans la société maure." In *Nomades et commandants: Administration et sociétés nomades dans l'ancienne A.O.F.,* edited by E. Bernus, P. Bouilley, J. Clauzel, and J-L. Triaud. 1993.

SAVAGE, ELIZABETH, ed. *The Human Commodity: Perspectives on the Trans-Saharan Slave Trade.* 1992.

WEBB, JAMES L. A., JR. "The Horse and Slave Trade between the Western Sahara and Senegambia." *Journal of African History* 34 (1993): 221–246.

E. Ann McDougall

North Carolina

North Carolina was one of the original thirteen colonies, a slave state as early as the seventeenth century, and by the nineteenth century a chief supplier of slaves to the new slave states west of the Appalachian Mountains.

Founded as a proprietary English colony in 1663, North Carolina was a fertile land with a mild climate, covered with trees, and populated by Indians who had practiced agriculture since 1200. Scotch-Irish and Quakers were the first European settlers in the area. By 1720 about eight thousand of North Carolina's sixteen thousand people were slaves of African descent. A prime slave hand (male) sold for as much as twenty-five British pounds in 1745. Slave workers grew tobacco, cotton, rice, corn, livestock, and forest products and engaged in mining operations. Especially in the northeast part of the state, the slaves raised tobacco to sell in Europe. By 1780 slaves continued to sell for fifteen to twenty-five English pounds per head. North Carolina settlers preferred American-born slaves, although such "seasoned" slaves commanded higher prices. North Carolina became a state on 23 November 1789.

In 1790 North Carolina had 100,572 slaves, over 5,000 free blacks, and 288,204 whites. But the slave population became overcrowded after tobacco and corn farming exhausted the soil in much of North Carolina. Over 200,000 whites left for Tennessee and the lower South by 1850, taking thousands of slaves with them.

By 1860 in North Carolina slaves could be hired for $100 to $150 and sold for over $800, especially in the western counties, where prices and demand for slave exports were high. In Norfolk the hired slaves were required to wear badges. Among its 661,563 whites in 1860, North Carolina had 34,658 slave owners (29 percent of its white families) holding 331,059 slaves. The average slaveholding was 9.7 slaves. A few Native Americans in western North Carolina owned some slaves, but generally Indians and blacks had good relations, perhaps because both were oppressed people. By 1860 some 33.4 percent of North Carolina's people were slaves, and sixteen counties were more than half populated by blacks.

Table 1.   Slave and Free Population of North Carolina, 1790–1860.

	1790	1800	1810	1820	1830	1840	1850	1860
Free blacks	5,041	7,043	10,266	14,712	19,543	22,732	27,463	30,463
Slaves	100,572	133,296	168,824	204,917	245,601	245,817	288,563	331,059
Whites	288,204	338,000	367,000	419,000	473,000	485,000	553,000	629,942
Owners	–	–	–	–	–	–	28,303	34,658

Source: The Negro in the United States, 1790–1915 (1968).

Few slaves lived in western North Carolina's fifteen mountainous counties. The state's Appalachia area had 14,395 slaves (11.5 percent) in 1860. Only 11.1 percent of the blacks in Appalachia, near the Tennessee border, were free. The slaves there were used to mine gold, farm, and work as servants in hotels, shops, and professional offices. This region of North Carolina placed fewer legal restrictions on slaves than was the case elsewhere. Some slaves even received reading lessons in the homes of benevolent or religious masters. Although few highland families owned slaves, the slaveholders' wealth dominated business and politics in North Carolina's highland society.

Work gangs were not common in the upper South, where most slaves were owned by persons holding fewer than twenty slaves. Most plantations had owner-managers, not overseers. But in the cotton and tobacco-growing areas gangs were used more often than the task system. The types of slaves included field hands (80 percent women; 75 percent men), house servants, artisans, and industrial and urban slaves. Slaves began work at sunup and returned to their quarters after sundown. Especially in the cotton, forest, and tobacco industries, the slaves worked through Saturday afternoon.

Where the holdings were really small, the slaves slept on the kitchen floor, in a loft, or out back in a small shed. Otherwise, four to five slaves usually lived in one-room cabins of about two hundred square feet, with a central fireplace for heat and cooking. Straw or feather pallets on the floor served as bedding, but occasionally crude post beds were made by the slaves. Clothing consisted of two hats, two pairs of shoes, and two pair of pants and two shirts (wool and cotton) or

Slaves thresh grain on a rice plantation near Cape Fear River, North Carolina. [Library of Congress/Corbis]

wool or calico dresses, issued once per year. The food supply was similar to the owner's, except that slaves received smaller rations and lower-quality items.

Besides losing personal liberty, slaves could not gather in groups, hunt, own firearms, or travel without passes from their owners. They were punished with whippings or by having their ears cut off; capital offenses were punished by hanging. On certain occasions the slaves were rewarded by being given permission to fish, dance, hunt, swim in nearby rivers and creeks, play ball games, visit nearby relatives on holidays (i.e., Christmas), and attend church. North Carolina slaves were allowed to keep hogs, sheep, cattle, and small gardens until 1741, after which such ownership was prohibited.

North Carolina's slaves protested their bondage by stealing food, making trouble on the plantation, causing horses and mules to go lame, committing arson, sometimes murdering the master, slowing the work in the fields, talking back to the mistress, and running away. The swamp area was a favorite place for runaways to build houses, plant and harvest crops, and raise their families.

Many slaves purchased their freedom or gained manumission from their masters. Although slaves outnumbered free Negroes twenty to one, North Carolina had one of the country's largest free black populations: 30,463 (8.4 percent of its black population) by 1860. Only Maryland and Virginia had more free blacks than North Carolina. Free Negroes could not vote or marry whites, and their children could be bound out for apprenticeships.

North Carolina had active antislavery movements. The white antislavery leaders included Benjamin S. Hedrick, Hinton R. Helper, Eli Washington, the Quakers, and the North Carolina Manumission Society. David Walker, a free Negro from North Carolina, wrote his famous *Appeal . . . to the Colored Citizens* (1829) to inspire rebellion against slavery.

In May 1861 North Carolina joined the Confederacy. Many slaves were used by their masters in the Confederate army. However, some 5,035 blacks from North Carolina joined the Union army. Slavery was abolished throughout the United States by ratification of the Thirteenth Amendment to the national Constitution in December 1865.

See also CONFEDERATE STATES OF AMERICA; DEMOGRAPHY OF SLAVES IN THE UNITED STATES; SEASONING; WALKER, DAVID.

BIBLIOGRAPHY

BALL, CHARLES. *A Narrative of the Life and Adventures of Charles Ball, a Black Man.* 1834.
FRANKLIN, JOHN HOPE. *The Free Negro in North Carolina, 1790–1860.* 1943.
INSCOE, JOHN C. *Mountain Masters, Slavery, and the Sectional Crisis in Western North Carolina.* 1989.
LEFFLER, HUGH T., and A. R. NEWSOME. *The History of a Southern State: North Carolina.* 1973.
RAWICK, GEORGE P., ed. *The American Slave: A Composite Autobiography.* 41 vols. 1972–1979. Volumes 14 and 15 have North Carolina slave narratives.

Bobby L. Lovett

Northeast Africa

This entry includes the following articles: Upper Nile Region; Ethiopia. *Related articles may be found at the entries* Africa; Central Africa; East Africa; North Africa; Ottoman Empire; Slave Trade; Southern Africa; West Africa. *See also the note accompanying the entry* Africa *for further information about the organization of these entries.*

Upper Nile Region

The needs of rulers, combined with the growing power of merchants, fueled the expansion of slavery and the slave trade in the upper Nile—the region drained by the Nile River and its main tributaries above the First Cataract. The Egyptian pharaohs raided Nubia, the northernmost region of the upper Nile, to capture slaves. For almost a millennium after the decline of pharaonic Egypt, the main raiding and trading frontier remained relatively stable geographically while shifting in social definition. After the rise of Islam, from about 700 to 1300, the Christian kings of medieval Nubia sent probably small numbers of slaves to Egypt's Muslim rulers, as part of customary Nubian diplomatic exchange. At the same time, private merchants encroaching on royal prerogatives exported Nubian slaves to Egypt. The boundary between Muslim and non-Muslim domains thus began to coincide with the raiding and trading frontier. In Nubia itself, members of the local nobility owned slaves; rulers probably supervised and drew revenues from slave raiding and trading.

State control of large-scale slave raiding and trading continued even as kingdoms in the sub-Saharan Nile valley, or Sudan, pushed the raiding frontier southward. By the seventeenth century the sultans of Sinnar demanded slaves as tribute from their southern hinterland, stretching from the Blue Nile hills in the east to the Nuba Mountains in the west. Some slaves entered the royal household, bureaucracy, or army; others were dispatched on state-sponsored caravans, mainly to Egypt.

The ancient pattern of state control began to crumble in the eighteenth century, when slave raiding and trading increasingly fell into the hands of Muslim merchants and their warrior allies. Nonetheless, warriors and merchants aggrandized themselves in the context of state dynamics, whether disintegration or consolidation. Rebelling against the Sinnar's sultans, warrior lords conducted raids and forwarded their captives to an emerging Muslim merchant middle class. The exploitation of slaves intensified and spread. Both rebel and royal armies absorbed slaves; the sultans' slaves also farmed land around the capital. Merchants not only traded slaves but also put them to work in their households. To the west, the sultans of Darfur centralized their rule by cultivating a new elite of slave officials, Muslim teachers, and Muslim merchants. Slaves labored on estates granted by the sultan to his allies, as well as on royal domains. Granted raiding rights by the sultans and supplied by merchants, warriors raided Darfur's southern periphery. In both Sinnar and Darfur, newly powerful Muslim scholars and traders regarded non-Muslims as legitimate targets of war and enslavement. Heightened raiding produced more slave exports. For most of the eighteenth century, caravans probably brought an average of three thousand slaves annually from the upper Nile to Egypt, while an

A group of slaves rests at Korti, Nubia. [Historical Picture Archive/Corbis]

unknown number went to Red Sea ports. After 1790, Egypt received as many as five thousand to six thousand slaves yearly from Darfur's caravans alone.

A nineteenth-century conquest regime, known as the Turkiyya, triggered the explosive growth of slave raiding, slave trading, and slave labor in the Upper Nile. In 1820, partly because he wanted slave soldiers, the Ottoman viceroy of Egypt ordered the invasion of the Sudan. Quickly conquering Sinnar, the invaders immediately raided the southern hinterland. Massive annual government slave raids continued for about twenty years. Even after official raids ceased, the number of slave exports sharply increased. Although estimates are tenuous, perhaps one-fifth (351,000) of all slaves imported into Egypt from the upper Nile between 1400 and 1900 arrived between 1820 and 1869. In the 1830s alone, Egypt received perhaps as many as ten thousand Sudanese slaves yearly. The number of upper Nile slaves crossing the Red Sea had also begun to increase in 1800, perhaps reaching 1,000 to 1,200 annually until 1879.

The Turkiyya encouraged its Sudanese subjects to raid, trade, and own slaves. Because the government at first accepted slaves as tribute, Sudanese herders raided to fulfill tax requirements. The government paid and fed its soldiers by selling such tribute-slaves or slaves captured by the soldiers themselves. Relatively cheap slaves flooded local markets. The first profiteers belonged to the commercial middle class of the northern Sudan: they were traders who invested in slaves and farmers who, for the first time, put slaves to work on irrigation agriculture. By midcentury, the agricultural use of slaves expanded to the central rainlands.

The local demand for slaves, as well as the expansion of elephant hunting and ivory trading, impelled raiding and trading yet farther southward. Merchants, who often commanded armed bands, pushed the violent commercial frontier up the White Nile, then west along its tributaries. Eventually meeting overland traders from Darfur, merchants built fortified communities that served as trade depots and military centers. As had government soldiers in the first years of the Turkiyya, slave soldiers belonging to merchants raided for yet more slaves. For their part, merchants parlayed their control over cash and armed men into government office. The man who eventually conquered Darfur for the Turkiyya in 1874 began his career as an ivory and slave trader.

The Turkiyya collapsed in 1881 under the tensions of the violent raiding and religious frontier, competitive merchant officials, and increasing class divisions. Sudanese Muslims sought relief by turning to a militant Islamic theocracy, known as the Mahdiyya. Although slave exports sharply decreased, non-Muslims on the southern frontier continued to be enslaved during the Mahdiyya.

Conquering the Sudan in 1898, the Anglo-Egyptian regime affirmed its opposition to the slave trade. The Sudan's new rulers, however, feared that ending slavery itself would result in a drastic decline in agricultural production, increased vagrancy in the towns, and the hostility of the Sudanese elite on whom they depended. The government thus reinforced the authority of masters over their slaves. The slave trade within the Sudan also continued, although on a reduced scale. Slavery itself slowly faded only in the 1930s, largely because of the struggles of slaves themselves, the rise of a pool of wage laborers, the pressure of international opinion, and a few committed antislavery activists in the colonial government.

In a tragic postscript, slavery revived in the 1980s and 1990s. Religious and racial violence—legacies of the Turkiyya, Mahdiyya, and related nineteenth-century raiding—broke out in the southern Sudan. Government soldiers and private militia fighting against rebels captured slaves, mainly women and children. Information reaching the international community indicated that many of these slaves suffered brutal conditions.

See also AFRICA; PLANTATIONS; WEST AFRICA.

BIBLIOGRAPHY

EWALD, JANET J. *Soldiers, Traders, and Slaves: State Formation and Economic Transformation in the Greater Nile Valley, 1700–1885.* 1990.

JOHNSON, DOUGLAS H. "The Structure of a Legacy: Military Slavery in Northeast Africa." *Ethnohistory* 36 (1989): 72–88.

O'FAHEY, R. S. *State and Society in Dar Fur.* 1980.

SIKAINGA, AHMAD ALAWAD. *Slaves into Workers: Emancipation and Labor in Colonial Sudan.* 1996.

SPAULDING, JAY. *The Heroic Age in Sinnar.* 1985.

———. "Medieval Christian Nubia and the Islamic World: A Reconsideration of the *Baqt* Treaty." *International Journal of African Historical Studies* 28, no. 3 (1995) 577–594.

———. "Slavery, Land Tenure, and Social Class in the Northern Turkish Sudan." *International Journal of African Historical Studies* 15 (1982): 1–20.

Janet J. Ewald

Ethiopia

The basic pattern of slavery in Ethiopia, variations of which prevailed until the first decades of the twentieth century, began to emerge in the first millennium. Perhaps as early as the trading empire of Aksum (ca. A.D. 100–1000), slaves supported a succession of states based in the highlands and ruled by elites made up of military aristocrats and Christian clerics. Empires extracted wealth, including slaves, from their frontiers. Sometimes tributary rulers forwarded slaves to the imperial center; imperial armies also captured slaves in their frontier campaigns. Slaves provided state revenues as taxable commodities channeled, along with other frontier wealth, through long-distance trade routes to the Nile valley or to ports on the Red Sea and the Gulf of Aden. Slave exports rose particularly when commerce flourished in the Indian Ocean basin. In the 1500s, perhaps several thousand Ethiopian slaves annually entered markets in the Muslim world, including India, and even east Asia. Ethiopian slaves became known throughout these regions as soldiers, servants, and concubines. Other slaves remained in the highlands, where they labored in elite households and on agricultural estates, and served in armies. Peasant farmers probably also owned slaves who helped produce crops, some of which went to the elite as tribute.

In the mid-eighteenth century slavery and the slave trade expanded even while central political institutions disintegrated. Slave raiding shifted to the south, where contentious rulers of independent kingdoms warred and raided, increasing the supply of slaves. At the same time the Indian Ocean trade revived. Muslim traders traveled deep into the interior, seeking slaves to satisfy an Indian Ocean basin demand for laborers, business agents, craft workers, and servants, as well as units of exchange in the trade network itself. Between 1800 and 1850, perhaps 15,000 people annually fell into slavery in southern Ethiopia. Of these, about 7,600 left Ethiopia and 4,400 to 5,400 were absorbed in the highland principalities of northern Ethiopia. The remaining 2,000 to 3,000 remained in southern Ethiopia, where slaves assumed new importance in the economy and society as agents, soldiers, servants, and concubines of the elite. Others labored in the fields of both aristocrats and small-hold farmers. Still others were weavers, tailors, metalworkers, and carpenters.

The old imperial pattern re-emerged in the last half of the nineteenth century when a newly expanding highland empire again drew wealth from slaves. The raiding frontier pushed still deeper into the south and southwest, as soldiers of the emperor or his tributaries captured slaves and sent them north. In some newly subjected regions, governors from the north settled with their armed entourages, supporting themselves from the tribute of local farmers. But these southern peasants themselves sometimes fell into slavery: if they could not pay taxes, their overlords seized their children as slaves. Other times, governors and soldiers returning to the center of the empire simply carried

Three nineteenth-century Ethiopian slaves are held in chains. [Hulton-Deutsch Collection/Corbis]

peasants away as slaves. Ironically, some local people resorted to capturing slaves and selling them for the guns necessary to resist imperial rule. The decline of the export trade after about 1880, resulting from international abolitionist pressures on the Ottoman imperial markets and reduced demand from the Indian Ocean basin perhaps depressed slave prices and reduced incomes from imports, thus increasing the exploitation of slaves held in the highlands. In some parts of the north, peasants invested in slaves as a strategy to hold onto their land; slaves provided insurance against labor shortages, which by reducing production threatened them with debt and foreclosure.

Slavery gradually ended in the 1920s and 1930s because of economic changes and Haile Selassie's abolitionist policies, which he manipulated to present himself as progressive to a European audience while undermining his domestic political rivals. Curbing the power of military governors in the south, the emperor suppressed their raiding and trading. At the same time the southern elite turned to producing export commodities, especially coffee. Instead of sending slaves to the north, they tried to keep workers on their own estates. As the supply of slaves from the south declined, the prices of slaves increased in the north. The conservative oligarchy, as well as poor peasants, lost slave labor. Enabled by Haile Selassie's antislavery measures to leave their owners, slaves sought to work for wages for wealthy peasants and government bureaucrats, who prospered from access to their labor. Deprived of workers and followers, the old oligarchy declined; poor peasants who lost slaves also lost their land, sometimes joining ex-slaves in a new, landless, labor force. New forms of stratification thus emerged in both northern and southern Ethiopia even as slavery ended.

See also AFRICA; PLANTATIONS; SLAVE TRADE.

BIBLIOGRAPHY

ABIR, MORDECHAI. *Ethiopia: The Era of the Princes.* 1968.
DONHAM, DONALD, and WENDY JAMES, eds. *The Southern Marches of Imperial Ethiopia: Essays in History and Social Anthropology.* 1986.
FERNYHOUGH, TIMOTHY. "Slavery and the Slave Trade in Southern Ethiopia in the Nineteenth Century." In *The Economics of the Indian Ocean Slave Trade in the Nineteenth Century,* edited by William Gervase Clarence-Smith. 1989.
McCANN, JAMES. "'Children of the House': Slavery and Its Suppression in Lasta, Northern Ethiopia, 1916–1935." In *The End of Slavery in Africa,* edited by Suzanne Miers and Richard Roberts. 1988.

Janet J. Ewald

Northwest Ordinance

In July 1787 Congress, operating under the Articles of Confederation, passed its most significant piece of legislation: the Northwest Ordinance, which provided for the organization of territories, and eventually states, in the area north and west of the Ohio River. Article VI of the Ordinance declared:

> There shall be neither slavery nor involuntary servitude in the said territory, otherwise than in the punishment of crimes, whereof the party shall have been duly convicted: provided always, that any person escaping into the same, from whom labour or service is lawfully claimed in any one of the original states, such fugitive may be lawfully reclaimed, and conveyed to the person claiming his or her labour or service as aforesaid.

This clause was added at the last possible moment, after the bill had been read twice in Congress. The provision was added without serious discussion and with no debate. The main impetus for the clause may have been the demands of Manassah Cutler, representing a group of Massachusetts investors who had formed the Ohio Land Company. That company planned to buy millions of acres of land from the national government as soon as the Ordinance was passed. The investors, especially Cutler, were opposed to slavery and may have felt that the land would be more attractive to settlers if slavery was excluded.

At the time the Ordinance was adopted, the slave states had an overwhelming majority in Congress because of the absence of the delegations from Pennsylvania, New Hampshire, Connecticut, and Rhode Island. However, the South did not see Article VI as a threat to slavery, because southerners expected the Northwest to be sympathetic to southern issues even if it had no slaves. Also, by banning slavery in the Northwest, the Ordinance implied that the Southwest would remain open to slavery. William Grayson, a delegate from Virginia, wrote to James Madison, explaining that the prohibition of slavery "was agreed to by the Southern members for the purpose of preventing Tobacco and Indigo from being made" in the Northwest (William Grayson to James Monroe, 8 August 1787, in Edmund C. Burnett, ed., *Letters of Members of the Continental Congress*, 8 vols., 1921–1936, VIII, 631–633).

Although it seemed to ban slavery in the region, the Ordinance did not specify how the ban was to be implemented or if it applied to the many slaves already living in what later became Indiana, Illinois, and Michigan. These slaves were mostly owned by French settlers who had been in the region since before the

Seven Years' War (1756–1763) or to Virginians who had moved into the region after the Revolution. In fact, some blacks remained in bondage in the region well into the 1840s.

In the antebellum period the Ordinance took on special meaning to opponents of slavery, particularly the Republicans. As the historian David Brion Davis points out, "It provided the core of the Republican party's ideology, an ideology that seemed convincing to millions of northerners who had no sympathy for the abolitionist cause." Thus in the 1850s northern Republicans, who had no interest in interfering with slavery in the South, nevertheless adopted the notion implicit in the Ordinance that slavery should not be allowed in the western territories. The Ordinance also helped set the stage for the emergence of five free states in the region. By discouraging slaveowners from moving into the region, the Ordinance helped create a white majority in the Northwest that was hostile to slavery. This proved crucial in Illinois, where in 1823 and 1824 opponents of slavery led by Governor Edward Coles soundly defeated an attempt to amend the Illinois Constitution of 1818 to allow slavery (Davis, p. 89).

See also ILLINOIS; INDIANA; LAW; MICHIGAN.

BIBLIOGRAPHY

DAVIS, DAVID BRION. "The Significant of Excluding Slavery from the Old Northwest in 1787." *Indiana Magazine of History* 84, no. 1 (May 1988): 75–89.

FINKELMAN, PAUL. *Slavery and the Founders: Race and Liberty in the Age of Jefferson.* 1996.

GRIFFIN, J. DAVID. "Historians and the Sixth Article of the Ordinance of 1787." *Ohio History* 78 (Autumn 1969): 252–260.

HUNTER, LLOYD, ed. *Pathways to the Old Northwest.* 1988.

ONUF, PETER S. "From Constitution to Higher Law: The Reinterpretation of the Northwest Ordinance." *Ohio History* 94 (Winter-Spring 1985): 5.

———. *Statehood and Union: A History of the Northwest Ordinance.* 1987.

WILLIAMS, FREDERICK D., ed. *The Northwest Ordinance: Essays On Its Formulation, Provisions, and Legacy.* 1989.

Stephen Middleton
Paul Finkelman

Norway

See Scandinavia.

Nott, Josiah Clark   [1804–1873]

Physician and racial theorist.

Josiah Clark Nott, the brother of Henry Junius Nott, was born 31 March 1804 in Columbia, South Carolina. After graduating from South Carolina College in 1824, he received an M.D. from the University of Pennsylvania medical school in 1827. He also studied in Paris from 1835 to 1836.

Upon his return from Paris, Nott moved to Mobile, Alabama. He became a prominent physician, and throughout his life he wrote on medical subjects, ultimately becoming well-known for his theories on yellow fever. Nott's Mobile practice included many slaves, and in the 1850s he ran a slave infirmary in the city. In his writings he argued that African-Americans suffered less from yellow fever and inflammatory diseases but were more susceptible to smallpox, cholera, the plague, and typhoid. He was best-known, however, for his writings on race and his defense of slavery. Beginning in the mid-1840s, Nott achieved a major reputation as a racial theorist in the United States and Europe. Nott maintained that there were innate differences between the races, that Caucasians were superior to all others, that African-Americans were best off as slaves, and that the American Indians were doomed to extinction. He enjoyed baiting the clergy and angered them and many others by his defense of multiple creations (polygenesis). His most influential work, written with George Gliddon, was *Types of Mankind* (1854). At great length, this volume defended the idea of multiple creations and innate differences between a variety of human races, and maintained that the inferiority of nonwhite races was permanent.

In the Civil War Nott served in the medical department of the Confederacy, but in 1867, disgusted at the freeing of the slaves and Northern occupation, he moved north, first to Baltimore and then to New York, where he established a successful medical practice. He died in Mobile on 31 March 1873.

See also CONFEDERATE STATES OF AMERICA; PERSPECTIVES ON SLAVERY.

BIBLIOGRAPHY

HORSMAN, REGINALD. *Josiah Nott of Mobile: Southerner, Physician, and Racial Theorist*. 1987.
STANTON, WILLIAM. *The Leopard's Spots: Scientific Attitudes toward Race in America, 1815–1859*. 1960.

Reginald Horsman

Nubia

See Egypt; Northeast Africa.

Nutrition

See Health.

Ohio

The early settlement of Ohio reflected sectional tensions in the young nation. Southerners flocked into the area along the Ohio River while settlers from New England and New York headed to the Western Reserve along Lake Erie. Free blacks and fugitive slaves were also attracted by the economic opportunity and liberty of the region, where slavery was formally banned by the Northwest Ordinance of 1787.

The debate over statehood in 1802–1803 raised questions of race and civil rights. The state Constitution of 1803 banned slavery but also had sanctions for free blacks entering the state. Until 1849 Ohio kept its punitive "black laws" in place, although enforcement was sporadic and usually took place only in the southern part of the state. In northern Ohio blacks were often afforded a great measure of equality. One black, John Mercer Langston, was admitted to the bar in 1854 and in 1855 became the first elected black official in the nation. In 1849 a small number of Free Soil representatives in the state legislature held the balance of power and managed to leverage their few votes to gain a repeal of most of Ohio's discriminatory legislation. By the 1830s northern Ohio, and especially Oberlin College, was a center of antislavery activity.

While no slaves ever lived in Ohio, the state was central in the controversy over fugitive slaves. *Jones v. Van Zandt* (1847) was the second fugitive-slave case to reach the Supreme Court. In 1858 students and faculty at Oberlin College went en masse to nearby Wellington to rescue a fugitive slaves. Litigation over the "Oberlin-Wellington rescue" nearly led to a confrontation between the government of Ohio and the United States. In the end most of the rescuers were released from federal custody with only token fines, which for the most part were never paid. In *Kentucky v. Dennison* (1861) the Supreme Court upheld Ohio's refusal to send a free black back to Kentucky to face trial for helping a slave woman escape to Ohio. One fugitive slave drowned her children rather than allow them to be taken from Ohio.

By the eve of the Civil War Ohio was famous for its role in the Underground Railroad and for the many fugitive slaves who had found sanctuary there. The presence of fugitive slaves in Ohio influenced Harriet Beecher Stowe, who grew up in the state. In *Uncle Tom's Cabin* the fictional Eliza escapes to Ohio, where she is eventually taken to a Quaker abolitionist, loosely modeled on John Van Zandt. At Oberlin College, a sculpture of a railroad track now emerges from the ground on the campus, symbolizing the place where the Underground Railroad surfaced. Salmon P. Chase, who, in the 1850s, served as governor of the state and as its U.S. Senator, argued so many fugitive cases that he became known as the "attorney general for fugitive slaves." Chase served as Secretary of the Treasury from 1861 to 1864, before Lincoln appointed him Chief Justice of the United States.

See also FUGITIVE SLAVE LAWS, U.S.; UNDERGROUND RAILROAD.

BIBLIOGRAPHY

CAYTON, ANDREW. *Frontier Republic: Ideology and Politics in the Ohio Country, 1780–1825.* 1986.

CHEEK, WILLIAM, and AIMEE LEE CHEEK. *John Mercer Langston and the Fight for Black Freedom,* 1829–1865. 1989.

GERBER, DAVID. *Black Ohio and the Color Line, 1860–1915.* 1976.

MIDDLETON, STEPHEN. *The Black Laws in the Old Northwest: A Documentary History.* 1993.

RODEABROUGH. "The Negro in Ohio." *Journal of Negro History* 31 (1946).

Stephen Middleton
Paul Finkelman

Oklahoma

Slavery in Oklahoma is dated from the resettlement of the five so-called civilized tribes—the Creeks, Cherokees, Seminoles, Choctaws, and Chickasaws—in the region in the 1830s. They were moved from their original homelands east of the Mississippi River, where they had adopted African slavery under European influence. Before contact with Europeans, some of these Native Americans had developed a social practice that the newcomers, using the closest European analogue called "slavery"; but it was more accurately a condition of kinlessness that existed when war captives were not adopted by their captors and were therefore without protection. This was not primarily an economic relationship and thus differed significantly from the European practice. The Native Americans had an egalitarian concept of property and community, so the personal accumulation of excessive material wealth was unacceptable to them, and the European notion of slavery as an institution conductive to such wealth was unimaginable. When these Native American groups adopted staple agriculture and plantation culture as a feature of their increasing involvement in a European exchange economy, including individual material aggrandizement, these characteristics were considered signs of their progress toward "civilization," and their establishment of a slave society was part of that development.

Even so, cultural change was contested and caused divisions among many of the groups; the traditionalists objected to Europeanization, including slavery. Moreover, many Native Americans who owned slaves, particularly among the Seminoles, treated them more often as tributary allies than as mindless labor units. Among the Creeks, Cherokees, Choctaws, and Chickasaws, the treatment of slaves, even on large plantations, was such that slaves generally preferred their

A former slave and her child live free in Oklahoma, known at the time (ca. 1900) as Indian Territory. [National Archives/Corbis]

situation to a similar one among whites. Still, there was occasional cruelty and harsh treatment by Native Americans—as by whites—and the stringency of treatment generally increased in the movement from the east to Indian territory, as Oklahoma was designated. Certainly legal structures were tightened. Though they had originally felt no racial prejudice toward Africans, Native Americans later absorbed prejudice as part of their acculturation and, particularly among the Choctaws, Chickasaws, Cherokees, and Creeks, adopted laws forbidding intermarriage between their people and blacks or mulattos and denying people with African genes formal positions of influence in their nations. Slaves were limited in their rights of property and in access to freedom and literacy. But these strictures were often ignored. For example, despite legal restrictions, slaves owed livestock, and literacy and miscegenation were not uncommon. The slaves' family life was often respected. Generally, there was more equality between master and slave, particularly among full-blooded Indians more imbued with traditional notions, and slaves pretty much went their own way once their required tasks were done.

Among the Indians, slaves raised cotton, wheat, corn, and other staples; herded livestock; and performed domestic and other chores. They were quick to learn Indian tongues and frequently acted as translators. This skill, and others, gave them significant influence. They were often conduits of increasing Europeanization, but they also assimilated Indian ways, and a few spoke little or no English; perhaps most often they combined African, Indian, and European cultures and outlooks. They developed a reputation of being ruined as good slaves for white people because of their relative independence. But slaves did run away in Indian Territory, and because of lawlessness in the region there were frequent kidnappings of slaves and free blacks for sale to other states.

The tribes were divided in their allegiance during the Civil War, but many, as slaveholders, sided with the Confederacy. When the Confederacy was defeated, the tribes were forced to give up slavery and grant certain rights to freedpersons.

See also NATIVE AMERICANS.

BIBLIOGRAPHY

LITTLEFIELD, DANIEL F., JR. *Africans and Creeks: From the Colonial Period to the Civil War.* 1979.
———. *Africans and Seminoles: From Removal to Emancipation.* 1977.
———. *The Chickasaw Freedmen: A People without a Country.* 1980.
PERDUE, THEDA. *Slavery and the Evolution of Cherokee Society, 1540–1866.* 1979.

Daniel C. Littlefield

Onesimus   [fl. ca. 60 C.E.]

Christian slave.

After fleeing from his master Philemon in Colossae, in Phrygia, Onesimus was baptized by the Apostle Paul and sent back to Philemon. In the Epistle of Paul to Philemon, the master, a Christian, is urged to set Onesimus free so that he can assist Paul in spreading the Gospel. Some scholars believe that Onesimus was emancipated and became bishop of Ephesus (in present-day Turkey) around 110.

During the early 1800s, proslavery polemists in the United States cited this epistle as a biblical sanction for slavery. The fact that Paul addresses Philemon as a "dearly beloved . . . partner" indicates that slave owners were permitted to remain in the early church. Furthermore, Paul does not order Philemon to free Onesimus, thus acknowledging implicitly a slave owner's rights to his slave's labor. Most importantly, Paul urges Onesimus to return to Philemon even though Paul has need of his services, demonstrating that conversion to Christianity did not dissolve the ties binding slaves to masters and that fugitive slaves were to be returned to their rightful masters posthaste.

Abolitionists rebutted this argument by declaring that Onesimus was not a slave but a servant, as he is identified in the epistle; that Paul did not force Onesimus to return to Philemon, indicating that servants could not be forced to return to their masters; and that Paul entreats Philemon to "receive [Onesimus] . . . as . . . a brother beloved," indicating that involuntary servitude and Christianity are incompatible.

Neither line of reasoning has convinced more than a handful of people to change their minds regarding the morality of slavery.

See also CHRISTIANITY.

BIBLIOGRAPHY

ARMSTRONG, GEORGE D. *The Christian Doctrine of Slavery.* 1857. Reprint, 1969.
BARNES, ALBERT. *An Inquiry into the Scriptural Views of Slavery.* 1855. Reprint, 1969.

Charles W. Carey Jr.

Opposition to Slavery

See Perspectives on Slavery.

Oregon

Prior to Oregon's admission to the Union, the territory endeavored to limit the number of African-Americans in the region by passing a bill prohibiting free blacks and mulattos from settling in the territory. This edict differed from an exclusion bill of 1844 insofar as it ordered transgressing blacks to leave Oregon in forty days rather than in two years. Unable to completely restrict the number of blacks in Oregon, the region was eventually forced to confront slavery, an institution inextricably linked with African-Americans in the minds of most Oregon pioneers. By 1861 Oregon was one of four western states admitted to the union. Despite its peripheral status, the state found itself in the middle of the slavery controversy. Oregon country was saved from slavery, however, by the political maneuvering of white free-soilers, who outnumbered proslavery advocates and slaveholders, not by geography or by any substantive devotion to human freedom by westerners.

During the 1850s slavery encroached upon Oregon politics, prompting debate and legislative maneuvering. The state's proslavery advocates could never overcome political and social barriers to the institution. The first provisional government of Oregon invoked the Northwest Ordinance of 1787 to prohibit slavery. Nonetheless, a small number of blacks brought to the Pacific Northwest between 1840 and 1860 were, in fact, slaves. The most compelling evidence of slavery in Oregon came in 1857, one month after the territory's voters had approved a ban on the practice. William Allen, a representative from Yamhill County, listed slaves in Benton, Lane, Polk, and Yamhill counties in his unsuccessful attempt to obtain legislation to protect slave property.

The major legal challenge to slavery in Oregon was *Holmes v. Ford*. In 1844 Nathaniel Ford, a Missouri farmer, brought a slave couple, Robin and Polly Holmes, to Oregon. Ford reneged on his promise to free the Holmeses upon their arrival in Oregon in 1844. In 1849 Ford freed Robin and Polly and their newborn son but refused to free their four other children, three of whom had been born in Oregon Territory. Robin Holmes filed suit against Ford in 1852 to acquire custody of the couple's children. *Holmes v. Ford* lay stagnant in various courts for eleven months. In July 1853 George A. Williams, chief justice of the territorial supreme court, ruled against Ford, declaring that slavery could not exist in Oregon without specific legislation to protect it. The Holmes case was the last attempt by Oregon's proslavery settlers to protect slave property through the judicial process.

See also NORTHWEST ORDINANCE, *as well as the individual entries on the other states of the United States.*

BIBLIOGRAPHY

TAYLOR, QUINTARD, JR. *In Search of a Racial Frontier.* 1998.
———. "Slaves and Free Men: Blacks in the Oregon Country, 1840–1860." *Oregon Historical Quarterly* 83, no. 2 (Summer 1982): 153–170.

Matthew C. Whitaker

Ottoman Empire

Slavery in the Ottoman Empire was widespread and long-lived, existing in many areas from the empire's founding in the late thirteenth century until the slave trade was officially abolished in 1909. Ottoman slavery took several forms: in all but one, it was a temporary juridical status which could and most often did change to freedom within a set period of time. Most slaves were imported from beyond the empire's frontiers, through either purchase or capture in time of war. They were employed primarily in domestic service or in small artisan enterprises. Few worked on the land. The one exception to temporary slavery were the *kuls*, who were taken by the government most often from within the empire and included all slaves used in government service, both civil and military. Legally *kuls* were the sultan's slaves, and they remained so until their death. Because they occupied official positions in the government and on occasion owned slaves of their own, *kuls* were not "slaves" in our normal use of the term. Slaves were imported, yet at any one time the number of slaves within the system was relatively small. Ottoman policies toward manumission, inherited from Islamic traditions, meant that the number of new slaves seldom exceeded the number of existing slaves manumitted.

Kul System

The Ottomans developed a system of recruitment (*devshirme*) for military and administrative staffs that had many characteristics of slavery, though the Ottomans themselves viewed it as a form of tax or levy. As Halil Inalcık (1979) portrayed it, *devshirme* was "one of the extraordinary services imposed by the state in an emergency." The "emergency" was a growing shortage of men for palace and military service, produced by the expansion of the state in the fourteenth and fifteenth centuries. Boys were chosen from the sultan's Christian subjects, primarily in the Balkan provinces, converted to Islam, trained in Istanbul, and employed in a variety of state activities: construction, military service, and administrative posts. Those who demonstrated ability were selected for service in the sultan's own *kapi-kulu* (household or palace administration); others were janissaries, the sultan's elite military corps. The number of *devshirme*-originated *kapi-kul* grew from fifteen thousand in 1481 to sixty thousand in 1568 to one hundred thousand in 1609. The *devshirme* ceased to be a source of Ottoman officialdom by the end of the seventeenth century, however. While in many respects the *kul* and *devshirme* systems resembled slavery, those taken into the governmental civil and military systems occupied genuine elite status, and some of them became members of the ruling circles of the empire. As a result, these "slaves" of the sultan must be considered separately from other slaves within Ottoman society. The discussions below will concern non-*devshirme* slaves.

Supply and Numbers

Slaves entered the Ottoman Empire in two ways: as captives taken in military campaigns and as individuals purchased in the slave markets of Crimea and Egypt. The Ottomans inherited a vigorous slave trade in al-

A nineteenth-century slave market in Egypt. [Historical Picture Archive/Corbis]

most all the lands they conquered. Italians in the Black Sea region, Byzantines in the Balkans and Mediterranean, and Mamluks in Egypt provided the Ottomans with established centers of supply as well as urban slave markets and depots (Constantinople itself, Kaffa in the Crimea, Tana-Azov in the northeast corner of the Black Sea, and Alexandria and Cairo in Egypt).

Although we cannot yet provide a count of slaves imported through either captivity or purchase over the period of Ottoman rule, governmental tax registers studied to date allow estimates of imported slaves from markets during some periods (taxes were collected on slave purchases and were noted in tax registers for each market). The Ottomans conducted periodic cadastral surveys of all provinces, which listed slaves owned within each province. And upon the death of an Ottoman official or grandee, a register of the deceased's property was made, and any slaves owned were enumerated. A great many tax registers, cadastral surveys, and registers of property of deceased Ottomans have survived, though only a fraction of these have been studied.

The Kaffa slave market produced the largest number of slaves for Ottoman buyers until the late seventeenth century. Primarily of Slavic origin, these slaves were generated by Crimean Tatar raids (in Crimean terms, "harvests" of the steppe). Estimates of numbers passing through the Kaffa market range from 1 million to 2.5 million during the period from 1500 to 1700.

In 1578 more than 17,500 slaves were sold there. Slaves were also imported from the Caucasus and Africa, though no evidence of numbers has come to light. Evidence for the first half of the nineteenth century, at the end of the Ottoman institution of slavery, indicates a continuation of slave imports, though fewer in number and no longer from the Slavic north.

These numbers should indicate a very large slave population in the empire at any given time before the eighteenth century. Yet, census figures show that at no time did slaves exceed five percent of the total population. The explanation for this apparent discrepancy comes from the Ottoman policy of manumission, which encouraged the freeing of privately owned slaves after a set period of time.

The Ottomans' Use of Slaves

The vast majority of Ottoman slaves, male and female, were employed in domestic service. Outside of the government, few individuals were sufficiently wealthy to own a large retinue of such slaves, and most households with any slaves had no more than two or three. Females were concubines of the owner or servants for his wives, while male slaves served as stewards.

Managers of artisan industries often used slaves in production, most often in textile and silk weaving before the advent of machinery in the nineteenth century. Such highly skilled activities justified the expense of buying slaves. The degree of expertise and the length of time that was necessary for the completion of brocades and velvets, especially, made slave labor the most efficient and economical way to accomplish the task. Scribes, bakers, spice merchants, and wax producers also occasionally owned slaves, who served as trusted stewards and occasionally as managers of small businesses.

In the early years of the empire, slaves were occasionally employed in agriculture. Mehmed II, the conqueror of Constantinople, used slave labor to populate and exploit abandoned land around the city soon after its conquest. In frontier regions agricultural slaves also were used. War captives were plentiful and thus inexpensive, and farming had been disrupted by war.

Finally, the Ottoman government frequently used slave labor in large state-managed construction projects. In the sixteenth century the building of large mosques, hospitals, schools, and marketplaces required the employment of thousands of government-owned slaves, derived from the wars of expansion in the first fifty years of that century.

Numbers and Ethnic Origin of Slaves

Until more Ottoman records are examined by historians, it is impossible to estimate the numbers of slaves imported, used, and freed within the empire at any particular time. We do know that at the main points of entry (Kaffa in the Crimea and Alexandria in Egypt) between 10,000 and 20,000 slaves were purchased each year by Ottoman buyers in the sixteenth and seventeenth centuries, with much larger numbers coming through the Crimea than Egypt. Most slaves were "white"—Russian, Ukrainian, Polish, Hungarian, Circassian. Fewer were "black"—from Nubia and sub-Saharan Africa. Registers were kept of taxes paid when slaves were purchased, and censuses, regularly taken in Ottoman provinces, listed the names and often the origins of slaves. Registers of estates of deceased Ottomans also often listed slaves by name, value, and "occupation."

Manumission

The particular characteristic that distinguished slavery in the Ottoman Empire, and in the Muslim world in general, from slave systems in the rest of the Western world was the prevalence and ease of manumission. The Koran encouraged pious Muslims to manumit their slaves. From the Ottoman records it is possible to separate these "pious" manumissions into a number of categories:

1. Unconditional, that is, genuinely pious manumission (*mevla*) made while the owner was alive.
2. Conditional manumission (*tedbir*) granted for some particular act or event, for example, "after my death" or "if I die from this illness."
3. Contractual manumission (*mukataba*), which was the most common. This manumission usually involved a payment by the slave to the owner. It could result from a financial arrangement between them in which the slave agreed to pay a set sum for manumission, or it could result from an agreed-upon period of labor or even a certain amount of production, as the weaving of a certain amount of cloth.
4. The freeing of a female slave who bore her master a child (*umm-i veled*). According to Islamic law, this was to be one of the most common ways for a slave to achieve manumission. Both mother and child were supposed to be freed. The main limiting factor was the requirement that the owner admit the parentage of the child.
5. There was also court-ordered manumission resulting from some misbehavior by an owner toward a slave. Ottoman court records contain many such instances. For example, a court ordered the manumission of a slave who had apparently been promised freedom on his owner's death, but the owner's son had broken the promise. Occasionally individuals who had been illegally enslaved were freed by court order.

Manumission served both to limit the total slave population and to provide a way for slaves to join Ottoman society as freed persons. It reflected the Ottoman view that slave status was only legal and juridical, and that it could be changed or voided just as easily as it could be created. By the time slavery came to an end in the empire, the number of Ottoman subjects whose ancestors had once been slaves must have been enormous.

Ottoman Slavery in the Nineteenth Century

By the end of the eighteenth century slavery no longer was a significant institution in the Ottoman Empire. The *devshirme* came to an end in the mid-seventeenth century (under circumstances still not discovered by historians), and both civilian and military officials ceased to be slaves of the sultan; henceforth, civilian officials were recruited and military officials conscripted from Ottoman free society. Slaves could no longer be imported from the north, which had been the main source of slaves before the eighteenth century, as Russia became a powerful adversary that could and did prevent cross-border raids for slaves. Prisoners of war no longer were enslaved (in law, with the Crimean War, in practice 150 years earlier when the Ottomans no longer won battles). Those few Ottoman industries that had earlier employed slave labor found new methods and sources of labor that were economically preferable. Finally, wealthy Ottomans discovered new ways to distinguish themselves from the less well-to-do in society: Western clothing, home, and furnishings, and travel abroad.

Slavery persisted at a lower level throughout the nineteenth century, limited by one official act after another, until it was officially abolished with the collapse of the empire at the end of World War I. The slave market in Istanbul was closed in 1846. With the Tanzimat (Westernizing) reforms of the 1850s and 1860s, legal distinctions between Ottoman subjects were eliminated and with them those of freeman and freedman, Muslim and non-Muslim, and, ultimately, free and slave. Under British pressure the Ottoman government prohibited the trade in black slaves in 1857. In the 1870s, because of a large influx of Circassian refugees fleeing Russian "ethnic cleansing" in the Caucasus, the government suppressed the enslavement of Circassians, since they were now Ottoman subjects. Finally, the Young Turk government abolished the trade in slaves anywhere under its jurisdiction, though the institution remained legal according to Islamic law. Kemal Atatürk's dissolution of the empire and abolition of the caliphate in the early 1920s brought slavery to an end.

See also EUNUCHS; HAREM; ISLAM; JANISSARIES; MILITARY SLAVES; PALACE SLAVES.

BIBLIOGRAPHY

CAHEN, CLAUDE. "Note sur l'esclavage musulman et le devshirme ottoman, à propos de travaux récents." *Journal of the Economic and Social History of the Orient* 13 (1970): 211–218.

ERDEM, Y. HAKAN. *Slavery in the Ottoman Empire and Its Demise, 1800–1909.* 1996.

FISHER, ALAN. "Chattel Slavery in the Ottoman Empire." *Slavery and Abolition* 1, no. 1 (1980): 25–45.

———. "The Sale of Slaves in the Ottoman Empire: Markets and State Taxes on Slave Sales, Some Preliminary Considerations." *Boğaziçi Üniversitesi Dergisi* 6 (1978): 149–174.

———. "Studies in Ottoman Slavery and Slave Trade, II: Manumission." *Journal of Turkish Studies* 4 (1980): 49–56.

INALCIK, HALIL. "Servile Labor in the Ottoman Empire." In *The Mutual Effects of the Islamic and Judeo-Christian Worlds: The East European Pattern,* edited by Abraham Ascher, Tibor Halasi-Kun, and Béla K. Király. 1979.

MÉNAGE, V. L. "Devshirme." In *The Encyclopaedia of Islam* 2nd ed., vol. 2, pp. 210–213. 1965.

SAHILLIOĞLU, HALIL. "Slaves in the Social and Economic Life of Bursa in the Late Fifteenth and Early Sixteenth Centuries." *Turcica* 17 (1985): 43–112.

TOLEDANO, EHUD. *The Ottoman Slave Trade and Its Suppression.* 1982.

WITTEK, PAUL. "Devshirme and Shari'a." *Bulletin of the School of Oriental and African Studies, University of London* 17 (1955): 271–278.

Alan Fisher

Overseers

In the antebellum southern United States, planters who owned thirty or more slaves generally employed an overseer to manage their labor force. Most slaves were held by such planters; and on these plantations, success depended on their proper handling. Apparently, however, few men of ability became overseers, and the planters were frequently dissatisfied with their overseers' performance. Still, the planters themselves were unwilling either to do the disagreeable and demanding work the overseer performed or to give up their leisure time. Because they distrusted their overseers, planters often supplied detailed written instructions regarding the overseer's duties and

An overseer of a plantation sits astride his horse and watches the slaves hoe the cotton fields. [Library of Congress/Corbis]

responsibilities. These instructions could cover everything from the conduct of the overseer himself to the care and handling of the slaves, including performance standards and individual work assignments. Nevertheless, the historical record provides many examples of planters' complaints against overseers, and seldom was an overseer retained for more than a season or two.

Dealing with a demanding planter was perhaps the least of the overseer's difficulties. Often, he was the only white man with whom the slaves had direct contact, and as Kenneth Stampp has noted, planters found slaves a "troublesome property." When slaves did contact the planter, the planter and the overseer had to demonstrate agreement in all matters, lest the slaves exploit any differences to their own advantage. Therefore, planters typically ignored slaves' complaints—but even so, frequent complaints could undermine a planter's confidence in an overseer. Planters and overseers agreed that force was often necessary to control the slaves, but the planters frequently included prohibitions against brutality in their instructions and specified the degree and types of punishment an overseer might use. Planters, of course, did not want their valuable slaves injured by excessively harsh discipline, but overseers knew that reemployment depended not upon the condition of the slave force but upon the size of the crop. Overseers were therefore under pressure to meet crop quotas that could be produced only by excessive driving, and they often ignored instructions, preferring to control the slaves by physical force rather than by positive incentives or other forms of coercion. It was not uncommon for an overseer to be discharged for cruelty.

Although many planters considered firm but humane overseers to be the most efficient, the available evidence suggests that such overseers were rare. In fact, some planters believed that brutality and cruelty were necessary qualities in an overseer, and in the minds of these planters, it was the overseer's duty to produce large crop yields, whatever the cost. Other planters, however, did dispense with the services of an overseer, depending solely on a trusted slave for the routine operation of the plantation. Free blacks also worked as overseers.

Whether white or black, the overseer on a large plantation generally employed black slave drivers to help manage the labor force; on some plantations there was a head driver, almost a sub-overseer; on other plantations, the drivers were directly under the overseer. These black drivers might or might not work alongside the other slaves, depending on conditions. White overseers, however, never worked in the fields, although they always had to be present.

See also DISCIPLINE AND PUNISHMENT.

BIBLIOGRAPHY

BREEDEN, JAMES O. *Advice among Masters: The Ideal in Slave Management in the Old South.* 1980.

FELDSTEIN, S. *Once a Slave: The Slaves' View of Slavery.* 1971.

JOYNER, CHARLES. *Down by the Riverside: A South Carolina Slave Community.* 1984.

SCARBOROUGH, WILLIAM KAUFFMAN. *The Overseer: Plantation Management in the Old South.* 1966.

STAMPP, KENNETH M. *The Pecular Institution: Slavery in the Ante-Bellum South.* 1956.

VAN DEBURG, WILLIAM L. *The Slave Drivers: Black Agricultural Labor Supervisors in the Antebellum South.* 1979.

Al McDermid

P

Pacific Island Societies

Chattel slavery was minimal in the indigenous societies of the Pacific Islands (Polynesia, Micronesia, Melanesia), and where it did exist, only small numbers of people were involved. However, other systems of obligations and deference institutionalized hierarchies of power, especially in Polynesia and parts of Micronesia. Most of these entailed reciprocal duties, rather than outright ownership of one human being by another. But there were some instances of slavery, and in practice even reciprocal burdens could be unequal.

The two categories of people most vulnerable to such exploitation were war captives and castaways. Both were at the mercy of their hosts and had to serve in order to survive. The Maori of Aotearoa (New Zealand) often ate defeated enemies, mainly as an ultimate debasement (that is, transforming them into excrement), but they took a few captive. Sometimes enemy leaders would be targeted as prospective captives before battle. The struggle to take them prisoner might itself injure or kill them, but a victorious warrior could save a defeated enemy by throwing his mat over him. A chief's daughter could even select a future mate, who would be a slave, this way. Bound prisoners might be eaten during the army's journey home, killed by vengeful widows when they arrived, or sacrificed later by their owner if they lost his goodwill.

Some European explorers who visited New Zealand in the late eighteenth and early nineteenth centuries accepted Maori slaves who wanted to escape into their ship crews as workers or guides. But few ever tried to go home again because their own kin regarded them as socially dead. The life of Maori slaves, while insecure, was not oppressive. They were not restricted physically, could marry (offspring by a free wife were considered free), generally ate well, and were not expected to overwork themselves. They did menial tasks like cooking, paddling canoes, fetching wood and water, and acting as arms bearers during war. Some were called pets, as a reminder of their lowly status, but they helped their masters accumulate wealth. People in most Maori tribes categorized themselves either as descendants of chiefly ancestors or as captives whose kin ties had been broken.

In Tahiti, as well, defeated enemies might be made into slaves, and the Samoan language had a word for "slave," but that status was not common. Even on Easter Island (Rapanui), the workers who toiled to put up the stone heads were not slaves; they were members of a low-status tribe who exchanged their stonecutting skill and labor for food from the high-status tribe who wanted their ancestors glorified. The two groups intermarried. However, deforestation produced an ecological crisis in the fifteenth century, the statue-building arrangement collapsed, and rival groups fought and enslaved each other. This power struggle became more organized in an annual competition in which young warriors competed to acquire the first bird's egg of spring; the winner's sponsor would then rule Rapanui for the next year.

Ancient Hawai'i had a small, unusual class of people called *kauwā*, meaning "outcast" or "slave." The term could be used figuratively for someone burdened with service, but it was normally a negative epithet. True *kauwā* lived apart from the rest of society, providing for their own needs by fishing and farming. They did not have to serve anyone, but from time to time a high priest might call on them to provide a victim of their own choosing for human sacrifice at a war temple. The chosen man would bid farewell and then voluntarily drown himself. Such people were considered by others to be polluting and could not marry outside their group. Hawaiian historian David Malo said they were descended from a *kauwā* who belonged to the founder of the Hawaiian people, Wakea. When Wakea deserted his wife, Papa, she lived with his *kauwā* and begat a line of such outcasts. But the abolition of traditional Hawaiian prohibitions in 1819 enabled the *kauwā* to leave their reservations and merge with the common people.

Polynesians generally ranked people according to their degree of *mana*, or "godliness," and in very hierarchical societies like Hawai'i, commoners were not permitted even to walk across the shadow of a chief, on pain of death. Chiefs claimed *mana* through their genealogies and could augment it by winning battles. They might hold life-and-death power over their subjects; a Tongan ruler displayed such absolute authority when he had the left arms of all his cooks amputated just to make them different from other chiefs' cooks. Tongan chiefs were considered so sacred that they often imported highborn Samoans as "neutral" servants, rewarding them with land and status, because a Tongan commoner would be polluting (and a potential rival). Because the sister of a Tongan chief had higher sacred rank than he did, he often married her off to a Fijian to eliminate political rivalry from her children. Tahitian and Hawaiian commoners could not marry chiefs and had to provide tribute in exchange for protection and land. In such a caste-like social system, the difference between being a "free" commoner and a slave is debatable.

Micronesia, in the northwest Pacific, had hereditary chiefs and, at least on larger islands, class distinctions. On Yap, for example, people were divided into two castes, each of which had four or five subclasses. The upper caste owned the land and referred to their lower-caste tenants as their "sons." The terms for lower-caste groups are sometimes translated as "servants" or "serfs," and their members were considered impure. They had to bury the dead, an unclean task; however, their impurity spared them from having to provide food for their landlords (though they might have to repair the roofs of their landlords' houses). Pohnpei (Ponape) and the Marshall Islands also had finely graded hierarchies, and in both Palau (Belau) and Kiribati, chiefs either killed castaways who arrived on their beaches or claimed them as landless depen-

dents until, after many generations of service, their descendants could finally escape the stigma of being outsiders. Even local-born commoner families often lived as "wards" of other families descended from the first settlers.

Probably the most egalitarian region of the Pacific was Melanesia, in the southwest, the largest island of which is New Guinea. Small polities often alternated violent conflict with economic exchanges built on reciprocal, kinlike bonds between trade partners. Leaders, generically called "big men" in the anthropological literature, were usually self-made entrepreneurs who could not pass on the status they achieved to their offspring, thus making for an open social system without hereditary rankings. Yet competition for success as farmers, traders, or feast givers created classes of big men and "rubbish" men. Moreover, big men built their reputations on the accumulation of service obligations from kin and clients. Perhaps the best way to sum up this system, and those in many other Pacific Island societies, is the Samoan word *tautua*, or service, the goal of which is to earn favor from the powerful and, ultimately, higher rank.

See also BLACKBIRDING IN THE PACIFIC ISLANDS; HAWAII; MAORI.

BIBLIOGRAPHY

ALKIRE, WILLIAM. *An Introduction to the Peoples and Cultures of Micronesia.* 1977.
HOWE, K. R. *Where the Waves Fall.* 1984.
MALO, DAVID. *Hawaiian Antiquities.* 1951.
OLIVER, DOUGLAS. *Oceania: The Native Cultures of Australia and the Pacific Islands.* 2 vols. 1989.
Ongka: Self-Account by a New Guinea Bigman. 1979.
VAYDA, ANDREW. "Maori Warfare." In *Law and Warfare*, edited by Paul Bohannan. 1967; pp. 359–380.
WALKER, RANGINUI. *Ka Whawhai Tonu Matou: Struggle without End.* 1990.

David A. Chappell

Painting

See Arts.

Palace Slaves in the Middle East

Premodern royal families found it difficult to staff their administrations and households with competent individuals at an affordable cost. In the Middle East most kings, emperors, caliphs, and sultans adopted a system of palace and household slavery to solve the problems of expenditure and effectiveness. In contrast to the post-Roman West, where rulers were forced to share power with the church, landowners, and the nobility, Middle Eastern rulers were able to sustain an autocratic power that made it possible to control their governments to an extent resembling actual ownership.

Even in the ancient Middle East, the Assyrian and Akkadian monarchs had resources sufficient to create vast palaces with large households, staffed largely by slaves. Assurnasirpal II at Nimrud is said to have owned more than two thousand slaves, who managed his palace and administered his government.

Sources that could tell us about the staffing of palaces for regimes in the Middle East over the next millennium are fragmentary, though from the evidence of archaeological remains of capital cities and government buildings, historians believe that most followed the lead of their ancient predecessors. The great Sassanian palaces in Iran, particularly the Taq-i Kisra in Ctesiphon, Dastagird, and Qusr-i Shirin, provided living space for large staffs of household slaves. The Sassanian emperors used free Zoroastrian officials as administrators.

The one Muslim palace for which we have evidence about internal staffing and administration is the Ottoman Topkapı Sarayı in Istanbul. Historians assume that comparable palaces in Isfahan, Baghdad, Tabriz, Konya, Fatehpur Sikri, Granada, and Cairo were similar.

Studies by Leslie Pierce, Halil Inalcık, and Gülru Necipoğlu provide a picture of a vast Ottoman slave establishment in the palace, numbering as many as five thousand in the seventeenth century. Women and men, including eunuchs, made up the sultan's household and maintained the internal administration of the palace, which was in fact the government.

The women lived in the harem portion of the palace, provided heirs to make the imperial succession secure, educated the sultan's children, and often took part in political decision making in the administration. They formed alliances with male political factions, on occasion advised the sultan about personnel and administrative matters, and provided the domestic services in his household. Virtually all of the them had entered the system as slaves. Some were purchased in markets in Crimea; others were given to the sultan by Ottoman and foreign individuals hoping for increased influence over affairs of state.

The harem was directed by the sultan's mother, who maintained a large staff of female and male slaves (the males were almost exclusively black eunuchs) responsible for the day-to-day affairs of the sultan's family household. Well educated in the harem, often in the arts and literature, these women were the most privileged in Ottoman society, though in fact legally the sultan's slaves. There were occasions when a sultan was incompetent and these women actually controlled

A cook (doubtless a slave) at the Topkapı Palace. [Historical Picture Archive/Corbis]

affairs of state. At other times, though, the women were abused by a sultan—in the early seventeenth century, for instance, all women in the harem were killed and replaced by a new harem.

The male slaves, called *ghulam* in Persian (*gilman*, singular) and by the Turkish term *kul*, entered the palace household staff in three ways. First, eunuchs, both white and black, were purchased in slave markets in Crimea and Egypt. Second, young Christian boys were taken as tribute from Ottoman Balkan provinces through the *devshirme* (or *devşirme*, a Turkish word meaning "collection" or "roundup") system, converted to Islam, and educated in the palace so that they could enter both military and civil administrative service. And third, on occasion men captured in military action who demonstrated unusual talent entered the sultan's household.

In the palace, the *ghulam* were organized—in early Ottoman practice—into five divisions: the chamber, treasury, commissary, royal falconers, and gatekeepers. By the end of the empire the divisions had grown to ten. Boys entering the palace were designated "pages" until they "graduated" from their training to join one of the major divisions. There was housing for as many as fifteen hundred *ghulam*. Large palace kitchens were required to provide the meals for the household; an infirmary, bath, mosque, library, and exercise ground were also provided.

While there were several hundred eunuchs in the palace, only six occupied positions of authority. White eunuchs included the cupbearer, who was in charge of the sultan's private apartments; the chief treasurer; the head of the commissary; the chief falconer; and the head of the stables. The chief black eunuch managed security for the harem. Each of these eunuchs had his own staff, and on more than one occasion eunuchs had slaves of their own.

Although modernization of the Ottoman administration in the nineteenth century replaced many of these slave administrators with professional free officials, the sultans maintained a slave household until the sultanate was abolished following the defeat of the Ottomans in World War I. The last sultan, who left Istanbul with the departing British after 1918, took with him his remaining slaves: women and eunuchs.

See also EUNUCHS; HAREM; ISLAM; JANISSARIES; OTTOMAN EMPIRE.

BIBLIOGRAPHY

FISHER, CAROL G., and ALAN FISHER. "Topkapı Sarayı in the Mid-Seventeenth Century: Bobovi's Description." *Archivum Ottomanicum* X (1985): 5–81."

INALCIK, H., D. SOURDEL, C. E. BOSWORTH, and P. HARDY. "Ghulam." In *The Encyclopaedia of Islam*, 2nd ed., vol. 2.

NECIPĞLU, GÜLRU. *Architecture, Ceremonial, and Power: The Topkapi Palace in the Fifteenth and Sixteenth Centuries.* 1991.

PEIRCE, LESLIE. *The Imperial Harem: Women and Sovereignty in the Ottoman Empire.* 1993.

Alan Fisher

Palmares

Slave uprisings and the formation and defense of runaway slave communities (called *quilombos* or *mocambos* in Brazil) were common facts of Brazilian slavery. *Quilombos* occurred at every moment during the history of slavery and everywhere in the vast territory of Brazil. The most famous of those fugitive communities was Palmares, located in the present-day state of Alagoas in the Brazilian northeast. Palmares had an estimated population of between 11,000 and 20,000 souls. It survived attacks from colonial forces for almost one hundred years, from about 1605 to 1694, when it was destroyed. Palmares seems to have grown considerably by adopting slaves who escaped plantations and villages during the wars between the Portuguese and the Dutch, who occupied the sugar-producing captaincy of Pernambuco, where the famous *quilombo* was located.

Palmares was in fact formed by several settlements, well protected by palisades, and ruled by a "king" who lived in a larger village called Macaco (Monkey). There are signs of a royal lineage (the last leader, Zumbi, was said to have been the nephew of the Palmares ruler Ganga Zumba), but lesser leaders apparently chose the supreme chief by acclamation.

The *quilombo's* population included mostly Africans from present-day Angola and neighboring Kongo. Some of its military and political organization has recently been linked to a warriors' initiation society (called *ki-lombo*) of Imbangala bands in sixteenth-century Angol and the surrounding regions. The economy was based on slash-and-burn agriculture and periodic raids into nearby villages, farms, and sugar plantations. The people of Palmares often exchanged surplus produce for arms, ammunition, and food in local markets or through traveling merchants.

Little is known of Palmares's social organization, but it seems to have been hierarchical, based on military distinction, control over people, and access to land. A kind of temporary slavery for captives taken in raids has been reported, but those who spontaneously joined the rebels apparently were never enslaved. As Palmares expanded, it became clear to the Portuguese government that it threatened slavery and even colonial rule in the northeast. Numerous expeditions were sent against the rebels, who tried to reduce the military pressure through peace proposals. In 1678 the rebel leader Ganga Zumba (an appellation considered by some a political/religious title rather than a personal name) signed a treaty with the colonial government promising to be loyal to the Portuguese crown and to return any future fugitive slaves. The treaty, which the Portuguese failed to honor, divided the rebels. Ganga Zumba's nephew, Zumbi, apparently had his uncle killed and became the ruler. Zumbi made no concessions to colonial authorities, who responded by keeping Palmares under constant military pressure during the 1680s.

In the early 1690s, the government decided to employ forces from the southern captaincy of São Paulo, under the leadership of *bandeirantes,* who were Indian hunters and experienced explorers of the colony's backlands. After several failed attempts, Palmares was finally defeated by *bandeirante* leader Domingos Jorge Velho in a bloody battle in February 1694. Having escaped the massacre, Zumbi was killed in November 1695.

No *quilombo* like Palmares would ever again be allowed to develop in Brazil. But smaller fugitive slave communities, which sometimes survived for many years, appeared repeatedly near sugar plantations in the northeast, including the area where Palmares once existed, and throughout other regions of Brazil. Like Palmares, they were hidden in well-protected mountainous country and combined subsistence agriculture with road robberies and raids against plantations and villages. More often, these runaway groups were small in number and short-lived. They were dismantled by assault troops or slave-hunting officers (*capitães-do-mato*) specially created to combat them after Palmares. But as quickly as they were destroyed, others were formed, and the history of *quilombos* in Brazil would only end with the emancipation of the slaves in 1888.

See also BRAZIL; MAROONS; REBELLIONS AND VIOLENT RESISTANCE.

BIBLIOGRAPHY

ALVES FILHO, IVAN. *Memorial dos Palmares.* 1988.

ANDERSON, ROBERT NELSON. "The *Quilombo* of Palmares: A New Overview of a Maroon State in Seventeenth-Century Brazil." *Journal of Latin American Studies* 28 (1996): 545–566.

CARNEIRO, EDISON. *O quilombo de Palmares.* 4th ed. 1988.

ENNES, ERNESTO. *As guerras nos Palmares.* 1938.

FREITAS, DÉCIO. *Palmares, a guerra dos escravos.* 5th ed. 1984.

KENT, R. K. "Palmares: An African State in Brazil." In *Maroon Societies,* edited by Richard Price. 1973.

REIS, JOÃO JOSÉ, and FLÁVIO DOS SANTOS GOMES GOMES, eds. *Liberdade por um fio: história dos quilombos no Brasil.* 1996.

SCHWARTZ, STUART B. "Rethinking Palmares: Slave Resistance in Colonial Brazil." In *Slaves, Peasants, and Rebels.* 1992.

João José Reis

Panics

The first Africans brought to British North America worked alongside white indentured servants, and their status was not clearly defined by law or by race. In the early 1600s, therefore, an African servant might gain freedom in much the same manner as a white servant, and so the motivation to revolt was limited, although rebellious servants, both black and white, were not unheard of. After about 1660, when the Africans' status as slaves was legally set, however, the possibility of resistance increased. This in turn engendered fear of the Africans—fear that was not totally unfounded. During the colonial period, for example, a number of limited revolts brought death to both blacks and whites. The most spectacular of these occurred at Stono, South Carolina, in 1739; it resulted in the death of as many as twenty-five whites and about fifty blacks. Also during this period several conspiracies were exposed before the slaves involved could actually revolt. In the wake of the "Great Negro Plot" of 1741, which may or may not have been an actual conspiracy, and

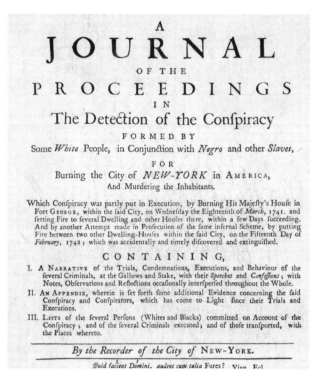

Title page from the official report of the investigation of the 1741 "Great Negro Plot" in New York City. [Corbis-Bettmann]

quite possibly arose out of white hysteria, thirty blacks and four whites were executed in New York City.

Military action, whether directed against the Dutch, Spanish, French, or Native Americans, further exacerbated whites' fears. This was especially true during the American Revolution, when the rhetoric of freedom inspired many slaves, and the British freed and enlisted slaves to fight against the colonists. After the Revolution, a number of the newly independent states were motivated, in part by fear of the growing number of blacks, to abolish the slave trade. The federal government followed suit in 1808. By this time also, the locus of fear shifted to the South where, unlike the North, slavery thrived. As one observer noted, there were men in the old South who feared neither God nor other white men, but who trembled at even the rumor of a slave rebellion. In fact, fear of blacks was so pervasive in the South that an isolated act of rebellion in one part of the region could lead to panic in other, distant parts, and white southerners came to believe that military preparedness was the only means of assuring domestic security. And although slave revolts were rare, localized, and easily put down by the superior numbers and firepower of the better organized whites, southerners still feared the black bondsmen. This fear led to increased militarization and a progressive strengthening of the slave codes. These new laws restricted the movements of both slaves and free blacks, especially black seamen from northern and foreign ships; limited or forbade the education of blacks; and set strict conditions for manumission.

The early part of the nineteenth century was rife with revolts, conspiracies, and rumors. Gabriel's rebellion (1800), the 1811 attempted march on New Orleans, Denmark Vesey's conspiracy (1822), and the revolt led by Nat Turner in 1831, along with a host of other minor incidents, all worked to heighten southerners' fear of slaves. Even such occurrences as unexplained fires, a rash of runaways, or reports of a gathering of blacks could spark rumors of insurrection. White southerners responded to these real and imagined plots with severe reprisals, including summary executions and the indiscriminate killing of slaves. Many slaves innocent of any wrongdoing were also killed or were removed to other parts of the South. Turner's rebellion, although short-lived and limited in scope, was especially traumatic, and the image of "Nat" came to represent an ever-present fear of another serious uprising.

In the thirty years between Turner's rebellion and the outbreak of the Civil War, no slave plot would again arise in the South, but the fear of such plots continued to shape the thinking of the southern white community. The rise of the clearly sectional Republican Party to national prominence exacerbated southerners' fears, and during the fall of 1856 rumors of an extensive uprising, set for Christmas day, could be heard throughout the South. Following John Brown's raid on Harper's Ferry in 1859, fear of slave insurrections again swept the South, leading to increased vigilance and new laws that further restricted both slaves and free blacks. In Georgia and South Carolina, there was even some talk of reenslaving free blacks, while Arkansas moved to expel all free blacks from the state. The historian Eugene Genovese has argued that, in part, fear of slave revolts drove the South to secede. Those fears were only magnified during the war, as slaves left the plantations to follow the invading Union armies.

See also BROWN, JOHN; GABRIEL; GABRIEL'S REBELLION; LAW; REBELLIONS AND VIOLENT RESISTANCE; TURNER, NAT; VESEY REBELLION.

BIBLIOGRAPHY

DAVIS, THOMAS J. *A Rumor of Revolt: The "Great Negro Plot" in Colonial New York.* 1985.

EGERTON, DOUGLAS R. *Gabriel's Rebellion: The Virginia Slave Conspiracies of 1800 and 1802.* 1993.

FINKELMAN, PAUL, ed. *Slavery and the Law.* 1997.

FREEHLING, WILLIAM W. *Prelude to Civil War: The Nullification Controversy in South Carolina, 1816–1836.* 1965, 1966.

JORDAN, WINTHROP D. *Tumult and Silence at Second Creek: An Inquiry into a Civil War Slave Conspiracy.* 1993.

LOFTON, JOHN. *Denmark Vesey's Revolt: The Slave Plot That Lit a Fuse to Fort Sumter.* 1983.

Al McDermid

Papacy

See Christianity.

Patterson Thesis

In *Slavery and Social Death* (1982) Orlando Patterson offered a "preliminary definition . . . on the level of personal relations" that has become the starting point for most subsequent general studies: "*Slavery is the permanent, violent domination of natally alienated and generally dishonored persons*" (p. 13, Patterson's italics). The book demonstrated a corollary proposition that has also become associated with Patterson's name: that slavery has occurred throughout human history and, by extension, may be incipient in all human societies.

Patterson's is a highly personalistic theory, focusing on the experience of the slave rather than on the initiative of the master and understanding slavery as a relationship with its core in the Hegelian master-slave dyad. It is also highly ironic, exploring both the fundamental contradiction of masters' attempting to gain honor through domination of social nonentities who cannot resist, or whose resistance does not count, and the ultimate power that the slave gains through the master's utter dependence on him or her—a paradox that Patterson terms "human parasitism." Patterson's intimately personal understanding of slavery differs from previous definitions emphasizing its legal aspect (slaves as "property") or its economic aspect (slaves as exploited labor). Rather than seeing slavery as a special case of property or economic dominance, Patterson held that notions of property evolved in conjunction with the experience of slavery. Extending Moses Finley's classic definition of slaves as "kinless outsiders," he argued that humans can become property because they have experienced "social death."

From Patterson's ironic viewpoint, the tragedy of slavery is crucial to the emergence of freedom. In his book *Freedom* (1991) the central thesis is that "the very ideal and valuation of freedom was generated by the existence and growth of slavery" (p. xiv). Patterson points out that in many societies values other than freedom have been paramount—for example, pursuit of glory, filial piety, valor in warfare, equality, and material progress. Hence the emergence of freedom as the preeminent ideal in Western culture requires explanation.

While slavery was widespread and usually stimulated some notion of freedom, only in Western culture did it become transformed into a widely held institutional value. This occurred initially in ancient Athens. Here large-scale slavery created an urban class of people who were neither slaves nor aristocrats and hence took pride in their freedom. They were not economic dependents of the aristocracy, and they frequently owned slaves themselves. Because slaves were assigned much of the heavier work, women became more confined to the household and were in close contact with slaves. Consequently, women frequently became a voice for personal freedom both in everyday life and in Greek drama. These structural developments of large-scale slavery and differentiated gender roles interacted with political democracy and the elevation of rationality in Greek philosophy. While this combination of circumstances made possible the social construction of freedom, large-scale slavery was the crucial stimulus. Most of Patterson's book is devoted to tracing how developments in ancient Greece, ancient Rome, early Christianity, and medieval European society led to the establishment of freedom as Western culture's paramount value.

See also FINLEY, MOSES I.; FREEDOM.

BIBLIOGRAPHY

FINLEY, MOSES I. "Slavery." In *International Encyclopedia of the Social Sciences,* edited by David L. Sills. Vol. 14, pp. 307–313. 1968.
PATTERSON, ORLANDO. *Freedom.* Vol. 1, *Freedom in the Making of Western Culture.* 1991.
———. *Slavery and Social Death: A Comparative Study.* 1982.

Murray Milner, Jr.

Peculium

In Roman law the term *peculium* denotes the property of a person, such as a slave or child-in-power, who is legally deemed incapable of legal ownership. In theory, since slaves belonged to masters, so did all of their possessions. Thus *peculium* was a voluntary and reversible grant, automatically revoked at the slave's death. Although custom sanctioned a living slave's rights to his or her *peculium,* Pliny (ca. A.D. 61–112) in *Epistle* 8.16 is exceptional in affirming the testamentary dispositions of his slaves—if only within his household.

Traditional respect for a slave's *peculium* was paradoxically seconded by law. A slave might be required to pay money to a deceased master's heir to attain manumission, but, in theory, the heir owned both the slave and the money already. The *peculium* gained its traditional and eventually quasi-legal status as a way of rewarding slaves' good behavior and because it enabled slaves to conduct business for their masters.

At their owners' discretion, the institution of *peculium* allowed slaves the use of property, unlimited in source and amount, occasionally including the use of other slaves. Although the use of their savings to buy freedom is most conspicuous, slaves also spent their money for personal expenses.

Slaves managed businesses and farms for masters, who automatically gained rights and property through their slaves. The existence of a *peculium* allowed slaves to incur financial obligations as well, a necessity for any business. Third parties could sue a master for up to the value of a slave's *peculium,* even for transactions performed without the master's knowledge.

Peculium, originally a Roman term, survived the fall of the empire along with Roman law. The term and concept of *peculium* resurfaced in slave systems in Latin America.

See also ANCIENT ROME; MANUMISSION; SELF-PURCHASE.

BIBLIOGRAPHY

KIRSCHENBAUM, AARON. *Sons, Slaves, and Freedmen in Roman Commerce.* 1987.
WATSON, ALAN. *Roman Slave Law.* 1987.

Peter Hunt

Pennsylvania

In 1681, when William Penn of the Society of Friends (Quakers) began his "holy experiment" in Pennsylvania, slavery had long existed under the Dutch and Swedes in the Delaware Valley and was well established in other English colonies. That many wealthy Quakers in early Pennsylvania, including Penn himself, quickly purchased enslaved Africans, despite opposition to the practice among some Friends, demonstrates how deeply slavery was already embedded in the Anglo-American economy and culture. Some of the earliest immigrants to the Quaker colony came from the West Indies, bringing enslaved Africans and connections for establishing trade in foodstuffs, livestock, and lumber, in return for West Indies sugar, molasses, and slaves, a trade that became the mainspring of the Pennsylvania economy. Many slaves lived and worked in Philadelphia, where their estimated percentage of the population peaked at 17 percent in 1701–1710, then declined. Most slaves in Pennsylvania were Africans, whom Philadelphia merchants imported in small consignments from the West Indies. Briefly, around 1760, slave traders brought shiploads of enslaved people directly from Africa, until the legislature curtailed the trade with its prohibitive duty of 1761. A few Pennsylvanians owned enslaved Indians, probably imported from South Carolina.

During the colony's first half-century, its government, dominated by wealthy Friends, gradually formalized a system of slavery that, while less brutal than the plantation regimes to the south, nevertheless constituted a caste society based upon perceptions of race. Neither Penn's *Frame of Government* nor early legislation mentioned slavery; before 1700, enslaved Africans were subject to the same courts and laws as whites. Then the Pennsylvania legislature established separate courts without juries for enslaved and free blacks and ruled that African-Americans but not whites would be executed for raping a white woman, buggery, and burglary. Black men would be castrated for attempted rape. In 1726, the assembly passed a comprehensive slave code that, in addition to limiting the activities of slaves, required manumission bonds and threatened free blacks with reenslavement for vagrancy or for marrying a white.

These restrictions on free blacks were in part a reaction against growing abolitionism in the colony. In 1688, four Germantown Quakers had issued the first antislavery petition in North America, followed by protests from numerous Pennsylvania Friends, including William Southeby, who in 1712 petitioned the assembly for general emancipation. Table 1 demonstrates the decline after 1720 in the percentage of slaves in the population of Pennsylvania, as manumission by will gradually became more common, especially among Friends, and employers took advantage of the influx of German and Scots-Irish immigrants to purchase bound servants or hire free laborers instead of buying slaves. Enslaved African-Americans, particularly during the American Revolution and its aftermath, further undercut the institution by escaping from their masters. In 1780, the Pennsylvania assembly, influenced by Revolutionary ideals, passed the first abolition act in the United States; but it freed only the children of slaves born after March 1, 1780, and further required that until they reached age twenty-eight, they would be bound servants to the owners of their mothers. Nevertheless, many Pennsylvania slaveholders followed the spirit of the law and freed their bondspeople after a term of years, seriously undermining the institution decades before the commonwealth outlawed slavery entirely in 1847.

In the early nineteenth century Pennsylvania became a mecca for freed and escaped slaves, as the Pennsylvania Abolition Society and the courts offered some protection against kidnappers and pursuing masters. A thriving black community developed in Philadelphia. After 1820, however, African-Americans in the state faced increasing racism and violence, declining economic opportunity, and (in 1838) loss of suffrage. Even so, black and white Pennsylvanians were among the most active, influential leaders of the abolitionist movements after 1815.

See also PENNSYLVANIA SOCIETY FOR THE ABOLITION OF SLAVERY; QUAKERS.

BIBLIOGRAPHY

NASH, GARY B. *Forging Freedom: The Formation of Philadelphia's Black Community, 1720–1840.* 1988.

NASH, GARY B., and JEAN R. SODERLUND. *Freedom by Degrees: Emancipation in Pennsylvania and Its Aftermath.* 1991.

WINCH, JULIE. *Philadelphia's Black Elite: Activism, Accommodation, and the Struggle for Autonomy, 1787–1848.* 1988.

Jean R. Soderlund

Table 1.   Decline of Slaves in the Population of Pennsylvania.

Year	Number of Slaves	Percent of Total Population
1720	2,000	6.5
1750	2,872	2.4
1770	5,561	2.3
1780	6,855	2.1
1790	3,760	0.9
1800	1,706	0.3
1810	795	0.1

Sources: For 1720 to 1780: U.S. Bureau of the Census, *Historical Statistics of the United States, Colonial Times to 1970* (1975), 2:1168; numbers reduced by estimates of 200 free blacks in 1770 and 1,000 free blacks in 1780. For 1790 to 1810: U.S. Bureau of the Census, *A Century of Population Growth from the First Census of the United States to the Twelfth, 1790–1900* (1909): 57, 133.

Pennsylvania Society for the Abolition of Slavery

In April 1775 in Philadelphia, a group consisting mostly of Quaker craftsmen and shopkeepers founded the Society for the Relief of Free Negroes Unlawfully Held in Bondage. Their initial purpose was to prevent the enslavement of Dinah Nevill and her three children. When the society lost its lawsuit to win the family's liberty, Quaker tailor Thomas Harrison, the group's linchpin for over thirty years, arranged the purchase of Nevill and two children, then freed them by manumission.

The society met only four times in 1775 and failed to reconvene until after the Revolution, yet its goals and *modus operandi* were already clear. The society reconstituted itself in 1784, after news circulated that two free blacks in Philadelphia had committed suicide, and it had become evident that African-Americans required legal assistance to enforce the provisions of the 1780 Pennsylvania gradual abolition act. To expand the society's influence, the Quaker founders recruited men of other religions; by late 1785, Friends held a scant majority of members. While most of the group ranked among the wealthiest one-third of Philadelphians, only a few were very rich.

During this early phase, the society—true to its name—emphasized relief to free blacks held illegally as slaves. Instead of seeking an end to slavery by judicial decree, as had been achieved in Massachusetts in 1783 with the Quock Walker cases, the society's lawyers worked, without pay, to amplify the scope of the 1780 act. They assisted blacks individually rather than at-tacking the institution as a whole. The society gained freedom for slaves whose masters failed to register them as the 1780 law required, and secured liberty for blacks brought into Pennsylvania and held there over six months—longer than the abolition act allowed. In one such case, George Washington protested that the society was too aggressive: when an out-of-state slave owner "whose purse will not measure with that of the Society . . . loses his property for want of means to defend it," he wrote, "it is oppression" (quoted in Finkelman, p. 51).

Rather than bow to such pressures from slaveholders, the society in 1787 enlarged its mission, changing its name to reflect the more ambitious goals. Now called the Pennsylvania Society for Promoting the Abolition of Slavery, and the Relief of Free Negroes, Unlawfully Held in Bondage (hereafter PAS), the organization recruited wealthy, high-profile Philadelphians including Benjamin Franklin, elected as PAS president; Quaker merchant James Pemberton, elected vice president; Philadelphia mayor Hilary Baker; and revolutionary pamphleteer Thomas Paine. The PAS probably hoped these men could

While representing Pennsylvania at the Constitutional Convention of 1787, Benjamin Franklin (seated second from the left) was also the president of the Pennsylvania Society for the Abolition of Slavery. [Corbis-Bettmann]

influence the Constitutional Convention, which met in Philadelphia that year. Indeed, the society provided Benjamin Franklin, a delegate to the convention, with a petition against the slave trade, which he failed to present out of deference to representatives from the lower South. The PAS also published antislavery tracts and urged newspapers to stop advertising slaves for sale. And it provided indentures for blacks whose masters freed them from slavery but recouped some of their monetary loss by arranging sale for a term of years. A ringing PAS success was its campaign to strengthen the 1780 Pennsylvania abolition act. In March 1788, the assembly approved a law to free immediately any slave brought into Pennsylvania by a new resident, banned the outfitting of ships for the slave trade, and prohibited masters from sending pregnant enslaved women to have their babies out-of-state.

In 1789 the PAS expanded its goals further, establishing the Committee to Improve the Condition of Free Blacks, which located jobs, established schools, offered legal support, and assumed responsibility to "superintend the morals, general conduct, and ordinary situation of the Free Negroes, and afford them advice and instruction, protection from wrongs, and other friendly offices" (quoted in Nash and Soderlund, p. 128). The committee persuaded parents in financial difficulty to bind out their children as apprentices to white families who would assist their "moral" as well as practical education.

During the 1790s, after the wealthier, more renowned PAS members died or drifted away, most of its core activists were young, middle-class Friends. With Thomas Harrison and another Quaker tailor, Isaac Hopper, at the helm, the society petitioned the Pennsylvania legislature to abolish slavery on the basis of the 1790 state constitution, which said "all men are born equally free and independent" (quoted in Nash and Soderlund, p. 132). The PAS also pursued abolition judicially with the case *Flora v. Graisberry,* but the court decided that slavery was constitutional in Pennsylvania because the state constitution did not specifically abolish it. Despite ongoing PAS efforts, slavery remained legal in Pennsylvania until 1847.

The first antislavery organization in the United States, the PAS secured freedom for hundreds of imperiled African-Americans and expanded the scope of the 1780 abolition act, yet retained the moderate, paternalistic approach of its Quaker members. In 1833 the conservative leaders of the PAS refused when William Lloyd Garrison asked them to cooperate in forming the new American Anti-Slavery Society for immediate abolition. The older society, instead, concentrated on education for African-Americans and legal assistance for blacks accused of escaping slav-

ery. While the PAS still exists, its resources and activities declined during the 1830s and 1840s as the new Garrisonian organizations attracted the support of young dedicated abolitionists.

See also ABOLITION AND ANTISLAVERY MOVEMENTS; PENNSYLVANIA; QUAKERS.

BIBLIOGRAPHY

EBERLY, WAYNE J. "The Pennsylvania Abolition Society, 1775–1830." Ph.D. diss., Pennsylvania State University, 1973.

FINKELMAN, PAUL. *An Imperfect Union: Slavery, Federalism, and Comity.* 1981.

NASH, GARY B., and JEAN R. SODERLUND. *Freedom by Degrees: Emancipation in Pennsylvania and Its Aftermath.* 1991.

ZILVERSMIT, ARTHUR. *The First Emancipation: The Abolition of Slavery in the North.* 1967.

Jean R. Soderlund

Pens, Slave

See Barracoons.

Peonage

This entry includes the following articles: United States; Latin America.

United States

Peonage, "a status or condition of compulsory service, based upon the indebtedness of the peon to the master" (*Clyatt v. U.S.,* 1904), entered U.S. law in its particular civil form from the New Mexico Territory. It was defined by the Territorial Court in *Jaramillo* in 1857. In March 1867 the U.S. Congress, under the authority of the Thirteenth Amendment, outlawed this labor status in the Anti-Peonage Act.

Yet after Reconstruction, peonage functioned in place of slavery in the South as a way to control black labor in the countryside. States used laws governing agricultural contracts, along with the convict lease system, vagrancy laws, and other means, as a matrix of compulsions which ensured that large landowners had sufficient low-cost black labor to produce export commodities profitably. From agriculture, the system expanded into industries like logging and turpentine rendering.

Vigorous federal prosecution of peonage in the early twentieth century was due chiefly to diplomatic entanglements that arose when European immigrants were held as peons in the deep South. The U.S. Justice Department investigated peonage in 1907–1908 and concluded that it existed mainly in rural extractive industries, but actually the major litigation between 1903 and 1914 involved African-American farmhands in the cotton belt of Alabama.

The case of Alonso Bailey, a black peon in Alabama, came before the Supreme Court twice. In *Bailey v. Alabama* (1911), the Court, by a 7–2 majority, struck down the state law under which Bailey had been made a peon; the authority cited was the Thirteenth Amendment, along with the Anti-Peonage Act. After 1914, antipeonage litigation in the United States revived in cycles, with a spate of cases in the 1940s involving black peons, and a flurry of activity involving Latino and African immigrant peons in the 1980s and 1990s. Peonage, a kind of retail slavery, appears to constitute a permanent aspect of labor relations in the United States.

See also LABOR SYSTEMS; LAW.

BIBLIOGRAPHY

BICKEL, ALEXANDER, and BENNO C. SCHMIDT, JR. *The Judiciary and Responsible Government, 1910–1921.* 1984.
DANIEL, PETE. *The Shadow of Slavery: Peonage in the South, 1901–1969.* 1972.

Harold S. Forsythe

Latin America

Debt peonage was only one of many coercive labor forms in Latin America; others included Indian draft labor and slavery, in addition to free wage labor. Indians once satisfied Spanish tribute demands by their labor service. Debt peonage became a widespread method of compelling Indians to work as a response to native depopulation, labor shortages, and poverty, in an economy increasingly oriented to cash.

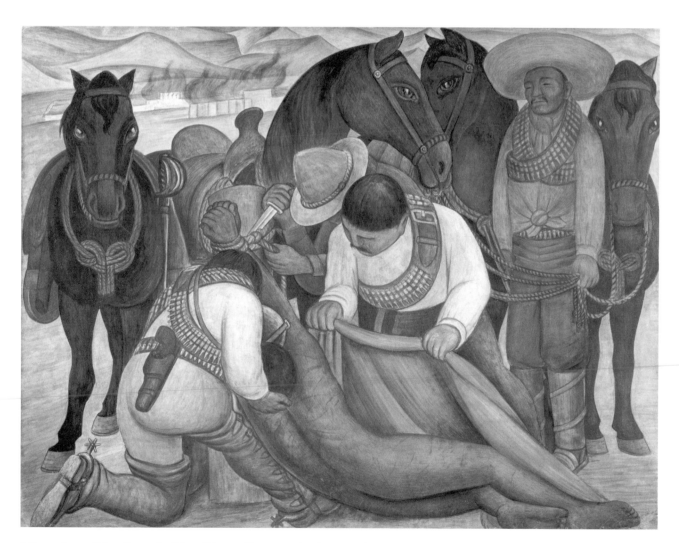

Liberation of the Peon *by Diego Rivera illustrates the fact that for many peons the only end to servitude was death.* [Philadelphia Museum of Art/Corbis]

Despite its great mineral wealth, colonial Latin America was generally currency-poor and even elite Spaniards conducted much economic activity on credit. Lower-class Indians and blacks also had to operate on credit, but their poverty often left them unable to satisfy their debts.

Employers who needed additional labor would hire poor Indians, mestizos, free blacks, and mulattos at a below-subsistence daily wage and advance them money for food and other necessities before they earned the promised wage. When employers demanded repayment and peons could not pay, they had to work off what they owed in urban sweatshops, on rural estates, or in the mines. The workers were often illiterate and fully dependent for their livelihoods upon unscrupulous creditor-employers who might never clear their accounts. In effect, peons became permanently tied to the employer to whom they were indebted. Bourbon administrators of the eighteenth century recognized debt peonage with laws requiring debtors and Indian tributaries to pay or work.

In his study of Jesuit estates, historian Nicholas Cushner called debt peonage "the Indian analogue of black slavery." While the perpetual and abusive nature of the two systems might be comparable, debt peonage lacked the racial character of slavery. In addition, indebted persons were not the property of their employer and could not be legally sold. Nor were debt peons legally subject to punishments that Africans endured under the slave codes.

See also DEBT PEONAGE; LABOR SYSTEMS; SPAIN.

BIBLIOGRAPHY

CUSHNER, NICHOLAS. *Lords of the Land: Sugar, Wine, and Jesuit Estates of Coastal Peru, 1600–1767.* 1980.

SEMO, ENRIQUE. *The History of Capitalism in Mexico: Its Origins, 1521–1763.* 1993.

Jane G. Landers

Persia

See Ancient Middle East; Modern Middle East.

Perspectives on Slavery

This entry includes the following articles: Definitions; Etymology and Semantics; Sociology of Slavery; Opposition to Slavery; Defenses of Slavery; African-American Perspectives, 1865–1965.

Definitions

A common definition of slavery says that it is "the ownership of a person by another person, group, or institution." For all its seeming clarity, the definition is not unproblematic on a global scale. It is founded on a set of distinctly Western assumptions as well as the most recent Western experience of slavery in the New World. Take "ownership" and the related idea of "property." These terms focus on the link between owner and object, in which the owner has total control over the object. But the control is, in fact, seldom total. Even in the West, the owner of a house or a piece of land cannot use it entirely at will: at the very least, the owner cedes some control to the state, which enforces zoning laws and the owner's legal responsibilities to neighbors and passersby. In reality, property almost always involves more than owner and object, encompassing a bundle of social relationships between the owner and other persons and institutions pertaining to an object. Thus, in Britain, the state is a party to the ownership of a piece of land, with rights to the minerals underneath it that supersede those of the landowner. And even in the United States, where the owner owns the minerals, the state interferes with free mining on, say, a residential lot. In many cultures, a single parcel of land may be allocated as farming land to one party, as hunting territory to another, and as a fruit-gathering area to a third. In such cases, to understand land as property one must also understand the entire system of rights in which that land is enmeshed.

In comparing societies and in developing definitions that can stand up cross-culturally, anthropologists have found it necessary to avoid such terms as "ownership" and "property," resorting instead to an analysis of specific constellations of rights in objects. And as with objects, so with people. In any social system, cultural notions of rights and obligations define the relationships among people, groups, and institutions. In most Western nations, the husband-wife relationship involves mutual rights to marital fidelity and to economic support—rights that the state upholds through the legal system. Similarly, children hold rights in their parents to be nourished, cared for, and educated by them, and these entail a claim to the fruits of the parents' labor. None of these rights of persons in other persons make us think of these family obligations as partaking of slavery.

In ancient Rome, however, a father had the right of life and death over his children, and he could also sell them. These rights do indeed remind us of slavery because we tend to see a person's vulnerability to being legally sold or killed by another as a criterion of being a slave. But in the Roman instance, we resist the label. Why? Because the existing kinship relationship overshadows our criteria of slavery. We see kinship and slavery as belonging to different and incompatible spheres: a legally fully recognized offspring cannot also be a slave of the parent. By the same token, once the Roman child has been sold to a stranger, the same set of rights, now transferred from father to a non-kinsman, makes us see the child as a slave. The facts of purchase, salability, and the power of life and death become the defining criteria of slavery. But what if the purchase of the Roman child had led to immediate adoption? This reintroduction of kinship puts us back in a quandary. Yet in places such as the premodern Middle East or Africa, kinship and slavery coexisted without difficulty. Marriage with slaves was widely practiced, and the children, who were simultaneously their fathers' slaves and kinsmen, could become the founders of a branch of slave-relatives.

The Western Cultural Model of Slavery

The crux of the matter, then, is this: what are the criteria, implicit and explicit, that make a modern Westerner (and scholars trained in the Western tradition) comfortable or uncomfortable in labelling a social relationship "slavery"? What, in short, is the contemporary Western cultural model of slavery? The model is, of course, rooted in what the West has been calling "slavery" in its own history. The term evokes an array of images, mainly from the modern (i.e., post-fifteenth-century) period and from the New World, and involves for the most part people brought from sub-Saharan Africa. In this model, the rights of owners in the slaves are explicitly and legally patterned on the Western notion of property rights—rights that historically were most expansive in the English-speaking world. It was in Britain and its dependencies that the triumphant liberalism of the Enlightenment, joined to traditional concepts of English freedoms, made the law most intolerant of restrictions on the property rights of freeborn Englishmen, including rights in human beings. Modern Western slavery—essentially synonymous with New World slavery—was a particular historical phenomenon, with cultural peculiarities that set it apart from the slave systems of other times and places.

The Peculiarities of Modern Western Slavery

The specialized nature of New World slavery is apparent in its notably narrow use of slaves, confining them primarily to household, farm, and plantation labor (even though, as recent research has been stressing, the variety of uses was greater than is popularly assumed). This narrow focus was dictated by an emerging modern world economy that favored the large-scale specialized production of commodities such as sugar and cotton. But the specific adaptation of New World plantation economies was also conditioned by the nature of the labor force.

The acquisition of slaves from afar, from physically and culturally different African populations, made slavery and race mutually reinforcing concepts. It rooted the slave identity in physique and made it easy to restrict slavery to a narrow range of occupations. This was, again, especially true of the British; positioned at the margins of Europe, they were largely unacquainted with the darker-skinned Mediterranean world and had little experience of the gradualness of the "racial" continuum between Africa and Europe.

The linkage of physique and slavery stands in contrast to the slave systems of most other times and places. Before the fifteenth century, most of the contacts between major world areas were by land, between peoples who were not radically different from one another. Under these conditions, the sources of slaves were not far across the ocean but in neighboring societies or within one's own society. And the absence of starkly different physiques meant that the slaves or their descendants could usually merge into the local population.

This was as true of the premodern West as of most other regions. Through the Roman period, Germanic and Celtic areas supplied slaves to the Mediterranean area. Medieval Muslim Spain got many of its slaves from the British Isles. From the Dark Ages until the early modern period, large numbers of slaves came from the Slavic lands, going first to western and southern Europe and then to the Muslim Middle East. North African pirate-states preyed on Mediterranean shipping for their European captives and slaves into the nineteenth century. And elsewhere, from the Middle East and Central Asia to India, China, and southeastern Asia, most slaves came from areas nearby. Most of these imported populations left no long-lasting enclaves in the host societies, having disappeared into the local population, and they failed to encourage linkages among slave status, exploitation, and physique.

Moreover, in most societies in history, a large proportion of slaves came from within the local population. These were prisoners captured in internal conflicts, people kidnapped in feuds between neighboring communities, travelers seized on the road, lost children picked up and incorporated into the finders' families, miscreants expelled from their own communities and sold off, relatives traded in times of famine or given to other groups in payment of debts and damages. Again, these slaves and their descendants blended easily with the host population.

Another peculiarity of modern Western slavery was imposed by Christianity, with its insistence on obligatory monogamy. In addition, the Protestant societies of northwestern Europe (and their New World derivatives) were especially markedly hostile to any public

This proslavery cartoon from 1850, originally published by someone called J. Haven, constrasts black slaves in the South with impoverished English factory workers. A standard part of the proslavery argument was the claim that slaves were happy (note that the cartoon depicts them as singing and dancing), while free workers were all miserable. [Library of Congress/Corbis]

recognition of sexual unions outside of marriage. Hence, for men engaged in building up social networks, marriage was a scarce social resource and public concubinage an unrealizable strategy. Almost all other areas of the world were different in this respect: plural marriage and public concubinage with both slaves and nonslaves could be used—freely, repeatedly, even exuberantly—to establish political alliances and expand one's circle of relatives. This provided a bridge between the spheres of slavery and kinship. To be sure, there was also interbreeding between masters and slaves in the West, but the offspring of these unions were placed outside the formally recognized boundaries of kinship.

To gauge the importance of these two factors—physical differences and monogamy—one need only imagine an American South where the slaves were all white, having been captured in the Appalachian hills or sold locally by their families, and where, for good measure, female slaves could be publicly acknowledged as their polygynous masters' mates and commonly bore members of the family circle. These features would not have prevented mistreatment and exploitation (for those were harsh times), and they would not have prevented trafficking in human beings. But surely the historical course of such a southern "peculiar institution" would have been very different from what in fact occurred.

The main purpose of New World slavery was economic and, in the Western image, this made slavery in general a "labor system." (Curiously, in this image, the main nonlabor facet of slavery became that of uncontrolled sexuality, giving the slave metaphor a singular niche in Western sexual fantasy.) The fact that slave labor was both hard and involuntary put slaves at the very bottom of the labor hierarchy, and the quintessential slave was seen as someone who was harshly treated in every respect. This made mistreatment a major criterion in deciding whether an institution could be called "slavery" and in providing a marker of metaphorical slavery. Thus, Marxists had their notion of wage-slavery, while the popular press has been quick to speak of slavery when reporting on illegal immigrant sweatshops. Finally, all the disabilities of the slave status were easily subsumed under the Western notions of "freedom" and "unfreedom"—ideas whose modern meaning was shaped by the eighteenth-century Enlightenment precisely at the time when New World slavery was coming to maturity.

These peculiarities of the recent Western experience of slavery have made for a constellation of features that became its popular definition: a "slave" is someone who is unfree, the property of the owner, bought and sold like any other property, acquired for economic reasons to furnish labor and give surplus labor value to the owner, exploited and mistreated, and placed in the lowest social stratum.

Applying the Western Model of Slavery

This bundle of features by which Westerners define and recognize slavery is held together by a unique historical logic. It is not surprising, then, that problems arise as soon as we take the bundle outside of its historical context. For example, should payment in child adoption (which may be described as "buying a child") be regarded nowadays as a kind of slavery and is it therefore not to be tolerated? Most states in the United States answer "yes" and have made such adoptions illegal and void. Similarly, in the United States in the middle of the twentieth century, there was the practice of what was popularly referred to as the "buying" and "selling" of actors and athletes, that is, trading their contracts between studios and sports teams. Eventually, the courts declared the practice illegal, because it involved trafficking in involuntary servitude. While not everyone agreed with these court rulings, it is significant that the argument has been not about the abhorrence of slavery (which was taken for granted) but about the appropriateness of the slave metaphor in specific cases.

When, however, we take the slavery model outside the West, it is the very nature of slavery that comes into question. We discover institutions that exhibit some but not all of the model's criteria, giving rise to unresolvable arguments about whether they are to be called "slavery." These arguments are not trivial. Once an institution is classified as slavery, it is put into the general hopper of "varieties of slavery" and provides thereafter data for discussions about the origins, functions, processes, and definitions of slavery.

In general, to Westerners, any indication that people are somehow "bought" suggests the presence of slavery, as in the case of adoption with payment, which in most cultures is regarded as simply a matter of equity. Another powerful indicator of slavery is "involuntary labor." Western scholars have often been faced with the issue of how to characterize the widespread practice of human "pawning." In this custom, whose logic is the same as in the pawning of objects in the West, the recipient of a loan gives the lender a person (usually a relative) as a pledge of repayment. The pawn comes under the full temporary control of the lender, living with him and usually working for him. But if the debt is not repaid, the pawn is permanently transferred to the lender. Is pawning as an institution in the same class as slavery? Is the pawn a species of slave from the very start, even before he or she is forfeited? To Westerners, any commercialized transaction in human beings—especially one involving rights to their labor—smacks of slavery, and most Western colonial governments, with the support of the League of Nations and the United Nations, banned pawning together with slavery. Both are seen to belong to the class of "servile" institutions, marked by labor obligations that are not freely given and that cannot be freely withdrawn. Usually, the class also includes serfdom, bonded and fixed-term contract physical labor, forced labor and judicially imposed hard labor, and even certain forms of apprenticeship. In all of these, "unfree" labor is the defining feature of "servility." But the boundary between metaphor and substance is not always clear, as witness the recent arguments in the United States over whether work requirements imposed on welfare recipients are a form of slavery.

The Enslavement Process

What lessons may we draw from all this as we search for a universal definition of slavery? One way of overcoming the conundrum is to shift our perspective away from considerations of what slavery "is," to focus on the features of the process that have led to various forms of enslavement. The process was least problematic in its initial stages and can be regarded as universal. It began with what Orlando Patterson has aptly called "social death," in his *Slavery and Social Death: A Comparative Study* (1982). When stripped of primary social identity in the natal group, an enslaved person ceased to be a social being and in effect became an object. It was in this desocialized state that, upon purchase or capture, slaves were transported and traded as if they were things.

But normally, social death was—had to be—followed by some sort of social resurrection. Once a society had brought in such desocialized people, it faced the question of what was to be done with them. Unless they were immediately killed (e.g., when acquired for a sacrifice), they had to be put to some suitable long-term use, and this required that they be given by fiat some kind of primary social identity. It is at this point in the process, when resocialization begins to usher in the subsequent career of the acquired person, that the myriad cross-cultural variations in slavery overwhelm our analysis. Generalizations become difficult, assumptions crumble, and the definition of slavery remains ever more elusive.

If the captive's new identity merely replicates the old one, as happens in adoption, we are not sure whether we should call this "slavery." But when the newly imposed social identity differs from the old one (and especially if it is socially inferior to it), we feel that enslavement has probably taken place. But to be fully convinced, we turn to the other elements of the Western model: harsh treatment, possibilities of resale, use as labor, restrictions on autonomy, and so on. The more we see of these, the more persuaded we become of the appropriateness of the "slavery" label. One problem with this procedure is that we may neglect to put each of these elements in its context. We may, for example, find treatment to be despicable, but is it despicable by modern Western standards or by those prevailing in the society? Was it applied equally to slaves and nonslaves? We may attribute the sale of a slave in times of famine to his slave status, when in fact "free" offspring were also commonly sold under the same circumstances. Or we may attribute to slavery the abuse of a slave-wife when such abuse commonly occurred in many marriages.

The Various Uses of Slaves

How a person, once acquired, could be used depended, of course, on the possibilities offered by the social and economic structure of the society. The simpler societies held out fewer possibilities than the more complex ones.

Hunting-gathering societies, made up of small mobile bands with little role differentiation and no effective overarching authority beyond the band, could offer to a stranger the same few niches that they had for their own members. They could not impose on newcomers, acquired or voluntary, a status substantially different from that of other members, and they lacked the institutional means of easily exploiting, mistreating, or controlling them. Like anyone else in the band, an unhappy newcomer could walk away and join another band. Since status here was a matter of age, talent, and character, it was only through these attributes that one could improve one's condition. For a stranger, a successful career was to make oneself an appreciated member of the band. In such simple societies, acquired persons were treated so benignly that we hesitate to call them "slaves," unless we formally, consistently, and resolutely make capture or purchase the only criteria of slavery.

At the other end of the scale of complexity were large societies, such as those of antiquity and premodern Asia or Africa. Their economies were multifaceted enough to allow an exploitative use of slave labor, but they did not enjoin such use. Their social structures offered a great variety of social niches and their affluence permitted unprofitable or luxury uses. Here, the career possibilities for acquired persons could vary enormously, encompassing almost the entire range of the occupations in the social hierarchy. In the hands of a king, slaves could end up as elite troops, palace retainers, bureaucrats, generals, ministers, royal wives and concubines, or harem eunuchs, as well as galley-slaves or maltreated workers in the royal mines. With other masters, opportunities were somewhat fewer but still quite varied: household servant, farm laborer, artisan, trading agent, wife, or family retainer. For a slave, social mobility lay in taking advantage of the connections of one's position rather than in detaching oneself from that position by seeking "freedom."

What of the innumerable societies of moderate complexity—societies that anthropologists call "tribal" or "middle-range"? In these, some specialized roles existed, but they were few, often part-time, and usually enmeshed in the structure of kin groups that framed the social organization. In their competition with one another, kin groups sought success as much by expanding their human resources as by controlling material ones. Newcomers were best used as adherents, retainers, and relatives; and women were valued as potential mates who could produce additional kinsmen. For a slave, social mobility called for an ever deeper incorporation as a quasi-relative into the master kin group.

Slavery and Kinship

When a society publicly recognized and legalized sexual unions between masters and slaves, slavery became entangled with kinship. The rights-in-persons governing relations among kinsmen could be merged with the rights-in-persons that defined the master-slave relation. For example, in most African societies, when a man married, he paid money, tools, luxury goods, or animals to his wife's kinsmen. The husband and his kin group thereby acquired (in effect, bought) certain precise rights in the woman; they did not, however, buy her in the sense of obtaining all the rights in her as a total person. The husband usually secured the exclusive rights to sexual cohabitation and to the wife's domestic labor and at least some of her food production. The rights to her offspring were variously allocated between the wife's and the husband's kin groups.

One can easily see the intermeshing between slavery and kinship by comparing marriage to a "free" woman with marriage to a "slave," for in both the same rights in persons were variously exchanged for material goods. In the case of a slave woman belonging to the husband's kin group, the totality of rights in her were already held by the group, so that no marriage payment was necessary. And if she bore children, all the rights in them, rights that normally would be divided between her own group and her husband's, were now held exclusively by the one group that legally stood for them both, namely the husband's. But when a man married a woman who was the slave of a kin group other than his own, the transactions were the same as in an ordinary marriage between the "free." The usual payments were made by the husband to her master's kin group, and the rights to her offspring were allocated between the husband and her master's group in the usual way. In sum, a single unified logic governed all these transactions, with adjustments within the same set of rights-in-persons. Kinship and slavery operated as parts of the same system.

Such arrangements pose a special challenge to the Western understanding of African marriage and slavery. The apparent one-for-one exchange of a woman for goods or money has led many Western observers to object to African marriages as a form of slavery. The marriage payment was quickly dubbed "bride-price," implying that the wife was "bought." This interpretation has been disputed by anthropologists, who offer the more neutral term "bridewealth," but with mixed success.

For the modern West, slavery is an extreme instance of the instrumental use of human beings, while kinship symbolizes the realm of positive sentiments—and indeed of little else, partly, no doubt, because individualism and social mobility through personal capacity have drained Western kinship of much of its past preoccupation with property and social advantage. When Westerners are faced with an institution, such as African marriage, that partakes so seamlessly of kinship, rights to people, and calculating material transactions, the response is to try to fit it into one or the other exclusive realm—that of voluntary sentiments or that of involuntary slavery.

The view of kinship as belonging to the realm of sentiment can intrude in other ways. When an acquired person is ritually inducted ("adopted") into the group and is addressed by such terms as "son" or "niece," a Westerner is tempted to see a kind of slavery that is so much like kinship that it must be benign and therefore not "real" slavery. But through most of human history, and this is also true of the premodern West, kinship has been regarded differently. It has been about property, power, and control no less than about kindness and affection—like Macbeth and Hamlet no less than Romeo and Juliet. Hence, harshness (as opposed to benignity) or crass calculation (as opposed to sentiment) cannot by themselves provide useful criteria for a cross-cultural definition of slavery.

The Question of Treatment

The possibilities existing in a society for using slaves conditioned their treatment and set the limits to viable variations in it. In those economies that allowed slaves to be used as labor, crass exploitation became one of the options. This was predominantly the case in the New World, though even here there were differences in the treatment of field-slaves and house-slaves, exemplified by the stereotypic image of the slave-nanny as quasi-relative. In most other complex societies, however, the purpose of holding slaves was not so focused on production, and their treatment varied widely. In the middle range, in tribal societies, the dominant purpose of kin groups was to build up social and political capital by maximizing the number of one's kinsmen and adherents. To keep their loyalty, one had to resort to methods rather different from those used to extract a maximum return on labor. One obtained pseudo-relatives in various ways: by reproduction through normal marriages, by adoption, and by capture or purchase of slaves. And one made them stay by magic, moral injunctions, rather ineffective intimidation, and above all by acceptable treatment and integration into the group. In the society at large, the status of such slaves reflected the status of the masters. Slaves did not represent a separate social body, or a class or stratum, or a group of common identity and interests. Their relation to social stratification was mediated by their masters: they were attached to the local hierarchy at its side, so to speak, rather than at its bottom rung. This is one of the reasons why, in spite of the ubiquity of slavery in human history, slave rebellions have been so rare.

The Question of Freedom

What of that most commonly mentioned criterion of slavery—the slave's lack of "freedom"? To define slavery as "unfreedom" is to force our analysis into the straitjacket of Western debates about slavery. Originally, "freedom" in the West marked a particular civil status, that of a "freeman" in northwestern European societies and of "citizen" in ancient Mediterranean cities. The status served to separate legally the polity's insiders from foreign residents and slaves. To be a freeman was to enjoy specific and positively defined rights, such as the right to vote in an assembly, to possess property, or to hold public office. In later centuries, the notion of freedom was taken in a more abstract and existential direction; it was conceived of negatively, as freedom from social restraints, and it is this conception that became embodied in the modern Western ideal of freedom as social autonomy, self-determination, and self-realization (including the freedom to make these terms mean whatever one wishes).

When the notion of freedom is transported to other cultures, it must necessarily be stripped of its culturally specific legal content. What is left, then, is the negative aspect: the lack of social restraints and obligations. But in premodern societies, this kind of freedom was inconceivable, unconceived, undesirable, and unattainable. Here, one's survival, livelihood, and status were ensured by one's ties to a kin group, a social network, or a patron—in brief, it was ensured by one's social connections. What people sought was not autonomy but the opposite—the safety one finds in social bonds (a term that, significantly, conveys the idea of both social fulfillment and constraint). By belonging *in* a group one also belonged *to* it. The group "owned" its own members, and this could mean control of their possessions and activities, the right of life and death, and sale. To modern Western sensibilities, these are onerous violations of personal freedom, evocative of "slavery." But once again, such culture-bound judgments are of little value in devising a cross-cultural definition.

The Usefulness of the Term "Slavery"

Can we, then, define slavery in a manner that would deal with all these difficulties? At the root of the problem is the fact that one can focus on one or the other point: either on how the slaves are inducted (purchase, capture, status inheritance) or on their subsequent careers (onerous treatment, low status, etc.). But the content of neither one determines the other; a definition specifying one leaves the other open.

Should we then abolish the term altogether for lack of any possibility of a consistent cross-cultural definition? No call is less likely to be answered than a call to redefine or abolish words of everyday usage. For all its imprecision, the word *slavery* will doubtless remain with us. The practical question is how to use it. If it is to be a serviceable rather than a confusing word, we should lower our expectations of what it can do for us analytically. As a generic concept, it is subject to endless debate. Yet it can continue to serve as it has in fact served—pragmatically, as a pointer to certain kinds of phenomena well worth understanding. But once analysis of these phenomena is launched, one should not expect any heuristic value from the term itself. A fruitful analysis must step down on the ladder of abstraction to more tangible and precise phenomena. For example, while we can detect no invariant relationship between the existence of slavery and a type of society or economy, we do see one between socioeconomic complexity and the range of variation in the treatment and status of acquired persons. Indeed, by rejecting an exclusive definition of slavery—for instance, as a kind of labor system—we can make useful distinctions, such as between slaves as social capital and slaves as economic capital. We can also see that the fact that a person is "bought" says little about the uses to which that person is then put. For such analytical exercises, the term "slavery" can usefully delineate a significant universe of careful investigation and discussion.

See also ENSLAVEMENT, METHODS OF; HISTORIOGRAPHY OF SLAVERY; LITERATURE OF SLAVERY; SLAVERY, CONTEMPORARY FORMS OF; SLAVE SOCIETIES.

BIBLIOGRAPHY

CRATON, MICHAEL, ed. *Roots and Branches: Current Directions in Slave Studies.* 1979.

DAVIS, DAVID BRION. *The Problem of Slavery in Western Culture.* 1966.

DONALD, LELAND. *Aboriginal Slavery on the Northwest Coast of North America.* 1997.

ENGERMAN, STANLEY L. "Some Considerations Relating to Property Rights in Man." *Journal of Economic History* 33 (1973): 43–65.

FINLEY, M. I. "Slavery." In *International Encyclopedia of the Social Sciences.* 1968; pp. 307–313.

GENOVESE, EUGENE D. *Roll, Jordan, Roll: The World the Slaves Made.* 1974.

HELLIE, R. *Slavery in Russia, 1450–1725.* 1981.

KOPYTOFF, IGOR. "Slavery." *Annual Review of Anthropology* 11 (1982): 207–230.

LASKER, BRUNO. *Human Bondage in South-East Asia.* 1950.

MEILLASSOUX, CLAUDE. *The Anthropology of Slavery: The Womb of Iron and Gold.* 1991.

MIERS, SUZANNE, and IGOR KOPYTOFF, eds. *Slavery in Africa: Historical and Anthropological Perspectives.* 1977.

MILLER, JOSEPH C. *Slavery and Slaving in World History: A Bibliography, 1900–1991.* 1993. Reprint, 1997.

———. *Slavery and Slaving in World History, 1992–1996.* 1997.

Slavery and Abolition. Continuing annual supplements.

VERLINDEN, CHARLES. *L'esclavage dans l'Europe médiévale.* 1955.

WATSON, JAMES L., ed. *Asian and African Systems of Slavery.* 1980.

WINKS, ROBIN W., ed. *Slavery: A Comparative Perspective.* 1972.

Igor Kopytoff

Etymology and Semantics

Over time, words for "slave" changed; and when such words remained the same, their meanings changed.

Slaveholders frequently asserted that the power of the master was absolute. This assertion approached reality when masters were dealing with recent captives far removed from their own people, like the African captives brought to early America. Similarly, the *servi* of the Roman republic and early empire were at first nearly helpless. Captives could not speak the language of their purchasers or often even that of fellow slaves. They understood neither the customs nor the psychology of their owners. Each *servus* stood virtually alone against the organized power of the exploiting class.

But conditions changed. The *servi* soon performed services upon which their masters depended. Later generations became more knowledgeable, informed by a far-reaching network of relatives and coreligionists that included both slaves and free people. Secular and religious authorities, seeking social stability, regulated their treatment. Amidst the chaos of the later Roman empire and early Middle Ages, masters were so occupied with fighting that they had little time to manage their estates. They left agriculture largely to their *servi*, who were now providing part of the harvest and certain labor services to a military class in return for protection. The rural *servus* was no longer a slave but a serf.

Yet slavery arose anew in the cities of the later Middle Ages. Latin Christendom's wars of expansion into eastern Europe produced fresh captives, who worked in urban households or in public employment. Many spoke Slavic languages. The debasement of these *slavi*, or *sclavi*, contrasted sharply with the mitigated servitude of the *servi*. Hence the modern languages of western Europe derive most of their words for "slave" from the ethnic term *Slav* and their words for mitigated forms of servitude from *servus*.

Beginning in the mid-fifteenth century, another shift in terminology occurred. It resulted from two developments: Turkish expansion into southeastern Europe constricted the flow of Slavic captives to European markets; and the Portuguese opening of a sea route to a new slave export area, Guinea, replaced Slavs with Africans. "Slave" no longer meant "Slav" but "African." "Black" or "negro," the color of the captives from Guinea, became a common synonym for "slave."

In the United States, over the generations, as brown-skinned slaves arrived from other parts of Africa and as slaves mated with Europeans and native Americans, the meanings of *black* and *negro* expanded to include people, slave or free, who were black, brown, or tan—and even those of European appearance if known to have some African ancestry.

Words for slaves also came from ideology justifying slaveholding societies. One such belief was paternalism, associated primarily with household slavery, the predominant form of the institution in the Old World. In an inversion of reality, slaveholders saw their slaves, upon whom they depended, as their "dependents," just as their own children were dependents. In the ancient, medieval, and modern world, people referred to adult slaves as "boys" or "girls." Like children, slaves were low-ranking members of a household, "almost" members of the family. Even in the less paternalistic and more market-driven slavery of the United States, older slaves were sometimes addressed as "aunt" or "uncle." Yet, although actual ties of blood sometimes linked bonded and free, this was language of fictitious kinship that confirmed rank among slaves rather than respect.

Paternalism flourished in the household slavery of Europe and in the northern colonies, where wealthy families wanted Christian slaves assimilated to European ways. For these, loyal service could mean freedom. But from Brazil to Maryland, most slaves worked in mines or on plantations. Here, harsher words for slaves appeared. Latin American planters wanted *boçais* or *bozales*, "muzzled" or "haltered" captives directly from Africa. English planters called them "outlandish blacks." They were cheaper and had no traditional claims to Christian usage or eventual freedom.

In the plantation colonies also, color words became loaded with new messages about status, the lighter skin colors suggesting power, wealth, and blood ties to conquerors; the darker shades, defeat, captivity, and debasement.

See also DEMOGRAPHY OF SLAVES IN THE UNITED STATES.

BIBLIOGRAPHY

KAHANE, HENRY, and RENÉE KAHANE. "Notes on the Linguistic History of Sclavus." In *Studi in onore di Ettore Lo Gatto e Giovanni Maver*. 1962.
PATTERSON, ORLANDO. *Slavery and Social Death: A Comparative Study*. 1982.
STEPHENS, THOMAS M. *Dictionary of Latin American Racial and Ethnic Terms*. Part 1, *Spanish American Terms*. Part 2, *Brazilian Portuguese Terms*. 1989.

William McKee Evans

Sociology of Slavery

Recent discussions of slavery have posed these questions: Did slavery ever contribute to human progress (Davis, 1984)? Was it an inefficient labor system that inhibited technological advance (Conrad and Meyer, 1958)? Was it harsher than other types of social subordination? What was the impact of slavery on society?

In 1848 Marx projected a theory of history in which slavery was one step in humanity's rise from lower to higher forms of social organization, passing from primitive communalism through slavery, feudalism, and capitalism to socialism and finally to communism. Greco-Roman slavery was thus at first "progressive," permitting an escape from the limitations of primitive communalism. Defeated warriors were no longer slaughtered. Instead they were enslaved, giving rise to a leisured class that created the world's first science, the key to future progress.

But slaves worked efficiently only at simple tasks. They made poor use of the techniques provided by the new learning. Lacking practical application for their work, scientists fell into empty speculation. Their science, and the ancient world itself, fell into decay, preparing the way for humankind's next step.

Marx's followers applied this concept of progress worldwide. The slavery phase, however, convinced few when applied outside the Greco-Roman world. Meanwhile, Marx himself concluded that, besides slavery, humanity had advanced from tribal communalism by other routes. In Asia, though he notes similar developments in ancient Mexico and Peru, "oriental despotisms" arose, in which rulers and their bureaucracies managed production. In northern Europe tribal society became feudal owing to a "German" transition: common warriors were settling down as farmers. Fighting was becoming the specialty of an elite, who protected the farmers from invading tribes from the east and exacted part of their harvest and certain labor services as payment. In eastern Europe a "Slavonic" transition combined elements from both the German and the oriental patterns. These ideas were only in notes and did not become part of the dialogue on slavery until they were published in the mid-twentieth century (in English, 1964).

In the nineteenth-century struggle over slavery, Marx took the abolitionist position that, compared with free-labor capitalism, slavery was retrogressive. But modern slavery had defenders. The southerners John C. Calhoun and George Fitzhugh, like Marx, thought that the achievements of civilization had resulted from the division of society into exploiting and exploited classes but denied that free-labor capitalism was an advance over slavery (Hofstadter, 1960; Fitzhugh, 1854). Northern capitalists invested in labor, southern planters in laborers. The planters' material stake in their workers gave rise to paternalism, the basis for a stable society. The irresponsibility of capitalists toward workers led to strikes, riots, and revolutions. Calhoun also insisted that slavery was not technologically retrogressive, nor did it stigmatize most types of manual labor. In the twentieth century Fogel and Engerman (1974) have argued that southern slaves were comparatively well compensated, worked efficiently, and could utilize advanced technology. And Genovese (1974) has found that the master-slave relationship was more paternalistic than that between capitalist and wage earner.

The idea that slavery was adaptable to modern technology, however, appeared incompatible with a study showing that urban slavery declined in the Old South (Wade, 1964). In the pre–Civil War South—as earlier in the colonial North—as cities grew, their black populations shrank relatively, and urban blacks increasingly were becoming freed people. Those who argue for the adaptability of slavery to modern conditions reply that this relative decline of urban slavery was due not to a lack of demand for slaves in the cities but rather to a stronger demand for them in the cotton fields. Also, they cite one city where slavery did not decline: Richmond, the most industrialized city in the Old South (Goldin, 1992). There, at the Tredegar metallurgical complex, slaves performed sophisticated industrial tasks. That industrial slaves often received "extra-work" payments is seen as evidence for the adaptability of slavery to change (Starobin, 1970).

Patterson (1982), by taking a worldwide look, sheds light on the potential of slaves for performing complex tasks. In most slaveholding societies, slavery was not a fixed but an upwardly mobile condition. Most masters used a system of rewards, promotions, and the prospect of freedom to transform rebellious captives into reliable servants, indeed, even into slave elites who performed skilled tasks. If Arab generals and Turkish secretaries of the treasury were still legally slaves, they were actually nearing their freedom.

But in the New World, the slaves' prospects for upward mobility and freedom became sharply curtailed. In the early colonial period, America's annihilating disease environment made labor scarce. Scarcest of all was free labor. Only the lure of riches brought free European labor. Spanish and Portuguese planters and mine operators enslaved many American natives, but they died in apocalyptic numbers. Such labor was largely unavailable upon the arrival of the English planters. They tried temporary white servants and convicts, of whom perhaps two-thirds died before their terms were completed. Those who survived became free in a world of opportunity: Their labor was much in demand, and land was cheap or free.

Meanwhile, as it became evident that many more Africans survived the plantation diseases than either American natives or Europeans, the African slave trade expanded dramatically (Curtin, 1968). Thus a racial division of society evolved: Europeans were self-employed or held skilled or supervisory jobs. Africans were slaves.

In the American tropics, the white-black polarization of society was held in check by the very scarcity of Europeans. Slaves continued to fill some skilled jobs. As in the Old World, masters frequently enhanced the competence of these workers by offering the prospect of freedom. Furthermore, the few sixteenth-century European immigrants were overwhelmingly males who mated with American native or African women and fathered children of intermediate color and status. Gradually, a population of free dark-skinned families arose that became as numerous as the slaves and more numerous than the whites.

The presence of both racial slavery and interracial free families confused the use of "color" words in these colonies: "black" might mean slave, but it also might mean one's relative, even one's child. Latin Americans, therefore, expressed color prejudice inconsistently, and as a result no strident racial defense of slavery emerged.

The ideology and practice of slavery in England's mainland plantation colonies took a different turn. There, in the late seventeenth century, health conditions improved remarkably, and large numbers of free Europeans arrived while the importation of African slaves continued apace. Two endogamous populations were emerging. But there was not yet a complete racial division of labor. For slavery still retained some Old World features that offered upward mobility and, sometimes, freedom: as late as 1715, South Carolina used slaves as soldiers in the Yamassee war, much as the Spaniards had used military slaves in Mexico and Peru. Also, the larger plantations had slave elites of carpenters, blacksmiths, and other craftspeople. But labor remained scarce, and free Europeans were recruited for the more privileged jobs, but not as field hands. Thus free whites began to displace skilled slaves.

In the nineteenth century the abolitionist challenge accelerated the decline of elite slavery. White unity became critical to the planter South's survival. To give a black a job that a white wanted was to undermine the belief that sustained black slavery in the Old South: all southern whites, as Calhoun stated it, "the poor as well as the rich, belong to the upper classes." Prosperous yeoman farmers, guardians of the planter South's stability, increasingly were becoming "poor whites." Cities were growing. Pressures were mounting to accommodate white workers and forestall a free-labor challenge to slavery like that in New England during the American Revolution. Strikes by white workers in Richmond and other local areas resulted in some being replaced by slaves. Yet, even in these places whites kept the best jobs. Little remained of elite slavery, with its potential for freedom. A field hand's prospects for upward mobility had virtually disappeared. In the United States slaves were becoming a permanent racial underclass, and ideas flourished about the fixed inferiority of Africans and their descendants.

One relic of elite slavery remained. Household slaves cared for the master and the master's family and property. They were in a position to poison the tea or ignite the roof. Their loyalty was important. As in the Old World and Latin America, there were sometimes ties of kinship—rarely acknowledged—between these

Slaves undergo the trauma of separation when a child is sold away from his mother. [Corbis-Bettmann]

slaves and their owners. During the late antebellum years the few slaves still being emancipated were overwhelmingly house servants.

What was the influence of slavery on the customs and personalities of slaveholders? Some studies stress the Protestant and Victorian attitudes shared by the free-labor North and the slave-labor South. But Thomas Jefferson thought that slavery was a school for tyranny. A clergyman of the Old South characterized young planters as "idle, dissipated, vicious, with pistols in their pockets and the fumes of liquor in their brains." Planters' values of "honor" and manhood constricted the lives of free women. As an indignant plantation wife confided to her diary, "Like the patriarchs of old our men live all in one house with their wives & their concubines." Similar observations have been made about the influence of slavery on Latin American society.

More sharply debated in the United States has been the impact of slavery on the slaves themselves. In few societies did slaves have normal families or leave behind many children. But in the Old South, especially after the invention of the cotton gin and the closing of the foreign slave trade elevated prices of the slaves, masters encouraged reproduction. Although southern courts never recognized in law the existence of the slave family, thus allowing owners to sell family members at will, planters nevertheless encouraged or tol-

erated a de facto family, which also served to control potential slave rebels.

How rebellious were New World slaves? In Latin America and in the West Indies, massive slave revolts erupted. Aptheker (1943) writes of several slave revolts in the Old South and waves of hysterical terror against suspected conspirators. Elkins (1959), by contrast, argues that slavery engendered a psychological passivity that debilitated resistance. Like some inmates in the Nazi concentration camps, slaves came to see themselves through the eyes of their oppressors, as childlike, fawning, irresponsible, and clownish "Sambos." Elkins's critics deny the validity of the comparison between concentration camps and plantations, since the one functioned to annihilate people, the other to preserve people who produced commodities and who were valuable commodities themselves. While these critics conceded that there could be Sambo-like behavior, they also said that for most slaves "Sambo" was a mask to be discarded at the first opportunity.

See also ECONOMICS OF SLAVERY; ELKINS THESIS; MARXISM.

BIBLIOGRAPHY

APTHEKER, HERBERT. *American Negro Slave Revolts.* 1943.
CONRAD, ALFRED H., and JOHN R. MEYER. "Economics of Slavery in the Ante Bellum South." *Journal of Political Economy* 66 (1958): 95–130, 442–443.

CURTIN, PHILIP D. "Epidemiology and the Slave Trade." *Political Science Quarterly* 83 (1968): 190–216.

DAVIS, DAVID BRION. *Slavery and Human Progress*. 1984.

ELKINS, STANLEY M. *Slavery: A Problem in American Institutional and Intellectual Life*. 1959.

FITZHUGH, GEORGE. *Sociology for the South*. 1854.

FOGEL, ROBERT WILLIAM, and STANLEY L. ENGERMAN. *Time on the Cross: The Economics of American Negro Slavery*. 1974.

GENOVESE, EUGENE D. *Roll Jordan Roll: The World the Slaves Made*. 1974.

GOLDIN, CLAUDIA D. "An Explanation for the Relative Decline of Urban Slavery." In *Without Consent or Contract: The Rise and Fall of American Slavery*, edited by Robert William Fogel and Stanley L. Engerman. 1992.

HOFSTADTER, RICHARD. "John C. Calhoun: The Marx of the Master Class." In *The American Political Tradition and the Men Who Made It*. 1960.

MARX, KARL. *The Communist Manifesto*. 1848.

———. *Pre-Capitalist Economic Formations*, edited by Eric J. Hobsbawm. 1964.

PATTERSON, ORLANDO. *Slavery and Social Death: A Comparative Study*. 1982.

STAROBIN, ROBERT S. *Industrial Slavery in the Old South*. 1970.

WADE, RICHARD C. *Slavery in the Cities*. 1964.

William McKee Evans

Opposition to Slavery

Slavery has existed since ancient times, but until recently it had few critics. Euripides, as well as the Epicureans, Cynics, and Stoics, praised individuals who freed slaves. But these occasional critics never questioned slavery as the natural condition for certain classes. In ancient and medieval times, masters did manumit slaves, but again on an individual basis, as when a Christian or a Muslim freed slaves as a gesture of benevolence. In the ancient world, slaves were often transported long distances for sale, but observers failed to report extraordinary suffering by slaves in transit—in contrast to those who, much later, gave accounts of the transatlantic shipments of slaves.

Periodic revolts suggest that slave workers conceptualized and valued freedom, as, for example, did the thousands who rose against their Sicilian owners in 135–133 B.C. and the thousands led against Roman legions by Spartacus, a former gladiator. Similarly, in the ninth century, Zanj slaves from East Africa, employed in gangs to clear swampland in the southern Tigris-Euphrates valley, revolted against their Muslim masters. As with other slave revolts, evidence is fragmentary, leading most historians to conclude that these were sporadic, localized events and not part of a movement to end slavery. Slavery in ancient times ended, as some modern slavery did, when slaves were gradually replaced by other workers and not, as in most modern cases, through legislation or revolution.

Sustained opposition to slavery is a modern phenomenon concentrated in the late eighteenth century and the nineteenth century, but continuing, with a focus on Africa and the Middle East, into the twentieth century. In Haiti masses of slaves emancipated themselves; but elsewhere, the eighteenth-century abolition movements developed as Quakers and their evangelical allies began pressuring legislatures to shut down the transatlantic slave trade. These first abolitionists, most of whom lived in Great Britain or its American colonies, published attacks on slavery and by the 1780s had formed societies that lobbied for a ban on slave trading, both as a humanitarian measure and as a means of ending slavery gradually. By the 1820s it became apparent that this first movement had eradicated slavery only where slaves worked in a small part of the economy. Reformers then organized a second movement, this time focused on the prosperous and politically powerful cotton, sugar, tobacco, rice, and coffee slaveholdings in the United States, the Caribbean, Cuba, and Brazil. Only after these New World forms of slavery were abolished did international reformers and European leaders turn some attention to other forms of slavery in Asia, Africa, and the Middle East. However, Europeans viewed slavery in African and Ottoman cultures as less harsh than the plantation slavery of the Americas. Consequently this new antislavery movement, though persisting through most of the twentieth century, was sporadic, diffuse, and often ineffective.

Roots of Antislavery

Historians still differ on whether antislavery movements were more deeply rooted in religious and philosophical ideas or in the economic changes accompanying the rise of capitalism. Eric Williams argued in *Capitalism and Slavery* (1944), for example, that the profitability of "free trade" and its attendant "free labor" system encouraged capitalists to abandon slavery as outmoded and cumbersome. But since cliometricians have shown that slavery was profitable, abolitionists more probably acted for the reason they expressed: that slavery was inconsistent with their belief in universal or Christian brotherhood. Howard Temperley and David Brion Davis both emphasize the power of antislavery ideas and note that, in keeping with abolitionists' argument that their movement was linked with progress, reformers chose antislavery tactics which they believed would strengthen rather than undercut economic development.

Before anyone could organize this type of antislavery program, an intellectual framework for questioning slavery had to emerge. This type of questioning first appears in the context of European colonization of the Americas. In *Report of the Destruction of the West Indies* (1523), Bartolomé de Las Casas described the suffering and death of West Indian slaves and suggested that rulers' obligation to promote Christian virtues might require them to condemn this labor system. The earliest philosophical attack on slavery was Jean Bodin's *Les Six Livres de la République* (1576), which argued that the existence of two kinds of subjects, some free and some slave, undermined good government. But neither Bodin nor Las Casas, who later questioned African slavery as well, attracted many to their antislavery ideas.

Similar criticism appeared in the seventeenth century, for example, in petitions against the African slave trade that were sent to the Lisbon government by Capuchin Brothers in Brazil. Early Quaker protests were equally ineffective, including the Germantown (Pennsylvania) Meeting's "Remonstrance Against Slavery and the Slave Trade" (1688) and George Keith's *An Exhortation and Caution to Friends Concerning Buying or Keeping of Negroes* (1693). The Puritan Samuel Sewall's *The Selling of Joseph* (1700) also met with little success. These writers argued that the Christian idea of brotherhood would require them to help slaves gain freedom. The Germantown Quakers were ignored at first, but thousands of later abolitionists agreed with a sentiment expressed by the Germantown Meeting: "There is a saying that we should doe to all men like as we will be done ourselves; making no difference of what generation, descent or colour they are."

In the eighteenth century, many more writers issued both religious and philosophical attacks on slavery. The more philosophical critics included Charles Montesquieu (*Spirit of the Laws*, 1748), Francis Hutcheson (*System of Moral Philosophy*, 1755), and George Wallace (*A System of the Principles of the Law of Scotland*, 1760). Wallace is notable for his argument that slaves brought into British territory should be automatically freed and that property in human beings was contrary to natural law.

This "enlightened" view was incorporated by the American Quakers John Woolman and Anthony Benezet into several antislavery tracts and by Louis de Jaucourt into an article on the slave trade for the widely circulated *Encyclopédie* (Paris; 1765); it was also incorporated in a landmark decision—the *Somerset* case of 1772. In this case Lord Chief Justice Mansfield ruled that a slave of a British customs official was free because the common and "natural" view of slavery was that it was so "odious, that nothing can be suffered to support it, but positive law," i.e., an English statute specifying that property in slaves was legal. Overlooking the laws governing slavery in British territories, Lord Mansfield ruled that because England did not have a slave code, Somerset, as soon as he set foot in England, could not be legally held in bondage.

While most writers attacked slavery for violating both moral and natural rights, Adam Smith (*Theory of Moral Sentiments*, 1764), John Millar (*The Origin of the Distinction of Ranks*, 1771), and Abbé Raynal (*Histoire des deux Indes*, 1770) argued that slave labor was also suspect because it was inefficient and unprofitable. This broad, diverse approach makes it difficult to pinpoint the origins of popular antislavery thought, particularly since eighteenth-century arguments for liberty were much more apt to focus on disputes about which elites deserved the liberty to hold property or political power, not on universal liberty or emancipation of slaves.

Slaves themselves were less distracted than whites by these varied arguments. Many developed a heightened sense of personal liberty from the revolutionary atmosphere. Some petitioned colonial assemblies for their freedom, and many more took advantage of colonies' struggles for independence to flee to whichever army had advertised liberty for slaves, usually in exchange for military service. For example, Lord Dunmore's proclamation of 1775, freeing slaves who bore arms for the British during the American war for independence, prodded colonials and their assemblies to manumit slaves, on the condition that the blacks would join the colonial military. As Winthrop Jordan (*White over Black*, 1968), Edmund Morgan (*American Slavery, American Freedom*, 1975) and Gary Nash (*Race and Revolution*, 1990) argue, some revolutionary leaders, who described themselves as struggling for freedom as a natural right, felt obliged to consider abolition as part of that program. If the war was a war for freedom, and if it was being fought against several forms of tyranny, perhaps African slavery—not just the slavery of being colonials—was incompatible with free, republican government.

Seeing a possible connection between revolutionary ideology and their own bondage, some African-Americans assumed that emancipation was a logical result of the enlightenment belief that all humans possessed natural rights, including reason, and also of the evangelical assumption that Christians must take their message of universal redemption to all "creatures." Some presented their request for freedom to revolutionary assemblies, declaring, for example, in a petition to the Connecticut legislature in 1779: "Your Honours . . . are nobly contending, in the Cause of Liberty; . . . [and] altho our Skins are different in Colour, . . . Yet Reason & Revelation join to declare, that we are the Creatures of that God, who made of one Blood, and Kindred, all the Nations of the Earth; we perceive . . . that we are endowed with the same

Faculties with our masters, . . . and the more we Consider of this matter, the more we are Convinced of our Right (by the Laws of Nature and by the whole Tenor of the Christian Religion . . .) to be free . . ." (Gary B. Nash, *Race and Revolution*, 1990, p. 175).

Historians continue to debate how this kind of humanitarian and religious argument interacted with economic and political reasons for ending slavery, particularly since we now know what neither the abolitionists nor the antiabolitionists acknowledged, that slavery was extremely profitable. Not surprisingly, elites resisted emancipation more strenuously when they perceived their wealth and way of life as dependent on slaves. To counter this economic concern, abolitionists drew from the stock of secular enlightenment ideas about freedom and progress and stressed the incompatibility of slavery with either progressive government or economic practices. Never were these enlightenment ideas about universal freedom more powerful than in the context of the revolutionary struggle for freedom from colonial rule.

The First Emancipation

This focus made many people decide that slaveholding was incongruous with freedom from tyranny. Still, in the Anglo-American context, religious arguments remained the most powerful. Quakers both initiated and set the terms of debate. When the founder of Methodism, John Wesley, read Benezet's *Some Historical Account of Guinea* (1770), he was moved to pen his own tract, the widely read *Thoughts on Slavery* (1774). Benezet and a fellow Quaker, John Woolman, pressed their antislavery agenda at meetings of Friends on both sides of the Atlantic, and by the 1780s the Society of Friends had eradicated slaveholding among most of its members. American Quakers then refocused their antislavery efforts, forming manumission societies that would promote abolition more broadly: for example, the Pennsylvania Abolition Society (1784), the New York Manumission Society (1785), the Providence (Rhode Island) Abolition Society (1789), and the New Jersey Society for Promoting the Abolition of Slavery (1793). Abolitionists in Maryland, Delaware, and Virginia also formed societies and participated in legislative debates about the best ways to phase out slavery. In 1794 representatives from several state groups met in Philadelphia, petitioning the U.S. Congress to control the slave trade and pressing each group to lobby for antislavery laws in its state legislature.

Whether they agreed with the ideological and religious assumptions in petitions or simply wanted to gain the support of black subjects, Revolutionary-era legislators from South Carolina to Rhode Island discussed plans to end imports of slaves, and many also discussed plans for gradual emancipation. By 1804 all the northern states had passed legislation to end slavery, either immediately or in the next generation. Maryland and Virginia continued to debate various schemes for abolition, but these debates in the end went nowhere.

Quaker and evangelical critiques of slavery were even more central to the related British campaign to end slave trading and slavery within its colonies. As in America, founding and core members of the British Society for Effecting the Abolition of the Slave Trade (1787) were Quakers. The successful campaign for this legislation began with the efforts of two leaders, Granville Sharp and Thomas Clarkson, who—together with the Rev. John Newton (a former slaver)—persuaded the Quaker William Wilberforce to join them in lobbying Parliament. Whether they focused on Methodist, Quaker, or general humanitarian concerns, these British reformers shared the belief that slavery was a sin requiring repentance and eradication: for them, complete abolition was both a patriotic and a religious mission, although initially they hoped that a legal ban on the international trade in slaves would result fairly quickly in a complete end to slavery. With slaves increasingly portrayed as Christian brothers and sisters, charity toward both the enslaved and the newly emancipated was also required.

In 1807 the political and humanitarian concerns of this first generation of abolitionists triumphed over the interests of West Indian planters when Parliament passed legislation forbidding British involvement in slave trading, long considered the worst feature of slavery. In 1815, when British forces prevailed in the Napoleonic wars, the European powers at the Congress of Vienna also agreed to stop their involvement in slave trading; the Danes, the Swedes, and the Dutch followed England in legislating an end to the slave trade in their colonies. English pressure on all European powers to make slave trading illegal was effective in large part because British shipping dominated most sea routes, and British military patrol vessels could take the lead in enforcement. At the same time, in 1858, humanitarian, economic, and prudential forces coalesced, leading the U.S. Congress to ban the importation of slaves.

First Caribbean and Latin American Emancipations

This British triumph—and its counterpart in the United States—signaled the end of the first international movement against slavery. A pause in diplomatic maneuvers against slavery, however, did not stop continued rebellions by slaves, particularly slaves who were able to observe anticolonial independence movements and who conflated rumors of political and personal independence. These rebellions, however, failed to elicit support from the elites, who in Latin America remained focused on achieving freedom from colonial rule, not from the institution of slavery.

The singular exception to this pattern was the French sugar island Saint Domingue–Haiti, which achieved independence from France when slaves rose up against their French masters. The French Revolution and enlightened views of human nature and equality clearly played a role in igniting this revolution. A group of Parisian intellectuals, the Société des Amis des Noir ("Friends of Black People"), had formed in 1788 and had corresponded with the Englishman Thomas Clarkson and with manumission societies in the United States. This group had dissolved before the French proclamation of emancipation in 1794 (later revoked); but some French revolutionaries, like the Americans earlier, had come to see slavery as the antithesis of morality and progressive politics.

While ideology was important to members of the French Convention who voted for emancipation and citizenship for freedmen, this vote was also a pragmatic attempt to retain some control over a valuable territory. Despite repeated military efforts to reassert French control over its former colony, Haitian independence had been won. In the next century, the existence of a self-declared black republic inspired abolitionists, but it more often caused panic, particularly among elites who lived near or in a plantation area with a black majority.

This contagion of liberty could not easily be stopped, as Toussaint-Louverture and other black jacobins had proved when they seized control of Saint Domingue. Those who ruled elsewhere in the Americas consoled themselves that the Haitian Revolution was not their problem but rather an extension of the bloody but aberrant French Revolution. Some abolitionists did warn, however, that if people wished to prevent another bloody revolution, they must emancipate their slaves. Spanish colonials who ruled the eastern half of Hispaniola (i.e., Spanish Santo Domingo) learned this lesson twice: first in 1801, when Louverture invaded and freed slaves (though these were later reenslaved by the Spanish); and again in 1822, when Haitians forces invaded and emancipated slaves—this time without a reversal of the emancipation by subsequent invaders.

While Anglo-Americans worried most about slavery and violence by slaves in the West Indies, the enthusiasm for independence was infecting both leaders and the slave population in other Latin American countries. As in the United States, colonial freedom

Simón Bolívar. [Corbis-Bettmann]

from European empires and abolition of slavery were commonly, if not always effectively, paired. In Venezuela and Chile, respectively, Simón Bolívar and José de San Martín promised freedom to slaves who joined their armies. When Bolívar's initial effort failed, he found refuge in Haiti; in 1816, its black rulers provided arms, supplies, and men for his next expedition. Bolívar in turn promised to incorporate the abolition of slavery into his revolutionary agenda.

Elsewhere in Latin America, freedom for slaves came more slowly, as the newly independent states focused on what they considered more pressing issues. As in British America, states with relatively small slave populations acted most quickly. Chile abolished slavery in 1823, and the short-lived United Provinces of Central America did so in 1824—an action never reversed by subsequent governments. Mexico abolished slavery in 1829.

Elsewhere gradual, compensated emancipation was popular, with some version being adopted in Argentina (1813), Columbia (1821), Venezuela (1821), and Paraguay (1842). This system was similar to post-nati emancipation in New Jersey and New York, where slaves born after a set date were free but were required to compensate their owners by working a prescribed number of years. In Venezuela, for example, this meant that a slave would labor for twenty-one years before gaining freedom. In the 1840s and 1850s, most of these states passed laws emancipating remaining slaves unconditionally, although Paraguay waited until 1870 to do this.

The New Abolitionism

Slavery and gradual abolition continued to be of sporadic interest in these Latin American states, but during the 1820s and 1830s a new kind of abolitionism emerged in both Great Britain and the United States. This second movement called for an immediate, unconditional end to slavery. It began in the United States, with reformers who were concerned that the southern slave population was rapidly increasing while manumissions had virtually stopped. In England, too, the second movement developed out of earlier organizations, with aging abolitionists determined to take whatever action seemed necessary to enact emancipation.

After an extended tract war with slaveholding planters, British abolitionists in 1833 succeeded in passing a bill emancipating all slaves in the West Indian colonies. On what is still celebrated as emancipation day, the "First of August" 1834, only children younger than six were freed without conditions. For a six- to eleven-year "apprenticeship" period, all other slaves were required to pay for the promised freedom by spending three quarters of their time as bound laborers for former masters. When reformers realized that this apprentice system, designed to aid in the transition to free labor, was in fact being abused by planter elites, they pressed for additional legislation. The handful of abolitionists in the Americas, who were achieving only slow and partial success, praised Britain and its reformers, and for decades they continued to compare their own struggle with the swift end of slavery in the West Indies.

This focus on American successes and failures, however, obscures the longer-term but less publicized difficulties of English reformers in British India, where slavery remained legal until 1862. Whether labor conditions changed, even at this date, remains doubtful, since (like elites in the Americas) the rulers of British India wished to avoid social disruption. So while fairly sudden emancipation, partially compensated and administered by British administrators and missionaries, remained for most abolitionists the most successful model, British administrators in India, and later in African territories, often adopted the laissez-faire attitude of other colonial elites, overlooking the continued existence of slavery in their jurisdictions.

It may seem ironic that Britain and other European powers were acquiring new African territories, complete with slave populations, just when they were abolishing slavery in most of their other colonies. Yet as Howard Temperley points out, many English reform-

ers felt that acquiring this territory was simply part of the wave of modern progress that had emancipated slaves in the New World. Colonial powers voiced humanitarian concerns for African peoples, but economic considerations and political expedience meant that antislavery laws and policies were often unenforced. Especially in areas where slaves produced money crops or served to bolster the status of local rulers, colonial administrators were reluctant to undermine the stable, profitable status quo. So at the very time that slavery was dead or dying in Britain and its protectorates, European states were acquiring new territories in Africa, where slavery remained legal well into the twentieth century.

The emancipation of Russian serfs was similarly prolonged. Atlantic-world reformers did not classify Russian serfs as slaves, but some scholars have done so. Peter Kolchin (*Unfree Labor*, 1987) contrasts the peaceful emancipation of Russian serfs, through an edict issued by the czar on 3 March 1861, with the bloody war that was required to free the slaves in the United States. In the decades prior to this edict, peasants periodically revolted against their landlords. Unlike slaveholders elsewhere, however, these masters accepted the necessity of emancipation as a step toward greater agricultural and industrial productivity. The plan was for gradual emancipation, which required former serfs to remain on their traditional lands and earn the compensation that the government plan allowed their former masters. Complete legal emancipation was delayed for decades, coming in the aftermath of the 1905 revolution.

Legislated emancipation in Latin America, particularly in the British West Indies—not in Russia or even in India—remained the model for most abolitionists. Reformers generally contrasted the peaceful transition to freedom under British rule with emancipation in Haiti, where blacks created their republic through bloody rebellion and wars, but most reformers stopped short of arguing that Haiti could serve as a desirable model for other slave societies, and some suggested that concern for preventing another Haiti should influence legislators to support emancipation. In contrast to Great Britain, abolitionists in the United States did not easily build on the success of the Revolutionary generation. While slavery was being phased out in northern states, and the U.S. Congress had agreed to ban international slave trading after 1808, the large slave population in the southern states continued to grow, from less than 1 million at the time of the American Revolution to 4 million in the 1860s, when slavery ended in the United States. Only then, after two years of civil war, did President Lincoln issue his Emancipation Proclamation, freeing slaves in the rebellious states, and only after the war did constitutional amendments free the remaining slaves and grant citizenship, including voting rights, without regard to race or previous servitude.

This second, more protracted fight for emancipation in the United States grew most intense during the 1830s, when antiabolitionists rioted against blacks and mobbed reformers, including William Lloyd Garrison and the Englishman George Thompson. These new abolitionists were responding, loudly and publicly, to the complaints of African-Americans like James Forten, a merchant in Philadelphia, who with other black leaders had long been holding meetings to discuss how to combat race prejudice. First black and then white abolitionists condemned the American Colonization Society, founded in 1817, for pressuring African-Americans, some of whom were veterans of the Revolutionary War, to leave the United States. Garrison had previously supported colonization, but in 1831 he published a detailed refutation, arguing that it was a cover for racism. Instead of gradual abolition or colonization, Garrison concluded, immediate and unconditional emancipation was the only tenable position. To publicize this new position outside the black community, he started a semiweekly newspaper, the *Liberator* (1831–1865), and published a tract, *Thoughts on Colonization* (1832), thereby launching a radical movement for immediate abolition of slavery and acceptance of blacks as full citizens.

This drive for unconditional abolition, the example of Haiti, and the success of emancipation in the British West Indies encouraged younger, more vocal reformers to organize a new movement dedicated to immediate abolition. In 1833 these new abolitionists gathered in Philadelphia to form the American Anti-Slavery Society. This group helped form several hundred local antislavery societies and sponsored the publication and mass distribution of antislavery tracts and newspapers. It also recruited young missionary agents, at one point dubbed "the Seventy," who spoke at meetings from the Ohio valley to Maine, as far south as Philadelphia and as far north as the Canadian border. The new movement met strong opposition in the north, where conservatives feared the implications of radical antislavery, and also in slaveholding states, where community leaders complained that pamphlets mailed to local elites were really intended to start slave rebellions. This new abolitionist movement gained the greatest following in sections of northeastern states that had experienced both evangelical revivals and economic prosperity—i.e., where a growing middle class saw slavery as at odds with religious beliefs and as incompatible with its own free labor system.

Encouraged by recent events in Saint Domingue and by the British Emancipation Act of 1833, these new American reformers saw their cause as linked to antislavery efforts elsewhere. In 1840, more than fifty of them journeyed to London for the World Anti-Slavery Convention, called by the new British and Foreign Anti-Slavery Society. This group, formed with the blessing of elderly reformers like Thomas Clarkson, mobilized a younger generation of reformers to monitor and aid both abolition and postemancipation reforms around the world. They discussed conditions in the West Indies, the United States, and Brazil, where the condition of the newly emancipated and, particularly, of those millions still enslaved elicited keen interest. The convention also heard reports on the smaller slave populations in Spanish, French, Dutch, Danish, and Swedish colonies and the prospects for their emancipation. In addition, these abolitionists estimated that millions were now enslaved in British India, Asia, and Africa. As important as the global scope of this group was its longevity: the British and Foreign Anti-Slavery Society (renamed Antislavery International) remains active today, and its published reports on slavery and antislavery movements in the monthly *Antislavery Reporter* (1840–1909) remain a valuable record of its broad concerns.

The scope of the British and Foreign Anti-Slavery Society, however, was not matched by a comparable range in the delegates attending the 1840 convention. Over 80 percent of the 530 official delegates were English; 50 individuals were from British territories (Scotland, Ireland, and the British Caribbean), and another 50 were from the United States. Single delegates from Haiti, Spain, and Switzerland, along with 4 from France, constituted the rest of this "world" convention. Still, the thirteen-day conference gathered reports on slavery worldwide and passed resolutions for presentation to governments in Latin America, the Middle East, the United States, and Europe. Convention leaders also selected antislavery addresses for publication and distribution as tracts.

Until 1865, the global concerns of this group were overshadowed by the antislavery controversy in the United States. Legal cases involving more than one country drew international interest, as did the efforts to settle claims about the legal status of slaves being carried on the ships *Amistad* (1939) and *Creole* (1841). While not new, diplomatic disputes about slave trading, and the publicity given to the complicated legal maneuvers to free the "cargo" of these ships, generated sympathy for both slaves and abolitionists.

Treaty agreements notwithstanding, the transatlantic slave trade obviously continued to feed the slave economies in Cuba and Brazil, and to a lesser extent the U.S. South. So while British abolitionists, aided by diplomats and official patrol ships, continued to pressure other countries to begin antislavery measures, reformers on both sides of the Atlantic directed most of their attention to the United States. In addition to their many legal battles, abolitionists worked to influence the opinion of both ordinary and leading citizens. In the 1830s, most radical abolitionists viewed their position as religious, with emancipation being a logical step as soon as one saw slaves as one's Christian brothers and sisters.

For this reason, the American Anti-Slavery Society began its crusade by employing ministers as agents and holding as many meetings as possible in churches. Denominations and local congregations were generally cautious, however, and a series of antiabolitionist riots between 1834 and 1837 persuaded most church leaders, even among the more egalitarian Baptists and Methodists, to avoid controversy by banning antislavery speeches and even announcements from their meeting houses. This informal "gag" infuriated radical reformers, who saw it as a proslavery position. More helpful to the cause was a formal gag rule, seen by many as an attack on free speech, which between 1836 and 1844 prevented members of the U.S. House of Representatives from discussing petitions mentioning slavery.

Stymied in their effects to convert church leaders, many abolitionists leaders concluded that James G. Birney was correct in titling one of his pamphlets *The American Churches, the Bulwarks of American Slavery* (1836). Abolitionists still had religious motives, but religious institutions became less important to them, and many decided that they needed to press for change—as the British had done—through political parties and legislation. This new emphasis on political processes coincided with the split of Garrison's "old organization," the American Anti-Slavery Society, and the formation of a new organization, the American and Foreign Anti-Slavery Society, whose members supported the new Liberty Party in both 1840 and 1844, when Birney stood as the party's candidate for president. After 1844 the party became moribund; and in 1848 most of its supporters threw their votes to the new Free Soil Party.

However, a core of radicals, convinced that a proslavery constitution made political abolitionism futile, remained loyal to Garrison's "moral sausion" tactics. They wrote, read, and circulated the *Liberator* and other antislavery tracts. Most also attended antislavery meetings and annual fairs, which functioned as an antislavery church. At such fairs, leaders collected funds and mingled with the faithful, many of whom enjoyed the informal sociability as much as the antislavery objects that were for sale.

Actually, neither moral nor political abolitionism attracted much popular support in the two decades before the Civil War, and colonization of free blacks

An antislavery poem published in William Lloyd Garrison's Liberator. *[Corbis-Bettmann]*

outside the United States remained the program favored by most whites as the long-term solution to slavery and race relations. The American Colonization Society had been started in 1817 mostly by southerners convinced that free blacks were a threat to whites, and by the 1830s agents of colonization had found broad interregional support that would last into the 1860s. The American Colonization Society and particularly state colonization societies had the endorsement of major denominations in their plans for resettling free blacks in Haiti or Liberia. Supporting colonization—even if that support consisted only of speaking time for agents of colonization at denomination meetings—kept church leaders free of any radical taint or any major financial commitment, and at the same time allowed them to envision repatriated blacks as a means of spreading Christianity to Africa. British abolitionists also found coloniza-tion attractive; the British and Foreign Antislavery Society and the later Christian Missionary Association recorded attempts, continuing well into the twentieth century, to found or stabilize colonies of former slaves in cultures as varied as Sierra Leone and Uganda.

Black abolitionists, including many former slaves, often became impatient with the ineffectiveness of white organizations and focused more on aiding fugitive slaves. While continuing to work with whites, Frederick Douglass helped promote conventions for blacks, who began meeting in the 1840s to develop their own programs for dealing with slavery and race prejudice. Black abolitionists like Douglass remained effective speakers for northern audiences lacking experience with slavery. Black agents drew significant support, not just in the northern United States but also when they toured Great Britain, Ireland, and Scotland. Among the more popular speakers were William and Ellen Craft, Henry "Box" Brown, and William Wells Brown. Each was skilled at depicting the horrors of slavery, and they all sold personal narratives and gathered funds to support further tours and publications, and sometimes to buy family members out of slavery.

More than most white reformers, these black abolitionists bridged divisions among reformers. Both Douglass and Sojourner Truth, for example, attracted a wide variety of admirers. Douglass maintained working relations with all abolitionists, even after he broke with the American Anti-Slavery Society in order to found his own newspaper. The diversity of the topics in Douglass's weekly, begun with British funds as the *North Star* in 1845 and later renamed *Frederick Douglass' Newspaper*, reflects several strands of antislavery ideology as well as a wide range of tactics. Like Garrison in the *Liberator*, Douglass reported on court cases—outrageous cases of abuse or racial discrimination—and on speeches and debates at meetings sponsored by the American Anti-Slavery Society or its local auxiliaries. But he also followed the black convention movement more closely than other antislavery newspapers, reporting on suggestions from within black communities on how to combat legal, educational, and economic discrimination. Douglass also reported any mention of slavery by party leaders, and he attended both Liberty and Free Soil party meetings, speaking in support of each party's stand against the extension of slavery.

By this time opposing the expansion of slavery into new western territories had popular support in the North; in most cases distracting northerners from plans for complete abolition. Unlike the relatively short campaigns of British abolitionists, which began with attempts to ban slave trading and climaxed when Parliament abolished slavery in the West Indies, the campaign against slavery in the United States had no central focus. Americans assumed that the Constitution left this issue to state governments and that the U.S. Congress could abolish slavery only in territories or in the federally administered District of Columbia. Leaders of the American Anti-Slavery Society continued to rail against all manifestations of the "slavocracy," which they saw as conspiring to limit the rights of free northerners. Moderates like Douglass and the Tappans continued nibbling at slavery, through court cases like that of the *Amistad* or legislative and party battles over the extension of slavery in places like Texas and Kansas. Slaves themselves argued with their feet; thousands fled to free territory. These rebellious acts by slaves, together with his own experiences fighting slaveholders in Kansas, convinced the maverick John Brown that armed assault on slavery was the only path to freedom left open. Ironically, freedom came only after much more violence and through the actions of President Lincoln, a supporter of colonization.

Abolition Movements after 1865

For the rest of the nineteenth century, the antislavery movement focused on how to end slavery in Cuba and Brazil, the two remaining plantation economies in the Americas. The longer process of emancipation in both countries was characterized by less discussion about morality and more about the social and economic necessity of slavery. But economic pressures worked against these slave economies—more so than in the United States, where the number of American-born slaves had continued to multiply until emancipation. This was not true in Cuba and Brazil, so that the closing down of the transatlantic slave trade cut off the usual source of workers. While it was difficult to shut down completely, the importing of slaves from Africa was increasingly attacked by British reformers, who in 1830 successfully pressured Brazil to legislate against further importations and Spain to pass similar measures in Cuba. For some time, though, these measures proved unenforceable.

In Brazil the ban was effectively ignored until 1850, when British ships blockading Brazil's slave ports actually entered harbors, seized slaves they found, and destroyed the carrier ships. Faced with this effective force and perhaps softened by arguments published in several leading newspapers, the Brazilian legislature acted to make slave trading piracy, and by 1853 Brazil's importation of slaves had stopped altogether. Emancipation in the United States further impressed Brazilians that slavery was a regressive, dying institution. In 1871 the national assembly passed legislation freeing all babies born to slave women. Antislavery reformers were aware that the nations with whom Brazil traded disapproved of slavery, that the number of slaves was declining, and that in some places the remaining slaves had revolted, but these reformers were nevertheless so scattered that no movement emerged until 1882. Then, anxious to modernize country's political and economic structure, these middle-class reformers petitioned the national assembly to legislate incentives for free laborers; they also sponsored occasional antislavery newspaper articles. In a short but effective campaign, the reformers organized rallies, published plans for manumission, and in certain provinces coordinated the work of agents who guided many of the thousands of slaves making a run for freedom. Heralded by street festivals and parades, complete abolition was legislated in 1888.

British blockades of the slave trade were never as effective in Cuba as they were in Brazil. Consequently, Cuban slaveholders continued to expand their sugar production well into the 1870s, supplementing slave labor with Chinese immigrants. The political struggle to end slavery was also much longer in Cuba than in Brazil. In 1868, rebels whose primary goal was to end Spanish colonial rule denounced slavery. Spanish authorities countered by approving a plan for gradual emancipation, the Moret Law of 1870. This increased the pressure for emancipation, both from nationalist leaders and from self-emancipating slaves. In 1880 all slaves were declared free, although they were required to serve an eight-year apprenticeship; and finally, in 1886, a government edict ended slavery unconditionally.

With emancipation in the Americas complete, the British *Antislavery Reporter* focused increasingly on African and Ottoman slavery. Yet in these areas—in contrast to the pressure they exerted on Latin American leaders—British reformers and the British government appeared confused and hesitant to press their abolitionist policy on various African and Ottoman allies. British officials as well as reformers cautioned that such Old World slavery, often in family households, seemed quite different from the plantation slavery that had predominated in the Americas. Clearly this hesitancy was similar to that displayed a bit earlier in India, where British officials obviously feared that anything but slow, gradual steps toward emancipation would undermine public order and the economy.

See also ABOLITON AND ANTISLAVERY MOVEMENTS; EMANCIPATION; EMANCIPATION IN THE UNITED STATES.

BIBLIOGRAPHY

BENDER, THOMAS, ed. *The Antislavery Debate: Capitalism and Abolitionism as a Problem in Historical Interpretation.* 1992.

BERLIN, IRA, et al. *Slaves No More: Three Essays on Emancipation and the Civil War.* 1992.

BLACKBURN, ROBIN. *The Overthrow of Colonial Slavery, 1776–1848.* 1988.

BLANCHARD, PETER. *Slavery and Abolition in Early Republican Peru.* 1992.

BOLT, CHRISTINE, and SEYMOUR DRESCHER, eds. *Anti-Slavery, Religion and Reform: Essays in Memory of Roger Anstey.* 1980.

CONRAD, ROBERT. *The Destruction of Brazilian Slavery, 1850–1888.* 1972.

DAVIS, DAVID BRION. *The Problem of Slavery in the Age of Revolution, 1770–1823.* 1975.

———. *The Problem of Slavery in Western Culture.* 1966.

———. *Slavery and Human Progress.* 1984.

DRESCHER, SEYMOUR. *Capitalism and Antislavery.* 1987.

DUMOND, DWIGHT L. *Antislavery: The Crusade for Freedom in America.* 1961.

ERDEM, Y. HAKAN. *Slavery in the Ottoman Empire and Its Demise, 1800–1909.* 1996.

FREEHLING, WILLIAM W. *The Reintegration of American History: Slavery and the Civil War.* 1994.

MIDGLEY, CLARE. *Women against Slavery: The British Campaigns, 1780–1870.* 1992.

MIERS, SUZANNE, and RICHARD ROBERTS. *The End of Slavery in Africa.* 1988.

NASH, GARY B., and JEAN R. SODERLUND. *Freedom by Degrees: Emancipation and Its Aftermath in Pennsylvania.* 1990.

RIPLEY, C. PETER. *The Black Abolitionist Papers.* Vols. 1–5. 1985–1992.

SCOTT, REBECCA J. *Slave Emancipation in Cuba: The Transition to Free Labor, 1860–1899.* 1985.

STEWART, JAMES B. *Holy Warriors.* Rev. ed. 1997.

TEMPERLEY, HOWARD. *British Antislavery, 1833–1870.* 1972.

TURLEY, DAVID. *The Culture of English Antislavery, 1780–1860.* 1991.

ZILVERSMIT, ARTHUR. *The First Emancipation.* 1967.

Deborah Bingham Van Broekhoven

Defenses of Slavery

In book 1, chapter 5 of the *Politics*, Aristotle writes, "It is clear then that by nature some are free, others slaves, and that for these it is both just and expedient that they should serve as slaves." Aristotle's discussion of slavery represents one of the earliest defenses of slavery in the West, and it remained one of the most frequently cited defenses down through the U.S. Civil War. But the defense of slavery in the West, like slavery itself, evolved over time and, in response to changing contexts and changing attacks, appealed to historical, anthropological, economic, scientific, and religious arguments, as well as philosophical ones, to insist that slavery was either "just" or "expedient" or both.

Plato actually preceded Aristotle in viewing slavery as a natural relation. Both Plato and Aristotle understood slavery as but one of many hierarchical relations that characterized the entire universe. Plato's ordered universe depended on the rational controlling the irrational; Aristotle's household, which included slaves, required that inferiors—wives, children, and slaves—obey superiors: husbands, fathers, and masters. By locating slavery among the natural relations, Plato and especially Aristotle sought to counter any, such as the egalitarian Sophists, who argued that slavery was a human invention, "one of convention only" in Aristotle's words, "based on force . . . and therefore not just." In responding to those unnamed ancient critics of slavery, Aristotle anticipated the proslavery argument of the modern era, which also developed in large part in response to attacks on slavery. Aristotle's insistence that "there are some who are slaves everywhere," notwithstanding his inability to devise a means of determining who, exactly, were slaves by birth, assured him a privileged place in proslavery thought. His belief in natural inequalities enabled later defenders of slavery to argue that subordination and superordination characterized all human relations. It is hardly surprising that the most forceful proponent of slavery in the old South, George Fitzhugh, urged southern colleges to make Aristotle's *Politics* a required text. The historian William Sumner Jenkins concludes, in *Pro-Slavery Thought in the Old South* (1935), that "probably to no other thinker in the history of the world did the slaveholder owe the great debt that he owed to Aristotle."

Neither ancient Rome nor early Christianity weakened slavery in the West, and in the absence of any serious threat, defenses of slavery remained largely implicit. Roman jurists did suggest, contrary to Aristotle, that slavery was not natural and therefore could not be defended by appeals to natural law. But those same jurists acknowledged that slavery was ubiquitous and thus part of the common law of nations. And Roman civil law, culminating in Justinian's *Institutes*, also recognized the legitimacy of slavery. Christianity elevated all men to the same level in the eyes of God but did little to undermine the legal and moral basis of slavery. Building upon Old Testament passages that condoned slavery—especially Noah's curse on Canaan (Genesis 9: 25), "And [Noah] said, 'Cursed be Canaan; a servant of servants shall he be unto his brethren'"—the authors of the New Testament maintained the moral legitimacy of slaveholding. Paul's famous declaration in the letter to Ephesians that slaves should obey "them that according to the flesh are your masters, with fear and trembling, in a singleness of heart, as unto Christ," reflects early Christianity's acceptance of slavery even as it embraced slaves as fellow children of God. Although nineteenth-century abolitionists and defenders of slavery would engage in a heated debate over Christianity's relation to slavery, Christian-

ity itself did not pose a significant challenge to the practice of slavery until the later eighteenth century.

The early church fathers, led by Augustine, emphasized that freedom and slavery were to be understood spiritually, not corporeally; one could find true freedom in Christ even if one were a slave on earth. Perhaps more important, the early leaders of Christianity viewed slavery as evidence of man's fallen state, as punishment for sin. As such, slavery not only was unavoidable but actually served to fulfill God's will—it restrained sinful, corrupt humans as did other institutions, notably government. Christianity thus reinforced the classical emphasis on slavery as part of the order of the universe, as an institution that, if not natural in the sense that it existed from the beginning of humanity—was necessary given the universal participation in original sin.

The medieval and early modern Christian eras posed no challenge to slavery per se, and, therefore, defenses of slavery continued to appeal to familiar classical and Christian justifications. Some writers, such as Thomas Aquinas, elaborated upon earlier explanations, but they did little to alter the dominant notion that slavery did not conflict with Christian ethics or violate God's will. In the late medieval era, enslaving fellow Christians was condemned, but even this did little to undermine slaveholding—in fact, it encouraged the enslavement of Muslim and pagan peoples, since such enslavement furthered the cause of Christianity. Nor did the Reformation produce notable modifications of traditional defenses of slavery. The veneration of classical texts in the Renaissance served mainly to reinforce the Greco-Roman acceptance of slavery. The great political thinkers of the early modern period, including Hugo Grotius, Thomas Hobbes, and John Locke, did not challenge the legitimacy of slavery, although some of their arguments—and arguments by others—did emphasize its secular and pragmatic bases, as opposed to the classical focus on natural origins and the Christian emphasis on original sin. Indeed, many early modern justifications of slavery tended to focus on its "expedience" more than its "justice," although some argued that a practice that had existed in so many societies for so long had demonstrated its essential legitimacy. In this era defenses of slavery begin to show a strong appeal to history, to past and current human practices—for example, victors enslaving rather than killing conquered opponents—as a means of justifying slavery. Although this secular appeal developed, in part, as a result of the expansion of slavery in the New World and, consequently, discussed slavery less as an abstract concept and more as an actual practice with serious economic and geopolitical implications, proslavery thought did not dispense with moral arguments that emphasized the inherent justness of slavery. As the modern age dawned, and slavery dramatically expanded in the New World, its European and American defenders had a long and rich intellectual tradition to draw upon, and they utilized it to build on all of the previous arguments. They also developed new justifications that reflected the context and character of slavery in the New World.

Proslavery thought during the colonization of the Americas expanded and diversified in reaction to the emergence of critiques of slavery. One of the first occasions of this recurring phenomenon took place in Valladolid, Spain, in the middle of the sixteenth century. The famous debate between Bartolomé de Las Casas and Juan Gines de Sepulveda prompted Sepulveda to defend both the means employed to capture slaves and slavery itself. He asserted that Indians were barbarians and idolaters and thus fit Aristotle's notion of natural slaves, arguing in terms of Indian cultural practices more than inherited racial traits. Slavery also exposed Indians to Christianity, thereby providing another good. Both nature and expedience condoned the enslavement of natives. As Africans replaced Indians as slaves, masters easily applied the same logic that justified Indian slavery. As it would elevate Indians, so too would slavery elevate barbaric heathen Africans, while also producing wealth for the colonizing nation.

A further elaboration of proslavery sentiment followed the publication of one of the first modern antislavery pamphlets, Samuel Sewall's *The Selling of Joseph*, which appeared in Boston in 1700 and posited that "all men, as they are sons of Adam, . . . have equal right unto liberty, and all other outward comforts of life." In 1701, John Saffin, a prominent Boston merchant, responded to Sewall's attack. Building his case primarily on the scriptures, Saffin appealed to what would become standard biblical passages to support slaveholding: Leviticus 24: 44–46, in which God authorizes the Israelites to hold slaves; the curse on Canaan; and I Corinthians 12: 13–26, in which Paul lays out the divine basis of secular orders and ranks. But he also focused on the slaves' African background and came close to asserting a racial argument to justify their enslavement. Expedience, in this case the Africans' inability to govern themselves and the impossibility of racial integration, required that slavery continue. In appealing to both scripture and the specter of racial conflict brought on by emancipation, Saffin anticipated much of subsequent proslavery thought. Here, as in the nineteenth-century American debate over the Bible and slavery, literalist defenders, appealing to the word of God, easily de-

feated the opponents of slavery, who rested their case on a highly subjective and interpreted "spirit" of the Bible.

The eighteenth-century Enlightenment brought forth the first clear attacks on slavery, and consequently also the emergence of self-consciously defensive proslavery thought. Rousseau, in the famous chapter "Slavery" in *The Social Contract*, leveled the most complete attack on slavery yet seen in the West. Maintaining that "no man has a natural authority over his fellow, and force creates no right," he rejected the right of conquerors to reduce the conquered to slavery, denied that people could sell themselves into slavery, and concluded that "from whatever aspect we regard the question, the right of slavery is null and void." Montesquieu's *The Spirit of the Laws* dismissed Aristotle's notion of natural slaves, claiming that "as all men are born equal, slavery must be accounted unnatural." But Montesquieu provided ammunition for apologists for slavery as well. In a passage that proslavery thinkers would frequently cite, Montesquieu acknowledged that "there are countries where the excess of heat enervates the body, and renders men so slothful and dispirited that nothing but fear or chastisement can oblige them to perform any laborious duty: slavery is there more reconcilable to reason." The idea that tropical and semitropical climates required slavery introduced a new argument that combined expedient economic concerns with ideas about environmental necessity. Defenders of slavery in the New World turned to this climatic argument often, claiming that free European laborers could not withstand the tropical climate that nurtured sugar, rice, and cotton plantations.

Other Enlightenment figures, especially David Hume, similarly rejected traditional justifications for slavery while providing new grounds in their stead. Hume and others, including Thomas Jefferson, formulated some of the eighteenth century's most notable discussions of racial differences. For these men, faith in an emerging view of humanity based on scientific observation and empirical facts replaced a Christian faith that emphasized human universality derived from a common created being. Asserting that some humans, for instance Africans, had traits that suited them for labor and supervision by more advanced groups, these men helped establish the basis for the defense of slavery in the New World on racial grounds that appealed to evidence of Africans' barbarism and cultural inferiority. Hume, notwithstanding his opposition to slavery, reasoned in this essay "On National Characters" that "there scarcely ever was a civilized nation of that complexion, nor even any individual eminent either in action or speculation, . . . [n]o ingenious manufactures amongst them, no arts, no sciences." He concluded, "I am apt to suspect the negroes to be naturally inferior to the whites." For slaveholders in the New World, such reasoning provided grounds for defending slavery as beneficial to Africans, who through it would be exposed to civilizing influences. Jefferson's *Notes on the States of Virginia* not only asserted that "it is not their [Africans'] condition then, but nature, which has produced the distinction" between their abilities and those of whites, but also expressed the fear that, among other factors, "the real distinctions that nature has made" meant that emancipation would "produce convulsions which will probably never end but in the extermination of the one or the other race." Thus, once slavery became established in the New World, its defenders argued that given the natural differences between the races, only the continuation of slavery could restrain African barbarism and prevent a racial bloodbath. Self-preservation, that most powerful of arguments based on expedience, increasingly appealed to observable, self-evident "facts" of nature. Although not based on classical or Christian defenses of slavery, the developing racial justification reinforced certain common features found in those earlier arguments. The notion that some peoples were meant to be ruled by others differed little from the classical and Christian ideas that the order of the universe required each part of the hierarchically arranged whole to play its proper role. Thus, although the Enlightenment did lead to some direct challenges to slavery, it also encouraged the development of scientific racism, which would emerge forcefully in the generation before the U.S. Civil War.

The American Revolution generated its own direct challenges to slavery. But like the Enlightenment, the Revolution did not by any means uniformly condemn slaveholding. Although some Americans saw a fundamental contradiction between the causes of the Revolution and slavery, others saw no conflict between fighting for liberty from Britain and practicing slavery at home. Nonetheless, the Revolution's focus on the legitimacy of slavery forced its defenders to once again justify a practice that increasing numbers of people in the West viewed as morally wrong and politically and economically inexpedient.

For many southern slaveholders during the era of the American Revolution, slavery was a temporary expedient, a necessary evil. Much like Jefferson, they saw little alternative to maintaining slavery. Not only racial self-preservation but economic viability and political reality made emancipation prohibitively costly. But the growing chorus of opponents of slavery, which included Quakers, many Methodists, some Baptists, and those influenced by natural-rights philosophy, en-

countered defenders who differed significantly from those who apologized for slavery on the basis of inheritance and economic expedience. In a series of petitions submitted to the Virginia legislature in 1784 and 1785 that protested attempts to encourage and expand slave manumission, proslavery Virginians asserted the righteousness and benefits of slavery. The petitions reflect the myriad of justifications present in revolutionary America and reveal how central the notion of property rights was to the defenders of slavery. Borrowing from the rhetoric of the Revolution, slaveholders insisted on their right to their property—slaves—and reminded the legislature that they had fought to protect that right. The petitioners also appealed to the Bible, citing the familiar Old and New Testament passages and asserting that the only freedom proclaimed in the scriptures was "freedom from the bondage of sin and Satan, and from the dominion of men's lusts and passions." Implicitly evoking Jefferson's fears, the opponents of manumission and emancipation warned of "the horrors of all the rapes, murders, and outrages" that freed slaves would commit. These petitions deny that slavery was an evil, necessary or other. For these slaveholders, slavery conformed to God's word and maintained order and prosperity; the right to "the full, free, and absolute enjoyment of every species of our property," a right "sealed with our blood," was what the Revolution had been about. Rather than weakening slavery in the South, the Revolution added to the arguments already available by emphasizing that "we risked our lives and fortunes, and waded through seas of blood" so that "our property might be secure, in future."

The debate in Britain in the 1780s and early 1790s over the legitimacy of the Atlantic slave trade and, by extension, of slavery in the West Indies, generated some of the most vociferous defenses of slavery to be found up to that time. The defenders of West Indian slavery provided models for subsequent proslavery arguments. In addition to utilizing the familiar arguments—that slavery was a ubiquitous feature of civilizations throughout history, that the Bible condoned slavery, and that tropical regions could not be cultivated without slavery—they asserted that slavery was a positive good because it Christianized and civilized African heathens and ensured practical economic benefits for the empire. They also appealed to what would become one of the most effective of all proslavery arguments. In the course of defending slavery in the West Indies, these advocates favorably contrasted the conditions of slaves with those of poor laborers in Britain. As the agricultural and industrial revolutions transformed Britain, supporters of slavery turned from traditional arguments to sober critiques of the consequences of "free" labor, especially the

A British political cartoon from 1789 represents the kinds of arguments that defenders of slavery were forced to counter or ignore in their fight to preserve the institution of slavery. [Library of Congress/Corbis]

material deprivation of peasants and mine workers. Subsequent proslavery writers would elaborate upon this, eventually suggesting that the adoption in "free" societies of something resembling slavery would actually improve the condition of laborers.

The proslavery arguments formulated regarding the West Indies arose in the midst of an attack on slavery. Even when antislavery agitation was politically and culturally insignificant, however, defenders of slavery demonstrated that slavery was not simply a necessary evil but, more important, a desired element of a just and orderly society. In the United States in the 1790s, for example, ministers from every Christian denomination (except the Quakers) asserted that the relation of master and slave, like that of husband and wife or parent and child, was divinely ordered and vital to the maintenance of a stable, harmonious household. For these ministers and their followers, households,

like society itself, consisted of unequal, hierarchical relations that required those who occupied assigned stations of life to recognize that their duties and obligations, as well as their rights, derived from the stations they occupied. Distancing themselves from the emerging notions of human equality and universal rights, these defenders of slavery strengthened the paternalistic ethos that urged masters to look upon their slaves as dependent, subordinated members of their households, to whom they owed certain duties, especially to convey God's word. Slavery was not simply an economic relation, but a social and moral one, supported by the Bible and part of a properly ordered Christian society. The religious justification of slaveholding remained central to proslavery arguments into the 1860s.

In the late eighteenth and early nineteenth centuries advocates of slavery appealed repeatedly to experience, especially contemporary experience, as well as the Bible to defend slavery as both necessary and good. One factor in this emphasis on reality, observation, and pragmatism over idealism, speculation, and abstract theorizing was the rise of wage labor in Britain and in northern U.S. cities. Defenders of slavery increasingly contrasted the order, harmony, and justice of slavery with the chaos, conflict, and exploitation of capitalist-labor relations. In its critique of free labor, proslavery thought attained some of its most sophisticated and self-confident arguments.

As we have seen in the British debates over the slave trade and slavery in the 1780s and 1790s, even before the rise of Dickensian images of industrial cities, slaveholders and their allies (for there were many who defended slavery but did not practice it) pointed to the material condition of "free" laborers as evidence of the superiority of slavery. But it was the industrial revolution, and the conditions it produced, that led the defenders of slavery to accentuate its benefits in contradistinction to the miseries of freedom. Robert Walsh's *An Appeal from the Judgements of Great Britain Regarding the United States of America* (1819), the "most formidable defense of slavery prior to the rise of abolition" (Tise, *Proslavery*, 1987), boldly asserted that slaves in the American South were less exploited than British wage laborers. Walsh's assertion soon became one that southerners frequently echoed. Oftentimes drawing from British government documents that described life and labor in manufacturing centers, advocates of slavery argued that free labor necessarily placed labor and capital in conflict. Antagonism characterized capitalist social relations. Slavery, they posited, united labor and capital. Since masters owned slaves, they naturally and logically had an interest in their slaves' welfare that simply did not exist in capitalism, in which the employer purchased merely labor, not the laborer. Southerners loved to contrast the image of an old slave, long past being productive yet still receiving care from a benevolent master, with the sick or old or injured wage laborer cast out of work and forced to live in squalor or in the shame of the poorhouse.

One of the most impassioned examples of this defense of slavery, which emphasized the positive good of slavery as a system of labor relations potentially applicable to all societies regardless of racial composition, appeared in 1845, in a public letter from the South Carolinian James Henry Hammond to the British abolitionist Thomas Clarkson. After reiterating familiar arguments appealing to the Bible, property rights, and the natural inequality of men, Hammond declared that "in Great Britain the poor and laboring classes of your own race and color, not only your fellow-beings, but your *fellow citizens*, are more miserable and degraded, morally and physically, than our slaves." Hammond, who had in this same letter defended southern slavery partially on racial grounds, then revealed how far his, and many of his fellow southerner's, understanding of slavery transcended narrow racial justifications. "To be elevated to the actual condition" of southern slaves, he maintained, "should be to these, *your fellow-citizens*, a most glorious act of *emancipation*." Hammond quoted extensively from British parliamentary commissioners' reports to illustrate the horrors of free labor, which he contrasted with the gentle, paternalistic benevolence of southern slavery. He then took the moral high ground, as did increasing numbers of southern ministers, statesmen, and intellectuals. Although by 1845 slavery had been abolished by nearly every nation in Western Europe and the Americas, southern slaveholders and, to a lesser extent, slaveholders in Cuba and Brazil boldly accused "free" society of crimes against humanity. "When you look around you," Hammond thundered at Clarkson the humanitarian, "how dare you talk to us before the world of Slavery. For the condition of your wretched laborers, you, and every Briton who is not one of them, are responsible before God and man. If you are really human, philanthropic, and charitable, here are objects for you. Relieve them. Emancipate them. Raise them from the condition of brutes, to the level of human beings—of American slaves, at least." In passages such as this, defenders of slavery went on the offensive, praising slavery in the abstract as a superior form of economic and social organization, one that was more just and humane than free labor.

The attack on free labor and the poverty and suffering it produced increased in intensity as the abolitionist attack on slavery grew stronger in the generation before the U.S. Civil War. Some of the most uncompromising advocates of slavery, including George Fitzhugh of Virginia, Henry Hughes of Mississippi, and the Reverend James Henley Thornwell of South Carolina, developed their arguments in direct response to the rise of a threatening antislavery movement. By the 1850s, when they produced their most important works, most proslavery arguments boldly and defiantly juxtaposed slave and free societies. Proslavery southerners believed not only in the right to hold slaves, but also that slavery and the values it endorsed—order, hierarchy, and the subordination of the individual to the community—provided the only stable basis of civilization. Thus proslavery thought, especially in the decades immediately before the U.S. Civil War, represented a repudiation of the market society (although not of a market economy) and the values associated with it—personal liberty, equality, and individualism. Defenders of slavery continued to rely on traditional arguments, but they employed those arguments, and new ones, in an escalating contest between competing visions of what constituted the good society. Refusing to admit that slavery was an evil, they contended that it was rather the basis of the most civilized, just, and stable society humankind would and—given the impossibility of human perfection—could ever know. For most advocates of slavery denounced as cruelly utopian the notion of social perfectibility. As they had in the past, those justifying slavery emphasized the harsh but by no means hopeless reality of life. In their view slavery was not an evil but rather the best means available of providing the necessities of life to masses who could not do as well for themselves.

For those who advocated the extension of slavery to all societies, regardless of racial composition, climate, or nature of economic activity, the virtue of slavery was its ability to provide subsistence and security to all laborers, and this demonstrated its essential justness. They insisted that free labor, which suffered from the iron law of wages, was inherently incapable of satisfying the basic needs of all members of society. Unlike slavery, which bound each laborer to a master, free labor relied on market forces to unite labor and capital. But the logic of the market produced an overabundance of labor, thereby driving wages down, even below subsistence. Thus free labor produced, in George Fitzhugh's words, a "competitive society" in which "the unprotected masses, without masters to provide for them, are left to the grinding, unfeeling oppression of skill and capital, which starve them by the million." The solution to the crisis of free labor was obvious: "We must teach that slavery is necessary in all societies, as well as to protect, as to govern the weak, poor, and ignorant." Henry Hughes was equally blunt: "Men must not be free-laborers. For if they are[,] some must starve."

The arguments of Fitzhugh, Hughes, and others who defended slavery in the abstract may have represented the broadest form of proslavery thought, but some continued to defend slavery on more narrow and particular grounds. Two of the most popular arguments were economics and race. Supporters of slavery in the New World had always praised its economic benefits, especially the production of valuable tropical staples. In the United States, the enormous southern cotton boom of the 1850s encouraged the proliferation of economic defenses of slavery. Among the most notable of these were "Cotton Is King" (1860) by David Christy and *Southern Wealth and Northern Profits* (1860) by Thomas Kettell. Christy and Kettell,

revealingly, were both northerners who feared that the growing antislavery sentiment in the North threatened national prosperity. Eschewing moral arguments regarding whether or not slavery was inherently just, both men pointed to the importance of cotton to the American and world economies. Slavery, they maintained, was a practical, beneficial system; without it, America would suffer economic collapse. The centrality of cotton to the American economy emboldened some southerners, such as James Henry Hammond, to boast in the U.S. Senate in 1858, "No, you dare not wage war on cotton. No power on earth dares make war on it. Cotton is King!" As long as slavery was identified as an essential component of the nation's economic health, some defenders did not believe it was necessary to appeal to broader arguments. The demonstrated success of slavery in the cotton South took precedence over abstract claims of its moral superiority or Christian legitimacy.

Although race had appeared in earlier arguments for slavery, several developments in the nineteenth century led its defenders to add new dimensions. The violence and decline in production that accompanied emancipation in the West Indies provided much ammunition for those who maintained that peoples of African descent were incapable of self-government or productive economic activity. The revolution in Saint Domingue in the 1790s, proslavery writers asserted, demonstrated the barbarism that only slavery could contain. Frequent references to the brutalities of the revolution, especially the slaughter of whites in its aftermath, and the subsequent decline of the island's economic productivity filled southern periodicals. The abolition of slavery in the British West Indies in the 1830s and the dramatic drop in sugar production as ex-slaves abandoned plantations for subsistence agriculture resulted in countless declarations that emancipation could produce only economic catastrophe and moral degeneracy. Slavery, in these arguments, was not the only just basis for society, but it was the proven means of controlling an inferior race and making that race economically worthwhile. Many who appealed to racial arguments, like Albert Taylor Bledsoe, specifically denied that whites should ever be slaves. Slavery was appropriate only for racial groups who could not otherwise live in civilized society. According to Bledsoe, for instance, the southerner "vindicates the institution of slavery on the ground that it finds the Negro race already so degraded as to unfit it for a state of freedom." Try as they might, Fitzhugh, Hughes, and others who insisted that slavery had to be defended on grounds other than race continued to confront southerners who supported slavery as first and foremost the proper and necessary status for people of African descent. The growth of scientific racism in the latter decades of the antebellum era further strengthened this defense of slavery.

Racial defenses of slavery were not new in the nineteenth century, but from the 1830s onward, as the abolitionist threat grew, radical arguments increasingly appealed to science, particularly the new science of "ethnology," to justify Negro slavery. Whereas many earlier writers had embraced an environmentalist explanation for racial differences, contending that climate and other factors had created distinctions within the single human family, the scientific racists of the antebellum period insisted that humankind actually comprised several different species—products, some suggested, of different creations. Scientific racism was by no means confined to those areas that practiced slavery; two of its most important early proponents, Samuel Morton and George Gliddon, hailed from the North and from England, respectively. Through what appeared to many as objective empirical research on skulls and other physical features, scientific racists concluded that physical differences were so great that the notion of a common set of ancestors was untenable. Some southerners, eager for a justification of slavery that rested on seemingly irrefutable scientific grounds, adopted this emerging explanation of "types of mankind." Two of the most prominent southern students of ethnology were two physicians, Josiah Nott of Alabama and Samuel Cartwright of Louisiana. Both of these men believed in polygenesis—multiple creations. Blacks were inferior not simply culturally, as most slaveholders in the New World had believed since the sixteenth century, but biologically and thus irremediably. In one sense, this new argument placed a modern scientific gloss on Aristotle's age-old adage about some men being born slaves. Slavery was thus right not because it provided the basis for a civilized and just social order, nor because it proved to be economically suited to plantation agriculture, nor because it was ordained by the Bible. Slavery was right because it conformed to the laws of nature, because it placed an inferior species securely under the control of a superior one. And because the relation between black and white derived from biological law, it could not be altered by human will. As Nott and Gliddon proclaimed in their influential book, *Types of Mankind*

In this Reconstruction-era cartoon, the defenders of slavery put forth the stereotypical image of a government run by an inferior race given to laziness and drink. [Corbis-Bettmann]

(1857), "no philanthropy, no legislation, no missionary labors can change this law: it is written in man's nature by the hand of his Creator."

Nott and Gliddon's allusion to God as the author of the different human species could not obscure the greatest problem of ethnology: it contradicted conventional religious beliefs. The vast majority of white southerners, although racist, believed in monogenesis. However much blacks differed from whites, all men descended from one set of ancestors. To accept polygenesis, most believed, meant rejecting the Bible. Throughout the 1850s, defenders of slavery debated the merits of scientific racism, and no group argued against polygenesis more effectively than the clergy. They were joined by defenders of slavery on social and economic grounds, such as Henry Hughes and George Fitzhugh, who believed that to defend slavery narrowly on racial grounds undermined the notion that slavery was the best arrangement possible between labor and capital, regardless of the racial makeup of a society. But the clergy, led by the Lutheran John Bachman and the Presbyterian James Henley Thornwell, made the most effective critique. In doing so, they also advanced what became the most influential defense of southern slavery: masters had a duty before God to provide for and protect their slaves, their fellow human beings whom God had placed in their care. By emphasizing the common humanity that linked masters and slaves, the southern clergy not only rejected the notion of separate species and separate creations, which to their minds encouraged masters to brutalize their "inferior beings," but also strengthened the belief that the legitimacy of slavery rested not on racial grounds but on the word of God.

On the eve of the Civil War, southerners defended slavery as an expeditious system of growing cotton for the world market, as a necessary stage in the civilizing of a still barbaric and potentially violent people, as the natural relation between different and unequal types of humankind. But they above all embraced two arguments that reinforced one another. The defense of slavery in the abstract and the religious defense of slavery both rejected the emerging modern orthodoxies of individual freedom and social equality and asserted instead that slavery constituted the only practical and just basis for Christian civilization. Both ministers and laypeople contended that only slavery, in one form or another, could save free societies from the chaos capitalism would soon produce. As southerners defended their social system, they did so believing not only that it was superior to free society, but also that, in the words of the celebrated Baptist minister James Furman, "We who own slaves honor God's law." Ultimately, proslavery thought revealed itself most forcefully in the confidence of southerners who saw their society as the last best hope for a stable, Christian social order, and who were thus prepared to fight to the death to preserve it.

See also ARISTOTLE; BLEDSOE, ALBERT TAYLOR; CHRISTIANITY; CLARKSON, THOMAS; ENLIGHTENMENT; FITZHUGH, GEORGE; HAMMOND, JAMES HENRY; HOBBES, THOMAS; HUGHES, HENRY; LOCKE, JOHN; MONTESQUIEU; NOTT, JOSIAH CLARK; PLATO; ROUSSEAU, JEAN-JACQUES; SEWALL, SAMUEL; THORNWELL, JAMES HENLEY.

BIBLIOGRAPHY

AMBROSE, DOUGLAS. *Henry Hughes and Proslavery Thought in the Old South.* 1996.

DAVIS, DAVID BRION. *The Problem of Slavery in the Age of Revolution.* 1975.

———. *The Problem of Slavery in Western Culture.* 1966.

———. *Slavery and Human Progress.* 1984.

FARMER, JAMES OSCAR, JR. *The Metaphysical Confederacy: James Henley Thornwell and the Synthesis of Southern Values.* 1986.

FAUST, DREW GILPIN. "A Southern Stewardship: The Intellectual and the Proslavery Argument." *American Quarterly* 31 (1979): 63–80.

———, ed. *The Ideology of Slavery: Proslavery Thought in the Antebellum South.* 1981.

FITZHUGH, GEORGE. *Cannibals All! or, Slaves without Masters.* 1857.

FOX-GENOVESE, ELIZABETH. *Within the Plantation Household: Black and White Women of the Old South.* 1988.

FOX-GENOVESE, ELIZABETH, and EUGENE D. GENOVESE. "The Divine Sanction of Social Order: Religious Foundations of the Southern Slaveholders' World View." *Journal of the American Academy of Religion* 55 (1987): 201–223.

FREDRICKSON, GEORGE. *The Black Image in the White Mind: The Debate on Afro-American Character and Destiny, 1817–1914.* 1971.

GENOVESE, EUGENE D. *The Slaveholders' Dilemma: Freedom and Progress in Southern Conservative Thought, 1820–1860.* 1992.

———. *"Slavery Ordained of God": The Southern Slaveholders' View of Biblical History and Modern Politics.* 1985.

———. *The World the Slaveholders Made: Two Essays in Interpretation.* 1969.

HORSMAN, REGINALD. *Josiah Nott of Mobile: Southerner, Physician, and Racial Theorist.* 1987.

HUGHES, HENRY. *Treatise on Sociology, Theoretical and Practical.* 1854.

JENKINS, WILLIAM SUMNER. *Pro-Slavery Thought in the Old South.* 1935.

KOLCHIN, PETER. "In Defense of Servitude: American Proslavery and Russian Proserfdom Arguments, 1760–1860." *American Historical Review* 85 (1980): 809–827.

MADDEX, JACK P., JR. "'The Southern Apostasy' Revisited: The Significance of Proslavery Christianity." *Marxist Perspectives* 2 (1979): 132–141.

MCCARDELL, JOHN. *The Idea of a Southern Nation: Southern Nationalists and Southern Nationalism, 1830–1860.* 1979.

SCHMIDT, FREDRIKA TEUTE, and BARBARA RIPEL WILHELM. "Early Proslavery Petitions in Virginia." *William and Mary Quarterly* 30: 3rd Series (1973): 133–146.

SNAY, MITCHELL. *Gospel of Disunion: Religion and Separatism in the Antebellum South.* 1993.

STANTON, WILLIAM. *The Leopard's Spots: Scientific Attitudes Toward Race in America, 1815–1859.* 1960.

THORNWELL, JAMES HENLEY. *The Rights and Duties of Masters.* 1850.

TISE, LARRY E. *Proslavery: A History of the Defense of Slavery in America, 1701–1840.* 1987.

WYATT-BROWN, BERTRAM. "Modernizing Southern Slavery: The Proslavery Argument Reinterpreted." *In Region, Race, and Reconstruction: Essays in Honor of C. Vann Woodward,* edited by J. Morgan Kousser and James M. McPherson 1982.

Douglas Ambrose

African-American Perspectives, 1865–1965

Though the Thirteenth Amendment declared chattel slavery illegal in 1865, during the century after emancipation African-Americans identified the spirit of slavery in many aspects of American life. A broad range of black writers, including teachers, clergymen, editors, and historians, considered slavery their race's special history. In their writings African-Americans lashed out against slavery and the racism that surrounded them. In doing so, early black writers anticipated the focus and conclusions of much later scholarship.

As they witnessed the overthrow of Reconstruction, the rise of late-nineteenth-century racial violence, and the gradual implementation of rigid segregation, black intellectuals recalled the "peculiar institution" with a sense of frightening immediacy. Some had been enslaved and vividly remembered slavery's indignities and sufferings. Almost all considered slavery the source of their ongoing second-class citizenship. Whereas white polemicists and proslavery historians in the years from 1865 to 1920 interpreted slavery as paternalistic and benign and the slaves as abstractions, most African-Americans emphasized slavery's darkest sides and recognized the slaves' humanity. Unlike whites, who generally considered the slaves to be uncivilized, backward, and docile, blacks viewed the bondsmen and bondswomen as skilled but discontented laborers.

African-Americans underscored slavery's brutality and its long-term ill effects of both races. Blacks also noted the ways that the postwar conditions of labor for African-Americans—sharecropping, peonage, the convict lease system, chain gangs, Jim Crow laws—drew heavily for their existence upon slavery's heritage. The impassioned attacks on slavery by blacks provided both valuable insights into the workings of the "peculiar institution" and vital, firsthand critiques of postwar proslavery ideology.

In 1865, for example, the Reverend Henry H. Garnet proclaimed that God had never intended for blacks to wear the yoke of slavery. Death, he said, was preferable to enslavement. In 1882 another black clergyman, the Reverend Issac McCoy Williams, blamed slavery for retarding the progress of his race, socially and intellectually. The following year, John M. Langston, a former slave and later an educator and diplomat, blasted slavery as a system of endless torture. Under its all-consuming control, the black man could not protect himself, his family, or his property. Once emancipated, Langston complained, blacks still were denied basic civil and political rights accorded whites. Frederick Douglass agreed. In 1895 the former slave and abolitionist wrote bitterly that while whites no longer could regulate blacks with the lash, they concocted new ways to maintain their hegemony. Whether by accusing black men of raping white women or by terrorizing blacks with threats of lynching, white Southerners continued to define blacks as slavelike inferiors.

Slavery, more than any other theme, dominated early black historical scholarship. In his *History of the Negro Race in America from 1619 to 1880* (2 vols., 1882), George Washington Williams denounced biblical defenses of slavery, championed ancient African cultures, and attacked slavery as cruel and inhumane. William T. Alexander described African-American slavery in *History of the Colored Race in America* (1887) as more severe than any previous system of servitude worldwide. Alexander also held slavery responsible for degrading southern white labor and discouraging immigration into the region. Even Booker T. Washington, ever careful to mask his true feelings in order not to alienate whites, spoke of slavery's severity. Washington, an ex-slave, credited the bondsmen with transforming the "peculiar institution" to serve their own special needs.

Among blacks in this period, W. E. B. Du Bois, the first African-American to receive a Ph.D. in the field of history, made the most significant contributions to slavery scholarship. In 1891, while a graduate student at Harvard, Du Bois presented a paper on the Atlantic slave trade before the American Historical Association. He argued that between the 1808 enactment of the congressional prohibition on African slave importations and 1862, whites nonetheless imported over 250,000 African slaves into the United States. Du Bois blamed the large volume of illegal slave imports on the greed of southern planters and northern capitalists. Because both profited handsomely from slavery, he said, there was little commitment on the part of the federal government to enforce the slave trade laws. In 1896 Du Bois elaborated upon this thesis in *The Suppression of the African Slave-Trade to the United States of America, 1638–1870.* Detailing the lax enforcement of the slave trade law, Du Bois com-

Booker T. Washington. [Corbis-Bettmann]

plained that there was seemingly no limit to the whites' constant compromising with slavery. He also insisted that slaves, far from being passive victims, resisted their bondage whenever possible. Not surprisingly, Du Bois said, whites feared insurrections such as that led by Toussaint-Louverture in Haiti in 1791. In his many books, articles, and editorials Du Bois identified slavery at the core of America's divisive race problem. He also contributed pathbreaking studies on slave culture and religion.

Like Du Bois, another Harvard-trained Ph.D., Carter G. Woodson, examined slavery critically and prefigured later scholarship. In 1916 Woodson, the most influential propagandist for African-American history, founded the *Journal of Negro History,* which published numerous articles, documents, and book reviews on slavery from the slaves' point of view. In 1919 Woodson challenged Ulrich B. Phillips's defense of slavery as a paternalistic institution in *American Negro Slavery* (1918). Phillips, Woodson insisted, undervalued slavery's harshness because he viewed the "peculiar institution" from the perspective of the big house, not the slave cabin. In *The Education of the Negro Prior to 1861* (1916), Woodson argued that bondsmen

worked actively to gain education and be free. Though whites were determined to keep blacks uneducated and dependent, Woodson concluded that roughly 20 percent of the slaves acquired a basic education before 1835, and 10 percent received some schooling before the Civil War.

Influenced by Du Bois and Woodson, over the next two decades black scholars chipped away at elements of Phillips's paternalism thesis. In *The Collapse of the Confederacy* (1937), for example, Charles H. Wesley, also a Harvard Ph.D. in history, argued that the South's commitment to slavery ultimately worked to undermine the Lost Cause. The Confederacy's last-gasp decision to arm the slaves, Wesley charged, disproved theories of black racial inferiority. In his writings on the African-American family, especially *The Negro Family in the United States* (1939), sociologist E. Franklin Frazier blamed slavery and economic exploitation, not inherent cultural or racial inferiority, for the long-term instability of black families. Slavery, he said, destroyed long-established African familial and cultural traditions.

During the 1940s, African-American historians looked carefully at the status of free blacks and contrasted their circumstance to that of the slaves. In *Free Negro Labor and Property Holding in Virginia, 1830–1860* (1942), Luther P. Jackson documented the economic success of free blacks in Virginia. They prospered, Jackson said, in spite of proscription and abuse by whites. Like Jackson, in *The Free Negro in North Carolina, 1790–1860* (1943), John Hope Franklin emphasized the level of discrimination directed at free blacks in a slave society. In the first edition of his textbook *From Slavery to Freedom* (1947), Franklin critiqued apologists like Phillips, highlighted the productivity of large plantations, and stressed the breadth of slave resistance. In *Frederick Douglass* (1948), Benjamin Quarles interpreted slavery as the antithesis of the American dream for Douglass as well as for all African-Americans. In his writings Quarles described how blacks thirsted for freedom and organized to overthrow the "peculiar institution."

Though during the century after emancipation white scholars often ignored their work, by the 1960s the writings of black historians entered the mainstream of revisionist scholarship on slavery. The results of their work took on new meaning during the civil rights era and provided important prototypes for later generations of scholars.

See also DOUGLASS, FREDERICK; DU BOIS, W. E. B.; GARNET, HENRY.

BIBLIOGRAPHY

FRANKLIN, JOHN HOPE. *George Washington Williams: A Biography.* 1985.

———. "On the Evolution of Scholarship in Afro-American History." In *The State of Afro-American History: Past, Present, and Future*, edited by Darlene Clark Hine. 1986.

GOGGIN, JACQUELINE. *Carter G. Woodson: A Life in Black History.* 1993.

LEWIS, EARL. "To Turn As on a Pivot: Writing African Americans into a History of Overlapping Diasporas." *American Historical Review* 100 (June 1995): 765–787.

MEIER, AUGUST. "Benjamin Quarles and the Historiography of Black America." Introduction to *Black Mosaic: Essays in Afro-American History and Historiography*, by Benjamin Quarles. 1988.

MEIER, AUGUST, and RUDWIDK, ELLIOT. *Black History and the Historical Profession, 1915–1980.* 1986.

SMITH, JOHN DAVID. "A Different View of Slavery: Black Historians Attack the Proslavery Argument, 1890–1920." *Journal of Negro History* 65 (Fall 1980): 298–311.

———. *An Old Creed for the New South: Proslavery Ideology and Historiography, 1865–1920.* 1985.

John David Smith

Peru

See Amerindian Societies; Spain.

Philippines

Slavery was an integral part of the precolonial societies in the islands that later became known as the Philippines, although the assumption of Spanish colonizers that it was equivalent to their own institution of chattel slavery was incorrect. Some historians argue that indigenous slavery in this region was more akin to debt bondage and sharecropping and should not be described as slavery at all. However, it was akin to slavery in many other parts of Southeast Asia and should be recognized as such.

Accounts of indigenous slavery exist only from the period of early colonial rule in the late sixteenth century, and so its origins and previous development over time are unclear. There were no major ports or building projects requiring forced labor as in other parts of precolonial Southeast Asia, and slaves do not appear to have been imported from outside. The existence of slavery reflected rather the inequality of power between and within local societies. Some slaves were obtained as war captives or through raids on neighbors, particularly in the warrior Visayan and Mindanao societies. In the sixteenth century these captives included Spanish soldiers and shipwreck survivors. Some captives were used for sacrifices, but many were absorbed into the host society. Enslavement was also a judicial punishment and served as a commuted sentence of death. In most cases slaves entered into the subservient relationship with their owners through indebtedness, sometimes to relatives and for only short periods, if the debt was repaid. Usually, however, debt slavery was more permanent; the debt could not be repaid and the bond was inherited by the children.

By the time of Spanish administration over the northern and central parts of the Philippines in the seventeenth century, many categories and gradations of slavery existed in indigenous Philippine societies. Spanish magistrates distinguished between slaves in both Tagalog and Visayan communities who were individual members of their master's household (*alipin sa gigilid,* or "hearth slaves," in Tagalog) and those who lived with their families in their own homes while working land belonging to their masters (*alipin namamahay,* or "householder slaves"). The Spanish viewed hearth slaves as more akin to chattel slaves, since they were directly under the control of their masters and could be bought and sold, whereas householder slaves had a greater degree of independence and security. Yet the distinction was not absolute: both *alipin sa gigilid* and *alipin namamahay* could redeem themselves from slavery by payments made through the profits of trading, raiding, or hunting; and *alipin sa gigilid* could marry and establish themselves as *alipin namamahay.* Descendants of both categories usually obtained higher status if one of their parents was a nonslave.

There is little evidence of the number or proportions of slaves in indigenous societies of the region. Slaves hunted, fished, farmed, and carried out domestic work, but these activities were also carried out by nonslaves. In many cases the slaves' importance was less in their economic role than in the status they gave to their owners, since control of people was of greater significance than that of land or production of surplus. Status among slaves was also defined by the status of their owners. Slaves themselves could own slaves—who had the lowest rank of all.

Royal decrees forbade the Spanish in the Philippines from owning local people as slaves. In the sixteenth century they brought a small number of Africans from Mexico and obtained other slaves from Portuguese African and Indian markets and from elsewhere in Southeast Asia. Some of these slaves they exported in turn to Mexico, but by the seventeenth century the majority were manumitted and lived as freed people in Manila. The enslavement of Moro (Muslim) raiders from the southern Philippines was authorized in 1570, but few such slaves were obtained. More significant to the Spanish was the use of local draft labor (*polo*), obligatory for all Filipino men except chiefs and slaves and used particularly during the Hispano-Dutch wars (1580–1648).

In 1679 the Spanish crown attempted to restrict indigenous slaveholding in areas of the Philippines under their control, mainly because slaves were exempt from paying colonial tribute. But protests both by local chiefs and by mestizo landlords led to the suspension of this edict. In fact, debt slavery in indigenous Filipino societies intensified in the eighteenth century as colonial taxes and tribute demands increased economic hardship. Such forms of slavery survived until well into the nineteenth century.

In the Islamic parts of the southern Philippines, debt slavery was also prevalent, but captives from outside played a more significant role. Muslim conflicts with the Spanish in the eighteenth century led to the capture and enslavement of thousands of coastal peoples from Luzon and the Visayas. Male slaves were used as workers in forest clearing, fishing, and raiding and females as concubines and wives; both males and females were used as objects of exchange in commercial economies where coinage was lacking. Slave labor was central to the maritime and forest extraction economy of the nineteenth-century Sulu sultanate, and slave raiding for the Sulu market greatly intensified in the central and northern Philippines and throughout Southeast Asia between 1780 and 1870, being finally suppressed only in 1900.

See also SLAVE TRADE; SOUTHEAST ASIA; SPAIN.

BIBLIOGRAPHY

PHELAN, JOHN L. *The Hispanization of the Philippines.* 1959.
SCOTT, WILLIAM HENRY. *Slavery in the Spanish Philippines.* 1991.
WARREN, JAMES FRANCIS. *The Sulu Zone, 1768–1898: The Dynamics of External Trade, Slavery and Ethnicity in the Transformation of a Southeast Asian Maritime State.* 1981.

Nigel Worden
Kerry Ward

Phillips, Wendell   [1811–1884]

Orator and U.S. abolitionist.

Born into one of the leading families of Boston, Wendell Phillips made his dramatic entrance into the abolitionist movement in 1837 with an eloquent speech defending the antislavery editor Elijah Lovejoy, who had been murdered by a mob in Alton, Illinois. Thereafter, Phillips became increasingly recognized across the nation by supporters and detractors alike as perhaps the most gifted orator of the entire Civil War era and the abolitionists' most persuasive advocate for immediate emancipation of the slaves.

Before the Civil War, Phillips aligned himself with the doctrines of William Lloyd Garrison, particularly with the view that the United States Constitution fully

Wendell Phillips. [*Gleason's Pictorial Drawing Room Companion*/Corbis]

supported slavery and that abolitionists therefore should not vote in elections but should agitate for a repeal of the federal union and transform public opinion in favor of racial equality. Like Garrison, he also endorsed women's rights, though he rejected Garrison's stress on pacifism and religious perfectionism. Phillips advocated the use of violence by slaves and their sympathizers in order to seize and defend their liberty.

After the slave states seceded 1861, Phillips reversed his views on northern disunion and fervently supported war to preserve the Union while insisting on emancipation. Throughout the war he used his formidable oratory to link the cause of abolition to racial equality by supporting the mobilization of black regiments and legislative measures to protect those emancipated. After the war, he campaigned ceaselessly for the passage of the Fourteenth and Fifteenth Amendments, designed to extend citizenship and civil rights to African-Americans, and in his final years he became prominent in workingmen's politics and urban reform.

See also ABOLITION AND ANTISLAVERY MOVEMENTS; GARRISON, WILLIAM LLOYD; LOVEJOY, ELIJAH P.

BIBLIOGRAPHY

STEWART, JAMES BREWER. *Wendell Phillips: Liberty's Hero.* 1986.

James B. Stewart

Philo of Alexandria   [ca. 13 B.C.–ca. A.D. 50]

Hellenistic philosopher and Jewish theologian.

Philo of Alexandria, also known of Philon and as Philo Judaeus, partook of the rich mixture of Jewish and Hellenistic culture in Alexandria. His many philosophical treatises influenced Neoplatonism, the Jewish theological tradition, and the biblical hermeneutics of both Judaism and Christianity—especially in regard to allegorical interpretation.

His major works can be divided into three general categories: the general philosophical-theological tracts, such as "On the Changelessness of God," "On the Virtues," "On the Contemplative Life," "On the Eternity of the World," and "On Providence"; the general hermeneutical texts, such as "Allegorical Interpretation"; and specific exegetical works, such as "The Life of Moses," "On the Creation," "The Decalogue," "On Joseph," and "The Special Laws."

In "Every Good Man Is Free" Philo distinguished between the wicked man who is a slave to his passions and to his attachments to the world and the virtuous man. The virtuous man who is indifferent to the world (especially if he be fearless of death) is incapable of being enslaved.

Of chattel slavery Philo observed that it was contrary to nature, since all men are equal, but the covetousness and injustice of some men caused them to prefer inequality and to oppress the weak. In his allegorical readings of Scripture, furthermore, Philo took the requirement that the slaves held by the Hebrews be circumcised (Gen. 17.12) as symbolic of the need for instruction of the slave to cut away his ignorance.

In regard to the mandate that Hebrew slaves be freed in the seventh year, Philo opined that six years of labor was properly sufficient to repay any debt owned to lenders. The biblical rules against cruelty to slaves were justified, according to Philo, by the fact that slave and master shared the same human nature, although fortune had reduced the slave to an inferior status in the world. Gentleness and humanity ought always to guide the master in all dealings with his servants.

See also CHRISTIANITY; JUDAISM.

BIBLIOGRAPHY

PHILO. *The Works of Philo.* Edited by David M. Scholer. Translated by C. D. Yonge. 1993.

Patrick M. O'Neil

Philosophy

This entry includes the following articles: An Overview; Greek and Hellenistic Philosophy; Roman Philosophy.

An Overview

The history of what philosophers have had to say about slavery is as sorry, although of course not as tragic, as the history of slavery itself. Philosophers have been no better or worse than other people in assessing slavery, so that prior to the Enlightenment there were few, if any, abolitionists among the philosophers. Even when thinkers such as Bodin or Montesquieu refuted traditional justifications of slavery, they did not move from there to the conclusion that slavery must be abolished; rather, they concluded that while slavery was in itself wrong, it was justified, or excused, by historical or climatic necessity. In fact, the overall movement to abolition consisted partly of a shift from justifying slavery to excusing it. To the extent that it was a phenomenon worth talking about, slavery was explained and justified either in terms of some trait of the slave—such as sin or an inherent incapacity for freedom—or in terms of how slaves come to be slaves, through war and conquest. Philosophers have only rarely been interested in slavery, and when they address it at all, the discussion is almost always on behalf of freedom. With most ancients, freedom was defined in opposition to slavery, and freedom was made secure by widening the gap between slave and free. With most moderns, freedom has been defined in opposition to absolute rule; and, since slavery was the paradigm of absolute rule, freedom is made secure by abolishing slavery.

To repeat, however: slavery as such has almost never been a subject of primary interest for philosophers. As Finley (p. 117) puts it with regard to ancient philosophy, "The only surviving ancient attempt at an analysis of slavery is in the first book of Aristotle's *Politics.*" Modern analyses are only slightly more common. Usually, discussions of slavery have been metaphorical—for example, using the relationship between master and slave as a symbol for the relationship of soul and body, or as a rhetorical device suggesting that "wage slaves" are no freer than chattel slaves.

Basically, then, to the extent that philosophers have discussed slavery at all, it has been as a term contrasting with, highlighting, or developing ideas about freedom. Thus, in the ancient world the institution of slavery was upheld because it was through a contrast to slavery that freedom could be realized, or because the institution of slavery was a reminder of a more fundamental moral or psychological slavery, in which passions rule reason. Moderns defended slavery on the ground that arguments against slavery could be used equally well against all forms of obedience and inequality. Beginning with the Enlightenment, slavery was attacked because showing that slavery was unnatural and wrong is a way to show that all inequality or coercion is a violation of human rights. The existence of slavery made freedom less secure. Whether slavery is justified or attacked—and when—depends on how best to uphold the value of freedom.

Thus Plato and Aristotle praised Greek political arrangements that increased the distance between free men and slaves, to the benefit of all citizens compared with barbarian systems. Thus Aristotle notes, as one mark of the superiority of Greeks over barbarians, that the Greeks distinguish the mastery of slaves from political rule and from the rule a husband exercises over his wife, while the barbarians assimilate all these forms of authority (*Politics* I.2.1252b4–9). Because some men deserve to be masters and others slaves, it is also justifiable to hunt and acquire slaves. Even some differences between Plato and Aristotle are a function of this overall desire to secure freedom through contrast with slavery. Where Plato in the *Laws* (777e) insists that slaves should be commanded, Aristotle says they should be admonished, thus appealing to their reason (*Politics* I.13.1260b3–7). In Plato, the citizen is distinguished as far as possible from the slave. Aristotle's civic freedom depends on separating the polis from the household as the economic unit. The polis is the realm of freedom and equality, the household the realm of inequality, domination, and necessity, including slavery. Precisely because slaves fall outside political consideration, they can be treated in a more friendly fashion—an idea contrary to Plato. This argument survived into colonial America, where one reason for preferring black slaves to white servants and workers was that it made secure the status of white gentlemen.

When, as was the case for most of the ancient world, freedom could be increased by contrast to slavery, the institution of slavery was upheld. When, as in many modern situations, the existence of slavery threatened the freedom of all but a few despotic rulers, then the interests of freedom required and sometimes generated attacks on slavery. Slavery is then seen as merely an extreme form of domination and inequality, which can be attacked not for the sake of abolition but in pursuit of equality. The Enlightenment stressed the power of empirical scientific and historical research, and equally the authority of rational inquiry. Davis rightly points out (*Problem of Slavery*, pp. 391–392) that all these ideas, and all prior philosophical ideas, such as natural law, could be turned into a defense of slavery. But readers were quick to see that the arguments of thinkers such as Locke, Montesquieu, and Rousseau could be turned into an argument against slavery itself.

Similarly, when slavery became a moral problem, the solution was, in part, to distinguish between slavery and the slave trade. The Enlightenment made it easier to separate questions of history from questions of right, and therefore to separate issues of slavery from issues of the acquisition of slaves. For example, Locke regards slavery itself as unjust (*Two Treatises of Government*, I.1), but he defends the acquisition of slaves under carefully specified circumstances—a "just" war. Such arguments were deployed in the opposite direction when the slave trade was seen as more unjust than slavery itself and so was first to be abolished. For Aristotle, the suitability of some people for slavery made capture and trade in slaves right; but for most moderns, it was the other way around: if someone was justly enslaved, then holding that person in captivity was therefore also just. (The symmetry is actually more complicated than this, since it was argued that some people deserved to be enslaved because they were pagans and idolaters, and it did *not* always follow that the purpose of slavery was conversion.)

During the long period when slavery was accepted as just, or at least necessary and inevitable, philosophers argued that slavery could not be attacked without undermining authority and political rule in general. Once people became committed to abolishing the slave trade and slavery itself, philosophers faced a specific philosophic problem: how to attack slavery without, as in Rousseau, attacking all forms of authority and inequality. Fortunately, abolitionism did not wait for philosophers to solve the problem. Once slavery became indefensible, philosophers such as Hegel, Marx, and Engels turned to explaining its role in history, in particular the history of freedom.

See also ARISTOTLE; LOCKE, JOHN; MONTESQUIEU, CHARLES-LOUIS DE SECONDAT DE; PERSPECTIVES ON SLAVERY; ROUSSEAU, JEAN-JACQUES.

BIBLIOGRAPHY

DAVIS, DAVID BRION. *The Problem of Slavery in the Age of Revolution, 1770–1823*. 1975.
———. *The Problem of Slavery in Western Culture*. 1966.
FINLEY, M. I. *Ancient Slavery and Modern Ideology*. 1980.
GARNSEY, PETER. *Ideas of Slavery from Aristotle to Augustine*. 1996.

Eugene Garver

Greek and Hellenistic Philosophy

Apart from Plato and Aristotle, who are treated in separate articles, the evidence for philosophers' discussions of slavery before the Hellenistic period is extremely limited. Aristotle's is the only systematic analysis of slavery that has survived, and probably the only systematic analysis of slavery written in the Greek world. Democritus, the founder of atomism, says that slaves are instruments to be used like the different organs of one's body (Fragment 270). According to Robert Schlaifer (1941, p. 199), all criticism of slavery (as opposed to criticism of its abuses) in Hellenic philosophy is limited: "There are only three surviving scraps: a sentence of Alcidamus, a reference in Aristotle, and an echo in Philemon," the last being a dramatist. Alcidamus (fl. 360 B.C.E.), a pupil of Gorgias and so a Sophist, is quoted by a scholiast in Aristotle's *Rhetoric*: "God has set all men free. Nature has made no man a slave" (1373b). Without context, we cannot determine whether this claim is an ideological thesis or merely a debating point, made starkly and controversially in order to enhance the speaker's reputation.

As Finley puts it,

> Aristotle and the classical *polis* died at about the same time. Henceforth the search for wisdom and moral existence concentrated on the individual soul so completely that society could be rejected as a secondary and accidental factor. (*The Ancient Greeks*, 1964: 113–114)

The period after the deaths of Alexander the Great (d. 323 B.C.E.) and Aristotle (d. 322 B.C.E.) is called Hellenistic rather than Hellenic.

Hellenistic philosophers, unlike Plato and Aristotle, denied that our moral obligations and relations with others stopped at the boundaries of citizenship and the polis. We can have moral relations with all mankind. Therefore they recognized the moral status of slaves as human beings. From this it might be thought to follow that slavery was a crime against nature that should be abolished, but this implication was never drawn. Because our morality is not limited to political relations, contemporary ethics and politics become separated, as they were not for Plato and Aristotle. Ethics then withdrew from the political realm, and slavery—as opposed to the humane treatment of slaves—was beyond the reach of ethical reasoning.

For Plato and Aristotle, hierarchy was natural, orderly, and harmonious. The Stoics asserted a natural equality of mankind quite alien to the philosophy of Plato and Aristotle. Because of this natural equality, all forms of inequality are unnatural and coerced, and so all kinds of inequality are really forms of slavery. Slavery is unnatural because all forms of property are conventional and so unnatural. Thus, Chrysippus is reported by Philo (ca. 13 B.C.E.–ca. 50 C.E.) to have said that "no human is a slave by nature" (cited by Garnsey; pp. 129–130).

More important is the connection asserted between chattel and moral or psychological slavery. Slavery is transformed as an issue by Epicurus and the Stoics, when freedom in the sense of free will becomes an issue for the first time. Diogenes Laertius in his *Lives of the Philosophers*, which is one of our principal sources for knowledge about Greek and Hellenistic philosophy, reports that the Stoics understood freedom and slavery this way:

> The wise man alone is free, the morally bad are slaves. For freedom is the power of independent action, whereas slavery is the absence of independent action. There is a second form of slavery that consists in subordination and a third which consists in both possession and subordination. The opposite of this is mastery; this too is bad. (7.121–122)

While one can be virtuous—and in that sense free—while a slave, one cannot be virtuous and free while a master.

Zeno (335–263 B.C.E.), founder of the Stoics, is reported by Philo to have said the wise man cannot be coerced because his soul is so strengthened by right reason that it is invincible. A later Stoic such as Epictetus (late first century to early second century C.E.) can argue that both master and slave are arguably morally wrong about what is good. The slave desires the wrong things and therefore subordinates himself to another, and the master too desires things he should not desire and employs slaves to help secure them. There is thus a connection between psychological or moral slavery and chattel slavery. Moral slavery leads men to enslave and to be enslaved.

See also ANCIENT GREECE; ARISTOTLE; PLATO.

BIBLIOGRAPHY

ERSKINE, ANDREW. *The Hellenistic Stoa: Political Thought and Action*. 1991.

GARNSEY, PETER. *Ideas of Slavery from Aristotle to Augustine*. 1996.

SCHLAIFER, ROBERT. "Greek Theories of Slavery from Homer to Aristotle." In *Harvard Studies in Classical Philology*, supp. vol., pp. 451–470. 1941. Reprinted in *Slavery in Classical Antiquity*, edited by M. I. Finley. 1960; pp. 93–132.

WIEDEMANN, THOMAS. *Greek and Roman Slavery*. 1981.

Eugene Garver

Roman Philosophy

The Roman Empire contained schools of virtually every philosophy known to the ancient world, but Stoicism was the only foreign philosophy which the Romans truly made their own, and Ciceronian philosophy was the only philosophy which they originated. The Roman character seemed to eschew speculative philosophy, preferring the practical disciplines of ethics and political philosophy.

Stoicism originated in Greece, in late fourth-century B.C. Athens, where Zeron gave formal lectures from the Painted Porch (*Stoa Poikile*). Stoics borrowed Heraclitlus's theories of physics and his notion of individual subordination to the law of nature. They also borrowed the Cynics' ideas of cosmopolitanism, the superiority of nature over cultural convention or law, and the autonomy of the virtuous man. Early Stoics included Zeno of Citium, Cleanthes of Assos, and Chrysippus of Soli in the Greek east. Figures of the Middle Stoa included Diogenes of Seleucia, Panaetius of Rhodes, and Posidonius of Apamea. Diogenes spent time in Rome with an Athenian delegation, while Panaetius influenced many young Roman nobles through his teaching.

Under Panaetius, Stoic doctrine moved from the ideal of "apathy" towards a greater concern with the external world and its goods. The Stoic concept of natural law in the Roman context came to be used to refine legal institutions and to judge the justice of the positive law.

Seneca (ca. 1 B.C.–A.D. 65), a statesman under Caligula and Claudius and the tutor to the young Nero, achieved the heights of power, but was forced to commit suicide when implicated in a plot against Nero. His major extant works include the *Moral Essays*, the *Moral Letters*, and the *Apocolocyntosis*, as well as a series of tragedies.

For Seneca, true slavery consisted in the free acceptance of vice, while chattel slavery was merely a status in life to which fortune might consign any soul. True nobility came from virtuous actions alone. His admonitions against anger and fury extended to retribution against slaves. A slave, despite his lowly station, was quite capable of virtue, of greatness of mind, and of doing a favor for his master. Seneca condemned any cruelty of masters toward their servants, specifically comparing the tyrant of the state to the cruel master of a household.

Epictetus (ca. A.D. 50–120), who came to Rome as the slave of Epaphroditus, a favorite of Nero, preached a more orthodox Stoicism. His works include the *Discourses* and the *Manual*.

In ethics generally, and in political philosophy especially, Epictetus preached a doctrine of submissiveness to the inexorable, seeing all events as God's will and as gifts from God. Since Zeus has created men free, tyrants could only enslave their bodies, but their spirits can persevere in righteousness. The tyrant or master attempts to show himself as all-powerful by his excesses, but they only show him to be the real slave.

The Neostoicism of Epictetus was eventually taken up by the emperor Marcus Aurelius Antoninus (A.D. 121–180), who has left one major work, his *Meditations*. Marcus Aurelius produced little that was original in his philosophy, but the circumstances of his life—his emperorship and the tragic circumstances that afflicted him, including the deaths of all but one of his sons, plagues and natural disasters, army mutinies, and barbarian assaults—added interest to his writings, as did their highly personalized character. Interestingly, he compared the man who feels vexation, anger, or fear, to the runaway slave who flees the will of his master.

Marcus Tullius Cicero (106–43 B.C.), a Roman statesman and orator, studied under the four main schools of Greek philosophy in his day—the Epicureans, the Stoics, the Peripatetic School, and the Academy—but the Stoa and the Academy dominated his thinking.

Cicero accepted slavery as a socioeconomic necessity in ancient society, and he shared the common Greco-Roman bias against manual labor as being suited only to the slave. He did, however, regard slaves as human beings, part of the universal human community, and in his *On Duties* (*De Officiis*), he advised a master to treat his slaves as employees. Unlike the Stoics, however, he saw slavery not as resulting from simple misfortune, but rather as a reflection of natural inferiority.

The Roman Stoics and Cicero have had important influences upon Christian theology. Boethius's *Consolations of Philosophy* and much of Augustine's work owe a debt to the Stoa, and Stoic conceptions exerted important influences on medieval scholastic thought on slavery.

See also ANCIENT ROME; EPICTETUS; LAW.

BIBLIOGRAPHY

AURELIUS, MARCUS. *The Meditations of Marcus Aurelius.* Translated by George Long. 1945.

CICERO, MARCUS TULLIUS. *De Officiis.* Translated by Walter Miller. 1968.

———. *De Re Publica/De Legibus.* Translated by Clinton Walker Keyes. 1977.

EPICTETUS. *The Moral Discourses of Epictetus.* Translated by Elizabeth Carter and Thomas Wentworth Higginson. 1964.

SENECA, LUCIUS ANNAEUS. *Seneca: Moral and Political Essays.* Edited and translated by John M. Cooper and J. F. Procope. 1995.

WOOD, NEAL. *Cicero's Social and Political Thought.* 1988.

Patrick M. O'Neil

Plantations

This entry includes the following articles: Ancient Rome; United States; Brazil; Caribbean Region; Sokoto Caliphate and Western Sudan; Cape Colony; Zanzibar and the Swahili Coast.

Ancient Rome

Plantation slavery, involving large numbers of field slaves laboring on large estates, is often portrayed as key to the development of agricultural production in Roman Italy from the second century B.C.E. onward. The Romans themselves talked about these great estates, called *latifundia*, as ruining Italy. Spartacus, the leader of a revolt in the first century B.C.E., who drew much of his support from rural slaves, has become one of the best-known figures from Roman history. Karl Marx and Friedrich Engels defined a slave mode of production as the basis of the ancient Roman economy, and modern Marxist scholars in Russia, Western Europe, and the United States have worked hard to reconstruct a picture of Roman society where plantation slavery was central.

Research on any aspect of Roman slavery, and especially on the slaves on rural latifundia, is difficult. The written sources are limited in quantity and quality, and slaves, like most of the conquered and oppressed in antiquity, did not speak for themselves. The comments of Roman authors, many of them masters, were often colored by the economic, political, and ideological debates of the period. Some writers, such as Cato in the second century B.C.E. or Varro in the first century B.C.E., discussed rural slavery in the context of an ideal rural economy. Other Romans feared that the spread of slave-based estates would undermine the military and social fabric of the free Roman citizenry. Inscriptions referring to slaves, especially on tombstones, have survived in large numbers, but they almost never refer to rural field slaves. The realities of ancient agricultural slavery did not find their way into artistic representation. Archaeological exploration of slavery is difficult even for the early modern period, and almost impossible for antiquity, where documents and artifacts cannot be closely related in the way that is possible for a North American plantation. A few collars incised with the names of slaves are the major certain physical evidence that we have bearing on ancient slavery.

The uncritical employment of historical analogy and projections of modern ideology have often proved misleading for the interpretation of Roman plantation slavery. It has seemed logical to draw parallels between ancient Rome and the better-documented world of plantation slavery in the U.S. South. However, major differences existed between Mediterranean and North American crops and climate, the ancient and much larger capitalist economies, and the racial character of modern slavery.

The influential Marxist interpretation of ancient slavery, best represented in the Anglo-American world by the late Moses Finley of Cambridge University,

Prisoners of war were often incorporated into the slave-based plantation system of ancient Rome. [David Lees/Corbis]

made a "slave mode of production" central to its interpretation of Roman economic history. However, while no one wishes to deny the existence of ancient plantation slavery, a growing number of scholars question the centrality that Finley attributed to the institution for Roman economy and society. The more generally accepted historical reconstruction accepts slavery as part of Roman society from its very beginnings. Issues associated with slaves are considered in our first Roman legal document, the Laws of the Twelve Tables of the mid-fifth century B.C.E. However, plantation slavery appeared only with Rome's rapid conquest of the Mediterranean during the first half of the second century B.C.E. These wars, first against Carthage in North Africa and then throughout the eastern Mediterranean, produced a large number of captives, including many suited to forced labor in Italian agriculture. These wars also resulted in high Roman casualties, particularly among the small farmers of Italy, who formed the backbone of the traditional Republican army. As a result of deaths or the prolonged absences of heads of households on military service, many small farms were deserted or threatened with economic ruin.

The wars also concentrated enormous wealth in the hands of the military class of the city of Rome. They saw land as the most secure form of investment and used their new wealth to buy slaves and land, forcing the remaining small farmers off the land and into the cities. The Romans also learned techniques of slave-based plantation agriculture from their former enemies, the Carthaginians in North Africa.

The combination of abundant slaves, cheap land, and borrowed expertise led by the second century B.C.E. to the development of latifundia, estates worked by newly imported slaves who labored under brutal conditions and were kept locked in *ergastula,* or barracks. Most of these slave plantations were concentrated in south-central Italy and Sicily, where large tracts of land were available and the conditions were well-suited to the development of latifundia.

Investment in latifundia seemed a secure way for the elite to obtain a guaranteed income at a time when growing cities increased the demand for agricultural products. However, not all members of the Roman ruling class favored those developments. By the 130s B.C.E. some politicians feared that the spread of the latifundia was destroying the free peasantry that had formed the backbone of the Roman army and was creating a large, restless poor population in the cities. Two tribunes, Tiberius and Gaius Gracchus, proposed land redistributions to restore the small farmer-soldiers, but they were killed by slaveholder-inspired mobs. Concern extended to fears of the enslaved strangers aroused by slave revolts in Sicily during the periods 145 to 132 and 104 to 101 B.C.E., and that of Spartacus in south Italy between 73 and 71 B.C.E. The Sicilian revolts in particular grew out of the resentment of the newly enslaved at their sufferings. The leaders of the revolts showed military skill and charismatic leadership, and Roman forces suppressed the uprisings only with difficulty.

Roman plantation slavery reached its high point in the late second and early first centuries B.C.E. An archaeological site that may represent the type of slave estate of this era is the Roman villa called Sette Finestre, located on the west coast of Italy about one hundred miles north of Rome. Excavations revealed luxurious living quarters but also evidence of wine and oil production and even small rooms that seemed suitable for slave quarters. The archaeologists who excavated the site saw it as an embodiment of the ancient slave mode of production and interpreted it by free use of analogies with North American slavery.

Many proponents of the plantation model acknowledge stresses in the system of rural slavery starting in the first century B.C.E. The Northern European wars of that later period generally did not produce large numbers of captives suited for plantation work as slaves under hot, dry Mediterranean conditions. Gauls, captured by Caesar in the 50s B.C.E., would not have had the endurance of the Mediterranean peasants enslaved in the wake of earlier wars. Moreover, many settled slaves were earning their freedom by taking advantage of relatively liberal Roman manumission laws. Declining supplies of slave labor put pressure on a system of agriculture profoundly dependent on them. Some effort at slave breeding was made on plantations, but that was an expensive and risky process. More profits were to be made by selling these children as household slaves than in keeping them as field hands. Shifting markets for wine and olive oil threatened the profitability of Italian estates as production grew in newly conquered outlying provinces. Significantly, the villa at Sette Finestre was abandoned in the second century C.E., when the Roman Empire was at its height.

More fundamental doubts have been raised about the importance or even the feasibility of plantation slavery in the Roman economy. Roman agriculture did not develop crops such as tobacco or cotton that lent themselves to concentrated production by slave labor. In antiquity grain was produced more efficiently by small farmers than by slave gangs. Both olives and grapes, the other major cash crops in the Roman world, required specialized labor, but often of a highly seasonal nature unsuited to permanently resident slaves. The ancient sources, moreover, indicate that many of the latifundia were given over to sheep raising, an activity that required only limited numbers of armed, free-roaming slave shepherds.

Recent archaeological research on the countryside of Roman Italy has raised doubts also about the extent to which the great slave estates dominated the rural economy. The rise of the latifundia was once supposed to have destroyed small farmers and to have led to the abandonment of their farms. However, recent settlement studies show that a significant number of small farms persisted in many areas from the second century B.C.E. to the first century C.E., when the great estates were supposed to have dominated the countryside.

Archaeology cannot reconstruct the legal relationships among the various residents of rural sites excavated, and it is probable that many small producers were not slaves but citizen renters or sharecroppers attached to large estates. Some may have been former slaves freed by estate masters. Plantation labor was probably a complex combination of specialized slaves engaged in household and skilled farming activities and dependent farmers who provided the master with cash and crop income as well as seasonal labor at the time of ploughing, planting, and harvest. True latifundia were probably developed mainly in marginal land more suited to pasturage and would have had few slaves.

This model of mixed rural labor forces suits better what we know about agriculture during the later Roman Empire. That era saw the persistence of large estates, many of which eventually came into the hands of the church. Rural slavery persisted, but the lack of massive fresh supplies of war captives meant that slaves performed only limited, specialized roles. The major change was the increased legal bondage of the peasantry to the great estate owners. Some historians have seen predecessors of the serfs of medieval times in these bound peasants, or *coloni*, of the late Roman Empire. Given the disruptive arrival of new Germanic groups with their own social institutions in the early Middle Ages, such strong continuities are unlikely.

See also ANCIENT ROME; ECONOMICS OF SLAVERY.

BIBLIOGRAPHY

BRADLEY, KEITH. *Slavery and Rebellion in the Roman World 140 B.C.–70 B.C.* 1989.
———. *Slavery and Society at Rome.* 1994.
CARANDINI, ANDREA. *Settefinestre: Una villa schiavistica nell'Etruria romana.* 1985.
DYSON, STEPHEN L. *Community and Society in Roman Italy.* 1992.
FINLEY, MOSES. *Ancient Slavery and Modern Ideology.* 1980.
———, ed. *Classical Slavery.* 1987.
HOPKINS, KEITH. *Conquerors and Slaves.* 1978.
STE. CROIX, G. E. M. *The Class Struggle in the Ancient World from the Archaic Age to the Arab Conquest.* 1981.

Stephen L. Dyson

United States

The term *plantation* has many connotations. In its most literal sense, it refers to the action of placing plants in the soil; therefore any agricultural unit or stand of planted trees can be a plantation. The term can also refer to a settlement of people in a new or conquered locale. Thus, the English referred to their Ulster plantation in Ireland and their Virginia plantation in America. Another common meaning, as in "to send to the plantations," implied penal service in a colony. Finally, "plantations" refer to estates, often in tropical locales, on which sugar, tobacco, cotton, coffee, or rice are grown, chiefly by means of servile labor. This last sense, while incorporating some of the other meanings, is most relevant to this article.

Plantations as estates normally shared a number of features. First, they were agricultural units. Second, they generally operated on a fairly large scale, although the scale varied over time, across space, and by crop; size was typically evident in acreage, capital equipment, and workforce. In the mid-nineteenth-century United States, a plantation was defined as a unit operating with twenty or more slaves, whereas in the seventeenth and eighteenth centuries many plantations had used far fewer slaves. Third, plantations commonly supplied a distant market with a specialized product; although many plantations devoted some acreage to subsistence crops, they were primarily export oriented. Fourth, labor was intensive, generally low-skilled, engaged in routine tasks, and largely coerced—force being a major feature of plantations. Fifth, labor was often imported, although in some cases the labor force became self-reproducing.

As early as the seventh century, plantations with at least some of these five characteristics existed in the eastern Mediterranean, especially in the Levant. Europe came into contact with these plantations at the time of the Crusades. The Crusaders inaugurated a westward movement of sugar plantations, first to Cyprus; then to Sicily, southern Iberia, and parts of North Africa; and finally to various Atlantic islands such as the Madeiras and Canaries. These last were the crucial stepping-stones to carry the plantation regime from the Mediterranean to the Americas. The Spanish first established plantations in Hispaniola, and later in Jamaica, Puerto Rico, and coastal Mexico. The Portuguese, with their domination of the African coast and thus access to a ready supply of forced labor, had far greater success in establishing plantations in Brazil. By the time the British settlement of North America began, plantations had a long history in both the Old and the New World.

The first North American plantations were in the Chesapeake region. The introduction of a commercially successful variety of tobacco from the West Indies in the 1610s proved the saving of Virginia. A booming export sector, fueled by initially spectacular prices for tobacco, lured large numbers of immigrants to the colony. From the mid-1610s to the 1680s, the Chesapeake tobacco economy experienced a period of general growth. Although the initial boom lasted less than a decade, planters were able to earn adequate profits despite falling tobacco prices by lowering their costs and improving their productivity. Most tobacco was raised on owner-operated units by small planters with the help of family members and occasional indentured servants, largely poor immigrants who signed contracts or indentures in England agreeing to work a specified number of years in the Chesapeake in return for free passage. Consequently, this period has been dubbed the age of the small planter. From a population of just under 1,000 in 1620, the population of Virginia and Maryland had increased to 60,000 by 1680. This population was primarily white and comprised many servants; the black population numbered only about 4,000.

Chesapeake plantations underwent major changes in the late seventeenth and early eighteenth centuries. The most important transformation was that tidewater tobacco planters began to substitute African slaves for white servants. As the supply of servants dwindled, largely because of improved conditions in England, and the supply of slaves rose, because ships direct from Africa began visiting the Chesapeake, those planters with sufficient capital switched to black labor. The transformation in the labor force occurred at a time of slow growth, even stagnation, in the Chesapeake tobacco economy. Rising costs and a failure to capture substantial gains in productivity account for the slump, which lasted from about 1680 to 1715. Prosperous families weathered the long depression better than poorer whites and could more readily afford the high price of slaves. A gentry class and large-scale agricultural units began to emerge; the era of the small planter ended. The white population was now growing by natural increase and imports of African slaves were on the rise; thus, by 1710 the Chesapeake population stood at 124,000, of whom 22,000 were now black.

From 1715 to the American Revolution, the Chesapeake economy experienced another sustained period of growth. Growth, however, was now slower than during the seventeenth century. Tobacco output per laborer declined and growth was demand-led rather than supply-driven. Yeoman planters still grew tobacco, but increasingly tenant farms and modest plantations worked by slaves dominated production. Tobacco cultivation expanded from the tidewater into the piedmont. The typical plantation was about two hundred acres, and the typical slaveholder owned three or four

Slaves from the early Chesapeake plantations prepare a shipment of tobacco to be sent back to England. [Library of Congress/Corbis]

adult slaves. Even the greatest planters who owned thousands of acres and hundreds of slaves divided their operations into numerous quarters where the workforce rarely exceeded a dozen or so slaves. About half of all householders owned no slaves, and about half owned no land.

Diversification was a marked feature of the Chesapeake's eighteenth-century economic development. Wheat became an important second crop in many older tidewater counties, and in the backcountry an economy of small farms and mixed grain-livestock husbandry emerged. The Chesapeake economy was increasingly notable for a larger range of crops, a wider diffusion of craft skills, more orchards, more dairying, and more textile production. Slaves served more often as farm workers than as plantation hands. Population surged, as now the black population joined the white in becoming self-sustaining. By 1720, the black population began to grow faster from natural increase than through slave imports. The less strenuous labor demands of tobacco than were required by many other staples, and the ready supply of corn due to the diversified Chesapeake economy, help explain why this region's slave population was the first in the New World to reproduce itself. By 1780 the Chesapeake population numbered 786,000, of whom 304,000 were black.

The Revolutionary era set in train developments that would characterize the Chesapeake plantation economy down to the Civil War. First, European demand for tobacco failed to keep pace with production. Tobacco cultivation became increasingly tenuous in much of the Chesapeake tidewater, in part because of extensive deterioration of the soil; by 1800 the crop was grown largely in southern Maryland and the southern Virginia piedmont. Because of their reduced labor requirements, tidewater slaveholders often hired out their slaves. Second, in part because of evangelical religion, revolutionary ideology, and the decline of tobacco, some tidewater planters began manumitting their slaves. The Chesapeake region began to fragment as blacks acquired more independence, opportunity, and nominal freedom in Maryland than in Virginia. By 1860 Maryland was only a semislave state where, in some places, a majority of blacks were free; in contrast, just one in ten blacks was free in Virginia. Third, the American Revolution freed whites to evict Indians from lands west of the Allegheny Mountains, and tobacco cultivation moved west with settlers to Kentucky, Tennessee, and Missouri. The Chesapeake region became the primary seedbed of the Southwest interior, as thousands of Chesapeake whites and their slaves migrated into Kentucky and further south. By the middle of the nineteenth century, about 16,000 tobacco plantations existed in the United States; and more tobacco production occurred west of the Appalachians than east. In Kentucky and Missouri an additional 8,000 plantations grew hemp, which was used principally for cordage and bale cloth, required by upland cotton planters. In 1850 an estimated 350,000 slaves grew tobacco and another 60,000 grew hemp; the average tobacco plantation and hemp plantation therefore numbered 22 and 7 slaves respectively.

The second plantation region to emerge in North America was the lowcountry of South Carolina, and later the Cape Fear district of North Carolina, Georgia, and northern Florida. In part an outgrowth of the Caribbean plantation system—because many white Barbadians migrated to early South Carolina with their slaves—the lowcounty established itself as a plantation region when, in the 1690s, it began the successful commercial cultivation of rice. At first, cattle-ranching and naval stores occupied most slaves. But once rice became the mainstay, output grew rapidly, particularly when planters learned to increase yields and control weeds by flooding fields with dammed water from nearby swamps. Perhaps African slaves, some of whom knew how to grow rice in their homelands, helped teach white South Carolinians some of the techniques of rice growing, although many African cultivation methods differed significantly from those employed in the lowcountry. What is indisputable is that by the first decade of the eighteenth century, South Carolina, after experiencing considerable use of free, indentured, and Indian slave labor, became the only North American colony with a black majority. In 1710 just over half of South Carolina's 10,000 people were black, and the black population of the Lower South continued to grow extremely rapidly until 1740, when it numbered 50,000, at the time the white population was about 25,000.

The 1740s—when war between Spain and England disrupted shipping, rice prices dropped, and slave imports temporarily halted, in part because of heightened fears of slave revolt generated by the Stono rebellion of 1739—was a period of stagnation in the Lower South's economy. Since the slump was more short-lived than that experienced earlier in the Chesapeake, and since large planters were already firmly in control, no great shakeout ensued. Some planters experimented with import substitution, greater self-sufficiency, and diversification, but the primary experiment was the development of a second staple, indigo, particularly valuable because it required less shipping than rice. At a time when Chesapeake planters were turning to grains, which in turn reduced labor demands, lowcountry planters were adding another labor- and capital-intensive staple to their agricultural repertoire. In addition, lowcountry planters at mid-century began experimenting with the tidal flooding of fields on coastal plantations. Tidewater cultivation, which would become the dominant production method, increased labor demands during the winter months but also resulted in significant improvements in crop yields.

The middle of the eighteenth century to the American Revolution were years of exceptional prosperity for Lower South planters. Some specialized in tidewater cultivation along the coast; others on the sea islands and in the middle country had their slaves growing primarily indigo; and yet others grew rice in their inland swamps and indigo on the adjoining uplands. Rice culture spread from South Carolina northward into Cape Fear and southward into Georgia and later east Florida. By the Revolution, rice output per laborer was 40 percent higher than early eighteenth-century levels. Just before the Revolution the lowcountry slave population began to grow—but only slowly—through natural increase. The region still relied heavily on the Atlantic slave trade; the arduousness and unhealthiness of rice cultivation and restricted food supplies due to a highly specialized economy help account for this delay in developing a self-sustaining slave population. By 1780 a typical lowcountry district was 90 percent black; a majority of slaves lived on units of fifty or more slaves and on plantations of more than a thousand acres. In 1780 the Lower South population stood at over 500,000, of whom 208,000 were black.

The post-Revolutionary era saw considerable change in the Lower South plantation world. Soon after the Revolution, indigo lost importance as a commercial crop and was succeeded by a new staple, the black-seeded long-staple cotton, soon known as sea-island cotton. More difficult to produce and yielding less than its upland counterpart, but bringing substantially higher prices, sea-island cotton was a luxury product confined to the littoral of South Carolina, Georgia, and middle Florida. In addition, rice cultivation became more and more specialized, increasingly confined to the seventeen tidal rivers extending from the Cape Fear River in southeastern North Carolina to the Saint Johns River in northern Florida. In 1850 the U.S. census counted only 551 plantations growing rice. They were also the largest in North America, averaging 226 slaves.

The third plantation system in North America took a long time to take root. Founded at the very end of the seventeenth century, French Louisiana was never a true plantation colony, but rather a rough-and-tumble, violent world of military outposts, maroon camps, and interracial alliances that made it one of the most racially flexible societies in the Americas. A few plantations producing tobacco and indigo did exist, but exports were of minor significance. Under Spanish rule, the slave population grew sharply, primarily from slave imports—from about 5,000 in the mid-1760s to 24,000 in 1800—and plantations cultivating tobacco and indigo grew more numerous. Experiments in sugar cultivation occurred, but the permanent establishment of a sugar industry had to wait until the 1790s, when immigrants from Saint Domingue introduced improved varieties of sugarcane and techniques for crystallizing the juice.

Only from the 1820s onward did sugarcane become the principal crop in Louisiana, and only about half the state's parishes—a southern tier with access to the rich alluvial lands of the Mississippi and its tributaries—contained sugar plantations. Some sugarcane was grown on lowcountry plantations, particularly of Florida, but most of the North American crop was produced in southern Louisiana. The work of a sugar plantation was exceptionally onerous, particularly during harvest; in Louisiana the labor demands also included ditch-digging, levee-building, and a fierce work pace because of the race against late-year frosts. Louisiana sugar plantations had a reputation as the worst work environment in the American South, although their slaves, unlike many in the Caribbean, did increase by natural means. From about 1820 to 1860 the number of Louisiana sugar estates increased sevenfold from about 200 to 1,400, and the slaves on those estates increased at about the same rate from about 20,000 to 130,000. By the middle of the nineteenth century, 2,681 sugar plantations existed in the United States, and an estimated 150,000 slaves cultivated the crop. The average sugar plantation therefore numbered 55 slaves, the second largest plantation type in the United States.

The last plantation system to arise in the United States was by far the largest. The cultivation of green-seeded short-staple cotton took off in earnest in the 1790s. It would eventually sprawl across a huge southern interior, a fertile crescent of rich land stretching from upcountry Carolina through Georgia and Alabama to the Mississippi Delta and Texas—an area of about 4000,000 square miles. Waves of development drew settlers to the region: the invention of an improved cotton gin in 1793 proved a catalyst for the opening of backcountry Georgia and South Carolina; major growth in Alabama and Mississippi occurred after the War of 1812; and rapid expansion on slavery's last frontier took place after Texas became a republic and was admitted to the Union. During every decade between 1810 and 1860 more than 100,000 slave migrants moved into this vast region.

The initial boom was long-lived, but, as with all staples, it did not last. The search for productivity gains became insistent. One became available in the 1820s

Slaves on a southern cotton plantation use a cotton gin to separate the cotton seeds from the soft fibers of the plant, a task done by hand prior to the nineteenth century.
[Library of Congress/Corbis]

after planters in the lower Mississippi Valley cross-bred short-staple cotton with a Mexican strain. This new variety, known as Mexican or Petit Gulf cotton, tripled the amount of fiber that workers could harvest during a picking season. Falling cotton prices in the late 1830s and 1840s provided the impetus for other changes. Cotton planters turned heavily to mechanization: with the aid of a range of horse-drawn equipment, a slave became, on average, able to cultivate twenty acres in cotton and corn, as well as grains, vegetables, and fruits.

These and other changes made cotton king in the antebellum South. At the beginning of the nineteenth century, about one in ten United States slaves lived on cotton plantations; by 1860 two in three did. In the middle of the nineteenth century, an estimated 1,815,000 slaves worked in cotton on seventy-four thousand plantations. An average cotton plantation, therefore, numbered 24 slaves, making it somewhat larger than a typical tobacco plantation but much smaller than a sugar or rice plantation.

Four distinct, contrasting, and evolving plantation systems therefore inhabited the United States in 1860. The core was the cotton kingdom, but on the margins were tobacco (and hemp) in the upper South, rice (and sea-island cotton) in the lower southeast, and sugar in southern Louisiana. Different as these plantation regimes were, they had much in common. A considerable measure of coercion was one element, embodied in the ubiquitous whip, whether it was in the hands of a master, overseer, or driver—or all three. A high labor participation rate, with most men, women, children, and the elderly put to work, was another. A regimented and highly supervised form of labor, the gang system, was widely used, although task labor was common in the rice regime and became more widespread, along with other incentives, in all crop regimes over time. A greater intensity of labor per day, a speeding of the work process, also seems to have distinguished slave labor on plantations from free labor on farms. In all of these ways, the success of United States plantations was bought at the expense of the slaves who built them.

Although the plantation was an oppressive institution, it provided some compensations. Some large planters in particular developed a paternalistic conception of their role, and their boasts of the good treatment of their slaves, while often self-serving, sometimes had merit. Slaves on plantations were often better fed, housed, and clothed than their counterparts on farms. More important, slaves on plantations had greater opportunities to form families and participate in a community life than slaves on farms. Especially on large plantations, many slaves married within the estate, formed extensive kin ties, and developed strong feelings of solidarity. Plantations were key sites in the growth of robust slave families and distinctive cultural experiences among slaves.

The plantation system even survived emancipation, although much transformed. It lasted in modified form well into the twentieth century. Planters continued to own large amounts of land, to retain some control over production decisions, and to achieve scale economies from centralized management and marketing. The greatest transformation was the ending of slavery. Freedpeople gained a greater measure of control over their own lives: they refused to work in gangs, resisted efforts to subjugate them to the old plantation discipline, and moved onto family farms. But they were still entrapped by their plantation landlords.

See also LABOR SYSTEMS; STONO REBELLION; UNITED STATES.

BIBLIOGRAPHY

COCLANIS, PETER. *The Shadow of a Dream: Economic Life and Death in the South Carolina Low Country, 1670–1920.* 1989.

CURTIN, PHILIP D. *The Rise and Fall of the Plantation Complex.* 1990.

DETHLOFF, HENRY C. *A History of the American Rice Industry, 1685–1985.* 1988.

FOGEL, ROBERT WILLIAM. *Without Consent or Contract: The Rise and Fall of American Slavery.* 1989.

GRAY, LEWIS C. *History of Agriculture in the Southern United States to 1860.* 2 vols. 1933.

HALL, GWENDOLYN MIDLO. *Africans in Colonial Louisiana: The Development of Afro-Creole Culture in the Eighteenth Century.* 1992.

HOPKINS, JAMES F. *History of the Hemp Industry in Kentucky.* 1951.

KULIKOFF, ALLAN. *Tobacco and Slaves: The Development of Southern Cultures in the Chesapeake, 1680–1800.* 1986.

MCCUSKER, JOHN J., and RUSSELL R. MENARD. *The Economy of British America, 1607–1789.* 1985.

MCDONALD, RODERICK A. *The Economy and Material Culture of Slaves: Goods and Chattels on the Sugar Plantations of Jamaica and Louisiana.* 1993.

MOORE, JOHN HEBRON. *The Emergence of the Cotton Kingdom in the Old Southwest: Mississippi, 1770–1860.* 1988.

MORGAN, PHILIP D. *Slave Counterpoint: Black Culture in the Eighteenth-Century Chesapeake and Lowcountry.* 1998.

RANSON, ROGER L., and RICHARD SUTCH. *One Kind of Freedom: The Economic Consequences of Emancipation.* 1977.

SITTERSON, JOSEPH C. *Sugar Country: The Cane Sugar Industry in the South, 1753–1950.* 1953.

THOMPSON, EDGAR T. *Plantation Societies, Race Relations, and the South: The Regimentation of Population.* 1975.

WRIGHT, GAVIN. *Old South, New South: Revolutions in the Southern Economy since the Civil War.* 1986.

Philip D. Morgan

Brazil

Brazilian plantations were large privately owned agricultural properties where—under unequal and involuntary labor conditions initially applied to captive Indians and then to African slaves—a commercial tropical crop was produced for sale in distant markets, often overseas. Immediate origins derive from the Atlantic islands, specifically Madeira at the end of the fifteenth century and São Tomé a century later. In the Atlantic islands Portuguese and foreign producers and merchants, mainly Italian, adapted and modified earlier Mediterranean and Iberian techniques of sugar production, estate management, and commercialization of sugar to meet local growing conditions. Labor was provided by enslaved Africans procured from trading forts that had been established at Axim and São Jorge da Mina on the West African coast. By the time of its transfer to Brazil in the sixteenth century, the fully formed sugar mill complex of the Atlantic islands had elements of a capitalist agricultural estate that drew on noncapitalist social relationships.

Slaves and Sugar Production

Portuguese and foreign merchants in the Atlantic islands trade supplied cane cuttings, cultivation techniques, and African slaves to recipients of crown land grants in the Brazilian coastal donataries of São Vicente and Pernambuco, where the first fully developed plantation systems emerged after 1570, though at this time they were never actually referred to as "plantations." The unit of production in the sugar industry was the *engenho*, named for the processing mill which came to represent the complex of land, coerced labor, technical skills, and capital that was the focus of social and economic organization. The *engenho* was mainly located along Brazil's narrow coastal strip, near to sources of water, timber, and stone. Its layout varied in size and complexity, but it was largely self-contained. The great house, with nearby fruit groves and vegetable gardens for provisions, was the social hub of the estate; there the owner presided over his family, a small patriarchal community that included a chaplain, the foremen, retainers—who received the protection of the landlord and assistance in return for a variety of services—and male and female slave laborers. Domestic slaves lived in the great house; all other slaves were housed in separate *senzalas*, or slave quarters, near to sheds, stables, processing units for maize and manioc, and the animal-powered or, on large estates, the water-powered mill. Separate facilities existed on the grounds for foremen, administrators, retainers, and their families. Grazing areas and fields of cane extended outward to forested reserves that held supplies of wood for the mill and for brickmaking and tile manufactures.

Sugar production involved predominantly imported African slave labor after 1580; and although the size of the slave labor force varied with the size and complexity of the estate, an average *engenho* held between sixty and one hundred slaves. The scale of slaveholding is suggested by import estimates of 4,000 slaves per year between 1570 and 1640. In 1600 the total African slave population was 13,000 to 15,000, and it continued to expand as levels of imports increased to 7,000 to 8,000 per year, reaching 150,000 in 1680. The negligible rate of increase in Brazil's slave population was due to a limited diet, crowded housing, disease, brutal working conditions, and harsh punishment, factors that for the average field slave on a sugar plantation meant survival for only seven years after arriving from Africa. A sexual imbalance that was aggravated by the preference of planters for male and adult African slaves in the regular transatlantic shipments, mistreatment, low birthrates, and high rates of infant mortality also kept reproduction rates negative. Although some planters rewarded productive and cooperative slaves with incentives that included portions of sugar, cane whisky, small payments, time off to farm garden plots for provision of food, and in limited cases, manumission, few considered improving living conditions

Two slaves plant sugarcane under the supervision of a whip-wielding overseer. [Corbis-Bettmann]

for slaves, since the average slave on a sugar plantation would recover his or her cost in less than two years of labor. Continuous supervision and surveillance by armed retainers hindered slaves' attempts to resist the brutality of the plantation labor regime. Suicides, revolts, escapes, and personal attacks on overseers and owners and their families, in addition to destruction of machinery, killing of draft animals, and burning of canefields, were some of the ways in which slaves, individually or collectively, opposed the institution of slavery.

Sugarcane was a unique commodity that required both agricultural skills and highly technical and costly refining to produce. The initial sugar crop took about a year and a half to mature, but successive crops every nine months kept the same field productive for three or four years without replanting. The sugar cycle was determined by the harvest, which in Bahia could run as long as three hundred days, from late July to late May. During the harvest cycle a slave man was expected to begin at dawn and to cut forty-two hundred canes a day. These would be bound in bundles of ten canes by a woman partner in the fields and carted for processing to the mills, which began operation at 4 P.M. and ended at 10 A.M. the following day. Because canes were perishable, milling and manufacture of a crude crystal sugar had to take place amid the cane fields themselves. The bulky cane was fed into rollers, and the squeezed-out juice was moved through copper kettles where it was boiled, skimmed, and purified over a raging fire that was stoked by slaves. Cooled syrup was poured into conical pottery molds and placed on racks in a purging house to allow molasses

to drain off and leave the sugar to crystallize. After slave women separated white from dark or *muscavado* sugar, the sugar was crated for market and a tithe extracted.

Slaves who were skilled artisans and those experienced in the stages of processing sugar benefited from supervisory and managerial positions in the mills. On most *engenhos* there was also a small cadre of salaried technicians, overseers, and artisans who were vital to the different stages of sugar production and processing. *Mestres* oversaw the milling of the estate cane. Semiautonomous tenant farmers, sharecroppers, renters, or landowners, called *lavradores de cana*, depended on nearby *engenhos* for refining and processing cane under a variety of arrangements that included paying half of the value of the processed sugarcane to the mill owner. Most *lavradores* were white, and some owned land and slaves; but they were generally considered a social cut beneath the planters, with whom they shared the risks and costs of planting, poor harvests, and low international market prices. Some *lavradores* became wealthy members of the local elite and established their own mills; many cemented formal labor relationships to prominent landowners with informal ties such as godparenthood or service in the estate militia.

The early sugar mills used presses until the first quarter of the 1600s, when a three-roller mill reduced to a handful the numbers of slaves needed at the mill, increased the average production of each slave from 0.25 ton to 0.5 ton of cane a year, and was adaptable to animal, water, or wind power. A further innovation was the replacement of a single cauldron for boiling by a battery of cauldrons in descending order of size and variable degrees of heat to control the process of clarification and evaporation.

Brazilian sugar production was the highest in the world under Spanish rule, from 1580 to 1640; but the Dutch occupied Bahia from 1624 to 1625 and controlled Pernambuco and much of the rich sugar-producing region from 1630 to 1654, and this enabled them to transfer cane agriculture and the technical advances of the vertical three-roller mill to holdings in the Caribbean. Sugar production thereafter continued to expand in Brazil, where this highly capitalized and commercialized product still accounted for high numbers of slave imports and as much as 90 percent of colonial exports. Brazil's monopoly was gradually eclipsed by expanding Caribbean competition, although other important factors included reduced capital resources available to planters, droughts, heavy rains, lower staple prices, rising costs of slaves, and a general slowdown of Portuguese commercial activity after 1650.

Alternative Plantation Staples

Slavery also influenced social organization and production in alternative agricultural activities, such as cattle ranching and tobacco, cotton, cacao, rice, ginger, dyewood, and indigo production. Cattle ranches initially developed to supply the coastal sugar industry with oxen, tallow, hides, and meat, but they rapidly expanded into backlands areas to meet increasing demands from the export sector. Slaves on cattle ranches generally worked alongside free people of color as cowboys; some slaves were also involved in herding cattle to regional markets, in slaughtering, in tanning hides, and in production of tallow. Slaves replaced Indians in the cultivation of tobacco, an associate crop of sugar that a less wealthy class of white planters grew in areas unsuited to cane production in Bahia and Pernambuco. High-grade tobacco was destined for European markets; lesser grades were soaked in molasses and increasingly sold along the West African coast as a commodity to be traded for slaves.

Supplied by the reform-minded marquis of Pombal's monopoly companies in the late eighteenth century and aided by British demand, planters imported large numbers of slaves to cultivate cotton in Pará, Moranhão, and the interior arid areas of Bahia and Pernambuco; this new source of revenue placed cotton second on Brazil's export list, after sugar. Some slave labor was employed in shipments of cacao from Parã, but since the cacao was a wild plant and was gathered by Indian laborers, plantations of the Venezuelan variety did not develop there. New plantation products did, however, engage large numbers of slaves as indigo and rice production responded to government efforts to diversify plantation agriculture in the central south. It was Brazilian coffee, introduced in the seventeenth century as an item of household consumption, that surpassed all other plantation staples as international attention focused on the high grade produced in the Paraiba Valley highlands inland from the capital city and court of Rio de Janeiro.

New Identities: Coffee, the Late Sugar Plantation, and Emancipation

By the 1830s coffee brought in more foreign exchange than sugar, shifting the postindependence economic axis from the sugar-producing northeast to Brazil's central south. The *fazenda*, organized as a large privately owned landed estate for raising crops or cattle, became associated in the nineteenth century with the large coffee estates, owned by elite merchant-planters holding titles in the bourgeois empire of the era with close ties to the corridors of power in the Brazilian

court. The *fazenda* borrowed much from the *engenho* in terms of organization and widespread reliance on slave labor. *Fazendas* were all located near sources of water, timber, and stone, but their size and layout varied as much as the capital, land, labor, and social status of their sugar-producing counterparts. The great house, chapel, and gardens of the owner, his family, and their servants and dependents looked out on a broad, flat coffee terrace, surrounded by processing units, stables, managers' dwellings, and slave quarters. Slave quarters on Brazilian coffee estates were generally located near the great house, although this did not suggest any corresponding social proximity. Slave quarters varied in style, ranging from thatched-roofed wattle-and-daub freestanding huts, reminiscent of West African village styles, to multiple-family units. On large estates slave housing consisted of wooden barracks constructed around the coffee terrace; this arrangement allowed for close surveillance of a sizable slave labor force.

On most coffee *fazendas*, slaves numbered between two hundred and five hundred, although holdings of slaves reached one thousand or more on complex diversified units of production. Male slaves were preferred, although the labor requirements of coffee accommodated slave children, elderly men and women, and increasing numbers of locally recruited free farming families. Space and gender were factors in the specific duties of field labor. Weeding was handled in gangs that separated older people from younger, more able-bodied men and women. Men and women shared in planting, hoeing, weeding, and harvesting activities. On the basis of interviews with ex-slaves, Stanley Stein (1985, pp. 163–164) described one such gang labor system, termed *corte e beirada*, in which the best hands were spread out in flanks, with the cutter and backup at end of a flank and two more lead-row men at the other end. These four among them set the work pace for slower workers, who worked between them as they moved up the rows of coffee, urged on by whip-wielding overseers.

For slave and some free field laborers, specialized tasks not related to coffee production were gender-related. Slave men with special training worked with free men felling trees, burning and clearing forests, digging ditches, mending fences, overseeing and supervising other slaves, serving as bodyguards and estate militia for the landowner, and driving and guiding mule trains. They generally handled the taming and training of horses and the construction and maintenance of fences and corrals. Pasturing and "shepherding" were tasks for women and children, as was the care of animals belonging to resident farmers and to slaves.

In the 1840s and 1850s the coffee economy reached its apex in the western Paraiba Valley, were coffee production for the international market was initially concentrated. Railroads increasingly replaced mule trains and provided cheaper alternatives to precarious fluvial and overland transport between coastal ports and the hinterland. In the following decades expansion into neighboring provinces threatened eventual overproduction and, together with falling prices and stocks unsalable in international markets, aggravated credit shortages at home.

Coffee production, like that of other plantation staples that depended on abundant and inexpensive sources of slave labor, was irreversibly affected by the Euzebio de Queiroz Law that suspended the transatlantic slave trade in 1850. Ushering in the transition from slave to free labor, gradual measures ensued which reflected increased public dissatisfaction with slavery. In 1869 laws prohibited the separation of slave mothers from their infants. Two years later, the Rio Branco Law declared all babies born of slave mothers to be conditionally free. Intensifying abolitionism radiated inland from Brazil's urban centers in the 1870s and 1880s, fueling growing resistance movements by slaves. When a law in 1886 outlawed whipping of slaves, they responded by gradually abandoning the plantations and the masters who had held them in lifelong captivity. On 13 May 1888, the approximately 700,000 remaining slaves were officially emancipated by the *Lei Aúrea* (Golden Law).

The Euzebio de Queiroz law set in motion a refashioning of labor on Brazilian plantations. The drain of slaves through the interprovincial slave trade to the coffee areas of the central south forced many northeastern planters to recruit locally available free labor. Except for recalcitrant coffee planters who resisted labor alternatives to slavery, similar practices were adopted in Rio de Janeiro, Minas Gerais, and Espírito Santo as rising costs and diminishing supplies of slaves compelled planters to replace aging male African field slaves with native-born slaves, including larger proportions of women and children, and to engage ex-slaves and local free farming families as sharecroppers or tenant farmers.

In the expanding coffee areas of São Paulo and in certain other southern localities, the formation of the free labor market was managed through the employment of indentured Chinese laborers and hundreds of thousands of European immigrants, called *colonos*, who, under often coercive conditions, took up the tasks of clearing land and planting, weeding, cultivating, harvesting, and processing coffee beans that had traditionally been handled by slaves.

Diversification of agriculture and modernization of the rural sector were primary goals of the republic that replaced the monarchy on 15 November 1889. Coffee and sugar continued to be the postemancipation mainstays of the export economy, and lacking government incentives to implement major structural changes such as land reform, planters' responses to modernization and mechanization were very mixed. Shortages of credit, high tariffs, and market insecurity, compounded by the planters' resistance to changing long-established traditions of large landholdings, dependence on slavery, and monoculture, contributed to their resistance to technological advances. On *engenhos* reorganization involved the establishment of central processing factories, or *usinas*, but only a few planters took advantage of related improvements such as new and better varieties of sugarcane, steam power, linked horizontal three-boiler units, vacuum pans to lower the boiling point of the cane juice, and centrifuges that used high-speed rotation to separate the molasses from the crystals. On progressive coffee *fazendas* machines were imported to dry, roast, and burnish harvested coffee beans, but in the fields the labor-intensive methods of cultivation remained unchanged. On the whole, technological improvements were adopted by only a small number of *usina* and *fazenda* owners, who, despite official subsidies, modernized their estates with their own resources.

Plantations survived emancipation and continue to be large privately owned landholdings where cattle raising and the production of coffee and other staples are carried out with cheap and abundant labor, perpetuating the unequal social relations that characterized the plantation complex since early times.

See also BRAZIL; ECONOMICS OF SLAVERY.

BIBLIOGRAPHY

DEAN, WARREN. *Rio Claro: A Brazilian Plantation System, 1820–1920.* 1976.

EISENBERG, PETER. *The Sugar Industry in Pernambuco: Modernization without Change, 1840–1910.* 1974.

FURTADO, CELSO. *The Economic Growth of Brazil: A Survey from Colonial to Modern Times.* 1963.

GALLOWAY, J. H. *The Sugar Cane Industry: An Historical Geography from Its Origins to 1914.* 1989.

GREENFIELD, SIDNEY M. "Plantations, Sugar Cane and Slavery." In *Comparative Perspectives on Slavery*, edited by Vera Rubin and Arthur Twiden. 1977.

LOCKHART, JAMES, and STUART B. SCHWARTZ. *Early Latin America.* 1983.

NARO, NANCY PRISCILLA. "Customary Rightholders and Legal Claimants to Land in Rio de Janeiro, Brazil, 1870–1890." *The Americas* 48, no. 4 (1992): 485–517.

———. "The Transition from Slave to Migrant Labour in Rural Brazil." *Slavery and Abolition* 15 (1994): 185–196.

SCHWARTZ, STUART B. *Slaves, Peasants, and Rebels.* 1992.

———. *Sugar Plantations in the Formation of Brazilian Society.* 1985.

STEIN, STANLEY. *Vassouras. A Brazilian Coffee County, 1850–1900.* 1985.

Nancy Priscilla Naro

Caribbean Region

Spain's loss of territory throughout the Caribbean basin in the seventeenth century to its more commercially oriented European rivals, most notably the British, French, and Dutch, set the stage of the development of a sugar plantation complex based on the labor of African-born slaves and their Afro-Caribbean descendants. For over two centuries, slave-worked plantations made the region the world's dominant producer of sugar, the richest plantation crop in the Americas during the slavery era and also the most valuable commodity of world trade by the eighteenth century.

The Caribbean's tropical maritime climate—frost-free and equable year-round temperatures and abundant, well-distributed rainfall—and its fertile soil provided optimal conditions for growing sugarcane, and cultivation of it spread throughout the Greater and Lesser Antilles and adjacent mainland territories, especially the Guianas. This natural potential provided conditions in which Europe's commercial nations brought modern, capitalist agriculture into being through development of the slave-worked plantation. On-site processing of the cane, through crushing in a large central mill and a carefully controlled process of boiling the sweet, crystalline residue from its juice, made very large, integrated enterprises the most efficient way to organize sugar production. England's island colonies led production through the seventeenth century as the core characteristics of this plantation complex took shape. The output increased through the eighteenth century, by the end of which, joined by the production of the French, Dutch, and Danish colonies, it had reached its peak. By the nineteenth century plantations in the Spanish Caribbean—Cuba, Puerto Rico, and Santo Domingo—provided most of the world's slave-grown sugar.

Mature Caribbean sugar plantations achieved economies of scale with workforces and landholdings far larger than those found in other American colonies and exacted more onerous labor than any of the other major staple crops. Slavery, which let planters disregard workers' welfare because of the ready availability of cheap replacements through a flourishing traffic in new captives, allowed unprecedented levels of technological sophistication in the agro-industrial organization of Caribbean plantations and developed labor-intensive production of an export-oriented tropical staple destined for consumption in the metropolis based on the sugar economy's access to banking and credit, efficient transportation, and integrated markets. Plantation-organized slavery made the sobriquet "sugar revolution" an apt description of the plantation era in the Caribbean.

The plantation complex reached the Caribbean during the mid-seventeenth century, when the Dutch introduced its basic features to the English colony of Barbados in the 1640s, using their experience with slave-grown sugar in northeastern Brazil. Local planter elites transformed the then-small settler colonies of the Lesser Antilles by buying up arable land and consolidating it into great estates devoted exclusively to cultivation of sugar. Growing importations of slaves facilitated by the Royal African Company (chartered in 1672) and a steady out-migration of poor whites dispossessed of their smallholdings left these islands with populations, 75 percent of whom were enslaved Africans, that anticipated the demographic profile of later Caribbean plantation societies. Within decades 80 percent of Barbados—essentially all the arable acreage—was in sugar.

British Jamaica and French Saint Domingue, the two much larger islands in the Greater Antilles, consolidated sugar plantation slavery in the Caribbean in the eighteenth century and steadily outstripped the production of the smaller Lesser Antillean colonies. British and French planters and their Dutch counterparts also expanded sugar cultivation into the mainland regions of the Guianas; even the tiny Danish Virgin Islands joined what had become a sustained sugar boom. When slave revolt, competing sources of sugar, and emancipation crippled these plantations in the nineteenth century, the plantation complex relocated to the Spanish islands, especially Cuba.

The coerced labor of million of slaves made the Caribbean's sugar plantations viable. The Atlantic slave trade grew dramatically in the eighteenth century, as small independent "free" traders replaced the monopoly chartered companies that had financed its start-up investments in slave labor forces. The islands' appetite for enslaved African workers remained voracious beyond even the expansion of lands devoted to sugar because of the failure of Caribbean slave populations to sustain their numbers through reproduction. During the eighteenth-century reign of King Sugar, at least four million Africans—some sixty percent of the entire transatlantic traffic for the period—landed in the Caribbean, with the British and French colonies taking more than two-thirds of them. The Spanish Caribbean's continued involvement in the slave trade through the first two-thirds of the nineteenth century, after suppression of the transatlantic traffic elsewhere in the region, brought an additional

Moulin. 2 Fourneaux 3. Formes. 4. Vinaigrerie. 5. Cannes SVCRERIE 6. Gros 7. Latanir. 8 Pajomirioba 9. Choux 10. Cafes ti Figuir. 131.

An engraving of a seventeenth-century sugar plantation in the West Indies. [Library of Congress/Corbis]

three-quarters of a million slaves, or more, most of them destined for Cuba. Although new imports from Africa (called *bozales* in the Spanish islands) were thus constantly introduced into sugar estate workforces, the percentage of slaves born in Caribbean (termed *creoles*) grew throughout the plantation era, particularly as rising prices for new captives in the late 1700s encouraged plantation managers to try fostering reproduction rather than continue to build their labor forces through purchases. The demographic profile of imported Africans reflected planters' preference for men over women (at a ratio two to one) and for slaves of prime working age, but over time reproduction shifted Caribbean plantation slave communities toward more normal population proportions.

The plantation achieved its efficiency largely through its strict discipline of the slaves working in the cane fields. The work regime featured gang labor geared to sugarcane's fourteen- to eighteen-month growing cycle. Hand implements, particularly the hoe and cutlass, remained the basic tools. Slaves covertly resisted adaptations to more sophisticated production: fears of slaves sabotaging expensive equipment, for example, increased planters' reluctance to invest in even such modest technological innovations as the plow. The growth of a population of trained, skilled creole slaves did allow some technological advances in the key central operations of processing the raw cane to semifinished sugar. Flat, low-lying Barbados replaced animal-powered mills with windmills, while more mountainous colonies harnessed the power of fast-flowing streams with water mills, but slave workers on each estate still had to plant and harvest the crops. In the Spanish Caribbean slavery survived into the era of steam power in the middle third of the nineteenth century, which allowed even greater concentration of sugar processing. Centralized factories, or *centrales*, also used such other nineteenth-century technological advances as vacuum dryers and railroads, and although some planters and mill owners preferred free or indentured labor for the more mechanized job assignments, slaves' work schedules too were adapted to accommodate such work, in addition to their field labor.

The gang system usually assigned male and female slaves at peak working ability to the first (or "great") gang, augmented with lesser "second" and "third" gangs of physically less capable younger and older slaves. "Pickaninny" or "hogmeat" gangs introduced slave children to regimented labor at very early ages. Some British planters lightened the workload of pregnant women and mothers with newborn children by introducing "sucklers'" gangs, as they attempted to foster natural reproduction among their slaves after closure of the slave trade in 1808. Not all plantation slaves worked in gangs, however, and "colored" creole slaves of mixed African and European ancestry did so rarely, if ever. Domestic servants attended to the estates' white residents, and skilled slaves worked in trades and other essential services, particularly in the sugar mills and boiling houses, and as drivers and craftsmen. Male slaves dominated these elite positions, and with fewer opportunities for non-fieldwork, women were disproportionately represented in the gangs. On mature plantations up to 20 percent of slaves were not field hands. Only a handful of whites, almost all men and headed by the planter-owners or their agents and managers, lived on the plantations, directing and supervising slave work.

The plantation imposed a brutal labor regime on the slaves. During planting and tending seasons ("out-of-crop") field slaves worked a sunup-to-sundown schedule, extended by "before-day" and "after-day" preparatory and cleanup jobs. During harvest ("in-crop") processing the sugarcane in the mill followed (or preceded) the field labor throughout the night, burdening slaves with eighteen- to twenty-hour work-

days. This timetable underwent little change even after nineteenth-century mechanization in the Cuban sugar industry. Slaves had only Sundays and occasional holidays free from the otherwise relentless pace of plantation production, and they had to spend considerable amounts of this respite growing provisions to supplement the meager protein rations provided by their owners. By the later eighteenth century slaves' marketing of their surplus provisions was providing most of the islands' fresh produce and had become a central component of the slaves' independent economic systems.

Elaborate and solid stone-built great houses and the sugar mill and boiling houses dominated the plantation landscape. Indeed, ruined or restored mansions and white residents' housing, water- and windmills, aqueducts, and boiling and curing houses still dot the Caribbean countryside. Although some planters assumed responsibility for providing slave housing, for the most part slaves had to build their own huts, mostly family dwellings, using local materials. Some huts housed unrelated slaves of the same sex, however, and during Cuba's more highly industrialized sugar boom some planters constructed large same-sex barracks.

An 1830 watercolor of the Caribbean Island of Saint Lucia; note the slave village with farm plots on the right. [Beinecke Lesser Antilles Collection at Hamilton College]

The debilitating work and the inadequate food, housing, clothing, and medical care that Caribbean plantations imposed on slaves resulted in high infant mortality, ill health, despair, and shortened life expectancies. In these conditions planters could rely only on violence to coerce labor, which kept their grim arsenal of weapons, such as whips, shackles, and chains, in constant use. Slaves nonetheless resisted and struggled to transcend the wretchedness of their lot. Their strategies of challenging the conditions of their bondage ranged from overt, organized rebellion to covert, individual opposition. They also created community and family lives of their own with an extraordinary tenacity that the discipline of plantation slavery could not suppress. The millions of men and women who toiled, lived, and died enslaved in the Caribbean thus confronted the rigor of early capitalist plantation labor exploitation with resourcefulness, aspiration, dignity, courage, and humanity.

Successful planters increasingly escaped the harsh realities of plantation life by opting for residence back in the metropolis, leaving only a tiny number of whites living in the Caribbean. A manager or overseer would take the place of an absentee planter, heading a small cadre of white supervisors permanently attached to the estate. Slaves vastly outnumbered Europeans: by the middle of the eighteenth century, Jamaican estates had slave-to-white population ratios of fifty or sixty to one, and even greater disparities occurred later in the century in Saint Domingue. Very few white women lived on plantations, and sexual liaisons between the white men and slave women, sometimes consensual but often coerced, prevailed. Sexual licentiousness thus characterized plantation life, where debauched and degraded white men routinely took slave women and girls as their concubines, while defiling and raping others without compunction. The children born of these unions made up the plantations' growing "colored" populations of slaves and grew up to work as domestics and artisans, or in other skilled jobs, but never as field hands. They also had greater, if still remote, chances of being manumitted.

A comparatively limited number of plantations in the Caribbean grew crops other than sugar. Saint Domingue, for example, led the world in the production of coffee, as well as of sugar, by the second half of the eighteenth century, and Jamaica also raised coffee and minor staples like pimiento, cotton, and indigo. These estates were organized on considerably smaller scales and employed fewer slaves in less arduous labor regimens. They exhibited the same preferences for male rather than female slaves, for gang labor, and for creoles rather than *bozales*. Slaves there resisted their bondage in ways similar to those of their sugar-plantation counterparts.

The Caribbean has sometimes been described as a pure plantation economy, a totally monocultural system oriented solely toward exports to metropolitan markets. Sugar cultivation most closely approached this degree of dominance in Barbados, but it was never achieved. Although sugar production for export remained dominant, the large scale of these plantation economies generated domestic production and local exchanges—livestock pens and produce farms, as well as slave-marketing networks—to support the plantations or to sustain the urban civilian and military populations of the region.

Caribbean populations also depended on integrated trade networks throughout the Atlantic basin, other than with the metropolis, for food and clothing for the slaves, and for livestock, wood, metal, and manufactures to process the sugar crop. Beyond consumer markets for the sugar they produced and swift transportation to get it there, the metropolitan countries principally provided financing for these capital-intensive endeavors.

The mature plantation system in the Caribbean shaped an integrated local colonial society around maximizing the export economy's profitability. The planter elite and their representatives controlled local politics and headed a white community, living mostly in the colonies' port towns, whose livelihood depended nonetheless on the rural plantation economy. Planter interests dominated the colonial administrations. The significant metropolitan military presence in the Caribbean colonies served as much against the persistent threat of slave revolt as to guard against attacks by colonial rivals. A close correlation between class and color shaped the colonies' hierarchical social orders, derived, of course, from the dominance of white owners over enslaved blacks on the plantations. The free colored urban populations present in all parts of the Caribbean grew from the plantation-based sexual control of white males over female slaves. Thus, the classic eighteenth-century slave-based plantation system throughout the region created a hierarchy of caste and race, as well as gender, with planters heading a tiny white and predominantly male population at the apex of the societal pyramid, with coloreds, free blacks, and slaves—creoles and African *bozales*—classified beneath them by status as free or slave and by gradations of color.

The black majority of enslaved plantation workers, once freed in the nineteenth century to pursue their own interests rather than those of their owners, destroyed, diminished, or transformed the plantation complex in the Caribbean. The successful slave revolt in Saint Domingue in 1791 led to the creation of the independent republic of Haiti in 1804, and the former slaves of the erstwhile French sugar and coffee

A map from A True and Exact History of the Island of Barbados *by Richard Ligon (1657) identifies several plantations in existence at the time.* [Beinecke Lesser Antilles Collection at Hamilton College]

plantations there overwhelmingly rejected further involvement with plantation labor in favor of family peasant production. Subsequent efforts to rebuild the island's sugar economy around plantations failed to overcome the population's determination to work for themselves. The end of the apprenticeship accorded the slaves of the British Caribbean full freedom in 1838, and emancipation came to the French islands in 1848, with similarly corrosive effects on plantation production formerly dependent on coercing labor. Planters attempted various initiatives to replace the former slaves with tractable workforces of other sorts, but with only limited success: for example, they tried to keep the former slaves dependent on plantation employment by limiting access to land of their own, and so checking the development of an independent peasantry. They also imported indentured Chinese and East Indian coolies under contracts that imposed terms of employment comparable to servitude. However, emancipation irrevocably eroded the labor discipline on which the plantation system had thrived,

introducing steady, sometimes dramatic, decline in the export economy everywhere throughout the Caribbean. Yet in today's highly mechanized but economically precarious Caribbean plantation complex, the coercion of poverty has driven the descendants of the slaves to provide most of its limited labor needs, in a bitter legacy of the system that held their ancestors in thrall to that "sweet malefactor," sugar.

See also CARIBBEAN REGION; ECONOMICS OF SLAVERY; SPAIN.

BIBLIOGRAPHY

BECKFORD, GEORGE L. *Persistent Poverty: Underdevelopment in Plantation Economies in the Third World.* 1972.

BEST, LLOYD. "Outlines of a Model of a Pure Plantation Economy." *Social and Economic Studies* 17 (1968): 283–326.

BIEBER, JUDY, ed. *Plantation Societies in the Era of European Expansion.* 1997.

CURTIN, PHILIP D. *The Rise and Fall of the Plantation Complex: Essays in Atlantic History.* 1990.

DUNN, RICHARD. *Sugar and Slaves: The Rise of the Planter Class in the English West Indies, 1624–1713.* 1972.

MINTZ, SIDNEY W. *Sweetness and Power: The Place of Sugar in Modern History.* 1985.

MORENO FRAGINALS, MANUEL. *The Sugar Mill: The Socioeconomic Complex of Sugar in Cuba, 1760–1860.* 1976.

RUBIN, VERA, and ARTHUR TUDEN, eds. *Comparative Perspectives on Slavery in New World Plantation Societies.* 1997.

SHERIDAN, RICHARD B. *Chapters in Caribbean History: The Development of the Plantations to 1750; An Era of West Indian Prosperity, 1750–1775.* 1970.

———. *Sugar and Slavery: An Economic History of the British West Indies, 1623–1775.* 1974.

SOLOW, BARBARA, ed. *Slavery and the Rise of the Atlantic System.* 1991.

SOLOW, BARBARA, and STANLEY L. ENGERMAN, eds. *British Capitalism and Caribbean Slavery: The Legacy of Eric Williams.* 1988.

WILLIAMS, ERIC. *Capitalism and Slavery.* 1944.

Roderick A. McDonald

Sokoto Caliphate and Western Sudan

Large-scale agricultural estates, often using slavery and sometimes corvée labor, were common in the western and central Sudan at least since the medieval empires of Songhay and Kanem-Borno dominated this region. In the sense used here, plantations were a type of agricultural organization that exploited slave labor, sometimes in combination with corvée labor, on a large scale. The scale of production was increased through the use of force. Sometimes called slave villages or slave estates, slave settlements ranged in size from a few score to hundreds and even thousands of people. Slaves often worked on the main fields in gangs, under overseers, in patterns that were comparable to the organization of labor on plantations in the Americas in the same period. It should be noted that the importance of plantations in the Islamic regions of western Africa, particularly in the Sokoto Caliphate in the nineteenth century, demonstrates that a slave-based economy developed in western Africa in parallel with the evolution of slavery in the Americas. This indigenous Islamic tradition of plantation organization reflects developments that were largely independent of the transatlantic slave trade.

Nonetheless, plantation production in the Islamic regions of the western and central Sudan was similar to that in the Americas with respect to the amount of land under cultivation and the concentration of land in units that could be worked on a large scale. As in the Americas, plantations were far from uniform. Muslim-owned plantations were sometimes small and compact, but others consisted of dispersed holdings, where slaves moved along fields that could be some distance apart. Overseers were often trusted slaves or former slaves; some masters resided on their estates

for only a portion of the year, if at all. Punishment for failure to work adequately or for other reasons was often in the form of whipping, exposure to the sun, and, in extreme cases, sale.

The crops grown on plantations in the western and central Sudan included grain, particularly bulrush millet and sorghum, cotton, tobacco, and indigo. The concentration of agricultural production in the rainy season left slaves who had been settled on estates for some time to work on their own account during the long dry season, paying regular amounts of money to their masters in the local currency—cowries in the Sokoto Caliphate and cloth strips in the far western Sudan. Some slaves engaged in irrigated farming on lowlands or were engaged in long-distance trade. Slaves often had access to separate plots of land for their own use. While these practices varied widely in the Islamic regions of western Africa, the installation of Muslim governments generally encouraged the spread of practices that incorporated slaves into society.

There were three types of plantations in the Sokoto Caliphate. First, there were those belonging to aristocratic families, often deriving from land grants made at the time of the jihad. The jihad leadership wrote numerous books and treatises on land tenure. As Islamic law was interpreted, land was distributed among the victorious Muslims. Second, there were smaller plantations developed by merchants and other wealthy commoners, many of whom were immigrants; officials awarded land as an inducement to settle, in return for annual homage and political support. These land grants often came with some form of tax exemption. Third, there were official estates, administered by royal slaves, that belonged to the government. Slaves on these royal estates technically belonged to the emir, the chief official of the provinces making up the caliphate, and these slaves could not be sold. Slave girls from all types of plantations were selected for concubinage, however, and strong boys were pressed into the military or administrative service.

Plantations were a central feature of Islamic countries in the western and central Sudan. State policy promoted demographic consolidation and expansion through the enslavement of independent or rebellious communities. Annual raiding and jihad thereby generated a steady stream of the newly enslaved or re-enslaved. Plantation development depended upon this influx of slaves. In connection with this military policy as it was implemented in the Sokoto Caliphate, frontier garrisons were settled at fortified *ribat*—walled towns that became the nucleus of agricultural and craft production. Land grants and favorable taxation were then implemented to encourage nomadic cattle herders to settle down. They were enticed further by the prospect of exploiting slave labor recruited through annual military campaigns into unsubjugated areas or against communities considered to be in arrears in tax payments. Fronter settlements thereby became centers of slave-based agricultural production. New captives were also settled in the central emirates of the caliphate, where they were engulfed in Hausa society because they were required to speak Hausa and demonstrate at least a nominal commitment to Islam. Nonetheless, their ethnic traits persisted, and facial and body markings helped identify individuals according to free or servile status.

See also ISLAM; WEST AFRICA.

BIBLIOGRAPHY

LOVEJOY, PAUL E. "Plantations in the Economy of the Sokoto Caliphate." 19, no. 3 (1978): 341–368.
———. *Transformations in Slavery: A History of Slavery in Africa.* 1983.
MEILLASSOUX, CLAUDE, ed. *L'esclavage en Afrique précoloniale.* 1975.

Paul E. Lovejoy

Cape Colony

There were no plantations in the Cape Colony. At no point during the two-hundred year history of slavery at the Cape of Good Hope (1652–1838) was farming organized around large-scale capitalist enterprises, nor did the farms produce a specialized staple crop for export to distant markets. The colony's largest agricultural enterprises, the wine and grain farms of the arable southwest, were too small and were insufficiently export-oriented to qualify as plantations. But like the plantations that arose elsewhere in the Atlantic trading system, Cape wine and grain farms relied on slave labor, although in holdings small by Caribbean standards. In the 1830s, when the slave population was at its height, the average wine or grain farmer possessed only eight slaves, and only one in twenty-two farmers owned twenty or more slaves. In contrast to other Atlantic slave societies, the Cape economy was not export-driven until late in its history, after 1810. Little of the wine and grain the Cape produced was sent overseas, except during the first decades of the nineteenth century. Most was sold locally, either to the settler population or to the hundreds of ships that stopped annually at the port of Cape Town to be reprovisioned.

The climate and soils of the Cape dictated that, to be profitable, arable farming would have to depend on forced labor. When it established the colony in 1652, the Dutch East India Company (DEIC) hoped that its employees would be able to supply fresh fruit and vegetables to its ships plying the trading routes to and from Asia. The plan failed, and the DEIC decided instead to release a few employees from their contracts and create a small community of free farmers. The free farmers quickly discovered that the scanty rain and poor soils of the Cape made intensive agriculture on small farms impossible. The vineyards and grainfields would have to be extensive, and both would require large inputs of labor. In neither case were the farms ever profitable enough to allow the farmers to offer wages and conditions that could attract free labor. Imported Asian and African slaves, who were first brought to the Cape in 1657, and to a much lesser extent forcibly indentured indigenous Khoikhoi and San, formed the farms' workforce.

Viticulture at the Cape dated from the late seventeenth century, when the DEIC imported vines from Europe and established model farms. The local market for wines grew steadily during the eighteenth century and was supplemented after 1813 by a flourishing export market based on the imperial tariff preference granted to Cape wines by the colony's British overlords, newly installed since 1806. Of the winter cereals produced in the southwestern Cape—wheat, barley, oats, and rye—wheat was by far the most important. Grain farmers, like the winemakers, had been able to count on a steadily, if only gradually, increasing market throughout the eighteenth century. While the division of Cape farms into wine and grain sectors is somewhat artificial, since farmers often produced both wine and grains and often ran cattle as well, there is no denying the prosperity of many of these farmers. By the end of the eighteenth century, the wealthier among them constituted a self-conscious colonial gentry.

By the middle of the eighteenth century the arable farming district extended 50 to 100 miles east and north of Cape Town, to the points at which inadequate rainfall made cultivation impossible. Without the labor of slaves, the wine and grain farms could not have developed or prospered. Two-thirds of the total colonial slave population lived on the arable farms. At the beginning of the nineteenth century, for instance, the population of this region was 32,000. Of this number, 15,000 were slaves, 11,000 were white settlers, and 6,000 were indigenous San and Khoikhoi. Over two-thirds of the slaves were male, reflecting the greater number of males imported into the Cape. After the suppression of the overseas slave trade in 1808, the gender ratio among the slaves began to even.

The effective emancipation of the slaves in 1838 created a short-lived labor crisis as freedpeople left the farms of the southwestern Cape, hoping to find better conditions and more autonomy in the colony's towns and villages or as independent farmers. These hopes were dashed, however, by the limited opportunities that the colonial economy provided, by the scarcity of unoccupied land, and by the return of coerced labor in the form of the Masters and Servants Ordinance of 1841. For the freedpeople of the Cape Colony, the legacy of slavery was poverty and dependence.

See also NETHERLANDS AND THE DUTCH EMPIRE; SOUTHERN AFRICA.

BIBLIOGRAPHY

MASON, JOHN. *Social Death and Resurrection: Slavery and Emancipation in South Africa.* 1998.

VAN DUIN, PETER, and ROBERT ROSS. "The Economy of the Cape Colony in the Eighteenth Century." *Intercontinenta* 7 (1987).

VAN ZYL, D. J. *Kaapse Wyn en Brandwyn, 1795–1860: Die Geskiedenis van Wynbou en Wynhandel in die Kaapkolonie.* 1974.

WORDEN, NIGEL. *Slavery in Dutch South Africa.* 1985.

John Edwin Mason

Zanzibar and the Swahili Coast

Plantation slavery developed along the Swahili coast—roughly, the coastline of modern Kenya and Tanzania—from around 1830, as rapidly expanding commerce drew the region into the world economy. The principal landowners and slave owners were Omani Arabs, the wealthy elite of an expanding but ill-defined commercial and political empire that moved its base from Oman to Zanzibar island during the 1830s. Investment in plantation agriculture was in part an attempt at diversification by merchant interests apprehensive of the risks involved in the profitable but uncertain trade in ivory and slaves from the mainland that had first impelled Zanzibari commercial growth. They turned to plantations also in response to restrictions placed by Britain on the export slave trade by treaties signed in 1822 and 1847; no longer able to sell slaves, the wealthy turned rather to exporting the products of slaves they bought.

The principal product involved was cloves. In 1839 Zanzibar and the neighboring island of Pemba exported 315,000 pounds of cloves; in 1870 they exported 8,715,000 pounds. The labor used to clear land, plant clove trees, and—most of all—pick the cloves was very largely that of slaves.

There had long been an export of slaves from East Africa, and in the settlements of the islands and mainland coast, slavery was a well-established institution, located within a hierarchy of servitude. The expansion of clove production, however, called for a much larger number of slaves. This demand was met from the East African mainland, where an expanding

commercial frontier, constantly pushed forward by caravans searching for ivory and other luxury goods, left a trail of disruption that produced a ready supply of newly enslaved women and men. In the 1850s and 1860s about fourteen thousand slaves a year were arriving on Zanzibar island, and of these around ten thousand each year were put to work there and on neighboring Pemba. Beginning in the 1860s plantations were also established along the mainland coast, growing sugarcane in the Pangani River delta and grain around Malindi. By 1873 Malindi was importing six hundred slaves a year from Zanzibar.

Plantation agriculture required changes in the organization of slaves' labor and time. Evidence is limited, but it would seem that, formerly, agricultural slaves either gave a portion of their food crops to their masters (as other kinds of dependents did also) or worked on their masters' fields for a set number of days per week, working small plots on their own account the rest of the time.

Clove agriculture called for even more direct control, particularly at harvesttime. Slaves still grew their own food and built their own houses but also worked in groups on their masters' crops under the supervision of overseers. Mainland sugarcane and the grain plantations of Malindi demanded even tighter control of the labor force. Slaves there were organized in gangs with a work-task set for each day. They were expected to feed and house themselves but often were allowed only one day each week to work their own fields. The distinction between labor expected from men and that from women—respected in clove work—was not maintained in these plantations: women and men worked on the same tasks.

This transformation was not abrupt, nor was it complete. The state was weak, and slaves who felt themselves unfairly treated often ran away—especially on the coast. Around Mombasa, while the use of slaves in agriculture expanded, the organization of their labor did not change. Elsewhere, while many of the plantation slave owners were recent Omani immigrants heedless of local conventions, others were longer-established landowners, and their slaves invoked certain rights and privileges through reference to former patterns of servitude. As they did so, recent arrivals appropriated some of the forms of coastal culture. It would be quite inappropriate to characterize slavery on the plantations of the East African coast as "benign," but slaves exerted a degree of negotiating power.

Plantation slavery on the Swahili coast went into a prolonged crisis during the 1880s, precipitated in the first instance by an increasing difficulty in securing supplies of new slaves on which the plantations relied, as anti–slave trade treaties slowly reduced sup-

The house of a rich slave trader (Zanzibar, ca. 1900) exhibits the luxuries accruing from investment in plantation agriculture as restrictions on the slave and ivory trade increased in the nineteenth century. [Bojan Brecelj/Corbis]

plies. By the early 1890s the imposition of effective British and German colonial rule along the whole of what had been the Zanzibari sphere ended large-scale trade in slaves. Colonial administrations were concerned for the future of the plantations, and some local officials sought to delay the final abolition of slavery; but by 1913 the legal status of slavery itself was abolished all along the coast. With varying degrees of support from colonial officials, landowners sought to maintain their plantations with new forms of servile labor, often relying on squatters. Only on Zanzibar and Pemba were they successful in maintaining a large-scale form of plantation agriculture.

See also AFRICA; EAST AFRICA.

BIBLIOGRAPHY

COOPER, F. *From Slaves to Squatters: Plantation Labor and Agriculture in Zanzibar and Coastal Kenya, 1890–1925.* 1980.
———. *Plantation Slavery on the East Coast of Africa.* 1977.
GLASSMAN, J. *Feasts and Riot: Revelry, Rebellion, and Popular Consciousness on the Swahili Coast, 1856–1888.* 1995.
MORTON, F. *Children of Ham: Freed Slaves and Fugitive Slaves on the Kenya Coast, 1873–1907.* 1990.
SHERIFF, A. *Slaves, Spices, and Ivory in Zanzibar: Integration of an East African Commercial Empire into the World Economy, 1770–1873.* 1987.

Justin Willis

Plato   [428–347 B.C.]

Greek philosopher; formative influences on Western culture.

Plato was not interested in whether or not slavery was a good thing. Slaves were obviously human beings. The extant works of Plato are in the form of dialogues depicting philosophical conversations between his teacher, Socrates, and a variety of others. In the *Meno* Socrates shows that even a slave has knowledge of higher mathematics, but he does not take this demonstration to have any ethical implications. That slaves exist in the ideal state constructed in the *Republic* seems to Plato to have been too obvious to be worth proving. One of the things that makes the Republic the ideal state is that it has very few laws, but one of those few is a bar against owning slaves of Greek stock

(V. 469c). The second-best state, constructed in the *Laws,* has many regulations about slaves, the general tendency of which is to increase the difference between free people and slaves and so to make free people secure in their freedom. For example, slaves who do wrong should be punished and whipped, while citizens who do wrong should in the first instance be warned and taught. The purpose of this distance is not to degrade slaves—Plato seems to have no interest in whether they are degraded or not—but to dignify free citizens by removing all slavishness from their character.

In other dialogues "slavishness" is a derogatory predicate indicating behavior incompatible with moral goodness: to be slavish is to be concerned with petty matters (*Symposium* 210d), worried about practical affairs rather than theoretical investigations (*Theaetetus* 173a), unable to control desire and passion (*Crito* 52c, *Rep.* IX, 577cd), or unable to follow a rational principle (*Laws* IV, 720b, *Statesman* 309a). In general, political relations, such as the relation of master and slave, become in Plato metaphors for the more important internal relations within the soul of the good person. Reason should rule desire as a master rules his slaves (*Laws* V.726, *Rep.* IV, 444b7), and the soul should stand to the body as master to slave (*Phaedrus* 79e–80a, *Timaeus* 34c, 44d).

See also ANCIENT GREECE; ARISTOTLE; PHILOSOPHY.

BIBLIOGRAPHY

MORROW, GLENN R. "Plato's Law of Slavery in Its Relation to Greek Law." *Illinois Studies in Language and Literature* 25 (1939): 11–40.
VLASTOS, GREGORY. "Slavery in Plato's Thought." In *Platonic Studies.* 1973; pp. 147–163. Originally published in *Philosophical Review* 50 (1941): 289–304.

Eugene Garver

Pleasants v. Pleasants (Va., 1799)

In the 1770s John Pleasants and his son Jonathan, both devout Quakers, died. Their wills provided freedom for their slaves when they turned thirty, if "the laws of the land will admit them to be set free, without their being transported out of the country." John Pleasants specified, "I direct my executors, or their successors, to free my slaves, or the descendants of my slaves, if and when the state of Virginia allows manumissions." Jonathan's will contained similar language. In 1782 Virginia passed legislation allowing for the private manumission of slaves within the state. By this time the slaves of John and Jonathan Pleasants had been distributed among various heirs. Robert Pleasants—the son of John and the brother of Robert—then began a suit to compel his various relatives to free the slaves they had inherited according to the terms of the bequest. In the Court of Chancery, Judge George Wythe, one of the few opponents of slavery in Virginia politics at that time, agreed with Robert Pleasant and ordered the slaves freed. The other Pleasants heirs appealed Wythe's ruling to Virginia's highest court.

Both wills probably violated an important legal doctrine, known as the rule against perpetuities. The wills were "perpetuities" because there was no way of knowing when Virginia might pass a manumission law, and the legal system could not allow a will to dictate that sometime in the distant and unknown future, the descendants of the original Pleasants slaves would become free. The judges of Virginia's highest court, although all slave owners, were nevertheless sympathetic to the freedom claims of the slaves and also supportive of their colleague Wythe. Thus, the judges explained away and ignored the rule against perpetuities to free the slaves. *Pleasants v. Pleasants* was a rare example of a southern court bending the law to free a slave.

See also LAW; MANUMISSION; VIRGINIA.

BIBLIOGRAPHY

COVER, ROBERT. *Justice Accused: Antislavery and the Judicial Process.* 1977.
FINKELMAN, PAUL. *The Law of Freedom and Bondage: A Casebook.* 1985.

Paul Finkelman

Poetry

See Literature of Slavery.

Politics

The struggle over slavery was as old as the American republic itself. The framers of the Constitution had suppressed their differences over slavery by avoiding any direct reference to it in the text. Yet slavery shaped numerous provisions. On the question of how to count the population of the slave states as a basis for representation in Congress and the electoral college and for levying direct taxes on the states, the framers decided to enumerate only three-fifths of slaves. They forbade Congress to outlaw the slave trade before 1808. They required the free states to return fugitives "on claim" and guaranteed federal assistance to states in suppressing slave uprisings. By requiring three-fourths of the states to ratify any amendment to the Constitution, the framers gave the slave states a perpetual veto. After the publication in 1840 of James Madison's notes of the debates in the Constitutional Convention, many northern abolitionists condemned the Constitution as a proslavery "covenant with death." Followers of William Lloyd Garrison even called for dissolution of the Union.

For a time the triumph over Britain in the Revolution fostered a sense of national identity throughout the young republic. Sectional differences were in abeyance. The Confederation Congress had prohibited slavery north of the Ohio River under the famous Northwest Ordinance of 1787, yet slavery lingered there for decades.

But the ordinance had said nothing about slavery in the new territory west of the Mississippi River, and when, in 1819, Missouri applied for admission to the Union as a slave state, it raised anew the question of slavery's expansion. When Representative James Tallmadge of New York proposed an amendment to establish a program of gradual emancipation in Missouri as a condition for its admission, he triggered the first Congressional debate on the morality of slavery. Congress was deadlocked over Missouri until Representative Jesse Thomas of Illinois proposed what became known as the Missouri Compromise, under which Missouri was admitted in 1820 as a slave state and Maine, heretofore a part of Massachusetts, was admitted as a free state, thus preserving sectional balance in the Senate. Slavery was prohibited in the remainder of the Louisiana Purchase north of 36 degrees, 30 minutes, the latitude of the southern boundary of Missouri. A second compromise proposed by Henry Clay of Kentucky made Missouri's admission conditional on its revoking a provision in its constitution excluding free blacks from the state. But southerners' fears for the security of slavery and northerners' concern about its spread remained. During the controversy, an aged Thomas Jefferson wrote, "This momentous question, like a fire-bell in the night, awakened and filled me with terror."

Inspired in part by the evangelical fervor of the Second Great Awakening, in the 1830s a militant form of antislavery erupted in the north. Calling for immediate, uncompensated emancipation, these "immediatists" pronounced slavery a mortal sin and strove to awaken the conscience of slave owners through strident propaganda. Abolition in Mexico and the British Empire put slavery on the defensive, and African-Americans found a voice in David Walker's "Appeal to Colored Citizens of the World," the convening of annual conventions of black abolitionists,

Frederick Douglass's newspaper, and Nat Turner's desperate rebellion in Virginia. By 1838 the American Anti-Slavery Society claimed a total membership of 250,000 in the North.

But to southerners the abolitionist crusade could serve only to incite slaves to rebel. Southern politicians banned abolitionist literature from the mails and after 1836 kept petitions for abolition from the floor of the House of Representatives until 1844 with a "gag rule." Despite growing numbers, by the late 1830s abolitionists recognized that they had failed to convert the North, where antiabolitionist mobs attacked lecturers and destroyed presses. The failure of moral suasion induced abolitionists in New York to organize the Liberty Party in 1839, but it attracted few voters in the presidential elections of 1840 and 1844. Many abolitionists eventually narrowed their objectives to opposing only the spread of slavery into the territories, in hope of killing it indirectly. In 1848 an expedient form of antislavery found expression in the founding of the Free-Soil Party, whose objective was to save the territories for free white labor, not to free the slaves.

The war with Mexico thrust the "territorial question" once more to the fore. When in 1846 President James K. Polk asked Congress for funds to purchase lands that might be acquired after the war, Congressman David Wilmot, a disgruntled Pennsylvania Democrat, proposed an amendment to an appropriations bill to exclude slavery altogether from such territories. The Wilmot Proviso, as the amendment became known, passed the House on several occasions only to be defeated in the Senate. Eventually Polk got his money, but the Wilmot Proviso soon became a rallying point for Free-Soilers and later a fundamental principle of the new Republican party. Northern legislatures endorsed it while southern legislators pledged to fight it as an affront to southern honor. Some southern congressmen threatened disunion.

The Wilmot Proviso promoted political realignment. In 1845 the Whigs had objected to the annexation of Texas, where slavery had been established by American migrants, but Whig opposition, concentrated in the northeast, was based primarily on the party's philosophy that the improvement of existing territory was a safer means of ensuring liberty than extension of the nation's borders. Creating territories from the Mexican Cession of 1848, northern Whigs and their allies now feared, might introduce slavery where it had not been legal under Mexican law.

Americans in both sections believed that the future of republican institutions everywhere was dependent upon the status of slavery in the new territories. In the election of 1848 both the Democrats and the Whigs suffered defections as "Barnburner" Democrats joined

"Conscience" Whigs and Liberty Party men to nominate the former president Martin Van Buren, once a "doughface" (prosouthern) Democrat, as their candidate. Proclaiming their allegiance to "Free Soil, Free Speech, Free Labor, and Free Men," they failed to prevent the Whig candidate, General Zachary Taylor, ironically a Louisiana slave owner, from winning the presidency by carrying seven northern states and most of the South.

Thus as Congress met in 1850 sectional issues would again obscure party lines. A plan to extend the Missouri Compromise line through the new territories was quickly discarded. A complex compromise proposal offered by Senator Henry Clay, the "Great Pacificator" of 1820 and 1833, also failed. But following President Taylor's sudden death, Illinois Senator Stephen A. Douglas, Lincoln's future rival, was able to mastermind passage of key provisions of Clay's compromise with the aid of President Millard Filmore, who persuaded many legislators to absent themselves for difficult votes. The result was less a compromise, as the historian David Potter observed, than an armistice.

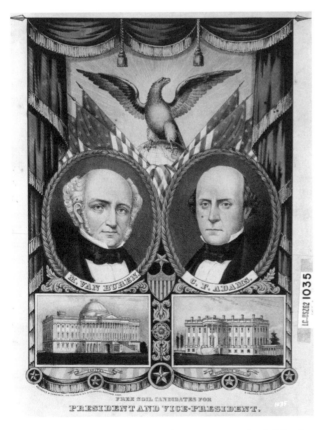

A campaign poster for the 1848 election puts forth Martin Van Buren and Charles Francis Adams as the Free-Soil Party candidates for president and vice president, respectively. [Library of Congress/Corbis]

California was admitted as a free state without a territorial stage, and in separate bills the territories of New Mexico and Utah were organized without reference to slavery. Moderate Democrats rallied behind Michigan Senator Lewis Cass, who proposed a doctrine of "popular sovereignty"—the idea of permitting residents in the territories to determine for themselves whether or not they wanted slavery. Although condemned by some historians as no solution, popular sovereignty was consistent with traditional principles of the Democratic Party—expansion, decentralized government, and local control. Yet in practice it was unclear at what stage the territorial government might lawfully include or exclude slavery. Northerners and southerners would interpret popular sovereignty in partisan ways. Ironically, both New Mexico and Utah adopted slave codes, but scarely any slaves appeared in either territory. California adopted a free-state constitution but elected representatives and senators who voted with the South.

The most controversial of the five bills constituting the Compromise of 1850 adjusted the Texas–New Mexico border in favor of New Mexico and compensated Texan investors claiming losses on the disputed land. Two other laws in the Compromise boded ill for the future. Legislators forbade the importation of slaves into the District of Columbia for the purpose of sale or transfer but did not end trading in slaves belonging to residents. The law satisfied no one. A new Fugitive Slave Law passed with little debate, even though it denied due process to blacks arrested in the free states as runaways. In the 1850s the plight of fugitives seized in the streets of northern cities led some free states to adopt personal liberty laws providing jury trials for suspected fugitives and requiring attorneys to defend them. The rendition of Anthony Burns in 1854 by federal troops brought many conservative Bostonians to the cause of abolition.

The widespread northern hostility to the Fugitive Slave Law strengthened sentiment in the North and propelled radical antislavery Whigs into office. Unionist Whigs and moderate Democrats in Georgia gave the Compromise qualified support, but President Taylor's alleged "betrayal" of southern interests prompted several leading Whigs to go over to the Democrats. In 1852 the Democrats regained the presidency by turning to a pro-Compromise dark horse, Franklin Pierce of New Hampshire, a doughface, after twenty-seven agonizing ballots. Equally split, the Whigs nominated General Winfield Scott—a Virginian and the conqueror of Mexico—over Fillmore after fifty-two ballots. The Free-Soil Party denounced the Compromise, demanded repeal of the Fugitive Slave Law, and condemned slavery as "a sin against God and a crime against man." Scott carried only two slave states as southern Whigs defected en masse.

After sweeping the North, Pierce squandered his credibility there by making the acquisition of Cuba his primary goal in foreign policy and flirting briefly with filibustering expeditions. The so-called Ostend Manifesto was a dispatch from three American ambassadors meeting in Ostend, Belgium, who pledged that if Spain refused to sell Cuba to the United States, "Then, by every law, human and divine, we shall be justified in wresting it from Spain." Although Secretary of State William Marcy repudiated the manifesto, the antislavery men were convinced that Pierce's administration had been captured by the "slave power conspiracy." When in 1853 Pierce's minister to Mexico, James Gadsden, purchased 45,000 square miles of Mexico bordering the United States, Pierce's opponents declared it a victory for slavery.

Pierce's mismanagement of the strife in Kansas confirmed the fears of the antislavery forces. In 1854 Senator Douglas's Committee on Territories had reported out a bill to organize the vast Nebraska Territory on the basis of popular sovereignty. Yielding to powerful southern senators, Douglas created a separate Kansas Territory and accepted an amendment repealing the provision of the Missouri Compromise that prohibited slavery north of 36 degrees, 30 minutes latitude. Pierce reluctantly supported the amendment, thus sealing his own political fate. The bill passed the House 113 to 100, with 91 percent of northerners voting nay.

Rallies protesting the Kansas-Nebraska Act greeted Douglas everywhere in the North. During the spring and summer of 1854, Free-Soilers and antislavery Whigs and Democrats joined with supporters of the anti-Catholic Know-Nothing Party to form anti-Nebraska coalitions. Soon these organizations took the name Republican. Dominated by native-born Yankees from New England and its cultural outposts throughout the upper North, the Republicans saw themselves as the party of progress, enterprise, and reform, as well as a party against slavery and Catholicism. The Republicans who had voted for the Kansas-Nebraska Act suffered a disaster in the fall elections, leaving their party strong only in the South.

A desperate competition to win Kansas swept settlers westward from Missouri, the Midwest, and New England. In Kansas local quarrels over land claims and timber and water rights quickly took on a sectional character. Nearly five thousand Missourians crossed into Kansas to elect a proslavery territorial legislature. That body promptly enacted a slave code and limited officeholding to avowed proslavery candidates. When free-staters created a rival legislature at Topeka, Pierce condemned it as illegal. In May 1856 civil war erupted when a proslavery territorial posse composed largely of Missouri "border ruffians" attacked the free-state town of Lawrence. Three days later, John Brown led a small band of northern irregulars in a retaliatory midnight foray on Pottawatomie Creek, where they hacked five unsuspecting proslavery settlers to death with broadswords. During the next four months guerrilla fighting along the Kansas-Missouri border left two hundred dead. In desperation, Pierce appointed a new governor who, aided by federal troops, was finally able to disarm the guerilla bands just two months before the national elections.

In Washington, meantime, Congressman Preston Brooks beat Senator Charles Sumner of Massachusetts savagely on the floor of the Senate with a cane to defend the honor of a cousin, Senator Andrew Pickens Butler of South Carolina, whom Sumner had denounced in his speech, "The Crime against Kansas." Brooks was applauded throughout the south and reelected unanimously to the House. Despite winning reelection in 1857, the injured Sumner was absent from the Senate for three years. In the fall of 1856 the slogans "Bleeding Kansas" and "Bleeding Sumner" won thousands of new Republican voters in the North. Young Republicans marched by torchlight in support of their candidate, John C. Frémont, chanting "Free Soil, Free Labor, Free Men, Frémont."

The Democrats passed over Pierce and Douglas, who were associated with the Kansas-Nebraska fiasco, to nominate the "consummate doughface," James Buchanan, who had been out of the country for three years as minister to Great Britain. The remnant of the American Party nominated Millard Fillmore. When southern "fire-eaters" threatened succession if Frémont won, conservative northerners rallied behind Buchanan. Carrying only five of sixteen free states, Buchanan won by sweeping the Democratic South, becoming the first president not to win election in both sections.

The cautious Buchanan proved helpless before the sectional whirlwind in Kansas. He went beyond the inflammatory ruling in the Dred Scott case by arguing that even as a state Kansas could not prohibit slavery. As northern migration to Kansas made this a hollow claim, Buchanan blundered further. His new territorial governor, Robert J. Walker, threw out twenty-eight hundred fraudulent proslavery votes in the October 1857 election for the territorial legislature, revealing that Free-Soilers now constituted a large majority. The Kansas constitutional convention then sitting at Lecompton nonetheless produced a proslavery constitution. To satisfy Buchanan's pledge to Walker that any constitution would be submitted to the voters, the Lecompton convention provided for a referendum

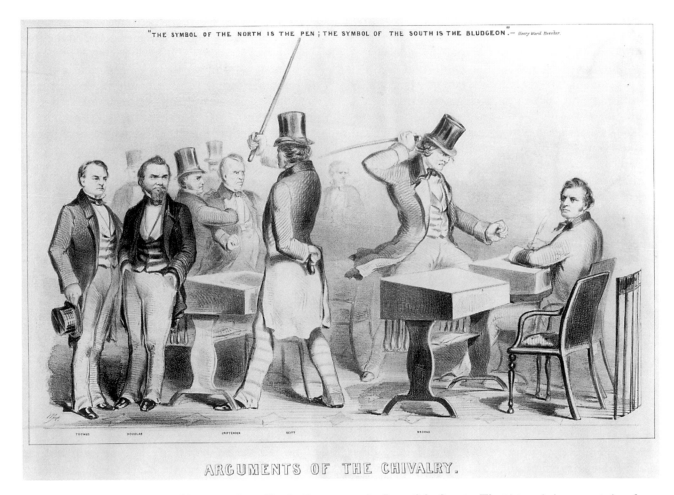

"THE SYMBOL OF THE NORTH IS THE PEN; THE SYMBOL OF THE SOUTH IS THE BLUDGEON." — *Henry Ward Beecher.*

ARGUMENTS OF THE CHIVALRY.

Preston Brooks prepares to use his cane to beat Charles Sumner on the floor of the Senate. The picture is inaccurate insofar as Brooks attacked Sumner from behind. [Library of Congress]

on a single, artfully worded article relating to slavery. Free-state voters boycotted the "Lecompton swindle" and later rejected the whole constitution in a referendum of their own devising. But Buchanan nonetheless decided to submit it to Congress with his endorsement. Because the Lecompton constitution was a mockery of popular sovereignty, Stephen A. Douglas broke with Buchanan and led the fight to defeat it, thus alienating his southern supporters within the Democratic Party and ensuring a divided national convention in 1860.

Any remaining hope for sectional reconciliation was dampened by John Brown's October 1859 raid on Harpers Ferry. "Old Brown" had left a trunk of letters sent to him by prominent people in the North, and after publishing the letters, Virginia authorities pictured him as the agent of a northern conspiracy. When Brown himself was hanged on December 2, northern sympathizers confirmed southerners' suspicions by depicting him as a martyr to the cause of freedom. Senator James Mason of Virginia launched a Senate investigation of the Harpers Ferry incident in an effort to link Brown to the "black Republican" party. Although Republican leaders condemned Brown's attack, the party's platform of 1860 reaffirmed its opposition to the extension of slavery into the territories. In 1860 the Republican candidate, Abraham Lincoln, running against the divided Democrats in a field of four, won the presidency with less than 40 percent of the popular vote and without carrying a single district in the South. Secession followed, creating an unprecedented constitutional crisis that neither Buchanan nor Lincoln could resolve. When on April 12 Confederates fired on the Union garrison at Fort Sumter in Charleston Harbor, Lincoln called for volunteers to suppress a "rebellion."

In the 1830s an expanding electorate had given its allegiance to Andrew Jackson's Democratic Party or his Whig opponents largely on the basis of religious and ethnic affiliations. Local issues like Sabbathbreaking, temperance, and public schools had preoccupied voters. But the question of slavery, as the historian David Potter observed, "structured" and "polarized" sectional quarrels of the antebellum decades, transforming politics from a "process of accommodation to a mode of combat."

Historians have debated the causes of the Civil War endlessly, but many have agreed with Lincoln, who declared during its final days that slavery was, "somehow, the cause of the war."

See also ABOLITION AND ANTISLAVERY MOVEMENTS; AMERICAN ANTI-SLAVERY SOCIETY; BROWN, JOHN; CALIFORNIA; CIVIL WAR, U.S.; COMPROMISE OF 1850; DOUGLAS, STEPHEN A.; DOUGLASS, FREDERICK; DRED SCOTT V. SANDFORD; FUGITIVE SLAVE LAWS, U.S.; GARRISON, WILLIAM LLOYD; KANSAS-NEBRASKA ACT; LINCOLN, ABRAHAM; MISSOURI COMPROMISE; NORTHWEST ORDINANCE.

BIBLIOGRAPHY

ASHWORTH, JOHN. *Slavery, Capitalism, and Politics in the Antebellum Republic*, vol. 1, *Commerce and Compromise, 1820–1850*. 1995.

BIRKNER, MICHAEL, ed. *James Buchanan and the Political Crisis of the 1850s*. 1996.

CARWARDINE, RICHARD J. *Evangelicals and Politics in Antebellum America*. 1993.

FREEHLING, WILLIAM W. *The Road to Disunion*, vol. 1, *Secessionists at Bay, 1776–1854*. 1990.

HOLT, MICHAEL F. *Political Parties and American Political Development from the Age of Jackson to the Age of Lincoln*. 1992.

MILLER, WILLIAM LEE. *Arguing against Slavery: The Great Battle in the United States Congress*. 1996.

MORRISON, MICHAEL A. *Slavery and the American West: The Eclipse of Manifest Destiny and the Coming of the Civil War*. 1997.

POTTER, DAVID. *The Impending Crisis, 1848–1861*. 1976.

STAMPP, KENNETH M. *America in 1857: A Nation on the Brink*. 1990.

STEGMAIER, MARK J. *Texas, New Mexico, and the Compromise of 1850: Boundary Dispute and Sectional Crisis*. 1996.

Robert E. McGlone

Portugal

This entry includes the following articles: Slavery in Portugal; Atlantic Islands Slavery; Colonies and Empire.

Slavery in Portugal

Unlike in its overseas holdings, slavery played a limited role in metropolitan Portugal. It rose to significance in the second half of the fifteenth century and reached its peak in the sixteenth, only to suffer a subsequent decline. While in the sixteenth century slaves played an important role in the Portuguese labor supply and constituted a significant demographic segment of the population, by the eighteenth century slaveholding was reduced to a marginal element of domestic service.

In medieval Portugal slaves were a by-product of the Christian-Muslim conflict. Muslims captured in war or in sea raids were subject to enslavement, which could become permanent if the victims were not ransomed. The same fate awaited Christians captured by the Muslims. The early Portuguese expeditions into the Atlantic reflected this pattern: these were corsairing expeditions intent on raiding non-Christian territories down the African coast. This situation changed soon after the arrival of the Portuguese in sub-Saharan Africa in the 1440s. The military prowess of the newly encountered peoples and the ready availability of slaves for purchase there turned slaving into a commercial pursuit. The influx of slaves into Portugal and its island outposts in the Atlantic increased dramatically, from about 900 slaves a year in the 1450s to 4,500 by 1520.

Portugal experienced an intense labor shortage in the fifteenth century. Slaves constituted a highly appreciated addition to the supply of domestic laborers and other workers. The *Cortes* (parliament) even petitioned the crown to employ slaves in repopulating less desirable areas of the Portuguese countryside, which had been devastated by epidemics and wars. The crown and other principal slave traders, however, preferred to reexport many of the slaves abroad (primarily to Spain and northern Italy), an option which yielded higher and more immediate profits than domestic repopulation projects.

Despite the reexports, a sizable slave population built up in Portugal between 1450 and 1550. It made a profound impression on many foreign visitors, who tended to exaggerate its size, claiming that large parts of Portugal were inhabited by blacks. However, assuming that they constituted about 2.5 percent of the overall population of 1.5 million, there would have been only some 37,500 slaves in Portugal at any given time. In the sixteenth century North African and black African slaves were joined by captives from Brazil, India, Southeast Asia, China, and Japan. Asian slaves, especially Japanese and Chinese, were much more highly regarded than slaves from sub-Saharan Africa, who in turn were valued and trusted more than Muslim slaves from North Africa.

Slaves were heavily concentrated in Lisbon and along the lower Tagus River, with secondary clusters in the urban centers of southern Portugal. Substantially fewer slaves are documented north of the Douro River, with the exception of Porto. Hardly any slaves lived in northeastern Portugal. Most were found in cities or in the vicinity of cities, rather than in the

A former slave market building at Lagos, in the Algarve province of Portugal. [Tony Arruza/Corbis]

countryside. Royal estates were the only significant exception.

Slavery was thus largely an urban matter and, accordingly, the slaves performed urban occupations. Numerous slaves served rich households, both noble and bourgeois. Large slave retinues were a mark of wealth and social status. Household slaves were treated on a par with free servants in terms of duties and apparel. Many masters trusted non-Muslim slaves with weapons, despite legal restrictions. Slaves who had won the favor of their masters were not only well treated and often manumitted but sometimes, if rarely, adopted into the family. The majority of slaves, however, were owned for their labor value and the profit they could bring their owners. A slave, as a rule, was a good investment. The purchase price could be amortized within two years, and skilled slaves amortized even faster. In the first half of the sixteenth century even persons of modest means could afford slaves.

Slaves worked side by side with free people. They were often trained as artisans and tradesmen, to aid their masters or to be hired out. Male slaves worked as clerks, traders, and peddlers. They also manned the barges on the Tagus River, worked in royal foundries and baking ovens, and were engaged in garbage removal and the cleaning of city streets and sewers. Female slaves worked mostly as domestic servants or as street vendors of water, fresh produce, and hot meals. They were also hired out as day-laborers and sometimes forced into prostitution.

Slavery was a matter of legal status. In Portuguese law a slave was a human being who was also a thing, in that he or she could be sold and bought. However, to kill a slave was to commit murder. The rape of a female slave invoked the same penalty as the rape of any other woman. The right of a master to punish a slave was essentially the same as his right to punish non-slave dependents. The church sought to protect the slaves' right to marriage, spiritual well-being, and religious instruction. Any rights that slaves might have, however, were severely curtailed by the fact that slaves could not testify against a free person, except before the Inquisition.

It appears that in the seventeenth and eighteenth centuries the slave population gradually diminished, owing to the combined effect of demographic recovery of the local population, decline in wages, and the increased prices of slaves in competition with Brazil. Slaves from sub-Saharan Africa remained predominant. A subculture specific to black slaves and freedmen developed that took on the form of religious confraternities, cultural events and performances, and a dialect of Portuguese, the *fala da Guiné.* The persistence of the *fala* and its representations in theater and literature in the eighteenth and early nineteenth centuries puts the date of the decline of African slave population in Portugal in some doubt.

In 1761 Marquis de Pombal made the first attempt to abolish slavery in metropolitan Portugal. The impact of his measure is uncertain. In the nineteenth century slavery in Portugal and within its empire had to be abolished step by step from 1816 to 1869, when abolition of slavery finally became law. Opposition to outlawing slavery and the slave trade was driven by African and Brazilian investment interests dependent on slave labor and by nationalist feelings against British abolitionist pressures rather than by significant lingering ownership of slaves in Portugal itself.

See also BRAZIL; SLAVE TRADE; URBAN SLAVERY.

BIBLIOGRAPHY

CAPELA, JOSÉ. *As Burguesias Portuguesas e a Abolição do Tráfico de Escravatura, 1810–1842.* 1979.

———. *Escravatura, Empresa de Saque: O Abolicionismo (1810–1875).* 1974.

ELBL, IVANA. "The Volume of the Early Atlantic Slave Trade, 1450–1521." *Journal of African History* 38 (1997): 31–75.

SAUNDERS, A. C. DE C. M. *A Social History of Black Slaves and Freedmen in Portugal, 1441–1555.* 1982.

TINHORÃO, JOSÉ RAMOS. *Os Negroes em Portugal: Uma Presença Silenciosa.* 1988.

Ivana Elbl

Atlantic Islands Slavery

Through a combination of territorial conquest, navigational expertise and commercial opportunism, the Portuguese pioneered the Atlantic slave trade and plantation slavery during the fifteenth and sixteenth centuries. Exploration along the African coast commenced in earnest after the Portuguese capture of Ceuta (in modern Morocco) from the Moors in 1415. Although militarily successful, the Portuguese never achieved one of the mission's main objectives, control of the Sudanese gold trade. Unable to dislodge Moorish traders from other northwestern African cities, the Portuguese pursued a seaborne strategy to gain direct access to Sudanese gold and proceeded gradually along the northwestern and western African coast, reaching Cape Bojador in 1434, Cape Verde in 1444, Sierra Leone in 1460, the Gold Coast and São Tomé in 1471, Principe in 1472, and the Congo River in 1483. These voyages laid the foundation for Vasco da Gama's rounding of the Cape of Good Hope and his arrival in India in 1498. In 1500 Pedro Álvares Cabral repeated da Gama's voyage, but not before storms pushed his fleet far enough into the western Atlantic to reach a previously unknown land, Brazil.

During their southerly progression along the African coast, the Portuguese captured and purchased Moors and Sudanese, perfecting these practices into a lucrative slave trade. By 1441 Portuguese explorers at the Rio de Ouro were kidnapping Moorish nobles and their Sudanese slaves, holding the nobles for ransom (usually gold or more Sudanese slaves), and selling the Sudanese in the European slave market. Shortly afterward, the Portuguese started bartering with Moorish nobles, exchanging European merchandise for gold and Sudanese slaves. Within a decade, the Portuguese and Moors were trading at a permanent post on Arguim Island.

Reaching the Senegal River opened a new phase in the gold and slave trade; the Portuguese now could deal directly with the Sudanese, thus bypassing Moorish middlemen. African kingdoms commonly welcomed Portuguese traders, prompting the latter to operate trading posts (*feitorias*) along the Sudanese coast. The most significant *feitoria*, the fortified castle of El Mina, erected on the Gold Coast in 1482, attracted African merchants from the interior, who traded gold for a variety of European merchandise and slaves, whom the Portuguese imported from other coastal regions, most notably Benin. Between 1450 and 1500 the total number of West Africans trafficked by the Portuguese, for both the European slave market and the African coastal trade, numbered in the tens of thousands, perhaps even as high as 150,000.

Although modest by later standards, the fifteenth-century slave trade gave the Portuguese vital experience to go along with their African footholds and trading relationships.

Development of the plantation system in the eastern Atlantic coincided with the early Portuguese slave trade. As early as the first decade of the fifteenth century, southern Portugal was exporting sugar to other European markets. The introduction of sugar initiated changes in Portuguese slavery. During the previous century, Portugal's relative abstinence from religious wars had limited the slave population to domestic servants and urban tradesmen. In contrast, sugar plantations employed a more rigorous productive routine, depended on greater numbers of slaves, and relied exclusively on African captives. As the Portuguese expanded sugar production to eastern Atlantic islands, these changes became more pronounced and finely tuned to the demands of emerging capitalist markets.

Three islands figured prominently in Portuguese sugar plantation development. After 1450 the Portuguese on Madeira introduced irrigation methods and sugar mills that greatly improved productivity while increasing the demand for slaves. To meet that demand, the Portuguese imported Guanche slaves from the Canary Islands along with African slaves. By the early seventeenth century, however, sugar production on Madeira was in full decline. Sugar production on Cape Verde had an even shorter life span because of various geographic, climatic, and political factors. During the sixteenth century the island became an important provisioning station for slave ships headed for the Americas. Through São Tomé's development as a plantation island, the Portuguese had achieved a fair degree of standardization in sugar cultivation and refinement based on exhaustive and extensive African slave labor. São Tomé also displayed two by-products common to future Portuguese plantations in Brazil. First, the racial and sexual balance fostered a class composed of free people of color, or mulattoes. Second, a significant fugitive slave population harassed the Portuguese from the 1560s until well after the island's sugar production tailed off during the early seventeenth century.

The Portuguese transplanted their plantation techniques into Brazil during the sixteenth and seventeenth centuries. Moreover, their involvement in the slave trade meshed neatly with Brazilian plantation requirements. Soaring European demand for Brazilian sugar and the unsuitability of Amerindian slave labor led to extensive imports of African slaves after 1570. São Tomé's location, between the Guinean and Central African coasts, encouraged its transition to the main Portuguese slave entrepôt along the African coast. At any time thousands of slaves, gathered from the Congo, Angola, Mozambique, Benin, Guinea, and Senegambia, awaited shipment to the Americas from São Tomé. Their principal Brazilian destinations were Pernambuco, Bahia, and Rio de Janeiro.

Portugal's Atlantic slave trade lasted well into the nineteenth century. Northern European competitors, primarily the Dutch, did expel the Portuguese from El Mina and other points along the Gold Coast and Slave Coast during the mid-seventeenth century. Nevertheless, throughout the following century Portuguese traders from Bahia continued to acquire slaves from Whydah and other points along the Slave Coast. Legal abolition of Portugal's slave trade in 1836 foreshadowed the activity's demise, although some Portuguese dealt in the Atlantic trade for nearly two decades afterward.

See also AFRICA; BRAZIL; PLANTATIONS; SLAVE TRADE.

BIBLIOGRAPHY

BLAKE, JOHN WILLIAM. *West Africa Quest for God and Gold, 1454–1578.* 1977.
BOXER, C. R. *Race Relations in the Portuguese Colonial Empire, 1415–1825.* 1963.
———. *The Portuguese Seaborne Empire, 1415–1825.* 1969.
CURTIN, PHILIP D. *The Rise and Fall of the Plantation Complex: Essays in Atlantic History.* 1990.
SCHWARTZ, STUART B. *Sugar Plantations in the Formation of Brazilian Society Bahia, 1550–1835.* 1985.
VOGT, JOHN. *Portuguese Rule on the Gold Coast, 1469–1682.* 1979.

John J. Crocitti

Colonies and Empire

Slavery and slave ownership played an important role in most areas of the Portuguese overseas empire, from its beginnings in the fifteenth century to the official abolition of slavery and the slave trade in the nineteenth century. On the economic level slaves were sources of profit and labor; on the social level they helped to define the owners' social status, prestige, and power.

Some Portuguese outposts and colonies focused primarily on export and reexport of slaves. The crown trading outposts in West Africa, the settlers of Cape Verde Islands, and the Portuguese traders in Kongo and Angola supplied the Atlantic slave trade, whereas Mozambique exported slaves throughout the Indian Ocean, Southeastasia, and East Asia and to Brazil in the nineteenth century. Most slaves were obtained through trade, except for those coming from Portuguese holdings in North Africa, who were often prisoners of war or victims of Portuguese raids. The same

was true, to some degree, of slaves acquired in West Central Africa.

The export and reexport of slaves created elaborate infrastructures and a demand for services that involved not only Portuguese expatriates but also a complex network of Luso-African and African agents and independent traders, who themselves used slaves. The labor demands created by the necessity to transport, house, and feed the transiting slaves on the one hand, and to cater to the needs of the colonial settlers and trading personnel on the other, resulted in the rapid growth of resident slave populations in all slave-exporting outposts. Slaves came to outnumber free residents by a factor of ten and more, except in the North African locations, where the chronic hostilities demanded the prevalence of a free soldiery of Portuguese origin.

Portuguese insular societies in the African Atlantic region, particularly the main islands of the Cape Verde archipelago and São Tomé and Príncipe, became dependent on slaves from the very beginning, in terms of both the domestic economy and the export trade. São Tomé, in addition to its supplier role in the Atlantic slave trade, became a heavy consumer of slave labor in the sixteenth century because of its booming sugar plantations. In the seventeenth century, competition from Brazilian sugar undermined the São Tomé economy but not its dependence on slavery.

Unlike the islands in the tropical African Atlantic, the temperate Madeiras and Azores did not develop a lasting dependence on slavery. The slave population of the Azores was insignificant and derived primarily from the Canaries and North Africa. The Madeiras also showed a pronounced preference for slaves from these two nearby areas, although Madeira, during its sugar boom in the late fifteenth and first half of the sixteenth century, imported slaves from sub-Saharan Africa as well. Madeira's sugar production was exceptional for the period in that it did not rely heavily on slave labor. Most Madeiran slaves were employed in urban settings as domestic servants. As in Portugal, slave ownership declined in Madeira in the seventeenth and eighteenth centuries in favor of wage labor.

The most important slave-importing parts of the Portuguese overseas empire were Brazil and the Asian outposts. Of the two areas, Brazil was by far the more significant player as a result of the essential productive role slaves played in its plantation and mining economy. While enslaved native people filled some of the labor needs of Portuguese settlers in Brazil until 1570 or so, the massively growing sugar plantations—and in the eighteenth century the gold and diamond mines of the interior—created a voracious demand for imported slave labor, drawn largely from Angola.

Victims of slave hunters are marched in chains toward the West African coast, probably to be sold to Portuguese slave traders. [Library of Congress/Corbis]

Brazil absorbed more than 40 percent of the ten million African slaves who crossed the Atlantic in the four centuries of the slave trade's duration and 60 percent in the nineteenth century, when it was the main American purchaser of slaves. African slaves were the defining factor in the demographic makeup of colonial Brazil, and slavery was one of the key institutions that shaped it.

In the Indian Ocean basin slaves were important both as a commodity in Luso-Asian trade and as a source of labor in Portuguese outposts. The Portuguese temporarily stationed or permanently settled in Asia possessed large numbers of slaves. The households of the rich and powerful were served by hundreds of slaves, and even the moderately well-off could afford to own dozens of Africans and Asians. These slaves performed primarily domestic and social tasks, and their backgrounds showed much greater racial, ethnic, and cultural diversity than in other parts of the Portuguese seaborne empire.

Slavery played three distinct but interconnected roles in the Portuguese overseas empire: it was a significant source of commercial profits, a key source of labor, and one of the sources of social power. Where the three functions were closely integrated, slavery

proved to be very enduring—this was particularly true in West Central Africa and Brazil. The acquisition, transport, and employment of slaves continued to provide one of the principal links among Portugal's far-flung colonial territories until well into the nineteenth century. Even after the abolition of most slaving in the 1850s, there remained a pervasive sense of Portuguese cultural—if not also racial—superiority. In the modern Portuguese empire wealth and power remained largely in the hands of the heirs of the masters. Slavery and slave trade thus left a deep-rooted legacy.

See also BRAZIL; SLAVE TRADE; SOUTHEAST ASIA.

BIBLIOGRAPHY

BOXER, CHARLES. *Portuguese Society in the Tropics: The Municipal Councils of Goa, Macao, Bahia, and Luanda, 1510–1800.* 1965.

CAPELA, JOSÉ. *Escravatura, Empresa de Saque: O Abolicionismo (1810–1875).* 1974.

CLARENCE-SMITH, GERVASE. *The Third Portuguese Empire, 1825–1975: A Study in Economic Imperialism.* 1985.

DUNCAN, T. BENTLEY. *Atlantic Islands: Madeira, the Azores, and the Cape Verde Islands in Seventeenth-Century.* 1972.

GARFIELD, ROBERT. *A History of São Tomé Island, 1470–1655: A Key to Guinea.* 1992.

MARCÍLIO, MARIA LUIZA. "The Population of Colonial Brazil." In *The Cambridge History of Latin America*, vol. 2, *Colonial Latin America*, edited by Leslie Bethell. 1989.

MILLER, JOSEPH C. *The Way of Death: Merchant Capitalism and the Angolan Slave Trade, 1730–1830*. 1988.

PINTO, JEANETTE. *Slavery in Portuguese India, 1510–1842*. 1992.

RUSSELL-WOOD, A. J. R. *The Black Man in Slavery and Freedom in Colonial Brazil*. 1982.

THORNTON, JOHN. *Africa and Africans in the Making of the Atlantic World, 1400–1680*. 1992.

VIERA, ALBERTO. "Slaves with or without Sugar: Madeira's Case." In *Slaves with or without Sugar: Registers of the International Seminar*. 1996.

Ivana Elbl

Prehistoric Societies

Although slavery was common to many early human societies, its precise origins remain obscure. Most likely, the archetypical slave was, as Gerda Lerner (1986) has argued, a female forcibly incorporated into her captor's household. But the rise of slavery may also have hinged on factors connected to the "neolithic revolution": the shift, some ten thousand years ago, from hunting and gathering—the prevailing mode of production for most of human history—to a new form of subsistence, agriculture.

While agriculture can support many more people per acre than hunting and gathering, this increased productivity comes at a cost: heightened inputs of labor to clear and plant fields, to harvest crops, and to watch over flocks of livestock. In the face of such needs, the bargain at the heart of slavery—sparing a captive's life in exchange for the promise to serve his or her master—would have acquired far greater value. Slaves could have met the increased demand for labor either by working directly in their masters' fields or, if the first slaves were indeed women, by bearing children, enlarging the labor pool.

Another reason for the expansion of slavery during the neolithic revolution may have been the growth in warfare that occurred at this time. Although warfare itself probably predated agriculture, farming created new stockpiles of goods, providing fresh reasons for combat. Hunter-gatherers rarely store food for more than a few days; rather, they exploit whatever natural resources are most prevalent during a given season. Agriculturalists, on the other hand, utilize a far narrower spectrum of foodstuffs. Because of the resulting need to make harvests last for much longer, the adoption of agriculture is signaled in the archaeological record by the construction of granaries, corrals, and other storage systems. Such surpluses would have proven alluring targets for raiders, who by seizing crops and animals could reap the benefits of a season of labor without doing any work themselves. Increased raiding would, in turn, have created more opportunities for the taking of captives, who could then be enslaved.

Most significantly, the neolithic revolution doubtless provided the model of domination that lay at the heart of slavery. A key component in the rise of agriculture was the domestication of sheep, goats, cattle, pigs, and other wild animals—a process that required pastoralists to assert direct daily control over often uncooperative animals. To achieve this control, humans developed a whole tool kit of whips, chains, collars, and brands. First used on animals, these same mechanisms were later applied to enslaved humans.

There was more to the process of enslavement, however, than simply the transfer of such techniques from animals to humans. Slavery also pivoted upon the recategorization of humans as animal-like "others." Indeed, the bestialization of the enslaved was a recurrent theme in slave societies. Aristotle, for instance, wrote of the ox as the "poor man's slave," observing that "the use which is made of the slave diverges but little from the use made of tame animals." Likewise, in the American south, apologists for slavery argued that blacks were a separate species, less than truly human. In these and similar cases, the logic was the same: only by implying that the enslaved were akin to beasts could slave owners justify treating fellow human beings like domestic animals.

See also CHAINS AND RESTRAINTS; PERSPECTIVES ON SLAVERY.

BIBLIOGRAPHY

JACOBY, KARL. "Slaves by Nature? Domestic Animals and Human Slaves." *Slavery and Abolition* 15 (April 1994): 89–99.

LERNER, GERDA. *The Creation of Patriarchy*. 1986.

Karl Jacoby

Prices of Slaves

Scholars have gathered prices of slaves from a variety of sources, including censuses, probate records, plantation accounts, slave traders' accounts, and proceedings of slave auctions. The largest source of information is a data set for New Orleans compiled by Robert Fogel and Stanley Engerman, but the structure of slave prices has been analyzed for many societies.

Throughout history, the price of a slave depended on two things: the characteristics of the individual slave and conditions in the slave market. Important individual features included age, sex, childbearing capacity for females, physical condition, temperament, and skills. In addition, the supply of slaves, life expectancy, costs of capture and transportation, demand for products produced by slaves, and seasonal factors helped determine market conditions and therefore prices.

Prices for both male and female slaves tended to follow similar life-cycle patterns. Prices rose through puberty as productivity increased. In nineteenth-century New Orleans, for example, prices peaked at about age twenty-two for females and age twenty-five for males. After the peak age, prices declined slowly for a time, then fell off rapidly as slaves' ability to work disappeared. Girls cost more than boys, up to age sixteen in Brazil, Cuba, and the United States and up to age twenty in Peru. The sexes then switched places in terms of value. Women were worth 90 to 95 percent as much as men in Cuba, 80 to 90 percent as much in the United States and the West Indies, and 70 to 80 percent as much in Brazil.

Selling Females by the pound.   Page 88.

A young slave sits on one side of a balance as slave traders put weights on the other side to determine her weight and price. [Library of Congress/Corbis]

One characteristic in particular set females apart: their ability to bear children. In the United States, fertile females commanded a premium. But in medieval Italy, a man who impregnated a slave had to pay her master compensation because of the high likelihood that she would die in childbirth. The bond between mother and child also proved important in a different way: people sometimes paid a premium for intact families.

Besides age and sex, skills helped determine a slave's price. The premium paid for skilled workers interacted with mortality rates and rates of depreciation for different characteristics. The United States had a relatively low slave mortality rate, and skilled workers sold for a premium of 40 to 55 percent. Slave owners in areas with higher death rates could not reap as large a benefit from their skilled workers. In Peru, the premium for a skilled slave was about 35 percent; in Cuba, it was about 10 to 20 percent. Because the human capital associated with strength drops off more quickly as people age than the human capital associated with skills and training, prices for unskilled slaves in the Spanish colonies also fell more rapidly than prices for skilled slaves.

Physical traits, mental capabilities, and other qualities contributed to price differentials as well. Crippled and chronically ill slaves sold for a steep discount. Slaves who proved troublesome—runaways, thieves, layabouts, drunks, slow learners, and the like—also sold for lower prices. Taller slaves cost more, perhaps because height indicates nutritional status. In New Orleans, light-skinned females (who were more popular as concubines) sold for a 5 percent premium.

Prices of slaves fluctuated with market conditions as well as with individual characteristics. The supply mattered. Prices dropped dramatically in fourth-century Egypt when the sale of babies became legal. In the Old World, prices rose sharply after the Black Death more than decimated the population, particularly the servile portion. In the United States slave prices fell around 1800, as the Haitian revolution sparked a movement of slaves into the southern states. Less than a decade later, slave prices climbed when the international slave trade was abolished, cutting off legal external supplies.

Demand also helped determine prices. In most slave societies, the demand for slaves derived from the demand for the commodities and services that slaves provided. Changes in slaves' occupations and variability in prices for slave-produced goods therefore created movements in slave prices. For example, a slave cost about a year's keep in early Athens, but prices rose significantly as the use of slaves expanded to include managerial and civil-service work. As slaves replaced increasingly expensive indentured servants in the New World, their prices went up. In the period from 1748 to 1775, slave prices in British America rose nearly 30 percent. As cotton prices fell in the 1840s, slave prices in the South also fell. But as the demand for cotton and tobacco grew after about 1850, the price of slaves increased. The connection between commodity and slave prices is not confined to the American South. Some scholars have speculated that slavery was abolished in Cuba because sugar prices had fallen too low to make it worthwhile.

Demand sometimes had to do with the time of year a sale took place For example, slave prices in the New Orleans market were 10 to 20 percent higher in January than in September. Why? September—harvest time—was a busy period for planters: the opportunity cost of their time was relatively high. Prices had to be relatively low for them to be willing to travel to New Orleans during the harvest.

One additional demand factor loomed large in determining slave prices: the expectation of continued legal slavery. As the United States Civil War progressed, slave prices dropped dramatically because people could not be sure that the peculiar institution would survive. In New Orleans prime male slaves sold on average for $1381 in 1861 and for $1116 in 1862. Burgeoning inflation meant that real prices fell considerably more. By the war's end slaves sold for a small fraction of their price in 1860.

See also ECONOMICS OF SLAVERY; UNITED STATES.

BIBLIOGRAPHY

FINLEY, MOSES, ed. *Classical Slavery*. 1987.

FOGEL, ROBERT. *Without Consent or Contract*. 1989.

FOGEL, ROBERT, and STANLEY ENGERMAN. *Time on the Cross*. 1974.

FRIEDMAN, GERALD, and RICHARD MANNING. "The Rent and Hire of Slaves." In *Without Consent or Contract: Evidence and Methods*, edited by Robert Fogel, Ralph Galantine, and Richard Manning. 1992.

GALENSON, DAVID. "The Atlantic Slave Trade and the Barbados Market, 1673–1723." *Journal of Economic History* 42 (1982): 491.

KOTLIKOFF, LAURENCE. "The Structure of Slave Prices in New Orleans, 1804–1862." *Economic Inquiry* 17 (1979): 496.

MARGO, ROBERT, and RICHARD STECKEL. "The Heights of American Slaves: New Evidence on Slave Nutrition and Health." *Social Science History* 6 (1982): 51.

MORENO FRAGINALS, MANUEL, HERBERT KLEIN, and STANLEY ENGERMAN. "The Level and Structure of Slave Prices on Cuban Plantations in the Mid Nineteenth Century: Some Comparative Perspectives." *American Historical Review* 88 (1993): 1201.

NEWLAND, CARLOS, and MARIA JESUS SAN SEGUNDO. "Human Capital and Other Determinants of the Price Life Cycle of a Slave: Peru and La Plata in the Eighteenth Century." *Journal of Economic History* 56 (1996): 694.

SCHMITZ, MARK, and DONALD SCHAEFER. "Paradox Lost: Westward Expansion and Slave Prices Before the Civil War." *Journal of Economic History* 41 (1981): 402.

Jenny Bourne Wahl

Prigg v. Pennsylvania (1842)

Prigg v. Pennsylvania was the first Supreme Court decision to interpret the constitutionality and meaning of the Fugitive Slave Act of 1793. The case involved four Marylanders, including Edward Prigg, who in 1837 entered Pennsylvania and seized Margaret Morgan and her children, claiming them as fugitive slaves. A justice of the peace denied their request for certificates of removal under Pennsylvania's 1826 personal liberty law because there was strong evidence that Morgan was in fact a free black. Without any legal authority, Prigg and his companions then removed the Morgans to Maryland. Pennsylvania convicted Prigg of kidnapping under the same law of 1826, and Prigg appealed to the United States Supreme Court. While the appeal was pending, Morgan's owner sold her and her children to slave traders, who removed them to the deep South.

In a decision that was overwhelmingly favorable to the South, the Supreme Court overturned Prigg's conviction. Speaking for the Court, Justice Joseph Story held that (1) the federal Fugitive Slave Law of 1793 was constitutional; (2) laws in the free states that interfered with the law of 1793 were unconstitutional; (3) the fugitive slave clause in the United States Constitution gave masters a common-law right to capture a fugitive slave without complying with the federal law of 1793, if such a capture could be done without a breach of the peace; and (4) all state judges and other officials ought to enforce the federal law, but the national government could not force them to do so because the federal government had no power to require state officials to act.

Chief Justice Roger B. Taney concurred with the result in *Prigg*, but he objected to Story's conclusion that state judges did not have to enforce the Fugitive Slave Act. He believed that state judges should be compelled to enforce the law. In his concurrence (which read more like a dissent) Taney misrepresented Story's opinion by claiming that it prohibited state officials from enforcing the Fugitive Slave Law, when in fact Story had actually urged state officials to enforce the law, though conceding that the federal government lacked the power to require them to do so.

Throughout the North judges and legislatures ignored Justice Story's admonition to the free states to cooperate in the return of fugitive slaves. Soon after this case some northern judges refused to hear cases involving fugitive slaves; some state legislatures also prohibited state officials from aiding in the return of fugitive slaves and from using state facilities for incarcerating alleged fugitive slaves or holding hearings over their status. Story's son claimed that his father's opinion was an antislavery decision because it allowed the free states to refuse to participate in fugitive slave cases. However, in private correspondence Story urged Congress to create federal commissioners to enforce various federal laws, including the 1793 act. In the Fugitive Slave Act of 1850 Congress adopted Story's recommendation, creating a system of federal commissioners to help slave owners recover their runaways.

See also FUGITIVE SLAVE LAWS, U.S.; LAW; TANEY, ROGER B.

BIBLIOGRAPHY

FINKELMAN, PAUL. "*Prigg v. Pennsylvania* and Northern State Courts: Anti-Slavery Use of a Pro-Slavery Decision." *Civil War History* 25 (1979): 5–35.

———. "Story Telling on the Supreme Court: *Prigg v. Pennsylvania* and Justice Joseph Story's Judicial Nationalism." *Supreme Court Review* 1994 (1995): 247–294.

Paul Finkelman

Profit

See Economics of Slavery; Prices of Slaves.

Prosser, Gabriel

See Gabriel.

Prostitution

Prostitution is promiscuous sexual intercourse in return for payment. Prostitutes can be of either sex and of any race or creed. Anyone can become a prostitute; even small children serve pedophiles. No special training is required, although some prostitutes are taught to make themselves alluring and are given pornographic literature by their procurers.

Opinions differ radically as to whether or not prostitution itself is a form of slavery. Some, particularly feminist groups, believe that it is sexual slavery and violates women's rights. Against this extreme view, there is the argument that if prostitutes are voluntarily recruited, remain in prostitution of their own volition, and control their own earnings, they are free; but if they are forcibly recruited or are kept against their will and do not control their earnings, they are slaves. The great difficulty is to draw a hard and fast line between forced and voluntary prostitution. It can be argued that all child prostitutes are slaves, since they cannot control their lives. In the case of adults, it seems logical to define as slaves only those subjected to physical or psychological force. However, the boundaries are not always clear. Should the drug addict exploited by a supplier, or a woman who is psychologically dependent on her pimp, be classed as a victim of force? These problems are an ongoing debate. However, there is general agreement that trafficking in prostitutes against their will is akin to slave trading.

Whether forced for not, prostitution differs from classic or chattel slavery in that the victims are recruited only for their sexual services. They are legally free and theoretically can leave when they wish. They are not property and cannot be bought or sold. Their status is neither lifelong nor hereditary.

Persons in forced prostitution can be of either sex. The majority, however, are female. Most of the males are children or adolescents. Quantification is impossible, not only because the practice is illegal but because between prostitutes who are virtual slaves and those who are free, there are unknown numbers in various degrees of servitude.

Prostitutes are recruited in a variety of ways. In the cases most like classic slavery, they are kidnapped and then sold. They may be held as prisoners and subjected to various forms of "softening up," including physical and mental abuse and even forced impregnation, until they cooperate. Many children are sold into prostitution or given to creditors by poverty-stricken or simply greedy parents or guardians. Some prostitutes are fraudulently recruited, particularly for work away from home or in a foreign country. They may be promised well-paid jobs that do not materialize or find that they are in debt, as they have to repay their fares. They may even be married by a procurer posing as a suitor. They may be married by mail order, only to find on arrival that they are forced into prostitution. At the other end of the scale, many prostitutes enter the profession willingly, lured by visions of glamour or easy money, and then fall into the hands of exploiters.

There are many reasons why people cannot escape from forced prostitution. Frequently they are intimidated by threats of beating, death, disfigurement, or prosecution for debt. Many become ensnared in an escalating cycle of debt. They are charged exorbitant sums for transportation, clothes, food, and accommodation. These debts may be passed from creditor to creditor; thus in practice, if not in theory, the prostitute is sold. Some prostitutes become psychologically dependent on their exploiters or depend upon them for drugs. Prostitutes sent to work in a foreign country may find that they have been brought in as illegal aliens, subject to imprisonment or deportation if they go to the authorities. Even legal immigrants fear deportation if they are found to be prostitutes. Some prostitutes accept their situation because they have dependent families. Others are reluctant to return home for fear of ostracism or rejection, in view of the odium in which prostitution is held. Those sold by their parents sometimes feel it is their filial duty to work until they can repay their purchase price—a time that may never come.

Historically, prostitution, called "the world's oldest profession," has always existed in some form, if only on a small scale. But it has proliferated in the last two centuries, with the spread of urbanization, poverty, and unemployment; with more women working outside the home; with the greater mobility of labor; with the increase in migrant labor; and with the toleration of pornography. These factors have also provided new opportunities for the exploitation of prostitutes. Poor women, for instance, may be tricked into pros-

titution in migrant labor camps. Sex tourism allows pedophiles and sexual deviants to find gratification aboard, where prosecution is less likely. Dealers import mail-order brides. Procurers offer impoverished families money for their children, or creditors take children in lieu of payment. The possibilities are endless.

Laws to suppress or control prostitution, passed in response to public outrage or to protect clients, have had the unforeseen effect of increasing forced prostitution. Whether states outlaw all prostitution, or whether they allow licensed, medically inspected brothels but criminalize soliciting on the streets, the impact has been to make prostitutes more dependent on procurers, pimps, or brothel keepers to find them a clientele, provide them with necessities, and protect them from harassment or arrest by the police. As a result, prostitution has become more and more of a business enterprise, often controlled by organized crime operating internationally as well as nationally.

Treaties for the suppression of the trade in females for prostitution, then generally called the "white slave trade," were signed in 1904 and 1910. The League of Nations appointed a permanent committee dedi-

Several women give testimony to police officials that a 1926 beauty contest was really a plot to force the girls into prostitution. [UPI/Corbis-Bettmann]

cated to suppressing prostitution, negotiated further treaties in 1921 and 1933, and drafted a more comprehensive treaty in 1937. In 1949 the United Nations consolidated and extended these earlier agreements in the Convention for the Suppression of the Traffic in Persons and the Exploitation of the Prostitution of Others. This convention does not prohibit prostitution as such, but to the end of rehabilitating prostitutes, it commits signatories to punish anyone who procures or entices a person into prostitution or who owns or runs a brothel or traffics in prostitutes. Success has been very limited. There is no mechanism for enforcing the treaty, or even for monitoring. Many countries have not ratified it. Many of those that have ratified it have not enforced it or have enforced it only selectively. In some developing nations prostitution has been encouraged as a legitimate source of foreign currency, brought in by sex tourism or by remittances from prostitutes working abroad.

Despite active propaganda from nongovernment organizations—notably the International Abolitionist Federation, the Coalition Against Trafficking in Women, and the Global Alliance Against Trafficking in Women—as well as the efforts of Interpol, despite changes in the laws of some countries, and despite a number of prosecutions, forced prostitution and trafficking in prostitutes continue to flourish. The large profits are a powerful incentive; and the involvement of organized crime, the complicity of officials, and the difficulty of getting evidence from frightened victims all make it hard to secure convictions. Added to this, there is no consensus among reforming groups, or among governments, as to the most effective means of combating prostitution. Some organizations, such as the Dutch prostitutes' union (the Red Thread), believe that legalizing prostitution, pimping, and brothel-keeping will decrease exploitation and give prostitutes the same protection as other workers. Steps in this direction in Sweden, however, resulted in active marketing of prostitution without decreasing the numbers of prostitutes or improving their lot. Feminists see legalizing prostitution as a step backward in the movement to improve the social and economic position of women. Many people believe that the exploitation of prostitutes can be ended only by a restructuring of class and gender systems to end inequalities. This issue is inextricably tied to larger questions of social and economic reform as well as to changes in attitudes toward sex and individual freedom.

See also COMFORT WOMEN IN WORLD WAR II; CONCUBINAGE; GENDER RELATIONS; SEXUAL EXPLOITATION.

BIBLIOGRAPHY

BINDMAN, JO. *Redefining Prostitution as Sex Work on the International Agenda.* 1997.

CONFERENCE ON TRAFFIC IN PERSONS. *Conclusions.* Utrecht and Maastricht, 15–19 November 1994.

ENNEW, J. *Children in Especially Difficult Circumstances: The Sexual Exploitation of Children, Prostitution and Pornography.* 1997.

EUROPEAN COMMISSION TO THE COUNCIL AND THE EUROPEAN PARLIAMENT ON THE TRAFFICKING IN WOMEN FOR THE PURPOSES OF SEXUAL EXPLOITATION. *Communication.* 1996.

INTERNATIONAL ABOLITIONIST FEDERATION. *Reports.* Annual.

UN COMMISSION ON HUMAN RIGHTS. *Annual Reports* of the Working Group of Experts on Contemporary Forms of Slavery of the Sub-commission on the Prevention of Discrimination and Protection of Minorities. 1976–1996.

WIJERS, MARJAN, and LIN LAP-CHEW. *Trafficking in Women: Forced Labour and Slavery-like Practices in Marriage, Domestic Labour and Prostitution.* 1997.

Suzanne Miers

Protestantism

See Bible; Christianity. *See also entries on specific Protestant denominations.*

Psychology

Probing the psychology of slavery and slaveholding deeply disturbs the twentieth-century mind. Psychoanalysis arouses suspicion, and the means for studying the inner workings of the mind are admittedly speculative. Moreover, critics contend that proposing any slave pathologies risks confirming racial prejudices best allowed to disappear. In any event, with few exceptions, the emotional dimension has received scant historical treatment.

Relations between master and slave, however, underline the corrupting effects of absolute power and powerlessness. As the sociologist Orlando Patterson (1982) has observed, slavery has always consisted of "social death." While slaveholders received honor in the public arena and abject obedience in their households, by whim or circumstance their human property could be rendered nameless, kinless, penniless, defenseless, hopeless, and reliant solely on an owner's mercy. In his *Notes on the State of Virginia* (1987, p. 162), Thomas Jefferson remarked, "The whole commerce between master and slave is a perpetual exercise of the most boisterous passions, the most unremitting despotism on the one part, and degrading submissions on the other." He added, "The parent storms, the child looks on, catches the lineaments of wrath, puts on the same airs" in tormenting slaves, and develops lifetime habits of tyranny stamped "with odious peculiarities." Even so, a myth of masterly constraint and rationality took hold, and despite emancipation, this popular legend of patriarchal benignity flourished in the American mind, culminating in romantic screen representations, notably *Jezebel* (1938) and *Gone with the Wind* (1939).

In subsequent twentieth-century history, however, the interrelationship of master and slave psychology became palpably obvious in the revelations of the Nazi Holocaust. At Auschwitz and other concentration camps, Nazi guards treated their prisoners as vermin to be exterminated or worked them to death. Bearing these atrocities in mind, Stanley Elkins in *Slavery* (1959) argued that utter helplessness, intensified by the brutalities of the middle passage, would have distorted the mental well-being of the African slave—just as unrestrained power twisted the master's mind. Elkins introduced a typological figure, the amoral, obsequious "Sambo." Outraged by the insulting image, African-American and liberal white intellectuals repudiated his findings altogether. Indeed, Elkins wrote before recent psychiatric work on mental depression and post-traumatic stress—work that has analyzed the despair and paralysis of will of people who are stripped of their former identity. Still, Elkins justly stressed the tragedy of psychological dependency. That phenomenon was neither racial nor peculiar to American slavery but is embedded in the structure of power itself. In 1977, a study of nursing home patients found that those denied normal ways to control their environment adopted "learned helplessness" (Friedan, 1993, pp. 88–90). With regard to other slave societies, a British traveler reported that bondsmen in Africa "cringe up and place their hands on each side of their master's hand" to signify submissiveness (Patterson, p. 83).

Historians have preferred to emphasize self-assertive options—resistance and rebellion. But unless the social order were to collapse, as, for instance, during the U.S. Civil War, rational slaves would recognize the hopelessness of those choices. The determination, vigilance, numbers, and armament of their oppressors were ample deterrents. Ritual behavior provided a more dependable way to survive and gain an advantage: obey orders in seeming compliance but without necessarily meeting the spirit of the task. The historian Eugene Genovese (1974) argues for a subtle interchange between master and slave of accommodation and passive yet stubborn resistance. Slave parents taught their young how to navigate in the shoals of unpredictability, an exercise that made prevarication a virtue and an articulate tongue a prized talent. But anger, frustration, and humiliation—repressed out of fear—had to find an outlet. Sometimes these emotions erupted in violence against fellow slaves or prompted

acts of irresponsibility that also served as sabotage. In positive ways, too, the slave found self-identity in family and communal ties, special skills, pride in African ancestry, deeds of undetected defiance, creation and recital of song and story, and even slave work well performed. Nonetheless, slaves had to be watchful for signs of peril. They often wore a mask, as it were, that observers found impenetrable. As the historian Moses I. Finley suggested, "Nothing is more elusive than the psychology of the slave" (1983, p. 108). This assessment is likely to remain true in the future.

See also FAMILY, U.S.; STEREOTYPES, SLAVISH.

BIBLIOGRAPHY

ELKINS, STANLEY. *Slavery: A Problem in American Institutional and Intellectual Life.* 1959.
FINLEY, MOSES I. *Economy and Society in Ancient Greece.* Edited by Brent D. Shaw and Richard P. Saller. 1982.
FRIEDAN, BETTY. *The Fountain of Age.* 1993.
GENOVESE, EUGENE D. *Roll, Jordan, Roll: The World the Slaves Made.* 1974.
JEFFERSON, THOMAS. *Notes on the State of Virginia.* Edited by William Peden. 1964.
PATTERSON, ORLANDO. *Slavery and Social Death: A Comparative Study.* 1982.
WYATT-BROWN, BERTRAM. "The Mask of Obedience: Male Slave Psychology in the Old South." *American Historical Review* 93 (December 1988):1228–1255.

Bertram Wyatt-Brown

Public Works

Unfree labor has been intimately connected with public works projects from ancient times. In ancient Babylon the vast bulk of work on the irrigation canals and levees was accomplished by corvée (forced) labor, as was the case in ancient China, India, Egypt, and the other regimes that Karl Wittfogel labeled "hydraulic societies"—that is, economies that were primarily dependent on extensive control of limited water resources and that had to be organized socially to provide the extensive labor required for the construction and maintenance of the physical structures necessary for the control of these water resources. Slaves were also used in public works construction, but on a limited basis and primarily in the larger cities.

Ancient Egypt in the Old and Middle Kingdoms, and to a lesser extent in the New Kingdom, relied on the corvée labor of peasants not only for the building of the irrigation structures that were essential for the proper utilization of the Nile's fructifying overflow but also for the creation of religious and governmental structures—for example, the pyramids, temple complexes, and royal tombs.

In ancient Greece many city-states, such as Athens, maintained a core of slaves owned by the government, who were cared for out of public funds and who were used in the construction of public works such as temples, courts, the agora, and amphitheaters. Sometimes such slaves were purchased from private sources, but in general they were prisoners of war captured by Athenian forces.

In the Roman Empire private contractors were regularly entrusted with the construction of roads and aqueducts. These contractors kept numerous slaves for use in such construction, and in the case of larger-than-usual contracts, they might be expected to buy or rent more slaves from other contractors, from slave markets, or even from agricultural sources.

In some societies where the corvée was common, a special levy of peasants might also be used for extraordinary public works projects. The creation of the Great Wall of China and the establishment of a new Russian capital in St. Petersburg are two of the best-known historical examples of projects that used these special levies.

In the second half of the third century B.C., the Ch'in emperor of China, Shih Huang Ti, began the construction of the Great Wall of China, which was designed to protect the northern provinces from raiding nomads. Levies of peasants from the northern regions of China, were pressed into forced labor, building the wall in its earliest configurations. In the first half of the fifteenth century A.D., under the Ming dynasty, the wall was largely rebuilt, taking on most of the characteristics one encounters in the late twentieth century. This massive reconstruction project was also accomplished by forced levies of peasant labor.

In 1703 Peter the Great, Romanov czar of Russia, decreed the creation of a new capital on the Baltic as a "window to the West." The construction of this new city—St. Petersburg—required the filling in of swamps and tidal pools and the construction of some thirty-five thousand buildings, ranging from elaborate palaces, monasteries, and cathedrals to humble homes. Levies of peasant labor were conscripted from large areas of Russia to work on this project. In the cold, damp climate of the site of the city, the death rates were astonishingly high.

Wherever slavery or any other form of unfree labor has existed, governments have claimed the right to employ that forced labor for the needs of the state—in a certain manner and under certain conditions. In France, up to the time of the Revolution, peasants were required to work on the repair of the roads under the corvée system. Slaves in the New World were sometimes rented and sometimes commandeered for work on public projects, especially in time of war. During the U.S. Civil War, for example, Confederate slaves were often employed to build fortifications and dig trenchworks and to load and drive supply wagons for the army.

In the postbellum South, even into the middle decades of the twentieth century, convicts organized in chain gangs made up an important source of labor for road construction and maintenance. The European colonial powers often employed corvée labor in their public works in their transmarine empires. Practices varied, of course, regarding the conscription of colonial labor for public works, but the British and French imperial authorities tended to use already existing customs and the authority of native rulers for the legal framework.

See also ANCIENT GREECE; ANCIENT ROME; CHINA; EGYPT; RUSSIA; UNITED STATES.

BIBLIOGRAPHY

BILLINGTON, JAMES H. *The Icon and the Axe: An Interpretive History of Russian Culture.* 1970.
DANDAMAEV, MOHAMMAD A. *Slavery in Babylonia—from Nabopolassar to Alexander the Great (626–331 B.C.).* Translated by Victoria A. Powell and edited by Marvin A. Powell and David B. Weisberg. 1984.
LATOURETTE, KENNETH SCOTT. *The Chinese: Their History and Culture,* 4th ed. 1964.
WITTFOGEL, KARL A. *Oriental Despotism: A Comparative Study of Total Power.* 1981

Patrick M. O'Neil

Punishment

See Discipline and Punishment.

Puritans

Puritans were English Protestants of the late sixteenth and seventeenth centuries who sought to reform the Church of England along Calvinist lines. Puritans founded and led several New England colonies in the seventeenth and eighteenth centuries, and they participated in the colonization of the Chesapeake, Bermuda, the West Indian sugar islands, and the short-lived Providence Island colony off the Mosquito Coast of Central America.

In all of these colonies some puritans held slaves despite tensions between the desire to evangelize slaves and the vision that the true church should be composed of voluntarily gathered saints. In New England, where there were enough white laborers to grow grain and raise livestock, African slaves seldom exceeded 5 percent of the population. In Barbados and St. Kitts Puritans were among those who traded in slaves and used them on sugar plantations. In the 1630s the Providence Island Company, directed by such English Puritan notables as John Pym, saw Providence Island briefly become the first English colony to have a majority of its people black and enslaved and the first to witness a slave rebellion (1638).

New England Puritans did enslave Indians in the aftermath of wars to acquire new territory, such as the Pequot War of 1636 or King Philip's War of 1675–1677. Many of the captives were sold to planters in the West Indies, where New England slave traders in turn acquired enslaved Africans or Indians of the Caribbean region. One such slave woman transplanted to New England, Tibuta, was at the center of the Salem witchcraft accusations.

The Puritans, in their dealings in slaves, followed the doctrine that non-Christians taken captive in just wars could be lawfully enslaved. Some Puritans, such as Richard Baxter (1664) and Samuel Sewall (in *The Selling of Joseph,* 1700), argued that Africans were kidnapping victims and that traders and the slaveholders who purchased from them were sinners. But these writers, along with Cotton Mather, nonetheless held that slaves had a duty to obey the "God in man" represented by a master's authority. In this regard, slaves were no different from other dependent members of the patriarchal household that was the Puritans' ideal.

Puritan theologians like Mather, William Ames, and William Perkins also believed that masters had obligations to their slaves that had to be fulfilled for the good of the master's soul. Above all, slaveholders must acknowledge that blacks had eternal souls and try to convert them, as Mather argued in *The Negro Christianized* (1706). Mather acted on his beliefs, operating a school for religious instruction of blacks, but in general, New England Puritans were unsuccessful in evangelizing their slaves. In the Caribbean Puritans, like other slaveholders, feared that preaching to slaves might foment disorder and rebellion; the Providence Island Company rebuked one of its colonists, Samuel Rishworth, for doing so. In addition,

Cotton Mather. [Corbis-Bettmann]

few Puritans believed that baptism should bring about emancipation, subscribing instead to the view that Christian liberty applied to the spirit but not the body. One measure of the ambivalence of the Puritan legacy on slavery is that while New England's states were among the first to abolish slavery in the United States in the late eighteenth century, its merchants were also among the most vigorous and active slave traders during the same period.

See also BIBLE; CHRISTIANITY; UNITED STATES.

BIBLIOGRAPHY

BLACKBURN, ROBIN. *The Making of New World Slavery, 1492–1800.* 1997.
DAVIS, DAVID BRION. *The Problem of Slavery in Western Culture.* 1966.
KUPPERMAN, KAREN. *Providence Island, 1630–1641.* 1993.

T. Stephen Whitman

Q

Quakers

The Society of Friends, which originated in northern England around 1650, was the first religion in the Atlantic world to oppose slavery. Though Quakers shared many Christian tenets, their central concept of the Inner Light set them apart. Friends believed that the Holy Spirit could enter anyone who sought to live without sin, regardless of gender, ethnic background, social class, or education. Everyone had the potential to become a Quaker minister, for lay preachers spoke God's words, not their own. Emanating from these core beliefs in the Inner Light and sanctity of all humans came the Friends' rejection of violence, tithes, oaths, and rituals of deference such as doffing one's hat to persons in authority, and their commitment to simplicity and work.

Though individual Quakers protested against slavery as early as the late seventeenth century, no Friends' meeting banned the practice until the 1770s. For many years, most Friends failed to perceive the inconsistency of slaveholding with their religion, and, indeed, many colonial Quakers—from the West Indies to New England—bought enslaved Africans and participated in the Atlantic slave trade. George Fox, considered the founder of Quakerism, first raised the issue of slavery in 1657, when he reminded his slave-owning brethen to treat their Indian and black bondpeople well. He went somewhat further in 1671, after witnessing firsthand the degradation of enslaved Africans in Barbados. There he preached to the slaves, warned masters to educate them in Christianity, and suggested freeing them "after a considerable term of years, if they have served . . . faithfully; and when they go, and are made free, let them not go away empty-handed" (Drake, p. 6). A few years later, the Irish Quaker missionary William Edmundson visited Barbados, then traveled to Rhode Island, where in 1676 he issued the first Anglo-American statement that slavery was sin, "an Agrivasion, and an Oppression upon the Mind" (Frost, p. 68).

Pennsylvania, where Quaker leader William Penn in 1681 attempted to establish a model society, or "holy experiment," became the center of Quaker abolitionism during the colonial period. Because many Delaware Valley Friends owned slaves and some Quaker merchants imported Africans from the Caribbean and West Africa, however, the process of reaching agreement within Philadelphia Yearly Meeting (hereafter PYM) to oppose slavery proved to be contentious and slow.

Before 1754, PYM leaders, many of them slaveholders, refused to approve the publication of antislavery tracts or to condemn slavery as sin. They did, over the course of seventy years, gradually strengthen the meeting's discipline against the slave trade. In 1688 four members of the Germantown Meeting petitioned the Yearly Meeting, without success, to take measures against slavery and the slave trade, arguing that these practices encouraged the division of families, adultery, and violence. The model Quaker society in Pennsylvania was a mockery, they thought:

> to bring men hither, or to rob and sell them against their will, we stand against. In Europe there are

William Penn. [Corbis-Bettmann]

many oppressed for conscience sake; and here there are those oppressed wh[o] are of a black colour . . . . This makes an ill report in all those countries of Europe, where they hear off, that the Quakers doe here handel men as they handel there the cattle. (printed version in Friends Historical Library, Swarthmore College)

Five years later, some followers of the schismatic George Keith published *An Exhortation and Caution to Friends Concerning Buying or Keeping of Negroes.*

While most orthodox Quakers ignored the Keithian essay, the issue gained greater attention in the late 1690s, as slave importation swelled in the English mainland colonies, including Pennsylvania. In response to papers by Pennsylvania Friends William Southeby and Cadwalader Morgan in 1696, PYM warned members to "be Careful not to Encourage the bringing in of any more Negroes." While unprepared to denounce slaveholding altogether, the meeting advised "such that have Negroes be Careful of them, bring them to Meetings, . . . & Restrain them from Loose, & Lewd Living" (quoted in Nash and Soderlund, p. 44). Nevertheless, some Quaker merchants continued to import blacks, prompting Pentecost Teague of Philadelphia to denounce slave auctions in the public market. A wealthy merchant and slaveholder himself, Teague demonstrated the ability of Friends who

took a moderate position during this early period to distinguish slavery from the slave trade. If they treated their slaves well, these Quakers apparently thought that they were not tainted by the sin of violence that besmirched the slave trade.

During the early eighteenth century, individual Friends continued to speak out. In 1712 William Southeby petitioned the Quaker-dominated Pennsylvania legislature for emancipation of all slaves within the colony. The assembly refused, and—echoing the PYM earlier—attacked the slave trade instead. The lawmakers placed a prohibitive duty on slaves imported into the province, a measure Queen Anne subsequently annulled. A few years later, when a traveling Friend from England, John Farmer, enjoined all Quakers to free their slaves, the Newport (Rhode Island) and Philadelphia meetings condemned him for causing division among Friends. Leaders of the society sought to control the publication of antislavery tracts by requiring members to submit their writings to a committee of overseers of the press. If antislavery activists failed to get permission and published anyway, or went to print without seeking leave, meetings disciplined them for disunity or "acting contrary to good order," not specifically for their antislavery beliefs.

In 1729 Ralph Sandiford of Philadelphia challenged the meeting when he became concerned about a recent rise in slave importation. He submitted his pamphlet to the overseers of the press; when denied permission, he published despite their refusal and was condemned for disunity. Benjamin Lay—who had emigrated with his wife, Sarah, first from England to Barbados, then later (1732) to Philadelphia—was outraged by slavery in the West Indies, shocked to find the institution flourishing in the Quaker province, and appalled by Friends' treatment of Sandiford. Lay took direct action to dramatize the injustice of slavery, "kidnapping" a young boy for several hours to demonstrate the emotional distress of African families who lost their children to slave traders. At the 1738 Yearly Meeting, to underscore the violence inherent in perpetual bondage, Lay plunged a sword into a hollowed-out book disguised as a Bible and filled with pokeberry juice, sprinkling "blood" on the weighty Friends nearby.

Before 1754, though Friends like Southeby, Sandiford, and Lay lacked success in convincing the Society of Friends to prohibit slaveholding, abolitionism made some progress within the meeting. After 1716, in response to repeated petitions from Chester County (Pennsylvania) Friends, PYM banned the buying and selling of Indian slaves, importing enslaved Africans, or buying imported blacks. London Yearly Meeting in 1727 censured the slave trade, and two years later,

OBSERVATIONS

On the Inflaving, importing and purchafing of

Negroes;

With fome Advice thereon, extracted from the
Epiftle of the Yearly-Meeting of the People called
QUAKERS, held at *London* in the Year 1748.

Anthony Benezet

*When ye fpread forth your Hands, I will hide mine
Eyes from you, yea when ye make many Prayers I
will not bear; your Hands are full of Blood. Wafh
ye, make you clean, put away the Evil of your Doings
from before mine Eyes* Ifai. 1, 15.

*Is not this the Feaft that I have chofen, to loofe the
Bands of Wickednefs, to undo the heavy Burden, to
let the Oppreffed go free, and that ye break every
Toke, Chap.* 58, 7.

Second Edition.

GERMANTOWN:
Printed by CHRISTOPHER SOWER. 1760.

*Title page of a pamphlet by Anthony Benezet presented at
the Yearly Meeting of Quakers in London, 1760.* [Library
of Congress/Corbis]

Chester Monthly Meeting once again demanded a more stringent prohibition against purchasing imported slaves. Friends continued to import blacks, though in declining numbers, for PYM refrained from designating involvement in the slave trade a disownable offense. Beginning in the 1720s, however, abolitionism gained sway among some Friends, for in Philadelphia, eastern New Jersey, and elsewhere, Quaker slave owners began to free their bondpeople by will. In 1735 even Isaac Norris, Quaker slave trader and longtime PYM clerk of meeting (presiding officer), indicated his concern at his death by emancipating his Indian slave, Will.

Change arrived in PYM in the 1750s, when a new group of leaders took control. Most important were abolitionists John Woolman and Anthony Benezet, who connected their crusade to end slaveholding to a broader reform movement among Friends. Woolman, of Burlington County, New Jersey, realized the injustice of slavery when asked by his employer to write a bill of sale for an enslaved woman. In 1746 he traveled to Maryland, Virginia, and North Carolina, witnessing, as he wrote in his journal, "so many vices and corruptions increased by [the slave] trade and this way of life that it appeared to me as a dark gloominess hanging over the land" (Moulton, p. 38). He wrote his first essay against slavery soon after his return, yet waited to submit it to the PYM overseers of the press until a change of membership on that committee ensured his success. Unlike Benjamin Lay, Woolman avoided confrontational methods, using gentle persuasion instead. When he published a second antislavery essay in 1762, he paid the costs of publication to avoid criticism from Quaker slaveholders that meeting funds subsidized his tracts. Woolman traveled throughout the British mainland colonies to convince Friends and their neighbors of the evils of slavery. Closer to home, with other abolitionists, he visited slaveholding families in Pennsylvania and New Jersey to convince them to free their slaves.

Anthony Benezet, who had been born in France and became a Friend after immigrating to Philadelphia, was Woolman's chief collaborator in convincing PYM to ban slaveholding. In 1750 he opened an evening school for African-Americans in his home. He served as one of the overseers of the press who approved Woolman's 1754 essay and wrote the initial draft of PYM's first denunciation of slavery, *An Epistle of Caution and Advice, Concerning the Buying and Keeping of Slaves* (1754). The *Epistle* condemned slaveholding itself, not just the slave trade, warning slaveholders that "to live in Ease and Plenty by the Toil of those whom Violence and Cruelty have put in our power, is neither consistent with Christianity, nor common Justice."

While the *Epistle* of 1754 marked PYM's acceptance that slavery was a sin, its leaders were not yet ready to disown members who refused to emancipate their slaves. Step by step, over the next twenty-two years, the Yearly Meeting moved toward that goal. In 1758 PYM instructed local meetings to exclude from meeting business (but not disown or restrict from attending meetings for worship) Friends who imported, bought, or sold slaves. At the same time, PYM appointed a five-man committee including Woolman to visit every slaveholder within the meeting's compass. By excluding slave traders from places of influence and convincing many members to emancipate their bondpeople, PYM gradually reached a consensus (in Quaker terms, a sense of the meeting) to prohibit slaveholding. In 1774 the Yearly Meeting ruled that Friends who bought or sold slaves should be disowned and those who refused to free their enslaved blacks should be excluded from leadership. Two years later, PYM prohibited slaveholding outright, directing local meetings to disown members who refused to manumit their slaves. Though some monthly meetings dragged their heels, by 1780 most Delaware Valley meetings were clear of slaveholding. Under duress, many Quaker owners freed hundreds of slaves, while more obstinate Friends—a minority of the slave owners—chose to be disowned from the society.

While PYM's *Epistle* of 1754 and the 1758 ban on trading in slaves placed Pennsylvania and New Jersey Friends in the vanguard of abolitionism, other yearly meetings promptly followed suit. In 1758 London Yearly Meeting renewed its condemnation of the slave trade; a few years later it recommended disownment for members who persisted "in the unchristian traffick." New England Yearly Meeting took longer than PYM to deny the Christianity of slaveholding, then acted promptly—in 1773—to ban the practice entirely. North Carolina Yearly Meeting moved more slowly, in part because of extensive personal involvement in slavery, in part because state law prohibited manumission except with judicial consent. When Friends proved unable to convince the North Carolina assembly to change the law, they helped emancipated blacks leave the state. Indeed, many Quakers themselves abandoned eastern North Carolina for Pennsylvania and Ohio.

With the battle against slavery within the meeting largely won, antislavery Friends sought to eradicate the institution in the larger society. Anthony Benezet played a major role in this transition, encouraging Pennsylvania legislators in 1780 to pass the first abolition act in the United States and internationalizing antislavery discourse by corresponding with like-minded men in Great Britain and France. In 1783 PYM petitioned the Confederation Congress to end the slave trade. Friends also provided the core membership of the Pennsylvania Society for the Abolition of Slavery and similar groups founded on its model in New Jersey, New York, New England, North Carolina, and elsewhere. The abolition societies encouraged and recorded manumissions, circulated petitions against slavery and the slave trade, and entered lawsuits to free African-Americans illegally held as slaves.

At the same time Quakers furnished much of the initiative for abolitionism in Great Britain. At PYM urging, London Yearly Meeting in 1783 presented a petition against the slave trade to Parliament and formed committees to circulate petitions, lobby government officials, and publicize their campaign. The Quaker network of local meetings throughout the country provided the basis for rank-and-file support of the budding abolitionist movement, which broadened in May 1789 when a coalition of Friends and non-Friends formed the Society for the Abolition of the Slave Trade. The organization forged links with abolition societies in the United States and the Société des Amis des Noirs in France, hoping to cooperate internationally to end the trade. The French Revolution and the outbreak of war between Great Britain and France cut short negotiations. Nevertheless, British abolitionists, funded largely by Friends, mobilized public opinion through mass meetings, petitions, and publications, eventually convincing Parliament, in 1807, to ban British participation in the international slave trade. Sixteen years later, Quakers again were prominent among the founders of the Society for the Mitigation and Gradual Abolition of Slavery throughout the British Dominions. This group and another, the Agency Committee, depended on Quaker financial support and, to a considerable extent, on Quaker leadership to obtain Parliament's approval of emancipation in the West Indies.

In the United States during the nineteenth century, particularly after the Garrisionian movement heated up in the 1830s, Quaker meetings—including both the Orthodox and Hicksite branches following the 1827 separation—discouraged antislavery activities. Most Friends believed that William Lloyd Garrison's demand for immediate abolition would exacerbate sectional tensions and lead to war. Nevertheless, committed Quaker abolitionists such as Lucretia Mott, John Greenleaf Whittier, and many lesser known activists joined the new American Anti-Slavery Society and its affiliates, ran free produce stores, sought ways to prevent southern bounty hunters from kidnapping free blacks, and supported the network known as the Underground Railroad to assist escaped slaves. The issue of slavery continued to divide Friends in the antebellum United States, just as it had in the colonial period, between conservative leaders fearful of disunity and of bringing disgrace upon Friends and Quakers whose consciences led them to more radical action, regardless of personal consequences.

See also AMERICAN ANTI-SLAVERY SOCETY; GARRISON, WILLIAM LLOYD; LAY, BENJAMIN AND SARAH; SOCIÉTÉ DES AMIS DES NOIRS; WOOLMAN, JOHN.

BIBLIOGRAPHY

BROOKES, GEORGE S. *Friend Anthony Benezet*. 1937.
DAVIS, DAVID BRION. *The Problem of Slavery in the Age of Revolution, 1770–1823*. 1975.
———. *The Problem of Slavery in Western Culture*. 1966.
DRAKE, THOMAS E. *Quakers and Slavery in America*. 1950.
FROST, J. WILLIAM, ed. *The Quaker Origins of Antislavery*. 1980.
JAMES, SYDNEY V. *A People among Peoples: Quaker Benevolence in Eighteenth-Century America*. 1963.

JENNINGS, JUDITH. "Mid-Eighteenth Century British Quakerism and the Response to the Problem of Slavery." *Quaker History* 66 (1977): 23–40.

MOULTON, PHILLIPS P., ed. *The Journal and Major Essays of John Woolman.* 1971.

NASH, GARY B., and JEAN R. SODERLUND. *Freedom by Degrees: Emancipation in Pennsylvania and Its Aftermath.* 1991.

SODERLUND, JEAN R. *Quakers and Slavery: A Divided Spirit.* 1985.

TEMPERLEY, HOWARD. *British Antislavery, 1833–1870.* 1972.

WORRELL, ARTHUR J. *Quakers in the Colonial Northeast.* 1980.

Jean R. Soderlund

Quran.

See Islam.

R

Race, Racism, and Racial Theories

See Enlightenment; Perspectives on Slavery.

Ramsey, James   [1797–1884]

U.S. proslavery author.

James Ramsey was born and raised in Tennessee, where he practiced medicine and engaged in business. An ardent apologist for slavery, he wrote newspaper articles and letters to editors in support of reopening the slave trade between the United States and Africa, which Congress had abolished in 1807. At the Knoxville Southern Commercial Convention in 1857, he was appointed to a committee chaired by Leonidas W. Spratt, editor of the Charleston (South Carolina) *Southern Standard*, which was to report to the 1858 Southern Commercial Convention in Montgomery, Alabama, concerning the advisability of reopening the African slave trade. Although Ramsey attended neither convention, he wrote seven letters to Spratt outlining his views on this subject. These letters, which Ramsey stipulated must be kept out of the committee's report and were to be returned to him after the convention (presumably because of their semitreasonable content), were evidently intended to provide Spratt, whom one historian called "the philosopher of the new African slave trade," with additional ammunition for his radical proslavery campaign.

Ramsey argued that the South's greatest industrial necessity, a sufficient labor force, could best be satisfied by resuming the importation of Africans. He prefigured Ulrich B. Phillips, one of the first historians to write about slavery, by arguing that the South's climate and the natural inferiority of blacks made slavery "humane, benevolent, scriptural, Christian, patriotic, and perhaps politic and expedient." Although the committee's report in favor of reopening the trade was tabled at Montgomery, it was adopted at the 1859 Southern Convention in Vicksburg, Mississippi.

See also SLAVE TRADE.

BIBLIOGRAPHY

HESSELTINE, WILLIAM B. *Dr. J. G. M. Ramsey: Autobiography and Letters.* 1954.
TAKAKI, RONALD T. *A Pro-slavery Crusade: The Agitation to Reopen the African Slave Trade.* 1971.

Charles W. Carey Jr.

Raynal, G.-T.-F. de, Abbé   [1713–1796]

French polemicist and antislavery advocate.

As a young man, Guillaume-Thomas-François Raynal was ordained a Roman Catholic priest and joined the Jesuits; he later left the order to become a writer. By far his most popular work was the six-volume *Philosophical and Political History of the Settlements and Trade of the Europeans in the East and West Indies* (1770, 30th ed. 1789). A considerable portion of this work's Volume 4 is devoted to a discussion of slavery in the European colonies of North and South America. Raynal declared that slaves in the New World were universally overworked, underfed, scantily clothed, and cruelly oppressed. He spoke out forcefully for the abolition of both the slave trade and slavery itself by appealing to the "sovereigns of the earth . . . [to] bring about this revolution" (vol. 4: 128) and predicted that, should emancipation not take place in the near future, a bloody slave revolution would occur. In the meantime, he called upon slave owners to alleviate the misery of their slaves by providing them with sufficient food, shelter, and clothing as well as "festivals, games, and rewards" (vol. 4: 104). He further urged slave owners to correct the gender imbalance that prevailed throughout the Caribbean sugar islands so that slaves might enjoy "the pleasures of love" (vol. 4: 107).

Raynal's antagonistic stance toward the Roman Catholic hierarchy and the French monarchy throughout this work caused it to be banned by the church in 1774 and burned by the French government in 1781. Nevertheless, it contributed in part to the abolition of slavery throughout the French empire following the French Revolution in 1789.

See also ABOLITION AND ANTISLAVERY MOVEMENTS; CARIBBEAN REGION; PERSPECTIVES ON SLAVERY.

BIBLIOGRAPHY

RAYNAL, GUILLAUME-THOMAS-FRANÇOIS. *A Philosophical and Political History of the Settlements and Trade of the Europeans in the East and West Indies.* Translated by J. O. Justamond. 1770. Reprint, 1969.

Charles W. Carey Jr.

Rebellions and Violent Resistance

The discussion that follows is distinct from but related to that in the entry Resistance, Day-to-Day, *which the reader is urged to consult for further information.*

Demographic realities and power relationships in the British mainland colonies and later, following independence, in the United States, militated against the type of large-scale slave conspiracies that took place in South America and the Caribbean. The presence of a heavily armed white majority in every state except South Carolina (and, toward the very end of the antebellum period, Mississippi), the lack of an impregnable hinterland in which to create maroon colonies from which runaways could besiege plantations, the relatively dispersed nature and small size of slaveholding, and the fact that the landlord class was in residence (not absentee) combined to make massive slave rebellions far less common than day-to-day resistance or individual acts of self-threat. In the years after the Revolution, as harsher forms of colonial patriarchalism began to metamorphose into paternalism—a

complex and ongoing process of negotiation and brutality that many scholars regrettably reduce to a simplistic model of accommodation—slaves achieved enough living space to build stable families and rich spiritual communities. Given the odds against success, it is hardly surprising that the handful of slaves bold enough to rise for their freedom found their rebellions reduced to unsuccessful conspiracies and their fellows doomed to die in combat or on the gallows.

Despite persistent attempts by historians to force a uniformity of vision and goals on rebel leaders, insurgent slaves in the eighteenth and nineteenth centuries differed from one another fully as much as white revolutionaries in the same era. Jemmy, a Angolan who led an agrarian uprising near Stono River, South Carolina, tried to hasten his African followers across the border into Spanish Florida. Caesar, who only two years later conspired to burn New York City, lived in one of North America's largest urban centers with an Irish wife. Gabriel, a young, secular rebel who had turned away from African traditions, hoped to stay and work in a more egalitarian Virginia. Denmark Vesey, an aged free black who bought his freedom the year before Gabriel died, expected to achieve a limited exodus for his family and followers, out of Charleston to Haiti. Vesey and his chief lieutenant, "Gullah" Jack Pritchard, an East African priest, fused African theology with the Old Testament God of wrath and justice, whereas Nat Turner relied on Christian millennial themes and hoped to bring on the day of jubilee for black Virginians. Beyond their obvious abilities as leaders and their equally obvious desire to breathe free, bond rebels in the United States fit no simple pattern.

If slave rebellions in North America correspond to any one model, it is that they proliferated during times when the white majority was divided against itself in significant ways. Colonial insurgents in South Carolina and New York City turned to violence at a time when their masters were at war with France and Spain. Gabriel, the most politicized of all the slave rebels, formulated his plans during the divisive election of 1800, when Federalists and Republicans threatened to take up arms against one another. The rebels in the Tidewater area of Virginia, despite the memory of the repression that followed Gabriel's death, began to organize again during the chaos of the War of 1812. Having read of the Missouri debates in Charleston newspapers, Vesey prayed that northern whites would prove tardy in riding to the rescue of the estranged southerners. Slaves near Natchez, Mississippi, began to plan for their freedom in 1861, following the outbreak of the Civil War.

Most of all, slaves, who well knew what they were up against and rarely contemplated suicidal ventures, plotted for their freedom only when safer avenues had been closed to them. For most of the seventeenth century, for example, when the high death rate in the southern colonies made inexpensive white indentured servants far more numerous than costly African slaves, enterprising bondpersons relied more on self-purchase than the sword. The economic possibilities in early Virginia produced more runaways than rebels; the practice of buying one's own body even produced several black entrepreneurs—such as Anthony Johnson, a former slave who became a wealthy planter and who named his estate Angola after the land of his birth. It was only after landless whites and hard-used white indentured workers under the command of Nathaniel Bacon burned Jamestown in 1676 that southern planters made a concerted effort to replace white servants with African slaves. The comprehensive Virginia Slave Code of 1705, the first of its kind in colonial North America, crushed the hope of industrious slaves that they might be upwardly mobile. Only then, as North American racial walls rapidly hardened, did desperate slaves turn to physically hazardous paths toward freedom. During the last days of Queen Anne's War in April 1712, a determined band of twenty-five Africans and Native Americans burned several buildings in New York City and killed nine whites. (Unfree labor had been legalized in New York by the Duke's Law of 1665.) Having made a commitment to unfree labor, equally determined whites revenged themselves on the rebels. Several rebels committed suicide before they could be captured, but those taken alive were broken on the wheel and hanged in chains as a warning to future rebels.

In the early eighteenth century, even though the constant threat of war between Britain and its continental neighbors provided endless opportunities for daring slaves, mainland revolts rarely posed much real danger to the slaveholding regime. Because the Atlantic slave trade was at its peak, every colony included large numbers of native Africans who sought to escape from bondage by building isolated maroon communities. Most runaways fled into the hinterland, where they established maroon colonies and tried to re-create the African communities they had lost. Even the two most significant rebellions of the period— that of Stono, South Carolina, in 1739 and the subsequent attempt to burn New York City in 1741—were led by Africans who dreamed only of ending their own bondage, not of ending unfree labor in general. Aware of Spanish promises of freedom in colonial Florida, Angolan soldiers under Jemmy tried to escape across the border. To the north, New York City bondmen planned to torch the wooden city and flee to French Canada, which was then at war with the rebels' masters. The price of failure was high. New York authorities ordered Caesar and twelve of his followers

burned alive; eighteen others were hanged—two of them in chains—and seventy more bondmen were banished from the colony.

The American Revolution alternately discouraged and stimulated slave rebellions. Although the British invasion and the animosity between patriots and Tories presented slaves with a unique opportunity to organize, most slaves chose instead to take advantage of the dislocation of war to escape with their families into the growing cities or behind British lines. (The Revolution was the one time in North American history when as many female slaves as males ran away.) Because the aggressive bondmen who cast their lots with the military forces of King George were precisely the sort of bold, determined slaves who normally tended to organize slave conspiracies, the bloody fighting in the southern states after 1778 actually diminished the prospect that a mainland counterpart of Toussaint-Louverture would rise out of the tobacco plantations.

Nonetheless, as Eugene D. Genovese suggests in his influential study *From Rebellion to Revolution* (1979), the age of revolution, and especially the slave revolt in Saint Domingue in 1791, marked a change in patterns in black resistance. The Caribbean rebels under the leadership of Boukman and Toussaint-Louverture sought not only to destroy the power of their Parisian absentee masters but to join the societies in which they lived on equal terms. For black Americans determined to realize the egalitarian promise of the American Revolution, the news from the Caribbean reminded them that it they dared, the end of slavery might be within their reach. Whereas Jemmy and his African recruits hoped only to escape the chains of colonial South Carolina, the slave Gabriel of Virginia, born in the year 1776, wanted to join political society on equal terms. Gabriel and his lieutenants, who instigated the most extensive plot in Virginia history, hoped to force the white patriot elite to live up to its stated ideal: that all men were created free and equal. Leading a small army of slaves in Henrico County, the young blacksmith planned to march into Richmond under a banner emblazoned with the words "Death or Liberty." He assured one supporter that "poor white people," who had no more political power than the slaves, "would also join" them in the struggle for equality. Although trial testimony makes little mention of events in Saint Domingue, white authorities like Governor James Monroe harbored no doubts that Toussaint-Louverture's victories had an enormous "effect on all the peoples of colour" in the early national South.

In several cases, bondmen who had been carried from revolutionary Saint Domingue by their masters participated in North American slave revolts. In 1792

Toussaint-Louverture participates in a revolt against the French power in Saint Domingue. [Corbis-Bettmann]

slaves on Virginia's eastern shore proposed to "blow up the magazine in Norfolk, and massacre its inhabitants." Norfolk County had a white majority, but Northampton and Elizabeth City counties, just across the Chesapeake bay, had an enslaved majority. Although the rebel leader Caleb, a favored servant and driver, was evidently American-born, several of his recruits were Haitian refugees, and all—according to the trial testimony—had been inspired by the example of Saint Domingue. Two decades later, in 1811, one of the most extensive conspiracies in the history of the United States erupted in southern Louisiana, only a few miles upriver from New Orleans. Slaves led by a mulatto driver named Charles Deslondes, reputedly a refugee from Saint Domingue, announced their intention of marching on the city "to kill whites." Eyewitness accounts placed the number of rebels at 180 to 500.

After Gabriel's execution and the death of twenty-five of his followers in the fall of 1800, slave rebellions on the eastern seaboard became both less common and less politically conscious. Slaves who worked along the rivers in southern Virginia and Halifax County, North Carolina, under the leadership of Sancho, a ferryman, formed a highly decentralized scheme to rise on Easter Monday of 1802. But Sancho, despite having been involved in Gabriel's plot, shared little of Gabriel's dream of a multiracial republic. The lack of an ideological dimension appeared even when the dislocation brought on by the War of 1812 and a second British invasion of the Chesapeake once more gave bondmen in Virginia an opportunity to rise for their liberty. Gloucester County authorities jailed ten slaves in March 1813, and the following month found rebels in Lancester County and Williamsburg "condemned on a charge of conspiracy & insurrection." By the late summer and early fall, rumors of revolt unnerved inhabitants of Norfolk and Richmond as well.

If the relative ease with which white authorities crushed these isolated rebellions did not extinguish the desire for freedom, it nonetheless reminded leaders in the slave community that the determined white majority in the American South presented insurgents with a formidable obstacle. Denmark Vesey of Charleston, perhaps the most pragmatic of all the rebel leaders, realized that Gabriel's dream of forcing mainland elites to accommodate blacks' aspirations to freedom and economic justice was impossible. Vesey plotted, therefore, not to end slavery in South Carolina, but instead to lead a mass escape from Charleston to the Caribbean, where he had lived and worked as a boy. Hoping to take control of the city on the night of 14 July 1822, Vesey's recruits—many of them Africans—intended to slaughter the inhabitants of the city and seize bank reserves before fleeing to Haiti, an embattled black republic sorely in need of capital and skilled labor. If Vesey, a prosperous freeman, doomed those who remained behind to renewed repression by whites, he can scarcely be faulted: he understood that his followers had virtually no hope of bringing down the peculiar institution in South Carolina.

Even Vesey's unsuccessful exodus, which may be regarded more as mass flight than a revolution, indicated the difficulties of planning an effective strategy amidst large numbers of ever-vigilant whites. Like virtually all rebel leaders in the United States, Vesey recognized the danger of openly recruiting in the countryside. Word of the Charleston plot probably reached several thousand slaves—which is not to say that even half that number committed themselves to the struggle—and there was always a danger that a black Judas would hear the whispers and inform the master class. White authorities had long ago perfected the art of dividing the slave community by offering a tempting reward—freedom—to those who would turn their coats. Like Jemmy and Gabriel before him, Vesey, whose army had more officers than soldiers, planned to rise quickly and present the low country's black majority with a fait accompli. The victorious armies would not be recruited or armed in advance but raised by the captains as they marched.

Ironically, the bloodiest slave revolt in the United States took place in the decade after Vesey's failure, at a time when rebellion—as opposed to other forms of resistance—had become virtually suicidal. The slaves in Southampton County, Virginia, who rose with Nat Turner in 1831 shared neither Gabriel's trust in a second American Revolution nor Vesey's hope of fleeing to the Caribbean. Although Turner may have hoped to establish a maroon colony in the vast Dismal Swamp, his plot gave little evidence of planning or rational preparation. Most likely, the messianic Turner hoped that God would protect and guide his army as the Lord had guided the Israelites. At least fifty-seven whites perished in the revolt, but local militiamen easily routed the ill-equipped rebels; three companies of federal artillery, together with seamen from two warships in the Chesapeake, reached Southampton only three days after the insurrection began.

Although the secession of the southern states in the winter of 1860–1861 presented militant blacks with precisely the sort of division that rebel leaders typically tried to take advantage of, the Civil War channeled black resistance into patterns acceptable to the politicians of the free states. During the first year of the conflict, as Confederate soldiers repulsed northern invasions, militant slaves across the cotton-growing South saw few options but to pull down the rebel government from within. The plot in Natchez, Mississippi, still shrouded in mystery, stands as but one example of collective resistance during the months before the Confederate debacle at Antietam Creek. Rumors of black resistance spread in New Orleans and Columbia, South Carolina. Seven slaves swung from the gibbet in Charleston in April 1861. The Confederate brigadier general R. F. Floyd urged the governor of Florida to declare martial law in the hope of eradicating a "nest of traitors and lawless negroes."

Most slaves, however, understood, as Herbert Aptheker suggested in his definitive work *American Negro Slave Revolts* (1943), that "the Army of Lincoln was to be the Army of Liberation." Aged slaves with long memories counseled patience and waited for the arrival of northern forces. Following the Emancipation Proclamation, northern freemen and southern runaways, eager and willing to fight, donned blue uniforms in the name of liberty for blacks. Despite the Confederates' threat to execute black soldiers as slave insurgents, thousands of bondmen fled the countryside, planning to return and liberate their families. By the end of the war, 180,000 African-Americans (one out of every five males in the republic) had served in Union forces. Those former slaves who marched back toward the plantations of their birth singing "General Gabriel's Jig" rightly understood themselves to be a part of the largest slave rebellion in the history of the United States.

See also GABRIEL'S REBELLION; PANICS; TOUSSAINT-LOUVERTURE; TURNER, NAT; VESEY REBELLION.

BIBLIOGRAPHY

APTHEKER, HERBERT. *American Negro Slave Revolts.* 1943.
DAVIS, T. J. *A Rumor of Revolt: The "Great Negro Plot" in Colonial New York City.* 1985.
EGERTON, DOUGLAS R. *Gabriel's Rebellion: The Virginia Slave Conspiracies of 1800 and 1802.* 1993.
FREY, SYLVIA R. *Water from the Rock: Black Resistance in a Revolutionary Age.* 1991.
GENOVESE, EUGENE D. *From Rebellion to Revolution: Afro-American Slave Revolts in the Making of the Modern World.* 1979.

HINKS, PETER P. *To Awaken My Afflicted Brethren: David Walker and the Problem of Antebellum Slave Resistance.* 1997.

JORDAN, WINTHROP D. *Tumult and Silence at Second Creek: An Inquiry into a Civil War Slave Conspiracy.* 1993.

OATES, STEPHEN B. *The Fires of Jubilee: Nat Turner's Fierce Rebellion.* 1975.

PAQUETTE, ROBERT. *Life and Death along the Levy: The Great Louisiana Slave Revolt of 1811.* 1998.

WOOD, PETER H. *Black Majority: Negroes in Colonial South Carolina from 1670 through the Stono Rebellion.* 1974.

Douglas R. Egerton

Reconstruction, U.S.

The Civil War began as a Confederate rebellion but ended as a Republican revolution that overthrew the power of the planters and liberated four million slaves. Thus, what was "reconstructed" was the southern regional and, indeed, the national power structure, with a different economic orientation, a different kind of society and labor system in the South, and a new status for African-Americans.

Virtually from the war's first shot debate broke out among Unionists about Reconstruction, or "war aims." "Conservatives" wanted to restore the Union "as it was, the Constitution as it is." But "Radicals" thought the nation could enjoy little stability until the national government abolished slavery and obtained more power over the "sovereign" states. The Radicals began gaining support, even among many who wanted to restore the old Union, because their approach seemed the way to win the war: by freeing and arming the slaves and by prosecuting the war more aggressively.

This drift toward radicalism intensified both the determination of the Confederates and the rage of the antiwar, or pro-Confederate, "copperheads" in the North. In face of such sharpening opposition, Lincoln's government passed measures that invigorated old friends and won over new ones. Industrialists received unprecedented tariff protection. Bankers who had once financed southern planters now bought war bonds with interest that was tax-exempt and payable in gold. The government began a distribution of federal lands in the West. The Homestead Act (1862) provided land for the landless. The railroad acts appropriated land to subsidize railroads that would open the West to settlers and open new markets for business. The Morrill Act (1862) granted land to create agricultural and engineering colleges accessible to ordinary citizens that would modernize agriculture and provide technical expertise to industry.

For millions this legislation inspired visions of personal success that only Union victory could fulfill. Meanwhile, Congress's Second Confiscation Act

(1862) and President Abraham Lincoln's Emancipation Proclamation (1863), along with the recruitment of 200,000 African-American soldiers and sailors, made the struggle a war on slavery. Revolutionary measures thus brought the prospect of both victory and a new Union.

But the assassination of Lincoln placed Andrew Johnson in the White House. Sustained by a postwar resurgence of conservatism, he set out to restore in the South as much as possible of the old Union. He reduced the federal military to a shadow and returned local power to the former Confederates. Despite Radical warnings that presidential Reconstruction was becoming rebel reconstruction, most Republicans, having made slavery unconstitutional with the Thirteenth Amendment, saw little reason for further transformation of the South.

Meanwhile, the moment most favorable to fundamental change in the South was slipping away. During the closing months of the war slavery had collapsed. In the spring of 1865, African-American squatters were cultivating plantation fields. In the Piney Woods of the eastern Carolinas and Georgia, black and white squatters were producing tar and turpentine for the market. It appeared that the now poor and marginalized plain whites of the Old South might be joined by a black yeomanry with similar interests.

But the antebellum leaders, clothed with legal authority by the president, acted quickly. They commanded battle-hardened Confederate veterans, who

Recently freed slaves line up at the Freedmen's Bureau to receive rations. The Freedmen's Bureau was originally created in 1865 to serve as a federal social service agency for former slaves during the period of emancipation and reconstruction. [Library of Congress/Corbis]

wore the uniforms of the state militia, or, if their mission was illegal, the white sheets of the Ku Klux Klan. They drove squatters from field and forest, reestablishing the old regime's control over land and resources. State legislatures reenacted "black codes," including laws that turned over freed people to planters as "apprentices" or "leased" to them those convicted of often fictitious crimes. Because of the Thirteenth Amendment and, especially, the restless movements of the freed people, planters could not recover individual property in slaves. Instead, they created a half-free racial labor pool.

Until late 1865 the Republicans debated but failed to unite against the president's policies. But then the newly elected southern congressional delegation arrived in Washington. It was much like the one that had seceded in 1861 and included the Confederate vice president himself. These "rebels," with their northern "copperhead" allies, seemed about to resume their prewar control of Congress. They could repeal every revolutionary measure passed by the Lincoln administration.

From right to left, the Republicans united behind their Radical faction. They refused to seat the "rebels." They passed the Civil Rights Act (1866), making blacks citizens and affirming their equal rights. To prevent this law from being thrown out by a conservative Supreme Court, they initiated the Fourteenth Amendment to incorporate the substance of the act into the Constitution. They passed the Reconstruction Acts (1867), requiring the president to send the army back into the South to organize new elections based on a new electorate that enfranchised African-Americans and excluded the old Confederate elite.

Black and plain white voters elected state conventions that wrote new constitutions, which included such innovations as the election of local officials, who previously had been appointed, and free public school education where none had existed before even for whites. The heretofore elitist University of North Carolina was declared to be part of the "free public school system." In Florida the Seminole Indians were given a seat in each house of the legislature. Flogging and branding were abolished as legal punishments. African-Americans participated in every level of government from the local community to Congress.

But in 1868 the Radical bloc to Congress disintegrated, torn apart by conflicting views about labor, farmers, and women. Business-oriented Republicans took charge. Support weakened for the Radical governments in the South, which one by one were being overthrown by terrorist bands.

The new Republican leaders were taking a fresh look at the South; planters were no longer the force they had been before the war and appeared still to be in 1866. Stripped of half their capital by emancipation, they had become more dependent than ever upon credit, which ultimately came from northeastern banks. Planters could no longer dominate the Democratic Party, now controlled by business interests similar to those supporting the Republicans. Even in the South they had to share power with officials of northern-owned railroads and merchants dependent upon northern financiers.

Between 1869 and 1877 a political convergence emerged. Democrats, North and South, unable to oppose the Republican economic revolution, had become its enthusiastic advocates. And the new Republican leaders, their economic goals secured, were now ready to bargain on civil rights. But, although the party's original northern base was growing rapidly, they still needed votes in the South. In 1868 President Ulysses S. Grant had won by only 300,000 popular votes. Yet in the South, despite the reign of terror, he had received 500,000 black votes. Election arithmetic thus counseled some further support for civil rights. Republicans therefore launched the Fifteenth Amendment (1870), guaranteeing the right of African-Americans to vote.

Congress also passed the Enforcement Acts and the Ku Klux Acts (1870–1871). But prosecution of terrorists in southern courts and a reluctance to use the army weakened enforcement of these acts. In Jackson county, Florida, for example, where local Republicans had reported 179 political murders during the previous five years, only fourteen suspects were tried and one convicted. In Monroe county, Mississippi, 28 people were convicted of murder, and all were given suspended sentences. Since the Ku Klux Acts had made white sheets an issue, the southern "Redeemers" launched the Mississippi Plan (1875): armed bands, sometimes in military uniform, sometimes in civilian dress, continued overthrowing local governments and taking over polling places. Under these conditions Congress' passage of the Civil Rights Act (1875), which prohibited discrimination in public accommodations and in jury selection, was only an election gesture. Redeemer violence also led to the disputed elections of 1876 in which the Republican presidential contender, Rutherford B. Hayes, in exchange for Redeemer support, agreed to withdraw the troops that protected the last three Radical governments in the South.

The victory of the New South Redeemers was neither immediate nor total. As late as 1896, North Carolina elected a Radical governor, and the last African-American did not leave Congress until 1901. Redeemer laws finally disfranchised virtually all blacks as well as many plain whites and imposed legal segregation. The new authorities often permitted peonage,

An 1867 political cartoon critical of the southern response to Reconstruction highlights the Black Codes, violence against former slaves, racially biased murder trials, lynchings, and shootings. [Corbis-Bettmann]

or debt servitude, but failed to make it legal or even respectable. Most former slaves continued to exercise their newly won mobility and thus punished the worst landlords with a labor shortage. And labor often was made scarcer and better compensated by the withdrawal of wives and children from the labor force. Sharecroppers, even peons, were better compensated than slaves, and their families were not broken up.

A stronger, legally recognized African-American family emerged from Reconstruction. Marriages, broken and remade by slavery, had sometimes created uncertainty about who was one's proper partner. The Freedmen's Bureau courts helped resolve some of this confusion. Parents recovered children. Under the new sharecropper system, a family worked as a team. An independent black church emerged from Reconstruction as the core of the African-American community. Some semblance of free schooling continued for both blacks and whites.

The Redeemers achieved power but never constitutional legitimacy, for Reconstruction had changed the Constitution fundamentally. The Thirteenth Amend-ment had abolished slavery. The Fourteenth Amendment made African-Americans citizens. The Fifteenth Amendment gave them the right to vote. The last two amendments were the sleeping giants of Reconstruction that the civil rights movement of the next century would awaken.

See also CODE NOIR; CONFISCATION ACTS, U.S.; ENFORCEMENT ACTS, U.S.; FREEDMEN'S BUREAU; PEONAGE.

BIBLIOGRAPHY

DU BOIS, W. E. B. *Black Reconstruction in America.* 1938.

EVANS, WILLIAM MCKEE. *Ballots and Fence Rails: Reconstruction on the Lower Cape Fear.* 1967.

FONER, ERIC. *Reconstruction: America's Unfinished Revolution.* 1988.

MCPHERSON, JAMES M. *Battle Cry of Freedom: The Civil War Era.* 1988.

TRELEASE, ALAN W. *White Terror: The Ku Klux Klan Conspiracy and Southern Reconstruction.* 1971.

WOODWARD, C. VANN. *Reunion and Reaction: The Compromise of 1877 and the End of Reconstruction.* 1956.

William McKee Evans

Redemption of Captives

Several religious orders had as their goal the liberation of Christians captured in war or by Muslim pirates and held in North Africa. The redemption of captives was related to the Christian military struggle against Muslims in the Mediterranean basin from the Middle Ages to the eighteenth century.

The earliest such order was the Order of Montjoie, established in 1180; it was united to the military order of Calatrava in 1221. In 1198, Pope Innocent III approved the Order of the Holy Trinity for the Redemption of Captives. (Usually called Trinitarians, the members of this order were called Mathurins in France.) Founded by John of Matha (1160–1213), the order had houses throughout western Europe. In 1218, Peter Nolasco (1189–1256) founded the Order of Our Lady of Mercy (its members were called Mercedarians) under the patronage of the King of Aragon. Pope Gregory IX approved the order in the 1230s. The Mercedarians were dedicated to the ransom of Christian captives and the conversion of Muslims to Christianity.

The orders collected money, usually in those areas of Spain and southern France most affected by piracy and war, and often from the families of captives. As part of their fund-raising efforts, the Trinitarians sponsored theatrical representations of the sufferings of captives and testimony from freed captives. Laypeople were involved in supporting the orders as collectors of money and as members of confraternities. The Trinitarians divided their income into three parts: a third for support of the order, a third for the poor in Europe, and a third for the ransom of captives. This division caused severe strains on their finances.

Members traveled to Muslim territories—the Trinitarians focused their efforts on Tunis and Algiers, the Mercedarians on Morocco—to seek out captives. They favored captives belonging to families who had donated money or who came from provinces in Europe where the order had collected money. If they did not have the amount demanded by the Muslims, members of both orders were willing to offer themselves as hostages to obtain the captives' freedom. Some were killed and are considered martyrs by the Roman Catholic Church. The most famous captive freed by the Trinitarians was the Spanish writer Miguel de Cervantes, who was held prisoner in Algiers between 1575 and 1580. Cervantes was buried in the habit of the Trinitarians.

The Trinitarians claimed to have freed about 140,000 captives throughout their history, 90,000 of them from the fourteenth to early seventeenth cen-

Miguel de Cervantes Saavedra. [Library of Congress/ Corbis]

turies. The Mercedarians claimed to have freed about 70,000 captives.

Although largely replaced by parish ministries in the eighteenth century, the work of redeeming captives continued, albeit on a lesser scale. Mercedarians traveled with Christopher Columbus to the Americas as missionaries. Mercedarians also occasionally redeemed captives from the Indians in Mexico in the eighteenth century, and some died as martyrs. A French captive in Algiers begged the assistance of the Trinitarians of Limoges, France, in the 1740s. As the American minister to the French court, Thomas Jefferson requested the help of the Trinitarians in freeing American sailors held prisoner in Algiers in 1787.

The goal of both orders was the redemption of Christian captives, not the abolition of slavery. Neither order took any position concerning slavery or the issue of non-Christians enslaved by Christians. John Greenleaf Whittier, however, used the example of the Trinitarians in his antislavery polemic "The Mantle of Saint John of Matha" in 1865.

See also FREEDOM; NORTH AFRICA; WHITE SLAVERY.

BIBLIOGRAPHY

DESLANDRES, P. *L'Ordre des Trinitaires pour le rachat des captifs.* 2 vols. 1903.

HEIMBUCHER, MAX. *Die Orden und Kongregationen der katholischen Kirche.* 2nd ed. 1907. Vol. 2, pp. 69–78 on the Trinitarians; pp. 212–218 on the Mercedarians.

PLACER LOPEZ, GUMERSINDO. *Bibliografia mercedaria.* 1963.

VÁZQUEZ, G. *Manual de historia de la Orden de N. Señora de la Merced.* 1931.

Stephen Wagley

Religion

See Redemption of Captives; Religious Groups, Slave Ownership by; Society for the Propagation of the Gospel. *See also the entries on specific religious denominations.*

Religious Groups, Slave Ownership by

Almost from the beginning of recorded history, religious groups have acquired and held slaves, whether captured in wars, sacrificed for ritualistic purposes, or used to maintain worship sites and "priestly" figures. In the wars between Christians and Muslims during the Middle Ages and after, each side enslaved captives, and insomuch as Christians felt any need to rationalize such actions, they did so by invoking the "just war" doctrine. In the western world, slavery went unquestioned by the major religious groups until the eighteenth century. Scripture did not condemn slavery as an institution—a fact that proslavery advocates in the United States would use in their defense of slavery during the nineteenth century.

Beginning in the late seventeenth century and intensifying during the next century, several small pietistic sects, especially the Society of Friends (Quakers), began to criticize slavery as a violation of the New Testament, an act of kidnapping, and a corruption of human relations. By the late eighteenth century the Quakers in North America no longer accepted slaveholders into their meetings, and they moved into the public sphere to call for general emancipation.

In British North America, the Baptists and Methodists both harbored antislavery sympathies as they evangelized among blacks and whites and preached a new birth in Christ that respected no human condition. The Anglican Society for the Propagation of the Gospel in Foreign Parts also tried to bring the Gospel to the slaves in British North America, but it met stiff resistance from slaveholders who feared that Christian slaves might be less obedient than "heathen" ones and that a baptized slave would have a different standing in law.

Anglican clergy in the southern colonies often owned slaves and proved largely indifferent to such missionary efforts. Elsewhere in the New World, the Catholic church, which acknowledged that slaves were humans with immortal souls needful of Christian conversion, baptized slaves and ministered to them to the extent that masters would allow, but conversion did not much affect the slaves' status in law or practice. By the early nineteenth century, the Baptists and Methodists operating in the American South largely forsook their antislavery reputation so as to be able to preach freely among whites.

Black slaves and free blacks used evangelical messages of an imminent Judgment Day and their own religious gatherings to mount resistance to bondage. This was especially true in Gabriel's Rebellion in Virginia in 1800, Denmark Vesey's Conspiracy in Charleston, South Carolina, in 1822, and Nat Turner's Rebellion in Virginia in 1831. The use of religion in resistance movements convinced white southerners that further controls on slave religion were necessary and that any hint of antislavery sentiment coming from white churches was dangerous.

By the late antebellum period, southerners had launched a campaign to bring the Gospel to the slave quarters, as a means to fulfill their duties as Christian masters and to control slave religion. In doing so, they also were responding to the increasingly vocal antislavery preachments of northern churches, which eventually led to the sectional break among Baptists, Methodists, and Presbyterians.

In 1844 slaveholding by clergy had precipitated both the Methodists' schism when northern Methodists objected to slave owning by Bishop James Osgood Andrew of Georgia and the Baptists' schism when Alabama Baptists objected to efforts to get a Baptist missionary to resign his post to the Cherokee Nation because he owned slaves. Episcopalians broke along sectional lines during the Civil War but reunited after Appomattox. Catholics, Lutherans, and Jews in the United States avoided crack-ups on the slavery question by accommodating to local social and political conditions in order to focus on building their own religious infrastructures.

The various churches' positions on slavery as an institution and on slaves as having souls capable of conversion shaped the practice of those churches as slaveholders. Quakers, Wesleyan Methodists, and numerous individual congregations prohibited slaveholding outright in the United States. As slavery was gradually abolished in the northern states, slaveholding among congregations and clergy there became a moot question. In the American South, however, it was not uncommon for individual clergy to own or hire slaves or for the boards of trustees of particular churches, as the titleholders to the property, to own slaves in the churches' name. Given the significant degree of congregational autonomy among the major Protestant denominations in the South, practices varied according to local customs, need, and resources. But the major church bodies exercised no control over the treatment or legal standing of slaves owned by individual churches or clergy.

Various church protocols urged ministers to baptize, catechize, and confirm slaves, and to provide places for them at worship (which often meant segregated seating). But southern Protestant churches endorsed the southern law that forbade slaves to learn to read and write, to assemble without a white presence, or to move about freely. The churches accepted the preeminent right of the master to dispose of his or her property without regard to slave marriages or family ties.

Hierarchically organized churches followed similar lines. Catholic slaveholders, for example, included prelates and religious orders throughout the New World. Indeed, in Brazil the Benedictines and Carmelites were great landed proprietors and slaveholders. Although individual priests and nuns tried to ameliorate the condition of slaves and follow the church's charge to bring slaves into the Catholic fold through baptism and catechism, the church overall bolstered slavery by insisting on respect for authority and obedience to masters. The church did not take the lead in antislavery activism anywhere in the New World. Critics of slavery in Brazil told tales of priests taking sexual liberties with their slaves and other scandals, much to the embarrassment of church authorities. By the mid-nineteenth century, the religious orders in Brazil began to move toward manumission. Indeed, in 1866, the Benedictines, who owned two thousand slaves, decided to free all children thereafter born to slaves held by the order. When the Benedictines and Carmelites began freeing slaves in the 1870s, their move helped spur many private manumissions from Catholic laypeople. In North America, Catholic religious orders were unique among slaveholding churches or clergy in that they sometimes held significant numbers of slaves. This was true in the case of the Jesuits, who ran plantations in Maryland before selling most of their slaves by the 1830s, and the Vincentians in Missouri, who also were unusual in allowing their slaves to veto a sale. Otherwise, Catholic religious orders and clergy conformed to southern custom and law regarding slaveholding. By all accounts, religious groups and clergy who owned slaves, regardless of denomination or location, were no better or no worse than other slaveholders in treatment of slaves, likelihood of manumission, or other interactions with bondage and bondspeople.

The number of slaves owned by southern churches and clergy was not large, but the involvement of clergy in slaveholding committed them further to upholding the institution, even as they called for a "humane" Christian oversight of slaves. Owning slaves heightened the clergy's acceptance in southern society generally, and made possible their critique of other aspects of southern morality. Slaveholding also thrust clergy to the forefront of defending slavery, as, for example, in the case of New York–born John Bachman, who became the leading Lutheran minister in the South and a proslavery apologist, and Episcopal bishop Leonides Polk, who owned a Louisiana sugar plantation and fought for slavery as a general in the Confederate army. During the Civil War, amid southern defeat, slaveholding clergy joined their nonslaveholding brethren in blaming Confederate reverses, in part, on a failure to live up to the responsibility of being Christian masters. But until emancipation came by force of arms, slaveholding clergy continued to buttress the peculiar institution by word and by holding on to their slaves. When freedom came, the slaves of slaveholding clergy and churches joined in the exodus from white churches to churches of their own.

See also CHRISTIANITY; PERSPECTIVES ON SLAVERY; SLAVE RELIGION.

BIBLIOGRAPHY

KOLCHIN, PETER. *American Slavery, 1619–1877*. 1993.
MATHEWS, DONALD G. *Religion in the Old South*. 1977.
MILLER, RANDALL M., and JOHN DAVID SMITH, eds. *The Dictionary of Afro-American Slavery*. Rev. ed., 1997.
MILLER, RANDALL M., and JON WAKELYN, eds. *Catholics in the Old South: Essays on Church and Culture*. 1983.
RABOTEAU, ALBERT J. *Slave Religion: The "Invisible Institution" in the Antebellum South*. 1978.
SNAY, MITCHELL. *Gospel of Disunion: Religion and Separatism in the Antebellum South*. 1993.

Randall M. Miller

Reparations

The legacy of the transatlantic slave trade has had a great impact upon the lives of Africans and the African diaspora. Many people of African descent feel that reparations to African descendants are warranted because of the negative effects of the slave trade and slavery on African peoples.

Leaders of the reparations movement cite several factors to strengthen their claims. In the United States black incomes are disproportionately below the poverty level. Many believe this is a result of slavery and its legacy, which led to political disenfranchisement and the economic dependence of blacks.

Institutionalized racism is cited as another reason why reparations are in order. The argument here is that the legacy of racism has prevented even the most capable blacks from progressing as their abilities warrant. Reparationists believe that the attempt to justify slavery by the negative depiction of blacks has severely tarnished the publicly held perception of black people today.

Violence against blacks is also an issue raised by reparationists in support of their argument. Police brutality and black-on-black crime is thought to result from the belief that a black life is not as valuable as a white one. The idea that blacks are inferior has also resulted in social degradation by some whites and blacks alike.

The movement for reparations gained considerable momentum in 1969, when James Forman of the National Black Economic Development Conference interrupted Sunday service at Riverside Church in New York City to demand five-hundred million dollars from the white community of churches and synagogues. The National Coalition of Blacks for Reparations in America is today one of most popular of the reparationist groups and is fervently pushing for reparations in the form of monetary payments to descendants of slaves.

Compensation in the form of money is not the only aim of reparationist groups, although it attracts the most attention. Some groups call for housing, educational improvements, and new jobs. Others call for formal apologies from western governments, acknowledgment of African contributions to civilization, and a more positive portrayal of black people.

In Africa the movement cites depopulation and colonialism as reasons for its call for reparations. Scholars believe that nine to fifteen million captives were taken from Africa as captives, but these numbers are often debated. Depopulation and colonialism are believed to have broken down the social structure of African nations by exporting Africans who were in their most productive years. Reparationists in Africa call for European nations to discontinue support of political tyrants and to provide aid in the democratization of their countries.

Reparation is not a topic that solely concerns African people. In the United States, victims and their families were awarded compensation for the internment of Japanese Americans during World War II. Native American groups are also attempting to reacquire lands lost during westward expansion. In 1996 the United Nations ordered Japan to pay reparations to Korean women held as sex slaves during World War II, often referred to as "comfort women." After World War II, the victorious Allied powers demanded payments from Germany for its mistreatment of prisoners of war and for the destruction of civilian property. Germany in fact paid reparations to Israel for atrocities committed against the Jewish people by Hitler.

Those who oppose the idea of reparations to blacks believe that because neither the victims nor the perpetrators of slavery are still alive, society is relieved from being held accountable and that the government did not, itself, take part in slavery. The belief that the movement for reparations fosters feelings of victimization among blacks and is detrimental to blacks' progress is also espoused by those who oppose the movement.

See also COMFORT WOMEN IN WORLD WAR II; NATIVE AMERICANS.

BIBLIOGRAPHY

ELLEN, DAVID. "Payback Time." *New Republic* 201 (1989): 10–11.
LECKY, ROBERT S., and H. ELLIOT WRIGHT, eds. *Black Manifesto: Religion, Racism, and Reparations.* 1969.
SOH, CHUNGHEE SARAH. "The Korean Comfort Women: Movement for Redress." *Asian Survey* 36 (1996): 1226–1240.

Perry L. Kyles Jr.

Repatriation to Africa

As the free black population grew after the Revolutionary War, abolitionist groups that included repatriation to Africa among their goals sprang up in England and the United States. In their efforts to check the slave trade, British philanthropists, with government support, shipped several hundred black Revolutionary War refugees—the first group traveling from Britain in 1787, the largest departing from Nova Scotia in 1792—to the West African territory of Sierra Leone, which in 1808 became a British crown colony. African-Americans, organized in African Union Societies in eastern cities, were not anxious to emigrate to places where they would be under white domination. Nor were British authorities eager to have Americans emigrate to or trade with Sierra Leone. An exception was made for Paul Cuffe, a New England sea captain of mixed black and Native American ancestry, who in 1816 was permitted to transport thirty-eight black emigrants from the United States to Sierra Leone, the vanguard of a movement he hoped would hasten universal emancipation as well as the development of a black Christian nation.

The movement to send African-Americans to Africa became institutionalized in 1816 with the founding of the American Colonization Society (ACS), an organization combining practicality and idealism. The ACS was headed largely by border-state slaveholders and politicians like Henry Clay and General Andrew Jackson who wanted the South rid of free blacks, whom they feared would cause rebellion and insurrection. The ACS was managed largely by Presbyterian ministers who were dedicated to the "Christianization and civilization" of Africa. After several years of searching, the ACS purchased from native chieftains territory on the west coast of Africa adjacent to Sierra Leone and named the colony Liberia. The first colony settled at Cape Mesurado in January 1822. The ACS transported three thousand African-Americans to Liberia in the 1820s and 1830s; except for the early 1850s, this was the heyday of colonization.

Many who later became antislavery leaders began as colonizationists. Mirroring the rise and decline of colonization was the career of James G. Birney, a Kentucky-born slaveholder who freed his slaves as an act of Christian benevolence around 1830. In 1832 he became the colonization society's southwest agent; in 1833 he organized an ill-starred shipment of blacks from New Orleans to Liberia; by the mid-1830s he had become disenchanted with colonization, as was reflected in his *Letter on Colonization*, and converted to emancipation; in 1840 and again in 1844 he was the antislavery Liberty Party candidate for president of the United States. In response to the Fugitive Slave Law of 1850 and proslavery decisions by the U.S. Supreme Court, Birney countenanced individual migration but remained adamantly opposed to group colonization.

Among the small African-American elite, interest in emigration intensified in the 1850s, as the future for free blacks appeared increasingly bleak in the United States. Representative of this group was a New York-born clergyman, Alexander Crummell (1819–1898), who after graduating from Queens' College, Cambridge, in 1853, emigrated to Liberia as a Protestant Episcopal Church missionary and became an influential promoter of African-American emigration in the 1850s and 1860s. Crummell's interest in Africa was long-standing. His father was born in Sierra Leone. Among his father's friends was John Russwurm, the first black to graduate from an American college and cofounder of the first black newspaper in the United States. In 1829 Russwurm emigrated to Liberia, where he was a civic and political leader until his death in 1851. Crummell's mentor, the Reverend Peter Williams Jr., had worked actively with Paul Cuffe to encourage African-American emigration and trade

with Africa. At the 1840 Negro Convention in Albany, Crummell was one of only two delegates to oppose a resolution condemning the Colonization Society.

Once in Liberia, Crummell embarked on his mission of black-Christian nation building, "During my residence in Africa," he later noted, "I was pastor; Master of the High School; Professor in Liberia College; School Farmer; Missionary." He was also a public teacher, repeatedly urging upon his countrymen the need for economic development, political restraint, and above all Christian benevolence. In the 1860s he made two extended visits to the United States, with ACS support, to promote colonization and to stimulate philanthropic interest in Liberian education. He also publicized colonization through his letters in the ACS journal, *African Repository,* and in his first book, *The Future of Africa* (1862). His Liberian years were not smooth, however. He ran afoul of his white church superiors in an abortive attempt to establish a separate black diocese in Monrovia. He also become involved in the political struggle between mulatto and black Americo-Liberians, siding with the blacks, and was forced to flee the country. Discouraged, he returned permanently to the United States

Members of the Presbyterian church in Liberia pose in front of their banner for the "stranger mission" around 1900. [Library of Congress/Corbis]

in 1872, calling on Britain or the United States to establish a protectorate in Liberia.

That Crummell lived in Liberia for nearly twenty years lent authority to his views on African emigration. Two contemporaries with whom he interacted were the Reverend Henry Highland Garnet, his boyhood friend, and Martin R. Delany, both of whom made arrangements for the selective emigration of black Americans to West Africa on the eve of the Civil War. The war cut short these plans, but the failure of Reconstruction rekindled their interest in Africa. In 1881, Garnet was chosen over Delany, who had ACS support, as American minister to Liberia. Crummell also influenced a handful of activists in the succeeding generation. African Methodist Episcopal church leader Henry M. Turner, the most prominent colonizationist in late-nineteenth-century America, attributed much of his early interest in Africa to Crummell. John E. Bruce and William H. Ferris, Crummell's protégés, were important members of Marcus Garvey's "Back-to-Africa" movement in the 1920s.

African-American emigration was a response to slavery and racial bigotry in the United States. Given the energy expended, the results were unimpressive. Down to the century's end, the ACS dispatched only 15,300 emigrants to Liberia. Like most newcomers, these Americans in Africa were culture-bound. The notion of "Christianization and civilization" was itself very American. The emigrants' "city on a hill" was to be modeled after what they had left behind in their American homeland. This meant bringing with them Anglo-American ideas regarding race, color, caste, and religion. Untenable then, their position is irrelevant in the present postnational age of globalism.

See also AMERICAN COLONIZATION SOCIETY; BIRNEY, JAMES G.; GARNET, HENRY; LIBERIA; SIERRA LEONE.

BIBLIOGRAPHY

FLADELAND, BETTY. *James Gillespie Birney: Slaveholder to Abolitionist.* 1955.

MILLER, FLOYD J. *The Search for a Black Nationality: Black Colonization and Emigration 1787–1863.* 1975.

MOSES, WILSON J. *Alexander Crummell: A Study of Civilization and Discontent.* 1989.

SCRUGGS, OTEY M. *We the Children of Africa in This Land: Alexander Crummell.* 1972.

STAUDENRAUS, P. J. *The African Colonization Movement 1816–1865.* 1961.

Otey M. Scruggs

Resistance, Day-to-Day

The discussion that follows is distinct from but related to that in the entry Rebellions and Violent Resistance, *which the reader is urged to consult for further information.*

"Day-to-day resistance" refers to a wide variety of indirect, masked, or passive acts by which individual slaves in their daily lives protested their enslavement. Throughout the history of slavery, slaves to varying degrees have deserted estates, willfully dragged their feet or sat down in the field, mutilated themselves, poisoned food, smashed tools, torched crops and buildings, abused stock, filched property, habitually lied, aborted pregnancies, practiced infanticide, and committed suicide. Recent scholarship on the development in the Americas of slave economies and internal markets and on the process of creolization and the forging of slave subcultures has expanded the concept of day-to-day resistance to cover virtually any means short of open revolt by which slaves have survived their enslavement.

Scholarship in the United States on day-to-day resistance grew out of a larger debate during the first half of the twentieth century on the essential nature of master-slave relations and on the personality of the typical slave. For decades, Ulrich Bonnell Phillips, a white southern-born historian who was the grandson of a Georgia plantation owner, dominated the field, depicting a largely benign, paternalistic institution that had acted to civilize an innately inferior race and to raise acquiescent and contented slaves. In this context, Phillips and his followers pointed to the relative infrequency and small size of slave revolts in the old South.

Leading African-American scholars such as W. E. B. Du Bois and Carter G. Woodson challenged the essentials of Phillips's view from the beginning. Initially, the white academic establishment ignored or dismissed their views. But their numerous writings on African-American life and culture included scattered commentary on slaves' initiatives and accomplishments, and this proved crucial, by the 1940s, to the first focused studies of day-to-day resistance as an alternative form of protest for persistent slave rebels—when open revolt, given the gross imbalance of forces, amounted to suicide. Woodson's *Journal of Negro History* published articles by Harvey Wish on slaves' disloyalty in the Confederacy (1938) and by Herbert Aptheker on fugitive slaves in the United States (1939). Then, in 1942, it featured a groundbreaking essay on day-to-day resistance by Raymond and Alice Bauer, two anthropologists who had studied under the pioneering Africanist Melville Herskovits. Aptheker also had a chapter on "Individual Acts of Resistance" in his *American Negro Slave Revolts* (1943), a classic attack on the stereotype of slave docility and still the indispensable starting point for the study of slave rebellion in the United States.

After World War II, in a rapidly changing political and social climate, Kenneth Stamp's systematic assault on the Phillips interpretation was warmly received. In a chapter on slaves as "A Troublesome Property" in *The Peculiar Institution* (1956), Stampp strengthened the case for day-to-day resistance by citing plantation records and planters' correspondence. Many acts of resistance, Stampp concluded, represented conscious decisions; others welled up without conscious intent, in response to the degradation of slavery. To justify at least some kinds of day-to-day resistance, slaves developed their own moral code, making a distinction, for instance, between taking from the master and stealing from fellow slaves. They ran away and made mischief to such an extent that the prominent southern physician Samuel Cartwright invented two "Negro diseases"—drapetomania (running-away disease) and dysaethesia aethiopica (mischief-making disease)—to explain their behavior. Stampp believed that the acts of day-to-day resistance occasionally reached dangerously high levels in the antebellum South, although the coercive nature of the institution guaranteed its continued profitability.

Writing in 1959, Stanley Elkins applauded Stampp's scholarship, but on the specific question of slaves' resistance, he came closer to Phillips by acknowledging infrequent revolts and acts of day-to-day resistance. Unlike Phillips, however, Elkins linked the alleged docile behavior of slaves in the antebellum South not to racial characteristics but to a system of slavery so "closed and circumscribed" that it resembled a Nazi concentration camp. Elkins saw a much more open and fluid system of slavery in Latin America. There, he argued, slaves revolted more often and in greater numbers; they enjoyed rights and protections guaranteed by the Spanish crown and the Catholic church; and they had relatively easy access to manumission. Elkins maintained (erroneously) that Latin American slavery produced nothing equivalent to "Sambo," his pejorative stereotype of blacks as indolent, infantile, and submissive. Although critics pointed out serious problems in Elkins's theory (the comparability of a system of labor with a system of extermination) and method (overreliance on secondary sources, which caused him to confuse Latin American law with Latin American reality), his heuristic book sparked considerable empirical research on the daily life of slaves, which tended to confirm the prevalence of day-to-day resistance wherever slavery existed.

Subsequent debate on day-to-day resistance centered on what slaves meant by these acts and what results they achieved. Writing in 1967, George Frederickson and Christopher Lasch questioned whether specific instances of noncooperation by individual slaves could legitimately qualify as resistance. For these authors, resistance, to be worthy of the name, had to have political content. Slaves who engaged in political resistance, as individuals or as groups, acted consciously on behalf of a larger collective interest to effect a redistribution of power from the haves to the have-nots. Thus, for the label to fit, "resistance" requires an understanding of the slave's conscious mind, which is often unknowable in the myriad cases of day-to-day resistance.

Sidney Mintz, a specialist in Caribbean anthropology, and Eugene Genovese, a historian, advanced the debate in their cross-fertilized scholarship on slavery. Mintz (1971) called for greater attention to day-to-day resistance as part of a multilevel struggle against enslavement. Preoccupation with violent resistance deflected attention from other strategies that slaves developed to deal with their daily hardships. "Considerable resistance," Mintz pointed out in a much-cited observation, "involved as its precondition some processes of culture change, of adaptation, on the part of the slaves themselves. . . . The house slave who poisoned her master's family by putting ground grass in the food had first to become the family cook."

Genovese, in *Roll, Jordan, Roll* (1974), argued that all slave societies reveal a continuum of "resistance in accommodation and accommodation in resistance." Of the wide-ranging forms of individual and collective resistance, only flight and revolt offered examples of a dramatic departure from the process of accommodation. Even insurrection itself might aim merely at redressing violations of local ground rules on a given plantation, rather than at any fundamental challenge to slavery per se. Genovese acknowledged that some writers had defined insurrection "as the only genuine resistance since it alone directly challenged the power of the regime." In contrast, day-to-day resistance appeared to "qualify at best as pre-political and at worst as apolitical."

Yet Genovese found those distinctions unsatisfactory. All forms of resistance asserted the slaves' essential humanity against the dehumanizing logic of slavery. Wherever slavery existed, masters had to make concessions to slaves who never became a pure embodiment of the master's will. In slave societies masters and slaves, in a dialectic of resistance and accommodation, constructed unequal relations of mutuality with a strong ethical dimension—in short, a moral economy. Contested terrain invariably remained, however, to feed day-to-day resistance. Over time, what masters regarded as privileges slaves regarded as rights. What masters saw as rascality slaves saw as amusement. In this conflict-ridden context, slaves' initiatives, whether singing spirituals or spinning folktales, could be called political in that they contributed to the cementing of social bonds that countered the divisive features of paternalism, and in that they created a barrier to casual violations of the unwritten standards embedded in the historically conditioned relations of power. Thus, for Genovese, day-to-day resistance could have political content without intentionality, although generally within a framework of accommodation.

However, in disagreement with Genovese, a number of recent students of resistance have appealed to the work of James Scott, a political scientist, who borrowed from the literature on slavery to explain day-to-day resistance by Asian peasants. Actually, Scott confuses Genovese's position with that of Frederickson and Lasch, but he nevertheless restores political content to acts of day-to-day resistance and exalts their cumulative potential to force redistributions of power and even to transform systems. In Scott's formulation of political resistance, leadership, premeditation, and coordination count for little. Spontaneity, selfishness, and anonymity count for more. Immanent in day-to-day resistance is revolution: "Any relaxation in surveillance and punishment and foot-dragging threatens to become a declared strike; folktales of oblique aggression threaten to become face-to-face defiant contempt, millennial dreams threaten to become revolutionary politics."

Without historical grounding, no act of day-to-day resistance can easily qualify as a conscious blow against power, and even when there is such grounding, the available documentation rarely states what the slave had in mind. Nor can the conclusions of white observers about slaves' cognition be readily trusted. A planter's diary, for example, might disclose a tragic incident of a slave mother who smothered her infant, when, as medical historians now believe, the more likely explanation was sudden infant death syndrome or a deficiency disease. Without evidence of slaves' intent, acts of day-to-day resistance might be explained not by the inherent injustice of the slave system but by slaves' rising expectations, produced by a generous master or by the slaves' own human frailty. Every society in human history has produced innumerable examples of noncooperation by the laboring classes that could be classified as day-to-day resistance. On one hand, the total impact of these acts, combined with the inefficiency of the elite in responding to them, may have unintended consequences that challenge the system. On the other hand, such acts may have bolstered the prevailing system by, say providing an outlet that siphoned off more serious insurrectionary pressures. Slaveholders may not have appreciated the irony, but as long as day-to-day resistance was kept within certain bounds, it may have conduced to the maintenance of the slave system, if not to the profit of certain masters. Notably, in the eighteenth-century Caribbean, revolutionary slave movements emerged on several islands only after planters, by

clearing all cultivable land, had closed off the escape routes for slaves who deserted.

To some, suicide by slaves stands out as the ultimate statement of protest against a heinous institution. But the suicide of an able slave leader might also diminish the collective capacity of an entire slave community to resist. Throughout the Americas African-born slaves committed suicide at higher rates than creole slaves, whether because of the trauma of the Middle Passage and forced acculturation or because certain West African religions sanctioned suicide for prisoners of war. Yet in colonial Cuba, the rate of suicide among slaves, though high enough to prompt a government inquiry in 1847, was only one-fourteenth of the rate among imported Chinese coolies, according to census data for 1862. The rate of suicide among slaves in the antebellum South was only one-third of the rate among the white population, according to data in the U.S. census of 1850.

Instances of abortion and infanticide by slaves have occurred in every slave society. Yet in the antebellum South the slave population still grew naturally at a rate comparable to the white population. Even in the notorious sugar regions of the Caribbean, the natural decrease in the slave population had more to do with lactation practices and the duration of childbearing years than with the cumulative impact of day-to-day resistance by slave women. At any rate, abortion and infanticide never won broad support in the slave quarters as legitimate forms of protest.

Malingering by slaves might reflect self-indulgence as well as political resistance. Malingerers might have consciously sought to make bad masters suffer, but other slaves knew that these masters might suffer so much that their debts would mount, forcing sales of slaves and thus separating slave families. As to the magnitude of malingering, the economic historians Robert Fogel and Stanley Engerman have calculated, using a sample of fifteen plantations in the antebellum South in the 1850s, an average loss of twelve workdays per year due to illness—a lower rate than for certain categories of twentieth-century laborers.

Running away ranks among the most common and most conspicuous forms of day-to-day resistance. In some of the more forbidding locations in the Americas, permanent desertion (*grand marronnage*) led to the formation of fortified enclaves that shielded scored of fugitives who formed autonomous communities. Short-term absenteeism (*petit marronnage*) afflicted all slaveholding societies and could reach epidemic proportions during civil wars and imperial conflicts. Young slave men accounted for more than three-quarters of all runaways in the major slaveholding regions of the Americas. Slaves tended to run away as individuals or with a partner, a pattern that seems to have been most

THE MODERN MEDEA—THE STORY OF MARGARET GARNER.—Photographed by Brady, from a Painting by Thomas Noble.—[See Page 318.]

The "Modern Medea" was a woman who, having been tracked down after her escape, would kill her own children rather than have them returned to a life of slavery. [Library of Congress/Corbis]

pronounced in the antebellum South. African-born slaves deserted more frequently than creole slaves and headed more mass desertions. Skilled slaves, excluding drivers, show up as fugitives in disproportionate numbers. Most fugitives deserted for a short time within a small radius of the master's estate; they usually returned within one or two weeks. Masters fully expected a certain number of runaways and often reacted rather casually. Months might pass before a master posted advertisements in newspapers for a runaway slave. On the Caribbean island of Saint Vincent a slave was called a runaway only after having been gone for five years. Besides personal liberation, the leading cause of desertion included avoiding punishment, meeting with relatives or loved ones, supplementing provisions, and escaping harvesttime or other periods of intense labor.

Fugitive slaves and other day-to-day resisters stretched and pushed the slave system, but by themselves they did not end slavery anywhere. Throughout the Americas, the institution remained profitable until the moment of emancipation. In truth, what the incumbents failed to do often proves to be far more

important in explaining the impact of resistance than what the insurgents themselves did. At those rare moments when day-to-day resistance reached debilitating proportions, external rivalries or civil war had already deeply divided the domestic elite and had thereby loosened the bonds of internal control. Every slave code in the history of the Americas reflected the concern of the elite with controlling day-to-day resistance. Laws were written to regulate provisioning; hours of work; leisure time and amusements; care of pregnant and lactating women; dwellings for slave families; assembly; travel; access to alcohol, tools, and weapons; manumission by self-purchase; and punishment. Enforcement tended to tighten during times of trouble, and theft was the most frequently punished of crimes committed by slaves.

On plantations and in towns and cities, masters more directly countered day-to-day resistance with chilling displays of coercion that could readily slip into cruelty. But they also instituted imaginative systems of rewards and incentives. They doled out presents, paid bonuses and wages, promoted stable slave families, permitted unlicensed travel, distributed garden plots, dangled the prospect of manumission, served as godparents to slave children (especially in Latin America), and elevated dutiful slaves to privileged positions. To a much greater extent than in the Caribbean, where slave-run internal markets flourished, masters in the antebellum South purchased the surplus produced from slaves' provision grounds and even served as bankers for slaves' earnings. In this respect, acts of day-to-day resistance in all slave societies can be seen more realistically as factors of varying significance within a larger arena where masters and slaves were continually negotiating the terms of the relationship.

Slaves who engaged in day-to-day resistance ultimately wielded a two-edged sword. Subjugated people, understandably, tend to romanticize those among them who by their actions boldly deny internalized consent to the powers that be. Thieving, lying, and general rascality could send a powerful message to abusive masters when a slave community had few or no alternative options. Yet despite the slaves' own distinctions, such as the difference between taking and stealing, nihilistic day-to-day resistance—for which there is ample evidence—created serious problems for slave leaders who aspired to build their own counter-hegemonic moral and social order, especially when the values of the slave community were interpenetrated by the values of a resident master class.

See also DU BOIS, W. E. B.; ELKINS THESIS; INSURRECTIONS.

BIBLIOGRAPHY

APTHEKER, HERBERT. *American Negro Slave Revolts.* 1943.

BAUER, RAYMOND A., and ALICE H. BAUER. "Day to Day Resistance to Slavery." *Journal of Negro History* 28 (1942): 338–419.

ELKINS, STANLEY M. *Slavery: A Problem in American Institutional and Intellectual Life.* 1959

FOGEL, ROBERT WILLIAM, and STANLEY L. ENGERMAN. *Time on the Cross: The Economics of American Negro Slavery.* 1974.

FREDERICKSON, GEORGE M., and CHRISTOPHER LASCH. "Resistance to Slavery." *Civil War History* 13 (1967): 315–329.

GENOVESE, EUGENE D. *Roll, Jordan, Roll: The World the Slaves Made.* 1974.

LICHTENSTEIN, ALEX. "'That Disposition to Theft, with Which They Have Been Branded': Moral Economy, Slave Management, and the Law." *Journal of Social History* 21 (1988): 413–440.

MINTZ, SIDNEY W. "Toward an Afro-American History." *Journal of World History* 13 (1971): 317–332.

PAQUETTE, ROBERT L. "Slave Resistance and Social History." *Journal of Social History* 24 (Spring 1991): 681–685.

SCOTT, JAMES C. *Domination and the Arts of Resistance.* 1990.

STAMPP, KENNETH M. *The Peculiar Institution: Slavery in the Ante-bellum South.* 1956

Robert L. Paquette

Réunion

See Mauritius and Réunion.

Rhode Island

A law of 1652 forbidding residents of Rhode Island to hold "negers" longer than ten years suggests reservations about slavery, but by 1708, a tax on imported Africans and a census count of 426 "Negroes"—or 5.9 percent of the population—reveals that Rhode Islanders had overcome their hesitancy. Some Indians were also enslaved, although more were sold in the West Indies, and colonial census records do not distinguish between free and enslaved "Negroes" and "Indians." Lorenzo Greene, in *The Negro in Colonial New England* (1942), found Rhode Island's legal controls over its slave population the harshest in New England, reflecting their greater numbers, especially in towns like South Kingston, where slaves were one-third of the population. The slave population of Newport, the urban center of slave trading and slaveholding between 1725 and the Revolution, peaked in 1755 at 18.3 percent (1,234).

Jay Coughtry, in *The Notorious Triangle: Rhode Island and the African Slave Trade, 1700–1807* (1981), states that by 1725 Newport had also become the home port for most slave traders in the mainland colonies. Since the city kept this position until Bristol muscled into the trade after the Revolution, slavery remained at the center of Rhode Island's economy.

Roger Williams voiced concern about African (though not Indian) slavery, but not until 1760 did Quakers—the Society of Friends—begin lobbying for restrictions on slavery. By 1773 the Friends had made slaveholding, not just trading, a cause for disownment. Eventually the legislature responded to petitions, and to a revolutionary zeal for freedom, by passing a bill freeing all slaves born after March 1784 and requiring slaveholders to educate those manumitted. Leaders were the Baptist George Benson, the Congre-

Table 1.   Slavery in Rhode Island, 1756–1790.

Year	Slave Population	% of Total Population
1756	4,697	11.6
1774	3,668	5.8
1790	958	1.4

gationalist Samuel Hopkins, and the Quaker Moses Brown, founders of the Providence Abolition Society (1789), and Newport Gardiner of the African Union Society (1780)—all lobbying for an end to slavery and for education for blacks.

By 1810, only 108 blacks remained in slavery (0.1 percent of the population), although their opportunities remained limited. In 1824, when a race riot leveled the black neighborhood of "Hard Scrabble" in Providence, Gardiner concluded that remaining to fight for racial equality was "vain" and along with thirty-two other Rhode Islanders joined an expedition of the American Colonization Society to Liberia.

Most of those concerned about race relations, however, welcomed the immediate abolition program of William Lloyd Garrison as promising both racial equality and a complete end to slavery. Spread through the state in 1831 and 1832 by Alfred Niger and George Willis's circulation of *The Liberator* and Arnold Buffum's lectures, the new abolitionism had by 1833 won enough converts to form a new abolition society in Providence. Support came from the now aged Moses Brown; two mavericks, Elder Ray Potter (Baptist) and Reverend Thomas Williams (Congregationalist); and a black educator, the Reverend John Lewis. Two thousand young people, including many women, formed auxiliaries and joined in distributing literature and petitioning, activities that persuaded legislators in 1836 and 1837 to reject a proposed ban on antislavery speech and literature.

By 1840, there were too few reformers to sustain rival societies, and so most ignored the schisms that opened up elsewhere in antislavery politics. Bigger drains were the economic depression of 1837–1842 and the political divisions of the Dorr War (1842–1843), a fight over the extension of democracy in which abolitionists divided on racial lines.

Rhode Islanders did view the Fugitive Slave Act of 1850 as an attack on states' rights, countering with a personal liberty bill that guaranteed a jury trial to blacks accused of being runaways. In 1854 the extension of slavery into Kansas aroused great public concern about the liberties of whites. A few reformers worked to integrate schooling and public transportation, perhaps understanding that most whites would agree with the legislature's resolution of 1861 to accept the extension of slavery in order to prevent disunion.

See also AMERICAN COLONIZATION SOCIETY; FUGITIVE SLAVE LAWS, U.S.; GARRISON, WILLIAM LLOYD; WOMEN IN THE ANTISLAVERY MOVEMENT.

BIBLIOGRAPHY

BARTLETT, IRVING H. *From Slave to Citizen: The Story of the Negro in Rhode Island.* 1954.

KIVEN, ARLINE RUTH. *Then Why the Negroes: The Nature and Course of the Anti-slavery Movement in Rhode Island: 1637–1861.* 1973.

VAN BROEKHOVEN, DEBORAH BINGHAM. *Abolitionists Were Female: Rhode Island Women and the Antislavery Network.* 1998.

Deborah Bingham Van Broekhoven

Rights of Man

Between 20 and 26 August, 1789, the French National Assembly adopted the seventeen articles which make up the Declaration des Droits de l'Homme et du Citoyen—the Declaration of the Rights of Man and the Citizen. In later years, the declaration became the preamble for the French constitution of 1791 and for the constitution of 1793.

The philosophical antecedents of the declaration were numerous and varied: natural rights doctrine from John Locke and the writers of the *Encyclopédie,* the inviolability of property from the Physiocrats, natural sovereignty and the general will from Jean-Jacques Rousseau, separation of powers from the baron de Montesquieu, and actual provisions from the state charters of New Hampshire and Virginia.

In retrospect, it is easy to see the revolutionary potential of the Declaration of the Rights of Man for slave populations, beginning with the fact that the declaration spoke of universal human rights, not merely the political rights of the citizens of the homeland. In a few instances, the declaration placed restrictions upon political rights—for example, public office was open only to middle-class males (Article 17) and the right to participate in legislation was differentiated into direct and indirect participation (Article 6).

In its universally applicable principles, best termed natural rights, the declaration proclaimed that "all men are born free and equal" (Article 1), endowed with rights of liberty, property, inviolability of person, and resistance to oppression (Article 2). In addition, persons were to be free from arrest without judicial warrant (Article 7) and were to enjoy freedom of speech (Article 11) and of religion (Article 10), consistent with public order. All of these rights could easily be seen as undermining the legitimacy of slavery; to counterbalance them, a defender of slavery could point only to the inviolable right of property (Article 17).

Many of the members of the National Assembly recognized the revolutionary potential of the Declaration of the Rights of Man, but they envisioned it as spreading revolt among the masses in the less progressive states of continental Europe.

The ideology of the declaration produced its effects in the virtual abolition of the feudal order. On 15 March 1790, the remnants of the feudal system, with its central feature of unfree labor, were abolished by the National Assembly. Compulsory labor for feudal overlords was done away with, as were the *banalités*—the minor feudal duties imposed on the lower orders.

On 2 March 1791, the National Assembly moved to eliminate aspects of unfree labor within commerce and manufacturing. All corporations were abolished, primarily because they enjoyed monopolies and special privileges. The medieval guilds, with their mastership system and their elaborate rule of production, were eliminated. Finally, on 14 June 1791, the Le Chapelier law forbade labor unions. From the modern perspective, this law might be seen as restricting workers' freedom, but in the bourgeois ideology of free labor which prevailed at this stage of the French Revolution, it was seen as enhancing the right of contract enjoyed by laborer and capitalist like.

Little thought was given, however, to the possibility that the declaration would inspire servile insurrection in France's colonies. By 1791, a complex, many-sided civil war had broken out in the French colony of Saint Domingue (Haiti), with whites fighting whites for control of the colony and with revolts by both the free colored and slave populations. Slave revolts were endemic in the Caribbean, largely because of the ill treatment of slaves, but the revolt in Haiti seems to have been especially fueled by the ideology of the French Revolution, and particularly by the Declaration of the Rights of Man.

French colonists had used the rhetoric of the declaration to argue for their own emancipation from restrictive mercantilist trade regulations and for a significant degree of colonial self-government. Quite naturally, though, they desired to exclude mulattoes and slaves from its provisions. But copies of the declaration and of various writings supporting the revolutionary goals of "liberty, equality, fraternity" were widley circulated throughout the French colonies, and in Haiti there was a large free mulatto population with a significant percentage of persons literate in French who absorbed these ideas and who communicated them to the slave population of the colony.

The desire of left-wing Jacobins to end slavery throughout the empire was restrained by the fear that planters would turn colonies over to British forces rather than accept general emancipation. By the time the National Convention outlawed slavery in 1794, Haiti was effectively lost to France, and later attempts by Napoleon to reannex the territory ended in inglo-rious failure. Haiti became the second independent republic of the Western Hemisphere, its first Afro-American state, and the first slave society of the New World to end slavery.

See also CARIBBEAN REGION; ENCYCLOPÉDIE; LOCKE, JOHN; MONTESQUIEU, CHARLES-LOUIS DE SECONDAT DE; REBELLIONS AND VIOLENT RESISTANCE; ROUSSEAU, JEAN-JACQUES.

BIBLIOGRAPHY

KNIGHT, FRANKLIN W. *The Caribbean: The Genesis of a Fragmented Nationalism.* 2nd ed. 1990.
SCHAMA, SIMON. *Citizens: A Chronicle of the French Revolution.* 1989.
SOBOUL, ALBERT. *A Short History of the French Revolution, 1789–1799.* Translated by Geoffrey Symcox. 1965.

Patrick M. O'Neil

Rights of Slaves and Freedmen

See Freedmen; Law.

Roma

The Roma—called by others Romani or Gypsies—entered southeastern Europe in the last quarter of the thirteenth century as part of the Ottoman expansion into that area. Originating in India as a composite, non-Aryan military population assembled to resist the Muslim incursions led by the Ghaznavids, they left through the Hindu Kush during the first quarter of the eleventh century, moving through Persia, Armenia, and the Byzantine Empire toward the West.

Early accounts of the Romani presence in medieval Europe are scant, but it appears that the first Roma in the Balkan principality of Wallachia (now part of Romania) arrived as free people, who found an economic niche for the skills in metalworking, carpentry, and entertaining that they had brought from India and the Byzantine Empire. Wallachian society at the time the Roma first encountered it was technologically backward and agriculturally centered, in part because of the depleting effects of the Crusades in earlier centuries. As this peasant economy gradually shifted to a market economy, it came to depend more and more upon the artisan skills of the Roma (Gheorghe, 1983). With the increasing need for their labor in rural agricultural production, the Romanian peasantry, though not enslaved, became serfs. The skills of the Roma allowed them to move into otherwise vacant artisan niches in the economy—though whether they were "free" at the time is open to question. Some may have been; others were probably prisoners of the Turks.

Roma, who had at first established only loose working relationships with the feudal landlords, became associated with particular estates and by the early 1300s were being included in parcels of property given by one owner to another and to the monasteries; the earliest documentation refers to such tributes being made to monasteries before 1350. If Roma were enserfed by the Turks, it was possibly because they weren't Muslims and certainly because they had valuable skills. The latter reason would hold true for Romania, too. The condition defined as slavery, however, emerged later, out of the increasingly stringent measures taken by the landowners, the court, and the monasteries to prevent their Romani labor force from leaving their principalities—as Roma were beginning to do in response to the ever more burdensome demands upon their skills—and from the shift of their "limited fiscal dependency upon the Romanian princes" to an "unlimited personal dependency on the big landlords of the country, the monasteries, and the boyars" (Gheorghe, 1983, p. 23). The Code of Basil the Wolf of Moldavia, dated 1654, contained references to the treatment of slaves, including the death penalty for a Rom who raped a white woman. (The same offense committed by a non-Rom warranted no punishment.)

Gheorghe saw the enslavement of the Roma as an abuse committed by the feudal landlords, without any legal base or legitimation. Certainly their status as outsiders deprived the Roma of any power to resist, and according to the Islamic worldview of the occupying Ottomans, dominated non-Muslim populations were "fit only for enslavement" (Sugar, 1964, p. 103). By the 1500s, the term *tsigan*, originally a neutral ethnonym applied by the Europeans to the first Roma, had become synonymous with "slave." The fact that in 1995 *tsigan* was adopted by the Romanian government as the official designation for Roma in that country has generated much pain and anger, and it is indicative of the ongoing racism against the Romani minority in contemporary Romania (see Szente, 1996; Zenk et al., 1991).

Other words for "slave" were *rob*, *sclav*, and *scindrom*. Slaves were broadly divided into field slaves (*tsigani de ogor*) and house slaves (*tsigani de casatsi*). The latter were further divided into two groups: (1) slaves of the crown or state, that is, those of the noblemen (the *sclavi domneshti*), the court (*sclavi curte*), and householders (*sclavi gospod*); and (2) slaves of the church (*sclavi monastiveshti*). The field slaves were likewise divided into two groups, those of the *boyars* or landbarons, called the *sclavi coeveshti*; and those of the small landowners, the *sclavi de moshii*. The slaves of

Basil the Wolf, Prince of Moldavia. [Hulton-Deutsch Collection/Corbis]

the crown had three principal occupations, all skilled: gold washer, bear trainer, and spoon maker. In addition, there were slaves known as *layeshi* who were allowed to move about the estates practicing a variety of crafts, including those of musician, farrier, whitewasher, sieve-maker, blacksmith, and coppersmith. Slaves of the church were grooms, cooks, and coachmen; among the house slaves were *skopitsi*, males castrated so as not to threaten defilement of the "pure" noblewomen whom they served.

Field slaves lived in *shatras*—clusters of reed and mud huts on the outskirts of the estates, seldom visited by their owners. They were not allowed to have musical instruments for their own amusement, and they were bought and sold in lots, also called *shatras*, *chetas*, or *salashes*. Groups of slaves remained under the supervision of a *vatav* (also called a *chokoi*) or overseer, who was sometimes brutally cruel; and although it was forbidden by law to kill a slave, punishment frequently led to death.

House slaves were forbidden to speak Romani, and their descendants, the *Beyash*, now speak a variety of Romanian, a Latin-based language, rather than Romani.

Female house slaves were provided to visitors for sexual entertainment (Colson, 1839); the half-caste children of such unions inherited the slave status of their mothers. In the sixteenth century, a Romani child sold for the equivalent of forty-eight cents. By the nineteenth century, slaves were sold by body weight, at the rate of one gold piece per pound. Punishment of slaves included flogging, cutting off the lips, burning with lye, and clamping on a three-cornered spiked iron collar called a *cangue*. Slaves were able to escape periodically and take refuge in maroon communities in the Carpathian mountains; these are called *netotsi* in the literature.

By 1800 the 1654 laws codified by Basil the Wolf had been forgotten, and the treatment of slaves had become subject to the whims of those in charge of the estates or the monasteries. The Ottoman court attempted to make the laws more stringent and in its 1818 Wallachian penal code incorporated all Romani as slaves. But Ottoman rule was thwarted by a takeover by the Russians in 1826, and Paul Kisseleff was appointed governor in 1829. He was firmly opposed to slavery, but because of pressure from the boyars, among other things, he did not abolish it. Instead, in 1833 he incorporated stringent, conservative revisions in the Moldavian civil code, including the following: §II(154) "Legal unions cannot take place between free persons and slaves"; §II(162) "Marriage between slaves cannot take place without their owner's consent"; §II(174) "The price of a slave must be fixed by the Tribunal, according to his age, condition and profession"; §II(176) "If anyone has taken a female slave as a concubine, she will become free after his death. If he has had any children by her, they will also become free."

By the nineteenth century, the efficiency of mechanization, introduced as a result of the Industrial Revolution, both in America and in southeastern Europe, was making the ownership, care, and feeding of slaves a liability rather than an asset. Western abolition movements, brought into Romania by students returning from abroad, provoked self-examination. Moldavia and Wallachia were eager to be regarded as a part of the new Europe and took France as their model, seeing slavery increasingly as a barbaric and inhumane anachronism.

By the 1830s calls for abolition began to be heard. But smaller landowners were not able to afford mechanization and still relied on their slaves; they continued to oppose abolition vigorously. In 1837, however, Governor Alexandru Ghica freed the slaves on the estates under his jurisdiction and allowed them to speak Romani and practice their own customs. This was merely a drop in the bucket, since it affected only a tiny fraction (perhaps one-hundredth) of the total slave population. Nevertheless, it stimulated similar actions on the part of others: Mihai Sturdza, the prince of Moldavia, freed his slaves in 1842, and in 1847 the Wallachian church did likewise. On 25 September 1848, students demonstrated publicly in Bucharest and tore up a copy of the Russian statutes relating to slavery (Russia had occupied Romania from 1826 to 1834). They replaced the government with a provisional party, which immediately called for abolition. This freedom was short-lived, for less than three months later the provisional government was overthrown by the Russian-Turkish Convention, which promptly reinstituted many of the old laws, including those legalizing the ownership of human beings. It is likely that many of the slaves had remained unaware of their brief emancipation; but for those who knew, their return to enslavement must have been a terrible blow.

On 23 December 1855, however, the Moldavian General Assembly voted unanimously for abolition, and the bill was passed. The Wallachian Assembly did likewise on 8 February 1856. Complete legal freedom came in 1864, when Prince Ioan Couza, ruler of the now-united principalities, restored the Roma, as "free" people, to the estates where they had worked. In this context, "free" means only "no longer enslaved"; the Roma are still not truly free in Romania.

While the enslavement of Roma in the Balkans is the most extensively documented, Gypsies have also been enslaved at different times in other parts of the world. In Renaissance England King Edward VI passed a law stating that Gypsies be "branded with a *V* on their breast, and then enslaved for two years," and if they escaped and were recaptured, they were then branded with an *S* and made slaves for life. In Spain, according to a decree issued in 1538, Gypsies were enslaved in perpetuity to individuals as a punishment for escaping. (Spain had already begun shipping Gypsies to the Americas in the fifteenth century; three were transported by Columbus to the Caribbean on his third voyage in 1498.) Spain's later *solución americana* involved the shipping of Gypsy slaves to its colony in eighteenth-century Louisiana. An Afro-Gypsy community today lives in St. Martin's Parish, and reportedly there is another one in central Cuba, both descended from intermarriage between the two enslaved peoples. In the sixteenth century Portugal shipped Gypsies as an unwilling labor force to its colonies in Maranhão (now Brazil), Angola, and even India—the Roma's country of origin, which they had left five centuries earlier. In the eighteenth century they were made "slaves of the crown" in Russia during the reign of Catherine the Great; in Scotland they were employed as virtual slaves in the coal mines. England and Scotland had shipped Roma to Virginia and the Caribbean as slaves during the seventeenth and eighteenth centuries.

J. A. Vaillant, writing in 1857, dedicated his book to Alexandru and Grigore Ghica with the words, "Those who shed tears of compassion for the Negroes of Africa, of whom the American Republic makes its slaves, should give a kind thought to this short history of the Gypsies of India, of whom the European monarchies make their Negroes. These men, wanderers from Asia, will never again be itinerant; these slaves shall be *free*."

See also ENSLAVEMENT, METHODS OF; MEDIEVAL EUROPE, SLAVERY AND SERFDOM IN; PERSPECTIVES ON SLAVERY; SLAVES, SALE OF; SLAVE TRADE.

BIBLIOGRAPHY

ASCHER, ABRAHAM, TIBOR HALASI-KUN, and BÉLA KIRÁLY, eds. *The Mutual Effect of the Islamic and Judeo-Christian Worlds: The East-European Pattern.* 1979.

BECK, SAM. "The Origins of Gypsy Slavery in Romania." *Dialectical Anthropology* 14 (1989): 53–61.

COLSON, FÉLIX. *De l'état présent et de l'avenir des principautés de Moldavie et de Valachie.* 1839.

CROWE, DAVID. "The Gypsy Historical Experience in Romania." In *The Gypsies of Eastern Europe,* edited by David Crowe and John Kolsti. 1991.

GHEORGHE, NICOLAE. "The Origin of Roma's Slavery in the Romanian Principalities." *Roma* 7, no. 1 (1983): 12–27.

HANCOCK, IAN. *The Pariah Syndrome: An Account of Gypsy Slavery and Persecution.* 1987.

İNALCIK, H. "Servile Labor in the Ottoman Empire." In *The Mutual Effect of the Islamic and Judeo-Christian Worlds,* edited by Abraham Ascher, Tobor Halasi-Kun, and Béla Király. 1979; pp. 25–52.

PRODAN, DAVID. "The Origins of Serfdom in Transylvania." *Slavic Review* 49, no. 1 (1990): 1–17.

SUGAR, PETER F. *Southeastern Europe under Ottoman Rule, 1354–1804.* 1964.

SZENTE, VERONIKA L., *Sudden Rage at Dawn: Violence against Roma in Romania.* 1996.

VAILLANT, J. A. *Histoire vraie des vrais Bohémiens.* 1857.

ZENK, TED, et al. *Destroying Ethnic Identity: The Persecution of Gypsies in Romania.* 1991.

Ian Hancock

Roman Catholicism

See Bible; Christianity; Thomas Aquinas.

Rome, Ancient

See Ancient Rome; Concubinage; Education of Slaves; Freedmen; Gladiators; Law; Manumission; Miners; Philosophy; Plantations; Slave Trade; Spartacus; Torture in Ancient Rome.

Roots

See Film and Television, Slavery in.

Rousseau, Jean-Jacques [1712–1778]

French philosopher and author.

The first chapter of the first book of Rousseau's *Social Contract* begins

> Man is born free, yet everywhere lives in chains. He who believes himself the master of others does not escape being more of a slave than they. How did this change take place? I have no idea. What can render it legitimate? I believe I can answer this question.

This transformation is legitimate only if all those who join and constitute a society exchange their natural equality and freedom for conventional justice through a social contract. Rousseau revives the idea—at least as old as Herodotus and the Hebrew bible—that true freedom is slavery to the law, and grafts it onto the quite different postulate of natural equality.

To uphold the principles of equality and freedom, Rousseau shows that all forms of domination are illegitimate and no different from slavery. In the *Discourse on the Origins of Inequality* he reverses the usual conception of historical order and progress. He argues that the first stage in the history of inequality is the establishment of law and the right to property, the second stage the institution of political rule, and only the final stage the transformation from legitimate to arbitrary power in the relation of master to slave. Slavery has importance in his argument just because it is a means of showing that all forms of inequality are unjust. If there were a right to slavery based on a right of conquest then, a fortiori, people would have no right to complain if they were oppressed by despots in ways that fell short of actual slavery. Therefore chapter 4 of book I is devoted to slavery. He has previously shown that "no man has a natural authority over" another and that might does not make right, so that there are no rights based on conquest. He then declares that it follows that all legitimate authority and justice are conventional and contractual. In the chapter on slavery he demonstrates that slavery can never be voluntary, even in conditions where someone offers a choice between killing someone defeated in war or enslaving that person, and therefore is always

Jean-Jacques Rousseau. [Library of Congress/Corbis]

unjust. Similarly, in the *Discourse on the Origins of Inequality* he argues against Samuel Pufendorf that voluntarily becoming a slave is impossible, since life and liberty are natural, while property is conventional, and therefore there can be no property in another's life and liberty. Moreover,

> . . . since liberty is a gift [children] receive from nature in virtue of being men, their parents had no right to divest them of it. Thus, just as violence had to be done to nature in order to establish slavery, nature had to be changed in order to perpetuate this right.

Since all legitimate moral and political relations are based in a voluntary contract and an association of equals, no despotism can be just. The distinction between natural and civil equality and freedom moves Rousseau to note a connection between kinds of freedom and moral or psychological slavery. Moral freedom is possible only in society, not in the state of nature, because only in society can man be the "master of himself. For to be driven by appetite alone is slavery, and obedience to the law one has prescribed for oneself is liberty." (I.8)

See also NATURAL LAW; PHILOSOPHY.

BIBLIOGRAPHY

ELLENBURG, STEPHEN. *Rousseau's Political Philosophy: An Interpretation from Within.* 1976.
RILEY, PATRICK. *Will and Political Legitimacy: A Critical Exposition of Social Contract Theory in Hobbes, Locke, Rousseau, Kant, and Hegel.* 1982.
SHKLAR, JUDITH N. *Men and Citizens: A Study of Rousseau's Social Theory.* 1969.

Eugene Garver

Royal African Company

The Royal African Company (RAC), founded in 1672, was Britain's main entry in an international race among European power to integrate overseas trading networks by granting monopoly privileges to favored investors in large limited societies. In chartering the RAC Britain imitated earlier Dutch commercial successes with its East and West India Companies. The charter of the RAC covered the entire Atlantic coast of Africa, where it expected to acquire slaves, and the West Indian islands of Barbados and Jamaica, just then converting to large-scale production of sugar based on the African labor it would deliver. The company did not anticipate carrying sugar back to England but concentrated on sending English manufactures to Africa and supplying labor to the plantations in America. It built or acquired several costly fortified coastal trading stations in Africa, notably Cape Coast Castle on the Gold Coast (modern Ghana).

In terms of the history of English (later British) slaving, the RAC represented an early phase in which well-placed investors—in this case including King Charles II and other members of the royal family—sought to overcome the high risks of an unknown business by sharing them under the protection of royal privileges. It provided significant financing in both Africa and the West Indies at a time when planters faced heavy start-up investments in their slave labor forces. The company supplied the first large cohorts of Africans sent to Barbados, particularly in the 1680s, but the credit that it had to extend to do so became a financial burden by the 1690s. Flexible small merchants, termed "interlopers" on the RAC monopoly, reaped the profits by replacing the slaves who died for payment in sugar and cash generated by the production capacity the company had created. An act of 1698 ended the RAC monopoly but allowed it to impose a 10 percent duty on its private competitors. It competed successfully with them only briefly and struggled to survive until termination of its charter in 1750. The RAC monopoly effectively launched British sugar and slavery in the Caribbean, but only at the cost of its own capital, contributed through the debts it never collected for the slaves it sold. "Free trade" thereafter became the order of the day, and free traders supplied the slaves who made Britain the leading producer of sugar in the world throughout the eighteenth century.

See also CARIBBEAN REGION; SLAVE TRADE.

BIBLIOGRAPHY

BURHARD, TREVOR. "Who Bought Slaves in Early America? Purchasers of Slaves from the Royal African Company in Jamaica, 1674–1704." *Slavery and Abolition* 17, no. 2 (1996): 68–92.

CARLOS, ANN M., and JAMIE BROWN KRUSE. "The Decline of the Royal African Company: Fringe Firms and the Role of the Charter." *Economic History Review* 49, no. 2 (1996): 291–313.

DAVIES, K. G. *The Royal African Company.* 1957.

GALENSON, DAVID W. "The Slave Trade to the English West Indies, 1673–1724." *Economic History Review* 32, no. 2 (1979): 241–49.

———. *Traders, Planters and Slaves: Market Behavior in Early English America.* 1986.

LAW, ROBIN C. C. *The English in West Africa, 1681–1699: The Local West African Correspondence of the Royal African Company of England.* 1999.

Joseph C. Miller

Russia

Slavery was a very important social institution in Rus' between, say, A.D. 800 and 1725. Initially, slaves were one of the "forest products" harvested by Vikings making their way on the "route from the Varangians to the Greeks," the Eastern European river route (from the Baltic Sea into the Neva to Lake Ladoga, to the Volkov, to the Shelon', to the Dnepr, into the Black Sea) between Sweden and Constaninople. The Vikings picked up slaves and hauled them (along with wax, honey, and furs) to Constantinople in exchange for luxury goods. No one knows the numbers of slaves there were after the formation of the Kievan Russian state (882–1132), but it is assumed that most of these slaves had come from raids on other non-Slavic people.

After the Kievan Russian state began to disintegrate in 1132, slaves became much more numerous as inhabitants of neighboring East Slavic principalities (much of the territory between Poland-Lithuania and the Volga River) became fair game for enslavement and the political jurisdictions fell into civil war and raided one another almost continuously. Landownership developed after 1132, and some estates were

farmed by slaves kept in barracks. Other slaves served in their owners' households. There were also debt slaves throughout medieval Russian history—people who could not repay obligations or who fell into servitude because they could not pay fines levied as penalties for crimes committed. There was a slave market in Kiev, and almost certainly others grew up in the capitals of every principality. Particularly important was the slave market in Novgorod, which provided East Slavic slaves for the Baltic, the European Atlantic coast, and North Africa. Jewish merchants took East Slavic slaves from Novgorod to these western destinations. Other East Slavic slaves were continuously "harvested" by the Turkic peoples inhabiting the southern and eastern frontiers of Rus' and subsequently sold to buyers in Byzantium, the Mediterranean world, and the Arab countries.

The Mongol invasions into Rus' from 1236–1240 accelerated the disintegration of Kievan Rus' that had commenced in 1132. Thirteen major principalities became fifty, then more than one hundred. Raiding to obtain East Slav slaves intensified and was compounded by the Mongal invasions, which may have resulted in the immediate enslavement of 10 percent of the populace and their deportation as slaves to Asian destinations as far away as Karakorum in Mongolia. Continuous Mongol slave raids replaced those of the pre-1240 Turkic peoples who had roamed the Ukranian steppe. In these centuries the Western European word "slave" was borrowed from the ethnonym "Slav."

During the ensuing period of the "Tatar yoke" (1237–1480), the export of slaves through Novgorod continued and the Novgorodian slave market at the intersection of Slave and High Streets was the most active business locale in the entire Republic of Novgorod, which encompassed much of Russia north of the Volga to the White Sea. Labor was an extraordinarily scarce commodity owing to the very low population densities on the east European plain. Meanwhile the demand for Slavic slaves remained high throughout much of Eurasia, the Middle East, and North Africa. Almost any person encountered by a raiding enemy band was liable to be seized and sold into slavery as a prize of war. Toward the end of this period, Moscow consolidated the northern East Slavic lands, and the institution of slavery continued to develop apace.

A new form of slavery evolved, a variety of antichresis (a kind of mortgage contract), in which a native Russian took a loan for a year and agreed to work for the creditor for the interest. He or she became a limited-service contract slave (*kabal'nyi kholop/kabal'naia raba*). A borrower who defaulted fell into permanent hereditary slavery. By the end of the 1850s, *kabal'noe kholopstvo* became a very common institution, which may have engulfed anywhere from 5 to 15 percent of the native Russian population. Almost no one ever repaid the loans, with the result that nearly all became perpetual slaves. This situation, in which a fair portion of the population consisted of natives who had sold themselves into slavery, was nearly unique in world history. This violated a "rule" of the social sciences—that the slave must be an outsider, that no society could withstand the tension of enslaving its own people. How or why the Russians managed to violate this rule on such a grand scale has been the subject of speculation but remains undetermined. The best explanation seems to be that almost anybody could be a "Russian" because of the large numbers of peoples involved in the ethnogenesis of the Russians (East Slavs, Balts, Finnic peoples, Iranian peoples, and Turkic peoples).

Because seemingly almost anybody could become a Russian, the boundary between "insiders" and "outsiders" was very permeable. In the institution of slavery, this could have meant that the Russians could have enslaved no one, or everyone. Because there was no concept of "human rights" and because of the shortage of labor, they elected to make everyone eligible for enslavement.

The 1580s and the 1590s were a period when Russian serfdom became entrenched. In the second half of the fifteenth century, peasants had been gradually limited to moving from estate to estate around the time of Saint George's Day (November 26), and then in the 1580s and in 1592 all peasants were temporarily forbidden to move on Saint George's Day. "Temporarily" lasted until 1906. The issue in the beginnings of the institution of serfdom, at least until 1650, was always a perceived shortage of labor by those who petitioned the government to solve their personnel problems by forbidding peasants to move, either from one lord to another or from the center of the Muscovite state to one of the frontiers. The serf was bound to the land, while the slave was bound to the person of a lord, a distinction which may have made little difference to most Russian peasants. The major objective difference was that the peasant always had to pay taxes, whereas many slaves did not. Taxes in Muscovy were onerous, so tax avoidance was a matter of consequence, and the ranks of the limited-service contract slaves began to swell. As a result, in the 1590s the government changed the nature of the "limitation" in limited-service contract slavery from a limit of a year and upon default to lifetime slavery to a limit of the lifetime of the owner with no possibility of repayment of the loan, something which, as was noted, was hardly ever done anyway. This resulted in two expropriations: the slave was expropriated of his

A pair of angels watches over a serf as he drives a horse-drawn plow. [Dean Conger/Corbis]

right to repay his loan (buy himself out of slavery) at the end of the first year, and the slaveowner was expropriated of his hereditary property, which he could no longer bequeath to his heirs. The government was gambling that at least once every generation the limited-service contract slave would become a freedman and go back on the tax rolls. What was not anticipated was that being enslaved created a mentality of dependency, in response to which the freedperson had little option but to sell himself back into slavery, often to the heir of the deceased owner.

Limited-service contract slavery, which was primarily a private welfare system in a society that provided few public alms, experienced several legal changes in the seventeenth century. Sometime in the 1620s the government established a fixed price of 2 rubles for a *kabal'nyi kholop*; in the 1630s this price was raised to 3 rubles. In 1678–1679 slaves engaged in farming were put on the tax rolls and converted into serfs by a state very apprehensive about its tax receipts. In the early 1720s the remaining household *kholopy* were converted into house serfs for the same reason, primarily because new censuses revealed a decline in the "peasant/serf" taxpaying population and a rise in the number of tax-exempt house serfs. Slavery in Muscovy was primarily a male institution: two-thirds of both adult and child slaves were males.

Although limited-service contract slavery assumed the central place in late Muscovite slavery, there were other types as well. Hereditary slaves were those who had been enslaved for a generation or more, perhaps Russians who had sold themselves, perhaps outsiders impressed in various ways. Military captives—especially Poles and Swedes but also Tatars—could be enslaved. (Poland and Sweden abolished slavery in these years, but the Crimean Tatars made a living by raiding Muscovy and Poland and annually kidnapping thousands of slaves whom they typically sold to other Muslims.)

Ordinary debt slavery persisted, and a formula specified that such slavery was to be worked off at a rate of 5 rubles per year by adult males, 2.50 rubles by adult females, and 2 rubles by minors over the age of ten. There was also indentured slavery, in which a person sold himself or herself to another for a period of years and upon expiration of the term was to be freed. Finally, there was an elite form of slavery in which an estate manager had to become a slave in order to hold the job. All of these people were "slaves" in the sense that they were so-called *kholopy* of various types, they were subject to the Moscow Slavery Chancellery (Russia was one of the few countries in the world ever to have a central governmental office whose sole responsibility was slaves), and they were all discussed at length in chapter 20 ("The Judicial Process for Slaves") of the great Law Code (*Sobornoe Ulozhenie*) of 1649.

Muscovite slavery was primarily a household slave system and was very mild by comparison with productive slave systems. Muscovite slave owners were primarily estate owners and holders who served in the cavalry. The higher one rose in the cavalry, the more likely he was to own more slaves. Other slave owners were merchants and craftsmen. Until the second quarter of the seventeenth century, it was even possible for elite slaves to own other slaves. Most slave owners kept their chattel as household menials and as status symbols of wealth, but military personnel often took some along as body servants to guard the baggage train and even to fight on horseback. Others used slaves to manage their estates or to aid merchants in their trade, including long-distance trade. At various times, some slaves performed governmental tasks as extensions of their owners in government service. As Muscovite society became rigidly stratified in the seventeenth century, it became nearly impossible for anyone to hire free workers, for the law specified that an employer who employed someone for more than three months could convert that person into a slave upon application by the employer.

Slavery was abolished by Peter the Great in the early 1720s, but its legacy lingered long. It had a direct impact on Russian serfdom, which was mentioned together with slavery increasingly frequently already in the seventeenth century and borrowed a number of its norms from slavery. Russian serfdom by the end of the eighteenth century had many of the features of slavery. This in turn led to the slavelike features of the Soviet Gulag and the general absence of human rights in the Soviet Union.

See also RUSSIA, SERFDOM IN.

BIBLIOGRAPHY

HELLIE, RICHARD. *Enserfment and Military Change in Muscovy.* 1971.

———. *Muscovite Society.* 1970. See especially chapter 8, "Bondage in Muscovy."

———. *Slavery in Russia, 1450–1725.* 1982.

———, ed. and trans. *The Muscovite Law Code (Ulozhenie) of 1649.* 1988. See especially chapter 20, "The Judicial Process for Slaves."

IAKOVLEV, A. I. *Kholopstvo i kholopy v Moskovskom gosudarstve XVII v.* 1943.

KOLYCHĒVA, E. I. *Kholopstvo i krepostnichestvo (konets XV–XVI v.).* 1971.

PANEIAKH, V. M. *Kabal'noe kholopstvo na Rusi v XVI veke.* 1967.

———. *Kholopstvo v pervoi polovine XVII v.* 1984.

———. *Kholopstvo v XVI-nachale XVII veka.* 1975.

ZIMIN, A. A. *Kholopy na Rusi (s drevneishikh vremën do kontsa XV v.).* 1973.

Richard Hellie

Russia, Serfdom in

Serfdom refers to the ties of dependence of servile or unfree peasant family farmers to their landlords. In its numerous local and regional variants, serfdom existed in one place or another in Europe for over a thousand years, from at least the ninth century to the nineteenth.

In all of preindustrial Europe (prior to the nineteenth century), agriculture was the primary pursuit of the overwhelming majority of the population. It is important to realize that in medieval and much of modern Europe all peasants, both free and unfree, had lords and paid rents. But the free peasants could choose their lords, whereas serfs were restricted in their movement by ties of personal dependency that were socially degrading, legally incapacitating, and economically burdensome.

Some historians hold that the key attribute of serfdom was the particular means by which landlords extracted wealth from their serfs. Most serfs had access to arable land and provided for their own subsistence; thus for lords to obtain an income from them, they had to resort to noneconomic or extraeconomic forms of compulsion. In contrast, slaves, like domestic livestock, depended completely on their owners for survival. Slaves could be deprived of their means of subsistence if they failed to perform as desired. Free peasants, on the other hand, sold their labor or its product in the marketplace. Their relationship with their landlords, though unequal, was primarily economic and contractual. Restricting freedom of movement, imposing an elaborate system of fines, confiscating serf property, levying poll taxes and inheritance taxes, and limiting marriage only to serfs tied to the same lord to gain the labor of their children—all these were ways by which landlords gained a substantial income from serf labor.

Numerous scholars have found this interpretation of extraeconomic coercion wanting. Some historians have even called into question the usefulness of serfdom as a concept in comprehending medieval European and imperial Russian society. In their view, peasants were first and foremost subsistence-oriented farmers living on land specifically allotted for their family's use. This, it is argued, gave them a degree of autonomy which neither dependency nor lordship could significantly penetrate. Subsistence farming left them free at times from a master's supervision and allowed them to control the intensity of their labor. In fact, many of the peasants' obligations to their lords were fixed by custom and not readily changed. Peasants could sell and exchange their produce, inherit property, and marry within their own group. Moreover, they formed small rural communities, which advanced and protected the interests of the members and exercised rights over common and arable lands. In a word, these "serfs" were not part of a distinctly feudal society but were rather peasant farmers in a stable, preindustrial economy in which family-oriented subsistence values regulated behavior and attitudes. The key distinction between cultivators was not a matter of freedom or servitude; the important difference

A number of serfs gather in their village, Goumnist, Russia, around 1861. [*Illustrated London News*/Corbis]

was between those who had access to enough land to provide for their family's subsistence needs and those who did not.

In Russia, serfdom was in place by the end of the sixteenth century. By the end of the eighteenth century, slightly over half of the total population of the Russian empire were serfs. When serfdom was abolished in 1861, over 22 million serfs were freed.

Serfdom served the interests of both the Russian state and the serf-owning nobility. Russia did not participate in the great economic expansion which took place in much of Western Europe following the age of discovery and the increase in trade and wealth that resulted. Consequently, Russia lacked the means to pay its military servitors and bureaucrats by levying vast new taxes on commerce and cities as was the case to the west. To compete militarily, Russia resorted to serfdom. Elites engaged in state service were paid with land, and peasants were bound to this land as serfs. Serfdom provided the class of nobles with an income—lessening, if not eliminating, the need for a salary from the financially precarious Russian state. As David Moon has noted, "Serfdom may not have been the most efficient way of organizing agricultural production, but, in most years, Russian servile agriculture provided enough food to feed the peasant population and sufficient surplus to support the nobility, the state, and the armed forces."

Serfdom was, of course, economically exploitative. It existed, after all, to support the owners. But while serfdom was imposed from above, it had to be maintained from below. To avoid the labor problems involved in exercising authority, many serf owners in Russia required only that their serfs give them an annual cash payment or quitrent, known as *obrok*. But in the nineteenth century, two out of three serfs paid their lord in obligatory labor or *barshchina*, usually working three unpaid days a week on the lord's land, a system in many ways akin to slavery. Among the serfs, laziness, negligence, apathy, and absenteeism were common responses to the labor dues expected of them. At times, the owners responded by imposing fines, inflicting floggings, exiling serfs to Siberia, and sending serfs into the army.

More often, however, serfdom did not mean relentless exploitation or coercion. The serf owners' intervention in rural Russia is best regarded as a matter of compromise and collusion with at least some of the serfs. Moreover, being tied to a lord as serfs implied an entitlement to use of the lord's land—not necessarily a bad arrangement for subsistence-oriented peasants. Finally, in times of need (crop failures, livestock blights, and the like), lords provided their serfs with assistance.

In all, Russian serfdom proved to be a viable institution for three centuries, addressing the vital needs of the state, the nobility, and the serfs and the prevailing economic and social constraints.

See also RUSSIA.

BIBLIOGRAPHY

BLUM, JEROME. *Lord and Peasant in Russia from the Ninth to the Nineteenth Century.* 1961.

HOCH, STEVEN. *Serfdom and Social Control in Russia: Petrovskoe, a Village in Tambov.* 1986.

KOLCHIN, PETER. *Unfree Labor: American Slavery and Russian Serfdom.* 1987.

MOON, DAVID. "Reassessing Russian Serfdom." *European History Quarterly* 26 (1996): 483–526.

Steven L. Hoch

S

Saint-Domingue

See Abolition and Antislavery Movements; Caribbean Region; Plantations; Slave Religion.

Sambo

See Elkins Thesis; Perspectives on Slavery.

Sandiford, Ralph [1693–1733]

Quaker merchant and abolitionist.

Born in Liverpool, England, to Anglican parents, Ralph Sandiford joined the Society of Friends (Quakers) as a young man. He immigrated to North America, where he worked for some time in South Carolina; he then pursued a successful mercantile career in Philadelphia. Though wealthy enough to own slaves and engage in the Atlantic slave trade, Sandiford became furious that Friends, whose religion he believed taught differently, imported and held Africans as slaves. Shortly after the Quaker-dominated Pennsylvania Assembly reduced the provincial duty on imported slaves in 1729, and importation rose as a result, Sandiford wrote an antislavery tract entitled *A Brief Examination of the Practice of the Times* (1729). Published by Benjamin Franklin, who omitted his own name as printer, the book attacked leading Friends who were enmeshed "in the most arbitrary and tyrannical oppression that hell has invented on this globe" (p. 9). Because Sandiford published the tract without permission of the Quaker overseers of the press, Philadelphia Monthly Meeting expelled him from membership. In 1730 he issued a second edition, entitled *The Mystery of Iniquity; in a Brief Examination of the Practice of the Times*, in which he added an appeal to London Yearly Meeting for help against the growing corruption of slavery in America.

While Sandiford failed to convince Quaker authorities to abolish slavery or the slave trade in Pennsylvania, he reinvigorated the antislavery movement within Philadelphia Yearly Meeting, as several local Quaker meetings called for more stringent rules against importing and purchasing enslaved blacks. Perhaps most important, Sandiford inspired the radical Benjamin Lay to begin his abolitionist campaign. When Sandiford died in 1733, on a small farm outside Philadelphia, Lay considered him a martyr to the cause.

See also ABOLITION AND ANTISLAVERY MOVEMENTS; LAY, BENJAMIN AND SARAH; QUAKERS.

BIBLIOGRAPHY

DRAKE, THOMAS E. *Quakers and Slavery in America.* 1950.
SANDIFORD, RALPH. *The Mystery of Iniquity; in a Brief Examination of the Practice of the Times.* 1730.

Jean R. Soderlund

Sandoval, Alonso de [1576–1652]

Spanish Jesuit missionary who ministered to slaves.

Born in Spain, Alonso de Sandoval became a Jesuit in Lima and worked in Cartagena, then the major slave trading port of Spanish South America. In 1605 he began boarding newly arrived slave ships to care for the physical and spiritual needs of the captives. Over the next forty-seven years, Sandoval baptized thousands and administered last rites to people dying from the rigors of the Middle Passage. He also catechized and baptized blacks kept in holding pens while awaiting sale to planters. Eventually, Sandoval employed up to eighteen assistants, including interpreters of African languages.

In 1627 Sandoval published a book on the conversion of Africans, reissued in 1647 as *De instauranda Aethiopum salute.* He condemned the harshness of the slave trade but did not question the legitimacy of slavery. Sandoval's correspondence with Portuguese missionaries in Angola led him to accept claims that most slaves deserved their fate as war captives or criminals. He also endorsed the notion that blacks descended from Noah's son Ham and grandson Canaan and had inherited Noah's curse of slavery on Canaan. Sandoval did argue that God had given Africans (as He gave everyone else) immortal souls and called for more Jesuit ministries to Africa, underlining his focus on blacks' spiritual needs. The tenor of *De instauranda* was such that the Spanish Council of the Indies cited it in justifying the slave trade in 1685.

Sandoval eventually lost favor with the Jesuits and was replaced as rector of their college in Cartagena, but he continued his dockside missions to slaves until his death in 1652.

See also MIDDLE PASSAGE; PERSPECTIVES ON SLAVERY.

BIBLIOGRAPHY

BLACKBURN, ROBIN. *The Making of Colonial Slavery, 1492–1800.* 1997.

T. Stephen Whitman

Saudi Arabia

See Modern Middle East.

Scandinavia

The Scandinavian countries of Denmark, Norway, Sweden, and Iceland all incorporated slavery in their social systems during the Middle Ages. We know about it from their provincial law codes, mainly written down during the thirteenth century, and from Icelandic "family sagas," stories written in their current form during the thirteenth century but describing events that took place during the tenth and eleventh centuries.

During the eighth through eleventh centuries, Danes, Norwegians, and Swedes ranged over the North and Baltic seas as traders and raiders (and in the later part of the period as settlers)—indeed, occasionally as far as the Mediterranean, and overland as far as Byzantium (later Constantinople). These raiders came to be known as Vikings (in Eastern Europe, Varangians). Among the items they captured in their raids, and sold at various entrepots at home and abroad, were slaves. The Vikings enslaved not only outsiders (Irish slaves captured by Norwegians and Icelanders were especially common) but also each other: it was not unheard of for Vikings from one region to raid another part of Scandinavia and take captives as slaves. We do not know whether it was the availability of slaves by capture that first introduced slavery to Scandinavia, because there are no written records about the social system in Scandinavia before the time of the Vikings. Archaeology provides some information but does not reveal exact gradations of

The Oseberg Ship at the Viking Ship Museum in Oslo is one of the best-preserved Viking longships. [Richard T. Nowitz/Corbis]

status. None of the Scandinavian countries ever became a slave society—that is, a society in which the entire economy was based on slavery. In parts of Norway and Denmark there is some evidence for use of slaves in large-scale, plantation agriculture, but only on a few of the largest estates. Most of the region, especially Norway and Iceland, was divided into smallholdings rather than large estates or manors. The picture derived from the sagas is that families would typically have one or two slaves to help with agricultural and domestic duties. There is no hard evidence as to numbers of slaves in any region at any particular time; a maximum of 10 percent of the population would be a rough, impressionistic estimate.

Although slaves were not very significant numerically, or in the economy, the existence of slavery was quite important to the otherwise egalitarian ideological superstructure of society. This can be seen especially in Norway and Iceland, where the sagas suggest a conflict between a myth of inclusive politics and the realities of aristocratic rank and landed wealth. Norway had a king (earlier, many regional kings) and Iceland did not, until it came under the Norwegian crown in the 1260s; in both countries assemblies (*things*) of free men played an important role in governance. Some *things* included all free men of a region, and some were representative. The key, however, was that participation was open to all free men. There was no legal distinction between nobles and commoners in the earlier period. Of course, some men were more powerful than others; there were magnates who controlled a good deal of land and had many clients. The existence of slavery, however, indicated that it meant something even to be a poor and powerless free man. It permitted the myth, particularly in Iceland, of broad-based political participation.

The law of slavery, as codified in the various regional laws of Denmark, Norway, and Sweden, and the national laws of Iceland, made sharp distinctions between slaves and free people in a number of areas. Slaves had greatly restricted inheritance rights. They had no right to compensation (*wergeld*) for acts committed against them, as a free person did, although slaveowners might have a right to compensation for damage to their human property. The laws provided rules for determining the status of slave and nonslave unions. They also provided procedures for manumission, which was apparently quite common. Freedmen and freedwomen remained in a dependent status with regard to their former owners. It is difficult to say how much these laws, codified late, represent ancient Scandinavian custom and how much they were influenced by Roman and canon laws after the Christianization of the Scandinavian lands in the years around 1000. Certain features—such as the child following the status of the mother, in some Swedish codes—resemble Roman law, but Roman law did not include the compensation system, which is prominent in the Scandinavian laws, and Scandinavian law did not adopt the Roman custom of the *peculium*.

One often-cited, though not well-documented, feature of Scandinavian slavery was the sacrifice of slaves. Poems set in the legendary past (the Sigurð cycle) depict large numbers of slaves being killed for a royal burial. An account by the tenth-century Arab traveler Ibn Fadlan describes the killing of a slave woman to accompany her master in the afterlife; this incident took place among the Rus' traders on the Volga, whom many scholars believe to have been Scandinavians. Several graves from the Viking period, in Denmark and Norway, contain one corpse with fine weapons or jewelry and another with no artifacts but with a broken neck; it has been suggested that the latter was a slave killed to accompany his or her master. In the absence of corroborating written evidence, however, such archaeological finds are ambiguous.

Literary evidence indicates that medieval Scandinavians believed that slaves had inherently slavish characteristics, which were retained even after a slave was freed. These characteristics were not, however, necessarily connected to race. One story tells of a queen whose children were small and dark; she exchanges them for the brawny blond child of her slave women, but the slave child reveals his ancestry through his cowardly behavior. Irish slaves were perhaps the most common ethnic group, at least in Iceland and Norway, but the attitude toward these slaves was not generalized to the Irish as a people.

The institution of slavery may have been responsible for a large admixture of Irish in the Icelandic gene pool. Iceland was uninhabited (except perhaps for a few hermits) until the latter part of the ninth century, when it was settled by Norwegians. Not all the Norwegians who settled there came directly from Norway, however; many had been living in the Northern Isles of Scotland (Shetland and Orkney), the Hebrides, or Ireland. In those areas they had intermarried with the local populations. They also captured or purchased slaves from those local populations and continued to do so after their colonization of Iceland.

Christian ideas of monogamous marriage made relatively slow headway in Iceland, even after its nominal conversion in the year 1000 and the establishment of bishoprics and monasteries. That is to say, people did marry in the Christian manner, but concubinage outside of marriage was widespread, particularly among the wealthy. These concubines were not always slaves but might be. Their children were acknowledged and considered free, although the Church considered them illegitimate, and the law required the consent of the legitimate heirs to give the child of a concubine a share in the inheritance. One of the most famous Icelandic sagas, *Laxdæla saga*, features as one of its main characters Óláfr pái, the son of such a union. His mother, Melkorka, a slave whom his father purchased at a market in Norway, turns out to be the daughter of an Irish king. This story cannot have been a common one—few Irish slaves were royal—but it reflects typical practice in that a wealthy man has set up a favored slave woman in her own household and treats her son as he does the sons of his legal marriage.

Melkorka resisted slavery by remaining mute for years, from the time of her capture, through her purchase—when her muteness was noted as a defect—until her owner caught her secretly speaking to her son. Other slaves in the sagas also resisted their enslavement in various ways, sometimes violently. In Iceland, however, an escaped slave would have difficulty finding anywhere to go in the inhospitable countryside, so flight was probably not common.

It is impossible to put a date on the end of slavery in Scandinavia except in two provinces of Sweden: the Skara Ordinance of 1335 established that everyone born in those provinces should henceforth be free. In the other parts of Scandinavia we can date the end of slavery only by the issuance of law codes that do not refer to it: in Iceland and Norway its decline can be placed in the late twelfth to thirteenth century, and such a date seems plausible for Denmark as well. In Sweden it continued into the fourteenth century. The reasons for the decline of slavery include the influence of the Church, as testamentary manumission was considered beneficial to the soul. Economic reasons also played a role: as the population grew and there was less free land, it was no longer necessary to enslave people to keep them working for someone else, and tenant farming became more common. Increasing social differentiation among the free, too, meant that not all free men shared the same political rights, and slavery was no longer needed as a category against which free people could measure themselves.

See also CHRISTIANITY; LAW; MEDIEVAL EUROPE, SLAVERY AND SERFDOM IN; PECULIUM; THRALLDOM.

BIBLIOGRAPHY

FOOTE, PETER. "Þrælahald á Íslandi." *Saga* 15 (1977): 41–74.

IVERSEN, TORE. "Den gammelnorske trelldommen og dens avvikling." *Historisk Tidsskrift* 64 (1985): 158–179.

———. *Trelldommen: norsk slaveri i middelalderen.* 1997.

KARRAS, RUTH MAZO. *Slavery and Society in Medieval Scandinavia.* 1988.

———. "Concubinage and Slavery in the Viking Age." *Scandinavian Studies* 62 (1990): 141–162.

NEVÉUS, CLARA. *Trälarna i landskapslagarnas samhälle: Danmark och Sverige.* 1954.

SAWYER, BIRGIT, and PETER SAWYER. *Medieval Scandinavia: From Conversion to Reformation, circa 800–1500.* 1993.

SKYUM-NIELSEN, NIELS. "Nordic Slavery in an International Setting." *Medieval Scandinavia* 11 (1978–1979): 126–148.

WILDE-STOCKMEYER, MARLIS. *Sklaverei auf Island. Untersuchungen zur rechtlich-sozialen Situation und literarische Darstellung der Sklaven im skandinavischen Mittelalter.* 1978.

Ruth Mazo Karras

Science Fiction and Fantasy, Slavery in

In some science fiction works and in much of fantasy literature, slavery is present as an element within the story development but usually it plays no significant role. It is often present merely as part of the window dressing of fantasies set in worlds with feudal societies, where slavery must naturally take its place beside the monarchy, the aristocracy, and serfdom, along with elves, witches, and wizards.

In the generic Norse fantasies of Elizabeth Boyer, for example, thralls are clearly part of the attempt to create authenticity and verisimilitude. Likewise, in the classic film *Robinson Crusoe on Mars* (1964), interplanetary slavery is a necessary element to introduce the "man Friday" character. In a rather absurd plot twist an advanced alien race with intergalactic spaceships, land-shattering rays, and other technological wonders mines rare minerals beneath the Martian surface using slaves equipped with merely primitive tools.

The science fiction of time travel often includes slavery as a necessary element of those ages into which the chrononauts venture. Perhaps one of the most interesting instances of this is one of the originals of the genre, H. G. Wells's *The Time Machine,* wherein the slavelike conditions of the working class have caused them to evolve into strong but monstrous Morlocks, while the rich have, through their luxury and idleness, evolved into the Eloi, the effete prey of the anthropophagous Morlocks.

In Mary Doria Russell's *The Sparrow,* a piece of space-travel science fiction, coevolution plays a role, as a Jesuit astrophysicist discovers signals from a distant star system where two races have evolved in unholy parallel—one race of lupine monsters, who feed upon the other species, which are their virtual slaves.

Sometimes, as in Robert Heinlein's *Farnham's Freehold,* the writer tries to explore human nature and social dynamism. Heinlein pictures a postcatastrophe world where blacks are the masters and whites are their slaves, and this distinctly dystopian tale preaches a decidedly libertarian social philosophy. In H. G. Wells's *The Island of Dr. Moreau* and in its cinematic representations, such as *The Island of Lost Souls* (1932), there is depicted a society of therianthropes (i.e., beast-men), created by surgery and painful conditioning, who are the slaves of the diabolic doctor.

Another subgenre of science fiction is alternative or counterfactual history. In Philip K. Dick's *The Man in the High Castle,* set in the United States, the Axis powers have won World War II and divided the world among themselves. Besides the genocide of certain selected groups, the masses of the population are held in a state resembling slavery. In C. M. Cornbluth's *Two Dooms* a scientist working on the Manhattan Project who has developed serious qualms about the creation of the A-bomb falls asleep and awakens in an Axis-dominated world where slavery flourishes.

Harry Turtledove, in *The Two Georges,* presents a counterfactual history in which the North American colonies did not separate from the British Empire, but had become in effect, its first dominion, under Governor-General George Washington. Slavery was abolished in 1833, as it was in reality throughout British colonial territory, and on that account, America did not have a race problem. Freed blacks were not seen as the effects, much less the cause, of a war of Northern aggression in the eyes of Southerners, so most have become middle class, forming a politically conservative and highly religious element within society. Turtledove's *The Guns of the South* is an alternative history rather more centered on the slavery question than *The Two Georges.*

S. M. Sterling's alternative history trilogy—*Marching Through Georgia, Under the Yoke,* and *The Stone Dogs*—presents a variant history in which Tory Loyalists fleeing the American Revolution ended up in South Africa, rather than Canada. Combining with the Boers, they form the Draka—a planter aristocracy which conquers and enslaves all of Black Africa.

More philosophical than most is H. Beam Piper's *A Slave Is a Slave,* wherein a rising galactic empire annexes a planet where a slavocracy rules, but the situation proves deceptive, for although a few hundred families nominally control the vast planetary population, the government is run by nominal slaves who pretend to rule on behalf of the master class, which they are careful to keep in idle luxury.

Cordwainer Smith's "Norstrilia" tales present a world with a slave caste of "underpeople," who have been surgically altered to suit them to their servile station. They manage to free themselves eventually through an alteration of their religious consciousness. In Julian May's multivolume *The Sage of Pliocene Earth* space aliens enslaved all of mankind in the far past, but the inevitable revolution destroys the xenocracy. In the science-fiction flick *The Mole People* (1956), as in H. Rider Haggard's *She,* the remnant of a high civilization established an outpost of its culture in a faraway place, relying on slaves for sustaining the enterprise.

The theme of the alien enslavement of mankind is a common one, as in Gordon R. Dickson's *The Way of the Pilgrim,* or the famous SF movie *Invaders from Mars* (1952), where the would-be Martian conqueror utilizes an implant at the base of the human skull to master his earthly slaves while he controls his Martian mutant slaves by mental telepathy. In the feature film *This Island Earth* (1955) the beings from the planet Metaluna control earth scientists with a mental-ray machine and on their planet have slaves that have been mutated from enormous, erect insect creations.

The war of the sexes does not escape such treatment either, for in Margaret Atwood's *Handmaid's Tale* segments of the female population are virtual fertility slaves obliged to bear offspring for the upper classes. In Poul Anderson's *Virgin Planet,* on the other hand, all males are in such a subservient role in the matriarchal order that they are virtual slaves.

On occasion, science fiction stories of slavery raise questions of what it is to be human. In John Brunner's *Into the Slave Nebula* servile androids are revealed to be humans who have been kidnapped, painted blue, drugged, and brainwashed. In Jack Williamson's *The Humanoids* men have conquered the stars, but they are served by robots who protect and serve them and have, thereby, been turning mankind into pampered slaves.

In the SF film *Creation of the Humanoids* (1962) an interesting twist enters, with the servant androids of a postnuclear world. These "clickers," as they are derisively called, serve man in all ways, even functioning as sexual partners. The Council of Flesh and Blood seeks restrictions upon the clickers, even their banning, but the head of the council learns by the movie's end he is himself an advanced robot.

Finally, the actual tendency in nature of ants and certain other insects to take slaves as well as the rigid hierarchical ordering of their monarchical societies, is utilized in motion pictures such as *Empire of the Ants* (1977) and *Phase IV* (1973), where humans are the ultimate targets for enslavement.

In the horror genre slavery—at least of a metaphorical kind—plays a vital role. The evil that threatens man from outside—from hell, from the grave, from another dimension—often desires his utter destruction, but just as often it seeks to enslave him. In the movie *Phantasm* (1979) humans are transmitted to another dimension to serve as slaves.

In *The Exorcist* and its imitators the phenomenon of demonic possession is presented, wherein devils take over the bodies of helpless energumina (i.e., possessed persons), enslaving them.

In much vampire literature since the appearance of Bram Stoker's *Dracula,* one of the central features of the tale has been the enslavement of the vampire's prodigies, that is, those who have been exsanguinated and transmogrified into vampires themselves. Ironically, this part of the vampire story is the literary creation of Stoker and the screen writers of the vampire cinema. In the real folklore of vampirism, vampiric attacks do not create new vampires. Traditionally, those who have led extraordinarily wicked lives are the true candidates for vampirism after death: suicides, excommunicates, werewolves, witches, and sorcerers.

Manmade human creatures, such as Frankenstein's monster, might be seen as intended for slavery, although in both Mary Shelley's classic and its Hollywood imitations this slave quickly turns rebel. Similarly, the Golem of Jewish legend, in both its literary incarnations and its films, such as *Der Golem* (1920) and *IT* (1967), is created as a servant for the Jewish ghetto by a learned rabbi, but it eventually runs amok.

Finally, the perfect slaves of the horror genre are the zombies—dead persons brought back from the grave to serve the voodoo priest or zombie master. *White Zombie* (1932), *I Walked with a Zombie* (1943), *The Plague of Zombies* (1968), and *The Serpent and the Rainbow* (1987), all explore this supernatural slavery, which is geographically centered in the former slave cultures of the West Indies.

See also FILM AND TELEVISION, SLAVERY IN; LITERATURE OF SLAVERY.

BIBLIOGRAPHY

CLUTE, JOHN. *SF—Science Fiction: The Illustrated Encyclopedia.* 1995.
HARDY, PHIL, ed. *The Overlook Film Encyclopedia: Horror.* 1994.
———. *Science Fiction: The Aurum Film Encyclopedia.* 1991.

Patrick M. O'Neil

Scientific Racism

See Enlightenment; Perspectives on Slavery.

Scott, Dred

See Dred Scott v. Sandford.

Scottish Antislavery Movement

The antislavery movement in Scotland was late in flowering. During the eighteenth century Scots moralists and writers such as Francis Hutcheson, John Millar, and Adam Smith spoke out forcefully against slavery. In proportion to their population the Scots probably contributed more to the Enlightenment critique of slavery than any other people. And in due course Scots expatriates, among them Zacharay Macaulay, James Stephen, and James Ramsay, played an important role in the campaigns against both the slave trade and slavery. Yet Scotland's own contribution to these efforts remained modest, for although most literate Scots disapproved of slavery, few of them manifested that evangelical zeal which transformed Englishmen into antislavery activists.

It was not, in fact, until *after* the passage of the Emancipation Act of 1833 that Edinburgh, Glasgow, and Aberdeen established antislavery societies on the English model. They did so in response to a fundraising tour by George Thompson, a fiery British lecturer fresh from his struggles over West Indian slavery, who was intent on capitalizing on the success of the British movement by launching a similar campaign in the United States. There is no doubt that many saw this as an opportunity to carry the crusade to the world at large. The result, however, was that the fortunes of the Scottish antislavery movement—if by that is meant a body of activists and an organizational structure—were from the first closely linked to those of the movement in the United States. The Scots provided platforms for visiting American speakers and collected funds on their behalf. They also formed alliances with rival U.S. antislavery factions and quarreled bitterly with one another over the role of women in the movement and other issues that divided abolitionists across the Atlantic. In Edinburgh the women's organization busied itself collecting on behalf of William Lloyd Garrison's American Antislavery Society and the men's organization on behalf of Garrison's antislavery opponents, while in Glasgow there were both male and female groups for and against Garrison. With the advent of the American Civil War the backbiting and rancor that had characterized the movement gradually evaporated, allowing Scots of formerly opposing views to cooperate in raising some $50,000 in aid of freedmen.

See also ABOLITION AND ANTISLAVERY MOVEMENTS; AMERICAN ANTI-SLAVERY SOCIETY; EMANCIPATION ACT, BRITISH; SMITH, ADAM.

BIBLIOGRAPHY

BOLT, CHRISTINE. *The Anti-Slavery Movement and Reconstruction, 1833–1877.* 1969.
RICE, C. DUNCAN. *The Scots Abolitionists, 1833–1861.* 1981.

Howard R. Temperley

Sculpture

See Arts.

Seasoning

The "seasoning" of slaves meant a period of time during which slaves fresh from Africa (called *bozales* in Spanish) became acclimatized and acculturated. Because a significant percentage did not survive this physiological and psychological tempering, planters also used the term as an accounting concept—writing off in advance the percentage of the new arrivals who would die.

In Cuba, seasoning mortality was placed at between seven and twelve percent during the first year. In Brazil, seasoning was thought of in terms of four years, and mortality was said by some to approach fifty percent. In 1811, a Jamaican physician and planter put the seasoning toll at about twenty-five percent within a period of three to four years. This was probably close to the norm for most slave societies in the Americas, most of the time. This physician listed the major killers during seasoning as: diseases born of the Middle Passage; a change of climate; a change of diet; hard labor; severe treatment; and suicide.

It is no coincidence that disease was listed first. Persons from many African disease environments were suddenly gathered together and crowded below the decks of slave ships for weeks on end, where they were not only exposed to a wide variety of pathogens but also debilitated by the effects of malnutrition and dehydration. Their major killer after arriving in the Americas was the "bloody flux" or amoebic dysentery. This disease was acquired aboard ship but had such a lengthy period of incubation that it generally struck the slaves only after they reached their respective plantations to begin the seasoning ordeal.

See also HEALTH; MIDDLE PASSAGE; MORTALITY IN THE NEW WORLD.

BIBLIOGRAPHY

COLLINS, ROBERT. *Practical Rules for the Management and Medical Treatment of Negro Slaves in the Sugar Colonies.* 1811.
KIPLE, KENNETH F. *The Caribbean Slave: A Biological History.* 1984.

Kenneth F. Kiple

A 1784 advertisement for the private sale of thirty slaves prominently displays the fact that they have already been seasoned. [Library of Congress/Corbis]

Segregation

See Law; United States.

Self-Purchase

In many slave societies, masters allowed slaves to acquire wealth and purchase their freedom or that of family members. Self-purchase typically involved installment payments in cash or kind, or the purchasing of a replacement slave. These agreements served to stabilize master-slave relations pending the arrival of freedom, provide public recognition of a partly-free slave's status, and regulate future dealings between former masters and freedmen. Self-purchase by payment of a lump sum could also legitimize the freedom of an escaped slave, as in Frederick Douglass's case. In legal form, self-purchase agreements ranged from contracts enforceable by law to voluntary and revocable acts of masters.

In colonial Cuba, slaves could ask a court to set a purchase price and then pay this price in installments. This procedure, called *coartación*, originated as custom in the seventeenth century, was codified in the eighteenth century, and spread to Louisiana after its transfer to Spain in 1763. *Coartación* drew upon the

Roman law concept of the *peculium*, property accumulated and disposed of by a slave. Masters were not compelled to allow a slave to amass a *peculium*; rather, concession of that privilege and respect for property thus acquired created an incentive for hard work that benefited master as well as slave.

A slave who was allowed to work land for his own gain might be expected to produce some or all of his food. Urban slaves permitted to hire themselves out for wages might be required to maintain themselves on the sums left over after the master received a portion of their earnings. Should a slave die before completing his self-purchase, the master retained payments that had already been made. In this regard, gradual self-purchase operated as a kind of insurance, lessening the financial risk associated with a slave's untimely death.

Freedpeople could assist slaves who wished to buy themselves out, both monetarily, and legally: a freedman or woman could enter into a binding contract to obtain the freedom of a spouse or relation. In such instances, a master might sell a slave to a kinsman on credit, holding title to the person to be freed as security for the debt. However the self-purchase agreement was constructed, masters could drive hard bargains: self-purchase prices frequently exceeded market prices for slave sales.

In the United States, courts did not formalize a slave's right to self-purchase, or generally treat agreements as enforceable contracts, but some legal protection of installment payment arrangements was afforded. Slaveholders could bind themselves to honor an agreement, either through registering it in court, or by making the promise of freedom part of a contract with a white person. Such actions could make their promises credible to slaves who might then enter wholeheartedly into the self-purchase bargain.

Most societies permitting self-purchase regulated the ages and conditions of those to be set free, both to prevent masters from dumping old or infirm slaves, and to limit the growth of a population of freedpeople. Typically, the slave that was promised freedom was no longer wholly a slave, but was not possessed of all the rights or duties of a freeborn person. *Coartados*, black Cubans who had partly purchased their freedom, could not be held responsible for debts, nor made to serve in the militia. In imperial Rome, most ex-slaves were classified as "Junian Latins," a status short of full citizenship in the empire that nonetheless gave them some important property rights, such as the right to make a will. In the United States, prospectively free slaves could still be bought and sold, but often could not legally be transported out of their state and thus beyond court supervision of their right to eventual freedom.

Some societies made freedom by self-purchase a reversible condition: Roman and Cuban slaveholders could re-enslave former chattels who failed to show appropriate deference to former masters, or who did not perform ongoing duties that had been stipulated as part of the freedom bargain. Americans typically enjoyed no such right.

As an avenue to freedom, self-purchase varied in importance according to general societal attitudes towards manumission. Where populations of freedpeople became substantial—for example, in imperial Rome, in Brazilian and West Indian cities from the late eighteenth century onward, or in the Upper South of the United States after 1790—self-purchase was fairly common. In contrast, self-purchase was a negligible factor in places where slaves prices were rising and freedpeople were few, such as the Cotton Belt of the nineteenth-century South.

See also COARTACIÓN; EQUIANO, OLAUDAH; FREEDOM; MANUMISSION; PECULIUM.

BIBLIOGRAPHY

BRADLEY, K. R. *Slaves and Masters in the Roman Empire: A Study in Social Control.* 1987.
KLEIN, HERBERT S. *Slavery in the Americas: A Comparative Study of Virginia and Cuba.* 1967.
MORRIS, THOMAS D. *Southern Slavery and the Law, 1619–1860.* 1996.

T. Stephen Whitman

Seminole War

The Seminole wars were a series of conflicts between Native Americans and white settlers in Florida and are generally related as two events: the First Seminole War (November 1817–April 1818) and the Second Seminole War (December 1835–August 1842). Both had to do with white Americans' land hunger and the threat that runaway slaves sheltered among the Indians posed to the institution of American slavery. The Seminoles, related to the Creeks in language and culture, were breakaway factions who settled in the Florida region and formed a society of their own. Along with other fugitives, free blacks fled or migrated to Florida and existed in a sometimes easy, sometimes troubled relationship with their Indian neighbors but united with them in opposition to encroachment by white Americans. Moreover, the Seminoles acquired African slaves or sheltered runaways as slaves, who settled among them and lived in a tributary relationship. Among the Indians, African-Americans—unlike slaves owned by whites—had only to surrender a portion of their crops or their labor to their masters and were otherwise virtually autonomous. They lived in separate settlements, and miscegenation was limited. Nevertheless, there was a cultural interchange between the two groups, and the blacks assumed particular importance as translators and advisers, having intimate knowledge of both white and red peoples' cultures.

The presence of an Indian sanctuary for runaway Africans, whether slave or free, was a prospect that white Americans viewed with alarm, particularly as these fugitives were least receptive to white encroachment, often steeled an Indian inclination to resist it, and were among the most determined fighters in opposition to it. The First Seminole War was caused by mutual raids across the border between United States and Spanish territory in which each side stole slaves and cattle. The United States succeeded in destroying the Seminoles' prosperity and curbing their power, but a fierce rearguard action by black fighters permitted some Indian villages to be successfully evacuated in face of an American advance. Spain ceded the region to the United States as a consequence of the conflict, but fugitive slaves remained an irritant. The Second Seminole War was provoked by an attempt to move the Seminoles to the trans-Mississippi West. It was longer, more bloody, and more expensive, and blacks were more heavily involved. General Thomas S. Jesup called it "a negro not an Indian war." It was pushed with obstinacy because slavery in the lower South could never be secure if a refuge for blacks remained. Many blacks were captured and sold to whites during the conflict, but some secured the right to migrate West with the Seminoles.

See also FLORIDA; MAROONS; NATIVE AMERICANS.

BIBLIOGRAPHY

MAHON, JOHN K. *History of the Second Seminole War, 1835–1842.* 1967.
MULROY, KEVIN. *The Seminole Maroons in Florida, the Indian Territory, Coahuila, and Texas.* 1993.
PORTER, KENNETH W. *The Black Seminoles: History of a Freedom-Seeking People.* 1996.

Daniel C. Littlefield

Senegambia

See West Africa.

Serfdom

See Medieval Europe, Slavery and Serfdom in; Russia, Serfdom in.

Seven Divisions, The

See Siete Partidas.

Sewall, Samuel   [1652–1730]

Merchant, colonial magistrate, diarist, and early antislavery figure.

Samuel Sewall was the son of Henry Sewall and Jane Dummer Sewall. He married Hannah Hull, with whom he had fourteen children; later, he married a widow, Abigail Woodmansey Tilley, and after her death, Mary Gibbs. Sewall served as a councilor for the colony of Massachusetts; as a commissioner of the Society for the Propagation of the Gospel in Foreign Parts, a missionary organization to Native Americans and African slaves; and as a chief justice for the superior court of judicature. Sewall was a judge for the Salem witch trials, a fact for which he later offered a public apology. He wrote a number of pamphlets; and his voluminous diary is a key source for the daily lives of late-seventeenth-century Puritans.

In 1700 he published a pamphlet called "The Selling of Joseph," one of the first antislavery appeals. In it, he challenged the idea of biblical support for enslavement of Africans. Made uneasy by the growing numbers of African slaves in Massachusetts province

Samuel Sewall. [*Dictionary of American Portraits*]

and—more likely—by the wholehearted participation of many Puritans in the Atlantic slave trade, Sewall observed that the fact that enslaved Africans were continually "aspiring after their forbidden Liberty, renders them Unwilling Servants"—doubtless a reaction to the frequency of runaway slaves locally. Sewall was already sorrowful about his participation in the witch trials, and his conscience was pricked by the slave trade and by petitions from enslaved Africans for their freedom. In subsequent years, his was an early and determined voice for the equality of all humans under God and against the sin of enslavement.

See also MASSACHUSETTS; PURITANS; SOCIETY FOR THE PROPAGATION OF THE GOSPEL.

BIBLIOGRAPHY

SEWALL, SAMUEL. *The Selling of Joseph, a Memorial.* Edited with notes and commentary by Sidney Kaplan. 1969.

Graham Hodges

Sexual Exploitation

Sexual exploitation of slaves is as old as slavery itself. Those who were born slaves or enslaved as captives were taught not only that they had no right to their labor or their families, but also that their bodies were subject to the desire and will of the slaveowner. In ancient Greece temple prostitutes were often slaves; in ancient Rome, slave men and women staffed urban brothels.

Sexual abuse was one means of controlling slaves. Owners asserted their authority by subjecting women to rape or sexual coercion and by forcing men to give sexual favors; slave men were also degraded by their inability to protect their female kin. Some masters continued a medieval custom, *jus prima noctae,* the "right of the first night" (also known as *droit de seigneur,* or right of the master): the lord of the manor, master of the household, was permitted to cohabit with a woman of the subordinate class on the day of her wedding, before her husband bedded her.

The practice of taking African women as concubines was well established in slaveowning cultures in Europe before the conquistadors set sail for the Americas; between the thirteenth and fifteenth centuries, the Venetians had imported into Europe thousands of slaves from Ethiopia, the Sudan, and Morocco. Such traditions of sexual exploitation were then brought to the New World by European settlers.

The Spanish colonizers had sexual liaisons with the Indian women they enslaved in the Americas. In fact, sexual relations among the native inhabitants, the imported Africans, and the colonizers created extraor-

dinary racial mixtures, and the Spaniards devised a system of fifty-five different racial categories. Offspring of women of African descent and men of European descent, for instance, were what the Spanish called *mulato.* Racial prejudice and concerns about racial purity were reflected in a proverb, popular from Florida to Argentina: "White women for marriage, mulatto women for f—ing, black women for work."

The French empire attempted to curb sexual exploitation and concubinage among its colonists in the Americas. In 1685 a series of statutes known as the *Code Noir* provided that a free man who impregnated a slave would be fined two thousand pounds of sugar, and a master who impregnated a slave would be deprived of both the woman and her child. The code also provided for the manumission of a slave woman upon her legal marriage to a free man and the free status of their subsequent children. But extramarital interracial liaisons continued in Haiti and other French settlements; in 1774 a Haitian census found that of seven thousand women of color, five thousand were concubines. By 1724 France prohibited intermarriage; thus slave women could no longer become free by marrying.

Slavery could be, and was, used to promote licentiousness for profit. At the beginning of the nineteenth century, a traveler to Martinique reported, "The slave women are so encouraged by their masters in their disorderly inconstancy, that often they give the slave woman the liberty of their own time, provided she bring in the day's price, that is, the proceeds of her prostitution." Not just prostitution but the sale of slave women for sex flourished in the British West Indies. A visitor to Antigua mentioned that a black mother received sixty pounds, a gallon of rum, and two slaves in exchange for her mulatto daughter.

In the British West Indies, which had a climate of debauchery, a colored concubine was considered a "necessary appendage" for any white male colonial, married or single. One newcomer to Jamaica noted, "When visitors stay all night on an estate they are accustomed, on going to bed, to desire the domestic [who] attends them to bring them a girl with almost as little ceremony as they would ask for a candle." This may have been partly because in all of the Caribbean colonies, white women were greatly outnumbered by white men (a condition that persisted well into the twentieth century), but in slaveowning cultures a taste for exploitation was bred into white males from an early age. A Jamaican observed, "As early as at fifteen years of age, it is quite common for a boy to select for himself a mistress and this is usually done from among the waiting maids of his mother or sister"—a practice that could have dire consequences, since the women chosen might be his half-sister. Violent abuse was also common; as one visitor complained, "White bookkeepers kick black women in the belly from one end of Jamaica to another."

Yet, brutality and indulgence seemed to exist side by side. Many white men provided handsomely for their slave concubines and their offspring. In his will, a white master was likely to emancipate one or more favorite concubines; and some white fathers of mulattos were so generous that in 1762 the Jamaican assembly passed a law voiding bequests by whites to "Negroes and the issue of Negroes" exceeding two thousand pounds. Some of these sexual liaisons, then, whatever the initial motivation, must have evolved into genuine and lasting affection.

In any case, though, liaisons with slaves, and sexual promiscuity in general, left no stain on a man's honor. When he visited Barbados, the Duke of Clarence—the future King William IV of England—frequented the Royal Naval Hotel, which was owned by a black woman who reportedly supplied her male guests with black women as bedmates.

Sexual exploitation of slaves on the American mainland has a complex and diverse history. The early records of Virginia are replete with examples of white men exploiting slaves for sexual purposes. The British colonists formulated creative laws to accommodate the sexual exploitation of slaves by white males. One of the first statutes appeared in 1662, when Virginia—defying several centuries of English tradition—declared that mulatto children of slave mothers would inherit the mother's status. Maryland, and indeed all the English mainland colonies, soon followed suit. This law gave all free men an incentive to take slave women rather than free women as paramours.

By contrast, colonial legislators panicked at any sexual defiance by white women, who were scarce in the English settlements. In 1691, citing a fear of "abdominable mixture and spurious issue," Virginia established a steep fine for any white woman who gave birth to a mulatto or a sentence of five years of servitude if she could not pay it. These legislative measures did little to prevent mixed births. In 1822 a Southerner observed that "more than half the slave population are mixed with white." By 1864, politicians had given a name to interracial liaisons: miscegenation. From the colonial period onward, "tainted" bloodlines were a social and psychological threat to white Southerners; this issue is sensitively explored in Kate Chopin's short story, *Desirée's Baby*.

African-American women had a persistent problem with sexual abuse: defiance of resistance resulted in severe punishment. One woman, Harriet Jacobs—whose powerful memoir, *Incidents in the Life of a Slave Girl*, was published in 1861—did defy her master, but she was a rare exception. Most women surrendered or were broken. One slave described his sister's plight:

The master "tried to force my sister to submit to his wishes. This she defeated by a resistance so obstinate that he, becoming enraged, ordered two of his men to take her to a barn, where he generally whipped his slaves; there to strip off her clothes and whip her, which was done, until the blood stood in puddles under her feet." A slave woman fought back at her peril; raising a hand against a white, whatever the circumstances, could be considered a capital crime. When a slave girl named Celia murdered her master—her tormentor—in 1855 in a rural county in Missouri, the case made the headlines. But her death by hanging was a foregone conclusion, although her lawyers could demonstrate that, despite her attempts to fight him off, he had raped her continually from the time he bought her when she was fifteen.

The law protected white men—and even black men—who preyed on slave women. As an antebellum Southern lawyer explained, "The crime of rape does not exist in the State between African slaves. Our laws recognize no marital rights as between slaves; their sexual intercourse is left to be regulated by their owners. . . . The violation of a female slave by a male slave would be a mere assault and battery." The rape of a female slave by a white man would be assault and battery only if her owner had any objection—which he never would if he was the rapist.

African-Americans had to contend with cruel and capricious laws and practices. In North America the most controversial claim was that slaves were forced to breed. U. B. Phillips argued in 1918 that there was "no shred of supporting evidence," but we know that slaveowners valued fertile women, and that the rearing of slaves was important in the economy of the antebellum South. Also, although infant mortality among American slaves was roughly 25 percent at this time, the slave population grew 2.5 percent a year. In interviews conducted by the Works Progress Administration (WPA), some ex-slaves mentioned "stockmen" and "breeding niggers," terms suggesting that forced mating was not uncommon. One interviewee, Luisa Everett, reported that her master brought a man before her and forced him to strip: "He told us what we must git busy and do in his presence, and we had to do it." Sexual exploitation took many forms in the old South.

One legacy of sexual abuse is the enduring pain of the loss of racial identity. But the burden has weighed most heavily on African-American women. As W. E. B. Du Bois wrote in a moving personal essay, "The Damnation of Women," published more than fifty years after emancipation, "I shall forgive the white South much in its final judgment day. . . . But I shall never forgive, neither in this world nor the world to come, its wanton and continued and persistent insulting of the black womanhood which it sought and seeks to prostitute to its lust." Sexual exploitation created emotional and psychological tangles, and behavioral and political ramifications, that remain with us today.

See also PROSTITUTION; SLAVERY, CONTEMPORARY FORMS OF; WHITE SLAVERY.

BIBLIOGRAPHY

JOHNSON, JAMES HUGO. *Race Relations in Virginia and Miscegenation in the South, 1776–1860.* 1970.
REUTER, EDWARD BYRON. *The Mulatto in the United States.* 1918.
ROGERS, JOEL AUGUSTUS. *Sex and Race: Negro-Caucasion Mixing in All Ages and All Lands.* 1967

Catherine Clinton

Sharecropping

See Labor Systems; United States.

Sharp, Granville   [1735–1813]

English abolitionist.

In 1767 Granville Sharp, a British government clerk, made the chance acquaintance of Jonathan Strong, a slave who had been abused and worn out by David Lisle, a planter on Barbados, and then abandoned on the streets of London. Two years later, after Sharp restored Strong's health and found him employment, Lisle reclaimed Strong and sold him to James Kerr, a planter in Jamaica. Sharp's attorneys advised him that English law disallowed a slave's emancipation by virtue of his having been brought to England; indeed, approximately 15,000 slaves were living at that time in England, the vast majority of them the personal servants of their colonial masters. Undaunted by this advice and his complete lack of legal training, Sharp began seeking a way to help Strong and found in Blackstone's *Commentaries* (1765) the opinion that the moment a slave set foot on English soil he became free. After Sharp publicized this opinion in *The Injustice of Tolerating Slavery in England* (1769), Lisle and Kerr abandoned all claims to Strong. .

Sharp continued to intervene in cases similar to Strong's. Largely because of Sharp's efforts, in 1772 William Murray, Lord Mansfield and Chief Justice of England, ruled in *Somerset v. Stewart* that slavery could not exist legally in any form in England.

In 1772 Sharp began campaigning against slavery in England's colonies (after 1787 as chairman of the Committee for Effecting the Abolition of the Slave-Trade) and in 1786 he helped to settle over a thousand free blacks in Sierra Leone.

Granville Sharp. [Corbis-Bettmann]

See also ABOLITION AND ANTISLAVERY MOVEMENTS.

BIBLIOGRAPHY

LASCELLES, EDWARD CHARLES PONSONBY. *Granville Sharp and the Freedom of Slaves in England.* 1928.

Charles W. Carey Jr.

Sierra Leone

Sierra Leone occupies a unique place in the history of the transatlantic slave trade in that it was both a principal source of slaves and a place of return and refuge for Africans who managed to escape slavery in the New World. Located along the west coast of Africa, Sierra Leone and Upper Guinea as sources of slaves are often coupled as one contiguous zone, differentiated from Senegambia to the north and the lower Guinea Coast to the south and east. As many as a third of Africans exported by sea in the sixteenth century came out of Upper Guinea and Sierra Leone. This percentage would become negligible during the seventeenth century, but the number of captives exported out of the zone sharply increased from the 1720s through the 1740s, and again in the last two decades of the eighteenth century. Even so, captives from Upper Guinea and Sierra Leone contributed less than 5 percent of the overall volume of slave exports in the eighteenth century.

Sierra Leone, in the centuries characterized by the transatlantic slave trade, was the home of numerous groups of varying populations, including the Mende, Susu, Yalunka, Vai, Temne, Sherbro, Bulom, Kissi, Gola, and many others. Sierra Leone's nineteenth-century role in receiving the repatriated will provide the context for the ethnogenesis of the Krio, or Saro, whom we will return to shortly. The Portuguese in the fifteenth and sixteenth centuries would refer to the coastal populations of Sierra Leone generally as the Sapes, distinguishing them from the Manes of the interior. The Manes were southern Mande speakers who, near the middle of the sixteenth century, launched waves of invasions into the coastal area. Referred to as the Mane Wars, these hostilities resulted in numerous captives for export by way of the Portuguese, qualifying Upper Guinea–Sierra Leone as a key early supplier of the trade into the Atlantic. The English and Dutch would arrive in Sierra Leone at the beginning of the seventeenth century. The first half of the eighteenth century would see the trade dominated by the French, who were followed by the English in the second half. It is a matter of speculation as to the extent to which the population of Sierra Leone was diminished by the transatlantic trade. According to Patrick Manning, the general African population could well have declined briefly, in some areas, after 1730 owing to the trade.

In contrast to the large centralized states of Senegambia to the north or the expansive towns of the Yoruba to the east (in what is now southwestern Nigeria), Sierra Leone was characterized by small-scale, at times loosely confederated polities, each of which was made up of several villages together with surrounding farm and hunting land. Rice was a staple of the Mende and others, and it was cultivated along with cassava, guinea corn, millet, cotton, indigo, sweet potatoes, and other crops. That various populations in Sierra Leone were knowledgeable about cultivating rice and cotton was significant to North American planters, who would take advantage of such experience for their own survival and profit in the New World.

The question of domestic slavery within Sierra Leone is a controversial one, with implications for the rest of sub-Saharan Africa. It was in fact Walter Rodney's research on Upper Guinea that led to a call for the reevaluation of assumptions about the antiquity of domestic slavery in Africa. Rodney contended that domestic slavery in Upper Guinea–Sierra Leone, and by extension all of sub-Saharan Africa, either did not exist or was an institution of minor importance—and of little magnitude relative the general population—prior to the rise of the transatlantic slave trade; and that domestic slavery escalated in significance and volume in conjunction with the introduction and proliferation of European slaving interests along the coast.

Scholarship has subsequently divided over Rodney's thesis. Arguments in support of it are drawn from the oral traditions of the Sherbro, which indicate that domestic slavery was not clearly established until the eighteenth century. The Sherbro referred to domestic slaves as *wono* and considered them to be heritable property, or *lok*. Free individuals were reduced to slavery for the most part by warfare and kidnapping, while others were enslaved through purchase, gift-giving, inheritance, or punishment for crimes. At least in the nineteenth century, slaves in Sherbro society engaged mainly in agricultural, while simultaneously bolstering the status of important slaveholders—men and women—by virtue of their numbers. In this regard, women slaves were particularly valuable because they both provided labor, their own and their children's, and were sexually exploited. Women and girls were married either to male slaveholders or to other enslaved males for purposes of procreation. Slaves had certain rights in the society, which included humane treatment and a measure of respect. They could expect enough land to meet their own subsistence needs, and they would be protected from raiding if their owners had sufficient power. By the latter half of the nineteenth century, domestic slaves and clients of important people in Sherbro society greatly outnumbered the free population. It is testimony to the vicissitudes of the period that relatively few Sherbro slaves ventured to Freetown or British Sherbro (established toward the end of the nineteenth century) to escape their captivity.

Research on the Vai of Sierra Leone reaches a conclusion at variance with Rodney's thesis. The data suggest that this northern Mande-speaking group brought well-established notions of servile order with them as they began, around 1500, to move from the savanna of what is now the Republic of Guinea (Conakry) to the coast of Sierra Leone. Three categories of the "unfree," or *jonnu*, existed in Vai society: indentured workers who labored until their debts were paid; pawns, usually the nephews and nieces of maternal uncles placed in the employ of the uncle's creditor until payment was made; and domestic slaves who, in contrast to the first two categories, rarely became free. The Vai produced domestic slaves through the same mechanisms as the Sherbro, and the slaves performed essentially the same tasks. The Vai's participation in the transatlantic slave trade was unremarkable until after the British abolition of the trade in 1808, resulting in a sharp rise in the price of captives (to meet the ongoing demand of the Portuguese, Spanish, and Brazilians) that stimulated Vai interest. The Vai's acquisition of captives for export then accelerated to the point that, according to one estimate in 1826, three-fourths of the twelve to fifteen thousand Vai population was "un-

Ships crowd the anchorage in the harbor off Sierra Leone around 1850. [*Illustrated London News*/Corbis]

free." British and American naval squadrons brought an end to the Vai's slave exporting in 1850.

Sierra Leone remains distinctive in the history of the transatlantic slave trade in that it became the site of an effort to resettle the victims of transatlantic trade at the same time that the Vai and others were expanding it. As part of the resettlement effort, Freetown was established in 1787 by 341 black men and 70 white women from England. It was an independent settlement with a constitution written by the British abolitionist Granville Sharp. More than 1,000 blacks from Nova Scotia arrived in 1792; many of them loyalists who had supported the British in the American War of Independence. In 1800, 550 Maroons from Jamaica joined the settlement, also by way of Nova Scotia. Sierra Leone became a British colony in 1808, and eventually some 74,000 African repatriates would settle in Freetown, most rescued from Portuguese, Brazilian, and Spanish slave ships between 1808 and 1864. This Krio—or Creole—population, then, was quite diverse in origin. A substantial proportion, if not the majority, of the repatriates were Yoruba, and beginning in 1839 a number of these began efforts to leave Sierra Leone for southern Nigeria and other destinations in West (and even South) Africa. In these ways, Sierra Leone represents the profound disruption of the transatlantic slave trade.

See also LIBERIA; REPATRIATION TO AFRICA; SHARP, GRANVILLE; SLAVE TRADE; WEST AFRICA.

BIBLIOGRAPHY

DIXON-FYLE, MAC. "The Saro in the Political Life of Early Port Harcourt, 1913–1949." *Journal of African History* 30 (1989): 125–138.

FYFE, C. *A History of Sierra Leone.* 1962.

HOLSOE, SVEND E. "Slavery and Economic Response among the Vai (Liberia and Sierra Leone)." In *Slavery in Africa: Historical and Anthropological Perspectives,* edited by Suzanne Miers and Igor Kopytoff. 1977.

MACCORMACK, CAROL P. "Wono: Institutionalized Dependency in Sherbro Descent Groups (Sierra Leone)." In *Slavery in Africa: Historical and Anthropological Perspectives,* edited by Suzanne Miers and Igor Kopytoff. 1977.

RODNEY, WALTER. *A History of the Upper Guinea Coast, 545–1800.* 1970.

WISE, AKINTOLA J. G. "The Sierra Leone Krios: A Reappraisal from the Perspective of the African Diaspora." In *Global Dimensions of the African Diaspora,* edited by Joseph E. Harris. 1993.

Michael A. Gomez

Siete Partidas (The Seven Divisions)

The *Siete Partidas* was an elaborate law code produced in the kingdom of Castile in the thirteenth century. One of the most important legal developments for slavery in the Middle Ages and after was the recovery and assimilation of Roman law into the legal systems of most of Europe. The slave laws contained in the Code of Justinian and other Roman legislation could easily be applied when new conditions called for them beginning in the fifteenth century.

In the eleventh century the Italian legal scholar Irnerius had begun the academic study of the Roman code, and during the next two centuries knowledge and application of Roman law spread widely in western Europe. In the mid-thirteenth century, King Alfonso X of Castile and his legists produced a new code for his kingdom, known as the *Siete Partidas*, with heavy influences derived from Roman law. The *Siete Partidas* had a significant influence on late medieval and early modern legislation in Spain, both for the home country and for the American colonies, and thereby ensured that many Roman rules for slavery entered Spanish law.

The *Siete Partidas* was a heavily theoretical work inspired by Roman and canon law. Among its provisions were several important regulations regarding slaves, their ownership, their rights and legal disabilities, and their emancipation. The code's authors were especially concerned to propose regulations for slave holding in a multicultural society made up of a Christian majority and Jewish and Muslim minorities. They distinguished between *presos*, prisoners of war captured by those of the same religion, and *cautivos*, prisoners of war whose captors differed in religion. They provided for only limited slave ownership by Jews, who could not hold Christians as slaves and whose Jewish or Muslim slaves could obtain their freedom, with no compensation for the master, by converting to Christianity. Important sections of the *Siete Partidas* address marriage, family life, and inheritance, and contain commentary regarding the complexities that servile status created in all those areas.

Scholars argue over just when and to what extent the *Siete Partidas* became law. Some suggest that it was in force during Alfonso X's lifetime (he died in 1284); others say that it was not formally promulgated until 1348, during the reign of Alfonso XI. Regardless of its official inception, Alfonso X's code influenced the slave laws of colonial Spanish America and in its general principles has remained influential in Spain and the Spanish world until the present day.

See also LAW; SPAIN.

BIBLIOGRAPHY

CRADDOCK, JERRY R. "The Legislative Works of Alfonso el Sabio." In *The Emperor of Culture: Alfonso the Learned and His Thirteenth-Century Renaissance,* edited by R. I. Burns. 1990.
MACDONALD, ROBERT A. "Law and Politics: Alfonso's Program of Political Reform." In *The Worlds of Alfonso the Learned and James the Conqueror: Intellect and Force in the Middle Ages,* edited by R. I. Burns. 1985.

William D. Phillips, Jr.

Slave Codes

Slave codes were provisions of law that defined the relationship between the master and slave and provided a means of resolving disputes that arose among masters, third parties, and the government in reference to slaves. Slave codes were a part of Roman law. In modern times France enacted the *Code Noir* for its slave colonies, and the code for Spanish slaveholding was contained in *Las Siete Partidas*. In the common-law legal systems, case law—decisions in cases—augmented the codes in establishing the law of slavery.

Slave codes generally defined slaves as the master's personal property, or chattels. This definition cut slaves off from claims of legal rights. At the same time, the law had to recognize slaves as people who retained their human character, but it did so in ways that were consistent with the definition of slaves as property.

The accommodation of slavery into the law presented difficult problems in western legal systems. This law usually distinguished between persons and things by recognizing that people can have legal rights and duties in reference to their actions, and in reference to their relative rights to control things. Things, however, can be only the objects of actions and merely embody the relative rights of persons and the government. Things cannot have rights. The slave codes and legal decisions accommodated slavery within the law through the definition of slaves as human property, and from this definition followed the slave's lack of legal rights.

This can best be seen by the treatment of the rights and duties of slaves and masters. Slavery was distinguishable from other forms of social and legal inequality by the power and authority possessed by the slave's master. According to an opinion by Thomas Ruffin, a justice of the North Carolina Supreme Court, in *State v. Mann* (13 N.C., 2 Dev., 263, 1829), the relationship between master and slave has as its end "the profit of the master, his security and the public safety." Slaves were required to labor but could never "reap the fruits" of their toil. Thus, a master could not be held liable for assault or battery on a slave; this "uncontrolled authority over the body" was found to be necessary to "render the submission of the slave perfect."

The codes also legitimized the master's power to commit assault and battery upon a slave, though they did limit the master's powers through provisions that criminalized cruel and unusual punishment of slaves and wanton and unprovoked killings of slaves by masters. These restrictions, as Sir Moses Finley argued in *Ancient Slavery and Modern Ideology* (1980), were consistent with the idea of slaves as property because they represented governmental regulations of the master's property rights, which are always subject to legal regulation, but in only the most extreme and unnecessary cases of violence.

The criminal law did not generally afford third-party strangers the same rights to correct and kill slaves. Nevertheless, overseers and even strangers were granted more legal rights to inflict violence upon slaves than upon nonslaves, obviously in the interest of controlling slaves. In the South, slave patrols also were authorized by the codes to discipline slaves. Masters had the right, however, to sue those who caused damage to slave property, and thus could be compensated if a slave was unjustifiably killed or maimed. The law also criminalized extreme violence and unprovoked killings by nonmasters, thus providing masters with even greater security and preserving property rights.

The criminal law also had a longer list of crimes for slaves than for free people, and for crimes that could be committed by slaves or free people, the punishments imposed upon slaves were often more severe. The most extreme example was a principle of Roman law called *senatus consultum silaninum*. According to this doctrine, when a master was murdered by one of his slaves, all the slaves who lived with the master were tortured and then condemned to death. This doctrine was not adapted outside of Rome.

When slaves were tried in the criminal courts, the master's interest in the slave often came into conflict with the interests of society at large. Thus, the degree of procedural "fairness" in criminal trials of slaves posed an interesting conflict of interests that was resolved in different ways at different times. Some slave codes gave slaves swift summary trials, while others accorded slaves most of the procedural safeguards that free people enjoyed. Scholars debate whether concern for slaves' rights or the master's property in the slaves on trial was the predominant interest in these cases. Nevertheless, an opinion by U.S. Supreme Court Chief Justice Roger B. Taney given in *United States v. Amy*, (24 F. Cas. 792, C.C.D. Va. 1859, No. 14, 445) recognized society's right to punish slaves "for its own safety, although the punishment may render the property of the master of little or no value."

The slave codes also recognized the slave's status as property through the legitimization of commercial dealings by masters and third parties. Masters had the right to buy and sell slaves, and this included the right to divide slave families. Some codes limited the master's right to sell children under ten years of age away from their mothers, but the otherwise unlimited slave market in human flesh was one of the cruelest reflections of the slaves' condition. Masters also hired slaves out, mortgaged slaves in financing transactions, and otherwise treated slaves as various forms of property. Slaves generally could be devised by a master's will and thus were the subjects of disputes surrounding inheritances.

The law of manumission also varied greatly. The slave codes of ancient Rome generally allowed masters to free their slaves. In the U.S. South, however, as the nineteenth century progressed the slave codes and case law first restricted and eventually banned manumissions. Roman law also accorded slaves the right to acquire a property right known as the *peculium*, which could be used to purchase freedom. Slaves in the U.S. South had no right to a *peculium* or any other ownership of property.

The codes in the South also sought to ensure the slaves' permanent status by banning education of slaves, limiting slave gatherings, requiring slaves to exhibit passes when at large, and forbidding slaves to earn income or to own property. The codes of most Southern States contained provisions prohibiting the teaching of slaves to read and write.

Unlike Roman law, the slave laws of the Americas based slavery on considerations of race. Even free blacks were subjected to slave code provisions that denied them the rights and legal status afforded to whites.

See also CODE NOIR; LAW; MANUMISSION; PECULIUM; SIETE PARTIDAS.

BIBLIOGRAPHY

FEDE, ANDREW. *People without Rights: An Interpretation of the Fundamentals of Slavery in the U.S. South.* 1992.
HIGGINBOTHAM, A. LEON. *In the Matter of Color: Race and the American Legal Process: The Colonial Period.* 1978.
MORRIS, THOMAS D. *Southern Slavery and the Law, 1619–1860.* 1996.
SCHAFER, JUDITH KELLEHER. *Slavery, the Civil Law, and the Supreme Court of Louisiana.* 1994.
TUSHNET, MARK V. *The American Law of Slavery, 1810–1860: Considerations of Humanity and Interest.* 1981.
WATSON, ALAN. *Roman Slave Law.* 1987.
———. *Slavery in the Americas.* 1989.

Andrew T. Fede

Slave Grace

In 1827, in *The Slave, Grace,* a case in the British High Court of Admiralty, Justice William Scott, Lord Stowell, ruled that Grace, a slave held in Antigua, was not a free woman by virtue of having previously resided in England. Grace had accompanied her mistress to Britain, where they resided for some time, after which she had returned voluntarily to the colony. Years later, Grace sued for her freedom.

Lord Stowell admitted that, under the precedent of *Somerset v. Stewart* (1772), a slave resident in Britain was free, but he maintained that slave status became reattached when a slave returned to a slaveholding colony without having claimed freedom in Britain.

Although Lord Stowell dismissed Lord Mansfield's observations in *Somerset* on the injustice and the unnatural character of slavery as *obiter dicta,* he readily admitted that Grace would have been freed had she sued while in England. He ignored the question of a slave forcibly repatriated to a colony to prevent such a suit, nor did he consider the status of a slave, abandoned or judicially liberated, who independently returned to the colony.

In the United States, although *Somerset* was a precedent, *The Slave, Grace,* decided long after American independence, was only learned commentary, and disputes over this doctrine recurred in American cases. Some state courts recognized residency in a free state as conferring freedom whenever and wherever claimed, while others, such as the Missouri Supreme Court in *Scott v. Emerson* (1852)—an earlier stage of *Dred Scott*—insisted that freedom had to be claimed while a slave was a resident in free territory.

See also DRED SCOTT V. SANDFORD; SOMERSET V. STEWART.

BIBLIOGRAPHY

Dred Scott v. Sandford, 19 Howard (U.S.) 393 (1857).
FINKELMAN, PAUL. *An Imperfect Union: Slavery, Federalism, and Comity.* 1981.
Scott v. Emerson, 15 Mo. 576 (1852).
The Slave, Grace, 2 Haggard Admiralty (G.B.) 94 (1827).
Somerset v. Stewart, Loft (G.B.) 1 (1772); 20 Howell St. Tr. (G.B.) 1 (1772).

Patrick M. O'Neil

Slave Narratives

Slave narratives constitute a very important category of source material for understanding matters of race and slavery in the United States. These narratives, of three types, had varying origins.

The first type appeared during slavery times, especially in the 1840s and 1850s. Written by people who had spent time in slavery but were now free, these narratives permitted Frederick Douglass, Harriet Jacobs, William Wells Brown, and others to tell what they had experienced in slavery and how they had escaped and made their way to freedom. Some, like Anthony Burns, told their stories through a white writer's pen, while others, like Frederick Douglass and Harriet Jacobs, told their stories themselves. Though many escaped slaves told their stories to live audiences, the published accounts, especially Frederick Douglass's, enabled them to reach vast audiences.

These antebellum narratives served multiple purposes. Northern abolitionists and the former slaves themselves intended these stories to reach people with the abolitionist message. Former slaves had an authenticity, as witnesses of slavery, that permitted them to speak, whether at a meeting or in a book, in dramatic and compelling terms of their personal experiences. Moreover, the stories could raise funds. Earnings from Anthony Burns's narrative, for example, helped pay his way to college and seminary in his quest to become a trained minister.

Those narratives continue to be read today. Students and scholars alike encounter Frederick Douglass's description of his Maryland owner's punishing efforts to break the slave's will. They read William Wells Brown's account of the destruction that slavery and the slave trade could wreck on the slave family. They learn from Harriet Jacobs that women's experience under slavery could differ from men's. And, from Henry "Box" Brown, they find a description of slavery under the best of conditions in Richmond, Virginia, followed by an account of how his wife and their three children had been suddenly sold away and how, now that "my family were gone," he contrived a way to have himself shipped out of slavery in a crate.

A second category of narrative was published sometime after 1865 and constitutes a variant of memoirs by Americans. The best known example is Booker T. Washington's *Up from Slavery: An Autobiography* (1901). Washington had little memory of slavery, for he was born only in 1857, and by the time he wrote he had no need to convince Americans to become active abolitionists. His book nonetheless had a political objective, and he addressed two audiences as he sought to ease the way for freedpeople in a racist society. He designed his book to serve as a guide to African-Americans by presenting the story of an exemplary citizen leading the way and demonstrating that success could be had through hard work. He also intended it to gain a favorable hearing among white Americans so that they might support his educational objectives at Tuskegee Institute.

The third type of narrative dates from the 1920s and 1930s. In the late 1920s people at Fisk University conducted two hundred interviews. On a much larger scale a New Deal agency, the Works Progress Admin-

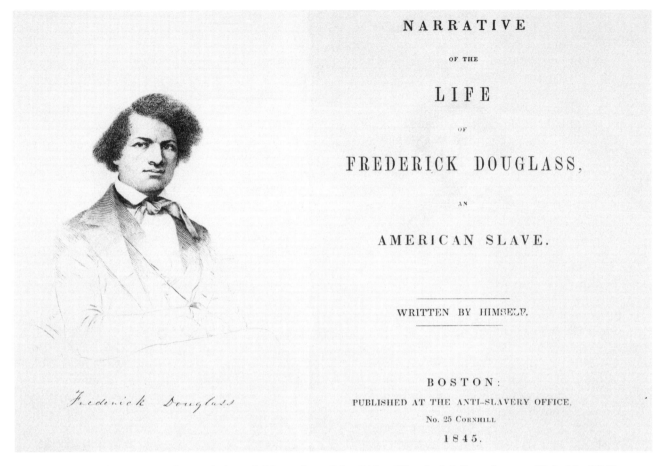

NARRATIVE

OF THE

LIFE

OF

FREDERICK DOUGLASS,

AN

AMERICAN SLAVE.

WRITTEN BY HIMSELF.

BOSTON:
PUBLISHED AT THE ANTI-SLAVERY OFFICE,
No. 25 CORNHILL
1845.

The title page and an engraved portrait from the Narrative of the Life of Frederick Douglass, *published in 1845.*
[Corbis-Bettmann]

istration (WPA), employed writers to interview Americans in various walks of life, thus supplying employment for writers while obtaining a vast collection of materials about Americans' diverse experiences through the late nineteenth and early twentieth centuries. One assignment called for interviewing former slaves and obtaining their recollections of slavery. Interviewers had a schedule of questions to guide them in their work. Thus former slaves were routinely asked questions about such matters as worship and punishment under slavery, and what they remembered about the end of slavery. By contrast, most were asked very little about their long lives since slavery had ended. Because few of them had reached adulthood as slaves, they were asked more about what they knew least and less about what they knew best, yet they nonetheless supplied remarkable recollections.

The WPA slave narratives opened windows through which one can still see vivid depictions of the American past. One former slave remembered that, though times had been hard since freedom came, at least the slave trade was gone, while another saw the end of

the threat of a whipping as the greatest single measure of what distinguished freedom from slavery. Asked whether he had ever gone to school as a slave, yet another respondent exclaimed, "No 'm, slave people jus' got somethin' in their stummicks an' somethin' on their backs. . . . But I schooled ever' one o' mine. I sure did."

There are WPA narratives from every former slave state. Some interviewers did a better job than others, and their results are more useful today. Subjects responded more candidly to black interviewers than to white ones, so that Susie Byrd, for example, obtained some particularly revealing responses from old black men and women living in the 1930s in Petersburg, Virginia.

By the 1970s, both principal kinds of narratives, those from the pre–Civil War years and those from the 1930s, were becoming more widely available, for both teaching purposes and research, than ever before. Gilbert Osofsky, for example, edited three antebellum narratives in a volume he called *Puttin' On Ole Massa: The Slave Narratives of Henry Bibb, William*

Wells Brown, and Solomon Northup (1969). George P. Rawick edited most of the 1930s WPA narratives in many volumes, *The American Slave: A Composite Autobiography* (1972–1979). Separately published were the WPA narratives from Virginia, edited by Charles L. Perdue Jr. and others, in *Weevils in the Wheat: Interviews with Virginia Ex-Slaves* (1976).

Many modern works on race, slavery, and the American South have relied on one set of slave narratives or another. John W. Blassingame relied heavily on the two sets of nineteenth-century narratives for *The Slave Community: Plantation Life in the Antebellum South* (1972), though he neglected the 1930s materials (Rawick's collection having itself appeared in 1972) and focused on slave men. Works relying primarily on the WPA narratives are George P. Rawick, *From Sundown to Sunup: The Making of the Black Community* (1972), and Paul D. Escott, *Slavery Remembered: A Record of Twentieth-Century Slave Narratives* (1979).

The critical literature on slave narratives emphasizes the antebellum writings. In view of the political objectives of the early narratives and the distant memories and self-censorship that could compromise the 1930s interviews, all three collections of materials must be used with care. Yet much of what was recounted in the narratives can be verified, and they remain a matchless source for historical research.

See also DOUGLASS, FREDERICK; JACOBS, HARRIET; LITERATURE OF SLAVERY; MEMORY AND HISTORY.

BIBLIOGRAPHY

ANDREWS, WILLIAM L. *To Tell a Free Story: The First Century of Afro-American Autobiography, 1760–1865.* 1986.

———, ed. *African American Autobiography: A Collection of Critical Essays.* 1993.

DAVIS, CHARLES T., and HENRY LOUIS GATES, JR., eds. *The Slave's Narrative.* 1985.

FOSTER, FRANCES SMITH. *Witnessing Slavery: The Development of Ante-Bellum Slave Narratives.* 1979. Reprint, 1994.

JACKSON, BLYDEN. *A History of Afro-American Literature.* Vol. 1, *The Long Beginning, 1746–1895.* 1989.

SEKORA, JOHN, and DARWIN T. TURNER, eds. *The Art of Slave Narrative: Original Essays in Criticism and Theory.* 1982.

SPINDEL, DONNA J. "Assessing Memory: Twentieth-Century Slave Narratives Reconsidered." *Journal of Interdisciplinary History* 27 (Autumn 1966): 247–261.

STARLING, MARION WILSON. *The Slave Narrative: Its Place in American History.* 1988.

Peter Wallenstein

Slave Religion

This entry includes the following articles: United States; Latin America; Caribbean Region.

United States

Slave traders uprooted men and women from highly ritualized African religious communities and carried them to servitude in a Christian world. Slave owners uniformly discouraged traditional African religious practices, including Islamic rites, but disagreed sharply over what, it any, Christian doctrine to preach to their bondspeople. Slaves responded discerningly to the shifting gospel preached to them by white divines. Few, in fact, converted to Christianity until revivalist fervor swept up both whites and blacks in the 1740s. Then, thousands upon thousands of slaves offered qualified assent to the gospel as preached by southern whites: yes to personal salvation, no to the doctrine of divinely sanctioned chattel slavery.

The "invisible church"—or worship meetings kept secret from whites—gave slaves a forum in which to negotiate between African traditions, proslavery elements of slaveholder piety, the message of Christ's sacrifice, and other aspects of scripture, including the story of Exodus. At these clandestine gatherings, slaves could sort out the information that they had received from itinerant ministers, from services at their masters' churches or at a fully supervised African-American church, from revivals, and from remembered African practices. Influenced by both the visible and the invisible church, many slaves accepted Christianity and reinterpreted its message to affirm, rather than denigrate, their humanity.

Contested Souls: 1619–1745

The first slaves encountered extraordinary obstacles to the maintenance of their African belief systems, although initially the European tradition against holding Christians in perpetual bondage protected them from proselytization. The terror of the Middle Passage, their masters' censure of open rituals, and the haphazard conglomeration of different peoples and languages on a single estate threatened the continuity of African faith. Owners denied Muslim slaves the guidance of their holy book, the Koran; and displaced devotees of Yoruba and other African systems could not visit their religion's holy sites or practice its rites. Several scholars, especially E. Franklin Frazier, have argued that these destructive factors virtually eliminated African religions.

But a steady flow of new African slaves with fresh memories of their spiritual heritage guarded slave communities against such spiritual bankruptcy. Colonists passed a sequence of laws against Islam and other nonwestern religious practices, proof that coherent African beliefs had endured the middle passage. Vigilant slave owners eventually curtailed the collective practice of most rituals, but the underlying tenents of African faith, including a belief in the presence of immanent spiritual forces, survived. Significantly, certain modes of worship common to African religions found renewed expression in a Christian context during the revivals of the mid-eighteenth century—for example, dances known as "ring shouts," ecstatic behavior during spirit possession, and immersion in water during baptism. These actions incorporated both Christian devotion and practices from the African past.

Civil and ecclesiastical authorities worked to assure slaveholders that they did not have to fear Christianity's impact on their property. Several states—including New York (1664), Virginia (1667), the Carolinas (1670), and Maryland (1671)—adopted laws explicitly denying that baptism liberated slaves or changed their civil status in any way. Sharing this conviction, the Anglican church formed the Society for the Propagation of the Gospel in Foreign Parts in 1701. The society's first missionary, Rev. Samuel Thomas, worked among slaves for several years and taught at least twenty how to read the Bible. Notwithstanding the efforts of Thomas and dissenting Quaker, Baptist, and Lutheran ministers, many planters remained concerned about the legal ramifications of baptism. The bishop of London published an official letter in 1727, asserting the biblical basis of perpetual slavery and thereby helping to allay slaveowners' fears. Catholics in nearby Florida and Louisiana needed no such prompting; the French and Spanish were already baptizing slaves and allowed them access to the sacraments.

The Society for the Propagation of the Gospel spearheaded Anglican efforts to convert slaves to Christianity and to inspire owners to proselytize their slaves. Education was the cornerstone of the society's efforts; in 1704, Elias Neau founded a school in New York City for black and Indian slaves that eventually enrolled approximately 1,500 students. From Neau and others, slaves learned about their new country's language and institutions, but few accepted the proslavery Anglican catechism and converted. In comparison, the missionaries' secondary strategy, to inculcate a missionary impulse in slaveowners, bore considerable fruit. In addition to reprinting thousands of copies of the bishop's letter of 1727, the society repeatedly published a sermon of 1711 by William Fleetwood, who forcefully argued that conversion granted only spiritual, not temporal, freedom. Through such propaganda, the society broke down whites' reluctance to spread the Christian faith and prepared slaveowners for an age of revival.

An Evangelical Faith: 1740–1822

A modest Anglican revival led by George Whitfield in 1740 marked the rise of Evangelical Protestantism among white Christians, an event with profound spiritual consequences for slaves. Decades of propaganda finally convinced the majority of masters that conversion did not interfere with a slave's civil status, and ministers from every denomination invited slaves to share their Christian faith. Baptists and Methodists committed the most resources to slave evangelization, and by the turn of the century, thousands of slaves had converted to Christianity.

Evangelical Protestant missionaries reached so many slaves because of the content of their message and favorable circumstances in the slave community. Around 1725, native-born slaves had begun to outnumber new African arrivals, and these "creolized" slaves responded more openly to the Christian message. Moreover, those who did remember tribal rituals found evangelical Protestant worship, especially as presented at revival meetings, more familiar than the extended catechism of the Anglicans. For these slaves, episodes of spirit possession and group singing recalled similar behavior across the sea.

To this more receptive audience, ministers preached the possibility of immediate conversion and the brotherhood of man. The doctrine of immediate conversion empowered slaves to enter into a personal relationship with God, and commitment to brotherhood led many divines to preach against slavery, or at least against its excesses. The rhetoric of the American Revolution fueled this radical message, and some Methodists and Baptists advocated general emancipation until the nineteenth century. In 1784, the Methodist general conference declared slavery an "abomination," and in 1789 Baptists in Virginia lamented the "violent deprivation of the rights of nature." Though political pressure and the desire to convert more southern whites soon compelled Evangelical Protestants to compromise on this, the flicker of abolitionist faith had given slaves the vision of an empowering belief system.

After conversion, enslaved Baptists and Methodists experienced empowerment within the institutional church. Slaves, whether in churches with their masters or in all-black congregations supervised by whites, obeyed denominational rules that validated them as moral agents. Furthermore, a few gifted slaves gained the right to preach, pray, or exhort in the church. Most often, such slave leaders worked within the slave population. On the plantation, for example, missionaries designated certain slaves as "watchmen" and relied upon them to minister to the needs of other bondspeople. Many slaves preached to racially mixed audiences at revival meetings or at mixed churches, however, and experienced genuine spiritual responsibility. Several especially famous slaves, including Bishop Francis Asbury's companion, Harry

Hosier ("Black Harry"), traveled through the country with white itinerants and gained a large following.

Several of these slave leaders worked to form independent black churches. George Léile, for example, baptized dozens along the Savannah River during the Revolutionary War, both before and after his master's death. One of his converts, Andrew Bryan, founded Savannah's First Colored Baptist Church in 1788, well before white Baptists established a presence in the area. Bryan purchased his freedom after beginning his pastorate, and he guided his church through intense persecution by carefully appeasing Savannah whites. He granted land that he had purchased for the church to white trustees, petitioned the town council to officially sanction his worship, and allowed for constant white supervision. Augusta (Georgia), Williamsburg and Petersburg (Virginia), and several other southern cities also supported independent black churches by the turn of the century. There, slaves and free blacks worshiped in relative autonomy. Additionally, dozens of former slaves played crucial leadership roles in the free black churches of the North. Richard Allen and Abasolm Jones, founders of the African Methodist Episcopal (AME) church, had purchased their freedom; their friend Daniel Coker had escaped from bondage in Maryland, as had Henry H. Garnet and James W. C. Pennington, abolitionist lecturers and pastors.

These runaway ministers dramatized the liberating effect of slave theology. Slaves identified themselves as the enslaved children of Israel in the book of Exodus and predicted confidently that a new Moses would lead them out of bondage. During the long wait for temporal salvation, Christian teaching comforted slaves by promising a restful afterlife and by giving them a firm moral ground for criticizing slaveholding whites. One indignant slave proclaimed: "White folk's got a heap to answer for the way they've done to colored folks! So much they won't never pray it away!"

The Persecuted Church: 1822–1865

By the early nineteenth century, the success of Evangelical Protestantism had created new racial dynamics. Sensitivity to the interests of converted slaveowners and to expanding African-American church membership compelled white churchgoers to reexamine their attitude toward slave Christianity. Intimidated by predominantly black congregations, influential black preachers, and the realized threat of religiously motivated slave revolts, southern whites divested their theology of any remotely abolitionist content. Baptist and Methodist congregations, once supportive of emancipation, expelled antislavery ministers. Nationwide, the Presbyterian, Baptist, and Methodist churches split into northern and southern factions (in 1837, 1845, and 1845, respectively). Leaders of the southern churches crafted doctrines that strengthened, rather than threatened, their precious institution. The proslavery ministers argued that slavery was consistent with the word of God and that blacks were "chosen" by God to be slaves. These proslavery ministers also asserted that slavery was a positive good because it introduced new peoples to Christianity, a proposition they attempted to validate by sending scores of missionaries into the slave community.

Denmark Vesey's failed rebellion in 1822, organized through networks within Charleston's AME Church, gave local whites grounds for reorganizing slave religion within their community. In 1817, slaves and free blacks had withdrawn from the city's Methodist churches to form an independent AME congregation. When white officials discovered Vesey's plot, they disbanded the black church and exiled its pastor, Morris Brown. Brown, like many other southern blacks, escaped further persecution by fleeing to black churches in the North.

Nat Turner's religiously inspired revolt nine years later, in Southampton, Virginia, accelerated a trend among southern white churches to limit the religious autonomy of slaves. A slave himself, Turner claimed

Richard Allen. [Corbis-Bettmann]

divine guidance for his violent rebellion, confirming the suspicions of many slaveowners that religion, improperly supervised, could serve as a powerful inducement to insurrection. Following this 1831 rebellion, Virginia led the southern states in passing a rigorous code against the black church that stripped all African-Americans of the right to preach, even informally, and prescribed the whip for any slaves who attempted to meet without white guidance.

White churchgoers compensated for this crippling blow to slave religion by sending hundreds of missionaries to slave communities. These missionaries fought for the amelioration, rather than abolition, of slavery and included obedience in their message to slaves. Charles Colcock Jones, foremost in this new legion of evangelists, became the first missionary for the Association for the Religious Instruction of Negroes in 1832. His innumerable plantation visits and myriad publications, including a special catechism for slaves and a manual for planters entitled *The Religious Instruction of the Negroes in the United States* (1842), exemplified the furious energy that white churchgoers poured into slave evangelism in the nineteenth century. Milton Sernett explained this explosion of evangelical activity as the balm applied to the southern conscience.

In the institutional church, slaves experienced additional changes in their religious life. For a variety of reasons, including discomfort with joint worship and pressure from free blacks, many white pastors divided their congregations along racial lines. White clergymen or superintending committees officially supervised each of the separate black churches, judging the slaves and free blacks incapable of managing their own faith. Complete control of these churches, however, proved impossible. While careful whites managed the church's long-term goals and preached from the pulpit, blacks, including slaves, learned about the day-to-day disciplinary and financial arrangements of the church and seized opportunities to exhort, encourage, and even preach from the floor. Skirting the law in the name of faith, slaves at Richmond's First African Baptist church, separated from the racially mixed First Baptist Church in 1841, learned to read, contributed funds to purchase blacks out of slavery with ministerial gifts and rented out their building for political rallys and social events.

After emancipation by U.S. troops, which slaves hailed as the biblical "day of jublilee," freed people from diverse Christian backgrounds converged on these separate black churches. Their prayer that God would deliver them from their bonds had been answered, and African-Americans from the secret glens of the invisible church and from the halls of racially mixed congregations met under the aegis of Christianity to embark upon their communal enterprise of freedom.

See also ANGLICANS; BAPTIST CHRISTIANITY; CHRISTIANITY; EXODUS; METHODISM; SOCIETY FOR THE PROPAGATION OF THE GOSPEL; VESEY REBELLION.

BIBLIOGRAPHY

BOLES, JOHN B. *Masters and Slaves in the House of the Lord: Race and Religion in the American South, 1740–1870.* 1988.
FINKELMAN, PAUL, ed. *Articles on American Slavery,* vol. 16: *Religion and Slavery.* 1989.
FRAZIER, E. FRANKLIN. *The Negro Church in America.* 1963.
GENOVESE, EUGENE D. *Roll, Jordan, Roll: The World the Slaves Made.* 1972.
HERSKOVITS, MELVILLE J. *The Myth of the Negro Past.* 1941.
LEVINE, LAWRENCE W. *Black Culture and Black Consciousness: Afro-American Folk Thought from Slavery to Freedom.* 1977.
MATHEWS, DONALD G. *Religion in the Old South.* 1977.
RABOTEAU, ALBERT J. *Slave Religion: The "Invisible Institution" in the Antebellum South.* 1978.
SERNETT, MILTON C. *Black Religion and American Evangelicalism: White Protestants, Plantation Missions, and the Flowering of Negro Christianity, 1787–1865.* 1975.
SOBEL, MECHAL. *Trabelin' On: The Slave Journey to an Afro-Baptist Faith.* 1979.

Charles F. Irons

Latin America

Religion allowed Africans to survive the dehumanizing effects of the slave trade and escape the alienation of living in a hostile New World environment. The blacks imported to Latin America came from diverse regions of Africa with different religious beliefs. African religions made a less absolute distinction between the sacred and the profane than does modern Western thought. Africans were highly religious in the sense that they saw the spiritual dimension everywhere. Some common religious beliefs came to the New World on the slave ships, such as ancestor worship, faith healing, spirit possession, and divination. The slave trade shattered families, clan religion, and village culture. However African gods and goddesses survived the exile of the African diaspora in the guise of Catholic saints in the Spanish and Portuguese Americas. The question of how Africans re-formed their religious beliefs in an alien environment has intrigued scholars for over a century.

Slaves created autonomous cultures and communities in the plantations and cities of Latin America. Since Roman Catholicism was forcibly imposed on slaves in the colonies of Latin America, slaves clung to their ancestral beliefs as a protest against the controls of slavery. African magical charms and spells were a liberating force, as the slaves used the power of the spirits to overcome oppression and to frighten the masters and overseers.

Religious improvisation and syncretism was based on the collective memory of religion in such specific West African areas as those of the Yoruba, Fon, and Dahomeans. Bantu-speaking peoples of west-central Africa carried other religious beliefs to places like Brazil, Haiti, and Cuba. Africans, like Indians, appropriated Christianity and its values to serve their local needs and shaped it into forms of their own. Religious syncretism and parallel religious cult houses emerged throughout the long history of Latin American slavery.

The millions of diasporan Africans facing cruelty and sudden death on plantations and in mines sought escape in religious ritual and magic. Slaves in the African cult houses in Cuba and Brazil preserved African religion and culture to escape marginality by remaining faithful to their ancestral beliefs.

Sex roles differed in African religions. Female slaves were the healers and mothers of the saints, while males were often *brujos,* or sorcerers, who used magic against their white oppressors and led fugitive slave communities in places as diverse as Colombia, Cuba, Haiti, and Brazil.

For many Africans, religion was inseparable from efficacious magic, and so they used Catholic articles of faith such as rosary beads as amulets or fetishes, along with holy water, prayers, and statues of the saints. For the same reason the miraculous powers attributed to the Catholic saints appealed to the slaves, who identified them with their ancestral gods. Several syncretistic folk religions emerged in Latin America in colonial times, and they have survived to the present day. They can be seen most clearly in Brazilian cults of the Catholic saints, which reflect the power of the African gods in exile.

The African cult practices of Candomblé in Bahia (northeastern Brazil) have been studied by the physician Nina Rodriques (1900), Melville J. Herskovits (1941), and Roger Bastide (1967). African ritual in Brazil expressed itself in song and dance, with spirit possession as the ultimate religious experience. Nina Rodrigues and Arthur Ramos investigated the therapeutic value of the trances induced during the cult rituals.

As to the reason why African religion survived better in Brazil than in North America, Roger Bastide noted that American slaves lived mostly on small farms and worked side by side with whites, so they became more acculturated than slaves in Latin America, where larger populations of Africans lived on plantations or mines in rural areas where they had closer and longer contact with recently arrived Africans and therefore remained in closer touch with African beliefs. The

African slave trade lasted from the 1530s to 1850 in Brazil and resulted in the shipment of between 3.5 and 4 million slaves to work in the sugar and coffee plantations and mines. The areas of Latin America where African religions survived were the regions where African slaves were in the majority.

Beyond the areas with large African populations, African religion survived in those regions of Latin America where the Catholic Church was weak, missionaries were few, and slaves were baptized only nominally, without thorough religious instruction. Religious syncretism was permitted by the colonial church in order to aid in converting the slaves. The church also sought to transform African cults by permitting the veneration of black saints, such as Benedict the Moor, Anthony, and King Balthasar, and black Madonnas, such as Nossa Senhora da Aparecida. So popular was African religion that it influenced the Portuguese Christians and led to what Roger Bastide described as "black Catholicism."

According to José Honorio Rodrigues, the Africanization of Brazil began in the sixteenth century with the arrival of the first slaves in 1538 and continued until the cession of the slave trade in the 1850s. From the seventeenth through the nineteenth centuries, Brazil had closer contact with Angola and parts of the coasts of western African than it did with Portugal, so much so that the seventeenth-century Portuguese Jesuit Antonio Vieira said, "Brazil has its body in America and its soul in Africa."

Arthur Ramos classified Brazilian slaves by culture into four groups: (1) a "Sudanese" civilization of West Africans composed of Yoruba (Nagô), Ketu, Dahomeans, the Gégé (Fon), and Fanti/Ashanti; (2) Islamic people of West Africa, including "Mandingos" (Mande) and Hausas; (3) Bantu-speakers from Angola and the Congo; and (4) Bantu-speakers from East Africa. The leveling of all these ethnic backgrounds by slavery was an obstacle to the preservation of any of the African religions in a pure form. Slaves of one ethnic group were thrown together with those of other ethnic groups in the plantations and cities of colonial Brazil. Since ethnic identities were relatively fluid in Africa, Bastide feels that shifting sources of slaves in Africa led to reconstitution of various religion tradition as Africans adapted to New World conditions. In the various cities of colonial Brazil, different groupings of slaves preserved different African languages and cultures. Even in the hostile environment of the New World, shipmates and slave brothers shared ritual knowledge of West and Central African religious traditions on the plantations and in the cities. Sidney Mintz and Richard Price have described this sharing, in emerging diasporan communities, as the innovative and creative beginnings of new religions and cultures of African derivation. Although these emerging slave communities venerated collective ancestors and African gods, they also incorporated beliefs derived from Indian and European cultures.

The African cult houses that survived in the late twentieth century emerged in the late eighteenth and nineteenth centuries. The Candomblé practices of Bahia are considered closest to West African roots. The Bahian city of Salvador has had a large African presence from colonial times to the late twentieth century. As in other coastal cities of Brazil with large African populations, it was natural for slaves to preserve African religion there. In Recife, Xangô was the most popular African religion, while Macumba was popular in Rio de Janeiro. Batuque emerged in Porto Alegre and the Casa das Minas in São Luís do Maranhão. Umbanda emerged out of Macumba and French spiritism in the twentieth century and was attractive to both rural Afro-Brazilian immigrants to urban areas and to European immigrants who sought its mutual aid benefits in the anomie of modern urban life.

African religious expression in Brazil always took the form of music and dance. Originally the names Candomblé and Macumba referred to dances with certain musical instruments, according to Arthur Ramos. The tribal gods of Yoruba and Dahomean slaves survived in the African cult practices of Brazil: Obatalá, the overlord; Shangô, god of lightning and storms; Ogun, the war deity; Eshu, a devil-like figure; and Yemanjá, Oshun, and Yansen, water spirits who might be found in rivers, seas and lakes. Religious persecution and legal prohibitions against large gatherings of slaves forced Afro-Brazilian devotees of these faiths to worship at night in secret places, like the bush arbors of North American plantations.

Worship of the African gods in Bahia takes place in special temples known as *terreiros* (terraces, public squares), which feature altars to the African gods and local *pegis*, or Indian shamans. The leading priest of the temple is the *babalão*, or *pai do santo* (father of the saint), who is both respected and feared by the local population for being a witch doctor. The priest is a repository of the secrets of tradition and interprets beliefs for the followers.

Many Afro-Brazilian cult houses are presided over by a woman known as the *mãe do santo* (mother of the saint), who takes care of the gods and the altars and directs temple worship. Devotion to the African gods in Brazil, Cuba, and Haiti includes animal sacrifice, sacred music from African drums, dances and songs from initiates known as *filhas do santo* (daughters of the saint), who often drift into ecstatic trances induced by the long hours of drumming and dancing. During these trances the African *orishas* (spirits) are said to mount the initiates and take possession of their spirits and bodies. The *filhas do santo* have their heads shaved and undergo fasts and long periods of study. The priest or priestess usually begins the religious ceremony with *despachos,* or banishments, of the devil Eshu before the dance can begin. Religious ceremonies in the Candomblé cult houses usually go on long into the night, with dances and prayers to the gods and spirit possession of initiates.

According to Ramos, the Macumbas of Rio de Janeiro have more syncretic religious practices than the Candomblés of Bahia and conform more closely to African practices. On the altars of Macumba temples, images of Catholic saints represent African gods and goddess. Saint George represents Ogun, while Saint Michael symbolizes Shangô. The Bantu traditions of Angola and the Congo region are more prevalent in the Macumba temples. The altars are surrounded by images of the Catholic saints, candles, pictures, swords, and flags. The colors white and red are preferred in most of the Afro-Brazilian temples, since these colors symbolize the African gods. The *filhas do santo* often wear white or red and white costumes to symbolize their loyalty to the *orishas*.

The Afro-Brazilian nations are symbolized by three colors believed traditionally African: white, black and red. Sacred stones are also placed on the altars. In the Macumba ceremonies Indian spirits known as Curupira also appear, showing *caboclo* (a person of Indian descent) influences.

At the end of the twentieth century, Umbanda was the most popular Afro-Brazilian religion in the coastal cities of Brazil. It is an amalgamation of African, Indian and European influences and it has been very popular with whites and new immigrants. Cross-fertilization of religious cultures was common among creole slaves born in Brazil and among freed slaves. American Indian religious beliefs influenced the religions that emerged in northeast and northern Brazil and were popular with the *caboclos,* people of mixed Indian and white heritage. Both Umbanda and Macumba involve worship of the family spirits of the Bantu-speaking peoples of West Central Africa.

As the newest Afro-Brazilian religion, Umbanda showed extreme religious improvisation as it emerged in Rio de Janeiro and Niteroi in the 1920s and 1930s and then spread throughout Brazil during the Getulio Vargas dictatorship (1937–1945) because its Europeanized practices made it acceptable to the white middle class. This religion embraces African gods, Catholic saints, and spirit possession trances and adds *Pretos Velhos* (dead African slaves) and *Caboclo* spirits to a pantheon that includes even the spiritism of Kardec. It shows acceptance of diluted African beliefs by a significant minority of the population: at least 30 million practitioners of Umbanda out of a population of over 150 million Brazilians. The cultural dynamism of Umbanda has flowed into diverse forms, such as Umbanda Kardecista following the spiritism of Kardec, Umbanda Africana (African Umbanda), and Umbanda Culto de Nação (native Umbanda). Leaders and initiates of Umbanda wear nurses' uniforms and experience spirit possession; they also act as mediums for the gods and give advice and assistance in personal problems. Spiritual cleansings and herbal baths are prescribed to solve spiritual and emotional problems. Spirit possessions in Macumba and Umbanda are more sedate affairs than in the Candomblés of Bahia. Séances occur in both Umbanda and Macumba temples in Rio de Janeiro. The vitality of these modern popular religions in Brazil certainly reflects the creativity with which slaves combined inspiration from diverse sources.

Even nominally Catholic lay religious brotherhoods established in the colonial period may have ensured the survival of African religions, since the brotherhoods were organized by race, social class, and ethnic background. Religious confraternities were created by the Catholic Church to aid in the conversion of African slaves, but they became popular among the slave and freed populations of Latin America, who treated them as similar to the secret societies of West Africa, and used them to gain informal power, social status, and prestige. In Recife and Bahia Afro-Brazilian cults survived in the shadows of these brotherhoods. Brotherhood members were also prominent in Afro-Brazilian cult houses, and brotherhood membership became a key ingredient in cult organization.

Fidelity to an African past made sacred by distance and by suffering made African religious survival integral to the diasporan communities in South America. The protean character of African religious expression was based on common beliefs, collective memories of religion at home, and common oppression. The African gods in exile survived to a greater extent in Brazil than elsewhere because of Brazil's longer experience with the slave trade. Religion functioned as a form of social capital, empowering poor people to overcome exploitation and allowing the slaves fuller participation in social life.

Retaining African religious practices helped ameliorate the painful separation from families and ancestral homelands that African slaves experienced. Sister religions survived in Haiti as voodoo and in the Spanish Caribbean in the form of Santeria and Ifá. They shared similar practices, such as animal sacrifices, divination with cowrie shells, trances, and spirit possessions, and similar fidelity to the African gods. Santeria, according to Joseph Murphy, functioned as an "alternative religion" of resistance to the ideology of slavery. African religion survived through the oral traditions of the slaves out of a shared experience of "difference."

See also BRAZIL; SLAVE TRADE; VIEIRA, ANTÓNIO.

BIBLIOGRAPHY

BASTIDE, ROGER. *The African Religions of Brazil: Toward a Sociology of the Interpenetration of Civilizations.* 1978.
———. *Les Americques noires: Les Civilisations africaines dans le nouveau monde.* 1967.
FERNANDES, FLORESTAN. *The Negro in Brazilian Society.* 1969.
IRELAND, ROWAN. *Kingdoms Come: Religion and Politics in Brazil.* 1991.
MINTZ, SIDNEY W., and RICHARD PRICE. *The Birth of African-American Culture: An Anthropological Perspective.* 1992.
MULVEY, PATRICIA A. "Black Brothers and Sisters: Membership in the Black Lay Brotherhoods of Colonial Brazil." *Luso-Brazilian Review* (Winter 1980).
———. *The Black Lay Brotherhoods of Colonial Brazil: A History.* Ph.D. diss. City University of New York. 1976.
———. "Slave Confraternities in Brazil: Their Role in Colonial Society." *The Americas* (July 1982).
MURPHY, JOSEPH M. *Santeria: An African Religion in America.* 1988.
RAMOS, ARTHUR. *The Negro in Brazil.* 1939.
RODRIGUES, JOSÉ HONORIO. *Brazil and Africa.* 1965.

Patricia A. Mulvey

Caribbean Region

Few aspects of the cultures of enslaved Africans and their descendants in the Americas have traditionally commanded as much attention as has religion. Documentary evidence of Afro-Caribbean religious practices reaches back to the 1530s in the case of the Spanish Caribbean. By the eighteenth century most major French, English, and German accounts by missionaries, travelers, or residents of the region featured descriptions of slave belief and ritual. Legislation concerning the slaves' religious activities likewise appeared early on. By the late seventeenth century both Spanish and French slave codes contained explicit instructions concerning the formal Christianization of slaves. Though rarely enforced by planters and urban magistrates, such laws mandated baptism and participation in church sacraments, guaranteed (at least in theory) freedom from work on church holidays, and made provisions for Christian marriages and burials. In the British colonies organized missionary endeavors did not commence before the end of the eighteenth century. However, in the aftermath of a massive Jamaican uprising in 1760, in which priests of African-derived religions were supposed to have played a leading role, the British colonies began to incriminate the practice of African-derived forms of religion in their so-called obeah laws. On some islands, these laws remained in effect until well into the twentieth century. Several major Caribbean slave rebellions appear to have had a religious component, and it is, perhaps, not accidental that in both Haitian national mythology, and in the Western popular imagination, a *vodou* ceremony is held to mark the beginning of the 1791 uprisings which culminated in the Haitian revolution.

Despite a relative wealth of published and documentary sources, however, the study of Caribbean slave religion is fraught with problems and ironies. The theme of Christianization served as a nominal justification for the slave trade from Africa to the Spanish and French islands and later underwrote abolitionist efforts in the British Caribbean to create a black rural proletariat. But by the early twentieth century the search for "Africanisms" in the religious lives of the descendants of Caribbean slaves provided the touchstone for the first sustained inquiries into the lasting cultural effects of the slave trade to the Americas.

Several contemporary Caribbean folk religions— *regla ocha* (Santería), *abakuá*, and the *reglas de congo* in Cuba; *revival* and *cumina* in Jamaica; Haitian *vodou*—

are characterized by representations, practices, and ideational complexes of African origin to such a degree that they are incomprehensible in both form and content unless viewed in light of transatlantic cultural continuities. Their unquestionable African heritage must be balanced analytically against complex local histories of cultural creativity and transformation under slavery, but the ways of doing so are not open to easy generalizations. All too often scholars have operated on the presumption that the results of centuries of conjunction between diverse and historically mutable African local traditions and various forms of Christianity under changing Caribbean social conditions could be broken down into separate "African" and "European" elements. The outcome of such presuppositions is a tendency to construe Christianity and "traditional African religion" into ideal types that thus assume the form of historically static, and internally undifferentiated, opposites.

Hence, there has existed a longstanding polarization of studies of Caribbean slave religion into institutional histories of colonial forms of Christianity on the one hand, and attempts to elucidate the African

Vodou practitioners perform a ritual before a candlelit altar. Such ceremonies, first performed in the time of slavery, express retained elements of the practitioners' African heritage. [Morton Beebe/Corbis]

contribution to the complex spectrum of religious forms that evolved in the region on the other. Studies of the first type have tended to elide the growth of African-influenced folk traditions among the enslaved as epiphenomenal to the history of Christian denominations in the Caribbean. Yet the latter perspective often enough assimilates its object to similarly reductionist projects. Geared towards foregrounding the Africanness of the beliefs and practices in question, such studies have too often relied on assertions of formal similarity between modern descriptions of African and Caribbean religions without offering convincing evidence that would allow for the historicization of such linkages as may actually exist.

In his highly influential work, Melville Herskovits posited a model for the origins of African-American cultures out of processes of acculturation that resulted in a spectrum of cultural forms gradable on a scale from complete retention of African "traits" through various stages of syncretism and reinterpretation, to complete loss. Hypothesizing that a deeply religious psychological orientation was the hallmark of Africanness, Herskovits held that the "purest" African "survivals" would be found in the field of practices oriented towards ideas of the sacred, where resistance to acculturation would prove strongest. It was a model of religious change, the ultimately mechanistic nature of which is only too obvious today.

In the 1970s Sidney Mintz and his colleague Richard Price authored a powerful alternative model purporting to historicize the origins of New World slave cultures. According to their views, Caribbean slave religions did not emerge from a mechanical transfer, and subsequent acculturative erosion, of ethnically traceable African cultural templates. They rather represented the historical creations of culturally heterogeneous populations adapting to the conditions of New World slavery. Though largely based on data pertaining to Suriname, where new African-American cultures emerged from a synthesis of heterogeneous African traditions and some European and Amerindian cultural elements within a remarkably short time, Mintz and Price's so-called rapid early synthesis, or creolization model has had a wide impact on scholarship concerned with the emergence and traditionalization of New World slave cultures.

Since its first publication, Mintz and Price's thesis has elicited a variety of reactions. These include attempts to interpret African-derived religions in the New World as truly novel, entirely synthetic phenomena but also endeavors geared towards substantiating both African and European influences on Caribbean slave religions in a manner responsive to the questions they raised—not just about verifying the provenience of cultural forms, but historically retracing processes of cultural transmission, reproduction, and transformation. Given the extremely repressive circumstances under which Caribbean slaves forged social communities, integrated, at least in part, by shared conceptions of the sacred, the issue of origins appears historically less relevant than the question of how, and under what conditions, certain religious forms imparted meaning and moral salience to the lives of the enslaved. Rather than opposing ideal-typical constructs of "Christianity" and "traditional African religion," scholars are now beginning to attend to the actual processes whereby enslaved and free individuals negotiated, accepted, or contested religious ideologies, disciplines, and symbolic idioms within concrete historical settings.

The historical process is particularly obvious in respect to the role world religions may have played in the religious syntheses that evolved in Caribbean slave societies. In Jamaica, for example, Christianity began to take hold among the slaves on a significant scale only after a handful of African-American Baptists carried it to the island in the wake of the American Revolution. Still, forms of Afro-Jamaican Christianity were widespread by the 1840s. Universalistic creeds and their ideologies and practices of conversion and recruitment, apparently made world religions such as Islam and Christianity useful to enslaved immigrants for the forging of social linkages across ethnic, linguistic, and other boundaries. The focus of research in this respect will lie in investigation, not of the—hypothetical—counterhegemonic inspiration or emotional consolation slaves may have found in adherence to belief systems professing (in however qualified a manner) notions of human secular equality, or otherworldly rewards for suffering, but in the concrete social uses slaves may have derived from them.

The historical experience of slavery also illuminates the more obviously "African" end of the spectrum of religious forms found in the Caribbean. In part, advances in Africanist research have made untenable many the presuppositions about the stability and ethnically discrete distribution of African cultures that Americanists have traditionally assumed in comparing Old and New World religious cultures. Even though researchers are increasingly able to pinpoint historical connections between specific New World areas and the African source regions from which they drew slaves at various times, the hope that more detailed data applied to old models of "culture transfer" will give us unambiguous insights into the religions of regional slave populations in the Americas is fast becoming tenuous. If, as, for example, Paul Lovejoy (1997) has claimed, African-American cultural history should be written as an Atlantic prolongation of African history, it should be expected that Africans in the New World would exhibit the same kind of volatility and fluidity of cultural and religious allegiance as existed in Africa during the period of the slave trade.

No less important, however, are insights accruing from a reevaluation of the theoretical tools for understanding slave religions. Contrary to Herskovits (and even Mintz and Price's) assumptions, it is now known, for example, that African forms of thinking about, and acting toward, the sacred proved easier to perpetuate and reproduce socially in urban, rather than rural, environments; within social institutions unwittingly provided by the masters, rather than separate from them; under the eyes of institutionally "blind" authorities, rather than in defiance of them (Palmié, 1991). Thus, it seems clear that in Spanish Caribbean the state- and church-sponsored Catholic brotherhoods—"ethnic" voluntary associations such as the *cabildos de nación*—played a crucial role in allowing their members to reconstitute African forms of ethnic and religious identification. Such voluntary associations of native Africans recruiting their members among individuals construing New World identities along the lines of situational interpretations of African models of ethnicity occupy a conspicuous place in governmental or ecclesiastical documents.

Still, the copious records of folk belief and practice on the mainland of the Americas produced by the Spanish Inquisition, for example, mainly describe actions recognizable as "incriminable"—blasphemy, or aberrations from Catholic sexual codes—under the precepts of an institution dedicated to persecuting heretics and backsliders. They remain silent on forms of religious practice that the Roman Catholic Church—tacitly or explicitly—condoned. Similar problems plague the study of obeah in the British Caribbean. For here, a legalistically inscribed catchall for—potentially—counterhegemonic, non-Christian religious activities ultimately obscures the precise ideological content of the practices in question. Although scholars have made a case for the continuity of a belief in obeah in Jamaica between 1760 and the revivalistic outbreaks of the 1840s, no one knows whether the term "obeah," as encoded in the British records, meant the same to Jamaican slaves in 1760 as it meant to the freedpeople who stormed churches, engaged in ecstatic mass baptisms, and roamed the countryside digging up charms in the 1840s.

Beyond such methodological quandries, however, the theoretical problems marking the study of Caribbean slave religion are only beginning to come into focus. Studies may ultimately have to consider African and American forms of slavery—and the cultures, belief systems, and ritual complexes that evolved among the victims as well as beneficiaries of such institutions—

as part of a larger, single "Atlantic" zone of cultural interchange defined by political-economic mechanisms. If Africanists now recognize the need to deconstruct analytical distinctions between "traditional" African religion and missionary Christianity on a level of local belief and practice, drawing the Americas into such a debate will invariably reveal even more complex, "Atlantic" ecologies of collective representations.

See also CHURCHES, AFRICAN-AMERICAN; SPIRITUALS.

BIBLIOGRAPHY

GEGGUS, DAVID. "The Bois Caiman Ceremony." *Journal of Caribbean History* 25 (1991b): 41–57.
LOVEJOY, PAUL E. "The African Diaspora: Revisionist Interpretations of Ethnicity, Culture, and Religion under Slavery." *Studies in the World History of Slavery, Abolition, and Emancipation* 2 (1997): 1–24.
MINTZ, SIDNEY W., and RICHARD PRICE. *The Birth of African-American Culture.* 1976. Reprint, 1992.
MINTZ, SIDNEY W., and MICHEL-ROLPH TROUILLOT. "The Social History of Haitian Voudou." In *Sacred Arts of Haitian Voudou,* edited by Donald J. Cosentino. 1995.
MORGAN, PHILIP D. "The Cultural Implication of the Atlantic Slave Trade: African Regional Origins, American Destinations, and New World Development." *Slavery and Abolition* 18 (1997): 122–145.
PALMIÉ, STEPHAN. *Das Exil der Götter: Beschichte und Vorstellungswelt einer afrokubanischen Religion.* 1991.
PEEL, J. Y. D. "The Pastor and the Babalawo: The Interaction of Religions in Nineteenth-Century Yorubaland." *Africa* 60 (1990): 338–369.
REIS, JOÃO JOSÉ, and PAULO F. DE MORAES FARIAS. "Islam and Slave Resistance in Bahia, Brazil." *Islam et sociétés au sud du Sahara* 3 (1989): 41–66.
RICHARDSON, DAVID, and DAVID ELTIS. "The 'Numbers Game' and Routes to Slavery." *Slavery and Abolition* 18 (1997): 1–15.
THORNTON, JOHN K. *Africa and Africans in the Making of the Atlantic World, 1400–1680.* 1992.
WRIGHT, DONALD R. *The World and a Very Small Place in Africa.* 1997.

Stephan Palmié

Slave Republics

The concept of "slave republics" derives from the perspective of a particular master class—one that defines a set of human beings primarily as slaves and imagines free government (even that of rebels or runaways) as synonymous with republican political principles. Enslaved Africans and African-Americans did not necessarily share such views. Rather, throughout the Americas, significant numbers of enslaved people escaped to the forests, mountains, and swamps—thus becoming maroons—and, banding together, forged new identities and new political systems based in part on African antecedents. Many such maroon societies survived for decades and sometimes centuries, and their descendants form distinct communities in several parts of the Americas today.

To be viable, the initial communities of maroons had to be inaccessible, and villages were typically located in remote, inhospitable areas. For example, in the southern United States swamps were a favorite setting, and maroons often became part of Native American communities; in Jamaica, some of the most famous maroon groups lived in the intricately accidented "cockpit country," where deep canyons and limestone sinkholes abound but water and good soil are scarce; and in the Guianas, seemingly impenetrable jungles provided maroons with a safe haven. At the same time, maroon communities remained dependent on plantation society for numerous manufactured items (guns, pots, tools, cloth) as well as for new recruits, especially women. Maroons, who had excellent intelligence networks among slave populations, developed great expertise in hit-and-run raids on plantations. Throughout the hemisphere, maroons were renowned for their skills in guerrilla warfare. To the bewilderment of their colonial enemies, whose rigid and conventional tactics had been learned on the open battlefields of Europe, these highly adaptable and mobile warriors took maximum advantage of local environments, striking and withdrawing with great rapidity, making extensive use of ambushes to catch their adversaries in crossfire, fighting only when and where they chose, and often communicating by drums and horns.

In many cases, wars between maroon communities and their former masters led the colonists, however reluctantly, to propose peace treaties. In return for an agreement on the part of the maroons to cease raiding plantations and taking new recruits, the colonists generally promised to grant maroons their freedom and recognize their territorial integrity. We know of the existence of such treaties in Brazil, Colombia, Cuba, Ecuador, Hispaniola, Jamaica, Mexico, Panama, Peru, Suriname, Venezuela, and elsewhere.

The internal government of maroon communities varied but, at least in their early wartime years, military authority was strictly maintained. Early maroon societies adopted African-style monarchical models. In the Brazilian maroon state of Palmares, which flourished for a century until it was annihilated in 1695, King Ganga Zumba and his relatives formed a dynasty; the sixteenth-century Venezuelan maroon leader El Rey Miguel was said to have a royal court and royal cabinet; at the same time in Panama, King Bayano was being treated with all the trappings of royalty; and the seventeenth-century maroon leader Domingo Bioho in Colombia styled himself Rey del Arcobuco or Rey Benkos. In maroon societies that have lasted into the present, such as those in Suriname, French Guiana, and Jamaica, internal authority continues to be asserted through a combination of centralized official roles (often hereditary and king-like in an African sense) and complex religious activities (including the consultation of oracles and other forms of divination).

Because the maroons who formed nascent communities along the fringes of plantation America came from diverse West and Central African societies, they were forced to create for themselves new institutions (from languages and religions to politics and kinship systems), and they accomplished this largely through processes of inter-African cultural syncretism, combining and adapting their various African heritages in their radically new environments, which were often wartime settings. For example, the political system of the great seventeenth-century Brazilian maroon kingdom of Palmares, which R. K. Kent ("Palmares: An African State in Brazil," 1965) has characterized as an "African" state, "did not derive from a *particular* central African model, but from several." In the development of the kinship system of the Ndyuka Maroons of Suriname, writes André Köbben ("Unity and Disunity: Cottica Djuka Society as a Kinship System," 1967), "undoubtedly their West-African heritage played a part . . . [and] the influence of the matrilineal Akan tribes is unmistakable, but so is that of patrilineal tribes, . . . [and there are] significant differences between the Akan and Ndyuka matrilineal systems." Likewise for the more purely cultural realm—historical and anthropological research has revealed that the magnificent woodcarving of the Suriname Maroons, long considered "an African art in the Americas" on the basis of many formal resemblances, is (in the words of Jean Hurault, *Africains de Guyane,* 1970) in fact a fundamentally new African-American art "for which it would be pointless to seek the origin through direct transmission of any particular African style." And detailed investigations—both in museums and in the field—of a whole range of cultural phenomena among the Saramaka Maroons of Suriname have confirmed the dynamic, creative processes that continue to animate these societies.

Maroon cultures do show a remarkable number of direct and sometimes spectacular continuities from particular African peoples, ranging from military techniques for defense to recipes for warding off sorcery. These are, however, of the same type as those that can be found, if with lesser frequency, in African-American communities throughout the hemisphere. In stressing these isolated African "retentions," there is a danger of neglecting far more significant cultural continuities. Roger Bastide divided African-American religions into those he considered "preserved" or "canned"—like Brazilian *candomblé*—and those that he considered "alive" or "living," like Haitian *vaudou*. The former, he argued, represent a kind of "defense mechanism" or "cultural fossilization," a fear that any small change may bring on the end, while the latter have a more secure future and are freer to adapt to the changing needs of their adherents. More generally, it can be shown that tenacious fidelity to "African" *forms* is, in many cases, an indication that a culture has finally lost meaningful touch with the vital African past. Certainly, one of the most striking features of West and Central African cultural systems is their internal dynamism, their ability to grow and change. The cultural uniqueness of the more developed maroon societies (e.g., those in Suriname) rests firmly on their fidelity to "African" cultural principles at these deeper levels—whether aesthetic, political, religious, or domestic—rather than on the frequency of their isolated "retentions." With a rare freedom to extrapolate African ideas (from a variety of societies) and adapt them to changing circumstance, maroon communities included (and still include today) what are in many respects at once the most meaningfully African and the most truly "alive" and culturally dynamic of all African-American cultures.

The best known historic maroon societies—communities of former slaves who governed themselves while slavery still continued—are Palmares in Brazil, Palenque de San Basilio in Colombia, the Maroons of Jamaica, and the Saramaka and Ndyuka of Suriname.

Because Palmares was finally crushed by a massive colonial army in 1695, after a century of success and growth, actual knowledge of its internal affairs remains limited, based as it is on soldiers' reports, the testimony of a captive under torture, archaeological work, official documents, and the like. As a modern symbol of black (and anticolonial) heroism, Palmares continues to evoke strong emotions in Brazil; Carlos Diegues's two well-known films—*Ganga-Zumba*, which emphasized the theme of "freedom"; and *Quilombo*, which emphasized "utopia"—are good examples. State-of-the-art scholarship on Palmares is included in *Liberdade por um fio*, listed in the bibliography.

Palenque de San Basilio, whose inhabitants are proud to be descendants of maroon warriors, boasts a history stretching back to the seventeenth century. In recent years, historians, anthropologists, and linguists—working in collaboration with Palen-

queros—have uncovered a great deal about continuities and changes in the life of these early Colombian freedom fighters. For an excellent illustrated introduction, see De Friedemann and Cross, *Ma ngombe.*

The Jamaica Maroons, who continue to live in two main groups centered in Accompong (in the hills above Montego Bay) and Moore Town (deep in the Blue Mountains), maintain strong traditions about their days as freedom fighters. Two centuries of scholarship, some written by Maroons themselves, offer diverse windows on the ways these men and women managed to survive and build a vibrant culture within the confines of a relatively small island. A useful entree into the relevant literature is provided in *Maroon Heritage.*

The Suriname Maroons now constitute the best-documented case of how former slaves built new societies and cultures, under conditions of extreme deprivation and hardship, in the Americas—and how they developed and maintained semi-independent societies that persist into the present. From their origins in the late seventeenth century and the details of their wars and treaties to their ongoing negotiations, once officially free, with colonial authorities, much is now known about these peoples' extraordinary historical achievements, in large part because of the extensive recent collaboration by Saramakas and Ndyukas with scholars. The relevant bibliography now numbers in the thousands; useful points of entry are the works by the Prices, and by Thoden van Velzen and van Wetering.

See also ESCAPE; MAROONS; PALMARES; REBELLIONS AND VIOLENT RESISTANCE.

BIBLIOGRAPHY

AGORSAH, E. KOFI, ed. *Maroon Heritage: Archaeological Ethnographic and Historical Perspectives.* 1994.
DE FRIEDEMANN, NINA S., and RICHARD CROSS. *Ma ngombe: Guerreros y ganaderos en Palenque* (Ma ngombe: Warriors and Cowherds in Palenque). 1979.
PRICE, RICHARD. *Alabi's World.* 1990.
———. *Maroon Societies: Rebel Slave Communities in the Americas,* 3rd ed. 1996.
PRICE, SALLY, and RICHARD PRICE. *Afro-American Arts of the Suriname Rain Forest.* 1980.
REIS, JOÃO JOSÉ, and FLÁVIO DOS SANTOS GOMES. *Liberdade por um fio: Historia dos quilombos no Brasil* (Precarious Freedom: History of Quilombos in Brazil). 1996.
SMITHSONIAN INSTITUTION. "Maroon Cultures in the Americas." *Festival of American Folklife* (1992): 54–80.
THODEN VAN VELZEN, H. U. E., and W. VAN WETERING. *The Great Father and the Danger: Religious Cults, Material Forces and Collective Fantasies in the World of the Surinamese Maroons.* 1988.

Richard Price

Slavery, Contemporary Forms of

"Contemporary forms of slavery" refers to present-day human rights violations that approximate slavery. Since 1975 a United Nations organization called the Working Group of Experts on Contemporary Forms of Slavery has met regularly to hear evidence on these practices and to recommend measures to suppress them. No satisfactory definition of slavery has yet been devised to cover the wide range of institutions that have been called by that name. The League of Nations defined it very broadly in the Slavery Convention of 1926 as the status of "a person over whom all or any of the powers attaching to the right of ownership were exercised." The United Nations adopted this definition in the 1956 Supplementary Convention on the Abolition of Slavery, the Slave Trade and Institutions and Practices Similar to Slavery. The institutions "similar to slavery" were identified as debt bondage, serfdom, forced marriage, and the exploitation of child labor by persons other than their legal guardians. Since 1956 a wide range of other practices have also been considered contemporary forms of slavery.

Many of these bear little resemblance to the classic or chattel slavery long practiced in Europe and which existed in the Americas until the late nineteenth century and in parts of the Muslim world and a few other areas well into the twentieth century. Chattel slaves are property. Owners have complete control over their lives, their labor, their marriage, and their progeny. They can be bought, sold, inherited, or given away. In some societies owners held powers of life and death over them. Elsewhere, slaves had limited legal protection, and in many non-Western societies the second and later generations were rarely sold, and a few slaves attained positions of trust and power. But the status was normally lifelong and hereditary, and advancement or manumission was at the discretion of the owner. Chattel slaves were acquired by purchase or capture, or were born into slavery.

Chattel Slavery

Contemporary forms of slavery still include chattel slavery, but this practice was outlawed everywhere in the course of the nineteenth and twentieth centuries and is now rare. It may be developing again in Sudan as a by-product of the war there between northern Muslims and the non-Muslim southerners. In the 1980s and 1990s northern Sudanese militias were accused of capturing southern women and children in raids and either holding them for ransom or sending them north, where some were sold. Children have been forced to convert to Islam, girls have been forced to marry, and most have been used for domestic and agricultural work. Both the northern and southern armies have also conscripted young boys to serve in their militias. Since the government denies these abuses, it is not possible at this time to predict whether or not these captives will become chattel slaves. This will depend on whether such captivity and coercion, which died out in the Sudan only in the 1930s, acquires legal recognition. Ominously the war has taken on the complexion of a jihad, or holy war, in which the enslavement of non-Muslim captives is permitted by Islamic law, but it seems unlikely that the civil government will actually restore the legal status of slavery.

So-called vestiges of chattel slavery—discrimination against persons of slave descent—persist in many societies in which slavery was formerly practiced, and particularly where, as in the African Sahel, it remained legal into the twentieth century. In some cases these vestiges are oppressive. Thus in Mauritania, although slavery has been outlawed a number of times, the descendants of slaves form a depressed, despised caste. They suffer discrimination over access to land and ownership of property. The descendants of their former owners often demand a share of their crops or wages and sometimes abduct or sell their children. Elsewhere the vestiges of slavery may amount to discrimination in matters of inheritance, marriage, and the participation in religious rituals. Although socially demeaning, these practices are less economically exploitative if persons of slave descent have equal economic and educational opportunities and the same political rights as other sections of the population. Generally speaking vestiges of slavery are disappearing as the result of growing opportunities for wage labor, public education, and inclusive national politics, as well as, sometimes, the active resistance of the descendants of slaves.

Other Forms of Slavery

Most contemporary forms of slavery differ from this chattel or classic slavery in significant ways. Victims are legally free. Their bondage is often for a limited time or purpose, and in many cases they unwittingly volunteer. Their position is analogous to slavery not because they are actually owned by another person but because they cannot escape from the form of exploitation in which they find themselves entrapped. In some cases the restraints end naturally, as when child slaves grow up, or a victim of forced prostitution grows old. Most of these practices have been forbidden by international treaties and outlawed by governments.

The contemporary forms of slavery which most resemble chattel slavery include not only those identified in 1956—debt bondage, serfdom, child labor, and forced marriage—but also forced prostitution and forced labor. Forced prostitution was condemned, not for the first time, in the United Nations Convention for the Suppression of the Traffic in Persons and the Exploitation of Prostitution of Others, signed in 1949. Forced labor was the subject of treaties negotiated by the International Labor Organization in 1930 and 1957. These categories of servitude are not mutually exclusive. A child slave, a serf, or a peon may also be in debt bondage, or be forced into prostitution.

Debt Bondage

Debt bondage is at least as old and perhaps older than chattel slavery, and it can be oppressive. It is defined by the United Nations as the condition of a person whose services have been pledged as security for debt for an indefinite time and whose work does not count equitably toward the liquidation of the debt. The debtor, who usually has no other assets, may pledge himself, but often he offers a substitute—usually his child. This type of servitude takes many forms and is widespread. Thousands of victims, many of them children, and even entire families are entrapped by debt and are working in hazardous conditions in factories, quarries, mines, plantations, and farms. Debt bondage is particularly rife in the Indian subcontinent and in Latin America where much of the agricultural labor is performed by peons bound to the land by various forms of indebtedness to the landowner. The debts are often unavoidable, incurred as the result of some family disaster, or the need to raise money for a wedding, a funeral, or a dowry, or they may arise through sharecropping arrangements which favor the landowners. Some are the result of drug addiction. Frequently, however, victims are tricked into debt. Contract workers in, for example, Brazil are promised well-paid jobs away from home but find on arrival at the worksite that they are charged exorbitant rates for their transport, their food and lodging, and even the tools with which to work. They thus arrive in debt without the means to return home, and the debts are manipulated in such a way that they can never be repaid. Since the debts have legal force, there is no escape. Those who try to flee are often beaten up or otherwise intimidated or sent to prison. In many cases the debts are inherited by the children of the debtor, who are thus born into lifelong servitude. In India whole families have been enslaved for five or even more generations. Peons in parts of Latin America face the same fate. Debts may also be passed from one creditor to another, thus giving rise to transfers of persons reminiscent of slave trading.

Serfdom

Serfdom was defined in 1956 as the condition of a tenant who is by law, custom, or agreement bound to live and work on land belonging to another, is required to perform services for the landlord, and is legally unable to change his status. These arrangements had a long history, but cases of serfdom are rarely raised today, possibly because the term has fallen out of use. Certain forms of peonage and debt bondage and what are called slavelike practices of slavery in Mauritania may well fall into the definition of serfdom.

Child Labor

Child labor is widespread in the poorer areas of the world. It is not considered a form of slavery, however, if, in accordance with the 1949 United Nations Declaration of the Rights of the Child, he or she is above the minimum working age, is provided with adequate food, lodging, recreation, medical care, and social security benefits, and is given an education and raised in a loving, healthy environment. In all too many cases, however, children are subjected to long hours of toil in grueling conditions, often far from home, and are neither paid nor educated. They are thus not only exploited but also condemned to lifelong poverty.

Many examples of child slavery can be cited. Children are employed in deplorable conditions, for instance, in carpet factories in the Indian subcontinent, in quarries in India and Nepal, in sweat shops in Thailand, and together with their parents as charcoal burners in the forests of the Amazon. Small Indian boys are used as jockeys in camel races in Arabia. Rural children in West Africa are often sent to towns to work as domestic servants or apprentices with promises of an education. These wards often end up as unpaid household drudges or unpaid apprentices. Many children work in conditions which generate disease. Some are crippled by being chained to looms or forced to carry heavy burdens. Under-age boys are forced to serve as soldiers.

Among the more heartrending cases are the children sold or forced into prostitution. Some are sent out by their parents to serve tourists near home, in Thailand or the Philippines, for instance. Others are sent far afield. Burmese girls become prostitutes in Thailand. Nepalese girls are sent to brothels in India. Boys from the Caribbean have reportedly been sold for prostitution in New York. Many of these children end up with sexually transmitted diseases and are

Two children weave a rug on an upright loom in a carpet factory. [Janet Wishnetsky/Corbis]

then likely to be thrown out onto the streets because they are often not accepted back by their home communities.

Children become victims of all the other types of contemporary slavery condemned by human rights watchdogs. Many child slaves are sold by their own parents, either because the parents cannot support them, need to repay a debt, or want money to buy drugs. Some are simply sent out to work as debt peons by their poverty-stricken families. Others are acquired by creditors and become victims of debt bondage.

Forced Marriage

Three distinct types of forced marriage were defined in the 1956 convention: the marrying of a woman without her consent in return for a payment, monetary or otherwise, to her kinsmen; a marriage which gives the husband the right to transfer his wife to another person without her agreement; and the inheritance of a widow by her dead husband's kinsmen. The United Nations Declaration on the Elimination of Discrimination against Women went much further, entering into the terms of marriages of any sort and

binding signatories to give women the same rights as men to property, inheritance, divorce, and custody of their children. Activists maintain that marriage without these rights places women in a state of servitude. The Convention on Consent to Marriage, Minimum Age for Marriage, and Registration of Marriages of 1962 and a Recommendation of 1965 were aimed at preventing the marriage of any child under fifteen and at ensuring that in all marriages the consent of both partners was voluntary. Since in many non-Western societies women and children are customarily betrothed without their consent and brideprice or dowry is paid to their kinsmen, and since women usually do not have equal rights with men when it comes to custody and divorce and sometimes rights to property, the definition of forced marriage raises the difficult question as to whether practices considered normal in many societies can or should be condemned internationally as slavery. Ultimately these standards raise the question as to whether or not a universal standard of human rights can apply to all societies.

A clear case of servile marriage, however, is practiced today in China, where women and girls are kidnapped and then sold as wives. Many are poorly educated peasant girls unaware of their rights, who are sent far from home. The more recalcitrant are often kept under lock and key until they have had a child, when they are less likely to try to escape. The traffic in females in China is ancient, but it was stamped out by the communist regime. It resurfaced in the 1970s and escalated in the 1980s in the hands of organized crime as the traditional brideprice became more expensive. The Chinese government has prosecuted thousands of people for their involvement in this trade and freed thirty-thousand women in 1989 and 1990 alone. Some of the kidnappers have been executed, but the trade continues because profits are high.

Forced Prostitution

Forced prostitution is another form of contemporary slavery, and found all over the world. Although some feminist groups consider all female prostitution to be sexual slavery, prostitution is not a form of bondage if the prostitute volunteers his or her services, is able to leave at will, and controls his or her own earnings and conditions of work. However, in many instances, prostitutes, usually female, work for brothel owners, pimps, boyfriends, or husbands under severe constraints. Many are recruited through kidnapping. Others are victims of fraud. They may be lured to China from Vietnam or to Japan from the Philippines by the promise of lucrative jobs, only to find on arrival that the employment awaiting them is as prostitutes. Usually without the means to return home but with families there relying upon their earnings, they are unable to escape. Many also fall into debt-bondage. Some women are fraudulently married by procurers or recruited through advertisements for mail-order brides. In developed countries young runaways are particularly liable to turn to prostitution to earn a living and then find that they cannot escape the clutches of their pimp.

Women are kept in forced prostitution by various methods. Some are intimidated. Others depend on a pimp or brothel owner to bring them customers, to supply accommodation, to protect them from police harassment, or to supply them with drugs. Some become psychologically dependent upon their exploiters; others have been forcibly turned into drug addicts. Illegal aliens are often entrapped because they dare not seek help from the authorities for fear of being deported.

Contract Labor and Migrant Workers

Although contract laborers and migrant workers are not slaves, some of them find themselves in servitude, particularly if they are far from home and family. Blatant examples of this are to be found in Brazil, where workers from areas of high unemployment have been promised jobs and even property in Amazonia, arriving only to find that wages are low and land is unavailable. Many are forced into debt bondage and compelled to renew their contracts indefinitely. Similarly, workers from the Philippines, particularly women, accept contracts to works in the Persian Gulf states, and when the well-paid jobs they were promised by unscrupulous recruiters prove to be nonexistent, they have to take what work they can get, even at exploitive wages, or risk being deported and charged for their fares home. In the Gulf states and in other rich countries, including the United States, Britain, and other European countries, aliens are often admitted with visas, which allow them to work only for a specified employer. Some of them, usually female domestic servants, have been kept as virtual prisoners, ill-treated, undernourished, and even raped. Afraid to go to the authorities for fear of being deported, their only recourse is to go into hiding as illegal aliens, and inevitably many end up as prostitutes.

Forced Labor

Forced labor differs from other types of servitude in that victims are conscripted by governments. According to the conventions against forced labor, governments may legitimately call out their citizens only in the national interest for services such as military duty, national emergencies, and public works, and they may employ penal labor. However, forced labor is never to be conscripted for private enterprises, as punishment for political offences, as a method of social, racial, national, or religious discrimination, or for economic development. Conscripts must be males between eighteen and forty-five, they must be paid fairly, their term of service must be limited, and their health must be protected. Some governments have been notorious for forcing people, often from minorities or opposition groups, to perform unlimited forced labor without pay. The government of Myanmar, for instance, has conscripted villagers of both sexes and all ages, often from dissident ethnic groups, to work on construction projects, sometimes for private companies, or as porters for the army. The conscripts may be kept away from home for months, in some cases years, and are neither paid nor fed, and some have suffered brutal punishments. Until recently the Soviet Union exploited the labor of dissidents and others in the gulags. In China political and religious dissidents are sentenced to "re-education through labor," and prisoners are believed to be forced to make goods for export.

From these examples it will be clear that although chattel slavery has largely disappeared, the conditions that gave rise to it—the demand for a cheap, pliant work force—are very much alive, particularly in economically marginal sectors of developed economies and in capital-starved economies in the Third World. This demand is being met today in an ever-changing variety of ways, many of them arguably crueler than chattel slavery. Chattel slaves were valuable assets, and although at sometimes and in certain areas they were worked to death, many were cared for in childhood and sometimes in sickness and old age, for reasons of morale if not humanity. The modern slave is generally more expendable. He or she can be acquired with minimum capital outlay when already capable of working, can be fired at will, and is not protected by the self-interest of an owner but is denied laws and benefits that shelter most workers in the developed world.

Steps to End Contemporary Slavery

It remains to consider what steps are being taken to end these abuses at the international and national level. Most of these modern forms of slavery have long been condemned in international treaties and outlawed by most states, but neither the laws nor the treaties are enforced. There are many reasons for this. There is no mechanism for enforcing the treaties, and many states have not signed or ratified them. Moreover, they impose no time limit for the introduction of reforms. At the national level, some governments are too poor or too weak to apply their own laws. Others are in the grip of the vested interests that profit from these abuses or are unable to control corrupt law enforcement officials or unscrupulous recruiting agencies or to suppress organized crime. Some states need the hard currency generated, for instance, by the export of cheap carpets or other products of sweatshops, or by the remittances of contract workers from abroad, or even by tourists attracted by travel agents catering to all forms of sexual gratification. Some governments, such as those of Brazil and Myanmar, allow or perpetrate abuses as a means of developing new areas quickly or, as in Myanmar, as a method of crushing ethnic resistance. In the developed countries of the Western world, immigration laws designed to protect their own workforces may compel illegal aliens or persons on restricted visas to take work on any terms they can get in less-than-reputable enterprises.

The pressure to suppress these forms of slavery comes mainly from nongovernmental agencies, or NGOs, the most active of which has been the British-based Anti-Slavery International. Such organizations operate on small budgets and have little political clout. The United Nations Working Group relies on their evidence, and because its meetings are public, it provides the NGOs with their most potent weapon—publicity. NGOs try to rally international support, and when the direct approach fails they attempt to shame governments into action through media attention. This strategy has had limited success. The media report only the most sensational cases. Governments ignore or deny charges, or promise action they do not take, or, seeking to disconcert their critics, ask for financial help to execute their own laws. The Working Group makes recommendations to the Sub-Commission on the Prevention of Discrimination and Protection of Minorities, but it has no powers to carry them out. The Working Group has always been heavily politicized. During the Cold War its deliberations were often dominated by the political posturing of the global powers. Moreover, because the word *slavery* immediately attracts attention, some of the evidence presented to the group concerns certain practices that, horrendous as they are, are difficult to consider forms of slavery. These include female circumcision or genital mutilation, the killing of people in order to sell their organs, and the killing of Muslim girls by their relations because they have disgraced them. The rationale for calling these practices slavery is that the victims have lost control over their own bodies. With more reason, and to get wider support for the formation of the Working Group, apartheid and colonialism were also designated as forms of "collective" slavery.

Another factor mitigating the suppression of contemporary forms of slavery, as already mentioned, is that some practices are simply not regarded as slavery in the cultures in which they occur. Thus, forced marriage and the denial of equal rights to women is perceived as right and normal by many peoples. A little girl working in a carpet factory in, say, Morocco, may not be exploited in the eyes of her parents. On the contrary, as they see it, she is assured of one meal a day and is not deprived of an education since as a female she would not be sent to school under any circumstances. A little household drudge in Lagos or children working exorbitant hours in a hotel in Katmandu may think that a hard life in town is preferable to toiling with their families in the fields, while their parents may believe that the children are on their way to a better life in the cities. The woman working in a sweatshop in Indonesia or the illegal alien earning a pittance in the United States may be glad just to have the job. Similarly the parents in Ghana who dedicate their children to a shrine to atone for their own sins may see this as an act of piety and not, as it seems to some activists, the consigning of innocent girls to a lifetime of servitude to the priest.

In the past, resentments and suspicions have arisen because most NGOs presenting evidence to the Working Group were European-based, while many of the institutions they sought to end were practiced in the developing world. Calls on the public in the richer nations to boycott goods made with child or sweatshop labor could be seen as attempts to limit competition. In the 1990s this problem has lessened with the formation of local NGOs and resistance organizations by exploited groups such as debt bondsmen in India and Pakistan and the descendants of slaves in Mauritania. These groups are now bringing their own cases to the United Nations, often with the aid of the older European NGOs.

Thanks to the activities of these organizations and of the Working Group, public awareness of contemporary forms of slavery has greatly increased. However, although most have been condemned in international conventions, problems of enforcement remain and are likely to continue for as long as there is poverty, ignorance, and unequal distribution of wealth and opportunity between individuals and among nations.

See also ANTI-SLAVERY INTERNATIONAL; COMFORT WOMEN IN WORLD WAR II; LABOR SYSTEMS; PERSPECTIVES ON SLAVERY; PROSTITUTION; SLAVERY AND CHILDHOOD.

BIBLIOGRAPHY

Annual Report of the Working Group of Experts on Contemporary Forms of Slavery of the Sub-Commission on the Prevention of Discrimination and Protection of Minorities of the United Nations Commission on Human Rights. 1976–1996.

Annual Reports of the Committee of Experts on the Application of Conventions and Recommendations—Conventions 29 and 105 of the International Labor Office.
Reports and newsletters of Anti-Slavery International (these cover a wide range of subjects).
Reports of other NGOs, including the International Catholic Child Bureau, the International Abolitionist Federation, and the reports of the various committees of Human Rights Watch.

Suzanne Miers

Slavery and Childhood

When Africans were brought to the Americas in the seventeenth and eighteenth centuries, high mortality rates and skewed sex ratios (many more men than women) made it difficult for them to form families. In the Caribbean colonies of England, France, and Spain, as well as in Portuguese Brazil and Dutch Surinam, mortality was so high that the enslaved population could be maintained only by continued importation. From 1700 to 1740, when almost one hundred thousand slaves were brought to the North American mainland, an ideal shipload contained about twice as many males as females. Nevertheless, by the 1730s, for example, a native-born population came of age in the Chesapeake tobacco region, the sex ratio balanced out, and births outnumbered deaths. As population growth through natural increase continued throughout the southern United States, an increasingly large proportion of the enslaved were children. By 1860, of the almost four million slaves counted by the U.S. Census, 56 percent were under age twenty.

On plantations in the tidewater Chesapeake and in low country Carolina, children grew up in relatively stable slave communities. About half of the young children lived with both parents, and those whose fathers lived nearby remained with mothers or other relatives. Slave boys were often named for absent fathers, thus confirming the paternal tie. Children were also named for grandparents, aunts, or uncles. These kinship ties were reinforced by shared daily life. In log or clapboard cabins children slept with siblings in lofts, on pallets, or in trundle beds. Sharing a common yard, slaves cooked and ate communally, serving the children from a single skillet or a wooden trough. Chesapeake children were put to work between the ages of five and ten—chasing crows, helping stack wheat, or picking worms off tobacco plants. Boys minded cows or chickens, toted drinking water to the fields, and guided oxen when fields were plowed. Girls dusted, cleaned silver, or set the table at the big house; at about age ten they became nurses for other slave children or their master's children. Carolina slaves were given a task to be performed each day, and youngsters of twelve or thirteen became three-quarter-task hands, helping to plant and harvest rice or hoeing and picking cotton.

Slave and white Chesapeake children grew up playing together. Boys wrestled and got into mischief, while girls made doll clothes and played house. Enslaved children first learned their status from this kind of play, white girls playing house relegated the black slave children to their quarters, or playing mistress, whipped them for learning to read. In Carolina coastal parishes slaves outnumbered whites by forty to one, and anxious parents drew a firm line between their own children and those of their slaves. In both areas enslaved children also played by themselves in the quarters or in the woods, fishing and hunting for possum, or playing ring games based on songs they improvised much as their parents and kinfolk did.

Interaction with white culture could create psychological conflict for enslaved children. In 1824, when six-year-old Frederick Douglass left his grandmother's cabin for Colonel Edward Lloyd's plantation on Maryland's Eastern Shore, he entered a self-sufficient community embracing thirteen farms and five hundred slaves. Yet he gravitated toward the great house, which he associated with an abundance of food. Sitting in on lessons with Lloyd's son Daniel, Fred learned the power of literacy and cultivated English speech. Sent to Baltimore at age ten, he bribed white boys with bread to teach him his letters, and he taught himself to read. Douglass would someday flee slavery and become a distinguished speaker and writer. Yet, even while he emulated the genteel values of the great house, he also regarded it with mixed anxiety and deep resentment.

Although eighteenth-century planters considered small children a nuisance and of little market value, by the early nineteenth century southeastern planters began to recognize the value of these surplus slaves. As seaboard agriculture declined in productivity, the planters or their sons migrated west, transporting a labor force as young as ten to fourteen years of age. When Congress ended the Atlantic slave trade in 1808, the demand of the cotton frontier for labor accelerated the domestic trade. As southeastern planters sold their slaves to professional traders, enslaved children increasingly became a commodity. Attitudes toward childbearing women also shifted, for a woman who bore a child every two years was as profitable as a prime field hand.

Ignoring fathers who lived off the plantation and networks of kin, planters and traders defined a slave family as a mother and her children. Although infants and toddlers were sold with their mothers, older children could be sold individually. These painful separations brought despair and disorder to the new labor forces assembled in the Southwest; families and communities similar to those in the southeastern states did not take shape until the 1840s and 1850s. As kinship groups worked the fields together, children as young as age five learned to work with the hoe and went to the fields with their parents during the cotton harvest. These children felt the whip, administered by the overseer or driver, if they failed to keep up in the cotton fields. They also knew about other kinds of punishment of slaves, and when family members were punished, they cried, ran in circles, and sometimes threw rocks at their masters. Throughout the South enslaved children feared punishment from a cruel master's wife, who might pummel their bare backs or whip them with a leather strap.

After the Civil War, freed parents searched for children from whom they had been separated. Many walked long distances, resorted to placing newspaper advertisements, or sought help from the Freedmen's Bureau. Families might locate some but rarely all of their scattered offspring. Orphans often stayed with other kinship groups until they could provide for themselves. Yet dangers still remained for the freed children, for former slave owners sought to bind them in various forms of apprenticeship. Even after emancipation the formerly enslaved children were highly valued for their labor.

See also DOUGLASS, FREDERICK; FAMILY, U.S.

BIBLIOGRAPHY

Federal Writers Project Interviews with Former Slaves. Southern Historical Collection, University of North Carolina Library, Chapel Hill. 1930s.

JOYNER, CHARLES. *Down by the Riverside: A South Carolina Slave Community.* 1984.

KING, WILMA. *Stolen Childhood: Slave Youth in Nineteenth-Century America.* 1995.

KULIKOFF, ALLAN. *Tobacco and Slaves: Development of Southern Cultures in the Chesapeake, 1680–1800.* 1986.

MALONE, ANN PATTON. *Sweet Chariot: Slave Family and Household Structure in Nineteenth-Century Louisiana.* 1992.

MCFEELY, WILLIAM S. *Frederick Douglass.* 1991.

REINIER, JACQUELINE S. *From Virtue to Character: American Childhood, 1775–1850.* 1996.

Jacqueline S. Reinier

Slavery Convention (1926)

The Slavery Convention was promulgated by the Assembly of the League of Nations after a Temporary Slavery Commission reported to the assembly that slavery continued to exist in some parts of the world.

In 1925, a draft convention submitted by the British government was recommended for approval by the Assembly and forwarded for recommendations to all league members as well as to nonmembers including Afghanistan, Ecuador, Egypt, Germany, Russia, the Sudan, Turkey, and the United States. Observations were incorporated into another draft, which was adopted by the Assembly on 25 September 1926 and immediately signed by twenty-five member nations. Pursuant to the convention's terms, it entered into force on 9 March 1927 but remained open for signature until April 1927, by which time eleven more nations had signed. By 1937 twenty-nine nations had ratified the convention and were therefore bound by its terms. However, it had been acceded to by fifteen additional nations, which, although not signatories, thereby became parties to the convention. In 1953 it was adopted by the United Nations and remains in force. As of 1986 sixty-seven nations were parties to the convention.

The convention was the first international agreement to define slavery and the slave trade. It defines slavery as the "status or condition of a person over whom any or all of the powers attaching to the right ownership are exercised." It defines the slave trade as "acts involved in the capture, acquisition or disposal of a person with intent to reduce him to slavery." These definitions encompass the acquisition of a slave, the sale of a slave, and the trade or transport in slaves.

The convention contains a separate provision regarding forced labor because members of the League disagreed on the extent of the similarities between slavery and forced labor. It states that "compulsory or forced labor may only be exacted for public purposes" and that the signatories will seek to prevent forced labor from "developing into conditions analogous to slavery." Although the United States acceded to the convention, it did so subject to a reservation regarding this last provision because the United States opposed the use of forced labor even for public purposes.

The convention provides that each nation must take necessary steps with respect to the "territories placed under its sovereignty, jurisdiction, protection, suzerainty or tutelage" to suppress the slave trade, but it does not outlaw the status of slavery. Because many nations were concerned about hardships and social upheavals that might be created if all slaves were suddenly liberated, some nations suggested that freed slaves be forced to continue to work for a certain time under contract for their former masters. Germany suggested that slave owners be compensated for their losses. As a compromise, the nations agreed to "bring about, progressively and as soon as possible, the complete abolition of slavery in all its forms." There are only two enforcement provisions in the convention. Article Seven provides that each nation forward to the League any laws and regulations that are enacted pursuant to the convention. Under Article Eight, each nation may bring any dispute regarding the implementation of the convention to the Permanent Court of International Justice. No nation has ever done so.

Significantly, the convention does not outlaw the slave trade as an act of piracy, a status that would give nations the right to stop and board vessels of other nations if such vessels were suspected of carrying slaves. Each nation only agreed to "adopt all appropriate measures with a view of preventing and suppressing the embarkation, disembarkation, and transport of slaves in their territorial waters and upon all vessels flying their respective flags." They also agreed to promulgate a convention creating mutual rights and duties similar to those found in the Convention on Supervision of International Trade in Arms and Ammunition and in Implements of War of 17 June 1925. That convention gave certain nations the right to stop and search certain vessels within specified zones if there was good reason to believe that the vessel was transporting illegal arms. A similar convention was never promulgated with respect to the slave trade.

In 1932 a permanent Advisory Committee of Experts on Slavery, consisting of seven experts of different nationalities, was charged with studying and compiling the reports received from nations pursuant to Article Seven. The committee met every two years and submitted reports until 1938. The committee's powers were limited due to concerns over encroachment on the sovereignty of nations. It could study and make recommendations regarding the means to eradicate slavery but it could not supervise the process in individual countries. It could not take depositions, nor could it communicate directly with nongovernment persons or organizations; all communication had to be through governments.

The committee's reports track the progress of individual countries in eradicating slavery and the slave trade. In 1932 it reported that only Nepal, Burma, and Anglo-Egyptian Sudan had manumitted all slaves. The status of slavery was still legal in the Hejaz and Nejd (now known as Saudi Arabia), Yemen, the sultanates of Hadhramuth, Oman, Koweit (Kuwait), and Abyssinia (now known as Ethiopia). However, the last report in 1938 indicated that the status of slavery had been outlawed in most countries and was at least weakened in others.

From 1932 to 1938 the committee reported that it was difficult to effectively fight the transportation of slaves in the Red Sea, the Persian Gulf, the Indian Ocean, and along the Arabian Coast because a convention providing for the detainment of foreign ves-

sels had never been promulgated. However, in 1932, it reported that the British government had entered into treaties with several Arab nations that granted British warships the right to pursue vessels suspected of slave trading in the Arab nations' territorial waters. European nations also took measures to prevent the traffic of slaves during pilgrimages to the holy sites in Arabia. These actions were apparently successful, for in 1938 the committee forwarded the Sudanese report that there was no evidence of slave trading in the Red Sea, and reported that the slave trade no longer existed across the Persian Gulf.

See also LABOR SYSTEMS; LEAGUE OF NATIONS; SLAVERY, CONTEMPORARY FORMS OF; SLAVE TRADE.

BIBLIOGRAPHY

BURTON, MARGARET ERNESTINE. *The Assembly of the League of Nations.* 1941.

REDMAN, RENEE COLETTE. "The League of Nations and the Right to Be Free from Enslavement: The First Human Right to Be Recognized as Customary International Law." *Chicago-Kent Law Review* 70, no. 2 (1994): 759.

Renee C. Redman

Slaves, Sale of

As human property, slaves were liable to absolute sale. The Atlantic slave trade, with its dealers and markets, represents perhaps the most horrifying aspect of the institution of slavery. But most slave sales took place outside formal markets in transactions involving one, two, or a few individuals.

Public Sales

A substantial proportion of sales was generated by judicial process. Sheriffs sold debtors' slaves to satisfy creditors' claims or sold recaptured runaways unclaimed by their masters to recoup jail fees. Probate courts ordered estate administrators to sell slaves to pay an estate's debts or facilitate its division among heirs. Orphans' courts directed guardians to sell slaves to provide income to support minor heirs. The exigencies of public sale were most likely to result in the separation of husbands, wives, and children, though market considerations frequently dictated separations in private sales as well.

Private Sales

Masters selling slaves privately could do so directly with relatives or neighbors, or sell to itinerant brokers who roamed the countryside, or advertise through newspapers. Direct sales could shade into transactions such as gifts from parent to child, conditional sales, or mortgages. In the latter cases the nominal seller might be in fact a borrower offering up a slave as security for a debt. The terms of direct sales often involved credit and installment payments. By contrast, brokers usually paid cash to sellers, in order to bargain for price discounts and to avoid any restrictive conditions on the sale. Sellers working through advertisements usually directed buyers to printing offices, taverns, or like gathering places to obtain further information or make offers for slaves. Private sellers might also place slaves in public jails, or in a slave dealer's private jail, where prospective buyers could see them.

Restrictions on Sale and Slave Involvement

Enslaved people, aware of the disruption that sale might bring, sometimes ran away before a sale could occur; masters, whether selling privately or under court order, sought to reduce such flights. One approach was for sellers to restrict sale to buyers in their own state or county or to engage in two-tiered pricing, accepting less from a local buyer. Or sellers could authorize a slave to find a new master to his or her liking, subject to seller and buyer agreeing on terms. A third possibility was that of trial sale, with the buyer able to return the slave to the seller as much as six months after the sale. Finally, masters, particularly in urban settings, could allow a slave to purchase his own freedom, either immediately with cash earned from extra work or via a delayed manumission in return for productive and reliable service over a term of years (often called self-purchase). Whether or not these palliatives were offered, many buyers sought to talk to slaves before purchase to assess their health, character, and willingness to work for a new master. All of these strategies sought to obtain acquiescence to sale by allowing enslaved people a degree of control over the process.

If some masters mitigated conditions of sale to engage a slave's cooperation, the converse could also apply. The threat of distant sale, away from home and family, could be employed to make enslaved people compliant; a troublesome slave could be sold far away or to a "bad" master as an exemplary punishment.

The Price Factors

However a sale took place, the price of slaves depended on assessments of a slave's size, strength, health, mental abilities, and character. Growing children were often sold by the pound, given uncertainty about slaves' birthdates and ages. Prices for women

A buyer examines the physical condition of a slave being sold in Virginia in 1830. [Library of Congress/ Corbis].

fluctuated according to their perceived or proven capacities as childbearers. The slaves most desired by buyers typically fell into three categories: young males, aged about eight to fifteen; prime male hands, generally in their twenties; and women in their first childbearing years, from about sixteen to twenty-five. Nonetheless, slaves of all ages and conditions could be and were sold, from infants to men and women in their seventies. Once a slave's general worth was determined, buyers and sellers looked to local market conditions to determine a sale price, with prices prevailing at recent local public sales as a guideline.

Buyers generally assumed the legal risks of acquiring physically or mentally unsound slaves; sellers frequently offered warranties of a slave's good health as a way to encourage buyer confidence and obtain a higher price. A dissatisfied buyer could obtain rescission of a sale if the seller had knowingly concealed a "defect," such as a slave's disease or a record of frequent running away, about which the buyer had inquired at time of purchase.

See also DISCIPLINE AND PUNISHMENT; PRICES OF SLAVES; SELF-PURCHASE; SLAVE TRADE.

BIBLIOGRAPHY

MORRIS, THOMAS D. *Southern Slavery and the Law, 1619–1860.* 1996.
TADMAN, MICHAEL. *Speculators and Slaves: Masters, Traders, and Slaves in the Old South.* 1989.

T. Stephen Whitman

Slave Societies

Slave societies are communities in which the institution of slavery defines the overall character of social and economic organization, and in which slavery permeates all, or most, aspects of life completely. They are whole societies, based on slavery but including slave owners, free people who do not own slaves, and freed people, as well as slaves. The slave society concept was adumbrated in the late nineteenth century, particularly in *The Slave Power* (1862) written by John E. Cairnes, and became common currency among popularizers of the Marxist slave mode of production. It was, however, first fully directed at the historiography of slavery in Frank Tannenbaum's *Slave and Citizen* (1946). Because of the fundamental nature of the institution's influence, argued Tannenbaum, it is better not to speak of "slave systems" or "slave economies" but rather to recognize the totality of a slave society. Thus he saw slavery as affecting all classes, free as well as slave, and all institutions of social and cultural life, all aspects of economy and polity, patterning life in a way peculiar to itself. Underlying his argument was the understanding that cultural influences move vertically, from below as well as above, even within a rigid social structure and even without conscious action. Tannenbaum believed this process could be observed wherever slavery existed, though he confined his argument to the Americas.

The slave society concept received substantial refinement in the 1960s in the work of Moses Finley. He distinguished between "genuine slave societies"—classical Greece and Rome, the American South, Brazil, and the Caribbean—and those many other "slave-owning societies" in which slaves were present but the institution was not foundational. Only where "the economic and political elite depended primarily on slave labor for basic production" could a slave society emerge, he argued. Although Finley claimed not to want to enter the "numbers game," ultimately his identification of slave societies depended on slaves making up roughly one-third of the population of a significant region over a long period of time. Other writers have reduced this qualification to one-fifth. Paul Lovejoy has argued that the Sokoto Caliphate qualifies as a sixth genuine slave society.

Apart from the demographic test, some historians argue that it is necessary to ask how important a role slaves played in the economy in terms of the "location" of their owners in the system and in the society at large. Where slaves dominated large-scale production, generated a major share of revenue, and were held in mass by the upper classes, there were slave societies. Application of this test produces the same results as that for the demographic test, yielding only five genuine slave societies in world history. Some, however, argue slave societies may exist even where slavery is simply one of a variety of forms of dependent or unfree labor from which the propertied classes may extract surplus, so long as the wealthy derive most of their revenue from this broader class of unfree labor.

As Keith Bradley (1994) notes, all of these tests depend on economic rather than social variables, and strict application of the tests reduces the existence of true slave societies to quite small areas and brief time spans. Brazil was a slave society for three hundred years, but the other qualified cases persisted for periods ranging from one hundred to two hundred years, depending on how the regional boundaries are drawn. The distinction between "genuine" slave societies and those in which slaves were simply present, holds Bradley, is a modern rather than an ancient concept and is therefore of limited utility except in attempts to comprehend the significance of slavery for contemporaries. As a society in which status, esteem, and authority were highly valued, argues Bradley, "Rome was always a slave society." This emphasis on status closely resembles the influential version of the slave society concept advanced by Elsa Goveia (1965) in which she contended that slave owners in the British Caribbean clung to their slaves for reasons of social status even when they could no longer extract economic profit from the system.

Critics of the slave society model sometimes prefer to talk of "social formations" rather than "societies," arguing that the idea of society suggests a false uniformity where a diversity of modes of production may co-exist in any particular situation. Orlando Patterson holds that a concentration on "genuine slave societies" or "large-scale slave societies" limits the potential of comparative studies of slavery and advocates analysis of "the entire range of slave-holding societies." In general, it seems the usefulness of the concept of slave society has been devalued by the increasingly common practice among historians of seeing slave societies almost everywhere they see slavery, and using the label interchangeably with slave system, slave economy, and slave community.

See also ANCIENT GREECE; ANCIENT ROME; BRAZIL; CARIBBEAN REGION; UNITED STATES.

BIBLIOGRAPHY

BRADLEY, KEITH. *Slavery and Society at Rome.* 1994.
FINLEY, MOSES. *Ancient Slavery and Modern Ideology.* 1980.
GOVEIA, ELSA V. *Slave Society in the British Leeward Islands at the End of the Eighteenth Century.* 1965.
PATTERSON, ORLANDO. *Slavery and Social Death.* 1982.
TANNENBAUM, FRANK. *Slave and Citizen.* 1946.

B. W. Higman

Slave Trade

This entry includes the following articles: An Overview; Ancient Mediterranean; Medieval Europe; Islamic World; Africa; Transatlantic; United States; Brazil; China; Coolie Trade; Southeast Asia; Indian Ocean; Twentieth-Century Trade. *Related articles may be found at the entry* Africa.

An Overview

No system of slavery has persisted on a significant scale unless supported by continuing systematic introductions of fresh captives: strangers brought into the slaveholding society without the cultural knowledge of seasoned slaves, not to mention the inherited rights accorded locally born members of the host community. Trade as a source of such newcomers has the specific connotation of purposive investment in—and organized movements of—people, by merchants in a commercialized economy. Otherwise, small numbers of dependent newcomers might enter localized communities through occasional, ad hoc transfers from neighbors, below the threshold of such an organized "trade." Distressed persons have offered themselves or their children directly into the hands of masters in times of economic and social collapse, usually associated with drought in seventeenth- and eighteenth-century Africa and India. However, voluntary subordination of this sort often entailed residual rights, thus resembling clientage or pawnship more than slavery, except in Africa amid the disorders provoked by slave-buying merchants from Europe.

At the core of economies systematically dependent on slave labor, the principal alternative to trade as a source of new captives was direct raiding, in which warlords or powerful military states systematically seized people from surrounding, smaller, decentralized communities unable to defend themselves, whom they then kept and employed as slaves. Slaves in such cases arrived without commercial intermediaries since victorious commanders and their followers claimed their human booty directly from the field of battle. The captives taken in raids of this sort might become mercenaries and retainers of the warlords. However, extracting captives by warfare to support such regimes had inherent limits, since the assaulted populations learned to defend themselves, or, if they did not, were eventually depleted, or fled beyond the reach of the attackers. Trade thus frequently backed even the most bellicose slave-acquisition strategies, and such plundering persisted in the long run only on the peripheries of commercialized, consumer markets for slave-produced commodities, and—often—also for some of the slaves themselves.

Thus, all the world's largest slave-consuming economies began in violence, and they increased in size and duration to the extent that commercialized trade supported, and—in modern times—also financed them. The slaves numerous in Athens, and subsequently in other city-states throughout the Hellenic eastern Mediterranean, originated as captives in local wars, but slavery there may have survived through commercial networks similar to those that later supplied captives to Islamic cities in the same region. Subsequent Roman military expansion in southern Europe, southwestern Asia, and northern Africa captured most of the slaves who supplemented, and for a century or so may have replaced, peasants on the grain, wine, and olive estates of late republican and early imperial Italy. Then Rome's empire reached its limits, conquests died out, and rural slavery declined for lack of continuing supplies of new captives. The military conquests attending the first centuries of Muslim Arab expansion similarly converted captives into slaves without their passing through merchants' hands. But subsequent consolidation of the vast commercial economy of the Islamic world supported consumer markets for trade-supplied slaves for urban public and private domestic services in cities all around the Mediterranean. Merchants and their governments—Greeks from the time of ancient Athens and Romans importing skilled slaves from Hellenistic cities, before the Muslims—both operated and employed the products of this enduring trade in slaves at the conjunction of Africa, Europe, and Asia.

Merchants obtained captives from processes that operated beyond, and independently of, the commercial sphere within which they traded. Fragmented overpopulated regions, often under military pressures or as a result of failures of their agriculture, were particularly vulnerable. A tendency toward marauding persisted for more than a millennium, from the eighth

A small felucca transports slaves along the coast of Africa in 1852. [*Gleason's Pictorial Drawing Room Companion/* Corbis]

through the nineteenth centuries, around the borders of Ethiopia and along the southern margins of the Sahara Desert, the so-called Sudanic latitudes of Africa. There cavalry forces under Muslim, or—in Ethiopia—Christian, rulers preyed on the "pagan" and "infidel" farmers living on their borders (where horses could not be used) to build up domestic slave populations and supply the cities in the Islamic heartlands of northern Africa and southwest Asia, as well as Saharan mines and oases. Muslim merchants not only provided secondary markets for the captives taken but also financed the imports of horses that made raiding so productive there. They may have conducted as many slaves across the Sahara Desert and the Red Sea as later reached the Americas, at lower annual volumes but over a longer period of time. Wealthy Islamic cities in northwestern Africa and Egypt, Arabia, Syria, and Iran at the peak of their prosperity also

purchased Christian slaves from Europe, from Vikings in the eleventh and twelfth centuries and from Italians from the thirteenth to the fifteenth centuries, as well as through Muslim commercial channels that tapped seemingly inexhaustible reservoirs of surplus people around the shores of the Black Sea.

Mercantile initiative extended further still in the Atlantic slave trade from the 1570s to the 1860s, to make it the largest, most geographically extensive, and most systematically organized trade in slaves ever. In the course of this trade, merchants from capitalistic Europe, aided by American counterparts, delivered some ten to eleven million live Africans to North and South America, where slaves became majority populations and supplied the labor force at the base of many American economies throughout the Caribbean, in most of Brazil, and in the southern colonies of English North America. The leading merchant nations of Europe succeeded one another at the leading edge of Atlantic slaving as they extended their commercial investments throughout the world: Italians backed the Portuguese in the late sixteenth century, until the Dutch replaced them in Brazil after about 1570, and the British and the French dominated the eighteenth-century trade. North Americans, Brazilians (sometimes with indirect English participation), and Cubans financed the maritime commerce in human beings as it declined, under abolitionist pressures from northern Europe, in the nineteenth century. In Africa, European merchants invested trade goods in the continent's largely non-capitalist economies to stimulate the sustained conflict and violence, beyond that provoked by occasional drought and other ephemeral disruptions, that generated massive regional movements of refugees as well as captives, of whom many were sold to satisfy debts owed to European merchants on the coast.

The Atlantic trade in slaves thus acquired a distinctively commercial logic, combining the classic economic factors of production—African labor with European capital and open American lands nearly emptied of their native populations by sixteenth-century disease and conquest—to fuel rapid economic expansion around the Atlantic until well after 1800. Although Atlantic slaving still carried labor from relatively stable economies outside the sphere of Atlantic law, contract, and civil society to rapidly growing sectors within it, European investment allowed secondary mercantile sectors in Africa to replace warfare and drought, violence and distress at the start of the processes generating slaves. Europeans gave merchandise in "trust" to African suppliers, which allowed them to finance chains of indebtedness that ended in insolvent borrowers condemned to sale by courts (some developed especially for the purpose), or compelled to offer children or other dependents as hostage-like "pawns" (who were sometimes sold upon default as slaves), or forced them to kidnap strangers or maneuver to condemn rivals to satisfy lenders—or they were simply seized themselves by outlaw creditors. Behind all these strategies, involving degrees of coercion usually short of outright violence, lay financial liabilities created by the financial strengths of the modern trade itself.

Mercantile networks supplying slave labor for primary nodes of economic expansion frequently spawned secondary trades. The Italians sold the Slavs they acquired from around the Black Sea throughout the Christian cities of the western Mediterranean, and this trade in turn prompted the Portuguese to develop slave supplies of their own along Africa's Atlantic coast for sale in Lisbon and Seville. Transatlantic

shipments of slaves developed in the sixteenth century primarily to supply enslaved Africans to cities in Spain's silver-producing American colonies, before the Portuguese used improved techniques of trans-oceanic transport to put still more Africans to work growing sugar in Brazil. Slaves first reached the poorer tobacco and rice colonies of temperate North America when English slavers supplying the sugar-growing tropical American extended beyond West Indian primary markets to these higher latitudes. American slavers in Brazil and Rhode Island entered the Atlantic trade with local commodities salable for captives in Africa, to undercut colonial mercantilist policies. In Africa slavery became a prominent—in some areas dominant—method of labor mobilization and community formation by the end of the nineteenth century because the African raiders and merchants who sold people to the Europeans, and later to Muslims from the Sahara Desert and the Indian Ocean, had kept at least as many captives as they sold.

As the growing global economy stimulated them, "trades" involving a similar range of worker volition developed to supply demand for labor in parts of nineteenth-century Asia. The violence and ownership characteristic of a trade in slaves was most prominent where supply systems crossed major cultural boundaries, particularly that between the Ottoman Empire and non-Muslim eastern and northeastern Africa. Ottoman commercial prosperity in the nineteenth century, deriving from trade with industrializing Europe, extended Muslim purchases of slaves into Africa south of the Sahara and down the Indian Ocean coast.

The Indian Ocean, India, Southeast Asia, and the islands of Melanesia constituted a commercial sphere comparable to the Atlantic, but one that had seldom grown at rates outpacing local supplies of labor and so had not stimulated coerced transfers of labor on scales that would support commercial investment in buying and selling slaves. Dutch merchants in the Indian Ocean mostly carried spices but in the eighteenth century also delivered small numbers of captive Asians to the Cape of Good Hope. The English and French trading companies active in the area developed sources for slaves to the plantation islands of Mauritius (Bourbon) and Réunion in East Africa and Madagascar. Muslim-financed merchants diverted these African sources to Ottoman markets when the Christian nations withdrew from buying and selling humans after 1807. The English, in particular, exploited growing distress in India at the same time to "contract" large numbers of workers for sugar plantations on Mauritius. In Southeast Asia and Melanesia, beyond the sphere of European colonial control, Asian raiders and traders carried Chinese and other workers from poorer, overpopulated zones to areas that were building a capacity to produce commodities for European markets, and renegade participants in these movements raided and captured other people whom they sold as slaves.

By the modern era, capitalist merchants and the trades in slaves that they financed and facilitated thus promoted economic growth through the use of enslaved laboring forces. So sensitive was slavery to their stimulus that European governments reacting to domestic pressures unrelated—in fact, sometimes contrary—to short-term commercial and colonial prosperity almost always ended American, African, and Asian slavery by outlawing, and in some cases actively suppressing, the trades that supplied it.

The violence and direct compulsion at the start of these trades in slaves distinguished them from more voluntaristic movements of "free" or "contracted" labor recruited in within more recent times. The suppression of the Atlantic trade in slaves between 1807 and about 1870 coincided with the further, industry-driven consolidation of a world economy. On its peripheries after about 1850, contracts replaced capture at the point of departure for new labor, drawn into its dynamic mining and plantation sectors as alien workers. These new workers were mostly young men from Asian lands that were then falling under formal European colonial control. Population movement also characterized the world economy's industrialized core in Europe and North America, where cities growing up around factories and nodes of transportation that supplied them and moved their output drew families of "free" emigrants from rural regions closer to home into the cities until well into the twentieth century. Industries—often mines—and plantations in the colonies attracted single, usually male "migrant" workers, and pass systems and other restrictions kept their families in increasingly impoverished rural homelands. Colonial migrant-labor systems were not formal (chattel) slavery, since workers were subject to government law (however repressive) rather than the permanent, exclusive authority of their employers. They resembled earlier trades in slaves in the force they employed (however veiled in "regulations") to separate workers from the societies that nurtured them (however temporarily), in their dependence on continuing infusions of new recruits, and in the sub-subsistence levels of wages they paid.

Since World War II, the elimination of colonial restraints on population movement, improved transportation, and growing inequalities between economies supplying and those consuming raw materials have extended these modern patterns of voluntary emigration, both of oscillating male migrants and of permanently relocating families, to global scales. When contemporary emigrants seeking jobs generated in growing economies pass national or cultural boundaries—whether as unauthorized "undocumented aliens" or officially registered *Gastarbeitern,* both thus designated, like slaves, as "outsiders"—they frequently survive unrecognized, or ignored, by governments, in the shadows of the regulated economy, subject to private employers under conditions of semirightlessness that may approach the subjugation of slaves. The general absence of forced removal and third-party investment in ownership during transit distinguish these modern population movements from earlier trades in slaves.

See also AFRICA; MAURITIUS AND RÉUNION; OTTOMAN EMPIRE.

BIBLIOGRAPHY

ELTIS, DAVID. *Economic Growth and the Ending of the Transatlantic Slave Trade.* 1987.
ENGERMAN, STANLEY L. "Coerced and Free Labor: Property Rights and the Development of the Labor Force." *Explorations in Economic History* 29 (1992): 1–29.
———. "Servants to Slaves to Servants: Contract Labor and European Expansion." In *Colonialism and Migration: Indentured Labour Before and After Slavery,* edited by Pieter C. Emmer. 1986.
GALLOWAY, JOHN. *The Sugar Cane Industry: An Historical Geography from Its Origins to 1914.* 1989.
LOVEJOY, PAUL E. *Transformations in Slavery: A History of Slavery in Africa.* 1983.
MEILLASSOUX, CLAUDE. *The Anthropology of Slavery: The Womb of Iron and Gold.* 1991.
MILLER, JOSEPH C. *Way of Death: Merchant Capitalism and the Angolan Slave Trade, 1730–1830.* 1988.
PATTERSON, ORLANDO. *Slavery and Social Death: A Comparative Study.* 1982.
PHILLIPS, WILLIAM D., JR. *Slavery from Roman Times to the Early Transatlantic Trade.* 1985.
WALLERSTEIN, IMMANUEL. *The Modern World System.* 3 vol. 1974–1989.
WOLF, ERIC. *Europe and the People without History.* 1982.

Joseph C. Miller

Ancient Mediterranean

Large-scale slave trading developed from the sixth century B.C. with the rise of chattel slavery in some Greek city-states, such as Athens, Aegina, Corinth, and Chios. The abolition of debt bondage in Athens and the Greek preference for slaves of non-Greek origin created substantial demand for imports. Roman military expansion outside Italy from the third century B.C. onwards fuelled the slave trade that supplied the urban centers and rural estates of peninsular Italy and Sicily—regions that imported several million slaves during the final two centuries B.C. The slave trade remained important, though on a less dramatic scale, until the fall of the Roman empire.

Among the main sources of the trade, warfare commonly eclipsed piracy. Armed conflicts between Greek city-states, between Greek colonists and native populations throughout the Mediterranean, and later between Hellenistic kingdoms regularly entailed the enslavement of captives. Much larger numbers of slaves were taken in various Roman campaigns: the subjugation of Italy in the fourth and third centuries B.C. and the operations in Spain, North Africa, Greece, and Asia Minor (present-day Turkey) in the second century B.C., in Gaul (present-day France), the Balkans, and the Middle East in the first century B.C., and in Britain, central Europe east of the Rhine and north of the Danube, and Mesopotamia during the following centuries. As with the modern transatlantic slave trade, orderly purchase from foreign sources was the most important source overall, augmented by the enslavement of newborn babies who had been exposed by their parents in parts of the Mediterranean.

The Greek slave trade first centered on the lower Danube region, mainly on Thracia and Dacia (present-day Bulgaria and Romania), and the hinterland of the Black Sea, with principal markets in Tanais at the mouth of the Don and in Byzantium on the Bosphorus. In the fifth and fourth centuries B.C., its focus shifted to the western parts of Asia Minor, first to Caria and then to Lydia, Phrygia, and Mysia, while the share of Black Sea slaves decreased. Ephesus was also an important entrepôt, but no one market dominated.

From the third century B.C., Rhodes, Tyre in Phoenicia (Lebanon), and Alexandria emerged as centers of the trade, and Syria became a major supplier. The Aegean island of Delos was proverbial as a major slave-market in the second and first centuries B.C. At the same time, large-scale slaving raids staged by pirates based in Cicilia (southeastern Turkey) and Crête swelled the slave trade until their suppression by the Romans in 67 B.C.

Under Roman rule, the trade shifted back to the Black Sea region, drawing on the Ukraine and the Caucasus. Roman conquests in western Europe opened up new sources of slaves, first trade in Celts from Gaul across the Alps to Italy, and later imports of Germans across the Rhine and the Danube. Information on slave dealers (called *andrapodokapelos* and *somatemporos* in Greek, *mango* in Latin) is scarce. Greek and Roman dealers would trail armies on military campaigns and purchase war captives on the spot. Many were nonspecialist merchants who also traded in other goods. Greek and Roman elite authors expressed contempt for the occupation of the slavedealer, which had a reputation for dishonesty. Yet many of the slavedealers attested in the Roman period were Roman citizens and were sometimes associated with the upper elite. Nothing specific is known about financing, though aristocrats could provide resources and patronage.

When transferred by dealers, slaves were chained together at the neck; long-distance transport was by ship. Permanent slave markets were limited to large cities and usually integrated into general market areas, such as the Forum Romanum in Rome. Slaves were also sold in periodic markets held at fairs and festivals. At auctions, slaves were presented on raised platforms and subjected to close scrutiny; newly imported slaves had their feet whitened with chalk. Greek and Roman law required sellers to disclose defects and salient characteristics of their slaves and protected the buyer from fraudulence.

See also ANCIENT GREECE; ANCIENT MIDDLE EAST; ANCIENT ROME.

BIBLIOGRAPHY

FINLEY, MOSES I. "The Slave Trade in Antiquity: The Black Sea and Danubian Regions." In *Economy and Society in Ancient Greece,* edited by Brent D. Shaw and Richard P. Saller. 1981.

GARLAN, YVON. *Slavery in Ancient Greece.* 1988.

HARRIS, WILLIAM V. "Towards a Study of the Roman Slave Trade." In *The Seaborne Commerce of Ancient Rome,* edited by John H. D'Arms and E. Christian Kopff. 1980.

Walter Scheidel

Tourists examine the remains of the ancient slave market of Delos. [Roger Wood/Corbis]

Medieval Europe

Although slave trading continued throughout the European Middle Ages, the main slave markets were outside western Europe—primarily in the Muslim world and secondarily in the Byzantine Empire.

One of the earliest groups of medieval European slave dealers were the Frisians on the North Sea coast. Flourishing in the seventh and eighth centuries, they traded into Scandinavia and the British Isles. They purchased prisoners of war in Anglo-Saxon London, along with other commodities, and sold them to France and Germany.

A major route followed by the Frankish slave dealers started in the lands of the pagan Slavs, from whom the Western languages derived their words for slave. From eastern Europe, one Frankish slave route traveled west through Bavaria and crossed the Alps to Venice, from where the Italians transported slaves by sea to Byzantine and Muslim markets. A second route went west from Germany and entered France, passing through Verdun. From there the slaves were taken down the Rhone to Arles and Marseilles, a main nexus of the Mediterranean slave trade. From these points the slaves were shipped to Spain, either by sea or land routes. Spanish Muslims purchased many of the slaves, while others were sold in North Africa or sent on to Egypt.

By the ninth century, the Venetians prospered from their sea trade with the Muslims. Before the early ninth century their slaves were other Italians. Thereafter, the Venetians looked farther afield, to Dalmatia, where they purchased slaves and conducted their own raids to obtain more. They also purchased slaves in eastern Europe and brought them to Venice.

The most westerly component of the early medieval slave trade in Europe was the British Isles. Up to the eleventh century the Vikings and the English were active slave traders. They also traded children who had been sold by destitute English parents. From Ireland the Vikings took slaves and sold them in Muslim Spain and in Scandinavia. The English also sold some Irish slaves across the Channel, to Frankish slave dealers.

In the twelfth and thirteenth centuries, the Italian slave trade remained vigorous. Genoa's slave trade was based on the western Mediterranean and in Muslim slaves that came from North Africa. In the thirteenth century, both the Venetians and the Genoese began to trade in the Black Sea region, where they obtained Russians, Circassians, and other eastern Europeans.

By the mid-fourteenth century, a catastrophic population decline owing to famine and epidemics changed the European labor market. Workers who survived found good jobs easily and could not be induced to become household servants. The rich who survived became richer, as fortunes were consolidated through inheritance. It is not surprising that slavery grew as a result and that it provided supplemental workers and domestics. In 1363 the Florentine government allowed the unrestricted importation of slaves from outside Italy, stipulating only that they be of non-Christian origin. Venice took a different course, probably because of the large influx of slaves over the preceding two decades, and prohibited slave auctions in 1366 in an effort to reduce sales. Venetians could still import slaves, but sales had to be accomplished by private contract.

Russian and Circassian slaves continued to enter Italy in the fourteenth and fifteenth centuries, but their numbers declined in the second half of the fifteenth century, after the Ottoman conquest of Constantinople denied them access to the Black Sea. In response, the Italians turned back to the western Mediterranean. Muslim slaves came to be purchased in increasing numbers in North Africa, Spain, and Portugal. A few Guanche slaves from the Canary Islands and some sub-Saharan Africans also found their way to Italy.

The slave trade also remained active in late medieval Spain. Catalan and Valencian merchants were active throughout the Mediterranean and into the Black Sea. They, together with Italian merchants, brought slaves from distant regions to Spain. For a time in the fourteenth century, Greeks appeared in the kingdom of Aragon as slaves. The Greeks, however, were Orthodox Christians, and efforts by Church officials freed many enslaved Greeks and eventually stopped that trade. Sards came on the market in relatively small numbers during the Aragonese conquest of Sardinia. In the fourteenth and fifteenth centuries, Italian merchants brought eastern Europeans to Spain. Muslim prisoners of war constituted the main supply of slaves for Spain, although a few Canarians and more sub-Saharan Africans entered Spain as the Middle Ages ended. By then, the traditional eastern European slaving grounds were closed, and in the early modern period Africa came to serve as the main focus of the European slave trade.

See also MEDIEVAL EUROPE, SLAVERY AND SERFDOM IN; PRICES OF SLAVES; SLAVES, SALE OF.

BIBLIOGRAPHY

PHILLIPS, WILLIAM D., JR. *Slavery from Roman Times to the Early Transatlantic Trade.* 1985.

VERLINDEN, CHARLES. *L'esclavage dans l'Europe médiévale.* Vol. 1, 1955. Vol. 2, 1977.

William D. Phillips Jr.

Islamic World

Slave trading in the "Islamic world" usually refers to the commerce and trade that integrated the lands in southwest Asia and parts of the Mediterranean world including northern Africa that were conquered by Muslim Arabs in the seventh century A.D. Later other lands in central Asia, Iberia, and southeastern Europe were added by Persian, North African, and Turkish successors claiming political leadership in the Muslim world. Earlier "Arabs"—in the linguistic sense of pastoralist inhabitants of the Arabian peninsula—probably bought few slaves, although the commercial towns of their homeland, at the nexus of major trading networks in the Indian Ocean, Red Sea, Persian Gulf, and Mediterranean Sea, were sites of slave markets serving the empires of the ancient world and employers of slaves in urban households, municipal services, and maritime and commercial enterprises.

Slaves probably figured among the commodities bought and sold in seventh-century Arabian towns, including Mecca and Medina, where the prophet Muhammad gathered Arab followers into the religious movement that became Islam (A.D. 610–632). For a century or more after that, the military conquests of his Islamic followers provided lands and captive local populations that met the conquerors' needs for labor. As Islamic law took shape, it justified the enslavement of non-Muslims who resisted the call of the prophet to the true faith, although it compelled masters to treat those slaves with compassion (as all Muslims had an obligation to "protect the weak"). Arab merchant families adopted the prevailing pan-Mediterranean habit of employing slaves as domestics, bodyguards, and skilled craftsmen.

As the era of violent Arab conquests merged into relatively peaceful economic integration of the far-flung Islamic domains, urban merchants added enslaved "infidels" (*kaffirs*) to the trading networks they developed to acquire commodities from the periphery of a growing Arab world economy. North African caravan traders seeking the gold of sub-Saharan west Africa were selling slaves in central Islamic markets by the eighth century. By the ninth century, Arab and Persian mariners had developed the Indian Ocean trade of gold, ivory, and construction materials from eastern Africa (whose coastal lands they knew as "Zandj") and had set the stage for the only mass slave uprising known in the Arab world by importing slaves from the region to drain the marshes at the headwaters of the Persian Gulf. The central Islamic cities of Syria and Mesopotamia bought Slavs and other Europeans from Vikings coming south down the Don and Volga Rivers to the Black and Caspian Seas. Muslim-Christian hostilities across the Mediterranean produced captives on both sides, and—in the wake of the Crusades and Europe's growing demand for Muslim-supplied Asian spices in the thirteenth century—merchants in Renaissance Italy became systematic suppliers of Slavs from the Black Sea to Arab-Muslim markets in the eastern Mediterranean, especially Egypt.

In general terms, Muslim merchants added slaves to the returns of commercial ventures they initiated beyond the tropical frontiers of Islam, particularly ventures aimed at gold from Africa; others with spices of the tropics to sell bought slaves from temperate-latitude Europeans eager for their merchandise. The prominence of demand for domestic servants, including concubines, kept the numbers of women high. Although specialized merchants distributed these slaves to their final owners through the marketplaces of Islamic cities, the purchase and transport of slaves seldom structured the external supply networks, unlike the later, finely tuned Atlantic trade from Africa.

By the thirteenth century, the major Arab-Islamic states began to rely more and more on enslaved men, particularly Caucasians and other captives from the Asian-European borderlands, as key—often high-ranking—military forces and administrative officers in their regimes. The Fatimid caliphate (A.D. 969–1171) in Egypt, pressed by crusading Christians, led the way; the slave soldiers they trained succeeded them as rulers in the *mamluk* (enslaved ones) period that followed, from A.D. 1250 to 1517. The Delhi sultans (A.D. 1206–1555) maintained control of similar forces as the "slave kings" of northwestern India, and Sultan Murad I (1360–1389) created the slave forces that became the janissaries of the Ottoman Turkish state by seizing young Christian boys from the Balkans. Shah 'Abbas in sixteenth-century Persia trained slave youths from Georgia, called *ghulams,* in similar ways. These regimes acquired such "white" males more from tribute and forced taxation than through the commercial networks, which tended to feature girls and women sold as domestic servants and concubines. Some trading systems concentrated on acquiring eunuchs, boys castrated by non-Muslim suppliers, since Islamic law prohibited Muslims from performing the operation.

By the sixteenth century, regular supply routes from southeastern Europe, central Asia, and western and eastern Africa brought thousands—perhaps tens of thousands—of slaves into the cities of the Arab world each year. The informality of the trade meant that only scattered and indirect evidence could hint at its volume, the ratios between the sexes of the people it brought, or the increasingly structured financial and management methods that merchants used to conduct their business in human commodities. The business became sufficiently defined that slave traders—sometimes Muslims, but also Christians and Jews—in Persia, Turkey, Egypt, and North Africa organized themselves in commercial guilds (*sinf*) and drew credit from moneylenders to finance their operations. Some sent caravans capable of bringing slaves by the hundreds across the wastes of the Sahara desert, and maritime traders transported their captives by fleets of *dhows* in the Indian Ocean and across the Mediterranean in galleys.

Nineteenth-century commercial prosperity in the Arab world, by then largely under the nominal authority of the Ottoman sultanate in Istanbul, allowed merchants to increase the numbers of slaves acquired through these networks by a significant amount, perhaps tripling the volume of the African sources most clearly documented by the 1850s. Muslim holy wars (*jihads*) in western Africa provided numerous captives at low cost, and firearms added to the ability of the government in Egypt, Muslim merchants along the Upper Nile, and Omani and Indian merchants based at Zanzibar to provoke violence that increased the volume of slaves acquired from eastern and northeastern Africa.

The resulting "boom" in slaves brought to the Ottoman heartland from 1820 to 1880 coincided with increasingly aggressive European—particularly British—interference in the affairs of the Arab world. Humanitarians in Britain, fresh from victories over the Atlantic slave trade and slavery in the colonies, emphasized the horrors of "Arab slaving" in justifying European imperialism as a humanitarian abolitionist crusade. Muslim regimes, under pressure from foreign abolitionists but also concerned to control the slavers' involvement with contraband and black markets in world currencies, gradually declared slave trading illegal; Tunisia and Persia issued antislaving decrees in 1846; the Ottoman regime followed in 1854, and Egypt in 1877. Although a smaller underground slave trade continued into the twentieth century, mostly from Africa, the World Muslim Conference held in Mecca in 1926 addressed the need for comprehensive legislation against it, and the Mogadishu Conference reissued antislaving resolutions in 1946. Laws in Saudi Arabia in 1962 and in Mauritania in 1980 ended, at least on paper, slave trading in the Arab and Muslim African worlds. A European stereotype of Arabs as incorrigible slavers, surviving from the antislaving campaigns of the nineteenth century, still sometimes inaccurately generalizes these scattered modern continuations of Muslim trading in slaves.

See also ENSLAVEMENT, METHODS OF; ISLAM; JANISSARIES; LAW; MEDITERRANEAN BASIN; NORTH AFRICA; OTTOMAN EMPIRE; SLAVS; TRIBUTE, SLAVES AS; WEST AFRICA; ZANJ.

BIBLIOGRAPHY

CLARENCE-SMITH, W. GERVASE, ed. *The Economics of the Indian Ocean Slave Trade in the Nineteenth Century.* 1989.

ERDEM, HAKAN. *Slavery in the Ottoman Empire and Its Demise, 1800–1909.* 1996.

GORDON, MURRAY. *Slavery in the Arab World.* 1989.

LEWIS, BERNARD. *Race and Slavery in the Middle East: An Historical Enquiry.* 1990.

PIPES, DANIEL. *Slave Soldiers and Islam: The Genesis of a Military System.* 1981.

RICKS, THOMAS M. "Slaves and Slave Traders in the Persian Gulf, Eighteenth and Nineteenth Centuries: An Assessment." *Slavery and Abolition* 9, no. 3 (1988): 60–70.

SAVAGE, ELIZABETH, ed. *The Human Commodity: Perspectives on the Trans-Saharan Slave Trade.* 1992.

TOLEDANO, EHUD R. *The Ottoman Slave Trade and Its Suppression, 1840–1890.* 1982.

Thomas M. Ricks

Africa

In his foreword to the English translation of Claude Meillassoux's *The Anthropology of Slavery,* Paul Lovejoy reminds us that it "is perhaps common sense, however often overlooked, that the African slaves who were brought from Africa [to the Americas] were slaves before they left Africa." He also goes on to suggest that "there were certainly more slaves in Africa in the nineteenth century than there were in the Americas at any time." Building on estimates made in his *Transformations in Slavery,* Lovejoy has since given substance to these claims of widespread nineteenth-century African slavery by coauthoring with Jan Hogendorn a detailed study of slavery and its abolition in the Sokoto caliphate in northern Nigeria. According to Lovejoy and Hogendorn the Sokoto caliphate had a "huge slave population" by 1897, numbering at least 1 million—and perhaps more than 2.5 million. This slave population, it is suggested, had grown through warfare and slave raiding and was sustained by a trade in slaves "of considerable proportions." The exact scale of these activities is incalculable, but it is clear that slave raiding and payments of slaves as tribute remained important features of the slavery system in the Sokoto caliphate well into the twentieth century.

Slavery in Africa was not, of course, confined to the Sokoto caliphate. Nor was Sokoto the only system of slavery in Africa to depend on slave raiding and trafficking to sustain its growth. For example, it is clear from Meillassoux's *Anthropology of Slavery* that in the Sahelo-Sudanese region of West Africa, slavery and slave trading dated from at least the seventh century and continued to exert a powerful influence on the history of the region throughout the following thirteen hundred years. Indeed, according to Meillassoux, states of the Sahelo-Sudanese region such as Ghana and Mali were "first and foremost instruments for the supply of slaves," and from the fourteenth century onward slave trading was one of the main functions of their political and military institutions. For such states and institutions, the seizure of slaves through warfare or raiding was often a corollary of trading in slaves, a pattern that was to be repeated in other parts of Africa. In the Sudan many of the slaves were transported across the Sahara to the Mediterranean, but large numbers were also retained within the Sahel-Sudan, thereby supporting the expansion of local slave regimes. Evidence relating to the early history of slave trading in the Sahelo-Sudan is sketchy and sometimes indirect. It becomes, however, much more abundant in the nineteenth century as the scale of slavery and slave trading in the region probably grew and as European powers, with antislavery agendas, came to exert greater political control over the region.

Analysis of evidence relating to western Sudan after 1800 has led Martin Klein to highlight the critical role played by the town of Banamba as the hub of a Sahel slave trade route that ran from Timbuktu in the east to Medine and Nioro in the west and that may have delivered over ten thousand slaves to Senegalese buyers in some years in the late nineteenth century. From his analysis of the western Sudan, Klein concludes that, while the trans-Saharan traffic in slaves probably stimulated the use of slaves within the medieval Sahel-Sudan, by the nineteenth century that traffic had become "incidental to the trade within Africa." Moreover, most of the slaves taken north from the Sahel-Sudan, he argues, were by this time retained within the desert rather than transported across it. In effect, therefore, the trans-Saharan slave trade had become subordinate to slave trades within the desert and the Sahel-Sudan after 1800.

There is little doubt that slavery and slave trading preceded the arrival of Europeans along the west coast of the continent in the rest of sub-Saharan Africa. As with the trans-Saharan slave traffic, it is probable that the rise of the Atlantic slave trade and the income it helped to generate for some groups in Africa encouraged further expansion of slavery in those areas most closely associated with the export slave trade. From Senegal in the north to Benguela in the south, major

Nineteenth-century slaves on the island of Zanzibar are held in chains. [Bojan Brecelj/Corbis]

suppliers of captives for export—kings, state officials, and merchants alike—became themselves owners of large retinues of slaves. Moreover, some historians have argued that, as the export slave trade declined in the nineteenth century under external pressures, slaveholding and slave trading within West and West-Central Africa probably grew to unprecedented levels. Such claims have been the source of some debate. Even though the scale of trafficking in slaves within these regions is difficult to measure, evidence from contemporary reports and travel accounts has revealed the existence of various active slave markets within West Africa years after the Atlantic slave trade had ended. Of these, perhaps the best known is that at Salaga in modern Ghana, whose trade in slaves in the last quarter of the nineteenth century has been closely studied by Marion Johnson. As elsewhere, precise figures on slave sales at Salaga are unavailable, but it is quite possible that between 1870 and 1890 several thousand slaves a year reached the town in the trade caravans arriving there. According to Johnson, some were sold to local buyers, but many were sold on to places further afield. It is possible that levels of slave sales were greater at Salaga than at other interior markets; but there is evidence that, before Salaga's rise to prominence, slaves were regularly sold throughout Asante as well as other states in West and West-Central Africa. We also know that slaves, sometimes in the guise of contract labor, were still being shipped from Angola, Gabon, Dahomey and mainland centers to the islands in the Gulf of Guinea after 1870. Moreover, between the 1820s and 1890s a lively traffic is known to have sent many slaves to Zanzibar and Pemba Island, just off the East African coast, from the area of Lake Malawi and other places. Precise quantification of these slave trades is again impossible. But the indications are that demand for slaves within West and West-Central Africa was strong in the nineteenth century and that by 1860 as many as nineteen thousand mainland captives were sold each year in Zanzibar and Pemba Island. It is more than likely, therefore, that, as in the Sahel-Sudan, the use of slaves in other areas, and the level of internal slave trading needed to support such use, did reach unprecedented levels in this period.

We still know relatively little about the reproduction of slaves under coerced labor regimes in Africa (compared to the slave systems of the Americas) and thus little about how much such regimes depended on regular supplies of new slaves. European powers seeking to destroy slave regimes in Africa after 1870 believed that it was necessary to curb slave trafficking; this suggests that, as in much of the Americas, slave trading was an essential aspect of African systems of institutionalized slavery. In studying African slavery, historians have often emphasized lineage systems, whereby slaves were absorbed into the households of their owners. To the extent that such systems assimilated slaves, the continued existence of slavery rested on supplies of new captives, whether by capture or by purchase through trade. By largely eliminating raiding as a direct source of slaves, colonialism by Europeans was in time to make African slavery vulnerable to interdiction through suppression of slave trafficking.

Students of African slavery have also emphasized female slavery, and in particular the roles of women and pubescent girls as concubines and household servants in Muslim societies. That there was a strong demand for females, especially young women, in some parts of Africa is indicated by patterns of the prices prevailing in the trade. Research has shown that, while it is unlikely that slave raids produced far more males than females, market prices of females aged thirty or less were normally significantly higher than those of males of similar ages in the western and central Sudan in the nineteenth century. Moreover, the highest prices for females and the greatest age-specific differentials were to be found in the case of pubescent girls. In this respect, price patterns for slaves in Sudanese markets were similar to those in North Africa but differed from those along the Atlantic coast of Africa where, during the era of the slave export trade to America, prices of male slaves were usually higher than those of females. Such market differentials in prices encouraged slave dealers in central Sudan to move adult male slaves south while retaining females for local sale or for shipment north across or into the desert. Some integration of internal and external markets for slaves within West Africa may, therefore, have occurred by the early nineteenth century, if not earlier.

It would be misleading, however, to attribute the high price of female slaves in these African markets purely to their role as providers of sexual or other personal services to their owners. Recent literature has reminded us that slaves of both sexes were, in fact, employed in a wide range of activities in Africa and that the range of tasks performed by slaves may have expanded from the late eighteenth century onward. It is clear, for example, that large numbers of male slaves served as soldiers in state armies and that, in some cases, such slaves rose to positions of command. Insofar as warfare was an important source of slaves as Meillassoux reminds us, slave soldiers were instruments in the continuing regeneration of coercive labor regimes in Africa. Equally importantly, however, it is evident that, as in the Americas, in many parts of Africa male and female slaves were central to production processes and to the commercialization and diversification of economic activity. Thus, for instance, we know that in the nineteenth century slaves were employed to produce gum in Senegal, gold in Asante, kola and foodstuffs in the Sudan, salt in the desert and Sahel, palm oil in the Bights of Benin and Biafra, ivory and wild rubber in West-Central Africa, and cloves and grain in East Africa. Local and regional slave trades were, in part, supported by such activities.

The units of production upon which slaves were employed in commercial activities were generally smaller than those that characterized sugar production in the West Indies under slavery. But large-scale units of production employing slaves were not unknown in both West and East Africa. Much of the output of these slave-based activities was consumed locally or was exchanged between regions or societies within Africa. But in some cases, notably where regions had earlier been heavily involved in selling slaves to Europeans or Muslims in exchange for imported goods, the expansion and diversification of local slave-based activities was motivated by the desire of commercial and political elites to sustain a capacity to import European goods. The Efik of Biafra and the Ovimbundu of central Angola, for example, made the transition in the nineteenth century from slave exporters to exporters of slave-produced goods. Moreover, these shifting patterns of activity seem often to have depended heavily on changing external markets for African goods and on imports of European and Muslim capital and credit. It is a sad fact, therefore, that, while advocates of abolition of the slave trade from Africa sometimes sought to remind their audience that the continent had great commercial potential in pursuits other than slaving, the development of such potential in the nineteenth century probably contributed to an expansion and transformation of patterns of slaveholding and slave trading across much of Africa itself.

See also AFRICA; EAST AFRICA; NORTH AFRICA; WEST AFRICA.

BIBLIOGRAPHY

COOPER, FREDERICK. *Plantation Slavery on the East African Coast.* 1977.

ELTIS, DAVID. *Economic Growth and the Ending of the Transatlantic Slave Trade.* 1987.

HEYWOOD, LINDA M. "Slavery and Forced Labor in the Changing Political Economy of Central Angola, 1850–1949." In *The End of Slavery in Africa,* edited by Suzanne Miers and Richard Roberts. 1988.

JOHNSON, MARION. "The Slaves of Salaga." *Journal of African History* 27 (1986): 341–362.

KLEIN, MARTIN A. "The Slave Trade in the Western Sudan during the Nineteenth Century." In *The Human Commodity: Perspectives on the Trans-Saharan Slave Trade,* edited by Elizabeth Savage. 1992.

LOVEJOY, PAUL E. *Transformations in Slavery.* 1982.

LOVEJOY, PAUL E., and JAN S. HOGENDORN. *Slow Death for Slavery: The Course of Abolition in Northern Nigeria, 1897–1936.* 1993.

LOVEJOY, PAUL E., and DAVID RICHARDSON. "Competing Markets for Male and Female Slaves: Prices in the Interior of West Africa, 1780–1850." *International Journal of African Historical Studies* 28, no. 2 (1995): 261–293.

MANNING, PATRICK. *Slavery and African Life: Occidental, Oriental and African Slave Trades.* 1990.

MEILLASSOUX, CLAUDE. *The Anthropology of Slavery: The Womb of Iron and Gold.* Translated by Alide Dasnois. 1991.

David Richardson

Transatlantic

From the fifteenth to the nineteenth centuries the roughly twelve million slaves shipped from Africa and the roughly ten and a half million who arrived in the Americas constituted the largest intercontinental migration then known to the world. The Atlantic was the first ocean in the history of the world to be regularly crossed, and the lands that bordered it came to have a common history. Slavery was a central feature of this emergent Atlantic system. It was the cornerstone of a vast Atlantic labor market, and at the heart of Atlantic slavery was the slave trade, a vast co-ordinated system for the coerced migration of Africans often from homelands hundreds of miles in the interior of the continent to virtually every corner of the Americas. Before 1820 perhaps three times as many enslaved Africans crossed the Atlantic as Europeans. Both Europeans and Africans participated in the trade, and four continents were deeply influenced by it.

The slave trade was a constantly changing process over four centuries, always responding to varying sources of supply, fluctuating demand, and shifting political, social and economic imperatives felt throughout the Atlantic system. The trade began about the mid-fifteenth century with slaves being exported from the African coast to various Atlantic islands (particularly the Canaries and Madeiras), São Tomé, and Europe. The first African slaves to reach the New World arrived in Hispaniola at the beginning of the sixteenth century. Spanish America began receiving Africans on a regular basis in the second quarter of the sixteenth century; and by the second half of the century, Spanish America and Brazil were importing about three-quarters of the slaves leaving Africa. The seventeenth century saw a striking increase in transatlantic slaving, with the emergence of new slave markets in the Caribbean; about 1.5 million Africans reached the Americas between 1600 and 1699. But by far the most massive increase in the Atlantic slave trade occurred during the eighteenth century, as Brazil continued to be a major market and as demand in the Caribbean islands pushed its volume to unprecedented levels. Between 1700 and 1810 over 6 million slaves, or about 60 percent of the overall number, reached the Americas; more than half went to the Caribbean. Despite its long and tortuous history, the Atlantic slave trade was primarily an eighteenth-century phenomenon.

But the slave trade lasted well into the nineteenth century; just as the ghastly traffic was born gradually, so it died gradually. The Danish were the first Europeans to abolish the trade, in 1805; the British and North American abolition acts took effect three years later. During the Spanish American wars of independence, attempts to abolish the trade occurred in Venezuela and Mexico in 1810, in Chile in 1811, and in Buenos Aires in 1812. But a definitive end to slave trading awaited the establishment of republican governments in the 1820s and increased British pressure to outlaw the trade. Nevertheless, formal abolition rarely meant an end of the traffic: Spain, Portugal, France, the United States, and Brazil were all lax in enforcing their own legislation. Even after international agreements were made to end the trade in the 1830s and 1840s, an active clandestine commerce sustained transatlantic and intra-American transfers of slaves until the 1870s. The main destinations were the coffee zones of Brazil and the sugar plantations of Cuba. From 1811 to 1870 the best estimate is that about 2 million Africans landed in the Americas, with Brazil the largest importer at about 60 percent and Cuba the next most important at about 30 percent. During the nineteenth century, various anti–slave-trade squadrons intercepted illegal slavers and dropped off the slaves "recaptured" from them usually in Sierra Leone or Liberia. This diversion of the nineteenth-century slave trade back to Africa is thought to have involved about 160,000 captives.

For most of its history, the slave trade was not considered morally reprehensible but was rather a routine commercial fact. Not until the late eighteenth century did the system arouse any real protest. The extraordinary waste of life associated with the slave trade was one reason it was targeted. Regulations of the traffic— such as Britain's Dolben's Act of 1788, which was the first major legislated attack by that nation on slave-ship mortality—attempted to curtail losses by limiting the number of slaves that could be carried per tonnage of ships. But what inspired people to focus on the trade as an inhumane and inefficient system were developments in sectarian and evangelical Protestantism. In its origin, the movement to outlaw the slave trade was overwhelmingly religious in character.

The participants in the Atlantic slave system ranged from Arabs to Portuguese, Asante to Italians, English to Swedes, Americans to Spaniards, and Danes to Yoruba. Jewish involvement in the slave trade, which some allege to have been vital, was in fact minimal. Christians, pagans, and Muslims initiated the European slave trades. The trading companies that came to dominate the Atlantic slave trade in the seventeenth century were exclusive monopolies, organized and headed by Christian rulers. Among private traders who ran the trade in the eighteenth century, Jews were marginal. Only in the Dutch slave trade and associated Portuguese slaving in the seventeenth century did Jews play a limited role. In the four most substantial Atlantic slave trades—the British and French flows of the late seventeenth and eighteenth centuries and the Brazilian and Cuban trades of the eighteenth and nineteenth centuries—Jews played almost no role.

The efficiency of the Atlantic slave trade changed dramatically over time. Early on, it might take nearly three years to complete a round-trip slave voyage; by the trade's end, some slave vessels took just three months to complete their voyages. In the early sixteenth century, the average Middle Passage (the leg from Africa to the Americas) lasted two to three months; three centuries later, slave ships routinely crossed to Bahia in less than three weeks and to Cuba in five. Shipping productivity, however, could fall as well as rise. One downturn occurred from the first to the third quarter of the eighteenth century when growing European demand exceeded African supply and almost doubled the time spent acquiring slaves on the African coast. Efficiency gains were most marked in the nineteenth century, when the transoceanic costs of transporting slaves declined significantly.

The profitability of the slave trade has aroused much controversy. Individual European merchants certainly grew rich on slaving profits, but returns varied greatly depending on loading rates of slaves in Africa, mortality in the Middle Passage, and payment recovery rates in the Americas. Annual returns from some British slaving voyages averaged about 8 to 10 percent, a respectable though by no means spectacular level of profit. Capital accrued through the slave trade was probably not crucial to the financing of the British or French or New England industrial expansions, although it certainly helped, directly and indirectly, to enrich important sections of those mercantile societies and the multiplier effects were important on key sectors of the broader economies.

Why did Africa become the source of the slaves carried in the trade? Part of the answer resides in the demographic catastrophe that occurred in the Americas. As Europeans invaded the New World, roughly ninety percent of native Americans died within the first century of contact. As a result, labor in the Americas was in short supply and demand could not be met from indigenous populations. Another part of the answer lies in the unwillingness of most Europeans to do the kind of labor that was required in the Americas. Essentially, it was cheaper to buy slaves and ship them to America than to pay wages to attract free laborers—and, in any case, European free laborers were reluctant to migrate to the New World in adequate numbers. It would certainly have been cheaper to enslave Europeans and ship them direct to the New World rather than carry people from the much more distant Africa, but by the early modern era nobody seriously proposed enslaving large numbers of Western Europeans. Thus, the final part of the explanation must be sought within Africa itself. Fortunately for Europeans and tragically for many Africans, West and Central Africa offered a ready supply of affordable, if not cheap, slave labor. Long before the earliest Portuguese voyages to West Africa, Arab and Berber merchants had constructed a slave trade across the Sahara desert that delivered hundreds of thousands of black slaves to North Africa, the Mediterranean, and the Persian Gulf. Although slavery in Africa rarely

entailed single-minded exploitation of labor for profit, most African states and societies knew a variety of forms of servitude and had developed sophisticated methods for recruiting captives and bartering slaves. Europeans tapped into these already-existing trading networks, even as they revolutionized them with their demand, much larger than domestic and Saharan markets.

For all these reasons, the African slave trade became an indispensable part of the European expansion and settlement of the New World. Most Atlantic ports in Western Europe, Africa, and the Americas participated in the business at some time or another. All the major European powers with an Atlantic outlet played a role in the trade. Britain was the major player, accounting for twice as many slave voyages as its nearest rival, France. Liverpool became the most successful port of the eighteenth-century Atlantic world, owing in part at least to its proximity to the emerging cotton textile industry in Lancashire, and it launched more

Europeans carry out slave-trading activities along the coast of Africa in the late eighteenth century. [Library of Congress/ Corbis]

transatlantic slaving voyages than any other city. It was followed closely by London and Bristol. Nantes was the fourth most important European port on the basis of slave trading voyages accomplished; other significant French ports were La Rochelle, Le Havre, Bordeaux, and Saint-Malo. Ownership of slave vessels tended to be widely distributed; small investors were quite numerous. The reasons for British preeminence lay in the efficiency of its shipping: British slavers carried more slaves per crew member and per ton, and their voyages were faster than those of other West European slave traders. A large proportion of slaving voyages—at least a third and probably more—originated in the Americas, not Europe. Rio de Janeiro, Salvador in Bahia (Brazil), Havana in Cuba, Newport in Rhode Island, and Bridgetown in Barbados were all prominent ports of departure for transatlantic slaving voyages. The notion of a triangular trade with Europe as the only departure point is inaccurate.

Not all regions of West and Central Africa participated equally in the trade. The largest supplier was West-Central Africa, a large region south of the equator and incorporating sites near the mouth of the Zaire river as well as the Portuguese towns of Luanda and Benguela, which provided about 40 percent of the slaves entering the Atlantic trade. West Africa accounted for most of the other Africans sent across the Atlantic, with three regions dominant: the Bight of Benin, otherwise and appropriately known as the Slave Coast, contributed about 22 percent of the Africans to the trade; the Bight of Biafra another 15 percent; and the Gold Coast 11 percent. The Windward Coast and Senegambia together supplied about 9 percent. In general, the slave trade of each African region was heavily centered at one, two, or possibly three principal ports. Ouidah on the Slave Coast may well have supplied more than a million slaves to the trade, making it probably the single most important port for slaves in sub-Saharan Africa; Cabinda, Benguela, and Luanda were the principal ports of West-Central Africa, and all three were in the top five African ports for embarking slaves; Bonny and Calabar accounted for about four-fifths of the slaves leaving the Bight of Biafra; and three-quarters of the Africans departing the Gold Coast went from either Cape Coast Castle or Anomabu.

Trading on the African coast was a partnership between African rulers and merchants and European ship captains and factors. Europeans had to adapt to established West African patterns of trade. Africans retained sovereignty over European forts and factories, collected customs dues and business fees, and organized systems of delivery and marketing. Europeans found the disease environment of the African littoral lethal; as a result, they rarely attempted colonization.

Except for a few trading posts, European establishments on the African mainland did not exist; permanent bases were confined to islands. Even small African polities could lay siege to the largest forts, although in general Europeans and Africans worked out relationships that, if uneasy, were at least not disruptive. Europeans possessed certain advantages in their dealings with Africans, but they could not easily dictate to native suppliers; instead, they entered into an alliance with them. African preferences—for certain types of textiles, for example—had to be met. Prices for slaves rose rapidly in Africa, faster than in the Americas. Europeans were forced to pay more and more goods and cash for the slaves they bought. Over time, the terms of trade shifted in favor of Africa.

The destinations of African slaves who ventured into the Atlantic were extraordinarily wide-ranging. American destinations encompassed a much wider span of landscapes, climates, and environments than the coastline of West and West-Central Africa. Brazil was the largest single recipient of Africans in the Atlantic slave trade, accounting for about 40 percent. The Caribbean—divided into British, French, Spanish, Dutch, and Danish components—was the most important regional destination, for it received about 45 percent of the imported slaves. Of far less numerical significance, and in declining order of importance, were Spanish America, North America (which received about 5 percent of the slaves delivered), and the Old World. Another way to think about destinations is to note that about 70 percent of all the Africans who survived the Atlantic voyages landed in a sugar colony. Europe's sweet tooth largely determined the extent, the timing, and the distribution of the Atlantic slave trade. The eighteenth century, the slave trade's peak, was when the output of sugar grew most dramatically.

The belief that men predominated among slaves carried across the Atlantic is false. To be sure, men were the largest single category of Africans to cross the Atlantic, but they were in fact a minority, outnumbered collectively by women, boys, and girls, who made up just over half (51 percent) of transported Africans. Furthermore, the proportion of both boys and girls increased over time. The rise in the percentage of children entering the trade was particularly steep in the nineteenth century. One explanation for the sharp increase in the numbers of children, who were lower-valued slaves, is the significant decline in shipping costs. Higher prices for slaves in the Americas and lower costs of transportation across the Atlantic made it possible to sell children profitably. Whatever the reason, not only were African men in the minority overall in the trade, their relative share of slave shipments declined over time as children took their place. Compared with the age and sex structure of indentured servant and convict trades, the slave trade comprised a remarkably large number of women and children. In fact, a larger share of children left Africa than left Europe. The sex and age ratios of the Atlantic slave trade were comparable to free, not contractual, migrant flows.

The proportion of women varied quite markedly both between African regions of embarkation and American regions of arrival and over time. From the perspective of African regions, the ratio of male to female slaves varied from about 75:25 in upper Guinea to about 55:45 at the Bight of Biafra. Calculated by American regions, much larger shares of women were carried to the British areas than elsewhere, with women and men arriving in almost equal numbers in early Barbados and Jamaica, whereas between two and three times more men than women arrived in Cuba and in Brazil. Over time, the share of women among African arrivals fell uniformly across their African region of origin. From one region to the next, the proportion of women dropped by well over 50 percent from the seventeenth to the nineteenth centuries. After 1810 women constituted a quite small proportion of Africans from every coastal region.

The proportions of children also fluctuated widely. West-Central Africa, and to a lesser extent Upper Guinea and the Bight of Benin, exported more children than other African regions. After 1810 over half of those leaving South-East Africa and West-Central Africa and just under half of those from Upper Guinea were children. The number of children carried in the Atlantic slave trade rose in all regions, but it was most pronounced at the most northerly and southerly extremes of the African continent. From the perspective of receiving regions, South-Central Brazil imported the most children, accounting for half of all arriving Africans; Cuba received 38 percent, Bahia 35 percent, and the French Caribbean and North America about 25 percent. At the other extreme, only about 10 percent of the slaves who arrived in the British Caribbean were children.

Mortality in the Atlantic slave trade averaged about 13 percent over all. In other words, of the roughly 12 million shipped, about 1.5 million people died in the Atlantic crossing. The average for the trade as a whole masks significant changes over time. Slave mortality in the Atlantic crossing tended to decline after 1700 as a result of technical and organizational changes in the trade. In the late eighteenth century, the British appear to have been the most efficient in keeping slaves alive. Despite the overall decline, mortality rates on board slave ships both for captives and crews remained much higher than for other contemporary oceanic migrations. Mortality rates were highly unpredictable between one voyage and the next. Very

high mortality rates tended to be associated with unexpectedly long voyages or with unusual outbreaks of disease. Dehydration seems to have been the major cause of death. Outbreaks of smallpox and measles were exceptional on voyages; more common were dysentary, vomiting, and sweating, all of which were not deadly in themselves but caused severe dehydration, which was.

Average mortality rates also mask considerable variations among African regions. In general, mortality owed more to pre-embarkation experiences in Africa than to shipboard mistreatment. In spite of the horrific images like the sketch of the slave ship *Brookes,* showing slaves packed together like sardines, little apparent connection existed between dense overcrowding and mortality rates. Rather, mortality varied markedly according to African region of origin, suggesting that malnutrition, intestinal disorders stemming from changes in diet, and diseases contracted by slaves moving into new epidemiological conditions were critical in determining death rates. Ships from the Bight of Biafra had by far the worst mortality records and ships from West-Central Africa the best.

Mortality in the whole enslavement process, rather than just the Middle Passage, was staggering. One 1840 estimate of mortality losses—from original seizure in Africa through forced march to the coast and detention in shoreside barracoons, the Middle Passage itself, to landing and "seasoning" in the New World—reckoned a 70 percent loss of life. By this estimate, the Middle Passage accounted for 18 percent of the deaths, while 72 percent occurred within Africa. A modern study on the Angola trade comes to roughly similar conclusions. For every 100 people seized in the Angolan interior, about 64 would have arrived six months later at the coast. After a month spent in the barracoons, only about 57 would have embarked. An average Middle Passage to Brazil delivered about 51 Africans alive. Deaths during full "seasoning" in the New World—about four years—left only about thirty alive. The Angolan trade may have been an extreme case, in part because of the lengthy march from interior to coast, the longest of any African region. In addition, Brazil had an extremely high rate of seasoning deaths. But whatever the African or New World region, slaves were in much greater risk of death on the march to the coast, in the coastal barracoons, in their loading, and during their first few years in the New World than during an average Atlantic crossing.

Whatever the scale of the mortality, the Middle Passage was unquestionably a traumatic event. Loading was often a protracted affair: in shore trade, a vessel might pick up slaves at a number of forts and factories; in ship trade, the captain would more than likely drop anchor at various points along the coast and either send boats ashore or invite canoes to approach the ship in order to put together a full cargo. The typical duration of trading by slave vessels ranged from four to six months along the Windward Coast to six to ten months on the Gold Coast. In many places, slaves were purchased singly or in pairs, rather than by the dozen or the score. A few days before embarkation, the slaves usually had their heads shaved. They were often branded with their owner's initials and were inspected to ensure physical suitability. Olaudah Equiano, an enslaved Igbo transported to Barbados and then Virginia and eventually freed, recalled how, when he was first carried on board ship, he "was immediately handled, and tossed up, to see if I were sound." Equiano vividly recalled his terror: "When I looked round the ship too, and saw a large furnace or copper boiling, and a multitude of black people of every description chained together, every one of their countenance expressing dejection and sorrow, I no longer doubted of my fate; and, quite overpowered with horror and anguish, I fell motionless on the deck and fainted." The slaves were usually stripped naked, apparently to facilitate cleanliness, were chained in pairs, and segregated by sex in holds. The space between the decks averaged four to five feet. The effects of this close confinement, stench, and general despair led many slaves, like Equiano, to avoid food and wish for death.

No specialized slave fleets existed. Slave vessels were drawn from the regular merchant marine and transported a varied cargo. As a result, vessels clearing for Africa often had temporary platforms to accommodate slaves that were then removed on the next leg of the journey. During the eighteenth century, British slaving vessels averaged about a hundred tons, although the size increased later in the century. Brigs and snows, which were two-masted, middling-sized craft, were the most popular slaving vessels. American slavers tended to use smaller craft, often sloops and schooners. The average number of slaves on board a ship as it left Africa was about 330, and 290 when it arrived in the Americas, but cargo size varied considerably from one African region to another. Ships usually carried twice as many slaves from West-Central Africa than from Senegambia or the Windward Coast. Over time, ships tended to become larger and more specialized, as merchants responded to the need for speed and bulk. In the 1770s, slave captains were the first to introduce copper sheathing on the hulls of their vessels. This innovation reduced the costs of maintenance and increased the speed of ships.

Slavers were well armed, and their crews were sixty percent larger than on regular merchant ships. Feeding, supervising, nursing, and, most important, guarding slaves required many hands: a rule of thumb was

A slave revolt breaks out aboard an eighteenth-century slave ship. [Corbis-Bettmann]

one sailor for every ten to fifteen slaves. Security concerns certainly merited the presence of a large crew, for one on-board slave rebellion occurred every four and a half years (or every fifty-five voyages) in the Rhode Island trade; while the British trade saw a slave rebellion every two years. Attacks on slave vessels by shore-based Africans and on-board slave rebellions (most of which occurred at the port of lading or within a week of setting sail) were not randomly distributed by region. Rather, such incidents were much more likely to occur on ships leaving Senegambia than on ships leaving the Niger Delta or Angola. What explains these regional differences is not yet apparent, but the effects seem transparent. The regions with the strongest records of resistance were the regions with the smallest number of slave departures.

Most African regions funneled a majority of their forced emigrants to a single region in the Americas. Thus, three-quarters of those leaving Southeast Africa went to South-Central Brazil; two of three Africans from the Bight of Biafra left for the British Caribbean; 60 percent of the Bight of Benin's forced emigrants went to Bahia; half of those leaving Senegambia went to the French Caribbean; half of West-Central Africa's forced emigrants went to South Brazil; and half of those leaving the Gold Cost and Windward Coast went to the British Caribbean. To be sure, all the regions of Africa sent slaves to almost all the regions of the Americas, but people tended to flow in one dominant channel, with, in some cases, a subsidiary stream.

Equally regular patterns emerge when the transatlantic links are examined from the perspective of American regions of disembarkation. What stands out are two extremes. First, the two main regions of Brazil—Bahia and Rio de Janeiro—drew heavily on a single region of Africa. In Bahia's case about nine in ten Africans came from the Bight of Benin; in South-Central Brazil about eight in ten came from Angola and other West-Central African ports. Second, at the other extreme, was much of the Caribbean and North America, with no dominant African provenance zone. No region of Africa, for example, supplied more than about 30 percent of arrivals to either Cuba, Barbados, Martinique, Guadaloupe, or the Danish islands. Between the two extremes were some major destinations that received about half of their arrivals from one African coastal region: St. Domingue from West-Central Africa, the British Leeward Islands from the Bight of Biafra, and the Guyanas and Suriname from the Gold Coast. In each of these American destinations—from St. Domingue to Suriname—the other half of their African influx came from a number of regions. Brazil, then, was exceptional in drawing slaves heavily from one region, while most other parts of the Americas drew on a wider mix of African peoples, even if in some cases up to half of slaves came from one region.

These broad summaries of aggregate patterns disguise marked shifts over time. A dynamic, diasporic approach reveals that slaves coming to any one New World region originated from a changing series of African coastal regions. Even within a single African coastal region, marked shifts often occurred in the peoples forcibly expelled. The supply of slaves to the Bight of Benin, for example, changed drastically from the eighteenth to the nineteenth centuries. Down to the late eighteenth century, when the Oyo (Yoruba) were principal suppliers of slaves to the Slave Coast, peoples from the north and west of Oyo—Nupe, Borgu, Hausa, and various Ewe-speaking peoples—were readily available. In the nineteenth century, after the collapse of the Oyo empire, Yoruba-speaking peoples dominated the flow leaving Bight of Benin ports, while the emergence of the Sokoto caliphate in Hausa regions near the Sahara generated a growing secondary stream of slaves from the Central Sudan. By

the early nineteenth century, at least two demographically distinct streams channeled slaves to the Bight of Benin: one brought males from the distant interior to the coast and another siphoned off men, women, and children from the coast itself. Thus it is somewhat misleading to say that Bahia received virtually all its slaves from the Bight of Benin, the ports of embarkation there imply some uniformity over time in the captives' origins in the interior.

African ports drew on a wider range of hinterlands as the volume of slaving grew, which again increased the diversity of people shipped across the Atlantic. For example, slaving in West-Central Africa came to cover a wider range of coastline and drew on an area extending hundreds of kilometers from the coast, a region of 2.5 million square kilometers, or an area larger than the United States east of the Mississippi River. At least three, sometimes four, distinct commercial networks drew slaves from this vast area toward the Atlantic shores. The mix of peoples flowing from that region grew more, not less, heterogeneous. Different ports within a single coastal region might draw upon distinct and fluctuating streams of peoples. Thus, along the early nineteenth-century Bight of Biafra coast, Igbo-speakers dominated slaves shipped from Bonny, Ibibio-speakers comprised 40 percent of slaves shipped from Old Calabar, and slaves from much further inland—Nupe, Kakanda, and Hausa, for example—formed between 5 and 25 percent of the exported slaves from various Biafran ports. Thus, although some Africans in the New World shared common languages and cultural backgrounds that helped them survive in a hostile setting, most New World slaves embarked in situations of extraordinary ethnic diversity.

That Africans drew on their homeland cultural resources even as their forced migration to the New World denied them so much illuminates the agency that slaves retained even within constraints of the Atlantic slave trade. African strategies were evident in the differential regional participation in the trade, the varied composition slave shipments from each region, and the contrasting regional rates of rebellions. The ability of Africans to mold the structure of the slave trade should not be underestimated. But most Africans involved in slaving were unwilling participants at the mercy of forces shaping the early modern Atlantic world. These forces included the technology of shipping, efficiency gains made in the organization of trade, the horrendous mortality levels, and the transatlantic connections that drew slaves from particular regions of Africa to specific American regions. In the final analysis, decisions about how the trade was conducted, who entered it, where slaves boarded and landed, and when the repugnant traffic began and ended arose from complex exchanges between Europeans, Americans, and Africans. The slave trade, in short and in sum, was part of an increasingly interconnected Atlantic world.

See also ABOLITION AND ANTISLAVERY MOVEMENTS; BRAZIL; CARIBBEAN REGION; CENTRAL AFRICA; CUBA; UNITED STATES; WEST AFRICA.

BIBLIOGRAPHY

COHN, RAYMOND L. "Maritime Mortality in the Eighteenth and Nineteenth Centuries: A Survey." *International Journal of Maritime History* 1 (1989): 159–191.

COUGHTRY, JAY. *The Notorious Triangle: Rhode Island and the African Slave Trade, 1700–1807.* 1981.

CURTIN, PHILIP D. *The Atlantic Slave Trade: A Census.* 1969.

ELTIS, DAVID. *Economic Growth and the Ending of the Transatlantic Slave Trade.* 1987.

ELTIS, DAVID, and STANLEY L. ENGERMAN. "Was the Slave Trade Dominated by Men?" *Journal of Interdisciplinary History* 23 (1992): 237–257.

———. "Fluctuations in Sex and Age Ratios in the Transatlantic Slave Trade, 1663–1864." *Economic History Review* 46 (1993): 308–323.

ELTIS, DAVID, and DAVID RICHARDSON. "Productivity in the Transatlantic Slave Trade." *Explorations in Economic History* 32 (1995): 465–484.

———, eds. *Routes to Slavery: Direction, Ethnicity and Mortality in the Transatlantic Slave Trade.* 1997.

HAINES, ROBIN, RALPH SHLOMOWITZ, and LANCE BRENNAN. "Maritime Mortality Revisited." *International Journal of Maritime History* 13 (1996): 133–172.

HOGENDORN, JAN. "Economic Modelling of Price Differences in the Slave Trade between the Central Sudan and the Coast." *Slavery and Abolition* 17 (1996): 209–222.

INIKORI, JOSEPH E., and STANLEY L. ENGERMAN, eds. *The Atlantic Slave Trade: Effects on Economies, Societies, and Peoples in Africa, the Americas, and Europe.* 1992.

KLEIN, HERBERT S. *The Middle Passage: Comparative Studies in the Atlantic Slave Trade.* 1978.

LOVEJOY, PAUL E. "The Volume of the Atlantic Slave Trade: A Synthesis." *Journal of African History* 23 (1982): 473–501.

McGOWAN, WINSTON. "African Resistance to the Atlantic Slave Trade in West Africa." *Slavery and Abolition* 11 (1990): 5–29.

MILLER, JOSEPH C. *Way of Death: Merchant Capitalism and the Angolan Slave Trade, 1730–1830.* 1988.

POSTMA, JOHANNES M. *The Dutch in the Atlantic Slave Trade, 1600–1815.* 1990.

RAWLEY, JAMES A. *The Transatlantic Slave Trade: A History.* 1981.

REYNOLDS, EDWARD. *Stand the Storm: A History of the Atlantic Slave Trade.* 1985.

RICHARDSON, DAVID, ed. *Bristol, Africa and the Eighteenth-Century Slave Trade to America.* 4 vols. 1986–1996.

STECKEL, RICHARD H., and RICHARD A. JENSEN. "New Evidence on the Causes of Slave and Crew Mortality in the Transatlantic Slave Trade." *Journal of Economic History* 46 (1986): 57–77.

THOMAS, HUGH. *The Slave Trade: The Story of the Atlantic Slave Trade, 1440–1870.* 1997.

THORNTON, JOHN. *Africa and Africans in the Making of the Atlantic World, 1400–1680.* 1992.

Philip D. Morgan

United States

Internal slave trading was widespread in the Americas but was particularly prevalent in the United States after the African slave trade was outlawed in 1808. However, the primary cause of the growth of the domestic slave trade was a large increase in cotton production in the early decades of the century. This development produced a huge demand for slaves, as farmers in newer regions of the South and West turned for their labor to the older, less prosperous states, particularly Virginia and Maryland, where agriculture was less productive and slaves were abundant and relatively inexpensive. The result was the emergence of a large-scale internal trade that amply supplied the labor needs of the lower South until the Civil War.

The day-to-day operations of this traffic began as a rule in small towns and rural districts of slave-exporting areas, which eventually included such states as Kentucky, Tennessee, and Missouri. The initial acquisition of slaves was the work of local dealers who induced slaveowners to part with their human property for ready cash. In the 1830s, for example, fifteen or more large buyers were active in Cambridge, Maryland, along with many petty traders, agents, and helpers. Dealers were particularly abundant on Maryland's eastern shore, wrote historian Frederic Bancroft in *Slave Trading in the Old South* (1931), because nowhere else were slaves so cheap; slaves purchased in that part of the state could be sold in the deep South for twice their original purchase price.

Transfers of slaves within states were also common, and, as economic or demographic conditions changed, sections of states became net slave exporters, whereas other sections were net buyers. The origins of transferred slaves thus varied over the years in response to changing conditions. As a British traveler, J. S. Buckingham, explained in *The Slave States of America* (1842), Virginia slaves were being transferred from places "where their labour is not in demand, to the rising states and territories, in which labour is in request." Thus, he added, in the Augusta [Georgia] and Washington newspapers, "every day are to be seen advertisements offering 'Cash for Likely negroes.'"

Slave buyers made ample use of newspaper advertisements, giving posterity insights into their aims

Slave buyers bid on a family placed on the auction block in Virginia. [Leonard de Selva/Corbis]

and methods. Often employing tiny engravings of slaves to attract the attention of the slaveholding public, these notices typically contained such information as the ages and genders of the slaves desired, the preferred method of payment (normally cash), the buyer's name or firm, and the hotel, tavern, or other location where he carried on his business. These advertisements reveal that the slaves most in demand were the young and the very young, with a clear preference for males and women of reproductive age who might contribute both labor and children to planters in slave-buying areas. Typical of advertisements placed in newspapers were the following, published by Harriet Beecher Stowe in *The Key to Uncle Tom's Cabin* (1852), the first from the *Daily Virginian* of Lynchburg, the second from the *Natchez Courier* of Mississippi:

Negroes Wanted

The subscriber, having located in Lynchburg, is giving the highest cash prices for negroes between the ages of 10 and 30 years. Those having negroes for sale may find it to their interest to call on him at the Washington Hotel, Lynchburg, or address him by letter. All communications will receive prompt attention.

J. B. McLendon

Negroes

The undersigned would respectfully state to the public that he has leased the stand in the Forks of the Road, near Natchez, for a term of years, and that he intends to keep a large lot of NEGROES on hand during the years. He will sell as low or lower than any other trader at this place or in New Orleans. He has just arrived from Virginia with a very likely lot of Field Men and Women; also House Servants, three Cooks, and a Carpenter. Call and see. . . .

Natchez, Sept. 28, 1852.   *Thomas G. James*

After a local trader had bought a collection of slaves, driven them to a major trading center, and there disposed of them by sale, his erstwhile property underwent additional misery, insults, and distress before setting out on yet another journey to a distant and unknown place. Prominent among such centers of abuse and mistreatment was the city of Washington, D. C., where large-scale slave trading was the result of the city's favorable location in the heart of the most active slave-exporting region, as well as its proximity to Alexandria, then a major port and prime location for initiating both coastwise and overland slave shipments. Washington's involvement in the trade aroused constant disapproval until the business was finally banned in the District of Columbia as part of the Compromise of 1850. Most distasteful to its critics were the many manifestations of slave trading in and about the District: gangs of chained or bound slaves driven through city streets, the use of private slave pens and even public prisons for housing slaves, the tragic spectacle of public auctions, incessant slave advertising, and, perhaps most offensive, the federal government's open sanctioning of slave trading in the nation's capital. As the educator and congressmen Horace Mann pointed out in the House of Representatives in 1849, "By authority of Congress, the city of Washington is the Congo of America."

Slaves were sent to their destinations in a variety of ways. Some were transported down the Ohio, Missouri, and Mississippi Rivers on flat boats and river steamers. Many thousands more were marched overland in slave gangs or "coffles" (from Arabic, *qafilah*, a caravan). This was the most grueling form of travel, since distances were often great and the danger of flight or rebellion required a burdensome use of chains and manacles. Finally, many slaves were shipped by sea from East Coast ports to places like Mobile, New Orleans, and Galveston. Some slave-trading firms had specially constructed ships for transporting slaves by sea. Typical cargoes consisted of perhaps 150 slaves, though some ships carried 200 or more. Overloading and long voyages sometimes brought illness or death, but most slaves who experienced a coastal voyage arrived at their destinations in much better condition than those brought from Africa. Nevertheless, observers sometimes encountered conditions on U.S. coastal ships resembling those of the African trade. A British traveler, Basil Hall, who had witnessed conditions on a slave ship at Rio de Janeiro, later described a brig docked in New Orleans after arriving from Baltimore with more than 200 slaves. "Her decks," he wrote in *Travels in North America* (1829), "presented a scene which forcibly reminded me of Rio de Janeiro. In the one case, however, the slaves were brought from the savage regions of Africa; in the other, from the very heart of a free country. To the poor negro the distinction is probably no great matter!"

How many slaves experienced the internal trade? Historians Herbert Gutman and Richard Sutch, in *Reckoning with Slavery* (1976), calculated that between 1790 and 1860 over a million slaves were taken across state borders by the traffic, constituting one of the largest forced migrations in history. This figure, however, omits slaves transferred within states, and thus their estimate does not tell the full story.

The traffic had grim consequences: It broke up countless families. It encouraged kidnapping and the enslavement of free people. It was a source of fear and anxiety among slaves of all ages. High slave prices encouraged sexual manipulation, including the granting of special favors to prolific women, involuntary mating based on favorable physical attributes, and the hiring of "stockmen" or studs to improve the quality of potential property. Defenders of slavery often denied the existence of slave breeding, but many documents, including the testimony of former slaves, prove that organized procreation of slaves was common, both to increase holdings and to obtain superior slaves for eventual sale, and that for many slaveowners this was an acceptable means of increasing their personal fortunes.

See also CAPITALISM AND SLAVERY; DEMOGRAPHY OF SLAVES IN THE UNITED STATES; ECONOMICS OF SLAVERY; FAMILY, U.S.; UNITED STATES.

BIBLIOGRAPHY

BANCROFT, FREDERIC. *Slave Trading in the Old South.* 1931.
DEYLE, STEVEN. "The Irony of Liberty: Origins of the Domestic Slave Trade." *Journal of the Early Republic* 12, no. 1 (1992): 37–62.
LIGHTNER, DAVID L. "The Interstate Slave Trade in Antislavery Politics." *Civil War History* 36, no. 2 (1990): 119–136.
STAMPP, KENNETH M. *The Peculiar Institution: Slavery in the Ante-bellum South.* 1956.
STOWE, HARRIET BEECHER. *The Key to Uncle Tom's Cabin.* 1854.
TADMAN, MICHAEL. *Speculators and Slaves: Masters, Traders, and Slaves in the Old South.* 1989.

Robert E. Conrad

Brazil

Brazil was the first slave plantation society to be developed in America. Forced to populate this valuable colony or lose it, the Portuguese in the 1550s brought sugarcane production and slave labor to Brazil. By the 1620s the plantations of Pernambuco and Bahia had a majority of African slave labor, though Indians were also enslaved until the middle of the century. Brazil was then the world's largest producer of sugarcane and was engaged in the world's largest and longest-running slave trade.

It was the Portuguese who first dominated the Atlantic slave trade from its initiation in the 1440s, and the opening up of Brazil to slave labor allowed them to supply their own needs from four African regions: Senegambia, the Lower Guinea coast, Congo-Angola, and finally Mozambique in the nineteenth century. By 1600, some 50,000 Africans had been brought to Brazil, and in the period to 1700 another 560,000 arrived. Although the Portuguese trade was severely disrupted when the Dutch seized Pernambuco from 1630 to 1654, and eventually lost its dominant position on the world sugar market to new West Indian producers in the second half of the seventeenth century, the opening up of the gold fields in the interior Brazilian province of Minas Gerais after 1700 created a new and greater demand for slaves. In the first two decades of the century some 15,000 slaves per annum were arriving, a figure which peaked at 30,000 slaves per annum in the last two decades of the century.

Though gold production declined from the 1750s, alternative uses for African slave labor developed. The south central provinces of Rio de Janeiro and São Paulo had become major sugar producers by the eighteenth century and in the early nineteenth century became the world's largest producers of coffee. In fact, there was no region or industry in Brazil where African slaves were not employed.

Although the Brazilian government was forced to deny legality to the trade after 1830, it continued until 1850, when direct British blockage finally forced an effective termination. During the nineteenth century, arrivals remained high, averaging 33,000 per annum in the 1810s and 43,000 per annum in the 1830s. It was still over 30,000 per annum in its last two illegal decades. By the end, some 3,980,000 Africans had been brought to Brazil, and in the first national census of 1872, Brazil counted 1.5 million slaves and 4.2 million free people of color, out of a total population of 8.4 million. A third of the population were slaves and a third of the free persons were slave owners, a pattern not dissimilar from what occurred in the United States, except that the majority of the free persons in Brazil were people of color, and a large number of them were slave owners.

The Brazilian slave trade was unique in many ways. Because of sailing conditions, it was virtually impossible to maintain a three-point trading pattern, and the slave ships simply plied a direct route between Africa and Brazil. This resulted in often very close relations between specific regions in Africa and in Brazil. The tightest such connection was between the province of Bahia, at its port of Salvador, and the Bight of Benin, but this also occurred between Rio de Janeiro and the ports of Luanda and Benguela in Angola. Although Brazilian traders bought East Indian textiles and cowry shells brought by Portuguese traders from the Indian Ocean to sell in Africa for slaves, the Brazilians also produced tobacco, gold, liquor, gunpowder, and other products that could be used to buy slaves, and they thus were more involved in African commerce than merchants from any other American region. The Brazilian Portuguese slavers were also unique in their use of Brazilian slaves as members of the crew. For almost half of the 350 slave ships which arrived in the port of Rio de Janeiro between 1795 and 1811, Brazilian slaves were listed as crew members, and in these cases they made up half of the crews. In all other aspects, from the manner of feeding, caring for, and carrying the slaves, to the types of ships used and the mortality suffered by the slave cargoes, the Portuguese Brazilian slavers differed little from their contemporaries in all the other regions participating in the Atlantic slave trade.

See also BRAZIL; PORTUGAL.

BIBLIOGRAPHY

CONRAD, ROBERT EDGAR. *World of Sorrow: The African Slave Trade to Brazil.* 1986.
FREYRE, GILBERTO. *Casa-grande e senzala.* 1933. Translated by Samuel Putnam as *The Masters and the Slaves: A Study in the Development of Brazilian Civilization.* 1946.
SCHWARTZ, STUART B. *Slaves, Peasants, and Rebels: Reconsidering Brazilian Slavery.* 1992.

Herbert S. Klein

China

In traditional Chinese society, the lowest rung of the social ladder was occupied by a group of people called *nu bi,* a term that can be rendered as "slaves" or "servants" in English. While most scholars believe that *nu bi* were truly slaves or quasi slaves, a few argue that their condition was actually much better than that of the slaves of the ancient Mediterranean world. Still others hold that *nu bi* had a different social status during different dynasties: they were sometimes slaves, sometimes serfs, and sometimes commoners. It is difficult to generalize about the status and condition of *nu bi* in traditional China; however, it is safe to say that from the Shang dynasty (sixteenth to eleventh centuries B.C.) to the Qing dynasty (A.D. 1644–1911), they were the members of Chinese society whose life was invariably closest to that of slaves.

There are two ways to classify the *nu bi* in traditional China: one is to group them into state *nu bi* and pri-

Two Chinese laborers. [Hulton-Deutsch Collection/ Corbis]

vate *nu bi;* the second is to divide them into *nu bi* engaged in production and those engaged in domestic service. But *nu bi* never seem to have played a dominant role in agricultural production. The sources of *nu bi* usually included prisoners of war, criminals, poor people who had to sell themselves or their children to survive, and men and women kidnapped by smugglers. Normally prisoners of war and criminals became state slaves, while the poor and the victims of kidnapping were sold as private slaves. The total number of *nu bi* and their proportion of the total population varied in different periods. During Qin and Han dynasties (221 B.C.–A.D. 220), their number is believed to have been so great that some historians feel it appropriate to describe Qin and Han China as slave society. Dynasties set up by conquerors from the north, including the Northern Wei of Xianbei (A.D. 386–534), the Yuan of the Mongols (A.D. 1260–1368), and the Qing of the Manchus, seem to have had more *nu bi* than their predecessors. These conquerors are believed to have had a stronger tradition of slavery than the contemporary Han Chinese at the time of conquest, and they imposed this tradition on Chinese society.

The legal status of the *nu bi* also changed over time. Early, during the Shang dynasty, owners had freedom to kill their *nu bi.* They were later deprived of that freedom, during and after the Qin and Han dynasties. Still later, during the Qing dynasty, the condition of the *nu bi* deteriorated relative to the previous period; it is believed that this was because the Manchu slave system was crueler than the Chinese system. Usually *nu bi* could be sold and exchanged as gifts. *Nu bi* sta-

tus could be hereditary, but there were also many ways for *nu bi* to become free: they could be freed by the order of the emperor or through manumission by their owner, or they could buy their freedom.

See also CHINA; HISTORIOGRAPHY OF SLAVERY.

BIBLIOGRAPHY

LI, JI-PING. *The Slave System of the Tang Dynasty.* 1986.
LIU, WEI-MIN. *Servitude in Ancient China.* 1975.
WEI, QING-YUAN, WU QI-YAN, and LU SU. *The Slave System of the Qing Dynasty.* 1982.

Han Xiaorong

Coolie Trade

The word coolie, which refers to unskilled cheap labor from Asia, is believed to have its origin in India, Turkey, or Africa. Its translateration in Chinese means "bitter labor." The term has been widely adopted to describe the Chinese who moved to foreign lands as contract laborers or indentured laborers in modern times. However, some scholars have rightly limited its use to the Chinese contract laborers who were brought to Latin America from the 1840s to the 1870s. The Chinese coolie trade was triggered by two events that occurred during the same period: the Opium War, which forced China to open several seaports to the West; and the abolition of the Atlantic slave trade, which drove many western countries to seek alternative sources of labor. The coolie trade started in the mid-1840s in southern China. It first flourished in Xiamen (Amoy) and then spread to other cities in southern and eastern China, including Hong Kong, Macao, Shantou (Swatow), Guangzhou (Canton), and Shanghai. Foreign companies monopolized the coolie trade, working through Chinese agents—the so-called coolie crimps, who were paid for each coolie they recruited. Countries whose territories or ships were involved in the trade included Britain, the United States, Spain, Peru, Italy, France, and Portugal. Cuba and Peru were the two largest markets for Chinese coolies. It has been estimated that from 1847 to 1874, 143,000 coolies were shipped to Cuba and 120,000 to Peru. Other destinations included the British colonies in Latin America, Brazil, Panama, Chile, and Ecuador.

Both contemporary observers and present researchers have frequently mentioned the similarities between the Chinese coolie trade and the African slave trade. Many coolies were first deceived or kidnapped and then kept in barracoons (detention centers) or loading vessels in the ports of departure, as were African slaves. Their voyages, which are sometimes called the Pacific passage, were as inhumane and dangerous as the notorious Middle Passage. Mortality was very high.

For example, it is estimated that from 1847 to 1859, the average mortality for coolies aboard ships to Cuba was 15.2 percent, and losses among those aboard ships to Peru were 40 percent in the 1850s and 30.44 percent from 1860 to 1863. At their destinations, they were sold like animals and were taken to work in plantations or mines under appalling living and working conditions. The duration of a contract was typically five to eight years, but many coolies did not live out their term of service because of the hard labor and mistreatment. Those who did live were often forced to remain in servitude beyond the contracted period. The coolies who worked on the sugar plantations in Cuba and in the guano beds of the Chinchas (the islands of Hell) of Peru were treated brutally. Seventy-five percent of the Chinese coolies in Cuba died before fulfilling their contracts. More than two-thirds of the Chinese coolies who arrived in Peru between 1849 and 1874 died within the contract period. Among the four thousand coolies brought to the Chinchas in 1861, not a single one survived! Because of these unbearable conditions, Chinese coolies often revolted against their Chinese and foreign oppressors at ports of departure, on ships, and in foreign lands.

However, there are also significant differences between the Chinese coolie trade and the African slave trade. First, despite the many recorded cases of deceiving and kidnapping coolies, probably not all coolies were forced into bondage, though it is difficult to know what percentage of the total number was represented by voluntary coolies. Owing to famines, wars, and shortages of land, many southern Chinese chose to go overseas to seek a better life. Second, not all coolies remained in bondage for life. Some of them became free men after serving out their contracts; a few even managed to return to China. Third, coolies received wages, although usually they were paid much less than local workers. Fourth, although there are reports of ships carrying women and children, the great majority of the Chinese coolies were men. Finally, the Chinese government, although not able to give the coolies as much protection as they needed, showed concern for them. Both central and local governments tried continuously to regulate and curb the coolie trade; at one point, the central government even sent inspectors to America to investigate conditions and intervene on the coolies' behalf. The Chinese government also took an active part in the final elimination of the coolie trade in 1874.

The flow of coolies to Latin America was not the only emigration of laborers from China in the nineteenth century. However, Chinese emigration to other parts of the world took varying forms. The Chinese in Southeast Asia were mostly free immigrants and indentured laborers brought to that region through the so-called *zhuzai* ("human pigs") trade system. Although there were cases in which the zhuzais were forced to work under miserable conditions, the zhuzai system differed from the coolie trade in several ways: it was run by the Chinese themselves; the zhuzais signed their contracts after they arrived in Southeast Asia rather than before the voyage; the duration of indenture was much shorter (usually no more than three years); and because the voyages were much safer, revolts seldom occurred on the zhuzai ships.

In the United States, Canada, and Australia, the so-called credit-ticket system was adopted as the major form of immigration. This differed from the coolie trade even more than the zhuzai trade because immigrants to these countries were usually sponsored by Chinese companies or organizations based in China, the immigrants were admitted individually, and much more effort was made to ensure that immigration was voluntary.

It is generally agreed that the Chinese coolies in Latin America in the nineteenth century, particularly those in Cuba and Peru, suffered much more than other Chinese immigrant workers.

See also CHINA; LABOR SYSTEMS; SLAVE TRADE.

BIBLIOGRAPHY

FARLEY, FOSTER M. "The Chinese Coolie Trade, 1845–1875." *Journal of Asian and African Studies* 3(3–4): 257–270, 1968.

HAN-SHENG, CHEN, ed. Preface. In *Collected Materials about Overseas Chinese Laborers*, vol. 1. 1985.

MEAGHER, ARNOLD JOSEPH. *The Introduction of Chinese Laborers to Latin America: The "Coolie Trade," 1847–1874.* Ph.D. diss., University of California, Davis, 1975.

PAN, LYNN. *Sons of the Yellow Emperor: The Story of the Overseas Chinese.* 1990.

WEI-REN, CHEN, *The Coolie Trade.* 1992.

Han Xiaorong

Southeast Asia

The widespread existence of slavery in Southeast Asia meant that slaves were a frequent commodity in the extensive trading networks of the region. In addition, some slaves were imported from Africa and South Asia, and between the seventeenth and nineteenth centuries Southeast Asia slaves were transported to colonial settlements in Sri Lanka, South Africa, and the Mascarene islands.

A long-established means of acquiring slaves in many Southeast Asian states was through capture or purchase from adjacent weaker societies, such as stateless hill peoples and hunter-gatherers. In numerical terms this was the most important form of slave acquisition, although detailed information is often lacking. It was the most regular source of slave supply to

Angkor in Cambodia from the ninth to the fifteenth centuries, and hill dwellers were highly valued as slaves in the lowland states of Cambodia, Thailand, Burma, and Malaya until well into the nineteenth century. Raiding was usually carried out by outsiders, although in some cases locals traded unwanted or impoverished people in return for textiles or guns. The impact on upland societies could be devastating, particularly when women and children were chief targets, such as among the Orang Asli hill peoples of nineteenth-century Malaya. In the insular regions non-Moslem peoples of the interior, such as the upland Toraja of Sulawesi, the Batak of Sumatra, the Dayak of Borneo, and the inhabitants of Luzon in the Philippines, were traded to the Islamic coastal lowlands, either for local use or for export elsewhere.

Southeast Asian seaborne merchants also traded in slaves, but they usually carried captives as one cargo among many in a complex network of trading routes that existed primarily for other purposes. Numbers are therefore difficult to estimate. Merchants from Java, Thailand, Sumatra, Sulawesi, and South Asia brought slaves on this basis to Islamic port cities such as Melaka (Malacca), Banten, and Patani from at least the fifteenth century. The Javanese sultanates stopped exporting slaves after their Islamization in the sixteenth century, but alternative supplies were obtained from regions such as Nias, the Moluccas, and the Sunda Islands. By the sixteenth century some sultanates, such as Sulu, Banda, and Tidore, began to specialize in the sale of slave captives from the eastern Indonesian and Philippine islands to city ports farther west. Major slave entrepôts in the seventeenth century included Aceh in northern Sumatra and Makassar in Sulawesi.

A few slaves were also imported into the region via the Islamic slave markets of the Middle East and India. In the fifteenth century slaves from Madagascar and the East African coast were brought to Aceh by Bengali traders and from the Maldives to Melaka by Banten merchants. Sixteenth-century Portuguese traders sold African slaves throughout the region, in the seventeenth and eighteenth centuries the Dutch and English trading companies brought slaves obtained in Madagascar or Surat in relatively small numbers to their Southeast Asian base at Batavia, and eight hundred at most to their base at Benkulen in Sumatra. Increasing commercial competition in the seventeenth century, accentuated by the presence of European traders, led to an intensified slaving in Southeast Asia. Sometimes the impact was dramatic: in 1621 the Dutch East India Company captured Banda, sent several thousand of its inhabitants into slavery in Batavia, and set up its own clove plantations with slaves from New Guinea, Ceram, Timor, and Borneo. But usually it changed only the scale and focus of preexisting trade.

This was especially true in the city ports where free labor was in short supply. The Portuguese used local debt slaves as well as imported slaves from Sumatra, Sunda, and the Maldives to build their fortress at Melaka after 1511. The Dutch East Indian Company headquarters at Batavia (Jakarta) imported slaves throughout the seventeenth and eighteenth centuries, both for local use and for reexport to its settlements in the Moluccas, Sri Lanka, and Cape Town. Areas of supply included Makassar—the center of a major indigenous trading network in the eastern parts of the region, from which at least two hundred slaves a year were supplied by Buginese and Makassarese merchants—and the island of Bali, from which some twelve hundred slaves were exported annually, mainly by Batavian Chinese traders. From 1810 to the 1830s, English and French merchants exported some five hundred Balinese slaves annually to Mauritius and Bourbon (Réunion).

Although the Makassar slaving entrepôt declined in the late eighteenth century, slaving increased markedly after the 1770s as a result of commercial growth in the Sulu sultanate (now in the southern Philippines and eastern Borneo), centered on Jolo Island. This area was a source of marine and forest products (such as birds' nests) sold for guns and opium to English East India Company traders, who used them in the China tea trade, or directly to Chinese merchants in Jolo. Collection of this produce relied on slave labor and heightened demand in the Sulu region for new supplies of slaves. Expeditions of perahu fleets regularly captured coastal inhabitants (including some Europeans) from the Philippines, Borneo, and Sulawesi and penetrated to northern Java, Sumatra, the Melaka Straits, the Gulf of Thailand, and the Bay of Bengal. (A perahu, or prau, is a type of Indonesian sailing vessel.) The historian James Warren has estimated that between two hundred thousand and three hundred thousand captives reached Sulu between 1770 and 1870. In addition, a very great many died on board ship. The expeditions were manned by Samal from Balangini Island and Iranun from Mindanao—sometimes themselves former captives, who usually obtained boats, ammunition, and credit from the Taosug Sulu rulers in return for their slave cargoes. Women and young men brought the highest prices. This activity was weakened by Spanish attacks on Jolo and Belangini in the mid-nineteenth century but was finally ended only by U.S. conquest of the area in 1900.

Elsewhere in Southeast Asia, slave trading continued for as long as slavery itself survived. Chinese traders imported slave women to work as prostitutes in Singapore and the Malayan tin mines up to at least the 1870s. Inland hill raiding in Burma and Borneo continued out of the sight of coastal colonial officials into the twentieth century. And the selling of children for prostitution continues in Southeast Asia today.

See also MAURITIUS AND RÉUNION; PHILIPPINES; PLANTATIONS; SOUTHEAST ASIA; SOUTHERN AFRICA.

BIBLIOGRAPHY

REID, ANTHONY, ed. *Slavery, Bondage, and Dependency in Southeast Asia.* 1983. See especially chapters 1, 2, 10, 12, 14, and 15.

WARREN, JAMES FRANCIS. *The Sulu Zone, 1768–1898: The Dynamics of External Trade, Slavery and Ethnicity in the Transformation of a Southeast Asian Maritime State.* 1981.

YOUNG, ROBERT J. "European Interests and the Eighteenth-Century Slave Trade to South and Southeast Asia." Paper presented at the Symposium on the Long Distance Trade in Slaves across the Indian Ocean and the Red Sea in the Nineteenth Century, School of Oriental and African Studies, University of London, December 1987.

Nigel Worden
Kerry Ward

Indian Ocean

The slave trade in the Indian Ocean consisted of three distinct regional networks. The first and oldest route worked from the East African coast north toward Egypt and the Middle East and into India. A second, rather complicated network in the eighteenth and nineteenth centuries involved East Africa, Mozambique, southern Africa, Madagascar, and several Indian Ocean islands: Mauritius, Réunion, the Seychelles, the Comoros Island, and Rodrigues. A third network centered on Madagascar, mostly in the nineteenth century, considered separately as both an exporter and an importer of slaves. A fourth route, important after about 1810, took slaves from Mozambique and eastern Africa out of the Indian Ocean and across the Atlantic to the Americas. All came under pressure from British abolitionism after 1810 before yielding slowly to naval patrols and to a round of anti–slave-trade treaties that marked the entry of European imperial control into the western Indian Ocean. Compared with the Atlantic trade, none of this Indian Ocean flow of captive labor, legal or illegal, has been well researched, and there are no conclusive quantitative studies of its volume.

The "Northern" Slave Trade

The export of East African slaves toward North Africa, the Middle East, and India originated in antiquity, and after about the eighth century it was mainly controlled by Muslim traders—Arabs and Persians. Western Asia, present-day Iraq, received the bulk of these slaves from before A.D. 800. Tens of thousands of them, known as Zanj, worked in salt pans near Basra at the head of the Persian Gulf and became famous for instigating rebellions in the late ninth century. In India, African ex-slaves formed distinct communities, such as the Siddis, who were sailors established on the northwestern coast as early as A.D. 1100 and who worked later for the Moghul emperors of the seventeenth and eighteenth centuries. In the fourteenth and fifteenth centuries, the Indonesian Muslim sultanate of Tidore developed a slave trade from New Guinea to the east, as far as China. Although the Portuguese intruded on the flow of labor to India after they established trading posts along the Mozambique coast in the sixteenth century, this northern trade continued as late as 1809, when one traveler observed some 500 slaves on their way from Africa to India.

Omani Arabs, operating under Busaidi sultans established at Zanzibar from late in the eighteenth century, and often working with Indian commercial capital, multiplied the volume of this trade toward the Persian Gulf and the Red Sea in the nineteenth century in response to commercial prosperity in southwestern Asia. Supplemented by captives from Ethiopia and the Gulf of Aden, the principal suppliers of slaves in the Red Sea area, slaves from East Africa supplied labor to expand data production in Oman and engaged in maritime activities: 30 percent of the pearl divers in the Persian Gulf were enslaved Africans by the 1880s and 1890s, and other slaves were members of dhow crews. A small proportion of slaves served as domestics and concubines in prospering cities in the Ottoman Empire, which then controlled the region. Some were also incorporated into armies outside the core Ottoman areas—for example, under the Busaidi sultans in mid-nineteenth-century Zanzibar. The northern slave route created what has been called a "cultural corridor" between Africa and Asia and led to an African diaspora in the northwestern Indian Ocean.

The early phases of this Arab and Indian trade established the maritime routes that other merchants would later use to obtain African gold and ivory. A long-distance trade in ivory had reached well up the Limpopo River valley and onto the Zimbabwe plateau by the eleventh century, and Zimbabwean gold exports apparently sustained the famous Shona stone-building tradition that culminated at Great Zimbabwe. Arabs and Indians thrived as purchasers of ivory as far south as Mozambique in the eighteenth century.

Slaving to the Islands of the Southwestern Indian Ocean

In the mid-eighteenth century, slave exports to the north were dwindling; but the south grew, becoming the principal area of slaving from what is now southern Tanzania and northern Mozambique, as French traders supplanted the Omani Arabs in the search for slaves in the southwestern Indian Ocean. Only Kilwa, the "entrepôt of the slave trade," continued to supply the northern route. Southern slaving developed after the French colonized the Mascarenes islands (Mauritius, which they renamed Île de France, and Réunion) in 1715 and as Dutch colonization at the Cape of Good Hope turned to vineyards and wheat farms in need of enslaved labor. Between 1652 and 1808 Dutch and French trading companies delivered some 63,000 slaves to South Africa from the Indonesian archipelago and from India, as well as from Madagascar and mainland East and East-Central Africa. In the Mascarenes, the French East India Company chartered to conduct French business in the region first attempted to bring slaves from West Africa, but the long journey resulted in high mortality among the slaves and the company abandoned the effort. French traders also sought Madagascar slaves in these early days but obtained only uneven supplies from the island, partly because of the importance of internal demand for slaves there. Governor Labourdonnais, who administered the Mascarenes from 1735 to 1746, sought supplies of slaves from Portuguese-claimed parts of the Mozambique coast, even though such trading operated in nominal illegality, since the Portuguese did not allow foreign ships in their ports. The French found the Afro-Portuguese commercial class there only too eager to meet their needs for slave labor in return for French goods, particularly foodstuffs, which were always in short supply. Since this business proved so advantageous for all, Portuguese governors turned a blind eye to the law they were appointed to enforce and often profited personally.

Anglo-French wars from 1753 to 1810 disrupted slave trading on the East African coast, particularly to the Mascarenes. Nevertheless, slaving from East Africa to the Mascarences reached its peak in the last quarter of the eighteenth century. From 1784, French traders from the Caribbean joined their commercial counterparts in the Indian Ocean at Mozambique, making it one of the most diversified and international slave markets in the world. Despite the Napoleonic wars and the ensuing British naval blockage of the Mascarenes after 1803, this trade continued at a certain level with the active participation of French "corsairs," who carried written permission from the French government (*lettres de marque*) to attack British ships but who operated independently as pirates.

Britain extended its efforts to abolish maritime Atlantic slaving into the Indian Ocean after a Parliamentary act of 1807. Governor Farquhar, the first British governor of Mauritius after its capture in 1810, developed contacts with rulers throughout the region to end the slave trade, but he did not want it terminated in fact until he found alternative sources of labor to develop the island's economy. Ironically, just as British attempts to suppress the Atlantic slave trade north of the Equator had led to increased slaving in the Southern Hemisphere, trading in slaves in the Indian Ocean thrived after the 1820s in spite of patrols stationed there by the Royal Navy.

The Omani mercantile class based on Zanzibar had begun to transform the economy of the coast by the late eighteenth century by supplying slaves from East Africa for Indian Ocean markets. When the British captured Mauritius in 1810, the Zanzibar trade to the island virtually stopped, forcing the Omanis to look for new markets, or new employment, for their slaves. They then developed a new slave plantation sector in Zanzibar itself, producing cloves for export to the eastern Indian Ocean. By the 1840s, of all the slaves brought down to the coast, only a third left Africa, and most remained in Zanzibar.

The Malagasy Slave Trade

The slave trade from Madagascar to the Mascarenes and the Seychelles was also significantly large, both in numbers and in its impact on exporting and importing societies. Of the 160,000 slaves believed to have reached the Mascarenes between 1720 and 1810, it is estimated that about 40 percent came from Madagascar. From Madagascar to the Mascarenes in the eighteenth century an "official" slave trade along the whole of the east coast, at least nominally monopolized by the king of France, competed with a "private" trade on the west coast, carried on by individual traders. The separation between these two spheres of trade was never strictly enforced, and an "illegal" trade also operated on the east coast in which Frenchmen of all sorts, even royal officials, were involved. The east coast was far easier for traders because of ease of navigation, the plentiful supply of slaves there, the availability of rice and meat to feed them, and the proximity of the Mascarenes. French traders shifted to Mozambique only when they failed to obtain the slaves they needed in Madagascar. After the British prohibited this trade in 1815, illegal trading continued, with traders hiding their cargoes in the Seychelles and on the islands of Rodrigues until they found it safe to travel to Mauritius. In general, small "bricks" were used for these short voyages, while much larger ships were engaged for trips to Mozambique.

Of the Malagasy sold as slaves, perhaps 70 percent came from the central highlands. After the 1780s the Merina kingdom emerged there from the wars that produced these captives, and by the early nineteenth century it controlled much of the island. For some years, the highland Merina passed these slaves through intermediaries down to the ports of Antongil, Foulpointe, and Tamatave on the east cost, but when the Merina rulers conquered the coastal areas too, they gained control of the whole of the slave trade to the Mascarenes. Exports dwindled by the late 1820s, mostly because the internal market for slaves expanded rapidly in the Merina kingdom to support royal programs of economic development. In 1817 a treaty, the fruit of Governor Farquhar's efforts to prohibit the slave trade, promised Radama I, the Merina ruler, financial compensation in exchange for prohibiting further exports of slaves from the island he by then controlled. The British also offered to subsidize a vast program of economic development in Imerina, to generate internal revenues that would make up for the profits Radama would lose from ending exports of slaves. The success of Radama's reforms increased internal slaving throughout Madagascar, an ironic effect similar to the consequences of Atlantic abolition in West Africa, with which the British did not concern themselves.

Another, smaller trade from Mozambique to the west coast of Madagascar also fed the growing labor market in Imerina after 1817. In addition, at the same season every year, the Saklava of northwestern Madagascar embarked in their swift, long boats and ransacked the island of Anjouan in the Comoros Islands, capturing men, women, and children. French firearms contributed to the violence of the political conflicts between different groups living on the island. It is believed that officials in Merina reexported some of the Mozambican slaves reaching their domains on to the Mascarenes, but the volume of this trade is not yet known. A measure of illegal reexportation also occurred between Mauritius and Réunion, but there are no reliable figures to establish its volume. Even more daunting is the attempt to assess the numbers of slaves caught in the Saklava raids. Nonetheless, it is probably safe to estimate that the trade of the nineteenth century more than doubled the volume of preceding years, in spite of Britain's attempts at suppression. This increase resulted from the incorporation of eastern and southern Africa into world economy, with the ensuing development of plantation production in the Mascarenes, as well as on Zanzibar and adjacent islands along the east African coast, and the consequent need for masses of cheap labor.

Slaves Sent to the New World

The Atlantic route developed when traders from the New World arrived along the southeast African coast in search of slaves for Brazil and Cuba, following British suppression of the Northern Hemisphere trade in the Atlantic. The area of slaving around Mozambique Island expanded toward the south, as far as Delagoa Bay, where exports of slaves jumped from a few dozen to several thousand after 1823; the British at that time were eager to control Delagoa Bay as much to exclude slavers as to secure its trade in ivory. The principal buyers were the Brazilians, who needed labor to supply the coffee plantations then spreading through the hills above Rio de Janeiro and São Paulo, and slavers from several nations supplying the fast-increasing sugar plantations in Cuba. Over 30,000 slaves from Mozambique entered the Atlantic in both 1828 and 1829, on the eve of Brazil's bow to British pressure to ban slaving in 1830. Portuguese authorities resisted Britain's suppression of the trade at first, and slavers moved to new sites throughout the region to escape detection. Exports to the Atlantic ended only with the closure of Brazil's ports to new slaves after 1850 and, finally, with the termination of the Cuban trade in the 1860s.

The growing volume of slave exports after 1823 came from increased violence in the southeast African interior, with large fortified settlements, private armies, and the destruction or abandonment of smaller, isolated communities, whose inhabitants fled to seek protection from stronger powers. Some areas were depopulated more by this flight than by losses to slave raiders. When guns began to be sold for slaves, those who could obtain firearms gained political power at the expense of holders of traditional forms of authority and of owners of the land. These disruptions sustained shipments of slaves to the coast for Zanzibari and other buyers for the northern trade into the 1870s.

Ending the Slave Trade

The British attempted to suppress the slave trade in the southwest Indian Ocean sending ships of the Royal Navy to patrol its slaving routes after 1810, but they achieved only partial success. During the hurricane season, British ships were hardly to be found in the area, and small local vessels took full advantage of their absence to engage in slaving. Even when present, they captured only a tiny percentage of the many small craft employed to carry the slaves. Furthermore, even when they captured a ship with slaves on board, they sent the "recaptives" to Mauritius, where they ended working on plantations under conditions very similar to the fate that would have befallen them had they been sold as slaves. Bilateral treaties with the larger political authorities in the region were more successful, such as the Anglo-Merina Treaty of 1817 and the Moresby Treaty of 1822 with Seyyid Said, sul-

Rescued slaves are kept in the hold of a British warship after being taken from slave traders sailing between Zanzibar and the African coast. [Bojan Brecelj/Corbis]

tan of Zanzibar, and a further agreement signed in 1845. But the agreement of 1828 with the Portuguese that took effect in 1830 had as little impact on the trade from Mozambique to Madagascar as it had on the Brazilian and Cuban trade to the Atlantic. British reports of slaves captured by the Royal Navy patrols numbering in the thousands seem, according to recent research, exaggerated.

The slave trade of the northern Indian Ocean dwindled in the 1840s, mainly because the clove plantations of Zanzibar absorbed most of the captives reaching the coast. Slave exports finally stopped after 1863 with the assent—however unwilling, under heavy British economic and diplomatic pressure—of sultan Barghash in Zanzibar. There, too, and also along the coast, suppression of the maritime trade indirectly stimulated heavier use of slaves to produce commodities, and even more extensive and violent slave raiding in the interior. The trade in slave-produced cloves replaced the exports of slaves themselves.

Slavery ended on British-held islands in 1834, followed by a brief period of bound "apprenticeship" for the slaves thus freed. Slavery on French islands ended in 1848. But a new movement of labor to the Mascarenes developed then—the transport of hun-

dreds of thousands of indentured laborers, mostly from India. From the 1860s on, other Indians were taken to Natal, the British colony in southeastern Africa, to plant and harvest sugar. Abolition of the trade in slaves thus did not diminish the volume of labor moving across the Indian Ocean but only replaced Africans with Indians and other Asians. Nor did it end slaving in Madagascar or on the African mainland; slavery there declined only slowly, finally ending during the first decades of colonial rule in the twentieth century. The British in Kenya and elsewhere continued the outflow of indentured labor from India until World War I. These technically free laborers aroused less moral outrage on the part of antislavery societies in Europe, but few of the people transported arrived under conditions much superior to what the slaves who preceded them had faced.

See also ABOLITION AND ANTISLAVERY MOVEMENTS; BRAZIL; CUBA; EAST AFRICA; INDIAN SUBCONTINENT; INDONESIA; MAURITIUS AND RÉUNION; ZANJ.

BIBLIOGRAPHY

ALPERS, EDWARD. "The East African Slave Trade." *Historical Association of Tanzania.* Paper no. 3.
———. *Ivory and Slaves in East-Central Africa.* 1975.

BISSOONDOYAL, U., ed. *Slavery in the South West Indian Ocean.* 1989.

CAMPBELL, GWYN. "Madagascar and the Slave Trade 1810–1895." *Journal of African History* 22: (1981): 203–227.

ELDREDGE, ELIZABETH. "Delagoa Bay and the Hinterland in the Early Nineteenth Century." In *Slavery in South Africa: Captive Labour in the Dutch Frontier,* edited by E. Eldredge and Fred Morton. 1994.

LARSON, PIER. "A Census of Slaves Exported from Central Madagascar to the Mascarenes between 1775 and 1820." Paper presented at the Conference Commemorating the Abolition of Slavery, Antananarivo. 1995.

NEWITT, MALYN. *A History of Mozambique.* 1995.

RASHIDI, RUNOKO. "Black Bondage in Asia." In *African Presence in Early Asia,* edited by Ivan Van Sertina. 1988.

SHERIFF, ABDUL. *Slaves, Spices, and Ivory in Zanzibar.* 1987.

TOUSSAINT, AUGUSTE. *La Route des Îles.* 1967.

Vijaya Teelock

Twentieth-Century Trade

By 1900 the trade in chattel slaves was mainly limited to Africa and the Middle East. In Africa, the gradual elimination of the Atlantic slave trade during the nineteenth century and the curtailing of the trade to the Muslim world after 1870 had stimulated indigenous slavery, already widespread, and a slave trade within the continent itself to support it. In the last decade of the nineteenth century and the first decade of the twentieth, however, the European colonial powers conquered most of Africa. As they established their rule over areas where in the past wars and raids had annually thrown up a rich harvest of slaves, and where slavery itself was endemic, the traffic declined. All the colonial powers were bound by the Brussels Act of 1890 to suppress the trade, and they outlawed it early in their administrations, although they often could not enforce their laws for many years. In time, however, the imposition of peace, the abolition of the legal status of slavery, and the political controls and wage labor that accompanied colonial rule eroded the market for slaves as well as the supply.

As late as 1920, however, raiding and trading continued in the remoter areas of the colonial empires, and it was reported to be still possible to buy a slave in the Sahara at the time of African independence in the 1960s. In the less remote regions, even in those under close control, the slave trade, although soon driven underground, remained active at least through the 1930s. By this time, however, it became largely a traffic in children, surreptitiously conducted by dealers who took them in small groups to sell in secret hideouts.

In the independent empire of Ethiopia, slave trading on an impressive scale continued virtually unchecked in the 1920s and early 1930s, fed by raids in the west and southwest of the country. Many of these raids were launched by ill-paid governors and other officials who were forced to live off the land. Slaves were also exported to Sudan and Arabia in the late 1920s. This situation ended when the Italians conquered the country in 1936 and announced the abolition of slavery. The institution was dealt the final coup de grace in 1942, when the newly restored Emperor Haile Selassie ended its legal status. Thereafter, only isolated instances of slave trading were reported.

In Arabia slavery was legal until the 1960s. The dimensions of the twentieth-century traffic in the peninsula are unknown. The import trade, which under Ottoman rule had been much reduced by 1914, revived after the withdrawal of the Turks during the First World War. Slaves were imported from both Africa and the eastern shores of the Persian Gulf and Indian Ocean. From the east, youthful victims—often kidnapped, but sometimes sold by their own parents—came from Baluchistan and even India to the Hijaz and Nedj (later Saudi Arabia), Yemen, Muscat and Oman, the Hadramaut, and the sheikhdoms on the western shores of the Persian Gulf, particularly the Trucial States. This traffic was active in the 1920s and early 1930s, and there were reports that it continued in the 1960s on a very small scale. In the 1920s and early 1930s greater numbers of slaves arrived from Ethiopia and Sudan across the Red Sea and the Gulf of Aden. Many came through Tajura, in French Somaliland, which the French barely policed, but they also came through Italian Eritrea and the Anglo-Egyptian Sudan. The British navy patrolled the Red Sea and Persian Gulf in the interwar years, and other powers made sporadic efforts to police their coastal waters. Nonetheless, this traffic, carried on in small craft from remote creeks and inlets often sheltered by coral reefs, was almost impossible to suppress as long as the Arabian market for slaves remained buoyant. The dimensions of this trade are unknown, but it may have amounted to several thousand victims a year in the early 1920s, while the British believed it had been reduced to a thousand a year, at most, by 1930. A few cases were reported in the 1950s.

Another important source of slaves for Arabia was the pilgrimage to the holy cities of Mecca and Medina. The convergence of the large retinues of wealthy, pious Muslims provided a unique opportunity not just for the sale of slaves but also for their purchase and subsequent re-export by their new owners. Slaves came by this route from as far away as West Africa and China, and presumably were taken back to destinations all over the Muslim world. Destitute pilgrims sold off their wives, children, and slaves. Some unfortunates fell into debt and sold themselves. Others were kidnapped, or tricked into slavery. Women, for instance, were married by seemingly devout husbands and taken on pilgrimages from which they never returned. Some parents sent their children to Arabia for religious education, consigning them to third persons, who sold them. Although the colonial powers tried to supervise the parties of pilgrims at the ports of embarkation and along the routes, there were always victims who slipped through the net.

In 1919 the colonial powers believed that the slave trade in Africa and the export traffic to the Middle East was so reduced that the Brussels Act—the first truly international act against the African slave trade—was abrogated. In the early 1920s, however, the recrudescence of slaving in Ethiopia and Arabia attracted sufficient public attention for the League of Nations to negotiate the Slavery Convention of 1926. This treaty called for the immediate suppression of the slave trade, but it contained no provisions for its enforcement and was not adhered to by Arabian rulers. A supplementary convention, negotiated by the United Nations Organization, followed in 1956, but again there was no way it could be enforced even on powers who signed it.

During the 1950s and early 1960s, slavery and slave trading in Arabia attracted attention in the European press. Changing economic and political conditions in the Middle East, however, led to a breakthrough, when Saudi Arabia ended slavery in 1962. The Gulf states, under increased British pressure, followed suit, and finally Muscat and Oman abolished it in 1970.

However, although the traffic in so-called chattel or classic slaves was virtually ended, dealing in persons continues. These transactions supply a demand for practices labeled analogous to slavery. They include trafficking in women and girls for prostitution, child labor for domestic and other work, dealing in illegal aliens, contract labor, and passing the obligations of persons in debt bondage from one creditor to another. Strictly speaking these are not slave trading since theoretically the victims are only in bondage for a limited period—children, for instance, until they grow up—and they are not directly owned like the chattel slave. But these transactions, which also have a long history and formerly existed side by side with the true slave trade, have now replaced it and are found in almost all areas of the world. In some cases the borderline between such dealings and slave trading is not clear. Thus Sudan, in the course of its war with the south (since 1983, in its current phase), has been accused of allowing women and children to be captured, taken north, and sold. But whether these captives are treated as chattel slaves is unknown. Similarly, the fate of children reportedly sold by dealers in western Africa may or may not approximate to slavery. In China, thousands of women have been kidnapped and sold as brides. Initially procured and kept

by force, many may come to accept their fate and be treated as other wives acquired by less coercive means. Since 1975 the U.N. Working Group on Contemporary Forms of Slavery has conducted inquiries and published reports on such cases.

See also DEBT PEONAGE; MODERN MIDDLE EAST; PROSTITUTION; SLAVERY, CONTEMPORARY FORMS OF; SLAVERY CONVENTION.

BIBLIOGRAPHY

Anti-Slavery Reporter. Continuing.
DERRICK, JONATHAN. *Africa's Slaves Today.* 1975.
LEAGUE OF NATIONS. *Report of the Temporary Slavery Commission of 1924–1925.* A.19.1925.VI.
———. *Reports of the Advisory Committee of Experts on Slavery.* CCEE.138.C159, M.113 1935.VI.
MIERS, SUZANNE. "Britain and the Suppression of Slavery in Ethiopia." *Slavery and Abolition* 18, no. 3 (1997): 257–288.
———. "Diplomacy versus Humanitarianism: Britain and Consular Manumission in Hijaz, 1921–1936." *Slavery and Abolition* 10, no. 3 (1989): 102–128.
———. "Slavery and French Rule in the Sahara." *Slavery and Abolition* 19, no. 2 (1998).
WORKING GROUP ON CONTEMPORARY FORMS OF SLAVERY. *Reports.* 1975–continuing.

Suzanne Miers

Slave Trials

See Trials of Slaves.

Slavs

The Slavs are a people whose name became synonymous with servile status. Through many centuries of their history, they served as slaves: in west and southwest Europe, in the Mediterranean region, and in the lands of Islam. The Arabic term *sakaliba* came to be used in the medieval West to denote all categories of Slavic slaves, though in Arabic it meant only castrated male slaves (eunuchs). Its origin was the Arabic transcription of the word *Slav*.

When and why the Slavic lands (north and west of the Black Sea, and including Russians, Ukrainians, Belorussians, Bulgarians, Serbs, Slovenians, and Ruthenians) became a source of slaves is debated by scholars. Pritsak (p. 23) argues that it was the "pseudo-Avars," a small band of Altaic and Iranian nomads who, in the mid-sixth century, used Slavs as slaves, and "thus introduced the Slavs into history." Pritsak demonstrates that for the nomads of Central Asia "The vast territory that lay beyond the cultural world of that time, east of the Elbe River and west and north of the Syr Darya River, was recognized as a reservoir of potential slaves." Small communities of farmers, outside of the various state and imperial structures of the time, had no means to protect themselves from the nomads' "harvesting" of people to be used and sold as slaves. This harvesting continued until the Slavs were incorporated into early modern state systems, such as Poland-Lithuania and Russia.

We know that in Byzantium (the later eastern Roman Empire) Slavs appeared often as slaves in both military and civil service. The great palace of the emperors, for example, employed Slavic eunuchs, often in high positions of state. What we do not know is the process by which they were enslaved.

In his study of slavery in the medieval west, Charles Verlinden has shown the important role of Jewish traders and merchants called the Rhadonites, centered in southeast Germany, in importing Slavic slaves to southern France and the Iberian peninsula, the latter under Muslim rule. In the ninth and tenth centuries, the "slave *par excellence* is the Slav" (1955 p. 618).

At this time the prime market for Slavic slaves was Muslim Spain. In the early ninth century the Spanish Caliph al-Hakam I (ruled 796–822) commanded a large slave military corps of more than five thousand men, which included many Slavs. Muslim historians argued that two peoples in particular proved to be excellent soldiers, even as slaves: Turks (who served primarily in the Muslim Middle East) and Slavs (in the Muslim West).

In the tenth century the Umayyad palace of Madinat az Zahra in Spain employed 3,750 *sakaliba,* some of whom held high positions in the caliph's administration. Evidence suggests that the vast majority, perhaps all, were of Slavic origin. In the latter part of the tenth century, Islamic Spain exported *sakaliba* to the Maghreb, Baghdad, and Egypt, where their reputation as soldiers and administrators won them positions of importance in caliphal courts and armies. In the late tenth century the caliphal court at Baghdad employed hundreds of Slavic *sakaliba.*

With the Mongol invasions of east Slavic lands, Slavic slaves became even more readily available than before. Italy and the Mediterranean islands were the most common destinations for these slaves in the thirteenth and early fourteenth centuries (between 1414 and 1423 ten thousand were sold in Venice itself), though Venice also established a large trading center in Alexandria, which imported Slavic slaves (as many as two thousand a year) to Egypt.

Two developments in the fourteenth century in east Slavic lands generated another vast increase in the numbers of Slavic slaves: the growth of the Ottoman Empire with its conquest of most of the Slavic Balkans and the establishment of the Crimean Tatar khanate whose economic life centered on the slave trade. The Italians were expelled from the Black Sea region by the Ottomans in 1475.

Thousands of Slavic boys were taken by the Ottoman government from the Balkans through the *devşirme* (Turkish for "roundup" or "collection") system, converted to Islam, and were trained to become soldiers and government officials. Legally slaves, these men nevertheless occupied important positions in society. In addition, the Ottomans purchased male and female Slavic slaves in large numbers from the Crimean khanate. Estimates of the number of these slaves imported by the Ottomans in the fifteenth through seventeenth centuries reach in excess of two million. Some attained almost the top positions in the government: Hurrem, of Ruthenian origin, and purchased in the Crimean slave market, became Sultan Süleyman I's only wife and the mother of his successor, Selim II.

The growing power of Russia in the seventeenth and eighteenth centuries, particularly under Peter I and Catherine II, ended the export of Slavic slaves in lands under their control. The Crimean khanate was eliminated at the end of the eighteenth century and annexed to Russia. The Ottoman Empire replaced the *devşirme* system in the early seventeenth century with recruitment of free individuals for government service, removing the need for slave imports.

While slavery was not abolished in Ottoman lands until the beginning of the twentieth century, the source of slaves was no longer the Slavic lands to the north and west; rather the Ottomans looked increasingly to the Caucasus and Africa.

See also BYZANTIUM; EUNUCHS; MEDIEVAL EUROPE, SLAVERY AND SERFDOM IN; MEDITERRANEAN BASIN; MILITARY SLAVES; RUSSIA.

BIBLIOGRAPHY

FISHER, ALAN. "Muscovy and the Black Sea Slave Trade." *Canadian-American Slavic Studies* 4 (1972): 575–594.

PRITSAK, OMELIAN. *The Origin of Rus',* vol. 1: *Old Scandinavian Sources other than the Sagas.* 1981.

VERLINDEN, CHARLES. *L'esclavage dans l'Europe médiévale,* vol. 1: *Péninsule ibérique.* 1955; vol. 2: *Italie—colonies italiennes du Levant—Levant latin—empire byzantin.* 1977.

Alan Fisher

Smith, Adam   [1723–1790]

Scottish philosopher and founder of political economy.

Impressed by the ethnographic writings of European travelers about the aboriginal peoples of North America and Africa, Adam Smith contrasted the virtues of these "savages" with the corruption of civilized societies. In *The Theory of Moral Sentiments* (1759), he criticizes their enslavement by European colonists: "Fortune never exerted more cruelly her empire over mankind, than when she subjected those nations of heroes to the refuse of the jails of Europe, to wretches who possess the virtues neither of the countries which they came from, nor of those which they go to" (v.2.9.).

In his *Lectures on Jurisprudence* in the early 1760s, Smith observed that, although the master's power over his slaves was everywhere absolute, the condition of the slave was in fact better in a poor, barbarous society than in a rich, polished one. In a poor country the number of slaves is small in relation to the number of freemen, and slaves are a valuable asset and represent no threat to their masters. In a rich country, slaves are more numerous than freemen, and they constitute a continuous danger. Smith illustrates this point by contrasting the relative humanity with which the colonists of continental America treated their slaves and the harshness shown by slaveowners in the West Indian islands.

In his *Inquiry into the Nature and Causes of the Wealth of Nations* (1776), Smith argues that all historical evidence shows that slave labor is less profitable than free labor. Slaves have no incentive to work harder than they are forced to do, and their masters have no incentive to introduce machinery, since that would reduce the value of slaves. Slave cultivation, in Smith's view, is thus feasible for sugar, and perhaps tobacco, but not for corn.

See also ECONOMICS OF SLAVERY; PERSPECTIVES ON SLAVERY.

BIBLIOGRAPHY

ROSS, I. S. *The Life of Adam Smith.* 1995.
SMITH, ADAM. *An Inquiry into the Nature and Causes of the Wealth of Nations.* Edited by R. H. Campbell and A. S. Skinner. 1976. Originally published 1776.
———. *Lectures on Jurisprudence.* Edited by R. L. Meek, D. D. Raphael, and P. G. Stein. 1978.
———. *The Theory of Moral Sentiments.* Edited by D. D. Raphael and A. L. Macfie. 1976. Originally published 1759.

Peter G. Stein

Smith, Gerrit   [1797–1874]

Abolitionist and antislavery activist.

The heir to one of the largest fortunes in New York, Gerrit Smith was one of the most important philanthropists and reformers in antebellum America. He supported temperance, schools for poor girls, indigent adults, numerous colleges and seminaries, and various

Gerrit Smith. [*Frank Leslie's Illustrated Newspaper/* Corbis]

churches. Issues of race and slavery ultimately drew most of his attention. He gave land in upstate New York to free blacks, supported many different antislavery organizations, and sent financial aid to fugitive slaves in Canada.

Although Smith was an advocate of peace, in 1851 he helped plan and execute the "Jerry rescue" in Syracuse, New York, which led to the liberation of a fugitive slave then in the custody of the U.S. marshal. Similarly, in 1854 he supported the use of violence in Kansas and spent at least $14,000, a huge sum at the time, helping northern opponents of slavery settle in Kansas from 1854 to 1856. He later gave funds to John Brown for his violent raid on Harpers Ferry, Virginia, although after the raid failed Smith claimed that he had not known his money would be used to support violence. While always friendly with William Lloyd Garrison, Smith rejected Garrison's disunionist theories and his disdain for politics.

Smith was an active leader of the Liberty Party, unsuccessfully running as its candidate for governor of New York in 1840. In 1848 he declined the party's presidential nomination. In 1852 he won a seat in Congress as an antislavery independent, but he resigned before his term expired. In 1858 he unsuccessfully ran for governor of New York on the "People's State Ticket." He supported the Union cause after 1861 and actively campaigned for Lincoln in 1864 and Grant in 1868. Quirky and eccentric, Smith was one of the nation's most prominent abolitionists and reformers.

See also ABOLITION AND ANTISLAVERY MOVEMENTS; BROWN, JOHN; GARRISON, WILLIAM LLOYD.

BIBLIOGRAPHY

ROSSBACH, JEFFREY. *Ambivalent Conspirators: John Brown, the Secret Six, and a Theory of Slave Violence.* 1982.
STEWART, JAMES B. *Holy Warriors: The Abolitionists and American Slavery.* 1996.

Paul Finkelman

Société des Amis des Noirs

The Société des Amis des Noirs (Society of Friends of Blacks) was an upper-class French antislavery club founded in 1788 by Jacques-Pierre Brissot de Warville, Étienne Clavière, the Comte de Mirabeau, and others. They were inspired by the abolition efforts of United States and English Quakers and the London Abolition Committee, with which, for a time, they were loosely affiliated. Members included the Marquis de Condorcet, the Marquis de Lafayette, Abbé Sieyès, the Duc de La Rochefoucauld d'Anville, Antoine Lavoisier, the Comte Destutt de Tracy, and Abbé Henri Grégoire. Many members were associated with the moderate-republican Girondist party during the French Revolution.

Brissot and Lafayette maintained contact with abolitionists in London, Philadelphia, and New York, and the Amis des Noirs included foreign members. Among these was William Short, secretary of the U.S. embassy in Paris, who had been personal secretary to the U.S. minister Thomas Jefferson. Jefferson himself had declined an offer of membership.

The group advocated an immediate end to the slave trade and gradual emancipation of slaves in the French colonies. Campaigning by the group led to the inclusion of antislavery petitions in third-estate grievance lists presented at the Estates General of 1789. However, efforts in the revolutionary assemblies to end the slave trade were blocked by the better-organized proslavery party.

The doctrines of the Amis des Noirs spread to the colonies, especially Saint Domingue (Haiti), and fed unrest among the slaves and mulattoes (the latter were free, though second-class citizens, and held property, including slaves).

By the summer of 1791, the Amis des Noirs had been absorbed into other Girondist groups. They continued to publish abolitionist articles, but the antislavery cause took a back seat to other concerns involving the governance of France and the defense of the revolution. Brissot, Condorcet, and others shared the tragic fate of Girondist leaders. In 1793 they lost a power struggle with Maximilien Robespierre and his Jacobin "Mountain" faction. Robespierre then had many of the Girondist leaders executed during the reign of terror. Other members of the society, like Lafayette, survived the French Revolution and continued their opposition to slavery. But even those who did not survive the terror had helped prepare the ground for subsequent abolition efforts.

See also ABOLITIONIST AND ANTISLAVERY MOVEMENTS; FRANKLIN, BENJAMIN, AND THE MARQUIS DE CONDORCET; GRÉGOIRE, HENRI, BISHOP.

BIBLIOGRAPHY

DAVIS, DAVID BRION. *The Problem of Slavery in the Age of Revolution, 1770–1823.* 1975.
ELLERY, ELOISE. *Brissot de Warville: A Study in the History of the French Revolution.* 1915.
KATES, GARY. *The Cercle Social, the Girondins, and the French Revolution.* 1985.
POPKIN, RICHARD H. "Condorcet, Abolitionist." In *Condorcet Studies I,* edited by Leonora Cohen Rosenfield and Richard H. Popkin. 1984.
STEIN, ROBERT LOUIS. *The French Slave Trade in the Eighteenth Century: An Old Régime Business.* 1979.

Marquis de Condorcet. [Corbis-Bettmann]

Charles E. Williams

Society for the Propagation of the Gospel

The missionary arm of the Anglican church, the Society for the Propagation of the Gospel was formed in 1701 to educate and reform the inhabitants of England's "Plantations, Colonies, and Factories beyond the Seas." In the church's opinion, the need for such work was urgent, since many of the island nation's "Loving Subjects" lacked ministers to administer the sacraments, and were therefore being drawn to "Popish Superstition and Idolatry." The society supported 329 missionaries, 82 schoolmasters, and 18 catechists before its last United States missionary departed in 1783. Through the society the Anglican Church also reached out to the islands of the Caribbean, where English subjects had been dispatched by an expanding monarchy. The society's seal effectively reflected its zeal: on it, natives cried "come over and help us" to a ship bearing a man with a Bible in his outstretched hand.

Once in the colonies, some society parsons purchased slaves; others used workers provided by their parishioners. The society instructed their slaves in reading and religion, and encouraged colonists to follow their example. The church argued that slaves, once converted to Christianity, would be more docile and diligent. Owners, however, remained wary of the society's plans. For them, the state of enslaved souls held little, if any, concern. Conversion to Christianity, planters worried, might make a slave free; literacy might encourage disobedience and rebellion. Here Christian duty and ownership prerogative clashed. Between 1664 and 1706 acts were passed or reinforced in Maryland, Virginia, North and South Carolina, New York, and New Jersey that stipulated that slave baptism and freedom were not at all related. Other laws forbade teaching slaves to read, effectively squelching the society's efforts.

For the Society of the Propagation of the Gospel, slavery was an accepted part of life's social and economic fabric. In contemporary opinion, Christianity and slavery were compatible. The society was supported in part by donations made by slave owners and by the profits of two Barbados sugar plantations, staffed by three hundred slaves, that Christopher Codrington bequeathed to it in 1710. Although it owned slaves, purchased Africans for its plantations, and profited from their labor, the Society viewed "the Instruction and Conversion of the *Negroes,* as a principal Branch of their Care." It was "a great Reproach," the Society argued in 1730, that "so many Thousands of Persons" lived in "*Pagan* Darkness, under a Christian Government." Missionaries vividly described slavery in the colonies, recording the cruel treatment of slaves by masters and the widespread opposition to religious instruction and conversion. While the society urged that slaves should be treated humanely, it ultimately viewed them as a means of production. Although they were "very capable of receiving Instruction," slaves were property. The society never suggested that they be otherwise. Many planters, meanwhile, argued simply that the society's work was useless, because "the *Negroes* had no Souls."

While other religious groups, such as the Quakers, argued for the abolition of slavery, the Anglican church maintained that Christianity and slavery were compatible. Freed by the Emancipation Act of 1833, slaves remained on the society's Codrington plantations as apprentices until 1838, when the Barbadian legislature freed them.

See also ANGLICANISM; CARIBBEAN REGION; CHRISTIANITY; MISSIONARIES.

BIBLIOGRAPHY

BENNETT, J. HARRY, JR. *Bondsmen and Bishops: Slavery and Apprenticeship on the Codrington Plantations of Barbados, 1710–1838.* 1958.

CALAM, JOHN. *Parsons and Pedagogues: The S.P.G. Adventure in American Education.* 1971.

HUMPHREYS, DAVID. *An Historical Account of the Incorporated Society for the Propagation of the Gospel in Foreign Parts.* 1730. Reprint, 1969.

PASCOE, C. F. *Two Hundred Years of the S.P.G.* 1901.

Jennifer Davis McDaid

Society of Friends

See Quakers.

Sociology of Slavery

See Perspectives on Slavery.

Soldiers, Slaves as

See Military Slaves.

Solomon, Job Ben   [ca. 1701–1773]

African Muslim enslaved in North America.

Job Ben Solomon was born Ayuba b. Sulayman Diallo in the upper Senegal valley of West Africa, in the land of Bundu (a part of the borderland between Senegal and Mali). A Muslim of Fulbe ethnicity, he will henceforth be referred to as Ayuba. The story of his enslavement, manumission, and subsequent repatriation to West Africa was an early and well-known African traveler's tale in Europe, having been first published

Job Ben Solomon. [New York Public Library, Research Libraries]

in 1734 by Thomas Bluett, to whom the account was given.

Captured by slave traders in West Africa in 1730 and taken to Maryland in 1732, Ayuba was put to work cultivating tobacco on Kent Island in the Chesapeake. When it became clear to his owner, a Mr. Tolsey, that he was unsuited for such labor, Ayuba was assigned to tend cattle. It was at this juncture that Ayuba's Muslim background became a factor and dramatically changed his circumstances, for he would often go into the woods to pray in seclusion. Constant harassment by a local white youth caused Ayuba to flee the Tolsey estate, but he was apprehended in what is now Kent County, Delaware. Unable to speak English, Ayuba began to write in Arabic for his captors and onlookers, who were astonished at the fact that an African was literate. Still in custody, Ayuba sent a letter to his father back in West Africa, pleading for him to intervene. The letter came to the attention of certain Englishmen, who arranged for Ayuba to be emancipated and to travel to England. Ayuba remained in England from April 1733 to July 1734, when he returned to West Africa.

At this point Ayuba's story becomes more complicated, for he returned to his native land not simply as a son of the soil but as an agent for a British trading establishment, the Royal African Company. It was the intention of the British to gain access to the slave, gold, and gum trades of the upper Senegal and upper Gambia valleys, and Ayuba was seen as someone whose influence could help direct the traffic in these trades toward the British along the Gambia River and away from the French operating in the lower Senegal. From the Gambia, Ayuba was accompanied to Bundu by Thomas Hull, a relative of the governor of British interests in Gambia, Richard Hull. The data suggest that Ayuba was very active in promoting British commercial interests in the upper Senegal, much to the consternation of the French. Mention of Ayuba in the records of the Royal African Company does not continue beyond the 1740s.

Ayuba b. Sulayman Diallo is significant as an example of the great diversity in background and experience of Africans imported as slaves into the Americas. There were many Africans who—like Ayuba—had practiced monotheism before arriving in the New World, whether they were Muslims or Christians. (For example, many slaves from Kongo in West Central Africa were Catholics.) There was also significant diversity in occupational expertise and propensities, as evidenced by Ayuba's inability to adjust to tobacco farming. Finally, there were Africans who had achieved substantial literacy and had come from circumstances of privilege and power. Such important information, crucial to understanding the origins and development of the African-American population, tends to go undetected in uncritical inquiries into American slavery.

See also ISLAM; ROYAL AFRICAN COMPANY.

BIBLIOGRAPHY

AUSTIN, ALLAN D. *African Muslims in Antebellum America: A Sourcebook.* 1984.

CURTIN, PHILIP D. "Ayuba Suleiman Diallo of Bundu." In *Africa Remembered: Narratives from the Era of the Slave Trade,* edited by Philip D. Curtin. 1977.

GRANT, DOUGLAS. *The Fortunate Slave: An Illustration of African Slavery in the Early Eighteenth Century.* 1968.

Michael A. Gomez

Somerset v. Stewart (1772)

The case of *Somerset v. Stewart* was decided in 1772 by the Court of King's Bench of England, sitting at Westminster Hall in London. The decision was a momentous step toward the abolition of slavery in England. Some expressions in the opinion given by the chief justice of the court, Lord Mansfield, became famous:

slavery is "so odious that nothing can be suffered to support it but positive law"; slavery "must be construed strictly" and "is not to be introduced by inference from principles either natural or political." These statements, in fact, helped create a popular belief that, by his opinion, Lord Mansfield had freed the slaves in England.

The scope of *Somerset* was in truth quite narrow. The case involved a habeas corpus petition procured by the abolitionist Granville Sharp on behalf of James Somerset, a slave who was at the time manacled in irons on board a ship lying in the Thames, bound for Jamaica. The captain of the ship had been instructed by Somerset's owner, Charles Stewart, that Somerset was to be taken to Jamaica to be sold. When the habeas corpus petition was heard, it came out that Somerset had been acquired by Stewart in Virginia and had lately been brought by Stewart to England, where Somerset had absconded, only to be spotted later by Stewart and retaken. The issue that was placed before the court was whether it was legal for Stewart, in England, to capture Somerset and forcibly take him out of the country. The court held that this was not allowed by English law. As Lord Mansfield himself later explained, the principles established by *Somerset* and earlier authorities "go no further than that the master cannot by force compel [his slave] to go out of the kingdom."

Before the *Somerset* case, the law of England on slavery was both unclear and confusing. Cases in the late seventeenth and early eighteenth century acknowledged that a master could have a special property interest in his slave sufficient to justify a trespass action, as would also be true of an indentured servant, but beyond this the law looked upon slaves "as on the rest of mankind." The question of the nature of slavery in English law did not arise in very many cases, but occasional attempts were made in the eighteenth century before *Somerset* to get a court to declare that masters had unqualified property rights in their slaves. These attempts were unsuccessful, though not so much because the courts were able to reject them outright as because the courts avoided being boxed into a corner where they would have to decide the question of property.

When the *Somerset* case arose, however, avoidance was no longer possible. Both sides—the abolitionist intensity of Granville Sharp for Somerset and the unified West Indian merchants on behalf of Stewart—insisted on taking the case to a final decision. The case was argued by talented barristers, John Dunning for Stewart and Francis Hargrave for Somerset. Dunning's heart was not in the case for the defense, and Hargrave was catapulted into prominence by his meticulous, intellectual presentation for Somerset (which he

later expanded and published as "*An Argument in the case of James Sommersett, a Negro, wherein it is attempted to demonstrate the present unlawfulness of Domestic Slavery in England,*" [London, 1772; Boston, 1774]. While the case was pending, Stewart, in a letter to an acquaintance, described "how the Negro cause goes on," stating that he had not attended the most recent hearings, but "am told that some young counsel flourished away on the side of liberty, and acquired great honor. Dunning was dull and languid, and would have made a much better figure on that side also."

Dunning emphasized what some viewed as the potentially harsh economic consequences of any declaration that slavery in England was no longer legal—consequences that would become catastrophic if any such declaration were extended to the colonies. The strongest legal argument for Stewart was that slavery was but an incremental step away from venerable practices that everyone in England accepted, that is, apprenticeship, indentured servitude, and villeinage (an ancient, extreme form of servitude connected to the land and deriving from the feudal era). Some attempt was made to say that if a servant could indenture himself for life by contract, then contract theory could be used to support the institution of slavery, but during an intermediate phase of the case, Lord Mansfield rejected this notion, as "utterly repugnant and destructive of every idea of a contract between the parties."

In arguing for Somerset, Hargrave showed how villeinage had fallen into complete disuse in England and could no longer carry any weight as a precedent. He went into the history of slavery in England and other countries, and he addressed the rather flimsy contractual theory as well as the question of what law applied to the case.

In the end, even though the actual ruling of the court in *Somerset* was technically narrow, the case quickly became folklore and gave considerable momentum to the march toward emancipation. Lord Mansfield was credited with more than he actually decided, as some historians have been at pains to explain. Nevertheless, the decision was of great contemporary importance to the population at large. Perhaps this is nowhere better illustrated than by a letter dated 10 July 1772 to Stewart from one John Riddell at Bristol Wells. Complaining to Stewart about the disappearance of a slave named Dublin, Riddell wrote: "But I am disappointed by Mr. Dublin who has run away. He told the servants that he had rec'd a letter from his Uncle Sommerset acquainting him that Lord Mansfield had given them their freedom & he was determined to leave me as soon as I returned from London which he did without even speaking to me."

See also LAW; SHARP, GRANVILLE.

BIBLIOGRAPHY

DAVIS, DAVID BRION. *The Problem of Slavery in the Age of Revolution, 1770–1823.* 1975.
FIDDES, EDWARD. "Lord Mansfield and the Sommersett Case." *Law Quarterly Review* 50 (1934): 499–511.
FINKELMAN, PAUL. *An Imperfect Union: Slavery, Federalism, and Comity.* 1981.
GERZINA, GRETCHEN. *Black London: Life before Emancipation.* 1995.
OLDHAM, JAMES. "New Light on Mansfield and Slavery." *Journal of British Studies* 27 (1988): 45–68.
——. *The Mansfield Manuscripts and the Growth of English Law in the Eighteenth Century.* 1992; chap. 21.
STEWART PAPERS, MS 5027, National Library of Scotland, Edinburgh.
WIECEK, WILLIAM M. *The Source of Antislavery Constitutionalism in America, 1760–1848.* 1977.

James Oldham

Sotho

See Southern Africa.

South America

See Amerindian Societies; Brazil; Caribbean Region; Plantations; Portugal; Spain.

South Carolina

South Carolina's proprietors envisioned slavery in the colony at its inception in 1663. They sought to attract settlers from, among other places, Barbados who were being pushed out of the island by the sugar revolution; and an early document suggested head rights of 20 acres for each male and 10 for every female African slave brought into the colony within the first five years. Many of the original settlers did come from Barbados, and they brought with them concepts of slavery as it had started to develop in the island. These included the idea that slaves were freehold rather than chattel property, who owed service but were not, at least in theory, absolutely transferable at will. Slaves had significant autonomy and provided much of their own livelihood. This autonomy was reinforced in the first years of Carolina's settlement, as frontier conditions fostered slaves' initiative and, occasionally, a rough working equivalence among small planters and their slaves as they struggled together to build a new society in the wilderness. These conditions did not, perhaps, obscure the slaves' servile status but may have fortified their sense of self-worth. Their position had deteriorated by the second half of the eighteenth century,

however, and chattel slavery and the planters' hegemony were secure.

In its early years, the colony engaged in extractive industries, cutting lumber and timber, refining tar and turpentine, and curing deerskins for transport overseas. It also provided auxiliary support for Barbados, shipping meat and other foodstuffs to the island. In some of these pursuits the contribution of slaves went beyond the labor they provided. Knowledge acquired in Africa facilitated the slaves' mastery of Carolina's river systems, and fishing methods and the practices of free grazing and nighttime pinning of cattle all had African analogues. But the slaves' greatest contribution to Carolina's development is to be found in the know-how Africans brought to rice cultivation, the crop that came to dominate the region's staple production. In perhaps no other region have scholars suggested that an African component was so important to success.

Rice cultivation secured the colony's wealth and eventually made South Carolina the richest of Britain's North American colonies. It maintained this distinction as a state into the nineteenth century. The largest slave owners and richest planters lived in South Carolina, which also had the greatest gulf between rich and poor. Unlike tobacco or cotton, which could be grown in small units by poor farmers without slaves, rice required an initial outlay of significant amounts of cash and an optimum labor force of at least thirty slaves. These requirements limited the number of rice planters and gave the social structure a more aristocratic cast than existed in, for example, the Chesapeake. The rice and sea-island cotton regions along the coast were distinguished by use of the task system of labor organization, which assigned slaves a specific acreage requirement for cultivation but allowed them to control their own time if they completed their assignment before the day's end. This system permitted a few slaves to accumulate significant property of their own, made it possible for individuals to reinforce the male role in the slave family, and facilitated mutual exchange among slaves that recalled, if it never quite duplicated, the internal systems of slave marketing that prevailed in the West Indies.

Charleston became the largest slave entrepôt in eighteenth-century North America; it was the point of entry for approximately 40 percent of all the slaves who entered North America. Several prominent merchant planters dealt in the Atlantic slave trade and served as local slave distributors, including the revolutionary patriot Henry Laurens, who also ran successful plantations in South Carolina and Georgia. The American Revolution interrupted the trade, but it was revived thereafter, and although South Carolina banned it in 1787, the state's opposition to the ban

Henry Laurens. [Library of Congress/Corbis]

along with that of Georgia prevented the slave trade's abolition at the Constitutional Convention. These two states were responsible for the compromise that was reached whereby the federal government could take no action on the traffic before 1807. South Carolina shocked the nation when it reopened the trade in 1803 to beat the deadline of its certain termination in 1808, thus becoming the last state to legalize the practice. It imported about ten thousand slaves annually in that interim.

While slave society focused on the seaboard during the colonial period, the advent of short-staple cotton spurred the spread of slavery into the backcountry during the second half of the eighteenth century and changed the demographics of the region. From the second decade of the century, lowland rice-growing parishes had exhibited a demographic disproportion of two to one in favor of blacks. This was the only region in mainland British North America where that degree of racial disparity existed; upland regions, by contrast, remained demographically white. The success of short-staple cotton changed this situation, and the black population grew significantly between 1790 and 1850, bringing economic, social, and political unity in its wake. The wealthiest districts of rice production, however, remained overwhelmingly black

until after the Civil War, a fact that was significant in the development of regional culture.

The region was also the scene of significant slave rebellions. The Stono Rebellion—the largest in Britain's North America colonies—occurred in 1739 several miles outside of Charleston, when slaves from the Angolan region of Africa, the predominant group in the colony at the time, fled toward the promise of freedom in Spanish Florida. The revolt, in which several planters were killed, was initially successful. When the slaves stopped to celebrate and draw others to their banner, however, they were surrounded and dispersed by colonial militia. In the rebellion's aftermath, South Carolina restricted the slave trade, tightened slave laws, and encouraged white immigration to offset the imbalance between whites and blacks. Denmark Vesey's 1822 slave conspiracy was betrayed before any white people were killed as in the Stono uprising, but it evoked no less fear. Vesey was a former slave who had purchased his freedom after winning a lottery and who was influenced by Christian beliefs modified by African outlooks and practices. He was emboldened by the example of a successful revolution in Haiti and encouraged by antislavery sentiments expressed in Congressional debates over the Missouri Compromise. He planned to conquer Charleston and perhaps flee to the West Indies. When authorities learned of the plot, they reacted swiftly and hanged thirty-five slaves including Vesey (most of them in a mass execution) and banished over forty others. They then banned worship in Charleston's African Methodist Episcopal Church, where Vesey had preached and gained support, and passed the Negro Seamen's Act, which called for imprisonment of black sailors while in port, in an attempt to insulate the black populace from undesirable outside influences.

This concern about the integrity of slavery influenced South Carolina's leading politicians and made them strident in defense of a states' rights position, which they deemed essential to slavery's security. An expansive federal system, particularly after 1830 when abolitionism gained increasing notoriety and northern free-soil sentiment challenged the South's proslavery desires in the nation's western territories, caused southern leaders like South Carolina's John C. Calhoun to forsake nationalism early and become firm proponents of regional outlooks and institutions. The state was home to some of the earliest and most obdurate "fire-eaters"—those who championed disunion and southern independence. Congressman Preston Brooks, who gained celebrity in his native state as a result of his near-fatal caning of Massachusetts' antislavery Senator Charles Sumner in 1856, declared that he had "been a disunionist from the time I could think." And Robert Barnwell Rhett willingly acknowl-

Table 1.   South Carolina's Population, Slave and Free, 1700–1860.

| | Black | | |
Year	Free Blacks	Slaves	White
1700		2,444	3,260
1710		5,768	5,115
1720		11,868	6,525
1730		20,000	10,000
1740		39,155	20,000
1750		40,000	25,000
1760		53,000	36,740
1770		75,178	49,066
1780		97,000	83,000
1790	1,801	107,094	140,178
1800	3,185	146,151	196,255
1810	4,554	196,365	214,196
1820	6,826	258,475	237,440
1830	7,921	315,401	257,863
1840	8,276	327,038	259,084
1850	8,960	384,984	274,563
1860	9,914	402,406	291,300

Sources: Peter Coclanis, *The Shadow of a Dream* (1989), p. 64; Henry Chase and C. H. Sanborn, *The North and the South* (1857), pp. 155–157; *Eighth Census of the United States, 1860,* vol. 1.

edged that the acute perception of dishonor involved in a southern submission to what many South Carolinians saw as northern tyranny derived from their command of slaves. Congressman Laurence M. Keitt connected the slaying of his brother by disgruntled bondsmen to northern influence and described the election of 1860 as more than just another election: "With us," he explained, "it is life or Death." These were among the considerations that caused South Carolina to leave the Union in December. Although slavery was not the only issue that motivated the state's people and politicians and brought disunion and civil conflict in its wake, it was the most basic.

See also ECONOMICS OF SLAVERY; STONO REBELLION; VESEY REBELLION.

BIBLIOGRAPHY

CLOWSE, CONVERSE D. *Economic Beginnings in Colonial South Carolina, 1670–1730.* 1971.

COOPER, WILLIAM J. *The South and the Politics of Slavery, 1828–1856.* 1978.

HUDSON, LARRY E., JR. *To Have and To Hold: Slave Work and Family Life in Antebellum South Carolina.* 1997.

JOYNER, CHARLES. *Down by the Riverside: A South Carolina Slave Community.* 1984.

KLEIN, RACHEL N. *Unification of a Slave State: The Rise of the Planter Class in the South Carolina Backcountry, 1760–1808.* 1990.

LITTLEFIELD, DANIEL C. *Rice and Slaves: Ethnicity and the Slave Trade in Colonial South Carolina.* 1981. Reprint, 1991.

WALTHER, ERIC H. *The Fire-Eaters.* 1992.

WOOD, PETER H. *Black Majority: Negroes in Colonial South Carolina from 1670 through the Stono Rebellion.* 1974.

Daniel C. Littlefield

Southeast Asia

Slavery existed widely throughout both mainland and insular Southeast Asia, with origins that preceded documentary evidence. Most historians analyze slavery as an integral part of the hierarchical social fabric of early Southeast Asian societies, so embedded that many Southeast Asian languages use first person pronouns as the common words for slave or bondsperson. Many of these societies also had creation myths legitimating these unequal relationships among kings, commoners, and slaves.

Slavery was part of the process of state formation in Southeast Asia. Methods of obtaining slaves included capture in war or raids on neighbouring peoples and judicial punishment for crimes or inability to pay fines. The commonest form of slavery, however, derived from debt bondage, which individuals or clans negotiated with creditors. Legal systems codified laws governing slavery in great detail, reflecting the importance of control over labor—rather than land—as the source of wealth and power within early Southeast Asian societies. The basic principles governing relationships of rank and precedence were therefore debt and obligation. Sometimes debt slavery to a powerful owner was deliberately chosen to obtain his protection or to escape from state corvée or tax obligations. Many such bondspeople were allowed to earn their own livings as cultivators, fisherpeople, artisans, and laborers while repaying their debt to their master from a percentage of their income. These bonds were fixed in monetary terms and were transferable, both characteristics of European ideas of chattel slavery. Although Southeast Asian slavery involved a commercial relationship of social claims and obligations, slaves retained legal rights as members of society. This differed from European and New World slavery, where masters owned slaves as disposable property without social or legal recognition of slaves' rights as people.

The oldest evidence of slavery in Southeast Asia comes from inscriptions such as those at Angkor in Cambodia, the earliest from the ninth century, which depict temple slaves as artisans, warriors, war captives, and laborers. Temple slaves in Buddhist societies labored in fields and on construction projects, and traded on behalf of the Buddhist monkhood (*sangha*), who were thus freed for their religious functions. Unlike secular slaves, *sangha* slaves were not liable for royal corvée labor. Historians debate whether Buddhist rulers attempted to coopt *sangha* slaves for corvée. By early modern times, secular debt slaves owned by individuals were also increasingly shielded from government corvée and taxes, and Burmese, Thai, and Vietnamese rulers actively tried to reduce their numbers.

Anthony Reid categorizes Southeast Asian slavery into "open" and "closed" systems, maintaining that both existed simultaneously and could change from one to the other over time. Closed systems involved immutable separation between categories of nobility, free and slave. Slave status was hereditary and ritualized, particularly in terms of forced labor duties for the dominant class. These societies included Nias, Toba Batak, and the Melanau of Sarawak, where the major distinctions were between slaves who worked in cultivation with a degree of independent livelihood and domestic slaves who were more intimately linked to their master's household. Among the Mandar and the Sa'dan Toraja of Sulawesi, the main distinction was between inalienable lineage slaves and other slaves who could be sold. Slaves in such closed systems were permanently unequal and their status emphasized in ritual practice. In the Nias language, the word for slave also meant child. Proportions of slaves in the population are estimated at 10 percent for the Melanau, 15 percent for Nias, and 30 percent for the Batak.

Open systems of slavery involved greater flexibility of people being absorbed as slaves into the society and their ability to change their status. Slaves could become free through manumission or over generations as bondage obligations weakened. Slavery in this sense mainly functioned as a way to initially obtain labor. Open systems became more common from the fifteenth century as commercialization and urbanization increased in Southeast Asia. There was no free labor market in the entrepôt city-states like Melaka in the fifteenth century and Aceh and Makassar from the sixteenth and seventeenth centuries. Slaves were considered the most important commodity within these societies, and the labor market consisted of hiring slaves from their masters. Theoretically, slaves could manumit themselves through repayment, but interest rates were so high that few managed to do so. Slaves seeking to escape manual labor and maximize their freedom would instead spend their income buying bondspeople of their own to take over their labor obligations. In this way they were absorbed into the

A relief sculpture from Bayon, Cambodia, depicts slave labor. [Kevin Morris/Corbis]

free population by virtue of escaping manual labor. Formal manumission as a legal recognition of freedom was not necessary or desirable. A shift from one system to the other within particular societies occurred with the social and economic changes of commercialization. For example, with increasing trade in the seventeenth century, Nias began to export its own people as slaves thereby shifting from a closed to an open slave system.

The introduction of Islam to some Southeast Asian societies altered slavery by incorporating concepts of Muslim insiders and outsiders as a distinction more important than slave and free. Islamization could also result in a shift from a closed to an open system of slavery. For example, the conversion to Islam of the Bugis ruler in South Sulawesi was accompanied by large-scale emancipation of hereditary slaves. Although debt bondage remained, this characterised a more open system of slavery. Islamization, however, also changed the pattern of the slave trade and ownership in other ways by forbidding the selling of Muslims as slaves. Islam allowed slavery but encouraged the conversion of non-Muslim slaves. Women slaves bought as concubines and their children were eventually assimilated into the free Muslim population through this process. Animist peoples of the interior were also gradually incorporated into the Muslim coastal societies through their enslavement and subsequent conversion.

From the sixteenth century European colonialism increased the number of slaves overall and strengthened racial differentiation in the region. Chattel slavery was legalized, and assimilation of slaves into the free colonial population became increasingly rare. While Europeans were enslaved only in small numbers in Southeast Asian societies, they engaged in a large-scale slave trade of indigenous Southeast Asians and differentiated between them according to racial characteristics attributed to them. Europeans did not enslave all Southeast Asian ethnic groups, but some groups were ascribed inherent traits that determined their suitability for enslavement and for different kinds of labor. The Dutch East India and English East India Companies and their employees traded and exported slaves as chattel. Europeans bought women as concubines, used others for domestic and rural labor, and in some cases employed them as plantation workers producing valuable spices (for example, cultivating nutmeg on the Banda Islands). Colonial slavery hardened the legal concept of slaves as chattel, though earlier forms of indigenous slavery continued, particularly the use of slaves for cultivation and as displays of individual wealth in colonial cities like Batavia. Following the example of Southeast Asian men, Eu-ropeans bought slave women as concubines, despite company sanctions against the practice.

Emancipation in Southeast Asia emerged from the nineteenth-century antislavery movements in Europe, although indigenous slavery was not eradicated in practice until the twentieth century. Debt slavery continued in some of the Malay states, the Sulu sultanate, and parts of Borneo. In Siam, which was never colonized, slavery was abolished in theory by royal edict in 1874—and accomplished by 1915.

The continuation of slavery in Southeast Asia in the twentieth century is a matter of great contention. Current investigations are examining Japan's use of slave labor during World War II, particularly the sexual exploitation of "comfort women." The United Nations held a convention condemning slavery in 1956, acknowledging that many forms of slavery described above still existed. Burma in particular has been singled out as practicing forms of state slavery through forced removals and conscripted labor of ethnic minorities. Human Rights Watch has documented the selling of Burmese female children for prostitution in Thailand as one example of contemporary slavery through sexual exploitation existing in Southeast Asia in the late 1990s.

See also BUDDHISM; COMFORT WOMEN IN WORLD WAR II; INDONESIA; ISLAM; PHILIPPINES; SLAVE TRADE; THAILAND.

BIBLIOGRAPHY

MIERS, SUZANNE. "Contemporary Forms of Slavery." *Itinerario* 17, no. 3 (December 1996): 238–246.
REID, ANTHONY. *Southeast Asia in the Age of Commerce, 1440–1680*, vol. 1: *The Land below the Winds*. 1988.
———, ed. *Slavery, Bondage, and Dependency in Southeast Asia.* 1983.
TARLING, N., ed. *Cambridge History of Southeast Asia.* 1992.

Kerry Ward
Nigel Worden

Southern Africa

This entry includes the following articles: Cape of Good Hope; Sotho/Nguni. *Related articles may be found at the entries* Africa; Central Africa; East Africa; North Africa; Northeast Africa; Plantations; Slave Trade; West Africa. *See also the note accompanying the entry* Africa *for further information about the organization of these entries.*

Cape of Good Hope

Slavery came to the Cape of Good Hope with European colonization. No indigenous forms of slavery existed in the region, although a well-established system of patronage bound some *San* (hunter-gatherers) as clients to *Khoikhoi* (pastoralists) patrons. A few enslaved body servants were among the possessions brought to the Cape of officials of the Dutch East India Company (DEIC) when they planted a small settlement on the shores of Table Bay in 1652. That this tiny enclave grew to become the port city of Cape Town, the capital of an extensive settler colony, was almost accidental. That the colony evolved into a slave society was not.

The DEIC intended the settlement to be more than a way station servicing its ships on trading voyages to and from Asia. The company supposed that barter with the Khoikhoi would provide cattle and sheep and that company employees, toiling in company gardens, would furnish fresh fruit and vegetables. This scheme proved unworkable. Khoikhoi chiefdoms could not supply livestock in the requisite numbers, and the company's employees showed no enthusiasm for farm labor. In 1655 the settlement's commander suggested that the DEIC release a small number of employees from their contracts and grant them land to cultivate as independent farmers. The way station was transformed into a colony of settlement.

Company officials at the Cape complained about scarce and inefficient labor from the first days of the settlement. The decision to create a community of free farmers aggravated the shortage. Company policy blocked local proposals to enslave the San and Khoikhoi and to import Chinese as indentured servants but allowed the importation of slaves. The first cargoes of Africans arrived in 1658 and were among the very few slaves of West African origin to reach the Cape. Some of these slaves became the property of the DEIC; others were sold to the free farmers. Thereafter the trade to the Cape, until it ended in 1808, drew on the Indian Ocean basin, bringing 62,000 slaves to the colony in approximately equal proportions from four broad geographical regions: the Indonesian archipelago, the Indian subcontinent and Sri Lanka, Madagascar, and East Africa north of Delagoa Bay. By the first decade of the eighteenth century, slaves constituted over half the population and supplied the bulk of the workforce in the two largest sectors of the economy, the port of Cape Town and the arable farming districts of the southwestern Cape. Slavery as an institution shaped the colony's laws and mores. The Cape had become a slave society.

Between 1750 and 1834 roughly half of all adult male settlers owned slaves. Private slaveholdings varied considerably in size but were generally small compared with other European slave societies of the Atlantic world. The largest were in Cape Town and in the intensively cultivated wine and wheat farming districts of the southwestern Cape. In the years just prior to formal emancipation in 1834, when the slave population totaled about 35,000, the average farmer of arable land had owned just under eight slaves; only a small minority, one in twenty-two farmers, possessed twenty or more slaves. Urban slave owners in Cape Town held an average of five slaves. In the northern and eastern cattle-raising districts, the average holding was about half the size of those in the arable southwest.

Throughout the slave era, 80 to 90 percent of the slave population was concentrated in Cape Town and the nearby arable farming districts. This distribution of slaves reflected southwestern slaveowners' need for a larger workforce and their ability to buy one. Arable farming was labor-intensive, and slaves filled every position on the farms from the least to the most skilled, including those of vintner, distiller, and occasionally overseer. Slave-produced wine, wheat, and brandy formed the basis of settlers' wealth. In Cape Town slave owners employed their slaves in every sector of the urban economy: on the docks as stevedores; in commerce as porters and warehousemen; in the trades as carpenters, blacksmiths, masons, fishermen, whalers, seamstresses, and laundrywomen; and of course in domestic service. Urban slave owners routinely rented slaves to farmers during peak labor seasons. A small number of slaveowners in Cape Town were free blacks. Their motives for purchasing slaves were diverse. Some bought friends and family members in order to free them. Others purchased slaves simply to profit from the exploitation of their labor. Most sheep and cattle farmers struggled economically and found it difficult to purchase slaves. These farmers tended to rely on hired or forcibly indentured San and Khoikhoi workers.

Male slaves always outnumbered females at the Cape, though the gap narrowed considerably in the nineteenth century. This hindered but by no means prevented the formation of slave families. Although the laws of the Cape recognized slave marriages only from the 1820s, slaves had long formed lasting unions among themselves, and it was common for slave men to take Khoikhoi women as wives. Slave women, especially those of Asian descent, occasionally married poor white men. The families that slaves created provided a fragile shelter from the storms of slavery and were an institutional basis for an emerging sense of communal identity.

Slaves at the Cape staged no large rebellions, yet less spectacular forms of resistance were endemic. Malingering, theft, and disobedience were daily events in virtually every slaveholding. Arson and assault were the forms of resistance slaveowners feared the most and punished the most severely, while escape was the most common. Slaves ran away singly and in groups, hoping to reach mountain hideaways or independent African societies on the colonial frontier. Escape was easiest in the northern and eastern ranching districts, where the population was scarce and African societies were near. There almost two slaves in every hundred were fugitives.

Antislavery sentiment in the Cape was weak and poorly organized and played no role in abolition. Emancipation was the work of the British Parliament, which in 1833 voted to end slavery in its Atlantic colonies. The formal abolition of slavery in 1834 was followed, however, by a four-year period of "apprenticeship," which Parliament eventually acknowledged was little more than slavery under another name. Apprenticeship came to an end on 1 December 1838, and with it, effectively, slavery at the Cape of Good Hope.

See also AFRICA; SLAVE TRADE.

BIBLIOGRAPHY

MASON, JOHN. *Social Death and Resurrection: Slavery and Emancipation in South Africa.* 1999.

ROSS, ROBERT. *Cape of Torments: Slavery and Resistance in South Africa.* 1983.

SCULLY, PAMELA. *Liberating the Family? Gender and British Slave Emancipation in the Rural Western Cape, 1823–1853.* 1997.

SHELL, ROBERT C.-H. *Children of Bondage: A Social History of the Slave Society at the Cape of Good Hope.* 1994.

WORDEN, NIGEL. *Slavery in Dutch South Africa.* 1985.

John Edwin Mason

Sotho/Nguni

Forms of subordination and servitude among the Sotho-speaking (Sotho, Tswana, Pedi) and Nguni-speaking (Xhosa, Zulu, Swazi) peoples in southeastern Africa arose from conquest and incorporation during a period, beginning in the seventeenth and eighteenth centuries, when political units were expanding in scale. They incorporated newcomers as dependent clients, obliged to provide tribute in labor and in kind, but given access to land and cattle. Generally, the subsequent development of kinship links through marriage eliminated the original social distinctions, and no permanent class of servants or slaves emerged in these societies.

Sotho and Nguni otherwise developed a wide range of patron-client relationships with each other and with neighboring KhoiSan hunter-gatherers prior to the nineteenth century. The obligations of these clients—*bathlanka* (SeTswana)/*bahlanka* (SeSotho)—

varied over time and region. Tswana farmers and herders established their dominance over San hunter-gatherers in the seventeenth century, initiating an increasingly harsh servitude. Children that the Tswana captured in war became servants, and their descendants inherited that status. Such captives could be ransomed by their parents with payment of one or two head of cattle, and although they were sometimes transferred from one master to another, they could not be bought or sold, nor did their captors ever transfer them or sell them to other groups. With the emergence of large Tswana kingdoms in the nineteenth century, the San (Basarwa, Balala) experienced a permanent reduction in status. The conditions of *bathlanka* clientage deteriorated steadily after the 1830s or 1840s, and by the late nineteenth century Basarwa living among the Tswana inherited their *bathlanka* status, enjoyed few legal protections, and were subject to compulsory, uncompensated labor. From the 1850s through the 1870s, Tswana sold *bathlanka* children to Boer slavers for settler farmers in the Transvaal. Such sale of *bathlanka* appears to have declined by 1910, but their status continued to be equated with slavery well into the twentieth century.

Sotho and Nguni incorporated voluntary clients and defeated populations on a massive scale during a prolonged period of environmental, social, and political disruption after the 1820s, but they do not seem to have traded, bought, or sold these clients or captives after they were attached as servants to a master or to the rulers of several new polities that emerged at the time. The BaSotho nation, under Moshoeshoe, took shape through wholesale voluntary submissions of existing chiefdoms, and no permanent class of *bahlanka* servants emerged. Among the Zulu, beginning in the time of Shaka, around 1818, a warrior who captured boys and girls was permitted to keep them as servants, if they did not have to be turned over to the king. Girls, treated as children of their captors, would eventually be eligible for marriage to their male master, and no stigma of social inferiority remained for them. Boys could be redeemed by their relatives only upon payment in cattle. Boys not redeemed served a chief until they became warriors at adolescence and eventually established their own homesteads as adult clients. The Swazi similarly took children as booty in war and attached them to homesteads, especially to the royal capitals.

As white settlement expanded after the 1840s, Europeans captured Sotho and Nguni as forced laborers. Africans distinguished persons thus enslaved by Europeans from indigenous forms of servitude by adopting the Dutch word *ingeboekte,* or "registered" (slave), which became *ikhoboka* (Xhosa/Zulu) and *lekhoba* (Sotho/Tswana). A market for these captives developed after the late 1700s in the Cape colony, and Ordinance 49 of 1828 allowed for the employment of so-called foreigners and thus encouraged a hunt for captive laborers from beyond the Cape frontier. From the 1790s some Griqua and Khoi communities along the lower Orange River joined outlaw Europeans and Dutch-speaking settlers there in capturing Tswana and Sotho, especially children, for sale into the Cape colony. The British, who had assumed political control at the Cape in 1806, tolerated the practice into the 1850s, as Boer settlers would participate in commando operations needed to defend the frontier only upon the promise that they could keep children they captured as booty. That such captive laborers, notably children, continued to be bought and sold among white settlers suggests their de facto status as slaves long after official emancipation of registered slaves in the Cape in 1838.

The movement of Dutch-speaking settlers beyond the Cape frontier after about 1835 expanded the catchment area for such forced laborers to the Tswana, Swazi, Pedi, and Zulu, especially children, under the guise of apprenticeship, at least through the 1870s. Further to the northeast, the violence fueling the Delagoa Bay slave trade reached its peak in the 1830s–1840s but affected only the Tsonga and remnant groups of Nguni who had migrated into southern Mozambique; the Sotho and Nguni living to the south and west were beyond the reach of this trade. However, the northern Transvaal became a catchment area for so-called apprentices—*inboekelinge,* usually children, sold into other parts of the Transvaal and the Orange Free State into the 1870s; laws prohibiting the exchange, sale, or purchase of these captives were not observed or enforced. White settlers accused the Swazi of selling captive children, but their allegations are highly suspect.

The Sotho and Nguni began a transition to wage labor in the 1880s, with a rapid growth of diamond and gold mines able to pay cash to compete with the forcible methods of labor recruitment prevailing among European farmers. Harshly enforced contracts, pass laws, and migrancy laws continued to tie laborers and their families to unpaid labor on rural farms, where use of child labor, harsh conditions of work, and the frequent failure of farmers to pay their workers created conditions akin to slavery—for example, on the sugar plantations that thrived in Natal after the 1860s. Up to the end of apartheid in 1994, farmers in the Transvaal and the Orange Free State kept Sotho and Nguni families in debt bondage.

See also NETHERLANDS AND THE DUTCH EMPIRE.

BIBLIOGRAPHY

ELDRIDGE, ELIZABETH A. "Sources of Conflict in Southern Africa, circa 1800–1830: The 'Mfecane' Reconsidered." *Journal of African History* 33, no. 1 (1992): 1–35.

ELDRIDGE, ELIZABETH A., and FRED MORTON. *Slavery in South Africa: Captive Labor on the Dutch Frontier.* 1994.

Elizabeth A. Eldredge

Spain

This entry includes the following articles: Slavery in Spain; African Slavery; Colonies and Empire.

Slavery in Spain

Although slavery persisted in the Iberian peninsula throughout the medieval and early modern periods, most labor was free. Nevertheless, the Iberian kingdoms were frontier states, and non-Christians living across the borders could be captured and legally enslaved. Accordingly, slavery persisted in the peninsula more vigorously than elsewhere in Christian Europe, except for Italy. In the eighth to the eleventh centuries the enslavement of Christians gradually declined, and Muslims began to predominate in the slave population. Muslim prisoners at that time were frequently baptized and often became amalgamated into the lower rungs of Christian society. The rural Christian slaves became dependent workers. Like slaves, they were subject to a lord and tied to their land, but they had security of tenure and could not be sold or moved to another place. The remaining true slaves worked the land or served as servants, shepherds, or artisans.

Christians were frequently captured in Muslim raids and held for ransom or enslaved, and the Christian states devised means of ransoming them. Families could exchange Muslim slaves for their relatives. Later, specialized officials and members of religious orders arranged the exchanges.

The kingdom of Aragon, in eastern Iberia, shared a common pattern of slavery and slave holding with Italy and southern France. In this pattern urban and domestic slaves were more common than rural slaves, and women were more frequently enslaved than men. By the thirteenth century, North African Muslims became predominant. They were obtained primarily through trade but also through piracy and raids on land. After the Black Death sharply reduced populations in the mid-fourteenth century in Mediterranean Spain, Spanish and Italian merchants increasingly imported slaves from distant regions. Greeks, Sards, Tatars, Russians, Caucasians, Turks, Armenians, and various Balkan peoples were among those targeted.

A relief sculpture at the twelfth-century monastery of Santo Domingo of Silos in Burgos, Spain, depicts the freeing of Christian slaves. [Manuel Bellver/Corbis]

Slaves in late medieval Castile, the central region of Iberia, were almost exclusively Muslim in origin. Castilian slavery was fed by the Reconquest and the raids into Muslim territory. Muslim slaves were more numerous in the frontier regions and less frequently seen in the northern parts of Castile. Before the fifteenth century, slaves were only rarely purchased from merchants there.

By the mid-fifteenth century, the traditional areas of slave supply in eastern Europe fell to the Ottoman Turks and were no longer open to Europeans, at a time when demand for more labor in Europe's new colonial areas began to rise. The Turks effectively barred European merchants from buying slaves in the Black Sea's slaving grounds. Castile's conquest of Granada removed the last reservoir of potential Muslim slaves in Europe.

To replace them, Europeans began to tap Africa south of the Sahara. The trans-Saharan trade provided only a few slaves for the Iberian peninsula. Europeans gradually became aware of and sought to tap the riches of sub-Saharan Africa, gold and slaves above all. Castilian seamen were interested in the Atlantic coast of Africa for fishing and trade, but Castile, before 1492, was too concerned with internal problems and the conflict with Granada to invest its resources in African exploration. Consequently, Portugal became the leader in Atlantic Africa and after 1479 obtained a monopoly on West African trade.

By then Castile had taken over the Canary Islands and introduced sugar production. For a time Canary Islanders were used both as laborers and as commodities for sale elsewhere. The natives were enslaved, either legally in the case of the conquered groups or illegally in the case of the bands that signed treaties. In the sixteenth century the Canarians increasingly assimilated European culture and intermarried with the colonists. Because native workers never adequately filled the labor needs of the Canaries, other workers arrived, including free Iberian settlers as well as slaves from North and West Africa.

The Portuguese and Spanish activities in Africa meant that a trade in black slaves developed in the peninsula. Outside Portugal, Seville probably held Europe's greatest number of African slaves in the fifteenth and sixteenth centuries. Slavery had been a feature of the life of Seville since Roman times and during Islamic control. Until the mid-fifteenth century, most of the slaves in Seville were Muslims. Black slaves became more common in the fourteenth century as Christian merchants purchased them in North African ports. After the mid-fifteenth century black slaves arrived in Seville by sea or overland from Portugal.

Most slaves in Seville were domestic servants. Others served as artisans, porters, longshoremen, retailers, and assistants for shopkeepers and merchants. Some acted as agents for their merchant-owners. Slaves were excluded from membership in the crafts guilds, although some did work as helpers for guild masters.

Muslim and converted Muslim slaves were considered recalcitrant, hostile, and liable to run away. African slaves, on the other hand, had a much better reputation, mainly because they usually became faithful Christians, devout, pious, and active in religious matters.

Slavery flourished in other cities of Mediterranean Spain during this period, even if not as prominently as in Seville. One was Valencia, an important center for slavery. Slaves were less numerous in Valencia than in Seville, but they were more varied in their ethnic origins, reflecting the pattern of slavery in the medieval Mediterranean. Most were Muslim in origin, either from Spain itself or from North Africa. Non-Muslim slaves came from many other places, brought to Valencia by the slave traders. Elsewhere in Spain, slaves were less numerous.

In the seventeenth and eighteenth centuries slaves were no longer important in Mediterranean Europe's economy. Without an economic justification, slavery in Spain gradually declined, and slaves increasingly were rarities after the seventeenth century. Those who remained were usually domestic servants and, occasionally, assistants in the artisan workshops. Slavery might have totally died out, but a continuing influx of Muslim captives from North Africa offered opportunities for the government and private owners to employ slaves. By the eighteenth century Spain and the North African states began to agree to exchanges of captives. Although corsair activities continued into the nineteenth century, the raids ceased to be an important part of the Spanish experience. In metropolitan Spain slavery died a natural death by the beginning of the nineteenth century.

See also MEDIEVAL EUROPE, SLAVERY AND SERFDOM IN; MEDITERRANEAN BASIN; REDEMPTION OF CAPTIVES; SIETE PARTIDAS; SLAVE TRADE.

BIBLIOGRAPHY

BONNASSIE, PIERRE. *From Slavery to Feudalism in Southwestern Europe.* 1991.
FRANCO SILVA, ALONSO. *La esclavitud en Andalucía, 1450–1550.* 1992.
PHILLIPS, WILLIAM D., JR. *Historia de la esclavitud en España.* 1990.
SOLANO, FRANCISCO DE, and AGUSTÍN GUIMERÁ, eds. *Esclavitud y derechos humanos.* 1986.
VERLINDEN, CHARLES. *L'esclavage dans l'Europe médiévale.* Vol. 1, *Péninsule Ibérique—France.* 1955.

William D. Phillips, Jr.

African Slavery

Spain played a marginal role in Africa, except for its development of the Canary Islands early in the history of European exploration of the Atlantic off Africa's northwestern coast, and much later in the nineteenth century, with its control of the island of Fernando Po (now Bioko) in the Gulf of Guinea. In the nearly three intervening centuries, Spain's colonial enterprises in the Atlantic were confined to the Americas, west of a midocean line of demarcation established by Pope Alexander VI in 1493, the year after Christopher Columbus had discovered the Americas (and established definitively by the Treaty of Tordesillas in 1494). Spain therefore had to procure slaves for its American possessions by licenses (*asientos*) given to merchants from Portugal, in whose geographical sphere the agreement placed Africa, and later to northern Europeans.

Spain had followed Portugal out into the Atlantic in the fifteenth century, managing to control the Canary archipelago, where Europeans had for some time been raiding and enslaving the native Guanche population, related to the Berber peoples of the adjacent mainland. Guanche slaves were sent to sugar estates on Portuguese Madeira or sent back to Seville, where they entered the multiethnic urban slavery of Renaissance Iberia. Under Spanish rule German investors developed small sugar holdings on the large island of Grand Canary that, for two or three decades after 1500, led world production of cane. Grand Canary, briefly, then became one of the major destinations of Portuguese slavers returning from the coasts of western Africa, although the slaves on the island never approached the majorities that later characterized New World plantation islands.

The rich silver of Peru and Mexico, and the Native American labor available in Spain's mainland colonies, gave little reason to regret this arrangement until the late eighteenth century, when the Spanish crown (under Carlos III, 1759–1788) relaxed long-standing mercantilist restrictions and opened its waning colonial trade monopolies to private merchants in the 1780s. These traders began to buy slaves in Africa, particularly for Spain's colonies along the Plata estuary in far southern America, making their base on the islands of Fernando Po and Annobón, acquired from

Portugal in 1788. When Cuban sugar developed in the nineteenth century, Cuban and Spanish ships—as well as Portuguese and United States vessels sailing under Spanish colors—became common among the slavers from several nations that defied British efforts to suppress Atlantic slaving and made Cuba, along with Brazil, one of the two major destinations for African slaves of that era. In Africa, where virtually no other hard currency circulated, Spanish silver dollars found a particular welcome among other European merchants, particularly the Portuguese. The Spanish government managed only minimal occupation of Fernando Po until Spain abolished slavery there in 1859 and the illegal slave trade wound down in the 1860s. For a time, the British occupied the island as a naval base for their squadrons patrolling against the slave trade.

The rich volcanic soil of Fernando Po and the two neighboring Portuguese islands, São Tomé and Príncipe, made the Gulf of Guinea the world's leading producer of cocoa in the 1870s, when improvements in processing cocoa beans made African varieties palatable and popular in Europe. In the ensuing local cocoa boom, planters on Fernando Po, many of them descendants of Sierra Leoneans who had settled during the period of British occupation, could not draft the local Bubi population, whose numbers were in any case declining precipitously from diseases. They imported West Africans, especially from Liberia and Sierra Leone and later from Nigeria, as "contract laborers" under conditions very akin to what slaves had suffered. This "modern slavery," which the Portuguese in São Tomé and Príncipe developed on a much larger scale with captives brought from their mainland colony in Angola, became internationally notorious in the 1890s, owing to publicity brought by British antislavery humanitarians. After 1900 Britain's colonial authorities on the mainland, compelled to rationalize their conquest of Africa as a "civilizing mission," found it easier to protect contract laborers moving to a Spanish island than to abolish slavery in their own territories. Since the British controlled most of the West African regions from which these workers came, they were in a strong position to terminate this recruiting. The corrupt independent government in Liberia left recruitment unregulated until a treaty with Spain in 1914.

Although rising production of cocoa in the British Gold Coast (Ghana) eclipsed Fernando Po and lessened pressures on the island's laborers at about this time, Spanish authorities nonetheless attempted to save the island's economy by bringing in penal labor and by recruiting Asians, especially from the Philippines. In 1913 authorities imposed a code of forced labor on local populations. The development of coffee plantations on the island brought a modest economic recovery in the 1920s, but prosperity came at the cost of substandard working conditions that prompted the League of Nations to investigate the situation as "slavery" in 1930. Independence in 1968 as Bioko—part of the nation of Equatorial Guinea, based on the larger mainland province of Rio Muni—turned into a dictatorship so brutal that most citizens survived in conditions at least metaphorically described as "slavery," until at least the 1980s.

Spain repeatedly resorted to slavery and successor forms of coerced labor to compensate for its economic weaknesses in Africa. Compulsion populated or repopulated all of the islands in the Gulf of Guinea, Portuguese as well as Spanish, from the first European occupation in the early sixteenth century. The slaves, slavelike contracted workers, and, finally, populations confined on the islands and subject to government forced-labor laws repeatedly made the islands leading producers of sugar, then cocoa, and then coffee, as well as objects of international condemnation. For their sacrifices, their heirs received only a lasting burden of slavelike poverty and political oppression.

See also ASIENTO; PORTUGAL; SLAVE TRADE; TORDESILLAS, TREATY OF.

BIBLIOGRAPHY

CLARENCE-SMITH, W. GERVASE. "Cocoa Plantations and Coerced Labor in the Gulf of Guinea, 1870–1914." In *Breaking the Chains: Slavery, Bondage, and Emancipation in Modern Africa and Asia,* edited by Martin A. Klein. 1993; pp. 150–170.

———. "The Portuguese Contribution to the Cuban Slave and Coolie Trades in the Nineteenth Century." *Slavery and Abolition* 5, no. 1 (1984): 25–33.

LOBO CABRERA, MANUEL. *La esclavitud en las Canarias orientales en el siglo XVI (negros, moros y moriscos).* 1982.

———. "Esclavitud y azúcar en Canarias." In *Escravos com e sem açúcar,* coordinated by Alberto Vieira. 1996; pp. 103–117.

STEVENS-ARROYO, ANTHONY M. "The Inter-Atlantic Paradigm: The Failure of Spanish Medieval Colonization of the Canary and Caribbean Islands." *Comparative Studies in Society and History* 35, no. 3 (1993): 515–543.

SUNDIATA, I. K. *From Slaving to Neoslavery: The Bight of Biafra and Fernando Po in the Era of Abolition, 1827–1930.* 1995.

Joseph C. Miller

Colonies and Empire

African slaves and free people of African descent were present in Spain's American colonies from the time of conquest and colonization. *Ladinos* (Hispanicized slaves) and *libertos* (freedmen) took part in the earliest campaigns to pacify Hispaniola and the other Antilles. At this stage of the colonial enterprise, however, most slaves were Amerindians taken as war prisoners and enslaved in accordance with principles of "just war" laid down in the Iberian peninsula during the Christian advances against the Moors. In the early Caribbean colonizing experience, which proved disastrous for the Amerindian population, some Spaniards began to distinguish between people who could be enslaved and those who could not. The humanitarian impulse of people like the Dominican friar Bartolomé de las Casas helped sharpen such distinctions. Although Las Casas later retreated from this position, his advocacy of an African slave trade to ease the burden on the native population was an important factor in the extension to the Caribbean of the slave trade already in place between West Africa, the Atlantic islands occupied by Iberians (São Tomé, Madeira, and the Canaries, among others), and the Iberian peninsula.

Replacing Taíno workers (Caribbean aborigines) with African slaves did not occur easily, however, for the trade from Africa implied great risks for all involved. Once it became clear that the number of Amerindians available for labor declined drastically after contact with Europeans, the settlers' first impulse was to raid for Amerindian slaves in territories not yet occupied by Europeans. Most of these locales offered little in the way of mineral wealth. But when this intraregional slave trade did not fully satisfy demand for labor, in 1518 the emperor, Charles I, authorized direct imports of *bozxles* (un-Hispanicized slaves) from Africa. This decision marks the beginning of a trade that eventually introduced an estimated 1.6 million people into the Spanish American colonies before it ceased well into the second half of the nineteenth century. From the 1520s to the 1580s, tens of thousands of slaves were imported into the Caribbean, where they worked primarily on estates producing sugar for export to Europe. By the time competing Brazilian sugar began to eclipse the Spanish Caribbean industry around 1580, signaling its eventual demise, all of the islands and many of the surrounding continental settlements had numerical majorities of African-born people and their descendants. Most of these endured slavery under the Spaniards, but a growing number had managed to escape and were known as *cimarrones* (maroons). These rebels lived on the fringes of European settlements, harassing the Spanish residents and sometimes forging alliances with their European enemies. Thus, for instance, when in 1573 the English privateer Sir Francis Drake ransacked the strategic Spanish entrepôt at Nombre de Dios on the isthmus of Panama, an alliance he had forged with the cimarrones ensured the success of his effort to capture Spanish treasure.

As the Spanish Caribbean islands faded in economic importance in the late sixteenth century, the locus of slave exploitation shifted to the mainland colonies of New Spain and Peru. The Amerindian demographic collapse in these vastly richer colonies ensured that there would be a high demand for African slaves, even in areas where indigenous labor had at first seemed inexhaustible. An inverse correlation between Amerindian populations and imports of Africans played itself out most clearly in New Spain, where the peak of slave imports occurred between 1580 and 1625. This surge coincided not only with the lowest ebb in the Amerindian population curve but also with a period of rapid expansion in silver production. In addition to working in mines, many of the slaves imported into New Spain worked in plantation agriculture, especially on sugar-producing estates located in the semitropical districts of Veracruz and Morelos. Others were engaged in the all-important carrying trades and in an array of urban occupations, from personal service to craft industries requiring a high degree of skill.

While the number of Africans in early colonial Peru was not initially as large as New Spain's, it grew considerably during the course of the seventeenth century, easily surpassing the northern viceroyalty as the region with the highest concentration of slaves. Accordingly, slaves and freed people of African descent constituted an increasingly important group within the overall *república de españoles*, the Spanish polity, of the Andean region. As in New Spain, slaves were active in wide array of occupations. Along Peru's warm coastal valleys, for instance, they formed the backbone of an important sugar industry which developed in the sixteenth century to satisfy a variety of urban markets in South America. They also labored in silver, gold, and copper mines scattered about the viceroyalty, and in artisanal and service occupations in the main urban centers. In key strategic outposts like Cartagena, on the northern coast of New Granada (modern Colombia), enslaved workers accomplished the grinding work of building the massive fortresses that helped Spain maintain the security of its scattered imperial holdings.

In Peru as elsewhere in Spanish America, slaves occupied an ambiguous social position. In a society organized according to strict rules of status and privilege, their legal standing was the lowest of all, below that of Amerindians, who were accorded some privileges, such as exemption from certain taxes. But because of their position in the labor hierarchy, which often involved skilled work, and their greater assimilation to Spanish customs, language, and dress, African and Afro-creole slaves were poised to gain material advantages and to achieve higher prestige than the

Spanish soldiers beat and torture Native American slaves around 1600. [Library of Congress/Corbis]

Amerindians. Dark skin color and other stigmatized features associated with African origin severely restricted their social advancement, but these traits did not prevent some individual slaves from accumulating wealth and earning prestige.

One of the distinctive features of African slavery in Spanish America is the unusually high rates of manumission, thanks to laws (some dating back to medieval Iberia) that allowed slaves to purchase their own freedom. The legal mechanism was known as *coartación;* this was a legal principle that obligated a master to grant an individual slave freedom upon payment of a sum of money stipulated in advance. *Coartación* existed in all of the Spanish colonies throughout the colonial period, although it appears to have reached its most highly developed legal form in nineteenth-century Cuba.

Because of *coartación* and other limits that the law imposed on the masters' power, some scholars have

claimed that slavery was generally more humane in Spanish America than in the British, French, and Dutch colonies. They point to the beneficial effects of *coartación* and other mitigating factors, such as the church's insistence that slaves be accorded the benefits of a Christian upbringing like any other of God's children. But other scholars counter that wherever plantation slavery thrived, no humane law or principle could mitigate the harshness of slave life. They point to nineteenth-century Cuba, whose slave-based sugar plantation economy developed into the world's largest after about 1830, fueling an illegal slave trade that brought several hundred thousand Africans between 1820 (the date of its prohibition by international treaty) and 1867 (the year of final importations). Neither *coartación* nor the more humane laws and church doctrine could ease the pain of Cuba's plantation slaves, who endured a regimen as exploitative as any in New World history. Spain's protective legislation proved incapable of countering the capitalist drive toward production and efficiency in the plantation environment.

See also CARIBBEAN REGION; COARTACIÓN; CUBA; LAS CASAS, BARTOLOMÉ DE; MANUMISSION; MAROONS; PLANTATIONS; SLAVE TRADE.

BIBLIOGRAPHY

ANDREWS, K. R. *The Spanish Caribbean: Trade and Plunder, 1530–1560.* 1978.

BERGAD, L. W., F. IGLESIAS GARCÍA, and M. D. C. BARCIA. *The Cuban Slave Market, 1790–1880.* 1995.

BOWSER, F. P. *The African Slave in Colonial Peru, 1524–1650.* 1974.

CURTIN, P. D. *The Atlantic Slave Trade: A Census.* 1969.

DAVIS, D. J., ed. *Slavery and Beyond: The African Impact on Latin America and the Caribbean.* Jaguar Books on Latin America, no. 5. 1994.

FRANCO SILVA, A. *La Esclavitud en Andalucia, 1450–1550.* 1992.

KNIGHT, F. W. *Slave Society in Cuba during the Nineteenth Century.* 1969.

LOCKHART, J. *Spanish Peru, 1532–1560: A Colonial Society.* 1969.

MELLAFE, R. *La esclavitud en Hispanoamérica.* 1964.

PALMER, COLIN. *Slaves of the White Gods: Blacks in Mexico, 1570–1650.* 1976.

TANNENBAUM, F. *Slave and Citizen: The Negro in the Americas.* 1946.

VILA VILAR, E. *Hispanoamérica y el comercio de esclavos.* 1977.

Francisco A. Scarano

Spartacus   [?–71 B.C.]

Leader of a great slave rebellion in republican Rome.

The forces of Spartacus, initially small but growing to perhaps seventy thousand, marched up and down the length of Italy for two years and defeated several Roman armies before finally being annihilated.

Background

Spartacus was probably brave and resourceful; conditions were also propitious for a slave rebellion. The late Roman republic saw three such insurrections: in addition to Spartacus's uprising much of the Sicilian countryside was overrun on two occasions (ca. 136–132 and ca. 104–100 B.C.). Analogies to modern slave rebellions and contemporary accounts, albeit moralistic, help explain the ability of Roman slaves to revolt during this particular period. As Rome conquered the Mediterranean basin, slaves were numerous and included a large proportion of first-generation slaves, a typically rebellious group. In Italy many free farmers were displaced by large estates owned by absentee owners and worked by slaves. Slave herdsmen, selected from the biggest and strongest men, were notorious for being poorly controlled semibrigands. The great slave uprisings took place in the context of repeated civil wars and general lawlessness: piracy was rampant, and senators did not travel through Italy without armed guards. Nevertheless, although the Roman republic was divided and slow to act, in the long run its military organization and weaponry, its wealth, and its manpower spelled the eventual defeat of any slave revolt.

Course of the Revolt

Spartacus was a slave from Thrace, who may have seen military service with the Roman auxiliary forces. He and seventy followers broke out of a gladiatorial training camp in Capua in the summer of 73 B.C. and set up a base on Mount Vesuvius. Although the slaves may have hoped only for a maroonlike escape from slavery, their growing numbers and pillaging attracted attention. Increasingly substantial Roman forces were sent against Spartacus and defeated. Over the winter, the rebels' activities spread throughout Campagnia and into southern Italy. Some discontented peasants and deserters may have joined Spartacus, but the movement remained essentially a slave revolt. Both of the new year's consuls, the highest rank of Roman official, were assigned to fight Spartacus, an indication of the seriousness of the revolt. Their armies probably totaled four legions with perhaps 20,000 legionaries as well as auxiliary troops. After a series of battles with varied but generally unfavorable results, the consuls retired to Rome in disgrace.

Having marched the length of Italy, Spartacus also defeated the governor of Cisalpine Gaul. At this point Spartacus and his followers could have left Italy. Dispersal, however, would have left his followers powerless and vulnerable to reenslavement; for slaves to return "home" after many years was often neither easy nor safe, and sometimes not even possible. If Spartacus's substantial troops had stayed together, they would have been unwelcome inside or outside the Roman empire and its sphere of influence. Instead, they turned back into Italy, with fatal consequences.

Late in 72 Crassus was given an extraordinary command against Spartacus with ten legions—as large as the army with which Julius Caesar conquered Gaul. After in initial defeat, Crassus's officers overcame detachments of the rebels. By the winter of 72–71, Crassus began to cut Spartacus off in the peninsula of Bruttium. After Spartacus finally broke off, he was forced to turn and fight Crassus, when Lucullus, recalled from a successful campaign in the eastern Mediterranean, landed with his army at Brundisium. Spartacus was defeated and killed. Six thousand slave captives were crucified along the road from Capua to Rome. Nevertheless, Crassus did not claim a "triumph" for a victory over the slaves; he was criticized for accepting even the lesser honor of an "ovation." Pompey, on his return from Spain with yet another army, defeated a final small detachment of slaves.

Spartacus's Leadership

Plutarch described Spartacus as "extremely brave and strong" and "smarter and more humane" than one would expect a slave to be. In addition to these qualities, Spartacus's wife, a prophetess who foretold his successes, lent his leadership a religious aura. Despite occasional dissension, especially between the Thracian and the Gallic or Germanic contingents, the slaves achieved remarkable successes against the most powerful army of the time.

Given his time and culture, the Communist appropriation of Spartacus as a hero must be considered metaphorical. Equally baseless, however, are dogmatic claims that he was not opposed to slavery: he left no writings and the motivations for his actions—vengeance, opposition to some or all slavery, and self-preservation—are impossible to disentangle.

See also ANCIENT ROME; INSURRECTIONS; MAROONS.

BIBLIOGRAPHY

BRADLEY, KEITH R. *Slavery and Rebellion in the Roman World: 140 B.C.–70 B.C.* 1989.
YAVETZ, ZVI. *Slaves and Slavery in Ancient Rome.* 1988.

Peter Hunt

Spirituals

Spirituals were the first philosophical creations of Africans in English North America. They are a large set of religious songs, existing in multiple forms, by groups of slaves throughout America, and they remained an oral tradition until after emancipation. Their anonymous collective authorship marks them as myths, and their manifest biblical content confirms their role in an evolving black Judeo-Christian tradition of worship. Enslaved Africans, brought "naked and thingless" to the Atlantic shores of the colonies, produced children who wrought a sonorous hymnody with amazing grace. These, the "sorrow songs," assimilated the history of ancient Israel and immanent Christian salvation into a contemporary and miserable reality—enslavement in a strange land.

The novel but obvious relevance of ancient Israel to African-Americans is memorably expressed in "Go Down, Moses":

When Israel was in Egypt's land,
Let my people go;
Oppressed so hard they could not stand,
Let my people go;
Go down, Moses, 'way down in Egypt's land;
Tell ole Pharaoh
Let my people go.

The conflation of Israel's bondage and black slavery marks the beginning of a revolutionary biblical fundamentalism among African-Americans. Slaves were permitted to sing explicitly about slavery and emancipation only through the metaphor of Israel. That metaphor, drawn from a very different civilization, resonated for the slaves of America. When they sang "Didn't my Lord deliver Daniel, then why not every man?" they too stood in a fiery furnace, praying for the God of Israel to bless and free them.

The transformation of the hierarchical world of enslavement through Christian eschatology is powerfully promised in "Git on Board, Little Chillen":

Git on board, little chillen, Git on board, little chillen,
Git on board, little chillen, Dere's room for many a mo!
De gospel train's a comin', I hear it just at han;
I hear de car wheels movin', an' rumblin' thro de lan'.
Git on board, etc.
De fare is cheap, an' all can go, de rich an' poor are here,
No second class aboard dis train, no diffrunce in de fare.

These lyrics, drawn from the first African-American compilation of spirituals (Johnson and Johnson, 1925) depicts an egalitarian future, without scarcity ("Dere's room for many a mo!"). And while the gospel is the message, its vehicle is one of the technological wonders of antebellum America, the railroad. The image of a steam engine "rumblin' thro de lan,'" a conveyance in which class distinction and moneyed privilege are abolished, encapsulates the social liberation that African-Americans expected from Christian salvation. All those working cotton or tobacco near the railroad tracks were transported by this image, and through song, they evangelized while sharing information with other slaves about a new technology.

It is neither quaint nor disrespectful to quote the lyrics of spirituals in the transitional vernacular in which Johnson and Johnson found them. Part of the elusive heritage of African-Americans is the complex of spiritual traditions so evident in the Caribbean and Brazil—tradition that originated in Africa. Spirituals rendered in standard English mark an endpoint of evolution or an extreme on a continuum: spirituals in their original form, in Black English, Gullah, or some other creole African language, may document the syncretism of African sacred traditions with Judeo-Christian forms. Certainly the original lyrics were shaped to be sung, but were they also encrypted?

When Harriet Tubman, a hero of the Underground Railroad, sang, "Steal away, steal away, steal away to Jesus," she embedded a code for physical escape in a metaphor of spiritual conversion. The open militancy in many of the spirituals should puzzle students of the slave South. What are we to make of lyrics such as "What a you say, brothers, About dat Gospel war, An I will die in the fiel'"; or of the spiritual "Singin' Wid a Sword in Ma Han'"? How did white preachers and slave masters accommodate themselves to any hymn about Joshua, knowing that he fulfilled Moses' prophetic mission by conquering the promised land for the heirs of the liberated Hebrew slaves? The spirituals provide some of the best evidence that the moral and temporal boundaries of slavery were highly con-

tested terrain, over which slaves as well as masters had a say.

The mythic elements of the spirituals were manifested as the United States approached its greatest internal crisis. The Civil War, from the perspective of the slaves, was the encounter between the prophet Moses and Pharaoh. They could sing "Ride on, Moses, I know de Lord would pass dat way" and make the line simultaneously a sacred image and political commentary.

The Civil War struck America like a plague, and out of it—though many of the firstborn died—came emancipation. The historian Margaret Washington argues, "The moment of freedom, more than any event, bound Africa-Americans to Christianity." Certainly, the prophecy had been fulfilled; the victors' "eyes had seen the glory of the coming of the Lord." For 4 million freedpeople, God had once again freed slaves who had kept the faith. And the spirituals, which had plaintively and magisterially commanded Moses to go tell Pharaoh to let the people go, become both anachronistic and the substance of a revitalized faith.

See also MUSIC BY SLAVES; SLAVE RELIGION; TUBMAN, HARRIET; UNDERGROUND RAILROAD.

BIBLIOGRAPHY

JOHNSON, JAMES WELDON, and J. ROSAMOND JOHNSON. *The Books of American Negro Spirituals.* 1925, 1926, 1969.

JONES, ARTHUR C. *Wade in the Water: The Wisdom of the Spirituals.* 1993.

LEVINE, LAWRENCE W. *Black Culture and Black Consciousness: Afro-American Folk Thought from Slavery to Freedom.* 1977.

Harold S. Forsythe

A young woman sings a spiritual as she walks along. [Corbis-Bettmann]

State v. Mann (N.C., 1829)

In this case Chief Justice Thomas Ruffin of the North Carolina Supreme Court reversed the assault and battery conviction of John Mann, who had shot and wounded Lydia, a slave he had rented from Lydia's owner, Elizabeth Jones. Lydia had "run off" from Mann to avoid a whipping. She was not trying to escape bondage at the time; she tried only to escape punishment. Mann shot her in the back with a rifle. While Jones might have easily sued Mann for damaging Lydia, instead she filed a criminal complaint, asserting that Mann's action violated the law.

Chief Justice Ruffin agreed that if a stranger had shot Lydia, a criminal prosecution would be in order. But, in this case Ruffin asserted that Mann, as a renter, had the same rights over Lydia as an owner. Thus, Ruffin asked whether an owner had a right to punish a slave in any manner he or she might choose. Ruffin concluded that a master did have such a right, as long as the punishment did not lead to death. Ruffin asserted that "the power of the master must be absolute to render the submission of the slave perfect." Ruffin acknowledged that the law seemed to force a harsh conclusion, and that "as a principle of moral right, every person in his retirement must repudiate it." But he asserted, "in the actual condition of things, it must be so." He found that such a "discipline belongs to the state of slavery. They cannot be disunited, without abrogating at once the rights of the master, and absolving the slave from his subjection." Such a conclusion was "inherent in the relation of the master and slave."

Mann agreed that in "particular instances of cruelty and deliberate barbarity" the "conscience of the law might properly intervene." But, he argued, it was impossible to anticipate in the abstract when that might be. "The truth is, that we are forbidden to enter upon a train of general reasoning on the subject. We cannot allow the right of the master to be brought into discussion in the Court of Justice. The slave, to remain a slave, must be made sensible, that there is no appeal from his master; that his power is in no instance usurped; but is conferred by the laws of man at least, if not by the law of God."

Harriet Beecher Stowe, in her book *The Key to Uncle Tom's Cabin,* commented that "No one can read this decision, so fine and clear in expression, so dignified and solemn in its earnestness, and so dreadful in its results, without feeling at once deep respect for the man and horror for the system." She regretted that "such a man, with such a mind, should have been merely an *expositor,* and not a *reformer* of law." Ruffin in fact provided in this case the most important statement written by a southern judge on the extent of the legal power of the master over the slave. Short of deliberately killing a slave, or punishing a slave in ways (like maiming) that were prohibited by statute, Ruffin declared that masters had absolute authority to punish a slave in any way they chose, without regard for the humanity of the slave or the conscience of the community.

See also STOWE, HARRIET BEECHER.

BIBLIOGRAPHY

MORRIS, THOMAS D. *Southern Slavery and the Law, 1619–1860.* 1996.
TUSHNET, MARK. *The American Law of Slavery, 1810–1860: Considerations of Humanity and Interest.* 1981.

Paul Finkelman

Status of Slaves, Legal

See Law.

Stereotypes, Slavish

Although the stereotypes associated with slaves are varied and, in some cases, contradictory, there is an underlying theme firmly rooted in the ideology of the master class. This theme, as presented in the writings of philosophers as different as Aristotle, W. G. F. Hegel, and John Locke, held that the capture of prisoners in war was justification for their enslavement. The man who surrendered was regarded as lacking a sense of honor.

To be without honor was to possess certain traits, and among the most obvious was cowardice. So thoroughly was this stereotype accepted that all the historical instances to the contrary could not shake the conviction with which it was held. History presents, after all, innumerable instances of acts of bravery by slaves—for example, the majority of the gladiators of ancient Rome were of the slave class; the slave Spartacus and his band of rebels (mostly slaves) stood up against three Roman armies acting in concert before they were overcome; the Mamluks of Islamic Egypt were known to be fearless as well as fearsome slave soldiers; and the slave rebels of Haiti defeated the armies that Napoleon sent to reduce them to servitude.

So invincible was the stereotype of cowardice in the character of the slave that it was thought to affect succeeding generations born into servitude, including those who had themselves never submitted to capture by an enemy in war.

Another slavish stereotype was dishonesty. Since the slave was thought to lack honor, it followed that he or she had no commitment to truth. The lying slave appeared as a stock character in comedies from ancient times to the present, as did the thieving slave.

The lazy slave was a well-worn cliché as well, but here one may be confronting, not the issue of loss of honor, but the logic of a slave's status. As Adam Smith observed in his great economic treatise *The Wealth of Nations* (1776), it is in the slave's interest to do as little as possible and to eat as much as possible. Smith's point does not concern the character of the slave but rather the logic of the situation of enslavement. The slave had to be concerned not to antagonize his master so as not to be beaten, but unlike a free laborer, the slave had little to gain by a conscientious application of industry.

Another alleged characteristic of the slave was extreme sexual promiscuity and predatoriness. New World slavery primarily refered to black slavery, and the sexual mythology surrounding blacks may have complicated the slavish stereotypes surrounding sex. A look at the portrayal of slaves in the ancient world, where the vast majority of slaves were Caucasians, demonstrates that the sexual stereotype associated with slaves was not primarily based on race. For example, Juvenal, the imperial Roman poet, warned that one should beware of Greek slaves in one's household, because their presence opened one's wife, parents, and children of both sexes to the dangers of debauchment.

In part, the image of sexual licentiousness associated with slaves was a further development of the notion of the slave as a person without honor. As the slave could not overcome his fear of death in order to avoid enslavement, it was thought that he would lack the character to restrain the sexual impulse. In reality, the position of a slave within a household was often eroticized, for the slave might better his or her condition by catering to the sexual tastes of the master or some member of the master's family. In like manner, for the master and his family, a slave represented an easily obtained sexual partner. It is not absurd to speculate that larger households may have acquired some slaves specifically for sexual purposes. In Suetonius's *Lives of the Twelve Caesars,* the debaucheries of the Emperor Tiberius at his retreat on Capri are recounted in shocking detail, with various slaves trained to perform specific sexual functions for the monarch.

The book of Genesis relates perhaps the most famous incident illustrating sexual exploitation of slaves. Sarah, concerned that she has grown old without producing a child for her husband, Abraham, offers him the opportunity to beget a child upon her bondswoman, Hagar the Egyptian. Significantly, the biblical text seems to emphasize the noble sacrifice of Sarah in this arrangement. Yet, the conduct of Hagar is interesting, too, for when she becomes pregnant, she subtly mocks her mistress, who has been unable to provide an heir.

The sexual mystique surrounding slaves in the Old South is well illustrated by a famous passage from the diaries of Mary Chesnut:

> God forgive us, but ours is a monstrous system, a wrong and iniquity. Like the patriarchs of old, our men live all in one house with their wives and their concubines; and the mulattoes one sees in every family partly resemble the white children. Any lady is ready to tell you who is the father of all the mulatto children in everybody's household but her own. Those, she seems to think, drop from the clouds.

Perhaps the most ignoble stereotype to arise from slavery was that of the "Sambo." The Sambo image at once conveyed childishness and buffoonishness, with cheerfulness, optimism, musicality, and ignorance thrown in. Physically, the Sambo was usually portrayed grinning. Degrading as the Sambo stereotype was, it no doubt served to reassure the masters. The slave was happy—how could slavery be regarded as a great evil? The slave was childish—would he not always, therefore, need the guidance of the master's firm but paternalistic hand? The Sambo was a chronic liar and thief—was not the chastisement of the slaves a necessary and proper measure?

Like so many of the other stereotypes engendered while slavery prevailed, the Sambo image—reinforced by portrayals on the stage, in print, and on the screen—would continue to plague freed blacks well into the twentieth century.

Another aspect of stereotyping concerns the conception of slave intelligence. One side of the stereotype emphasized the stupidity of the slave. This emphasis may be seen as another aspect of the image of the slave as a man without honor, his lack of intelligence reinforcing his undervaluation of honor. In the New World, where black slaves from Africa were deliberately kept from all education and where in many jurisdictions teaching a slave to read was a criminal offense, the stereotype of the ignorant slave was easily maintained. And although not absent from the Old World, there the stereotype had to coexist with the fact that some slaves acted as tutors of the classics and even as imperial administrators (though freedmen more commonly held such offices). Nor should it be forgotten that many slaves may have found it advantageous to feign ignorance or stupidity to escape unwanted responsibilities and to divert the suspicion of the master and his overseers.

Coexisting with the image of the stupid slave was the image of the slave imbued with a dangerous cunning, a trait that, while not precisely identified with intelligence, seems strangely at odds with the image of slavish stupidity. In literature the very embodiment of this cunning is Babo, the organizer of the shipboard slave mutiny in Herman Melville's "Benito Cereno," a slave who is remorseless in his hatred and defiance of whites, cunning as a serpent, and vicious in the extreme.

It may not be farfetched to see in a character such as Babo a projection of the fears of the master class. The cruelties and humiliations visited upon slaves produced a natural and corresponding guilt and fear in their oppressors. Babo was the dream figure who haunted the sleep of the masters.

See also EDUCATION OF SLAVES; ELKINS THESIS; LITERATURE OF SLAVERY.

BIBLIOGRAPHY

BOSKIN, JOSEPH. "Sambo." In *Dictionary of Afro-American Slavery,* edited by Randall M. Miller and John David Smith. 1988.

ELKINS, STANLEY M. *Slavery: A Problem in American Institutional and Intellectual Life.* 2nd ed. 1968.

PATTERSON, ORLANDO. *Slavery and Social Death: A Comparative Study.* 1982.

Patrick M. O'Neil

Stewart, Maria W.   [1803–1879]

Black political activist and author.

A pioneering radical, Maria Stewart was born into a free black family in Hartford, Connecticut, and spent much of her career battling against the political and economic fetters keeping persons of African descent as second-class citizens. Orphaned at the age of five, Stewart worked as a domestic servant as a young girl before moving to Boston. She married a free black merchant involved in the shipping trade and was a member of the African Baptist Church.

Stewart was a contemporary of David Walker, whose *Appeal* (published in 1829) had a profound effect upon her. Her husband James's death, after less than three years of marriage, threw Stewart into a downward spiral. When she was cheated out of her legacy from her husband, the indigent Stewart launched a speaking career in 1832 to support herself. She was the first African-American woman to offer public lectures on political themes, and her tone and message were militant. Her speeches were printed in Garrison's *Liberator,* and two collections of her writing appeared in 1832 and 1835. She became a teacher and secured employment in New York City, Baltimore, and, finally, Washington, D.C. She remarried, but when her second husband, a Union veteran of the Civil War, died, Stewart was left alone a second time.

In 1879, shortly before her death, Stewart subsequently republished an expanded version of her first book, *Meditations.* A powerful and outspoken figure, Stewart's career paved the way for other abolitionists and feminists who followed.

See also WALKER, DAVID; WOMEN IN THE ANTISLAVERY MOVEMENT.

BIBLIOGRAPHY

RICHARDSON, MARILYN, ed. *Maria W. Stewart, America's First Black Woman Political Writer: Essays and Speeches.* 1987.

Catherine Clinton

Stono Rebellion (1739)

The Stono Rebellion erupted southwest of Charleston, South Carolina, before dawn on Sunday, 9 September 1739, when slaves from a road-repair crew broke into Hutchenson's store near the Stono River, beheading two persons and seizing weapons. Their leader, Jemmy, ranks with Gabriel Prosser, Denmark Vesey, and Nat Turner in managing to prompt a major uprising against the slave regime in North America. The rebels, shouting "Liberty" and beating drums, began marching toward Florida. They burned certain plantations, killed at least twenty whites, and soon added more than fifty recruits. But an armed posse attacked and dispersed the band, shooting, hanging, and gibbeting alive their prisoners. If Jemmy's troops had eluded authorities longer, they might have drawn an unstoppable number of enslaved Carolinians to their banner and disrupted the rice planters' world so thoroughly as to alter the course of American history.

Beyond the inhumanity of hereditary race-based slavery, specific factors helped spark the revolt. Blacks outnumbered whites in the colony almost two to one, and many were newly enslaved Africans from Angola. Some of these newcomers may have had prior military experience in Africa, and many knew that the Spanish in Saint Augustine were offering freedom to Carolinian slaves. Word of the start of war between Spain and England, the presence of an epidemic among whites, and fear of impending tighter controls on slaves may all have contributed to the desperate action. In its aftermath, South Carolina's white minority moved quickly to pass a stiffer slave code, temporarily halt new importations from Africa, and challenge the free black colony at Fort Mose in Spanish Florida.

See also REBELLIONS AND VIOLENT RESISTANCE; SOUTH CAROLINA.

BIBLIOGRAPHY

WOOD, PETER H. *Black Majority: Negroes in Colonial South Carolina from 1670 through the Stono Rebellion.* 1974.

Peter H. Wood

Stowe, Harriet Beecher   [1811–1896]

U.S. author.

Born Harriet Elizabeth Beecher, Stowe grew up in Connecticut, where in 1827 she became a schoolteacher. Five years later she accompanied her family to Cincinnati, Ohio, where her father became the head of Lane Theological Seminary. In addition to teaching, she joined a local literary society and began writing tales and sketches, many of which were published in magazines. In 1836 she married Calvin Ellis Stowe, a professor at Lane. During the course of the eighteen years that she lived in Cincinnati, she became familiar with slavery—which thrived just across the Ohio River in Kentucky—by frequently visiting a small plantation in Kentucky and by regularly talking with friends and family members whose travels took them into the South. She also conversed with runaway slaves, especially Josiah Henson and Henry Bibb, both of whom escaped to freedom via Cincinnati and wrote narratives of their adventures. She was deeply moved by the abolitionist literature of the 1830s and 1840s, which described in repugnant detail the vicious beatings administered to slaves for the most trivial reasons and the heartbreak caused when slave families were broken up by sale.

In 1850, her husband having accepted a position at Bowdoin College, Stowe moved with him to Brunswick, Maine. That same year she began writing one of the most important works in American literature, *Uncle Tom's Cabin; or, Life among the Lowly,* a novel about the horrors of slavery as they befall a family of slaves in Kentucky. Although several of these slaves reach freedom by escaping to Canada or being colonized in Africa, Uncle Tom is "sold down the river" to the vicious Simon Legree, who condemns Tom to a hellish existence on a Louisiana plantation before eventually having him beaten to death.

For years Stowe had felt increasingly driven to write something that, as she noted in the preface to *Uncle Tom's Cabin,* would "awaken sympathy and feeling for the African race, as they exist among us; to show their wrongs and sorrows, under a system so necessarily cruel and unjust." She was inspired at last to take up her pen by the passage of the Fugitive Slave Act of 1850, a most unpopular law in the North because it required northerners to cooperate with slave-catchers and thereby actively participate in the perpetuation of slavery. *Uncle Tom's Cabin* first appeared in serial form in the *National Era,* a small, moderately abolitionist newspaper published in Washington, D.C. Stowe's story had originally been scheduled to appear in ten issues in 1851, but its immediate popularity caused her to lengthen it to forty installments so that it ran well into 1852, thereby greatly enhancing the paper's reputation and helping to increase its circulation to 28,000. Later that year the story appeared in book form; it sold 10,000 copies the first week and more than 300,000 copies the first year. It was eventually translated into thirty-seven languages and has never been out of print.

Uncle Tom's Cabin depicts slaves as long-suffering, God-fearing individuals, thus making it the first American novel to present blacks as heroes. It portrays the South as a land where love of money and the corrosive effects of a slave culture caused white slave owners to pervert every good human emotion, especially the love that binds husband to wife and mother to child. Stowe's depiction of slavery as totally incompatible with Christianity made her a heroine in the North and a villain in the South. *Uncle Tom's Cabin* evoked such passionate responses on both sides of the Mason-Dixon Line that when Stowe met President Lincoln in 1863, he reportedly greeted her as "the little woman who wrote the book that made this great war."

In 1853 Stowe published *The Key to Uncle Tom's Cabin,* essentially a collection of documents describing the horrors of slavery. It was reminiscent of the antislavery literature of an earlier decade, and it served to outrage southern sensibilities even more than *Uncle Tom's Cabin.* In 1856 she published *Dred: A Tale of the Great Dismal Swamp,* her second antislavery novel. This hastily written, overwrought story about an unsuccessful fomenter of a slave rebellion never generated the same moral passion as *Uncle Tom's Cabin* and so had little effect on public attitudes.

Although Stowe continued to write until shortly before her death, she never published another novel about slavery. Despite her strong antislavery feelings, she played no role in the abolitionist movement other than as an author. Nevertheless, Stowe, more than any other single individual, compelled the northern middle class to embrace abolitionism.

See also ABOLITION AND ANTISLAVERY MOVEMENTS; HENSON, JOSIAH; LITERATURE OF SLAVERY.

Harriet Beecher Stowe. [Corbis-Bettmann]

BIBLIOGRAPHY

CROZIER, ALICE C. *The Novels of Harriet Beecher Stowe*. 1969.
HEDRICK, JOAN D. *Harriet Beecher Stowe: A Life*. 1994.
JOHNSTON, JOHANNA. *Harriet and the Runaway Book: The Story of Harriet Beecher Stowe and "Uncle Tom's Cabin."* 1977.

Charles W. Carey Jr.

Sub-Saharan Africa

See Central Africa; East Africa; Southern Africa; West Africa.

Sudan, Medieval Western

See Plantations; West Africa.

Suffrage

See Law; Reconstruction, U.S.

Sugar

See Plantations.

Suriname

After the loss of Brazil, the Dutch looked for a new colony to produce sugar. In 1667 they captured Suriname from the British, but because of war with Amerindians, it took some decades before the colony was pacified enough to set up plantations. That work started around 1690. Sugar, the most important commodity, grew in wet environments, and was extremely laborious to cultivate. In Suriname's hot and humid tropical climate, African slaves established plantations for their Dutch owners in the marshy territories along the rivers. The slaves excavated canals, raised levees, and constructed locks to regulate water levels in the resulting polders. Sugarcane, coffee, and cotton were the most important cash crops.

Apart from the Amerindians not involved in the slave economy, the population of Suriname in 1683 included approximately 800 whites (mostly Dutch Protestants and Portuguese Jews) and 4,281 African slaves. Twenty years later, in 1705, there were 10,000 unfree Africans, and sixty years after that, some 50,000 dispersed over Paramaribo and 591 plantations. Approximately 210,000 African slaves were sold to Surinamese planters between 1668 and 1826.

Table 1. Plantation Area in Cultivation, by Commodity, in 1770 and 1862.

Commodity	Acreage	
	1770	1862
Sugar	21,598	21,990
Coffee	46,873	3,712
Cotton	8,741	4,844

Source: Van Stipriaan (1993), p. 54.

Around 1750, 17,342 acres were dedicated to sugarcane growth; in 1770, 21,598 (see Table 1); in 1790, 16,981; and in 1862, 21,990. In that year sugar production reached 34,760,563 pounds (15,800,256 kg). Coffee became and important crop during the second half of the eighteenth century, and in the years between 1760 and 1790, coffee production exceeded (in market prices) the value of exported sugar.

The model plantation in the nineteenth century had between 100 and 150 slaves, with 60 percent working in agriculture. Of the colony's 213 plantations, 15 had an excess of 300 slaves in 1850, with the largest plantation controlling 599.

For a long time the religion of the slave population remained African, with a belief in higher and lower gods and in reincarnation of the soul. Ancestor worship also played an important role in this religion (*winti*). A need for peace on the plantation dictated a certain tolerance of the slaves' beliefs and the conversion of the slaves to Christianity was a relatively late occurrence. Only 5 percent of the slaves were Christian in 1826, but by 1863, at the time of abolition, approximately 80 percent of the slaves had become Christian.

Suriname is most renowned for the formation of maroon societies. Almost all plantations in Suriname were situated along rivers, bordering swamps and forests to the rear that extended far into Brazil, and desertion was not difficult, as very few whites or Indians lived inland. Since escape was relatively easy, desertion in Suriname seldom or never involved mass migration. Fugitive slaves fled alone or in small groups. As a result, slave rebellions were also infrequent.

The number of maroons was so large and the chance of tracking them so small that the Surinamese planters were compelled to make peace with the most important groups in 1760. But war once again broke out, though this time with other groups. About four hundred maroons fought a guerrilla war in East Suriname from around 1765 to 1793. These wars were named the Boni Wars after their most important leader, Boni. The Scottish soldier John Gabriel Stedman, who fought against the Bonis from 1773 to 1777, wrote the most famous contemporary account of slavery in Suriname.

As elsewhere in plantation America, a group of free mulattos and free blacks emerged. Because few European women resided in Suriname, sexual relationships between white masters and female slaves were quite common. Two-thirds of the manumitted slaves were women; a large number of those who were declared free were the mulatto children of those women. In 1830, for example, there were 3,947 free mulattoes, as compared with 1,094 free blacks. From 1832 onward, the number of manumissions was systematically recorded, and 6,364 slaves were freed between 1832 and 1863.

See also AMERINDIAN SOCIETIES; BRAZIL; CARIBBEAN REGION; MAROONS; NETHERLANDS AND THE DUTCH EMPIRE; PLANTATIONS.

BIBLIOGRAPHY

BEELDSNIJDER, RUUD. "Om werk van jullie te hebben." In *Plantageslaven in Suriname, 1730–1750.* 1994.

HOOGBERGEN, WIM. *The Boni-Maroon Wars in Suriname.* 1990.

KLINKERS, ELLEN. *Op Hoop van Vrijheid. Van slavensamenleving naar Creoolse gemeenschap in Suriname, 1830–1880.* 1997.

OOSTINDIE, GERT. *Roosenburg en Mon Bijou: Twee Surinaamse plantages, 1720–1870.* 1989.

VAN LIER, R. A. J. *Frontier Society: A Social Analysis of the History of Surinam.* 1971.

VAN STIPRIAAN, ALEX. *Surinaams contrast: Roofbouw en overleven in een Caraïbische plantage-kolonie, 1750–1863.* 1993.

Wim Hoogbergen

Swahili Region

See East Africa.

Sweden

See Scandinavia.

T

Taney, Roger B. [1777–1864]

U.S. Chief Justice.

Roger Brooke Taney, the son of a Maryland tobacco planter, inherited from his father several slaves, whom he then manumitted. He also worked during the early part of his legal career to protect the rights of freedmen and slaves. Despite his conviction that slavery was an evil institution, he did not believe blacks and whites could coexist peacefully as equals, and so he supported efforts to colonize freedmen overseas. He also held that the Constitution granted the power to abolish slavery in the states only, an opinion that informed his thinking while he served as chief justice of the U.S. Supreme Court from 1836 until his death.

Taney wrote the majority opinion in two important decisions involving slavery. *Dred Scott v. Sandford* (1857) concerned a Missouri slave who claimed his freedom by virtue of having been taken by his owner into territory that the Missouri Compromise made off-limits to slavery. Taney argued that the Court could not hear the case because the Constitution did not grant citizenship to blacks, who therefore could not sue in federal court. He further argued that Congress lacked the constitutional power to make slavery illegal in the territories and thus nullified the appropriate part of the Missouri Compromise. *Ableman v. Booth* (1859) concerned a decision by the Wisconsin Supreme Court that the Fugitive Slave Law of 1850 was unconstitutional. Taney overturned this decision, arguing that no state could interfere with a federal marshal

Roger B. Taney, from an engraving made while he was chief justice. [Corbis-Bettmann]

who was enforcing federal law. Both decisions infuriated Northerners and served to further polarize North and South on the question of slavery.

See also DRED SCOTT V. SANDFORD; FUGITIVE SLAVE LAWS, U.S.; MISSOURI COMPROMISE.

BIBLIOGRAPHY

SMITH, CHARLES W., JR. *Roger B. Taney: Jacksonian Jurist.* 1973.

Charles W. Carey Jr.

Tannenbaum, Frank   [1893–1969]

Scholar of slavery and Latin America.

Frank Tannenbaum, a native of Poland, taught for most of his academic career at Columbia University. Among his many books, a brief but influential one was *Slave and Citizen: The Negro in the Americas* (1946). Beginning with a quantitative presentation, he suggested the enormous magnitude of the slave trade from Africa to the Americas, and he concluded that the building of new societies in the New World was as much an African undertaking as it was European. He proceeded to a qualitative analysis to develop a comparison of slavery and race relations in Brazil, Spanish America, the British West Indies, and the United States. He focused on church and state, on religion and the law, to contrast the Iberian variants of slave-based societies with those of the English. In Brazil, he said, the Catholic Church and the legal system alike recognized slaves as humans with rights, fostered the slave family, and facilitated the manumission of individual slaves. Slaves in the American South, he said, had no such protection. Thus, when slaves obtained freedom in Brazil, they and their former owners had limited difficulty in equating black freedom with white freedom.

Tannenbaum's work proved to be the foundation and touchstone of future work on slavery and race relations in the New World, particularly in the United States. Some scholars criticized him for failing to distinguish among disparate features of the slave experience. Eugene Genovese urged scholars to distinguish among three broad categories of the "treatment of slaves"—day-to-day living and working conditions; slaves' families, religious life, and community; and the prospects for obtaining freedom. In comparisons emphasizing such objective phenomena as disease and diet as they affected physical survival, British North America might appear a better place to have been a slave. In studies focusing on the more qualitative aspects of slave life, especially the slave family, North America again might look preferable, in part because of the earlier end to the slave trade into the United States, which both resulted from and led to a sex ratio approaching parity.

Yet Tannenbaum's primary interest had been in the transition from slavery to freedom—not only the likelihood that a slave might obtain freedom but also that black freedom would approximate white freedom—and in that regard Brazil appeared to come off better. Tannenbaum raised crucial questions, and subsequent students of New World slavery, whether focusing on small areas or comparing vast regions, could follow in his footsteps and had to respond to his formulations. Such historians have included Carl Degler, George Fredrickson, and Peter Kolchin.

Tannenbaum himself provided afterthoughts to *Slave and Citizen.* In the early 1940s he had been writing at the dawn of the modern civil rights movement in the United States. When he published *Ten Keys to Latin America* (1962), much of the slow change that he had predicted for the United States was already coming to pass. In his new book he repeated his observations about law and religion under slaveholding conditions, but he now stressed other differences between post-emancipation race relations in Latin America and the United States.

Tannenbaum continued to see significant differences in race relations in various parts of the New World in the long aftermath of slavery. The descendants of Africans and Europeans—were they two groups or three? North American whites' greater failure to distinguish between blacks and mulattoes could translate into advantages for blacks in the United States and for mulattoes elsewhere. Emphasizing the critical role of mixed-race Americans outside the United States, Tannenbaum observed that "the pure black man" faced greater resistance to social and political advancement in Latin America than in the United States.

While mulattoes' African ancestry might play a greater role in inhibiting success in the United States than in Latin America, other, more structural factors loomed larger in shaping developments. Tannenbaum's travels and studies had now convinced him that—given the more hierarchical, less democratic nature of Latin American societies, where there was less wealth and where it, like political power, was less equally distributed—African-Americans typically had greater social, economic, and political opportunities in the United States (outside the Deep South) than in Latin America.

Tannenbaum's work helped shape the changes in American society that lay between the publication of *Slave and Citizen* and *Ten Keys.* Branch Rickey's signing of Jackie Robinson to a major league baseball contract in 1947 fostered change in American life. Rickey, encouraged by *Slave and Citizen* in his belief that the experiment could give him a great ballplayer and at the same time reduce racial prejudice, often quoted the book's last paragraph about how "physical proximity" and "slow cultural intertwining" could ease the salience of race.

See also ECONOMIC INTERPRETATION OF SLAVERY; HISTORICAL APPROACHES TO SLAVERY; HISTORIOGRAPHY OF SLAVERY; LITERATURE OF SLAVERY.

BIBLIOGRAPHY

DEGLER, CARL N. *Neither Black nor White: Slavery and Race Relations in Brazil and the United States.* 1971.

"Dr. Frank Tannenbaum, 76, Dies; Organized Columbia Seminars." *New York Times,* 2 June 1969.

EDER, DONALD GRAY. "The Tannenbaum Thesis: A New Black Legend?" Ph.D. diss., Ohio State University, 1970.

FONER, LAURA, and EUGENE D. GENOVESE, eds. *Slavery in the New World: A Reader in Comparative History.* 1969.

FREDRICKSON, GEORGE M. *The Arrogance of Race: Historical Perspectives on Slavery, Racism, and Social Inequality.* 1988.

JACQUITH, L. PAUL. "The University Seminars at Columbia University: A Living Monument to Frank Tannenbaum." Ed.D. diss., Columbia University, 1973.

TYGIEL, JULES. *Baseball's Great Experiment: Jackie Robinson and His Legacy.* 1983.

Peter Wallenstein

Tappan Brothers

Abolitionists, philanthropists, and businessmen.

The Tappan brothers, Arthur (1786–1865) and Lewis (1788–1873), were the sons of Benjamin and Sarah Holmes Tappan. Their mother influenced the brothers by her evangelical pietism, millennialism, and fervent belief in God and obedience to the teachings of Scripture. Arthur never married; in 1813 Lewis Tappan married Sarah Aspinwall, with whom he had six

Lewis Tappan (left) and Arthur Tappan. [Library of Congress]

children; in 1854 he was married once again, this time to Sarah J. Davis.

After a childhood in Northampton, Massachusetts, and early adult years in Boston, the brothers formed a prosperous partnership as silk merchants in New York City. Both were early supporters of the American Board of Commissioners for Foreign Missions, the American Bible Society, and the revivalist Broadway Tabernacle, and they funded Oberlin College, an early interracial school. At first, Arthur was a member of the American Colonization Society, but their association in 1830 with William Lloyd Garrison turned the brothers toward radical "immediatist" abolition. They gave financial and public support to the American Anti-Slavery Society, underwrote the newspaper *The Emacipator,* and assisted Prudence Crandall in her attempt to run an interracial school in Connecticut. In 1834 rioters in New York City wrecked Lewis's home. In 1839 both brothers were active in defense of the *Amistad* case.

In 1840 the Tappans parted from Garrison when he wished to broaden antislavery to include other reforms (especially women's equality). They then formed the American and Foreign Anti-Slavery Society and a similarly named newspaper. Working closely with African-American abolitionists, the Tappans actively campaigned for the Liberty Party's presidential candidate, James Birney, in 1844 and helped establish a national abolitionist newspaper, *National Era.* Both were active in forming the American Missionary Society, which employed innumerable black radicals. In 1850, although Arthur's health declined, Lewis was a key supporter of the Underground Railroad. At the same time the brothers formed the Mercantile Agency, which eventually became the national credit bureau Dun and Bradstreet. In the 1850s Arthur, convinced that slavery was illegal everywhere, started the Abolitionist Society to push federal action to abolish slavery under the Constitution. Their importance lies in their financial and moral support to the abolitionist movement, and in their uncompromising ideals.

See also AMERICAN AND FOREIGN ANTI-SLAVERY SOCIETY; AMERICAN ANTI-SLAVERY SOCIETY; AMISTAD; GARRISON, WILLIAM LLOYD.

BIBLIOGRAPHY

STEWART, JAMES BREWER. *Holy Wars: The Abolitionists and American Slavery.* Rev. ed. 1996.
WYATT-BROWN, BERTRAM. *Lewis Tappan and the Evangelical War against Slavery.* 1969.

Graham Hodges

Television

See Film and Television, Slavery in.

Temple Slaves in Ancient Greece and Rome

In ancient Greece and Rome, gods were considered the foremost residents of a city. Temples were their domiciles, where they also accepted their honors and sacrifices; these were not places for worshipers to meet. Thus temples and temple gear were consecrated as the gods' property, or at least reserved for their exclusive use. In both cultures slaves were among this equipment and were employed in various menial occupations, though Greek and Roman concepts and practices differed. Sacred slaves are found in ancient Greece since before 1200 B.C.E. At Pylos tablets inscribed in the Linear B script, in the formula *teojo (doero/doera),* record both male and female slaves of deities such as Poseidon, Artemis, or a goddess named Divia. But we know little of the nature of the services they performed.

From the classical period, and far more frequently from the Hellenistic era, a large number of inscriptions from the whole extent of the Greek world and a fair number of literary sources (especially Strabo) have preserved evidence of persons commonly known as *hierodouloi* (sacred slaves). Their servitude was effected in various ways: prisoners of war, often a tenth of the total number of captives, were given over by a victorious general in fulfillment of his vow to the deity responsible for the victory (especially to Apollo at Delphi); private individuals might make a gift of a slave or slaves to a god's temple; abandoned children left to a god's care at a sanctuary were raised for lifelong service there; and slaves could also be purchased outright.

Because a temple derived much of its revenue from rents or produce of adjoining lands, temple slaves were often occupied in working the land, as well as in all other kinds of domestic service. Sometimes they were allowed small plots to work for themselves, and even to own slaves. At temples of Aphrodite, especially in Corinth, the chief source of income was sacred prostitution, performed by female slaves, many of whom were gifts to the goddess from both men and women.

Rome, like other cities, owned a pool or *familia* of public slaves, the property of the people—not the god—and employed in all kinds of public business. Some of these were reserved for the common use of the principal priestly colleges, and certain religious fraternities charged with the care of a temple also kept their own slaves for this purpose. They are designated in inscriptions as *publici* (that is, *servi*), to which is added the priestly college to which they were assigned, for example, *publicus pontificum,* "public (slave of the college) of pontifices." They performed chiefly as couriers, records clerks, and assistants at sacrifices, but they were also found as temple custodians, called *aed-itu[m]i*, sometimes residing in the temple precinct (Tacitus, *Histories* 1. 43). Because a temple might contain precious items, however, this position was gradually more often held by trusted freedmen or, in the case of significant sanctuaries, by a free person of some importance.

See also ANCIENT GREECE; ANCIENT ROME; ENSLAVEMENT, METHODS OF.

BIBLIOGRAPHY

HEPDING, H. "Hieroduloi." In *Real-Encyclopädie der klassischen Altertumswissenschaft*, vol. 8, edited by A. Pauly, G. Wissowa, and W. Kroll. 1913; pp. 1459–1468.

JORDAN B. *Servants of the Gods.* 1979.

WISSOWA, G. *Religion and Kultus der Römer.* 2nd ed. 1912.

Peter Cohee

Tennessee

Tennessee became a state in 1796 with a population of 77,212, including 10,613 blacks. Slavery had existed in the territory since the late 1760s, when settlers and their slaves from the old eastern slave states of Virginia and North Carolina began to move into the area west of the Appalachian Mountains. The climate was mild in the west and middle counties and had some heavy snowfall in the mountainous eastern counties.

Tennessee's three geographical divisions had different effects on slavery. In western Tennessee, where the soil was deep and fertile, slaves (11 to 50 percent of the population) usually worked six days a week and produced cotton, sorghum, tobacco, and corn. In central Tennessee slaves (11 to 47 percent of the population) produced corn, tobacco, wheat, rye, oats, hay, livestock, and some cotton. In the iron rim counties

(Dickson, Hickman, Montgomery, and Steward) slaves mined iron, carrying baskets of ore and charcoal on their heads to feed the hillside furnaces. In eastern Tennessee—where only 10 percent of Tennessee's slaves lived and where most of Knoxville's 752 blacks were free by 1860—slaves worked as servants, laborers, miners, and farm workers who raised corn, wheat, rye, oats, hay, and livestock.

In 1860 some 36,844 owners (24.8 percent of white families) held 275,719 slaves (24.9 percent of Tennessee's population). Slaves cost $800 to $1,300 by 1862 and could be hired out for between $100 and $150 per year. Tennessee became a slave-exporting state between 1850 and 1860, annually selling thousands of its slaves to the Deep South. Memphis and Nashville were important slave markets in the upper South.

The types of slaves included field hands (80 percent women and 75 percent men), house servants, artisans, and industrial and urban slaves. Slaves began work at sunup and returned to their quarters after sundown. Four to five slaves usually lived in one-room cabins of about two hundred square feet, with a central fireplace for heat and cooking. In some cases, where the owner held only one or two slaves, they slept in the loft or kitchen. Bedding was straw or feather pallets on the floor, but crude post beds were sometimes made by the slaves. Annual issues of a slave clothing were typically two hats, two pairs of shoes, and two pair of pants and two shirts (cotton and wool) or wool or calico dresses.

Negro mortality was higher than that of whites, especially among the children, who accounted for most deaths among the slaves. Pneumonia, whooping cough, cholera, bowel disorders, and other contagious diseases were caused by hard work, poor housing, inadequate diet, and little if any health care. Food allowances consisted of fat pork, corn meal, molasses, some vegetables (peas, potatoes, and corn), and local fruits and wild game.

Table 1.   Slave and Free Population of Tennessee, 1790–1860.

	1790	1800	1810	1820	1830	1840	1850	1860
Free blacks	361	309	1,317	3,181	4,555	5,524	6,422	7,300
Slaves	3,417	13,584	44,535	80,105	141,603	183,059	239,459	275,719
Whites	31,913	91,709	215,875	347,713	535,865	640,627	763,258	834,023
Owners	–	–	–	–	–	–	33,864	36,844

Source: The Negro in the United States, 1790–1915 (1968).

The slave codes required slaves to get written permission to leave the farm, prescribed ten lashes for wandering away, and prohibited ownership of firearms and sales of alcohol and other items to them. Assemblies were forbidden among slaves and free blacks. The blacks could attend religious services only under white supervision. Slave patrols roamed the countryside to control and prevent plots and rebellions. Yet slave disturbances took place in 1833, 1835, and 1836. Although Tennessee courts generally were not harsh on slavery, many blacks were imprisoned and even hanged for capital offenses. Blacks resisted their enslavement by breaking tools, slowing the pace of work, making trouble in their quarters, feigning sickness, and committing violence toward whites. Whenever they had the opportunity, they took on extra work to earn money to buy their own freedom and that of relatives.

By 1850 free blacks constituted 23 percent of the 4,000 blacks living in Nashville, where they operated several schools and quasi-independent church congregations. But slavery was strictly controlled in western Tennessee, where blacks outnumbered whites in two counties, and in Memphis, where only 61 of 2,110 blacks were free by 1850. The urban slaves and free blacks were riverboat workers, laborers, craftsmen, barbers, hackmen, shoemakers, washerwomen, domestic workers, and railroad builders.

By 1817 antislavery societies and abolitionist newspapers operated in eastern Tennessee, and the American Colonization Society had chapters throughout the state. Yet the powerful interests that profited from slavery refused to release their hold.

Tennessee joined the Confederacy in June 1861, but was occupied by the Union army in February 1862. Some 20,133 blacks and 31,000 whites served in the Union army in Tennessee. Slavery officially ended in the state in March 1865 through an amendment to the state constitution and throughout the United States by ratification of the Thirteenth Amendment to the national Constitution in December 1865.

See also individual entries on the other states of the United States.

BIBLIOGRAPHY

CIMPRICH, JOHN. *Slavery's End in Tennessee, 1861–1865.* 1985.

LOVETT, BOBBY L. "The Negro in Tennessee, 1861–1866: A Socio-Military History of the Civil War Era." Ph.D. diss., University of Arkansas, 1978.

MOONEY, CHASE C. *Slavery in Tennessee.* 1957.

SCHWENINGER, LOREN. *From Tennessee Slave to St. Louis Entrepreneur: The Autobiography of James Thomas.* 1984.

Bobby L. Lovett

Texas

People of African descent arrived in Texas as early as 1528 with the Spanish explorers, but African slavery did not exist in colonial times. In Texas slavery really developed in the period from 1820 to 1865. After the Mexican revolt of 1821 and the arrival of American settlers, large numbers of slaves were brought into Texas. Stephen F. Austin's colony had 443 slaves by 1825. Although the Mexican government prohibited any new slave imports after 1827, the American settlers continued to import slaves illegally.

The American settlers revolted against Mexico in 1835, established a republic, and made slavery legal. Over two thousand slaves were shipped into Texas ports between 1836 and 1850. Galveston had one of the largest slave markets west of New Orleans. There were about twenty-seven thousand slaves in Texas in 1845, when the territory was annexed by the United States.

Texas was the last state admitted to the union to include the practice of slavery. Slavery grew so rapidly that some northerners feared that the settlement of Texas and the Mexican American War were a conspiracy to continue southern domination of national politics by the slavocracy—the slave-owning class.

The average slaveholding in Texas was 7.5 slaves in 1850 and 8.3 slaves in 1860. Some 21,878 (48.1 percent) white families in Texas owned slaves. Sixty percent of the slaves were held by owners who averaged ten or more slaves. The white and slave population of

Stephen F. Austin (standing center) brought slaves to Texas along with the white settlers pictured here receiving their grants from Baron de Bastrop, the land commissioner of the Mexican government. [Corbis-Bettmann]

Table 1.   Slave and Free Population in Texas, 1850–1860.

	1850	1860
Free Blacks	397	355
Slaves	58,161	182,566
Whites	154,431	421,649
Owners	7,743	21,878

Source: The Negro in the United States, 1790–1915 (1968).

Texas more than doubled between 1850 and 1860. Slaves were 27.4 percent of the population in 1850 by 30.2 percent of the 604,570 population by 1860.

The settlers in Texas came from old slaves states, especially Louisiana, Mississippi, and Tennessee. So many slaveholders left Mississippi for Texas that their worn-out, abandoned land became known as "gone to Texas" farms. Most slaves in Texas were brought from the former slave states by their masters. One ex-slave, George W. Harmon of Lamar City, recalled that his mother and father were born in Virginia and Tennessee, respectively. Richard H. Boyd recalled that in 1859, when he was fifteen, he, his mother, and his three sisters were moved by their masters from Mississippi to rich lands in Washington County, East Texas; they lived in log huts (chinked with mud) and grew cotton and raised cattle. Boyd's mother, Indiana, had been born in Virginia before being sold as a teenager to Georgia, then to Louisiana and Mississippi. By 1865, however, 63 percent of the state's slaves had been born in Texas.

Slave owners were attracted to Texas by cheap and plentiful land. In fact, land was so plentiful that many masters hired their slaves out to raise cash to buy more land. Sometimes a slave was used as collateral for a loan or was sold to pay debts. Slaves cost eight hundred to a thousand dollars and even more by 1861. The slaves were concentrated in the eastern counties where soil and vegetation were rich and rainfall was abundant. Depending on the county, slaves represented 1 to 53 percent of the population in various Texas locations. The chief concentration by 1850 was along the lower Colorado River. At least six counties in Texas had a black majority by 1850. There were no slaves in barren, arid West Texas. Slavery in East Texas came to mirror slavery in nearby Mississippi. The slaves produced huge amounts of corn and cotton in Texas.

Slave gangs were common in the deep South, including Texas, where slaves produced about 90 percent of the state's cotton. White overseers and Negro drivers supervised the slave gangs and made sure that everyone met the day's quota of work: at least 150 pounds of cotton for male adults and 100 pounds for women and teenage slaves. Slaves who could pick more than 150 pounds of cotton a day were highly valued. The cotton season lasted most of the year, so slaves got some relief only during the brief winter. Some Texas slaves worked in the cattle industry; but cotton was king in the slave areas. The "task system" (assigning individual slaves specific jobs each day, such as mending fences) was also used in Texas.

Slavery in Texas was primarily a labor system, but it was also a tyrannical social institution. One slave recalled that slave children sometimes served at the table for the white family and fanned away flies, cleaned the yards of the slave quarters, tended small gardens, and helped the mistress with her daily chores. Four or five slaves usually shared a one-room cabin of about two hundred square feet, with a central fireplace for heat and cooking. The beds were straw or feather pallets on the floor or occasionally crude post beds made by the slaves. A slave's clothing typically consisted of two hats, two pairs of shoes, and a pair of pants and one or two shirts or wool or calico dresses, issued once a year. Small children received a large shirt but no shoes or underwear.

Farms in Texas, unlike Mississippi, were self-sufficient with regard to food. Slaves ate salt pork (bacon), corn, molasses, cornmeal, snap beans, squash, and other vegetables. They had tin utensils and wooden spoons. They used parched corn and okra for coffee and syrup for sugar. Slaves stored potatoes, turnips, and beets in deep holes on mounds of sand; cornstalks and straw were piled above to preserve the food. Children picked pecans and other nuts for storage. The slaves also supplemented their diet with game, including fish and opossums. Mortality was higher among blacks than among whites. Most of the deaths among slaves were among the children, who suffered from pneumonia, whooping cough, cholera, bowel disorders, and other diseases. Excessive work, poor housing, inadequate diet, and little clothing and insufficient health care helped cause the high disease and death rates among the slaves. Because the slaves were seldom near enough to an urban center to get medicines, they used roots and herbs.

Slaves in Texas, as elsewhere, resisted their bondage in various ways: by breaking tools, making animals go lame, slowing down the work, pretending to be sick, and acting shiftless. Some earned money to buy freedom for themselves and their relatives. A few slaves ran away, but Texas's vast interior and the proximity of slave states minimized escapes. Some slaves joined Native Americans (Indians) in fights against the whites during the period from 1830 to 1840. At least three thousand slaves had escaped into Mexico by 1851. Yet

Texas had tough slave patrols, harsh slave codes, and a death penalty law whereby owners were paid for slaves who were hanged.

Probably because Texas was a state developed by slaveholders for slaveholders, the whites passed laws and committed themselves to racist practices that discouraged any increase among free Negroes in the state and any settlement of free Negroes from outside Texas. By 1860 about 10 percent of the blacks in the United States were free, but in Texas the proportion was less than 2 percent. The laws of Texas severely restricted the movement of free Negroes and required newly manumitted blacks to leave the state. Some free Negroes settled in Mexico with the Seminole Indians in 1849. Between 1850 and 1860 free Negroes in Texas declined by 10.5 percent.

In February 1861 Texas joined the Confederacy. Many slaves were forced to serve their masters in the Confederate army. Only forty-seven blacks got the chance to join the Union army. Hardly any fighting took place in Texas during the war. Not until the Union army landed at Galveston on 19 June 1986—"Juneteenth," as the Negroes named it—did the word spread through the vast interior of Texas that the war was over and slavery was ended. Slavery was officially abolished in Texas and throughout the United States by the ratification of the Thirteenth Amendment to the national Constitution in December 1865.

See also CONFEDERATE STATES OF AMERICA.

BIBLIOGRAPHY

BARR, ALWYN. *Black Texans: A History of Negroes in Texas, 1528–1971.* 1974.
CAMPBELL, RANDOLPH B. *An Empire for Slavery: The Peculiar Institution in Texas, 1821–1865.* 1989.
MERK, FREDERICK. *Slavery and the Annexation of Texas.* 1972.
PRATHER, PATRICIA S., and J. C. MONDAY. *From Slave to Statesman: The Legacy of Joshua Houston, Servant to Sam Houston.* 1983.
SILVERTHORNE, ELIZABETH. *Plantation Life in Texas.* 1986.
TYLER, RONNIE C., and L. R. MURPHY, eds. *The Slave Narratives of Texas.* 1971.

Bobby L. Lovett

Thailand

The origin of slavery among the Thais probably goes back to their migration into mainland Southeast Asia, which dates from the second half of the eleventh century A.D. During the eleventh, twelfth, and thirteenth centuries, the Thais took control of regions with long-established traditions of various forms of slavery. The oldest written Thai sources, dating back to the Sukhothai period (ca. 1250–1438), mention these forms of slavery, as do countless later sources up to the final abolition of slavery in the early twentieth century.

The most detailed descriptions of slavery in Thailand date from the mid-nineteenth century. Bishop Pallegoix, who traveled extensively in the country, estimated that at least one-third of the whole population had to be counted as falling under the label "slave." Among this enormous number of people it was possible to distinguish three different categories: war captives, fiduciary slaves, and "absolute" slaves.

Among the war captives were reckoned not only those who had been captured during a war but also the descendants of such captives. One of the major incentives for waging a war in traditional Southeast Asia was to depopulate hostile regions and to take virtually all inhabitants as war prisoners. After a successful campaign these prisoners were distributed by the king among his officers in accordance with their rank and merit. The laws provided that war captives who felt unhappy with their master could arrange to be transferred to someone more to their liking.

A fiduciary slave was somebody who was held as security for borrowed money. Some people willingly joined this category by joining the household of a high-ranking noble, thus avoiding the obligation to pay the greater tax burden of a freeman. Others temporarily sold their wives or children in order to cope with a sudden emergency or to lessen the pressure of poverty.

On an absolute slave more money was often borrowed than he or she was legally worth. In the second half of the nineteenth century an adult man could be pawned for sums of money of up to fifty-six baht. This was a large amount of money at the time, the baht being a piece of silver weighing fifteen grams. If an adult man required more than fifty-six baht, he became the absolute property of the lender. Similarly, an adult woman's maximum pawnable worth was set at forty-eight baht.

Both state and religious institutions were staffed largely by slaves. A prince's household depended for its manpower and upkeep upon a large number of such dependents. Some he would have inherited, some might have been presented to him by the king, and others he could have acquired himself. All high-ranking state officials would need a variety of bonded persons, while many Buddhist monasteries were endowed with a number of bonded households that provided labor and agricultural produce for the monks.

The status of each category of slave was clearly circumscribed in the traditional legal code, and the conditions of their bondage were usually laid down in a written contract. The slavery system was embedded in a large variety of laws that set out the rights and privileges of master and slave. For example, when a female fiduciary slave became pregnant by her master,

Rama V, who prompted the abolition of slavery in Thailand and is better known as King Chulalongkorn of Siam, is surrounded by a group of young students around 1900. [Hulton-Deutsch Collection/Corbis]

the birth of the child would automatically cancel her debt and she would be free.

Contrary to what is often thought, absolute slaves, who were otherwise their masters' property, nonetheless enjoyed a measure of protection by law. If a famine occurred and a master had allowed his slaves to take refuge with a freeperson who could feed them throughout the whole period of famine, ownership would automatically be transferred to the individual who provided refuge. Other laws dealt with the problem of runaway slaves. It was strictly forbidden to shelter such a fugitive; for every day that this rule was broken, a large fine could be imposed. If a person hired a slave from another master and the slave ran away, the one who hired the slave had to compensate the owner with the full legal value of the lost slave.

In 1873, King Chulalongkorn became twenty-one years old and formally took control of the Thai government. During the years when he was being prepared for the throne, Chulalongkorn had already made two extensive journeys to the Dutch East Indies, Singapore, Burma, and British India, and he was highly motivated to reform those aspects of the Thai government that were considered old fashioned by the Europeans. The abolition of slavery was an item high on his agenda, and the young king's first act concerned this issue. The king and his chief advisers decided to diminish the legal value of slaves by stages, beginning with those who had been born in 1868, so that over a period of time the value of all slaves gradually was reduced to nothing. By the early twentieth century legal slavery ceased to exist in Thailand.

See also BUDDHISM; SOUTHEAST ASIA.

BIBLIOGRAPHY

CHOMCHAI, PRACHOOM. *Chulalongkorn the Great.* 1965.

PALLEGOIX, BAPTISTE. *Description du Royaume de Siam.* 1854.

SMITH, SAMUEL J. *Siamese Domestic Institutions: Old and New Laws on Slavery.* 1880.

TERWIEL, BAREND. "Bondage and Slavery in Early Nineteenth Century Siam." In *Slavery, Bondage, and Dependency in Southeast Asia,* edited by Anthony Reid. 1983.

TURTON, ANDREW. "Thai Institutions of Slavery." In *Asian and African Systems of Slavery,* edited by James L. Watson. 1997.

WICHIENKEEO, AROONRUT, and G. WIJEYEWARDENE, eds. and trans. *The Laws of King Mangrai (Mangrayathammasart).* 1986.

Barend Jan Terwiel

Thomas Aquinas   [1224–1274]

Medieval philosopher and scholastic theologian.

Thomas Aquinas, whose ideas have dominated all subsequent theology of the Catholic Church and have been influential for natural law thinking in general, expressed his political ideas in a number of works, including *On Kingship* (*De Regimine Principum*), the *Summa Theologica, Commentary on Aristotle's "Nicomachean Ethics,"* and the *Commentary on the "Sentences" of Peter Lombard.*

Aquinas, like Augustine, saw slavery as punishment for sin—slavery in general came from original sin, while individual enslavement occurred as punishment for crime or participation in unjust war. Following Aristotle, Aquinas held slavery to be contrary to nature and only imposed as punishment by positive law. He viewed the slave as a living tool of the master's will who partook simultaneously in the properties of person and of possession. There were persons who might be called slaves by nature, but the ultimate justification of the enslavement of any individual rested on deeds, not natures.

The rule that status, whether slave or freeborn, derives from the mother was justified by the uncertainties of paternity. Thomas's acceptance of the slavery of the children of slaves rested upon a lesser-of-evils argument—without the hereditary status of slavery, masters would be unlikely to grant slaves the right to procreate or to provide sustenance to their children.

Following Stoic doctrine, Aquinas held that the slave was obliged to obey the master in externals only; his mind remained free. Even in regard to the body, the slave owed obedience only in his labor. In questions of procreation, sustenance, and the like, the slave had no moral duty to obey.

See also ARISTOTLE; NATURAL LAW; PHILOSOPHY.

BIBLIOGRAPHY

THOMAS AQUINAS. *Commentary on the Nicomachean Ethics.* 2 vols. 1964.

———. *The Political Ideas of St. Thomas Aquinas.* Edited by Dino Bigongiari. 1953.

———. *Summa Theologica.* 5 vols. 1948.

Patrick M. O'Neil

Thornwell, James Henley   [1812–1862]

Presbyterian minister, educator, and southern nationalist.

The son of an overseer, James Henley Thornwell was born on 9 December 1813. Though raised in poverty after his father's premature death, Thornwell proved an exceptional student and in 1831 graduated from South Carolina College at the head of his class. Converting to Presbyterianism, he briefly attended the Andover Theological Seminary and Harvard until New England's liberal atmosphere hastened his return to South Carolina. Known as the "Calhoun of the Church" for his commanding intellect, passionate oratory, and orthodox religious beliefs, Thornwell founded the *Southern Presbyterian Review* in 1847, accepted the presidency of his alma mater in 1851, and four years later became professor of didactic and polemic theology at the Presbyterian Seminary at Columbia, where he served until his death from consumption on 1 August 1862.

In numerous letters, essays, and sermons, several of which were widely circulated in pamphlet form, Thornwell insisted that "communities and States" might "honestly differ" on the "political question" of slavery, but "as a *moral* question, the Bible . . . [had] settled it." Human bondage was, in his estimation, divinely sanctioned so long as slaves were treated moderately and exposed to the saving grace of "Christian knowledge." Bitterly opposed to the scientific racism of Josiah Nott and other ethnologists, Thornwell contended that "the Negro . . . [was] of one blood with ourselves," and as late as 1860, he seriously contemplated gradual emancipation "as the only measure that would give peace to the country." Yet, with the election of Abraham Lincoln, Thornwell actively embraced secession and became a leading force behind the creation of a Confederate Presbyterian Church.

See also BIBLE; NOTT, JOSIAH CLARK; PERSPECTIVES ON SLAVERY.

BIBLIOGRAPHY

BISHOP, CHARLES C. "The Pro-slavery Argument Reconsidered: James Henley Thornwell, Millennial Abolitionist." *South Carolina Historical Magazine* 73 (Jan. 1972): 18–26.

FARMER, JAMES OSCAR, JR. *The Metaphysical Confederacy: James Henley Thornwell and the Synthesis of Southern Values.* 1986.

FREEHLING, WILLIAM W. *The Reintegration of American History: Slavery and the Civil War.* 1994.

THORNWELL, JAMES HENLEY. *The Rights and Duties of Masters.* 1850.

Eric Robert Papenfuse

Thralldom

The term *thralldom* is an Anglicization of the Old Norse *þrældómr*, from *þræll*, which meant "slave." Writers in both English and the Scandinavian languages have tended to use "thralldom" when discussing slavery in Scandinavia, especially Iceland, in the medieval period, perhaps to stress its distinction from slavery in other societies. Medieval Scandinavian society did not have large-scale plantation slavery, but the institution usually called thralldom fits easily within the broad spectrum of enslavement. Thralls were treated as property and subject to the same legal disabilities and personal stigma as slaves in many other societies. Most modern translators of medieval sources that use the term *þræll* now translate it as "slave," abandoning a deliberately archaic term and acknowledging that thralldom is not a distinct institution but simply the Old Norse word for slavery.

See also SCANDINAVIA.

BIBLIOGRAPHY

KARRAS, RUTH MAZO. *Slavery and Society in Medieval Scandinavia.* 1988.
WILLIAMS, CARL O. *Thraldom in Ancient Iceland.* 1937.

Ruth Mazo Karras

Tobacco

See Plantations.

Tordesillas, Treaty of

Spain and Portugal signed the Treaty of Tordesillas on 7 June 1494. Portugal had claimed the lands discov-

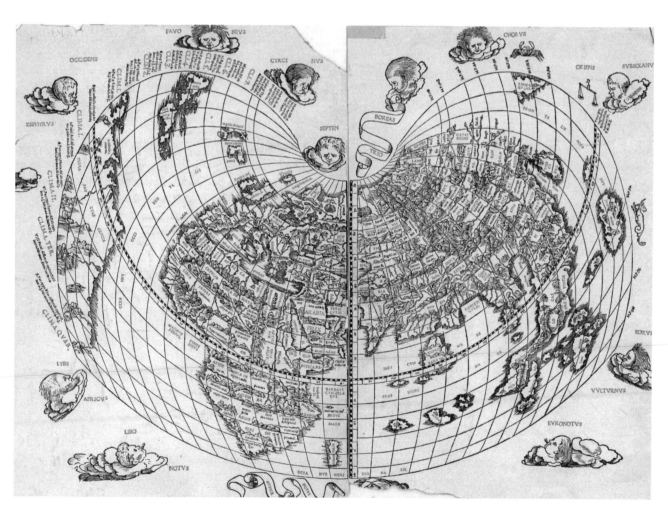

The 1511 edition of the Venetian World Map, which contains the first printed delineation of North America, illustrates the known world around the time of the Treaty of Tordesillas. [Corbis-Bettmann]

ered by Columbus on his voyage of 1492 in the service of Spain. Both sides appealed to Pope Alexander VI, who in his bull *Inter Caetera*, on 4 May 1493, drew a line of demarcation in the Atlantic Ocean, giving Spain the right to explore and colonize all the lands 100 leagues west and south of the Azores and the Cape Verde Islands. King João II of Portugal (reigned 1481–1495) found this unsatisfactory and opened negotiations directly with the Spanish rulers Ferdinand of Aragon (reigned 1479–1516) and Isabella of Castile (reigned 1474–1504). The treaty concluded at Tordesillas drew the line of demarcation from the North Pole to the South Pole 370 leagues west of the Cape Verde Islands. The region to the east of the line was reserved for Portugal; the west fell to Spain. The treaty was ratified by Spain on 2 July 1494 and by Portugal on 5 September. Pope Julius II confirmed the treaty in 1506. The placement of the line had the effect of giving Portugal claim to Brazil. Disputes between the two powers over Brazil and the islands in the Pacific continued for some time. Portuguese title to the Moluccas was acknowledged by the treaty of Zaragoza (Saragossa) in 1529; and the treaty of San Ildefonso, signed in 1777, fixed the western boundaries of Brazil and acknowledged the right of Spain to the Philippines.

The Treaty of Tordesillas did not explicitly speak of slavery or the slave trade, but it did open to exploration, colonization, and exploitation by both Spain and Portugal, conditions that soon involved the capture of slaves in Africa and their transport to the New World as well as enslavement of indigenous populations in America.

See also AMERINDIAN SOCIETIES; PORTUGAL; SPAIN.

BIBLIOGRAPHY

DAVENPORT, FRANCES. *European Treaties Bearing on the History of the United States and Its Dependencies to 1648.* 4 vols. 1917–1937; vol. 1, no. 9, pp. 84–100.
DIFFIE, BAILEY W., and GEORGE D. WINIUS. *Foundations of the Portuguese Empire, 1415–1580.* 1977.
El tratado de Tordesilla y su proyección. 2 vols. 1973.
PÉREZ EMBID, FLORENTINO. *Los descubrimientos en el Atlántico y la rivalidad castellano-portuguesa hasta el tratado de Tordesillas.* 1948.

Joseph F. O'Callaghan

Torts

See Law.

Torture in Ancient Rome

Torture, legally speaking, refers to judicial investigation—the discovery of evidence—rather than to the forcing of a confession, and still less to punishment. The Latin *quaestio* and the English "putting to the question" both stress this aspect. In the Roman Republic only slaves, not free persons (unless they were aliens, or *penegrini*), could be tortured. In the empire humble citizens also became liable to torture, and eventually everyone did in cases of treason.

Torture was deemed necessary because slaves as a group were thought untrustworthy. The Romans always associated honesty and virtue with high social status; the upper ranks of society became known as *honestiores* and the lower orders of citizens as *humiliores*. The formalization and deepening of this division led to the general assimilation of *humiliores* with noncitizens and slaves.

There were rules about taking evidence by torture. Certain forms of torture were forbidden; furthermore, torture was not supposed to kill. Pregnant women and children under the age of puberty were not normally liable to torture. On the other hand, torture was applied to slaves in cases of delict as well as crime, and even in civil cases—certainly in criminal cases—a slave was not to be believed without torture. The *Senatus-consultum Silanianum* of A.D. 10 laid down that all slaves in a household where the owner was found dead in suspicious circumstances were to be tortured to discover the perpetrator. Particular restrictions were placed on slaves giving evidence about their owners. In the republic slaves could be tortured about their owners only when the owner was charged with incest. After the reign of Emperor Augustus (A.D. 14) slaves could be tortured when the owner was charged with adultery but not with incest, unless the incest was also adulterous. By the later empire there was interrogation under torture of all the slaves in a household where adultery was alleged to have taken place, or one spouse was alleged to have murdered or attempted the murder of the other.

Torture is not legally concerned with punishment. A slave might be condemned to a deliberately painful death, but so too—if rather less often—were free citizens of the lower classes. There were no penalties specifically reserved for slaves; from the viewpoint of the Romans, Jesus and the two brigands were just foreigners.

See also ANCIENT ROME.

BIBLIOGRAPHY

BRUNT, P. "Evidence Given under Torture in the Principate". *Savigny-Stiftung Zeitschrift (Römanische Abteilung)* 97 (1981): 256–265.
ROBINSON, O. F. "Slaves and the Criminal Law". *Savigny-Stiftung Zeitschrift (Römanische Abteilung)* 97 (1981): 213–254.

O. F. Robinson

Toussaint-Louverture   [ca. 1743–1803]

Haitian revolutionary leader.

Toussaint-Louverture was born a slave on a sugar estate in Saint Domingue (modern Haiti), then the Caribbean's wealthiest colony. He died a statesman and general of international renown, having been swept into power by the largest—and only successful—slave insurrection in modern history. According to a nineteenth-century memoir by his son Isaac, Toussaint's father was an African of royal lineage, and Toussaint learned his language, Aja-Fon, as well as the local creole and eventually gained a basic command of French. He learned to read and, in middle age, to sign his name. Toussaint's experience of slavery was relatively benign; he seems to have worked as a stockman, coachman, and horse doctor. Living with his wife and children on the Bréda plantation until the great slave uprising of 1791, Toussaint was long assumed to be a member of the slave elite at the outbreak of the Haitian Revolution. Many of his contemporaries thought so, and this was the image he cultivated until his death. Documents published in 1978, however, showed that by 1791 he had been free perhaps twenty years and had rented land and slaves and even owned (and freed) at least one slave. He was thus a black freedman from the lower ranks of the free colored middle sector, similar to several other leaders of slave rebellions or conspiracies in these years. Toussaint's familiarity with African, creole, and European cultures helps explain his political acuity and versatility as a leader.

Although some believe Toussaint helped organize the 1791 uprising, as middle-man in a white counter-revolutionary plot against colonial democrats, it is more certain he belatedly joined the slave rebels' ranks and then slowly emerged as one of their top military commanders. Like most insurgents, he joined the invading Spanish forces that in 1793 sought to seize Saint Domingue from the French, and he immediately began to distinguish himself as a general and politician. Historians disagree to what extent Toussaint was a pragmatic opportunist or an idealist visionary. He occasionally supported a compromise peace with the colonists that would have forced most rebels back into slavery. Unlike other slave leaders, however, he did not sell black prisoners and noncombatants to the Spanish. It is not certain whether he championed general emancipation of all slaves before beleaguered French radicals in the colony took up that idea in August 1793. Yet it was about this time he adopted the name Louverture, with its cryptic connotation of a new beginning, and he soon became identified with the cause of freedom for all, even while fighting for the proslavery Spanish. He transferred his allegiance to the French Republic in the spring of 1794, around the time it officially declared slavery abolished.

During the following four years of constant warfare against Spanish and British invaders, Toussaint's ragged soldiers continually lacked food, clothing, and ammunition. They suffered terrible casualties, but in the process Toussaint forged a formidable army that eventually prevailed. In the bitter War of the South (1799–1800), he drove out the former free colored André Rigaud, his erstwhile ally and last remaining rival. The French perforce recognized him as captain-general in March 1801. Meanwhile, Toussaint had deftly outmaneuvered the French officials and generals sent to control him, and many of Saint Domingue's plantations passed into the hands of his ex-slave officers, who sequestered the abandoned property. Seeking to revive the plantation economy, Toussaint continued French republican policy of compelling ex-slaves to work on the plantations in return for a share of the produce, and he used the army to impose labor laws that included the use of corporal punishment. The policy was unpopular, as the masses preferred to become peasant smallholders. With no export economy, however, there would be no revenue to maintain the black army. And without the army, the gains of the revolution would be at the mercy of France's unstable politics.

Toussaint-Louverture. [Corbis-Bettmann]

Toussaint also encouraged the return of white planters. Some say this was because he believed in a multiracial future for Saint Domingue; others see it as hostage taking. While acting the role of loyal servant of France, Toussaint conducted his own foreign policy, signing in 1799 a nonagression treaty with Britain and the United States, which were then at war with France. He promulgated a constitution in July 1801 that made him dictator for life, but he stopped short of declaring independence, probably because it would have caused Britain and the United States to cut off the commerce on which his army depended. However, once both powers made peace with France, they were happy to see the new head of state, Napoleon Bonaparte, attempt to restore white supremacy and slavery. This precipitated the War of Independence (January 1802–December 1803). Defeated in a four-month campaign, Toussaint surrendered and was deported to France. He died in prison in April 1803 but left behind others to finally expel the French and found the state of Haiti.

See also CARIBBEAN REGION; INSURRECTIONS; REBELLIONS AND VIOLENT RESISTANCE.

BIBLIOGRAPHY

GEGGUS, DAVID. "Toussaint Louverture and the Slaves of the Bréda Plantations." *Journal of Caribbean History* 20 (1985–1986) : 30–48.

JAMES, C. L. R. *The Black James: Toussaint L'Ouverture and the San Domingo Revolution.* 1980.

PLUCHON, PIERRE. *Toussaint Louverture: Un Révolutionnaire noir d'ancien régime.* 1989.

David Geggus

Trials of Slaves

A slave's legal right to a "day in court" has never been seriously upheld in most societies. Most slave "trials" occurred before the master, who served as prosecutor, judge, jury, and occasionally executioner. Summary justice belonged to the owner, but even in cultures that promoted legal rights for bondsmen, slave trials could be hasty affairs, without defense attorneys or witnesses. In the Western Hemisphere, the volatile nature of slave justice descended from racial prejudice. In colonial Brazil, according to A. J. R. Russell-Wood, "blacks and mulattoes, slave and free, fell victims to the arbitrary and discriminatory form of justice meted out to coloreds. The colored person was often convicted without defense." The masters' virtually unlimited right to judge and punish their slaves gave them the upper hand, but the intimacy of the master-slave relationship might temper a master's justice with mercy and compassion. In addition to compassion, the master's financial interest in the slave might temper his punishment. Ironically, if a slave ever received anything like fair treatment, justice was more likely to come from the owner than from a judge or jury. In a courtroom, where procedures and punishments barely masked the slave-owning classes' disdain, slaves did not often receive fair trials.

Throughout the ancient world, masters were enjoined to treat their bondsmen fairly. Natural law or divine injunctions circumscribed the master's absolute power, by acknowledging the slave as a human being with some inalienable rights. The Ten Commandments in the Torah or Old Testament created moral precepts that persisted into the modern world about fair dealings between bond and free persons. Similarly, the Koran placed limits upon what masters could do to their slaves; the Islamic presumption of freedom gave slaves greater rights at trial than in any other culture. As interpretation of the Koran advanced, protections available to slaves at trial generally expanded. By the nineteenth century, Islamic law required a master to manumit his female slave upon his death, if he had fathered a live child by her; in a police trial in 1854, the slave Shemsigul confronted her former master, Deli Mehmet, and produced witnesses to attest to her pregnancy by him. The court accepted Shemsigul's testimony, which would ultimately give her freedom when Deli Mehmet died. Likewise, courts in both the Middle East and South America might compel an owner to accept a fair price for a slave's manumission. In cases that could lead to a slave's freedom, some courts enforced slave rights that masters preferred to ignore.

Cases leading to freedom were unusual, however: slave trials generally did not aid the oppressed. Aside from manumission suits, slaves could not initiate civil suits in most countries, but a slave could always be the defendant in a criminal trial. Several legal codes provided only for trials of slaves who stood accused of crimes against members of the master class. We know little about how justice dealt with crimes committed by one slave against another in ancient Rome, short of murder. In court, procedural rules almost always put the slave at a disadvantage relative to free men. In Rome, slaves could provide evidence in trials only after being tortured, and they could never give evidence against an owner unless he stood accused of treason. Under the *siete partidas,* a thirteenth-century codification of Castilian law (partly based on Roman law), slaves still could not testify in court. When the Spanish conquered much of Central and South America, they brought these harsh laws to the New World. As Europeans settled North America, they created similar disabilities for their African slaves: no slave testimony was admissible in court, a slave could not initiate a legal suit, and judges were usually slave owners themselves (not the most impartial lawgivers). Petty crimes did not require juries in the United States; justices (who, to repeat, were generally slave owners) would render judgment alone. In urban centers, the judge in slave trials might also be the mayor or chief of police. Appeals were usually unheard of, unless the slave stood convicted of a capital crime. Many legal systems allowed the convicted slave at least one round of appeals before a death sentence was imposed. In the United States most southern courts appointed lawyers to defend slaves if the master would not provide one. Some state supreme courts in the South also provided slaves with some procedural protections and on occasion overturned convictions of slaves based on coerced confessions, blatantly unfair trials, the enforcement of vague laws, or the failure to provide slaves with legal representation. A few southern courts even overturned the convictions of slaves who had killed whites, on the ground that these killings were legitimate forms of self-defense.

Slaves convicted of a crime could expect speedy punishment. Some American colonies permitted mutilation to indicate a slave's guilty status: branding, nose-slitting and ear-cropping could be inflicted upon a slave after conviction. In colonial and antebellum North America, the usual penalty for a slave was whipping, although a second or third offense could mean death. Incarceration or forced labor was rarely ordered for convicted slaves in North America, although it was common in nineteenth-century Rio de Janeiro, according to Leila Mezan Algranti. For offenses like murder, arson, or insurrection, a convicted slave could expect death in virtually every country. Some jurisdictions chose to deport rather than execute a dangerous slave. If the slave was killed or deported, colonial and antebellum U.S. courts typically reimbursed the slaveowner for his lost property, although rarely for the full value of the slave. This led some masters to avoid reporting crimes by slaves because a conviction of the slave might cost the master a valuable piece of property.

The rise of abolitionist sentiment around the globe in the nineteenth century, coupled with the popularity of graphic journalism, gave some slave trials unexpected notoriety. In the United States, the most famous slave trials occurred in the nineteenth century as sectional tensions pitted North against South. Harriet Beecher Stowe fictionalized a real-life slave trial that took place in North Carolina (*State v. Mann*, 1829) in one of her best-sellers, *Dred: A Tale of the Great Dismal Swamp* (1856). Arguably the most famous and influential slave trial of the century was *Dred Scott v. Sandford* (1857). In this case, the U.S. Supreme Court found that the Missouri slave Dred Scott was not entitled to freedom, even though his master had taken him to live for years in federal territories where slavery was prohibited. Chief Justice Taney used the opinion as a platform from which to issue highly inflammatory pronouncements that angered many northerners, who previously had little respect for the abolitionist movement. The *Dred Scott* decision briefly undermined respect for the Supreme Court, but more important, it was one of several factors that led to the Civil War only four years later.

See also ABOLITION AND ANTISLAVERY MOVEMENTS; LAW; SIETE PARTIDAS; STOWE, HARRIET BEECHER; TANEY, ROGER B.

BIBLIOGRAPHY

ALGRANTI, LEILA MEZAN. "Slave Crimes: The Use of Police Power to Control the Slave Population of Rio de Janeiro." *Luso-Brazilian Review* 25 (1988): 27–48.

CROOK, J. A. *Law and Life of Rome: 90 B.C.–A.D. 212.* 1967.

FEHRENBACHER, DON E. *The Dred Scott Case: Its Significance in American Law and Politics.* 1978.

LEWIS, BERNARD. *Race and Slavery in the Middle East: An Historical Inquiry.* 1990.

RUSSELL-WOOD, A. J. R. "Black and Mulatto Brotherhoods in Colonial Brazil: A Study in Collective Behavior." *Hispanic American Historical Review* 54 (1974): 567–602.

SCHWARZ, PHILIP. *Twice Condemned: Slaves and the Criminal Laws of Virginia, 1705–1865.* 1988.

WATSON, ALAN. *Slave Law in the America.* 1989.

Sally Hadden

Tribute, Slaves as

The purposes of the payment of tribute in the forms of slaves are numerous and varied. In some cases, of course, slave tribute is necessary because certain provinces may lack sufficient alternative forms of wealth to satisfy the demands of the ruling class of an imperial system. On the other hand, slaves may be regarded as simply another form of tribute to be supplied with a variety of other products, or individuals may be desired for their particular beauty or skills. In other instances, slaves may be needed for religious rituals. Finally, in the supplying slaves as tribute, outlying territories of an empire reaffirm their loyalty to the sovereign.

In the great Homeric epic poem *Iliad,* we see a hint of the tributary role of slaves in the confrontation of Achilles and Agamemnon, which proves central to the plot and the theme. When Agamemnon, the leader of the expedition against Troy, is forced by fear of the wrath of the god Apollo to return the daughter of Cryses, the priest of Apollo, who has been taken captive in a plundering raid on her father's temple, he demands and is grudgingly given Briseis, a slave girl that Achilles has been granted from the booty of a raid. Chryseis and Briseis are originally prizes of war, but King Agamemnon's insistence on the surrender of Briseis by the royal warrior Achilles is a demand for a kind of tribute from a nominal superior to a subordinate.

In the Old Testament Book of Esther, one finds an account of King Ahasuerus who, when he has deposed his queen, Vashti, for gross disobedience, orders beautiful young virgins to be collected from all the provinces of the Persian Empire so that he can select a queen from among them. This tribute of virgins has many of the aspects of slave tribute, given its involuntary character as well as the servile status of women in that age.

During the New Kingdom in Egypt, tribute in slaves was often paid by Ethiopia, Nubia, and certain Middle Eastern kingdoms to the court of the pharaoh. In the reign of Queen Hatshepsut (fifteenth century B.C.), the king of Punt sent gifts, including numbers of his subjects as slaves to the royal court. Likewise, in the reign of Thutmose III (also fifteenth century), Nubian slaves were sent in tribute by their ruler. After the Persian conquest of Egypt under the emperor Cambyses, the practice of slave tribute was restored. One year, in the reign of King Artaxerxes, the Ethiopians presented two measures of virgin gold, two hundred ebony logs, twenty elephant tusks, and five boys.

In classical Greek mythology, one finds the story of Theseus and the Minotaur, which suggests the existence of human tribute. Because Androgeus, the son of Minos, has been killed by a bull which was terrorizing the plains of Attica, Minos—the king of Crete—

imposes a penalty: seven youths and seven maidens are to be sent every nine years by Athens to face the monstrous bull-headed Minotaur in the Labyrinth of Crete, and be devoured. Theseus allows himself to be chosen as one of these youths in order to go to Crete to slay the monster, and thus end the tribute.

This tale is of special interest because murals and pottery found on Crete show young people of both sexes doing elaborate jumps and dances before charging bulls, suggesting a core of reality in the legend of the tribute. The Minoan civilization was a powerful thallasocracy—or seaborne empire—and may well have required its subordinate territories to supply young people for ritualistic purposes. Although the participants in the tribute, according to the myth, were not (and perhaps could not be) slaves at the time of their selection, it should be recognized that they assumed slave status in going to face the Cretan bull or bulls.

The use of slaves as tribute was not confined to Greece and the ancient Near East. Roman tax collectors gathered slaves from the eastern provinces for about two centuries, starting in 200 B.C.E. Various communities sent both adults and children as slave tribute to the government of the Ottoman Empire. Many of the Ottoman janissaries originated as children sent in tribute from Christian communities within the empire. In the thirteenth century Korea sent thousands of formerly free people as tribute to the Mongols. While records are fragmentary, there is strong evidence that the Aztec Empire demanded tribute in the form of slaves from outlying regions of Mexico and Central America.

Historians have disagreed about the mix of methods that political authorities in Africa employed to support state institutions, but it is clear that tribute was among them from very early times. Historians have likewise disputed the methods that slavers in Africa used to generate the captives whom they sold to Europeans from the sixteenth through the nineteenth centuries, but numerous reports confirm that these methods included tributes in slaves. Various African regions fell victim to the growing trade in slaves from occasional raids by armies of neighboring states; after a region was conquered and absorbed into the expanding political system, it then continued to provide slaves to the conqueror as tribute. The distinction between enslavement by violent outright kidnapping and enslavement as payment of tribute under threat of state violence would have been lost on the victims.

African state authorities receiving slaves in tribute kept the choice individuals, particularly girls and women and sold the others off for export. During the eighteenth and nineteenth centuries, when the use and exploitation of slaves reached a peak, provincial

A young female slave is presented as tribute to the ruler.
[Leonard de Selva/Corbis]

authorities and local communities built up stocks of enslaved individuals in order to avoid having to give up local people to state demands for tribute in slaves. By that time, slaving had become pervasive in many parts of Africa, and the movement of captives as political tribute would not have outranked default on commercial indebtedness, pawning of dependents against loans of trade goods, and continuing warfare as sources of slaves.

The submission of slaves (or of free persons assuming slave status) in tribute may be seen as a ritualistic assertion of, and submission to, imperial authority. Anthropologists, historians, and psychologists alike recognize that such rituals can be important in maintaining imperial relationships.

See also ANCIENT GREECE; ANCIENT MIDDLE EAST; BIBLE; EGYPT.

BIBLIOGRAPHY

BREASTED, JAMES HENRY. *A History of Egypt—from Earliest Times to the Persian Conquest.* 1964.
LOVEJOY, PAUL E. *Transformations in Slavery: A History of Slavery in Africa.* 1983.
MANNING, PATRICK. *Slavery and African Life: Occidental, Oriental and African Slave Trades.* 1990.
PATTERSON, ORLANDO. *Slavery and Social Death: A Comparative Study.* 1982.

Patrick M. O'Neil

Trinidad

See Caribbean Region.

Truth, Sojourner   [ca. 1797–1883]

Black U.S. abolitionist and freedmen's advocate.

Born into slavery in New York as Isabella, Sojourner Truth at an early age developed an intensely personal relationship with God that included seeing visions and hearing voices. In 1826 Isaac and Maria Van Wagenen bought her and immediately set her free; she adopted their last name in gratitude. Two years later she moved to New York City where she became a street missionary. In 1843 she answered a call from God by changing her name to Sojourner Truth and setting out on foot across southern New England, preaching the simple message that God loves mankind and so should man.

Later that year, Truth became an abolitionist after joining the Northampton (Massachusetts) Association, a utopian community that had been founded by abolitionists. For the next seven years she spoke against slavery throughout southern New England, and in

Sojourner Truth. [Corbis-Bettmann]

1845 she addressed the annual meeting of the American Anti-Slavery Society in New York City. In 1851 she began preaching the gospel of abolition throughout western New York and Ohio, supporting herself by selling copies of her life's story, which was written by Olive Gilbert. Over the next decade her colorful speaking style—a combination of simple observations, witty comebacks to hecklers, humorous gestures, and snatches of gospel songs, all of which she delivered with great earnestness in a husky voice with a Dutch accent—became a prominent part of antislavery meetings from Massachusetts to Indiana.

In 1861 Truth ceased speaking about abolition and instead promoted the use of black troops in the Union Army. She unintentionally incited a riot at a pro-Union meeting in Indiana by making this appeal while wearing a red, white, and blue uniform-like costume; she spent the next ten days in jail, during which time she was threatened repeatedly by racist mobs. When the First Michigan Colored Infantry Regiment was organized in 1863, she traveled throughout the Battle Creek area (where she had lived since 1857) collecting food and clothing for these soldiers while they were bivouacked in Detroit.

In 1864 Truth moved to Washington, D.C., where she worked as a resettlement counselor for the privately funded National Freedmen's Relief Association and the U.S. Freedmen's Bureau. For the next three years she helped find jobs in the North for former slaves from Virginia and Maryland who were living at Freedmen's Village in Arlington Heights, Virginia; she also worked to desegregate Washington's streetcars and toured the eastern United States, stumping for equal rights for blacks. Having decided that freedman should be resettled on federal land in the west in a manner similar to the reservations being set aside for native Americans, in 1870 she began circulating petitions to Congress and speaking throughout Kansas, Missouri, Iowa, and Wisconsin to drum up support for her idea. Although these efforts failed, in 1879 and 1880 many freedmen moved on their own from Louisiana, Mississippi, Texas, and Tennessee to Kansas in search of a more hospitable political climate, and Truth participated in the effort to sustain these refugees until they could begin farming for themselves.

See also ABOLITION AND ANTISLAVERY MOVEMENTS; WOMEN IN THE ANTISLAVERY MOVEMENT.

BIBLIOGRAPHY

PAINTER, NELL IRVIN. *Sojourner Truth: A Life, a Symbol.* 1996.
STETSON, ERLENE. *Glorifying in Tribulation: The Lifework of Sojourner Truth.* 1994.

Charles W. Carey Jr.

Tryon, Thomas   [1634–1703]

English primitivist writer.

Born near Cirencester, Thomas Tryon worked as a hatter and wrote popular tracts urging simple living and abstention from luxury. He was influenced by the mysticism of Jakob Boehme and by Anabaptist religious thought. His *Way to Health* (1682) served as Benjamin Franklin's model for "Poor Richard." As "Philotheos Physiologus" Tryon produced *Friendly Advice to the Gentlemen-Planters of the East and West Indies* (1684), which drew on a sojourn in Barbados in the 1660s. While this work deals with preserving health in tropical climates, Tryon also discussed slavery in a dialogue between "Sambo" and his master.

Tryon employed this vehicle to excoriate slave traders for separating mothers from children and husbands from wives, and to denounce the grinding work routines of the sugar islands. Sambo notes that planters cannot defend themselves by saying that they only buy men already enslaved: without American buyers the slave trade would not exist. Tryon's imaginary slave criticizes planter indolence, arguing that men released from healthy labor become in turn lazy, sinful, and sick. Throughout the tract, African simplicity and innocence are used as devices to condemn European luxury and immorality. Yet the dialogue closes with Sambo's reconciliation to his lot and his admission that if blacks had not violated the laws of nature, they would never have been enslaved. Ultimately, this depiction of slavery is but one part of a wide-ranging critique of late-seventeenth-century society, in which self-interest and consumerism were assuming dangerous proportions for an advocate of self-restraint and abstention such as Tryon.

See also LITERATURE OF SLAVERY.

BIBLIOGRAPHY

DAVIS, DAVID BRION. *The Problem of Slavery in Western Culture.* 1966.
STEPHEN, SIR LESLIE, ed. Dictionary of National Biography. 1885–1901.

T. Stephen Whitman

Tubman, Harriet   [ca. 1821–1913]

Black U.S. abolitionist.

Harriet Tubman was born into slavery in Maryland's Eastern Shore as Araminta. While still a slave she changed her name to Harriet and acquired her surname from her first husband. Around 1849, having worked most of the previous fifteen years cutting wood and plowing with oxen, she successfully ran away by hiding during the day and following the North Star at night until she reached Philadelphia.

In 1850 Tubman became a "conductor" on the Underground Railroad, a clandestine network of northern abolitionists and a few southerners, white and black, who helped runaway slaves reach Canada where they would be safe from the provisions of the Fugitive Slave Act. She made nineteen return visits to Maryland, on several occasions to rescue family members and friends. Many of these forays were financed by her earnings as a cook in a Philadelphia hotel. All of them were planned in advance by means of coded letters sent to free blacks or sympathetic whites. Her favorite ploy involved rounding up her "passengers" on a Saturday night (since many slaves had Sunday off, they would not be missed too soon), secreting them in their master's carriage or wagon, and then driving rapidly until late Sunday afternoon, when the vehicle would be abandoned. From that point on she navigated her charges through the woods by follow-

Harriet Tubman. [Library of Congress/Corbis]

ing the North Star until they reached Wilmington, Delaware. There, Thomas Garrett, a local Quaker, often took charge of them.

A cunning and fearless operator, Tubman put her complete faith in God. In tight situations she often reacted according to what she believed were messages from the Almighty. Usually her physical strength and endurance were enough to inspire her tired, sick, or scared passengers to continue their quest. When they did not, she threatened to shoot anyone who gave up short of reaching freedom. During the 1850s she personally led over 300 slaves to freedom without losing a single one to capture or desertion, a record that earned her the nickname "Moses."

Tubman spoke on several occasions at abolitionist gatherings throughout the North. She greatly admired John Brown, the militant abolitionist who called her "General Tubman," and she helped him plan his 1859 raid on the federal arsenal at Harpers Ferry, Virginia, which was intended to instigate a servile insurrection throughout the South. In addition to urging him to attack on the Fourth of July, she evidently intended to participate in the raid but was prevented from doing so by illness.

In 1862 Tubman joined Union forces in Port Royal, South Carolina, where she served variously as nurse, laundress, guide, scout, and spy. In 1863 she played a major role in planning and leading a Union raid up South Carolina's Combahee River that resulted in the liberation of over 750 slaves. After the war she worked to establish freedmen's schools in North Carolina and eventually returned to Auburn, New York, where in 1857 she had settled her aged parents. She spent her remaining years caring for orphaned and elderly blacks in her home, while working to establish a "John Brown Home" for indigent blacks.

See also UNDERGROUND RAILROAD.

BIBLIOGRAPHY

BENNETT, LERONE, JR. *Pioneers in Protest.* 1968.
BRADFORD, SARAH H. *Scenes in the Life of Harriet Tubman.* 1869. Reprint, 1971.

Charles W. Carey Jr.

Turkey, Ottoman

See Ottoman Empire.

Turkish Tribes

See Ottoman Empire; Slave Trade.

Turnbull, Gordon   [fl. 1785–1795]

Grenadian planter and proslavery pamphleteer.

A prominent British sugar planter from the West Indian island of Grenada, Gordon Turnbull was so enraged by the "specious and fallacious arguments" of antislavery "fanaticks" Anthony Benezet, Thomas Clarkson, and James Ramsay that he penned two influential tracts, *Letters to a Young Planter* (1785) and *An Apology for Negro Slavery* (1786), which vigorously defended the slave trade and idealized the plantation system. Blacks, wrote Turnbull, were an "inferior species of mankind . . . not at all fitted to fill the superior stations, or more elevated ranks in civil society." "Negro Slavery" in the Caribbean was "of the very mildest kind," and was "not only consistent with the principles of sound policy, but also with those of justice, and of humanity."

According to Turnbull, the "very cheerful and happy" West Indian slave was "perfectly reconciled to the white man." He was "comfortably lodged," ate "wholesome food," and frequently gathered to "sing and dance" in "joyous assemblies." Indeed, his pleasant situation was preferable to that of poor white English laborers, who, "obliged to toil for a scanty pittance," were little more than *slaves of necessity.*" In March 1795, Turnbull watched in horror as thousands of seemingly docile slaves took up arms against Grenada's white inhabitants. His *Narrative of the Revolt and Insurrection of the French Inhabitants in the Island of Grenada by an Eye-witness* (1796) can best be understood as the desperate attempt of an aging planter to come to terms with the causes of this failed sixteen-month rebellion and to accept its devastating social and economic consequences.

See also PERSPECTIVES ON SLAVERY.

BIBLIOGRAPHY

COX, EDWARD L. *Free Coloreds in the Slave Societies of St. Kitts and Grenada, 1763–1833.* 1984.

TURNBULL, GORDON. *An Apology for Negro Slavery; or, the West-India Planters Vindicated from the Charge of Inhumanity.* 1786.

                                    Eric Robert Papenfuse

Turner, Nat   [1800–1831]

Leader of a U.S. slave rebellion.

Nat Turner organized and led one of the largest and most important slave rebellions in United States history. On Sunday afternoon, 21 August 1831, Turner arranged a dinner gathering with six fellow conspirators (Hark, Henry, Nelson, Sam, Jack and Will) near Cabin Pond in Southampton County, Virginia. During the early morning hours of 22 August, the group began the rebellion at Turner's home farm, killing all members of the Joseph Travis family. They moved quickly from farm to farm, murdering all white inhabitants—men, women and children—and gathering slave recruits and arms as they moved along.

At some point during the afternoon of 22 August, Turner believed his force had become sufficiently strong to attempt an assault on the county seat of Jerusalem. However, by then the first white militia units had appeared on the scene, and in a series of skirmishes over the next several hours the rebels became disorganized and scattered. By the morning of 23 August, all organized slave resistance had ended. White militia units quickly killed or captured the other rebels, but Nat Turner eluded his pursuers for over two months, hiding most of the time near his home plantation. Turner was captured by local resident Benjamin Phipps on 30 October, tried in a Southampton County court of oyer and terminer on 5 November, and hanged on 11 November 1831.

Overall, the rebellion involved no more than sixty to eighty active rebels. The rebels killed fifty-seven to sixty whites. In the initial panic and confusion caused by the outbreak, Virginia Governor John Floyd responded with a force of over three thousand soldiers. However, he soon recognized this was an overreaction and arranged for their quick demobilization. Local militia units defeated the rebels in little more than twenty-four hours. Approximately two dozen slaves were either killed in skirmishes or hanged after quick trials. At least one hundred twenty (and probably many more) black "suspects" were summarily killed by white mobs and militia. As was the case with most United States slave rebellions, the encounter produced far more deaths among blacks than whites.

Most of what scholars know about the early life and thought of Nat Turner derives from a series of "confessions" delivered in his jail cell between 1 and 3

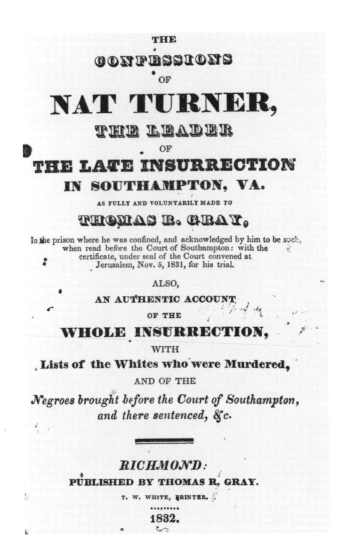

The title page from The Confessions of Nat Turner. [Library of Congress/Corbis]

November, 1831. Local lawyer Thomas R. Gray transcribed (and probably slightly altered) Turner's statements and published them on 25 November of that year in a widely circulated edition of *The Confessions of Nat Turner*. In addition to chronicling the events of the rebellion, these confessions describe the ways in which an African-American cultural and religious heritage nurtured a slave rebel. Turner grew up with a sense that he was different from other people and that he had unique abilities and powers. When he was three or four years old, his mother told him that he had memories of events that occurred before he was born. His family also noted marks on his head and chest which they believed indicated he was destined for greatness. As he grew up, Turner became a spiritual leader in his community. He cultivated a life of prayer, fasting, and preaching; placed himself apart from other men; and waited for the moment when he would fulfill the destiny that he believed awaited him.

At some point during the 1820s, Turner began to experience religious revelations. He saw visions of Christ in the heavens; he discovered drops of blood on the corn; he found hieroglyphic characters and other symbols written in blood on leaves in the woods. Ultimately, the "Spirit" came to him and revealed that "Christ had laid down the yoke he had borne for the sins of men" and that the burden of fighting "the Serpent" had passed into his hands. He interpreted a solar eclipse, and a "greenish sun," as final signs to fulfill his mission to begin a rebellion.

The Nat Turner slave rebellion had important short- and long-term consequences. Most immedi- ately, white Southerners took steps to prevent future rebellions. Free blacks in Southampton County came under suspicion as instigators of the revolt. Many were forced to flee the county; others accepted transportation to Liberia by the American Colonization Society. In addition, since Nat Turner was a religious leader, Virginia passed new legislation to repress the development of an independent African-American religion. Also in response to the rebellion, the Virginia legislature seriously considered, but ultimately rejected, a plan to abolish slavery.

Nat Turner's legacy was an object of contention during the antebellum period, and remains a source of controversy today. For many whites in the antebellum South, Turner and his rebellion represented the kind of insane brutality that would be released if slaves were exposed to abolitionist ideas. At the same time, blacks and sympathetic whites saw Turner as a noble hero who gave his life for the liberty of his people. Twentieth-century debates about Nat Turner involve a variety of issues, including whether he was insane, and whether his rebellion was a minor or major event in the larger history of resistance to slavery.

See also PANICS; REBELLION AND VIOLENT RESISTANCE.

BIBLIOGRAPHY

GREENBERG, KENNETH S. *The Confessions of Nat Turner and Related Documents.* 1996.

OATES, STEPHEN B. *The Fires of Jubilee: Nat Turner's Fierce Rebellion.* 1975.

TRAGLE, HENRY IRVING, ed. *The Southampton Slave Revolt of 1831: A Compilation of Source Material.* 1971.

Kenneth S. Greenberg

U

Uganda

See Central Africa.

Uncle Tom's Cabin

See Literature of Slavery; Stowe, Harriet Beecher.

Underground Railroad

Reference to the Underground Railroad evokes a picture of fugitive slaves being hidden by sympathetic abolitionists, then moved secretly from one northern site to another. Their destination was usually Canada, where slavery had been outlawed. Such aid, when available, was loosely organized and operated on a regional rather than national basis. Indeed, no national network or organization existed.

In the years following the Civil War, Underground Railroad activities developed into a popular northern legend, and many variations of that legend appeared in print and were repeated from lecture platforms. The legend popularized the use of such terms as "stations," "passengers," and "conductor" in connection with aid to fugitives. Those stories also exaggerated the role of the abolitionists and depicted the fugitives as helpless passengers rather than active participants in their own escape.

In every state, whether free or slave, some individuals were willing to assist escaped slaves. They included free African-Americans as well as whites with antislav-

ery views. Some abolitionists made such work a specialty. For example, in the early 1820s Levi Coffin and his wife undertook to organize such activity in the Newport, Indiana, area and later in Cincinnati. At about the same time, Thomas Garrett began his lengthy Underground Railroad career in Wilmington, Delaware. However, it was the Fugitive Slave Law of 1850 that sparked the greatest fugitive aid activity in the North. That law made returning fugitive slaves a federal responsibility and was weighted against any African-American who was claimed as a fugitive slave. It led abolitionists to organize vigilance committees that provided food, temporary housing, travel directions, and sometimes transportation to fugitive slaves passing through their communities. Occasionally the committees also prevented the kidnapping of free persons into slavery or helped rescue fugitive slaves from the custody of law enforcement officers.

New York City, Boston, Philadelphia, and several other northern cities had vigilance committees. They sometimes carried out nationally publicized acts of civil disobedience, such as the rescue in 1851 of Jerry Henry in Syracuse, New York, or Shadrach in Boston. On the other hand, the Boston committee failed to free Anthony Burns, who was returned to slavery under heavy military guard. Abolitionists later purchased and freed Burns. The chair of the Philadelphia committee was William Still, who years later published notes from his journals as well as many other documents valuable to historians.

Some fugitive-slave rescues, like the Oberlin-Wellington Rescue of 1858, were spontaneous. Soon after John Price was arrested as a fugitive near his home in Oberlin, Ohio, a crowd of African-Americans and abolitionists abducted him from his place of confinement and sent him to Canada. The federal government then indicted thirty-seven of the rescuers. The ensuing trials drew national attention and inspired demonstrations near the jail where some of the rescuers were held. When a county grand jury indicted the federal marshall and others for kidnapping Price, federal and state authorities reached an agreement to drop all charges.

The majority of slaves who ran away were courageous individuals who devised their own escape plans. While a very few rescuers, like the fearless Harriet Tubman or Calvin Fairbanks, went into the South to lead escaping slaves to safety, most fugitives found no such assistance. Many of them traveled on foot at night and hid out during the day. Ellen and William Craft were more ingenious, making a daring escape from Georgia with the light-skinned Ellen disguised as a

sick, elderly master and William as his loyal servant. Frederick Douglass, who borrowed a black sailor's free papers, refused to reveal his method of escape in prewar editions of his autobiography. Henry "Box" Brown literally had himself shipped from Richmond, Virginia, to the Philadelphia antislavery office. For the most part, fugitives who received help from the Underground Railroad had already completed the most dangerous part of their journey. All those who successfully ran away deserve a large share of the credit, as do abolitionists who risked liberty and property to assist their escapes.

Aiding a slave escape was clearly illegal, and at times secrecy was essential. Yet in some circumstances abolitionists were surprisingly open about their fugitive aid work. In 1844 a Chicago antislavery paper published a cartoon captioned "The Liberty Line," which illustrated and accompanied a story describing the underground line and even listed some participants. The authorities never arrested Levi Coffin,

Harriet Tubman (extreme left) stands with a group of slaves she assisted in escaping through the Underground Railroad. [Corbis-Bettmann]

though he made no secret of his sympathies or of his work on behalf of fugitive slaves. Slave rescues got widespread coverage in the press, and any violation of the civil liberties of citizens who aided escaping slaves served to deepen antisouthern sentiment in the North. Fugitive slaves were sometimes guests at antislavery gatherings. Some were even featured as speakers. Those caught aiding fugitives in the South, like Calvin Fairbanks, Alanson Work, and Delia Webster, often spent years in prison. While Henry "Box" Brown became a celebrity in the North after his escape, his white friend who shipped him in the box languished in a Virginia jail.

While abolitionists found Underground Railroad stories useful in spreading their message, southern slavery apologists used them to attack antislavery activity as a violation of the constitutional protection of private property. It is impossible to determine the exact number of slave escapes, though the census figure of about a thousand a year is probably much too low. Southern congressmen exaggerated the number of escapes and the monetary loss to southern planters. Trials under the Fugitive Slave Act gave both sides material for their propaganda. By 1855 the law had become virtually a dead letter in much of the North and a major source of irritation for the South.

It was in the years after the Civil War that the Underground Railroad became a national legend. Free-Soilers, who only favored containing slavery, as well as former abolitionists sometimes achieved inflated reputations as Underground Railroad agents. Hundreds of newspaper accounts associated anyone who had been opposed to slavery with local stories of the Underground Railroad. The reports were often gleaned from descendants or friends of abolitionists. Moreover, some leading abolitionists published memoirs that provided source material for the history of the Underground Railroad. While such memoirs contained important information, they were seldom supplemented by the narratives of fugitive slaves or by material from William Still's important book, *The Underground Railroad* (1883), which emphasized the significant role of the fugitives themselves. While the Underground Railroad helped many slaves to reach freedom, it was a far more complex institution than the simplistic legend suggests.

See also ABOLITION AND ANTISLAVERY MOVEMENTS; CANADA; ESCAPE; FUGITIVE SLAVE LAWS, U.S.

BIBLIOGRAPHY

BLOCKSON, CHARLES L. *The Underground Railroad: First-Person Narratives of Escapes to Freedom in the North.* 1987.
GARA, LARRY. *The Liberty Line: The Legend of the Underground Railroad.* Reprint, 1996.
SIEBERT, WILBUR H. *The Underground Railroad from Slavery to Freedom.* 1898.
STILL, WILLIAM. *The Underground Railroad.* 1883.

Larry Gara

Union Army, African-Americans in the

See Civil War, U.S.

United States

This entry includes the following articles: Colonial Period; The South; Breeding of Slaves; The North.

Colonial Period

One of the standard stories about colonial America describes the first African slaves arriving at Jamestown, Virginia, in 1619. Undoubtedly, black people did come on a Dutch ship that year and were the first to enter the mainland English colonies. But otherwise the story is almost entirely wrong. Blacks had come to the mainland decades earlier with Spanish explorers and colonizers. The probability is high that the Jamestown people were not Africans, but rather Western Hemisphere creoles. They may have been slaves when they boarded that vessel, but Virginia had no law of slavery. These pioneers of the African-American community probably became indentured servants, with a realistic hope of freedom at the indenture's end.

By 1650 there was a community of free black people on Virginia's eastern shore. They married legally, carried firearms, owned property, and claimed the protection of Virginia law. One, named Anthony Johnson, has become a historical icon, suggesting by his successful example a might-have-been of American history. Nonetheless, fifty years later slavery had become the defining condition of black people throughout British America. The northern colonies remained "societies with slavery," in which the institution existed but to which it was not basic. Maryland, Virginia, and South Carolina, however, were turning into "slave societies," fundamentally dependent on slave labor for the production of wealth and on slave law for the underpinning of all of social relations.

Unlike the Spaniards and Portuguese, the English arrived in the New World with no preset law of slavery and no direct acquaintance with the institution. Early modern English law did assume human inequality and did enshrine both the rights of masters and the obligations of servants. But it did not have room for the concept of "social death" that Orlando Patterson sees at the heart of enslavement. In the beginning some English people clearly took pride in this difference between themselves and their rivals for dominion over the Western Hemisphere. Yet many elements pointed toward the establishment of slavery in England's colonies, if not in England itself.

The most important was the availability of people for enslavement. "Race," as we now understand the concept, was not the central point. But Christian thinking did hold that "heathens" were fitting subjects for enslavement, especially if they rejected the Gospel when it was offered to them. Defeat in warfare could also justify the complete degradation and dishonor that enslavement entailed, a point codified late in the seventeenth century by the philosopher of English freedom, John Locke. Freedom itself was understood not as a human right but rather as a quality that went with specific social standing and community membership. The unspoken corollary was that the lack of any such standing and membership justified complete unfreedom. The social vision of all Europeans presumed some form of subjection. Slaves were merely the ultimate subjects.

For all these reasons, slavery was simply a fact of life in the world the colonizing English knew. Somewhat backhandedly, the Puritans of Massachusetts Bay recognized that point in 1641, when their law code excluded slavery except for those who might be "brought among us." It was the first explicit recognition of slavery in British North American law. Except for South Carolina, which imported the institution of slavery intact from Barbados, every other mainland colony followed Massachusetts in developing its own homegrown slave law. One result was considerable variation in what slavery meant.

As the English accommodated to the idea of American slavery, there was no particular reason to confine it to Africans. Indian enslavement did happen to a considerable degree. New Englanders enslaved Indians defeated in Metacom's ("King Philip's") war in 1676. The most famous seventeenth-century slave in Massachusetts, Tituba of Salem, was of Caribbean Indian ancestry. Slaving parties from South Carolina raided as far as Pawnee Indian country, beyond the Mississippi River. As late as 1776 a Carolina revolutionary leader was offering "disaffected" backcountry settlers the right to enslave defeated Indians as an inducement to join the American side. Yet Africa did become the prime source of American slaves, and African ancestry became prima facie evidence of slave status.

African slaves were readily available when English colonization began, but they were considerably more expensive than English indentured servants. When tobacco cultivation began in Barbados and Virginia, servants readily supplied the need for cheap, highly

exploitable labor. They made possible the development of the first forms of American plantation agriculture. In the long run, however, servitude could not sustain plantation life. Servants had an English frame of reference for judging their own harsh conditions. If they survived their indentures, they could claim places in free society. Moreover, the supply of people desperate enough to accept American servitude dwindled as word drifted back of what it entailed.

Barbados began the transition to massive slavery in the mid-seventeenth century, as sugar cultivation replaced tobacco. In Virginia there was no change of crop. Nor was there any specific moment when slavery appeared. Instead, a slow degradation of African labor took place after about 1650, combined with a greater availability of people fresh from Africa. Both black and white servants took part in Bacon's Rebellion of 1676, but by 1700 such collaboration was almost unthinkable. By that time white women did not work in the tobacco fields. Black women did. Blacks could not bear firearms or raise their hands against

A depiction of the arrival of the Dutch ship bearing the first group of blacks brought to Virginia, where they were sold as indentured servants. [Corbis-Bettmann]

white people. Black marriages had no legal standing. Blacks could not testify against whites in courts of law.

In terms of the Atlantic slave trade, North American slavery was a minor development. The roughly 360,000 people imported directly from Africa to the thirteen colonies and the young United States are dwarfed by the roughly 747,000 who went just to the island of Jamaica to grow sugar. Even tiny Barbados imported more than North America. Throughout the islands, the continuation of slavery depended on a wide-open slave trade. In Virginia, however, the slave population was self-increasing by the middle of the eighteenth century. Anxious to exclude Africans, who had direct experience of freedom and were more likely to revolt, Chesapeake planters began moving to cut off the African trade. By the time of the American Revolution (1775–1783) they were framing their opposition in moral terms. By then slaves accounted for two-fifths of all Virginians.

Nonetheless, the Chesapeake's creole black population emerged despite the conditions of enslavement—not because those conditions were intrinsically "milder" than in the West Indies. As in the islands, the ships brought far more men than women, making it difficult for slaves to form families. One of every four Africans imported to Virginia was dead within a year of arrival. When South Carolina began massive importations for rice production after 1710, it entered two decades when the death rate among slaves outstripped their ability to reproduce. As in the West Indies, it took massive importations to increase the actual number of slaves, so demanding was the situation that the slaves entered.

Yet those same conditions permitted the development in South Carolina of the most cohesive and perhaps the most self-determining black community in colonial America. Rice planters wanted not just strong bodies to provide labor but members of specific African communities, both for what planters saw as tribal character and for the knowledge those Africans had of rice production. By 1739 lowland Carolina was "more like a Negro country," where blacks far outnumbered whites and where African languages, religions, and customs survived to a considerable degree. One result was the greatest slave uprising that colonial America experienced, the Stono Rebellion of 1739. Frightened whites immediately moved to cut off the slave trade, though later they would reopen it several times. Another result was the emergence of long-term Gullah communities, whose distinctive language and culture became a permanent part of Carolina life.

The Stono rebels were not the only slaves who tried to throw off their bonds. For a time the Dismal Swamp on the boundary between Virginia and North Carolina harbored a community of runaway "maroons."

Slaves fled masters elsewhere, although there was no place where the natural fact of blackness was not also a badge of enslavement. Slaves in New York City formed the largest nonsouthern group of black colonials, accounting for as much as 20 percent of the population. They plotted a rebellion in 1712 and again in 1741. Each time they were fiercely repressed with punishments that included slow death by fire. Even in Massachusetts, where slaves never amounted to more than 3 percent of the population and where the law of slavery rested perhaps most lightly, the Puritan minister Cotton Mather inveighed against slaves' "fondness for freedom."

The colonial epoch accounts for roughly half the time that slavery endured in English-speaking North America. By its end most of the people involved were native-born, not imported form Africa. Against all odds, slaves had formed families. Different variations on the theme of African-American culture had appeared, their precise form depending on African origins, the ratio of blacks to whites, and the conditions slaves had to endure. Some slaves had been converted to the orthodox Protestantism of their colonies, such as Virginia Anglicanism. Others were finding a welcome among Methodists and Baptists. But no independent black church existed before 1774. A general acceptance that slavery was the most extreme form of inequality was on the point of yielding to the belief that race excluded all black people from American "equal rights." From this start would emerge both the strengthened slavery of the cotton-growing "Old South" and a postindependence free black community that would do all it could against slavery in the emerging American Republic.

See also DEMOGRAPHY OF SLAVES IN THE UNITED STATES; LABOR SYSTEMS; MAROONS; SLAVE TRADE; STONO REBELLION.

BIBLIOGRAPHY

BERLIN, IRA. "From Creole to African: Atlantic Creoles and the Origins of African-American society in Mainland North America. *William and Mary Quarterly*, 3rd ser., 53 (1996): 251–288.

JORDAN, WINTHROP D. *White over Black: American Attitudes toward the Negro, 1550–1812.* 1968.

KULIKOFF, ALLEN. *Tobacco and Slaves: The Development of Southern Culture in the Chesapeake, 1680–1800.* 1996.

MORGAN, EDMUND S. *American Slavery, American Freedom: The Ordeal of Colonial Virginia.* 1975.

PATTERSON, ORLANDO. *Slavery and Social Death.* 1982.

WOOD, BETTY. *The Origins of American Slavery: Freedom and Bondage in the English Colonies.* 1997.

WOOD, PETER H. *Black Majority: Negroes in Colonial South Carolina from 1670 through the Stono Rebellion.* 1974.

Edward Countryman

The South

Slavery in what became the U.S. South shaped social, economic, political, diplomatic, military, and cultural developments in North America for three and a half centuries, from the early 1500s until the 1860s, particularly during the final 150 years of that period. The Spanish introduced slavery into Florida and Louisiana, and the French brought it into the Mississippi Valley. But the English beginnings in the Chesapeake Bay region proved far more consequential and eventually spread south and west and absorbed the Spanish and French settlements.

Definition and Context

The U.S. "South" has not stood in one place. The region began in the Chesapeake and underwent continuous redefinition during the colonial period and the century after the American Revolution. At the 1787 Constitutional Convention, George Mason of Virginia complained that the "South," by which he meant Georgia and South Carolina, demanded special constitutional protection for the Atlantic slave trade. The Mason-Dixon Line gained its symbolic sectional significance, dividing North from South, only during and after the Revolution, as every state north of the line acted in one fashion or another to bring an end to slavery, while no state south of it did so. In the years that followed, The "South" spread south and west to Texas.

After eleven states seceded in 1860 and 1861 and formed the Confederate States of America, the "South" could be defined as the Confederacy. Yet slavery persisted for a time in the "North," in Maryland, Delaware, Kentucky, and Missouri, and the Confederacy itself was hardly unified, even on the white side of the great racial divide. Tens of thousands of black men, together with tens of thousands of white men, contested—and thwarted—the Confederacy's bid for independence.

Twentieth-century historians, when referring to the "South"—whether of the nineteenth century or the twentieth, before emancipation or afterward—have usually meant those states (Confederate or not) where slavery thrived into the 1860s, only to be followed by generations of racial segregation and disfranchisement. As the sectional delineator, the Mason-Dixon line (together with its western, more winding extension, the Ohio River) was established in the late eighteenth century and persisted two hundred years later.

The discussion in this essay focuses on slavery in North America, but it must be kept in mind that this is only a portion of the story of New World slavery. Of the millions of Africans who made a forced migration across the Atlantic during the four centuries after Columbus's first voyage to America in 1492, only perhaps 6 percent, or roughly 600,000, went to North America, most of these in the eighteenth century. For reasons having to do with such matters as gender ratios, birthrates, and death rates, however, a full third of all New World slaves in the mid-nineteenth century dwelled in the United States. By 1860, more than 300,000 slaves lived in each of seven different states in the U.S. South—topped by Virginia's 491,000 and Georgia's 462,000. Five others had more than 100,000.

Slavery in the Colonial South

In the areas that eventually formed the United States, slavery and its social and economic context varied depending on place and time. Similarly, African-American culture varied widely across time and space, but by the era of the American Revolution a number of key features had emerged. The variety stemmed in part from the diverse religious and linguistic traditions of Africa and in part from the great differences between life in New England, New Netherlands, the Chesapeake, South Carolina, and Spanish Florida.

African-Americans, though barely 2 or 3 percent of the populations of colonial New Hampshire, Massachusetts, and Pennsylvania, made up more than half of all residents, at least sometimes in the eighteenth century, in such places as eastern Virginia, South Carolina, and French or Spanish Louisiana. Everywhere, most North Americans of African ancestry remained slaves at least through the end of the colonial era.

The first Africans entered North America with Spanish explorers in the sixteenth century, long before English settlement at Jamestown or Plymouth. Some came with Ponce de Leon's expedition to Florida in 1513. African explorers played many roles that facilitated European exploration in the Americas, and their African experience in river navigation often made them especially valuable as crewmen.

In British North America the first African colonists appeared in the Chesapeake before 1620, and the first in New England before 1640. Their numbers remained scant, even in the South, until the late seventeenth century but grew rapidly in the first half of the eighteenth. Initially, some Africans in the colonies were indentured servants, and a few became landowners and even slave owners. By the 1640s, however, some black colonists were clearly slaves, and before many years had passed virtually all were.

If the seventeenth century laid the foundations of a slave society in the U.S. South, the eighteenth century brought its emergence. Slavery was born in the seventeenth century, had its adolescence in the eighteenth, and matured in the nineteenth. Across those years, two kinds of developments spurred the adoption and spread of slave labor. One kind might be called permissions to enslave human beings. The other might be termed inducements, or even imperatives, to adopt slave labor.

The seventeenth century, particularly the second half of the century, brought the legitimization of slavery in such colonies as Maryland and Virginia. A hardening of racial attitudes made it easier for whites to view blacks as suitable candidates for enslavement, a status that came to be defined as not only lifelong but inherited.

The seventeenth century also brought an agricultural system of commodity production that depended on a large and reliable labor force; a rise in wages in Europe and a decline in death rates in America that made the labor of black slaves cheaper than that of white servants; and a sharp rise in demand for labor that even a steady supply of European servants could not have satisfied. Meanwhile, an expansion of the slave trade made slaves more available to North Americans than in the early years of settlement.

The law of slavery reflected modifications of unfreedom already widely known in Europe. Indentures were contracts that specified the terms of unfreedom in the colonies, whether for apprentices or for indentured servants. The lives of servants may have been harsh, even short, but the prospect of freedom—ownership of their own labor and, beyond that, ownership of their own land—attracted servants by the tens of thousands. Slaves, by contrast, came to America involuntarily, and thus no concessions were necessary to induce them to make the commitment and the journey. The rights of Englishmen did not necessarily apply to people who, neither white nor Christian, were deemed unassimilable into political society.

Slavery proved a far more central institution in the southern colonies than in the North. This had little to do with the cultural imperatives of Puritans over Cavaliers, Yankees over Carolinians. Indeed, Puritans in the West Indies demonstrated an affinity for, rather than an aversion to, slavery as a means to produce great wealth.

Rather, the natural environment made the chief difference. New England had short summers and rocky soil. Agricultural producers could not generate sizable surpluses, so what was the point of putting additional hands to work? Producers had to eat through the long winters, even when there was much less to produce. In the South, by contrast, the soil and the climate conspired to render unfree labor highly attractive, even compelling. Workers there could produce far beyond what they required for consumption, and work conditions in the hot climate deterred the employment of free labor.

As a central part of social and economic life in North America, slavery had its beginnings in the Chesapeake colonies—Maryland and Virginia. By the mid-eighteenth century, and lasting as long as slavery did, entire counties in eastern Virginia had substantial black majorities. Measured in terms of slave percentages, the greatest slave society of the eighteenth century was South Carolina. Carolina was launched by settlers, slaves and their owners, who migrated to the mainland from Barbados, a Caribbean island that was a speck in the English empire. Through much of the eighteenth century, and again through most of the nineteenth, blacks in South Carolina outnumbered whites.

African-American Culture

When tens of thousands of Africans arrived in British North America, whether in Maryland and Virginia in the 1720s or in Georgia and South Carolina as late as the 1790s, they brought vivid memories of the world they had left behind. They spoke various languages and came from varied societies. Gradually they forged a new culture, one that incorporated key features of their legacies from Africa as well as significant aspects of European and even Native American cultures. Language and religion would long be the most obvious.

Africans did not make their way from Old World villages to New World plantations in clusters that remained intact. New slaves in Connecticut and Carolina alike had to find a new means of communication. Most quickly learned enough English vocabulary to get by—to understand orders from their masters and communicate with their fellows. The decline of the slave trade into all of British North America except Georgia and South Carolina by the 1750s meant few new immigrants from Africa encountering English for the first time. Yet in some areas, particularly along the rural coast of Georgia and South Carolina, African-born slaves remained so numerous and so routinely separate from whites that they and their descendants long continued to speak a dialect, known as Gullah, quite distinct from English.

Slowly through the colonial era, African-Americans in the British colonies began to embrace Protestant Christianity, just as their counterparts in French and Spanish America adopted Catholicism. The process was slow for various reasons. White settlers displayed reluctance to promote the gospel among blacks out of fear that conversion might render them in some ways

An advertisement announcing the auction of slaves from Guinea, 3 August 1774, tops a handbill printed in Savannah, Georgia. [Library of Congress/Corbis]

equal to whites or might compromise their status as slaves. Slaves themselves often failed to see the attractions of whites' religious beliefs, though the Great Awakening brought a more expressive form of religion that proved more attractive to whites and blacks alike. As late as the American Revolution, only a small minority of African-Americans had adopted Christianity, but the process continued to pick up strength until most, slave or free, came to identify themselves as Baptists, Methodists, or some other variant of Protestant faith.

In kinship and family relationships, African-Americans created a culture not altogether like that of either their former homelands or their white neighbors. Slaves had limited ability to protect themselves from decisions by their owners that could, without warning, split families forever. Parents might never again see children, or the children their siblings. Partly for that reason, and partly to create relationships that might replace lost members of former communities, African-Americans established broad kinship ties, whether based on blood and marriage or not, that could better promote a sense of community.

Whatever the specifics of family relationships, the end of the slave trade meant that most African-Americans could create long-term connections. The slave trade brought two or three men for each woman, but second-generation African-Americans, born in the colonies, included as many women as men. By the time of the American Revolution, slave communities were growing as fast as white communities through natural increase—more births than deaths. Black families were as successful in raising four, six, or eight children as were their white owners or neighbors.

The slave family proved to be a central feature of African-American life. The law nowhere recognized slave marriages or inheritance, nowhere effectively compelled owners to protect slave families from interruption by sale. But slaves themselves knew their own relationships. And their owners found that supporting the institution of the slave family, up to a point, served their own purposes. Slave men with families were far less likely to take violent action against their owners, far less likely to seek escape from slavery alone, and far less likely to succeed if they tried to take their families.

African-American culture at the end of the colonial era extended far beyond such emerging central features as family and community, the English language, and Protestant Christianity. In expressive culture, African-Americans introduced the banjo into American music and, with it and the European fiddle, created new musical forms that were neither entirely African nor entirely European. Various words, long since assimilated into the dominant language, originated in Africa, among them "OK" and "mumbo-jumbo," as did such culinary phenomena as deep-fat frying and gumbo.

In material culture, slaves brought their own distinctive design features to houses and furnishings. Archeologists in recent years have uncovered astonishing material evidence regarding the lives of slaves in the U.S. South. Such artifacts as bowls, spoons, and baskets demonstrate craftsmanship—artistic ability and pride in one's work—at the same time that they reveal spiritual beliefs and an aesthetic that can be traced back to Africa. The same is true of houses, shrines, and other things that the descendants of Africa built in the New World. Black Americans worked, ate, and slept in a world that was African as well as European. They contributed to creating an America that was neither African nor European.

People of African ancestry proved to be central players in the history of colonial America. South Carolina's coastal plantations make the point as well as any New World phenomenon. At first, many of the laborers in Carolina were European servants and Indian slaves, but African-American slaves soon made up most of the labor force. They made possible the massive cultivation of rice and indigo—the major crops of eighteenth-century South Carolina—through far more than their labor alone. Europeans knew nothing of growing rice; Africans knew everything about growing it. African culture—from such economic activities as river navigation, cattle raising, and rice cultivation to such expressive activities as dance and music—made life in British North America something radically different from Old World European patterns.

For African-Americans themselves, the world they made was composed of materials from Old World and New World alike. In language, family, religion, music, and various other ways, the African-American culture of the nineteenth century—and the twentieth—had gone a far distance toward taking shape by the time white Americans gained their independence from England.

The American Revolution

During the era of the American Revolution, large numbers of African-Americans—whether in Massachusetts or Virginia—gained their freedom from white ownership. More and more began to live lives that, no longer so desperately shadowed by slavery, gave them more space to shape their own futures. Virtually all slaves in New England and the Middle Atlantic states gained their freedom, but the number of freedpeople in Delaware, Maryland, and Virginia grew as large, even if nine out of ten black Virginians remained enslaved.

The Revolution created opportunities for some slaves to fight for their freedom. In 1775 Lord Dunmore, the last governor of the Virginia colony, offered slaves—and servants—their freedom if they would fight in support of the empire. Some Virginia slaves obtained their freedom in this way and, after the Revolution, retained it in Sierra Leone. Other slaves gained their freedom by fighting on the rebel side.

Such Virginia planters as Thomas Jefferson and George Washington may have been particularly sensitive—in view of the many slaves that labored on their plantations—to allegations that England was seeking to "enslave" the colonies. Regardless, the Revolutionary era brought many changes to the slave societies of what emerged as the United States of America. The new state of Virginia exemplified those changes when it enacted an end to the immigration of new slaves from outside the new nation or even outside the state, and when it established a means by which slaveowners could determine for themselves whether to manumit a few or even many of their slaves.

In freeing some slaves, white Virginians were responding to a variety of considerations, among them religious attacks on the ethics of slave ownership, a sense that squawking about England's efforts to "enslave" white Americans sounded hollow if those Americans enslaved others, and the economic disruptions of the era that, for a time, rendered slavery unprofitable.

The new nation had the capacity to regulate the future of slavery in some ways. It might do so in strengthening the institution—through facilitating owners' recapture of runaway slaves, obtaining more land into which the slave system might spread, and removing Indians from such lands, as in Mississippi and Alabama. Or it might do so in weakening slavery through measures that limited the expansion of the system, as with the Northwest Ordinance, or that diminished its profitability, as with a protective tariff on imported goods that planters brought.

Migration and Expansion, 1790–1860

In 1790, 293,000 slaves resided in Virginia, 42 percent of all the slaves in the United States. Three states—Maryland, North Carolina, and South Carolina—combined accounted for roughly as many more, and far smaller numbers lived in such states as Georgia, New York, New Jersey, Pennsylvania, and Delaware. By the 1790s, slavery had ended in much of New England, and it was under attack elsewhere in the North and even in Virginia. The cotton gin had only recently come into use, and the "Cotton Kingdom" had yet to emerge across the Deep South, so the huge slave trade out of the Chesapeake states had not yet begun.

A combination of factors led to the enormous growth of slavery in the years between the presidencies of George Washington and Abraham Lincoln. The cotton gin broke a production bottleneck that had curtailed the profitability of cultivating a short-staple cotton. But the cotton gin needed co-conspirators to transform the eighteenth-century South into the nineteenth-century version. There had to be mounting demand for raw cotton by textile manufacturers, whether in England or in New England.

And there had to be abundant land and a salubrious climate. Had there been no Gulf coast region in the South—had North America reached only to the Appalachians—or had the region remained unavailable to settlement by plantation owners and their slaves, there could have been no immense Cotton Kingdom of the sort that emerged in the last half-century of slavery. Yet the land was there, and it proved available. No European empire long prevented American expansion, and removal of the Indians eliminated the last obstacle. The Louisiana Purchase brought vast new lands, including those into which the Spanish

An 1824 engraving illustrates the great labor question from the southern point of view. [Corbis-Bettmann]

and French had brought slavery, and, more important in the near term, it supplied an area into which southern Indians from east of the Mississippi River could be removed.

Yet another crucial feature of the antebellum South was demographic. The legal end of the slave trade into the United States by 1808—not so very different from its actual end—meant that no new hordes of imported slaves could keep supplies of labor high and costs down. Slave owners and would-be slave owners had to depend on a finite stock of slaves for purchase and hire. Yet the demographic developments of the Old South—high rates of fertility, high rates of natural increase—led to a growth in the slave population that matched the increase in whites. The children of slave owners outnumbered their parents, but the children of each generation of slaves also outnumbered their parents. Unlike slaves through much of the rest of the New World, especially in the Caribbean, slaves in the American South survived and reproduced, more than replacing themselves.

Though the slave trade into the United States came to an end, the slave trade from one state to another certainly did not. Thus the actual number of slaves living in Virginia grew far less than natural increase would have predicted. By the tens of thousands,

Chesapeake-born slaves lived and worked much of their lives in the cotton South. There was never any confusion between slavery in the upper South and the Garden of Eden, but it nonetheless had its serpent, as the slave trade reached into slave families and communities and tore men, women, and children away from their loved ones and familiar surroundings.

Slave Society in the Old South

Slaves were never entirely powerless. Willful and resourceful, they worked with the materials at hand to forge as acceptable a way of life as slavery could afford. In effect, they negotiated over their work schedules, their days off, their provisions and housing, and their families, regardless of whether any of these was recognized in law or formal contract. They developed what came to be accepted on both sides as entitlements, and thus they created space for themselves within the institution.

Rarely did southern slaves engage in collective violence. Individuals might find themselves engaged in violence, though more subtle forms of resistance were more typical. Still, slave owners and their families knew that violence was always a possibility. The uprising in August 1831 in Southampton County, Virginia, was one example, as Nat Turner and more than fifty other black men launched an attack on white families. Perhaps the best other example from the antebellum years occurred in Florida, where the U.S. Army deployed thousands of men in the 1830s to fight the Second Seminole War against a combined force of Native Americans and African-Americans.

Slavery demonstrated its adaptability as slaves went to work in cities as well as on plantations, in industry as well as agriculture. Mining, historically a favored venue for forced labor, did not become a significant part of the American economy or the western landscape until after the Civil War—else the "natural limits," as they have been called, to the expansion of the Cotton Kingdom might have proved less significant than is sometimes argued. Through the end of the slave era, most southern slaves worked in agriculture, and a majority worked on what historians call "plantations," holdings of more than twenty slaves, though most holdings, it remained true, were of fewer than ten slaves.

Never were all black southerners slaves. By 1860 most black residents of Delaware were free, as were nearly half of those in Maryland and roughly one in ten in Virginia and North Carolina. By contrast, fewer than 1,000 black residents of Mississippi, Florida, Texas, or Arkansas were free. Moreover, black freedom should in no way be confused with white freedom. In no slave state in 1860 were black men permitted to vote, and in some states it was a crime to teach a black person, even if free, how to read or write. Increasingly by the late 1850s, free black southerners were offered the choice of leaving the state or losing their freedom. It is said, often and truly, that some free people of African ancestry in South Carolina and Louisiana, particularly in Charleston and New Orleans, found a more expansive definition of black freedom, but not only were most of them light-skinned (many had more European ancestry than African), their numbers were not large. The vast majority of all free black southerners lived in Delaware, Maryland, Virginia, and North Carolina.

Slaves along the periphery of the slave South had more opportunity than those elsewhere to escape to freedom. Slaves in Georgia had at one time made their way to Florida, but the U.S. reduced that opportunity by acquiring Florida and then winning the Second Seminole War. Black Texans sometimes fled to Mexico, and slaves from Virginia, Maryland, and Kentucky sometimes made their way north to the free states or, to escape the reach of the Fugitive Slave Act, to Canada. Slave owners in the upper South, in light of their greater proximity to free states, sought the practical guarantees of a stronger federal Fugitive Slave Act, just as their counterparts in the Deep South craved the symbolic assurance of a national government acting in support of slavery.

White southerners found themselves divided over slavery. The institution had a major presence in many states, but not in every section of most states. Only in pre–Civil War South Carolina, where slaves were a majority of all residents, was there no region where whites were in a large majority and where slaves and slave owners were few and far between. In parts—particularly the mountainous parts—of other states, whether in north Georgia, eastern Tennessee, or western Virginia, the plantation regime made much less headway. The whites of western Virginia mounted an effort in the state legislature, in the aftermath of Nat Turner's uprising, to launch the Old Dominion on a path toward a slaveless society. They failed, but the fissures in white society remained. To repeat: never was it true in the South that all blacks were slaves, even less that all whites owned slaves. And slaveless whites were unreliable proponents of the slave system.

In every state that joined the Confederacy, members of slaveholding families in 1860 and 1861 made up roughly 20 percent of all residents—slightly more in South Carolina, Georgia, and Mississippi, slightly less in the others. The states differed far more in the fractions of residents who were slaves or were nonslaveholding whites. In Arkansas, Texas, and Tennessee, white nonslaveholders—people who were neither slaves nor slave owners—outnumbered the other two groups combined. In South Carolina and Mississippi, by contrast, slaves outnumbered all other residents.

Developments in the slave South can be partly explained in terms of southern conditions and events. Yet the South depended on economic conditions and political relations outside the region. The demand for southern commodities makes the point, but the immense size of the new nation, and the growing sectional differences within the nation, played just as great a role.

North, South, and Southern Slavery

As forces external to the South continued to shape developments there, political forces in the early republic proved central. The most obvious had to do with such events as the Missouri crisis from 1819 to 1821, when a dispute over territory acquired in the Louisiana Purchase threatened to undo the new nation, and the secession crisis of 1860 and 1861, when South Carolina led the way out of the Union and other states followed. As a rule, white northerners were not so concerned about slavery within the South as they were about the threat it posed to themselves, whether in slaveholders' dominance in national politics or in the prospect that the slave system would expand into regions northerners had their eyes on.

Southern leaders demanded the safeguards they saw as necessary to protect their interests from interference by northerners. The Compromise of 1850 brought a stronger federal Fugitive Slave Act, though the costs of obtaining the rendition in 1854 of Anthony Burns from Boston back to Virginia, for example, demonstrated that the act still gave insufficient protection.

The fact that the Republican platform in the 1860 election disavowed abolition failed to satisfy slaveholders' anxieties. The Republicans were committed to ending the expansion of slavery into new territories. Moreover, from a proslavery perspective, the same voters who elected Lincoln had voiced their support of white abolitionist John Brown after his biracial band's raid a year earlier at Harpers Ferry, Virginia. A national government in Republican hands was not to be trusted.

Secession, Confederacy, and Civil War

The kinds of demands raised during the secession crisis indicated the sources of the political insecurity that slaveholders in the South felt in the face of indifferent or hostile public opinion elsewhere in the nation. The Virginia convention demanded amendments to the U.S. Constitution that would expressly deny Congress authority to legislate against slavery in any state, curtail the interstate slave trade, or impose discriminatory taxes on slave owners. The 36-degree, 30-minute line from the Missouri Compromise had to be extended farther west, and new territory could be acquired only with the consent of a majority of senators from the slave states as well as a majority from the nonslave states. These and other constitutional protections of slavery were to be amendable only with "the consent of all the States." Unable to secure guarantees for slavery, Virginia seceded and joined the Confederacy.

The Confederacy never was "the South," or it would have gained its independence. West Virginia broke away from Virginia, and Kentucky was a major slave state that remained in the Union. Tens of thousands of white men from the upcountry of east Tennessee wore blue instead of gray, as did countless men from Kentucky and West Virginia, and, doing so, they greatly weakened the Confederacy. Finally, from the plantation areas of the South, tens of thousands of slave men fought for and gained their freedom.

Had the Confederate states never seceded and never sought to form an independent nation, emancipation could not have come in the 1860s. Had the United States let the Confederate states go, there would have been no war and thus no emancipation at that time. Had the war been more quickly won by either side, little might have changed for many years. But the war ground on, and slavery came to a violent death.

President Lincoln could see that slave labor kept the Confederate army in the field, fed and clothed and relieved of many of the combat support duties that absorbed much of the North's manpower. Moreover, the United States needed more manpower to prosecute the war and break the stalemate. Therefore, as a war measure under his authority as commander in chief, Lincoln issued the Emancipation Proclamation at the beginning of 1863. After nearly two more years of war, in the presidential election of 1864, voters reelected him on a platform that demanded a constitutional amendment to outlaw slavery throughout the nation. Meantime, slaves left their masters' plantations and entered Union army lines, some even donning blue uniforms.

After Slavery

Yet freedom, when it came as a consequence of the Civil War, proved illusory. The postemancipation experience of former slaves in the South had been prefigured in the North, where widespread disfranchisement and proscription lasted for generations. It had also been prefigured in the "freedom" of free black residents in the South under slavery, though the end of slavery opened new opportunities for free people as well as freedpeople, as the working definition of black freedom grew more elastic, particularly for a few years.

In death as in life, southern slavery roiled national politics. During the decade after emancipation, Congress reflected the will of mainstream public opinion in the North that the death of slavery must be incontrovertible and guaranteed. Mississippi was one state that attempted to deny African-Americans access to land of their own, and landlessness doomed workers to work others' lands, much as they had under slavery. Congress sought to override such measures by enacting the Civil Rights Act of 1866 and by approving and seeking ratification of the Fourteenth Amendment. Former slaves had to have rights that clearly distinguished them from slaves.

Moreover, most northerners insisted, the death of slavery must not mean that white southern Democrats would regain power and dominate the national government. Yet the Three-Fifths Clause operated so that, now that slaves were "free," they would count at full value rather than only at three-fifths. The Fourteenth Amendment demanded that black men vote their representation or that black residents be ex-

An engraving by J. W. Watts entitled Reading the Emancipation Proclamation *shows a family of slaves in the South receiving news of their emancipation.* [Corbis-Bettmann]

cluded from the population count on which power in the House of Representatives and the electoral college was based. When ten of the eleven states of the former Confederacy rejected the amendment, Republicans in Congress forced the issue. Congressional reconstruction supplied the answer to the question, and thus, for a time, black men voted and even held political office.

The period called Reconstruction was brief, and the revolution went backward toward slavery. Northerners soon found themselves satisfied that the Union would remain together, that slavery could never again disrupt it, and that their own political and economic interests had adequate security. Insufficiently unified or committed to a transformation of the South, they let it go its own way. In the years to come, a postwar convict-lease system proved, for many black men, more deadly and exploitative than slavery had been, though it enveloped fewer black southerners than did its predecessor.

The long nightmare of slavery in the South was alleviated only in degree by the long nightmare of Jim Crow proscription that followed it—segregation, inequality, disfranchisement, poverty, and violence. Disfranchisement left black southerners largely powerless to shape developments in law and policy. Poverty left most of them dependent for their economic well-being on a sharecropping system that only grudgingly surrendered a subsistence and rarely supplied the

means to economic independence. Terror—violence and the threat of violence—underlay the entire system of political and economic repression.

Among the forces that eroded the system that followed slavery, one was surely a change in public policy by the national government in the middle third of the twentieth century. That change can be explained in various ways, but perhaps no explanation has more power than the consequences of migration, as black southerners moved to northern cities, picked up the right to vote, and began to influence the perspectives and behavior of policymakers in the federal government.

At the end of the twentieth century, southern slavery persisted as a touchstone of American life. African-Americans might call for reparations and a national apology for the evils and expropriations of slavery and its long aftermath—or demand that buildings memorializing slaveholders undergo name changes. Blacks might view every white as the descendant of a slaveholder, and whites and blacks alike might view every black as having slave ancestry, regardless of the historical probability or contemporary usefulness of such stereotypes. The institution of slavery, together with its entanglements in American economic development and political conflict, continued to draw platoons of talented historians to its study.

Various recurring cultural phenomena—the controversy over William Styron's novel *Nat Turner* in the

1960s, the television series *Roots* in the 1970s, and the movie *Amistad* in the 1990s—testified to the continued resonance for throngs of Americans, black and white and throughout the nation, of themes related to southern slavery.

See also DEMOGRAPHY OF SLAVES IN THE UNITED STATES; LABOR SYSTEMS; LAW; MATERIAL CULTURE IN THE UNITED STATES; SLAVE SOCIETIES; SLAVE TRADE.

BIBLIOGRAPHY

BERLIN, IRA, et al. *Slaves No More: Three Essays on Emancipation and the Civil War.* 1992.

CAMPBELL, EDWARD D. C., with KYM RICE, eds. *Before Freedom Came: African-American Life in the Antebellum South.* 1991.

COOPER, WILLIAM J., JR. *The South and the Politics of Slavery, 1828–1856.* 1978.

DAVIS, DAVID BRION. *The Problem of Slavery in Western Culture.* 1966.

FEHRENBACHER, DON E. *The Dred Scott Case: Its Significance in American Law and Politics.* 1978.

FERGUSON, LELAND. *Uncommon Ground: Archaeology and Early African America, 1650–1800.* 1992.

FREEHLING, WILLIAM W. *The Road to Disunion.* Vol. 1, *Secessionists at Bay, 1776–1854.* 1990.

HARRIS, J. WILLIAM. *Plain Folk and Gentry in a Slave Society: White Liberty and Black Slavery in Augusta's Hinterlands.* 1985.

JONES, NORRECE T., JR. *Born a Child of Freedom, Yet a Slave: Mechanisms of Control and Strategies of Resistance in Antebellum South Carolina.* 1990.

JOYNER, CHARLES. *Down by the Riverside: A South Carolina Slave Community.* 1984.

KING, WILMA. *Stolen Childhood: Slave Youth in Nineteenth-Century America.* 1995.

KOLCHIN, PETER. *American Slavery, 1619–1877.* 1993.

KULIKOFF, ALLAN. *Tobacco and Slaves: The Development of Southern Cultures in the Chesapeake, 1680–1800.* 1996.

MALONE, ANN PATTON. *Sweet Chariot: Slave Family and Household Structure in Nineteenth-Century Louisiana.* 1992.

MORGAN, EDMUND S. *American Slavery, American Freedom: The Ordeal of Colonial Virginia.* 1975.

MORRIS, THOMAS D. *Southern Slavery and the Law, 1619–1860.* 1996.

OAKES, JAMES. *Slavery and Freedom: An Interpretation of the Old South.* 1990.

ROSE, WILLIE LEE, ed. *A Documentary History of Slavery in North America.* 1976.

STAMPP, KENNETH M. *The Peculiar Institution: Slavery in the Ante-bellum South.* 1956.

STEPHENSON, BRENDA E. *Life in Black and White: Family and Community in the Slave South.* 1996.

TADMAN, MICHAEL. *Speculators and Slaves: Masters, Traders, and Slaves in the Old South.* 1989.

VAN DEBURG, WILLIAM L. *Slavery and Race in American Popular Culture.* 1984.

VLACH, JOHN MICHAEL. *By the Work of Their Hands: Studies in Afro-American Folklife.* 1991.

WALLENSTEIN, PETER. *From Slave South to New South: Public Policy in Nineteenth-Century Georgia.* 1987.

WALSH, LORENA. *From Calabar to Carter's Grove: The History of a Virginia Slave Community.* 1997.

WHITE, DEBORAH G. *Ar'n't I a Woman? Female Slaves in the Plantation South.* 1985.

Peter Wallenstein

Breeding of Slaves

Abolitionists claimed that planters systematically bred slaves for sale. Although scholars have debated the precise meaning of breeding, it traditionally involved systematic control over reproduction both by selection of fertile partners who would produce desirable offspring and by the rearing of children for sale. In the slave community, as in the livestock industry, the process was presumably guided by economic incentives.

Slave owners were placed on the defensive by these claims because they were impossible to disprove. The law of slavery undeniably gave owners considerable latitude in the control of their chattel: slaves could not legally marry (although informal plantation marriages were common); slaves were bought and sold at auction; and owners could apply force to achieve work and discipline. Individual owners and southern apologists could deplore the idea, but there was always the possibility that someone practiced slave breeding as a business.

Scholars of the twentieth century have taken a more sophisticated view, considering evidence and arguments. No serious scholar has claimed that breeding in its traditional meaning was common—or indeed anything but unusual. Actually, most scholars deny that it was even a rare practice, although a few have offered economic arguments and circumstantial evidence to suggest that it might have existed in parts of the South under particular situations.

One piece of circumstantial demographic evidence cited is the ratio of children to women of childbearing age. Unlike the situation for whites, this ratio was higher in the older slave states of the East relative to those of the West, and—consistent with the breeding thesis—large numbers of slaves were shipped from East to West. Moreover, slavery was less profitable on the older, exhausted soils of the East, which might have created an incentive for owners to engage in breeding and sell surplus labor. In addition, the slave population in the United States grew at rates that were remarkably high by worldwide historical standards.

However, this circumstantial evidence alone is weak when it is placed in perspective. The American white population also grew at a similarly high rate, and both the black and the white populations were significantly below a biological maximum, as revealed by age at menarche and microlevel study of evidence on age at first birth, child-spacing patterns, age at last birth, and the proportion of women who ever had children. Contradicting a breeding model, birthrates of slaves declined while prices roughly doubled from 1840 to 1860. Also, many slaves would have objected to forced mating, expressing their discontent in costly ways, such as shirking field labor, that would have lessened profits. In addition, proponents have yet to find such historical records as stud books or diaries to document breeding procedures.

Scholars generally agree that owners indirectly encouraged childbearing because a spouse and children promoted social stability. Owners established separate living quarters for families and, following a birth, gave clothing or household items. However, fertility on plantations was reduced by other aspects of management, such as discouraging marriage by slaves who lived off the farm.

See also DEMOGRAPHIC ANALYSIS OF SLAVES AND SLAVERY; DEMOGRAPHY OF SLAVES IN THE UNITED STATES; PLANTATIONS.

BIBLIOGRAPHY

FOGEL, ROBERT WILLIAM, and STANLEY L. ENGERMAN. *Time on the Cross: The Economics of American Negro Slavery.* 1974.
STECKEL, RICHARD H. *The Economics of U.S. Slave and Southern White Fertility.* 1985.
SUTCH, RICHARD. "The Breeding of Slaves for Sale and the Westward Expansion of Slavery, 1850–1860." In *Race and Slavery in the Western Hemisphere: Quantitative Studies,* edited by Stanley L. Engerman and Eugene D. Genovese. 1975.

Richard H. Steckel

The North

When the American Revolution began, there were about forty-six thousand slaves in Pennsylvania, New Jersey, New York, Massachusetts, Connecticut, Rhode Island, and New Hampshire, making up about 9 percent of the roughly five hundred thousand slaves in the thirteen colonies. New York's slave population of fifteen thousand was the North's largest, followed by Pennsylvania with ten thousand and New Jersey's roughly seven thousand. Slavery declined in Pennsylvania and New England beginning in the 1780s, as new state constitutions and judicial action led to immediate abolition in Massachusetts, New Hampshire, and Vermont, and legislation began a gradual emancipation in Pennsylvania (1780), Connecticut (1783), and Rhode Island (1784). Slavery continued to grow in New York and New Jersey until those states adopted gradual emancipation statutes in 1799 and 1804, respectively. At its peak slavery bound twenty thousand people in New York and twelve thousand in New Jersey.

Slavery gained a foothold in the Northwestern Territories, despite the Northwest Ordinance of 1787, which prohibited slavery in that region. French and Canadian residents who had lived north of the Ohio River before 1783 retained their slaves: Illinois reported some nine hundred slaves in the 1820 census and more than three hundred as late as 1840.

Slaves made up 5 percent or less of northern states' populations, but some locales had much greater concentrations. Kings County in New York, modern-day Brooklyn, may have had 30 percent enslaved people in its late-eighteenth-century population, for example. The North and Northwest collectively still had nineteen thousand slaves in 1820; four northern states reported about one thousand slaves in the 1840 census. In 1865 the passage of the Thirteenth Amendment set free fourteen "lifelong apprentices," former slaves, in New Jersey.

Slave-trade activity in New York during the seventeenth century is depicted in an 1895 illustration. [Corbis-Bettmann]

Slave Work, Family, and Culture in the North

Northern slaves worked primarily in agriculture, but also as craft workers or domestics in cities, or doing industrial work in the countryside. In New York and New Jersey, farmers employed slaves in their wheat fields and fruit orchards, especially in the Hudson valley and in eastern New Jersey, where many slaveholders were descended from Dutch settlers. Slaves in New England concentrated in the port cities, where they toiled as sailors and in the shipping trades, as well as serving as domestics. In Pennsylvania many slaves labored in iron mines, furnaces, and forges.

In cities throughout the Northeast, well-to-do merchants, manufacturers, and professionals of the late eighteenth century had slaves who took care of their houses, gardens, and stables, and who served as badges of their masters' status. These elite slaveholders sprang from a variety of ethnic groups, including a few free people of color who had fled Saint Domingue with their slaves in the 1790s, and included men and women of nearly all religions, except Quakers, who had largely purged their ranks of slaveholders by the 1780s. Even men of antislavery sentiment, such as New York's John Jay, sometimes owned slaves.

In the Northwest, slaves were largely found in counties bordering the Ohio River, where they worked on farms, in lead mines, or at salt works. The territorial legislatures of Indiana and Illinois facilitated the use of slaves, allowing them to be imported for up to a year at a time to work. After statehood Illinois permitted such importations for up to seven years at the salt works near Shawneetown, in the southeastern corner of the state. Most of the northwestern territories permitted southern immigrants to bring in blacks defined as indentured servants with terms of servitude up to ninety-nine years, effectively keeping them slaves for life. This practice only gradually ended after each territory became a free state.

Most slaveholders in the North and Northwest owned one or a few slaves, who were thus unlikely to live in family units, or to be able to refresh their links to African culture by contacts with recently arrived Africans. Northern slaves and free blacks sought to live in northern cities and towns so that they could find spouses, make friends, and worship among other blacks. Northern slaves developed culturally hybrid rituals and festivals combining African, European, and American elements, such as Pinkster. Originally deriving from the Dutch version of Pentecost, Pinkster was widely celebrated in New York well into the nineteenth century, where it came to be regarded as a black-dominated celebration, evoking a carnival-like atmosphere.

Emancipation in the North

Between 1777 and 1804 northern states began to curtail slavery. Vermont abolished slavery in its state constitution of 1777, the first polity in North America to do so; Ohio and Indiana would abolish slavery in a similar fashion in 1803 and 1816.

In 1780 Pennsylvania passed the first gradual emancipation law, which freed no slave then living, but promised freedom to children of slave mothers born after its passage, upon completion of a twenty-eight-year term of servitude. Rhode Island and Connecticut passed similar postnati laws in 1784, as did New York in 1799 and New Jersey in 1804. Some northern states eventually freed slaves born before the passage of their postnati laws: New York declared all such remaining slaves free in 1827, for example.

Supporters of emancipation included Quakers and Methodists, who saw slaveholding as sinful and demoralizing, as well as a broader group of people who regarded slavery as economically inefficient and politically inappropriate in a newly independent America. Antislavery activists formed local and state organizations, such as the Pennsylvania Abolition Society and the New Jersey Society for the Abolition of Slavery, founded in 1775 and 1786, respectively. These organizations petitioned legislators to end slavery, facilitated individual manumissions, and provided legal aid to blacks challenging their slave status in the courts.

Slaveholders rejected antislavery views, arguing that protection of property, including slave property, was central to the country's concept of liberty. Slaveholders blocked passage of gradual emancipation laws for twenty years in New York and New Jersey; thereafter, they strove to gain compensation for the expenses of bringing up slave children, and to dilute the laws' liberating intent by selling some blacks to the South.

In Massachusetts and New Hampshire the route to emancipation ran from state constitutions through the courts. In 1778 the Massachusetts town meetings rejected a proposed constitution because it allowed slavery and denied blacks suffrage. In 1780 the state adopted a constitution which declared all people born "free and equal"; New Hampshire's 1784 constitution contained a similar clause. Accordingly, when Quock Walker sought his freedom in a Massachusetts court in 1783 on grounds that his master had failed to honor a promise of manumission, the court found that slavery as an institution was contrary to the spirit of the state constitution. Slavery quickly decayed when deprived of the force of law: the 1790 census found no slaves in Massachusetts and only a handful in New Hampshire.

Blacks throughout the North helped bring about the end of slavery in a variety of ways. In New England from the 1770s onward slaves and free blacks petitioned state legislatures to abolish slavery; otherwise, they argued, the claims of the revolutionaries to love liberty and to be fighting for freedom would ring false. Individual slaves petitioned the courts for their freedom, either when promised manumissions were denied or when slaveholders attempted to hold or sell blacks illegally after the passage of postnati emancipation laws. Many more blacks put pressure on slavery by fleeing their masters and passing for free in northern cities, thereby helping to change the economic calculus that had rendered slavery in the North profitable even in the absence of a staple crop like tobacco or cotton.

During and after the ending of slavery in the North runaway slaves from southern slave states sought haven there. Southerners' efforts to recover such fugitives generated controversy, helping to fuel sectional conflict. Federal law authorized the return of runaways across state lines, beginning with the Fugitive Slave Act of 1793. But in many northern locales, courts, law-enforcement officials, and private citizens declined to assist slaveholders seeking to recapture fugitives. In fact, by the 1840s many northern states had passed personal-liberty laws, discouraging or banning public officials from participating in recapturing fugitives. The Fugitive Slave Act of 1850, designed to make rendition of fugitives more effective, heightened discontent. While the act was enforced to reenslave hundreds of blacks who had escaped from southern states, some of them many years before their recapture, many other recaptures were resisted. Slaves put in jail pending their return southward were rescued by crowd action in several northern cities, and in Christiana, Pennsylvania, fugitives shot and killed their former master to avoid returning with him to Maryland. The presence of slaves in the North would end completely only with the ending of slavery throughout the nation in 1865.

See also ABOLITION AND ANTISLAVERY MOVEMENTS; DEMOGRAPHY OF SLAVES AND SLAVERY IN THE UNITED STATES; LAW; URBAN SLAVERY.

BIBLIOGRAPHY

FINKELMAN, PAUL. *Slavery and the Founders: Race and Liberty in the Age of Jefferson.* 1996.

HODGES, GRAHAM. *Slavery and Freedom in the Rural North: African Americans in Monmouth County, New Jersey, 1665–1865.* 1997.

MCMANUS, EDGAR J. *Black Bondage in the North.* 1973.

NASH, GARY B., and JEAN SODERLUND. *Freedom by Degrees: Emancipation in Pennsylvania and Its Aftermath.* 1991.

WHITE, SHANE. *Somewhat More Independent: The End of Slavery in New York City, 1770–1810.* 1991.

T. Stephen Whitman

Universal Declaration of Human Rights (1948)

Article 4 of the Universal Declaration of Human Rights provides that "No one shall be held in slavery or servitude; slavery and the slave trade shall be prohibited in all their forms." The Declaration was adopted on 10 December 1948 by the General Assembly of the United Nations by a vote of forty-eight to zero, with eight abstentions that included several European communist nations as well as South Africa and Saudi Arabia. The communist nations expressly accepted the Declaration in 1975, however.

The Declaration was drafted in 1947 by a committee appointed by the newly formed Human Rights Commission. The committee initially consisted of Eleanor Roosevelt of the United States, Charles Malik of Lebanon, and P. C. Chang of China. It later added members from the Soviet Union, the United Kingdom, France, Australia, and Chile. Some members sought a binding convention that would provide international protection for individual victims. However, the representative from the Soviet Union urged that national institutions handle implementation. The committee settled on a compromise put forward by P. C. Chang: first a declaration would be adopted, then a convention would be adopted, and last provisions for implementation would be created.

By its own terms, the Declaration is a statement of a "common standard of achievement for all peoples and all nations, to the end that every individual . . . shall strive by teaching and education to promote respect for these rights and freedoms." The members of the United Nations are not expressly bound by it. Although the Declaration contains many equivocal provisions, the prohibition of slavery in Article 4 is among the strongest. In fact, Article 4 is considered by many to have since achieved the status of customary international law, a status that would make it binding on the world.

In 1976, twenty years later, two covenants entered into force pursuant to the Declaration. Both contain provisions whereby the Declaration's prohibitions against slavery and the slave trade became legal obligations. The Covenant on Economic, Social, and Cultural Rights, which went into force on 3 January 1976, indirectly outlaws slavery by guaranteeing the right to employment that the individual freely accepts. The

Covenant on Civil and Political Rights, which went into force on 23 March 1976, directly outlaws slavery and slavelike practices. Article 8 contains the same strong prohibitions as the Declaration against slavery, the slave trade, and servitude.

The Covenant on Civil and Political Rights also created a Human Rights Committee, which receives reports by nations on measures taken to effectuate the Covenant and in turn submits reports to the General Assembly. Under certain circumstances the Human Rights Committee accepts reports from one nation accusing another nation of violating the Covenant. Nations can elect to authorize the Human Rights Committee to receive claims by individuals.

In addition, the Supplemental Convention on the Abolition of Slavery, the Slave Trade, and Institutions and Practices Similar to Slavery went into force on 7 September 1956, in consideration of the Declaration as well as in recognition of the Slavery Convention adopted by the League of Nations in 1926.

See also SLAVERY, CONTEMPORARY FORMS OF; SLAVERY CONVENTION.

BIBLIOGRAPHY

LAUTERPACHT, H. *International Law and Human Rights*. 1950.
TOLLEY, HOWARD, JR. *The U.N. Commission on Human Rights*. 1987.

Renee C. Redman

Ur

See Ancient Middle East.

Urban Slavery

This entry includes the following articles: United States; The World.

United States

Never in the long history of slavery in North America did the phrase "plantation slavery" encompass the experience of all slaves or all slave owners. In the colonial era and the nineteenth century alike, slavery in the cities shaped much of the social and economic life.

Slavery emerged in New York before there was a Charleston, South Carolina, and it thrived in Philadelphia and ended in Boston before there was a Washington, D.C. At the time of the American Revolution, roughly as many slaves labored in New York City as in Norfolk, Virginia. Slavery came to an end in the northern cities by early in the nineteenth century—at about the time that it began to flourish in Memphis, Tennessee, and Louisville, Kentucky.

In the Old South, the social geography of black slavery differed from that of black freedom. Most slaves lived in rural areas. By contrast, free black residents of Georgia tended to live in Augusta or Savannah, even more than their counterparts in Virginia tended to live in Richmond, Norfolk, or Petersburg.

Slavery may have been slavery everywhere, but its characteristics varied by time and place. Urban slavery in the eighteenth century resembled urban slavery in the nineteenth—and slavery in New York resembled that in Norfolk—more than any of these resembled the rural varieties to be found on the North American plantations, colonial or antebellum, that grew cotton, tobacco, rice, or sugar.

Cities in the antebellum South provided a wider range of possible jobs than did farms and plantations, especially for men. Urban slaves worked in ironworks, textile mills, and tobacco factories, and on railroads and as stevedores.

More important than the types of employment available in the cities was the likelihood, especially in the Upper South, that slaves might hire themselves out. Those who found their own work had greater autonomy in their work lives than did most slaves, and when they also found their own housing they had more control over their social lives as well. Moreover, as Frederick Douglass reported in his observations of slave life in Baltimore, slaves who hired themselves out might, more likely than most slaves, save up money toward the purchase of their own freedom or that of family members.

Most urban slaves remained slaves into the 1860s. Moreover, most slave women in cities worked much as many of them might have on a plantation, as domestics. Women's responsibilities revolved around cooking, cleaning, and child care, though urban slavery added going to market as an important function.

Life as an urban slave did not protect one from the slave trade. The slave trade remained a threatening fact of life for slaves, whether they lived in Upper South cities like Baltimore and Norfolk or Deep South cities like Charleston and New Orleans. Living in Richmond, Henry Brown hired himself out, found his own housing, married, and had three children, but the slave trade reached into his happiness and sent his wife and children out of state. His previous advantages no longer of value to him, he grasped the only remaining advantage: the greater opportunity of successfully running away to freedom that life in an Upper South city afforded.

Urban slaves typically had greater freedom to engage in community activities than their plantation and farm counterparts. Slaves and free blacks alike lived in considerable numbers in southern cities, and both groups enjoyed greater freedom, including free-

Henry "Box" Brown rises out of a shipping crate amid men from the Underground Railroad after shipping himself out of the South to escape from slavery. [Corbis-Bettmann]

dom of movement, there than was possible in rural areas. Black churches arose in southern cities, and slaves and free blacks often worshiped together. African-American churches provided opportunities for organizational leadership, for learning how to read and write, and for establishing mutual aid and other benevolent societies. Black churches and other organizations—and the leadership experience that they fostered among black southerners—did not wait until slavery's end to become important parts of the social landscape in southern cities.

Urban slavery differed from rural slavery in its pattern of growth as well as in its conditions of life. The absolute and relative numbers of African-Americans living as slaves in cities declined in the nineteenth century even as the broader society underwent rapid urbanization. This was most evident in northern cities, where the overall population growth proved extraordinary but where slavery virtually vanished. It was generally true too in the South. The District of Columbia contained three cities in the early nineteenth century, and in all three—Georgetown, Alexandria, and Washington—the number of slaves peaked no later than the early 1830s, as did the ratio of slaves to free black residents and their percentage of all city residents. The same was true in Baltimore. Given the demand for plantation labor, slaves with few skills might well find themselves leaving the cities and working on farms or plantations near their cities of origin or somewhere far to the south and west.

Yet not everywhere did the numbers of urban slaves decline before the 1860s, and the numbers remained substantial for southern cities even where they dropped. The slave figure for New Orleans peaked with the 1840 census, but 13,385 slaves still resided there in 1860, and the figure for Charleston peaked in 1850, but 13,909 slaves still lived there in 1860. Richmond's figure for 1860—11,699—was the highest it ever recorded, and it placed third among all U.S. cities that year. Moreover, the numbers of slaves in major southern cities surged during the Civil War, as urban industries grew to meet Confederate military needs.

When emancipation came in the 1860s, three main groups of African-Americans emerged in greatly disproportionate numbers among black leaders. Free blacks—from the North and from southern cities—made up two of these groups. Former slaves in southern cities were the third. Slavery in the cities, restrictive though it was, provided slaves with opportunities and experiences that permitted them to acquire skills that served them and other African-Americans well when they finally came to own themselves.

See also DEMOGRAPHY OF SLAVES IN THE UNITED STATES; FREE PEOPLE OF COLOR; LABOR SYSTEMS.

BIBLIOGRAPHY

GOLDFIELD, DAVID R. "Black Life in Old South Cities." In *Before Freedom Came: African-American Life in the Antebellum South*, edited by Edward D. C. Campbell Jr., with Kym S. Rice. 1991.

GOLDIN, CLAUDIA DALE. *Urban Slavery in the American South, 1820–1860: A Quantitative History.* 1976.

GREEN, CONSTANCE MCLAUGHLIN. *The Secret City: A History of Race Relations in the Nation's Capital.* 1967.

MILLER, ELINOR, and EUGENE D. GENOVESE, eds. *Plantation, Town, and County: Essays on the Local History of American Slave Society.* 1974.

NASH, GARY B. *Race, Class, and Politics: Essays on American Colonial and Revolutionary Society.* 1986.

PHILLIPS, CHRISTOPHER. *Freedom's Port: The African American Community of Baltimore, 1790–1860.* 1997.

POWERS, BERNARD E., JR. *Black Charlestonians: A Social History, 1822–1885.* 1994.

WADE, RICHARD C. *Slavery in the Cities: The South, 1820–1860.* 1964.

WHITE, SHANE. *Somewhat More Independent: The End of Slavery in New York City, 1770–1810.* 1991.

Peter Wallenstein

The World

Two ancient institutions, town life and slaveholding, have been linked throughout recorded time. Since

A copper engraving depicts a spahi, one of a corps of irregular Turkish cavalry, and two janissaries, members of an elite slave military guard of the Ottoman Empire. [Chris Hellier/Corbis]

the earliest riverine settlements in the Fertile Crescent, elite urbanites have relied upon the nearby countryside for sustenance, and for corvée and captive labor for food, clothing, shelter, and a respite from the round of backbreaking toil that affords leisure to persons of means and status. This rarely happened without a supply of laborers who could be made to work for little or nothing. As towns came to symbolize sophistication, so were the activities of city dwellers invested with extra significance. Thus, city folk and those who have studied them have tended to stress skilled artisanry, occupational specialization, wide-ranging bureaucracies, and, where applicable, literacy.

Wherever human beings have coalesced into societies, some people have found ways to compel others to serve them. Although this has usually revolved around the control of another's labor power, slaves were also prized for their prestige value, exchange value, and use value, and as "play children" for the offspring of the master class. The conditions of enslavement differed considerably according to locale, climate, and the social structure of a given slave polity.

Urban life added a new texture to an old institution. In Egypt urbanization expanded the scale of slave use, as bonded persons were employed not only in the agriculture that fed the urban metropolises but also in the construction of royal monuments, as concubines and scribes, and as subjects of sacrificial rites.

But urban life was a double-edged sword for slave societies. Life in cities could encourage rebellions by large groups of slaves such as the "Zanj" of Baghdad, the janissaries of Egypt, or the architects of urban insurrections in the American colonies and the United States. Rebellions in New York City (in 1712 and the so-called New York Conspiracy of 1741), as well as those of Gabriel Prosser of Richmond, Virginia (1800), and Denmark Vesey of Charleston, South Carolina (1822), were urban. New World and Roman slaves often had greater freedom in cities, where they could not only escape the drudgery of country labor but also at times escape into the city itself. Even under medieval serfdom, a form of unfree labor, serfs could become free by residing in a city for a year.

The American example of Frederick Douglass in Fells Point in Baltimore reminds us that certain "favored" slaves frequently earned at least nominal wages; this was more likely in urban settings than in the countryside. At the same time, urban life in pharaonic Egypt was not likely to have benefited slaves residing there more than their rural counterparts unless they worked in prosperous households for generous and kind masters; all of these variables should be considered in any case.

Contrasts between urban and rural slavery gain significance with the passage of time. The ancient world left behind precious few records of early antislavery movements beyond occasional references to rebellions such as that of Spartacus; the point is that slaves had only each other to count on for support, and not always even that. With the seventeenth-century advent of a worldwide humanitarian thrust to curb slavery, whether mounted within a given religious community such as the Society of Friends, like John Woolman's 1754 dissertation, or in the context of the Second Great Awakening of the eighteenth century, urban areas might serve as havens for slave refugees, even in cities where slavery had gone on largely unchallenged. Thus, a considerable amount of the struggle waged against the slave power in the antebellum United States centers around the activities of abolitionists targeting urban populations with propaganda and with public appearances of various kinds. This was also true in Kansas at the time of the Kansas-Nebraska controversy.

Indeed, the Underground Railroad, while rooted in the countryside, flourished in a kind of symbiotic relationship with the urban and periurban areas of each state in which it functioned. Urban areas could afford the anonymity runaway slaves needed while on the move, provided that the heat was not on, as was the case when bounty hunters, patrollers, and vigilantes empowered by the Fugitive Slave Law of 1850 were on the prowl. Fugitive slaves often gravitated to cities such as Cincinnati, New York, Philadelphia, Boston, Rochester, and Syracuse, among others, because they offered a place to work, a black community that could aid them, and a place to hide. Many fugitive slaves, such as Henry "Box" Brown and Anthony Burns, as well as the aforementioned Douglass, used the city as the first step to "stealing themselves," or fomenting an escape to freedom.

Outside the Christian West, other mores pertained to slaves in urban areas. Fred Cooper has argued that the tenets of Islam gave a particular character to slave life in coastal East Africa. Similar points could be made regarding slaves in urban areas in other parts of the continent, though again the treatment of a slave was subject to more than simply an owner's interpretation of the Koran. If, as was often the case, an urban Muslim member of the elite was also pious and scrupulous in his religious practice, this was a fact that could be helpful to a slave under his control. On the other hand, the scale of one's slaveholdings could at times outweigh humanitarian instincts, as profit was of vital import. Nonetheless, in Christian and Islamic settings, the nature of urban life meant that the activities of masters and slaves tended to occur in the full view of large numbers of people and were thus subject to public opinion.

Urban slavery may also have provided the social space for some limited upward mobility. In *Africa Remembered,* the historian Philip Curtin presents a series of narratives drawn from Africans whose lives were changed by enslavement; some of these people were literate residents of cities. Several North American slave narratives were constructed around the lives of people laboring or living in or close to cities. Besides Frederick Douglass, Harriet Jacobs and Solomon Northup were two such people for whom urban life had critical value; again, all three were literate and skilled members of households.

Seaman Olaudah Equiano, although he was held on board ship for a considerable part of his early life, would still seem to fit this pattern, in part because for a crew member the ship might have functioned like a city of sorts, as it presented him with opportunities to travel, meet people, and become literate, and the time and space to reflect upon his circumstances. It was also a kind of preparation for life after slavery, for even though Equiano worked in the North American South and the Caribbean, he gained fame in the British humanitarian movement as a writer and speechmaker in the mold that Douglass would follow a generation later, speaking to churches and civic groups largely in metropolitan localities.

Robert Smalls (left) was made a wheelsman by the Confederate government while he was still a slave, but in May 1862 Smalls seized control of the CSS Planter *(right) and delivered it across Union lines to the U.S. Navy. Also on board were members of Smalls's family and a small group of other slaves.* [Corbis-Bettmann]

Urban visibility and participation could also enhance the general position of slaves as a whole. Frederick Douglass was a member of a literary group, the Baltimore Improvement Society, which catered to both slaves and free people, giving them opportunities to read and discuss works of literature and to practice public speaking, as well as to cultivate meaningful social contacts with peers. The greater variety of patterns of city life also made it more difficult for the average urbanite to think of slaves monolithically, whatever such a person may have opined about the black "race." It was no accident that many slaves came to revere city life as a ticket to the amelioration of their overall condition. Ease of movement, the availability of information, and access to learning all lent appeal to urban life, and slaves were no less aware of these potentialities than any other people.

Yet, as Solomon Northup's case makes clear, cities could just as well be the kiss of death for some slaves. After thirty-two free years in New York City, Northup was kidnapped in Washington, D.C., and spirited south to the area of the Red River in Louisiana, where he spent a dozen years in unlawful captivity. While unusual, such events could happen. Cities in border states were often hostile to the free and to relatively unfettered slaves who sought to take full advantage of the benefits they might offer. But urban life, whether in Cairo, Rabat, Memphis, St. Augustine, Annapolis, Wilmington, or Kingston, was no savior when it came to the auction block. Whether individually or collectively held or born into a hereditarily servile caste such as the *haratin* in Arab-ruled Mauritania, slaves were ever on their guard, in city and countryside alike. Esteban Montejo had both good and bad experiences in Cuba. Robert Smalls lived a relatively pleasant slave sailor's life in Charleston, and slave urbanites tended to do better in Brazil. But no one who has not walked in a slave's shoes can truly say what that was like, whether it was "good" or "bad," "better" or "worse," and especially if any term such as "happiness" applies, since for most free folk there is only imagination to work from.

See also DOUGLASS, FREDERICK; EQUIANO, OLAUDAH; JACOBS, HARRIET; MONTEJO, ESTEBAN; VESEY REBELLION.

BIBLIOGRAPHY

COOPER, FREDERICK. *Plantation Slavery on the East Coast of Africa.* 1977.

CURTIN, PHILIP D., ed. *Africa Remembered: Narratives by West Africans From the Era of the Slave Trade.* 1968.

DAVIS, T. J. *The Rumor of Revolt: The "Great Negro Plot" of Colonial New York.* 1985.

DOUGLASS, FREDERICK. *Narrative of the Life of Frederick Douglass, an American Slave, Written by Himself.* 1988.

HORSMANDEN, DANIEL. *The New York Conspiracy.* 1971.

JACOBS, HARRIET. *Incidents in the Life of a Slave Girl, Written by Herself.* 1987.

LITWACK, LEON F. *North of Slavery: The Negro in the Free States, 1790–1860.* 1961.

MONTEJO, ESTEBAN. *Autobiography of a Runaway Slave.* 1973.

NORTHUP, SOLOMON. *Twelve Years a Slave.* 1968.

UYA, OKON EDET. *From Slavery to Public Service: The Life of Robert Smalls, 1839–1915.* 1971.

WADE, RICHARD C. *Slavery in the Cities: The South, 1820–1860.* 1960.

David H. Anthony III

Utah

Slavery thrived among Utah's Native Americans more than three decades before the Mormon pioneers arrived in 1847. Between the 1830s and 1840s the slave trade in the Great Basin was dominated by Walkara, a Ute war chief, and his team of Ute, Paiute, and Shoshoni.

This form of the "peculiar institution" grew out of a desire for laborers, primarily children and young women, in the haciendas of New Mexico and California, which led to an expansion of trade relations between Spanish traders with the Ute and Navaho. In exchange for Paiute and Gosiute captives, Spanish traders gave the Native American captors horses, guns, blankets, and trinkets. Sometimes Paiute and Gosuite would even exchange their children and young women for horses or mules, which were then slaughtered and eaten.

From the beginning, sympathy for Indian captives frequently impelled Mormons to barter with the Ute. When the Mormons first arrived to settle the valley of the Great Salt Lake, the Ute offered them two young Paiute in exchange for guns and horses. Surprised, the Mormons refused—stunning the Indians, who informed them that the children would be killed if they were not purchased. When the Mormons purchased only the female Paiute, the Ute killed the male child.

Upon learning about increased numbers of Mexican slave traders in Utah territory, the Mormon leader and governor, Brigham Young, proposed legislation to eliminate the slave trade and enslavement of Native Americans, replacing that system with indentured servitude that, according to a probate judge or selectman, could not exceed a period of twenty years. Whites were obligated to provide access to schools (if available) and adequate clothing. Adopted in 1852, "The Act for the Further Relief of Indian Slaves and Prisoners" prevented Utah's Native Americans from being subjected to chattel slavery as African-Americans were. Mormons believed that Indians were one of the lost tribes of Israel and that they could be transformed and redeemed from a state of degradation.

By contrast, however, many Morman leaders and members accepted the biblical scriptures used by southern slaveholders to justify enslaving blacks. Consequently, African-American slaves were held by Mormons in Utah beginning in 1847. By 1850, approximately sixty-five slaves resided in the territory. A small number of the Mormon pioneers who came from the South brought their slaves with them, and this created a potential problem for the Mormons, who were seeking political recognition from the United States government after the end of the Mexican-American War in 1846. Aware of the tension over the issue of slavery in the territories acquired from Mexico, Mormon leaders sought to avoid antagonizing either the proslavery or the antislavery group. In Utah's petition for statehood, no mention was made of the presence of slaves. Given Utah's climate and geography, many members of Congress did not see slavery there as a serious issue; they did not consider the setting conducive to slavery. Utah was made a territory as part of the Compromise of 1850. Whether or not to permit slavery was left to its residents, who legally sanctioned the bondage of blacks by "An Act in Relation to Service" (1852), with Brigham Young's approval. The provisions of this act were mild in comparison with the laws of the southern slaveholding states. In Utah, the slaveholder's control over slaves was regulated, and owners were obligated to send their slaves to school if a school was available, and to provide adequate food, clothing, and shelter.

Slaves in Utah worked primarily on small farms, and a few worked in local businesses. They were also used to build shelters, perform household duties, and work on public and church buildings. One slave woman was a midwife for settlers in her vicinity. The possibility of being sold was a reality, and a few slaves fled in wagon parties going west. Some sought refuge in Brigham Young's home when abused by their owners. Although Young accepted the scriptural justification for slavery, he did not want slavery to flourish in Utah; he said that if Utah was granted statehood, it would be a free state. He also believed that slaves should be treated humanely. On one occasion Young freed a slave whose owner had left Utah. Although their number was small, some slaves developed relationships that led to courtship, marriage, and families.

Black slavery officially ended in Utah when Congress abolished slavery in the territories in 1862, approximately twenty-five years after the first African-American slaves had entered Utah.

See also COMPROMISE OF 1850; LABOR SYSTEMS; NATIVE AMERICANS.

BIBLIOGRAPHY

BAILEY, L. R. *Indian Slave Trade in the Southwest.* 1973.
COLEMAN, RONALD G. *A History of Blacks in Utah, 1825–1910.* 1980.
FOWLER, CATHERINE S., and FOWLER, DON D. "Notes on the History of the Southern Paiute and Western Shoshonis." *Utah Historical Quarterly* 39, no. 2 (1971): 95–113.

Ronald G. Coleman

Utopias and Slavery

Slavery is quite uncommon in utopian literature, for that genre's projection of perfection seems to militate against the inclusion of a "relic of barbarism." One of the major exceptions to this rule is Sir Thomas More's *Utopia.* Despite having given its name to the entire genre, More's *Utopia* is not itself, as Sir Arnold Toynbee observed, a truly utopian work.

More's "ideal society" was lacking in the otherworldly perfection characteristic of many other utopian works. Utopians face foreign threats, as well as domestic crime and sin. The institutions which King Utopus created for his people were designed to elevate and ennoble human nature, but not to abolish it.

S⟨R⟩ THOMAS MORE.

An engraved portrait of the English statesman, author, and saint Sir Thomas More, who was beheaded on the orders of Henry VIII for treason. More had refused to acknowledge Henry's ascendancy over the pope as the supreme head of the English church. [Library of Congress/Corbis]

In Utopia serious felons are sentenced to perpetual slavery because, More opines, criminals fear slavery as greatly as they fear death—but also because the work of the slave benefits the state. An enslaved criminal who resists the conditions of servitude is executed; but a slave who, after long labor, is truly penitent for the crime (rather than for the punishment) may be freed by a pardon.

As is often the case with utopian authors, More was holding up a mirror to his own time. In the England of Henry VII and Henry VIII, most felonies were punishable by death, often death by torture. The penal slavery envisioned in *Utopia* served as a humane critique of the savagery of early Tudor criminal law.

In many utopias, what is most notable is not the presence of slavery but the absence of traditional labor. Incredibly advanced science and technology and new social organizations free humankind from that scarcity which was alike the assumption of all economics and the curse of God upon the fallen Adam.

For that exceedingly rare subgenre, kakotopian literature, where the author's attempts to portray a utopia produce a vision that shocks and revolts the average reader, no works better exemplify the type than those of that satanic philosophe, the Marquis de Sade. In many of his writings, including *120 Days of Sodom,* the depraved French nobleman pictures a microcosmic world where bondage and degradation flourish, but the meaning cannot be attributed exclusively to the psychosexual pathology associated with the name de Sade. This work stands as well for his vision of the bestiality of human nature and the corrupt hypocrisy of human institutions.

It is in dystopias, however, that slavery truly holds center stage. If utopias may criticize current society by holding it up to standards of perfection, the dystopia takes the vices and evils of the current day (and of the human condition in general) and draws them out to a moral extreme.

Since in the Judeo-Christian heritage of the West, sin and vice have been held to be a kind of slavery, it is most appropriate that societies steeped in evil, such as dystopias usually involve, should be represented with a dominant motif of slavery.

Certainly the theological types that serve as the models for utopias and dystopias provide clues to the role of slavery in these genres. The Judeo-Christian concept of heaven serves as the obvious blueprint for the terrestrial paradise of utopia, and hell must be seen as the ultimate pattern for dystopia. Heaven enjoys a concordancy of all wills, with angelic and human wills having freely joined themselves to the divine, and the lesser freedom of the *liberum arbitrium* (the free choice between good and evil) translated into the *libertas* of the deity—the divine will that is always done.

Hell, on the other hand, is the ultimate realm of slavery. The damned, who have rejected the divine will, are held in an infernal hierarchy of terror and hate.

Orwell's *1984* presented a society in which all are enslaved by a totalitarian ideology and by the mechanism of modern dictatorship—torture, propaganda, and mind control. In Aldous Huxley's *Brave New World* and Yevgeny Zamyatin's *We,* the brutal aspects of slavery are less obvious but are nonetheless present at the core of the system. Orwell's brilliant slogan in *1984,* "Freedom is slavery," might well serve as the motto of the modern dystopia.

H. G. Wells's *The Time Machine* presented a topsy-turvy dystopia of the distant future when the brutal near-slavery of the working class had produced the animalistic, cannibalistic Morlocks, while the soft, dronelike existence of the upper classes had caused them to evolve into the effete Eloi.

Sometimes the theological patterns that inspired a dystopia are explored on the very surface, as in Robert Hugh Benson's *Lord of the World,* which relates the ultimate enslavement of humanity in the apocalyptic final days of the coming of To Mega Therion (the An-

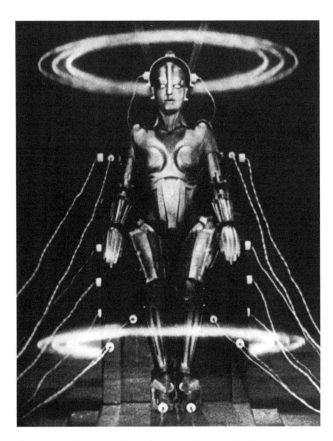

In a scene from the film Metropolis, *a robot is created to assist the Master of Metropolis in carrying out his plans for enslaving the workers of the city.* [Corbis-Bettmann]

tichrist); or in C. S. Lewis's *That Hideous Strength,* where the demonic "macrobes" directly command their slaves through a possessed severed head.

In H. G. Wells's *The Island of Dr. Moreau,* the forced evolution of the vivisectionist dystopia has produced the therianthropes, mindlessly reciting a law they cannot truly understand, in fear and trembling before the House of Pain.

Behind the dystopian vision lurks the common fear that all the technological progress that has promised liberation for humankind has led only to self-enslavement. The machines of the industrial age, which were thought to presage a golden age without physical labor, have turned their masters into mechanistic slaves, like the regimented workers of Fritz Lang's *Metropolis.*

Slavery is perhaps the essence of the dystopian vision, from the branded slaves of the Antichrist who bear the mark of the beast in their flesh to the brainwashed proles who scream in mad love for Big Brother. Thus, in *1984* O'Brien exults to Winston Smith in the Ministry of Love that the future is a boot stamping on a human face . . . forever.

See also SCIENCE FICTION AND FANTASY, SLAVERY IN.

BIBLIOGRAPHY

KUMAR, KRISHAN. *Utopia and Anti-Utopia in Modern Times.* 1987.
MANUEL, FRANK E., and FRITZIE P. MANUEL. *Utopian Thought in the Western World.* 1979.
MORE, THOMAS. *Utopia.* Edited by Edward Surtz. 1964.

Patrick M. O'Neil

V

Verbal Arts

See Arts.

Vermont

Vermont was the first state to abolish slavery directly and unequivocally in its constitution of 1777. Practically, this abolition was facilitated by the virtual absence of slavery within the state and by the disconnectedness of this landlocked state from the international slave trade in which its New England neighbors were intimately involved.

An ideological origin for this early opposition to slavery may rest in the fact that while Vermont reacted against British attempts to "enslave" it, as did other states, Vermont also found a crisis of identity unknown to them. Vermont was unrecognized by the other states—unrepresented in both the Continental Congress and the Constitutional Convention at Philadelphia. In addition, the "Green Mountain State" was nominally claimed in its entirety by New Hampshire and facing actual attempts by the state of New York to exercise sovereignty—including tax collection—within its borders.

In 1786 Vermont passed an act to forbid the exportation of negroes and mulattoes from the state, but repealed that act when it was admitted into the Union under the misapprehension that the act contradicted the fugitive slave clause of the U.S. Constitution.

In 1802 the board of selectmen of the town of Windsor sued Stephen Jacob for the cost of maintaining an aged, ill, black woman who had been purchased by Jacob and then later abandoned. The evidence against Jacob consisted in a bill of sale for the former slave, but Judge Royal Tyler found that the Vermont constitution's ban on slavery within the state made the bill of sale a legal nullity, whatever status it might enjoy in any other state. The only recognition of slavery the Vermont courts would make, Tyler insisted, was in enforcement of the fugitive slave clause of the U.S. Constitution. Stephen Jacob was held not to be liable for the upkeep of the elderly black lady.

Like many other Northern states Vermont passed personal liberty laws in reaction to the federal Fugitive Slave Acts of 1793 and 1850. Like Massachusetts, New Hampshire, Maine, and eventually Rhode Island, Vermont also gave blacks full political rights, including the right to vote on the same basis as whites.

See also FUGITIVE SLAVE LAWS, U.S.

BIBLIOGRAPHY

FINKELMAN, PAUL, ed. *An Imperfect Union: Slavery, Federalism, and Comity.* 1981.
Selectmen v. Jacob, 2 Tyler (Vt.) 192 (1802).

Patrick M. O'Neil

Vesey Rebellion (1822)

Perhaps the most extensive of all North American slave conspiracies, was the Vesey Rebellion in Charleston, South Carolina. The plot was organized by fifty-

Jean-Pierre Boyer was the president of Haiti at the time of the Vesey Rebellion. He encouraged black Americans to emigrate to Haiti, in part to halt the downward trend in that country's economy. [Gianni Dagli Orti/Corbis]

five-year-old Denmark Vesey, a former slave. Although Vesey had purchased his freedom with lottery winnings in December 1799, his wife Susan and his numerous children remained human property. Following the temporary closure of the Charleston African Methodist Episcopal (AME) Church in 1818, Vesey briefly considered emigrating to the English colony of Sierra Leone, but at length chose instead to orchestrate a rebellion followed by a mass exodus from Charleston to Haiti; President Jean-Pierre Boyer had recently encouraged black Americans to bring their skills and capital to his beleaguered republic.

Vesey planned the escape for nearly four years. His chief lieutenants included Peter Poyas; Rolla Bennett, the house servant of Governor Thomas Bennett; and "Gullah" Jack Pritchard, an East African priest purchased in Zinguebar (modern-day Zanzibar) in 1806. Although there are no reliable figures for the number of recruits, Charleston alone was home to 12,652 slaves. Jack Pritchard, probably with some exaggeration, boasted that he had 6,600 recruits on the plantations across the Cooper and Ashley Rivers. The plan called for Vesey's followers to rise on the night of Sunday, 14 July—Bastille Day, the day blacks in

Boston celebrated their freedom—slay their masters, and sail for Haiti, where Vesey had briefly worked as a child.

The plot unraveled in June 1822 when two slaves, including George Wilson, a fellow class leader in the AME church, revealed the plan to their owners. Mayor James Hamilton called up the city militia and convened a special court to try the captured insurgents. Vesey was captured at the home of Beck, his first wife, on 21 June and hanged on the morning of Tuesday, 2 July. Thirty-five slaves were executed; forty-two others were sold outside the United States. Charleston authorities also demolished the AME church and banished its leaders. The state assembly subsequently passed laws prohibiting the reentry of free blacks into the state; city officials enforced ordinances against teaching African-Americans to read.

See also PANICS; REBELLIONS AND VIOLENT RESISTANCE; SOUTH CAROLINA.

BIBLIOGRAPHY

EGERTON, DOUGLAS R. *He Shall Go Out Free: The Lives of Denmark Vesey.* 1998.
LOFTON, JOHN. *Insurrection in South Carolina: The Turbulent World of Denmark Vesey.* 1964.
STAROBIN, ROBERT S., ed. *Denmark Vesey: The Slave Conspiracy of 1822.* 1970.

Douglas R. Egerton

Vieira, António   [1608–1697]

Jesuit priest in Brazil; opponent of slavery.

António Vieira, who was born in Lisbon and died in Bahia, Brazil, was one of the great preachers, writers, and missionaries of the seventeenth century. Vieira, a Jesuit priest, served as court preacher and adviser to King John IV of Portugal (1640–1656) and continued to play an important role in Luso-Brazilian religious and political life throughout his career. Among the most notable aspects of Vieira's career was his effort, over the course of seventy years, to prevent the illegal enslavement of the Brazilian Indians.

Vieira served from 1653 to 1661 as Jesuit Superior in the Amazon, where the Portuguese crown had put the Jesuits in control of the distribution of Indian labor to the settlers. Vieira also had an additional charge—to bring under Jesuit control the notorious slaving expeditions that the settlers were conducting in the backlands. When the Jesuits' legal authority proved inadequate in the face of the settlers' continued slave raiding, Vieira returned to Lisbon to seek to strengthen the crown's Indian legislation in the Amazon. In 1655 he played the decisive role in the promulgation by John IV of laws that limited the enslavement of Indians to four sets of circumstances: when the crown ordered the enslavement; when the Indians had prevented the preaching of Christianity; when the Indians were captives of other tribes and at risk of becoming victims of ritual cannibalism; and when the Indians were captured by the Portuguese in a just war. These laws, and Vieira's efforts to enforce them, led to a protracted conflict between the Jesuits and the settlers that culminated in the settlers' expulsion of the Jesuits from the Amazon in 1661. Although Vieira never returned to the region, he was instrumental in the promulgation by King Pedro II in 1680 of a new set of laws governing Indian slavery and the Jesuit missions in the Amazon. As a result of his experience in the Amazon, Vieira demanded that Jesuit missionaries abandon their attempts to minister to both the Portuguese and the Indians. He argued that the only way to prevent the illegal enslavement of the Indians was to place all Indian communities under the control of the Jesuits and to permit only minimal contact between these communities and Portuguese settlers in Brazil.

Although Vieira was the most eloquent defender of the freedom of the Indians in the Luso-Brazilian world, he did not defend the freedom of African slaves in Brazil. In his first public sermon, preached in 1633 to a brotherhood of African slaves at a sugar mill near Bahia, Vieira lamented the hardships of slave labor but counseled the slaves to accept their lot and await their reward in heaven. Although Vieira did not systematically develop this argument, neither did he develop a critique of African slavery in Brazil comparable to his critique of Indian slavery. The Jesuits had dominated the missionary enterprise among the Indians since the establishment in 1549 of the first missions in Brazil, and Vieira viewed the strengthening of this enterprise as the Jesuits' primary responsibility, even if it meant limiting their ministries among other groups in colonial society. Vieira concluded early in his career that social and economic conditions in Brazil made some form of slavery inevitable; that Africans were physically better suited than Indians for slave labor; that the introduction of African slaves was an appropriate means of reducing the need for Indian labor; and that therefore, in order to ensure social peace and the success of the Jesuit missionary enterprise among the Indians, African slavery had to be tolerated in Brazil.

See also BRAZIL; PORTUGAL.

BIBLIOGRAPHY

BOXER, CHARLES. *A Great Luso-Brazilian Figure: Pe. António Vieira, S.J.* 1957.
COHEN, THOMAS M. *The Fire of Tongues: António Vieira and the Missionary Church in Brazil and Portugal.* 1998.
HEMMING, JOHN. *Red Gold: The Conquest of the Brazilian Indians.* 1978.

Thomas M. Cohen

Vietnam

See Slave Trade; Southeast Asia.

Vikings

See Scandinavia.

Virginia

Almost always the largest slave society in North America, Virginia, contained as many varieties of slaves and slaveholding as any other North American colony or state. The burgeoning (until the 1820s) slave population reflected significant natural reproduction as well as importation through the 1770s. (At least 70,500 enslaved people were carried to Virginia from 1699 to 1775, over half of them between 1727 and 1769.)

Its beginning was less decisive than its ending: slavery started as an exceptional phenomenon in Virginia based on practices in the Western Hemisphere and protected mostly by customary law. Slavery developed—slowly in comparison with the West Indies—into a social institution defended by force and by customary, civil, and criminal law. Social conventions initially defined the status of Africans, the first of whom perhaps arrived in early 1619. Whites dominated black laborers in ways that increasingly resembled slavery. Hardening and legalization of these practices as well as increased importation made Virginia a full-fledged slave society by 1700. In many counties, slaves became the majority by the 1730s and 1740s.

The American Revolution changed Virginia's peculiar institution. More owners allowed slaves to practice Christianity openly; legal reforms, including prohibition of slave importation (1778)—the first such law in the South—and a law of 1782 that allowed private manumission, improved conditions for some African-Americans. At the same time, however, the few abolition societies succumbed to heated opposition and inadequate support, more slaves were sold to locations farther from their loved ones than before, and the terms of manumission were made more onerous for freed people in 1806.

From the 1820s, Virginia's economic and political decline provoked a crisis of confidence. The "slavery

Table 1.   Slavery in Virginia, 1660–1860.

	1660	1710	1760	1790	1800	1810	1820	1830	1840	1850	1860[1]
Slaves	950	23,118	140,470	292,027	345,796	392,516	425,148	469,757	448,987	472,528	490,865
Free white	26,337	55,163	199,156	442,117	514,280	551,514	603,085	694,300	740,968	894,800	1,047,299
Free black			2,000	12,866	20,124	30,570	36,883	47,348	49,842	54,333	58,042
Total	27,287	78,281	341,626	747,010	880,200	974,600	1,065,116	1,211,405	1,239,797	1,421,661	1,596,206
Slaves (%)	3.5	29.5	41.1	39.1	39.3	40.3	39.9	38.8	36.2	33.2	30.8
Ratio of slaves to whites (%)	4	42	71	66	67	71	70	68	61	53	47
Slave growth (%)[2]		6.59	3.67	1.47	0.34	0.25	0.16	0.20	–0.09	0.10	0.08

1. Total population for 1860 does not include 112 enumerated Indians.
2. Average annual growth rate of slave population.

Sources: U.S. Census Office, *The Statistics of the Population of the United States.* Vol. 1, *Population and Social Statistics,* 1872; Jack P. Greene, *Pursuits of Happiness: The Social Development of Early Modern British Colonies and the Formation of American Culture,* 1988; author's estimates.

debates" in the session of the 1832 Assembly—a public discussion nearly unique in the South—revealed deep division over the future of bondage, mostly because western Virginians objected to the slaveholders' political power. Industrial employment of slaves, heavy exportation of slaves, and increased reliance on hiring helped bondage survive. Yet antebellum slavery in Virginia paled relative to the institution in the cotton states. The scene of many battles in the Civil War, the Old Dominion predictably was the setting of black fugitive Virginians' movements toward Union troops—a catalyst for the contraband crisis that helped lead to the Emancipation Proclamation.

Africans and African-Americans in Virginia developed extensive kinship groups and communities that interacted with one another more intensively over time. Slaveholders and African-American laborers created Virginian work patterns, agricultural techniques, and forms of cultural expression. Blacks and whites responded in unique ways to the requirements of tobacco, grain crops, and other produce; to each other's behavior; to the Old Dominion's climate; and to urban growth. The plantation culture of the upper South necessitated regular interaction among black and white Virginians, as is manifested in economic activity, religion, dress, speech, games, music, food, ar-

Table 2.   Virginia Slaveholders, 1790–1860.

	1790	1800	1810	1820	1830	1840	1850	1860
Slaveholders	34,026	39,075	44,354	48,042	53,083	50,736	55,063	52,128
Slave population	292,027	345,796	392,516	425,148	469,757	448,987	472,528	490,865
Free population	455,583	534,404	582,084	639,968	741,648	790,810	949,133	1,105,453
Ratio of slaveholders to slaves (%)	12	11	11	11	11	11	12	11
Ratio of slaveholders to free people (%)	7	7	8	8	7	6	6	5

Note: Estimate for 1800–1840 based on average 1790, 1850, 1860 ratio of slaveholding families to slaves. This is a somewhat, but certainly not completely, justifiable straight-line method of estimation because the ratios of slaveholders to slaves for 1790, 1850, and 1860 are so close to one another. Lee Soltow, "Economic Inequality in the United States in the Period from 1790 to 1860," *Journal of Economic History* 31 (December 1971): 822–839, estimates Virginia slaveholders in 1830 as 42,500, which appears to be too low. Given the escape or capture of slaves during the War of 1812 and other such intervening variables, these straight-line estimates can be only so accurate.

Sources: 1790 and 1850, U.S. Bureau of the Census, *Negro Population, 1790–1915,* 1918, p. 56. 1860: Inter-University Consortium for Political and Social Research, Study 00003: Historical Demographic, Economic, and Social Data: U.S., 1790–1970–http://icg.harvard.edu/census/. Population data: U.S. Census Office, *The Statistics of the Population of the United States.* Vol. 1, *Population and Social Statistics,* 1872, pp. 3–8.

Nat Turner was captured in the forest more than two months after leading an 1831 slave rebellion that left fifty-seven to sixty white people dead in Southampton County, Virginia. [Library of Congress/Corbis]

chitecture, dance, and folk customs. This interaction occurred within an oppressive social structure, with its concomitant potential for brutal discipline and the willingness of some enslaved people—notably Gabriel (1800) and Nat Turner (1831)—to defy or revolt against slave owners. Still, Virginia's African-Americans and European Americans interacted more with one another than was the case in some other slave societies.

See also GABRIEL; GABRIEL'S REBELLION; HEADRIGHT SYSTEM; HEMMINGS, SALLY; JEFFERSON, THOMAS; TURNER, NAT.

BIBLIOGRAPHY

DEW, CHARLES B. *Bond of Iron: Master and Slave at Buffalo Forge.* 1994.

DUNN, RICHARD S. "Black Society in the Chesapeake, 1776–1810." In *Slavery and Freedom in the Age of the American Revolution,* edited by Ira Berlin and Ronald Hoffman. 1983.

MINCHINTON, WALTER E., CELIA KING, and PETER WAITE. *Virginia Slave-Trade Statistics, 1698–1775.* 1984.

MULLIN, GERALD W. *Flight and Rebellion: Slave Resistance in Eighteenth-Century Virginia.* 1972.

VAUGHAN, ALDEN T. "The Origins Debate: Slavery and Racism in Seventeenth-Century Virginia." In *The Roots of American Racism: Essays on Colonial Perceptions and Policies.* 1995.

Philip J. Schwarz

Virginia Society for the Abolition of Slavery

Three abolition societies appeared in the Old Dominion in the 1790s. One, based in Winchester, is quite obscure. Motivated by Society of Friends and Methodist values and encouraged by Revolutionary ideals, a few Virginians founded the Richmond-based Virginia Society for Promoting the Abolition of Slavery, and the Relief of Free Negroes or Others Unlawfully Held In Bondage, and Other Humane Purposes in 1790. Quaker Robert Pleasants (1723–1801) led the group. Pleasants knew leading members of the Pennsylvania Abolition Society. His father, John Pleasants, had freed his bondspeople in his will. Robert, his brother Joseph, and other Quakers followed suit later.

Pleasants advertised the proposed society in the *Virginia Gazette* (January 1790). Soon, the Pennsylvania Abolition Society announced the new organization's birth to similar bodies in London and Paris. Overcoming hostility from some white Virginians, arguments over Robert Pleasants's insistence on excluding slave owners, and disputes about cooperation between Quakers and Methodists, the fledging organization published its constitution. Its membership rose to 147 by 1796. The four officers and nine-person "Acting Committee" were mostly Quakers, as well as some Methodists who joined with Bishop Francis Asbury's blessing. It is not clear whether women participated. The constitution stated the Society's limited objective of supporting freedom suits. There was no call to advocate general emancipation, except as a principle.

The Virginia Abolition Society successfully assisted some kidnapping and freedom suits, but Robert Pleasants explained in 1795 that the group could not afford major freedom suits. The Society subscribed to a 1791 petition to Congress in favor of gradual emancipation, supported a similar petition to the Virginia General Assembly advocating emancipation of enslaved children, corresponded with the Pennsylvania Abolition Society, and wrote to newspapers concerning the evils of slavery. Whether these activities exercised a long-term effect on later antislavery advocates in the Old Dominion is almost impossible to say.

The Alexandria Society for Promoting the Abolition of Slavery was founded by Archibald McLean and others in 1795. It reported a membership of sixty-two in 1796. Like the Richmond group, this society assisted slaves in freedom and kidnapping suits; it also successfully operated a school for over one hundred free African-Americans. About a year after the founding, however, local leaders campaigned against the Alexandria group on the grounds that it would sow rebelliousness among slaves. This assault bore legislative fruit: a 1795 state law forestalled abolitionist assistance in freedom suits, while a 1798 statute barred members of abolitionist societies from juries in freedom suit trials. The Richmond society's legal activism largely ended; the Alexandrian group could hardly begin to act.

At times, Robert Pleasants vainly searched for delegates for a Philadelphia meeting of abolitionist societies and struggled fruitlessly to attract members to meetings. The Alexandrian organization faced similar problems as its members succumbed to pessimism. Their opponents wielded Gabriel's Plot of 1800 as still another weapon to stymie antislavery activity. The Alexandrians judged it prudent to close their school for free blacks. The shadowy Winchester group, the Richmond society, and the Alexandrian organization were the last organized abolitionists to venture into the public arenas of Virginia for some time.

See also ABOLITION AND ANTISLAVERY MOVEMENTS; QUAKERS; VIRGINIA.

BIBLIOGRAPHY

FINNIE, GORDON ESLEY. "The Antislavery Movement in the South, 1787–1836: Its Rise and Decline and Its Contribution to Abolition in the West." Ph.D. diss., Duke University, 1962.

The Papers of the Pennsylvania Abolitionist Society, 1774–1916. Historical Society of Pennsylvania. Microfilm.

PLEASANTS, ROBERT. *Letterbook, 1754–1797.* (Transcript of original in the Haverford College Library, Quaker Collection.) The Valentine Museum Library, Richmond, Virginia.

VIRGINIA SOCIETY FOR PROMOTING THE ABOLITION OF SLAVERY. *The Constitution of the Virginia Society, for Promoting the Abolition of Slavery, and the Relief of Free Negroes, or Others, Unlawfully Held in Bondage, and Other Humane Purposes.* 1792.

Philip J. Schwarz

Visual Arts

See Arts.

Voodoo

See Slave Religion.

Voting Rights

See Law; Reconstruction, U.S.

W

Wage Slavery

See Labor Systems.

Walker, David [1785–1830]

Freeborn black U.S. abolitionist.

David Walker was born free in Wilmington, North Carolina, where he was raised and educated. He traveled throughout the South before settling in 1825 in Boston, where he joined the Massachusetts General Colored Association, a black organization that opposed slavery and racial discrimination. In addition, he served as an agent for *Freedom's Journal*, the first black newspaper in the United States. In 1827 he opened a used clothing store that catered to seamen; an enterprise that allowed him to smuggle antislavery pamphlets into the South. He stuffed the pamphlets in the pockets of the store's greatcoats because he knew many of the coats would be acquired by used clothing dealers in southern ports, who were mostly free blacks and who would distribute the pamphlets.

In 1829 Walker published *Appeal . . . to the Colored Citizens of the World*, which urged masters to free their slaves before the wrath of God overwhelmed them and urged slaves to murder their masters, if necessary, in order to obtain their freedom. White southerners were outraged; several slave states outlawed the distribution of literature espousing slave insurrection and toughened the laws against teaching slaves to read. Several Georgians put a price on his life, and in 1830 his dead body was found near his shop. Although poisoning was suspected, the cause of death was never determined. *Appeal*, the most radical pamphlet written by a U.S. abolitionist, was reprinted and distributed after Walker's death. However, black and white abolitionists alike rejected its advocacy of violence and it does not seem to have inspired Nat Turner's Rebellion in 1831 or any other rebellion.

See also ABOLITION AND ANTISLAVERY MOVEMENTS; FREE PEOPLE OF COLOR; PANICS; REBELLIONS AND VIOLENT RESISTANCE.

BIBLIOGRAPHY

PEASE, JANE H., and WILLIAM H. PEASE. *Bound with Them in Chains: A Biographical History of the Antislavery Movement.* 1972.

Charles W. Carey Jr.

Ward, Samuel Ringgold [1817–1866]

Black U.S. abolitionist, orator, and writer.

Born into slavery on Maryland's Eastern Shore, in 1820 Samuel Ringgold Ward escaped with his parents to New Jersey. In 1826 the family relocated to New York City, where Samuel received an education and became a teacher and Congregational minister. Between 1839 and 1850, Ward toured western and central New York as a traveling agent of the American and New York State antislavery societies and lectured against slavery from the Christian perspective of "love thy neighbor." In 1840 he joined the Liberty Party, which sought to abolish slavery by political means, and in 1844 he toured the North on behalf of James G. Birney, the party's presidential candidate. Ward's eloquence earned him the sobriquet "the black Daniel Webster."

Throughout the North, Ward spoke out forcefully against the Fugitive Slave Act of 1850, which greatly restricted the legal rights of blacks accused of being runaway slaves. In 1851 he became actively involved in the rescue of Jerry, a runaway slave, from a Syracuse, New York, jail. After this, Ward fled to Canada to avoid arrest. For the next two years he served as an American Anti-Slavery Society agent in Canada. He organized local chapters, spoke against racial discrimination in Canada, founded abolitionist newspapers, and helped to settle runaways who made it to Canada via the Underground Railroad. In 1853 he went to England to raise money for abolitionist activities in Canada and addressed a number of abolitionist groups including the British and Foreign Anti-Slavery Society. In 1855 he wrote *Autobiography of a Fugitive Negro: His Anti-Slavery Labours in the United States, Canada, and England.* He spent his last eleven years as a minister in Jamaica.

See also ABOLITION AND ANTISLAVERY MOVEMENTS; AMERICAN ANTI-SLAVERY SOCIETY; UNDERGROUND RAILROAD.

BIBLIOGRAPHY

SORIN, GERALD. *The New York Abolitionists: A Case Study of Political Radicalism.* 1971.
WARD, SAMUEL RINGGOLD. *Autobiography of a Fugitive Negro: His Anti-slavery Labours in the United States, Canada and England.* 1855. Reprint, 1970.

Charles W. Carey Jr.

War Service

See Manumission; Military Slaves.

Washington, George   [1732–1799]

First U.S. president.

George Washington's experience illustrates what David Brion Davis has called "the problem of slavery in the Age of Revolution." Born into the lesser gentry, Washington became a major Virginian farmer by acquiring land and the slaves to work it. His slave force rose from 49 in 1760 to 317 at his death. Approximately half were actually his; the rest were "dower slaves" belonging to his wife, Martha.

A lithograph depicts the first meeting of George Washington and the Marquis de Lafayette. Lafayette influenced Washington's decision to emancipate his slaves in his will. [Library of Congress/Corbis]

James Thomas Flexner describes Washington as "cheerfully insensitive" as he ordered the sale of a recalcitrant slave in 1766. One of his early acts as commander of the Continental Army in 1775 was to order the dismissal of black New England militiamen from service. He was as outraged as any white Virginian when Lord Dunmore rallied slaves against rebel masters that year. But on his own initiative he also reopened the American ranks to black men, lest they aid the British instead.

In 1778 Washington thought of freeing himself from slavery by selling his slaves. Five years later he responded favorably when the Marquis de Lafayette proposed that they jointly set up an estate where former slaves could become tenant farmers. He gave guarded encouragement when two British clergymen tried to bring an antislavery petition before the Virginia Assembly in 1785. As president, Washington opposed attempts to bring the slaves of federal officials under the coverage of Pennsylvania's gradual emancipation law. Nonetheless, his will freed all the slaves he owned, though not until his widow's death.

See also GRADUAL EMANCIPATION STATUTES.

BIBLIOGRAPHY

FLEXNER, JAMES THOMAS. *George Washington: Anguish and Farewell (1793–1799).* 1972.
MAZYCK, WALTER H. *George Washington and the Negro.* 1932.

Edward Countryman

Webster-Ashburton Treaty

The Webster-Ashburton Treaty of 9 August 1842 resolved many of the irritants between the United States and England that had fomented talk of war. The northeastern boundary dispute headed a long list of problems that included the *Caroline* and Alexander McLeod affair, the *Creole* slave revolt, and the African slave trade. Ambiguous phrasing in the Treaty of Paris, which ended the Revolutionary War in 1783, had caused Canadian boundary disagreements. Then, in the late 1870s, Americans violated their government's neutrality legislation by participating in Canadian rebellions against the British Crown, at one point diverting the steamer *Caroline* to transport goods and men across the Niagara River in New York. British loyalists burned the *Caroline*, with one American allegedly dying at the hand of Alexander McLeod. The result was a wave of Anglophobia that, by the fall of 1841, caused talk of war.

When these issues had reached crisis stage, Sir Robert Peel in London sent a special emissary to Washington with instructions to resolve all problems between the Atlantic nations. Lord Ashburton (Alexander Baring) met with Secretary of State Daniel Webster during the summer of 1842, emerging with a treaty that settled the northeastern boundary dispute, authorized an extradition agreement, and approved a joint squadron clause intended to end the African slave trade. The two diplomats resolved additional matters by an exchange of notes allowing each nation to state its argument for the record.

The Webster-Ashburton Treaty underwent bitter attack even though it proved to be a vital prologue to manifest destiny. To promote the boundary settlement, President John Tyler authorized Webster to draw from the president's secret service fund. Four years later, in 1846, Webster's political opponents accused him of illegal behavior and attempted to impeach him retroactively (he was no longer secretary of state at that time). The effort failed, primarily after former President Tyler assured the congressional committee that he had approved Webster's actions. The treaty awarded the United States seven-twelfths of the area in dispute, but four-fifths of its assessed value, including the strategically important entrance into Lake Champlain, along with an area west of Lake Superior that later proved to be rich in iron ore. The pact also established the mutual extradition of fugitives accused of nonpolitical crimes (excluding mutiny) and approved a joint squadron clause that authorized Anglo-American cooperation in suppressing the African slave trade. The overall settlement with England permitted Americans to focus on the west, while encouraging a mid-century rapprochment with Great Britain that has lasted to the present day.

See also AFRICA SQUADRON; CREOLE INCIDENT; SLAVE TRADE.

BIBLIOGRAPHY

JONES, HOWARD. "Daniel Webster: The Diplomatist." In *Daniel Webster: The Completest Man*, edited by Kenneth E. Shewmaker. 1990.
———. *To the Webster-Ashburton Treaty: A Study in Anglo-American Relations, 1783–1843.* 1977.
JONES, HOWARD, and DONALD A. RAKESTRAW. *Prologue to Manifest Destiny: Anglo-American Relations in the 1840s.* 1997.

Howard Jones

Weld, Theodore   [1803–1895]

U.S. abolitionist and evangelical Christian.

Born in Connecticut and raised in New York, Theodore Dwight Weld was converted to immediate abolitionism by Charles Stuart, a family friend and member

Theodore Weld. [*Dictionary of American Portraits*]

of the British Anti-Slavery Society, and Lewis Tappan, a reform-minded philanthropist. In 1832 Weld enrolled in Lane Seminary in Cincinnati, Ohio, where in 1834 he organized a debate on abolition between proponents of colonization and immediate emancipation. The rancor engendered by the debate induced him to leave Lane and become an agent for the American Anti-Slavery Society. His impassioned evangelical oratory recruited many gradualists and colonizers to immediatism, among them Gamaliel Bailey, Henry Ward Beecher, James G. Birney, Harriet Beecher Stowe, and Elizur Wright. In 1836 Weld organized and trained the "Band of Seventy" to preach immediatism throughout the North; their success ensured the vitality of northern abolitionism. Having injured his voice during this campaign, he began writing pamphlets such as *The Bible against Slavery* (1837) and *American Slavery As It Is* (1839). The latter quoted from southern newspapers to illustrate the horrors of slavery; next to Stowe's *Uncle Tom's Cabin* (which it inspired), it was the most widely read antislavery work published in the United States.

After a three-year hiatus from abolitionism during which he married Angelina Grimké, a fellow abolitionist, in 1841 Weld went to Washington, D.C., where he supplied information and advice to John Quincy Adams and other congressmen who worked to repeal the "gag rule" forbidding the discussion of antislavery petitions by Congress. In 1843 Weld retired from public life to spend time with his family.

See also ABOLITION AND ANTISLAVERY MOVEMENTS; GRIMKÉ, ANGELINA AND SARAH.

BIBLIOGRAPHY

ABZUG, ROBERT H. *Passionate Liberator: Theodore Dwight Weld and the Dilemma of Reform.* 1980.

Charles W. Carey Jr.

Wesley, John

See Methodism.

West Africa

This entry includes the following articles: Medieval Western Sudan; Senegambia; Forest Areas; Sokoto Caliphate. *Related articles may be found at the entries* Africa; Central Africa; East Africa; North Africa; Northeast Africa; Slave Trade; Southern Africa. *See also the note accompanying the entry* Africa *for further information about the organization of these entries.*

Medieval Western Sudan

This synopsis of slavery in the western Sudan will cover the period from the eighth century to the end of the sixteenth and will touch on conditions from the West African coast to the Lake Chad region, but it will not include Senegambia proper and will mention the central Sudan only for purposes of comparison. The northern perimeter of this expanse is the Sahara Desert; its southern boundaries lie at the fringes of the West African forest. This territory is a savanna: mostly level grassland with trees dispersed here and there.

In medieval western Sudan, a place and period characterized by such renowned empires as Mali and Songhay (or Songhai), proprietary notions of slavery do not consistently explain transactions in human beings; Orlando Patterson's reconceptualization of slavery as a condition of natally alienated and socially dishonored persons is much more useful to describe the various groups of individuals who were considered slaves.

To the extent that such slavery existed in medieval western Sudan, it was concentrated in three interrelated sectors. The first sector was domestic slavery. The second was an export trade in slaves into and across the Sahara to North Africa (al-Maghrib) and other parts of the Islamic world (dār al-Islām). The third sector, which appeared in the region at the end of the medieval period, consisted of captives seized for export into the Atlantic. In fact, the rise of the transatlantic slave trade in the fifteenth century helps to identify the close of the medieval period in the western Sudan.

Domestic slaves played a variety of roles in all aspects of life in the western Sudan. They were critical to productive, administrative, and military operations within the various polities of the region. In agriculture, slaves were for the most part utilized to work the land for royal families and were housed in separate slave settlements. It would appear that the use of agricultural slaves by nonroyal free persons was not extensive; in fact, in many societies a free person was identified by his or her involvement in cultivation. Slaves were also used for such domestic purposes as food preparation and housekeeping; and women were sexually exploited, and their offspring incorporated into lineage of the owner to increase its size.

The use of slaves in the military is a matter of speculation and, consequently, scholarly debate. First of all, it is not clear that all states maintained standing armies. Those that did not would have mobilized the peasantry in times of conflict. For states whose size assumed the proportions of an empire, a standing army would seem to be indispensable, but this expectation is not conclusively demonstrated in the literature. Even so, when armies (standing or not) do appear in the primary sources, slaves play the crucial role of foot soldiers, usually armed with bows and arrows. Medieval Sudanese armies were also composed of cavalry troops bearing short javelins, longer spears, and swords. This wing of the military was usually made up of free persons, nobility for the most part, who could afford the high costs for upkeep of horses imported from the desert in exchange for the slaves they sold there.

Domestic slavery in the ancient kingdom of Ghana (ca. 800–1060 C.E.), or Wagadu as it was called in oral traditions (or Kaya Magha, as designated in written sources from the area), is rather shadowy and poorly documented. For example, al-Bakrī (d. 1094) records that when the king of Ghana died, he was placed underneath a domed construction under which were also arranged his jewelry; his personal drinking and eating vessels, filled to capacity; and the men who served his meals. Such an account suggests that these men were royal slaves, especially since the dome was subsequently covered over with dirt, burying the attendants alive with the dead body of their lord. Ghana, a Serrakole or Soninke state, was either bordered by or synonymous with the even more obscure kingdom of "Farwiyyūn," concerning which al-Bakarī states that its ruler "owns an enormous number of women," a clear reference to slave concubines. Given the focus of contemporary observers on the royal court and other elites, it is difficult to extrapolate how far slaveholding extended elsewhere.

Slaves were also prominent at the later royal courts of the Sudan, and they were regularly named to administrative posts of great sensitivity and responsibility. As confidants and trusted advisors of the ruler, these slaves in some cases rose to positions of enormous power and privilege. Indeed, in certain empires of medieval western Sudan, there were numerous instances of slaves who served as governors over whole provinces, wielding authority over slave and free alike and answering only to the ruler. Slaves controlled key entrepôts, levied taxes, and disciplined members of nobility for infractions against the state. Indeed, the ruling Keita dynasty of the Malian empire was temporarily overthrown near the beginning of the fourteenth century by Sākurā, a former slave, and again by the slave Sandiki (or *Sandigi*, a title rather than a personal name) in 1387–1388. Viewing such varied conditions of enslavement, an observer from Europe would have been hard pressed to know who was servile and who was not by most modern definitions of the status.

Concerning the sector of slaves sold into Muslim lands, African captives from the savanna began to move into and through the Sahara Desert with regu-

larity early in the first millennium of the current era. The desert crossing was made possible by the introduction of the camel into North Africa sometime between 100 B.C.E. and 100 C.E. With a dependable means of transport available, caravans organized in North Africa began to develop long-distance trade networks into western Sudan by way of the lords of the desert oases, the Tuareg, who served as intermediaries in the commercial transactions between North and West Africa. The West African commodity of primary interest to North African merchants was gold, followed by a list of other items that included slaves. In turn, West Africans were interested in buying salt, a mineral mined in the Sahara, along with cowrie shells, horses, textiles of all kinds, and other North African manufactures.

Accounts of the trans-Saharan slave trade such as those in *Kitāb-al-Istibsār* (completed in 1191) confirm the transfer of captives from the Sudan. Discussing market conditions in Awdaghust, an entrepôt to the north of Ghana, this document states that Sudanese women were available for purchase, having established a reputation as superb cooks. Such anecdotal evidence is consistent with the view that the trans-Saharan slave trade was essentially a traffic in women, used for domestic work and male sexual gratification. West African male slaves were used to mine the salt in the desert, and formed enduring relations of servility to the Tuareg and other Berbers of the desert and *sāhil* (literally "shore," a transition zone between the desert and the savanna). The western Sudan was never a major supplier of slaves for the trans-Saharan trade to North Africa and the Islamic Mediterranean; that distinction was reserved for the central Sudan, which lacked gold to pay for arms and other imports. Contact between North African and Sub-Saharan Africa led to the term "Sudan," or "black," a term taken from the Arabic designation for the region as the *bilād as-Sūdān*, or "land of the blacks." The trans-Saharan slave trade therefore antedated its transatlantic counterpart and lasted even later, continuing well into the last quarter of the nineteenth century.

Anecdotal information concerning imperial Mali (fourteenth and fifteenth centuries) reveals rather extensive slaveholding at the court. Both al-'Umarī (d. 1349) and Ibn Battūta (d. 1368) comment on Malian domestic slavery, and by the time of their writings the ruling elites of the empire had adopted numerous Islamic political institutions. Al-'Umarī stated that thirty slaves (*mamlūk*) stood behind the king during an audience, and other courtiers are mentioned in a servile capacity. Al-'Umari claimed that the Malian army fielded about 100,000 soldiers, 10,000 of whom were cavalry. How many of the infantry may have been slaves is unknown, but Ibn Battūta reports seeing at least 300 armed slaves proceeding from the palace during one audience. Female slaves are mentioned as commodities of exchange or as gifts to luminaries for the purpose of ratifying political alliances or complementing diplomacy. Battūta also mentioned female slaves prominently in his account, including 200 seen leaving the royal palace one night during Ramadān. This source discusses various royal slaves, including thirty slave boys (*ghulām*) who were specially clothed in the ruler's presence. Al-'Umarī comments that male and female slaves provided the labor for copper mines near the sahelian town of Takedda.

In imperial, Islamized Songhay (fifteenth and sixteenth centuries), the ruling elite were also the principal slaveholders. Leo Africanus, visiting the capital of Gao around 1508, reported that the royal compound consisted of wives, concubines, slaves, and eunuchs—the eunuchs were used to guard the women. Women were frequently given as gifts by rulers to men of prominence. A substantial number of Songhay's infantry were either slaves or of servile origin, explaining how the rulers of the *askia* dynasty could take their soldiers' daughters as concubines. The Songhay cavalry, some 3,000 strong according to Leo Africanus, included a contingent of royal eunuchs. To feed the relatively large urban populations of the main trading towns, Gao and Timbuktu, royal settlements of slaves cultivated rice and other crops along the Middle Niger River. These agricultural slaves were supervised by slave officials. When all this is taken into consideration, along with correspondence wrangling over legal issues relating to slaves, it is possible to conclude that slavery was of tremendous importance to the Songhay state and to merchants in the area. Indeed, such a conclusion is inescapable when it is realized that every one of the *askia* rulers following *Askia* Muhammad (ruled 1493–1528) was the son of a concubine.

Although Songhay and Mali sold captives in the trans-Saharan slave trade, the volume of slaves exported from the western Sudan was much less than that generated in the central Sudan. It would in fact appear that whereas the western Sudan was principally an exporter of gold, the central Sudan trafficked heavily in the sale of captives. As early as 890, al-Ya'qubi describes Zawīla, a town in the Fezzan (modern Libya), as a major source of slaves coming out of the central Sudan. Perhaps the reputation of the central Sudan as a principal source of slaves increased over time, reaching an apex in the sixteenth century with the incessant military campaigning of *Mai* Idrīs Aloma (ruled 1564–1599) of Bornu, the largest state centered on Lake Chad. However, with the rise of the transatlantic slave trade, captives from the western Sudan would be funneled into both the transatlantic and the trans-Saharan trades.

See also ISLAM.

BIBLIOGRAPHY

HOPKINS, J. F. P., and NEHEMIA LEVTZION, eds. *Corpus of Early Sources for West Africa History.* 1981.
HUNWICK, J. O. "Notes on Slavery in the Songhay Empire. "In *Slavery and Muslim Society in Africa,* edited by J. R. Willis. 1985.
LEVTZION, NEHEMIA. *Ancient Ghana and Mali.* 1973.

Michael A. Gomez

Senegambia

Portuguese navigators moving down the West African coast during the early fifteenth century reached Senegambia in 1444. It was their first contact with black Africans. Portuguese captains, each of whom went further than their predecessors, had orders to bring home some local residents who could serve as interpreters for subsequent expeditions. Understandably, local people were hostile to subsequent Portuguese visitors, but within a few years formal trade ties had been established, and the Portuguese were buying slaves from Senegambian rulers. They were able to do so because the local people already owned slaves. The Portuguese ship captain Alvise Ca da Mosto tells us that the Buurba Jolof in the mid-fifteenth century put prisoners of war to work cultivating the land or exchanged them for horses.

Senegambia was on the edge of a world of large states. Tekrur, which straddled the lower Senegal River, was one of the first areas to convert to Islam and was an important bridge between the nomadic societies of the southern Sahara and the agriculturalists of the river valley and further south. Senegambian rulers there exchanged slaves for horses, which were crucial to their military power. Senegambia was thus already exporting slaves into the Saharan slave trade at the time of the Portuguese arrival. Most of northern Senegambia was controlled by the Jolof empire, which was, in turn, subject for a time to the more powerful Mali empire of the Niger River valley to the east. The area further south, around the Gambia, had been colonized by Mandinka from Mali and was an important source of sea salt for Mali. Thus, coastal Senegambia had trade ties with North Africa, with the Sahara, and with the Mali empire, in all of which areas slave labor was used. It is probable that slaves were traded all over the region because slaves had little value close to home, where they might easily escape.

During the fifteenth and sixteenth centuries Senegambia became one of the major sources of slaves for the Portuguese trade. Eventually, more densely

A slave merchant on Gorée Island at the end of the eighteenth century. [Gianni Dagli Orti/Corbis]

populated areas farther down the coast also became important, but New World slave data on origins of slaves there suggest that most of the slaves during this early period came from Senegambia and the upper Guinea coast. The increasing European demand for slaves had a number of effects in Senegambia. The first was that slave supply routes extended deeper and deeper into the interior. By the end of the seventeenth century, the English and French had replaced the Portuguese, and most slaves were coming from the upper Niger valley. The second result was the emergence of small European communities along the coast. Luso-Africans scattered along the coast speedily integrated themselves into Africa, but St. Louis and Gorée were French towns. There never were, however, more than several hundred French in Senegal. Both towns had slave majorities until the French abolished slavery in 1848. Slaves not only did most of the work within the towns but also manned the boats that sailed down the coast and up the Senegal river. Slaves also did most of the work in outposts linked to the European trade along the two rivers and along the Atlantic coast. The third result of the growing trade was to

break up the Jolof empire and increase conflict within the area, not only among the states but also between the pagan ruling class and a rising Muslim community of farmers and traders.

Fourth and finally, the Atlantic trade increased the use of slaves within the Senegambian states. This is most strikingly shown in the increased importance of slave warriors, called *ceddo,* among the Wolof and Fulbe. During the late seventeenth century, when demand from the Americas for slaves was increasing, the rulers of the Wolof and also nearby Sereer states increasingly centralized their personal power by relying more heavily on slave warriors. Being kinless, the ceddo were expected to serve the kings with total loyalty. Increasingly, power drifted from the chiefs of the free commoners to slave chiefs chosen from among the ceddo. Increasingly too, slaves performed more and more agricultural labor, especially within the Muslim community, which was more frugal than the warrior aristocrats, less involved in conspicuous consumption, and more systematic in its exploitation of slave labor. Slave exports from Senegambia rose until the first third of the eighteenth century. Then, from about 1740, in spite of constant efforts by Europeans to stimulate warfare and further slave exports, Senegal's export of slaves actually declined, probably as a result of increased domestic use of slave labor to produce food, both for the small urban market on the Senegalese coast and for the ships that departed Gorée and St. Louis for the Middle Passage or for Europe.

These slaves were generally exploited within a household or family economy and usually lived in either the master's compound or a slave quarter in the village. The newly captured or newly purchased slave was generally watched very carefully and worked full time on his master's lands. As slaves became part of the community, they were given spouses and, with marriage, a plot of land to support themselves. The slave generally worked five days a week on the master's land, the working day extending from shortly after sunrise until about two in the afternoon. Evenings and off days, the slaves worked their own fields. What they produced belonged to them. A first-generation slave could be sold but was most in danger of sale during his or her early years or when drought forced sacrifices of dependents for food. The slave born in the community was not supposed to be put on the market, though there was no real sanction against the master who did so except the disturbance of his other slaves and perhaps the disapproval of his neighbors.

Second-generation slaves were also often allowed to farm for themselves in exchange for a fixed obligation paid to their owner. They still owed respect to any noble, which meant that they had to greet their

The stairways of the historic slave house on Gorée Island. [Wolfgang Kaehler/Corbis]

superiors politely and could not sit in a chair in their presence. Slaves sat on the ground. During the dry season, slaves generally wove. They also were expected to repair houses and clean latrines and could be asked to carry messages. Manumission seems to have been relatively rare, though Islam regarded manumission as a pious act, and some aging Muslims freed trusted slave retainers. The most common form of manumission was probably for a woman to bear the child of her master. Such a woman could not be sold, and when her master died, she became free. A majority of the newly enslaved were women, probably over two-thirds of the adults. In a sense female slaves were the cement of the society. The more attractive were taken as concubines by noble men. Others were given to the slave warriors, who scorned manual labor and generally depended on their wives for their sustenance. Male slaves were also given female partners.

A hardworking male slave could save enough money to take a second wife. In fact, for a slave taking a second wife or buying his own slave was often a more advisable strategy than buying his own freedom. A freed man remained a dependent of his master and still had obligations, largely because he had no kin. He

then also had to save to free his spouse and his children. The essence of the slave's subjection lay in his kinlessness. The slave's child could be taken from him when the child was old enough to work. The child could be kept by the master or given to one of the master's children and, in any case, did not inherit the slave parent's property, which belonged to the master. The slave ménage's security lay in good relations with his master and if possible in acquiring a second wife or a more junior slave.

Though most Senegambians were nominally Muslim, the area was increasingly divided between a more orthodox Muslim community and the warrior elite of the Wolof and Mandinka states. The opposition between the communities led to a series of jihads that began in the Senegal river during the 1770s and continued until completion of the colonial conquest by the French and British in about 1890. In many cases the excesses of the slave trade were an issue. The Muslims were more sober and more frugal than the slave-raiding warriors. They resented demands made on them and most particularly the enslavement of Muslims. With the end of the Atlantic trade in the 1830s, they increasingly directed their slaves to the production of gum and peanuts. The success of the jihads generally led to the transformation of the Muslim community into militaristic slavers and exploiters of slave labor. The decline of the export trade led not to the decline of slavery within Senegambia but to a more rigorous exploitation of slaves to produce commodities for sale abroad. As peanut exports increased after the middle of the century, so too did the exploitation of slave labor.

See also PORTUGAL.

BIBLIOGRAPHY

BARRY, BOUBACAR. *Senegambia and the Atlantic Slave Trade.* 1998.

CURTIN, PHILIP. *Economic Change in Precolonial Africa: Senegambia in the Era of the Slave Trade.* 1975.

KLEIN, MARTIN. "Servitude among the Wolof and Sereer of Senegambia." In *Slavery in Africa,* edited by Suzanne Miers and Igor Kopytoff. 1977.

————. *Slavery and Colonial Rule in French West Africa.* 1998.

RENAULT, FRANÇOIS. "L'abolition de l'esclavage au Sénégal: L'attitude de l'administration française (1848–1905)." *Revue français de l'histoire d'outre-mer* 59 (1971).

SEARING, JAMES. *West African Slavery and Atlantic Commerce. The Senegal River Valley, 1700–1860.* 1993.

Martin A. Klein

Forest Areas

The West African forest region can be divided into two sections: the western forest (Upper Guinea), extending from southern Senegambia to Côte d'Ivoire; and the eastern forest (Lower Guinea), extending from the Ghana to the Bight of Benin and the Bight of Biafra. Before the twentieth century it embraced several cultural-linguistic regions, subregions, polities, and communities. In Lower Guinea the political formations included the Akan-speaking Asante (Ashanti) kingdom, the Fon-speaking Dahomey kingdom, the Edo-speaking Benin state, and, east of the lower Niger River valley, the Igbo-speaking polities. Slavery was an established institution and practice in this area well before 1500. The varying historical forms of this mode of social domination are the subjects of this article.

Introduction

The Lower Guinea social-political formations exercised control over, and were constituted by, different networks—bulk goods, prestige goods, political-military, and information—which were interwoven into systems of competing and cooperating polities and communities, areas of specialization, and modes of accumulation. The development of specialization in food and other kinds of material production, as well as in cultural and symbolic production, led to the continuous emergence of different sites of specialization. The boundaries between specialized sites formed "frontiers" which shifted across time and space, and these articulated in complex ways with the flow of people, services, and goods, with regimes of surplus accumulation, and with the institution and practice of slavery.

On the basis of their accumulation strategies, Lower Guinea polities and communities can be usefully described as *societies with slaves* or as *slave societies.* The main distinctions between these are that in slave-based societies, slavery was the principal mode through which dominant and ruling social strata gained the bulk of their surplus at a particular moment in history and slaves possessed relatively few rights and could be bought, sold, or inherited. In societies with slaves, slavery was only one among several other modes that generated surplus wealth for dominant elites. In addition, slaves appear to have enjoyed greater rights than their counterparts in slave societies, but they could still be bought, sold, and inherited. Within the Lower Guinea slave systems slaves were both chattel (property) and human. Historically, opposition and resistance by slaves assumed different forms: rebellion, maroonage, running away, suicide, and acts of sabotage.

According to some interpretations, the emergence and development of slave groups were an effect of either warfare and the emergence of military aristocracies (predation) or commerce and the emergence of professional merchants (trading capital). Both processes have been linked to state-building activities. Another interpretation maintains that slave groups appeared in association with towns and urbanization and that servile labor functioned as a mainstay of an urban economy which supported the high consumption culture of military aristocracies and merchants. West African urbanization, in one view, created a particular kind of distinction between "town" and "country." On the one hand, there were market and political-administrative centers with their immediate rural hinterlands of farms of indebted peasants and, importantly, plantations worked by servile labor. These centers with their hinterlands constituted the "towns." On the other hand, there were "deep rural" farming communities where peasants' indebtedness to urban-based merchants and money-lenders was relatively limited, and where social and political dependence on slave surplus production were socially and institutionally constrained. These communities constituted the "country," which comprised, at different historical moments, societies with slaves. In contrast, towns functioned as slave-based entities.

The earliest documentary references to slaves and slavery in Lower Guinea are to be found in Portuguese accounts dating from the second half of the fifteenth century. Descriptions of the Gold Coast (or Costa da Mina in Portuguese sources) indicate that when Portuguese factors and officials began trading there after 1471, they encountered a preexisting cabotage trade that connected the Gold Coast and market centers in the Benin kingdom and in the Niger Delta and Igboland. In 1483 the Portuguese built fort São Jorge da Mina in the coastal town of Elmina (Edina) and participated in this prestige-goods network. Slaves were an important commodity in this commerce. Portuguese ships transported slaves, male and female, to their Elmina fort, where they were sold to Akan-speaking traders from the coastal hinterland in exchange for gold. In the seventeenth century Akanland continued to import slaves, but these came mainly from Allada (Ardra), the dominant state on the eastern Slave Coast, and not from Benin and the Niger Delta and Igboland. Allada merchants obtained some of their slaves from the emerging Dahomey polity, which was located to the north of Allada.

In the central districts of Akanland there existed a continuous demand for labor among the rich and powerful (Akan: *abirempon;* sing., *obirempon*) for a period of possibly two hundred years or more. One study suggests that the demand for slaves was largely initiated not only by the requirements of the gold mining industry but by large-scale forest clearance in the Pra-Ofin river basin. Imported slaves were employed in creating farmland, which formed the productive base for a new kind of city-state polity—the *abirempondom*—in the central forest zone. The *abirem-*

A sixteenth-century illustration depicts the Fort of St. George at Elmina. [Library of Congress/Corbis]

pon are to be identified with the expanding fifteenth- and sixteenth-century "frontier" of specialized production: agriculture and gold. For the period 1500 to 1535, it has been estimated that the Portuguese imported 10,000 to 12,000 slaves into São Jorge. Benin and Igboland were among the main sources of this labor for a period of perhaps a century or more. In the case of Igboland, the long-distance trade in slaves dates back to the ninth century.

Akanland belonged to another prestige-goods network. In the fifteenth century and earlier it produced gold for the urban markets of the middle and upper Niger valley trading centers and received in exchange from Muslim Wangara caravan merchants slaves, Saharan salt, and other valued commodities. Wangara capital investments facilitated the emergence of the *abirempondom.* The wealth and presence of the Akan principalities were at the endpoint of the overland gold route from the middle Niger city of Jenne. This route transformed particular local "deep rural" communities into entrepôt towns—that is, market and administrative centers—for the Sudanic gold trade. The high-consumption culture of the towns' rich and powerful people was dependent on servile labor and, hence, on the importation of slaves from Benin, the Niger Delta-Igboland region, and Allada. Akanland was the meeting point of two long-distance prestige-goods networks. In the sixteenth and seventeenth centuries the reproduction of elite economic and political power was heavily dependent on servile labor, as producers and as household and court servants or attendants. The elite of central Akanland ruled slave-owning polities and communities.

Asante (Ashanti)

Several *abirempon*-dominated polities merged in the early 1680s to give rise to the Asante confederation. By this time, the Portuguese had been superseded on the Gold Coast by agents of Danish, Dutch, English, and other European trading companies. These had established trading stations in the various towns on the littoral. Beginning in the 1690s and continuing through the first half of the eighteenth century the federated Asante kingdom entered a period of territorial conquest, southward toward the coastal entrepôt towns and northward toward the Muslim market centers in the southern savanna. As it created a political-military network under its authority, Kumase (the capital) and other towns of central Asante acquired an extensive hinterland. Throughout the eighteenth century Asante traders and office-holders sold thousands of war prisoners at the European commercial posts in the entrepôt towns.

Within central Asante the state apparatus underwent a series of reforms from the second half of the eighteenth through the mid-nineteenth century. New political and military posts were created as Asante rulers expanded the scale of government through a process referred to by one historian as "bureaucratization." This process was linked to policies of royal centralization and to the "rationalization" of the state's political-military and information networks. One of its effects was a reduction in the political influence of the hereditary aristocracy and their replacement by royally appointed persons descended from slaves (and also from commoners). At the same time, new trading-administrative centers were founded in the provinces, each with its rural hinterland of slave and peasant-farmer producers. The different grades of servile status reflected the different social conditions of bondage that existed in eighteenth- and nineteenth-century Asante. These included: (1) *awowa*, one who had been placed as security in the hands of a creditor (pawn); (2) *akoa pa*, one who had been enslaved for criminal or antisocial activities; (3) *domum*, a war prisoner or one who had been received as part of a tribute payment; and (4) *odonko*, a slave sold or bought in the open market. These statuses predated the rise of Asante. The urban economy expanded relatively rapidly between 1750 and 1874 as increasingly large concentrations of wealth built up in the hands of officeholders and the rich. One consequence was that greater reliance was placed on the production and services of slaves and pawns.

In the nineteenth century the possession of slaves and pawns by matrilineages and commoner families became increasingly widespread in Asante. This was another consequence of the expansion of the urban economy, which allowed "ordinary" people to enter international markets through the Asante version of "legitimate commerce." The slaves were bought in the various Asante markets, but some were acquired through the patronage of an officeholder. Slaves were employed in the production of kola nuts, gold, and, from the 1880s, rubber. The descendants of these slaves were incorporated as cadet members of families and lineages. In the post-Atlantic slave trade economy of Asante, commoners' accumulation of slaves and other forms of wealth involved a relative decline in officeholders' share in foreign trade and general wealth. The abolition of slavery followed the establishment of British colonial rule in 1902.

Benin

The expansionist Benin kingdom of the fifteenth and sixteenth centuries had a great urban capital, a powerful dynastic monarchy, social and political hierarchies, large central markets, and a well-organized army. In and around the capital and in various parts of the kingdom and its tributaries were monumental constructions of different kinds. These societal features, linked to political-military, prestige-goods, and bulk-goods networks, presuppose the existence of a slave labor force. In the fifteenth and early sixteenth century the trading associations of Benin maintained a flourishing trade in slaves (and other commodities). By 1516 there were specific markets for male and female slaves. One result was a restriction on the export of male slaves, which in a few years developed into a total embargo. The prohibition—which, according to one interpretation, was based on indigenous religious precepts—remained in force for nearly two centuries. Compared with other Lower Guinea polities, Benin was never an active participant in the Atlantic slave trade.

War captives were usually the property of the king. However, most of them were allocated to military officers or to titled officeholders whom the king wished to reward. The ruler and the ranking military and political officials used their slaves to establish villages and farm centers that produced provisions for the masters' households. Although the villages or farm centers began by serving their founder, over time they attained the position of independent villages; that is, they paid their taxes directly to the king and not through their original founders (or their founders' families). The descendants of an original slave village eventually attained free status and merged with the population of free peasant-farmers. Emancipated slaves were eligible for admission into the urban-based craft guilds, particularly those that were waning in strength and numbers. When the king wished to form a new guild, freed slaves were placed in it. The descendants of slaves were incorporated into the population of free peasant-cultivators and artisans. The slave population, however, continued to be renewed, either through warfare or by purchase. One midcentury ruler, for example, is said to have purchased many slaves and to have founded many towns and villages for them to dwell in. For the most part, slave ownership was confined to the elite—royals, nobles, and rich commoners. Since the fifteenth century, Benin appears to have been a society with slaves rather than a slave-based society.

Wealthy privileged slaves served the Benin monarchy in different capacities. Slave officials were employed in various roles in the palace bureaucracies of the royal court. Such persons could also own slaves. Rulers were continually creating new titles in order to strengthen their positions vis-à-vis competing noble

In a depiction from the early eighteenth century, the Benin king stands next to two guards as a troop of soldiers on horseback marches past behind them. [Library of Congress/Corbis]

lineages, to weaken the influence and authority of great hereditary officials, and to reward their supporters. Slave officeholders played an important role in the royal policies of centralization.

During the era of "legitimate commerce" in the nineteenth century, Benin faced civil war, the loss of territory, general political and economic decline, and external military threats. It did not benefit in any significant way from the growth and development of the palm oil trade in neighboring countries. In 1897 the kingdom of Benin was conquered by a British expeditionary force and was incorporated into the emergent colony of Nigeria.

Igboland

Fifteenth-century Igboland exported slaves (and other goods) to the Gold Coast and was, thus, a participant in a long-range prestige-goods network. However, it is less clear what the role of slaves within the area might have been. Given the historical significance of expanding agricultural production, and increasing specialization in food crop production, and the need for labor by successful and wealthy farming families, slaves must have played a vital role in farmwork. However, until the later eighteenth or early nineteenth century, slave labor would seem to have supplemented rather than supplanted the labor of the freeborn. Pre-seventeenth-century Igboland would have been largely communities with slaves with relatively few slave-based communities. Perhaps a more important source of labor for rich farmers prior to 1600 was debt bondage: a debtor repaid an obligation with labor until the loan was repaid. This would have meant temporary servitude.

In the seventeenth and eighteenth centuries Igbo-speaking professional trading groups widened their business horizons, expanded the range of goods they handled, improved their organizational structure, and developed specialist services as smiths or as religious and medical specialists. Each trading group, like the Aro and the Awka, was associated with a particular shrine and its oracle. These groups did not seek to create large state systems comparable to Benin or Asante; rather, they sought to exercise control over different kinds of networks—prestige goods, bulk goods, and information (or culture)—and to expand these networks through alliances of different kinds and occasionally through warfare.

By the eighteenth century slaves had become the most important export of Igboland. The merchant specialists profited immensely from the traffic in slaves, gaining wealth and social ascendancy in the process. They established trading towns and collecting centers and promoted the prestige and influence of their particular shrine-oracles, for which they served as priestly agents. They encouraged the expansion of agricultural production through the introduction of new crops. Part of this production fed slaves during the Middle Passage. The trading groups would seem to have formed the social core of a kind of mercantile "commonwealth," or socioeconomic federation, in Igboland to which different groups—lineage, artisanal, military, titled, cult—made contributions. The traders owned numerous slaves, requiring slaves as porters, farm laborers, servants, attendants, and shrine functionaries, and as sacrifices on ritual occasions. Eighteenth-century Igboland had become a region of slave-based communities.

There were two classes of slaves: the *ohu* (also *oro* and *olu:* ordinary slaves), who had none of the rights of the freeborn, but were not socially loathed; and the *osu* (ritual slaves), who also lacked the rights of the freeborn and were abhorred as social pariahs. Enslavement could be a consequence of war, kidnapping, religious sanctions, or judicial sentencing. Slaves were bought, sold, and disposed of like any other property of a freeborn person.

The *ohu* were employed as domestic servants, soldiers, traders, and farm laborers. They could own property and even purchase slaves who would work for the owners as surrogates so that the slaveowners could pursue other economic activities. In some communities, slaves could redeem themselves if they had the means to do so; in others, manumission was not an option. A slave could not marry a freeborn person. In the eighteenth century in some parts of Igboland, segregated slave villages were placed around farmlands as sentries to watch out for raiders and armies. The slaves cultivated the land but were not permitted to carry weapons or to use them in defense of their masters' farms. In some places, they were incorporated into lineages as "pseudo kin." As permanent servile members of their owners' lineages, slaves had to work for their masters and had to subscribe to distinct ritual obligations and social restrictions and prohibitions.

The *osu* were attached to religious shrines, were dedicated to a god or goddess, and worked at the shrines as priests or priestesses, diviners, or prophets. They either assumed this role voluntarily or took the status by seeking refuge at a shrine to avoid being sold into Atlantic slavery. The shrines were, therefore, sanctuaries. The status of an *osu* was lifelong and hereditary. *Osu* were free to earn their living as they chose, and they often became wealthy. They were used to collect taxes on behalf of their particular shrine. Socially, they were at the bottom of society with no possibility of upward social mobility; they were shunned by the freeborn as "horrible and holy." They could marry only other *osu*. The Aro trading group included freeborn high priests who were responsible for the Aro Chukwu oracle-shrine. The religious functions of the *osu,* who served under them, were compatible with their status as property servicing the (ritual and religious) needs of the freeborn. The use of slaves permitted the delegation of powerful ritual and "metaphysical" powers to a politically and socially marginal group, thus ideologically and structurally separating the spiritual realm from secular political and social struggles.

In the eighteenth century wealthy families of merchant-farmers emerged as a new social class in the village-groups. For such families, slaves were an asset, a sign of wealth and status; they increased the size and reproductive power of a lineage. They also produced surplus food staples for local markets. With the rise of "legitimate trade" in the first half of the nineteenth century and the growing demand for palm oil and palm kernels in Europe, such families prospered. Palm oil plantations worked entirely by slave labor were set up in increasing numbers in the nineteenth century. Large retinues of slaves were deployed to transport tons of palm oil to the entrepôts. The labor-intensive nature of palm oil processing and transport stimulated the growth of domestic slavery among elite and nonelite alike. In some of the palm oil–producing districts slaves outnumbered the freeborn. The British military conquest of Igboland occurred between 1900 and 1920, and the abolition of slavery followed the imposition of British colonial rule.

Dahomey

Founded in the early seventeenth century, Dahomey became a recognized military power following its conquest of the coastal Allada and the Savi-Hueda kingdoms in the 1720s. In the course of the seventeenth century the kingdom had expanded from eighteen "countries," grouped around the capital Agbomey, to forty-two "countries" by the beginning of the eighteenth. In spite of its local military successes Dahomey itself became a tributary of the powerful expanding Oyo empire in the 1730s, and it remained subject to that state until the early 1820s. However, political subordination to Oyo did not put an end to the raids and military campaigns of the Dahomey army into neighboring polities.

Coercive state organizations such as the army and judicial courts functioned as instruments of enslavement. Male and female slaves were also bought from Hausa, Bariba, and Yoruba merchants from polities north of Dahomey. With respect to the slaves who were not sold to the European factors in the coastal entrepôts, the military and political elite and rich traders employed them as farm laborers, servants and attendants, concubines and wives, domestics in service to a deity, and sacrifices for ritual executions. The descendants of servants and attendants and of concubines and wives were incorporated into the families and lineages of their owners.

The great private merchants ("merchant-nobles"), who dominated Dahomey's export of slaves, owned large agricultural estates worked by slave labor. The produce supported the owners' households and was sold on local markets and to the slave ships. In the nineteenth century, these estates produced palm oil for export to Europe. The Dahomey state was also directly engaged in the production of food, both for consumption by the royal court establishment and for sale. In the eighteenth century slave labor was employed on the large royal plantations near Agbomey to produce provisions for the royal household. In the nineteenth new plantations were set up for the purpose of producing palm oil for export to Europe. The majority of slaves in Dahomey were engaged in agricultural production on state-owned plantations or on the family estates of rich merchant-farmers. The social situation of these slaves was hereditary: their descendants were also slaves. Nineteenth-century peasant communities also produced palm oil for export, but apparently without reliance on the labor of slaves or pawns. Instead, they developed a collective work organization (of free cultivators) which was known as *dokpwe*. The palm oil trade did not lead to the spread of slavery among free rural cultivators. In 1892–1893 France conquered Dahomey and slavery was abolished with the formal establishment of French rule.

See also ENSLAVEMENT, METHODS OF; HUMAN SACRIFICE; MANUMISSION; MAROONS; PORTUGAL.

An engraving from The History of Dahomey *depicts the celebratory preparation for human sacrifice.* [Historical Picture Archive/Corbis]

BIBLIOGRAPHY

AFIGBO, ADIECE. *Ropes of Sand. Studies in Igbo History and Culture.* 1981.

AKINJOGBIN, I. A. *Dahomey and Its Neighbours, 1708–1818.* 1967.

AKINJOGBIN, I. A., and S. O. OSOBA, eds. *Topics on Nigerian Economic and Social History.* 1980.

AUSTIN, GARETH. "'No Elders Were Present': Commoners and Private Ownership in Asante, 1807–1896." *Journal of African History* 37, no. 1 (1996): 1–30.

BROWN, CAROLYN A. "Testing the Boundaries of Marginality: Twentieth-Century Slavery and Emancipation Struggles in Nkanu, Northern Igboland, 1920–1929." *Journal of African History* 33, no. 1 (1996): 51–80.

COQUERY-VIDROVITCH, CATHERINE. "De la trait des esclaves à l'exportation del'huile de palm et des palmistes au Dahomey." In *The Development of Indigenous Trade and Markets in West Africa*, edited by Claude Meillassoux. 1971; pp. 107–123.

GLELE, MAURICE A. *Le Danxome. Du Pouvir Aja à La Nation Fon.* 1974.

ISICHEI, ELIZABETH. *A History of Nigeria.* 1983. Reprint, 1984.

OLANIYAN, RICHARD, ed. *Nigerian History and Culture.* 1985.

RYDER, ALAN. *Benin and the Europeans, 1485–1897.* 1969.
WILKS, IVOR. *Asante in the Nineteenth Century: The Structure and Evolution of a Political Order.* 1975.
———. *Forests of God.* 1993.

Ray A. Kea

Sokoto Caliphate

Slavery in the Sokoto caliphate, centered in modern northern Nigeria, was closely associated with the origins of the state. Founded as a result of a jihad that took place between 1804 and 1808, the Sokoto caliphate came into being as loose confederation of emirates owing allegiance to the spiritual and intellectual founder of this Islamic reform movement, Shehu Usman dan Fodio (1758–1817). Before the outbreak of the jihad, the shehu, his brother Abdullahi dan Fodio, and his son, Muhammad Bello (first caliph, 1817–1837) protested the enslavement of Muslims by the Hausa rulers of the region and restrictions on enslaved Muslims escaping to sanctuaries offered by the shehu and his followers; but subsequently the realities of political power and the inability to resolve labor problems without using slaves comprised this early concern over issues of freedom.

Caliph Muhammad Bello is associated with the stabilization of the jihad regime through social and economic policies that relied on settlement and assimilation of non-Muslim slaves. Inevitably, Muslims whose religious credentials were in doubt were also enslaved. The caliphate faced a contradiction involving the pursuit of jihad and the corresponding advancement of the boundaries of Islam, on the one hand, and the reliance on slavery as a means of conversion, on the other. The caliphate as a state encouraged enslavement and a reliance on slave labor through tribute requirements, credit and trade, military and administrative structures, procreation, and production. Slavery permeated the caliphate's society and economy. The aristocracy descended from the founding generation of jihadists, many of whom claimed Fulbe ancestors, those whose forebears had immigrated from the Senegambia region of the far western Sudan. The local Hausa term for these Fulbe was Fulani. The aristocracy in fact had a mixed ancestry and became more mixed through union with non-Fulbe slave concubines. Moreover, power was exercised through royal slaves, who acquired a degree of affluence, learning, and Islamic culture similar to that of the mamluks and janissaries in the contemporary Ottoman Empire. Slavery was royal and sexual, reinforcing military and aristocratic authority arising from Islamic traditions.

The Sokoto caliphate was also a slave society, in which much of the agricultural sector was organized around large concentrations of slaves working in conditions similar to slave plantations elsewhere. Probably a majority of slaves worked on farms and large estates, especially those belonging to the aristocracy, but also including many belonging to merchants and craftsmen. Annual slave raids, tribute in slaves, and the products of slave labor were essential to the prosperity and position of the aristocracy and the merchant class. Although it was not common, some aristocratic women owned estates with slaves, and certainly the more prosperous women and the wives of prosperous men had slaves as domestics.

The slave trade was an integral part of the caliphate's political economy. In the course of the nineteenth century, thousands of slaves were exported each year from the caliphate, including those, largely women and children, sent north into and across the Sahara as well as others, mostly males, sent south to the Guinea coast. Slaves from the Sokoto caliphate and the central Sudan in general were concentrated in Bahia, in northeastern Brazil. Slaves from the central Sudan were also found in the various Yoruba states, Dahomey, and Asante in West Africa. Because of the antislave trade activities of the British navy, liberated slaves from the central Sudan were also settled in Sierra Leone. Slaves who attained their freedom in Brazil and those who were liberated in Sierra Leone maintained connections with the central Sudan via the ports of the Bight of Benin. European abolition had its impact on the central Sudan through the commercial and cultural activities of these former slaves.

Through its wars of expansion, the Sokoto caliphate came to have one of the largest slave populations of any country in modern history. As many as 2.5 million people were slaves in 1900, perhaps a quarter of its total population. In the heavily populated districts around Sokoto, the great majority of the population were slaves. In Kano, the most densely populated emirate, perhaps half the population were slaves. In addition to the importance of slaves in agriculture, they were often allowed, even required, to work on their own account in the nonagricultural season, thereby securing for their masters a regular weekly or monthly cash payment in the cowrie currency of the caliphate. This opportunity for amelioration worked well in prosperous times, but bad health and famine often kept slaves dependent on their masters. Even freed slaves usually maintained ties of dependency with their former masters.

Slavery in Sokoto expanded in the course of the nineteenth century, despite the initial abolitionist nod toward protecting enslaved Muslims. Because the jihad spread throughout the central Sudan, many slaves who identified themselves as Muslims fled to camps of the jihadists and thereby became free—indeed, positioned to acquire booty to start a new life. After Usman dan Fodio launched his campaign in the Hausa state Gobir, the jihad spread westward as far as Massina in the middle Niger basin south of Timbuktu and southeastward to the highlands inland from the Bight of Biafra, from modern Mali to the Central African Republic. The shehu issued official flags to Muslims, usually Fulbe, who were staging loyal uprisings in Hausa states other than Gobir, thereby promoting the idea of an Islamic polity that transcended the boundaries of the old political order. Beyond the Hausa states of Kano, Katsina, Zazzau, Daura, and Kebbi, the jihad quickly spread to Borno, Nupe, Oyo, and the decentralized territories beyond these states.

Slaves in the Islamic polity of the Sokoto caliphate were by law property. The Islamic court system and the official correspondence among emirates within the caliphate operated to restrain the movements of slaves, defining their status in terms of religion and legal position, and this allowed masters to exploit the labor and the bodies of their slaves. Although some slaves were badly abused, religious orthodoxy, literary tradition, and local custom mitigated against overly harsh treatment, and encouraged the emancipation of slaves through deathbed grants and other pious acts and by allowing slaves themselves, their relatives, or other third parties to pay a ransom. The ideology of Islamic society promoted conversion and public religious observance. Nonetheless, some slaves ran away and otherwise resisted their enslavement. Acts of violence, including the assassination of masters by concubines, are well documented.

Except in the early years of the caliphate, when newly enslaved individuals were often Hausa in origin, slaves were often ethnically different from the predominant Hausa population and almost never ethnically identical with the ruling Fulani, or Fulbe. Slavery was a status associated with Habe, that is, the non-Fulbe. Consequently, ethnic origins were a factor in social control; designations such as Gwari, Warjawa, and Tangali indicated "pagan" or "niam niam" status as legitimate objects of enslavement.

The imposition of European colonial rule—British, French, or German in different parts of the former caliphate—undermined the slave economy of the Sokoto caliphate and challenged the primacy of slavery in determining social relations. To limit slavery, each colonial regime imposed its own solution with varying results. The majority of the soldiers conscripted into the European armies of conquest and occupation were in fact former slaves—often fugitives. Many slaves, perhaps several hundred thousand, fled their masters with the onset of colonial occupation. Female slaves frequently ran away to military barracks, seeking ties to males other than those imposed on them through slavery. The majority of slaves, nonetheless, stayed with their masters.

The colonial regimes tried to minimize the social impact of conquest because of threatened disorder and potentially higher costs that would inevitably result in quelling such disorders. The pervasiveness of slavery was clearly recognized, but slaves were not emancipated. Instead, enslavement and slave trading were made illegal, and children born under colonial rule were considered free. Slavery was "reformed" into extinction. Although officially committed to abolition, colonial governments overlooked many abuses. German Kamerun permitted local Muslim rulers to raid for slaves until 1914, and raiding continued even after British occupation of German territory in World War I. The Protectorate of Northern Nigeria stopped these raids for good in the early 1920s, but kidnapping remained common in some non-Muslim areas into the 1930s. In British portions of the Sokoto caliphate, the legal status of slavery was not formally abolished for all individuals until 1936, and Islamic courts continued to sanction slavery for several decades under colonial rule. As new slaves became hard to get, the conditions of slavery gradually improved, but slavery did not end. The colonial emphasis was conservative, attempting to eliminate the sources of slaves while allowing aristocrats to retain their large slave estates. Individuals with royal slave status dominated local administration, despite British efforts to limit their influence, and many ex-slaves continued to work on the plantations of their former masters until recent decades.

See also ISLAM; PLANTATIONS.

BIBLIOGRAPHY

LOVEJOY, PAUL E. "Slavery in the Sokoto Caliphate." In *The Ideology of Slavery in Africa*, edited by Paul E. Lovejoy. 1981.

LOVEJOY, PAUL E., and JAN HOGENDORN. *Slow Death for Slavery: The Course of Abolition in Northern Nigeria*. 1993.

MACK, BEVERLY. "Women and Slavery in Nineteenth-Century Hausaland." *Slavery and Abolition* 13 (1992).

MASON, MICHAEL. "Captive and Client Labour and the Economy of Bida Emirate, 1857–1901." *Journal of African History* 14, no. 4 (1973): 453–471.

O'HEAR, ANN. *Power Relations in Nigeria: Ilorin Slaves and Their Successors*. 1997.

Paul E. Lovejoy

West Virginia

Although slavery existed in the western part of Virginia, the people there were hostile toward the institution. People in the western counties were completely isolated, self-sufficient, and engaged in few activities that would profit from slave labor. The Piedmont region was thinly populated, and its backwoods farmers resented the wealth and political power of the slavocracy to the east. As early as 1830 representatives from western Virginia favored gradual emancipation of the slaves. Blacks composed about 20 percent of the population by 1860, with the largest black populations in Jefferson and Berkeley counties. Nearly one-third of the population near Harpers Ferry (where John Brown's raid took place) was black. Greenbrier, Hampshire, Hardy, and Monroe County had over 1,000 slaves each. The region's population in 1860 was 424,033 whites and 17,980 blacks, including 3,000 free persons of color. Slaves worked in the orchards, in coal and salt mines, on small farms, and in shops and homes.

West Virginia was not among the slave states in 1860 and did not exist as a state until the Civil War. On 11 May 1861 a convention at Wheeling—the western terminus of a railroad—repudiated the ordinance of secession that had been passed in a Virginia convention the previous April. Congress approved the petition of West Virginia to be admitted as a state on 10 December 1862, President Lincoln signed the bill on 19 April 1863, and the thirty-fifth state entered the Union on 20 June 1863. Although the 1863 constitution of West Virginia mandated gradual emancipation of the slaves, the white citizens mostly remained hostile toward freed slaves. Some 196 black West Virginians served in the Union army, but many freedmen left West Virginia when the army gave them permission to do so.

See also BROWN, JOHN; VIRGINIA.

BIBLIOGRAPHY

BALLAGH, JAMES C. *A History of Slavery in Virginia.* 1902.
EMMERTH, BARBARA L. "Slavery in Present West Virginia in 1860." *West Virginia History* 21 (1960): 275–277.
The Negro in the United States, 1790–1915. 1968. For statistics on the black population.

Federal troops storming the engine house at Harpers Ferry arsenal succeed in capturing John Brown and his men. [Corbis-Bettmann]

RAWICK, GEORGE P., ed. *The American Slave: A Composite Autobiography*. 41 vols. 1972–1979. See vol. 16 for Virginia slave narratives.

RICE, OTIS K. *West Virginia: A History*. 1985.

SQUIRES, WILLIAM H. T. *Unleashed at Long Last: Reconstruction in Virginia*. 1939. Reprint, 1970.

Bobby L. Lovett

Wet Nurses

Wet nurses suckle infants other than their own. Since ancient times wet nurses have been employed by new mothers. In the Old Testament Pharaoh's daughter hired a nurse for the infant Moses. In Egypt freeborn and slave women alike contracted to provide infants with "milk pure and untainted" in return for payment. In ancient Greece wet nurses were often slaves, entrusted with the total care of children in their charge. Free women also nursed, and enslaved nurses could earn their freedom. Not all wealthy women employed wet nurses; Roman mothers of all classes were encouraged to breast-feed. In most societies lactating women (whether mothers or wet nurses) were held in high regard since the survival of infants depended on them.

While historians have long believed that breast-feeding in the U.S. South was delegated to slaves, new research indicates that white women often nursed their own babies. In *Motherhood in the Old South* (1990) Sally G. McMillen argues that "a large proportion of middle- and upper-class southern women breast-fed their infants." Motivation to breast-feed was twofold: to promote children's health and to fulfill the maternal duties outlined in prescriptive literature. McMillen's examination of the letters and journals of southern women suggests that more than 85 percent of white mothers breast-fed their own children, handing their care over to slave nurses after the dangerous process of weaning had been accomplished.

Nineteenth-century travelers from the northern United States and Great Britain unfamiliar with the sight may have paid disproportionate attention to the suckling of white infants by slaves, thereby overstating the wet nurse's role. Interviews with former slaves contain little evidence of widespread wet-nursing, but some slaves, like Irene Robertson of Arkansas, remembered being "suckled . . . together" with a master's child whose mother had fallen ill.

Although Carl Degler and Orville Vernon Burton agree that women usually breast-fed their own infants, other historians like W. E. B. Du Bois and Eugene Genovese argue that slaves were of critical importance as wet nurses. While further research is needed to shed additional light on this important aspect of life for black and white women, it is certain that breast-feeding played an essential role in a baby's survival.

See also HOUSEHOLD SLAVES; SLAVERY AND CHILDHOOD.

BIBLIOGRAPHY

BURTON, ORVILLE VERNON. *In My Father's House Are Many Mansions: Family and Community in Edgefield, South Carolina*. 1985.

FILDES, VALERIE. *Breasts, Bottles, and Babies: A History of Infant Feeding*. 1986.

———. *Wet Nursing: A History from Antiquity to the Present*. 1988.

GENOVESE, EUGENE. *Roll, Jordan, Roll: The World the Slaves Made*. 1974.

MCMILLEN, SALLY G. *Motherhood in the Old South: Pregnancy, Childbirth, and Infant Rearing*. 1990. See especially Chapter 5, "So Sweet an Office: Maternal Breast-Feeding," and Table 4 in Appendix 1, "Infant-Feeding Practices."

POMEROY, SARAH B. *Goddesses, Whores, Wives, and Slaves: Women in Classical Antiquity*. 1975.

RAWICK, GEORGE P., ed. *The American Slave: A Composite Autobiography*. Vol. 10 (*Arkansas*), Part 5, p. 334.

Jennifer Davis McDaid

Wheatley, Phillis   [ca. 1753–1784]

U.S. slave and poet.

Born in West Africa, Phillis Wheatley was enslaved in 1761 and purchased by John Wheatley, a merchant tailor in Boston, Massachusetts, who apparently named her after the slave ship in which she arrived. She quickly learned to speak English and within sixteen months her master's family, who practically made her one of them, had taught her how to read the Bible. By 1765 she had taught herself to write, and in 1766 she began composing poetry in the style of the noted English poets Alexander Pope and Thomas Gray. In 1770, with the financial assistance of her master, she published "An Elegiac Poem, on the Death of the Celebrated Divine . . . George Whitefield."

Shortly thereafter Wheatley began corresponding with Selina Hastings, the Countess of Huntingdon, and several members of her coterie. In 1773 she visited England with Nathaniel Wheatley, her master's son; while there she created a sensation in London polite society. Later that year Lady Huntingdon sponsored the publication of Wheatley's *Poems on Various Subjects, Religious and Moral*, which inspired her master to emancipate her. By 1776, the year she dedicated a poem to General George Washington, she had earned a reputation throughout England and portions of British North America. Her work drew the praise of the *Boston Gazette* and the French philosopher Voltaire.

Phillis Wheatley. [Corbis-Bettmann]

Not surprisingly, given her upbringing and New England background, Wheatley's work dealt mostly with religious topics. Although lacking in originality, her work was equal to that of any colonial poet of the day. By 1800 her book of her poems had gone through five editions; it was republished in 1834 by abolitionists to prove that blacks were capable of attaining the same refined development and intellectual accomplishments as whites.

See also LITERATURE OF SLAVERY; SLAVE NARRATIVES.

BIBLIOGRAPHY

ROBINSON, WILLIAM H. *Phillis Wheatley and Her Writings.* 1984.

Charles W. Carey Jr.

Whips

See Discipline and Punishment.

White Slavery

White slavery has two meanings. It was the term commonly used in the past in the Western world to denote forced prostitution. This term had the advantage of branding forced prostitution as slavery, while dis-
tinguishing it from the slavery into which millions of Africans had been consigned. Under this name forced prostitution was widely attacked in the late nineteenth and early twentieth centuries by social reformers. Women and girls were warned of the danger of being kidnapped and sold into the "white slave trade." The term was a misnomer, as females of all races, including Africans could be forced into prostitution.

The term *white slave* was more correctly used in the nineteenth century to denote the non-African slaves of both sexes, many of them Georgians or Circassians, sold to the Muslim world. The most attractive of the girls were destined to be the concubines of the rich and often became mothers of rulers, while the boys became army officers, officials of state, or companions for the sons of the rich or they were employed in other positions of trust. Some were procured by raids and sold as captives. Often the Circassians were slaves in their homeland and were sold by their owners; sometimes they were free children sold by their parents, who believed that they were sending them to a more secure and privileged life. To enhance their chances, these children might be trained in domestic skills and taught to read the Koran.

This traffic in non-African slaves was attacked by the British and French in the 1850s during the Crimean War, when they were defending the Ottoman Empire against Russian encroachment and found that the slave trade across the Black Sea was alienating public opinion and endangering their alliance with the Turks. The sultan issued a law against the trade in 1854, and in the years that followed, both Russia and Turkey took steps to end the traffic of Georgians, who were Christian, and thus were wanted in the Russian but not the Ottoman Empire. Conversely, the Circassians, as Muslims, were not wanted in the Russian Empire, and as the Russians conquered the Caucasus in the 1860s, they forced half a million Circassians to emigrate to the Ottoman Empire. These immigrants included 150,000 slaves, many of whom were sold by their owners, while many destitute peasants also sold their children.

The result was a lively traffic in Circassian girls, many of them transported across the Black Sea in European steamers, bound for the harems of the Muslim world. The greatest buyers were the sultan and his officials; they bought good-looking girls over fourteen, who could be "socialized" in their harems. By the 1890s, however, this traffic had declined, as the Turks took steps to free slaves and depression reduced the buying power of the Ottoman elite. This branch of the slave trade thus petered out, and the demand for exotic girls was met from other areas of the world.

See also HAREM; OTTOMAN EMPIRE; PROSTITUTION.

BIBLIOGRAPHY

TOLEDANO, EHUD R. *Slavery and Abolition in the Ottoman Middle East.* 1997.
WORKING GROUP ON CONTEMPORARY FORMS OF SLAVERY. *Reports.* 1975–continuing.

Suzanne Miers

Whitney, Eli   [1765–1825]

U.S. inventor.

In 1792 Eli Whitney, who was born in Connecticut, moved to South Carolina to study law while working as a tutor. En route he met Catherine Greene, a plantation owner and widow of General Nathaniel Greene, who took him in when his tutoring position fell through. He showed his gratitude by using his natural mechanical abilities to fix things around the plantation. Impressed with his skill, Greene suggested that he invent a machine to remove the seeds from short-staple cotton. At the time this product was in great demand in English textile mills, a demand southern planters could not satisfy because it took one full day of manual labor to clean one pound of short-staple cotton. Within days Whitney developed the first prototype of the cotton gin (short for "engine"), a device that separated seeds from fibers by means of a wire-studded revolving cylinder. In 1793 he perfected this invention so that it could clean fifty pounds of cotton per day.

The cotton gin revolutionized southern agriculture by making possible the expansion of King Cotton and his loyal courtier, Slavery, into the rich bottom lands of the lower South. Prior to Whitney's invention, the United States exported less than 200,000 pounds of cotton yearly; by 1800 that figure had risen to almost 18 million pounds with an equal amount being processed in domestic mills. Ironically, Whitney profited not at all from his invention. Although he obtained a patent in 1794, southern courts refused to indict the builders of rival machines or the planters who purchased them. In 1802 South Carolina paid him a modest sum for the patent rights on behalf of

A replica of the cotton gin built by Eli Whitney in 1793. [Corbis-Bettmann]

its planters, as did Georgia, North Carolina, and Tennessee in later years. Altogether he received about $90,000 from these settlements, almost all of which went to pay legal fees.

Although Whitney's cotton gin did not "save" slavery in the United States—the institution was a lucrative practice for American slave owners throughout its history—it contributed materially to the spread of slavery and its entrenchment throughout the South.

See also PLANTATIONS; UNITED STATES.

BIBLIOGRAPHY

MIRSKY, JEANNETTE, and ALLAN NEVINS. *The World of Eli Whitney.* 1952.

Charles W. Carey Jr.

Wilberforce, William   [1759–1833]

British abolitionist.

William Wilberforce was born in Hull, Yorkshire, England, and served as a member of the House of Commons from 1780 to 1825. Following his conversion to evangelical Christianity in 1784, he became a leader of the movement in Parliament to abolish the slave trade. In 1787 he helped to found the Society for

A monument to William Wilberforce. [Angelo Hornak/ Corbis]

Effecting the Abolition of the Slave Trade, also known as the Anti-Slavery Society, and in 1791 he worked to make Sierra Leone a refuge for freed slaves. Most important, he served as the movement's chief debater and strategist in Commons, where he introduced a number of bills to curtail or restrict the participation of British subjects in the slave trade. After almost getting the slave trade abolished in 1796, he finally succeeded in 1807, the same year that the U.S. Congress forbade the importation of slaves into the United States. In that year Parliament passed his bill to abolish the slave trade between Africa and the British West Indies.

Wilberforce then turned his attention to ameliorating the lot of West Indian slaves. In 1815, this effort having achieved no results, he began a parliamentary campaign for complete emancipation. In 1823 he helped to found the Society for the Mitigation and Gradual Abolition of Slavery Throughout the British Dominions—again, also known as the Anti-Slavery Society—and published *Appeal to the Religion, Justice, and Humanity of the Inhabitants of the British Empire on Behalf of the Negro Slaves in the West Indies.* In 1833, shortly after his death, Parliament passed the Slavery Abolition Act, which emancipated all slaves in British colonies.

See also ABOLITION AND ANTISLAVERY MOVEMENTS.

BIBLIOGRAPHY

POLLOCK, JOHN. *Wilberforce.* 1977.

Charles W. Carey Jr.

Williams Thesis

First published more than fifty years ago (1944), *Capitalism and Slavery* by Eric Williams remains central to any discussion of the relation of plantation slavery in the West Indies to the historical development of Europe, North and South America, and Africa.

The Williams thesis comprises three separate themes: (1) modern slavery is economic in origin and not a consequence of race; (2) the English industrial revolution was financed from the profits of the slave trade and the plantation economy; and (3) the British slave trade and colonial slavery ended not because of British humanitarianism but because they conflicted with economic interests.

Mainstream American scholars, including Henry Steele Commager, Frank Pitman, and Lowell T. Ragatz, were warmly favorable to the book, though Pitman found that it contained little that was new. Indeed, standard history textbooks of the time taught that in the eighteenth century colonies mattered a lot to Europe, and slave colonies mattered most. English scholars such as Roger T. Anstey, J. D. Fage, and Douglas Fairlie opposed the thesis, emphasizing Williams's roots as a radical black colonial and accusing him of crude economic determinism; meanwhile they defended British humanitarianism.

Others criticized Williams's economic arguments. Some held that the ratio of the value of the slave trade and the plantation economy to British income and investment were too small to matter (Engerman). Others argued that Williams overestimated the importance of slavery through incorrect measurement (Thomas); or that Williams underestimated the importance of slavery in his view of "decline" (Drescher, Eltis). Debate has continued as more archival material and modern economic analysis and statistical techniques have become available.

Today these theses of Williams have both supporters and critics, but there may be grounds for thinking that a broad consensus exists: that Williams was excessive in his claims and incorrect in some of his arguments but sound in his intuition and his grasp of his subject. Thus it is the direction of his thinking and not the credibility of his detailed arguments that maintains his importance.

The view of slavery as an economic phenomenon commands widespread acceptance and has largely supplanted earlier notions that modern slavery is explained by race, climate, and geography. Racism is now widely seen as resulting from political and economic power relations, rather than some inherent characteristic of blacks.

The Williams thesis portrayed the West Indian slave economies as having been central to the Atlantic trading system from the later seventeenth to the early nineteenth century. Further, Williams argued that this Atlantic system had an important impact on European and North American—and especially British—economic development and industrialization. (Bailey, Engerman and O'Brien, Inikori, Richardson, Sheridan, Solow). He does not deny the endogenous roots of the British industrial revolution, but claims only that the Atlantic trade accelerated its timing and affected its pattern.

Williams's arguments on the economic determinants of abolition and emancipation seem especially weak, particularly in their failure to emphasize the role of British antislavery agitation. Some scholars today believe that the British inflicted serious damage on their economy by ending the trade and freeing the slaves (Drescher, Eltis). Others support the idea of a decline in the importance of the British West Indies, either because of American independence or because British economic growth in the nineteenth century depended more on capital investment and technological change than it had in the heyday of West Indian slavery. (References to the works and authors cited in the article can be found in Solow and Engerman, and Solow.)

See also ECONOMIC INTERPRETATION OF SLAVERY; GREAT BRITAIN, AFRICAN SLAVERY IN; HISTORICAL APPROACHES TO SLAVERY.

BIBLIOGRAPHY

SOLOW, BARBARA L., ed. *Slavery and the Rise of the Atlantic System.* 1991.
SOLOW, BARBARA L., and STANLEY L. ENGERMAN, eds. *British Capitalism and Caribbean Slavery: The Legacy of Eric Williams.* 1987.
WILLIAMS, ERIC. *Capitalism and Slavery.* 1944.

Barbara L. Solow

Wisconsin

As part of the old Northwest Territory, Wisconsin had few slaves, for the Northwest Ordinance (1787) had banned slavery north of the Ohio River, and the soil and climate of Wisconsin were not hospitable to that institution. In later years, however, especially after the Fugitive Slave Act of 1850 increased federal activity against escaped slaves, Wisconsin became one of the routes for slave flight into Canada.

In this context one of the most severe clashes ever between federal and state judiciaries arose in the aftermath of attempts to implement the Fugitive Slave Act of 1850 in Wisconsin.

In 1854 fugitive slave Joshua Glover was captured in Racine by his owner, a Mr. Garland, and U.S. Deputy Marshall Stephen Ableman. Both Garland and Ableman were arrested by the local sheriff for assault and battery but were freed on a writ of habeas corpus by the federal district court.

Glover was subsequently freed from jail by a mob incited by Sherman Booth and John Rycraft, who were then arrested but freed by a writ of habeas corpus issued by Judge A. D. Smith of the Wisconsin Supreme Court. In *In re Booth* (1854) Judge Smith held the Fugitive Slave Act of 1850 to be unconstitutional on the grounds that Article IV of the U.S. Constitution did not grant enforcement power to the federal government and because the act of 1850 denied due process and jury trial to Glover.

After his release Booth was rearrested by federal authorities, and the whole Wisconsin Supreme Court, in *Ex parte Booth* (1854), declined to interfere with the federal courts during the pendency of a federal criminal matter. After the federal conviction of Booth and Rycraft, however, the Wisconsin Supreme Court again ordered the pair freed on the basis of its original holding of the unconstitutionality of the act of 1850 in *In re Booth and Rycraft* (1855).

The U.S. Supreme Court sought review on a writ of error, but the clerk of the Wisconsin court, on judicial instruction, refused to comply with the writ. In *United States v. Booth* (1855) the U.S. Supreme Court directly instructed the clerk to comply. In *Ableman v. Booth* (1859) U.S. Chief Justice Roger B. Taney wrote the Court's decision, holding that state courts could not free federal prisoners through writs of habeas corpus. In the obiter dicta of the case, furthermore, Taney upheld the constitutionality of the act of 1850.

Although there was some further rhetorical resistance to federal authority in the Wisconsin state case of *Ableman v. Booth* (1861), wherein the state supreme court split evenly on whether to accede to the federal appellate power, in the civil suit of *Arnold v. Booth* (1861), the state court refused to attempt to interfere in the jurisdiction of the federal district court.

Ableman v. Booth rang the death knell for judicial resistance to federal judicial power in the arena of fugitive slave law, although the accession to that authority in *Arnold v. Booth* was accompanied by a defiant rhetoric of resistance.

See also FUGITIVE SLAVE LAWS, U.S.; NORTHWEST ORDINANCE.

BIBLIOGRAPHY

Ableman v. Booth, 11 Wis. 517 (1861).
Ableman v. Booth, 62 US (21 How.) 506 (1859).
Arnold v. Booth, 14 Wis. 195 (1861).
COVER, ROBERT M. *Justice Accused: Antislavery and the Judicial Process.* 1975.
Ex parte Booth, 3 Wis. 145 (1854).
FINKELMAN, PAUL. *An Imperfect Union: Slavery, Federalism, and Comity.* 1981.
———. *Slavery in the Courtroom: An Annotated Bibliography of American Cases.* 1985.
In re Booth, 3 Wis. 1 (1854).
In re Booth and Rycraft, 3 Wis. 157 (1855).
MORRIS, THOMAS D. *Free Men All: The Personal Liberty Laws of the North, 1780–1861.* 1974.
United States ex rel. Garland v. Morris, 26 F. Cas. 1318 (D. Wis. 1854) (No. 15, 811).
United States v. Rycraft, 27 F. Cas. 918 (D. Wis. 1854) (No. 15, 211).

Patrick M. O'Neil

Witchcraft

See Slave Religion.

Witnesses, Slaves as

In Roman law the testimony of a slave could be received in a trial only if it had been obtained under torture. The slave was believed to be naturally mendacious, but this could be overcome by the truth-inducing properties of pain.

In the U.S. South, as in the slave-holding colonies of the British Empire, the testimony of a slave could not be employed for or against a white. Some states also prohibited the testimony of a slave from being used for or against a free black. In the 1820s this began to change in British territory, but only emancipation ended that rule in the South.

Originally in the U.S. South, slave testimony could be used only against other slaves, but by the 1820s such evidence was admissible in most states in trials involving free blacks and Indians. In 1717 Maryland admitted such evidence in any case against a free black or an Indian that would not deprive the defendant of "life or member."

In 1777 North Carolina expanded the admissibility of such evidence to include capital cases, as did Mississippi in a statute of 1822, which also allowed slaves to take the stand in civil cases to which only persons of color were parties.

Slaves who had not been baptized and indoctrinated in the Christian faith might be excluded from giving testimony in any case whatsoever, since they could not meaningfully take the oath.

Even in those cases where the testimony of slaves was admitted, the problem of perjury arose. This was solved by substituting for the oath an admonition on the penalties for perjury by a slave. In colonial Virginia the punishment for a perjurious slave was to have his ears nailed to the pillory and then cut off, and finally to receive thirty-nine lashes.

In some states, such as Virginia and South Carolina, even when the testimony of slaves was admitted—as against other slaves—if the issue were a capital offense, there was a two-witness rule, eventually modified to allow single-witness testimony when "pregnant circumstances" existed. By 1740 South Carolina had abandoned the two-witness rule and the "pregnant circumstances" exception. Georgia followed suit in 1770 and Maryland in 1808. Georgia modified its statute in 1816 to allow for oaths of any who were Christians, and Louisiana also allowed administration of an oath.

In *State v. Ben* (1821) the North Carolina Supreme Court rejected the "pregnant circumstances" rule. Kentucky, Tennessee, Mississippi, and Alabama dropped the rule between the 1830s and the 1850s.

Although the administration of an oath to slaves was common only in Georgia and Louisiana, throughout the South corporal punishment for perjury by slaves was common, with between thirty-nine and one hundred lashes the rule. Alabama even followed the flogging by branding the slave with the letter *P*.

One clear area where slave testimony was needed and was commonly used was when conspiracy to servile insurrection was involved because, by the very nature of such an undertaking, all evidence had to be hidden from whites until rebellion broke out.

Finally, judicial torture was not unknown in the United States in regard to slave testimony. The civil law system in Louisiana sanctioned it, and in the common law jurisdictions of the other states, although formal judicial torture was not allowed, confessions of guilt, often implicating other blacks, were often obtained by the extrajudicial application of torture (such as sustained flogging) or by threats of force.

The ban on slave testimony often prevented the prosecution or conviction of whites who had murdered or illegally brutalized slaves. Even the proslavery legal theorist Thomas R. R. Cobb admitted that this was a major drawback of the legal system in the South.

See also LAW; TORTURE.

BIBLIOGRAPHY

MORRIS, THOMAS D. *Southern Slavery and the Law; 1619–1860*. 1996.
State v. Ben (a slave), 8 N.C. 233 (1821).

Patrick M. O'Neil

Women as Slaves

See Africa; Family, U.S.; Harem; Prostitution; Slavery, Contemporary Forms of; White Slavery.

Women in the Antislavery Movement

After the War of 1812, when organized antislavery gained momentum, women joined this movement in significant numbers. Quaker women often led the way, both because their denomination condemned slavery and because it encouraged female activism. In the 1820s Quaker Elizabeth Chandler wrote articles for Benjamin Lundy's colonizationist newspaper, *The Genius of Universal Emancipation*, under a special section entitled "Ladies Repository." Over time, she rejected the colonizationist approach and adopted the doctrine of immediate, uncompensated abolition espoused by William Lloyd Garrison.

Garrison took the lead in recruiting and encouraging female participation in antislavery. Understand-

ing the widely held nineteenth-century belief that women were morally and religiously superior to men, he realized that women might play a central role in the movement. His Boston-based newspaper, *The Liberator*, included a "Ladies Department" that featured a masthead of a female slave in chains over the caption "Am I not a Woman and a Sister."

The radical abolition movement spawned a host of new organizations, most of which affiliated with Garrison's American Anti-Slavery Society. Because it was considered socially improper for women and men to participate in the same societies, separate organizations evolved. One of the first female groups was the Boston Female Anti-Slavery Society, founded in 1833 by a racially mixed group of Unitarians, Quakers, Congregationalists, and Baptists. They selected Charlotte Phelps, wife of Reverend Amos Phelps, to be their president. The society focused on fundraising and petitioning. Because its radical goal of emancipation alienated many, the society's activities aroused considerable criticism in newspapers and occasional mob violence.

The Philadelphia Female Anti-Slavery Society evolved from a core of support within the Society of Friends. Lucretia Mott, who became a Quaker minister at the age of twenty-five, was one of its early lead-

Lucretia Mott. [Library of Congress/Corbis]

ers. From its inception, the Philadelphia society included African-American women from the city's sizable free black community. At least one third of the women who signed its first constitution were black women, including Charlotte Forten, wife of antislavery activist James Forten, and their daughters, Margaretta, Sarah, and Harriet. Like the Boston Female Anti-Slavery Society, the Philadelphia group raised money, some of which was used to open a school for black children. They canvassed for signatures on antislavery petitions and arranged public lectures.

The decade of the 1830s saw a substantial growth in female participation in the antislavery movement. Writers, including Lydia Maria Child, published pamphlets and essays condemning slavery. Women joined the ranks of antislavery orators, thereby opening to them a form of public expression never before available to women. The Grimké sisters of South Carolina, Sarah and Angelina, were among the first female orators. Members of an elite slaveowning family, they had rejected slavery after moving to Philadelphia and converting to the Quaker faith. Their New England lecture tour in 1837 opened the door for others, and soon numerous women accepted positions as paid lecturers for the American Anti-Slavery Society. Women speakers such as Quakers Abby Kelley Foster and Sallie Holley traveled widely, boarded with sympathetic families, and faced considerable verbal and even physical threats.

Black women faced even greater indignities. Isabella Van Wagener, a New York slave liberated by statewide emancipation, had a vision in which God told her to leave New York and adopt a new name. She chose Sojourner Truth. Illiterate throughout her life, her eloquence and firsthand knowledge of slavery's horrors made her one of abolition's most effective speakers. Tall and angular, she once bared her breasts to prove to a disbelieving member of her audience that she was a woman.

In 1837, 1838, and 1839, Antislavery Conventions of American Women met in Northeastern cities and drew activists from throughout the free states. These meetings reveal women's growing political consciousness ten years before the women's rights movement was formally launched in Seneca Falls, New York. Resolutions called upon women to reject their circumscribed role and along with antislavery activism to demand their own rights as citizens. Following this series of meetings, new antislavery societies began in northeastern and midwestern states.

Antislavery petitioning reached its peak in the late 1830s. Women represented the majority of both canvassers and signatories. Denied a formal role in the American political system, women found in petitioning a way to give voice to their political views.

In 1840 the radical antislavery movement founded by William Lloyd Garrison in the previous decade splintered. One cause was the role of women in the movement. Although Garrison welcomed women's participation and encouraged those who wished to inject a women's rights perspective, others did not. When Garrison appointed several women to leadership positions within the American Anti-Slavery Society, opponents broke away to form a separate organization. After 1840, the abolition movement would never again enjoy the unity that had characterized it during the 1830s, but the legitimacy of female participation and leadership was firmly established.

A number of American abolitionists attended the World Anti-Slavery Convention in London in 1840. When female American delegates were denied seats on the floor of the convention because of their gender, it would prove a catalyst for two of them—Lucretia Mott and Elizabeth Cady Stanton—to found the American women's rights movement several years later. Ironically, English women abolitionists did not embrace feminist activism after the 1840 meeting. Women were more powerful figures in the American antislavery movement because slavery itself occupied a more prominent place in the national spotlight. England had abolished slavery in 1833.

Elizabeth Cady Stanton and her infant daughter Harriet.
[Library of Congress/Corbis]

Harriet Beecher Stowe, whose *Uncle Tom's Cabin* (1852) became the most persuasive and popular antislavery novel in America, declined a formal association with antislavery organizations. Although she preferred to act as an independent voice for emancipation, women abolitionists found inspiration in her writing and pride in her success.

The antislavery and women's rights movements continued to be closely tied for the next several decades. During the Civil War, feminist abolitionists vowed to devote themselves to the single issue of eradicating slavery. Toward this end they founded the Woman's National Loyal League. With auxiliaries in every free state, its primary purpose was to collect signatures on a "mammoth petition" to Congress emphasizing the need for constitutional emancipation. Despite their publicly stated purpose, the League's leaders, Elizabeth Cady Stanton and Susan B. Anthony, interjected a feminist agenda in the League, including female suffrage. The two movements remained linked after the war, though the issue of female exclusion from the Fourteenth and Fifteenth Amendments divided activists.

See also CHILD, LYDIA MARIA; GARRISON, WILLIAM LLOYD; GRIMKÉ, ANGELINA AND SARAH; STOWE, HARRIET BEECHER; TRUTH, SOJOURNER.

BIBLIOGRAPHY

HEDRICK, JOAN D. *Harriet Beecher Stowe: A Life.* 1994.
HERSH, BLANCHE GLASSMAN. *The Slavery of Sex: Feminist Abolitionists in America.* 1978.
VENET, WENDY HAMAND. *Neither Ballots nor Bullets: Women Abolitionists and the Civil War.* 1991.
YEE, SHIRLEY. *Black Women Abolitionists: A Study in Activism, 1828–1860.* 1992.
YELLIN, JEAN FAGAN, and JOHN C. VAN HORNE, eds. *The Abolitionist Sisterhood: Women's Political Culture in Antebellum America.* 1994.

Wendy Hamand Venet

Woolman, John   [1720–1772]

Quaker abolitionist.

Born to a prosperous Quaker farming family in Burlington County, New Jersey, John Woolman rejected agriculture as his primary occupation and chose shopkeeping, tailoring, and schoolteaching instead. As told in his *Journal*, he turned early to spiritual matters, becoming a Quaker lay minister at age twenty-two. At about the same time, he awakened to the injustice of slave keeping when directed by his employer to write a bill of sale for an enslaved woman. Though slaveholding was common in his neighborhood, Woolman apparently gained inspiration for his

John Woolman. [*Dictionary of American Portraits*]

lifelong antislavery crusade during a 1746 ministerial journey to Maryland, Virginia, and North Carolina. Upon returning home, he penned "Some Considerations on the Keeping of Negroes; Recommended to the Professors of Christianity of Every Denomination" (1754), which he delayed submitting to the Philadelphia Yearly Meeting overseers of the press because of expected resistance from prominent slaveholding Friends. The essay gently reminded masters of the rule "not to do that to another which . . . we would not have done to us" (Moulton, p. 199), then warned prophetically of God's wrath if owners refused to free their slaves.

Woolman deserves substantial, but not sole, credit for the decision of North American Quakers to ban slaveholding among their members. From 1746 to 1772 he made numerous journeys throughout the mainland British colonies and collaborated with Anthony Benezet and other abolitionists to strengthen Friends' discipline against black bondage. Woolman published "Considerations on Keeping Negroes: Part Second" in 1762, then recommended monetary restitution to former slaves or their heirs in his remarkable essay, "A Plea for the Poor," published posthumously.

While Woolman addressed many issues in his writings and ministry, including education, injustice toward Indians, and the sinfulness of greed and ostentation, the central focus of his life and his enduring legacy remained his unstinted opposition to slavery.

See also ABOLITION AND ANTISLAVERY MOVEMENTS; QUAKERS.

BIBLIOGRAPHY

DRAKE, THOMAS E. *Quakers and Slavery in America.* 1950.
MOULTON, PHILLIPS P., ed. *The Journal and Major Essays of John Woolman.* 1971.

Jean R. Soderlund

Wright, Henry Clarke [1797–1870]

U.S. abolitionist.

In 1835 Henry Clarke Wright, a Congregational minister in Connecticut, joined the American Anti-Slavery Society in order to work for the immediate emancipation for slaves. In 1836 he resigned from the ministry to become a member of the society's "Band of Seventy," a group of salaried speakers who spread immediatism throughout the North. After briefly touring Maine, he was reassigned to New York City, where he preached abolition to children. In 1837 he went to Newburyport, Massachusetts, where—in addition to his own speaking engagements—he boarded, managed, and encouraged Angelina and Sarah Grimké, the abolitionist daughters of a prominent slaveholding Charleston, South Carolina family.

Wright's interests in reform extended beyond abolition to include radical views about peace, government, gender relations, and organized religion. These views shocked many in his audience because they smacked of political and religious anarchy. He insisted on discussing these views during abolition meetings in violation of the society's instructions, so in 1837 he was reassigned to Philadelphia, Pennsylvania, and then dropped as a traveling agent later that year.

For the next thirteen years Wright served as one of William Lloyd Garrison's trusted lieutenants and wrote numerous articles and letters for publication in Garrison's newspaper, the *Liberator*. In 1850 he became a representative of the New England Non-Resistance Society, which permitted him to speak his mind on any subject. His most important contribution to abolitionism was to denounce the clergy's conservatism because it protected slavery; he thus helped to remove a major impediment to the movement's success.

See also AMERICAN ANTI-SLAVERY SOCIETY; GARRISON, WILLIAM LLOYD.

BIBLIOGRAPHY

PERRY, LEWIS. *Childhood, Marriage, and Reform: Henry Clarke Wright, 1797–1870.* 1980.

Charles W. Carey Jr.

Z

Zanj

Black African slaves were imported into the Arab and Iranian Middle East from time immemorial, though no written statistical evidence exists. Arab traders were present in Ethiopia and Sudan before the advent of Islam in the mid-seventh century C.E., and they included slaves in the various goods that they purchased.

Arabs and Iranians used the term *zanj* for Bantu-speaking Africans at least by the mid 650s C.E., and because almost all of these black Africans were slaves, the term *zanj* came to mean black—not Ethiopian—slaves, with the negative connotation that "slave" evoked.

"Zanj" is not an Arabic word; its origin is the subject of an unresolved debate among scholars. The Ethiopian verb *zanega*, "to speak jubberish," the Persian Pahlevi term *zangik*, "black," and the Indian name *Zanzbar*, "country of the black man," have been suggested as origins of "zanj."

In the seventh to ninth centuries, tens of thousands of these black African zanj slaves were owned and employed by wealthy Arabs in southern Iraq preparing salt-polluted land for cultivation. Because the Sassanian canal system, which had allowed the drainage of land between Basra and the Gulf, fell into disrepair after the Arab conquests, large areas that had heretofore been productive agricultural land became nitrous-polluted wasteland. The Zanj were used to clear the top layer of soil, remove the nitrates and saltpeter pollutants, and return the area to cultivation.

All of the evidence that survives portrays a sitution of inhuman and miserable living conditions for these slaves. These intolerable conditions and the great numbers of slaves provided the raw material for slave revolts, needing only leadership to galvanize the slaves to action.

Two minor revolts of the Zanj occurred in 689–690 and 694–695, but the Arab Umayyad leadership was then powerful, and the revolts were suppressed with great loss of life and a deterioration of living conditions. For the next two centuries the Zanj continued to be imported and used in the southern Iraq salt flats. A major revolt broke out in 868, led by Ali ibn Muhammad, an Arab claiming descent from Ali, and lasted for fifteen years. The Arab Abbasid government with great difficulty finally suppressed the revolt in 883, massacring more than three-fourths of the Zanj rebels, amounting to tens of thousands killed. This catastrophe ended the effort to maintain the southern Iraq flats as an agricultural area, and the region returned to its salt marsh character soon thereafter.

"Zanj" continued to be a term with derogatory connotations used for blacks in the Arab Muslim world, though it no longer referred to a servile class. Black slaves remained a fixture in the Middle East, primarily in Arab households, not in agriculture.

See also EAST AFRICA; ISLAM; SLAVE TRADE.

BIBLIOGRAPHY

NÖLDEKE, THEODORE. "A Servile War in the East." In *Sketches from Eastern History*, translated by John Sutherland Black. 1963; pp. 146–175. Reprint of 1892 original.

Popovic, Alexandre. *La révolte des esclaves en Iraq au IIIe/IXe siècle.* 1976.

Alan Fisher

Zanzibar

See Plantations.

Zulu

See Southern Africa.

Zumbi

See Palmares.

Synoptic Outline of Entries

This outline provides a general overview of the conceptual structure of this encyclopedia. The outline is organized under nine major headings, most of which are divided into several subsections. The entries are organized alphabetically within each subsection.

Biographies
Definitions and Types of Slavery
Experience of Slavery
Geography of Slavery
Interpretations of Slavery

Law, Diplomacy, and War
Operation of Slavery
Religion
Theory and Politics of Slavery

BIOGRAPHIES

Defenders of Slavery

Bellon de Saint-Quentin, Jean
Bledsoe, Albert Taylor
Butler, Pierce Mease
Cobb, Thomas R. R.
Chesnut, Mary
De Bow, James D. B.
Dew, Thomas Roderick
Fitzhugh, George
Hammond, James Henry
Harper, Robert Goodloe
Holmes, George Frederick
Hughes, Henry
Jefferson, Thomas
Long, Edward
Melon, Jean-François
Nóbrega, Manuel da
Nott, Josiah Clark
Thornwell, James Henley
Turnbull, Gordon

Opponents of Slavery

Albornoz, Bartolomé de
Birney, James G.
Brown, John
Buxton, Thomas Fowell
Child, Lydia Maria
Clarkson, Thomas
Coles, Edward
Franklin, Benjamin, and the
  Marquis de Condorcet
Garnet, Henry
Garrison, William Lloyd
Godwyn, Morgan
Grégoire, Henri, Bishop
Grimké, Angelina and Sarah
Hepburn, John
Kemble, Frances Anne
  ("Fanny")
Lay, Benjamin and Sarah
Lovejoy, Elijah P.
Lundy, Benjamin

Mercado, Tomás de
Montesquieu, Charles-Louis de
  Secondat de
Nabuco de Araujo, Joaquim
Phillips, Wendell
Ramsey, James
Raynal, G.-T.-F. de, Abbé
Sandiford, Ralph
Sandoval, Alonso de
Sewall, Samuel
Sharp, Granville
Smith, Adam
Smith, Gerrit
Stowe, Harriet Beecher
Tappan Brothers
Tryon, Thomas
Vieira, António
Walker, David
Ward, Samuel Ringgold
Weld, Theodore
Wilberforce, William

Women in the Antislavery
  Movement
Woolman, John
Wright, Henry Clarke

Slaves
Ambar, Malik
Burns, Anthony
Cheng Ho
Cinqué
Douglass, Frederick
Ellison, William
Epictetus
Equiano, Olaudah
Gabriel
Gray, Simon
Hemings, Sally
Henson, Josiah
Jacobs, Harriet
Jefferson, Isaac
Montejo, Esteban
Onesimus
Solomon, Job Ben
Spartacus
Toussaint-Louverture
Truth, Sojourner
Tubman, Harriet
Turner, Nat

General
Baxter, Richard
Butler, Benjamin
Claver, Pedro
Columbus, Christopher
Douglas, Stephen A.
Hurd, John Codman
Las Casas, Bartolomé de
Lincoln, Abraham
Norris, Robert
Stewart, Maria W.
Washington, George
Wheatley, Phillis
Whitney, Eli

DEFINITIONS AND TYPES OF SLAVERY
Slavelike Statuses
Caste Systems
Comfort Women in World
  War II
Debt Peonage
Gulag
Labor Systems
Nazi Slave Labor
Peonage
Roma
Russia, Serfdom in
Slavs
Thralldom
White Slavery

Slavery
Chattel Slavery
Debt Slavery
Elite Slaves
Eunuchs
Gallery Slaves
Genocide, Slavery as
Gladiators
Harem
Janissaries
Military Slaves
Miners
Palace Slaves in the Middle East
Perspectives on Slavery:
  Definitions
Slavery, Contemporary Forms of
Temple Slaves in Ancient
  Greece and Rome
Urban Slavery
Wet Nurses

EXPERIENCE OF SLAVERY
Free People and Freedpeople
Contraband
Freedmen
Freedmen's Bureau
Free People of Color
Reconstruction, U.S.

Material Culture
Clothing, U.S.
Food and Cooking
Housing
Material Culture in the
  United States

Resistance and Rebellion
Christiana Slave Revolt (1851)
Creole Incident (1841)
Demerara Slave Revolt (1823)
Escape
Gabriel's Rebellion (1800)
Insurrections
Maroons
Palmares
Panics
Rebellions and Violent
  Resistance
Resistance, Day-to-Day
Slave Republics
Stono Rebellion (1739)
Underground Railroad
Vesey Rebellion (1822)
Zanj Slaves

Slave Arts
Arts
Dance
Music by Slaves

Slave Narratives
Spirituals

Slave Life and Death
Africa: Women as Slaves in
  Africa
Artisans
Concubinage
Demographic Analysis of Slaves
  and Slavery
Demography of Slaves in the
  United States
Education of Slaves
Familia Caesaris
Family, U.S.
Field Labor
Gender Relations
Health
Household Slaves
Human Sacrifice
Industrial Slaves
Miscegenation
Mortality in the New World
Names and Naming
Prostitution
Public Works
Seasoning
Sexual Exploitation
Slave Religion
Slavery and Childhood
United States: Breeding of
  Slaves

GEOGRAPHY OF SLAVERY
United States
Alabama
Arkansas
California
Connecticut
Confederate States of America
Delaware
Florida
Georgia
Hawaii
Illinois
Indiana
Iowa
Kansas
Kentucky
Louisiana
Maine
Maryland
Massachusetts
Native Americans
New Hampshire
New Jersey
New Mexico
New York
North Carolina

Timeline of Slavery

Year	Asia	Europe	Africa	Americas	North America
ca. 3000 B.C.E.	Slaves evident in Sumer		Pyramids built in Egypt employing corvée labor		
ca. 2000	Curse of Ham (?)				
1752	Hammurabi's Code defines slavery in Babylon				
ca. 1500	Slaves evident in Assyria, Babylon	Mycenean use of slaves	Military expansion in New Kingdom Egypt produces slaves, including Nubians		
1220s	Moses leads Jews in Exodus to freedom		Israelites enslaved in Egypt		
ca. 1000	Israelites develop laws of slavery				
621–20		Draco codifies slave law in Athens			
ca. 600	Intensive use of slaves in Persia	Spartan subjects held as helots			
ca. 550	Achaemenid conquests generate slaves in Persia				
ca. 500		Slavery prominent in Athens (Greece)		Evidence of slavery in Meso-America	
453		Slaves in Twelve Tables (Rome)			
ca. 200	Slavery already in existence in China intensified under Former Han dynasty	Roman conquests flood Italy with slaves			
136–32		Slave revolts, Sicily			
73–71		Spartacus's revolt			

Date				
1st c. B.C.E.		Slave laws tightened at Rome		
ca. 300 C.E.		Decline of agricultural slavery in Roman Italy		Extensive Mayan sacrificial use of slaves
ca. 500		Germanic invasions renew slavery		
late 7th c.	Development of Islamic law of slavery			
9th c.	(800–1400) Slavery flourishes at Angkor (Cambodia)	Slavery in decline; rise of feudalism	Muslims in North Africa develop trans-Saharan slaving	
883	Zanj slaves revolt along Persian Gulf			
10th c.	Samanids selling Turkic slaves in Muslim markets	German expansion into Slavic lands replaces Latin *servus* with ethnonym "slave"	Use of military slaves in Muslim Egypt	
	Palace (military) slaves in Islamic states	Vikings selling slaves to Muslim markets		
11th c.		Crusader states in Palestine adopt cultivation of sugarcane		
12th c. 1249	Slaves becoming numerous in Kievan Russia	*Las Siete Partidas* define Iberian law of slavery (Castile)	Military slaves in Egypt rule as Mamluk dynasty (until **1517**)	
ca. 1265				
1300s	Main period of slavery in Korea	Italians selling Slavs as slaves throughout the Mediterranean	Slavery prominent in western Sudan, exports north across Sahara	
		Italians develop sugar on Crete, Cyprus, Sicily		
1400s	Slavery growing in Muscovy	Sugar cultivation extended to Atlantic islands (Madeira, Canaries)		Lavish Aztec sacrifices of slaves
1444			First recorded purchases of Africans, by Portuguese	

Year	Asia	Europe	Africa	Americas	North America
1470s–80s			Portuguese establish contacts along Atlantic African coast, buying slaves as well as gold; Columbus gains maritime experience		
1495				Columbus sends Carib captives to Spain as slaves	
ca. 1500			Madeira sugar grown with slaves		
1502				Enslavement of Caribs in Spanish West Indies	
1513		First Spanish *asiento* to deliver slaves to American colonies		Africans first brought to Spanish Indies, via Spain	
1516			Benin restricts sales of male slaves	Direct shipments of Africans to Spain's American colonies, as slaves	
1520s			São Tomé sugar thrives, grown by central African slaves; Kongo king protests slaving		
1542				"New Laws" end enslavement of Spain's Amerindian subjects	
1544	Ottomans assume control of Black Sea slave trade, Slavs from Crimea				
1547–53		End of slavery in England			
1568			Slave revolt in São Tomé		
1570s			Drought in Angola generates inexpensive slaves	Large numbers of Africans growing sugar in Brazil as slaves	
1573	(1580s) Serfdom consolidated in Russia	Albornoz's attack on slave trade in Spain			
1590s	Malik Ambar rules in India				
1600	Blackbirding in the Pacific		Portuguese slaving post in Angola (Luanda)		
1603				*Ordenações filipinas* define law of slavery in Brazil	
1617					Tobacco grown in Virginia. with English indentured servants

Year	Asia/Pacific	Europe	Africa/Indian Ocean	Americas	North America/United States
1619		Synod of Dort extends rights to baptized slaves		(1620s) English settlers farming in Barbados	"20 and odd Negroes" landed at Jamestown; treated as indentured servants
1621		Dutch West India Co. chartered			
1629				First recorded sale of slave in Canada	Indentured labor contracts common in colonies
1630s		Dutch West India Company seizes Portuguese possessions; Brazil (1630–54); Curaçao (1634)			First evidence of enslavement of blacks (VA and MD)
1637				English turn to sugar and slaves in Barbados	New England militias capturing Amerindians as slaves, for sale in English plantation colonies
1640s			Dutch hold Angola (1641–48)		
1665				French establish colony in Saint Domingue	(1660s) Virginia passes laws defining slavery
1670s			Slaving expanded in West Africa; muskets imported	English begin converting Jamaica to sugar and slaves	Imports of slaves increase in Chesapeake for tobacco cultivation
1672		Royal African Company (RAC) chartered (England)	Moroccan dynasty using slaves as soldiers and for growing sugar	Palmares (*quilombo*, or escaped slave colony) flourishes in Brazil	
Year	Asia/Pacific	Europe	Africa/Indian Ocean	Americas	North America/United States
1685		French *Code Noir*			
1695				Defeat of Palmares	
1698		Free trade in slaves replaces RAC monopoly			
ca. 1700			Asante warfare produces slaves sold on Gold Coast	Gold boom in Brazil draws Africans as slaves (Minas Gerais)	Imports of slaves growing at Charleston (Carolina) to cultivate rice
1712					Slave rebellion, New York City
1720s				French imports of slaves grow at Saint Domingue	
1730s			Dahomey/Oyo wars generate captives sold at Ouidah (Slave Coast)		Slaves in Chesapeake achieve positive rates of reproduction
1739					Stono Rebellion (SC)

977

Year	North America/United States	Americas	Africa/Indian Ocean	Europe	Asia/Pacific
1740	Negro Act defines law of slavery in South Carolina				
1740s			Imports of slaves growing at Cape of Good Hope (wheat, wine)		
1741	New York slave conspiracy				
1742				French *Code Noir*	
1755		Nominal ending of Indian slavery in Brazil			
1760s	Quaker opposition to slavery (Philadelphia)	End of Brazilian gold boom (**ca. 1760**)	Slave exports increasing to all-time peaks	Quaker opposition to slavery in England	
1770s	Slavery flourishing in British Florida	Brazilian slaves employed growing sugar and cotton (**after 1770s**)	French develop slave trade to Mascarene Islands		
1772				Somerset case (UK)	
1775	First abolition society				
1780s	Gradual emancipation statutes in northern states (PA 1780, CT 1784, RI 1784, NJ 1804)	Peak imports of slaves in the Caribbean; growing autonomy of slave communities (**ca. 1780s**)	Barbary Wars (U.S./Algiers)		
1787	Constitution embeds slavery in the laws of the United States		British colony at Freetown (Sierra Leone) for freed American slaves		Penal colonies established in Australia
1788	Northwest Ordinance prohibits slavery northwest of Ohio River			*Société des Amis des Noirs* founded, Paris	
1789	(**1780s–90s**) U.S. conflict with Algiers over enslavement of captured sailors			Spanish *código negro*	
1791		Saint Domingue slave revolt			
1792				Denmark ends slave trading	
1793	Fugitive Slave Act				
1794	Invention of cotton gin by Eli Whitney	Efforts at amelioration in British colonies		(First) French emancipation decree	
1798			Mamluks in Egypt fall to Napolean		

978

Year					
1799					Gradual emancipation statute in New York
1800				First plantings of coffee in Brazil	Gabriel's Rebellion (VA)
1802		Napoleon reinstates slavery (France)	Sokoto *jihad* launches slaving wars in West Africa		
1803					Louisiana Purchase expands areas open to slavery in U.S.
1804				Independent Haiti	
1807		Britain abolishes slave trade, eff. **1808**			U.S. ends slave imports, **1808**
1815			(**1810s**) Busaidi sultans start to develop clove plantations at Zanzibar	Slavery restored in French colonies	(**1810s**) Cotton attracts U.S. slaves to antebellum South
1816				Barbados slave revolt	Am. Colonization Soc. founded
1819		(**1818**) Wallachian penal code treats Roma (Gypsies) as slaves	(**1810s**) Slaves employed in producing commodities in West Africa		
1820	(**1820s**) Ottoman imports of slaves from Africa growing			(**1820s**) Slaves brought to Cuba in growing numbers for sugar	Missouri Compromise; (**1821**) Christiana revolt; Vesey revolt (Charleston, SC)
1822			Freed U.S. slaves settle in Liberia		
1823		British Anti-Slavery Society founded	(**1820s**) Growing reliance on labor in Madagascar	Demerara slave revolt	(**1820s**) Sugar attracts U.S. slave owners to Louisiana
1831		Suppression of illegal French slave trade	(**1830s**) Muhammad Ali develops Egyptian slaving on upper Nile	Jamaica slave revolt	Garrison founds Am. Anti-Slavery Soc., *Liberator* published
1833	(**1830s**) Indentured workers leaving India for British colonies around the world	Britain emancipates slaves in colonies (eff. **1838**)	(**1830s**) British naval squadron operates against slaving ships off African shores	Brazil bans imports of slaves, to no effect	Nat Turner's revolt
1834				"Apprenticeship" in West Indies, Cape Col.	
1835				*Malê* revolt (Brazil)	(**1830s**) Five civilized tribes removed to Oklahoma
1836		Portugal ends slavery			
1839				*Amistad* revolt	

979

Year	Asia/Pacific	Europe	Africa/Indian Ocean	Americas	United States
1840s	Coolie trade from Asia increases		Slaves growing cloves in Zanzibar; exports throughout Indian Ocean region	Indentured workers replace slaves as plantation workers in British Caribbean	Sectional divisions growing
1841					*Amistad* decision
1842				Cuban laws of slavery codified	African Squadron created as Atlantic anti–slave trade patrol
1843	Slavery loses legal status (British India)		(1840s) British naval pressure against slaving in Atlantic waters	*La Escalera* slave conspiracy in Cuba	Supreme Court upholds Fugitive Slave Law (*Prigg v. Pa.*)
1845					Annexation of Texas expands territory for slavery expansion
1848				(Second) French emancipation in colonies	
1849			French freed-slave colony at Libreville (Gabon)		
1850					Fugitive Slave Law
1851				Effective end of slave imports to Brazil	Christiana revolt (Delaware)
1854	First Ottoman prohibition of slave imports	Portugal abolishes slavery in African colonies			Kansas-Nebraska Act opens territories to slavery; (1855–56) conflict in Bleeding Kansas
1855		(1855–56) Abolition of Roma slavery in Balkans	Slaves in Portugal's African colonies subject to *serviçal* apprenticeship	(1850s) Slaves from northeastern Brazil moved to coffee plantations in the south	
1857			(1850s) Egyptian slavers raiding along Upper Nile		Dred Scott decision
1859					John Brown's raid at Harpers Ferry (VA)
1861	Russia ends serfdom		(1860s) Slavers from Zanzibar move into Upper Congo region	(1860s) Free European immigration growing in Brazil	Civil War breaks out
1863	(1860s) Kidnapping (blackbirding) grows in the Pacific	(1864) Emancipation of Roma			Emancipation Proclamation (Lincoln)
1865					13th Amendment ends slavery
1866					Civil Rights Act
1867				(1868–78) Ten Years' War in Cuba weakens slavery	Antipeonage law
1870					Ratification of 14th and 15th Amendments

Year	Asia	Europe	Africa	Americas	United States
1871				Brazil enacts law of the "free womb"	
1873			Zanzibar abolishes slaving (Indian Ocean)		Civil Rights Act, last act of Reconstruction
1875	End of Pacific coolie trade				
1877			Egypt prohibits imports of slaves		
1878		Portugal ends "apprenticeship" in colonies		(1880) Brazilian Anti-Slavery Society	
1885		Berlin Conference declaration against slave trading	Colonial rule (Treaty of Berlin)—little effect on slavery in colonies	Brazil frees aged slaves	Foran Act outlaws contract labor
1886				Cuba frees slaves	
1888				Emancipation voted in Brazil (eff. **1889**)	
1890		Brussels Act (repression of slave trading in Africa)	(1890s) Development of slavelike indentured labor in Portuguese colonies		(1896) Publication of Du Bois's *Suppression of the African Slave-Trade*
20th c.			Colonial rulers slowly end trading in slaves		
1909		Anti-Slavery International established	Forced labor (*indigenato*) in Portuguese colonies		(1916) Carter G. Woodson founds *J. Negro History*
1920s	Soviet slavelike labor conditions		Sales of slaves to Arabia grow from Ethiopia		(1918) U. B. Phillips publishes *American Negro Slavery*
1924			League of Nations Temporary Slavery Commission		
1926	Pan-Islamic congress condemns slavery		League of Nations (anti-) Slavery Convention		
1930s	Japan uses comfort women as sex slaves	(1932) League of Nations Standing Committee of Experts on Slavery	League of Nations investigates labor conditions in Liberia	(1933) G. Freyre's *Casa grande e senzala* ("Masters and Slaves") published in Brazil	WPA slave narratives collected
1936	Nationalist China outlaws concubinage	Nazi Germany slavelike labor system			

Year	Asia	Europe	Africa	Americas	United States
1937			League of Nations treaty against prostitution		
1942			Haile Selassie ends slavery in Ethiopia		
1944				Williams's *Capitalism and Slavery* published	(**1947**) Tannenbaum's *Slave and Citizen* published; J. H. Franklin's *From Slavery to Freedom*
1948			United Nations Universal Declaration of Human Rights		
1949			UN Convention for the Suppression of the Traffic in Persons and the Exploitation of the Prostitution of Others		
1950	China Communist Party outlaws concubinage				
1954					*Brown v. Board of Education* accelerates Civil Rights movement
1956			UN Supplementary Convention on the Abolition of Slavery		(**1956**) Stampp's *Peculiar Institution* published
1962	Saudi Arabia abolishes slavery		UN Convention on Consent to Marriage, Minimum Age for Marriage, and Registration of Marriages		(**1959**) Elkins's *Slavery* published
1964		(**1968**) Finley's *Slavery* published	Mogadishu Pan-Islamic Congress condemns slavery	(**1969**) Curtin's *Atlantic Slave Trade* published	Civil Rights Acts; D. B. Davis wins Pulitzer for *Problem of Slavery in Western Culture*
1970	Muscat and Oman end slavery				
1970s	Servile marriage resurfaces as issue in China				(**1972**) Blassingame's *Slave Community* published; (**1974**) Genovese's *Roll, Jordan, Roll* and Fogel and Engerman's *Time on the Cross* published
1980s		(**1982**) Patterson's *Slavery* published	Reports of enslavement from Sudan		
1990s	Slavery alleged in Burma		Slavery alleged in Sudan, Mauritania	Slavery of Amerindians alleged in Brazil	

A Select Bibliography of Slavery

"Africans in Spanish American Colonial Society." In *Cambridge History of Latin America,* edited by Leslie Bethell, vol. 2, pp. 848–853. 1984. Bibliographical essay.

ALLISON, ROBERT J., ed. *The Interesting Narrative of the Life of Olaudah Equiano, Written by Himself.* 1995.

ANSTEY, ROGER T. *The Atlantic Slave Trade and British Abolition, 1760–1810.* 1975.

APTHEKER, HERBERT. *American Negro Slave Revolts.* 1943.

ARCHER, LÉONIE J., ed. *Slavery and Other Forms of Unfree Labour.* 1988.

AYALON, DAVID. *Islam and the Abode of War: Military Slaves and Islamic Adversaries.* 1994.

BAILYN, BERNARD. "Jefferson and the Ambiguities of Freedom." *Proceedings of the American Philosophical Society* 137, no. 4 (1993): 498–515.

BECKLES, HILARY McD. *Black Rebellion in Barbados: The Struggle against Slavery, 1627–1838.* 1984.

———. *Natural Rebels: A Social History of Enslaved Black Women in Barbados.* 1989a.

———. *White Servitude and Black Slavery in Barbados, 1627–1715.* 1989b.

BERLIN, IRA. "From Creole to African: Atlantic Creoles and the Origins of African-American Society in Mainland North America." *William and Mary Quarterly* 53, no. 2 (1996): 251–288.

———. *Making Slavery, Making Race: The First Two Centuries of African-American Captivity in Mainland North America.* 1998.

BERLIN, IRA, and PHILIP D. MORGAN, eds. *The Slaves' Economy: Independent Production by Slaves in the Americas.* 1991.

BLACKBURN, ROBIN. *The Making of New World Slavery: From the Baroque to the Creole.* 1996.

———. *The Overthrow of Colonial Slavery, 1776–1848.* 1988.

BLANCHARD, PETER. *Slavery and Abolition in Early Republican Peru.* 1992.

BLASSINGAME, JOHN W. *The Slave Community: Plantation Life in the Antibellum South.* 1972. Rev. ed. 1979.

BLIGHT, DAVID W., ed. *Narrative of the Life of Frederick Douglass, an American Slave, Written by Himself.* 1993.

BLOCH, MARC. *Slavery and Serfdom in the Middle Ages: Selected Essays.* Translated by William R. Beer. 1975.

BOLLAND, O. NIGEL. "Colonization and Slavery in Central America." In *Unfree Labour in the Development of the Atlantic World,* edited by Paul E. Lovejoy and Nicholas Rogers. 1994; pp. 11–25.

"Bondage, Freedom and the Constitution: The New Slavery Scholarship and Its Impact on Law and Legal Historiography." *Cardozo Law Review* 17, no. 6 (1996). Special issue.

BONNASSIE, PIERRE. *From Slavery to Freedom in South-Western Europe.* Translated by Jean Birrell. 1991.

BONTEMPS, ARNA W. *Great Slave Narratives.* 1969.

BOWSER, FREDERICK P. *The African Slave in Colonial Peru, 1524–1650.* 1974.

BRADLEY, KEITH R. " 'The Regular, Daily Traffic in Slaves': Roman History and Contemporary History." *Classical Journal* 87, no. 2 (1992): 125–138.

———. *Slavery and Society at Rome.* 1994.

BUSH, BARBARA. *Slave Women in Caribbean Society, 1650–1838.* 1990.

BUSH, MICHAEL L., ed. *Serfdom and Slavery: Studies in Legal Bondage.* 1996.

CARDOSO, CIRO FLAMARIÓN S. "The Peasant Breach in the Slave System: New Developments in Brazil." *Luso-Brazilian Review* 25, no. 1 (1988): 49–57.

CARROLL, PATRICK J. *Blacks in Colonial Veracruz: Race, Ethnicty, and Regional Development.* 1991.

CHAUHAN, R. R. S. *Africans in India: From Slavery to Royalty.* 1995.

CLARENCE-SMITH, W. GERVASE, ed. "The Economics of the

Indian Ocean Slave Trade in the Nineteenth Century." *Slavery and Abolition* 9, no. 3 (1988). Special issue.

"Colonial Brazil: Plantations and Peripheries." In *Cambridge History of Latin America*, edited by Leslie Bethell, vol. 2, pp. 856–864. 1984. Bibliographical essay.

CONRAD, ALFRED H., and JOHN R. MEYER. "The Economics of Slavery in the Ante Bellum South." *Journal of Political Economy* 66, no. 2 (1958): 95–130.

CONRAD, ROBERT EDGAR. *Children of God's Fire: A Documentary History of Black Slavery in Brazil.* 1994.

CONSTABLE, OLIVIA REMIE. "Muslim Spain and Mediterranean Slavery: The Medieval Slave Trade as an Aspect of Muslim-Christian Relations." In *Christendom and Its Discontents: Exclusion, Persecution, and Rebellion, 1000–1500,* edited by Scott L. Waugh and Peter D. Diehl. 1996.

COSTA, EMILIA VIOTTI DA. *Crowns of Glory, Tears of Blood: The Demerara Slave Rebellion of 1823.* 1994.

CRATON, MICHAEL M. *Searching for the Invisible Man: Slaves and Plantation Life in Jamaica.* 1977.

———. *Sinews of Empire: A Short History of British Slavery.* 1974.

CRONE, PATRICIA. *Slaves on Horses: The Evolution of the Islamic Polity.* 1980.

CURTIN, PHILIP D. *The Atlantic Slave Trade: A Census.* 1969.

DAVID, PAUL A., HERBERT G. GUTMAN, RICHARD SUTCH, PETER TEMIN, and GAVIN WRIGHT, with an introduction by Kenneth Stampp. *Reckoning with Slavery: A Critical Study in the Quantitative History of American Negro Slavery.* 1976.

DAVIS, DAVID BRION. *The Problem of Slavery in the Age of Revolution, 1770–1823.* 1975.

———. *The Problem of Slavery in Western Culture.* 1966.

———. *Slavery and Human Progress.* 1984.

DEGLER, CARL N. *Neither Black nor White: Slavery and Race Relations in Brazil and the United States.* 1971.

DOCKÈS, PIERRE. *La libération médiéval.* 1979. Translated by Arthur Goldhammer as *Medieval Slavery and Liberation.* 1982.

DOMAR, EVSEY D. "The Causes of Slavery or Serfdom: A Hypothesis." *Journal of Economic History* 30, no. 1 (1970): 18–32.

DONALD, LELAND. *Aboriginal Slavery on the Northwest Coast of North America.* 1997.

DOVRING, FOLKE. "Bondage, Tenure, and Progress: Reflections on the Economics of Forced Labour." *Comparative Studies in Society and History* 7, no. 3 (1965): 309–323.

DRESCHER, SEYMOUR. *Capitalism and Antislavery: British Mobilization in Comparative Perspective.* 1986.

———. *Econocide: British Slavery in the Era of Abolition.* 1977.

DU BOIS, W. E. B. *The Negro.* 1915. Reprint, with introduction by Herbert Aptheker, 1975.

———. *The Suppression of the African Slave Trade, 1638–1870.* Foreword by John Hope Franklin. 1969. Original edition, 1896.

EGYPT, OPHELIA SETTLE, J. MASUOKA, and CHARLES S. JOHNSON, eds. *Unwritten History of Slaves: Autobiographical Accounts of Negro Ex-Slaves.* 2nd ed., 1968.

ELDREDGE, ELIZABETH A., and FRED MORTON, eds. *Slavery in South Africa: Captive Labor on the Dutch Frontier.* 1994.

ELKINS, STANLEY M. *Slavery: A Problem in American Institutional and Intellectual Life.* 1959. 2nd ed., 1968. 3rd ed., 1976.

ELTIS, DAVID. *Economic Growth and the Ending of the Transatlantic Slave Trade.* 1987.

ELTIS, DAVID, DAVID RICHARDSON, STEPHEN D. BEHRENDT, and HERBERT S. KLEIN, eds. *The Atlantic Slave Trade: A Database on CD-ROM Set and Guidebook.* 1998.

ENGERMAN, STANLEY L. "The Extent of Slavery and Freedom throughout the Ages, in the World as a Whole and in Major Subareas." In *The State of Humanity*, edited by Julian Lincoln Simon. 1995; pp. 171–177.

———. "Slavery, Serfdom, and Other Forms of Coerced Labor: Similarities and Differences." In *Serfdom and Slavery: Studies in Legal Bondage*, edited by Michael L. Bush. 1996; pp. 18–41.

ENGERMAN, STANLEY L., and EUGENE D. GENOVESE, eds. *Race and Slavery in the Western Hemisphere: Quantitative Studies.* 1975.

ESCOTT, PAUL D. *Slavery Remembered: A Record of Twentieth-Century Slave Narratives.* 1979.

ESSAH, PATIENCE. *A House Divided: Slavery and Emancipation in Delaware, 1638–1865.* 1996.

EVANS, WILLIAM McKEE. "From the Land of Canaan to the Land of Guinea: The Strange Odyssey of the 'Sons of Ham,' " *American Historical Review* 85, no. 1 (1980): 15–43.

FEHRENBACHER, DON E. *The Dred Scott Case: Its Significance in American Law and Politics.* 1978.

FINKELMAN, PAUL. *Dred Scott v. Sandford: A Brief History.* 1997a.

———. *An Imperfect Union: Slavery, Federalism, and Comity.* 1981.

———. *The Law of Freedom and Bondage: A Casebook.* 1986.

———. *Slavery and the Founders: Race and Liberty in the Age of Jefferson.* 1996.

———, ed. *Slavery and the Law.* 1997b.

———, ed. *Slavery, Race, and the American Legal System, 1700–1872.* 16 vols. 1988.

FINLEY, MOSES I. *Ancient Slavery and Modern Ideology.* 1980.

———. "Slavery." In *International Encyclopedia of the Social Sciences*, edited by David L. Sills. Vol. 14, pp. 307–313. 1968.

FOGEL, ROBERT W. *Without Consent or Contract: The Rise and Fall of American Slavery.* 1989.

FOGEL, ROBERT W., and STANLEY L. ENGERMAN. *Time on the Cross: The Economics of American Negro Slavery.* 2 vols. 1974. Reissue, with new afterword by Fogel, 1989.

FOX-GENOVESE, ELIZABETH, and EUGENE D. GENOVESE. *Fruits of Merchant Capital: Slavery and Bourgeois Property in the Rise and Expansion of Capitalism,* 1983.

FRANTZEN, ALLEN J., and DOUGLAS MOFFAT, eds. *The Work of Work: Servitude, Slavery, and Labor in Medieval England.* 1994.

FREYRE, GILBERTO. *Casa grande e senzala.* 1933. Translated by Samuel Putnam as *The Masters and the Slaves: A Study in the Development of Brazilian Civilization.* 1946.

GARLAN, YVON. *Les esclaves en Grèce ancienne.* 1982. Revised and expanded edition translated by Janet Lloyd as *Slavery in Ancient Greece.* 1988.

GARNSEY, PETER. *Ideas of Slavery from Aristotle to Augustine.* 1996.

GASPAR, D. BARRY. *Bondmen and Rebels: A Case Study of Master-Slave Relations in Antigua with Implications for Colonial British America.* 1985.

GASPAR, DAVID BARRY, and DARLENE CLARK HINE, eds. *More Than Chattel: Black Women and Slavery in the Americas*. 1996.

GENOVESE, EUGENE D. *Roll, Jordan, Roll: The World the Slaves Made*. 1974.

———. *The World the Slaveholders Made: Two Essays in Interpretation*. 1969.

GILROY, PAUL. *The Black Atlantic: Modernity and Double Consciousness*. 1993.

GOMEZ, MICHAEL A. *Exchanging Our Country Marks: The Transformation of African Identities in the Colonial and Antebellum South*. 1998.

GORDON, MURRAY. *Slavery in the Arab World*. 1989.

GORDON-REED, ANNETTE. *Thomas Jefferson and Sally Hemings: An American Controversy*. 1996.

GOVEIA, ELSA V. *Slave Society in the British Leeward Islands at the End of the Eighteenth Century*. 1965.

GRAHAM, RICHARD, ed. *Brazil and the World System*. 1991.

GUTMAN, HERBERT G. *The Black Family in Slavery and Freedom, 1750–1925*. 1976.

———. *Slavery and the Numbers Game: A Critique of "Time on the Cross."* 1975.

HALL, GWENDOLYN MIDLO. *Africans in Colonial Louisiana: The Development of Afro-Creole Culture in the Eighteenth Century*. 1992.

HALL, N.A.T. *Slave Society in the Danish West Indies: St. Thomas, St. John, and St. Croix*. Edited by B. W. Higman. 1992.

HANCOCK, IAN F. *The Pariah Syndrome: An Account of Gypsy Slavery and Persecution*. 1987.

HANDLIN, OSCAR, and MARY HANDLIN. "Origins of the Southern Labor System," *William and Mary Quarterly*, 3rd ser., 7, no. 2 (1950): 199–222.

HARRIS, JOSEPH E. *The African Presence in Asia: Consequences of the East African Slave Trade*. 1971.

HARRIS, MARVIN. *Patterns of Race in the Americas*. 1964.

HELLIE, RICHARD. *Slavery in Russia, 1450–1725*. 1982.

HIGMAN, BARRY W. *Slave Population and Economy in Jamaica, 1807–1834*. 1976.

———. *Slave Populations of the British Caribbean 1807–1834*. 1984.

HÜNEFELDT, CHRISTINE. *Paying the Price of Freedom: Family and Labor among Lima's Slaves, 1800–1854*. 1994.

"Identifying Enslaved Africans: The 'Nigerian' Hinterland and the African Diaspora." Proceedings of SSHRC/UNESCO Summer Institute, 1997, coordinated by Paul E. Lovejoy and Robin C.C. Law. 1998.

INIKORI, JOSEPH E. "Ideology versus the Tyranny of Paradigm: Historians and the Impact of the Atlantic Slave Trade on African Societies." *African Economic History*, 22 (1994): 59–92.

———, ed. *Forced Migration: The Impact of the Export Slave Trade on African Societies*. 1981.

INIKORI, JOSEPH E., and STANLEY L. ENGERMAN, eds. *The Atlantic Slave Trade: Effects on Economies, Societies, and Peoples in Africa, the Americas, and Europe*. Selected chapters also appeared as "The Transatlantic Slave Trade," special issue of *Social Science History* 13, no. 4, and 14, nos. 1–3 (1989–1990).

JAMES, C. L. R. *The Black Jacobins: Toussaint l'Ouverture and the San Domingo Revolution*. 2nd rev. ed. 1963.

JOHNSON, LYMAN L. "The Competition of Slave and Free Labor in Artisanal Production: Buenos Aires, 1770–1815." *International Review of Social History* 40, no. 3 (1995): 409–424.

JORDAN, WINTHROP D. *White over Black: American Attitudes toward the Negro, 1550–1812*. 1968.

KARASCH, MARY C. *Slave Life in Rio de Janeiro 1808–1850*. 1987.

KARRAS, RUTH MAZO. *Slavery and Society in Medieval Scandinavia*. 1988.

KLEIN, HERBERT S. *The Middle Passage: Comparative Studies in the Atlantic Slave Trade*. 1978.

KLEIN, MARTIN L., ed. *Breaking the Chains: Slavery, Bondage, and Emancipation in Modern Africa and Asia*. 1993.

KNIGHT, FRANKLIN W. *Slave Society in Cuba during the Nineteenth Century*. 1970.

KOLCHIN, PETER. *American Slavery, 1619–1877*. 1993.

———. "More *Time on the Cross*? An Evaluation of Robert William Fogel's *Without Consent or Contract*." *Journal of Southern History* 58, no. 3 (1992): 491–502.

———. *Unfree Labor: American Slavery and Russian Serfdom*. 1987.

KONSTAN, DAVID. "Slavery and Class Analysis in the Ancient World." *Comparative Studies in Society and History* 28, no. 4 (1986): 754–766. A review of Ste. Croix, *Class Struggle in the Ancient Greek World*.

KOPYTOFF, IGOR. "The Cultural Context of African Abolition." In *The End of Slavery in Africa*, edited by Suzanne Miers and Richard Roberts. 1988; pp. 485–503.

———. "Slavery." *Annual Review of Anthropology* 11 (1982): 207–230.

LAL, K. S. *Muslim Slave System in Medieval India*. 1994.

LAMUR, HUMPHREY E. *The Production of Sugar and the Reproduction of Slaves at Vossenburg (Suriname), 1705–1863*. 1987.

LEWIS, BERNARD. *Race and Color in Islam*. 1971.

———. *Race and Slavery in the Middle East: An Historical Enquiry*. 1990.

LIGHTNER, DAVID L. "More Time on the Cross: Slavery and the Slave Trade. *Canadian Review of American Studies*. 21, no. 3 (1990): 363–368. Review essay: Fogel and Engerman, reissue of *Time on the Cross*; Fogel, *Without Consent or Contract*; Ransom, *Conflict and Compromise*; and Tadman, *Speculators and Slaves*.

LITTLEFIELD, DANIEL C. "From Phillips to Genovese: The Historiography of American Slavery before *Time on the Cross*." In *Slavery in the Americas*, edited by Wolfgang Binder. 1993; pp. 1–23.

LOVEJOY, PAUL E. "The Impact of the Atlantic Slave Trade on Africa: A Review of the Literature." *Journal of African History* 30, no. 3 (1989): 365–394.

———. *Transformations in Slavery, A History of Slavery in Africa*. 1983.

———. "The Volume of the Atlantic Slave Trade: A Synthesis." *Journal of African History* 23, no. 4 (1982): 473–501.

LOVEJOY, PAUL E., and NICHOLAS ROGERS, eds. *Unfree Labour in the Development of the Atlantic World*. 1994. Also reprinted as a special issue of *Slavery and Abolition* 15, no. 2 (1994).

LUENGO, JOSE MARIA SALUTAN. *A History of the Manila-Acapulco Slave Trade, 1565–1815*. 1996.

MANNING, PATRICK. *Slavery and African Life: Occidental, Oriental and African Slave Trades.* 1990.

MANNIX, DANIEL P., and MALCOLM COWLEY. *Black Cargoes: A History of the Atlantic Slave Trade, 1518–1865.* 1962.

MATTOSO, KÁTIA M. DE QUEIRÓS. *To Be a Slave in Brazil, 1550–1888.* Translated by Arthur Goldhammer with a new foreword by Stuart B. Schwartz. 1986.

MEILLASSOUX, CLAUDE. *Anthropologie de l'esclavage: Le ventre de fer et d'argent.* 1986. Translated by Alide Dasnois as *The Anthropology of Slavery: The Womb of Iron and Gold.* Foreword by Paul E. Lovejoy. 1991.

———. "The Role of Slavery in the Economic and Social History of Sahelo-Sudanic Africa." In *Forced Migration,* edited by Joseph E. Inikori. 1981; pp. 74–99.

MELLAFE, ROLANDO. *La esclavitud en Hispanoamérica.* 1964. Translated by J.W.S. Judge as *Negro Slavery in Latin America.* 1975.

MIERS, SUZANNE, and IGOR KOPYTOFF, eds. *Slavery in Africa: Historical and Anthropological Perspectives:* 1977.

MILLER, JOSEPH C. *Slavery and Slaving in World History: A Bibliography, 1900–1991.* 1993. 10,351 entries. Republished, with corrections, together with a second volume (3,897 entries), as *Slavery and Slaving in World History: A Bibliography, 1992–1996.* 1998. Current annual updates appear in *Slavery and Abolition.*

———. *Way of Death: Merchant Capitalism and the Angolan Slave Trade, 1730–1830.* 1988.

MINTZ, SIDNEY W., and RICHARD PRICE. *An Anthropological Approach to the Afro-American Past.* 1976. Republished as *The Birth of African-American Culture: An Anthropological Perspective,* 1992.

MONTEIRO, JOHN M. "From Indian to Slave: Forced Native Labour and Colonial Society in São Paulo during the Seventeenth Century." *Slavery and Abolition* 9, no. 2 (1988): 105–127.

MORENO FRAGINALS, MANUEL, FRANK MOYA PONS, and STANLEY L. ENGERMAN, eds. *Between Slavery and Free Labor: The Spanish-Speaking Caribbean in the Nineteenth Century.* 1985.

MORGAN, EDMUND S. *American Slavery, American Freedom: The Ordeal of Colonial Virginia.* 1975.

MORGAN, PHILIP D. "The Cultural Implications of the Atlantic Slave Trade: African Regional Origins, American Destinations, and New World Developments." *Slavery and Abolition* 18, no. 1 (1997): 72–98.

———. *Slave Counterpoint: Black Culture in the Eighteenth-Century Chesapeake and Low Country.* 1998.

MÖRNER, MAGNUS, ed. *Race and Class in Latin America.* 1970.

MORRIS, THOMAS D. *Free Men All: The Personal Liberty Laws of the North, 1780–1861.* 1974.

———. *Southern Slavery and the Law, 1619–1860.* 1996.

MORRISSEY, MARIETTA. *Slave Women in the New World: Gender Stratification in the Caribbean.* 1989.

MORTON, PATRICIA, ed. *Discovering the Women in Slavery: Emancipating Perspectives on the American Past.* 1996.

MUKHERJEE, SANDHYA N. "Slave Trade in Ancient India." *Indian Studies Past and Present* 8, no. 2 (1967): 211–214.

MUNRO, DOUG. "The Pacific Islands Labour Trade: Approaches, Methodologies, Debates." *Slavery and Abolition* 14, no. 2 (1993): 87–108.

NEEDHAM, RODNEY. *Sumba and the Slave Trade.* 1983.

NIEBOER, H. J. *Slavery as an Industrial System: Ethnological Researchers.* 1900. 2nd rev. ed., 1910.

NORTHRUP, DAVID, ed. *The Atlantic Slave Trade.* 1994.

PADGUG, ROBERT A. "Problems in the Theory of Slavery and Slave Society." *Science and Society* 40, no. 1 (1976): 3–27.

PALMER, COLIN. *Passageways: An Interpretive History of Black America, 1619–1863.* Vol. 1. 1998.

———. *Slaves of the White God: Blacks in Mexico, 1570–1650.* 1976.

PALMIÉ, STEPHAN, ed. *Slave Cultures and the Cultures of Slavery.* 1995.

PAQUETTE, ROBERT L. *Sugar Is Made with Blood: The Conspiracy of "La Escalera" and the Conflict between Empires over Slavery in Cuba.* 1988.

PARISH, PETER J. *Slavery: History and Historians.* 1989.

PATNAIK, UTSA, and MANJARI DINGWANEY, eds. *Chains of Servitude: Bondage and Slavery in India.* 1985.

PATTERSON, ORLANDO. *Freedom in the Making of Western Culture.* 1991.

———. *Slavery and Social Death: A Comparative Study.* 1982.

———. *The Sociology of Slavery: An Analysis of the Origins, Development, and Structure of Negro Society in Jamaica,* 1967.

PAUL, JÜRGEN. *The State and the Military: The Samanid Case.* 1994.

PELTERET, DAVID ANTHONY EDGELL. *Slavery in Early Mediaeval England: From the Reign of Alfred until the Twelfth Century.* 1995.

PHILLIPS, ULRICH B. *American Negro Slavery: A Survey of the Supply, Employment, and Control of Negro Labor as Determined by the Plantation Regime.* 1918. Reprint, 1966.

PHILLIPS, WILLIAM D., JR. *Slavery from Roman Times to the Early Transatlantic Trade.* 1985.

PIPES, DANIEL. *Slave Soldiers and Islam: The Genesis of a Military System.* 1981.

PRAKASH, GYAN. *Bonded Histories: Genealogies of Labor Servitude in Colonial India.* 1989.

RAGATZ, LOWELL J. *The Fall of the Planter Class in the British Caribbean 1763–1833: A Study in Social and Economic History.* 1928.

RAWICK, GEORGE P., ed. *The American Slave: A Composite Autobiography.* 19 vols. 1972.

———. *The American Slave: A Composite Autobiography, Supplement, Series II.* 1979.

RAWLEY, JAMES A. *The Transatlantic Slave Trade: A History.* 1981.

REID, ANTHONY, ed. *Slavery, Bondage, and Dependency in Southeast Asia.* 1983.

REIS, JOÃO JOSÉ. *Slave Rebellion in Brazil: The Muslim Uprising of 1835 in Bahia.* Revised and expanded edition, 1993.

REUCK, ANTHONY DE, and JULIE KNIGHT, eds. *Caste and Race: Comparative Approaches.* 1967.

ROBERTSON, CLAIRE C., and MARTIN A. KLEIN, eds. *Women and Slavery in Africa.* 1983.

ROUT, LESLIE B. *The African Experience in Spanish America: 1502 to the Present Day.* 1976.

RUSSELL-WOOD, A. J. R. *The Black Man in Slavery and Freedom in Colonial Brazil.* 1982.

STE. CROIX, G. E. M. DE. *The Class Struggle in the Ancient Greek World: From the Archaic Age to the Arab Conquests.* 1981.

———. "Slavery and Other Forms of Unfree Labour." In *Slavery and Other Forms of Unfree Labour*, edited by Léonie J. Archer. 1985; pp. 19–32.

SAUNDERS, A. C. DE C. M. *A Social History of Black Slaves and Freedmen in Portugal, 1441–1555*. 1982.

SAVAGE, ELIZABETH, ed. "The Human Commodity: Perspectives on the Trans-Saharan Slave Trade." *Slavery and Abolition* 13, no. 1 (1992). Special issue.

———, ed. *The Human Commodity: Perspectives on the Trans-Saharan Slave Trade*. 1992.

SCARANO, FRANCISCO A. *Sugar and Slavery in Puerto Rico: The Plantation Economy of Ponce, 1800–1850*. 1984.

SCHAFER, JUDITH K. *Slavery, the Civil Law, and the Supreme Court of Louisiana*. 1994.

SCHWARTZ, STUART B. *Slaves, Peasants, and Rebels: Reconsidering Brazilian Slavery*. 1992.

———. *Sugar Plantations in the Formation of Brazilian Society: Bahia, 1550–1835*. 1986.

SHARP, WILLIAM F. *Slavery on the Spanish Frontier: The Colombian Choco, 1680–1810*. 1976.

SHELL, ROBERT C.-H. *Children of Bondage: A Social History of the Slave Society at the Cape of Good Hope, 1652–1838*. 1994.

SHEPHERD, VERENE S., BRIDGET BRERETON, and BARBARA BAILEY, eds. *Engendering History: Caribbean Women in Historical Perspective*. 1995.

SHERIDAN, RICHARD B. *Sugar and Slavery: An Economic History of the British West Indies, 1623–1775*. 1974.

Slave Narratives: A Folk History of Slavery in the United States from Interviews with Former Slaves. 1941.

"Slavery in the Age of Washington." Conference, Mount Vernon, VA, 3–4 November 1994.

SMITH, JOHN DAVID, and JOHN C. INSCOE, eds. *Ulrich Bonnell Phillips: A Southern Historian and His Critics*. 1990.

SOBEL, MECHAL. *The World They Made Together: Black and White Values in Eighteenth-Century Virginia*. 1987.

SOLOW, BARBARA L., ed. *Slavery and the Rise of the Atlantic System*. 1991.

STAMPP, KENNETH M. *The Peculiar Institution: Slavery in the Ante-Bellum South*. 1956.

STANTON, LUCIA C. *Slavery at Monticello*. 1996.

STAROBIN, ROBERT S., ed. *Blacks in Bondage: Letters of American Slaves*. 1974. New edition with foreword by Ira Berlin, 1988.

———, ed. *Slavery As It Was: The Testimony of the Slaves Themselves While in Bondage*. 1971.

STEIN, ROBERT. *The French Sugar Business in the Eighteenth Century*. 1988.

STEIN, STANLEY J. *Vassouras: A Brazilian Coffee County, 1850–1900*. 1957.

STUCKEY, STERLING. *Slave Culture: Nationalist Theory and the Foundations of Black America*. 1987.

TADMAN, MICHAEL. *Speculators and Slaves: Masters, Traders, and Slaves in the Old South*. 1989. Paperback edition with new introduction, 1996.

TANNENBAUM, FRANK. *Slave and Citizen: The Negro in the Americas*. 1947.

THOMAS, HUGH. *The Slave Trade: The Story of the Atlantic Slave Trade: 1440–1870*. 1997.

THORNTON, JOHN K. *Africa and Africans in the Making of the Atlantic World, 1400–1680*. 1992. Revised and expanded edition, 1998.

TOLEDANO, EHUD R. *The Ottoman Slave Trade and Its Suppression, 1840–1890*. 1982.

———. *Slavery and Abolition in the Ottoman Middle East*. 1998.

TOMICH, DALE W. *Slavery in the Circuit of Sugar: Martinique and the World Economy, 1830–1848*. 1990.

TUSHNET, MARK V. *The American Law of Slavery, 1810–1860: Considerations of Humanity and Interest*. 1981.

UNESCO. *De la traite négrière au défi du développement: Réflexion sur les conditions de la paix mondiale*. 1998.

UNSWORTH, BARRY. *Sacred Hunger*. 1992.

WALLERSTEIN, IMMANUEL. *The Modern World System*. 3 vols. 1974–1989.

WARREN, JAMES F. *The Sulu Zone 1768–1898: The Dynamics of External Trade, Slavery, and Ethnicity in the Transformation of a Southeast Asian Maritime State*. 1981.

WASHINGTON, BOOKER T. *The Story of the Negro: The Rise of the Race from Slavery*. 2 vols. 1909.

WATSON, ALAN. *Roman Slave Law*. 1987.

———. *Slave Law in the Americas*. 1989.

WATSON, JAMES L., ed. *Asian and African Systems of Slavery*. 1980.

WIECEK, WILLIAM M. *The Sources of Antislavery Constitutionalism in America, 1760–1848*. 1977.

WIEDEMANN, THOMAS E. J. *Slavery*. 1992.

WILLIAMS, ERIC. *Capitalism and Slavery*. 1944.

WILLIAMS, GEORGE WASHINGTON. *History of the Negro Race in America*. 2 vols. 1882.

WILLIS, JOHN RALPH, ed. *Slaves and Slavery in Muslim Africa*. 2 vols. 1985.

WOLF, ERIC. *Europe and the People without History*. 1982.

WORDEN, NIGEL A. "Brazilian Slavery: A Survey from the Cape of Recent Literature in English." *Social Dynamics* 17, no. 2 (1991): 76–102.

———. *Slavery in Dutch South Africa*. 1985.

WORDEN, NIGEL, and CLIFTON CRAIS, eds. *Breaking the Chains: Slavery and Its Legacy in the Nineteenth-Century Cape Colony*. 1994.

YETMAN, NORMAN R., ed. *Life under the "Peculiar Institution": Selections from the Slave Narrative Collection*. 1970.

———, comp. *Voices from Slavery*. 1970.

Index

Note: Page numbers in **boldface** indicate main articles on subject. Those in *italic* indicate illustrations or tables

Beriberi, 232, 382, 388, 389

Berkeley, Sir William, 364

Berlin Conference (1885), **104**, 132
    (*see also* Brussels Act)

Bermuda. *See* Caribbean region;
    Plantations

Bertoa (Portuguese ship), 116

Best, Elsdon, 556

Best, Willie, 329

Betsimisaraka (polity), 267

Beulah Land (television program), 331

Biafra. *See* Bight of Biafra

Biard, Auguste-François, 95

Bibb, Henry, 530, 881

Bible, **104–112**
    African-American slave parallels, 91
    antislavery interpretations, 107–108,
        109, 192, 698, 795
    biblical law, 106, 107, 108, **110–112**,
        480, 779 (*see also* Judaic law)
    Epictetus parallels with New
        Testament, 313
    Exodus story, 319–320 (*see also*
        Exodus)
    film depictions of slavery in, 331
    as inspiration for black spirituals,
        618, 877, 878
    Jewish and Christian
        interpretations, **107–110**, 182,
        450, 451, 708, 894
    on eunuchs, 318
    on non-Hebrew slavery, 482
    on sexual exploitation of slave, 880
    on slaves as property, 477
    on treatment of slaves, 238, 614
    overview, **104–107**
    as slave literacy factor, 278
    as slave name source, 626
    slavery portrayed in, 64, 103–105,
        110, 238, 304–305, 900 (*see also*
        Exodus)
    slavery provisions in, 450
    slavery seen sanctioned in, 107, 108,
        115, 183, 184–185, 191, 192,
        451, 488, 696, 697, 699, 700,
        702, 703, 766, 806, 894, 929
    wet nurses in, 956
    See also specific books of the Bible

Bible against Slavery, The (Weld), 942

Bibliography of slavery, 398–403

Bight of Benin, 34, 35, 39, 161, 247,
    248, 837, 840, 841, 842, 843, 847

Bight of Biafra, 34, 161, 247, 248, 310,
    837, 842, 843

Bilali, 440, 441

Bilal ibn Rabah, 439

Binsse, Louis B., 191

Biography of a Runaway Slave
    (Montejo), 611–612

Bioho, Domingo, 815

Bioko (formerly Fernando Po),
    526–527, 872–873

Birney, James G., 47, 48, 50, **112–113**,
    693, 769, 942

Birth of African-American Culture (Mintz
    and Price), 152, 322

Birth of a Nation (film), 329, 581

Birth rates, table of slave-based
    societies in Americas
    (1633–1861), 380 (*see also* Fertility
    rates)

Bissette, Cyrille, 20

Black Belt (Alabama), 46

Blackbirding in Pacific Islands,
    113–115

Black Cargoes (publication), 585

Black churches. *See* Churches, African-
    American

Black Code (French). *See Code Noir*

Black Codes (U.S. South), 195, 196,
    299, 608, 763, *764*

Black Death, 574, 577, 743, 832, 879

Black drivers. *See* Drivers

Black English, 194

Blackface performers, 329, 567, 619,
    623

Black Family in Slavery and Freedom, The
    (Gutman), 397

Black Jacobins (James), 539, 560

Black language, 91

*Black Majority; Negroes in Colonial South
    Carolina from 1670 through the
    Stono Rebellion* (Wood), 397

Black nationalism, 605

Black People Making Merry in Surinam
    (Valkenburg), 94

Black Power movement, 581

Black Rangers, 596

Black Reconstruction in America (Du
    Bois), 406–407

Black Saturnalia, The (Dirks), 150

Black Sea, 136, 286, 610, 661, 831, 832,
    871, 957

Blacksmithing, 429, 446

Blackstone, William, 365

Blackstone's *Commentaries*, 365, 708

Black Yagers, 596

Blaer, Jan, 127

Blake, William, 95, 532–533, 538

Blakely, William, 86

Blake; or, The Huts of America (Delany),
    530

Bland, James, 620

Blankets, 565

Blassingame, John, 395, 397, 407, 410,
    805

"Blaxploitation" films, 331

Bleak House (Dickens), 533

Bledsoe, Albert Taylor, **115–116**, 701

"Bleeding Kansas," 7, 17, 131, 209,
    227, 510, 735

Blinded slave (2400 B.C.E.), 63

Blondi, Alpha, 620

Blow, Taylor, 262

Blowers, Sampson Salter, 141

Blues music, 618, 623

Bluett, Thomas, 861

Boas, Franz, 349

Bodin, Jean, 303, 304, 306, 612, 631,
    688, 708

Boehme, Jakob, 902

Boers, 294, 869, 870

Boethius, 711

Bogle, Paul, 579

Bograd, Mark, 87

Bohemia, 575

Bolívar, Simón, 69, 291

Bolivia, 291

Bolonha, José de, 189

Bomba (dance), 623

Bonaire, 167

Bonampak (city-state), 53

Bonaventure, Saint, 187

Bonded Histories (Prakash), 411

Bondi, August, 448

Bond-servanthood. *See* Debt slavery

*Bondsmen and Rebels: A Study of Master-
    Slave Relations in Antigua*
    (Gaspar), 431

Boni Wars (1765–1793), 884

Bonnaire, *637*

Bonny, 840, 843

Bontemps, Arna, 91, 531

Boogart, Ernst van den, 534

Book of American Negro Spirituals
    (Johnson), 531

Book of Mormon, 474

Book of Negro Folklore (Bontemps and
    Hughes), 531

Boorstin, Daniel, 386

Booth, Sherman, 508, 513, 960, 961

Borgu, 843

Borneo, 428, 546, 850, 867

Borno, 309, 954

Bornu, 591, 944

Borobudur temple complex (Java),
    427, *428*

Bossuet, Jacques, 188

Boston (Massachusetts)
    abolitionist activity, 17, 907, 962,
        963
    Attucks memorial, 582
    fugitive slave trials, 133–134,
        507–508, 734, 917
    Shaw Memorial, 578, *579*
    slaves in, 924, 956

Boston, John, 296

Chesnutt, Charles, 531
Chess Players, The (Flagg), 95
Chester County (Pennsylvania)
    Friends, 752, 753
Chiapas, 474
Chicago (Illinois), 91
Chichimec, 53
Chickasaws, 628, 658–659
Child, David Lee, 178
Child, Lydia Maria, 14, **178–179**, 369,
    962
Childbirth, 385–386 (*see also*
    Motherhood)
Child care, 61, 74, 121, 419
    wet nurses, 956
Child labor. *See* Slavery and childhood
Children. *See* Family; Infant mortality
    rates; Slavery and childhood
Chile, 291, 596, 690, 838
China, **179–180**
    Cheng Ho, 177
    class-based sumptuary laws, 477
    Communist forced relocations, 432
    Communist slave-labor camps, 467
    concubinage, 213–215
    contemporary forms of slavery, 467,
        819, 820, 836
    coolie emigration, 463–464
    corvée labor, 749
    debt peonage, 237
    eunuchs, 317
    full emancipation (1909), 180, 214
    historiographies of slavery, 411,
        412–413
    Japanese comfort women, 207, 208,
        468
    legal systems, 477–478
    public works projects, 748, 749
    slave inheritance pattern, 304
    slave sources, 179, 214, 307–308,
        848
    slave trade, 847–848, 850
    Southeast Asian slave trade from, 830
Chinese Communist Party. *See*
    Communist Party of China
Chinese coolie labor. *See* Coolies
Chinn, Wilson, *256*
Chios, 57, 306
Choctaw Nation, 54, 629, 658–659
Cholera, 381, 656
Chopin, Kate, 797
Choson. *See* Korea
Chou dynasty, 317
Christiana Slave Revolt (1851),
    180–181, 351, 923
Christian Director, A (Baxter), 103
Christianity, **181–193**
    abolitionism linked with, 4, 5, 8, 11,
        13–14, 687, 688–689, 692, 697,
        733

as African-American verbal
    influence, 91
ancient Rome and Byzantium, 76,
    137, 493
biblical antislavery interpretations,
    107–108, 192, 289, 659, 697,
    698
Caribbean region, 812–814
conversion as manumission basis,
    523
conversions as argument for
    enslavements, 698, 910
Council of Épaone, 312
Crusades, 229–230 (*see also as
    separate listing*)
early church, **185–186**, 711
Epictetus as influence on, 313
and Exodus significance, 319–320
freedom's valuation in, 671
Germanic slavery, 488
hierarchical beliefs, 185, 192
justifications for slavery, 11,
    103–104, 109, 183, 184–185,
    191, 192, 361, 364–365, 659,
    696, 698, 699, 700, 702, 860,
    910 (*see also* Bible; Just war)
liberation theology, 320
medieval West, **186–187** (*see also*
    Medieval Europe, slavery and
    serfdom in)
Mediterranean basin slavery,
    576–577
missionary activity, 603–605
monogamous ideal, 677, 679, 789
natural law and, 630, 894
opposition to slavery, 8, 13–14, 20,
    47, 108, 184, 294
Ottoman enslavement of young
    Christian boys, 660, 667, 833
overview, **181–185**
paternalistic ethos, 699, 750
as promising only spiritual freedom,
    106–107, 345, 346, 390, 750,
    894
Protestantism, **192–193** (*see also as
    separate listing*)
redemption of Christians captured
    by Muslims, 765
Roman Catholicism, **188–192** (*see
    also as separate listing*)
self-castrates, 318
slave converts, 3, 167, 189–190,
    806–808, 914 (*see also* Baptism
    of slaves; Churches, African-
    American; Slave religion)
slave spirituals, 877, 878
slave syncretism, 189–190, 193, 194,
    806, 809, 878
slave traders, 838
spiritual redemption belief, 106–107

Thomas Aquinas, 894
See also Jesus of Nazareth; *specific
    denominations and sects*
Christmas, 414
Christmas Rebellion (1831), 579
Christophe, king of Haiti, 26, 539
Christy, Cuthbert, 524
Christy, David, 701
Chryseis, 900
Chrysippus of Soli, 710
Chulalongkorn, king of Siam, 893
Churches, African-American, **193–194**
    African roots, 806
    Baptist evangelicalism, 100, 606
    as core of community, 764
    emergence of, 911
    Kentucky, 456
    Methodist, 193, 561, 583, 584
    Missouri, 609
    postemancipation perspectives on
        slavery, 704
    slave code restrictions, 808
    slave moral agency within, 806–807
    southern cities, 925
    verbal arts, 91
Church Missionary Society, 78
Church of England. *See* Anglicanism
Church of Ireland. *See* Anglicanism
Ciboney, 164
Cicero, Marcus Tullius, 73, 76, 77, 277,
    288, 490, 549, 710
    manumission of slave Tiro, 547
    on gladiator honor, 363
    on natural law, 630
    views on slavery, 711
Cicero, Quintus, 547
Cimarrons. *See* Maroons
Cincinnnati (Ohio), 617, 881, 882,
    907, 927
Cinqué (Joseph Cinqué), 55, 57, 96,
    195, 604
Circassians, 283, 284, 286, 309, 318,
    610, 662, 663, 832
    white slave traffic, 957
Circumcision, 458, 483
Cisalpine Gaul, 72
Cistercians, 472
Cities. *See* Urban slavery; *specific cities*
Citizenship
    of ancient Roman freed slaves, 71,
        73, 74, 75, 76, 77, 84, 176, 338,
        339, 484, 490, 492, 549
    as basis of Taney's *Dred Scott* ruling,
        262, 511, 523, 885
    denied to antebellum freed U.S.
        slaves, 12, 13, 227, 523
    first U.S. constitutional definition
        of, 195
    free blacks, 195, 117, 528, 763 (*see
        also* Fourteenth Amendment)

household slaves as, 683–684, 685–686, 738

Mamluks as, 283–284

in Russia, 783

southern racial consciousness and decline of, 685

Elizabeth I, queen of England, 273

Elizia (ship), 527

Elkins, Stanley, 125, 288, 349, 397, 407, *408*, 410, 686, 771

Elkins thesis, 125, **288**, 349, 397, 407, 417, 748, 771, 880

Elliot, Jonathan, 225

Ellison, Ralph, 625

Ellison, William, **288–289**

Elmina Castle (or El Mina; Ghana), 580, 616, 739, 740, 948

Elmore, Rush, 453

Eltis, David, 34, 128, 273, 345, 960

Emancipation, **289–293**

in Africa, 8, 28, 40–43, 949

associated with American gradual abolitionists, 1, 2, 12

in Brazil, 118, 123, 124, 130, 210, 245, 290–291, 409, 554, 625, 695, 722

in British empire, 2, 4, 7, 24, 41, 42, 73, 78, 136, 141, 158–159, 176, 245, 285, 289–290, 293–294, 368, 692, 959

British parliamentary battle, 135–136, 959

in Canada, 141, 293

in Caribbean region. *See under* Caribbean region

of central Asian slaves, 174

chain-breaking as symbol of, 175

in China, 180, 214

compensation provisions, 297

in Cuba, 146, 153, 165–166, 234, 245, 291, 292, 664, 695

in Danish colonies, 24, 153, 168, 292, 431

in Dutch colonies, 153, 167, 290, 637, 729

in East Africa, 245, 266, 269

and Enlightenment philosophy, 11, 688

European abolitionists' view of, 26

freedom vs., 345

in French colonies, 19–20, 24, 41, 153, 162, 163, 245, 269, 290, 776

in Hawaii, 377

in Islamic countries, 496

in Korea, 458

legal process

literature of, 530

in Malaya, 546–547

manumission vs., 243, 550

in Mauritius and Réunion, 570

in Ottoman Empire, 285, 496, 611, 663, 695

in Portugal, 290–291, 738

in Romania, 778

in Russia, 23, 174, 290, 576, 691, 749, 783

in Scandinavia, 176, 790

in Southeast Asia, 867

in Spanish colonies, 24, 165–166, 291–293, 873

stages in, 689–695

Thailand, 893

in United States. *See* Emancipation in the United States

See also Abolition and antislavery societies; Freedmen; Gradual emancipation statutes; Manumission

Emancipation Act, British (1833), 10, **293–294**, 692, 792

Emancipation Days, 415

Emancipation Group (Ball), 96

Emancipation in the United States, 293, **294–299**, 511, 691–692

artists' depictions of, 96

black churches and, 808

by Coles in Virginia, 205

Civil War, 3, 4, 18, 197–201, 227, 228, 245, 293, **296–299**, 528, 691, 918

Confiscation Acts, 220, 228

conflict-of-laws theory, 221–223

consequences of, 918–919

Delaware, 240

demographic analysis of, 244–245

festival commemorations, 415

first acts, 293, 754 (*see also* Emancipation Proclamation)

Freedmen's Bureau, 198, 342–343

Illinois, 423

Indiana, 424, 922

Maryland, 562

Massachusetts, 545, 563, 922

New Hampshire, 922

New York, 641, 642

North Carolina, 651

northern experience, 12, 293, **294–296**, 551, 689, 754, 922–923

Ohio, 922

personal naming patterns following, 626

procedure, 511

Rhode Island, 774–775

as slave memorial theme, 578–579

Tennessee, 890

Texas, 415, 892

of U.S. slaves-in-transit, 222

See also Abolition and antislavery movements; Gradual emancipation statutes; Manumission

Emancipation Monument (Washington, D. C.), 578

Emancipation Proclamation (1863; U.S.), 3, 4, 18, 45, 82, 96, 134, 197, 293, 297, 298, *346*, 511, 691, 762, *919*

congressional signatories, *292*

Lincoln on, 299

preliminary (1862), 196, 220, 297

reasons for, 918

Emancipator (abolitionist publication), 14, *15*, 888

Emecheta, Buchi, 537

Emerson, John, 261

Emerson, Ralph Waldo, 475

Emigration. *See* Repatriation to Africa

Emmer, Pieter, 534

Emmett, Dan, 619

Empire of the Ants (film), 791

Enchiridion (Epictetus), 313

Encomienda system, 275, 473–474

Encyclopédie, **299–300**, 302, 688, 775

Enforcement Acts, U.S. (1870, 1871), **300**, 763

Enfranchisement. *See* Voting rights

Engels, Friedrich, **300–301**, 409, 558, 709, 712

Engenhos (Brazilian sugar processing mills), 719, 720, 721, 722

Engerman, Stanley, 128, 145, 269–270, 273, 275, 408, 410, 684, 742, 772, 960

England. *See* Great Britain

England, John, 190

English common law, 497–502, 514, 572, 614–615

English East India Company, 425, 426, 427, 592, 850, 867

English in the West Indies; or, the Bow of Ulysses (Froude), 539

English Slave Trade Committee, 368

Enlightenment, **301–303**

as abolitionist inspiration, 3, 8, 11, 19, 20, 23, 301–303, 312, 688, 689, 697, 709

as Declaration of Independence influence, 505–506

defensive proslavery arguments, 697

Encyclopédie, 299

Éphémérides du Citoyen, 302, 312

Franklin, Benjamin, and the Marquis de Condorcet, 337–338

human rights as focus, 301, 312

Jefferson's slavery positions and, 447

and ending Egyptian slavery, 285, 286

industrial development seen financed by slavery profits, 149, 273, 560, 959, 960

lecture tours by former slaves, 694

literature of slavery, 314, 532–534, 902

Mauritius cession, 568, 569, 570

medieval slavery and serfdom, 562, 571, 832

naval campaign against slave trade, *102*, 103

Norman conquest, 485, 573

opposition to African slave trade, 1, 3, 5, 8–9, 10, 21, 752

opposition to Brazilian slavery, 21

Pacific islander "blackbirding," 114, 115

paintings depicting slavery, 93

penal colonies, 472

Puritans, 749–750

Quaker abolitionists, 5, 8, 9, 689, 754

repatriation advocates, 768

Roma enslavement, 778

Royal African Company, 780–781, 861

Scottish Enlightenment, 301–302

slavery and serfdom in, 307, 573 (*see also* Great Britain, African slavery in *as separate listing*)

slave trade, 176, 505, 780–781, 829, 832, 839–840, 842, 850

slave trade ban, 1, 3, 5, 7, 8–9, 21, 24, 28, 40, 45, 78, 176, 289–290, 293, 525, 689, 754, 838, 959

slave trade museum, 617

theological views on slavery, 103

trade, 149, 275

Utilitarianism, 413–414

Webster-Ashburton Treaty, 941

See also American Revolution; Ireland; London; Scottish antislavery movement

Great Britain, African slavery in, **366–368**

legal cases, 176, 221, 368, 497–498, 502

Great Depression (1930s), 28, 81, 581, 632

Great Dismal Swamp, 315, 911

Greater Antilles. *See* Jamaica; Haiti

"Great Negro Plot" of 1741 (New York City), 669, 758, 759

Great Wall of China, 749

Greece, ancient. *See* Ancient Greece

Greek Civil Code, 493

Greek mythology, 900

Greek Slave, The (Powers), 96, 175

Greek War of Independence (1820s), 175, 437

Green, Beriah, 14

Greenberg, Kenneth, 417

Greene, Catherine, 958

Greene, Lorenzo, 397

Greene, Nathaniel, 958

Grégoire, Henri, Bishop of Blois, 19, **368–369**, 535, 859

Gregory IX, pope, 765

Gregory XVI, pope, 190, 290

Gregory Nazianzen, 186

Gregory of Nyssa, 318

Grenada, 147, 148, 153, 157, 159

slave rebellion, 430, 904

Turnbull's proslavery tracts, 903–904

Grier, Robert C., 181, 508

Griffith, D. W., 329, 332

Griffith, Mattie, 530

Griffiths, William, 36

Grimké, Angelina and Sarah, 16, **369–370**, 531, 942, 963, 965

Griots, 90

Griqua, 870

Gross Rosen (Nazi concentration camp), 632

Grotius, Hugo, 504, 631, 696

Groves v. Slaughter (1841), 226

Guadeloupe

black armed corps, 596

black militia members, 595

emancipation, 20, 338

French colonization, 159, 160

plantations, table of, 161

as revolutionary activity center, 162

slave population, 161

slave trade to, 843

sugar plantations, 147, 159

Guadelupe-Hidalgo, Treaty of (1848), 54

Guam, 113

Guanche, 739, 832, 872

Guarani, 118

Guardian of Sally, a Negro v. Beaty (1792), 499

Guatemala, 53, 148

Guayaquil, 161

Guerrilleros negros, Los (Leante), 536

Guianas, 146, 147–148, 152, 157, 159, 303

Dutch. *See* Suriname

French penal colony, 472

maroon communities, 153, 557, 815

sugar plantations, 723

Guilds

Benin, 949

slave trader, 834

Guillén, Nicolás, 536

Guimarães, Bernardo, 539

Guiné, 116

Guinea. *See* Lower Guinea; Upper Guinea

Guizot, Françoise, 20

Gulag, 331, **370–371**, 432, 467, 473, 783, 820

Gulag Archipelago, 467

Gulag Archipelago, The (Solzhenitsyn), 370

Gulf of Guinea, 873

Gullah dialect and culture, 626, 911, 913

Gundrisse (Marx), 559

Guns of the South, The (Turtledove), 791

Gunston Hall (Virginia), 566

Guo Moruo, 413

Gurnah, Abdulrazak, 537

Guti, 66

Gutiérrez Alea, Tomás, 536

Gutman, Herbert, 325, 397, 410, 616, 846

Guyana

Demerara slave revolt, 3, 159, 240–241

emancipation, 338

Gypsies. *See* Roma

H

Habeas corpus writs, 961

Hadramaut (Hadramuth), 265, 266, 824, 855

Hadrian, emperor of Rome, 492

Hagar (Old Testament), 64, 880

Haggard, H. Rider, 791

Hague Convention, 632

Haidas, 52, 54

Haile Selassie, emperor of Ethiopia, 654, 855

Hairston, Jester, 619

Haislas, 54

Haiti (formerly Saint Domingue)

African religion, 190, 810, 811, *812*

as antislavery symbol, 25, 26, 690, 691

cacao plantations, 148

coffee plantations, 160–161, 726

concubinage, 796

Declaration of Rights of Man influence on, 776

Douglass as U.S. minister to, 260

freedmen colony (proposed), 544, 693

as French colony, 159, 160

as fugitive slave haven, 162

independence, 153, 159, 162, 164–165, 290, 897–898

indigo exports, 148

largest slave population, 149, 160, 726

Imerina (Madagascar), 267, 269, 853
Immigrants, U.S.
    as alternative to slave labor, 295
    antiblack bigotry, 13, 14
    Chinese laborers, 849
    as contract labor, 461
    headright system, 378
    as peons in deep South, 674–675
Imperial Abolition Act of 1833
        (Canada), 141
Impressment, 28, 219
    U.S. Civil War Confiscation Acts,
        197, 198, 220
Inalcık, Hilal, 411, 660, 667
Incas, 421, *421*
Incas: The Royal Commentaries (de la
        Vega), 538
Incidents of the Life of a Slave Girl
        (Jacobs), 443, 529–530, 797
Indentured servitude (contract labor),
        461–462
    Africa, 799
    ancient Greece, 61
    ancient Israelite slavery as similar,
        481
    as Brazilian slave replacement, 722
    Caribbean plantations, 147, 159
    as chattel slavery replacement, 830
    Chinese coolie, 463–464, 848–849
    as field labor, 326
    Hawaii, 377, 378
    headright system, 378
    Illinois, 423
    Indiana, 424
    indigenous Liberians, 526
    Maryland, 561
    migrant workers, 820
    in Mormon Utah, 476, 928
    New Mexico, 639–640
    Russia, 783
    in seventeenth-century North
        American colonies, 468–470,
        561, 910, 913
    slavery vs., 913
    in southeastern Africa, 854
    as step in gradual slave
        emancipation, 12
    as step toward debt peonage, 818
    West Africa, 40, 525
    See also Gradual emancipation
        statutes
Index of Forbidden Books (Roman
        Catholic), 189, 190
Indiana, **424–425**, 506, 655, 922
Indian Ocean, 40, 70
    contemporary slave trade, 824
    regional networks, 851–853
    slave trade, 247, 248, 265, 266–267,
        308, 425, 568–569, 636, 653,
        654, 740, 741, 833, 868

slave trade curbs, 132, 853–855
slave trade suppression attempts,
        852
transatlantic slave trade link, 851,
        853
See also East Africa; Mauritius and
        Réunion
Indians, American. *See* Native
        Americans
Indian subcontinent, **425–427**
    African former slave as ruler, 47
    British emancipation moves, 10, 41,
        290
    Buddhism, 132
    caste system, 168–169, 425–426
    child slavery, 818
    contemporary forms of slavery, 818
    debt peonage, 237, 818
    debt slavery, 238, 438
    East African slave trade, 265, 266,
        568, 851
    emancipation, 290, 691, 695
    forced labor, 468
    Hinduism, 392–393
    historiographies of slavery, 411
    indentured laborer emigrés, 471,
        472, 854
    indigo trade, 148
    Islam, 435, 436–437
    legal-status abolition, 245
    Mamluks, 435
    Portuguese shipments of Gypsy
        slaves to, 778
    public works projects, 748
    Roma origination in, 776
    slave system, 392–393
    slave trade, 265, 266, 568, 829, 850,
        851, 852
    slave trade to southern Africa, 868
Indian Territory. *See* Oklahoma
*Indigenous Races of the Earth, or, New
        Chapters of Ethnological Inquiry*
        (Nott), 386
Indigenous slavery, chattel slavery vs.,
        10, 53
Indigo plantations
    Caribbean region, 147, 148, 150,
        151, 160, 161, *161*
    Egypt, 286
    slave labor cost advantages, 143
    South Carolina and Georgia, 326,
        717, 915
    trade demands, 273
    work conditions, 151
Indio Esclavo, El (Las Casas), 188
Indonesia, **427–428**
    Dutch colonial imports of slaves,
        636
    Japanese World War II comfort
        women, 207, 208

slave trade by, 113, 851
slave trade from, 568, 852, 868
See also Malaya
Industrial Revolution, slavery profits
        seen financing, 149, 273, 560,
        959, 960
Industrial slaves, **428–429**
    Brazil, 122
    demographic analysis, 247–248
    Nazi forced labor, 633–635
    U.S. North, 922
    U.S. South, 684–685
    See also Miners
Infanticide, 75, 772 (*see also*
        Abandoned children)
Infant mortality rates
    Caribbean slaves, 150
    Cuban slaves, 232
    malnutrition and, 382
    U.S. slaves, 250, 382, 606, 797
Ingres, Jean Dominique, 93
Inikori, Joseph, 34, 273, 960
Injustice of Tolerating Slavery in England
        (Sharp), 798
*In My Father's House Are Many
        Mansions: Family and Community in
        Edgefield, South Carolina* (Burton),
        408
Inner Light (Quaker belief), 294, 751
Innocent III, pope, 765
Innocent IV, pope, 361
Inoculation, 385, 586, 613
In Old Kentucky (film), 329
In Ole Virginia (Page), 531
*Inquiry into the Law of Negro Slavery in
        the United States to which is prefixed,
        An Historical Sketch of Slavery*
        (Cobb), 204, 396
*Inquiry into the Nature and Causes of the
        Wealth of Nations* (Smith). *See
        Wealth of Nations*
Inquisition, 47, 738, 814
In re Anthony Burns (1854). *See* Burns,
        Anthony
In re Bates (1858), 509
In re Booth (1854), 508, 960
In re Booth and Rycraft (1855), 961
In re Lewis (1902), 81
In re Perkins (1852), 139
In re Thomas Sims (1851), 507–508
In re William Chaplin (1851), 509
Inscoe, John, 626
Inscriptions (ancient world), 83
Institutes (Justinian), 696
In Supremo Apostolatus (papal
        encyclical), 190
Insurrections, **429–431**
    conditions for, 429–430
    escapes linked with, 315
    Garnet's speech calling for, 357

North, U.S. (*cont.*)
    free black churches, 807
    free black migrations to, 919
    fugitive slave laws enforcement, 226–227
    fugitive slave laws opponents, 734, 923
    fugitive slave rescues, 907–909, 923
    gradual abolition statutes, 365, 689
    law, 512–513
    manumissions, 551
    personal liberty laws, 350, 513, 585, 734, 744, 775, 923, 933
    pro-Confederate copperheads, 762, 763
    slave field labor, 328
    slave population, 11, 249, 294, 911
    slaves-in-transit status, 222
    urban slavery, 924–925
    See also Abolition and antislavery movements; Civil War, U.S.; New England; *specific cities and states*
North Africa, **643–649**
    Barbary wars, 101–102
    central African slave sales to, 172
    East African slave trade to, 851
    French colonialism, 644–645, 647, 648
    galley slaves, 356
    harems, 376
    military slaves, 436, 590–591
    Morocco, **643–646** (*see also* Morocco *as separate listing*)
    Portuguese holdings, 740
    redemption of Christian captives in, 765
    as Roman province, 72, 712, 713
    Sahara region, 172, 436, 524, **646–649**, 855
    slaves in Spain, 870
    slave trade, 833, 872
    Slavic slaves in, 781
    sugar plantations, 714
    twentieth-century slave trade, 496
    See also Trans-Saharan slave trade
Northampton (Massachusetts) Association, 901
North Carolina, **649–651**
    antislavery leaders, 651
    black Union Army soldiers, 197
    as Confederate state, 218
    free blacks, 917
    headright system, 378
    legal cases, 500, 501, 514, 516, 520, 522, 616, 801, 878–879, 899
    maroon community, 315, 651
    mine slaves, 600
    murder-of-slave law, 615, 616
    Native American enslavement, 628

    plantations, 716
    Quakers, 649, 651, 754
    slave legal disabilities, 520, 521, 651
    slave rebellion, 760
    slavery practices, 649–650, 753, 754
    slave testimony, 961
North Carolina Manumission Society, 651
North Carolina Yearly Meeting (Quaker), 754
Northeast Africa, **651–654**
    Ethiopia, **653–654** (*see also as separate listing*)
    upper Nile region, **651–653**
    See also Egypt
Northern Methodist Episcopal Church, 584
Northrup, David, 34
Northrup, Solomon, 928
North Sea, 832
North Star, 902, 903
North Star, The (Douglass newspaper), 259, 694, 733
Northup, Solomon, 529, 927
Northwest Ordinance (1787), 227, 293, 350, 423, 584, **655**, 657, 733
    Jefferson (Thomas) draft of, 447
    Oregon slavery prohibtion under, 660
    provisions, 423, 424, 506, 585, 600, 655
    repeal efforts, 424
    slaveholding under, 921
    slavery in territories debate, 733
    Wisconsin slavery ban under, 960
Norway, 104, *788*, 789, 790 (*see also* Vikings)
Nossa Senhora da Apareçeda, 809
Nosy Be, 267
Notes on the State of Virginia (Jefferson), 446, 447, 698, 747
Notorious Triangle: Rhode Island and the African Slave Trade (Coughtry), 774
Nott, Henry Junius, 655
Nott, Josiah Clark, 237, 386, **655–656**, 702–703, 894
Novás Calvo, Lino, 536
Nova Scotia, 639, 641, 768, 800
Novels. *See* Literature of slavery; *specific titles*
Novgorod slave market, 781
Nozick, Robert, 541
Nuba Mountains, 651
Nu-bi (Chinese slaves), 179, 180, 847–848
Nubia, 305, 651, *652*, 662, 900
Nubi community (East Africa), 592
Nullification controversy (U.S.), 13
Nunes Garcia, José Maurício, 122

Nupe, 843, 954
Nuremberg International Military Tribunal (1946–1949), 468, 632, 635
Nutrition. *See under* Health

O
O Abolicionismo (Nabuco de Araujo), 625
Oakes, James, 145, 410
Oarsmen. *See* Galley slaves
"Oath helpers" (Germanic), 487
Oaxaca, 52–53
Obeah, 812, 814
Oberlin College, 14, 579, 657, 888
Oberlin-Wellington rescue (1858), 351, 657, 907–908
O'Connell, Daniel, 190–191, 434
Octoroons, 347
Odacer, 485
Odalisque with Slave (Ingres), 93
"Oh, Brothers, Don't Get Weary" (spiritual), 618
O'Higgins, Bernardo, 291
Ohio, **657–658**
    antiblack discrimination, 13
    antislavery societies, 14
    fugitive slave cases, 509, 513, 657, 907–908
    interstate comity breakdown, 222, 522
    Quaker society, 754
    slavery museums and memorial, 617, 657
    See also Cincinnati; Oberlin College
Ohio Land Company, 655
Ohio River, 293, 456, 655, 881, 912, 922, 960
Oiketes (Byzantine term for slave), 136
Oklahoma, 54–55, 629, **658–659**
Old Choson, 457
Old Kentucky Home (Negro Life in the South) (Johnson), 95, *96*
Old Mammy's Charge (film), 329
"Old Man River" (song), 620
Old Oak's Secret, The, 329
"Old Oligarch" (Athens), 61, 489
Old Plantation (anonymous painting), 95
Old Testament. *See* Bible; *specific books and personages*
O Libertador (journal), 22
Olivier de Sardan, Jean-Pierre, 411
Olmstead, Frederick Law, 273, 529
Omai (Pacific islander), 114
Oman, 265, 437, 496, 730–731, 824, 834, 851, 852, 855, 856
On Duties (Cicero), 711
O'Neall, John, 499

Buddhism, 132–133
contemporary forms of slavery, 177
corvée labor, 464–465
free Chinese immigrants, 849
historiography of slavery, 411
Portuguese slave trade, 740, 741
slave trade, 428, 829–830, 849–851, 867
See also Cambodia; Indonesia; Philippines; Thailand
Southeby, William, 752
Southern Africa, 247, 290, 293, 294, 620, **867–870**
Cape of Good Hope, **867–869** (*see also as separate listing*)
ILO forced labor inquiry, 432
Mormon integrated congregations, 476
slave trade, 849, 851, 852
Sotho/Nguni, **869–870**
Southern Baptist Bible Board, 100
Southern Baptist Convention, 101
Southern Presbyterian Review (journal), 894
Southern Review (journal), 116
Southern Standard (newspaper), 757
Southern Wealth and Northern Profits (Kettell), 701
Souther v. Commonwealth (1851), 520, 616
South Kingston (Rhode Island), 774
South Wulawesi, 428
Sovereign immunity, 517–518
Soviet slave labor, 276, 331, 432, 466
gulag system, 370–371, 467, 473, 783, 820
Spain, **870–876**
abolition of slavery, 24, 291–293
African military slaves in New World, 593, 594
African slavery, 176, **872–873**
Amerindian enslavement, 628
Amistad case involvement, 56
antislavery committee, 7
asiento, 97, 872
Berlin Act (1885), 104
blackbirding in Pacific Islands, 113
Brussels Act (1890), 132
colonies and empire, 11, 23, 24, 53–54, 97, 146, 149, 176, 247, **873–876** (*see also* Bioko; Caribbean region; Cuba; Hispaniola; Latin America; Mexico; New World; Philippines)
critics of slavery, 47
Dutch trade rivalry, 126
economic benefits of colonial slavery, 274
encomienda system, 275, 473–474

free black population, 553
illegal slave trade, 102, 165
Islamic conquest and slave trade, 309
legal codes, 251, 253, 255, 514, 551–552, 553, 800–801, 898
literature of slavery, 536–537
redemption of Christian captives, 765
Roma enslavement, 778
Roman Catholic views of slavery, 187, 190
Roman conquest of, 72
Roman law, 503
Roman mine slaves, 598, 599
self-purchase provisions, 151
slavery in Spain, 176, 832, **870–872**
slave traders, 272, 723–724, 832
as Slavic slave market, 857, 870
sugar plantations, 714
Treaty of Tordesillas, 603–604, 872, 895–896
types of slavery, 306
See also Seville
Spalding, Martin, 191
Spalding, Thomas, 420
Spanish-American War (1898), 597
Spanish Cocoa Plantation (Bioko), 526
Sparrow, The (Russell), 790
Sparta (Greek city-state), 57, 58, 59–60, 489
Spartacus, 73, 363, **876–877**, 879
crucifixion of followers, 253, 430, 877
rebellion, 430, 559, 614, 687, 712, 713
Spartacus (film), 331
Special Messenger, A (film), 329
Speer, Albert, 634, 635
Spelling Book (Webster), 279
Spice plantations, 867
Spielberg, Steven, 332, 581
Spinning wheels, 564–565
Spirit of the Laws (Montesquieu), 688, 697
Spirit possession, 808, 810, 811
Spirituals, 618, 622, **877–878**
"Sportsman's Sketches" (Turgenev), 23
Sprague, Pelag, 509
Spratt, Leonidas, 757
Spring Park Historic Site (Virginia), 579
Spy, The (Cooper), 529
Squatter labor, 731, 762, 763
Sri Lanka, 849, 850, 868
Srivijaya Empire, 427, 428
SS Economic and Administrative Main Office, 634, 635
Staël, Germaine de (Madame de Staël), 20, 535
Stalin, Josef, 370, 467

Stampp, Kenneth M., 270, 397, 398, 407, 410, 664, 770–771
Standing Committee of Experts on Slavery (League of Nations), 82
Stanton, Elizabeth Cady, 18, 963, 964
Stanton, Henry B., 16, 48
State-owned slaves
ancient Greece, 58, 59–60, 61, 749
Cambodia, 141
central Asia, 173–174
China, 179, 180
Japanese World War II comfort women, 207–208
Korea, 458
Morocco, 644
Nazi and Soviet, 276
Ottoman, 662
Roman Empire, 287–288
Romani, 777
Sparta, 59–60
Thailand, 892
See also Bureaucracy; Public works
States, U.S.
Compromise of 1850, 209, 510
constitutional basis of representation, 224
interstate slave traffic, 844–846
laws regulating slavery, 504–505, 512–523, 615–616
Missouri Compromise (1820), 227, 510, 609–610
popular sovereignty, 131, 209, 227, 258, 510, 610, 734, 735
slave vs. free states, 12, 13, 16, 225, 227, 929
See also Interstate comity; *specific states*
State v. Ben (North Carolina, 1821), 961
State v. Hoover (North Carolina, 1839), 520, 616
State v. Jones (Mississippi, 1812), 499
State v. Mann (North Carolina, 1829), 479, 514, 516, 801, **878–879**, 899
State v. Raines (South Carolina, 1826), 616
State v. Reed (North Carolina, 1823), 616
State v. Tackett (North Carolina, 1822 or 1829), 499, 616
Status of slaves, legal. *See* Conflict of laws; Disability, legal; Slave codes
Statute of Distributions of 1670 (England), 499
"Steal Away to Jesus" (spiritual), 622, 878
Stearns, Junius Brutus, *94*, 95
Stedman, John Gabriel, 95, 538, 596, 884
Stein, Stanley, 721